Psychology in Education

 WEB Visit the *Psychology in Education* Companion
Website at **www.pearsoned.co.uk/woolfolkeuro**
to find valuable **student** learning material
including:

- Self assessment questions to check your understanding
- Annotated links to relevant sites on the web
- Flashcards to test your understanding of key terms
- Voting system for the discussion points in the book

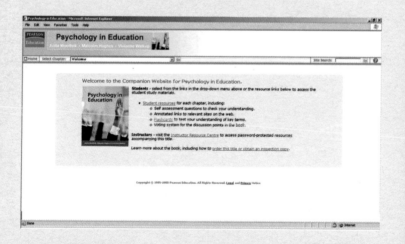

Brief Contents

Contents

Part 2 – Learning and Motivation

Part 3 – Teaching and Assessing

Supporting resources

Visit **www.pearsoned.co.uk/woolfolkeuro** to find valuable online resources

Companion Website for students

- Self assessment questions to check your understanding
- Annotated links to relevant sites on the web
- Flashcards to test your understanding of key terms
- Voting system for the discussion points in the book

For instructors

- Extra case studies
- Downloadable PowerPoint slides of all figures from the book

Also: The Companion Website provides the following features:

- Search tool to help locate specific items of content
- E-mail results and profile tools to send results of quizzes to instructors
- Online help and support to assist with website usage and troubleshooting

For more information please contact your local Pearson Education sales representative or visit **www.pearsoned.co.uk/woolfolkeuro**

Guided Tour

Focus on Practice

An important reason for studying psychology in education is to gain skills in solving problems in the learning situation. Often, texts give pages of theory and research findings but little assistance in translating theory into practice. This text is different. Included in every chapter after the first one are features called *Focus on Practice*. These are teaching tips and practical suggestions based on the theory and research discussed in the chapter. Each suggestion is clarified by two or three specific examples. Although the *Focus on Practice* features cannot cover every possible situation, they do provide the bridge needed between knowledge and practice, and should help you transfer the text's information to new situations.

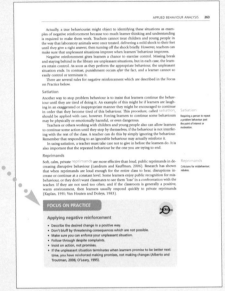

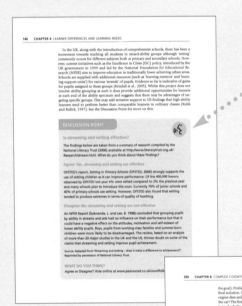

Discussion Points

In every chapter, a debate called *Discussion Point* examines two contrasting perspectives on an important question or controversy related to research or practice in education; issues such as 'brain-based' education, making learning 'fun', and questions such as 'Should pupils be discouraged from using calculators and spell checkers?', 'Should schools teach character and compassion?', and 'Is zero tolerance a bad idea?' are examples. Many of the topics considered in these *Discussion Points* are topical and central to the discussions of educational reformers.

Connect and Extend

Connect and Extend features appear in the margins several times throughout each chapter, linking content to research and professional journals and other useful resources for further reading and information.

Stop and Think

These features provide an opportunity for readers to stop and reflect upon the text in order to add depth to their understanding of it.

In the Classroom: What Would They Do?

At the end of each chapter practitioners working in different places and learning contexts offer their own comments upon and solutions to the problem presented by the 'In the Classroom' feature at the beginning of each chapter. This discussion gives you insights into the thinking of experienced practitioners and allows you to compare their solutions to the ones you came up with. Their ideas truly show psychology in education at work in a range of everyday situations.

Preface

There is no doubt that the application of psychology to education is rapidly becoming increasingly important across the UK and other European countries. The material in this book should be of interest to everyone who is concerned about education and learning, from the nursery school volunteer to the facilitator in a community programme for adults with learning difficulties. No background in psychology or education is necessary to understand this material. It is as free of jargon and technical language as possible, and many people have worked to make this edition clear, relevant, and interesting.

This book is an adaptation of a well-known and established text in the USA which aims to make the content more directly relevant and accessible to readers in the UK and Europe. The text emphasises the educational implications and applications of research on child development, cognitive science, learning, teaching, and assessment. Theory and practice are not separated, but are considered together; the text shows how information and ideas drawn from research in educational psychology can be applied to solve the everyday problems of teaching. To explore the connections between knowledge and practice, there are many integrated examples, case studies, practical applications and tips from experienced educational practitioners. Throughout the text you will be challenged to think about the value and use of the ideas in each chapter, and you will see principles of educational psychology in action.

In order to make this text relevant to European readers and not just those in the UK, pupil age rather than educational level has been referred to throughout. For further clarification, the table below gives the names and age groups for the phases of education in the countries of the United Kingdom and a selection of other European countries. Structure of Education in a selection of European Countries.

	Pre-School	Primary	Secondary	Tertiary
England and Wales	Foundation Stage Nursery 3–4 years Reception 4–5 years	5–11 years (or 5–12 years)	Middle School 9–13 years Secondary 11–16 years	Further Education 16–19 years 6th Form 16–18 years
Scotland source: http:// www.britishschool. nl/22_international _info/scotland.html	3–5 years	5–12 years	12–16 years	Upper Secondary 16–18 years
Northern Ireland source: http:// www.deni.gov.uk/	Nursery 3–4 years Reception 4–5 years	Primary 4–11 years	Grammar or Secondary 11–16 years	6th Form 16–18 years Further Education 16–19 years

	Pre-School	Primary	Secondary	Tertiary
Sweden source: http://www.estia.educ.goteborg.se/svestia/edu/edu_sys.html	förskola (pre-school) 1–5 years	pre-school class 6–7 years (not compulsory) *grundskola* *(comprehensive school)* 7–16 years		*gymnasieskola* (Upper secondary) 16–20 years
The Netherlands source: http://www.euroeducation.net/prof1/netherco.htm, and http://www.britishschool.nl/22_international_info/thenederlands.html.	Basisonderwijs (Primary School) 4–12 years	Secondary Education (HAVO) 12–17 years. Pupils head for HBO (practice-based university, former polytechnics) Preparatory Vocational Education (VMBO) 12–16 years. Pupils head for further education at MBO University Preparatory Education (VWO) 12–18 years		Middelbaar Beroepsonderwijs (MBO) Vocational Education 16–20 years
Norway source: http://www.euroeducation.net/prof/norco.htm	Barnehage (kindergarten) 3–6 years	Grunnskole, Barnetrinnet; Primary School 6–13 years	Grunnskole, Ungdomstrinnet; Secondary School 13–16 years	Videregående Skole; Upper Secondary School 16–19 years Vitnemål Fra Videregående Skole 16–19 years
Belgium http://www.britishschool.nl/22_international_info/belgium.html	Kleuter Onderwijs (pre-school) 2–6 years	Lager Onderwijs (primary school) 6–12 years	Secundair Onderwijs (secondary school) 12–18 years	
Denmark source: http://www.britishschool.nl/22_international_info/denmark.html	Kindergarten 3–6 years pre-school class 6–7 years (not compulsory)	Folkeskole (Primary and Lower secondary school) 7–16 years		Gymnasium, HF, HHX, HTX (Upper secondary) 16–19 years

The Plan of the Book

The introductory chapter begins with a discussion of the importance of psychology in education, and some of the methods that psychologists use to understand what is happening in classrooms and other site of learning. What is good teaching, and what does it take to become an excellent practitioner? How can educational psychology help to understand the process of learning and how to facilitate this?

Part One, 'Learners' focuses on how learners develop mentally, physically, emotionally, and socially, and how all these aspects fit together. Where do individual differences come from, and what do they mean for teachers and those working with learners? What does it mean to create a culturally inclusive classroom, one that makes learning accessible to all?

Part Two, 'Learning and Motivation' looks at learning and motivation from three major perspectives – behavioral, cognitive, and constructivist – with an emphasis on the last two. Learning theories have important implications for instruction at every level. Cognitive research is particularly vital right now and promises to be a wellspring of ideas for teaching in the immediate future. Engaged learning is the goal of all those working within learning environments.

Part Three, 'Teaching and Assessing' examines the creation of learning environments and, then, how to teach and assess. The material in these chapters is based on the most recent research in *real* classrooms. We examine many teaching strategies and different kinds of testing and grading.

Aids to Understanding

At the beginning of each chapter you will find an **Outline** of the key topics with page numbers for quick reference. Then you are presented with an example in 'What would they do?' about a real-life classroom situation related to the information in the chapter. By the time you reach the end of the chapter, you should have even more ideas about how to solve the problem raised, so be alert as you read. The chapter then begins with a quick **Overview** along with a list of **Questions** to focus your thinking about the upcoming pages.

Within the chapter, headings point out themes, questions, and problems as they arise, so you can look up information easily. These can also serve as a quick review of important points. When a new term or concept is introduced, it appears in bold type along with a brief margin definition. These **Key Terms** are also defined in a **Summary Table** at the end of each chapter. The **Summary Table** is an excellent resource for study and review. Throughout the book, graphs, tables, photographs and comments from practitioners on 'In the Classroom: What would they do?' features have been chosen to clarify and extend the text material – and to add to your enjoyment.

Text Features

Chapters include **Focus on Practice, Discussion Points, Connect and Extend, Stop and Think** and **In the Classroom: What Would They Do**?

Acknowledgements

The authors wish to thank Catherine Yates, Steven Jackson and Rhian McKay from Pearson Education for their support, expertise, professionalism and collective trust in the authors ability to complete this project; Jackie Day, Lee Card, Lisbeth Jonsson, Lizzie Meadows and Tessa Herbert for their expertise and willingness to react quickly to unrealistic demands for their responses; and finally to the review panel who contributed so much to the final product.

Malcolm Hughes would like to say 'thank you' to my wife Sue for all her practical and personal support in the preparation of the final manuscript for this book and for contributing to its research and scholarship. Without you, Sue, I could never have climbed this particular 'mountain'.

Vivienne Walkup would like to thank all those who contributed to and supported her through the writing of this, particularly her daughter Suzy and son Patrick.

Publisher Acknowledgements

The publishers would like to thank the following reviewers for their valuable input:

Anne-Marie Akerlund, Uppsala universitet, Sweden
Dr Tom Billington, Sheffield University, UK
Sofie Loyens, Erasmus University Rotterdam, Netherlands
Professor Brahm Norwich, University of Exeter, UK
Professor Colin Rogers, Lancaster University, UK
Professor Alec Webster, University of Bristol, UK
Dr Lisa Woolfson, University of Strathclyde, UK

The publishers are grateful to the following for permission to reproduce copyright material:

Table 2.2 adapted from Development of Private Speech among Low-Income Appalachian Children in *Developmental Psychology*, 20, pub APA, reprinted by permission of American Psychological Association and Laura E. Berk (Berk, L. E. and Garvin, R. A. 1984); Figures 2.3 and 3.1 adapted from *The Developing Person Through Childhood and Adolescence, 6th Edition*, Worth Publishers (Berger, K. S. 2003); Table 2.3 from Effective Teaching Redux in *ASCD Update* 32(6), Association for Supervision and Curriculum Development (O'Neil, J. 1990); Table 2.4 adapted from http://www.ldonline.org/ld_indepth/speech-language/lda_milestones.html, http://www.med.umich.edu/1libr/yourchild/devmile.htm, reprinted from LDOnLine.org, with thanks to the Learning Disabilities Association of America; Table 3.4 from Supporting Victims of Child Abuse in *Educational Leadership*, 50(4), Association for Supervision and Curriculum Development (Bear, T., Schenk, S. and Buckner, L. Dec. 1992/Jan. 1993); Table 3.6 reproduced with permission of Lawrence Erlbaum Associates, Inc., from Compliance to responsibility: Social and emotional learning, and classroom management by M. J. Elias and Y. Schwab in *Handbook of Classroom Management: Research, Practice, and Contemporary Issues* edited by C. Evertson and C. Weinstein, Copyright 2006; permission conveyed through Copyright Clearance Center, Inc.; Table 3.7 adapted from The Cognitive-Developmental Approach to Moral Education in *Phi Delta Kappan*, 56, Phi Delta Kappa International, Inc. (Kohlberg, L. 1975); Table 4.1 from *Education, Information and Transformation: Essays on Learning and Thinking, 1st Edition*, pub Prentice Hall, reprinted by permission of Dr. Howard Gardner (Kane, J. ed. 2002); Table 4.4 from Three facets of visual and verbal learners: Cognitive ability, cognitive style and learning preference in *Journal of Educational Psychology*, 95(4), pub APA, reprinted by permission of American Psychological Association and R. Mayer (Mayer, R. E. and Massa, L. J. 2003); Table 4.5 from *Child and Adolescent Development for Educators*, The McGraw-Hill Companies, Inc. (Meece, J. L. 1997); Table 4.6 adapted from *Diagnostic and Statistical Manual of Mental Disorders, 4th Edition, Text Revision*, Copyright 2000, American Psychiatric Association; Table 5.1 data from www.nomisweb.co.uk and Office for National Statistics reproduced under the terms of the Click-Use Licence; Figure 5.2 from *Ethnicity and Education: The Evidence on Minority Ethnic Pupils aged 5–16*. Research Topic Paper 0208-2006DOM-EN, reproduced under the terms of the Click-Use Licence (DfES 2006); Table 5.2 adapted from Figure 3, Copyright © The Attic Youth Center and Carrie Jacobs, PhD; Table 5.4 adapted from Literacy Instruction for Language-Minority Students: The Transition Years in *The Elementary School Journal*, 96, pub University of Chicago

Press, Copyright © 1996 by the University of Chicago Press (Gersten, R. 1996); Table 5.5 adapted from *Londoners on-line: An analysis of levels of home internet access from the London Household Survey 2002*, Greater London Authority (Mayor of London 2003); Table 6.2 and Figure 7.2 from *Learning Theories: An Educational Perspective, 4th Edition*, Pearson Education, Inc. (Schunk, D. H. 2004); Figure 7.3 from *Cognition, 3rd Edition*, Pearson Education, Inc. (Ashcraft, M. H. 2002); Table 7.3 adapted from *Cognitive strategy instruction that really improves children's academic performance, 2nd edition*, Brookline Books (Pressley, M. and Woloshyn, V. 1995); Figure 7.5 adapted from *Psychology, 4th Edition*, Worth Publishers (Gray, P. 2002); Figure 8.3 from http://cmapskm.ihmc.us/servlet/ SBReadResourceServlet?rid=1064009710027_1483270 340_27090&partName=htmltext at http://cmap.ihmc. us/, The Institute for Human and Machine Cognition; Figure 8.5 from *Mathematics with Reason: The Emergent Approach to Primary Maths*, reproduced by permission of Hodder & Stoughton Ltd. (Atkinson, S. ed. 1992); Figure 8.6 reproduced with permission of Lawrence Erlbaum Associates, Inc., adapted from Problem-Solving Strategies by M. L. Gick, *Educational Psychologist*, 21, 1986; permission conveyed through Copyright Clearance Center, Inc.; Figure 8.7 from *Torrance Tests of Creative Thinking*, Scholastic Testing Service, Inc. (Torrance, E. P. 1966, 2000); Figure 8.9 Institute for Human Machine Cognition Cmap Tools homepage from http://cmap.ihmc.us/. Reprinted with permission from the IHMC; Figure 8.10 from *Non-Fiction Case Studies: Y5 Non-chronological report writing*, The National Literacy Strategy, reproduced under the terms of the Click-Use Licence (DfES 2001); Figure 9.1 reproduced with permission of Lawrence Erlbaum Associates, Inc., adapted from Social-Self Interaction and Achievement Behaviour by D. H. Schunk, *Educational Psychologist*, 34, 1999; permission conveyed through Copyright Clearance Center; Figure 9.2 adapted from *Educational Psychology, 3rd Canadian Edition*, reprinted with permission by Pearson Education Canada Inc. and Philip Winne (Woolfolk, A. E. *et al.* 2006); Table 9.2 adapted from *Classroom Instruction and Management*, The McGraw-Hill Companies, Inc. (Arends, R. I. 1997); Table 9.3 adapted from *Instructional Conversations and Their Classroom Application*, pub National Center for Research on Cultural Diversity and Second Language Learning, reprinted by permission of Center for Research on Education, Diversity and Excellence (CREDE) (Goldenberg, C. 1991); Table 9.4 from Kneedler, P. (1985) California Assesses Critical Thinking (p. 277), in A. Costa (ed.) *Developing Minds: A Resource Book for Teaching Thinking*, Alexandria, Virginia: ASCD. Reprinted with permission. The Association for Supervision and Curriculum Development is a worldwide community of educators advocating sound policies and sharing best practices to achieve the success of each learner. To learn more, visit ASCD at www.ascd.org; Table 9.5 adapted from *Reconceptualizing Learning for Restructured Schools*. Paper presented at the Annual Meeting of the American Educational Research Association, April 1992, reprinted by permission of Hermine H. Marshall (Marshall, H. H. 1992); Figure 10.1 from *Motivation and Personality, 2nd Edition*, pub Harper and Row, reprinted by permission of Ann Kaplan (Maslow, A. 1970); Table 10.2 from *Motivation in Education: Theory, Research and Applications, 3rd Edition*, Pearson Education, Inc. (Pintrich, P. R. *et al.* 2008); Table 10.3 reproduced with permission of Sage Publications, Inc., adapted from *Human Motivation: Metaphors, Theories, and Research* by B. Weiner, Copyright 2005; permission conveyed through Copyright Clearance Center, Inc.; Table 11.1 from Learning from Peers: Beyond the Rhetoric of Positive Results in *Educational Psychology Review*, 6, Springer Science and Business Media (O'Donnell, A. M. and O'Kelly, J. 1994); Table 11.2 adapted from *Cooperative Learning*, copied and adapted with permission from Kagan Publishing (Kagan, S. 1994); Figure 11.3 from I just don't like the whole thing about war!: encouraging the expression of political literacy among primary pupils as a vehicle for promoting education for active citizenship. Paper presented at the European Conference on Educational Research, University of Crete, 22–25 September, reprinted by permission of Ross Deuchar and Henry Maitles, University of Strathclyde (Deuchar, R. and Maitles, H. 2004); Table 11.3 reproduced with permission of Lawrence Erlbaum Associates, Inc., adapted from Implications of cognitive approaches to peer learning for teacher education by A. Woolfolk Hoy and M. Tschannen-Moran in *Cognitive Perspectives on Peer Learning* edited by A. O'Donnell and A. King, Copyright 1999; permission conveyed through Copyright Clearance Center, Inc.; Figure 11.4 from Evaluating Classroom Charters from http://homepage.ntlworld.com/i-hedley/sen/chartstudy. htm, reprinted by permission of the author, Ian Hedley; Table 11.4 from Structuring Peer Interaction to Promote High-level Cognitive Processing in *Theory into Practice*, 41(1), College of Education, The Ohio State University (King, A. 2002); Tables 11.6 and 12.3 adapted from *Secondary Classroom Management: Lessons from Research and Practice, 2nd Edition*, The McGraw-Hill Companies, Inc. (Weinstein, C. S. 2003); Table 11.8 adapted from Warning Signs, http://apahelpcenter.org/featuredtopics/feature.php?

id=38, American Psychological Association; Table 11.9 from Making Violence Unacceptable in *Educational Leadership*, 56(3), Association for Supervision and Curriculum Development (Rembolt, C. 1998); Figure 12.1 from Peterhead Academy Behaviour Policy, http://www.peterheadacademy.aberdeenshire.sch.uk/assets/pdf/pages_policies_parents_001.pdf, reprinted by permission of Peterhead Academy; Tables 12.1 and 12.2 adapted from *Teachers' and Pupils' Days in the Primary Classroom. The Scottish Council for Research in Education. Research Report No. 93*, December, The Scottish Council for Research in Education (now part of The Faculty of Education, University of Glasgow) (McPake, J. *et al.* 1999); Figure 12.2 adapted from *Rediscovering Hope: Our Greatest Teaching Strategy*, Solution Tree (Curwin, R. 1992); Table 12.4 reproduced with permission of Lawrence Erlbaum Associates, Inc., from Tips for Managing a Computer Lab by C. M. Bolick and J. M. Cooper in *Handbook of Classroom Management: Research, Practice, and Contemporary Issues* edited by C. Evertson and C. Weinstein, Copyright 2006; permission conveyed through Copyright Clearance Center, Inc.; Table 13.1 adapted from *How to Write and Use Instructional Objectives, 6th Edition*, Pearson Education, Inc. (Gronlund, N. E. 2000); Figure 13.2 from http://www.feniton.devon.sch.uk/projects/teacher.htm, reprinted by permission of Feniton C. of E. Primary School; Table 13.4 from *Inspiring Active Learning: A Handbook for Teachers*, Association for Supervision and Curriculum Development (Harmin, M. 1994); Table 13.5 adapted from Questioning Skills in *Classroom Teaching Skills: A Handbook , 3rd Edition* edited by J. Cooper, Houghton Mifflin Company (Sadker, M. and Sadker, D. 1986); Table 14.4 adapted from Preparing adolescents with high-incidence disabilities for high-stakes testing with strategy instruction in *Preventing School Failure*, 49(2), pub Heldref Publications, reprinted by permission of the Helen Dwight Reid Educational Foundation (Carter, E. W. *et al.* 2005); Figure 14.5 adapted extracts from Staining CE Voluntary Controlled Primary School from QCA Online http://www.qca.org.uk/9115_9288.html, reprinted by permission of Qualifications and Curriculum Authority; Figure 15.1 from Paulson, F. L., Paulson, P. and Meyers, C. (1991) What Makes a Portfolio a Portfolio? *Educational Leadership*, 48(5), p. 63. Reprinted with permission. The Association for Supervision and Curriculum Development is a worldwide community of educators advocating sound policies and sharing best practices to achieve the success of each learner. To learn more, visit ASCD at www.ascd.org; Figure 15.2 from *Classroom Assessment: Concepts and Applications, 5th Edition*, The McGraw-Hill Companies, Inc. (Airasian, P. W. 2005); Table 15.2 adapted from *Classroom Assessment: Concepts and Applications, 5th Edition*, The McGraw-Hill Companies, Inc. (Airasian, P. W. 2005); Figure 15.3 adapted from Johnson, D. W. and Johnson, R. T. (1996) The Role of Cooperative Learning in Assessing and Communicating Student Learning (p. 41) in T. Guskey (ed.) *ASCD 1996 Yearbook: Communicating Student Learning*, Alexandria, Virginia: ASCD. Reprinted with permission. The Association for Supervision and Curriculum Development is a worldwide community of educators advocating sound policies and sharing best practices to achieve the success of each learner. To learn more, visit ASCD at www.ascd.org; Table 15.3 adapted from *Classroom Teaching Skills, 7th Edition*, Houghton Mifflin Company (Cooper, J. 2003); Figure 15.4 adapted from Lake, K. and Kafka, K. (1996) Reporting Methods in Grades K-8 (p. 104) in T. Guskey (ed.) *ASCD 1996 Yearbook: Communicating Student Learning*, Alexandria, Virginia: ASCD. Reprinted with permission. The Association for Supervision and Curriculum Development is a worldwide community of educators advocating sound policies and sharing best practices to achieve the success of each learner. To learn more, visit ASCD at www.ascd.org; Table 15.4 from Wiggins, G. W. (April, 1989) Characteristics of Authentic Tests, *Educational Leadership*, 46(7), p. 44. Reprinted with permission. The Association for Supervision and Curriculum Development is a worldwide community of educators advocating sound policies and sharing best practices to achieve the success of each learner. To learn more, visit ASCD at www.ascd.org.

We are grateful to the following for permission to reproduce the following texts:

Chapter 1, p. 4 adapted extract from What do Educational Psychologists Do? from http://www.aep.org.uk/Careers/body_careers.html, Association of Educational Psychologists; Chapter 1, p. 5 extract from http://www.politics.co.uk/issuebrief/education/schools/a-levels/testing-in-schools-$366569.htm accessed 16 December 2002, Adfero Ltd.; Chapter 1, p. 8 adapted extracts from My Best Teacher column in *Times Educational Supplement*, 24 November 2006, reprinted by permission of Heather Neill (Neill, H. 2006); Chapter 2 Discussion Point, Brain-based Education, abridged extract from In search of . . . brain-based education in *Phi Delta Kappan*, 80, Phi Delta Kappa International, Inc. (Bruer, J. T. 1999); Chapter 3 Discussion Point, What Should Schools Do to Encourage Learners' Self-Esteem? extracts from Beane, J. A. (1991) Sorting Out the Self-Esteem Controversy, *Educational*

Leadership, 49(1), pp. 25–30. Reprinted with permission. The Association for Supervision and Curriculum Development is a worldwide community of educators advocating sound policies and sharing best practices to achieve the success of each learner. To learn more, visit ASCD at www.ascd.org; Chapter 4 Discussion Point, Is streaming and setting effective? adapted extracts from Streaming and setting – does it make a difference to achievement? from http://www.literacytrust. org.uk/Research/stream.html, National Literacy Trust; Chapter 4, pp. 151–2 adapted extract from Assessments and Statements: CSIE Summary, updated June 2005, available at http://csie.org.uk, Centre for Studies on Inclusive Education (CSIE); Chapter 4, p. 152 extract from *Special Educational Needs*, reproduced under the terms of the Click-Use Licence (Teaching in England 2006); Chapter 4, p. 153 extract from *Valuing People: A new strategy for learning disability for the 21st century*, reproduced under the terms of the Click-Use Licence (Department of Health 2001); Chapter 4 Focus on Practice, Working with learners with Dyslexia, adapted from *Learning and teaching for dyslexic children*, reproduced under the terms of the Click-Use Licence (DfES 2005); Chapter 4 Focus on Practice, Working with children with dyscalculia, adapted extract from *Dyscalculia: School Support*, from http://www.snapassessment.com/INFdyscal.htm, reproduced by permission of Hodder & Stoughton Ltd. (SNAP 2006); Chapter 4, p. 173 extract from *Guidance on teaching gifted and talented pupils*, reproduced under the terms of the Click-Use Licence (DfES 2002); Chapter 4, p. 176 extract from *The National Curriculum for England*, Crown Copyright material is reproduced with the permission of the Controller of HMSO and the Queen's Printer for Scotland (DfEE/QCA 1999); Chapter 5, p. 186 extracts from *Ethnicity and Education: the Evidence on Minority Ethnic Pupils aged 5–16*. Research topic paper 0208-2006DOM-EN, reproduced under the terms of the Click-Use Licence (DfES 2006); Chapter 5, p. 187 extract from School, family and community relationships, with reference to families of Bangladeshi origin in the North East of England. Paper presented at the British Educational Research Association Annual Conference, Heriot-Watt University, 11–13 September, European Conference on Educational Research, University of Hamburg, 17–20 September and European Research Network About Parents and Education, University of Gdansk, 4 September, reprinted by permission of Gill Crozier (Crozier, G. 2003); Chapter 5, p. 193 extract from *Tackling poverty and extending opportunity: The modernization of Britain's tax and benefit system, no. 4*, reproduced under the terms of the Click-Use Licence (HM Treasury 1999); Chapter 5,

Zoe's Story extracts from article My smart school still failed me in *The Observer*, 12 September 2004, reprinted by permission of Zoe Smith (Smith, Z. 2004); Chapter 5 Discussion Point, Do Boys and Girls Learn Differently? extract from In search of . . . brain-based education in *Phi Delta Kappan*, 80, Phi Delta Kappa International, Inc. (Bruer, J. T. 1999); Chapter 5 Focus on Practice, Building learning communities, adapted extract from School/Family/Community Partnerships: Caring for Children We Share in *Phi Delta Kappan*, 76, Phi Delta Kappa International, Inc. (Epstein, J. L. 1995); Chapter 6 Discussion Point, Should Learners Be Rewarded for Learning? extract from Sticking Up for Rewards in *Phi Delta Kappan*, 74, Phi Delta Kappa International, Inc. (Chance, P. 1993); Chapter 6 Discussion Point, Should Learners Be Rewarded for Learning? extracts from Rewards versus Learning: A Response to Paul Chance in *Phi Delta Kappan*, 74, Phi Delta Kappa International, Inc. (Kohn, A. 1993); Chapter 8, p. 358 extract from *The Implementation of the National Numeracy Strategy*, reproduced under the terms of the Click-Use Licence (DfES 1998); Chapter 8 Focus on Practice, Developing expert pupils, adapted extract from Research Synthesis on Study Skills in *Educational Leadership*, 39(2), Association for Supervision and Curriculum Development (Armbruster, B. B. and Anderson, T. H. 1981); Chapter 9 Focus on Practice, Applying constructivist principles, adapted extract from Framing constructivism in practice as the negotiation of dilemmas; An analysis of the conceptual, pedagogical, cultural, and political challenges facing teachers in *Review of Educational Research*, 72, Sage Publications, Inc. (Windschitl, M. 2002); Chapter 10 Focus on Practice, Building on interests, extract from *Motivation in Education: Theory, Research and Applications, 2nd Edition*, Pearson Education, Inc. (Pintrich, P. and Schunk, D. 2002); Chapter 10, p. 468 abridged extract from An interview with Jere Brophy in *Educational Psychology Review*, 15, pp. 199–211, with kind permission from Springer Science and Business Media (Gaedke, B. and Shaughnessy, M. F. 2003); Chapter 11, p. 494 and p. 496 extract from King, A. (2002) Structuring Peer Interaction to Promote High-level Cognitive Processing. *Theory into Practice*, 41(1), pp. 34-35. Copyright 2002 by the College of Education, The Ohio State University. All rights reserved; Chapter 11, p. 508 extract from http://www.teachernet.gov.uk/casestudies/ reproduced under the terms of the Click-Use Licence; Chapter 11, p. 508 extract from Evaluating Classroom Charters from http://homepage.ntlworld.com/i-hedley/ sen/chartstudy. htm, reprinted by permission of the author, Ian Hedley; Chapter 11 Focus on Practice, Handling potentially explosive situations, adapted extract from *Secondary Classroom Management: Lessons from Research and Practice, 2nd Edition*, The McGraw-Hill Companies, Inc. (Weinstein, C. S. 2003); Chapter 15 Focus on Practice, Writing essay-type test items, adapted extract from *Assessment in Schools, 2nd Edition*, Blackwell Publishing Ltd. (Satterley, D. 1998); Chapter 15, p. 672 extract from Assessment in *Classroom Teaching Skills, 7th Edition*, edited by J. Cooper, Copyright © 2003 by Houghton Mifflin Company, reprinted with permission (TenBrink, T. D. 2003); Chapter 15, p. 690 adapted extracts from A factorial experiment in teachers' written feedback on pupil homework: Changing teacher behaviour a little rather than a lot in *Journal of Educational Psychology*, 77, pp. 162–73, pub APA, reprinted by permission of Maria Cardelle-Elawar and American Psychological Association (Elawar, M. C. and Corno, L. 1985); Chapter 15 Focus on Practice, Consultations, adapted extract from *The Successful Classroom: Management Strategies for Regular and Special Education Teachers*, Teachers College Press, Columbia University (Fromberg, D. P. and Driscoll, M. 1985).

Photographs: p2 Corbis/Gideon Mendel; p12 Corbis/Image 100; p14 Topfoto/Image Works; p19 Punchstock/Banana Stock; p27, Getty Images/Martin Riedal; p38 Getty Images/AFP; p54 Martyn Chillmaid; p62 Alamy/Sally & Richard Greenhill; p79 Corbis/James Grill; p90 Getty Images/Taxi; p100 Alamy/Photofusion; p132 Getty Images/Image Bank; p138 Report Digital/Ray Peters; p155 Alamy/Photofusion; p192 Report Digital/Jess Hurd; p197 Report Digital/Ray Peters; p209 Kobal/BEND IT FILMS/FILM COUNCIL/THE KOBAL COLLECTION/PARRY, CHRISTINE; p242 Getty Images/Nick Clements; p254 Corbis/Roy McMahon; p268 Alamy/Dennis McDonald; p272 Photo Edit Inc/Michael Newman; p312 Getty Images/Image Bank; p320 Alamy/Andrew Fox; p328 Corbis/Martyn Goddard; p339 Alamy/Ian Miles, Flashpoint Pictures; p347 Alamy/Ian Shaw; p357 Alamy/Janine Wiedel; p398 Topfoto/Topham Picturepoint; p400 Alamy/Janine Wiedel; p417 Report Digital/Paul Box; p440 Alamy/Apex News & Picture Agency; p452 Corbis/Thinkstock; p466 Corbis/LWA-Dann Tardif; p482 Getty Images/Stone; p486 Topfoto/Guidi; p500 Corbis/Don Hammond/Design Pictures; p523 Getty Images/Doug Corrance; p527 Report Digital/Joanne O'Brien; p544 Getty Images/Riser; p551 Report Digital/Paul Herrmann; p575 author photo; p585 Alamy/Paul Doyle; p600 Getty Images/Image Bank; p619 Getty Images/Taxi; p634 Corbis/BrynColton/Assignments Photographers; p650 Punchstock/Digital Vision; p661 Corbis/Thinkstock; p676 Corbis/Image 100; p689 Alamy/Photofusion.

In some instances we have been unable to trace the owners of copyright material, and we would appreciate any information that would enable us to do so.

Overview

Like many students, you may begin reading this text with a mixture of anticipation and wariness. Perhaps you are required to take psychology of education as part of a programme in teacher education, speech therapy, nursing, counselling or a course in applied psychology. You may have chosen a module or unit on the psychology of education from those considered appropriate for this part of your course. Whatever your reason for enrolling, you probably have questions about teaching, schools, pupils – or even about yourself – that you hope this text may answer. We have written this first edition of *Psychology in Education* with questions such as these in mind.

After a brief introduction to the world of the teacher, we will turn to a discussion of educational psychology itself. How can principles identified by educational psychologists benefit teachers, therapists, parents and others who are interested in teaching and learning? What exactly is the content of educational psychology, and where does this information come from?

By the time you have completed this chapter, you should be able to answer the following questions:

- **What is the connection between national standards and the *Every Child Matters* national agenda?**
- **Does teaching matter?**
- **What is good teaching?**
- **What do expert teachers know?**
- **What are the greatest concerns of beginning teachers?**
- **Why should I study the psychology of education?**
- **What roles do theory and research play in this field?**

In the Classroom

It is Nandini's second year as a teacher at Bushmore (4–13) Combined School. The local education authority (LEA) has just received money from a private foundation to give three awards (substantial travel bursaries) to staff at Bushmore for 'excellence in teaching'. The head teacher wants the teachers' recommendations for recipients of these awards, so a committee is formed, composed of experienced teachers and one 'beginner' – Nandini is asked by the head teacher to serve on the committee and she doesn't feel able to refuse. All week, the staff room has been buzzing with discussion about the awards. Some teachers are suspicious – they fear the decisions will be purely political. Others are glad to see individuals' efforts in teaching honoured. Names are mentioned as 'certain winners' and a few teachers who seldom speak to Nandini have become very friendly ever since the committee membership was announced. The first meeting is next week. Nandini knows she must be as objective as possible. What does she need to know about teaching to make a judgement here? What are the indicators of excellent teaching and do different styles of teaching provide different answers? How should she prepare for the meeting?

Group Activity

With three or four other members of your group, draw a concept map or web that graphically depicts 'good teaching'. For an example of a concept map, see Figure 8.3 on page 344.

Introduction

In this first chapter, we begin with education – more specifically, with teaching today and the kind of legislation and educational policies that impact on the work of every teacher. Teachers have been both criticised as ineffective and lauded as the best hope for young people. Do teachers make a difference in pupils' learning? What characterises good teaching? Only when you are aware of the challenges and possibilities of teaching and learning today can you appreciate the contributions of psychology to any study of education. It is worth noting at this point how we will use the terms *'educational psychology'* and *'psychology of education'*. In a UK setting we are wary of using the term educational psychology as it can refer to the broad area of training and work of educational psychologists who apply psychological theories, research and techniques to help children and young people who may have learning difficulties, emotional or behavioural problems.

Educational psychologists:

- *work with children and young people, mainly under 19 years old, experiencing difficulties (e.g. learning, emotional, behaviour problems) to promote their educational and psychological development;*

- *are employed mostly by local education authorities, but some are self-employed and work as consultants for social services departments, voluntary bodies, parents and others; and*

- *work mainly in consultation with parents, teachers, social workers, doctors, education officers and other people involved in the education and care of children and young people.*

Adapted from http://www.aep.org.uk/Careers/body-careers.html

In contrast, the psychology of education, is the study of how psychological theories and research inform and support the work of education professionals working across the whole range of teaching and learning settings. This text supports the study of the *psychology of education* rather than the specific knowledge and skills required for work as an educational psychologist.

Educational psychology

Refers to the broad area of training and work of educational psychologists who apply psychological theories, research and techniques to help children and young people who may have learning difficulties, emotional or behavioural problems.

Psychology of education

The discipline concerned with teaching and learning processes; applies the methods and theories of psychology to teaching and learning and has its own methods and theories as well.

National Standards of Attainment and *Every Child Matters*

Excellent teaching has to be defined within the national context of expectations about schools and teachers. Across the world, governments have made wide-ranging changes to the ways schools are governed and organised and, more particularly, the ways in which schools are held to account for the outcomes of the public investment in schooling. Historically, English schools have been held to account by the standards achieved by pupils at the ages of 11, 16 and 18 years old, in public examinations. As you can see from the quotation below, testing and assessment of pupils in England now takes place much more frequently. Such judgements about pupils, and thus schools and teachers, have been commonplace in schools in England and some other parts of the UK for many years.

Introduced under the Education Reform Act 1988 many pupils in the UK still undergo four sets of national tests, corresponding to attainment targets under four 'Key Stages'. Testing against Key Stage 1 targets takes place at age 7; testing against KS2 targets take place at 11; testing against KS3 targets takes place at age 14; and testing against KS4 targets, that is, GCSE or equivalent external examinations, takes place at age 16, the end of compulsory secondary education. Originally known as 'SATs' (Standard Assessment Tasks), since 1991 the tests have been formally called 'National Curriculum Tests'.

http://www.politics.co.uk/issuebrief/education/schools/a-levels/testing-in-schools-$366569.htm accessed July 2007

Furthermore, the *UK Government Circular 11/98* gave advice on implementing the regulations on target-setting for pupil attainment in the National Curriculum tests made under section 19 of the Education Act 1997 and the Education (School Performance Targets) (England) Regulations 1998/1532. The regulations applied to the governing bodies of all maintained schools in England, including special schools that, in the autumn term 1998, were required to set and publish targets for performance in the summer term 2000, and from September 2000, schools had to publish their annual performance against those targets. The education system in Scotland has marked differences to that in the rest of the UK, including a different series of school examinations based on a much less centralised curriculum. In the Netherlands secondary pupils progress each year from one class to the next or repeat a year if their end-of-year grades are 'not sufficient'. By law, Dutch secondary schools are also legally obliged to publish examination results and drop-out rates, and since 1998 have also received a report from the inspection services that includes comparisons with similar secondary schools in the region. This is another example of a government initiative attempting to provide parents with more information about standards and to promote what is seen as 'good practice' in schools.

Similar requirements in many European countries have had a profound effect upon the way in which schools and individual teachers are judged by parents, local communities and employers. In England, good teachers are judged to be those who contribute to the achievement of the targets set through the appropriate application of approved styles of teaching disseminated in a range of national teaching and learning strategies. Teachers who achieve or exceed their targets for pupil gains in public examinations, by teaching in the approved way, are often reclassified as advanced skills teachers (ASTs) or leading teachers, and have their salaries and professional standing enhanced.

Teachers also have to take on board a new initiative that will have an equally profound effect upon how society views the worth of their contribution. In 2003, the UK government published a green paper called *Every Child Matters*. This was published alongside the formal response to the report into the death of Victoria Climbié, a young girl who was horrifically abused and tortured, and eventually killed by her great aunt and the man with whom they lived. Following the consultation, the government published *Every Child Matters: the Next Steps*, and passed the Children Act 2004.

Every Child Matters: Change for Children (DfES, 2004) is a new approach in England to the well-being of children and young people from birth to age 19. Its main implication for teachers is that they are now viewed as a leading member of a professional team working in and through extended school provision. An excellent teacher is one who can work well as a member of a team of social workers, police officers and health workers, and who leads a classroom team of counsellors, advanced skills teaching and learning support staff, to ensure the well-being of children. *Every Child Matters* defines the rights of children to: be healthy; stay safe; enjoy and achieve; make a positive contribution; and achieve economic well-being. But how will this change the way we judge teachers and good teaching? One answer is through a personal anecdote. One of the authors attended a one-day conference in London on the implications of *Every Child Matters* for the design of initial teacher education (ITE) courses. A London primary school head teacher addressed an audience of other head teachers and ITE course leaders: 'On my staff is a teacher, an excellent classroom practitioner who is well-respected by her pupils and their parents. However, she finds it very difficult to work as a member of a team and so because of the changes brought about by *Every Child Matters*, I am going to have to let her go.'

In your Group Activity (see p. 3), did your group include 'achieving improvement targets for pupil attainment', or 'teamwork and team leading' in a concept map of what constitutes 'good teaching'? If so, you are already well on the way to considering the rapidly changing expectations of classroom teachers. If not, this is hardly surprising and you shouldn't feel too disappointed. We doubt that serving classroom practitioners have yet to appreciate the full implications for them and their schools of new attitudes to what constitutes excellent classroom practice.

Many teaching professionals are now questioning not only the changes to teaching brought about by the current testing, targets and school tables regime but also how such a regime is compatible with more recent initiatives in personalised learning, inclusion and collaboration. Rona Tutt, winner of the Leadership in Teaching Award 2003 and, in 2004, awarded an OBE for her services to special needs education, writes:

> It is hard to see how anyone can believe that the current testing regime and all that goes with it is compatible with the ECM agenda, which emphasises treating people as individuals, giving them an educational experience they will enjoy (and happier children, as we know, are more likely to learn), helping them to feel their contribution is valued, and that the education they receive will give them the start they need to play a full part in society as an economically independent adult. When it comes to personalised learning, the whole regime of tables, targets and tests becomes an even greater absurdity. (2006: 214)

We started the first chapter of this text describing the target regime and the *Every Child Matters* agenda, because they show the tensions in views held of what makes good teachers and what constitutes good teaching. As Tutt notes, 'it is impossible to implement ideas that are diametrically opposed to each other' (2006: 215) yet the good teacher is expected so to do. Given the amount of factors affecting how well young people do at school, we need to analyse the role of teachers and the theories of educational psychology that underpin excellent classroom practice. Before looking at what is good classroom teaching and defining good teaching, let's examine a more basic question: with all this testing, these targets, tables and agendas, do teachers make any difference?

STOP AND THINK

What are the (real and ideal) goals of education? What does it mean to be an educated person? What makes a teacher effective? Describe the most effective teacher you ever had. How do you learn best? What do you hope to gain from this course? Your answers will provide the basis for developing a philosophy of teaching.

Do Teachers Make a Difference?

For a while, some researchers reported findings suggesting that wealth and social status, not teaching, were the major factors determining who learned in schools (e.g. Coleman, 1966). In fact, much of the early research on teaching was conducted by educational psychologists who refused to accept these claims that teachers were pow-erless in the face of poverty and societal problems (Wittrock, 1986).

How could you decide if teaching really does makes a difference? You could look to your own experience. Were there teachers who had an impact on your life? Perhaps one of your teachers influenced your decision to take advantage of higher education. Your experiences provided a very useful benchmark when measuring the potential im-pact on lives of a good teacher and inspirational teaching. However, one of the pur-poses of educational psychology in general, and this text in particular, is to go beyond individual experiences and testimonies, powerful as they are, to examine larger groups. Three studies speak of the powerful effect of teachers on the lives of learners. The first explored how teachers ensured that Black Caribbean pupils did well. The sec-ond examined how teachers' beliefs about their ability to make a difference made a difference to the attainment of their pupils. The third was a large-scale study of thou-sands of pupils and teachers.

Achievement of Black Caribbean pupils

In an attempt to identify significant common themes for success in raising the achieve-ment in British schools of pupils from Black Caribbean backgrounds Feyisa Demie from the Research and Statistics Unit, Lambeth Education, London drew evidence from 13 case study schools (Demie, 2004). She identified teachers who had high ex-pectations of their pupils, who created 'a mesmerising curriculum' using creative intu-ition to deepen the quality of pupils' learning, who developed a highly inclusive curriculum, with strong links with the community, and who demonstrated a strong commitment to equal opportunities and a clear stand on racism. These teachers en-sured that Black Caribbean pupils did well and bucked the national trend. These teachers made a difference.

Collective teacher efficacy

Collective teacher efficacy (CTE) refers to the extent to which a school has a collective perception that teachers make a difference to the attainment of their pupils over and above the impact of the pupils' social circumstances. Karen Parker and Elizabeth Hannah of Dundee City Council, Scotland and Keith Topping of the University of Dundee (Parker *et al.*, 2006) studied 66 teachers in 15 primary schools. Significant re-lationships were found between socioeconomic status and attainment in reading and mathematics (but not writing) and, more excitingly, there was a significant relation-ship between how teachers collectively felt they could make a difference and their children's attainment in reading and writing (but not mathematics). Collec-tive teacher efficacy appeared to have a much stronger independent impact on children's attainment in writing than the children's socioeconomic status. Two up to the teachers!

Fifteen Thousand Hours

One of the most influential and respected studies of the impact of schools and teach-ers on the lives of young learners was published in 1979 and took its title from the av-erage amount of time children spend in schooling in the UK. *Fifteen Thousand Hours: Secondary Schools and their Effects on Children* is written by Michael Rutter and a group of research colleagues at the University of London, and gives a remarkable account of what goes on in schools and what the effects are likely to be. Although written over

⇄ Connect and Extend

For another perspective on teacher quality and teacher preparation, see Blanton *et al.* (2006), 'Models and measures of beginning teacher quality', in *Journal of Special Education*, *40*(2) (June), pp. 115–127, or Borko *et al.* (2000), 'Teacher education does matter: A situative view of learning to teach secondary mathematics', in *Educational Psychologist, 35*, pp. 193–206.

25 years ago, it is really timeless. The book classifies the effects of schools in four fields: achievement, attendance, behaviour and delinquency. Each of those fields is studied in the context of 12 inner-city schools. Through measurement and analysis of virtually every aspect of the school environment, Rutter and his colleagues help us to understand the impact of the smallest of teachers' behaviours. For example, attention is given to the setting and checking of homework; disciplinary interventions in lessons; expectations of pupil performance; interactions with whole classes and individual pupils; punctuality and standards of behaviour set; skills and styles; organisation and experience. It is clear that teachers can and do make a difference to the achievements of learners and their life chances. Game, set and match to the teachers!

Changing people's lives

After over 30 years working in classrooms you might think confronting the awesome opportunities and responsibilities of being a teacher might surprise us. Yesterday, Alex (a student who had just completed the teacher training programme I lead) came face to face with me in a university coffee bar. 'You know I wouldn't have done this without you?' she said in mock accusation. She had passed her final teaching practice at the second attempt and her face shone with pride, promise and pleasure.

> *I feel like this is the start of my life and it's because you believed in me. I came to you wanting to give up – it was too hard, too big a mountain to climb. You believed in me and you made me believe in myself. You saw the teacher in me. Now I am a teacher, a real teacher and I get the chance to do for others, what you did for me. Thank you!*
> *(Followed by a very big hug.)*

Did this make me special or extraordinary? Of course it did! But it is just one more example of how our pupils and students believe we can and do change their lives. Here's another. It is taken from a recent edition of the *Times Educational Supplement*. David Oyelowo is a young award-winning Shakespearean and television actor.

> *We went back to Nigeria when I was six for family reasons, but returned after seven years when the political situation changed. I then went to Highbury Grove Boys' School and joined the youth theatre group run by the National Theatre's Education Department. This prompted me to take theatre studies as an A-level subject when I moved to Islington Sixth Form College, and it was there that I was taken under the wing of Gill Poster. She was hugely encouraging. Gill was beautiful, tall and dark with a slight northern accent, and everyone fancied her. Other teachers were good, but they were battle-scarred; she was genuinely enthusiastic and I think that was infectious.*
>   *She cracked plays open in a way that related to me. She loved the theatre and would often direct productions outside school hours, not necessarily for public performance, but scenes, devised pieces that we worked on and showed to the school. She was always generous with her time. She said: 'Look, you should consider drama school,' and I got into the London Academy of Dramatic Art on a scholarship. Gill has come to see every single play I've done – and that really means something to me. She bubbles with pride over my acting. She also understands the craft of it. Gill is so special because she was the first person who saw a spark of any kind in me. (Adapted from TES, 24 November 2006)*

Effective teachers who establish positive relationships with their pupils appear to be a powerful force in learner's lives and those who have problems seem to benefit the most from good teaching. What makes a teacher effective? What is good teaching?

What is Good Teaching?

Educators, psychologists, philosophers, novelists, journalists, filmmakers, mathematicians, scientists, historians, policymakers and parents, to name only a few groups, have examined this question; there are hundreds of answers. And good teaching is not confined to classrooms – it occurs in homes and hospitals, museums and sales meetings, offices and summer activity weeks. In this book, we are primarily concerned with teaching in classrooms, but much of what you will learn applies to other settings as well.

What makes a good teacher? They must deal with a wide range of student abilities and challenges: different languages, different home situations and different abilities and disabilities. They must adapt instruction and assessment to pupils' needs. They must make the most abstract concepts, such as valency (in chemistry, the combining power of an atom) or logarithms (arithmetic exponents to aid calculation), real and understandable for their particular pupils. There is also the challenge of incorporating new connected technologies and techniques. Teachers must use them appropriately to accomplish important goals, not just to entertain the pupils. The whole time that these experts are navigating through the academic material, they also are taking care of the emotional needs of their pupils, propping up sagging self-esteem and encouraging responsibility. If we followed these individuals from the first day of class, we would see that they carefully plan and teach the basic procedures for living and learning in their classes. They can efficiently collect and correct homework, regroup pupils, give directions, distribute materials, collect lunch money and deal with disruptions – and do all of this while also making a mental note to find out why one of their pupils is so tired.

Connect and Extend

You will get a wider perspective on the issues addressed in this book by reading the respected educational press. One widely read periodical is the *Times Education Supplement*.

See the Companion **WEB** Website (Web Link 1.1).

So what is good teaching?

Is good teaching science or art, teacher-centered lecture or pupil-centered discovery, the application of general theories or the invention of situation-specific practices? Is a good teacher a good explainer or a good questioner, a 'sage on the stage' or a 'guide on the side'? These debates have raged for years. In your other education classes, you will probably encounter criticisms of the scientific, teacher-centered, theory-based, lecturing sages. You will be encouraged to believe in teachers as artistic, inventive, pupil-centered, questioning guides. Is this the right path? Let's see what the arguments are.

Is teaching theory-based science, inventive art form or serendipity?

One position is that teaching is a theory-based science. Psychologists have spent decades studying how children think and feel, how learning occurs, what influences motivation and how teaching affects learning. These general and abstract concepts apply to a wide range of situations. Why should teachers have to reinvent all this knowledge? Other educators believe that the mark of an excellent teacher is not the ability to apply theories, but the artistry of being reflective – thoughtful and inventive – about teaching (Schon, 1983). Educators who adopt this view believe teaching 'is specific with respect to task, time, place, participants, and content, and that different subjects vary in those specifics' (Leinhardt, 2001: 334). Thus, teaching is so complex, according to this view, that it must be reinvented with every new lesson and each new class.

To illustrate this continuous recreation of the act of teaching read the following accounts by two teachers of their best lesson. First, Roger Humphries (Key Stage 2

Reflective

Thoughtful and inventive. Reflective teachers think back over situations to analyse what they did and why and to consider how they might improve learning for their pupils.

Manager at St John's C of E Primary School in Hindley Green, Lancashire (*TES* magazine, 24 November 2006).

My best lesson was not actually my best, but someone else's. I was covering for a colleague in a mixed Year 3/4 class. They were a lovely lot and the absent teacher had said that I could read them Daft Jack and the Bean Stalk *from the Seriously Silly series at the end of the lesson as a treat, if they deserved it. The class had tried hard, and even though I didn't know the Silly series, I opened the book and began to read. By the fourth page, I was unable to continue. Tears of laughter were rolling down my cheeks and I could hardly force the words out.*

'Sir, you're rubbish,' Ashley called out, 'give me the book.' Pathetically, I handed it to him and he drew a chair to the front. He started again, at the beginning, while I sat giggling like an imbecile, paralysed by Laurence Anholt's offbeat humour.

The lesson was fantastic, led by Ashley – a nine-year-old. The children enjoyed and learned, while I corpsed in the corner. If stimulating an interest in reading had been my objective, I would have succeeded hands down. For the rest of the term, children from that class would appear at odd moments with a silly story and urge me to read it, as they thought that it was funnier than Daft Jack.

Second, Liam Murtagh (assistant head teacher at Kind Edward VI School, Morpeth) tells of his best lesson (*TES* magazine, 8 December 2006).

The lesson was not going well. All of my carefully crafted resources had been noisily rejected. The hubbub of conversation grew. My strident voice grew more impotent. They were not listening and Katie had moved from shouting to openly passing photographs around the classroom. I quickly snatched them from her hands. They were of a dog – her puppy. How rude, I thought. It was all I could do to avoid shredding them in front of her eyes. Instead, in a desperate, furious attempt to regain order, I held them high.

'Listen! Imagine Katie's puppy was . . .'

What exactly? Some thoughts ran through my mind. . . . Roadkill? Hacked to death by a mysterious cloaked figure? Baked in the oven with Mediterranean vegetables? Then inspiration. . . .

'Was being experimented on so that your make-up was safe to use.' The class fell silent.

'They couldn't do that, could they, sir?' said Katie, with a note of panic in her voice.

'Is it right,' I said, emphasising each word with thrusts of the photo, 'to test make-up or hairspray or medicines on animals?' I held my breath. We'd moved from potential anarchy to the whole class hanging on my every word.

'No, sir, that isn't right.'

'What if they were testing drugs that could stop cancer?' replied Jordan.

They were off. Debate raged. My only role became that of puppy photo bearer. At least one of these endless tough lessons with this seemingly apathetic group had taken flight.

Katie's dog – God bless you.

These two teachers, Roger Humphries and Liam Murtagh, were themselves inspired by what happened in their classrooms during the two lessons they have described. However, even inspired teachers can recall when matters take a turn for the worst and the most careful application of the science of teaching seems to fall apart. There may be no obvious explanation for when the worst that can happen, decides to happen. In the same article, Liam Murtagh now describes his worst ever lesson.

It is ironic that the lesson I would most like to forget involved amnesia. Mystery Mary was a story you wrote by piecing together who Mary – a victim of memory loss – was from her belongings. It could be used for coursework and my Year 11 (15- to 16-year-olds) group desperately needed coursework. I was their fourth teacher in a year and they had produced nothing. And that's exactly what I intended to produce this lesson, too. It was the last thing on a Wednesday and I was wallpaper. I had to act. I strode towards my desk and, with a lung-bursting scream of 'Listen!', karate-chopped the desk surface.

Silence.

A minute passed before the incredulous comment of: 'Look at sir's hand'. It had swollen to five times its normal size – and hurt like hell. They laughed long and very loud. Bedlam ensued. It was the longest hour of my life. Order was beyond me. Yet I kept trying and, as the bell sounded, I made one final attempt at control.

'No-one is leaving this lesson until all the pencils have been collected.'

I stood in front of the door. The mob obeyed my wishes. I counted each pencil into the box. 'Eleven and twelve,' I patted the lid on the box shut and proudly announced, 'At least something has been accomplished this lesson.'

Then the bottom of the box opened and the pencils tumbled out all over the floor. The class roared. I fell to my knees, clawing them back into the box while the pupils surged out of the door. Some even gave me gentle, consoling pats on the back. 'Never mind, sir.'

Beware of either/or choices

Most people agree that teachers must be both theoretically knowledgeable and practically inventive. They must be able to use a range of strategies, and they must also be able to invent new strategies. They must have some basic research-based routines for managing classes, but they must also be willing and able to break from the routine when the situation calls for change. Teachers need both general theories and context-specific insights. They need 'understandings of pupils in general – patterns common to particular ages, culture, social class, geography and gender; patterns in typical pupils' conceptions of the subject matter' (Ball, 1997: 773) and they also need to know their own pupils. 'Face to face with actual children who are particular ages and gender, culture and class, teachers must see individuals against a backdrop of sociological and psychological generalisations about groups' (Ibid., 773). The theories you encounter in this text should be used as cognitive tools to help you examine, inspect and interpret the claims you will hear and read about teachers and teaching (Leinhardt, 2001).

Connect and Extend

Growth as a professional relies on becoming a member of a community of practice by attending conferences, conventions and meetings to advance ideas, theories and practice. To get a feel for the British Psychological Society's approaches to issues related to professionalism and for excellent links to many online resources, see the Companion Website (Web Link 1.2).

Expert knowledge

Expert teachers have elaborate *systems of knowledge* for understanding problems in teaching. For example, when a beginning teacher is faced with pupils wrong answers in maths or history all of these answers seem about the same – they're wrong. However, for an expert teacher, wrong answers are part of a rich system of knowledge that could include how to recognise several types of wrong answers, the misunderstanding or lack of information behind each kind of mistake, the best way to reteach and correct the misunderstanding, materials and activities that have worked in the past, and several ways to test whether the reteaching was successful. In addition, expert teachers have clear goals and take individual differences into account when planning for their pupils. These teachers are reflective practitioners (Russell, 2005; Hudson, 2002; Hogan, Rabinowitz and Craven, 2003; Larrivee, 2000; Mullen, 2000).

Expert teachers

Experienced, effective teachers who have developed solutions for common classroom problems. Their knowledge of the teaching process and content is extensive and well organised.

What do expert teachers know that allows them to be so successful? Lee Shulman (1987) identified seven areas of professional knowledge. Expert teachers know:

1. The academic subjects they teach – their content knowledge is deep and interconnected.

2. General teaching strategies that apply in all subjects (such as the principles of classroom management, effective teaching and evaluation that you will discover in this book).

3. The curriculum materials and programmes appropriate for their subject and grade level.

4. Subject-specific knowledge for teaching: special ways of teaching certain pupils and particular concepts, such as the best ways to explain negative numbers to lower-ability pupils.

5. The characteristics and cultural backgrounds of learners.

6. The settings in which pupils learn – pairs, small groups, teams, classes, schools and the community.

7. The goals and purposes of teaching.

A key factor for expert teachers that may not be clear from the above list is the need to know their 'teacher-self' – their personal biases, strengths and blind spots as well as personal cultural identity. Only by having a clear sense of self can teachers understand and respect the cultural identity of their pupils (Warin *et al.*, 2006). Jay Dee and Allan Henkin (2002) note that teachers must be willing to explore beyond their own zone of comfort as members of the majority cultural status quo.

This is quite a list. Obviously, one course alone cannot give you all the information you need about teaching. In fact, a whole programme of courses won't make you an expert. That takes time and experience. But studying educational

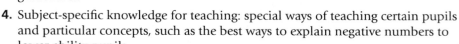

>
> **Connect and Extend**
>
> For some interesting perceptions of how trainee teachers view expert teaching read Olugbemiro *et al.* (2000), 'Trainee teachers' perception of their knowledge about expert teaching', in *Educational Research, 42*(3), pp. 287–308.

A really effective teacher is not only confident about the subject he/she is teaching but is also able to keep learners interested and involved

psychology can add to your professional knowledge because at the heart of educational psychology is a concern with learning wherever it occurs. To know about the psychology of education, you will need to know about *pupils* (Part 1 of this book), *learning and motivation* (Part 2) and *teaching and assessing* (Part 3).

The Role of Educational Psychology

For as long as educational psychology has existed – about 100 years – there have been debates about what it really is. Some people believe educational psychology is simply knowledge gained from psychology and applied to the activities of the classroom. Others believe it involves applying the methods of psychology to study classroom and school life (Brophy, 2003; Wittrock, 1992). A look at history shows the close connections between educational psychology and teaching.

Some interesting history

Psychology emerged as a distinct academic discipline in the 1880s and in its early stages was generally confined to teaching the subject and research in colleges and universities. However, in the mid-1900s, various strands of applied psychology emerged including educational psychology. As discussed earlier in this chapter the term *educational psychology* is sometimes misleading because it has two meanings, relating both to the role of educational psychologists who help children with learning and/or behavioural problems and to the psychology of education, which studies learning and teaching in order to improve educational practice. It is this latter meaning which this book is essentially concerned with.

In the 1940s and 1950s, the study of educational psychology concentrated on individual differences, assessment and learning behaviours. In the 1960s and 1970s, the focus of research shifted to the study of cognitive development and learning, with attention being paid to how individuals learn concepts and remember. Recently, educational psychologists have investigated how culture and social factors affect learning and development (Pressley and Roehrig, 2003).

What is educational psychology today? The view generally accepted is that *educational psychology* is a distinct discipline with its own theories, research methods, problems and techniques. Both in the past and today, educational psychologists study learning and teaching and, at the same time, strive to improve educational practice (Pintrich, 2000). However, even with this long history of interest in teaching and learning, are the findings of educational psychologists really that helpful for teachers? After all, most teaching is just common sense, isn't it? Let us take a few minutes to examine these questions.

Is it just common sense?

In many cases, the principles set forth by educational psychologists – after spending much thought, time and money – sound pathetically obvious. People are tempted to say, and usually do say, 'Everyone knows that!' Consider these examples.

Taking turns

What method should a teacher use when choosing learners to read aloud in a class of five-year-olds?

Common sense answer   Teachers should call on children randomly so that everyone will have to follow the reading carefully. If a teacher were to use the same order every time, the class would know when their turn was coming up.

These pupils are participating in real 'hands-on' co-operative learning. Will their knowledge of science improve using this approach? Are there better ways to learn in biology? Educational research should shed light on questions like these

Answer based on research   Years ago, research by Ogden, Brophy and Evertson (1977) found that the answer to this question is not so simple. In reading lessons with five-year-olds, for example, going around the circle in order and giving each child a chance to read led to better overall achievement than calling on children randomly. The critical factor in going around the circle may be that each child gets a chance to participate. Without some system for calling on everyone, learners can be overlooked or missed out. Research suggests there are better alternatives for teaching reading than going around the circle, such as the use of questions and answers to ensure understanding, but teachers should make sure that everyone has the chance for practice and feedback whatever approach is used (Tierney, Readence and Dishner, 1990).

Helping learners

When should teachers provide help for lower-achieving learners as they do classwork?

Common sense answer   Teachers should offer help often. After all, these lower-achieving learners may not know when they need help or they may be too embarrassed to ask for help.

Answer based on research   Research found that when teachers provide help before learners ask, the learners and others watching are more likely to conclude that the helped learner does not have the ability to succeed. The individual is more likely to attribute failures to lack of ability instead of lack of effort, so motivation suffers (Graham and Weiner, 1996)

Accelerated learning (fast-tracking)

Should a school encourage exceptionally bright learners to progress more quickly than peers or to apply for higher education early?

Common sense answer   No! Very intelligent learners who are a year or two younger than their classmates are likely to be social misfits. They are neither physically nor emotionally ready for dealing with older people and would be miserable in the social situations that are so important in school, especially in the later years.

Answer based on research   The research is inconclusive on this but one study in the US concluded, 'From early admissions to school to early admissions to college, research studies invariably report that children who have been accelerated have adjusted as well as or better than have children of similar ability who have not been accelerated' (Kirk, Gallagher and Anastasiow, 1993: 105). Whether acceleration is the best solution for a learner depends on many specific individual characteristics, including the intelligence and maturity of the person, and the other available options. For some learners, moving quickly through the material and working in advanced classes with older learners is a very good idea. A current example of this in practice is the decision taken by East Renfrewshire Council in Scotland that plans to allow pupils to take their first national exams a year early at the age of 14 in order to recognise individual differences and developmental rates in learners. The Scottish Secondary School's Teachers' Association secretary commented, 'The danger is that we put all young people in a year group together and say that they must all move at the same pace, at the same time, regardless of what their background has been or how able they are to learn' (BBC News, January 2006). See Chapter 4 for more on adapting teaching to learners' abilities.

Obvious answers?

Lily Wong (1987) demonstrated that just seeing research results in writing can make them seem obvious. She selected 12 findings from research on teaching; one of them was the 'taking turns' result noted above. She presented six of the findings in their correct form and six in *exactly the opposite form* to both teaching learners and experienced teachers. Both the learners and the teachers rated about half of the *wrong* findings as 'obviously' correct. In a follow-up study, another group of subjects was shown the 12 findings and their opposites, and was asked to pick which ones were correct. For eight of the 12 findings, the subjects chose the wrong result more often than the right one.

You may have thought that educational psychologists spend their time discovering the obvious. The preceding examples point out the danger of this kind of thinking. When a principle is stated in simple terms, it can sound simplistic. A similar phenomenon takes place when we see a gifted dancer or athlete perform; the well-trained performer makes it look easy. However, we see only the results of the training, not all the work that went into mastering the individual movements. It is also worth bearing in mind that any research finding – or its opposite – may sound like common sense. The issue is not what *sounds* sensible, but what is demonstrated when the principle is put to the test (Gage, 1991).

> **Connect and Extend**
>
> See the Companion Website (Web Link 1.3) to find many links to databases on educational systems and research. These include EURYDICE (Information network for European education) WEB and the British Education Index.

Using research to understand and improve learning

> **STOP AND THINK**
>
> Quickly list all the different research methods you can name.

Descriptive studies

Studies that collect detailed information about specific situations, often using observation, surveys, interviews, recordings or a combination of these methods.

Ethnography

A descriptive approach to research that focuses on life within a group and tries to understand the meaning of events to the people involved.

Participant observation

A method for conducting descriptive research in which the researcher becomes a participant in the situation in order to better understand life in that group.

Case study

Intensive study of one person or one situation.

Correlations

Statistical descriptions of how closely two variables are related.

Positive correlation

A relationship between two variables in which the two increase or decrease together. Example: calorie intake and weight gain.

Negative correlation

A relationship between two variables in which a high value on one is associated with a low value on the other. Example: height and distance from top of head to the ceiling.

Conducting research to test possible relationships is one of two major tasks of educational psychology. The other is combining the results of various studies into theories that attempt to present a unified view of such things as teaching, learning and development.

Descriptive studies

Educational psychologists design and conduct many different kinds of research studies. Some of these are 'descriptive', that is, their purpose is simply to describe events in a particular class or several classes. Reports of descriptive studies often include survey results, interview responses, samples of actual classroom dialogue or audio and video records of the class activities.

One descriptive approach, classroom ethnography, is borrowed from anthropology. Ethnographic methods involve studying the naturally occurring events in the life of a group and trying to understand the meaning of these events to the people involved. Researchers make detailed observations in the teachers' classes and analyse these observations, along with audio recordings and information from interviews with the teachers and sometimes the pupils in order to describe events within the learning situation.

In some descriptive studies, the researcher uses participant observation and works within the class or school to understand the actions from the perspectives of the teacher and the learners.

Researchers also employ case studies. A case study investigates in depth how a teacher plans lessons, for example, or how an individual tries to learn specific material.

Correlation studies

Often, the results of descriptive studies include reports of correlations. We will take a minute to examine this concept, because you need knowledge of correlations to fully understand the many correlations you will encounter in the coming chapters. A correlation is a number that indicates both the strength and the direction of a relationship between two events or measurements. Correlations range from 1.00 to –1.00. The closer the correlation is to either 1.00 or –1.00, the stronger the relationship. For example, the correlation between height and weight is about 0.70 (a strong relationship); the correlation between height and number of languages spoken is about 0.00 (no relationship at all).

The sign of the correlation tells the direction of the relationship. A positive correlation indicates that the two factors increase or decrease together. As one gets larger, so does the other. Height and weight of the human body are positively correlated because greater height tends to be associated with greater weight.

A negative correlation means that increases in one factor are related to decreases in the other. An example of this might be that as the weather becomes warmer (increase in temperature) we wear fewer clothes (decrease in clothing). Temperature and amount of clothing are negatively correlated because higher temperature tends to be associated with wearing fewer clothes. It is important to note that correlations do not prove cause and effect (see Figure 1.1). Height and weight are correlated – taller people tend to weigh more than shorter people but gaining weight obviously does not cause you to grow taller. Knowing a person's weight simply allows you to make a general prediction about that person's height. Educational psychologists identify correlations so they can make predictions about important events in the classroom.

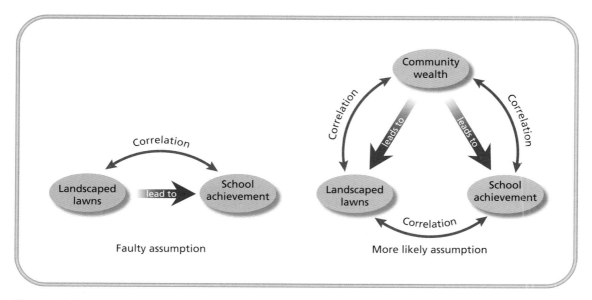

Figure 1.1
Correlations do not show causation

When research shows that landscaped lawns and school achievement are correlated, it does not show causation. Community wealth, a third variable, may be the cause of both school achievement and landscaped lawns.

Experimental studies

A second type of research – experimentation – allows educational psychologists to go beyond predictions and actually study cause and effect. Instead of just observing and describing an existing situation, the investigators introduce changes and note the results.

First, a number of comparable groups of participants are created. In psychological research, the term participants (also called subjects) generally refers to the people being studied – such as teachers or 12-year-olds.

One common way to make sure that groups of participants are essentially the same is to assign each person to a group using a random procedure. Random means each participant has an equal chance of being placed in any group.

In one or more of these groups, the experimenters change some aspect of the situation to see if this change or 'treatment' has an expected effect. The results in each group are then compared. Usually, statistical tests are conducted. When differences are described as statistically significant, it means that they probably did not happen simply by chance.

A number of the studies we will examine attempt to identify cause-and-effect relationships by asking questions such as this: If teachers ignore learners who are out of their seats without permission and praise those who are working hard at their desks (cause), will learners spend more time working at their desks (effect)?

In many cases, descriptive and experimental research occur together. In order to answer questions about the relationship between how five-year-old learners are chosen to read aloud and their achievement in reading, these investigators first observed learners and teachers in a number of classrooms and then measured the reading achievement of the children. They found that having learners read in a predictable order was associated, or correlated, with gains in reading scores. With a simple correlation such as this, however, the researchers could not be sure that the strategy

Experimentation

Research method in which variables are manipulated and the effects recorded.

Participants/ Subjects

People or animals studied.

Random

Without any definite pattern; following no rule.

Statistically significant

Not likely to be a chance occurrence.

was actually causing the effect. In the second part of the study, Ogden and her colleagues (Ogden *et al.*, 1977) asked several teachers to call on each learner in turn. They then compared reading achievement in these groups with achievement in groups where teachers used other strategies. This second part of the research was thus an experimental study – specifically, a *field experiment* because it took place in a real classroom setting and not a laboratory.

Single-subject experimental designs

Single-subject experimental studies

Systematic interventions to study effects with one person, often by applying and then withdrawing a treatment.

The goal of single-subject experimental studies is to determine the effects of a therapy or teaching method, or other intervention. One common approach is to observe the individual for a baseline period (A) and assess the behaviour of interest; try an intervention (B) and note the results; then remove the intervention and go back to baseline conditions (A); and finally reinstate the intervention (B). This form of single-subject design is called an ABAB experiment. For example, a teacher might record how much learners are out of their seats without permission during a week-long baseline (A), and then try ignoring those who are not seated, but praising those who are seated and recording how many are wandering out of their seats for the week (B). Next, the teacher returns to baseline conditions (A) and records results, then reinstates the praise-and-ignore strategy (B) (Landrum and Kauffman, 2006). Years ago, when this very intervention was tested, the praise-and-ignore strategy proved effective in increasing the time learners spent in their seats (Madsen *et al.*, 1968).

Microgenetic studies

Microgenetic studies

Detailed observation and analysis of changes in a cognitive process as the process unfolds over a several-day or week period of time.

The goal of microgenetic research is to intensively study cognitive processes in the midst of change – as the change is actually happening. For example, researchers might analyse how children learn a particular strategy for adding two-digit numbers over the course of several weeks. The microgenetic approach has three basic characteristics: (a) researchers observe the entire period of the change – from when it starts to the time it is relatively stable; (b) many observations are made, often using videotape recordings, interviews and transcriptions of the exact words of the individuals being studied; (c) the behaviour that is observed is 'put under a microscope', that is, examined moment by moment or trial by trial. The goal is to explain the underlying mechanisms of change – for example, what new knowledge or skills are developing to allow change to take place (Siegler and Crowley, 1991). This kind of research is expensive and time-consuming, so often only one or a few children are studied.

The role of time in research

Another distinction is useful in understanding research – a distinction based on time. Many things that psychologists want to study, such as cognitive development, happen over several months or years. Ideally, researchers would study the development by observing their subjects over many years as changes occur. These are called *longitudinal* studies. They are informative, but time-consuming, expensive and not always practical – keeping up with subjects over years as they grow up and move can be impossible. As a consequence, much research is *cross-sectional*, focusing on groups of children at different ages. For example, to study how children's conceptions of 'alive' change from ages three to 16, researchers can interview children of several different ages, rather than following the same children for 14 years.

Connect and Extend

Read the following account of applying cognitive psychology to learning mathematics. Leron, U. and Hazzon, O. (2006), 'The rationality debate: Application of cognitive psychology to mathematics education' in *Educational Studies in Mathematics*, 62(2), pp. 105–126.

Teachers as researchers

Research can also be a way to improve teaching in one classroom or one school. The same kind of careful observation, intervention, data gathering and analysis that occurs in large research projects can be applied in any classroom to answer questions

Observational methods
may be used by
researchers

such as, 'Which type of stimuli seem to encourage the best descriptive writing in a class?', 'When does Oliver seem to have the greatest difficulty concentrating on academic tasks?', 'Would assigning specific tasks in science groups lead to more equitable participation of girls and boys in the work?' This kind of problem-solving investigation is called action research. By focusing on a specific problem and making careful observations, teachers can learn a great deal about both their teaching and their learners.

Action research
Systematic observations or tests of methods conducted by teachers or schools to improve teaching and learning for their learners.

Theories for teaching

The major goal of educational psychology is to understand teaching and learning; research is a primary tool. Reaching this goal is a slow process. There are very few landmark studies that answer a question once and for all. Human beings are too complicated. Instead, research in educational psychology examines limited aspects of a situation – perhaps a few variables at a time or life in one or two classrooms. If enough studies are completed in a certain area and findings repeatedly point to the same conclusions, we eventually arrive at a principle. This is the term for an established relationship between two or more factors – between a certain teaching strategy, for example, and learner achievement.

Principle
Established relationship between factors.

Theory

Integrated statement of principles that attempts to explain a phenomenon and make predictions.

Another tool for building a better understanding of the teaching and learning processes is theory. The common sense notion of theory (as in 'Oh well, it was only a theory') is 'a guess or intuitive feeling'. However, the scientific meaning of theory is quite different. 'A theory in science is an interrelated set of concepts that is used to explain a body of data and to make predictions about the results of future experiments' (Stanovich, 1992: 21). Given a number of established principles, educational psychologists have developed explanations for the relationships among many variables and even whole systems of relationships. There are theories to explain how language develops, how differences in intelligence occur and, as noted earlier, how people learn.

Few theories explain and predict perfectly. In this book, you will see many examples of educational psychologists taking different theoretical positions and disagreeing on the overall explanations of such issues as learning and motivation. Because no one theory offers all the answers, it makes sense to consider what each has to offer.

So why, you may ask, is it necessary to deal with theories? Why not just stick to principles? The answer is that both are useful. Principles of classroom management, for example, will provide help with specific problems. A good *theory* of classroom management, on the other hand, will provide a new way of thinking about discipline problems; it will provide cognitive tools (or ways of thinking) for creating solutions to many different problems and for predicting what might work in new situations. A major goal of this book is to provide readers with the best and the most useful theories related to teaching – those that have solid evidence behind them. Although you may prefer some theories to others, consider them all as ways of understanding the challenges faced within the learning situation.

> **⬅️➡️ Connect and Extend**
>
> Read this article by Poulou, M. (2005), 'Educational psychology within teacher training', in *Teachers and Teaching: Theories and Practice*, 11(6), pp. 555–574 for a discussion about the dynamic relationship between educational psychology and teacher preparation.

DISCUSSION POINT

Should scientific methods be the only ones used in educational research?

Educational research is the subject of a range of different views and debates. Below are summaries of two that are particularly relevant to this book. The first calls for the coordination of European research whilst the second suggests that although this is desirable, caution about different meanings is needed when doing so.

Agree: Yes, it is the only way of ensuring accurate research findings

The European Educational Research Association (EERA) was formed in 1994 and includes representatives from Belgium, the Czech Republic, Denmark, Estonia, Finland, France, Germany, Iceland, Ireland, Lithuania, the Netherlands, Norway, Portugal, Spain, Sweden, Switzerland and the UK.

EERA was founded after two years of meetings and discussions between representatives from the various countries' research associations and institutes. The association has gathered strength and identifies the complexity of European education which contains distinct, diverse and changeable national policies. For example, countries such as Spain and Finland, which have traditionally employed highly controlled curricula, have switched to a more teacher-led and decentralised model. In contrast, countries such as the UK have moved towards a more prescriptive National Curriculum. There are similar differences in terms of approaches to teacher education or training with France moving towards more academic programmes and the UK and the Netherlands adopting more practically based training. However, the role of educational research is not always visible in these decisions.

It is critical, therefore, for educational research to inform these decisions and help develop knowledge and coordination between nations:

> . . . educational research is not, for the most part, well co-ordinated at international levels, and improved co-ordination might well lead to closer links to education policy and practice. . . . Educational research in some European countries is little developed, in some others it has little prestige or is undervalued. The co-ordination of research at a European level might serve to greatly enhance the way in which it is viewed, used and developed. www.eera.ac.uk.

Disagree: No, a range of methods should be used

Different cultures and contexts affect the meanings attached to research

Deborah Court, who researches educational cultures in Israel and other countries, also suggests that educational research should be shared between 'diverse communities of researchers, teachers and learners' but she stresses the importance of understanding the context and culture within which the research has been carried out.

In her article 'The quest for meaning in educational research', Court (2004) recognises that all researchers have similar aims. These encompass the development of effective programs and teaching methods to improve the learning process, the unearthing of variables between learning establishments and the investigation of cultural contexts of schools so that educational environments that are free from prejudice and inequality can be created.

However, she suggests that research is driven by the 'quest for meaning' which includes personal, contextual and shared meaning. Calling upon Vygotsky's (1962) emphasis upon the importance of language and meaning being part of the culture it belongs to and Polanyi's arguments about culture providing a 'frame of reference' for understanding (1962: 112), Court stresses the need to pay close attention to the cultural contexts within which educational research is located, without which there is a risk that the research may be misinterpreted, leading to inaccurate conclusions.

This has implications for sharing educational research across cultures regardless of the logic and methods used because the values underlying the research and the claims made from it, as well as the motivation for choosing certain research areas, is inseparable from the context within which it has taken place.

Sources: Court, D. (2004), 'The quest for meaning in educational research' in *Academic Exchange Quarterly, 8*(3), pp. 7–12; EERA (European Educational Research Association) The role of EERA. Available at http://www.eera.ac.uk/web/eng/all/about/key_documents/role/index.html

WHAT DO YOU THINK?
Agree or Disagree? Vote online at www.pearsoned.co.uk/woolfolkeuro.

The Contents of This Book

Part 1 of this text focuses upon the learners. In Part 1 we examine the ways in which learners develop. Because children may differ from adolescents and adults in their thinking, language and way of viewing themselves, they may require different kinds of teaching to allow them to learn and develop effectively. Teachers will want to take account of these mental, physical, emotional and social aspects of their learners.

Part 1 also discusses how children differ from one another in their abilities, previous learning, learning styles and preferences, and in the ways they have been prepared for school by their cultural experiences. Classrooms today are becoming more and more diverse and teachers are expected to work with a wide range of children and young people, from different backgrounds and with different abilities.

Part 2 focuses upon human learning and motivation and their application to teaching. Theoretical approaches to how and why learning occurs are explored and their relevance to the classroom discussed. There is no learning without attention and engagement so it is important for teachers to understand motivation and incorporate strategies that support active learning.

Part 3 is concerned with teaching and assessing. How do teachers manage their classrooms, not just to be orderly environments (important though that is) but also to be exciting and vivid places in which pupils are motivated to invest their time and effort in learning. The focus for any classroom setting is pupils' learning and teachers need to understand what children already know – to assess them – and to then teach them accordingly. Finally, teachers need to understand how effective their teaching has been, how much progress pupils have made in their classes, and be able to report that progress in a form that allows comparisons between pupils and schools.

Finally

Whatever your particular interests and requirements, there is no doubt that relating psychology to education is an important and rapidly increasing area both in the UK and other parts of Europe. We hope that you find this book useful, informative and challenging so that you are able to return to it as a point of reference for whichever direction you might take in your future.

SUMMARY TABLE

Do Teachers Make a Difference? (pp. 6–8)

What evidence is there that teachers make a difference?

Three studies speak to the power of teachers in the lives of learners. The first explored how teachers ensured that Black Caribbean pupils did well. The second examined how teachers' beliefs about their ability to make a difference made a difference to the attainment of their pupils. The third was a large-scale study of thousands of pupils and teachers.

In the study, observations were made of setting and checking homework; disciplinary interventions in lessons; expectations of pupil performance; interactions with whole classes and individual pupils; punctuality and standards of behaviour set; skills and styles; organisation and experience. It is clear that teachers can and do make a difference to the achievements of learners and their life chances.

What is Good Teaching? (pp. 9–13)

What do expert teachers know?

It takes time and experience to become an expert teacher. These teachers have a rich store of well-organised knowledge about the many specific situations of teaching. This includes knowledge about the subjects they teach, their pupils, general teaching strategies, subject-specific ways of teaching, settings for learning, curriculum materials and the goals of education.

The Role of Educational Psychology (pp. 13–22)

What is educational psychology?

The goals of educational psychology are to understand and to improve the teaching and learning processes. Educational psychologists develop knowledge and methods; they also use the knowledge and methods of psychology and other related disciplines to study learning and teaching in everyday situations.

What are descriptive studies?

Reports of descriptive studies often include survey results, interview responses, samples of actual classroom dialogue or records of the class activities. Ethnographic methods involve studying the naturally occurring events in the life of a group and trying to understand the meaning of these events to the people involved. A case study investigates in depth how a teacher plans courses, for example, or how a learner tries to learn specific material.

What are correlations and experimental studies?

A correlation is a number that indicates both the strength and the direction of a relationship between two events or measurements. The closer the correlation is to either 1.00 or –1.00, the stronger the relationship. Experimental studies can indicate cause-and-effect relationships and should help teachers implement useful changes. Instead of just observing and describing an existing situation, the investigators introduce changes and note the results.

What are single-subject and microgenetic studies?

In single-subject experimental designs, researchers examine the effects of treatments on one person, often by using a baseline/intervention/baseline/intervention or ABAB approach. Microgenetic studies take many detailed observations of participants to track the progression of change from the very beginning until a process becomes stable.

What is action research?

When teachers or schools make systematic observations or test out methods to improve teaching and learning for their learners, they are conducting action research.

Distinguish between principles and theories

A principle is an established relationship between two or more factors – between a certain teaching strategy, for example, and learner achievement. A theory is an interrelated set of concepts that is used to explain a body of data and to make predictions. The principles from research offer a number of possible answers to specific problems, and the theories offer perspectives for analysing almost any situation that may arise.

Glossary

Action research: Systematic observations or tests of methods conducted by teachers or schools to improve teaching and learning for their learners.

Case study: Intensive study of one person or one situation.

Correlations: Statistical descriptions of how closely two variables are related.

Descriptive studies: Studies that collect detailed information about specific situations, often using observation, surveys, interviews, recordings or a combination of these methods.

Educational psychology: Refers to the broad area of training and work of educational psychologists who apply psychological theories, research and techniques to help children and young people who may have learning difficulties, emotional or behavioural problems.

Ethnography: A descriptive approach to research that focuses on life within a group and tries to

understand the meaning of events to the people involved.

Experimentation: Research method in which variables are manipulated and the effects recorded.

Expert teachers: Experienced, effective teachers who have developed solutions for common classroom problems. Their knowledge of the teaching process and content is extensive and well organised.

Microgenetic studies: Detailed observation and analysis of changes in a cognitive process as the process unfolds over a several-day or week period of time.

Negative correlation: A relationship between two variables in which a high value on one is associated with a low value on the other. Example: height and distance from top of head to the ceiling.

Participant observation: A method for conducting descriptive research in which the researcher becomes a participant in the situation in order to better understand life in that group.

Participants/subjects: People or animals studied.

Positive correlation: A relationship between two variables in which the two increase or decrease together. Example: calorie intake and weight gain.

Principle: Established relationship between factors.

Psychology of education: The discipline concerned with teaching and learning processes; applies the methods and theories of psychology to teaching and learning and has its own methods and theories as well.

Random: Without any definite pattern; following no rule.

Reflective: Thoughtful and inventive. Reflective teachers think back over situations to analyse what they did and why and to consider how they might improve learning for their pupils.

Single-subject experimental studies: Systematic interventions to study effects with one person, often by applying and then withdrawing a treatment.

Statistically significant: Not likely to be a chance occurrence.

Theory: Integrated statement of principles that attempts to explain a phenomenon and make predictions.

CHECK YOUR LEARNING!

 WEB

In the Classroom: What Would They Do?

You may remember that Nandini, in her second year as a teacher, has been asked to sit on a committee which will decide who will get three travel bursary awards for excellence in teaching. What does she need to know about teaching to make a judgement here? What are the indicators of excellent teaching and do different styles of teaching provide different answers?

Here are some responses from practising school teachers:

Lee Card, primary school teacher, Bosbury Church of England Primary School

It is initially interesting that the recipients will be decided by colleagues only and through 'meetings'. Perhaps there needs to be a wider range of views and opinions taken into account here? In more publicised teacher awards, the local school community, including parents/governors/children, are often involved in some way. Nevertheless, Nandini is faced with basing her comments and decisions on a potentially vast range of criteria. There is, in my opinion, no tried and tested formula for an 'award-winning teacher'. However, there are indicators that excellent teaching is happening that Nandini could look out for; hopefully with the school granting her some observation time to make this possible. Some things to look for are quantitative. For example, assessment records through the year might illustrate greater than usual progress amongst the teacher's pupils. High standards of attainment in the classroom may be evidenced in pupils' books, or on

displays. For me, however, Nandini needs to be in the classroom sampling the 'feeling' of quality teaching that cannot be levelled or qualified by grades. Nandini will *know* quality teaching, and see the resulting learning that takes place, when she sees it and feels it. Children will be enthused; talking, questioning, learning, teaching, moving, shouting and laughing. The 'quality teacher' will be doing the same.

Jackie Day, special educational needs co-ordinator, The Ridge Primary School, Yate

Nandini needs to know that, while excellent teachers may differ hugely in personality and teaching style, they share common characteristics. First, they have a thorough knowledge of their subject, and are interested in extending that knowledge. They plan lessons carefully, with differentiation so that all can succeed. Excellent teachers constantly review their teaching, always aiming to teach more effectively next time. They know their pupils' strengths and weaknesses, and plan strategies to extend the learning of all ability groups. This will involve using innovative methods, using teaching assistants effectively communicating with parents. They are able to motivate and inspire children, use plenty of visual aids, and know how to target appropriate questions at different groups. All pupils are clear about what they need to do to improve their work. They have high expectations, which are reflected in measurable results. Excellent teachers will be recognised and trusted by both pupils and their parents, and their lessons will be inspirational. If I were Nandini I would prepare for the meeting by talking informally with pupils and parents to ascertain their perceptions. In addition, to make an objective, defendable decision I would compare value added pupil outcomes.

Lizzie Meadows, deputy head teacher, The Park Primary School, Kingswood, Bristol

In order to prepare for the meeting Nandini needs to equip herself with as much information about the teachers as possible. Given her position this should be done in as informal a way as possible, for example:

- What can she glean from visiting the teacher's classrooms, what is the environment like?

- What has she picked up about the relationships that the teacher has with the class from seeing them around school?

- What does behaviour look like in the classes in question?

It is probable that the more experienced members of the committee and management will have the relevant data at their disposal, so Nandini's contribution can be more anecdotal and relationship based. She is completely at liberty to make it known to people that she is not comfortable in this role, and ensure that she remains as impartial and discreet as possible.

Overview

Children beginning their formal schooling might understand a picture of a heart on a greetings card simply to be a 'pretty' familiar shape which they have encountered in 'sorting' and 'posting' toys. However, when entering secondary or later education at approximately 11 years of age they are likely to understand the romantic, perhaps embarrassing, connotations attached to receiving a card with a heart upon it. This clearly indicates that there are differences in children's understanding at various ages.

Think for a moment about how a six-year-old child might be helped to understand 'symbolic' concepts perhaps within a study of poetry. Would a similar method be suitable for 13-year-old learners? Do you have a clear understanding about the ways that younger and older children differ in their ways of thinking?

We begin with a discussion of the general principles of human development and take a brief look at the human brain. Then we will examine the ideas of two of the most influential cognitive developmental theorists, Jean Piaget and Lev Vygotsky. Piaget's ideas have implications for teachers about what their learners can learn and when they are ready to learn it. We will consider criticisms of his ideas as well. The work of Lev Vygotsky, a Russian psychologist, is becoming more and more in-fluential. His theory highlights the important role teachers and parents play in the cognitive development of the child. Finally, we will explore language development and discuss the role of the school in developing and enriching language skills.

By the time you have completed this chapter, you should be able to:

- **State three general principles of human development.**
- **Explain how children's thinking differs at each of the four stages of development Piaget described.**
- **Summarise the implications of Piaget's theory for facilitating learners of different ages.**
- **Recognise the similarities and differences between Piaget's and Vygotsky's ideas about cognitive development.**
- **Understand the implications of Vygotsky's theories for facilitating learners of different ages.**
- **Briefly describe the stages of language development.**
- **Suggest ways a teacher (or caregiver) can help children expand their use and comprehension of language.**

In the Classroom

A group of nine- to ten-year-old children are about to be introduced to the use of symbolism in poetry.

Martin, their teacher, is concerned that they will find this difficult to understand. In order to test this he asks the children what a symbol is:

'It's a big metal thing that they have on drums,' says Emma.

'Yes, my brother's got some and they make a lot of noise,' giggles Katy.

This tells Martin that they have taken the question literally and not followed the intended meaning so he tries again:

'I was thinking of a different kind of symbol, such as a ring as a symbol of marriage or a heart as a symbol of love.'

The children stare blankly at him but then Charlie tries:

'Do you mean like the Olympic torch?'

'Yes, well done. What do you think that symbolises, Charlie?'

'It is a torch,' replies Charlie.

Group Activity

In your groups discuss the following questions:
- **What do these reactions tell you about children's thinking?**
- **How would you approach teaching this to them?**
- **What more might be done to 'listen' to the children's thinking to facilitate their learning?**
- **How could the children be given 'hands on' concrete experiences to help their understanding?**
- **How could Martin decide whether or not they are developmentally ready for this learning?**

A Definition of Development

The discussion so far has looked at changes which take place as children's understanding develops. The term development in its most general psychological sense refers to certain changes that occur in human beings (or animals) between conception and death. The term is not applied to all changes, such as those caused by tiredness, mood or certain situations for example, but rather to those that appear in orderly ways and remain for a reasonably long period of time. Therefore a temporary change caused by a brief illness is not considered a part of development. Psychologists also make a value judgement in determining which changes qualify as development. The changes – at least those that occur early in life – are generally assumed to be for the better and to result in behaviour that is more adaptive, more organised, more effective and more complex (Mussen, Conger and Kagan, 1984).

Human development can be divided into a number of different aspects:

- Physical development, as you might guess, deals with changes in the body.

- Personal development is the term generally used for changes in an individual's personality.

- Social development refers to changes in the way an individual relates to others.

- Cognitive development refers to changes in thinking.

Many changes during development are simply matters of growth and maturation. Maturation refers to changes that occur naturally and spontaneously and that are, to a large extent, genetically programmed. Such changes emerge over time and are relatively unaffected by environment, except in cases of malnutrition or severe illness. Much of a person's physical development falls into this category. Other changes are brought about through learning, as individuals interact with their environment. Such changes make up a large part of a person's social development but what about the development of thinking and personality? Most psychologists agree that in these areas, both maturation and interaction with the environment (or nature and nurture, as they are

Development
Orderly, adaptive changes we go through from conception to death.

Physical development
Changes in body structure and function over time.

Personal development
Changes in personality that take place as one grows.

Social development
Changes over time in the ways we relate to others.

Cognitive development
Gradual orderly changes by which mental processes become more complex and sophisticated.

Maturation
Genetically programmed, naturally occuring changes over time.

Nature and Nurture

'Simon is such a bright lad – of course the whole family have done well at school so we expect it from him.'

Imagine that you have overheard this at a school parents' evening. What is the speaker implying about Simon's abilities? Are these being explained in terms of his genetics (nature) and assuming that Simon was born with the potential to be particularly bright or intelligent and that this has unfolded as he has matured? Or are they suggesting that because he has lived in an environment which encouraged and modelled 'brightness' he has learned to be intelligent (nurture)? Or perhaps the implication is that both are involved? In that case Simon's inborn tendencies developed within a setting that supported their continued growth and therefore they flourished in a way that they might not have otherwise (nature and nurture).

sometimes called) are important, but they disagree about the amount of emphasis to place on each one.

General principles of development

Although there is disagreement about both what is involved in development and the way it takes place, there are a few general principles almost all theorists would support.

1. *People develop at different rates.* In any classroom, there will be a whole range of examples of different developmental rates. Some learners will be larger, better coordinated or more mature in their thinking and social relationships. Others will be much slower to mature in these areas. Except in rare cases of very rapid or very slow development, such differences are normal and should be expected in any large group of learners.

2. *Development is relatively orderly.* People develop abilities in a logical order. In infancy, they sit before they walk, babble before they talk and see the world through their own eyes before they can begin to imagine how others see it. In school, they will master addition before algebra, Bambi before Shakespeare, and so on. Theorists may disagree on exactly what comes before what, but they all seem to find a relatively logical progression. But 'orderly' does not necessarily mean linear or predictable – people might advance, stay the same for a time period or go backwards.

3. *Development takes place gradually.* Very rarely do changes appear overnight. A learner who cannot manipulate a pencil or answer a hypothetical question may well develop this ability, but the change is likely to take time.

The brain and cognitive development

If you have studied biological psychology, you will have read about the brain and nervous system. You probably remember that there are several different areas of the brain and that certain areas are involved in particular functions. For example, the feathery looking cerebellum (*little brain* in Latin) which is located underneath the occipital and temporal lobes at the back of the brain, coordinates and orchestrates balance and smooth, skilled movements – from the graceful gestures of the dancer to the everyday action of eating without stabbing yourself in the nose with a fork. The cerebellum may also play a role in higher cognitive functions such as learning. The hippocampus (*seahorse* in Greek because of its curved shape) located inside the temporal lobe is critical in recalling new information and recent experiences, while the amygdala (an almond-shaped group of neurons) that directs emotions and the thalamus (Greek for *chamber* or *bedroom*) that is involved in our ability to learn new information, particularly if it is verbal, are both located deep within the brain. The reticular formation (part of the brain stem) plays a role in attention and arousal, blocking some messages and sending others on to higher brain centres for processing, and the corpus callosum moves information from one side of the brain to the other.

Some researchers have described the brain as a jungle of layers and loops, an interconnected and complex organic system (Edelman, 1992). Although complex it is useful to have some understanding of the structure and development of the brain when we come to study cognitive development as there are likely to be interconnections. The outer $\frac{1}{8}$-inch-thick covering of the cerebrum is the wrinkled-looking cerebral cortex – the largest area of the brain. The cerebral cortex allows the greatest human accomplishments, such as complex problem solving and language. In humans, this area of the brain is much larger than it is in lower animals. The cortex is the last part of the brain to develop, so it is believed to be more susceptible to environmental influences than other areas of the brain (Berk, 2005; Meece, 2002; Wood, Wood and Boyd, 2005). The cerebral cortex accounts for about 85% of the brain's weight in adulthood and contains the greatest number of neurons – the tiny structures that store and transmit information. Let's see how neurons develop.

Neurons

Nerve cells that store and transfer information.

Connect and Extend

To view accounts of current research in this area see the Companion Website (Web Link 2.1).

The developing brain: neurons

About one month after conception, brain development starts. In the tiny tube that is the very beginning of the human brain, neuron cells emerge at the amazing rate of 50,000 to 100,000 per second for the next three months or so. These cells send out long arm- and branch-like fibres to connect with other neuron cells and share information by releasing chemicals that jump across the tiny spaces, called synapses, between the fibre ends. By the time we are born, we have all the neurons we will ever have, about 100 to 200 billion, and each neuron has about 2,500 synapses. However, the fibres that reach out from the neurons and the synapses between the fibre ends increase during the first years of life, perhaps into adolescence or longer.

Synapses

The tiny space between neurons – chemical messages are sent across these gaps.

By age two to three, each neuron has around 15,000 synapses; children at this age have many more synapses than they will have as adults. In fact, they are *oversupplied* with the neurons and synapses that they will need to adapt to their environments. However, only those neurons that are used will survive, and unused neurons will be 'pruned' (Bransford, Brown and Cocking, 2000). This pruning might be compared to the act of producing a sculpture where the basic material is moulded and carved to fit the artist's vision. Those synapses which are unused are discarded and those which are retained are necessary and support cognitive development. In fact, some forms of mental retardation are associated with a gene defect that interferes with pruning (Cook and Cook, 2005).

Two kinds of overproduction and pruning processes take place. One is called *experience-expectant* because synapses are overproduced in certain parts of the brain during certain developmental periods, awaiting (expecting) stimulation. For example, during the first months of life, the brain expects visual and auditory stimulation. If a normal range of sights and sounds occurs, then the visual and auditory areas of the brain develop. But children who are born completely deaf receive no auditory stimulation and, as a result, the auditory processing area of their brains becomes devoted to processing visual information. Similarly, the visual processing area of the brain for children blind from birth becomes devoted to auditory processing (Nelson, 2001; Siegler, 1998).

STOP AND THINK

Do you think that the reading you have done so far helps to explain the fact that deaf or blind people develop stronger other senses?

Experience-expectant overproduction and pruning processes are responsible for general development in large areas of the brain. This may explain why adults have difficulty with pronunciations that are not part of their native language. For example, native Japanese speakers do not distinguish the different sounds of 'r' and 'l'. The capacity to hear these differences was available to the Japanese infants, but the neurons and synapses involved in recognising these differences may have been 'pruned' because they were not used to learn Japanese. Therefore, learning these sounds as an adult requires intense instruction and practice (Bransford, Brown and Cocking, 2000).

The second kind of synaptic overproduction and pruning is called *experience-dependent* sometimes referred to as 'use it or lose it'. Here, synaptic connections are formed based on the individual's experiences. Again, more synapses are produced than will be kept after 'pruning'. Experience-dependent processes are involved in individual learning, such as learning unfamiliar sound pronunciations in a second language you are studying. For example many native French speakers struggle with the 'th' sounds in English often pronouncing these as 'ze' and similarly native English speakers find the rolled French 'r' very difficult to master.

Stimulation is important in both development (experience-expectant processes) and learning (experience-dependent processes). In fact, animal studies have shown that rats raised in stimulating environments (with toys, tasks for learning, other rats, and human handling) develop and retain 25% more synapses than rats who are raised with little stimulation. Both social stimulation (interactions with other rats) and physical/sensory stimulation (toys and tasks) are important; some studies showed that toys and tasks alone did not lead to increased brain development (Bransford, Brown and Cocking, 2000). Age may also be a factor in this. Stimulating environments may help in the pruning process in early life (experience-expectant period) and support increased synapse development in adulthood (experience-dependent period) (Cook and Cook, 2005).

Early stimulation is important for humans as well. It is clear that extreme deprivation can have negative effects on brain development, but extra stimulation will not necessarily improve development for young children who are getting adequate or typical amounts of stimulation (Byrnes and Fox, 1998; Kolb and Whishaw, 1998). So spending money on expensive toys or baby education programmes probably provides more stimulation than is necessary. Pots and pans, blocks and books, sand and water all provide excellent, varied stimulation – especially if accompanied by caring conversations with parents, caregivers or teachers.

Even though the brain is developing rapidly during early childhood, learning continues over a lifetime. Early severe stimulus deprivation can have lasting effects, but because of brain plasticity or adaptability, some compensation can overcome deprivation or damage. Of course, many factors besides stimulus deprivation, such as the mother's intake of drugs (including alcohol and caffeine) during pregnancy, toxins in the infant's environment such as lead paint, or poor nutrition, can have direct and dramatic negative effects on brain development such as the actual size and growth of the brain (Perry and Pollard, 1997).

Another factor that influences thinking and learning is myelination, or the coating of neuron fibres with an insulating fatty covering. This process is something like coating bare electrical wires with rubber or plastic. This myelin coating makes message transmission faster and more efficient. Myelination happens quickly in the early years, but continues gradually into adolescence and is the reason the child's brain grows rapidly in size in the first few years of life.

The developing brain: cerebral cortex

Let's move from the neuron level to the brain itself. The cerebral cortex develops more slowly than other parts of the brain and parts of the cortex mature at different rates. The part of the cortex that controls physical motor movement matures first, then the areas that control complex senses such as vision and hearing, and last, the frontal lobe that controls higher-order thinking processes. The temporal lobes of the cortex that play major roles in emotions and language do not develop fully until the secondary school years and maybe later.

Neuroscientists are just beginning to understand how brain development is related to aspects of childhood and adolescence such as planning, risk-taking, decision

Plasticity

The brain's tendency to remain somewhat adaptable or flexible.

Myelination

The process by which neural fibres are coated with a fatty sheath called myelin which makes message transfers more efficient.

making and managing impulsive behaviours. Getting angry or wanting revenge when we are insulted or hurt are common human emotions. It is the job of the prefrontal cortex to control these impulses through reason, planning or delay of gratification. However, the impulse-inhibiting capacities of the brain are not present at birth (as all new parents quickly discover). An immature prefrontal lobe explains some of the impulsiveness and temper tantrums of two-year-olds. Emotional regulation is more difficult at this age. Many studies show advances in the prefrontal cortex around three to four years old, but it takes at least two decades for the biological processes of brain development to produce a fully functional prefrontal cortex (Weinberger, 2001). Thus, learners within statutory education still lack the brain development to balance impulse with reason and planning. Weinberger suggests that parents have to 'loan' their children a prefrontal cortex, by helping them set rules and limits and make plans, until the child's own prefrontal cortex can take over. Schools and teachers also can play major roles in cognitive and emotional development if they provide appropriate environments for these developing, but sometimes impulsive, brains (Meece, 2002).

Specialisation and integration

Different areas of the cortex seem to have different functions, as shown in Figure 2.1. Even though different functions are found in different areas of the brain, these specialised functions are quite specific and elementary. To accomplish more complex functions such as speaking or reading, the various areas of the cortex must communicate and work together (Byrnes and Fox, 1998).

Lateralisation

The specialisation of the two hemispheres (sides) of the brain cortex.

Another aspect of brain functioning that has implications for cognitive development is lateralisation, or the specialisation of the two hemispheres of the brain. We know that each half of the brain controls the opposite side of the body. Damage to the right side of the brain will affect movement of the left side of the body and vice versa. In addition, certain areas of the brain affect particular behaviours. For most of us, the left hemisphere of the brain is a major factor in language processing, and the right hemisphere handles much of the spatial-visual information and emotions (nonverbal information). For some left-handed people, the relationship may be reversed, but for most left-handers, and for females on average, there is less hemispheric

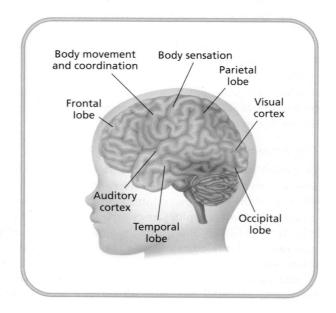

Figure 2.1
A view of the cerebral cortex

This is a simple representation of the left side of the human brain, showing the cerebral cortex. The cortex is divided into different areas, or lobes, each having a variety of regions with different functions. A few of the major functions are indicated here.

specialisation altogether (Berk, 2005; O'Boyle and Gill, 1998). Before lateralisation, damage to one part of the cortex often can be overcome as other parts of the cortex take over the function of the damaged area but after lateralisation, the brain is less able to compensate.

These differences in performance by the brain's hemispheres, however, are more relative than absolute; one hemisphere is just more efficient than the other in performing certain functions. Nearly any task, particularly the complex skills and abilities that concern teachers, requires participation of many different areas of the brain in constant communication with each other. For example, the right side of the brain is better at working out the meaning of a story, but the left side is where grammar and syntax are understood, so both sides of the brain have to work together in reading. 'The primary implication of these findings is that the practice of teaching to "different sides of the brain" is not supported by the neuroscientific research' (Byrnes and Fox, 1998: 310). Thus, beware of educational approaches based on simplistic views of brain functioning – what Keith Stanovich has called 'the left-brain–right-brain nonsense that has inundated education through workshops, inservices, and the trade publications' (1998: 420). Remember, no mental activity is exclusively the work of a single part of the brain – so there is no such thing as a 'right-brained learner' unless that individual has had the left hemisphere removed, a rare and radical treatment for some forms of epilepsy.

Learning and brain development

Research from animal and human studies shows that both experiences and direct teaching cause changes in the organisation and structure of the brain. For example, deaf individuals who use sign language have different patterns of electrical activity in their brains compared to deaf people who do not use sign language. Also, the intensive instruction and practice provided when someone suffers a stroke can help the person regain functioning by forming new connections and using new areas of the brain (Bransford, Brown and Cocking, 2000). Bennett Shaywitz and his colleagues (2004) reported a dramatic demonstration of brain changes in children following instruction. The researchers studied 28 children aged six to nine who were good readers and 49 children who were poor readers. A process known as functional magnetic-resonance imaging (MRI) showed differences in the brain activity of the two groups. The poor readers underused parts of their brains' left hemisphere and sometimes overused their right hemispheres. After over 100 hours of intensive instruction in letter–sound combinations, the brains of the poor readers started to function more like those of the good readers and continued this functioning a year later. Poor readers who received the standard support (used as a control/comparison group) did not show the brain function changes so this suggests that the improvement in those receiving intensive instruction were not simply due to natural developmental processes but as a result of the extra stimulation.

In other research, several studies have found that children and adults with ADHD (Attention Deficit Hyperactivity Disorder) have smaller frontal lobes, basal ganglia and cerebellums than people without ADHD. These areas are involved with self-regulation of behaviour, coordination and control of motor behaviour (Hallahan and Kauffman, 2006).

One clear connection between the brain and classroom learning is in the area of emotions and stress. As you will see in Chapter 10, anxiety interferes with learning, whereas challenge, interest and curiosity can support learning. If learners feel unsafe and anxious, they are not likely to be able to focus attention on academics (Sylvester, 2003). But if learners are not challenged or interested, learning suffers too. Keeping the level of challenge and support 'just right' is a challenge for teachers and helping learners learn to regulate their own emotions and motivation is an important goal for education (see Chapter 3).

Implications for teachers, caregivers and facilitators of learning

As you have seen, the brain and learning are intimately related, but what does this mean for teachers, caregivers and facilitators? Marcy Driscoll (2005) draws these implications:

1. Many cognitive functions are differentiated – they are associated with different parts of the brain. Thus, learners are likely to have preferred modes of processing (visual or verbal, for example) as well as different capabilities in these different modes. Using different modalities for instruction and activities that draw on different senses may support learning – for example, using drawings of shapes and solid objects to teach mathematical concepts.

2. The brain is relatively plastic, so enriched active environments and flexible instructional strategies are likely to support cognitive development in young children and learning in adults.

3. Some learning disorders may have a neurological basis, so neurological testing may assist in diagnosing, treating and evaluating the effects of treatments.

Much has been written lately about brain-based education. Many of these publications for parents and teachers have useful ideas, but beware of suggestions that oversimplify the complexities of the brain. As you can see in the Discussion Point below, however, there is little conclusive evidence of the effectiveness of many of these programmes.

DISCUSSION POINT

Are there clear educational implications from the neuroscience research on the brain?

Educators are hearing more and more about brain-based education, the importance of early stimulation for brain development, the 'Mozart effect' and right- and left-brain activities. In fact, based on some research findings that listening to 10 minutes of Mozart can briefly improve spatial reasoning (Rauscher and Shaw, 1998; Steele, Bass and Crook, 1999), a former governor of Georgia established a programme to give a Mozart CD to every newborn (Meece, 2002). Are there clear educational implications from the neuroscience research on the brain? Below are two differing views:

Agree: Yes, teaching should be brain-based

If you want to read about programmes, strategies and approaches that have been developed to be consistent with brain research, type 'brain-based education' into an Internet search engine. There is even a forum for teaching practitioners to discuss issues about the brain and learning that is indicative of the importance of the current debate in this area (Learning Sciences and Brain Research at www.teach-the-brain.org).

Schools should not be run based solely on the biology of the brain. However, to ignore what we do know about the brain would be equally irresponsible. Brain-based learning offers some direction for educators who want more purposeful, informed teaching.

Disagree: No, the implications are not clear

John Bruer, president of the James S. McDonnell Foundation, has written articles that are critical of the brain-based education craze (Bruer, 1999). He notes that many so-called applications of brain research begin with solid science, but then move to unwarranted speculation. He suggests that for each claim, the educator should ask, 'Where does the science end and the speculation begin?' For example, one claim that Bruer questions is the notion of right-brain, left-brain learning.

> 'Right brain versus left brain' is one of those popular ideas that will not die. Speculations about the educational significance of brain laterality have been circulating in the education literature for 30 years. Although repeatedly criticized and dismissed by psychologists and brain scientists, the speculation continues. David Sousa devotes a chapter of How the Brain Learns to explaining brain laterality and presents classroom strategies that teachers might use to ensure that both hemispheres are involved in learning. . . . Now let's consider the brain sciences and how or whether they offer support for some of the particular teaching strategies Sousa recommends. To involve the right hemisphere in learning, Sousa writes, teachers should encourage learners to generate and use mental imagery. . . . What brain scientists currently know about spatial reasoning and mental imagery provides counterexamples to such simplistic claims as these. Such claims arise out of a folk theory about brain laterality, not a neuroscientific one. . . . Different brain areas are specialized for different tasks, but that specialization occurs at a finer level of analysis than 'using visual imagery.' Using visual imagery may be a useful learning strategy, but if it is useful it is not because it involves an otherwise underutilized right hemisphere in learning. (Bruer, 1999: 653–654)

WHAT DO YOU THINK?

Agree or Disagree? Vote online at www.pearsoned.co.uk/woolfolkeuro.

The brain is a complex collection of systems working together to make sense of the individual's experiences. These change over time as maturation and development occur. Before we move to the next section check that you can answer the following:

STOP AND THINK

- What are the three principles that describe how development takes place?
- What part of the brain is associated with higher mental functions?
- Why is an understanding of the nature–nurture debate important in terms of brain development?

We turn next to examine this process of change with a theory of cognitive development offered by a biologist turned psychologist, Jean Piaget.

Piaget's Theory of Cognitive Development

Piaget carried out ground-breaking research which showed that there were qualitative differences involved in children's cognitive development

During the past half century Swiss psychologist Jean Piaget devised a model describing how humans go about making sense of their world by gathering and organising information (Piaget, 1954, 1963, 1970a, 1970b). We will examine Piaget's ideas closely, because they provide an explanation of the development of thinking from infancy to adulthood.

According to Piaget (1954), certain ways of thinking that are quite simple for an adult, are not so simple for a child. For example, a child might have difficulty understanding that she is English but also a Londoner because she is unable to classify one concept (London) as a subset of another (England). There are other differences between adult and child thinking such as a child's concepts of time may be different from your own. Children may think, for example, that they will some day catch up to a sibling in age, or they may confuse the past and the future.

Influences on development

As you can see, cognitive development is much more than the addition of new facts and ideas to an existing store of information. According to Piaget, our thinking processes change radically, though slowly, from birth to maturity because we constantly strive to make sense of the world. How do we do this? Piaget identified four factors – biological maturation, activity, social experiences and equilibration – that interact to influence changes in thinking (Piaget, 1970a). Let's briefly examine the first three factors. We'll return to a discussion of equilibration in the next section.

One of the most important influences on the way we make sense of the world is *maturation*, the unfolding of the biological changes that are genetically programmed. Parents, caregivers and teachers have little impact on this aspect of cognitive development, except to be sure that children get the nourishment and care they need to be healthy.

Activity is another influence. With physical maturation comes the increasing ability to act on the environment and learn from it. When a young child's coordination is reasonably developed, for example, the child can discover principles about balance by experimenting with a seesaw. Thus, as we act on the environment – as we explore, test, observe and eventually organise information – we are likely to alter our thinking processes at the same time.

As we develop, we are also interacting with the people around us. According to Piaget, our cognitive development is influenced by *social transmission*, or learning from others. Without social transmission, we would need to reinvent all the knowledge already offered by our culture. The amount people can learn from social transmission varies according to their stage of cognitive development.

Maturation, activity and social transmission all work together to influence cognitive development. How do we respond to these influences?

Basic tendencies in thinking

Organisation

Ongoing process of arranging information and experience into mental systems or categories.

As a result of his early research in biology, Piaget concluded that all species inherit two basic tendencies, or 'invariant functions'. The first of these tendencies is towards organisation – the combining, arranging, recombining and rearranging of behaviours and thoughts into coherent systems. The second tendency is towards adaptation, or adjusting to the environment.

Adaptation

Adjustment to the environment.

Organisation

People are born with a tendency to organise their thinking processes into psychological structures. These psychological structures are our systems for understanding and interacting with the world. Simple structures are continually combined and coordinated to become more sophisticated and thus more effective. Very young infants, for example, can either look at an object or grasp it when it comes in contact with their hands. They cannot coordinate looking and grasping at the same time. As they develop, however, infants organise these two separate behavioural structures into a coordinated higher-level structure of looking at, reaching for and grasping the object. They can, of course, still use each structure separately (Flavell, Miller and Miller, 2002; Miller, 2002).

Piaget gave a special name to these structures: schemes. In his theory, schemes are the basic building blocks of thinking. They are organised systems of actions or thought that allow us to mentally represent or 'think about' the objects and events in our world. Schemes can be very small and specific, for example, the sucking-through-a-straw scheme or the recognising-a-rose scheme. Or they can be larger and more general, for example, the drinking scheme or the categorising-plants scheme. As a person's thinking processes become more organised and new schemes develop, behaviour also becomes more sophisticated and better suited to the environment.

Schemes

Mental systems or categories of perception and experience.

Adaptation

In addition to the tendency to organise their psychological structures, people also inherit the tendency to adapt to their environment. Two basic processes are involved in adaptation: assimilation and accommodation.

Assimilation takes place when people use their existing schemes to make sense of events in their world. Assimilation involves trying to understand something new by fitting it into what we already know. At times, we may have to distort the new information to make it fit. For example, the first time many children see a fox, they call it a 'doggy'. They try to match the new experience with an existing scheme for identifying animals.

Assimilation

Fitting new information into existing schemes.

Accommodation occurs when a person must change existing schemes to respond to a new situation. If data cannot be made to fit any existing schemes, then more appropriate structures must be developed. We adjust our thinking to fit the new information, instead of adjusting the information to fit our thinking. Children demonstrate accommodation when they add the scheme for recognising foxes to their other systems for identifying animals.

Accommodation

Altering existing schemes or creating new ones in response to new information.

People adapt to their increasingly complex environments by using existing schemes whenever these schemes work (assimilation) and by modifying and adding to their schemes when something new is needed (accommodation). In fact, both processes are required most of the time. Even using an established pattern, such as sucking through a straw, requires some accommodation if the straw is of a different size or length than the type you are used to. If you have tried drinking fruit juice from a carton, you know that you have to add a new skill to your sucking scheme – don't squeeze the carton or you will force the juice up through the straw, straight up into the air and into your lap. Whenever new experiences are assimilated into an existing scheme, the scheme is enlarged and changed somewhat, so assimilation involves some accommodation.

There are also times when neither assimilation nor accommodation is used. If people encounter something that is too unfamiliar, they may ignore it. Experience is filtered to fit the kind of thinking a person is doing at a given time. For example, if you overhear a conversation in a foreign language, you probably will not try to make sense of the exchange unless you have some knowledge of the language.

Equilibration

Equilibration

Search for mental balance between cognitive schemes and information from environment.

Disequilibrium

In Piaget's theory, the 'out-of-balance' state that occurs when a person realises that his or her current ways of thinking are not working to solve a problem or understand a situation.

According to Piaget, organising, assimilating and accommodating can be viewed as a kind of complex balancing act. In his theory, the actual changes in thinking take place through the process of equilibration – the act of searching for a balance. Piaget assumed that people continually test the adequacy of their thinking processes in order to achieve that balance. Briefly, the process of equilibration works like this: if we apply a particular scheme to an event or situation and the scheme works, then equilibrium exists. If the scheme does not produce a satisfying result, then disequilibrium exists, and we become uncomfortable. This motivates us to keep searching for a solution through assimilation and accommodation, and thus our thinking changes and moves ahead. Of course, the level of disequilibrium must be just right or optimal – too little and we aren't interested in changing, too much and we may be too anxious or not ready to change. In order to maintain a comfortable balance between our schemes for understanding the world and the data the world provides we continually assimilate new information (using existing schemes) and accommodate (or change) our thinking whenever unsuccessful attempts to assimilate result in disequilibrium.

Four stages of cognitive development

Now we turn to the actual differences that Piaget hypothesised for children as they grow. Piaget believed that all people pass through the same four stages (sensorimotor, preoperational, concrete operational and formal operational) in exactly the same order. These stages are generally associated with specific ages, as shown in Table 2.1,

Table 2.1 Piaget's stages of cognitive development

Stage	Approximate age	Characteristics
Sensorimotor	0–2 years	Begins to make use of imitation, memory and thought. Begins to recognise that objects do not cease to exist when they are hidden. Moves from reflex actions to goal-directed activity.
Preoperational	2–7 years	Gradually develops use of language and ability to think in symbolic form. Able to think operations through logically in one direction. Has difficulties seeing another person's point of view.
Concrete operational	7–11 years	Able to solve concrete (hands-on) problems in logical fashion. Understands laws of conservation and is able to classify and seriate. Understands reversibility.
Formal operational	11–adult	Able to solve abstract problems in logical fashion. Becomes more scientific in thinking. Develops concerns about social issues, identity.

Source: From *Piaget's Theory of Cognitive and Affective Development* (5th ed.) by B. Wadsworth. Published by Allyn and Bacon, Boston, MA. Copyright © 1996 by Pearson Education.

but these are only general guidelines, not labels for all children of a certain age. Piaget noted that individuals may go through long periods of transition between stages and that a person may show characteristics of one stage in one situation, but characteristics of a higher or lower stage in other situations. Therefore, knowing a learner's age is never a guarantee that you know how the child will think (Orlando and Machado, 1996).

Infancy: the sensorimotor stage (birth to two years approximately)

The earliest period is called the sensorimotor stage, because the child's thinking involves seeing, hearing, moving, touching, tasting, and so on. During this period, infants develop object permanence, the understanding that objects exist in the environment whether they perceive them or not. This is the beginning of the important ability to construct a mental representation. As most parents discover, before infants develop object permanence, it is relatively easy to take something away from them. The trick is to distract them and remove the object while they are not looking – 'out of sight, out of mind'. The older infant who searches for the ball that has rolled out of sight is indicating an understanding that objects still exist even when they are not in view (Moore and Meltzoff, 2004). Recent research, however, suggests that infants as young as three to four months may know that the object still exists, but they do not have the memory skills to 'hold on' to the location of the object or the motor skills to coordinate a search (Baillargeon, 1999; Flavell, Miller and Miller, 2002).

A second major accomplishment in the sensorimotor period is the beginning of logical, goal-directed actions. Think of the familiar container toy for babies. It is usually clear plastic with a lid and contains several colourful items that can be emptied out and replaced. A six-month-old baby is likely to become frustrated trying to get to the toys inside. An older child who has mastered the basics of the sensorimotor stage will probably be able to deal with the toy in an orderly fashion by building a 'container toy' scheme: (1) get the lid off, (2) turn the container upside down, (3) shake if the items jam, and (4) watch the items fall. Separate lower-level schemes have been organised into a higher-level scheme to achieve a goal.

The child is soon able to reverse this action by refilling the container. Learning to reverse actions is a basic accomplishment of the sensorimotor stage. As we will soon see, however, learning to reverse thinking – that is, learning to imagine the reverse of a sequence of actions – takes much longer.

The early childhood years: the preoperational stage (two to seven years approximately)

By the end of the sensorimotor stage, the child can use many action schemes. As long as these schemes remain tied to physical actions, however, they are of no use in recalling the past, keeping track of information, or planning. For this, children need what Piaget called operations, or actions that are carried out and reversed mentally rather than physically. At the preoperational stage the child has not yet mastered these mental operations, but is moving towards mastery.

According to Piaget, the first type of thinking that is separate from action involves making action schemes symbolic. The ability to form and use symbols – words, gestures, signs, images, and so on – is thus a major accomplishment of the preoperational period and moves children closer to mastering the mental operations of the next stage. This ability to work with symbols, such as using the word 'horse' or a picture of a horse or even pretending to ride a horse to represent a real horse that is not actually present, is called the semiotic function.

In fact, the child's earliest use of symbols is in pretending. Children who are not yet able to talk will often use action symbols – pretending to drink from an empty cup or

Sensorimotor
Involving the senses and motor activity.

Object permanence
The understanding that objects have a separate, permanent existence.

Goal-directed actions
Deliberate actions towards a goal.

Operations
Actions a person carries out by thinking them through instead of literally performing the actions.

Preoperational
The stage before a child masters logical mental operations.

Semiotic function
The ability to use symbols – language, pictures, signs or gestures – to represent actions or objects mentally.

touching a comb to their hair, showing that they know what each object is for. This behaviour also shows that their schemes are becoming more general and less tied to specific actions. The eating scheme, for example, may be used in playing house. During the preoperational stage, there is also rapid development of that very important symbol system, language. Between the ages of two and four, most children enlarge their vocabulary from about 200 to 2,000 words.

As the child moves through the preoperational stage, the developing ability to think about objects in symbolic form remains somewhat limited to thinking in one direction only, or using *one-way logic*. It is very difficult for the child to 'think backwards' or imagine how to reverse the steps in a task. Reversible thinking is involved in many tasks that are difficult for the preoperational child, such as the conservation of matter.

Conservation is the principle that the amount or number of something remains the same even if the arrangement or appearance is changed, as long as nothing is added and nothing is taken away. You know that if you tear a piece of paper into several pieces, you will still have the same amount of paper. To prove this, you know that you can reverse the process by taping the pieces back together. A classic example of difficulty with conservation is found in the preoperational child's response to the following Piagetian task. Leah, a five-year-old, is shown two identical glasses, both short and wide in shape. Both have exactly the same amount of coloured water in them. She agrees that the amounts are 'the same'. The experimenter then pours the water from one of the glasses into a taller, narrower glass and asks, 'Now, does one glass have more water, or are they the same?' Leah responds that the tall glass has more because 'It goes up more here' (she points to higher level on taller glass).

Piaget's explanation for Leah's answer is that she is focusing, or centring, attention on the dimension of height. She has difficulty considering more than one aspect of the situation at a time, or decentring. The preoperational child cannot understand that decreased diameter compensates for increased height, because this would require taking into account two dimensions at once. Thus, children at the preoperational stage have trouble freeing themselves from their own immediate perceptions of how the world appears.

This brings us to another important characteristic of the preoperational stage. Preoperational children, according to Piaget, have a tendency to be egocentric, to see the world and the experiences of others from their own viewpoint. The concept of egocentrism, as Piaget intended it, does not mean selfish; it simply means children often assume that everyone else shares their feelings, reactions and perspectives. For example, if a little boy at this stage is afraid of dogs, he may assume that all children share this fear. Very young children centre on their own perceptions and on the way the situation appears to them. This is one reason it is difficult for these children to understand that your right hand is not on the same side as theirs when you are facing them.

Egocentrism is also evident in the child's language. You may have seen young children happily talking about what they are doing even though no one is listening. This can happen when the child is alone or, even more often, in a group of children – each child talks enthusiastically, without any real interaction or conversation. Piaget called this the collective monologue.

Research has shown that young children are not totally egocentric in every situation, however. Children as young as two describe more details about a situation to a parent who was not there compared to the descriptions they give to a parent who experienced the situation with them. It follows then that young children do seem quite able to take the needs and different perspectives of others into account, at least in certain situations (Flavell, Miller and Miller, 2002). In fairness to young children, even adults can make assumptions that others feel or think as they do. For example, have you ever received a gift that the giver loved but was clearly inappropriate for you? It is

Reversible thinking

Thinking backwards, from the end to the beginning.

Conservation

Principle that some characteristics of an object remain the same despite changes in appearance.

Decentring

Focusing on more than one aspect at a time.

Egocentric

Assuming that others experience the world the way that you do.

Collective monologue

Form of speech in which children in a group talk but do not really interact or communicate.

likely that the 'three mountains task' used by Piaget to measure egocentrism in young children was inadequate (McDonald and Stuart-Hamilton, 2002). The Focus on Practice gives ideas for working with preoperational thinkers.

FOCUS ON PRACTICE

Working with preoperational children

Use concrete props and visual aids whenever possible

Examples

1. When you discuss concepts such as 'part', 'whole' or 'one-half', use shapes on a felt board or cardboard 'pizzas' to demonstrate.
2. Let children add and subtract with sticks, rocks or coloured chips. This technique also is helpful for early concrete-operational learners.

Make instructions relatively short – not too many steps at once. Use actions as well as words

Examples

1. When giving instructions about how to enter the room after a class break and prepare for a social skills lesson, ask a child to demonstrate the procedure for the rest of the class by walking in quietly, going straight to his or her seat, and placing the text, paper and a pencil on his or her desk.
2. Explain a game by acting out one of the parts.
3. Show children what their finished work should look like. Use an overhead projector or display examples where they can easily be seen.

Help children develop their ability to see the world from someone else's point of view

Examples

1. Relate geography and history lessons about different people or places back to the children's experiences, pointing out similarities and differences.
2. Be clear about rules for sharing or use of material. Help children understand the value of the rules and develop empathy by asking them to think about how they would like to be treated. Avoid long lectures on 'sharing' or being 'nice'.

Be sensitive to the possibility that learners may have different meanings for the same word or different words for the same meaning. Children may also expect everyone to understand words they have invented

Examples

1. If a child protests, 'I don't want to have a nap. I'll lie down!' be aware that a nap may mean something such as 'changing into pyjamas and being in my bed at home'.
2. Ask children to explain the meanings of their invented words.

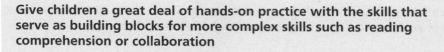

Give children a great deal of hands-on practice with the skills that serve as building blocks for more complex skills such as reading comprehension or collaboration

Examples

1. Provide cut-out letters to build words.
2. Supplement paper-and-pencil tasks in arithmetic with activities that require measuring and simple calculations – cooking, building a display area for class work, dividing a batch of flapjacks equally.
3. Allow children to clip from used magazines pictures of people collaborating – families, workers, educators and children all helping each other.

Provide a wide range of experiences in order to build a foundation for concept learning and language

Examples

1. Take field trips to zoos, gardens, theatres and concerts; invite storytellers to the class.
2. Give children words to describe what they are doing, hearing, seeing, touching, tasting and smelling.

Middle childhood: the concrete-operational stage (seven to 11 years approximately)

Piaget coined the term concrete operations to describe this stage of 'hands-on' thinking. The basic characteristics of the stage are the recognition of the logical stability of the physical world, the realisation that elements can be changed or transformed and still conserve many of their original characteristics, and the understanding that these changes can be reversed.

Look at Figure 2.2, which shows examples of the different tasks given to children to assess conservation and the approximate age ranges when most children can solve these problems.

According to Piaget, a learner's ability to solve conservation problems depends on an understanding of three basic aspects of reasoning: identity, compensation and reversibility. With a complete mastery of identity, the learner knows that if nothing is added or taken away, the material remains the same. With an understanding of compensation, the learner knows that an apparent change in one direction can be compensated for by a change in another direction. That is, if the glass is narrower, the liquid will rise higher in the glass. When an understanding of reversibility is gained, the learner can mentally cancel out the change that has been made. Leah apparently knew it was the same water (identity), but lacked compensation and reversibility, so she was moving towards conservation.

Another important operation mastered at this stage is classification. Classification depends on a learner's abilities to focus on a single characteristic of objects in a set (e.g. colour) and group the objects according to that characteristic. More advanced classification at this stage involves recognising that one class fits into another. A city can be in a particular county or area and also in a particular country. As children apply this advanced classification to locations, they often become fascinated with 'complete'

Concrete operations

Mental tasks tied to concrete objects and situations.

Identity

Principle that a person or object remains the same over time.

Compensation

The principle that changes in one dimension can be offset by changes in another.

Reversibility

A characteristic of Piagetian logical operations – the ability to think through a series of steps, then mentally reverse the steps and return to the starting point; also called reversible thinking.

Classification

Grouping objects into categories.

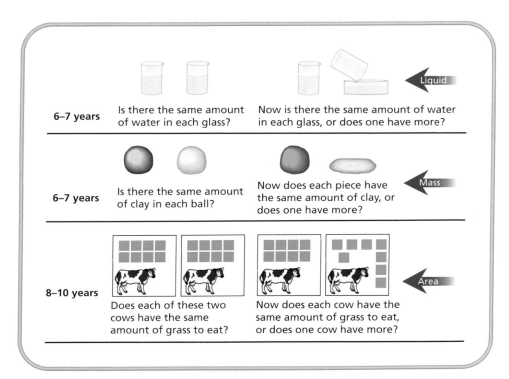

Figure 2.2
Some Piagetian
conservation tasks

In addition to the tasks
shown here, other
tasks involve the
conservation of
number, length,
weight and volume.
These tasks are all
achieved over the
concrete-operational
period.

Source: From *Child
Development* (4th ed.) by
Laura E. Berk. Published by
Allyn and Bacon, Boston,
MA. Copyright © 1997
by Pearson Education.

addresses such as Mr Lawrence Matthews, 349 Underwood Road, Allerton, Liverpool, Lancashire, England, United Kingdom, Northern Hemisphere, Earth, Solar System, Milky Way, Universe.

Classification is also related to reversibility. The ability to reverse a process mentally now allows the concrete-operational child to see that there is more than one way to classify a group of objects. The learner understands, for example, that buttons can be classified by colour, and then reclassified by size or by the number of holes.

Seriation is the process of making an orderly arrangement from large to small or vice versa. This understanding of sequential relationships permits a learner to construct a logical series in which A < B < C (A is less than B is less than C), and so on. Unlike the preoperational child, the concrete-operational child can grasp the notion that B can be larger than A but still smaller than C.

Seriation
Arranging objects in
sequential order according
to one aspect, such as size,
weight or volume.

With the abilities to handle operations such as conservation, classification and seriation, the learner at the concrete-operational stage has finally developed a complete and very logical system of thinking. This system of thinking, however, is still tied to physical reality. The logic is based on concrete situations that can be organised, classified or manipulated. Thus, children at this stage can imagine several different arrangements for the furniture in their rooms before they move any pieces. They do not have to solve the problem strictly through trial and error by actually making the arrangements. However, the concrete-operational child is not yet able to reason about hypothetical, abstract problems that involve the coordination of many factors at once. This kind of coordination is part of Piaget's next and final stage of cognitive development.

In any learning context, knowledge of concrete-operational thinking will be helpful (see the Focus on Practice below). In the early stages, the children are moving towards this logical system of thought. In the middle childhood years, it is in full flower, ready to be applied and extended by teachers and caregivers. Older learners and even adults still commonly use concrete operational thinking, especially in areas that are new or unfamiliar.

FOCUS ON PRACTICE

Working with concrete-operational children

Continue to use concrete props and visual aids, especially when dealing with sophisticated material

Examples

1. Use time lines in history and three-dimensional models in science.
2. Use diagrams to illustrate hierarchical relationships such as family trees or branches of government and the agencies under each branch.

Continue to give learners a chance to manipulate and test objects

Examples

1. Set up simple scientific experiments such as the following involving the relationship between fire and oxygen. What happens to a flame when you blow on it from a distance? (If you don't blow it out, the flame gets larger briefly, because it has more oxygen to burn.) What happens when you cover the flame with a jar?
2. Have learners make candles by dipping wicks in wax, weave cloth on a simple loom, bake bread or do other craft work that illustrates the daily occupations of people in earlier times.

Make sure presentations and readings are brief and well-organised

Examples

1. Choose stories or books with short, logical chapters, moving to longer reading assignments only when children are ready.
2. Break up a presentation with a chance to practise the first steps before introducing the next familiar examples to explain more complex ideas.

Make readings 'real'

Examples

1. Compare children's lives with those of characters in a story. After reading a story about a girl who grew up alone on a deserted island, ask 'Have you ever had to stay alone for a long time? How did you feel?'
2. Teach the concept of area by having learners measure two classrooms that are different sizes.

Give opportunities to classify and group objects and ideas on increasingly complex levels

Examples
1. Give children slips of paper with individual sentences written on each and ask them to group the sentences into paragraphs.
2. Compare the systems of the human body to other kinds of systems: the brain to a computer, the heart to a pump. Break down stories into components, from the broad to the specific: author; story; characters, plot, theme; place, time; dialogue, description, actions.

Present problems that require logical, analytical thinking

Examples
1. Use brain teasers and riddles.
2. Discuss open-ended questions that stimulate thinking: 'Are the brain and the mind the same thing?', 'How should the city deal with stray animals?', 'What is the largest number?'
3. Use sports photos or pictures of crisis situations (Red Cross helping in disasters, victims of poverty or war, senior citizens who need assistance) to stimulate problem-solving discussions.

For more ideas see http://chiron.valdosta.edu/whuitt/col/cogsys/piagtuse.html

Late childhood and adolescence: formal operations

Some learners remain at the concrete-operational stage throughout their school years, even throughout life. However, new experiences, usually those that take place in school, eventually present most learners with problems that they cannot solve using concrete operations. What happens when a number of variables interact, as in a science experiment? Then a mental system for controlling sets of variables and working through a set of possibilities is needed. These are the abilities Piaget called formal operations.

At the level of formal operations, the focus of thinking can shift from what is to what might be. Situations do not have to be experienced to be imagined. Ask a young child how life would be different if people did not sleep, and the child might say, 'People do sleep!' In contrast, the adolescent who has mastered formal operations can consider contrary-to-fact questions. In answering, the adolescent demonstrates the hallmark of formal operations – hypothetico-deductive reasoning. The formal thinker can consider a hypothetical situation (people do not sleep) and reason deductively (from the general assumption to specific implications, such as longer working days, more money spent on energy and lighting, smaller houses without bedrooms or new entertainment industries). Formal operations also include inductive reasoning, or using specific observations to identify general principles. For example, the economist observes many specific changes in the stock market and attempts to identify general principles about economic cycles. Formal-operational thinkers can form hypotheses, set up mental experiments to test them, and isolate or control variables in order to complete a valid test of the hypotheses. This kind of reasoning is necessary for success in many advanced learning contexts (Meece, 2002).

Formal operations

Mental tasks involving abstract thinking and coordination of a number of variables.

Hypothetico-deductive reasoning

A formal-operations problem-solving strategy in which an individual begins by identifying all the factors that might affect a problem and then deduces and systematically evaluates specific solutions.

The ability to consider abstract possibilities is critical for much of mathematics and science. Most mathematics is concerned with hypothetical situations, assumptions and givens: 'Let $x = 10$', or 'Assume $x^2 + y^2 = z^2$', or 'Given two sides and an adjacent angle . . .' Work in humanities and literature requires abstract thinking, too: 'What did David Lloyd George, the British prime minister, mean when he said of World War One, "This war, like the next war, is a war to end all wars"?', 'Identify some metaphors for hope and despair in Shakespeare's sonnets?', 'What symbols of old age does T. S. Eliot use in *The Waste Land*?', 'How do animals symbolise human character traits in Aesop's fables?' The organised, scientific thinking of formal operations requires that learners systematically generate different possibilities for a given situation. For example, if asked, 'How many different shirt/trousers/jacket outfits can you make using three of each kind of clothing?' the child using formal operations can systematically identify the 27 possible combinations. A concrete thinker might name just a few combinations, using each piece of clothing only once. The underlying system of combinations is not yet available.

Adolescent egocentrism

Assumption that everyone else shares one's thoughts, feelings and concerns.

Another characteristic of this stage is adolescent egocentrism. Unlike egocentric young children, adolescents do not deny that other people may have different perceptions and beliefs; the adolescents simply become very focused on their own ideas. They analyse their own beliefs and attitudes. This leads to what Elkind (1981) calls the sense of an imaginary audience – the feeling that everyone is watching. Thus, adolescents believe that others are analysing them: 'Everyone noticed that I wore this top/shirt twice this week.' or 'The whole class thought my answer was stupid!' You can see that social blunders or imperfections in appearance can be devastating if 'everybody is watching'. Luckily, this feeling of being 'on stage' seems to peak in early adolescence by age 14 or 15, although in unfamiliar situations we all may feel our mistakes are being noticed.

The ability to think hypothetically, consider alternatives, identify all possible combinations and analyse one's own thinking has some interesting consequences for adolescents. Because they can think about worlds that do not exist, they often become interested in science fiction. Because they can reason from general principles to specific actions, they often are critical of people whose actions seem to contradict their principles. Adolescents can deduce the set of 'best' possibilities and imagine ideal worlds (or ideal parents and teachers, for that matter). This explains why many young people at this age develop interests in utopias, political causes and social issues. They want to design better worlds, and their thinking allows them to do so. Adolescents can also imagine many possible futures for themselves and may try to decide which is best. Feelings about any of these ideals may be strong and idealistic.

Do we all reach the fourth stage?

Most psychologists agree that there is a level of thinking more sophisticated than concrete operations. But the question of how universal formal-operational thinking actually is, even among adults, is a matter of debate. The first three stages of Piaget's theory are forced on most people by physical realities. Objects really are permanent. The amount of water doesn't change when it is poured into another glass. Formal operations, however, are not so closely tied to the physical environment. They may be the product of practice in solving hypothetical problems and using formal scientific reasoning – abilities that are valued and taught in literate cultures, particularly within educational settings. Even so, about 50% of undergraduate learners fail Piaget's formal operational tasks (Berk, 2005).

Piaget himself (1974) suggested that most adults may be able to use formal-operational thought in only a few areas where they have the greatest experience or interest. Formal education fosters formal operational abilities in that subject, but not necessarily in others (Lehman and Nisbett, 1990). So it is likely that many middle and late childhood learners will have trouble thinking hypothetically, especially when they are learning something new. Sometimes, children and young people find shortcuts for dealing with problems that are beyond their grasp; they may memorise formulae or lists of steps. These systems may be helpful for passing tests, but real understanding will take place only if learners are able to go beyond this superficial use of memorisation. The Focus on Practice below may help to support the development of formal operations with young people.

FOCUS ON PRACTICE

Helping young people to use formal operations

Continue to use concrete-operational teaching strategies and materials

Examples
1. Use visual aids such as charts and illustrations as well as somewhat more sophisticated graphs and diagrams, especially when the material is new.
2. Compare the experiences of characters in stories to learners' experiences.

Give learners the opportunity to explore many hypothetical questions

Examples
1. Have learners write an argument for one side of a topical debate, then exchange these with the opposing side and discuss the issues raised – for example, the environment, educational reform, euthanasia.
2. Ask young people to write about their personal vision of a utopia; write a description of a universe that has no sex differences; write a description of Earth after humans are extinct.

Learners' opportunities to solve problems and reason scientifically

Examples
1. Set up group discussions in which young people design experiments to answer questions.
2. Ask learners to justify two different positions on animal rights, with logical arguments for each position.

Whenever possible, teach broad concepts, not just facts, using materials and ideas relevant to the young people's lives (Delpit, 1995)

Examples
1. When discussing World War Two, consider racism or other issues that are relevant to current issues in their own lives.

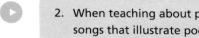

2. When teaching about poetry, encourage learners to find lyrics from popular songs that illustrate poetic devices, and talk about how these devices do or don't work well to communicate the meanings and feelings the songwriters intended.

For more ideas about formal operations, see http://chiron.valdosta.edu/whuitt/col/cogsys/piagtuse.html

Information-processing and neo-Piagetian views of cognitive development

As you will see in Chapter 7, there are explanations for why children have trouble with conservation and other Piagetian tasks. These explanations focus on the child's developing information-processing skills, such as attention, memory capacity and learning strategies. As children mature and their brains develop, they are better able to focus their attention, process information more quickly, hold more information in memory, and use thinking strategies more easily and flexibly. Siegler (1998, 2000) proposes that as children grow older, they develop progressively better rules and strategies for solving problems and thinking logically. Teachers can help pupils develop their capacities for formal thinking by putting the learners in situations that challenge their thinking and reveal the shortcomings of their logic. Siegler's approach is called 'rule assessment' because it focuses on understanding, challenging and changing the rules that children use for thinking.

Neo-Piagetian theories

More recent theories that integrate findings about attention, memory and strategy use with Piaget's insights about children's thinking and the construction of knowledge.

Some developmental psychologists have formulated neo-Piagetian theories that retain Piaget's insights about children's construction of knowledge and the general trends in children's thinking, but add findings from information processing about the role of attention, memory and strategies. For example, Robbie Case (1992, 1998) has devised an explanation of cognitive development suggesting that children develop in stages within specific domains such as numerical concepts, spatial concepts, social tasks, storytelling, reasoning about physical objects and motor development. As children practise using the schemes in a particular domain (e.g. using counting schemes in the number concept area), accomplishing the schemes takes less attention. The schemes become more automatic because the child does not have to 'think so hard' about it. This frees up mental resources and memory to do more. The child now can combine simple schemes into more complex ones and invent new schemes when needed (assimilation and accommodation in action).

Within each domain, such as numerical concepts or social skills, children move from grasping simple schemes during the early preschool years, to merging two schemes into a unit (between about ages four and six), to coordinating these scheme units into larger combinations, and finally, by about ages nine to 11, to forming complex relationships that can be applied to many problems (Berk, 2005; Case, 1992, 1998). Children do progress through these qualitatively different stages within each domain, but Case argues that progress in one domain does not automatically affect movement in another. The child must have experience and involvement with the content and the ways of thinking within each domain in order to construct increasingly complex and useful schemes and coordinated conceptual understandings about the domain.

Some limitations of Piaget's theory

Although most psychologists agree with Piaget's insightful descriptions of how children think, many disagree with his explanations of why thinking develops as it does.

The trouble with stages

Some psychologists have questioned the existence of four separate stages of thinking, even though they agree that children do go through the changes that Piaget described (Miller, 2002). One problem with the stage model is the lack of consistency in children's thinking. For example, children can conserve number (the number of blocks does not change when they are rearranged) a year or two before they can conserve weight (a ball of clay does not change when you flatten it). Why can't they use conservation consistently in every situation? In fairness, we should note that in his later work, even Piaget put less emphasis on stages of cognitive development and gave more attention to how thinking changes through equilibration (Miller, 2002).

Another problem with the idea of separate stages is that the processes may be more continuous than they seem. For example, rather than appearing all at once, object permanence may progress gradually as children's memories develop. The longer you make the infants wait before searching – the longer you make them remember the object – the older they have to be to succeed. Siegler (1998) notes that change can be both continuous and discontinuous, as described by a branch of mathematics called catastrophe theory. Changes that appear suddenly, like the collapse of a bridge, are preceded by many slowly developing changes such as gradual, continuous corrosion of the metal structures. Similarly, gradually developing changes in children can lead to large changes in abilities that appear to be abrupt (Fischer and Pare-Blagoev, 2000).

Underestimating children's abilities

It now appears that Piaget underestimated the cognitive abilities of children, particularly younger ones. The problems he gave young children may have been too difficult and the directions too confusing. His subjects may have understood more than they could demonstrate when solving these problems. For example, work by Gelman and her colleagues (Gelman, 2000; Gelman and Cordes, 2001) shows that preschool children know much more about the concept of number than Piaget thought, even if they sometimes make mistakes or get confused. As long as preschool children work with only three or four objects at a time, they can tell that the number remains the same, even if the objects are spread far apart or clumped close together. In other words, we may be born with a greater store of cognitive tools than Piaget suggested. Some basic understandings, such as the permanence of objects or the sense of number, may be part of our evolutionary equipment, ready for use in our cognitive development (Geary and Bjorklund, 2000).

Piaget's theory does not explain how even young children can perform at an advanced level in certain areas where they have highly developed knowledge and expertise. An expert nine-year-old chess player may think abstractly about chess moves, while a novice 20-year-old player may have to resort to more concrete strategies to plan and remember moves (Siegler, 1998).

Cognitive development and culture

One final criticism of Piaget's theory is that it overlooks the important effects of the child's cultural and social group. Children in Western cultures may master scientific thinking and formal operations because this is the kind of thinking required in Western schools (Berk, 2005; Geary, 1998). Even concrete operations such as classification may develop differently in different cultures. For example, when individuals from the Kpelle

Connect and Extend

For more information about Piaget see the Companion Website (Web Link 2.2).

people of Africa were asked to sort 20 objects, they created groups that made sense to them – a hoe with a potato, a knife with an orange. The experimenter could not get the Kpelle to change their categories; they said this is how a wise man would do it. Finally, the experimenter asked in desperation, 'Well, how would a fool do it?' Then the subjects promptly created the four neat classification piles the experimenter had expected – food, tools, and so on (Rogoff and Morelli, 1989).

There is another increasingly influential view of cognitive development. Proposed years ago by Lev Vygotsky and recently rediscovered, this theory ties cognitive development to culture.

Vygotsky's Sociocultural Perspective

Psychologists today recognise that culture shapes cognitive development by determining what and how the child will learn about the world. For example, young Zinacanteco Indian girls of southern Mexico learn complicated ways of weaving cloth through informal teachings of adults in their communities. In Brazil, without going to school, children who sell candy on the streets learn sophisticated mathematics in order to buy from wholesalers, sell, barter and make a profit. Cultures that prize cooperation and sharing teach these abilities early, whereas cultures that encourage competition nurture competitive skills in their children (Bakerman *et al.*, 1990; Ceci and Roazzi, 1994). The stages observed by Piaget are not necessarily 'natural' for all children because to some extent they reflect the expectations and activities of Western cultures (Kozulin, 2003; Rogoff, 2003).

Sociocultural theory

Emphasises role in development of cooperative dialogues between children and more knowledgeable members of society. Children learn the culture of their community (ways of thinking and behaving) through these interactions.

A major spokesperson for this sociocultural theory (also called sociohistoric) was a Russian psychologist who died in 1934. Lev Semenovich Vygotsky was only 38 when he died of tuberculosis, but during his brief life he produced over 100 books and articles and some of these translations are still available (Vygotsky, 1978, 1986, 1987a, 1987b, 1993 and 1997). Vygotsky's work began when he was studying learning and development to improve his own teaching. He went on to write about language and thought, the psychology of art, learning and development, and educating children with special needs. His work was banned in Russia for many years because he referenced Western psychologists. However, in the past 30 years, with the rediscovery of his work, Vygotsky's ideas have become major influences in psychology and education and have provided alternatives to many of Piaget's theories (Kozulin, 2003; McCaslin and Hickey, 2001; Wink and Putney, 2002).

Vygotsky believed that human activities take place in cultural settings and cannot be understood apart from these settings. One of his key ideas was that our specific mental structures and processes can be traced to our interactions with others. These social interactions are more than simple influences on cognitive development – they actually create our cognitive structures and thinking processes (Palincsar, 1998). In fact, 'Vygotsky conceptualized development as the transformation of socially shared activities into internalized processes' (John-Steiner and Mahn, 1996: 192). We will examine three themes in Vygotsky's writings that explain how social processes form learning and thinking: the social sources of individual thinking; the role of cultural tools in learning and development, especially the tool of language; and the zone of proximal development (Wertsch and Tulviste, 1992; Driscoll, 2005).

The social sources of individual thinking

Vygotsky assumed that 'every function in a child's cultural development appears twice: first, on the social level and later on the individual level; first between people (interpsychological) and then inside the child (intrapsychological)' (1978: 57). In other words, higher mental processes first are co-constructed during shared activities between the child and another person. Then the processes are internalised by the child and become part of that child's cognitive development. For example, children first use language in activities with others, to regulate the behaviour of the others ('No nap!' or 'Want drink.'). Later, however, the child can regulate her own behaviour using private speech ('careful – don't spill'), as you will see in 'The role of language and private speech' section later in this chapter. So, for Vygotsky, social interaction was more than influence, it was the origin of higher mental processes such as problem solving. Consider this example:

> *A six-year-old has lost a toy and asks her father for help. The father asks her where she last saw the toy; the child says 'I can't remember.' He asks a series of questions – did you have it in your room? Outside? Next door? To each question, the child answers, 'no.' When he says 'in the car?' she says 'I think so' and goes to retrieve the toy. (Tharp and Gallimore, 1988: 14)*

Who remembered? The answer is really neither the father nor the daughter, but the two together. The remembering and problem solving were co-constructed – between people – in the interaction. However, the child may have internalised strategies to use next time something is lost. At some point, the child will be able to function independently to solve this kind of problem. So, like the strategy for finding the toy, higher functions appear first between a child and a 'teacher' before they exist within the individual child (Kozulin, 1990: 2003).

Here is another example of the social sources of individual thinking. Richard Anderson and his colleagues (Anderson, Nguyen-Jahiel and McNurlen, 2001) studied how nine- and ten-year-olds in small-group classroom discussions appropriate (take for themselves and use) argument stratagems that occur in the discussions. An argument stratagem is a particular form such as 'I think [POSITION] because [REASON]', where the child fills in the position and the reason. For example, a child might say, 'I think that the foxes should be left alone because they are not hurting anyone'. Another strategy form is 'If [ACTION], then [BAD CONSEQUENCE]', as in 'If they don't kill the foxes, then the foxes will eat the chickens'. Other forms manage participation, for example, 'What do you think [NAME]?' or 'Let [NAME] talk'.

Anderson's research identified 13 forms of talk and argument that helped to manage the discussion, get everyone to participate, present and defend positions, and handle confusion. The researchers found that the use of these different forms of talking and thinking snowballed – once a useful argument was employed by one learner, it spread to other learners and the argument stratagem form appeared more and more in the discussions. Open discussions – learners asking and answering each other's questions – were better than teacher-dominated discussion for the development of these argument forms. Over time, these ways of presenting, attacking and defending positions could be internalised as mental reasoning and decision making for the individual learners.

Both Piaget and Vygotsky emphasised the importance of social interactions in cognitive development, but Piaget saw a different role for interaction. He believed that interaction encouraged development by creating disequilibrium – cognitive conflict – that motivated change. Thus, Piaget believed that the most helpful interactions were those between peers because peers are on an equal basis and can challenge each other's thinking. Vygotsky (1978, 1986, 1987a, 1987b, 1993), on the other hand, suggested that children's cognitive development is fostered by interactions with people who are more capable or advanced in their thinking – people such as parents and teachers (Leat and Nichols, 1997; Moshman, 1997; Palinscar, 1998). Of course, pupils

Co-constructed process

A social process in which people interact and negotiate (usually verbally) to create an understanding or to solve a problem. The final product is shaped by all participants.

can learn from both adults and peers who all use 'cultural tools' to support learning and the transmission of knowledge.

Cultural tools and cognitive development

Vygotsky emphasised the importance of the 'tools' that the culture provides to support thinking. He believed that all higher-order mental processes, such as reasoning and problem solving, are *mediated* by (accomplished through and with the help of) psychological tools, such as language, signs and symbols. Adults teach these tools to children during day-to-day activities and the children internalise them. Then the psychological tools can help learners advance their own development (Karpov and Haywood, 1998). The process is something like this: as children engage in activities with adults or more capable peers, they exchange ideas and ways of thinking about or representing concepts – drawing maps, for example, as a way to represent spaces and places. These co-created ideas are internalised by children. Thus, children's knowledge, ideas, attitudes and values develop through appropriating or 'taking for themselves' the ways of acting and thinking provided by both their culture and other members of their group (Kozulin and Presseisen, 1995).

Vygotsky believed that cultural tools, including material tools (such as printing presses, rulers and the abacus – today, we would add mobile phones, computers and the Internet) and psychological tools (signs and symbol systems such as numbers and mathematical systems, Braille and sign language, maps, works of art, signs, codes and language) play very important roles in cognitive development. For example, as long as the culture provides only Roman numerals for representing quantity, certain ways of thinking mathematically – from long division to calculus – are difficult or impossible. But if a number system has a zero, fractions, positive and negative values, and an infinite quantity of numbers, then much more is possible. The number system is a psychological tool that supports thinking, learning and cognitive development. This symbol system is passed from adult to child through formal and informal interactions and teachings.

In this exchange of signs and symbols and explanations, children begin to develop a 'cultural tool kit' to make sense of and learn about their world (Wertsch, 1991). The kit is filled with material tools such as pencils or rulers directed towards the external world and psychological tools such as concepts or problem-solving strategies for acting mentally. Children do not just receive the tools, however. They transform the tools as they construct their own representations, symbols, patterns and understandings. As we learned from Piaget, children's constructions of meaning are not the same as those of adults. In the exchange of signs and symbols, such as number systems, children create their own understandings (a fox is a 'doggy'). These understandings are gradually changed (a fox is a fox) as the children continue to engage in social activities and try to make sense of their world (John-Steiner and Mahn, 1996; Wertsch, 1991). In Vygotsky's theory, language is the most important symbol system in the tool kit, and it is the one that helps to fill the kit with other tools.

The role of language and private speech

Language is critical for cognitive development. It provides a way to express ideas and ask questions, the categories and concepts for thinking, and the links between the past and the future. Language frees us from the immediate situation to think about what was and what might be (Das, 1995; Driscoll, 2005). Vygotsky thought that:

> *the specifically human capacity for language enables children to provide for auxiliary tools in the solution of difficult tasks, to overcome impulsive action, to plan a solution to a problem prior to its execution, and to master their own behaviour. (1978: 28)*

Cultural tools

The real tools (computers, scales, rulers etc.) and symbol systems (numbers, language, graphs) that allow people in a society to communicate, think, solve problems and create knowledge.

Vygotsky stressed the importance of the tools which cultures provide to support thinking

If we study language across cultures, we see that different cultures need and develop different language tools.

Language and cultural diversity

In general, cultures develop words for the concepts that are important to them. For example, how many different shades of green can you name? When selecting a suitable colour for painting your living room there are hundreds of different shade cards available to choose from. English-speaking countries have over 3,000 words for colours. Such words are important in our lives for fashion and home design, artistic expression, films and television, and lipstick and eye shadow choices – to name only a few areas (Price and Crapo, 2002). Other cultures care less about colour. For example, the Hanunoo people of Midori Island in the Philippines and the Dani in New Guinea each have fewer than five words for colours, even though they can recognise many colour variations. Eskimos really don't have hundreds of words for snow, but the Ulgunigamiut Eskimo do have more than 160 words for ice, because they have to recognise ice at different stages of freezing in order to hunt and live safely in their environment. Cultures that care about feelings have many word tools to talk about emotion. Think of the variety of words in English for anger (rage, resentment, disgust, pique, wrath, fury, exasperation, ire, hostility, animosity, annoyance).

Languages change over time to indicate changing cultural needs and values. The Shoshoni Native Americans have one word that means 'to make a crunching sound walking on the sand'. This word was valuable in the past to communicate about hunting, but today, new words describing technical tools have been added to the language of the Shoshoni, as their life moves away from nomadic hunting. To hear hundreds of new 21st century tool words, listen to enthusiasts talk about computers (Price and Crapo, 2002).

Vygotsky placed more emphasis than Piaget on the role of learning and language in cognitive development. He believed that, 'thinking depends on speech, on the means of thinking, and on the child's socio-cultural experience' (Vygotsky, 1987: 120). In fact, Vygotsky believed that language in the form of private speech (talking to yourself) guides cognitive development.

Private speech: Vygotsky's and Piaget's views compared

It is commonly accepted that young children often talk to themselves as they play. Piaget called children's self-directed talk 'egocentric speech'. He assumed that this egocentric speech is another indication that young children can't see the world through the eyes of others. They talk about what matters to them, without taking into account the needs or interests of their listeners. As they mature, and especially as they have disagreements with peers, Piaget believed, children develop socialised speech. They learn to listen and exchange (or argue) ideas. Vygotsky had very different ideas about young children's private speech. Rather than being a sign of cognitive immaturity, Vygotsky suggested that these mutterings play an important role in cognitive development by moving children towards self-regulation: the ability to plan, monitor and guide one's own thinking and problem solving.

Vygotsky believed that self-regulation developed in a series of stages. First the child's behaviour is regulated by others using language and other signs such as gestures. For example, the parent says, 'No!' when the child reaches towards a candle flame. Next, the child learns to regulate the behaviour of others using the same language tools. The child says, 'No!' to another child who is trying to take away a toy, often even imitating the parent's voice tone. The child also begins to use private speech to regulate her own behaviour, saying 'No' quietly to herself as she is tempted to touch the flame. Finally, the child learns to regulate her own behaviour by using silent inner speech (Karpov and Haywood, 1998). For example, in any early years setting you

Private speech

Children's self-talk, which guides their thinking and action. Eventually, these verbalisations are internalised as silent inner speech.

might hear four- or five-year-olds saying, 'No, it won't fit. Try it here. Turn. Turn. Is this the one?' while they do puzzles. As these children mature, their self-directed speech goes underground, changing from spoken to whispered speech and then to silent lip movements. Finally, the children just 'think' the guiding words. The use of private speech peaks at around nine years then decreases, although there is research support (Berk, 1992) for Vygotsky's claim that private speech is used more when the task is difficult and that performance often improves after self-instruction (Berk and Spuhl, 1995). One study found that some learners from ages 11 to 17 still spontaneously muttered to themselves during problem solving (McCafferty, 2004; Winsler, Carlton, and Barry, 2000; Winsler and Naglieri, 2003).

This series of steps from spoken words to silent inner speech is another example of how higher mental functions appear first between people as they communicate and regulate each others' behaviour, and then emerge again within the individual as cognitive processes. Through this fundamental process, the child is using language to accomplish important cognitive activities such as directing attention, solving problems, planning, forming concepts and gaining self-control. Research supports Vygotsky's ideas (Berk and Spuhl, 1995; Emerson and Miyake, 2003). Children and adults tend to use more private speech when they are confused, having difficulties or making mistakes (Duncan and Cheyne, 1999). Inner speech not only helps us solve problems but also allows us to regulate our behaviour. Have you ever thought to yourself something like, 'Let's see, the first step is . . . ' or 'Where did I use my glasses last?' or 'If I work to the end of this page, then I can . . . '? You were using inner speech to remind, cue, encourage or guide yourself. In a really challenging situation, such as taking an important test, you might even find that you return to muttering out loud. Table 2.2 contrasts Piaget's and Vygotsky's theories of private speech. We should note that Piaget

Table 2.2   Differences between Piaget's and Vygotsky's theories of egocentric or private speech

	Piaget	**Vygotsky**
Developmental significance	Represents an inability to take the perspective of another and engage in reciprocal communication.	Represents externalised thought; its function is to communicate with the self for the purpose of self-guidance and self-direction.
Course of development	Declines with age.	Increases at younger ages and then gradually loses its audible quality to become internal verbal thought.
Relationship to social speech	Negative; least socially and cognitively mature children use more egocentric speech.	Positive; private speech develops out of social interaction with others.
Relationship to environmental contexts		Increases with task difficulty. Private speech serves a helpful self-guiding function in situations where more cognitive effort is needed to reach a solution.

Source: From 'Development of private speech among low-income Appalachian children' by L. E. Berk and R. A. Garvin, 1984, *Developmental Psychology, 20*, p. 272. Copyright © 1984 by the American Psychological Association. Adapted with permission.

accepted many of Vygotsky's arguments and came to agree that language could be used in both egocentric and problem-solving ways (Piaget, 1962).

Self-talk and learning

Because private speech helps learners to regulate their thinking, it makes sense to allow, and even encourage, pupils to use private speech in school. Teachers' insisting on total silence when young children are working on difficult problems may make the work even harder for them. If muttering increases when children are working, it could be a sign that they need help. One approach, developed by Donald Meichenbaum at the University of Waterloo, is called *cognitive self-instruction*. It teaches learners to use self-talk to guide learning. For example, children learn to give themselves reminders to go slowly and carefully.

The zone of proximal development

According to Vygotsky, at any given point in development, there are certain problems that a child is on the verge of being able to solve. The child just needs some structure, clues, reminders, help with remembering details or steps, encouragement to keep trying, and so on. Some problems, of course, are beyond the child's capabilities, even if every step is explained clearly. The zone of proximal development (ZPD) is the area between the child's current development level 'as determined by independent problem solving' and the level of development that the child could achieve 'through adult guidance or in collaboration with more capable peers' (Vygotsky, 1978: 86). This is the area where instruction can succeed, because real learning is possible. Kathleen Berger (2006) called this area the 'magic middle' – somewhere between what the learner already knows and what the learner isn't ready to learn (see Figure 2.3).

Zone of proximal development

Phase at which a child can master a task if given appropriate help and support.

Private speech and the zone

We can see how Vygotsky's beliefs about the role of private speech in cognitive development fit with the notion of the zone of proximal development. Often, an adult uses

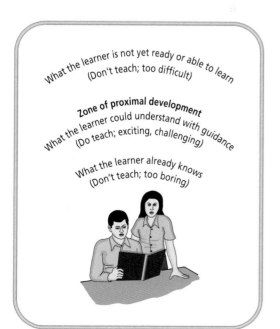

Figure 2.3
Teaching in the magic middle

The zone of proximal development is the teaching space between the boring and the impossible. In that space scaffolding from the teacher or a peer can support learning.

Source: Adapted from K. S. Berger (2003). *The Developing Person Through Childhood and Adolescence*, 6/E. New York: Worth Publishers, Fig. 2.5, p. 50.

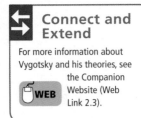

Connect and Extend

For more information about Vygotsky and his theories, see the Companion Website (Web Link 2.3).

verbal prompts and structuring to help a child to solve a problem or accomplish a task. This scaffolding can be gradually reduced as the child takes over the guidance, perhaps first by giving the prompts as private speech and finally as inner speech. Let's move forward to a future day in the life of the girl in the earlier example who had lost her toy and listen to her thoughts when she realises that a schoolbook is missing. They might sound something like this:

Where's my mathematics book? Used it in class. Thought I put it in my school bag after class. Dropped my bag on the bus. That idiot Matthew kicked my stuff, so maybe . . .

The girl can now systematically search for ideas about the lost book without help from anyone else.

The role of learning and development

Piaget defined *development* as the active construction of knowledge and *learning* as the passive formation of associations (Siegler, 2000). In other words children build (construct) their own understanding and base it upon what they already know. He was interested in knowledge construction and believed that cognitive development has to come before learning – the child had to be cognitively 'ready' to learn. He said that 'learning is subordinated to development and not vice-versa' (Piaget, 1964: 17). Learners can memorise, for example, that Geneva is in Switzerland, but still insist that they cannot be Genevan and Swiss at the same time. True understanding will take place only when the child has developed the operation of class inclusion – one category can be included in another. In contrast, Vygotsky believed that learning was an active process that does not have to wait for readiness. In fact, 'properly organized learning results in mental development and sets in motion a variety of developmental processes that would be impossible apart from learning' (Vygotsky, 1978: 90). He saw learning as a tool in development – learning pulls development up to higher levels and social interaction is a key in learning (Glassman, 2001; Wink and Putney, 2002). Vygotsky's belief that learning pulls development to higher levels means that other people, including teachers, play a significant role in cognitive development.

Limitations of Vygotsky's theory

Vygotsky's theory added important considerations by highlighting the role of culture and social processes in cognitive development, but he may have gone too far. As we have seen in this chapter, we may be born with a greater store of cognitive tools than either Piaget or Vygotsky suggested. Some basic understandings, such as the idea that adding increases quantity, may be part of our biological predispositions, ready for use to guide our cognitive development. Young children appear to figure out much about the world before they have the chance to learn from either their culture or teachers (Schunk, 2004). Also, Vygotsky did not detail the cognitive processes underlying developmental changes – which cognitive processes allow learners to engage in more advanced and independent participation in social activities? The major limitation of Vygotsky's theory, however, is that it consists mostly of general ideas; Vygotsky died before he could expand and elaborate on his ideas and pursue his research. His learners continued to investigate his ideas, but much of that work was suppressed until the 1950s and 1960s by Stalin's regime (Gredler, 2005; Kozulin, 1990, 2003). A final limitation might be that Vygotsky did not have time to detail the applications of his theories for teaching, even though he was very interested in instruction. So most of the applications described today have been created by others – and we don't even know if Vygotsky would agree with them.

Implications of Piaget's and Vygotsky's Theories for Teachers

Piaget did not make specific educational recommendations and Vygotsky did not have enough time to develop a complete set of applications. But we can glean some guidance from both men.

Piaget: what can we learn?

Piaget was more interested in understanding children's thinking than in guiding teachers. He did express some general ideas about educational philosophy, however. He believed that the main goal of education should be to help children learn how to learn so that they construct their own meanings and that education should 'form not furnish' the minds of learners (Piaget, 1969: 70). Even though Piaget did not design programmes of education based on his ideas, many other people have. For example, the Stepping Stones outlined within The Early Years Foundation Stage of the National Curriculum for England has guidelines for practitioners to plan activities which meet the needs of learners at different stages of development in the six areas of learning (personal, communication, mathematical, world knowledge, physical and creative). These are not age related but recognise developmental progression in children's learning thus reflecting Piaget's ideas. (DfEE/QCA, 2000).

Piaget has taught us that we can learn a great deal about how children think by listening carefully, by paying close attention to their ways of solving problems. If we understand children's thinking, we will be better able to match teaching methods to children's current knowledge and abilities.

Understanding and building on children's thinking

The learners in any class will vary greatly in both their level of cognitive development and their academic knowledge. A teacher or facilitator may wish to determine whether children are having trouble because they lack the necessary thinking abilities or because they simply have not learned the basic facts. To do this, Case (1985) suggests they need to observe learners carefully as they try to solve the problems they have been presented with. What kind of logic do they use? Do they focus on only one aspect of the situation? Are they misled by appearances? Do they suggest solutions systematically or by guessing and forgetting what they have already tried? If learners are asked how they tried to solve the problem and attention is paid to their answers, the kind of thinking and strategies they used will be revealed and help to explain their repeated mistakes or problems. Learners are the best sources of information about their own thinking (Confrey, 1990).

Implications of Piaget's theory for learning contexts

An important implication is what Hunt years ago (1961) called 'the problem of the match'. Children must be neither bored by work that is too simple nor left behind by teaching they cannot understand. According to Hunt, disequilibrium must be kept 'just right' to encourage growth. Setting up situations that lead to unexpected results can help create an appropriate level of disequilibrium. When pupils experience some conflict between what they think should happen (a piece of wood should sink because it is big) and what actually happens (it floats!), they may rethink the situation and new knowledge may develop. Capitalising on the unexpected is a basis for conceptual change teaching in science.

Many materials and lessons can be understood at several levels and can be 'just right' for a range of cognitive abilities. Classics such as *Alice in Wonderland* myths, and fairy tales can be enjoyed at both concrete and symbolic levels. It is also possible for a group of children to be introduced to a topic together, then work individually on follow-up activities matched to their learning needs. Often it makes sense to let pupils choose their own follow-up activities – with encouragement from the teacher to tackle challenges. Using multi-level lessons is called differentiated instruction (Tomlinson, 2005). We look at this approach more closely in Chapter 13.

Activity and constructing knowledge

Piaget's fundamental insight was that individuals construct their own understanding; learning is a constructive process. At every level of cognitive development, you will also want to see that children and young people are actively engaged in the learning process. In his words:

> *Knowledge is not a copy of reality. To know an object, to know an event, is not simply to look at it and make a mental copy or image of it. To know an object is to act on it. To know is to modify, to transform the object, and to understand the process of this transformation, and as a consequence to understand the way the object is constructed. (Piaget, 1964: 8)*

This active experience, even at the earliest school levels, should not be limited to the physical manipulation of objects. It should also include mental manipulation of ideas that arise out of class projects or experiments (Gredler, 2005). For example, after a lesson about different jobs, a primary teacher might show the class a picture of a woman and ask, 'What could this person be?' After answers such as 'teacher', 'doctor', 'secretary', 'lawyer', 'saleswoman', and so on, the teacher could suggest, 'How about a daughter?' Answers such as 'sister', 'mother', 'aunt', and 'granddaughter' may follow. This should help the children change dimensions in their classification and centre on another aspect of the situation. Next, the teacher might suggest 'English', 'athletic' or 'curly-haired'. With older children, hierarchical classification might be involved: it is a picture of a woman, who is a human being; a human being is a primate, which is a mammal, which is an animal, which is a life form.

All learners need to interact with teachers and peers in order to test their thinking, to be challenged, to receive feedback and to watch how others work out problems. Disequilibrium is often set in motion quite naturally when the teacher or another child suggests a new way of thinking about something. As a general rule, children should act on, manipulate, observe and then talk and/or write about (to the teacher and each other) what they have experienced. Concrete experiences provide the raw materials for thinking. Communicating with others makes learners use, test and sometimes change their thinking abilities.

The value of play

Maria Montessori once noted, 'Play is children's work' and Piaget would agree. We saw that the brain develops with stimulation and play provides some of that stimulation at every age. Babies in the sensorimotor stage learn by exploring, sucking, pounding, shaking, throwing – acting on their environments. Preoperational preschoolers love 'pretend' play and use pretending to form symbols, use language and interact with others. They are beginning to play simple games with predictable rules. Primary-school-age children also like fantasy, but are beginning to play more complex games and sports, and thus learn cooperation, fairness, negotiation, winning and losing, as well as developing more sophisticated language. As children grow into adolescents, play continues to be part of their physical and social development (Meece, 2002).

Piaget taught us that children do not think like adults. His influence on developmental psychology and education has been enormous, even though recent research has not supported all of his ideas. There is evidence also of a shift in child–teacher relationships since the introduction of Piaget's ideas into the arena of educational psychology (Cunningham, 2006).

Vygotsky: What can we learn?

There are at least three ways that cultural tools can be passed from one individual to another: imitative learning (where one person tries to imitate the other), instructed learning (where learners internalise the instructions of the teacher and use these instructions to self-regulate) and collaborative learning (where a group of peers strives to understand each other and learning occurs in the process) (Tomasello, Kruger and Ratner, 1993). Vygotsky was most concerned with instructed learning through direct teaching or by structuring experiences that support another's learning, but his theory supports the other forms of cultural learning as well. Thus, Vygotsky's ideas are relevant for those who teach directly and also create learning environments (Das, 1995; Wink and Putney, 2002). One major aspect of teaching in either situation is assisted learning.

The role of adults and peers

Vygotsky believed that cognitive development occurs through the child's conversations and interactions with more capable members of the culture – adults or more able peers. These people serve as guides and teachers, providing the information and support necessary for the child to grow intellectually. Thus, the child is not alone in the world 'discovering' the cognitive operations of conservation or classification. This discovery is assisted or mediated by family members, teachers and peers. Most of this guidance is communicated through language, at least in Western cultures. In some cultures, observing a skilled performance, not talking about it, guides the child's learning (Rogoff, 1990). Jerome Bruner called this adult assistance scaffolding (Wood, Bruner and Ross, 1976). The term aptly suggests that children use this help for support while they build a firm understanding that will eventually allow them to solve the problems on their own.

Assisted learning

Vygotsky's theory suggests that teachers, facilitators and caregivers need to do more than just arrange the environment so that children can discover on their own. Children cannot and should not be expected to reinvent or rediscover knowledge already available in their cultures. Rather, they should be guided and assisted in their learning – so Vygotsky saw teachers, parents and other adults as central to the child's learning and development (Karpov and Haywood, 1998).

Assisted learning, or guided participation in the classroom, requires the scaffolding described above – giving information, prompts, reminders and encouragement at the right time and in the right amounts, and then gradually allowing the learners to do more and more on their own (Table 2.3). Teachers and caregivers can assist learning by adapting materials or problems to children's current levels; demonstrating skills or thought processes; walking learners through the steps of a complicated problem; doing part of the problem (e.g. in algebra, the pupils set up the equation and the teacher does the calculations or vice versa); giving detailed feedback and allowing revisions; or asking questions that refocus learners' attention (Rosenshine and Meister, 1992). Cognitive self-instruction is an example of assisted learning. Cognitive apprenticeships and instructional conversations (Chapter 9) are other examples.

Connect and Extend

See the following research article that explores ways that current early years teachers view the influence of Piaget. Cunningham, P. (2006), 'Early years teachers and the influence of Piaget: evidence from oral history', *Early Years: Journal of International Research and Development, 26*(1) pp. 5–16.

Scaffolding

Support for learning and problem solving. The support could be clues, reminders, encouragement, breaking the problem down into steps, providing an example or anything else that allows the individual to grow in independence as a learner.

Assisted learning

Providing strategic help in the initial stages of learning, gradually diminishing as learners gain independence.

Connect and Extend

For a discussion of using scaffolding within the learning situation see the **WEB** Companion Website (Web Link 2.4).

Table 2.3 Assisted learning: strategies to scaffold complex learning

- *Procedural facilitators.* These provide a 'scaffold' to help pupils learn implicit skills. For example, a teacher might encourage pupils to use 'signal words' such as *who, what, where, when, why* and *how* to generate questions after reading a passage.

- *Modelling use of facilitators.* The teacher in the above example might model the generation of questions about the reading.

- *Thinking out loud.* This models the teacher's expert thought processes, showing pupils the revisions and choices the learner makes in using procedural facilitators to work on problems.

- *Anticipating difficult areas.* During the modelling and presentations phase of instructions, for example, the teacher anticipates and discusses potential pupil errors.

- *Providing prompt or cue cards.* Procedural facilitators are written on 'prompt cards' that students keep for reference as they work. As pupils practise, the cards

gradually become unnecessary. Think of these like the 'quick reference cards' that came with your computer or fax machine.

- *Regulating the difficulty.* Tasks involving implicit skills are introduced by beginning with simpler problems, providing for pupil practice after each stage and gradually increasing the complexity of the task.

- *Providing half-done examples.* Giving pupils half-done examples of problems and having them work out the conclusions can be an effective way to teach pupils how to ultimately solve problems on their own.

- *Reciprocal teaching.* Having the teacher and pupils rotate the role of teacher. The teacher provides support to pupils as they learn to lead discussions and ask their own questions.

- *Providing checklists.* Pupils can be taught self-checking procedures to help them regulate the quality of their responses.

Source: From O'Neil, J. (1990) 'Effective teaching redux', *ASCD Update, 32*(6), p. 5. Reprinted with permission. The Association for Supervision and Curriculum Development is a worldwide community of educators advocating sound policies and sharing best practices to achieve the success of each learner. To learn more, visit ASCD at www.ascd.org.

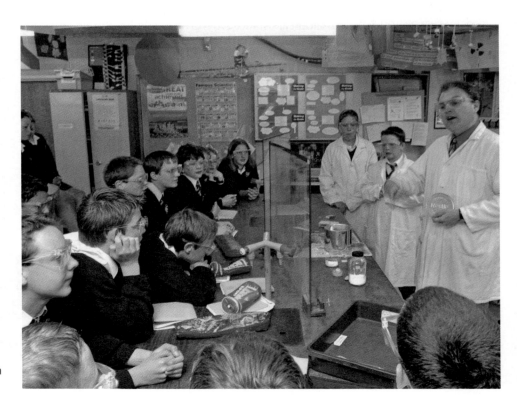

According to Vygotsky much of children's thinking is assisted by teachers and most of this guidance is communicated through language.

Teaching and the 'magic middle'

Both Piaget and Vygotsky probably would agree that learners need to be taught in the magic middle (Berger, 2006) or the place of the 'match' (Hunt, 1961) – where they are neither bored nor frustrated. Children should be put in situations where they have to reach to understand, but where support from peers or the teacher is also available. Sometimes the best teacher is another child who has just worked out how to solve the problem, because this child is probably operating in the learner's zone of proximal development. Children and young people should be guided by explanations, demonstrations and work with other learners – opportunities for cooperative learning. Having a child work with someone who is just a bit better at the activity would also be a good idea – both learners benefit in the exchange of explanations, elaborations and questions. In addition, children should be encouraged to use language to organise their thinking and to talk about what they are trying to accomplish. Dialogue and discussion are important avenues to learning (Karpov and Bransford, 1995; Kozulin and Presseisen, 1995; Wink and Putney, 2002). The Focus on Practice below gives more ideas for applying Vygotsky's ideas.

Piaget and Vygotsky would agree that language plays a major role in learning, both inside and outside the classroom. Let's look at this human capability more closely.

FOCUS ON PRACTICE

Applying Vygotsky's ideas in the learning situation

Tailor scaffolding to the needs of learners

Examples

1. When learners are beginning new tasks or topics, provide models, prompts, sentence starters, instruction and feedback. As the learners grow in competence, give less support and more opportunities for independent work.
2. Give learners choices about the level of difficulty or degree of independence in projects; encourage them to challenge themselves, but to seek help when they are really stuck.

Make sure learners have access to powerful tools that support thinking

Examples

1. Encourage learners to use learning and organisational strategies, research tools, language tools (dictionaries or computer searches) spreadsheets and word-processing programs.
2. Model the use of tools; show learners how you use a diary or electronic notebook to make plans and manage time, for example.

Build on the learners' cultural funds of knowledge (Moll *et al.*, 1992)

Examples
1. Identify family knowledge by having learners interview each others' families about their work and home knowledge (agriculture, economics, manufacturing, household management, medicine and illness, religion, child care, cooking, etc.).
2. Link assignments with these funds of knowledge and use community experts to evaluate assignments.

Capitalise on dialogue and group learning

Examples
1. Experiment with peer tutoring; teach learners how to ask good questions and give helpful explanations.
2. Experiment with cooperative learning strategies described in Chapter 11.

The Development of Language

All children in every culture master the complicated system of their native language, unless severe deprivation or physical problems interfere. This knowledge is remarkable. At the least, sounds, meanings, words and sequences of words, volume, voice tone, inflection and turn-taking rules must all be coordinated before a child can communicate effectively in conversations.

It is likely that many factors – biological and experiential – play a role in language development. One early view suggested that random babbling sounds made by the child (such as 'dadadada') are responded to by those caring for the child ('Yes, Daddy's home – what a clever girl!'). Thus the young child learns to say 'Daddy' because it has been rewarded by a positive response and probably plenty of attention. Children learn new words by imitating sounds that they hear and improve their use of language as they are corrected by those around them. However, children often manufacture their own words which they have certainly not heard used. For example, children will often over-generalise plurals incorrectly and refer to 'foots' and 'mouses' or they will create 'never heard' phrases such as 'all-gone dinner'. Reward and correction certainly play a part in helping children learn language but the child's thinking in putting together the parts of this complex system is very important (Rosser, 1994).

The important point is that children develop language as they build on other cognitive abilities by actively trying to make sense of what they hear and by looking for patterns and making up rules to put together the jigsaw puzzle of language. In this process, humans may have built-in biases, rules and constraints about language that restrict the number of possibilities considered. For example, young children seem to have a constraint specifying that a new label refers to a whole object, not just a part. Another built-in bias appears to lead children to assume that the label refers to a class of similar objects. So the child learning about the rabbit may assume that rabbit refers to the whole animal (not just its ears) and that other similar-looking animals are also rabbits (Markman, 1992). Reward and correction play a role in helping children learn accurate language use, but the child's thinking in putting together the parts of this complicated system is very important (Flavell *et al.*, 2002). Table 2.4 shows the

Table 2.4 Milestones in language in the first six years and ways to encourage development

Age range	Milestone	Strategies to encourage development
By age 1	Says 1–2 words; recognises name; imitates familiar sounds; understands simple instructions	• Respond to coos, gurgles and babbling. • Tell nursery rhymes and sing songs. • Teach the names of everyday items and familiar people. • Play simple games such as 'peek-a-boo' and 'pat-a-cake'.
Between 1 and 2	Uses 5–20 words, including names, says 2-word sentences; vocabulary is growing; waves goodbye; makes 'sounds' of familiar animals; uses words (like 'more') to make wants known; understands 'no'	• Reward and encourage early efforts at saying new words. • Talk about everything you're doing while you're with the child. • Talk simply, clearly and slowly. • Look at the child when he or she talks to you. • Describe what the child is doing, feeling, hearing. • Let the child listen to children's records and tapes.
Between 2 and 3	Identifies body parts; calls self 'me' instead of name; combines nouns and verbs; has a 450-word vocabulary; uses short sentences; matches 3–4 colours, knows 'big' and 'little'; likes to hear same story repeated; forms some plurals; answers 'where' questions	• Help and child listen and follow instructions by playing simple games. • Repeat new words over and over. • Describe what you are doing, planning, thinking. • Have the child deliver simple messages for you. • Show the child you understand what he says by answering, smiling and nodding your head. • Expand what the child says. Child: 'more juice'. You say, 'Chris wants more juice.'
Between 3 and 4	Can tell a story; sentence length of 4–5 words; vocabulary about 1000 words; knows last name, name of street, several nursery rhymes	• Talk about how objects are the same or different. • Help the child to tell stories using books and pictures. • Encourage play with other children. • Talk about places you've been or will be going. • Help the child sort objects and things (e.g. things to eat, animals).
Between 4 and 5	Sentence length of 4–5 words; uses past tense; vocabulary of about 1,500 words; identifies colours, shapes; asks many questions like 'why?' and 'who?'	• Teach the child how to use the telephone. • Let the child help you plan activities. • Continue talking about the child's interests. • Let the child tell and make up stories for you.
Between 5 and 6	Sentence length of 5–6 words; average 6-year-old has vocabulary of about 10,000 words; defines objects by their use; knows spatial relations (like 'on top' and 'far') and opposites; knows address; understands 'same' and 'different'; uses all types of sentences	• Praise children when they talk about feelings, thoughts, hopes, fears. • Sing songs, rhymes. • Talk with them as you would an adult.
At every age		• Listen and show your pleasure when the child talks to you. • Carry on conversations with the child. • Ask questions to get the child to think and talk. • Read books to the child every day, increasing in length as the child develops.

Source: Adapted from http://www.ldonline.org/ld_indepth/speech-language/lda_milestones.html
http://www.med.umich.edu/1libr/yourchild/devmile.htm. Reprinted from LDOnLine.org, with thanks to the Learning Disabilities Association of America.

milestones of language development, ages one to six, in Western cultures, along with ideas for encouraging development. The next section looks at theoretical explanations of language development as these may help us to anchor our own understanding.

Theories of language development

By about age three or four, most children have mastered the basics of their native language. This is a considerable achievement it itself but one which adults usually take for granted. It becomes even more impressive when the complexities of this process (including pronunciation, grammar, vocabulary and meaning, pragmatics and metalingual awareness) are considered. These aspects are discussed in the 'Language development in the school years' section which follows but before we look at these it is useful to think about some of the main theoretical explanations for language development.

The question of how children acquire language has intrigued philosophers for centuries and the debate still continues. Generally it is helpful to view these in the light of the nature–nurture debate referred to near the beginning of this chapter.

Nature or nurture?

Three key approaches have been suggested to explain language acquisition. These are behavioural theories (*nurture*), nativist theories (*nature*) and social interactionist theories (*combination of nature and nurture*).

Behavioural approaches were popular in the early and middle part of the 20th century and they proposed that children basically learn language through reinforcement (Skinner, 1957). Therefore an accidental babbling sound such as 'dadadada' from an infant would be responded to (reinforced) by the parent/caregiver perhaps with, 'Daddy? What a clever girl! You said "daddy" didn't you?' and so on. This makes the child more likely to repeat the sound again in order to gain the attention or recognition given. Many claims for this approach have not stood the test of time as there are frequent examples of children using words creatively which they have not heard or been reinforced for using before. An example of this is a toddler screaming, 'All-gone teddy' when he cannot find his cuddly toy. Further, the rules of grammar are very difficult and parents/caregivers rarely correct grammatical errors (Brown and Hanlon, 1970). However, whilst the behavioural approach cannot explain all aspects of language development it does provide insights into the importance of the environment and the influence of caregivers. Let us now look at the nativist approach to see whether it can answer some of the unanswered questions about language acquisition.

Nativist approaches suggest that children have an inbuilt facility for language and thus they are biologically programmed to develop language. The work of Noam Chomsky (1957) is the cornerstone of this *nature* approach, which is radically different from the behaviourist understanding. Chomsky argued that the reason children are able to unravel the complexities of their native language so easily is because they have an innate neural device (the *language acquisition device* or *LAD*) that allows them to absorb and decode language easily. This device is triggered by hearing language spoken and is flexibly able to adapt to any language.

Other theorists such as Lenneberg (1967) support Chomsky's nativist ideas about language acquisition although they take a less specific approach. Lenneberg suggests that there is a 'critical period' during childhood for language learning to happen. After this the brain has lost its flexibility and therefore learning a second language after this for example is very difficult. This is an interesting point when we consider that the majority of second language learning in UK schools takes place in secondary (post-11 years) education. Perhaps this accounts for the fact that English people are notoriously bad at speaking other languages fluently. What do you think?

> ### STOP AND THINK
>
> Think back to the section on the brain and cognitive development.
> - Are there ways in which Chomsky's ideas link with the overproduction of neurons and synapses?
> - Might this allow for the brain to adapt to the native language experienced and thus 'prune' those sounds which are not used?
> - Could this explain the difficulties with certain sounds from other languages we discussed earlier?

Whether or not Chomsky's LAD or Lenneberg's 'critical period' exists remains debatable but there seems little current argument that children are specially prepared to learn language and thus there are elements of 'nature' involved. Many contemporary theorists suggest a social-interactionist explanation.

Social-interactionist perspectives agree that humans are biologically prepared for language in a way that other species are not. However, they also see the environment as an important part of language development. Jerome Bruner (1983), for example, believed that the way language is presented to children helps them to engage with it more easily. He labelled that way that adults talk to infants (using high-pitched, simple, repetitive, exaggerated language) 'child-directed speech' and suggested that adults use this automatically to make language more accessible to young children. Similarly the ideas of Piaget and Vygotsky (earlier in this chapter) include an understanding of the role of interaction with the environment where development (including language) is concerned. As we said at the beginning of this section, the basics of language are acquired by three or four years of age and by the time children begin school they are generally fluent. Let's now look at the school years to see what happens next.

Language development in the school years

What remains then for the school-age child to accomplish?

Pronunciation

The majority of five- and six-year-olds have mastered most of the sounds of their native language, but a few may remain unconquered. The j, v, th and zh sounds are the last to develop. About 10% of eight-year-olds still have some trouble with s, z, v, th and zh (Rathus, 1988). Young children may understand and be able to use many words, but they may prefer to use the words they can pronounce easily.

Grammar

Children master the basics of word order, or syntax, in their native language early. However, the more complicated forms, such as the passive voice ('The car was hit by the bus'), take longer to master. By about five, many children can understand the meaning of passive sentences, yet they do not use such constructions in their normal conversations, unless the passive construction is common in their culture. Other accomplishments during primary school include first understanding and then using complex grammatical structures such as extra clauses, qualifiers and conjunctions. In adolescence, learners can understand and use more elaborate grammatical constructions – clauses, connecting words, longer sentences, and so on (Berk, 2005).

Vocabulary and meaning

The average six-year-old has a vocabulary of 8,000 to 14,000 words, growing to about 40,000 by age 11. In fact, some researchers estimate that children in the early school years learn up to 20 words a day (Berger, 2003). School-age children enjoy language games and jokes that play on words. In the early school years, some children may have trouble with abstract words such as justice or economy. They also may not understand the subjunctive case ('If I were a butterfly') because they lack the cognitive ability to reason about things that are not true ('But you aren't a butterfly'). They may interpret all statements literally and thus misunderstand sarcasm or metaphor. Fables are understood concretely simply as stories instead of as moral lessons, for example. Many children are in their preadolescent years before they are able to distinguish being teased from being taunted or before they know that a sarcastic remark is not meant to be taken literally. However, by adolescence, learners are able to use their developing cognitive abilities to decipher abstract word meanings and to use poetic, figurative language (Berk, 2005).

Pragmatics

Pragmatics

The rules for when and how to use language to be an effective communicator in a particular culture.

Pragmatics involves the appropriate use of language to communicate. For instance, children must learn the rules of turn-taking in conversation. Young children may appear to take turns in conversations, but if you listen in, you realise that they are not exchanging information, only talk time. In later primary school, children's conversations start to sound like conversations. Contributions are usually on the same topic. By middle childhood, learners understand that an observation can be a command, as in 'I see too many children at the pencil sharpener.' By adolescence, individuals are very adept at varying their language style to fit the situation. Thus, they can talk to their peers in 'slang' that makes little sense to adults, but it marks the adolescent as a member of the group. Yet these same young people can speak politely to adults (especially when making requests) and write persuasively about a topic in history. As learners grow older, they are more able to judge if their communications are clear to their audience. Interacting with adults, and especially peers who challenge unclear messages, helps develop this skill (Berk, 2005).

Metalinguistic awareness

Metalinguistic awareness

Understanding about one's own use of language.

Around the age of five, children begin to develop metalinguistic awareness. This means their understanding about language and how it works becomes explicit. They have knowledge about language itself. They are ready to study and extend the rules that have been implicit – understood but not consciously expressed. This process continues throughout life, as we all become better able to use language. One goal of schooling is the development of language and literacy.

Partnerships with families

Connect and Extend

See Letts, C. and Hall, E. (2003), 'Exploring early years professionals' knowledge about speech and language development and impairment.' *Child Language Teaching & Therapy, 19*, pp. 211–229 for a discussion of increasing demands upon early years staff to identify and accommodate language difficulties.

Especially in the early years, the child's home experiences are central in the development of language and literacy (Roskos and Neuman, 1993; Whitehurst *et al.*, 1994). In homes that promote literacy, parents and other adults value reading as a source of pleasure, and there are books and other printed materials everywhere. Parents read to their children, take them to bookshops and libraries, limit the amount of television everyone watches, and encourage literacy-related play such as setting up a pretend school or writing 'letters' (Pressley, 1996; Roskos and Neuman, 1998; Sulzby and Teale, 1991). Of course, not all homes provide this literacy-rich environment, but teachers can help by encouraging families to be involved in the child's goals and school activities. This might include, for example, sending regular news bulletins to homes which suggest home activities to support children's learning, inviting parents to take part in classroom activities when possible and encouraging family members to work with children at home. Let us now look at children using two languages to see how/whether this may impact upon language development.

Dual language development

Many school-aged children speak a language other than English at home. The number grows each year. It is a misconception that young children learn a second language faster than adolescents or adults. In fact, older learners go through the stages of language learning faster than young children. Adults have more learning strategies and greater knowledge of language in general to bring to bear in mastering a second language (Diaz-Rico and Weed, 2002). Age is a factor in learning language, but 'not because of any critical period that limits the possibility of language learning by adults' (Marinova-Todd, Marshall and Snow, 2000: 28). However, there appears to be a critical period for learning accurate language pronunciation. The earlier people learn a second language, the more their pronunciation is near-native. After adolescence, it is difficult to learn a new language without speaking with an accent (Anderson and Graham, 1994). Kathleen Berger (2006) concludes that the best time to teach a second language is during early or middle childhood, but the best time to learn on your own through exposure (and to learn native pronunciation) is early childhood.

Luckily, learning a second language does not interfere with understanding in the first language. In fact, the more proficient the speaker is in the first language, the more quickly he will master a second language (Cummins, 1984, 1994). For most children who learn two languages simultaneously as toddlers, there is a period between ages two and three when they progress more slowly because they have not yet worked out that they are learning two different languages. They may mix up the grammar of the two but researchers believe that by age four, if they have enough exposure to both languages, they sort things out and speak as well as native monolinguals, people who speak only one language (Baker, 1993; Reich, 1986). Also, bilingual children may mix vocabularies of the two languages when they speak, but this is not a sign that they are confused because their bilingual parents often intentionally mix vocabularies as well. It takes from three to five years to become truly competent in the second language (Berk, 2005; Bhatia and Richie, 1999).

There is no cognitive disadvantage for children who learn and speak two languages. In fact, there are benefits. Higher degrees of bilingualism are correlated with increased cognitive abilities in such areas as concept formation, creativity and cognitive flexibility. In addition, these learners have more advanced metalinguistic (language in which to think and talk about language) awareness; for example, they are more likely to notice grammatical errors. These findings seem to hold good as long as there is no stigma attached to being bilingual and as long as children are not expected to abandon their first language to learn the second (Berk, 2005; Bialystok, 1999; Galambos and Goldin-Meadow, 1990; Garcia, 1992; Ricciardelli, 1992). In addition, speaking English plus another language can be a considerable asset, for example when graduates enter the business world (Mears, 1998). Let us now look at cognitive development across cultures in order to understand any differences and similarities which may affect learning.

Cross-cultural differences in cognitive development

Research across different cultures has confirmed that Piaget was accurate in the sequence of stages he described, but there is diversity in the age ranges for the stages. Western children typically move to the next stage about two to three years earlier than children in non-Western societies. Careful research has shown that these differences across cultures depend on the subject or domain tested and how much the culture values and teaches knowledge in that domain. For example, children in Brazil who sell sweets in the streets instead of attending school appear to fail a certain kind of Piagetian task – class inclusion (Are there more daisies, more tulips, or more flowers in the picture?). However, when the tasks are phrased in concepts they understand – selling sweets – these children perform better than Brazilian children the same age who attend school (Ceci and Roazzi, 1994). When a culture or context emphasises a cognitive ability, children growing up in that culture tend to acquire the ability sooner. In another study that compared Chinese six- and seven-year-old, eight- and nine-year-old, and ten- and 11-year-old children to American learners of the same ages, the Chinese children mastered a Piagetian task that involved distance, time and speed relationships about two years ahead of American children. The Chinese education system puts more emphasis on mathematics and science in the early years of school (Zhou *et al.*, 2001).

We have also seen that there is diversity in language development. Some children learn two or more languages growing up, others only one. Children in every culture and context learn their native language, but they may learn a different set of rules for language use – pragmatics. For example, children brought up within Asian cultures may develop higher-level receptive language skills than children brought up within Western cultures who tend to have higher-level expressive skills. This may be because Asian cultures emphasise the listener's role in ensuring accurate communication whereas the responsibility rests with the speaker within Western cultures (Meesook, 2003).

Cross-cultural similarities in cognitive development

In spite of these cross-cultural differences in cognitive development, there are some convergences. Piaget, Vygotsky and more recent researchers studying cognitive development and the brain probably would agree with the following major ideas:

1. Cognitive development requires both physical and social stimulation.
2. To develop thinking, children have to be mentally, physically and linguistically active. They need to experiment, talk, describe, reflect, write and solve problems. However, they also benefit from teaching, guidance, questions, explanations, demonstrations and challenges to their thinking.
3. Play matters. It is the way children and adolescents try out their thinking and learn to interact with others.
4. Teaching what the learner already knows is boring. Trying to teach what the child or young person is not ready to learn (too difficult, too complex, too little background knowledge) is frustrating and ineffective.
5. Challenge with support will keep learners engaged but not fearful.

SUMMARY TABLE

A Definition of Development (pp. 30–38)

What are the different kinds of development?

Human development can be divided into physical development (changes in the body), personal development (changes in an individual's personality), social development (changes in the way an individual relates to others) and cognitive development (changes in thinking).

What are the three principles of development?

Theorists generally agree that people develop at different rates, that development is an orderly process, and that development takes place gradually.

What part of the brain is associated with higher mental functions?

The cortex is a crumpled sheet of neurons that serves three major functions: receiving signals from sense organs (such as visual or auditory signals), controlling voluntary movement and forming associations. The part of the cortex that controls physical motor movement develops or matures first, then the areas that control complex senses such as vision and hearing, and last the frontal lobe, which controls higher-order thinking processes.

What is lateralisation and why is it important?

Lateralisation is the specialisation of the two sides, or hemispheres, of the brain. The brain begins to lateralise soon after birth. For most people, the left hemisphere is the major factor in language, and the right hemisphere is prominent in spatial and visual processing. However, even though certain functions are associated with certain parts of the brain, the various parts and systems of the brain work together to learn and perform complex activities such as reading and to construct understanding.

Piaget's Theory of Cognitive Development (pp. 38–52)

What are the main influences on cognitive development?

Piaget's theory of cognitive development is based on the assumption that people try to make sense of the world and actively create knowledge through direct experiences with objects, people and ideas. Maturation, activity, social transmission and the need for equilibrium all influence the way thinking processes and knowledge develop. In response to these influences, thinking processes and knowledge develop through changes in the organisation of thought (the development of schemes) and through adaptation – including the complementary processes of assimilation (incorporating into existing schemes) and accommodation (changing existing schemes).

What is a scheme?

Schemes are the basic building blocks of thinking. They are organised systems of actions or thought that allow us to mentally represent or 'think about' the objects and events in our world. Schemes may be very small and specific (grasping, recognising a square), or they may be larger and more general (using a map when visiting a new place). People adapt to their environment as they increase and organise their schemes.

As children move from sensorimotor to formal-operational thinking, what are the major changes?

Piaget believed that young people pass through four stages as they develop: sensorimotor, preoperational, concrete-operational and formal-operational. In the sensorimotor stage, infants explore the world through their senses and motor activity, and work towards mastering object permanence and performing goal-directed activities. In the preoperational stage, symbolic thinking and logical operations begin. Children in the stage of concrete operations can think logically about tangible situations and can demonstrate conservation, reversibility, classification and seriation. The ability to perform hypothetico-deductive reasoning, coordinate a set of variables and imagine other worlds marks the stage of formal operations.

How do neo-Piagetian and information-processing views explain changes in children's thinking over time?

Information-processing theories focus on attention, memory capacity, learning strategies, and other processing skills to explain how children develop rules and strategies for making sense of the world and solving problems. Neo-Piagetian approaches also look at attention, memory and strategy use as well as how thinking develops in different domains such as numbers or spatial relations.

What are some limitations of Piaget's theory?

Piaget's theory has been criticised because children and adults often think in ways that are inconsistent with the notion of invariant stages. It also appears that Piaget underestimated children's cognitive abilities. Alternative explanations place greater emphasis on children's developing information-processing skills and ways that caregivers and teachers can enhance their development. Piaget's work is also criticised for overlooking cultural factors in child development.

Vygotsky's Sociocultural Perspective (pp. 52–58)

According to Vygotsky, what are three main influences on cognitive development?

Vygotsky believed that human activities must be understood in their cultural settings. He believed that our specific mental structures and processes can be traced to our interactions with others; that the tools of the culture, especially the tool of language, are key factors in development; and the zone of proximal development is the area where learning and development are possible.

What are psychological tools and why are they important?

Psychological tools are signs and symbol systems such as numbers and mathematical systems, codes and language that support learning and cognitive development – they change the thinking process by enabling and shaping thinking. Many of these tools are passed from adult to child through formal and informal interactions and teachings.

Explain how interpsychological development becomes intrapsychological development

Higher mental processes appear first between people as they are co-constructed during shared activities. As children engage in activities with adults or more capable peers, they exchange ideas and ways of thinking about or representing concepts. These co-created ideas are internalised by children. Thus children's knowledge, ideas, attitudes and values develop through appropriating, or 'taking for themselves,' the ways of acting and thinking provided by their culture and by the more capable members of their group.

What are the differences between Piaget's and Vygotsky's perspectives on private speech and its role in development?

Vygotsky's sociocultural view asserts that cognitive development hinges on social interaction and the development of language. As an example, Vygotsky describes the role of children's self-directed talk in guiding and monitoring thinking and problem solving, while Piaget suggested that private speech was an indication of the child's egocentrism. Vygotsky, more than Piaget, emphasised the significant role played by adults and more able peers in children's learning. This adult assistance provides early support while learners build the understanding necessary to solve problems on their own later.

What is a learner's zone of proximal development?

At any given point in development, there are certain problems that a child is on the verge of being able to solve and others that are beyond the child's capabilities. The zone of proximal development is the area where the child cannot solve a problem alone, but can be successful under adult guidance or in collaboration with a more advanced peer.

What are two criticisms or limitations of Vygotsky's theory?

Vygotsky may have overemphasised the role of social interaction in cognitive development – children work out many things on their own.

Also, because he died so young, Vygotsky was not able to develop and elaborate on his theories. His students and others since (such as Daniil El'konin and Daniel Luria) have taken up that work.

Implications of Piaget's and Vygotsky's Theories for Teachers (pp. 59–64)

What is the 'problem of the match' described by Hunt?

The 'problem of the match' is that learners must be neither bored by work that is too simple nor left behind by teaching they cannot understand. According to Hunt, disequilibrium must be carefully balanced to encourage growth. Situations that lead to errors can help create an appropriate level of disequilibrium.

What is active learning? Why is Piaget's theory of cognitive development consistent with active learning?

Piaget's fundamental insight was that individuals *construct* their own understanding; learning is a constructive process. At every level of cognitive development, learners must be able to incorporate information into their own schemes. To do this, they must act on the information in some way. This active experience, even at the earliest school levels, should include both physical manipulation of objects and mental manipulation of ideas. As a general rule, children should act, manipulate, observe and then talk and/or write about what they have experienced. Concrete experiences provide the raw materials for thinking. Communicating with others obliges learners use, test and sometimes change their thinking abilities.

What is assisted learning and what role does scaffolding play?

Assisted learning, or guided participation in the classroom, requires scaffolding – giving information, prompts, reminders and encouragement at the right time and in the right amounts, and then gradually allowing the learners to do more and more on their own.

Teachers can assist learning by adapting materials or problems to children's current levels, demonstrating skills or thought processes, walking learners through the steps of a complicated problem, doing part of the problem, giving detailed feedback and allowing revisions or asking questions that refocus learners' attention.

The Development of Language (pp. 64–70)

How are humans predisposed to develop language? What role does learning play?

Children develop language as they build on other cognitive abilities by actively trying to make sense of what they hear, looking for patterns and making up rules. In this process, built-in biases and rules may limit the search and guide the pattern recognition. Reward and correction play a role in helping children learn correct language use, but the child's thought processes are very important.

What are pragmatics and metalinguistic awareness?

Pragmatics is knowledge about how to use language – when, where, how and to whom to speak. Metalinguistic awareness begins around age five or six and grows throughout life.

Glossary

Accommodation: Altering existing schemes or creating new ones in response to new information.

Adaptation: Adjustment to the environment.

Adolescent egocentrism: Assumption that everyone else shares one's thoughts, feelings and concerns.

Assimilation: Fitting new information into existing schemes.

Assisted learning: Providing strategic help in the initial stages of learning, gradually diminishing as learners gain independence.

Classification: Grouping objects into categories.

Co-constructed process: A social process in which people interact and negotiate (usually verbally) to create an understanding or to solve a problem. The final product is shaped by all participants.

Cognitive development: Gradual orderly changes by which mental processes become more complex and sophisticated.

Collective monologue: Form of speech in which children in a group talk but do not really interact or communicate.

Compensation: The principle that changes in one dimension can be offset by changes in another.

Concrete operations: Mental tasks tied to concrete objects and situations.

Conservation: Principle that some characteristics of an object remain the same despite changes in appearance.

Cultural tools: The real tools (computers, scales, rulers etc.) and symbol systems (numbers, language, graphs) that allow people in a society to communicate, think, solve problems and create knowledge.

Decentring: Focusing on more than one aspect at a time.

Development: Orderly, adaptive changes we go through from conception to death.

Disequilibrium: In Piaget's theory, the 'out-of-balance' state that occurs when a person realises that his or her current ways of thinking are not working to solve a problem or understand a situation.

Egocentric: Assuming that others experience the world the way that you do.

Equilibration: Search for mental balance between cognitive schemes and information from the environment.

Formal operations: Mental tasks involving abstract thinking and coordination of a number of variables.

Goal-directed actions: Deliberate actions towards a goal.

Hypothetico-deductive reasoning: A formal-operations problem-solving strategy in which an individual begins by identifying all the factors that might affect a problem and then deduces and systematically evaluates specific solutions.

Identity: Principle that a person or object remains the same over time.

Lateralisation: The specialisation of the two hemispheres (sides) of the brain cortex.

Maturation: Genetically programmed, naturally occurring changes over time.

Metalinguistic awareness: Understanding about one's own use of language.

Myelination: The process by which neural fibres are coated with a fatty sheath called myelin which makes message transfer more efficient.

Neo-Piagetian theories: More recent theories that integrate findings about attention, memory and strategy use with Piaget's insights about children's thinking and the construction of knowledge.

Neurons: Nerve cells that store and transfer information.

Object permanence: The understanding that objects have a separate, permanent existence.

Operations: Actions a person carries out by thinking them through instead of literally performing the actions.

Organisation: Ongoing process of arranging information and experience into mental systems or categories.

Personal development: Changes in personality that take place as one grows.

Physical development: Changes in body structure and function over time.

Plasticity: The brain's tendency to remain somewhat adaptable or flexible.

Pragmatics: The rules for when and how to use language to be an effective communicator in a particular culture.

Preoperational: The stage before a child masters logical mental operations.

Private speech: Children's self-talk, which guides their thinking and action. Eventually, these verbalisations are internalised as silent inner speech.

Reversibility: A characteristic of Piagetian logical operations – the ability to think through a series of steps, then mentally reverse the steps and return to the starting point; also called reversible thinking.

Reversible thinking: Thinking backwards, from the end to the beginning.

Scaffolding: Support for learning and problem solving. The support could be clues, reminders, encouragement, breaking the problem down into steps, providing an example, or anything else that allows the individual to grow in independence as a learner.

Schemes: Mental systems or categories of perception and experience.

Semiotic function: The ability to use symbols – language, pictures, signs or gestures – to represent actions or objects mentally.

Sensorimotor: Involving the senses and motor activity.

Seriation: Arranging objects in sequential order according to one aspect, such as size, weight or volume.

Social development: Changes over time in the ways we relate to others.

Sociocultural theory: Emphasises the role in development of cooperative dialogues between children and more knowledgeable members of society. Children learn the culture of their community (ways of thinking and behaving) through these interactions.

Synapses: The tiny space between neurons – chemical messages are sent across these gaps.

Zone of proximal development: Phase at which a child can master a task if given appropriate help and support.

CHECK YOUR LEARNING! WEB

In the Classroom: What Would They Do?

Here is how one practising teacher dealt with the challenge of teaching abstract concepts such as 'symbols' to nine- and ten-year-old children.

Class teacher of nine- and ten-year-olds in rural primary school (UK)

To begin the lesson I would show the class a simple, outline drawing of a car or a house and ask them to identify it. When they had named it, I would ask them about different types of cars and houses and encourage them to understand that these simple drawings represented ALL kinds of cars and houses. This would allow me then to introduce the word 'symbol' as something representing all of these different categories. I would follow this with a practical map-making session – based upon the immediate area in which the school was located – and include in this the use of pictorial symbols to show where various things were located (e.g. telephones, bus-stops, road crossings etc.). Further work would be done on developing this concept of 'symbols' by using greetings cards (such as Valentine's Day, Christmas or Easter) and working with the children to construct a collage that included a variety of these (hearts, Christmas trees, Easter eggs and so on). This would be accompanied by a discussion of what these pictures mean/ symbolise to them and others and thus help them to understand the idea of something complex being represented/symbolised in this way.

Overview

Schooling involves more than cognitive development. As you remember your years in school, what stands out – memories about academic knowledge or memories of feelings, friendships and fears? In this chapter, we examine personal, social and emotional development.

We begin with a basic aspect of development that affects all the others – physical changes as children mature. Next, we turn to Sigmund Freud, Erik Erikson and Urie Bronfenbrenner, whose comprehensive theories provide frameworks for studying personal and social development. We then consider the three major influences on children's personal and social development: families, peers and teachers. Families today have gone through many transitions, and these changes affect the roles of teachers. Next, we explore ideas about how we come to understand ourselves by looking at self-concept and identity, including ethnic and sexual identity. Finally, we look at emotional and moral development. What factors determine our views about morality? What can facilitators of children's learning do to foster such personal qualities as honesty, cooperation and self-esteem?

By the time you have completed this chapter, you should be able to answer these questions:

- **How does physical development affect personal and social development in adolescence?**

- **How does an understanding of Freud's ideas help us to understand children's emotional development?**
- **What are Erikson's stages of psychosocial development, and what are the implications of his theory for learning contexts?**
- **How does Bronfenbrenner's framework describe the social systems that influence development?**
- **What are the roles of peers, cliques and friendships in learners' lives?**
- **What can teachers do to deal with aggression and bullying in schools?**
- **How do relationships with teachers support children's development?**
- **How can teachers help to foster genuine and appropriate self-esteem in their learners?**
- **How does ethnic identity develop?**
- **What are Kohlberg's stages of moral reasoning, and what are some of the challenges to his work?**
- **Which factors encourage aggression and cheating in classrooms, and how can these be responded to effectively?**
- **What are some of the risks and challenges which learners face today, and how are teachers involved in attempting to respond to these?**

In the Classroom

Think for a moment about how best to deal with a situation between a group of 12–13-year-old learners which seems particularly vicious. A clique of popular girls has made life miserable for several of their former friends – now rejects. The discarded friends have committed the social sins of not fitting in – they wear the wrong clothes or aren't attractive enough or aren't interested in boys yet. To keep the status distinctions clear between themselves and 'the others', the popular girls spread gossip about their former friends, often disclosing the intimate secrets revealed when the 'out' girls and the 'in' girls were *best* friends – only a few months ago. Then you discover that Sophie, one of the rejected girls, has written a long, confidential e-mail to her former best friend Alison, asking why Alison is 'being so cruel'. The now-popular Alison forwarded the e-mail to the entire school and Sophie is humiliated. She has been absent for three days since the incident.

This chapter will help to answer questions about how best to respond to the girls in this situation as well as inform your understanding of many other aspects of social and emotional development.

Group Activity

With at least two other people in your group, discuss your own experiences of being an adolescent at school. Did you have problems with being accepted and fitting in with peers? Were there others in your year group who did? How were issues resolved?

Physical Development

For most children, at least in the early years, growing up means getting bigger, stronger and more coordinated. It also can be a frightening, disappointing, exciting and puzzling time because not only are their bodies changing but the demands made upon them are also changing. They are faced with new environments and responsibilities and expected to mix with others, perhaps in preschool or nursery settings as well as finding responsibilities.

The preschool years

Preschool children are very active. Their gross-motor (large muscle) skills improve greatly over the years from ages two to five (see Table 3.1). Between ages two and about four or five, young children's muscles grow stronger, their balance improves and their centre of gravity moves lower, so they are able to run, jump, climb and hop. Most of these movements develop naturally if the child has normal physical abilities and the opportunity to play. Children with physical problems, however, may need special training to develop these skills. For young children, as for many adolescents and adults, physical activity can be an end in itself. It is fun just to improve. However, because they can't always judge when to stop, preschoolers may need interludes of rest scheduled after periods of physical exertion (Darcey and Travers, 2006).

Fine-motor skills such as tying shoes or fastening buttons, which require the coordination of small movements, also improve greatly during the preschool years (Table 3.1). Children should be given the chance to work with large paintbrushes, fat pencils and crayons, large pieces of drawing paper, large plastic building blocks and soft clay or play dough to accommodate their developing skills. During this time, children will begin to develop a lifelong preference for their right or left hand. By age five, about 90% of children prefer their right hand for most skilled work and 10% or so prefer their left hand, with more boys than girls being left-handed (Feldman, 2004). This is a genetically based preference which is best left to develop naturally.

Table 3.1 Motor skills in the preschool years

Pupils' motor skills improve throughout the preschool years

Approximate age	Gross-motor skills	Fine-motor skills
Birth to 3 years	Sits and crawls; begins to run	Picks up, grasps, stacks and releases objects
3 to 4.5 years	Walks up and down stairs; jumps with both feet; throws ball	Holds crayon; uses utensils; buttons; copies shapes
4.5 to 6 years	Skips; rides two-wheel bicycle; catches ball; plays sports	Uses pencil; makes representational drawing; cuts with scissors, prints letters

Children need opportunities to learn for themselves in order to develop initiative

The early school years

During the early school years, physical development is fairly steady for most children. They become taller, leaner and stronger, so they are better able to master sports and games. There is tremendous variation, however. A particular child can be much larger or smaller than average and still be perfectly healthy. Because children at this age are very aware of physical differences but are not the most tactful people, you may hear comments such as 'You're too little to be in this class. What's wrong with you?' or 'Why are you so fat?'

Throughout early and middle childhood, many girls are likely to be as large as or larger than the boys in their classes. Between the ages of 11 and 14, girls are, on the average, taller and heavier than boys of the same age (Cook and Cook, 2005). The size discrepancy can give the girls an advantage in physical activities, although some girls may feel conflict over this because it is counter to societal expectations about boys and girls and, as a result, downplay their physical abilities.

Adolescence

Puberty marks the beginning of sexual maturity. It is not a single event, but a series of changes involving almost every part of the body. The sex differences in physical development observed during the earlier years become even more pronounced at the beginning of puberty. Generally, girls begin puberty between ages 10 and 11, about two years ahead of boys, and reach their final height by age 16 or 17; most boys continue growing until about age 18, but both boys and girls can continue to grow slightly until about 25. The average age for girls in the UK and Europe to have their first menstrual period is just under 13. One tension for adolescents is that they are physically and sexually mature years before they are psychologically or financially ready to shoulder the adult responsibilities of marriage and childrearing.

The physical changes of adolescence have significant effects on the individual's identity. Psychologists have been particularly interested in the academic, social and

Puberty

The physiological changes during adolescence that lead to the ability to reproduce.

emotional differences they have found between adolescents who mature early and those who mature later. Early maturation seems to have certain special advantages for boys. The early maturers' taller, broader-shouldered body type fits the cultural stereotype for the male ideal. Early-maturing boys are more likely to enjoy high social status; they tend to be popular and to be leaders. However, they also tend to have more mental health problems, such as anxiety and depression, and engage in more delinquent behaviour as research from a variety of cultures has reported (Kaltiala-Heino *et al.*, 2003; Cota-Robles, Neiss and Rowe, 2002). This may be because they have less time to develop psychologically and academically before encountering the social and sexual challenges of adolescence. On the other hand, boys who mature late may initially have a difficult time because they are lagging behind their peers but benefit later. Some studies show that in adulthood, males who matured later tend to be more creative, tolerant and perceptive. Perhaps the trials and anxieties of maturing late teach some boys to be better problem solvers (Brooks-Gunn, 1988; Steinberg, 2005).

For girls, these effects are reversed. Maturing way ahead of peers can be a definite disadvantage. Being larger than everyone else in the class is not a valued characteristic for girls in many cultures (Jones, 2004). A girl who begins to mature early probably will be the first in her peer group to start the changes of puberty. Early maturation is associated with emotional difficulties such as depression, anxiety and eating disorders, especially in Western societies that define thin as attractive (Steinberg, 2005). Later-maturing girls seem to have fewer problems, but they may worry that something is wrong with them. All young people can benefit from knowing that the 'normal' range in rates of maturation is great and that there are advantages for both early and late maturers.

Adolescents going through the changes of puberty are very concerned about their bodies. This has always been true, but today, the emphasis on fitness and appearance makes adolescents even more likely to worry about how their bodies 'measure up'. Both boys and girls can become dissatisfied with their bodies during adolescence – boys because they do not match the muscular models they see and girls because they don't match the cultural ideals either. For girls, it also appears that conversations with friends about appearance can make dissatisfactions worse (Jones, 2004). For some, the concern becomes excessive. One consequence is eating disorders such as bulimia (binge eating) and anorexia nervosa (self-starvation), both of which are more common in females than in males. Recent research in Australia suggested that almost half of the 80 five- to eight-year-old girls interviewed wanted to be slimmer and most thought that being slimmer was likely to increase their popularity. Forty-five per cent of the girls said that they would diet if they gained weight (Dohnt and Tiggemann, 2005). The UK Eating Disorder Association commented that they were not surprised by this finding as children as young as eight had been diagnosed with anorexia in the UK (BBC News, 2005). Even more recently a report in the *Independent* highlighted the rise of websites known as 'pro-ana' which encourage extreme dieting and near starvation. These sites (over 1,000) include picture galleries of extremely thin celebrities such as Victoria Beckham and images of emaciated women who are near to death by starvation. It is suggested that children and young people are turning to these websites because of the conflicting messages they receive about diet and health. On the one hand there is an increased focus upon healthy eating and anti-obesity but on the other they are surrounded by advertisements for junk food and images of extremely thin females (Goodchild, 2006). Sadly eating disorders now affect more than one girl in every hundred and there are increasing signs of boys also being referred for treatment (Beat, 2007). Let us look at these disorders in more detail.

Bulimia

Eating disorder characterised by overeating, then getting rid of the food by self-induced vomiting or laxatives.

Anorexia nervosa

Eating disorder characterised by very limited food intake.

Bulimics often binge, eating a family-sized carton of ice cream or a whole cake. Then, to avoid gaining weight, they force themselves to vomit, or they use strong laxatives, to purge themselves of the extra calories. Bulimics tend to maintain a normal weight, but their digestive systems can be permanently damaged.

Anorexia is an even more dangerous disorder, for anorexics either refuse to eat or eat practically nothing while often exercising obsessively. In the process, they may lose 20% to 25% of their body weight, and some (about 20%) literally starve themselves to death. Anorexic learners become very thin, and may appear pale, have brittle fingernails and develop fine dark hairs all over their bodies. They are easily chilled because they have so little fat to insulate their bodies. They often are depressed, insecure, moody and lonely. Girls may stop having their menstrual period. These eating disorders often begin in adolescence and are becoming more common, particularly amongst girls. These young people usually require professional help and it is important to notice the warning signs as less than one-third of people with eating disorders actually receive treatment (Stice and Shaw, 2004). A teacher or facilitator of learning may be the person who begins the chain of help for learners with these tragic problems.

Connect and Extend

See Fairborn, C. and Harrison, J. (2003), 'Eating disorders', *The Lancet, 361*, pp. 407–416 for an informative discussion of eating disorders and their management available at http://dx.doi.org

The brain and adolescent development

Along with all the other changes in puberty come changes in the brain and neurological system that affect personal and social development. Throughout adolescence, changes in the brain increase learners' computational skills as well as their ability to control behaviour in both low-stress and high-stress situations, to be more purposeful and organised and to inhibit impulsive behaviour. However, these abilities are not fully developed until the early 20s, so adolescents may 'seem' like adults, at least in low-stress situations, but their brains are not fully developed. They may have trouble controlling emotions and avoiding risky behaviours. In fact, adolescents appear to need more intense emotional stimulation than either children or adults, so these young people are set up for taking risks or seeking thrills. Teachers can take advantage of their adolescent learners' intensity by helping them devote their energy to areas such as politics, the environment or social causes (Price, 2005), or by guiding them to explore emotional connections with characters in history or literature.

Other changes in the neurological system during adolescence affect sleep; teenagers need about nine hours of sleep per night, but many young peoples' biological clocks are reset so it is difficult for them to fall asleep before midnight. Yet in many places school begins by 8:30 a.m., so nine hours of sleep are impossible and learners are continually sleep-deprived. Classes that keep young people in their seats, taking notes for the whole lesson may literally send them to sleep. With no time for breakfast, and little for lunch, these learners' nutrition often is deprived as well (Sprenger, 2005).

We turn now to personal and social development and begin with the psychoanalytic theory of Sigmund Freud. We then consider the context of development with reference to the ideas of Erik Erikson and Urie Bronfenbrenner.

Freud: Stages of Individual Development

Sigmund Freud who moved from being a medical doctor to psychologist is probably the most famous and influential 20th-century thinker. His ideas are so well-known that they form part of popular culture, for example Freudian slips, the analysis of dreams and our understanding of the unconscious mind. He is probably

Id

The instinctive needs and desires of a person present from birth.

Ego

Responsible for dealing with reality and meeting needs of the id in a socially acceptable way.

Superego

Holds all the moral principles and ideals acquired from parents and society.

Conscience

Includes information about those things viewed as bad by parents and society – punishes with guilt.

Ego-ideal

Includes standards of good, desirable behaviour approved by parents and society – rewarded with feelings of pride.

Psychosexual stages

The stages through which humans pass as they develop their adult personality.

best known as the 'father' of psychoanalysis and it is his ideas about the development of personality which are of particular interest to us here. Freud described human personality as a dynamic mechanism consisting of the id, the ego and the superego.

The id is present at birth and is made up of the person's instinctive needs and desires which seek to maximise pleasure and minimise pain (sometimes known as the *minimax* principle). The newborn infant's personality consists solely of id as he or she seeks to have his or her needs for food, warmth and comfort met.

The ego develops as the part of personality concerned with reality. This finds ways of effectively meeting the needs of the id whilst also dealing with external demands, such as those from parents, caregivers or society in general. So the young child learns that smiling at mother is an effective way of gaining attention which may well result in his or her needs for food, warmth or comfort being met.

The superego is the moral, principled part of personality which acts as a kind of internalised parent, caregiver or teacher. It is made up of the conscience which punishes unacceptable thoughts, feelings and behaviours with guilt and the ego-ideal which provides us with a sense of how we should aspire to behave, rewarding us with a sense of satisfaction when we have behaved in ways consistent with these aspirations.

Freud suggested in *Three Essays on the Theory of Sexuality*, published in 1905, that development occurs through a series of psychosexual stages that are predetermined and differentiated (Fleud, 1962). Each stage involves conflicts between the id, ego and superego and is focused upon a different area of the body. The developing person encounters and must resolve these conflicts as he or she progresses through the stages. Table 3.2 presents a summary of these stages.

According to Freudian theory then, development involves resolving these conflicts in a way which is sufficiently balanced in order for healthy emotional growth to take place. If this does not occur then a person may become fixated at a certain stage and regress (go back to) when in stressful situations. For example a child who has been overindulged or deprived of being allowed to suck (oral stimulation) may continue to seek this

---

Table 3.2   Freud's psychosexual stages of development

Stage	Description
Oral (Birth–1 year approximately)	The mouth is the centre of pleasure here and thus the feeding and weaning process (where stimulation and interaction occur) is critical.
Anal (1–3 years approximately)	The anus becomes the focus of stimulation as toilet training is carried out.
Phallic (3–6 years approximately)	Attention moves to the genitals as the centre of stimulation. Gender role and moral development occur.
Latency (6–12 years approximately)	A period of little sexual activity as development is focused upon physical and intellectual issues.
Genital (12 years–adult)	Genitals are the focus of stimulation as puberty occurs and mature sexual relationships develop.

throughout life even though it might be unhealthy. People who overeat, are alcohol dependent or smoke heavily would then be fixated at the earliest stage of emotional development and those who manage to overcome these fixations but return to them when facing stressful situations have regressed to them. (I am aware that I am chewing gum as I write and wonder how many of you are biting your nails or pen as you read?)

Implications for those working with children

Although Freud's stages of development focus upon the years of early childhood they are relevant for a deeper understanding of the emotional life of older children and adolescents as well as adults. Freud himself is often criticised for basing his theories upon retrospective material and for having little professional contact with children (Eysenck and Wilson, 1973; Greenberg, 1986). Anna Freud (his youngest daughter) and Melanie Klein, however, applied psychoanalytical concepts directly to children arguing that they provide educators with insights into the inner conflicts for children (Freud, 1931; Klein, 1959). Generally, they suggest that formal education conflicts with and seeks to repress the child's natural desires for pleasure and stimulation and that teachers need to be therapists as well as educators of children. Anna Freud commented, 'in each period there is a different emotional reaction of the child to those around him . . .' (1963: 93). Teachers then should aim to provide for the emotional needs of children by providing safe, inclusive learning environments and avoiding unnecessary frustrations.

Another aspect of psychoanalysis relevant to the learning situation is the awareness of *transference* taking place. This is the idea, identified by Freud during work with his patients, that an authority figure might act as an unwitting target for unresolved issues with the original authority figures (parents) in a child's life (Freud, 1953) So, for example, a child who displays a strong emotional response, such as fear or anger, towards a teacher he or she has just encountered may be transferring these feelings from those felt towards the mother or father. A teacher who is aware of this possibility is much more likely to be able to deal effectively with this response than one who is simply hurt or bewildered by it.

So far we have discussed Freud's ideas and their relevance to those interested in understanding human development. However, there are many criticisms of his work which we will turn to here before moving to attachment theory.

Criticisms of Freud's theory

Although Freud's theories remain significant they have long been subjected to extensive criticism, mainly in terms of their lack of scientific legitimacy. These criticisms can be grouped into four general categories. First, critics contend that Freud's theory is *untestable* because it is difficult to prove or disprove, which means that it has little scientific value. So, for example, if you were biting your nails or pen as you read earlier, Freudian theory would suggest that you were orally fixated but this would be impossible to test scientifically. Second, Freud's ideas are criticised for lacking *empirical evidence* (experimental data) and relying too heavily on his therapeutic achievements. The sample Freud used was very small and consisted of his patients (suffering from psychological problems) who were mainly wealthy middle-class women in late 19th-century Vienna. Therefore, it is not realistic or scientifically legitimate to generalise these findings to other groups or populations but the theory is presented as one which is universally applicable. Third, Freud's theory has no *predictive value*, which is part of the criteria applied to scientific research. If, for example, a child had no mother figure, it would not predict the future development or behaviour of the child. Fourth, many of the interpretations Freud made of his patients' underlying problems were based upon his own *subjective* analysis and may well have been interpreted differently by

Fixated

A person remains fixed at a certain psychosexual stage and their personality reflects this throughout life.

Regress

A person returns to an earlier stage of development when in stressful situations.

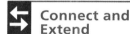

Connect and Extend

See the 'Sigmund Freud: his life and work' website at www.freudfile.org/ for more detailed information and links.

other therapists. For example, Freud's interpretations of dreams rely upon his own coding of symbols (such as towers or other cylindrical objects as phallic symbols) but these may well have many other meanings for individuals.

However, the fact that many of Freud's ideas have stood the test of time and remain the most widely known, suggest that, despite these limitations, they still have value in terms of providing an alternative or additional view of human development. A central aspect of Freud's work is the importance placed upon the early years of a child's life. This is seen as central principle in determining the kind of adults children become. We move here to a consideration of attachment theory in order to explore the nature and importance of a child's attachment to the mother or main caregiver.

Attachment Theory

Attachment

The emotional bond between an infant and a caregiver.

The development of an emotional bond or attachment is usually formed between an infant and his or her caregiver during the first year of life and is seen by many as an important base for future relationships. If this is the case then it is potentially important for the future social and emotional development of the child.

The most famous attachment theorist is John Bowlby (1907–1990) who argued that the need for attachment was an instinctive biological need and that mother love in infancy and childhood was as important for mental health as are vitamins and protein for the physical body (1951). Bowlby argued that babies who were separated from their mothers before becoming securely attached would find it impossible to bond with others and in later life suffer ill effects from this deprivation. Further, based upon his studies of delinquent boys in 1944, he suggested a link between maternal deprivation and juvenile crime.

Although much of his work is criticised because of its emphasis upon a *monotropic* attachment (innate tendency to become attached to *one* particular adult female) and on methodological grounds, Bowlby's theory was comprehensive and provided a foundation for research into the nature of early relationships.

Mary Ainsworth used Bowlby's ideas as a basis for measuring different attachment types and devised a laboratory-based 'strange situation' test (Ainsworth and Wittig, 1969). This involved providing an unfamiliar but interesting environment where the child (usually about a year old) was motivated to explore but needed to feel secure (an unfamiliar room with toys). An observer then recorded the child's responses to the departure and subsequent return of the mother. This research revealed significant differences between children's responses which Ainsworth categorised into three major *attachment types:*

1. **Anxious/avoidant** where the child may not be distressed by the mother leaving and may avoid or turn away from her when she returns.
2. **Securely attached** where the child is distressed by the mother's departure and easily comforted when she returns.
3. **Anxious/resistant (anxious/ambivalent)** where the child may be extremely 'clingy' during the first few minutes and become very distressed when she leaves. When she returns the child will seek comfort at the same time as distance from the mother, for example, crying and reaching up to be held but trying to wriggle away when picked up.

The importance of forming secure attachment has been indicated by many studies that have looked at connections between attachment type and later behaviour and development. These indicate that *securely attached children* are superior on a range of different measures including, persistence when solving problems, using symbolic play

(Matas, Arend and Stroufe, 1978), social and cognitive competence (Waters, 1978; Miens, 1997; Crandell and Hobson, 1999), engaging in successful problem solving (Frankel and Bates, 1990), and making friends at school (Lyons-Ruth *et al.*, 1997). On the other hand children classed as *insecurely attached* (avoidant or anxious/resistant) are less effective when mixing with others, succeed less when attempting to master challenging tasks and have more behavioural problems (van den Boom and Hoeksma, 1994).

Ainsworth suggests that the primary carer needs to provide a secure base from which the child can explore the world. If the child develops a sense of trust in the caregiver, he or she is more likely to become independent earlier. Sensitive responsiveness seems to be a key factor here so the child's needs are met. This includes attentiveness to the child, mutuality of interactions and the mother's ability to stimulate the child (Murray and Trevarthen, 1985; Brazleton *et al.*, 1975; Brazleton and Cramer, 1991).

There are implications here, as with the emphasis which Freudian theory places on early experiences, for those children entering day care at an early age and indeed for entering preschool or early years educational settings. Those children with insecure attachment types are not necessarily happy and secure and it makes it particularly important that emotional security is provided within the context of early years care and education.

Let us now move to the work of Erik Erikson, sometimes called a neo-Freudian, to see how the framework he proposed helps us to understand the developing learner further. Erikson amended and extended Freud's developmental framework to include an understanding of late childhood, adolescence and adulthood that provides further insight.

Secure base

The attachment figure provides a safe foundation for the child to explore the world.

Sensitive responsiveness

A mother/caregiver's ability to respond accurately, promptly and appropriately to an infant's needs.

Erikson: The Individual and Society

Like Piaget, Erik Erikson did not start his career as a psychologist. A meeting with Sigmund Freud in Vienna led to an invitation to study psychoanalysis. Erikson then emigrated to America to practise his profession and to escape the threat of Hitler. In his influential *Childhood and Society* (1963), Erikson offered a basic framework for understanding the needs of young people in relation to the society in which they grow, learn and later make their contributions. His later books, *Identity, Youth, and Crisis* (1968) and *Identity and the Life Cycle* (1980), expanded on his ideas, claiming that the individual's experiences of society and culture are impossible to differentiate from familial influences as they are all equally significant and interconnected.

Erikson's psychosocial theory has much in common with Freud's psychosexual one but the emphasis moves from sexual to social identity. Erikson emphasised the emergence of the self, the search for identity, the individual's relationships with others and the role of culture throughout life. Like Freud and Piaget, Erikson saw development as a passage through a series of stages, each with its particular goals, concerns, accomplishments and dangers. He concurred with Freud that the stages are interdependent and that accomplishments at later stages depend on how conflicts are resolved in the earlier years. Again like Freud, Erikson suggests that the individual faces a developmental crisis at each stage – a conflict between a positive alternative and a potentially unhealthy alternative. The way in which the individual resolves each crisis will have a lasting effect on that person's self-image and view of society. We will look briefly at all eight stages in Erikson's theory – or, as he called them, the 'eight ages of man' which continue until death rather than end at early adulthood as Freud's did. Table 3.3 presents the stages in summary form.

Psychosocial

Describing the relation of the individual's emotional needs to the social environment.

Developmental crisis

A specific conflict whose resolution prepares the way for the next stage.

The preschool years: trust, autonomy and initiative

Erikson identifies *trust versus mistrust* as the basic conflict of infancy. According to Erikson, the infant will develop a sense of trust if its needs for food and care are met

Table 3.3   Erikson's eight stages of psychosocial development

Stages	Approximate age	Important event	Description
1. Basic trust versus basic mistrust	Birth to 12–18 months	Feeding	The infant must form a first loving, trusting relationship with the caregiver or develop a sense of mistrust.
2. Autonomy versus shame/doubt	18 months to 3 years	Toilet training	The child's energies are directed towards the development of physical skills, including walking, grasping, controlling the sphincter. The child learns control but may develop shame and doubt if not handled well.
3. Initiative versus guilt	3 to 6 years	Independence	The child continues to become more assertive and to take more initiative but may be too forceful, which can lead to guilt feelings.
4. Industry versus inferiority	6 to 12 years	School	The child must deal with demands to learn new skills or risk a sense of inferiority, failure and incompetence.
5. Identity versus role confusion	Adolescence	Peer relationships	The teenager must achieve identity in occupation, gender roles, politics and religion.
6. Intimacy versus isolation	Young adulthood	Love relationships	The young adult must develop intimate relationships or suffer feelings of isolation.
7. Generativity versus stagnation	Middle adulthood	Parenting/mentoring	Each adult must find some way to satisfy and support the next generation.
8. Ego integrity versus despair	Late adulthood	Reflection on and acceptance of one's life	The culmination is a sense of acceptance of oneself and a sense of fulfilment.

Source: From *Psychology* (5th ed.) by Lester A. Lefton. Published by Allyn and Bacon, Boston, MA. Copyright © 1994 by Pearson Education.

with comforting regularity and responsiveness from caregivers. In this first year, infants are in Piaget's sensorimotor stage and are just beginning to learn that they are separate from the world around them. This realisation is part of what makes trust so important: infants must trust the aspects of their world that are beyond their control (Isabella and Belsky, 1991; Posada *et al.*, 2002).

Autonomy

Independence.

Erikson's second stage, *autonomy versus shame and doubt,* marks the beginning of self-control and self-confidence. Young children begin to assume important responsibilities for self-care such as feeding, toileting and dressing. During this period, parents must tread a fine line; they must be protective – but not overprotective. If parents do not maintain a reassuring, confident attitude and do not reinforce the child's efforts to master basic motor and cognitive skills, children may begin to feel shame; they may learn to doubt their abilities to manage the world on their own terms. Erikson believes that children who experience too much doubt at this stage will lack confidence in their own abilities throughout life.

For Erikson, the next stage of *initiative* versus *guilt* 'adds to autonomy the quality of undertaking, planning, and attacking a task for the sake of being active and on the move' (Erikson, 1963, p. 255). The challenge of this period is to maintain a zest for activity and at the same time understand that not every impulse can be acted on. Again, adults must tread a fine line, this time in providing supervision without interference. If children are not allowed to do things on their own, a sense of guilt may develop; they may come to believe that what they want to do is always 'wrong'. The Focus on Practice below suggests ways of encouraging initiative.

Initiative

Willingness to begin new activities and explore new directions.

FOCUS ON PRACTICE

Encouraging initiative in preschool children

Encourage children to make and to act on choices

Examples
1. Have a free-choice time when children can select an activity or game.
2. As much as possible, avoid interrupting children who are very involved in what they are doing.
3. When children suggest an activity, try to follow their suggestions or incorporate their ideas into ongoing activities.
4. Offer positive choices: Instead of saying, 'You can't have the strawberries now', ask, 'Would you like the strawberries after lunch or after naptime?'

Make sure that each child has a chance to experience success

Examples
1. When introducing a new game or skill, teach it in small steps.
2. Avoid competitive games when the range of abilities in the class is great.

Encourage make-believe with a wide variety of roles

Examples
1. Have costumes and props that go along with stories the children enjoy. Encourage the children to act out the stories or make up new adventures for favourite characters.
2. Monitor the children's play to be sure no one monopolises playing 'teacher', 'Mummy', 'Daddy' or other heroes.

Be tolerant of accidents and mistakes, especially when children are attempting to do something on their own

Examples
1. Use cups and jugs that make it easy to pour and hard to spill.
2. Recognise the attempt, even if the product is unsatisfactory.
3. If mistakes are made, show children how to clean up, repair or redo.
4. If a child consistently behaves in ways that are highly unusual or unacceptable, seek guidance from other professionals. The best time to help children deal with psychosocial problems is at an early age.

For more ideas, see http://www.vtaide.com/png/ERIK3.htm

The early and middle school years: industry versus inferiority

Erikson suggested that the next stage involved a conflict between industry and inferiority as they move into formal education. Between the ages of five and seven, when most children start school, cognitive development is proceeding rapidly. Children can process more information faster and their memory spans are increasing. They are moving from preoperational to concrete-operational thinking. As these internal changes progress, the children are spending hours every weekday in the new physical and social world of school. They must now reestablish Erikson's stages of psychosocial development in the unfamiliar school setting. They must learn to *trust* new adults, act *autonomously* in this more complex situation and *initiate* actions in ways that fit the new rules of school.

Industry

Eagerness to engage in productive work.

The new psychosocial challenge for the school years is what Erikson calls *industry versus inferiority*. Children are beginning to see the relationship between perseverance and the pleasure of a job completed. In modern societies, children's ability to move between the worlds of home, neighbourhood and school, and to cope with academic work, group activities and friends will lead to a growing sense of competence. Difficulty with these challenges can result in feelings of inferiority. Children must master new skills and work towards new goals but at the same time they are being compared to others and risking failure.

The way children cope with these challenges has implications for the rest of their school experience. Two of the best predictors of dropping out of school are poor achievement by seven- and eight-year-olds and being held back from progressing with peers (Paris and Cunningham, 1996). Good school performance matters more for children's future success in the early years of school than at any other time (Entwisle and Alexander, 1998: 354). Because schools tend to reflect middle-class values and norms, such as the type of language used and the focus upon the importance of formal learning, the transition to school may be especially difficult for children who differ economically or culturally. The achievement test score differences among children from high- and low-socioeconomic groups at five and six years old are relatively small, but by the time they are ten years old, the differences have tripled. These achievement gaps are discussed more fully in Chapter 5. The Focus on Practice below gives ideas for encouraging industry.

As children progress from the early to middle years of school they are likely to confront an increased focus on grades and performance as well as more competition on all fronts – academic, social and athletic. Just when they are eager to make decisions and assume more independence, these developing minds encounter more rules, required courses and assignments. They may move from a close connection with one teacher all year to more impersonal relations with many teachers in many different

FOCUS ON PRACTICE

Encouraging industry

Make sure that learners have opportunities to set and work towards realistic goals

Examples

1. Begin with short assignments, then move on to longer ones. Monitor learners' progress by recording progress.
2. Teach learners to set reasonable goals. Write down goals and have learners keep a journal of progress towards these goals.

Give learners a chance to show their independence and responsibility

Examples

1. Tolerate honest mistakes.
2. Delegate to learners tasks such as watering class plants, collecting and distributing materials, monitoring the classroom, keeping records of homework tasks, and so on.

Provide support to learners who seem discouraged

Examples

1. Use individual charts and contracts that show learner progress.
2. Keep samples of earlier work so learners can see their improvements.
3. Have awards for most improved, most helpful, most hardworking.

For more ideas, see http://www.vtaide.com/png/ERIK4.htm

---

subjects across the year and from being the most mature and highest status pupils in a small, familiar school to being the 'babies' in a larger, more impersonal school (Meece, 2002; Murdock, Hale and Weber, 2001; Rudolph *et al.*, 2001; Wigfield *et al.*, 1991).

Adolescence: the search for identity

As learners move into adolescence, cognitive processes are expanding as the young people develop capabilities for abstract thinking and the capacity to understand the perspectives of others. Even greater physical changes are taking place in the learners as they approach puberty. So, with developing minds and bodies, young adolescents must confront the central issue of constructing an identity that will provide a firm basis for adulthood. The individual has been developing a sense of self since infancy but adolescence marks the first time that a conscious effort is made to answer the now-pressing question, 'Who am I?' The conflict defining this stage is *identity versus role confusion*. Identity refers to the organisation of the individual's drives, abilities, beliefs and history into a consistent image of self. It involves deliberate choices and decisions, particularly about work, values, ideology and commitments to people and ideas (Marcia, 1987; Penuel and Wertsch, 1995). If adolescents fail to integrate all these aspects and choices, or if they feel unable to choose at all, role confusion threatens.

Identity

The complex answer to the question: 'Who am I?'

The search for identity is the key aspect of adolescent development. Adolescents 'try out' different roles and behaviours during this period

Identity statuses

James Marcia (1991, 1994 and 1999) suggests that there are four identity alternatives for adolescents, depending on whether they have *explored* options and made *commitments*. The first, identity diffusion, occurs when individuals do not explore any options or commit to any actions. They reach no conclusions about who they are or what they want to do with their lives; they have no firm direction. Adolescents experiencing identity diffusion may be apathetic and withdrawn, with little hope for the future, or they may be openly rebellious. These adolescents often go along with the crowd, so they are more likely to abuse drugs (Archer and Waterman, 1990; Berger and Thompson, 1995; Kroger, 2000).

Identity foreclosure is commitment without exploration. Foreclosed adolescents have not experimented with different identities or explored a range of options, but simply have committed themselves to the goals, values and lifestyles of others – usually their parents, but sometimes cults or extremist groups. Foreclosed adolescents tend to be rigid, intolerant, dogmatic and defensive (Frank, Pirsch and Wright, 1990).

Adolescents in the midst of struggling with choices are experiencing what Erikson called a moratorium. Erikson used the term moratorium to describe exploration with a delay in commitment to personal and occupational choices. This delay is very common, and probably healthy, for modern adolescents. Erikson believed that adolescents in complex societies have an *identity crisis* during moratorium. Today, the period is no longer referred to as a crisis because, for most people, the experience is a gradual exploration rather than a traumatic upheaval (Grotevant, 1998).

Identity achievement means that after exploring the realistic options, the individual has made choices and is committed to pursuing them. It appears that few young people achieve this status by the time they are 16 years old and often leaving school. Because so many people today go on to college or other continuing education after school, it is not uncommon for the explorations of moratorium to continue into the early 20s. About 80% of learners change their minds about the subjects they want to study and some adults may achieve a firm identity at one period in their lives, only

Identity diffusion

Uncentredness; confusion about who one is and what one wants.

Identity foreclosure

Acceptance of parental life choices without consideration of options.

Moratorium

Identity crisis; suspension of choices because of struggle.

Identity achievement

Strong sense of commitment to life choices after free consideration of alternatives.

to reject that identity and achieve a new one later. So identity, once achieved, may not be unchanging for everyone (Kroger, 2000; Nurmi, 2004).

Both moratorium and identity-achieved statuses are considered healthy. Schools that give adolescents experiences with community service, real-world work and mentoring help to foster identity formation (Cooper, 1998). The Focus on Practice below gives other ideas for supporting identity formation.

FOCUS ON PRACTICE

Supporting identity formation

Give learners many models for career choices and other adult roles

Examples
1. Point out models from literature and history. Have a calendar with the birthdays of eminent women, minority leaders, or people who made a little-known contribution to the subject you are teaching. Briefly discuss the person's accomplishments on his or her birthday.
2. Invite guest speakers to describe how and why they chose their professions. Make sure all kinds of work and workers are represented.

Help young people find resources for working out personal problems

Examples
1. Encourage them to talk to year tutors or school counsellors.
2. Discuss potential outside services.

Be tolerant of teenage fads as long as they don't offend others or interfere with learning

Examples
1. Discuss the fads of earlier eras (punk hair styles, powdered wigs, love beads).
2. Don't impose strict dress or hair codes.

Give learners realistic feedback about their work and support for improving. Adolescents may need many 'second chances'

Examples
1. When learners misbehave or perform poorly, make sure they understand the consequences of their behaviour – the effects on themselves and others.
2. Give learners model answers or show them the completed projects of others so they can compare their work to good examples.
3. Because learners are 'trying on' roles, keep the roles separate from the person. Criticise the behaviour without criticising the student.

For more ideas about working with adolescents using Erikson's theory, see http://www.cde.ca.gov/ls/cg/pp/documents/erikson.pdf

Beyond the school years

The crises of Erikson's stages of adulthood all involve the quality of human relations. The first of these stages is *intimacy versus isolation*. Intimacy in this sense refers to a willingness to relate to another person on a deep level, to have a relationship based on more than mutual need. Someone who has not achieved a sufficiently strong sense of identity tends to fear being overwhelmed or swallowed up by another person and may retreat into isolation. The next stage is *generativity versus stagnation*. Generativity extends the ability to care for another person and involves concern and guidance for both the next generation and future generations. While generativity frequently refers to having and nurturing children, it has a broader meaning and includes generating ideas, productivity and creativity as essential features. The last of Erikson's stages is *integrity versus despair*, coming to terms with death. Achieving integrity means consolidating your sense of self and fully accepting its unique and now unalterable history. Those unable to attain a feeling of integrity and fulfilment sink into despair.

Erikson's work helped start the life-span development approach, and his theories have been especially useful in understanding adolescence. However, feminists have criticised his notion that identity precedes intimacy, because their research indicates that for women, identity achievement is fused with achieving intimacy (Miller, 2002). It is also evident that some important issues, such as ethnic and racial identity, were not fully explored by Erikson. We will read about recent research which does this later on in the book.

Bronfenbrenner: The Social Context for Development

Erikson highlighted the role of social and cultural context in personal-social development, but Urie Bronfenbrenner went further to map the many interacting social contexts that affect development with his bioecological model of development (Bronfenbrenner, 1989; Bronfenbrenner and Evans, 2000). The *bio* aspect of the model recognises that people bring their biological selves to the developmental process. The *ecological* part recognises that the social contexts in which we develop are ecosystems because they are in constant interaction and influence each other (see Figure 3.1).

Every person lives within a *microsystem*, inside a *mesosystem*, embedded in an *exosystem*, all of which are a part of the *macrosystem* – rather like a set of Russian painted dolls with the person as the smallest doll nested inside the other slightly larger ones which themselves are part of the whole. More of this below.

In the microsystem are the person's immediate relationships and activities. For a child, it might be the immediate family, friends or teachers and the activities of play and school. This is the child's own little world. Within it relationships are reciprocal – they flow in both directions. The child affects the parent and the parent influences the child, for example. The mesosystem is slightly more distant from the child because they do not involve him or her directly but nevertheless they influence his or her life. It is the set of interactions and relationships among all the elements of the microsystem – the family members interacting with each other or with the teacher. Again, all relationships are reciprocal – the teacher influences the parents and the parents affect the teacher, and these interactions affect the child. The exosystem is another layer (or slightly larger Russian doll) which includes all the social settings that affect the child, even though the child is not a direct member of the systems. Examples are the teachers'

Generativity

Sense of concern for future generations.

Integrity

Sense of self-acceptance and fulfilment.

Bioecological model

Bronfenbrenner's theory describing the nested social and cultural contexts that shape development. Every person develops within a *microsystem*, inside a *mesosystem*, embedded in an *exosystem*, all of which are a part of the *macrosystem* of the culture.

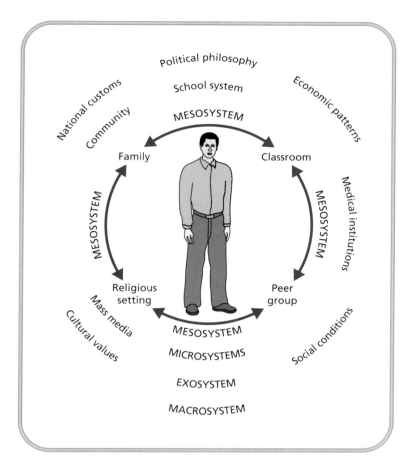

Figure 3.1
Urie Bronfenbrenner's bioecological model of human development

Every person develops within a *microsystem* (family, friends, school activities, teacher, etc.) inside a *mesosystem* (the interactions among all the microsystem elements), embedded in an *exosystem* (social settings that affect the child, even though the child is not a direct member – community resources, parents' work place, etc.); all are part of the *macrosystem* (the larger society with its laws, customs, values, etc.).

Source: Adapted from K. S. Berger (2003). *The Developing Person Through Childhood and Adolescence,* 6/E. New York: Worth Publishers, Fig. 1.2, p. 3.

relations with managers and the school governors; parents' jobs; the community resources for health, employment or recreation; or the family's religious affiliation. The macrosystem is the larger society – its values, laws, conventions and traditions all of which influence the conditions and experiences of the child's life. For another example, think of the teacher's own bioecological system. The teacher is influenced by the microsystem of the head teacher/principal, colleagues and pupils; the mesosystem of the interactions among those people; the exosystem of local and national educational policies, and the macrosystem of cultural norms and values (Woolfolk Hoy, Davis and Pape 2006).

Bronfenbrenner's theory has at least two lessons for teachers. First, influences in all social systems are reciprocal. Second, there are many dynamic forces that interact to create the context for individual development. Next, we look at three important social contexts – families, peers and teachers.

Families

The most appropriate expectation to have about your learners' families is no expectation at all. Increasingly, children today have only one or no sibling, or they may be part of blended families, with stepbrothers or stepsisters who move in and out of their lives. Some of your learners may live with an aunt, with grandparents, with one

Blended families

Parents, children and stepchildren merged into families through remarriages.

parent, in foster or adoptive homes, or with an older brother or sister. The best advice is to avoid the phrases 'your parents' and 'your mother and father' and to speak of 'your family' when talking to learners.

Parenting styles

If you spend time in staff rooms in schools, you may hear quite a bit of talk about learners' parents, including some blame for learners' problems. Actually, most current research in child development says it is not that simple. As Bronfenbrenner's bioecologial model tells us, there are many influences on children. However, the influence of parents is clearly still important so let us look more closely at the different styles of parenting.

Parenting styles

The ways of interacting with and disciplining children.

One well-known description of parenting styles is based on the research of Diane Baumrind (1991). Her early work focused on a careful longitudinal study of 100 (mostly European American, middle-class) preschool children. Through observation of children and parents and interviews with parents, Baumrind and the other researchers who built on her findings identified four styles based on the parents' high or low levels of warmth and control (Berger, 2006):

1. *Authoritarian* parents (low warmth, high control) seem cold and controlling in their interactions with their children. The children are expected to be mature and to do what the parent says, 'Because I said so!' There is not much talk about emotions. Punishments are strict, but not abusive. The parents love their children, but they are not openly affectionate.

2. *Authoritative* parents (high warmth, high control) also set clear limits, enforce rules and expect mature behaviour but they are warmer with their children. They listen to concerns, give reasons for rules and allow more democratic decision making. There is less strict punishment and more guidance. Parents help children think through the consequences of their actions (Hoffman, 2001).

3. *Permissive* parents (high warmth, low control) are warm and nurturing but they have few rules or consequences for their children and expect little in the way of mature behaviour because 'They're only children'.

4. *Rejecting/neglecting* parents (low warmth, low control) don't seem to care at all and can't be bothered with controlling, communicating or caring for their children.

Culture and parenting

Authoritarian, authoritative and permissive parents all love their children and are trying to do their best – they simply have different ideas about the best ways to parent. In broad strokes, there are differences in children associated with these three parenting styles. At least in European and American, middle-class families, children of authoritative parents are more likely to be happy with themselves and to relate well to others, whereas children of authoritarian parents are more likely to be guilty or depressed, and children of permissive parents may have trouble interacting with peers – they are used to having their own way. Of course, the extreme of permissiveness becomes indulgence. Indulgent parents cater to their children's every whim – perhaps it is easier than being the adult who must make unpopular decisions. Both indulgent and rejecting/neglecting parenting styles are harmful.

Cultures also differ in parenting styles. Research indicates that higher control parenting is linked to better grades for Asian and African American learners

(Glasgow *et al.*, 1997). Parenting that is strict and directive, with clear rules and consequences, combined with high levels of warmth and emotional support, is associated with higher academic achievement and greater emotional maturity for inner-city children (Garner and Spears, 2000; Jarrett, 1995). Differences in cultural values and in the danger level of some urban neighbourhoods may make tighter parental control appropriate and even necessary (Smetana, 2000). Additionally, it may be a misreading of the parents' actions to perceive their demand for obedience as 'authoritarian' in cultures that have a greater respect for elders and a more group-centred rather than individualist philosophy (Nucci, 2001).

Divorce

Currently the divorce rate in the UK is ranked third highest in the world with the US highest and New Zealand second (Berk, 2005). Some analysts estimate that between 40% and 50% of first-time marriages that took place in the 1990s will end in divorce (Amato, 2001). As many of us may know from experiences in our own families, separation and divorce are stressful events for all participants, even under the best circumstances. The actual separation of the parents may have been preceded by years of conflict in the home or may come as a shock to all, including friends and children. During the divorce itself, conflict may increase as property and custody rights are being negotiated.

After the divorce, more changes may disrupt the children's lives. The parent who has custody may have to move to a less expensive home, find new sources of income, go to work for the first time, or work longer hours. For the child, this can mean leaving behind important friendships in the old neighbourhood or school, just when support is needed the most. It may mean having just one parent, who has less time than ever to be with the children. About two-thirds of parents remarry and half of them divorce again, so there are more adjustments ahead for the children (Nelson, 1993). Even in those rare cases where there are few conflicts, ample resources and the continuing support of friends and extended family, divorce is never easy for anyone.

The first two years after the divorce seem to be the most difficult period for both boys and girls. During this time, children may have problems in school or avoid school, lose or gain an unusual amount of weight, have trouble sleeping or experience other difficulties. They may blame themselves for the breakup of their family or hold unrealistic hopes for reconciliation (Hetherington, 1999). Long-term adjustment is also affected. Sons of divorced parents tend to show a higher rate of behavioural and interpersonal problems at home and in school than either girls in general or boys from intact families. Daughters of divorced parents may have trouble in their dealings with males. They may become more sexually active or have difficulties trusting males. However, adjustment to divorce is an individual matter; some children respond with increased responsibility, maturity and coping skills (Amato, Loomis and Booth, 1995; Berk, 2005). Over time, about 75% to 80% of children in divorced families adapt and become reasonably well adjusted (Hetherington and Kelly, 2002). See the Focus on Practice below for ideas about how to help learners dealing with divorce.

Connect and Extend

See Kieman, K. (2003). *Cohabitation and Divorce across Nations and Generations*. Centre for Analysis of Social Exclusion (available from sticerd.lse.ac.uk) for a review of the effects of divorce across nine Western European countries (including the UK) and the US.

Peers

Peers and friendships are central to learners' lives. When there has been a falling-out or an argument, when one child is not invited to a party or sleep-over, when rumours are started and pacts are made to ostracise someone (as with Alison and Sophie at the beginning of the chapter), the results can be devastating. The immaturity and

FOCUS ON PRACTICE

Helping children of divorce

Take note of any sudden changes in behaviour that might indicate problems at home

Examples
1. Be alert to physical symptoms such as repeated headaches or stomach pains, rapid weight gain or loss, fatigue or excess energy.
2. Be aware of signs of emotional distress such as moodiness, temper tantrums, difficulty in paying attention or concentrating.
3. Let parents know about the learners' signs of stress.

Talk individually to learners about their attitude or behaviour changes. This gives you a chance to find out about unusual stress such as divorce

Examples
1. Be a good listener. Learners may have no other adult willing to hear their concerns.
2. Let learners know you are available to talk, and let the learner set the agenda.

Watch your language to make sure you avoid stereotypes about 'happy' (two-parent) homes

Examples
1. Simply say 'your families' instead of 'your mothers and fathers' when addressing the class.
2. Avoid statements such as 'We need mothers to volunteer' or 'Your father can help you'.

Help learners maintain self-esteem

Examples
1. Recognise a job well done.
2. Make sure the learner understands the assignment and can handle the workload. This is not the time to pile on new and very difficult work.
3. The learner may be angry with his or her parents, but may direct the anger at teachers. Don't take the learner's anger personally.

Find out what resources are available at your school. Be sensitive to both parents' rights to information

Examples
1. When parents have joint custody, both are entitled to receive information and attend parent–teacher conferences.

2. The noncustodial parent may still be concerned about the child's school progress. Check with the head teacher or principal about the rules around this.

Be aware of long-term problems for learners moving between two households

Examples

1. Books, assignments and sports clothes may be left at one parent's house when the child is currently visiting the other parent.
2. Parents may not appear for their turn to pick up their child at school or may miss a parent–teacher conference because the note never got home.

For ideas about helping children understand divorce, see http://muextension. missouri.edu/xplor/hesguide/humanrel/gh6600.htm

impulsiveness of the adolescent brain combined with the power of peer cultures can make these problems even more likely.

Peer cultures

Recently, psychologists have studied the powerful role of peer culture in children's development. Peer cultures are groups of learners who have a set of 'rules' about such things as how to dress, talk or style their hair. The group determines which activities, music or other learners are in or out of favour. For example, Mia, a 13-year-old girl in the UK, described the way her peer group worked:

We go to certain clubs [in school] which others in the group go to but not otherwise – not geeky things like maths and stuff because no-one else would go to that. You never wear big, clunky shoes because they don't look nice and they're not cool. Same with rucksacks – nobody would take one of those huge, big walking-type bags to school. They'd take a smaller, more fashionable kind of bag. If they did take one then you'd still be friends but the others wouldn't like it. They might say something – depends on who it is – some people are louder and they might say something to them or others might say something to someone else.

We can see that Mia is extremely conscious of the kind of clothing and behaviour which is acceptable within her peer group and that this influences what she chooses to do and wear. To understand the power of peers, we have to look at situations where the values and interests of parents clash with those of peers, and then see whose influence dominates. In these comparisons, peers usually win. However, not all aspects of peer cultures are bad or cruel. The norms in some groups are positive and support achievement in school. These might include initiatives such as the Duke of Edinburgh awards or sports and music clubs. Peer cultures are more powerful in defining issues of style and socialising. Parents and teachers still are influential in matters of morality, career choice and religion (Harris, 1998).

Beyond the immediate trauma of being 'in' or 'out' of the group, peer relationships play significant positive and negative roles in healthy personal and social development. Peer groups influence members' motivation and achievement in school (Ryan, 2001). In one study, 11- and 12-year-old learners without friends showed lower levels of academic achievement and positive social behaviours and were more emotionally distressed, even two years later, than children with at least one friend (Wentzel, Barry and Caldwell, 2004). The characteristics of friends and the quality of the friendships matter, too. Having stable, supportive relationships with friends who are socially competent and mature enhances social development, especially during difficult times such as parents' divorce or transition to new schools (Hartup and Stevens, 1999). Children who are rejected by their peers are less likely to participate in classroom learning activities; they are more likely to drop out of school as adolescents and may even evidence more problems as adults. For example, rejected aggressive pupils are more likely to commit crimes as they grow older (Coie *et al.*, 1995; Coie and Dodge, 1998; Fredricks, Blumenfeld and Paris, 2004).

Who is likely to have problems with peers?

Children and adolescents are not always tolerant of differences. New classmates who are physically, intellectually, ethnically, racially, economically or linguistically different may be rejected in classes with established peer groups. Children and young people who are aggressive, withdrawn and inattentive-hyperactive are more likely to be rejected. However, classroom context matters too, especially for aggressive or withdrawn learners. In classrooms where the general level of aggression is high, being aggressive is less likely to lead to peer rejection whereas in classrooms where solitary play and work are more common, being withdrawn is not as likely to lead to rejection. Thus, part of being rejected is being too different from the norm. Also, prosocial behaviours such as sharing, cooperating and friendly interactions are associated with peer acceptance, no matter what the classroom context. Many aggressive and withdrawn learners lack these social skills; inattentive-hyperactive learners often misread social cues or have trouble controlling impulses, so their social skills suffer, too (Coplan *et al.*, 2004; Stormshak *et al.*, 1999). A teacher should be aware of how each learner gets along with the group. Are there outcasts? Do some individuals play the bully role? Careful adult intervention can often correct such problems, especially at the earlier school levels. Let us now look at aggression amongst peers as this is often a key issue within the learning situation.

Peer aggression

There are several forms of aggression. The most common form is instrumental aggression, which is intended to gain an object or privilege, such as shoving to get in line first or snatching a toy from another child. The intent is to get what you want, not to hurt the other child, but the hurt may happen anyway. A second kind is hostile aggression – inflicting intentional harm. Hostile aggression can take the form of either overt aggression, such as threats or physical attacks (as in, 'I'm gonna beat you up!'), or relational aggression, which involves threatening or damaging social relationships (as in, 'I'm never going to speak to you again!'). Boys are more likely to use overt aggression and girls, like Alison in the opening case, are more likely to use relational aggression (Berk, 2005). Aggression should not be confused with assertiveness, which means affirming or maintaining a legitimate right. As Helen Bee explains, 'A child who says, "That's my toy!" is showing assertiveness. If he bashes his playmate over the head to reclaim it, he has shown aggression' (1981: 350).

Modelling plays an important role in the expression of aggression (Bandura, Ross and Ross, 1963). Children who grow up in homes filled with harsh punishment and family violence are more likely to use aggression to solve their own problems (Patterson, 1997). One very real source of aggressive models is found in almost every home in industrialised countries – television. Many TV programmes have at least

---

Instrumental aggression

Strong actions aimed at claiming an object, place or privilege – not intended to harm, but may lead to harm.

Hostile aggression

Bold, direct action that is intended to hurt someone else; unprovoked attack.

Overt aggression

A form of hostile aggression that involves physical attack.

Relational aggression

A form of hostile aggression that involves verbal attacks and other actions meant to harm social relationships.

some violence. The rate of violent acts within children's programmes is also high, particularly in cartoons, and in some of the violent scenes, the violence goes unpunished (Mediascope, 1996; Waters, 1993). Because most children spend more time watching television than they do in any other leisure activity (averaging two hours per day across UK and Europe: Livingstone and Bovill, 2001) the possible influence of television violence is a real concern for many people (Timmer, Eccles and O'Brien, 1988).

Does watching violent TV increase aggression? The debate about the relationship between television violence and aggression still rages. Generally, research findings from the US suggest that it does (Anderson and Bushman, 2001). Results of a recent longitudinal study indicate a clear, 'yes'. Rowell Huesmann and colleagues examined the relationship between exposure to violence on television from ages six to ten and aggressive behaviour in adulthood 15 years later for over 300 people. Their conclusion? 'Childhood exposure to media violence predicts young adult aggressive behaviour for both males and females. . . . These relations persist even when the effects of socioeconomic status, intellectual ability, and a variety of parenting factors are controlled' (Huesmann *et al.*, 2003: 201). When the children identified with aggressive TV characters (they said they acted like those characters) and when they thought the violence on TV was like real life, they were more likely to be violent as adults.

However, studies of this kind may be establishing *links* between children's viewing of television violence and later aggression rather than demonstrating that the first *causes* the second. Watching violent TV or films may be part of a range of complex social and emotional factors rather than a single causal factor. Professor David Buckingham, an internationally respected researcher in the area, commented: 'Children are not going to commit a violent act just because they see it on TV' (Buckingham, 2005). Further, studies in other parts of the world (including Holland, Australia, Israel and Poland) are less conclusive and challenge claims that viewing TV violence at an early age is a predictor of later aggression (Cumberbatch, 2004).

Whatever view you take, it is possible to reduce the negative effects of TV violence by stressing three points with children: Most people do not behave in the aggressive ways shown on television; the violent acts on TV are not real, but are created by special effects and stunts; and there are better ways to resolve conflicts, and these are the ways most real people use to solve their problems (Huesmann *et al.*, 2003). Also, avoid using TV viewing as a reward or punishment because that makes television even more attractive to children (Slaby *et al.*, 1995). However, television is not the only source of violent models. Many popular films and video games are also filled with graphic depictions of violence, often performed by the 'hero' who saves the day. Children growing up in the inner cities may see gang violence. Newspapers, magazines and the radio are filled with stories of murders, rapes and robberies.

Bullies

Aggressive children tend to believe that violence will be rewarded, and they use aggression to get what they want. They are more likely to believe that violent retaliation is acceptable: 'It's OK to shove people when you're mad' (Egan, Monson and Perry, 1998). Seeing violent acts go unpunished probably affirms and encourages these beliefs. In addition to being surrounded by violence and believing that a violent 'pay back' is appropriate when you are insulted or harmed, some children, particularly boys, have difficulty reading the intentions of others (Dodge and Pettit, 2003; Zelli *et al.*, 1999). They assume another child 'did it on purpose' when their block tower is toppled, they are pushed on the bus or some other mistake is made. Retaliation follows and the cycle of aggression continues.

Helping children handle aggression can make a lasting difference in their lives. For example, one study in Finland asked teachers to rate learners' aggression by answering

Aggressive children tend to believe that aggression will be rewarded and use aggression to achieve their goals. Early interventions are necessary to prevent this becoming a pattern in later life

'never', 'sometimes' or 'often' to statements such as 'hurts another child when angry'. Teacher-rated aggression when learners were age eight predicted school adjustment problems in early adolescence and long-term unemployment in adulthood (Kokko and Pulkkinen, 2000). Similar results were found in a study conducted in Canada, New Zealand and the US. Boys (but not girls) who were often physically aggressive in their early school years were at risk for continuing violent and nonviolent forms of delinquency throughout adolescence (Broidy *et al.*, 2003).

One of the best approaches for preventing problems with aggression later in life is to intervene early. For example, one study found that aggressive children whose teachers taught them conflict management strategies were diverted from a life path of aggression and violence (Aber, Brow and Jones, 2003). Sandra Graham (1996) has successfully experimented with approaches that help aggressive 10–12-year-old boys become better judges of others' intentions. Strategies include engaging in role play, participating in group discussions of personal experiences, interpreting social cues from photographs, playing pantomime games, making videos and writing endings to unfinished stories. The boys in the 12-session training group showed clear improvement in reading the intentions of others and responding with less aggression. We will look at all these approaches in depth in Chapter 12.

Relational aggression

Insults, gossip, exclusion, taunts – all are forms of relational aggression, sometimes called *social aggression* because the intent is to harm social connections. Both boys and girls take part in relational aggression, but after the first few years of school, girls tend to engage in relational aggression more than boys. This may result because as girls become aware of gender stereotypes, they push their overt aggression underground into verbal, not physical, attacks. This type of aggression can be even more damaging than overt physical aggression – both to the victim and the aggressor. Victims, like Sophie in the chapter opening, can be devastated. Relational aggressors can be viewed as even more problematic than physical aggressors by teachers and other learners (Berger, 2006; Crick, Casas and Mosher, 1997). As early as preschool, children need to learn how to negotiate social relations without resorting to aggression.

Victims

Some learners tend to be bullies; other children are victims. Studies from both Europe and the US indicate that about 10% of children are chronic victims – the constant targets of physical or verbal attacks. One kind of victim tends to have low self-esteem and to feel anxious, lonely, insecure and unhappy. These learners often are prone to crying and withdrawal; when attacked, generally they won't defend themselves. Recent research suggests that these victims may blame themselves for their situation. They believe that they are rejected because they have character flaws that they cannot change or control – no wonder they are depressed and helpless! There is a second kind of victim – highly emotional and hot-tempered learners who seem to provoke aggressive reactions from their peers. Members of this group are rejected by almost all peers and have few friends (Pellegrini, Bartini and Brooks, 1999).

Increasing numbers of children avoid school every day and thousands more drop out of school altogether because they are afraid of being bullied there. Children who have been chronic victims throughout school are more depressed and more likely to attempt suicide as young adults (Graham, 1998; Hodges and Perry, 1999) – we will examine suicide in Chapter 4. Moreover, learners who kill or injure others in schools are more often victims than bullies (Reinke and Herman, 2002a, 2002b). In the past years, we have seen tragic consequences when bullied learners turned guns on their tormentors in schools in the US and in Europe. Interviews with adolescents reveal how much these young people count on their teachers and other adults in the school to protect them. Even though they are moving towards independence, these learners still want and need your help (Garbarino and deLara, 2002). The Focus on Practice below provides ideas for handling aggression and encouraging cooperation.

Connect and Extend

See Ananiadou, K. and Smith, P. (2002), 'Legal requirements and nationally circulated materials against school bullying in European countries', *Criminology and Criminal Justice, 2*(4), pp. 471–491 for a discussion about anti-bullying legislation in schools.

FOCUS ON PRACTICE

Dealing with aggression and encouraging cooperation

Present yourself as a non-aggressive model

Examples
1. Do not use threats of aggression to win obedience.
2. When problems arise, model non-violent conflict-resolution strategies (see Chapter 11).

Ensure that your classroom has enough space and appropriate materials for every learner

Examples

1. Prevent overcrowding.
2. Make sure prized toys or resources are plentiful.
3. Remove or confiscate materials that encourage personal aggression, such as toy guns.
4. Avoid highly competitive activities and evaluations.

Make sure learners do not profit from aggressive behaviours

Examples

1. Comfort the victim of aggression and ignore the aggressor.
2. Use reasonable punishment, especially with older learners.

Teach directly about positive social behaviours

Examples

1. Incorporate lessons on social ethics/morality through reading selections and discussions.
2. Discuss the effects of antisocial actions such as stealing, bullying and spreading rumours.
3. Provide models and encouragement – role play appropriate conflict resolution.
4. Build self-esteem by building skills and knowledge.
5. Seek help for learners who seem especially isolated and victimised.

Provide opportunities for learning tolerance and cooperation

Examples

1. Emphasise the similarities among people rather than the differences.
2. Set up group projects that encourage cooperation.

Loneliness and children with disabilities

Jake is a 14-year-old with hearing problems. He has always been shy, but lately he seems more withdrawn. He has stopped going around with friends and seems more and more depressed. Maria is a ten-year-old with learning disabilities who is repeating Year 5. She feels alone and believes she has nothing in common with the other children – she has a strong wish for friends, but can't seem to find any. Both of these learners described by Shireen Pavri (2003) are lonely. Children with disabilities, especially those with learning disabilities and developmental delays, are especially vulnerable to feelings of loneliness (Pavri and Luftig, 2000). One reason is that children with disabilities may also have trouble reading and understanding cues from others, so they may respond inappropriately to their peers. Also, learners with disabilities often are separated from their peers for assessment and teaching, and thus not allowed full participation in all class activities, so they have fewer opportunities to form friendships

(Hallahan and Kauffman, 2006). What can be done? First, teachers can detect signs of loneliness. They are likely to notice who is rejected and who plays alone. They are able to talk to learners about their friends and to parents about their child's experiences with peers. In addition, Pavri (2003) suggests that teachers intervene in these ways:

- Provide social skills training for all learners in how to initiate and terminate interactions and manage conflict.

- Create opportunities for interactions through cooperative learning tasks, structured breaks and play times, peer tutoring opportunities and after-school activities such as boys' or girls' clubs or team sports.

- Capitalise on lonely learners' talents and strengths – use these abilities in classwork.

- Create an accepting classroom community (see Chapter 11).

- Teach adaptive coping strategies such as engaging in creative activities when alone or initiating contact with others when lonely.

- Enhance learners' self-esteem by giving them responsibilities in class and positive reinforcement for jobs well done.

Teachers

The first and most important task of the teacher is to educate, but learning suffers when there are problems with personal and social development, and teachers are the main adults in children's lives for many hours each week. Teachers have the opportunity to play a significant role in learners' personal and social development. For learners facing emotional or interpersonal problems, teachers are sometimes the best source of help. When children and young people have chaotic and unpredictable home lives, they need a caring, firm structure in school. They need teachers who set clear limits, are consistent, enforce rules firmly but not punitively, respect learners, and show genuine concern. Teachers can be available to talk about personal problems without requiring that learners do so.

Academic and personal caring

When researchers ask learners to describe a 'good teacher', three qualities are at the centre of their descriptions. Good teachers have positive interpersonal relationships – they care about their learners. Second, good teachers can keep the classroom organised and maintain authority without being rigid or unkind. Finally, good teachers are good motivators – they can make learning fun by being creative and innovative (Woolfolk Hoy and Weinstein, 2006). Pedro Noguera said that the children and young people in a 'last chance' school for older children told him they look for three things in a teacher: 'They look first for people who care. . . . Second, they respect teachers who are strict and hold learners accountable. Third, they like teachers who teach them something' (2005: 17–18). We will look at management in Chapter 12 and at motivation in Chapter 10, so for now let's focus on caring and teaching.

For the past 15 years, research has documented the value and importance of positive relationships with teachers for all learners within formal education (Davis, 2003). Tamera Murdock and Angela Miller (2003) found that 13–14-year-olds' perceptions that their teachers cared about them were significantly related to the children's academic motivation, even after taking into account the motivational influences of parents and peers. Learners seek respect, affection, trust, a listening ear, patience and humour in their relationships with teachers (Bosworth, 1995; Phelan et al., 1992; Wentzel, 1997).

Frequently, children's decisions about whether to cooperate are based on their liking for the teacher. As a young person in a study by Stinson commented: 'If I donlike 'em . . . I'm not gonna do anything for 'em' (1993: 221). Learners define caring in two ways. One is academic caring – setting high but reasonable expectations and helping learners reach those goals. The second is personal caring – being patient, respectful, humorous, willing to listen, interested in learners' issues and personal problems.

Table 3.4 Indicators of child abuse

The following are some of the signs of abuse. Not every child with these signs is abused, but these indicators should be investigated.

	Physical indicators	**Behavioural indicators**
Physical abuse	• Unexplained bruises (in various stages of healing), welts, human bite marks, bald sports • Unexplained burns, especially cigarette burns or immersion-burns (glovelike) • Unexplained fractures, lacerations or abrasions	• Self-destructive • Withdrawn and aggressive – behavioural extremes • Uncomfortable with physical contact • Arrives at school early or stays late, as if afraid • Chronic runaway (adolescents) • Complains of soreness or moves uncomfortably • Wears clothing inappropriate to weather, to cover body
Physical neglect	• Abandonment • Unattended medical needs • Consistent lack of supervision • Consistent hunger, inappropriate dress, poor hygiene • Lice, distended stomach, emaciation	• Regularly displays fatigue or listlessness, falls asleep in class • Steals food, begs from classmates • Reports that no caretaker is at home • Frequently absent or tardy • Self-destructive • School dropout (adolescents)
Sexual abuse	• Torn, stained or bloodied underclothing • Pain or itching in genital area • Difficulty walking or sitting • Bruises or bleeding in external genitalia • Venereal disease • Frequent urinary or yeast infections	• Withdrawn, chronic depression • Excessive seductiveness • Role reversal, overly concerned for siblings • Poor self-esteem, self-devaluation, lack of confidence • Peer problems, lack of involvement • Massive weight change • Suicide attempts (especially adolescents) • Hysteria, lack of emotional control • Sudden school difficulties • Inappropriate sex play or premature understanding of sex • Threatened by physical contact, closeness • Promiscuity

Source: From Bear, T., Schenk, S. and Buckner, L. (December 1992/January 1993) 'Supporting victims of child abuse', *Educational Leadership, 50*(4), p. 44. Reprinted with permission. The Association for Curriculum Development is a worldwide community of educators advocating sound policies and sharing best practices to achieve the success of each learner. To learn more, visit ASCD at www.ascd.org.

For higher-achieving learners, academic caring is especially important, but for learners who are placed at risk and often alienated from school, personal caring is critical (Cothran and Ennis, 2000; Woolfolk Hoy and Weinstein, 2006). Of course, learners need both academic and personal caring (Katz, 1999). In short, caring means not giving up on learners and their learning as well as demonstrating and teaching kindness in the classroom (Davis, 2003). In Chapter 11, you will learn about strategies and programmes for helping learners feel a sense of belonging in school.

Teachers and child abuse

Certainly, one critical way to care about learners is to protect their welfare and intervene in cases of abuse. Accurate information about the number of abused children is difficult to find; most experts agree that an enormous number of cases go unreported. Of course, parents are not the only people who abuse children. Siblings, other relatives and even teachers have been responsible for the physical and sexual abuse of children.

It is part of the teacher's role to alert the head teacher or principal, school psychologist or school social worker if abuse is detected. The legal definition of abuse has been broadened to include neglect and failure to provide proper care and supervision. Most laws also protect teachers who report suspected neglect in good faith (Beezer, 1985). It is important that teachers understand the laws in the country they are teaching in on this important issue, as well as their own moral responsibility. Some unfortunate children die of abuse or neglect because no-one would 'get involved' (Children's Defense Fund, 2005).

What should teachers and care-givers look for as indicators of abuse? Table 3.4 lists possible indicators.

Self-Concept: Understanding Ourselves

What is self-concept? Is self-concept different from self-esteem or identity? How do we come to understand other people and ourselves? You will see that the development of self-concept follows patterns similar to those noted in Chapter 2 for cognitive development. Children's understandings of themselves are concrete at first. Early views of self and friends are based on immediate behaviours and appearances. Children assume that others share their feelings and perceptions. Their thinking about themselves and others is simple, segmented and rule-bound, not flexible or integrated into organised systems. In time, children are able to think abstractly about internal processes – beliefs, intentions, values and motivations. With these developments in abstract thinking, then, knowledge of self, others and situations can incorporate more abstract qualities (Berk, 2005; Harter, 2003).

Self-concept and self-esteem

Psychologists' interests in all aspects of the self have grown steadily. In 1970, about one in every 20 publications in psychology was related to the self. By 2000, the ratio was one in every seven (Tesser, Stapel and Wood, 2002). In studying the psychology of education much research is focused on self-concept and self-esteem.

The term self-concept is part of our everyday conversation. We talk about people who have a 'low' self-concept or individuals whose self-concept is not 'strong', as if self-concept were the oil level in a car or your abdominal muscles. These actually are misuses of the term. In psychology, self-concept generally refers to individuals'

Self-concept

Individuals' knowledge and beliefs about themselves – their ideas, feelings, attitudes and expectations.

knowledge and beliefs about themselves – their ideas, feelings, attitudes and expectations (Pajares and Schunk, 2001). We could consider self-concept to be our attempt to explain ourselves to ourselves, to build a scheme (in Piaget's terms) that organises our impressions, feelings and beliefs about ourselves. However, this model or scheme is not permanent, unified or unchanging. Our self-perceptions vary from situation to situation and from one phase of our lives to another.

STOP AND THINK

How strongly do you agree or disagree with these statements?

- On the whole, I am satisfied with myself.
- I feel that I have a number of good qualities.
- I wish I could have more respect for myself.
- At times, I think that I am no good at all.
- I certainly feel useless at times.
- I take a positive attitude towards myself.

Self-esteem

The value each of us places on our own characteristics, abilities and behaviours.

The questions above are taken from a widely used measure of self-esteem (Rosenberg, 1979; Hagborg, 1993). Self-esteem is an affective reaction – an evaluative judgement of self-worth – for example, feeling good about your tennis or dance skills. If people evaluate themselves positively – if they 'like what they see' – we say that they have high self-esteem (Pintrich and Schunk, 2002). Can you see the evaluative judgements in the above questions?

Self-concept and self-esteem are often used interchangeably, even though they have distinct meanings. Self-concept is a cognitive structure, a belief about who you are – for example, a belief that you are a good tennis player or dancer. Sometimes self-esteem is considered one aspect of self-concept – the evaluative part. Self-esteem is influenced by whether the culture around you values your particular characteristics and capabilities (Bandura, 1997). In research, it has been difficult to find differences between these two concepts, so some writers use self-concept and self-esteem interchangeably. However, there is a conceptual difference.

The structure of self-concept

A learner's overall self-concept is made up of other, more specific concepts, including non-academic self-concepts about, for example, social relations or physical appearance, and academic self-concepts in English, mathematics, art and other subjects. These self-concepts at the second level are themselves made up of more specific, separate conceptions of the self. For example, self-concepts about social relationships might be made up of concepts about relations with peers, teachers, other adults and family (particularly parents) (Byrne and Shavelson, 1996; Vispoel, 1995; Yeung *et al.*, 2000). These conceptions are based on many experiences and events, such as sports or academic performances, assessment of one's body, friendships, artistic abilities, contributions to community groups, and so on. For older adolescents and adults, the separate, specific self-concepts are not necessarily integrated into an overall self-concept, so self-concept is more situation-specific in adults (Byrne and Worth Gavin, 1996; Marsh and Ayotte, 2003).

How self-concept develops

The self-concept evolves through constant self-evaluation in different situations. Children and adolescents are continually asking themselves, in effect, 'How am I doing?' They gauge the verbal and non-verbal reactions of significant people – parents and other family members in the early years and friends, schoolmates and teachers later – to make judgements (Harter, 1998).

Young children tend to make self-concept appraisals based on their own improvement over time. Researchers followed 60 schoolchildren in New Zealand from the time they started school until the middle of their third year (Chapman, Tunmer and Prochnow, 2000). In the first two months of school, differences in reading self-concept began to develop, based on the ease or difficulty children had in learning to read. Children who entered school with good knowledge about sounds and letters learned to read more easily and developed more positive reading self-concepts. Over time, differences in the reading performance of children with high and low reading self-concepts grew even greater. Thus, the early experiences with the important school task of reading had strong impact on self-concept.

During the middle and later school years, learners grow more self-conscious (remember adolescent egocentrism and Elkind's imaginary audience where young people believe that others are analysing them, discussed in Chapter 2).

At this age, self-concepts are tied to physical appearance and social acceptance as well as school achievement, so these years can be exceedingly difficult for learners such as Sophie, described at the opening of this chapter (Wigfield, Eccles and Pintrich, 1996). In school, learners compare their performance with their own standards – their performance in mathematics to their performance in English and science, for example – to form self-concepts in these areas. However, social comparisons are becoming more influential, too, at least in Western cultures. Learners' self-concepts in mathematics, for example, are shaped by how their performance compares to that of other learners in their mathematics class and even by comments their classmates make about them (Altermatt *et al.*, 2002; Pintrich and Schunk, 2002). Pupils who are good at mathematics in an 'average' school feel better about their mathematics skills than do learners of equal ability in high-achieving schools. Marsh (1990) calls this the 'Big-Fish-Little-Pond Effect (BFLP)'. Research that surveyed over 100,000 15-year-olds around the world found the BFLP effect in every one of the 26 participating countries (Marsh and Hau, 2003). Participation in a gifted and talented programme seems to have an opposite 'Little-Fish-in-a-Big-Pond' effect: learners who participate in gifted programmes, compared to similar learners who remain in regular classes, tend to show *declines* in academic self-concepts over time, but no changes in non-academic self-concepts (Marsh and Craven, 2002).

Self-concept and achievement

Many psychologists consider self-concept to be the foundation of both social and emotional development. Research has linked self-concept to a wide range of accomplishments – from performance in competitive sports to job satisfaction and achievement in school (Byrne, 2002; Davis-Kean and Sandler, 2001; Marsh and Hau, 2003). One important way self-concept affects learning in school is through course selection. Think back to your secondary (post-11 years) school. When you had a chance to choose subjects, did you pick your worst subjects – those where you felt least capable? Probably not. Herbert Marsh and Alexander Yeung (1997) examined how 246 boys in early high school (approximately 12–14 years old) in Sydney, Australia, chose their courses. Academic self-concept for a particular subject (mathematic, science, etc.) was the most important predictor of course selection – more important even than previous grades in the subject or overall self-concept. In fact, having a positive self-concept in a particular subject was an even bigger factor in selecting courses when self-concept in other subjects was low. The courses selected in secondary/high school (15–18 years old) put young people on a path towards the future, so self-concepts about particular academic subjects can be life-changing influences.

School life and self-esteem

We turn now to self-esteem – the learners' evaluations and feelings about themselves. Over 100 years ago, William James (1890) suggested that self-esteem is determined by how *successful* we are in accomplishing tasks or reaching goals we *value*. If a skill or accomplishment is *not* important, incompetence in that area doesn't threaten self-esteem. Learners must have legitimate success with tasks that matter to them. The way individuals explain their successes or failures also is important. Learners must attribute their successes to their own actions, not to luck or to special assistance, in order to build self-esteem.

For teachers, there are at least two questions to ask about self-esteem: (1) How does self-esteem affect a learner's behaviour in school? and (2) How does life in school affect a learner's self-esteem? In answer to the first question, it appears that learners with higher self-esteem are somewhat more likely to be successful in school, although the strength of the relationship varies greatly, depending on the characteristics of the learners and the research methods used (Ma and Kishor, 1997; Marsh and Holmes, 1990). In longitudinal studies, more positive self-beliefs are related to higher academic achievement, especially when the beliefs are specific to the subject studied. But the sizes of the relationships generally are small (Valentine, DuBois and Cooper, 2004). Of course, as we discussed in Chapter 1, knowing that two variables are related (correlated) does not tell us that one is causing the other. It may be that high achievement and popularity lead to self-esteem, or vice versa. In fact, it probably works both ways (Guay, Larose and Boivin, 2004; Marsh and Ayotte, 2003).

What about the second question of how school affects self-esteem: is school important? As you can see from the Discussion Point below, the school's role in learner self-esteem has been hotly debated. Studies such as those by Galbraith and Alexander (2005) in the UK and Theodorakou and Zervas (2003) in Greece would indicate that the kind of provision offered by schools has a significant impact upon children's self-esteem and subsequent progress. A study that followed 322 11–12-year-old learners for two years in the US (Hoge, Smit and Hanson, 1990) found that learners' satisfaction with school, their sense that classes were interesting and teachers cared, and teacher feedback and evaluations influenced learners' self-esteem. In physical education teachers' opinions were especially powerful in shaping learners' conceptions of their athletic abilities. Being placed in a low-ability group or being held back in school seems to have a negative impact on learners' self-esteem, but learning in collaborative and cooperative settings seems to have a positive effect (Covington, 1992; Deci and Ryan, 1985). Interestingly, special programmes such as 'Learner of the Month' or admission to advanced mathematics classes had little effect on self-esteem, perhaps because the learners concerned were no longer the most effective or outstanding learner in these groups ('Little-Fish-Big Pond Effect').

Teachers' feedback, grading/marking practices, evaluations and communication of caring for learners can make a difference in how they feel about their abilities in particular subjects. However, the greatest increases in self-esteem come when learners grow more competent in areas they value – including the social areas that become so important in adolescence. *Thus, a teacher's greatest challenge is to help learners achieve*

DISCUSSION POINT

Should schools provide programmes aimed at increasing self-esteem?

More than 2,000 books about how to increase self-esteem have been published. Schools and mental-health facilities continue to develop self-esteem programmes (Slater, 2002). The attempts to improve learners' self-esteem have taken three main forms: personal development activities such as sensitivity training; self-esteem programs where the curriculum focuses directly on improving self-esteem; and structural changes in schools that place greater emphasis on cooperation, learner participation, community involvement and ethnic pride. Below are differing views on this.

Agree: Yes, schools should provide programmes to increase self-esteem

Beyond the 'feel-good psychology' of some aspects of the self-esteem movement is a basic truth: 'Self-esteem is a central feature of human dignity and thus an inalienable human entitlement. As such, schools and other agencies have a moral obligation to help build it and avoid debilitating it' (Beane, 1991: 28). If we view self-esteem accurately as a product of our thinking and our actions – our values, ideas and beliefs as well as our interactions with others – then we see a significant role for the school. Practices that allow authentic participation, cooperation, problem solving and accomplishment should replace policies that damage self-esteem, such as tracking and competitive grading.

Beane suggests four principles to guide educators:

First, being nice is surely a part of this effort, but it is not enough. Second, there is a place for some direct instruction regarding affective matters, but this is not enough either. Self-esteem and affect are not simply another school subject to be placed in set-aside time slots. Third, the negative affect of 'get tough' policies is not a promising route to self-esteem and efficacy. . . . Fourth, since self-perceptions are powerfully informed by culture, comparing self-esteem across cultures without clarifying cultural differences is distracting and unproductive (1991: 29–30).

Psychologist Lauren Slater in her article, 'The trouble with self-esteem' suggests we rethink self-esteem and move towards honest self-appraisal that will lead to self-control:

Maybe self-control should replace self-esteem as a primary peg to reach for. Ultimately, self-control need not be experienced as a constriction; restored to its original meaning, it might be experienced as the kind of practiced prowess an athlete or artist demonstrates, muscles not tamed but trained, so that the leaps are powerful, the spine supple and the energy harnessed and shaped (1991: 47).

Disagree: No, there are many problems with this

Many of the self-esteem courses are US-based, commercial packages – costly for schools but without solid evidence that they make a difference for learners (Crisci, 1986; Leming, 1981). Some people have accused schools of developing programmes where the main objective is 'to dole out a huge heaping of praise, regardless of actual accomplishments' (Slater, 2002: 45). But Erik Erikson warned years ago: 'Children cannot be fooled by empty praise and condescending encouragement. They may have to accept artificial bolstering of their self-esteem in lieu of something better. . . .' Erikson went on to explain that a strong and positive identity comes only from 'wholehearted and consistent recognition of real accomplishment, that is, achievement that has meaning in their culture' (1980: 95).

Frank Pajares and Dale Schunk point to another problem. '[W]hen what is communicated to children from an early age is that nothing matters quite as much as how they feel or how confident they should be, one can rest assured that the world will sooner or later teach a lesson in humility that may not easily be learned. An obsession with one's sense of self is responsible for an alarming increase in depression and other mental difficulties' (2002: 16).

Sensitivity training and self-esteem courses share a common conceptual problem. They assume that we encourage self-esteem by changing the individual's beliefs, making the young person work harder against the odds. But what if the student's environment is truly unsafe, debilitating and unsupportive? Some people have overcome tremendous problems, but to expect everyone to do so 'ignores the fact that having positive self-esteem is almost impossible for many young people, given the deplorable conditions under which they are forced to live by the inequities in our society' (Beane, 1991: 27). Worse yet, some psychologists are now contending that low self-esteem is not a problem, whereas high self-esteem may be. For example, they contend, people with high self-esteem are more willing to inflict pain and punishment on others (Slater, 2002). Further, when people set self-esteem as a main goal, they may pursue that goal in ways that are harmful over the long run. They may, for example, avoid constructive criticisms or challenging tasks (Crocker and Park, 2004).

Source: From 'The trouble with self-esteem' by L. Slater, *The New York Times Magazine*, 3 February, 2002, pp. 44–47 and 'Sorting out the self-esteem controversy' by J. A. Beane, 1991, *Educational Leadership, 49*(1), pp. 25–30. Reprinted with permission.

WHAT DO YOU THINK?

Agree or Disagree? Vote online at www.pearsoned.co.uk/woolfolkeuro.

Table 3.5 Suggestions for encouraging self-esteem

1. Value and accept all pupils, for their attempts as well as their accomplishments.
2. Create a climate that is physically and psychologically safe for pupils.
3. Become aware of your own personal biases (everyone has some biases) and expectations.
4. Make sure that your procedures for teaching and grouping pupils are really necessary, not just a convenient way of handling problem pupils or avoiding contact with some pupils.
5. Make standards of evaluation clear; help pupils learn to evaluate their own accomplishments.
6. Model appropriate methods of self-criticism, perseverance and self-reward.
7. Avoid destructive comparisons and competition; encourage pupils to compete with their own prior levels of achievement.
8. Accept a pupil even when you must reject a particular behaviour or outcome. Pupils should feel confident, for example, that failing a test or being reprimanded in class does not make them 'bad' people.
9. Remember that positive self-concept grows from success in operating in the world *and* from being valued by important people in the environment.
10. Encourage pupils to take responsibility for their reactions to events; show them that they have choices in how to respond.
11. Set up support groups or 'study buddies' in school and teach pupils how to encourage each other.
12. Help pupils set clear goals and objectives; brainstorm about resources they have for reaching their goals.
13. Highlight the value of different ethnic groups – their cultures and accomplishments.

Sources: Information from 'Improving students' self-esteem' by J. Canfield. 1990, *Educational Leadership, 48*(1), pp. 48–50; *Teacher Behavior and Student Self-Concept* by M. M. Kash and G. Borich. 1978, Menlo Park, CA: Addison-Wesley; 'The development of self-concept' by H. H. Marshall, 1989, *Young Children, 44*(5), pp. 44–51.

important understandings and skills. Given this responsibility, what can teachers do? The recommendations in Table 3.5 are a beginning.

Diversity and Identity

Diversity and perception of self

A number of studies have found that girls tend to see themselves as more able than boys in reading and close friendships; boys are more confident about their abilities in mathematics and athletics. Of course, some of these differences in self-confidence may reflect actual differences in achievement – girls tend to be better readers than boys, for example. It is likely that confidence and achievement are reciprocally related – each affects the other (Cole *et al.*, 1999; Eccles, Wigfield and Schiefele, 1998; Wilgenbusch and Merrell, 1999). For most ethnic groups (except African Americans), males are more confident about their abilities in mathematics and science. Differences between males and females generally are small, but consistent across studies (Grossman and Grossman, 1994; Kling *et al.*, 1999). Unfortunately, there are currently no long-term studies of other ethnic groups, so these patterns may be limited to European Americans.

How do learners feel about themselves in general during the school years? Jean Twenge and Keith Campbell (2001) analysed over 150 samples of learners from studies conducted between 1968 and 1994, looking at general self-esteem, not subject-specific competence. They found that self-esteem decreased slightly for both girls and boys in the transition to junior high (approximately 11 years old). Boys' general self-esteem increased dramatically during their teen years, while girls' self-esteem stayed about the same, leaving girls with significantly lower general self-esteem than boys prior to leaving school. When these results are examined together with Marsh and Yeung's (1997) results that academic self-concept influences course selection, it seems that many learners make decisions about courses that forever limit their options in life, and often these decisions are not based on ability, but instead on 'illusions of incompetence'.

Ethnic and racial identity

People who belong to ethnic or racial groups are conscious of their ethnic identity as they negotiate being members of the larger culture as well. Because ethnic minority learners are members of both majority and minority group cultures it is complicated for them to establish a clear identity. Values, learning styles and communication patterns of the learner's ethnic culture may be inconsistent with the expectations of the school and the larger society. Embracing the values of mainstream culture may seem to require rejecting ethnic values. Ethnic minority learners have to 'sift through two sets of cultural values and identity options' to achieve a firm identity, so they may need more time to explore possibilities – a longer *moratorium* in Erikson's terms (Markstrom-Adams, 1992: 177). However, the exploration is important; some psychologists consider ethnic identity a 'master status,' one that dominates all other identity concerns when judging the self (Herman, 2004).

Ethnic identities: outcome and process

Jean Phinney (1990; 2003) describes four outcomes for ethnic minority youth in their search for identity. They can try *assimilation,* fully adopting the values and behaviours of the majority culture and rejecting their ethnic culture. At the opposite end, they can be *separated,* associating only with members of their ethnic culture. A third possibility is *marginality,* living in the majority culture, but feeling alienated and uncomfortable in it and disconnected from the minority culture as well. The final alternative is *biculturalism* (sometimes called integration), maintaining ties to both cultures. There are at least three ways to be bicultural. You could alternate between the two cultures, being fully 'majority' in your behaviour in one situation and fully 'minority' in another situation. Or you could blend the two cultures by finding values and behaviours that are common to both and acting on them. Finally, you could fuse the two cultures by truly merging them into a new and complete whole (Phinney and Devich-Nevarro, 1997). No matter what your identity outcome is, an important factor for good mental health seems to be having strong positive feelings about your own ethnic group (Steinberg, 2005). Ethnic identity then can be seen as an aspect of self-concept which develops in psychologically healthy individuals but it may also be that negative feelings may result in mental health problems. A growing number of researchers have explored this possibility suggesting that ethnic identity is directly related to a variety of negative health outcomes including drug use and violence (James, Kim and Armijo, 2000; Arbona *et al.*, 1999). The debate on this continues.

Some psychologists have used Marcia's identity statuses (discussed earlier in the section on 'Adolescence: the search for identity') to understand the process of forming an ethnic identity. Children may begin with an *unexamined ethnic identity,* either because they have not explored at all (diffusion) or because they have accepted the identity encouraged by others (foreclosure). Many European American adolescents could fit the unexamined category. A period of *ethnic identity exploration* (moratorium) might be followed by a *resolution* of the conflict (identity achieved).

Racial identity: outcome and process

The establishment of a racial identity is complex for those living within different racial groups. A survey of 34,000 pupils in predominantly white schools (at least 94%) in the UK reported that individuals in 14 schools indicated that aspects of their ethnicity were central to their self-identity (Cline *et al.*, 2002). However, there was considerable variation in how they would have liked to see their ethnic identity expressed at school. Clearly schools face a challenge in attempting to respect the range of views expressed.

Determining a racial identity may be even more complicated for biracial or multi-racial adolescents. The parent they live with, the make-up of their neighbourhood, their appearance and their experiences of discrimination or support can influence these adolescents' decisions about racial identity. Some psychologists think that these challenges help multiracial youth develop stronger and more complex identities, but other researchers argue that the challenges are an extra burden in an already difficult process (Herman, 2004). Perhaps the outcome depends in part on the support adolescents get in facing the challenges.

Racial and ethnic pride

For all learners, pride in family and community is part of the foundation for a stable identity. Special efforts to encourage racial and ethnic pride are particularly important, so that learners examining their identities do not get the message that differences are deficits (Spencer and Markstrom-Adams, 1990).

Each of us has an ethnic heritage. Janet Helms (1995) has written about stages in white identity development. Richard Milner (2003) has pointed to the importance of racial identity development and awareness, especially in teaching. When majority adolescents are knowledgeable and secure about their own heritage, they are also more respectful of the heritage of others. Thus, exploring the racial and ethnic roots of all learners should foster both self-esteem and acceptance of others (Rotherham-Borus, 1994).

Racial and ethnic pride

A positive self-concept about one's racial or ethnic heritage.

Emotional and Moral Development

As we seek our own identity and form images of ourselves, we are also learning to cope with emotions and trying to understand the 'significant others' around us. How do we learn to interpret what others are thinking and feeling?

Emotional competence

Understanding intentions and taking the perspective of others are elements in the development of emotional competence or the ability to understand and manage emotional situations. Beginning with the early interactions described by Murray and Trevarthen (1985) and developing throughout early childhood, children acquire the ability to interact effectively with those around them.

Social and emotional competences are critical for both academic and personal development. In fact, a number of studies that followed learners over several years in the US and in Italy have found that prosocial behaviours and social competence in the early grades are related to academic achievement and popularity with peers as many as five years later (Elias and Schwab, 2006). Table 3.6 describes four skills of emotional competence. How can teachers help learners develop emotional competence? The Focus on Practice below gives some ideas. In Chapter 9 we look at teaching strategies and programmes that encourage self-regulation of emotions.

Theory of mind and intention

By two or three years old, children are beginning to develop a theory of mind, an understanding that other people are people too, with their own minds, thoughts, feelings, beliefs, desires and perceptions (Flavell, Miller and Miller, 2002). Children need a theory of mind to make sense of other people's behaviour. Why is Sarah crying? Does she feel sad because no one will play with her? You will see in Chapter 4 that one

Theory of mind

An understanding that other people are people too, with their own minds, thoughts, feelings, beliefs, desires and perceptions.

Table 3.6 Essential social emotional skills

Here are examples of four important social/emotional skills and competences needed for each. The list was developed by the Collaborative for Academic, Social and Emotional Learning (CASEL) http://www.casel.org/home/index.php

Know yourself and others

- *Identify feelings* – Recognise and label feelings in yourself and others.
- *Be responsible* – Understand and act upon obligations to engage in ethical, safe and legal behaviours.
- *Recognise strengths* – Identify and cultivate positive qualities.

Make responsible decisions

- *Manage emotions* – Regulate feelings so that they aid rather than impede the handling of situations.
- *Understand situations* – Accurately understand the circumstances you are in.
- *Set goals and plans* – Establish and work towards the achievement of specific short- and long-term outcomes.
- *Solve problems creatively* – Engage in a creative, disciplined process of exploring alternative possibilities that lead to responsible, goal-directed action, including overcoming obstacles to plans.

Care for others

- *Show empathy* – Identify and understand the thoughts and feelings of others.
- *Respect others* – Act on the belief that others deserve to be treated with kindness

and compassion as part of our shared humanity.

- *Appreciate diversity* – Understand that individual and group differences complement one another and add strength and adaptability to the world around us.

Know how to act

- *Communicate effectively* – Use verbal and non-verbal skills to express yourself and promote effective exchanges with others.
- *Build relationships* – Establish and maintain healthy and rewarding connections with individuals and groups.
- *Negotiate fairly* – Strive to achieve mutually satisfactory resolutions to conflict by addressing the needs of all concerned.
- *Refuse provocations* – Convey and follow through effectively with decisions not to engage in unwanted, unsafe and unethical behaviour.
- *Seek help* – Identify your need for help and access appropriate assistance and support in pursuit of needs and goals.
- *Act ethically* – Guide decisions and actions by a set of principles or standards derived from recognised legal/professional codes or moral or faith-based systems of conduct.

Source: *Handbook of Classroom Management: Research, Practice, and Contemporary Issues* (Paper) by M. J. Elias and Y. Schwab. Copyright 2006 by Lawrence Erlbaum Associates, Inc – Books [T]. Reproduced with permission of Lawrence Erlbaum Associates Inc – Books [T] in the format Textbook via Copyright Clearance Center.

explanation for autism is that children with this condition lack a theory of mind to help them understand their own or other people's emotions and behaviours.

Around the age of two, children have a sense of *intention*, at least of their own intentions. They will announce, 'I wanna banana'. As children develop a theory of mind, they also are able to understand that other people have intentions of their own. Older preschoolers who get along well with their peers are able to separate intentional from unintentional actions and to react accordingly. For example, they will not get angry when another child accidentally knocks over the tower they have built with blocks. However, aggressive children have more trouble assessing intention. They are likely to attack anyone who topples their tower, even accidentally (Dodge and Pettit, 2003). As children mature, they are more able to assess and consider the intentions of others.

With a developing theory of mind, children are increasingly able to understand that other people have different feelings and experiences, and therefore may have a different viewpoint or perspective. This perspective-taking ability develops over time until it is quite sophisticated in adults. Being able to understand how others might think and feel is important in fostering cooperation and moral development, reducing prejudice, resolving conflicts and encouraging positive social behaviours in general (Gehlbach, 2004).

Robert Selman (1980) has developed a stage model to describe perspective-taking. As children mature and move towards formal-operational thinking, they take more information into account and realise that different people can react differently to the same situation. At some point between the ages of 10 and 15, most children develop the ability to analyse the perspectives of several people involved in a situation from the viewpoint of an objective bystander. Finally, older adolescents and adults can even imagine how different cultural or social values would influence the perceptions of the bystander. Even though children move through these stages, there can be great variation among children of the same age. Learners who have difficulty taking the perspective of others may feel little remorse when they mistreat peers or adults. Some training in perspective-taking from the teacher might help if the mistreatment is not part of a deeper emotional or behavioural disorder (Berk, 2005).

Moral development

Along with a more advanced theory of mind and an understanding of intention, children also are developing a sense of right and wrong. In this section we focus on children's moral reasoning, their *thinking* about right and wrong and their *active construction* of moral judgements. Some of the earliest moral issues in classrooms involve dividing and sharing materials or distributive justice (Damon, 1994). For young children (ages five to six), fair distribution is based on *equality*; thus, teachers often hear, 'Joshua got more than I did – that's not fair!' In the next few years, children come to recognise that some people should get more based on *merit* – they worked harder or performed better. Finally, around age eight, children are able to take need into account and to reason based on *benevolence*; they can understand that some children may get more time or resources from the teacher because they have special needs.

Another area that involves moral development is an understanding of rules. If you have spent time with young children, you know that there is a period when you can say, 'You are not allowed to eat in the living room!' and they accept this. For young children, rules simply exist. Piaget (1965) called this the state of moral realism. At this stage, the child of five or six believes that rules about conduct or rules about how to play a game are absolute and can't be changed. If a rule is broken, the child believes that the punishment should be determined by how much damage is done, not by the intention of the child or by other circumstances. So, accidentally breaking three cups is worse than intentionally breaking one, and in the child's eyes, the punishment for the three-cup offence should be greater.

As children interact with others, develop perspective-taking emotional abilities and see that different people have different rules, there is a gradual shift to a morality of cooperation. Children come to understand that people make rules and people can change them. When rules are broken, both the damage done and the intention of the offender are taken into account.

Kohlberg's theories of moral development

Lawrence Kohlberg's (1963, 1975, 1981) theory of moral development is based in part on Piaget's ideas, described above. Kohlberg built upon and extended Piaget's ideas evaluating the moral reasoning of both children and adults by presenting them with moral dilemmas, or hypothetical situations like the one below in which people must make difficult decisions and give their reasons.

Perspective-taking ability

Understanding that others have different feelings and experiences.

Moral reasoning

The thinking process involved in judgements about questions of right and wrong.

Distributive justice

Beliefs about how to divide materials or privileges fairly among members of a group; follows a sequence of development from equality to merit to benevolence.

Moral realism

Stage of development wherein children see rules as absolute.

Morality of cooperation

Stage of development wherein children realise that people make rules and people can change them.

Moral dilemmas

Situations in which no choice is clearly and indisputably right.

A man's wife is dying. There is one drug that could save her, but it is very expensive, and the drug company who invented it will not sell it at a price low enough for the man to buy it. Finally, the man becomes desperate and considers stealing the drug for his wife. What should he do, and why?

The reasoning put forward by the people taking part in the study formed the basis for Kohlberg's proposed, detailed sequence of stages of moral reasoning, or judgements about right and wrong. He divided moral development into three levels: (1) preconventional, where judgement is based solely on a person's own needs and perceptions; (2) conventional, where the expectations of society and law are taken into account; and (3) postconventional, where judgements are based on abstract, more personal principles of justice that are not necessarily defined by society's laws. Look at Table 3.7 to see how each of these three levels is then subdivided into stages. You might find it useful to see where your own reasons would be in this table.

Moral reasoning is related to both cognitive and emotional development. As we have seen, abstract thinking becomes increasingly important in the higher stages of moral development, as children move from decisions based on absolute rules to those based on abstract principles such as justice and mercy. The ability to see another's perspective, to judge intentions and to imagine alternative bases for laws and rules also enters into judgements at the higher stages.

Table 3.7   Kohlberg's theory of moral reasoning

Level 1. Preconventional moral reasoning

Judgement is based on personal needs and others' rules.

Stage 1   Punishment – obedience orientation.

Rules are obeyed to avoid punishment. A good or bad action is determined by its physical consequences.

Stage 2   Personal reward orientation.

Personal needs determine right and wrong. Favours are returned along the lines of 'You scratch my back, I'll scratch yours'.

Level 2. Conventional moral reasoning

Judgement is based on others' approval, family expectations, traditional values, the laws of society and loyalty to country.

Stage 3   Good boy–nice girl orientation.

Good means 'nice'. It is determined by what pleases, aids and is approved by others.

Stage 4   Law and order orientation.

Laws are absolute. Authority must be respected and the social order maintained.

Level 3. Postconventional moral reasoning

Stage 5   Social contract orientation.

Good is determined by socially agreed-upon standards of individual rights.

Stage 6*   Universal ethical principle orientation.

Good and right are matters of individual conscience and involve abstract concepts of justice, human dignity and equality.

*In later work Kohlberg questioned whether Stage 6 exists separately from Stage 5.

Source: Adapted from 'The cognitive-developmental approach to moral education' by L. Kohlberg, 1975, *Phi Delta Kappan, 56,* p. 671. Reprinted by permission of Phi Delta Kappan.

Criticisms of Kohlberg's theory

Even though there is evidence that the different levels of reasoning identified by Kohlberg do form a hierarchy, with each stage an advancement in reasoning over the one before (Boom, Brugman and van der Heijden, 2001), his stage theory has been criticised. First, in reality, the stages do not seem to be separate, sequenced and consistent. People often give reasons for moral choices that reflect several different stages simultaneously. Or a person's choices in one instance may fit one stage and his or her decisions in a different situation may reflect another stage. When asked to reason about helping someone else versus meeting their own needs, both children and adolescents reason at higher levels than when they are asked to reason about breaking the law or risking punishment (Arnold, 2000; Eisenberg *et al.*, 1987; Sobesky, 1983).

Second, in everyday life, making moral choices involves more than reasoning. Emotions, competing goals, relationships and practical considerations all affect choices. People may be able to reason at higher levels, but they may make choices at lower levels based on these other factors (Carpendale, 2000). Kohlberg emphasised cognitive reasoning about morality, but overlooked other aspects of moral maturity, such as character and virtue, that operate to solve moral problems in everyday life (Walker and Pitts, 1998).

Gender differences: the morality of caring

One of the most hotly debated criticisms of Kohlberg's theory is that the stages are biased in favour of Western male values that emphasise individualism. His stages do not represent the way moral reasoning develops either in women or in other cultures, because the stage theory was based on a longitudinal study of American men only (Gilligan, 1982; Gilligan and Attanucci, 1988).

Carol Gilligan (1982) has proposed a different sequence of moral development, an 'ethic of care'. Gilligan suggests that individuals move from a focus on self-interest to moral reasoning based on commitment to specific individuals and relationships, and then to the highest level of morality based on the principles of responsibility and care for all people (which is a bit like Kohlberg's stage 3). If women never reach what Kohlberg considers the higher stages of justice, are they morally immature?

Actually, recent studies find few significant differences between men and women, or boys and girls, in their level of moral reasoning as measured by Kohlberg's procedures (Eisenberg, Martin and Fabes, 1996; Turiel, 1998). Walker and his colleagues (Walker, 1991; Walker *et al.*, 1995) asked children, adolescents and adults to describe a personal moral problem and to analyse a traditional moral dilemma. For both types of problems, males and females revealed both a morality of caring *and* a concern with justice. When they read fables to six- and seven-year-old and eight- and nine-year-old boys and girls, Andrew Garrod and his colleagues (1990) found no differences in their moral reasoning. However, a few ten- and 11-year-old boys (but no girls) suggested solutions involving violence or tricks. So justice and caring seem to be important bases for moral reasoning for both genders. Even though men and women both seem to value caring and justice, there is some evidence that in everyday life, women feel more guilty about violating caring norms (being inconsiderate or untrustworthy) and men feel more guilty when they show violent behaviours (fighting or damaging property) (Williams and Bybee, 1994). Women are somewhat more likely to use a care orientation, but both men and women *can* use both orientations (Skoe, 1998).

Moral judgements, social conventions and personal choices

1. If there were no law against it, would it be acceptable to blind someone?
2. If there were no rule against it, would it be acceptable to chew gum in class?
3. Who should decide your favourite vegetable or how to style your hair?

We probably could agree that it is wrong to blind someone, wrong to break class rules, and wrong to dictate food preferences or hairstyles for other people – but it is a different kind of wrong in each case. The first question is about actions that are inherently immoral. The answer to the question is concerned with conceptions of justice, fairness, human rights and human welfare. Even young children know that it is not acceptable to hurt other people or steal from them – law or no law. However, some rules, like no gum chewing in question 2, are social conventions – agreed-upon rules and ways of doing things in a particular situation. Learners (mostly) avoid chewing gum when the class rules (conventions) say so. It is not inherently immoral to chew gum – it is just against the rules. Some classes – in further and higher education, for example – work well using different rules. It is not immoral to dislike broccoli (at least one hopes not) or to wear your hair long if you are a male; these are personal choices – individual preferences and private issues.

Other criticisms of Kohlberg's stages are that they mix up moral judgements with decisions about social conventions and also overlook personal choice. Larry Nucci (2001) offers an explanation of moral development that covers all three domains or areas: moral judgements, social conventions and personal choice. Children's thinking and reasoning develops across all domains, but the pace of development may not be the same in every area.

Social conventions

Agreed-upon rules and ways of doing things in a particular situation.

Moral v. conventional domains

For teachers, the most common 'right and wrong' situations involve the moral and conventional domains. In the moral domain, beginning with a few basic ideas about right and wrong ('It is wrong to hurt others'), children move through the following stages: a sense that justice means equal treatment for all, an appreciation of equity and special needs, a more abstract integration of equity and equality along with a sense of caring in social relations, and finally, a sense as adults that morality involves beneficence and fairness and that moral principles are independent of the norms of any particular group.

In the conventional domain, children begin by believing that the regularities they see are real and right – men have short hair, women have longer hair, for example, so that is the way it should be. As they mature, children see the exceptions (men with pony tails, women with very short cuts) and realise that conventions are arbitrary. Next, children understand that rules, even though they are arbitrary, are made to maintain order and that people in charge make the rules. But by early adolescence, learners begin to question these rules. Because they are arbitrary and made by others, maybe rules are 'nothing but' social expectations. As they move through adolescence, there is another swing – from understanding conventions as the appropriate way things have to operate in a social system to again seeing them as nothing but society's standards that have become set because they are used. Finally, adults realise that conventions are useful in coordinating social life, but changeable, too. So, compared to young children, older adolescents and adults generally are more accepting of others who think differently about conventions and customs.

Implications for teachers

Nucci (2001) offers several suggestions for creating a moral atmosphere in your classroom. First, it is important to establish a community of mutual respect and warmth with a fair and consistent application of the rules. Without that kind of community, all your attempts to create a moral climate will be undermined. Second, teachers' responses to learners should be appropriate to the domain of the behaviour – moral or conventional. For example, here are some responses to *moral issues* (Nucci, 2001: 146):

1. When an act is inherently hurtful or unjust, emphasise the harm done to others: 'John, that really hurt Jamal'.
2. Encourage perspective-taking: 'Nicola, how would you feel if someone stole from you?'

Here are two responses to rule or *conventional issues*:

3. Restate the rule: 'Lisa, you are not allowed to be out of your seat during registration'.
4. Command: 'Patrick, stop swearing!'

In all four cases, the teacher's response fits the domain. To create an inappropriate response, just switch responses 1 or 2 with 3 or 4. For example, 'James, how would you feel if other people got out of their seat during announcements?' James might feel perfectly happy with this. It is a weak response to a moral transgression to say, 'John, it is against the rules to hit'. It is more than against the rules – it hurts and it is wrong.

In the third domain, personal, children must sort out what decisions and actions are their personal choices and what decisions are outside personal choice. This process is the foundation for developing moral concepts related to individual rights, fairness and democracy. Here, different cultures may have very different understandings about individual choice, privacy and the role of individuality in the larger society. For example, some research has shown that both the parents in cultures that emphasise individualism and the parents in cultures that emphasise group membership believe that children need to be given choices to develop their ability to make good decisions. But middle-class parents tend to encourage making choices earlier, before adolescence. For children living in poverty, making too many choices early may be a bad idea, given the very real dangers they face in their neighbourhoods (Nucci, 2001).

Diversity in reasoning

There are a number of broad cultural distinctions that might influence moral reasoning. Some cultures can be considered more traditional, with greater emphasis on customs and rituals that change slowly over time. In contrast, traditions and customs tend to change more rapidly in modern cultures. Nucci (2001) suggests that in more traditional cultures, customs may become 'moralised'. For example, not wearing head coverings in some cultures may seem to be in the conventional domain to outsiders, but is closer to the moral domain for members of the culture, especially when religious beliefs are involved. Consider the findings of one study described by Nucci that asked devout Hindus to rate 35 behaviours that violated community norms. An eldest son eating chicken a day after his father's death was considered the worst violation and beating a disobedient wife was the least offensive. What seems like a convention (eating chicken) is a moral issue because the Hindus believed that the son's behaviour would prevent his father from receiving salvation – a terrible and eternal fate. So, to understand what is convention and what is moral, we need to know about the beliefs of the culture.

In cultures that are more family-centred or group-oriented, such as China or Korea (often called collectivist cultures), the highest moral value might involve putting the opinions of the group before decisions based on individual conscience. Research has found that children's reasoning about moral, conventional and personal domains is similar across cultures (Berk, 2005). Even in societies such as China that encourage deference to authority, Chinese children agree with Western children that adults have no right to dictate how children spend their free time. They think that people without authority, including children, should be obeyed when what they want you to do is fair and just, but disobeyed when what they dictate is immoral or unjust (Helwig *et al.*, 2003; Kim, 1998).

In the last years of his life, Kohlberg was studying moral behaviour in schools. We turn to that topic now.

Moral behaviour

As people move towards higher stages of moral reasoning, they also evidence more sharing, helping and defending of victims of injustice. However, this relationship between moral reasoning and moral behaviour is not very strong (Berk, 2005) because many other factors besides reasoning affect behaviour. Three important influences on moral behaviour are modelling, internalisation and self-concept. First, children who have been consistently exposed to caring, generous adult models will tend to be more concerned for the rights and feelings of others (Cook and Cook, 2005; Eisenberg and Fabes, 1998). Second, most theories of moral behaviour assume that young children's moral behaviour is first controlled by others through direct instruction, supervision, rewards and punishments and correction. However, in time, children internalise the moral rules and principles of the authority figures who have guided them; that is, children adopt the external standards as their own. If children are given reasons they can understand when they are corrected – particularly reasons that highlight the effects of actions on others – then they are more likely to internalise moral principles. They learn to behave morally even when 'no one is watching' (Hoffman, 2000).

Finally, we must integrate moral beliefs and values into our total sense of who we are or our self-concept.

> *The tendency for a person to behave morally is largely dependent on the extent to which moral beliefs and values are integrated in the personality, and in one's sense of self. The influence our moral beliefs have on our lives, therefore, is contingent on the personal importance that we as individuals attach to them – we must identify and respect them as our own (Arnold, 2000: 372).*

Let's consider a moral issue that may arise in classrooms – cheating.

Cheating

Early research indicates that cheating seems to have more to do with the particular situation than with the general honesty or dishonesty of the individual (Burton, 1963). A pupil who cheats in mathematics is probably more likely to cheat in other classes, but may never consider lying to a friend or shoplifting. Many pupils will cheat if the pressure to perform well is great and the chances of being caught are slim. In 1996, Steinberg reported that 66% of the adolescents in his study admitted to cheating on a test in the last year, and figures as high as 90% have been reported for university students (Jensen *et al.*, 2002). Currently, a new kind of cheating is emerging and we are surrounded by debates about plagiarism and 'buying' essays from the internet (Underwood and Szabo 2003).

There are some individual differences in cheating. Most studies of adolescent and university students find that males are more likely to cheat than females and lower-achieving learners are more likely to cheat than higher achievers. Learners focusing on performance goals (high grades, looking intelligent) as opposed to learning goals, and pupils with a low sense of academic self-efficacy (a belief that they probably can't do well in school) are more likely to cheat.

Cheating is not all about individual differences – the situation plays a role as well. In one study, the level of cheating decreased when pupils moved from mathematics

Internalise

Process whereby children adopt external standards as their own.

classes that emphasised competition and grades to classes that emphasised understanding and mastery (Anderman and Midgley, 2004). Learners also are particularly likely to cheat when they are behind or revising for exams or when they believe that their teachers do not care about them.

The implications for teachers are straightforward. To prevent cheating, they should try to avoid putting learners in high-pressure situations. They should make sure they are well prepared for tests, projects and assignments so they can do reasonably well without cheating. There should be focus on learning and not on grades, and encouragement to collaborate on assignments. Teachers can experiment with open-book, collaborative or tests that are taken home. It is possible for teachers to tell learners what concepts will be included in the test and to encourage them to discuss the concepts and their applications before the test. It is also helpful if teachers make extra help available for those who need it and having clear policies in regard to cheating, which are enforced consistently. Further, learners should know that they will be carefully watched throughout exams so that they are discouraged from attempting to cheat.

SUMMARY TABLE

Physical Development (pp. 78–81)

Describe the changes in physical development in the preschool, early and later school years.

During the preschool years, there is rapid development of children's gross- and fine-motor skills. Physical development continues throughout the early school years, with girls often ahead of boys in size. With adolescence comes puberty and emotional struggles to cope with all the related changes.

What are some of the consequences of early and late maturation for boys and girls?

Females mature about two years ahead of males. Early-maturing boys are more likely to enjoy high social status; they tend to be popular and to be leaders. However, they also tend to engage in more delinquent behaviour. Early maturation is not generally beneficial for girls.

What are some of the signs of eating disorders?

Anorexic learners may appear pale, have brittle fingernails and have fine dark hairs developing all over their bodies. They are easily chilled because they have so little fat to insulate their bodies. They often are depressed, insecure, moody and lonely. Girls may stop having their menstrual period.

Freud: Stages of Individual Development (pp. 81–84)

Why do Freud's ideas have importance for understanding children's emotional development?

Freud stressed the importance of the unconscious mind and ways in which the personality strives to meet the competing demands of the id, ego and superego. This provides insights into the emotional turmoil which some children experience as they struggle to control their impulses and develop a sense of personal morality.

What are Freud's psychosexual stages of development?

Freud believed that individuals develop emotionally as they pass through a series of stages (from birth to sexual maturity) which focus upon different areas of physical pleasure. The person's adult personality is affected by the balance between insufficient and excessive amounts of stimulation received at each stage (particularly the early stages).

Attachment Theory (pp. 84–85)

How does the notion of attachment help to explain difficulties in friendship formation and peer acceptance in later life?

Bowlby's suggestion that attachment is vital to healthy development, led to the categorisation of attachment types by Mary Ainsworth. Secure attachment relates to many positive aspects of development including peer acceptance and sociability.

Erikson: The Individual and Society (pp. 85–92)

Why is Erikson's theory considered a psychosocial perspective?

Erikson was interested in the ways that individuals developed psychologically to become active and contributing members of society. He believed that all humans have the same basic needs and that each society must accommodate those needs. Erikson's emphasis on the relationship between society and the individual is a psychosocial theory of development – a theory that connects personal development (psycho) to the social environment (social).

What are Erikson's stages of psychosocial development?

Erikson believed that people go through eight life stages between infancy and old age, each of which involves a central crisis. Adequate resolution of each crisis leads to greater personal and social competence and a stronger foundation for solving future crises. In the first two stages, an infant must develop a sense of trust over mistrust and a sense of autonomy over shame and doubt. In early childhood, the focus of the third stage is on developing initiative and avoiding feelings of guilt. In the child's early school years, the fourth stage involves achieving a sense of industry and

avoiding feelings of inferiority. In the fifth stage, identity versus role confusion, adolescents consciously attempt to solidify their identity. According to Marcia, these efforts may lead to identity diffusion, foreclosure, moratorium or achievement. Erikson's three stages of adulthood involve struggles to achieve intimacy, generativity and integrity.

Bronfenbrenner: The Social Context for Development (pp. 92–105)

Describe Bronfenbrenner's bioecological model of development

This model takes into account both the biological aspects internal to the individual and the nested social and cultural contexts that shape development. Every person develops within a *microsystem* (immediate relationships and activities) inside a *mesosystem* (relationships among microsystems), embedded in an *exosystem* (larger social settings such as communities); all of these are part of the *macrosystem* (culture).

What are some aspects of the family that affect learners in school?

Learners probably have experienced different parenting styles and these styles can influence their social adjustment. At least in European American, middle-class families, children of authoritative parents are more likely to be happy with themselves and relate well to others, whereas children of authoritarian parents are more likely to be guilty or depressed, and children of permissive parents may have trouble interacting with peers. However, cultures differ in parenting styles. Research indicates that higher-control parenting is linked to better academic achievement.

How does divorce affect learners?

During the divorce itself, conflict may increase as property and custody rights are being decided. After the divorce, the custodial parent may have to move to a less expensive home, find new sources of income, go to work for the first time, or work longer hours. For the child, this can mean leaving behind important friendships in the old neighbourhood or school just when support is needed the most, having only one parent who has less time than ever to be with them, or adjusting to new family structures when parents remarry.

Why are peer relations important?

Peer relationships play a significant role in healthy personal and social development. There is strong evidence that adults who had close friends as children have higher self-esteem and are more capable of maintaining intimate relationships than adults who had lonely childhoods. Adults who were rejected as children tend to have more problems, such as dropping out of school or committing crimes.

What are peer cultures and how can aggression develop?

Groups of learners develop their own norms for appearance and social behaviour. Group loyalties can lead to rejection for some learners, leaving them upset and unhappy. Peer aggression can be instrumental, which is intended to gain an object or privilege, or hostile, which is intended to inflict harm. Hostile aggression can be either overt threats or physical attacks or relational aggression, which involves threatening or damaging social relationships (as in, 'I'm never going to speak to you again!'). Boys are more likely to use overt aggression and girls, like Alison in the opening case, are more likely to use relational aggression.

How can teachers' academic and personal caring affect learners?

Learners value caring in teachers. Caring can be expressed as support for academic learning and as concern for personal problems. For higher-achieving and higher socioeconomic status learners, academic caring may be more important, but for learners who are alienated from school, personal caring may be more important.

What are some signs of child abuse?

Signs of abuse or neglect include unexplained bruises, burns, bites or other injuries, and fatigue, depression, frequent absences, poor hygiene, inappropriate clothing, problems with peers and many others. Teachers must report suspected cases of child abuse and can be instrumental in helping learners cope with other risks as well.

Self-Concept: Understanding Ourselves (pp. 105–111)

What are some of the consequences of early and late maturation for boys and girls? Distinguish between self-concept and self-esteem

Both self-concept and self-esteem are beliefs about the self. Self-concept is our attempt to build a scheme that organises our impressions, feelings and attitudes about ourselves. But this model is not permanent. Self-perceptions vary from situation to situation and from one phase of our lives to another. Self-esteem is an evaluation of who you are. If people evaluate themselves positively, we say that they have high self-esteem. Self-concept and self-esteem are often used interchangeably, even though they have distinct meanings. Self-concept is a cognitive structure and self-esteem is an affective evaluation.

How do self-concept and self-esteem change as children develop?

Self-concept (definition of self) and self-esteem (valuing of self) become increasingly complex, differentiated and abstract as we mature. Self-concept evolves through constant self-reflection, social interaction and experiences in and out of school. Learners develop a self-concept by comparing themselves to personal (internal) standards and social (external) standards. The self-esteem of middle and junior secondary school learners (9–14 year olds) becomes more tied to physical appearance and social acceptance. High self-esteem is related to better overall school experience, both academically and socially. Gender and ethnic stereotypes are significant factors as well.

Diversity and Identity (pp. 111–113)

Are there differences in self-concepts for girls and boys?

From five to 16 years old competence beliefs decline for both boys and girls in mathematics, English and sports. By 11–12 years of age boys and girls express about the same competence in mathematics, girls are higher in English and boys are higher in sports. In terms of general self-esteem, both boys and girls report a decline as they move from their first school (11–12 years of age) but boys' self-esteem goes up in the later years of education while girls' self-esteem stays down.

Describe the formation of ethnic and racial, and sexual identities

Ethnic and racial minority learners are confronted with the challenge of forming an identity while living in two worlds – the values, beliefs and behaviours of their group and of the larger culture. Most explanations for identity development describe stages moving from being unaware of differences between minority group and majority cultures, to different ways of negotiating the differences, finally to an integration of cultures.

Emotional and Moral Development (pp. 113–121)

What are the skills involved in emotional competence?

Emotionally competent individuals are aware of their own emotions and the feelings of others – realising that inner emotions can differ from outward expressions. They can talk about and express emotions in ways that are appropriate

for their cultural group. They can feel empathy for others in distress and also cope with their own distressing emotions – they can handle stress. Emotionally competent individuals know that relationships are defined in part by how emotions are communicated within the relationship. All these skills come together to produce a capacity for emotional self-efficacy.

What is a theory of mind and why is it important?

A theory of mind is an understanding that other people are people too, with their own minds, thoughts, feelings, beliefs, desires and perceptions. Children need a theory of mind to make sense of other people's behaviour. As children develop a theory of mind, they also are able to understand that other people have intentions of their own.

How do perspective-taking skills change as learners mature?

An understanding of intentions develops as children mature, but aggressive learners often have trouble understanding the intentions of others. Social perspective-taking also changes as we mature. Young children believe that everyone has the same thoughts and feelings they do. Later, they learn that others have separate identities and therefore separate feelings and perspectives on events.

What are the key differences among the preconventional, conventional and postconventional levels of moral reasoning?

Kohlberg's theory of moral development includes three levels: (1) a preconventional level, where judgements are based on self-interest; (2) a conventional level, where judgements are based on traditional family values and social expectations; and (3) a postconventional level, where judgements are based on more abstract and personal ethical principles. Kohlberg evaluated the moral reasoning of both children and adults by presenting them with moral dilemmas, or hypothetical situations in which people must make difficult decisions. Critics suggest that Kohlberg's view does not account for possible cultural differences in moral reasoning or differences between moral reasoning and moral behaviour.

Describe Gilligan's levels of moral reasoning

Carol Gilligan has suggested that because Kohlberg's stage theory was based on a longitudinal study of men only, it is very possible that the moral reasoning of women and the stages of women's development were not adequately represented. She has proposed an 'ethic of care'. Gilligan believes that individuals move from a focus on self-interests to moral reasoning based on commitment to specific individuals and relationships and then to the highest level of morality based on the principles of responsibility and care for all people. Women are somewhat more likely to use a care orientation, but studies also show that both men and women *can* use both orientations.

How does thinking in the moral and conventional domains change over time?

Beliefs about morality move from the young child's sense that justice means equal treatment for all to the adult's understanding that morality involves beneficence and fairness and that moral principles are independent of the norms of any particular group. In thinking about social conventions, children begin by believing that the regularities they see are real and right. After going through several stages, adults realise that conventions are useful in coordinating social life, but changeable too.

What influences moral behaviour?

Adults first control young children's moral behaviour through direct instruction, supervision, rewards and punishments and correction. A second important influence on the development of moral behaviour is modelling. Children who have been consistently exposed to caring, generous adult models will tend to be more concerned for the rights and feelings of others. The world and the media provide many negative models of behaviour. In time, children internalise the moral rules and principles of the authority figures who have guided them. If children are given reasons – particularly reasons that highlight the effects of actions on others – they can understand when they are corrected and then they are more likely to internalise moral principles. Some schools have adopted programmes to increase learners' capacity to care for others. In schools, cheating is a common behaviour problem that involves moral issues.

Glossary

Anorexia Nervosa: Eating disorder characterised by very limited food intake.

Attachment: The emotional bond between an infant and a caregiver.

Autonomy: Independence.

Bioecological model: Bronfenbrenner's theory describing the nested social and cultural contexts that shape development. Every person develops within a *microsystem,* inside a *mesosystem,* embedded in an *exosystem,* all of which are a part of the *macrosystem* of the culture.

Blended families: Parents, children and stepchildren merged into families through remarriages.

Bulimia: Eating disorder characterised by overeating, then getting rid of the food by self-induced vomiting or laxatives.

Conscience: Includes information about those things viewed as bad by parents and society punishes with guilt.

Developmental crisis: A specific conflict whose resolution prepares the way for the next stage.

Distributive justice: Beliefs about how to divide materials or privileges fairly among members of a group; follows a sequence of development from equality to merit to benevolence.

Ego: Responsible for dealing with reality and meeting needs of the id in a socially acceptable way.

Ego-ideal: Includes standards of good, desirable behaviour approved by parents and society – rewarded with feelings of pride.

Fixated: A person remains fixed at a certain psychosexual stage and their personality reflects this throughout life.

Generativity: Sense of concern for future generations.

Hostile aggression: Bold, direct action that is intended to hurt someone else; unprovoked attack.

Id: The instinctive needs and desires of a person present from birth.

Identity: Principle that a person or object remains the same over time.

Identity achievement: Strong sense of commitment to life choices after free consideration of alternatives.

Identity diffusion: Uncentredness; confusion about who one is and what one wants.

Identity foreclosure: Acceptance of parental life choices without consideration of options.

Industry: Eagerness to engage in productive work.

Initiative: Willingness to begin new activities and explore new directions.

Instrumental aggression: Strong actions aimed at claiming an object, place or privilege – not intended to harm, but may lead to harm.

Integrity: Sense of self-acceptance and fulfilment.

Internalise: Process whereby children adopt external standards as their own.

Moral dilemmas: Situations in which no choice is clearly and indisputably right.

Moral realism: Stage of development wherein children see rules as absolute.

Moral reasoning: The thinking process involved in judgements about questions of right and wrong.

Morality of cooperation: Stage of development wherein children realise that people make rules and people can change them.

Moratorium: Identity crisis; suspension of choices because of struggle.

Overt aggression: A form of hostile aggression that involves physical attack.

Parenting styles: The ways of interacting with and disciplining children.

Perspective-taking ability: Understanding that others have different feelings and experiences.

Psychosexual stages: The stages through which humans pass as they develop their adult personality.

Psychosocial: Describing the relation of the individual's emotional needs to the social environment.

Puberty: The physiological changes during adolescence that lead to the ability to reproduce.

Racial and ethnic pride: A positive self-concept about one's racial or ethnic heritage.

Regress: A person returns to an earlier stage of development when in stressful situations.

Relational aggression: A form of hostile aggression that involves verbal attacks and other actions meant to harm social relationships.

Secure base: The attachment figure provides a safe foundation for the child to explore the world.

Self-concept: Individuals' knowledge and beliefs about themselves – their ideas, feelings, attitudes and expectations.

Self-esteem: The value each of us places on our own characteristics, abilities and behaviours.

Sensitive responsiveness: A mother/caregiver's ability to respond accurately, promptly and appropriately to an infant's needs.

Social conventions: Agreed-upon rules and ways of doing things in a particular situation.

Superego: Holds all the moral principles and ideals acquired from parents and society.

Theory of mind: An understanding that other people are people too, with their own minds, thoughts, feelings, beliefs, desires and perceptions.

CHECK YOUR LEARNING! WEB

In the Classroom: What Would They Do?

Here is how some practising teachers responded to the situation presented at the beginning of this chapter about cliques among adolescents at school and the difficulties some learners face with 'fitting in'.

Science teacher at a large suburban school in the UK (11–16-year-olds)

I would begin by meeting the two girls individually to get their side of the story. I would make it clear to Alison that she was behaving in a hurtful and unacceptable way and that if she did not start to mend bridges she would be moved to a different class. I would then talk to Sophie and reassure her that she would not be made to feel embarrassed by what had happened. I would enlist the help of a friendly pupil in the year group and ask her to include Sophie in some of the activities which her group of friends took part in. This would help to integrate her into her peer group.

English teacher at an inner-city school in the UK (11–16-year-olds)

I see this behaviour as a form of bullying and would treat it as such. I would use some of the 'no blame' principles in dealing with this. I would first of all get an independent account of what had happened from both girls before inviting all those involved – including those who had witnessed but not taken part – to a meeting. This would not include Sophie. I would then present to the group the problems which Sophie had identified in her talk with me. This would be done in a neutral rather than 'telling off' way and would consist of presenting the facts about how Sophie is feeling. I would then ask the group for suggestions about ways of solving this problem and discuss with them strategies for changing things. This would mean that they were taking responsibility for changing things as they recognised that Sophie was unhappy and that this was a problem. No punishment would be given. The group would then be left to get on with it and told that there would be another meeting in two weeks to monitor progress. Meanwhile Sophie would be invited to talk to me and report progress. As things improved and the group dynamics changed Sophie herself would be invited to join with the group for meetings. Eventually I am confident that these would cease to be necessary. I have used this strategy many times and find it very effective. The only problem is that the parents often want retribution but this can make things worse for the child involved.

Overview

To answer the questions that follow, you need an understanding of individual differences. So far, we have talked little about individuals. We have discussed principles of development that apply to everyone – stages, processes, conflicts and tasks. Our development as human beings is similar in many ways, but not in every way. Even among members of the same family, there are marked contrasts in appearance, interests, abilities and temperament, and these differences have important implications for teaching and learning. In addition, there is probably at least one learner with special needs in each class, at whatever level. In this chapter, we explore both common and less frequently occurring learning problems that individuals may have. As we discuss each problem area, we will consider how a teacher might recognise problems, seek help and plan instruction.

By the time you have completed this chapter, you should be able to answer the following questions:

- **What are the potential problems in categorising and labelling learners?**
- **What is your personal concept of intelligence?**
- **What do you think about ability grouping?**
- **Should lessons be adapted for individuals with varying learning styles?**
- **What are the implications of policies to promote inclusive education in European countries (such as the resolution of the European Parliament relating to Equal Opportunities for People with Disabilities (2001) and the Special Educational Needs and Disability Act 2001 in the UK) for schools?**
- **In a classroom, how might learners with hearing, vision, language and behaviour problems, and specific learning difficulties, as well as those who are gifted, be identified and helped to learn?**

In the Classroom

It's a new school year and Christina has been informed that her new class includes four children with special educational needs. Whilst teachers know that they are going to have learners with a wide range of abilities, social skills and motivation for learning in their classrooms, Christina is now faced with a pupil with impaired hearing, two pupils who speak very little English and a pupil with severe learning difficulties. Within the European Union and internationally, legislation and policy have increased participation in mainstream education for pupils with special educational needs (Key Principles for Special Needs Education, 2003). In the UK, for example, the Special Educational Needs Code of Practice introduced in 2001 (DfES, 2001a) following the government's *Every*

Child Matters policy made teachers accountable for the learning and progress of all of their pupils which is monitored on at least an annual basis.

How would you expect Christina to be advised by the SENCO (Special Educational Needs Coordinator) or Special Educational Needs (SEN) advisor in order to meet the targets set out in the pupils' Individual Education Plans (IEPs)?

Group Activity

Working with two or three others suggest some strategies for teaching and monitoring the progress of all pupils.

Individual Differences in Intelligence

Because the concept of intelligence is so important in education, so controversial and so often misunderstood (in terms of how it is defined and measured) we will spend some time discussing it, but before we begin let's first examine the practice of labelling people based on differences such as intelligence, ability or disability.

Learner differences and labelling

Every child is a distinctive collection of talents, abilities and limitations. In that sense, all children are 'exceptional', but some have physical, intellectual or behavioural skills and abilities which differ substantially from the norm – either higher or lower. For example, they may have special abilities and talents, learning difficulties, communication disorders, emotional or behavioural disorders, intellectual disabilities, physical disabilities, impaired vision or difficulties hearing, autism, traumatic brain injury, or some combination (Hardman, Drew and Egan, 2005). Even though we will use terms like these throughout the chapter, a caution is in order: labelling learners is a controversial issue.

A label does not tell which methods to use with individual learners. For example, few specific 'treatments' automatically follow from a 'diagnosis' of intellectual disabilities; many different teaching strategies and materials are appropriate. So, for example, simply diagnosing a learner as being dyslexic, does not immediately inform teachers how to support the learning of this pupil. Further, the labels can become self-fulfilling prophecies. Everyone – teachers, parents, classmates, and even the learners themselves – may see a label as a stigma that cannot be changed. Finally, labels are mistaken for explanations, as in, 'Anthony gets involved in fights because he has a behavioural disorder.' 'How do you know he has a behavioural disorder?' 'Because he gets involved in fights.' This kind of circular reasoning is non-productive and negative because nothing is actually done to address the issues of Anthony being 'involved in fights'.

On the other hand, some educators argue that for younger learners, at least, being labelled as 'special' protects the child. For example, if classmates know a pupil has intellectual disabilities (sometimes called cognitive disabilities), they will be more willing to accept her behaviours. Of course, labels still open doors to some special programmes, useful information, special technology and equipment, or financial assistance. Labels probably both stigmatise and help learners (Hallahan *et al.*, 2005; Hardman, Drew and Egan, 2005). Anita Ho (2004) suggests that a commitment to inclusion and equality means that we should acknowledge the problems associated with categorisation or labelling and focus upon the construction of social and educational support systems rather than 'pathologizing children's learning difficulties' (2004: 86). So rather than applying the medical model (which involves seeing the condition as a biological one and assumes abnormality) we should be flexible and accommodating to the diversity we encounter amongst learners.

Person-first language

This caution about labelling also applies to many of the common descriptions heard in schools every day. Today, we rarely hear labels such as 'mentally handicapped' because describing a complex person with one or two words implies that the condition labelled is the most important aspect of the person. Actually, the individual has many abilities, and to focus on the disability is to misrepresent the individual. An alternative is 'person-first' language or speaking of 'learners with intellectual difficulties'. Here, the emphasis is on the learners first, not on the special challenges they face (Meece, 2002). Other examples might include:

A girl with special educational needs	NOT	An SEN girl
A person with epilepsy	NOT	An epileptic
A child with a physical disability	NOT	A crippled child
Children diagnosed with autism	NOT	Autistic children or autistics

Disorders, disabilities and handicaps

One more distinction in language is important. A disorder is a broad term – a general disturbance in physical or mental functioning, for example, a communications disorder. A disability is just what the word implies – an inability to do something specific such as pronounce words or see or walk. A handicap is a disadvantage in certain situations. Some educators have suggested that we drop the word 'handicap' altogether because the source of the word is demeaning. *Handicap* came from the phrase 'cap-in-hand', used to describe people with disabilities who once were forced to beg just to survive (Hardman, Drew and Egan, 2005).

Some disabilities lead to handicaps, but not in all contexts. For example, being blind (a visual disability) is a handicap if you want to drive a car but blindness is not a handicap when you are composing music or talking on the telephone. Stephen Hawking, the renowned physicist, sufferers from Lou Gehrig's disease and can no longer walk or talk. He once said that he is lucky that he became a theoretical physicist 'because it is all in the mind. So my disability has not been a serious handicap'. It is important that we do not *create* handicaps for people by the way we react to their disabilities.

Disabilities are part of the human condition. We can think of all human characteristics as being on a continuum, from very acute hearing to complete deafness for instance. We all fall somewhere on that continuum and we change over our lifetimes. As we age, for example, there are likely to be changes in hearing, vision, even some aspects of intellectual ability, as you will see later in this chapter. This relates to the points raised earlier about the complex nature of intelligence.

Intelligence is a widely used label in education and life in general. Let us begin with a basic question.

Disorder
A broad term meaning a general disturbance in physical or mental functioning.

Disability
The inability to do something specific such as walk or hear.

Handicap
A disadvantage in a particular situation, sometimes caused by a disability.

What does intelligence mean?

> **STOP AND THINK**
>
> Who was the most intelligent person in your secondary school? Write down a name and the first four or five words that come to mind when you see that person in your mind's eye. What made you pick this individual?

The idea that people vary in what we call intelligence has been with us for a long time. Plato discussed similar variations over 2,000 years ago. Most early theories about the nature of intelligence involved one or more of the following three themes: (1) the capacity to learn; (2) the total knowledge a person has acquired; and (3) the ability to adapt successfully to new situations and to the environment in general.

Intelligence
Ability or abilities to acquire and use knowledge for solving problems and adapting to the world.

During the past century, there was considerable controversy over the meaning of intelligence. In 1986, at a symposium on intelligence, 24 psychologists each offered a different view about the nature of intelligence (Neisser *et al.*, 1996; Sternberg and Detterman, 1986). More than half of the experts mentioned higher-level thinking processes such as abstract reasoning and problem solving as important aspects of intelligence and they added metacognition (being able to reflect upon your own thinking) and executive processes (monitoring your own thinking) to earlier views. The interaction of knowledge with mental processes, and the cultural context – what is valued by the culture – as elements of intelligence were also agreed upon but the psychologists disagreed about the structure of intelligence – whether it is a single ability or many separate abilities (Gustafsson and Undheim, 1996; Louis *et al.*, 2000; Sattler, 2001; Sternberg, 2004). Let us think about that question for a while.

Intelligence: one ability or many?

Some theorists believe intelligence is a basic ability that affects performance on all cognitively oriented tasks, from computing mathematical problems to writing poetry or solving riddles. Evidence for this position comes from study after study finding moderate-to-high positive correlations among all the different tests that are designed to measure separate intellectual abilities (Carroll, 1993; McNemar, 1964). What could explain these results? Charles Spearman (1927) the first psychologist to approach intelligence research scientifically, suggested there is one mental attribute, which he called *g* or general intelligence, used to perform any mental test, but each test also requires some specific abilities in addition to *g*. For example, memory for a series of numbers probably involves both *g* and some specific ability for immediate recall of what is heard. Spearman assumed that individuals vary in both general intelligence and specific abilities, and that together these factors determine performance on mental tasks.

Are these children/ young people using both general and specific abilities as they perform?

Another view that has stood the test of time is the Cattell-Horn theory of fluid and crystallised intelligence (Cattell, 1963; Horn, 1998). Fluid intelligence is mental efficiency that is essentially culture-free and non-verbal such as the individual's ability to think and act quickly, solve novel problems and store short-term memories. This aspect of intelligence increases until adolescence because it is grounded in brain development, then declines gradually with age. Fluid intelligence is sensitive to injuries. In contrast, crystallised intelligence, the ability to apply culturally approved problem-solving methods, can increase throughout the life span because it includes the learned skills and knowledge such as vocabulary, facts and how to read a timetable, sew on a button or study effectively at undergraduate level. By *investing fluid intelligence* in solving problems, we *develop our crystallised intelligence,* but many tasks in life such as mathematical reasoning draw on both fluid and crystallised intelligence (Finkel *et al.,* 2003; Hunt, 2000). Thus they require a mixture of nature (fluid intelligence) and nurture (crystallised intelligence).

The most widely accepted view today is that intelligence, like self-concept, has many facets and is a hierarchy of abilities, with general ability at the top and more specific abilities at lower levels of the hierarchy (Sternberg, 2000). Earl Hunt summarised the current thinking about the structure of intelligence this way:

> *After almost a century of such research, that structure is pretty well-established. There is considerable agreement for the bottom two levels of a three-tiered lattice model of intelligence. At the bottom are elementary information-processing actions, and immediately above them are eight or so secondary abilities. These are more broadly defined capabilities, such as holding and accessing information in short- and long-term memory and, most importantly, the trio of 'intellectual' abilities: crystallized intelligence, fluid intelligence, and visual-spatial reasoning ability [which] may be just the most visible of several abilities to manipulate information coded in a particular sensory modality (2000: 123).*

Look at Figure 4.1 to see an example of this three-level view of intelligence. John Carroll (1997) identifies one general ability, a few broad abilities (such as fluid and crystallised abilities, learning and memory, visual and auditory perception, processing speed) and at least 70 specific abilities such as language development, memory span and simple reaction time. General ability may be related to the maturation and functioning of the frontal lobe of the brain, which plays a part in impulse control, judgement, language, memory, motor function, problem solving, sexual behaviour, socialisation and spontaneity. The frontal lobes assist in planning, coordinating, controlling and executing behaviour while specific abilities may be connected to other parts of the brain (Byrnes and Fox, 1998). Some theorists, however, suggest that there are a number of separate types of intelligence or 'multiple intelligences' rather than a hierarchical structure.

Multiple intelligences

In spite of the correlations among the various tests of different abilities, some psychologists insist that there are several separate mental abilities (Gardner, 1983; Guilford, 1988). According to Gardner's (1983, 2003) theory of multiple intelligences, there are at least eight separate intelligences: linguistic (verbal), musical, spatial, logical-mathematical, bodily-kinesthetic (movement), interpersonal (understanding others), intrapersonal (understanding self) and naturalist (observing and understanding natural and human-made patterns and systems) (see Table 4.1). Gardner stresses that there may be more kinds of intelligence – eight is not a magic number. Recently, he has speculated that there may be an existential intelligence – the abilities to contemplate big questions about the meaning of life (Gardner, 2003).

Fluid intelligence

Mental efficiency, non-verbal abilities grounded in brain development.

Crystallised intelligence

Ability to apply culturally approved problem-solving methods.

Theory of multiple intelligences

In Gardner's theory of intelligence, a person's eight separate abilities: logical-mathematical, linguistic, musical, spatial, bodily-kinesthetic, interpersonal, intrapersonal and naturalist.

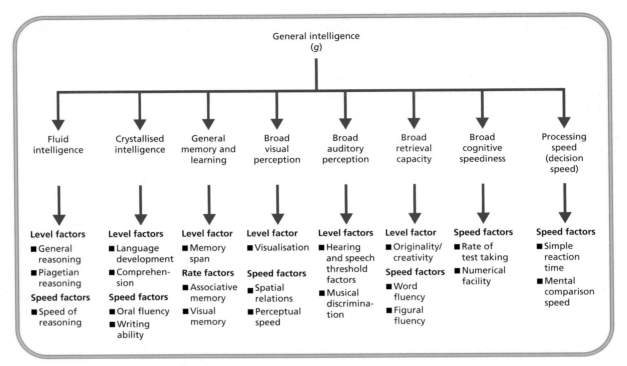

Figure 4.1
An example of a hierarchical model of intelligence

The specific abilities at the third level are just some of the possibilities. Carroll identified over 70 specific abilities.

Source: From 'The three-stratum theory of cognitive abilities' by J. B. Carroll. In D. B. Flanagan, J. L. Genshaft and P. L. Harrison (eds), *Contemporary Intellectual Assessment: Theories, Tests and Issues*. Copyright © 1996 by Guilford Publications, Inc.

Gardner bases his notion of separate abilities on evidence that brain damage (e.g. from a stroke) often interferes with functioning in one area, such as language, but does not affect functioning in other areas. It is also true that individuals may excel in one of these eight areas, but have no remarkable abilities in the other seven.

What are these intelligences?

Gardner (1998, 2003) contends that an intelligence is the ability to solve problems and create products or outcomes that are valued by a culture. Varying cultures and eras of history place different values on the eight intelligences. A naturalist intelligence is critical in farming cultures, whereas verbal and mathematical intelligences are important in technological cultures. In addition, Gardner believes that intelligence has a biological base. An intelligence is 'a biological and psychological potential; that potential is capable of being realised to a greater or lesser extent as a consequence of the experiential, cultural, and motivational factors that affect a person' (1998: 62). So an individual may or may not develop her or his potential intelligence depending upon environmental experiences.

Gardner's multiple intelligences theory has not received wide acceptance in the scientific community, even though it has been embraced by many educators. Some critics suggest that several intelligences are really talents (bodily-kinesthetic skill, musical ability) or personality traits (interpersonal ability). Other 'intelligences' are not new at all. Many researchers have identified verbal and spatial abilities as elements of

Table 4.1 Eight intelligences

Howard Gardner's theory of multiple intelligences suggests that there are eight kinds of human abilities. An individual might have strengths or weaknesses in one or several areas.

Intelligence	End states	Core components
Logical-mathematical	Scientist Mathematician	Sensitivity to, and capacity to discern, logical or numerical patterns; ability to handle long chains of reasoning.
Linguistic	Poet Journalist	Sensitivity to the sounds, rhythms and meanings of words; sensitivity to the different functions of language.
Musical	Composer Violinist	Abilities to produce and appreciate rhythm, pitch and timbre; appreciation of the forms of musical expressiveness.
Spatial	Navigator Sculptor	Capacities to perceive the visual-spatial world accurately and to perform transformations on one's initial perceptions.
Bodily-kinesthetic	Dancer Athlete	Abilities to control one's body movements and to handle objects skilfully.
Interpersonal	Therapist Salesman	Capacities to discern and respond appropriately to the moods, temperament, motivations and desires of other people.
Intrapersonal	Person with detailed, accurate self-knowledge	Access to one's own feelings and the ability to discriminate among them and draw on them to guide behaviour; knowledge of one's own strengths, weaknesses, desires and intelligence.
Naturalist	Botanist Farmer Hunter	Abilities to recognise plants and animals, to make distinctions in the natural world, to understand systems and define categories (perhaps even categories of intelligence).

Source: From *Education, Information and Transformation: Essays on Learning and Thinking,* 1st Edition, edited by J. Kane. Published by Prentice Hall 2002. Reprinted by permission of Dr Howard Gardner.

intelligence. In addition, the eight intelligences are not independent; there are correlations among the abilities. In fact, logical-mathematical and spatial intelligences are highly correlated (Sattler, 2001). So, these 'separate abilities' may not be so separate after all. Recent evidence linking musical and spatial abilities has prompted Gardner to consider that there may be connections among the intelligences (Gardner, 1998) so the theory is still developing.

Gardner (1998, 2003) has responded to critics by identifying a number of myths and misconceptions about multiple intelligences theory and schooling. One is that intelligences are the same as learning styles. (Gardner doesn't believe that people actually have consistent learning styles.) Another misconception is that multiple intelligences theory disproves the idea of 'g'. Gardner does not deny the existence of a general ability, but does question how useful g is as an explanation for human achievements. Let us now see how Gardner's theory relates to education.

Multiple intelligences go to school

An advantage of Gardner's perspective is that it expands teachers' thinking about abilities and avenues for teaching, but the theory has been misused. Some teachers embrace a simplistic version. They include every 'intelligence' or ability in every lesson, no matter how inappropriate. Table 4.2 lists some misuses and positive applications of Gardner's work.

Even though many teachers and schools are enthusiastic about Gardner's ideas, there is not yet strong research evidence that adopting a multiple intelligences approach will enhance learning. In one of the few carefully designed evaluations, Callahan, Tomlinson and Plucker (1997) found no significant gains in either achievement or self-concept for students who participated in a multiple intelligences approach in the US to identifying and promoting talent in students who were at risk of failing. Learning is still hard work, even if there are multiple paths to knowledge. Professor John White speaking at the Institute of Education, London voices similar concerns

---

Table 4.2 Misuses and applications of multiple intelligence theory

Recently, Howard Gardner described these negative and positive applications of his theory. The quotes are his words on the subject.

Misuses:

1. **Trying to teach all concepts or subjects using all intelligences:** 'There is no point in assuming that every subject can be effectively approached in at least seven ways, and it is a waste of effort and time to attempt to do this.'

2. **Assuming that it is enough just to apply a certain intelligence, no matter how you use it:** For bodily-kinesthetic intelligence, for example, 'random muscle movements have nothing to do with the cultivation of the mind'.

3. **Using an intelligence as a background for other activities,** such as playing music while pupils solve maths problems. 'The music's function is unlikely to be different from that of a dripping faucet or humming fan.'

4. **Mixing intelligences with other desirable qualities:** For example, interpersonal intelligence 'is often distorted as a license for cooperative learning,' and intrapersonal intelligence 'is often distorted as a rationale for self-esteem programmes'.

5. **Direct evaluation or even grading of intelligences without regard to context:** 'I see little point in grading individuals in terms of how "linguistic" or how "bodily-kinesthetic" they are.'

Good uses:

1. **The cultivation of desired capabilities:** 'Schools should cultivate those skills and capabilities that are valued in the community and in the broader society.'

2. **Approaching a concept, subject matter, discipline in a variety of ways:** Schools try to cover too much. 'It makes far more sense to spend a significant amount of time on key concepts, generative ideas, and essential questions and to allow students to become familiar with these notions and their implications.'

3. **The personalisation of education:** 'At the heart of the MI perspective – in theory and in practice – [is] taking human difference seriously'.

Source: Extracts from 'Reflections on multiple intelligences: myths and messages' by H. Gardner, 1998. In A. Woolfolk (ed.), *Readings in Educational Psychology* (2nd ed.), pp. 64–66, Boston: Allyn and Bacon. Copyright © 1998 by Phi Delta Kappan.

about Gardner's theories, concluding that there is no evidence for the existence of eight or nine intelligences. He questions therefore the assumptions which form the basis for school reforms (including 'shrink-wrapped' versions of multiple intelligences such as visual, auditory, kinesthetic approaches) although the reforms themselves might have positive effects:

> One question which intrigues me here is: what should be done if the theory is flaky but the use to which teachers put it seems to produce the goods – to give children more self-confidence and desire to learn? (White, 2004: 17–18).

Emotional intelligence

STOP AND REFLECT

Have you heard the term 'emotional intelligence'? If so what do you understand by it? Do you think it is possible to be emotionally intelligent but lack academic skills?

Howard Gardner's theory of multiple intelligences includes intrapersonal and inter-personal intelligences, or intelligence about self and others. Here we look at a related perspective – emotional intelligence.

We all know people who are academically or artistically talented, but unsuccessful. They have problems in school, in relationships and at work, and can't seem to improve the situations. According to some psychologists, the source of the difficulties may be a lack of emotional intelligence, first defined by Peter Salovey and John Mayer as the ability to process emotional information accurately and efficiently (Mayer and Cobb, 2000; Mayer and Salovey, 1997; Roberts, Zeidner and Matthews, 2001). Daniel Goleman (1995) popularised the idea of emotional intelligence (E-IQ or EQ) in his best-selling book *Emotional Intelligence* based on the work of Salovey and Mayer.

What is EQ?

At the centre of emotional intelligence (EQ) are four broad abilities: perceiving, in-tegrating, understanding and managing emotions (Mayer and Cobb, 2000). If you can't *perceive* what you are feeling, how can you make good choices about jobs, rela-tionships, time management or even entertainment (Baron, 1998)? Individuals who can *perceive* and *understand* emotions in others (usually by reading the non-verbal cues) and respond appropriately are more successful in working with people and often emerge as leaders (Wood and Wood, 1999). If you can't *integrate* your emotions into your thinking about situations and *understand* your own emotions, how can you com-municate your feelings to others accurately? Friends keep asking, 'What's wrong?' and you keep saying, 'Nothing!'

Emotional intelligence (EQ)
The ability to process emotional information accurately and efficiently.

Finally, you must *manage* your emotions, particularly negative emotions such as anger or depression. The goal is not to suppress feelings, but not to be overwhelmed by them either. Managing emotions includes the ability to focus energy, persist, con-trol impulses and delay immediate gratification. Emotional management is critical in school. For example, compared to four-year-old children who act on their impulses immediately, four-year-old children who can delay instant gratification become much more successful learners later (Shoda, Mischel and Peake, 1990).

Some researchers have criticised the notion of EQ, saying that emotional intelligence is not a cluster of capabilities, but rather a set of personality traits or the

Children need to develop emotional as well as cognitive intelligence if they are to be successful in life

application of general intelligence to social situations (Izard, 2001; Nestor-Baker, 1999). British researchers (Petrides, Frederickson and Furnham, 2004) suggest that the roots of emotional intelligence (EI) can be traced back to Thorndike's (1920) concept of 'social intelligence', which describes the ability of people to understand and manage others. They find that EI is related to scholastic achievement and deviant behaviour at school, suggesting that the inclusion of EI measures in assessments and intervention programmes might be useful to inform future research and social provision. So the question which remains from these differing views is does intelligence inform emotion so we are clever about managing our feelings and impulses, or does emotion inform intelligence so we make good decisions and understand other people? Probably both are true. The major point is that success in life requires more than cognitive skills, and teachers are important influences in helping pupils develop all of these capabilities.

EQ goes to school

Research in the US suggests that programmes designed to help children build their emotional competencies have beneficial effects, including an increase in cooperative behaviours and a reduction in anti-social activities such as the use of insults and bullying. For example, Norma Feshbach (1998, 1997) developed a 36-hour programme to help elementary (primary school) children become more empathetic or able to put themselves in the position of another and understand how they are feeling. The programme included exercises such as deciding what each person in your family would like most as a birthday present or determining how the world would appear to you if you were a cat. Children also retold stories from the perspective of the different characters in a story, then played the role of each character in videotaped performances of the stories. Children learned to analyse how people looked and sounded as they played each role. Sandra Graham's (1996) programme for helping aggressive boys learn to read the intentions of others also included role plays and practice in reading the emotions of others. The educational advantages of decreased pupil aggression and increased empathy are obvious, but these skills also prepare children and young people for life outside the classroom.

Cautions

One of the problems with innovations in educational psychology is that they are often inadvertently misinterpreted or ill-described in the popular media by writers and reporters who have limited backgrounds in both psychology and education. The concept of emotional intelligence is one innovation that seems to be facing that fate. Many reports use the term loosely or inaccurately, causing misunderstanding. Make sure that the sources you read are based on careful research not popular opinion.

Intelligence as a process

As you can see, the theories of Spearman, Cattell and Horn, Carroll, and Gardner, which define and measure intelligence, tend to describe how individuals differ in the *content* of intelligence – different abilities. Recent work in cognitive psychology has emphasised instead the thinking *processes* that may be common to all people. How do humans gather and use information to solve problems and behave intelligently? New views of intelligence are growing out of this work.

Robert Sternberg's (1985, 2004) triarchic theory of successful intelligence suggests that there are three aspects involved and is a cognitive process approach to understanding intelligence. 'Successful intelligence', according to Sternberg includes 'the skills and knowledge needed for success in life, according to one's own definition of success, within one's own sociocultural context' (Sternberg, 2004: 326). Sternberg prefers the term successful intelligence to stress that intelligence is more than what is measured by mental abilities tests – intelligence is about success in life. As you might guess from the name, this theory has three parts – analytic, creative and practical (see Table 4.3).

Analytic/componential intelligence involves the mental processes of the individual that lead to more or less intelligent behaviour. These processes are defined in terms of components – elementary information processes that are classified by the functions they serve and by how general they are. *Metacomponents* perform higher-order functions such as planning, strategy selection and monitoring. Executing the strategies selected is handled by *performance components*. Gaining new knowledge is performed by *knowledge-acquisition components*, such as separating relevant from irrelevant information as you try to understand a new concept (Sternberg, 1985).

Some components are specific; that is, they are necessary for only one kind of task, such as solving analogies (e.g. graceful is to clumsy as hot is to?). Other components are very general and may be necessary in almost every cognitive task. For example, metacomponents are always operating to select strategies and keep track of progress. This may help to explain the persistent correlations among all types of mental tests. People who are effective in selecting good problem-solving strategies, monitoring progress, and moving to a new approach when the first one fails are more likely to be successful on all types of tests. Metacomponents may then be a modern-day version of Spearman's *g* – general intelligence.

Connect and Extend

See Petrides, K.V. *et al.* (2004), 'The role of trait emotional intelligence in academic performances and deviant behaviour at school', *Personality and Individual Differences, 36,* pp. 277–293, for an examination of the relationship between EI, academic ability and deviant behaviour in British secondary schools.

Triarchic theory of successful intelligence

A three-part description of the mental abilities (thinking processes, coping with new experiences and adapting to context) that lead to more or less intelligent behaviour.

Table 4.3   Sternberg's triarchic theory of intelligence

Sternberg suggests that intelligent behaviour is the product of applying thinking strategies, handling new problems creatively and quickly, and adapting to contexts by selecting and reshaping our environment.

	Analytic	Creative	Practical
	Componential intelligence	*Experiential intelligence*	*Contextual intelligence*
Definition	Ability to think abstractly, process information; verbal abilities.	Ability to formulate new ideas and combine unrelated facts; creativity – ability to deal with novel situations and make new solutions automatic.	Ability to adapt to a changing environment and shape the environment to make the most of opportunities – problem solving in specific situations.
Examples	Solving analogies or syllogisms, learning vocabulary.	Diagnosing a problem with a car engine; finding resources for a new project.	Switching your mobile off or putting a 'do not disturb' sign on the door to limit distractions while studying.

Insight

The ability to deal effectively with novel situations.

Automaticity

The result of learning to perform a behaviour or thinking process so thoroughly that the performance is automatic and does not require effort.

Tacit knowledge

Knowing how rather than knowing that – knowledge that is more likely to be learned during everyday life than through formal schooling.

The second part of Sternberg's triarchic theory, *creative/experiential intelligence*, involves coping with new experiences. Intelligent behaviour is marked by two characteristics: (1) insight or the ability to deal effectively with novel situations; and (2) automaticity – the ability to become efficient and automatic in thinking and problem solving. Thus, intelligence involves solving new problems as well as quickly turning new solutions into routine processes that can be applied without much cognitive effort.

The third part of Sternberg's theory, *practical/contextual intelligence*, highlights the importance of choosing to live and work in a context where success is likely, adapting to that context and reshaping it if necessary. Here, culture is a major factor in defining successful choice, adaptation and shaping. For example, abilities that make a person successful in a rural farming community may be useless in the inner city or in a suburban area. People who are successful often seek situations in which their abilities will be valuable and then work hard to capitalise on those abilities and compensate for any weaknesses. Thus, intelligence in this third sense involves practical matters such as career choice or social skills. In a field study in a Russian city, Elena Grigorenko and Robert Sternberg (2001) found that adults with higher practical and analytical intelligence coped better both mentally and physically with the stresses caused by rapid changes in that part of the world.

Practical intelligence is made up mostly of action-oriented tacit knowledge. This tacit knowledge is more likely to be learned during everyday life than through formal schooling – it is 'knowing how' rather than 'knowing that' (Sternberg *et al.*, 1995). Recently, however, Sternberg and his colleagues have designed a programme for developing practical intelligence for school success by teaching learners effective strategies for reading, writing, doing homework and taking tests (Sternberg, 2002; Williams *et al.*, 1996). As you will see shortly, adaptive skills (similar to practical intelligence) are considered when identifying individuals with intellectual disabilities (British Psychological Society (BPS), 2000).

How is intelligence measured?

STOP AND THINK

What is the capital of France? How are a centimetre and a kilometre alike? What does *obstreperous* mean? Repeat these numbers backwards: 8 5 7 3 0 2 1 9 7. In what two ways is a lamp better than a candle? If a coat sells for half of the marked price at £70, what was the original cost of the coat?

The items in the Stop and Think are similar to the verbal questions from a common individual intelligence test for children. Another part of the test asks the child to tell what is missing in a picture, put pictures in order to tell a story, copy a design using blocks, assemble part of a puzzle, complete mazes and copy symbols. Even though psychologists do not agree about what intelligence is, they do agree that intelligence, as measured by standard tests, is related to learning in school. Why is this so? It has to do in part with the way intelligence tests were first developed.

Binet's dilemma

In 1904, Alfred Binet was confronted with the following problem by the minister of public instruction in Paris: how can children who will need special instruction and extra help be identified early in their school careers, before they fail in regular classes? Binet was also a political activist, very concerned with the rights of children. He believed that having an objective measure of learning ability could protect children from poor families who might be forced to leave school because they were the victims of discrimination and assumed to be slow learners.

Binet and his collaborator Theodore Simon wanted to measure not merely school achievement, but the intellectual skill which children needed to do well in school. After trying many different tests and eliminating items that did not discriminate between successful and unsuccessful learners, Binet and Simon finally identified 58 tests, several for each age group from three to 13. Binet's tests allowed the examiner to determine a mental age for a child. A child who succeeded on the items passed by most six-year-olds, for example, was considered to have a mental age of six, whether the child was actually four, six, or eight years old.

The concept of intelligence quotient (IQ), was added after Binet's test was taken to the US and revised at Stanford University to give the Stanford–Binet test. An IQ score was computed by comparing the mental-age score to the person's actual chronological age. The formula was:

Intelligence Quotient = Mental Age/Chronological Age × 100

So a child who had a mental age of six years and a chronological age of eight years would have an IQ of 75 as illustrated below:

$6/8 \times 100 = 600/8 = 75$ (100 is the average IQ)

The early Stanford–Binet test has been revised five times, most recently in 2003 (Roid, 2003). The practice of computing a mental age has proven to be problematic because IQ scores calculated on the basis of mental age do not have the same meaning as children get older. To cope with this problem, the concept of deviation IQ was introduced. The deviation IQ score is a number that tells exactly how much above or

Mental age

In intelligence testing, a score based on average abilities for that age group.

Intelligence quotient (IQ)

Score comparing mental and chronological ages.

Deviation IQ

Score based on statistical comparison of an individual's performance with the average performance of others in that age group.

below the average a person scored on the test, compared to others in the same age group, as you will see in the next section.

Group versus individual IQ tests

The Stanford–Binet is an individual intelligence test. It has to be administered to one person at a time by a trained psychologist and takes about two hours. Most of the questions are asked orally and do not require reading or writing. A child usually pays closer attention and is more motivated to do well when working directly with an adult.

Psychologists also have developed group tests that can be given to whole classes or schools although currently they are only used within a small number of UK local education authorities that still retain grammar schools and in some independent schools. Compared to an individual test, a group test is much less likely to yield an accurate picture of any one person's abilities. When learners take tests in a group, they may do poorly because they do not understand the instructions, because they have trouble reading, because their pencils break or they lose their place on the answer sheet, because other children distract them or because the answer format confuses them (Sattler, 2001). Teachers should be very wary of IQ scores based on group tests.

What does an IQ score mean?

Most intelligence tests are designed so that they have certain statistical characteristics. For example, the average score is 100; 50% of the people from the general population who take the tests will score 100 or above, and 50% will score below 100. About 68% of the general population will earn IQ scores between 85 and 115. Only about 16% will receive scores below 85, and only about 16% will score above 115. Note, however, that these figures are based upon UK norms and assume that English is the first language of the person taking the test. Whether IQ tests should even be used with learners from ethnic minority groups is hotly debated. The Focus on Practice below will help you interpret IQ scores realistically.

FOCUS ON PRACTICE

Interpreting IQ scores

Check to see if the score is based on an individual or a group test. Be wary of group test scores

Examples
1. Individual tests include the Wechsler Scales (WPPSI, WISC-III, WAIS-III, WAIS Abbreviated), the Stanford–Binet, the McCarthy Scales of Children's Abilities, the Woodcock–Johnson Psycho-Educational Battery, the Kaufman Assessment Battery for Children, the Kaufman Adolescent and Adult Intelligence Test (KAIT), and the Das–Naglieri Cognitive Assessment System.
2. Group tests include the Cognitive Abilities Test (CogAT – formerly the Lorge-Thorndike Intelligence Tests), the Analysis of Learning Potential, the Kuhlman–Anderson Intelligence Tests, the Otis–Lennon School Abilities Test (formerly the Otis–Lennon Intelligence Test), and the School and College Ability Tests (SCAT).

Remember that IQ tests are only estimates of general aptitude for learning

Examples

1. Ignore small differences in scores among learners.
2. Bear in mind that even an individual learner's scores may change over time for many reasons, including measurement error.
3. Be aware that a total score is usually an average of scores on several kinds of questions. A score in the middle or average range may mean that the individual performed at the average on every kind of question or that the person did quite well in some areas (e.g. on verbal tasks) and rather poorly in other areas (e.g. on quantitative tasks).

Remember that IQ scores reflect a learner's past experiences and learning

For more about interpreting IQ scores, see http://www.wilderdom.com/personality/L2-1UnderstandingIQ.html

The Flynn effect: are we getting more intelligent?

Ever since IQ tests were introduced in the early 1900s, scores in 20 different industrialised countries and in some more traditional cultures have been rising (Daley *et al.*, 2003). In fact, in a generation, the average score goes up about 18 points on standardised IQ tests – maybe you really are cleverer than your parents! This is called the Flynn effect after James Flynn, a political scientist who documented the phenomenon. Some explanations include better nutrition and medical care for children and parents, increasing complexity in the environment that stimulates thinking, smaller families who give more attention to their children, increased literacy of parents, more and better schooling and better preparation for taking tests. One result of the Flynn effect is that the norms used to determine scores (more about norms in Chapter 14) have to be continually revised. In other words, to keep a score of 100 as the average, the test questions have to be made more difficult. This increasing difficulty has implications for any programme that uses IQ scores as part of the entrance requirements. For example, some 'average' pupils of the previous generation now might be identified as having intellectual disabilities because the test questions are harder (Kanaya, Scullin and Ceci, 2003).

Flynn effect
Because of better health, smaller families, increased complexity in the environment, and more and better schooling, IQ test scores are steadily rising.

Intelligence and achievement

Intelligence test scores predict achievement in schools quite well, at least for large groups. For example, the *correlation* (or number which indicates the strength of a relationship between two measurements) is about 0.4 to 0.5 (a midway figure as correlation scores range between 1.00 to −1.00) between school grades and scores on a popular individual intelligence test, the revised Wechsler Intelligence Scale for Children (WISC-III). Correlations between standardised achievement test and intelligence test scores are higher, around 0.5 to 0.7 (Sattler, 2001). This isn't surprising because the tests were designed to predict school achievement. Remember, Binet threw out test items that did not discriminate between good and poor learners.

Do people who score high on IQ tests achieve more in life? Here, the answer is less clear. There is evidence that *g*, or general intelligence, correlates with 'real-world academic, social, and occupational accomplishments' (Ceci, 1991), but there is great debate about the size and meaning of these correlations (McClelland, 1993). People with higher intelligence test scores tend to complete more years of school and to have higher-status jobs. However, when the number of years of education is held constant, IQ scores and school achievement are not highly correlated with income and success in later life. Other factors such as motivation, social skills and luck may make the difference (Goleman, 1995; Neisser *et al.*, 1996; Sternberg and Wagner, 1993). However, these may be mutually influential, for example, you are likely to be more motivated to work harder at school if you achieve high scores/results and this may make it more likely that you are spotted as having potential, etc. Continued debate surrounds the whole area of intelligence, particularly the inherent or learned aspect of it.

Intelligence: heredity or environment?

Nowhere has the nature-versus-nurture debate raged so hard as in the area of intelligence. Should intelligence be seen as a potential, limited by our genetic makeup? Or does intelligence simply refer to an individual's current level of intellectual functioning, as influenced by experience and education? In fact, it is almost impossible to separate intelligence 'in the genes' from intelligence 'due to experience'. Today, most psychologists believe that differences in intelligence are the result of both heredity and environment, probably in about equal proportions for children (Petrill and Wilkerson, 2000). 'Genes do not fix behaviour. Rather they establish a range of possible reactions to the range of possible experiences that the environment can provide' (Weinberg, 1989: 101). Further, environmental influences include everything from the health of a child's mother during pregnancy to the amount of lead in the child's home to the quality of teaching a child receives.

For teachers, it is especially important to realise that cognitive skills, like any other skills, are always improveable. *Intelligence is a current state of affairs*, affected by past experiences and open to future changes. Even if intelligence is a limited potential, the potential is still quite large, and a challenge to all teachers. For example, Japanese and Chinese students know much more mathematics than American students but their intelligence test scores are quite similar. This superiority in mathematics probably is related to differences in the way mathematics is taught and studied in the three countries and to the self-motivation skills of many Asian students (Baron, 1998; Stevenson and Stigler, 1992). Further, an international survey by the Basic Skills Agency (1997) on the numeracy skills of adults in seven countries (France, Netherlands, Sweden, Japan, Australia, Denmark and the UK) found that the UK sample ranked the highest in percentage of outright refusal to answer (13%), while in other countries, the percentage of outright refusal was at most 6%. Indirectly, these results suggest there is a lack of interest in mathematics or a relatively higher tendency of mathematics avoidance among many of the UK adults which is clearly indicative of environmental differences in attitudes (Lip Chap Sam, 2002).

Now that you have a sense of what intelligence means, let's consider ways in which cognitive ability differences are managed within education.

Ability Differences and Teaching

STOP AND THINK

During your school years were you divided into ability groups? If so, what form did this take and how did you react to it? Was it made obvious that pupils were grouped in this way and if not, did children know about it?

In this section, we take forward the notion of differences in academic ability and consider alternatives for managing these. By the time you finish this section, you should have an answer to the question, 'Is ability grouping a solution to the challenge of ability differences?'

Streaming or between-class ability grouping

When whole classes are formed based on ability, the process is called streaming or between-class ability grouping which used to be a common practice in secondary schools and many primary schools in the UK (Jackson, 1964) although this is not the case in many European countries (Ireson and Hallam, 1999). Streaming is based upon the idea that learners have fairly fixed levels of ability. Indeed the 11 + system of selective secondary education placed children in different schools depending upon their ability and was still in place in the UK up until the 1970s. This system separated children at the end of their primary school years sending them either to 'grammar' (top ability range) 'secondary modern' (lower ability range) or less commonly 'technical' (middle range) schools depending upon their performance on a range of ability tests, known as the 11 + exam. Although this may seem on the surface to be an efficient way to teach it is commonly recognised as 'elitist' because it favoured children from wealthier backgrounds who were likely to receive coaching and better resources (Galindo-Ruada and Vignoles, 2005). Thus this system was replaced by a 'comprehensive' system of secondary education which did not require ability tests to be taken in order to gain a place. However, there is ongoing debate surrounding the effectiveness of this system and some areas in the UK retain grammar schools (Reynolds *et al.*, 1987; Scheerens *et al.*, 1989; Benn and Chitty, 1996).

> **Streaming or between-class ability grouping**
>
> System of grouping in which learners are assigned to classes based on their measured ability or their achievements.

Within other European countries there is a variety of provision for children as they move into the later stages of compulsory education. In Denmark mixed ability grouping operates throughout as the streaming for certain subjects, which did exist, was abolished in the 1994/5 school year. Similarly countries such as Finland, Norway, Portugal and Sweden provide comprehensive education throughout although there is currently a move towards ability grouping in Iceland (Eurydice at NFER, 2002). Let us look at some of the research findings about ability grouping to see how this informs our understanding of the debate.

Research in the US has consistently shown that although segregation by ability may benefit high-achieving learners, it causes a number of problems for low-achieving learners including low expectations and self-esteem (Castle, Deniz and Tortora, 2005; Garmon *et al.*, 1995). In the UK there have been relatively few studies into the impact of streaming or 'setting' (ability groups for different subjects such as maths, English and science) upon academic performance but Kerckhoff (1986) found some evidence of high ability group learners being slightly advantaged at the expense of considerable losses to low ability groups in ability grouped secondary school pupils. Boaler's ongoing studies (1997a, 1997b, 1997c; Boaler, William and Brown, 2000) are indicative that ability grouping is a significant factor in terms of ideas, responses and achievements in mathematics at secondary schools and that many learners are disadvantaged.

This may relate to findings in the US that suggest that low ability groups tend to receive lower-quality instruction in general. Teachers emphasise lower-level objectives and routine procedures, with less academic focus. Often, there are more pupil behaviour problems and, along with these problems, increased teacher stress and decreased enthusiasm. These differences in instruction and the teachers' negative attitudes may mean that low expectations are communicated to the class. Attendance may drop along with self-confidence. The lower ability groups often have a disproportionate number of minority-group and economically disadvantaged learners, so ability grouping, in effect, becomes segregation in school. Possibilities for friendships also become limited to others in the same ability range.

In the UK, along with the introduction of comprehensive schools, there has been a movement towards teaching all students in mixed-ability groups although 'setting' commonly occurs for different subjects both at primary and secondary schools. However, current initiatives such as the Excellence in Cities (EiC) policy, introduced by the UK government in 1999 and led by the National Foundation for Educational Research (NFER) aim to improve education in traditionally lower achieving urban areas. Schools are supplied with additional resources (such as 'learning mentors' and 'learning support units') for various 'strands' of pupils. Evidence so far is indicative of gains for pupils assigned to these groups (Kendall *et al.*, 2005). Whilst this project does not involve ability grouping as such it does provide additional opportunities for learners at each end of the ability spectrum and suggests that there may be advantages of targeting specific groups. This may add tentative support to US findings that high-ability learners tend to perform better than comparable learners in ordinary classes (Kulik and Kulick, 1997). See the Discussion Point for more on this.

DISCUSSION POINT

Is streaming and setting effective?

The findings below are taken from a summary of research compiled by the National Literacy Trust (2006) available at http://www.literacytrust.org.uk/Research/stream.html. What do you think about these findings?

Agree: Yes, streaming and setting are effective

OFSTED's report, *Setting in Primary Schools* (OFSTED, 2006) strongly supports the use of setting children as it can improve performance. Of the 400,000 lessons observed by OFSTED last year 4% were setted compared to 2% the previous year and many schools plan to introduce this soon. Currently 70% of junior schools and 40% of primary schools use setting. However, OFSTED also found that setting tended to produce extremes in terms of quality of teaching.

Disagree: No, streaming and setting are not effective

An NFER Report (Suknanda, L. and Lee, B. 1998) concluded that grouping pupils by ability in streams and sets had no influence on their performance but that it could have a negative effect on the attitudes, motivation and self-esteem of lower ability pupils. Boys, pupils from working-class families and summer-born children were more likely to be disadvantaged. The review, based on an analysis of more than 20 major studies in the UK and the US, throws doubt on some of the claims that streaming and setting improve pupil achievement.

Source: Adapted from 'Streaming and setting – does it make a difference to achievement?'. Reprinted by permission of National Literacy Trust.

WHAT DO YOU THINK?
Agree or Disagree? Vote online at www.pearsoned.co.uk/woolfolkeuro.

Within-class ability grouping and flexible grouping

> **STOP AND THINK**
>
> How can teachers prepare for classes who come to them with different knowledge and experience? Have you ever begun a new class to find that you have covered the work previously or that you are considerably behind some of the others?

Differences between pupils' experiences and levels of ability are common in most schools and classrooms but even if teachers decide to simply forge ahead and teach the same material in the same way to the entire class, they would not be alone. One study in the US found that in 46 different classrooms, 84% of the activities were the same for high-achieving and average-achieving learners (Westberg *et al.*, 1993). Differences in learners' prior knowledge are a major challenge for teachers, especially in subjects that build on previous knowledge and skills such as mathematics and science (Loveless, 1998).

Today, many primary-school classes are grouped for reading and maths, even though there is no clear evidence that this within-class ability grouping is superior to other approaches. Thoughtfully constructed and well-taught ability groups in maths and reading can be effective, but other approaches such as cooperative learning are available, too. The point of any grouping strategy should be to provide appropriate challenge and support – that is, to reach children within their 'zone of proximal development' (Vygotsky, 1997). Ability grouping which is flexible seems to work best (Dyson *et al.*, 2004). Let us now move on to consider different styles and preferences of learning.

Within-class ability grouping

System of grouping in which learners in a class are divided into two or three groups based on ability in an attempt to accommodate individual differences.

Learning Styles and Preferences

> **STOP AND THINK**
>
> What do you know about learning styles? Do you think you have your own preferred style/s of learning? Do you, for example, find it easier to understand diagrams or do you prefer text? Does it matter?

The way a person approaches learning and studying is known as his or her learning style. Although many different learning styles have been described, one theme that unites most of the styles is the differences between deep and surface approaches to processing information in learning situations (Snow, Corno and Jackson, 1996). Individuals who have a *deep-processing approach* see the learning activities as a means for understanding some underlying concepts or meanings. For example, those of you reading this book who take a deep-processing approach may be thinking, as you read, about situations and examples from your own experience which relate to what you are

Learning styles

Characteristic approaches to learning and studying.

reading in order to understand them properly. Deep-processing learners tend to learn for the sake of learning and are less concerned about how their performance is evaluated, so motivation plays a role as well. Learners who take a *surface-processing* approach focus on memorising the learning materials, not understanding them. So surface-processors may be trying to remember certain aspects of this book as you know you are having a test about learning styles. Surface-processing learners tend to be motivated by rewards, grades, external standards and the desire to be evaluated positively by others. Of course, the situation you are in can encourage deep or surface processing depending upon how interested you are in the material, how tired you are, how much time is available, and so on but there is some evidence that individuals have tendencies to approach learning situations in characteristic ways (Biggs, 2001; Coffield *et al.*, 2004; Pintrich and Schrauben, 1992; Tait and Entwistle, 1998).

Cautions about learning preferences

Learning preferences

Preferred ways of studying and learning, such as using pictures instead of text, working with other people versus alone, learning in structured or in unstructured situations, and so on.

Since the late 1970s, a great deal has been written about differences in individuals' learning preferences (Dunn, Dunn and Price, 2000; Dunn and Griggs, 2003; Gregorc, 1982; Keefe, 1982). Learning preferences are often called *learning styles* in these writings, but preferences is a more accurate label because the 'styles' are determined by your preferences for particular learning environments – for example, where, when, with whom or with what lighting, food or music you like to study. You may like to study and write in fairly short chunks with clear deadlines in place. You usually have some kind of a plan in your head about how long each piece of work will take and you try to stick to that, adjusting it accordingly if some things take more or less time. Then you may take a day off. When you plan or think, you often make a note of the main points so that you remember them clearly. A close friend of this co-author carries his plans in his head and is able to reactivate them when he is ready to use them. She also has a colleague who draws diagrams or 'mind maps' at meetings or when listening to a speaker or planning a paper. You may be very different to this profile, but we all may work effectively. The question is, are these preferences important for learning?

There are a number of instruments for assessing people's learning preferences: the *Learning Style Inventory* (Dunn, Dunn and Price, 2000), *Learning Style Inventory (Revised)* (Kolb, 1985) and the *Learning Style Profile: Examiner's Manual* (Keefe and Monk, 1986). However, tests of learning style have been strongly criticised for lacking evidence of reliability and validity (Snider, 1990; Wintergerst, DeCapua and Itzen, 2001). In fact, in an extensive examination of learning styles instruments, researchers at the Learning Skills Research Centre in England concluded, 'with regard to Dunn and Dunn (Section 3.2), Gregorc (Section 3.1) and Riding (Section 4.1), our examination of the reliability and validity of their learning style instruments strongly suggests that they should not be used in education or business' (Coffield *et al.*, 2004: 127).

Some proponents of learning styles believe that individuals learn more when they study in their preferred setting and manner (Dunn, Beaudry and Klavas, 1989; Lovelace, 2005) and there is evidence that very bright learners need less structure and prefer quiet, solitary learning (Torrance, 1986). However, most educational psychologists are skeptical about the value of learning preferences. 'The reason researchers roll their eyes at learning styles research is the utter failure to find that assessing children's learning styles and matching to instructional methods has any effect on their learning' (Stahl, 2002: 99). This leads to the question then, why are these ideas so popular? Part of the answer is, 'A thriving commercial industry has also been built to offer advice to teachers, tutors and managers on learning styles, and much of it consists of inflated claims and sweeping conclusions which go beyond the current knowledge base and the specific recommendations of particular theorists' (Coffield *et al.*, 2004: 127). Some of the teaching ideas may be useful, but not necessarily because they are based on learning styles.

So it is worth remembering that learners, especially younger ones, may not be the best judges of how they should learn. Sometimes, learners, particularly those who have difficulty, prefer what is easy and comfortable; real learning can be hard and uncomfortable. Sometimes, individuals prefer to learn in a certain way because they have no alternatives (e.g. they may prefer pictures because they are unable to read) and it is the only way they know how to approach the task. These learners may benefit from developing new – and perhaps more effective – ways to learn. One final consideration: many of the learning styles advocates imply that the differences in the learner are what matter but recent research points to the person in the context of the entire teaching-learning system as a better way to understand people's learning (Coffield *et al.*, 2004). We will examine this again in the next chapter when we consider culture and learning style but let us now examine one learning style in particular which does have some supporting evidence.

> ⬅➡ **Connect and Extend**
>
> See Franklin, S. (2006), 'VAKing out learning styles – why the notion of "learning styles" is unhelpful to teachers', *Education, 34*(1), pp. 81–87, for an exploration of the relevance of learning styles within education.

Visual/verbal distinctions

There is one learning styles distinction that has research support. Richard Mayer, known for his research-based approach to the use of multimedia in learning, has been studying the distinction between visual and verbal learners, with a focus on learning from computer-based multimedia. He is finding that there is a visualiser–verbaliser dimension and that it has three facets: *cognitive spatial ability* (which is measured to find whether low or high), *cognitive style* (visualiser v. verbaliser) and *learning preference* (verbal learner v. visual learner), as shown in Table 4.4 (Mayer and Massa, 2003). The picture is more complex than simply categorising a person as either a visual or a verbal learner. Individuals might have preferences for learning with pictures, but their low spatial ability (the ability to mentally manipulate two-dimensional and three-dimensional figures, for example, when doing puzzles or jig-saws) could make using

Table 4.4 Three facets of the visualiser–verbaliser dimension

There are three dimensions to visual versus verbal learning: ability, style and preference. Individuals can be high or low on any or all of these dimensions.

Facet	Types of learners	Definition
Cognitive ability	High spatial ability	Good abilities to create, remember and manipulate images and spatial information
	Low spatial ability	Poor abilities to create, remember and manipulate images and spatial information
Cognitive style	Visualiser	Thinks using images and visual information
	Verbaliser	Thinks using words and verbal information
Learning preference	Visual learner	Prefers instruction using pictures
	Verbal learner	Prefers instruction using words

Source: From R. E. Mayer and L. J. Massa (2003). 'Three facets of visual and verbal learners: Cognitive ability, cognitive style and learning preference.' *Journal of Educational Psychology*, *95*(4), p. 838. Published by APA, reprinted with permission.

pictures to learn less effective. These differences can be reliably measured, but research has not identified the effects of teaching to these styles. Certainly, presenting information in multiple modalities might be useful. (See the section later in this chapter about learners with dyslexia.)

The value of considering learning styles

Even though much of the work on matching learning styles and preferences to teaching is suspect, with unreliable measures and inflated claims, there is some value in thinking about learning styles. First, by helping learners think about how they learn, you can develop thoughtful self-monitoring and self-awareness. In upcoming chapters, we will look at the value of such self-knowledge for learning and motivation. Second, looking at individual learners' approaches to learning might help teachers appreciate, accept and accommodate learner differences (Coffield *et al.*, 2004; Rosenfeld and Rosenfeld, 2004).

Thus far, we have focused mostly on the varying abilities and styles of learners. For the rest of the chapter, we will consider what can interfere with learning. It is important for all teachers to be aware of these issues because of the laws and policy changes over the past 30 years. These have occurred both in the UK and other parts of Europe. Although there are varying definitions and provision across different countries (EADSNE, 2003) these have expanded teachers' responsibilities in working with all learners.

Inclusion

STOP AND REFLECT

Have you ever had the experience of being the only one in a group who had trouble doing something? How would you feel if every day in school you faced the same kind of difficulty, while everyone else seemed to find the work easier than you? What kind of support and teaching would you need to keep trying?

Inclusion

The integration of all learners, including those with severe disabilities, into mainstream classes.

In most European countries there is a national legal framework for identifying pupils with special educational needs and including them within mainstream education. This includes providing additional resources for their education (EADSNE, 2003.) Inclusion is the integration of all learners into mainstream classes. A core part of frameworks for inclusion has of course led to changes in the education of children with disabilities. The Special Educational Needs and Disability Act (SENDA) in 2001 brought significant amendments to the 1996 Education Act making discrimination against learners with disabilities in England and Wales illegal and strengthening the right of children with special educational needs (SEN) to be included within mainstream education (HMSO, 2001). The law now requires educational providers to treat children with disabilities as favourably as non-disabled learners and to make reasonable adjustments to their facilities and arrangements so that learners with disabilities are not unreasonably disadvantaged. Schools have a duty to inform parents where they are making SEN provision and have a right to request assessment of a pupil's SEN. The requirements of this law have direct implications for those working within the educational system so let us consider the Code of Practice that accompanies the legislation.

The Code of Practice

Schools and local education authorities (LEAs) have to have regard for the Code of Practice in England, Northern Ireland and Wales (Supporting Children's Learning Code of Practice in Scotland) when planning how to meet the needs of children with SEN, and these must be met throughout their school years. Most children with special needs will be educated in mainstream schools with the help of outside specialists where necessary. A graduated response to children with SEN is suggested by the Code which recognises that there is a continuum of needs that will bring increasing specialist involvement depending upon the severity of the difficulties experienced by the child. If these exist before the child starts school then both the LEA and health services should be involved. The Code emphasises that children with special educational needs, including those with statements (support plans already in place as a result of formal assessment usually by educational psychologists) should normally:

- be educated alongside other children in mainstream schools;

- have full access to a broad and balanced education including the National Curriculum.

Additionally, the role of the parents in terms of their knowledge, views and experience are seen as vital and tasks of assessing and meeting the needs of the children are seen as most successful when:

- the school, the LEA and other professionals work in partnership with parents;

- a child's wishes are taken into account in the light of his or her age and understanding;

- there is close cooperation between all agencies concerned and a multi-disciplinary approach is taken to resolving issues.

A graduated response which gradually increases interventions in teaching and the curriculum is referred to as School Action and School Action Plus or Early Years Action and Early Years Action Plus for younger children. This normally precedes the statutory assessment and statementing process but schools may customise this pattern appropriately as long as the various levels of needs, types of provision and responsibilities are taken properly into account. Parents and pupils should be fully consulted at all stages. The early stages of the assessment and meeting SEN should be based within the school setting. Below is a summary of this approach taken from the Centre for Studies on Inclusive Education website (http://inclusion.uwe.ac.uk/csie/):

1. **Identification** – The class teacher or form/year tutor identifies a child's SEN, based upon the child making inadequate progress despite differentiation of learning opportunities.

2. **School Action** – The school informs families that the child is considered to have SEN and the SEN Co-ordinator (SENCO) gathers information about the child including that from parents/family. The SENCO then organises special educational provision and ensures that an Individual Education Plan (IEP) is drawn up, working with the child's teachers to design and plan school-based interventions.

3. **School Action Plus** – The SENCO brings in outside specialists to advise on further changes that could be made within the school to meet the child's needs.

4. **Statutory Assessment** – The LEA considers the need for statutory assessment and, if appropriate, actions a multi-disciplinary assessment.

5. **Issuing a Statement** – The LEA considers a need for SEN statement and if appropriate issues a statement and arranges, monitors and reviews provision.

Source: Adapted extract from 'Assessments and Statements: CSIE Summary, updated June 2005'. Available at http://csie.org.uk

Let's examine further a key aspect of this process – the drawing up of the individual education plan – as this is of particular interest to those working with or interested in educational provision.

Individual Education Plan

All children who are placed on the register at the School Action stage are entitled to an Individual Education Plan (IEP) and it is the responsibility of the class teacher to draw up and review the plan at this stage. Although this is specific to England, Wales and Northern Ireland most European countries use individual educational planning when working with children with special educational needs (Scottish Executive, 2006). Strategies that are used to facilitate the child to progress should be included within the IEP and these should only record those which are different from or additional to those provided for the rest of the class or teaching group. Information should be clearly set out and relate to the following (as listed on the Teaching in England website).

- short-term targets set for/by the child;

- teaching strategies to be used;

- provision to be put in place;

- review date;

- success and/or exit criteria;

- outcomes (recorded at the review) (Teaching in England, 2006a).

The targets set should be specific to key areas in communication, literacy, mathematics, behaviour and physical skills and should take account of the individual pupil's strengths and successes. The IEP might also include what help parents/families could give to help support the child's learning. In some cases an IEP might not be written but a record would be kept by the school showing how the child's needs are being met in a different way, perhaps as part of lesson plans (DirectGov, 2006). The IEP should be reviewed at least twice a year (arranged by class teacher) and should include parental/family views as well as where possible the child's own input.

It can be seen then that the SENDA (Special Educational Needs and Disabilities Act) in 2001 and the Code of Practice which followed it have had considerable effects upon educational provision and practice, presenting additional challenges for those working within this area. Let us now turn to some of these.

Individual Education Plan (IEP)

This builds on the curriculum that a child with learning difficulties or disabilities is following and is designed to set out the strategies being used to meet each child's identified needs.

Connect and Extend

See Vislie, L. (2003) 'From integration to inclusion: focusing global trends and changes in the western European societies', *European Journal of Special Needs Education, 18*(1), pp. 17–35 for a discussion of distinctions between integration and inclusion and an examination of inclusion policies across 14 European countries.

The Most Common Challenges

Recent figures issued by the DfES (Department for Education and Skills) regarding children with Special Educational Needs in England report that 236,700 (2.9% of) pupils across all schools had statements of SEN (DfES, 2006). Of these children, 58.7% are placed in mainstream schools and 35% attend special schools. This means that most classes within nursery, primary and secondary education are likely to include a child or children with special educational needs.

About half of all learners receiving some kind of special education services in state schools are diagnosed as having *learning difficulties or disabilities* – by far the largest category of learners with disabilities.

Pupils with learning difficulties/disabilities

How do you explain a pupil who struggles to read, write, spell or learn mathematics, even though they may have normal vision, hearing and language capabilities? One explanation is that the individual has a learning difficulty/disability. This is a relatively new and controversial category which became popular in England following a speech to Mencap (the Learning Disability charity) by the Secretary of State for Health in 1996 (British Institute of Learning Disabilities, 2004). It is controversial because many people (including People First, an international advisory organisation) prefer the term 'people with learning difficulties' to describe specific problems with learning and it tends to be the preferred term in the UK, particularly within education, although both are used. There is no fully agreed-upon definition of a learning difficulty/disability but the *Valuing People* strategy presented to Parliament in 2001 lists the following:

- *A significantly reduced ability to understand new or complex information, to learn new skills (impaired intelligence), with;*

- *a reduced ability to cope independently (impaired social functioning);*

- *which started before adulthood, with a lasting effect on development.*

(Department of Health, 2001, 1.4)

This means that the person will have difficulties understanding, learning, remembering and generalising learning to new situations. They therefore may have difficulties with social contexts such as communication, self-care and health and safety awareness. There is still debate about the most effective way to measure 'significantly reduced ability' but psychometric tests as well as other information are commonly used.

Some educators and psychologists believe the learning difficulty/disability label is overused and abused. Researchers in the US suggest that many of the people called learning disabled are really slow learners in average schools, average learners in high-achieving schools, learners with second-language problems, or learners who are behind in their work because they have been absent frequently or have changed schools often (Finlan, 1994).

Learner characteristics

People with learning difficulties or disabilities are not all alike. The most common characteristics are specific difficulties in one or more academic areas; poor coordination; problems paying attention; hyperactivity and impulsivity; problems organising and interpreting visual and auditory information; disorders of thinking, memory, speech and hearing; and difficulties making and keeping friends (Hallahan and Kauffman, 2006; Hunt and Marshall, 2002). As you can see, many learners with other disabilities (such as attention-deficit disorder) and many ordinary learners may have some of the same characteristics. To complicate the situation even more, not all people with learning difficulties will have these problems, and few will have all of the problems. One person may be three years behind in reading but above average in mathematics, while another learner may have the opposite strengths and weaknesses and a third may have problems with organising and studying that affect almost all subject areas.

Learning
difficulty/
disability

Problem with acquisition and use of language; may emerge as difficulty with reading, writing, reasoning and mathematics.

Table 4.5 lists some of the most common reading problems, although these problems are not always signs of learning difficulties/disabilities. These difficulties appear to be caused by problems with relating sounds to letters that make up words, making spelling hard as well (Stanovich, 1994; Willcutt *et al.*, 2001). Mathematics, both computation and problem solving, is the second most common problem area for pupils with learning difficulties/disabilities. The writing of some of these learners is virtually unreadable, and their spoken language can be halting and disorganised. Individuals with learning difficulties/disabilities often lack effective ways of approaching academic tasks. They don't know how to focus on the relevant information, get organised, apply learning strategies and study skills, change strategies when one isn't working, or evaluate their learning. They tend to be passive learners, in part because they don't know *how* to learn. Working independently is especially trying, so homework and classwork are often left incomplete (Hallahan *et al.*, 2005).

Early diagnosis is important so that individuals with learning difficulties/disabilities do not become terribly frustrated and discouraged. The learners themselves may

---

Table 4.5 Common reading problems

Do any of your pupils show these signs? They could be indications of learning disabilities.

Poor reading habits

- Frequently loses his or her place
- Jerks head from side to side
- Expresses insecurity by crying or refusing to read
- Prefers to read with the book held within inches from face
- Shows tension while reading, such as reading in a high-pitched voice, biting lips and fidgeting

Word recognition errors

- Omitting a word (e.g. 'He came to the park,' is read, 'He came to park')
- Inserting a word (e.g. 'He came to the [beautiful] park')
- Substituting a word for another (e.g. 'He came to the *pond*')
- Reversing letters or words (e.g. *was* is read *saw*)
- Mispronouncing words (e.g. *park* is read *pork*)
- Transposing letters or words (e.g. 'The dog ate fast,' is read, 'The dog fast ate')
- Not attempting to read an unknown word by breaking it into familiar units
- Slow, laborious reading, less than 20 to 30 words per minute

Comprehension errors

- Recalling basic facts (e.g. cannot answer questions directly from a passage)
- Recalling sequence (e.g. cannot explain the order of events in a story)
- Recalling main theme (e.g. cannot give the main idea of a story)

Difficulties with social relationships are often present in pupils with learning disabilities

not understand why they are having such trouble, and they may become victims of learned helplessness. This condition was first identified in learning experiments with animals. The animals were put in situations where they received punishment (electric shocks) that they could not control. Later, when the situation was changed and they could have escaped the shocks or turned them off, the animals didn't even bother trying (Seligman, 1975). They had learned to be helpless victims. Pupils with learning difficulties may also come to believe that they cannot control or improve their own learning. This is a powerful belief. The individuals never exert the effort to discover that they can make a difference in their own learning, so they remain passive and helpless (Male, 1999).

Pupils with learning difficulties such as dyslexia may also try to compensate for their problems and develop bad learning habits in the process, or they may begin avoiding certain subjects out of fear of not being able to handle the work. To prevent these things from happening, the teacher should refer the learners to the appropriate professionals in the school as early as possible.

Learned helplessness

The expectation, based on previous experiences with a lack of control, that all one's efforts will lead to failure.

Teaching pupils with learning difficulties/disabilities

There is also controversy over how best to help these learners. A promising approach seems to be to emphasise study skills and methods for processing information in a given subject such as reading or mathematics. Many of the principles of cognitive learning from Chapters 7 and 8 can be applied to help all pupils improve their attention, memory and problem-solving abilities (Sawyer, Graham and Harris, 1992). The Focus on Practice below taken from Hardman, Drew and Egan (2005) provides some general guidelines for working with children with learning difficulties.

In teaching reading, a combination of teaching letter–sound (phonological) knowledge and word identification strategies appears to be effective. For example, Maureen Lovett and her colleagues (Lovett *et al.*, 2000) in Canada taught learners with severe reading disabilities to use the four different word identification strategies: (1) identifying words by analogy, (2) seeking the part of the word that you know,

FOCUS ON PRACTICE

Working with pupils with learning difficulties

Preschool years
- Keep verbal instructions short and simple.
- Match the level of content carefully to the child's developmental level.
- Give multiple examples to clarify meaning.
- Allow more practice than usual, especially when material is new.

Primary school years (5–11 year olds)
- Keep verbal instructions short and simple; have children repeat directions back to you to be sure they understand.
- Use mnemonics (memory strategies) in instruction to teach children how to remember.
- Repeat main points several times.
- Provide additional time for learning and practice – re-teach when necessary.

Secondary school (11–16 year olds)
- Directly teach self-monitoring strategies, such as cueing learners to ask, 'Was I paying attention/listening/watching?'
- Connect new material to knowledge learners already have.
- Teach learners to use external memory strategies and devices (tape-recording, note-taking, to-do lists, etc.).

(3) attempting different vowel pronunciations, and (4) 'peeling off' prefixes and suffixes in a multi-syllabic word. Teachers worked one-to-one with the pupils to learn and practise these four strategies, along with analysis of word sounds and blending sounds into words (phonological knowledge). Direct teaching of skills and strategies is especially important for learners with reading disabilities (as we see in the section on dyslexia and dyscalculia). Let us now look at some specific learning difficulties/disabilities: hyperactivity and attention disorders, dyslexia and dyscalculia, communication and intellectual disabilities/difficulties.

Learners with hyperactivity and attention disorders

You probably have heard and may even have used the term 'hyperactivity'. The notion is a modern one; there were no hyperactive children 50 to 60 years ago. Such children, like Mark Twain's Huckleberry Finn, were seen as rebellious, lazy, or 'fidgety' (Nylund, 2000). Today, if anything, the term is applied too often and too widely and many classes include pupils diagnosed as 'hyperactive'. Actually, hyperactivity is not one particular condition, but two kinds of problems that may or may not occur together – attention disorders and impulsive-hyperactivity problems.

Definitions

Today, most psychologists agree that the main problem for children labelled hyperactive is directing and maintaining attention, not simply controlling their physical activity. The American Psychiatric Association's definition (*Statistical Manual of Mental Disorders*, 4th edition – known as DSM-IV) is widely used in the UK to identify children with this problem and Table 4.6 lists some indicators of attention-deficit hyperactivity disorder (ADHD). The World Health Organization *International Classification of Diseases*, 10th Revision (1992) – known as ICD-10 is also used in the UK but this has a narrower definition than ADHD and applies to the most serious cases.

Children with ADHD are not only more physically active and inattentive than other children, they also have difficulty responding appropriately and working steadily towards goals (even their own goals). In addition, they may not be able to control their behaviour on command, even for a brief period. The problem behaviours are generally evident in all situations and with every teacher. It is difficult to know how many children should be classified as hyperactive and estimates vary depending upon the population sampled, the methods used and the criteria applied. Three studies of English populations have shown a prevalence rate of between 2% and 5%, depending on whether DSM-IV or ICD-10 criteria were applied (Taylor *et al.*, 1992; McArdle *et al.*, 1995; Merrell and Tymms, 2001).

About three to four times more boys than girls are identified as hyperactive, but the gap appears to be narrowing (Hallahan *et al.*, 2005). Just a few years ago, most psychologists thought that ADHD diminished as children entered adolescence, but now there are some researchers who believe that the problems can persist into adulthood (Hallowell and Ratey, 1994). Adolescence – with the increased stresses of puberty, transition to secondary school, more demanding academic work and more engrossing

ADHD (attention-deficit hyperactivity disorder)

Current term for disruptive behaviour disorders marked by over activity, excessive difficulty sustaining attention or impulsiveness.

Table 4.6   Indicators of ADHD: attention-deficit hyperactivity disorder

Problems with *inattention*

- Often does not give close attention to details or makes careless mistakes
- Has trouble keeping attention in tasks or play activities
- Does not seem to listen when spoken to directly
- Does not follow through on instructions and fails to finish schoolwork (not due to oppositional behaviour or failure to understand instructions)
- Has difficulty organising tasks or activities
- Avoids, dislikes or is reluctant to engage in tasks that require sustained mental effort (such as schoolwork or homework)
- Loses things necessary for tasks or activities
- Is easily distracted by extraneous stimuli
- Is forgetful in daily activities

Problems with *impulse control*

- Often blurts out answers before questions have been completed
- Has trouble awaiting his or her turn
- Often interrupts or intrudes on others in conversations or games

Hyperactivity

- Often fidgets with hands or feet or squirms in seat
- Often gets up from seat when remaining seated is expected
- Often runs about or climbs excessively in situations in which it is inappropriate (in adolescents may be limited to subjective feelings of restlessness)
- Often has difficulty playing or engaging in leisure activities quietly
- Often talks excessively
- Often acts as if 'driven by a motor' and cannot remain still

Source: Reprinted with permission from the *Diagnostic and Statistical Manual of Mental Disorders*, 4th ed., Text Revision, Copyright © 2000 American Psychiatric Association.

social relationships – can be an especially difficult time for young people with ADHD (Taylor, 1998).

Causes of ADHD

Numerous studies and scientific testing have suggested that ADHD is biological in nature and is related to chemical imbalances in the brain. Research carried out across various countries including the UK, Australia, Norway and the US, indicates that there are strong genetic factors involved. Although factors such as family environment, parental management skills and stressful life events influence the lives of those individuals with ADHD they are not enough, in themselves, to cause the disorder (Barklay, 2002).

Treating and teaching learners with ADHD

Today, there is an increasing reliance on drug therapy for ADHD. In fact, from 1990 to 1998, there was a 700% increase in the production of Ritalin in the US (Diller, 1998) and it is increasingly common in the UK. Ritalin and other prescribed drugs such as Adderall and Cylert are stimulants, but in particular dosages, they tend to have paradoxical effects on many children with ADHD. Short-term effects include possible improvements in social behaviours such as cooperation, attention and compliance. Research suggests that about 70% to 80% of children with ADHD are more manageable when on medication but the effects are short-lived and not a permanent cure. For many there are negative side effects such as increased heart rate and blood pressure, interference with growth rate, insomnia, weight loss and nausea (Friend and Bursuck, 2002; Hallahan *et al.*, 2005; Panksepp, 1998). In addition, little is known about the long-term effects of drug therapy, so caution is needed. Many studies have concluded that the improvements in behaviour from the drugs *seldom* lead to improvements in academic learning or peer relationships, two areas where children with ADHD have great problems. Because children and young people appear to improve dramatically in their behaviour, parents and teachers, relieved to see change, may assume the problem has been cured. It hasn't. They still need special help in learning (Doggett, 2004; Purdie, Hattie and Carroll, 2002). One large study in Australia concluded that using a variety of approaches is the best way forward:

> *Multimodal approaches to intervention have been found to be most effective in terms of lasting change. For most, but not all, children and adolescents, treatment with psychostimulants has beneficial effects, provided that it is accompanied by remedial tuition, counselling, and behaviour management by parents/teachers, as required. Thus, advice from several different professions may be necessary (van Kraayenoord et al., 2001: 7).*

In a similar vein, Steer's (2005) overview of current treatments for ADHD in the UK suggested that 'over medicalisation' of ADHD and its treatment at the expense of behavioural strategies should be avoided and stressed the pivotal importance of 'psychoeducation' (information, explanation and counselling) in supporting children and families.

What can teachers do? Long assignments may overwhelm pupils with attention deficits, so giving them a few problems or paragraphs at a time with clear consequences for completion may be helpful. Another promising approach combines instruction in learning and memory strategies with motivational training. The goal is to help learners develop the 'skill and will' to improve their achievement (Paris, 1988). They are also taught to monitor their own behaviour and encouraged to be persistent and to see themselves as 'in control' (Reid and Borkowski, 1987).

The notion of being in control is part of a new therapy strategy for dealing with ADHD, one that stresses personal agency. This approach originated in the US but is becoming known internationally. Rather than treating the problem child, David Nylund's (2000) idea is to enlist the child's strengths to conquer the child's problems – put the child in control. New metaphors for the situation are developed. Rather than seeing the problems as inside the child, Nylund helps everyone see ADHD, trouble, boredom and other 'enemies of learning' as outside the child – demons to be conquered or unruly spirits to be enlisted in the service of what *the child* wants to accomplish. The focus is on solutions. The steps of the SMART approach are:

- *Separating the problem of ADHD from the child;*
- *Mapping the influence of ADHD on the child and family;*
- *Attending to the exceptions to the ADHD story;*
- *Reclaiming special abilities of children diagnosed with ADHD;*
- *Telling and celebrating the new story (Nylund, 2000: xix).*

Those working with children can look for times when the learner is engaged – even short times – and examine what is different about these times. Discovering the learner's strengths and appreciating these may be helpful as well as adapting teaching so that this supports the changes the learner is trying to make. The above methods should be thoroughly tested with the learner before medication is used. Even if pupils are on medication, it is critical that they also learn the academic and social skills they will need to survive. Again, this will not happen by itself, even if behaviour improves with medication (Purdie, Hattie and Carroll, 2002).

Learners with dyslexia and dyscalculia

Dyslexia is a learning difficulty which involves problems with literacy. Recent estimates of people with dyslexia suggest that 2% to 15% of the population have forms of dyslexia (ranging from mild to severe) and that the figure for English speakers is higher than for most other languages perhaps because of the inconsistency of the letter-sound relationships (Parliamentary Office of Science and Technology, 2004).

There is considerable individual variation in types and levels of dyslexia but generally pupils with dyslexia have marked difficulties in learning to read, write and spell and this persists despite the fact that progress may be made in other areas. There may also be poor reading comprehension, handwriting and punctuation as well as difficulties in dealing with words (such as concentration, organisation and remembering word sequences). There may also be mispronunciation of commonly used words, with the reversal of letters and sounds within words occurring frequently (such as 'b' and 'd' or 'no/on'). The British Dyslexia Association's website includes more information on indications of dyslexia (http://www.bdadyslexia.org.uk).

There is continued debate about the causes (and even existence) of dyslexia but most agree that the areas of the brain associated with language processing are involved (Brookes, 1997).

Whatever the causes, however, the child's educational progress will be affected by dyslexia so parents or teachers who suspect that a child may be dyslexic can refer them to a learning difficulty clinic where an assessment will be carried out by an educational psychologist. This will involve gathering information from the child's parents/ family and teachers about family history, educational history and general health, and the child will be asked to complete a series of tests including reading, spelling, mathematics, visual and auditory perception, memory and sequential organisation. These are

Dyslexia

A learning difficulty which involves problems with literacy.

usually presented as games or puzzles to make the child feel comfortable and the ones commonly used in the UK are the Dyslexia Early Years Screening Test (DEST), the Dyslexia Screening Test (DES) and the Aston Index.

Teaching learners with dyslexia

The National Literacy Strategy (NLS) introduced in 1998 encourages 'phonics' teaching where children are encouraged to identify individual sounds (or phonemes) and blend them into words (Ofsted, 2002a). This is seen as helpful for children with dyslexia who commonly have difficulties with phonological aspects of language and includes within it three levels of support. Children who struggle to keep up with standard lessons (Wave 1) may be entered into small groups for teaching at a slower pace and with more individual attention (Wave 2) and if they still do not catch up with their peers they are given an individually targeted (Wave 3) intervention (funded by the school's SEN budget and designed by the SEN coordinator with other staff). Further support is likely to be necessary for children who are severely dyslexic, which is likely to be on an individual basis (Parliamentary Office of Science and Technology, 2004). Particular methods for supporting learners in primary schools with dyslexia are suggested by the DfES (2005), such as multi-sensory approaches, mind mapping, teaching specific memory skills (see Chapter 7 for more on these) and the use of ICT. Some examples of these (taken from the DfES Standards Website) are listed in the Focus on Practice below.

FOCUS ON PRACTICE

Working with learners with dyslexia

Methods	Activities
Multi-sensory approaches	Make learning *visual* by using coloured highlighters, pictures, charts and diagrams. Include mind maps to plan and organise work.
	Make learning *auditory* by using a range of speaking and listening strategies, perhaps including tapes and computers to record and play back sound. Include peer teaching to consolidate learning and use singing as a whole-class activity.
	Make learning *tactile* by having children trace over letters, words and numbers. Allow children to physically move (jump) on number-lines. Cut up information and ask children to rearrange it.
Mind mapping	Demonstrate and encourage the use of mind maps. Ask children to design their own mind map either individually, in pairs or groups and display the results. Encourage discussion of these. Choose a topic they are familiar with to allow them to grasp the idea (e.g. what we have learned about dyslexia/ our school, etc.) then integrate into new learning.

Memory strategies	Ask children how they remember things such as spellings, shopping lists, telephone numbers etc. and use the strategies they give (such as making pictures in their minds, mnemonics, writing notes to themselves) to try out these different ways in role plays. Discuss effectiveness of strategies with class.
ICT	Highlight the advantages of ICT for dyslexic learners: it allows organisation and planning of work, can use spelling and grammar checks and present work neatly; allows children to revisit, revise and amend earlier work. Encourage learners to take advantage of these resources.

Source: Adapted from Primary National Strategy: Learning and teaching for dyslexic children. DfES Publications Centre at http://www.standards.dfes.gov.uk/primary/publications/inclusion/1170961/pns_incl1184-2005dyslexia_s2.pdft

Within secondary schools support from the LEA is available for children already identified as dyslexic but there is more variability at this level than at primary school. On the whole, provision is likely to be for children and young people with severe and noticeable literacy difficulties but those who are not so obvious may be less well supported.

Dyscalculia is a condition that affects the ability to acquire arithmetical skills. Dyscalculic learners may have difficulty understanding simple number concepts, lack an intuitive grasp of numbers, and have problems learning number facts and procedures. They lack understanding and confidence of their skills with numbers (DfES, 2001a). Research into dyscalculia is at a fairly early stage and relatively few guidelines or strategies have so far been produced. Prevalence estimates are rather inconsistent depending upon the criteria used for identification but the best estimates are between 1% and 7% (Parliamentary Office of Science and Technology, 2004). Dyscalculia is thought to occur as a result of failure of certain brain areas (located in the parietal lobes) to develop properly (Landerl, Bevan and Butterworth, 2004) and this causes a failure to represent and process numbers in a normal way.

Usually methods used for assessment involve testing children across a range of ability and dyscalculia is diagnosed by a score lower than the cut-off point in mathematical tests without similarly low scores in other tests (Dowker, 2004) although a new method using computerised screening of basic numerical skills has been recently devised (Butterworth, 2002).

Dyscalculia
A condition that affects the ability to acquire arithmetical skills.

Teaching learners with dyscalculia

The National Numeracy Strategy (part of the Primary National Strategy) was introduced in 1999 and this emphasises the importance of a lively and interactive approach to teaching mathematics including both small group work and whole-class discussions (Ofsted, 2002b). This is thought to have had a positive impact upon numeracy teaching for children with special educational needs but those children with dyscalculia struggle with the daily mathematics lessons and may benefit from individual teaching. There is no specific support for children with dyscalculia beyond primary school.

Below in the Focus on Practice is a summary of advice about those working with children with dyscalculia provided by SNAP (Special Needs Assessment Profile).

Let us now look at another group of children who have special educational needs.

FOCUS ON PRACTICE

Working with children with dyscalculia

- Memory: Do not expect competent recall of number facts or tables – these will be hard for him or her.
- Processing: Encourage/allow use of a table square or calculator whenever possible.
- Use concrete rather than abstract examples to illustrate a problem.
- Ask the pupil to go over the 'working' to a problem – this can provide the opportunity of suggesting more efficient strategies.
- Precision is necessary for mathematics – remember that pupils with a global or more random way of thinking may find it demanding to focus on accuracy and detail.
- Allow more time for maths problems – break problems down into several steps, and allow time for checking and monitoring the progress throughout these steps.
- Language: The technical language of maths may be a difficulty – the pupil may understand the general meaning of words such as 'difference', 'evaluate', 'odd', 'mean' and 'product', but stumble over their quite different meanings in the context of mathematics.
- Motivation and self-esteem: Reassure the pupil that lots of famous and successful people have similar difficulties. Let the pupil know you are aware of his or her difficulty and that you are sympathetic – but that you have high expectations. Be specially generous with praise and cautious with criticism. Praise can be a natural motivator as long as the child feels the praise is genuine and deserved. It is important to let the pupil know why he or she is being praised rather than just to provide praise. In a behavioural reward system with extrinsic rewards such as stickers or points, the child can easily see why he or she is being praised. This can be an effective motivator, as long as the rewards are meaningful and appropriate. (See Chapter 6 for more about behavioural strategies.)

Source: Adapted from SNAP (Special Needs Assessment Profile) (2006) *Dyscalculia: School Support.* Available at http://www.snapassessment.com/INFdyscal.htm

Learners with communication difficulties

Communication difficulties or disorders are extremely common in children and young people and those working within education are highly likely to encounter children with some or all of these communication problems. A child with a hearing impairment will not learn to speak normally. Injuries can cause neurological problems that interfere with speech or language. Children who are not listened to, or whose perception of the world is distorted by emotional problems, will reflect these problems in their language development. Because speaking involves movements, any impairment of the motor functions involved with speech can cause language disorders and because language development and thinking are so interwoven, any problems in cognitive functioning can affect the ability to use language.

Speech and language difficulties

Children with specific speech and language difficulties (SSLD) have a primary language problem which is not explained by hearing loss, intellectual impairment or lack of language exposure (Leonard, 1997). About 5% to 7% of school-age children have some form of language difficulty (Law *et al.*, 1998) and this places them at risk of associated problems such as literacy difficulties, poor academic progress and social-emotional problems (Lindsay *et al.*, 2005). Articulation problems and stuttering or stammering are the two most common problems.

Articulation disorders include substituting one sound for another (*thunthine* for *sunshine*), distorting a sound (*shoup* for *soup*), adding a sound (*ideer* for *idea*), or omitting sounds (*po-y* for *pony*) (Smith, 1998). Keep in mind, however, that most children are six to eight years old before they can successfully pronounce all English sounds in normal conversation. The sounds of the consonants *l, r, y, s* and *z* and the consonant blends *sh, ch, zh* and *th* are the last to be mastered. Also, there are dialect differences based on geography that do not represent articulation problems. For example, a person from south-east England might pronounce *glass* as *glarse* whereas a person from the Midlands or north might use the flat 'a' sound as in 'ass' and this would be because of regional differences in pronunciation rather than articulation problems.

Stuttering generally appears between the ages of three and four. Causes of stuttering are unclear, but might include emotional or neurological problems or learned behaviour. Whatever the cause, stuttering can lead to embarrassment and anxiety for the sufferer. If stuttering continues more than a year or so, the child should be referred to a speech therapist. Early intervention can make a big difference in improving this condition (Hardman *et al.*, 2005).

Voicing problems, a third type of speech impairment, include speaking with an inappropriate pitch, quality or loudness, or in a monotone (Hallahan and Kauffman, 2006). A learner with any of these problems should be referred to a speech therapist. Recognising the problem is the first step so teachers and others working with children should be alert for learners whose pronunciation, loudness, voice quality, speech fluency, expressive range or rate is very different from that of their peers. It is also important to pay attention to those individuals who seldom speak. It may be that they are simply shy but they might have difficulties with language.

Articulation disorders
Any of a variety of pronunciation difficulties, such as the substitution, distortion or omission of sounds.

Voicing problems
Inappropriate pitch, quality, loudness and intonation.

Language disorders

Language differences are not necessarily language disorders. Learners with language disorders are those who are markedly deficient in their ability to understand or express language, compared with other pupils of their own age and cultural group (Owens, 1999). Children or young people who seldom speak, who use few words or very short sentences, or who rely only on gestures to communicate should be referred to a qualified school professional for observation or testing. Table 4.7 gives ideas for promoting language development for all learners.

Language disorders
A marked deficit in the ability to understand and express language.

Learners with intellectual disabilities

Intellectual disability is an alternative name for learning difficulty/disability but is used infrequently in the UK. It was formerly known as mental retardation in the US. A working definition used by the Open Society Mental Health Initiative UK (2005) suggests it relates to a lifelong condition, usually present from birth or which develops before the age of 18. It is permanent and characterised by 'significantly lower than average intellectual ability' resulting in significant limitations (EUMAP, 2005: 15).

Intellectual function is usually measured by IQ tests with a cut-off score of 70 (100 being the average score) as one indicator of learning problems. However, an IQ score

Intellectual disabilities
Significantly below-average intellectual and adaptive social behaviour, evident before age 18.

Table 4.7 Encouraging language development

- Talk about things that interest children.
- Follow the children's lead. Reply to their initiations and comments. Share their excitement.
- Don't ask too many questions. If you must, use questions such as *how did/do . . .* , *why did/do . . .* , and *what happened . . .* that result in longer explanatory answers.
- Encourage children to ask questions. Respond openly and honestly. If you don't want to answer a question, say so and explain why. (*I don't think I want to answer that question; it's very personal.*)
- Use a pleasant tone of voice. You need not be a comedian, but you can be light and humorous. Children love it when adults are a little silly.
- Don't be judgemental or make fun of children's language. If you are overly critical of children's language or try to catch and correct all errors, they will stop talking to you.
- Allow enough time for children to respond.
- Treat children with courtesy by not interrupting when they are talking.
- Include children in family and classroom discussions. Encourage participation and listen to their ideas.
- Be accepting of children and of their language. Hugs and acceptance can go a long way.
- Provide opportunities for children to use language and to have that language work for them to accomplish their goals.

Source: From *Language Disorders* (3rd ed.) by Robert E. Owens, Jr. Published by Allyn and Bacon, Boston, MA. Copyright © 1999 by Pearson Education.

below the 70 range is *not* enough to diagnose a child as having intellectual disabilities. There must also be problems with adaptive behaviour, day-to-day independent living and social functioning. This caution is especially important when interpreting the scores of learners from different cultures who may score low because of cultural differences.

Thus IQ ranges are not perfect predictors of individuals' abilities to function. In the UK the Department of Health uses the terms 'moderate', 'severe' and 'profound' to link IQ scores with levels of learning difficulties/disabilities and the AAMR (American Association on Mental Retardation) now recommends a classification scheme based on the amount of support that a person requires to function at his or her highest level (Taylor, Richards and Brady, 2005).

Teachers are likely to work with children with learning difficulties/disabilities probably in the moderate or severe categories but they are less likely to work with learners who have profound or 'profound/multiple' classifications (those with an IQ of less than 20 who will have great difficulty communicating and may also have more than one disability: MENCAP, 2004). In the early years, these children may simply learn, more slowly than their peers. They will need more time and more practice to learn, and have difficulty transferring learning from one setting to another or putting small skills together to accomplish a more complex task.

Learning goals for many children with intellectual disabilities between the ages of nine and 13 include basic reading, writing, arithmetic, learning about the local environment, social behaviour and personal interests. For these children in primary, junior and secondary school, the emphasis is on vocational and domestic skills, literacy for living (using the telephone book; reading signs, labels and newspaper ads; completing a job application), job-related behaviours such as courtesy and punctuality; health self-care; and citizenship skills. Today, there is a growing emphasis on preparing the person to live and work in the community. As you saw earlier in the chapter, the law requires that schools design an IEP, or individual education plan, for every child with disabilities and in Year 9 (13–14-year-olds) a transition plan is created. This aims to bring together relevant information to plan for the young person's move into adult life and is reviewed annually (DfES, 2001a).

Learners with emotional or behavioural disorders

Learners with emotional and behavioural disorders can be among the most difficult to teach in a regular class, and are a source of concern for many people who work with children. Professionals in education state that behavioural disorders are behaviours that deviate so much from the norm that they interfere with the child's own growth and development and/or the lives of others. Clearly, deviation implies a difference from some standard, and standards of behaviour differ from one situation, age group, culture, ethnic group and historical period to another. What passes for team spirit at a sporting event might be seen as disturbed behaviour in a bank or restaurant. In addition, the deviation must be more than a temporary response to stressful events; it must be consistent across time and in different situations and the learner must not have responded to direct interventions in general education (Forness and Knitzer, 1992).

> **Emotional and behavioural disorders**
>
> Behaviours or emotions that deviate so much from the norm that they interfere with the child's own growth and development and/or the lives of others – inappropriate behaviours, unhappiness or depression, fears and anxieties and trouble with relationships.

There are other definitions. The language used by education authorities in the UK is likely to be *emotional and behavioural difficulties* but Health Services may classify them as *mental disorders* (DfES, 2001b). Table 4.8 describes a few of the specific disorders

---

Table 4.8   Examples of emotional and behavioural disorders from the *Diagnostic and Statistical Manual of Mental Disorders*

- **Anxiety disorders.** Anxiety disorders occur when pupils experience an overwhelming sense of fear or dread. One example is obsessive-compulsive disorder (OCD) in which pupils cannot stop themselves from worrying excessively about a specific concern, for example germs. Other examples include phobias (fear of specific items, such as spiders, or fear of certain activities, such as going to school) and post-traumatic stress disorder (PTSD) in which pupils re-live in nightmares or flashbacks a traumatic event that they witnessed.
- **Disruptive behaviour disorders.** This category includes three types of disorders:
  - *Attention deficit-hyperactivity disorder* . . . is characterised by inattention, a high level of activity and impulsivity, or a combination of these. Note, though, that it often is not considered a disability.
  - *Oppositional defiant disorder* (ODD) is diagnosed when pupils are defiant with adults and vindictive or blaming with peers to an excessive degree over a long period of time.
  - *Conduct disorders* are diagnosed when pupils fight, bully, display cruelty to animals or people, or otherwise repeatedly break serious rules.
- **Eating disorders.** The most common eating disorder is anorexia nervosa in which pupils believe they are overweight and refuse to eat, even when they are near starvation.
- **Mood disorders.** Also called affective disorders, this group includes depression . . . and bipolar disorder, also called manic depression, in which pupils' moods swing from extreme highs (manic) to extreme lows (depression).
- **Tic disorders.** Tics are involuntary, rapid, stereotyped movements of specific muscle groups. Pupils with tics may blink their eyes or repeatedly sniff. The most well known tic disorder is Tourette syndrome, a disorder that ranges from mild to severe and includes both facial or other physical tics as well as vocal tics, often 'barking' or profanity.

Source: From 'Diagnostic and Statistical Manual of Mental Disorders' in *Special Education: Contemporary Perspectives for School Professionals* by M. Friend. Published by Allyn and Bacon, Boston, MA. Copyright © 2006 by Pearson Education.

covered by the *Diagnostic and Statistical Manual of Mental Disorders* (4th edition, revised) also called the *DSM-IV-TR*.

However defined, by the end of January 2004, learners with behavioural, emotional and social difficulties accounted for over 30% of all primary school and 38% of secondary school children identified as having special educational needs (DfES, 2004). As with learning difficulties and ADHD (attention-deficit hyperactivity disorder) there are more boys than girls diagnosed with these disorders perhaps because of genetic factors or differences in the socialisation of boys and girls. For behavioural disorders, the numbers are about six to nine times as many boys as girls.

Because learners with emotional and behavioural disorders frequently break rules and push the limits, teachers often find themselves disciplining them. Teachers are usually advised by the SENCO (special educational needs coordinator) who will offer guidance and support (Teaching in England, 2006a).

The range of possible emotional and behavioural disorders is wide and children with other disabilities – learning difficulties/disabilities, intellectual disabilities or ADHD, for example – may also have emotional or behavioural problems as they struggle in school. Methods from applied behavioural analysis (Chapter 6) and direct teaching of social skills (Chapter 3) are two useful approaches. Another possibility that has proved helpful for these learners is to provide structure, organisational tools and choices so that they are clear about what is expected and have some control over their environment.

Let's consider an area where teachers may be able to detect problems and make a difference – suicide.

Suicide

Of course, not every child or young person with emotional or behavioural problems will consider suicide, and many people without such problems will, but depression often is associated with suicide. Suicide accounts for the deaths of 20% of all young people aged 15–24 and is the second most common cause of death after accidental death for this age group (Samaritans, 1998). About 19,000 young people attempt suicide every year and about 700 die as a result (Mind, 2006). Young women (aged 15–19) are the most likely to attempt suicide but young men are much more likely to die as a result of their attempt, perhaps because of the methods they choose.

Substance abuse is thought to be a significant factor in the suicide of young people, along with academic pressure, family break-up and relationship problems. A history of family abuse often increases the risk of suicide or self-harm. A study in Avon in England (Vassilas and Morgan, 1997) suggested that many young male suicides were impulsive and American research found that having more than one of these risk factors is especially dangerous (Steinberg, 2005). In addition, there is concern today that some drugs prescribed for depression may increase the risk of suicide in adolescents.

Suicide often comes as a response to life problems – problems that parents and teachers sometimes dismiss. There are many warning signs that trouble is brewing. Professionals and families should watch for changes in eating or sleeping habits, weight, grades at school or college, disposition, activity level, interest in friends or activities that were once fun. Children or young people at risk sometimes suddenly give away prized possessions such as stereos, CDs, clothing or pets. They may seem depressed or hyperactive and may say things like 'Nothing matters anymore,' 'You won't have to worry about me anymore,' or 'I wonder what dying is like.' They may start missing school or stop doing work. It is especially dangerous if the young person not only talks about suicide, but also has a plan for carrying it out.

If those working with an individual suspect that there is a problem, it is advisable to talk to him or her directly. One feeling shared by many people who attempt suicide is that no one really takes them seriously. 'A question about suicide does not provoke suicide. Indeed, teens (and adults) often experience relief when someone finally cares enough to ask' (Range, 1993: 145). It is best to be realistic, not poetic, about suicide, ask about specifics, and take the person seriously. Also, it is worth reflecting that teenage suicides often occur in clusters. After one person acts or when stories about a suicide are reported in the media, other teens are more likely to copy the suicide (Lewinsohn, Rohde and Seeley, 1994; Rice and Dolgin, 2002). If there are serious concerns then the child should be encouraged to seek help from his or her family doctor and or a referral to healthcare professionals is recommended. Table 4.9 lists common myths and facts about suicide.

Drug abuse

Although drug abuse is not always associated with emotional or behavioural problems and people without these challenges may abuse drugs, many adolescents with emotional problems also abuse drugs. Modern society makes growing up a very confusing process. Notice the messages from films and adverts. 'Beautiful', popular people and 'celebrities' drink alcohol and smoke cigarettes with little concern for their health. We have over-the-counter drugs for almost every common ailment. Coffee wakes us up, and a pill or alcohol helps us sleep. This makes it difficult for adolescents to take the 'say no' to drugs message seriously.

For many reasons, not just because of these contradictory messages, drug use has become a problem for learners. Accurate statistics are hard to find, but estimates from the bulletin *Statistics on Young People and Drug Misuse: England, 2006* (National Statistics, 2006) suggest that 11% of secondary school children in England and Wales (2005) reported using drugs in the month prior to the survey. Among 11-year-olds, 4% had sniffed volatile substances in the last year and 1% had taken cannabis.

Table 4.9 Myths and facts about suicide

Myth:	People who talk about suicide don't kill themselves.
Fact:	Eight out of ten people who commit suicide tell someone that they're thinking about hurting themselves before they actually do it.
Myth:	Only certain types of people commit suicide.
Fact:	All types of people commit suicide – male and female, young and old, rich and poor, country people and city people. It happens in every racial, ethnic and religious group.
Myth:	When a person talks about suicide, you should change the subject to get his or her mind off it.
Fact:	You should take them seriously. Listen carefully to what they are saying. Give them a chance to express their feelings. Let them know you are concerned. And help them get help.
Myth:	Most people who kill themselves really want to die.
Fact:	Most people who kill themselves are confused about whether they want to die. Suicide is often intended as a cry for help.

Source: Extract from *Changing Bodies, Changing Lives: A Book for Teens on Sex and Relationships* (p. 142) by R. Bell, 1980, New York: Random House.

There are understandable concerns and debates about what can be done about drug use among learners. First, we should distinguish between experimentation and abuse. Many young people try something at a party, but do not become regular users. The best way to help pupils who have trouble saying no appears to be through peer programmes that teach them how to say no assertively. The successful programmes also teach general social skills and build self-esteem; are located in schools, but run by community agencies; give intensive, caring, adult attention to individual learners; involve the family; and provide opportunities for work experiences (Lerner and Galambos, 1998; Steinberg, 2005). Also, the older people are when they experiment with drugs, the more likely they are to make responsible choices, so helping younger people say no is a clear benefit.

Prevention

The key question here though is what works? Providing information or 'scare' tactics such as the DARE drug prevention programme (which was widely used in the UK and the US) seems to have little positive effect and may even encourage curiosity and experimentation (Dusenbury and Falco, 1995; Tobler and Stratton, 1997). See the Focus on Practice below for some suggestions.

FOCUS ON PRACTICE

Suggestions for preventing drug abuse

The most effective programmes include the use of:

- developmentally appropriate language and concepts;
- teaching children and young people to resist social pressure;
- providing accurate information about rates of behaviour (assuring young people that *not* everyone is doing it);
- using interactive teaching methods such as role-playing or small groups;
- providing training in skills that help in many situations such as the six-step problem-solving strategy described in Chapter 12;
- giving thorough coverage of the topic with follow-up; and practising cultural sensitivity.

It is important that all schools have a drugs education policy that sets out the school's role in relation to all drug matters. Guidance for schools is produced by the DfES (2004b) and many areas produce resources for teachers such as the 'Choices' packs that is currently being used in Derbyshire primary schools. This includes ideas for cross-curricular links so, for example, pupils would engage with discussions, activities and games in PSHE/Citizenship lessons, be taught about the role of drugs as medicines, and the effects of alcohol, tobacco and other drugs in National Curriculum science lessons, and engage with readings such as extracts from *George's Marvellous Medicine* by Roald Dahl in literacy. The pack also includes fact sheets, schemes of work, pictures of different drugs and details of relevant drugs policies and legislation (Health Promoting Schools, 2005). Initiatives such as this are still in their early stages and so their effectiveness remains to be seen but teachers are reacting positively to them.

Less Prevalent Problems and More Severe Disabilities

In this section, we focus upon learners with more severe disabilities including health impairments, physical disabilities, autism spectrum disorders and Asperger's syndrome. Let us begin with looking at learners who have physical limitations.

Learners with health impairments

Some learners must use special devices such as braces, special shoes, crutches or wheelchairs to participate in a normal school programme. If the school has the necessary architectural features, such as ramps, lifts and accessible rest rooms, and if teachers allow for the physical limitations of learners (by providing alternatives during PE lessons, for example) little needs to be done to alter the usual educational programme. Two other health impairments which may be encountered and may have a direct impact upon the child's learning experience are cerebral palsy and seizure disorders.

Cerebral palsy and multiple disabilities

Damage to the brain before or during birth or during infancy can cause a child to have difficulty moving and coordinating his or her body. The problem may be very mild, so the child simply appears a bit clumsy, or so severe that voluntary movement is practically impossible. The most common form of cerebral palsy is characterised by spasticity (overly tight or tense muscles). Many children with cerebral palsy also have secondary disabilities (Kirk, Gallagher and Anastasiow, 1993). In the classroom, these secondary disabilities are the greatest concern – and these are generally what the regular teacher can help with most. For example, many children with cerebral palsy also have visual impairments, speech problems or mild intellectual disabilities. The strategies described in the next section should prove helpful in such situations.

Seizure disorders (epilepsy)

A seizure is a cluster of behaviours that occurs in response to abnormal neurochemical activities in the brain (Hardman, Drew and Egan, 2005). People with epilepsy have recurrent seizures, but not all seizures are the result of epilepsy; temporary conditions such as high fevers or infections can also trigger seizures. Seizures take many forms and differ with regard to the length, frequency and movements involved. A partial or absence seizure involves only a small part of the brain, whereas a generalised or tonic-clonic seizure includes much more of the brain.

Most generalised seizures (once called *grand mal*) are accompanied by uncontrolled jerking movements that ordinarily last two to five minutes, possible loss of bowel or bladder control, and irregular breathing, followed by a deep sleep or coma. On regaining consciousness, the person may be very weary, confused and in need of extra sleep. Most seizures can be controlled by medication. If a learner has a seizure accompanied by convulsions in class, the teacher must take action so the person will not be injured. The major danger to someone having such a seizure is getting hurt by striking a hard surface during the violent jerking. The Focus on Practice feature below provides some information for those who might be working with learners with epilepsy.

Not all seizures are dramatic. Sometimes the person just loses contact briefly. The person may stare, fail to respond to questions, drop objects and miss what has been happening for one to 30 seconds. These were once called *petit mal*, but they are now referred to as absence seizures and can easily go undetected. If a child appears to daydream frequently, does not seem to know what is going on at times or cannot remember what has just happened when you ask, then health professionals should be

Cerebral palsy

Condition involving a range of motor or coordination difficulties due to brain damage.

Spasticity

Overly tight or tense muscles, characteristic of some forms of cerebral palsy.

Epilepsy

Disorder marked by seizures and caused by abnormal electrical discharges in the brain.

Absence seizure

A seizure involving only a small part of the brain that causes a child to lose contact briefly.

Generalised or tonic-clonic seizure

A seizure involving a large portion of the brain.

FOCUS ON PRACTICE

Working with learners with epilepsy

If a learner has a seizure, it is important for those working with him or her to stay calm and reassure the rest of the class. It is not advisable to try to restrain the child's movements as it is impossible to stop the seizure once it starts. It is usually best to lower the child gently to the floor, away from furniture or walls and to move hard objects away. Loosening scarves, ties or anything that might make breathing difficult is recommended as well as turning the child's head gently to the side and putting a soft coat or blanket under the learner's head. It is not advisable to ever put anything in the person's mouth – it is *not* true that people having seizures can swallow their tongues. Neither is it advisable to attempt artificial respiration unless the individual does not start breathing again after the seizure stops. It is useful to find out from the child's parents how they deal with seizures. If one seizure follows another and the individual does not regain consciousness in between, if the young person is pregnant or has a medical ID that does not say 'epilepsy, seizure disorder', if there are signs of injury, or if the seizure goes on for more than five minutes, then medical help should be called right away (Friend, 2006).

For more ideas and information, see the Epilepsy Research Foundation website at http://www.erf.org.uk/about_us/who_we_are.htm

consulted. The major problem for learners with absence seizures is that they miss the continuity of the class interaction – these seizures can occur as often as 100 times a day. If their seizures are frequent, learners will find the lessons confusing. Those working with them should question these learners to be sure that they are understanding and following the lesson and be prepared to repeat themselves periodically.

Learners who are deaf and hard of hearing

Sometimes the term 'hearing impaired' is used to describe these learners, but the deaf community and researchers object to this term, so here we will use their preferred terms, deaf and hard of hearing, which are used by the RNID (Royal National Institute for the Deaf, 2006). The number of deaf learners has been declining over the past three decades, but when the problem does occur, the consequences for learning are serious (Hunt and Marshall, 2002). Signs of hearing problems are turning one ear towards the speaker, favouring one ear in conversation or misunderstanding conversation when the speaker's face cannot be seen. Other indications include not following directions, seeming distracted or confused at times, frequently asking people to repeat what they have said, mispronouncing new words or names and being reluctant to participate in class discussions. Those learners who have frequent earaches, sinus infections or allergies may be worth monitoring by those working with them.

In the past, educators have debated whether oral or manual approaches are better for children who are deaf or hard of hearing. Oral approaches involve speech reading (also called lip reading) and training learners to use whatever limited hearing they may have. Manual approaches include sign language and finger spelling. Research indicates that children who learn some manual method of communicating perform better in academic subjects and are more socially mature than learners who are exposed only to oral methods. Today, the trend is to combine both approaches (Hallahan and Kauffman, 2006).

Another perspective suggests that people who are deaf are part of a different culture with a different language, values, social institutions and literature. Hunt and Marshall quote one deaf professional: 'How would women like to be referred to as male-impaired, or whites like to be called black-impaired? I'm not impaired; I'm deaf!' (2002: 348). From this perspective, a goal is to help deaf children become bilingual and bicultural, to enable them to function effectively in both cultures. Technological innovations such as speech-to-text (STT) reporters and the many avenues of communication through e-mail and the internet have expanded communication possibilities for all people, including those with hearing problems.

Learners who are blind or partially sighted

A survey of educational provision for blind and partially sighted children in England, Scotland and Wales in 2002 estimated that approximately 24,000 children up to the age of 16 were known to LEA Visual Impairment Services (Keill and Clunies-Ross, 2003). Thus they are the highest proportion of pupils with disabilities within mainstream schools (2.4 per 1,000 children). Learners who have difficulty seeing often hold books either very close to or very far from their eyes. They may squint, rub their eyes frequently, or complain that their eyes burn or itch. The eyes may actually be swollen, red or encrusted. Learners with vision problems may misread material on the board, describe their vision as being blurred, be very sensitive to light or hold their heads at an odd angle. They may become irritable when they have to do deskwork or lose interest if they have to follow an activity taking place across the room (Hunt and Marshall, 2002). Any of these signs should be reported to a qualified professional.

Special materials and equipment that help these learners to function in mainstream classrooms include large-print books; software that converts printed material to speech or to Braille; personal organisers that have talking appointment books or address books; tape recorders; special calculators; an abacus; three-dimensional maps, charts and models; and special measuring devices. For learners with visual problems, the quality of the print is often more important than the size, so care should be taken with handouts (RNIB, 2006). Visit the RNIB website which has plenty of guidance for the production of materials to be used with blind people (http://www.rnib.org.uk/).

The arrangement of the room is also an issue. Learners with visual problems need to know where things are, so consistency matters – a place for everything and everything in its place. It is advisable to leave plenty of space for moving around the room and make sure to monitor possible obstacles and safety hazards such as waste baskets in aisles and open cupboard doors. If the room is rearranged, those working with children should give learners with visual problems a chance to learn the new layout and make sure the learners have a partner/buddy for fire drills or other emergencies (Friend and Bursuck, 2002).

Learners with autism spectrum disorders and Asperger's syndrome

Almost four children in every 1,000 children have a severe learning difficulty/disability (approximately 200 in a typical local area) and many of these children will have autism or ASD (autistic spectrum disorder). Additionally, approximately 25 per 1,000 children in the UK have moderate learning difficulty and many of these will have ASD (NIASA, 2003). It is very difficult to obtain accurate estimates of ASD across European countries because of differing definitions although generally numbers are seen to be rising (European Commission Health and Consumer Protection, 2005).

Autism spectrum disorders

You may be familiar with the term 'autism'. In 1943 Leo Kanner, an Austrian-American psychiatrist, first described classic autistic syndrome and since then the concept of autistic disorders has broadened (National Autistic Society, 2006). The term preferred by professionals in the field, autism spectrum disorders, is used here to emphasise that autism includes a range of disorders from mild to major. From an early age, children with autism spectrum disorders may have difficulties in social relations. They do not form connections with others, avoid eye contact or don't share feelings such as enjoyment or interest with others. Communication is impaired and about half of these children are non-verbal; they have very limited or non-existent language skills. Others make up their own language. They may obsessively insist on regularity and sameness in their environments – change is very disturbing. They may repeat behaviours and have restricted interests, watching the same DVD over and over, for example. They may be very sensitive to light, sound, touch or other sensory information – sounds may be perceived as painful, for example. They may be able to memorise words or steps in problem solving but not use them appropriately, or be very confused when the situation changes or questions are asked in a different way (Friend, 2006).

Asperger's/Asperger syndrome is one of the disabilities included in the autistic spectrum. Children who have many of the characteristics described above but their greatest trouble is with social relations are often given this diagnosis. Their language is less affected than with autism and their speech may be fluent, but unusual, mixing up pronouns of 'I' and 'you', for example (Friend, 2006). Many learners with autism also have moderate-to-severe intellectual disabilities, but those with Asperger's syndrome usually have average-to-above average intelligence. The recent bestseller *The Curious Incident of the Dog in the Night-Time* by Mark Haddon (2003) gives insight into Asperger's syndrome through the main character and might be useful for those working with children to increase understanding of this condition. The book is written in the first-person by Christopher who is a 15-year-old mathematics genius with a photographic memory and keen powers of observation but little understanding of other humans with this condition.

Theory of mind

One current explanation for autism and Asperger's syndrome is that children with these disorders lack a theory of mind – an understanding that they and other people have minds, thoughts and emotions. They have difficulty explaining their own behaviours, appreciating that other people might have different feelings and predicting how behaviours might affect emotions. So, for example, a learner may not understand why classmates are bored by his constant repetition of stories or obscure facts about topics he finds fascinating. Or the learner may stand too close or too far away when interacting, not realising that he or she is making other people uncomfortable (Friend, 2006).

Interventions

Early and intense interventions that focus on communication and social relations are particularly important for children with autism spectrum disorders. For pre-school and primary school-aged children the Family Care Plan (FCP) and Individual Education Plan (IEP) must include clear ASD (autism spectrum disorders) management plans for staff and parents to use as well as access to specific individual or small group opportunities depending upon their clinical and developmental needs. Many local

Autism spectrum disorders

Developmental disability significantly affecting verbal and non-verbal communication and social interaction, generally evident before age three and ranging from mild to major.

Asperger's syndrome

Includes many of the characteristics of autism, but greatest problems lie in social relations.

areas have an ASD-trained teacher who can visit, advise and set up appropriate IEPs (NIASA, 2003).

As they enter school, many of these children will be in inclusive settings, others in specialised schools, and some in a combination of these two. Collaboration among teachers and the family is particularly important for these learners. Supports such as smaller classes, structured environments, providing a safe 'home base' for times of stress, consistency in instruction, assistive technologies and the use of visual supports may be part of a collaborative plan (Friend, 2006). Through adolescence and the transition to adulthood, life, work and social skills are important educational goals.

We end the chapter with another group that has special needs but in a different sense, highly intelligent or talented learners.

Learners Who Are Gifted and Talented

Consider this true account given by US researchers.

> Latoya was already an advanced reader when she entered 1st grade in a large urban school district. Her teacher noticed the challenging chapter books Latoya brought to school and read with little effort. After administering a reading assessment, the school's reading consultant confirmed that Latoya was reading at the 5th grade level. Latoya's parents reported with pride that she had started to read independently when she was 3 years old and 'had read every book she could get her hands on'.
>
> In her struggling urban school, Latoya received no particular accommodations, and by 5th grade, she was still reading at just above the 5th grade level. Her 5th grade teacher had no idea that Latoya had ever been an advanced reader (Reis et al., 2002).

Latoya is not alone. There is a group with special needs that is often overlooked by the schools in most countries: gifted and talented learners. In the past, providing an enriched education for extremely bright or talented learners was seen as undemocratic and elitist. Now, there is a growing recognition that gifted children are being poorly served by many schools. In July 2006, a National Register was launched by the government in the UK in order to identify and track the top 5% of pupils in ability range in schools across England (NAGTY, 2006). From 2006, all secondary schools have been asked to identify their gifted and talented learners in the Schools Census and this will be extended to primary schools in 2007.

Gifted and talented learner

A very bright, creative and talented pupil.

Who are these learners?

There are many definitions of gifted because individuals can have many different gifts. Remember that Gardner (2003) identified eight separate 'intelligences' (linguistic, musical, spatial, logical-mathematical, bodily-kinesthetic, interpersonal, intrapersonal and naturalist) and Sternberg (1997) suggests a triarchic model (thinking processes, coping with new experiences and adapting to context). Renzulli and Reis (2003) have a different three-part conception of giftedness which consists of above-average general ability, a high level of creativity and a high level of task commitment or motivation to achieve. In recent years the DfES (2002) has broadened its definition (below) to include a larger proportion of children and young people identifying:

- 'gifted' pupils as those who have abilities in one or more subjects in the statutory school curriculum other than art and design, music and PE;

- 'talented' pupils as those who have abilities in art and design, music, PE, or in sports or performing arts such as dance and drama.

Truly gifted children are not the ones who simply learn quickly with little effort. The work of gifted learners is original, extremely advanced for their age and potentially of lasting importance. These children may read fluently with little instruction by age three or four. They may play a musical instrument like a skilful adult, turn a visit to the grocery store into a mathematical puzzle, and become fascinated with algebra when their friends are having trouble 'carrying' in addition (Winner, 2000).

What do we know about these remarkable individuals? A classic study of the characteristics of the academically and intellectually gifted was started decades ago by Lewis Terman and colleagues (1925, 1947, 1959; Holahan and Sears, 1995). This huge project is following the lives of 1,528 gifted males and females in the US and will continue until the year 2010. The subjects all have IQ scores in the top 1% of the population (140 or above on the Stanford–Binet individual test of intelligence). They were identified on the basis of these test scores and teacher recommendations.

Terman and colleagues found that these gifted children were larger, stronger and healthier than the norm. They often walked sooner and were more athletic. They were more emotionally stable than their peers and became better-adjusted adults than the average individual. They had lower rates of delinquency, emotional difficulty, divorce, drug problems, and so on. Of course, the teachers in Terman's study who made the nominations may have selected children who were better adjusted initially. It is also worth noting that Terman's study just tells about academically gifted children. There are many other kinds of gifts including the ability to develop empathy and respect for others and to become an autonomous, responsible person (Stoll, Fink and Earl, 2004).

What is the origin of these gifts?

For years, researchers have debated the nature/nurture question about people with extraordinary abilities and talents. As usual, there is evidence that it takes both. Studies of prodigies and geniuses in many fields document that deep and prolonged practice is necessary to achieve at the highest levels. For example, it took Newton 20 years to move from his first ideas to his ultimate contribution (Howe, Davidson and Sloboda, 1998; Winner, 2000).

Bloom's study of talent (1982) is relevant here. His research team had interviewed, among others, the top tennis players in the world, their coaches, parents, siblings and friends. One coach said that he would make a suggestion, and a few days later the young athlete would have mastered the move. Then the parents told how the child had practised that move for hours on end after getting the coach's tip. So, focused, intense practice plays a role. Also, the families of prodigies tend to be child-centred and to devote hours to supporting the development of their child's gifts. Bloom's research team described tremendous sacrifices made by families: rising before dawn to drive their child to a coach in another city, having two jobs, or even moving the whole family to another part of the country to find the best teachers or coaches. The children responded to the family's sacrifices by working harder and the families responded to the child's hard work by sacrificing more – an upward spiral of investment and achievement.

However, hard work will never make this co-author a world-class tennis player or a Newton. There is a role for nature as well. The children studied by Bloom showed early and clear talent in the areas they later developed. As children, great sculptors were constantly drawing and mathematicians were fascinated with dials, gears and gauges. Parents' investments in their children came after the children showed early high-level achievement (Winner, 2000; 2003). Some recent research in the US suggests that gifted children, at least those with extraordinary abilities in mathematics, music and visual arts, may have unusual brain organisation – which can have both advantages and disadvantages. Giftedness in mathematics, music and visual arts appears to be associated with superior visual-spatial abilities and enhanced development of the right side of the brain. Children with these gifts are also more likely not to have right-hand dominance and to have language related-problems. These brain differences are evidence that 'gifted children, child prodigies, and savants are not made from scratch but are born with unusual brains that enable rapid learning in a particular domain' (Winner, 2000: 160). However, Winner herself concedes that the evidence is 'indirect' (2000: 159) and stresses the importance of nurturing these talents and gifts.

What problems do the gifted face?

In spite of Bloom's and Terman's findings, it would be incorrect to say that every gifted learner is superior in adjustment and emotional health. In fact, gifted adolescents, especially girls, are more likely to be depressed and to report social and emotional problems (Berk, 2005). Many difficulties confront a gifted child, including boredom and frustration in school as well as isolation (sometimes even ridicule) from peers. Schoolmates may be consumed with sport or worried about failing mathematics while the gifted child is fascinated with Mozart, focused on a social issue or totally absorbed in computers, drama or physics. Gifted children may be impatient with friends, parents and even teachers who do not share their interests or abilities. Because their language is well developed, they may be seen as show-offs when they are simply expressing themselves. They are sensitive to the expectations and feelings of others, so these children and young people may be very vulnerable to criticisms and taunts. Because they are goal-directed and focused, they may seem stubborn and uncooperative. Their keen sense of humour can be used as a weapon against teachers and classmates. Adjustment problems seem to be greatest for the most gifted, those in the highest range of academic ability (e.g. above 180 IQ) (Hardman, Drew and Egan, 2005; Robinson and Clinkenbeard, 1998).

Strategies for identifying and teaching gifted learners

Identifying gifted children is not always easy, and teaching them well may be even more challenging. Many parents provide early educational experiences for their children. Even very advanced reading ability in the early years of school does not guarantee that children will still be outstanding readers years later (Mills and Jackson, 1990). In secondary school, some very able learners deliberately earn lower grades, making their abilities even harder to recognise. Girls are especially likely to hide their abilities (Berk, 2005). This may relate to stronger peer acceptance needs. It seems that the fear of being seen as a 'geek' or a 'swot' and the desire to conform with peers are stronger motives than the desire to achieve academically for many adolescents.

Recognising gifts and talents

Clearly it is important to identify gifted and talented children in order to provide adequately for their learning. Several approaches are used for this including test scores and teacher observations. Teachers are successful only about 10% to 50% of the time in picking out the gifted children in their classes (Fox, 1981). Here are a few questions to guide identification, suggested by Marilyn Friend (2006). Who can easily manipulate abstract symbol systems such as mathematics? Who can concentrate for long periods of time on personal interests? Who remembers easily? Who developed language and reading early, like Latoya described at the beginning of this section? Who is curious and has many interests? Whose work is original and creative? These learners may also prefer to work alone, have a keen sense of justice and fairness, be energetic and intense, form strong commitments to friends – often older learners – and struggle with perfectionism. Other major sources of information for identifying gifted and talented children include information from parents, peers and the learners themselves (Eyre, 2002).

As well as formal test scores, other measures are helpful when recognising gifted and talented learners. These include looking at the pupil's work and using checklists such as those on the QCA website and within relevant academic literature (Eyre, 2002;

Tong, 2002; Wallace, 2000). There are also subject-specific checklists which means both should be used. However, research is at a relatively early stage and there are no definitive exclusive lists.

Many psychologists recommend a case study approach to identifying gifted children. This means gathering many kinds of information about the individual in different contexts: test scores, grades, examples of work, projects and portfolios, letters or ratings from community members, self-ratings, nominations from teachers or peers, and so on (Renzulli and Reis, 2003; Sisk, 1988). Especially for recognising artistic talent, experts in the field can be called in to judge the merits of a child's creations. Science projects, exhibitions, performances, auditions and interviews are all possibilities. Creativity tests may identify some children not picked up by other measures, particularly learners from ethnic minority groups who may be at a disadvantage on the other types of tests (Maker, 1987). It is worth remembering that learners with remarkable abilities in one area may have much less impressive abilities in others.

Teaching gifted learners

The National Curriculum for England (DfEE/QCA, 1999) makes it quite clear that adequate provision for gifted and talented learners should be made. In its statement on inclusion, it states the following:

> For pupils whose attainments significantly exceed the expected level of attainment within one or more subjects during a particular key stage, teachers will need to plan suitably challenging work. As well as drawing on materials from later key stages or higher levels of study, teachers may plan further differentiation by extending the breadth and depth of study within individual subjects or by planning work which draws on the content of different subjects.

There is considerable debate about the best ways of providing suitable educational provision. Some educators believe that gifted learners should be *accelerated* – moved quickly through the year group or through particular subjects. Other educators prefer enrichment – giving the learners additional, more sophisticated and more thought-provoking work, but keeping them with their age-mates in school. Actually, there may be a place for both (Torrance, 1986).

Many educationalists object to acceleration because of the fear that this practice might deprive learners of social and emotional interactions with children of their own age (Kirby and Townsend, 2005). However, research studies indicate that truly gifted learners who begin all stages of education early do as well as, and usually better than, non-gifted learners who are progressing at the normal pace. Social and emotional adjustment does not appear to be impaired. Gifted learners tend to prefer the company of older playmates and may be miserably bored if kept with children of their own age. Acceleration or skipping years may not be the best solution for a particular learner, but there are arguments in its favour (Jones and Southern, 1991; Kulik and Kulik, 1984; Richardson and Benbow, 1990). An alternative to skipping a year/s is to accelerate learners in one or two particular subjects or allow concurrent enrolment in advanced placement courses, but keep them with peers for most classes (Robinson and Clinkenbeard, 1998). For pupils who are extremely advanced intellectually (e.g. those scoring 160 or higher on an individual intelligence test), the only practical solution may be to accelerate their education (Hardman, Drew and Egan, 2005; Hunt and Marshall, 2002). Some writers comment, however, that acceleration is evidence of schools failing to provide for its most able pupils (Freeman, 1998).

Teaching methods for gifted pupils should encourage abstract thinking (formal-operational thought), creativity, reading of high-level and original texts and independence, not just the learning of greater quantities of facts. Freeman's research (1998) suggested that mixed-ability groups may not be beneficial for gifted and talented learners because teachers tend to focus upon the middle-ability range and have lower expectations. This can lead to the most able in the group underachieving and possibly to a lower self-concept. Gifted pupils tend to learn more when they work in groups with other high-ability peers (Fuchs *et al.*, 1998; Robinson and Clinkenbeard, 1998). However, there are indications that they can benefit from the interactions within mixed-ability groups as long as teachers are flexible and provide for their needs.

In working with gifted and talented learners, a teacher must be imaginative, flexible, tolerant and unthreatened by the capabilities of these children and young people. The teacher should ask questions such as: What do these children need most? What are they ready to learn? Who can help me to challenge them? Challenge and support are critical for all learners but challenging pupils who know more than anyone else in the school about history or music or science or mathematics can be a challenge! Answers might come from other sources of expertise such as nearby universities, retired professionals, books, museums or older pupils. Strategies might be as simple as letting the child do mathematics with the next year group. Other options are summer schools; courses at nearby colleges; classes with local artists, musicians or dancers; independent research projects; selected classes in higher level institutions and special-interest clubs (Mitchell, 1984).

In the midst of providing challenge, it is important to provide support for these learners. We all have seen the ugly sights of parents, coaches or teachers forcing the joy out of their talented children by demanding practice and perfection beyond the child's interest. This co-author witnessed this phenomenon recently at an under-12s tennis competition where several parents became almost hysterical as they argued a line-call decision by the coach. Just as we should not force children to stop investing in their talent ('Oh, Michelangelo, stop messing about with those sketches and go outside and play'), we also should avoid destroying intrinsic motivation with heavy doses of pressure and external rewards.

This has been a brief, selective look at the needs of children. If those working with children decide that children might benefit from special services of any kind, then the school's coordinator for gifted and talented children (who should have close links with the school's management team) would be involved in order to ensure appropriate provision is made.

SUMMARY TABLE

Individual Differences in Intelligence (pp. 130–144)

What are the advantages of and problems with labels?

Labels and diagnostic classifications of exceptional learners can easily become both stigmas and self-fulfilling prophecies, but they can also open doors to special programmes and help teachers develop appropriate instructional strategies.

What is person-first language?

'Person-first' language ('pupils with intellectual disabilities', 'learners placed at risk', etc.) is an alternative to labels that describe a complex person with one or two words, implying that the condition labelled is the most important aspect of the person. With person-first language, the emphasis is on the learners first, not on the special challenges they face.

Distinguish between a disability and a handicap

A disability is an inability to do something specific such as see or walk. A handicap is a disadvantage in certain situations. Some disabilities lead to handicaps, but not in all contexts. Teachers must avoid imposing handicaps on disabled learners.

What is g?

Spearman suggested there is one mental attribute, which he called *g* or general intelligence, that is used to perform any mental test, but that each test also requires some specific abilities in addition to *g*. A current version of the general plus specific abilities theory is Carroll's work identifying a few broad abilities (such as learning and memory, visual perception, verbal fluency) and at least 70 specific abilities. Fluid and crystallised intelligence are two of the broad abilities identified in most research.

What is Gardner's view of intelligence and his position on g?

Gardner contends that an intelligence is a biological and psychological potential to solve problems and create outcomes that are valued by a culture. These intelligences are realised to a greater or lesser extent as a consequence of the experiential, cultural and motivational factors in a person's environment. The intelligences are: linguistic, musical, spatial, logical-mathematical, bodily-kinesthetic, interpersonal, intrapersonal, naturalist and perhaps existential. Gardner does not deny the existence of *g*, but questions how useful *g* is as an explanation for human achievements. The concept of emotional intelligence, or EQ, is similar to Gardner's intrapersonal and interpersonal intelligences.

What are the elements in Sternberg's theory of intelligence?

Sternberg's triarchic theory of intelligence is a cognitive process approach to understanding intelligence. Analytic/componential intelligence involves mental processes that are defined in terms of components: metacomponents, performance components and knowledge-acquisition components. Creative/experiential intelligence involves coping with new experiences through insight and automaticity. Practical/contextual intelligence involves choosing to live and work in a context where success is likely, adapting to that context and

reshaping it if necessary. Practical intelligence is made up mostly of action-oriented tacit knowledge learned during everyday life.

How is intelligence measured, and what does an IQ score mean?

Intelligence is measured through individual tests (Stanford–Binet, Wechsler, etc.) and group tests (Cognitive Abilities Test, Analysis of Learning Potential, School and College Ability Tests, etc.). Compared to an individual test, a group test is much less likely to yield an accurate picture of any one person's abilities. The average score is 100. About 68% of the general population will earn IQ scores between 85 and 115. Only about 16% of the population will receive scores below 85 or above 115.

What is the Flynn effect and what are its implications?

Since the early 1900s, IQ scores have been rising. To keep 100 as the average for IQ test scores, questions have to be made more difficult. This increasing difficulty has implications for any programme that uses IQ scores as part of the entrance requirements. For example, learners who were not identified as having intellectual disabilities a generation ago might be identified as disabled now because the test questions are harder.

Ability Differences and Teaching (pp. 144–147)

What are the problems with between-class ability grouping?

Academic ability groupings can have both disadvantages and advantages for pupils and teachers. For low-ability learners, however, between-class ability grouping generally has a negative effect on achievement, social adjustment and self-esteem. Teachers of low-achievement classes tend to emphasise lower-level objectives and routine procedures, with less academic focus. Often, there are more learner behaviour problems, increased teacher stress, lowered expectations and decreased enthusiasm. Ability grouping can promote segregation within schools.

What are the alternatives available for grouping in classes?

Cross-age grouping by subject can be an effective way to deal with ability differences in a school. Within-class ability grouping, if handled sensitively and flexibly, can have positive effects, but alternatives such as cooperative learning may be better.

Learning Styles and Preferences (pp. 147–150)

Distinguish between learning styles and learning preferences.

Learning styles are the characteristic ways a person approaches learning and studying. The most common distinction is between deep and surface processing. Learning preferences are individual preferences for particular learning modes and environments. Even though learning styles and learning preferences are not related to intelligence or effort, they can affect school performance.

Should teachers match teaching methods to individual learning styles?

Results of some research indicate that pupils learn more when they study in their preferred setting and manner, but most research does not show a benefit. Many learners would do better to develop new – and perhaps more effective – ways to learn.

What learning style distinctions are best supported by research?

One distinction that is repeatedly found in research is deep versus surface processing. Individuals who have a *deep-processing approach* see the learning activities as a means for understanding some underlying concepts or meanings. Learners who take a *surface-processing* approach focus on memorising the learning materials, not understanding them. A second is Mayer's visualiser–verbaliser dimension that it has three facets: *cognitive spatial ability* (low or high), *cognitive style* (visualiser v. verbaliser) and *learning preference* (verbal learner v. visual learner).

Inclusion (pp. 150–152)

Describe the main changes resulting from the 2001 Special Educational Needs and Disabilities Act (SENDA)

The SENDA (2001) and the Code of Practice than followed it means that Local Education Authorities (LEAs) must plan for the needs of children with SEN. Learners with SEN should normally be taught within mainstream schools and have full access to a broad, balanced curriculum. Working with other professionals and families schools must provide a graduated response to the child's needs, gradually increasing appropriate support depending upon the degree of difficulty/need. An Independent Education Plan (IEP) will be drawn up by the class teacher for all children placed on the register of SEN and this will include targets and reviews of progress.

The Most Common Challenges (pp. 152–168)

What is a learning difficulty/disability?

Specific learning difficulties/disabilities are disorders in one or more of the basic psychological processes involved in understanding or using spoken or written language. Listening, speaking, reading, writing, reasoning or mathematical abilities might be affected. These disorders are intrinsic to the individual, presumed to be the result of central nervous system dysfunction, and may occur across the life span. Children and young people with learning difficulties/disabilities may become victims of learned helplessness when they come to believe that they cannot control or improve their own learning and therefore cannot succeed. A focus on learning strategies often helps pupils with learning difficulties/disabilities.

What is ADHD and how is it handled in school?

Attention-deficit hyperactivity disorder (ADHD) is the term used to describe individuals of any age with hyperactivity and attention difficulties. Use of medication to address ADHD is controversial, but currently on the rise. For many pupils there are negative side effects. In addition, little is known about the long-term effects of drug therapy. There also is no evidence that the drugs lead to improvement in academic learning or peer relationships. Two promising approaches are behaviour modification and techniques that combine motivational training with instruction in learning and memory strategies. The SMART approach that focuses on the abilities of children is another possibility.

What are dyslexia and dyscalculia?

Dyslexia relates to problems with literacy and includes difficulties with reading, writing, comprehension, organisation and memory. Dyscalculia affects competence with arithmetical skills and includes problems grasping number concepts and skills.

What are the most common communication disorders?

Common communication disorders include speech impairments (articulation disorders, stuttering and voicing problems) and oral language disorders. If these problems are addressed early, great progress is possible.

What defines intellectual disabilities?

Before age 18, learners must score below about 70 on a standard measure of intelligence and must have problems with adaptive behaviour, day-to-day independent living and social functioning.

What are the best approaches for learners with emotional and behavioural disorders?

Methods from applied behavioural analysis and direct teaching of social skills are two useful approaches. Learners also may respond to structure and organisation in the environment, schedules, activities and rules.

What are some warning signs of potential suicide?

Pupils at risk of suicide may show changes in eating or sleeping habits, weight, grades, disposition, activity level or interest in friends. They sometimes suddenly give away prized possessions such as stereos, CDs, clothing or pets. They may seem depressed or hyperactive and may start missing school or stop doing work. It is especially dangerous if the learner not only talks about suicide, but also has a plan for carrying it out.

Less Prevalent Problems and More Severe Disabilities (pp. 169–173)

How can schools accommodate the needs of learners with physical disabilities?

If the school has the necessary architectural features, such as ramps, elevators and accessible rest rooms, and if teachers allow for the physical limitations of learners, little needs to be done to alter the usual educational programme. Identifying a peer to help with movements and transitions can be useful.

How might an epileptic seizure be handled in class?

It is best not to restrain the child's movements. The child should be lowered gently to the floor, away from furniture or walls, and any hard objects moved away. The child's head should be turned gently to the side, and a soft coat or blanket placed under his or her head. Any tight clothing should be loosened. Nothing should be placed in the person's mouth. The pupil's parents should be consulted about how they deal with seizures. If one seizure follows another and the pupil does not regain consciousness in between, if the learner is pregnant or if the seizure goes on for more than five minutes, then medical help should be sought immediately.

What are some signs of hearing and visual impairment?

Signs of hearing problems are turning one ear towards the speaker, favouring one ear in conversation or misunderstanding conversation when the speaker's face cannot be seen. Other indications include not following directions, seeming distracted or confused at times, frequently asking people to repeat what they have said, mispronouncing new words or names and being reluctant to participate in class discussions. Frequent earaches, sinus infections or allergies may also be indications. Holding books very close or far away, squinting, rubbing eyes, misreading the chalkboard and holding the head at an odd angle are possible signs of visual problems.

How does autism differ from Asperger's syndrome?

Asperger's syndrome is one of the autism spectrum disorders. Many learners with autism also have moderate to severe intellectual disabilities, but those with Asperger syndrome usually have average to above average intelligence and better language abilities than other children with autism but they have problems with social relationships.

Learners Who Are Gifted and Talented (pp. 173–177)

What are the characteristics of gifted learners?

Gifted pupils learn easily and rapidly and retain what they have learned; use common sense and practical knowledge; know about many things that the other children don't; use a large number of words easily and accurately; recognise relations and comprehend meaning; are alert and keenly observant and respond quickly; are persistent and highly motivated on some tasks; and are creative or make interesting connections. Teachers should make special efforts to support underrepresented gifted pupils – girls, learners who also have learning difficulties/disabilities, and children living in poverty.

Is acceleration a useful approach with gifted learners?

Many people object to acceleration, but most careful studies indicate that truly gifted pupils who

are accelerated do as well as, and usually better than, non-gifted learners who are progressing at the normal pace. Gifted learners tend to prefer the company of older playmates and may be bored if kept with children their own age. Skipping years may not be the best solution for a particular learner, but for pupils who are extremely advanced intellectually (with a score of 160 or higher on an individual intelligence test), the only practical solution may be to accelerate their education.

Glossary

Absence seizure: A seizure involving only a small part of the brain that causes a child to lose contact briefly.

Articulation disorders: Any of a variety of pronunciation difficulties, such as the substitution, distortion or omission of sounds.

Asperger's syndrome: Includes many of the characteristics of autism, but greatest problems lie in social relations.

ADHD (attention-deficit hyperactivity disorder): Current term for disruptive behaviour disorders marked by over activity, excessive difficulty sustaining attention or impulsiveness.

Autism spectrum disorders: Developmental disability significantly affecting verbal and non-verbal communication and social interaction, generally evident before age three and ranging from mild to major.

Automaticity: The result of learning to perform a behaviour or thinking process so thoroughly that the performance is automatic and does not require effort.

Cerebral palsy: Condition involving a range of motor or coordination difficulties due to brain damage.

Crystallised intelligence: Ability to apply culturally approved problem-solving methods.

Deviation IQ: Score based on statistical comparison of an individual's performance with the average performance of others in that age group.

Disability: The inability to do something specific such as walk or hear.

Disorder: A broad term meaning a general disturbance in physical or mental functioning.

Dyslexia: A learning difficulty which involves problems with literacy.

Dyscalculia: A condition that affects the ability to acquire arithmetical skills.

Emotional and behavioural disorders: Behaviours or emotions that deviate so much from the norm that they interfere with the child's own growth and development and/or the lives of others – inappropriate behaviours, unhappiness or depression, fears and anxieties and trouble with relationships.

Emotional intelligence (EQ): The ability to process emotional information accurately and efficiently.

Epilepsy: Disorder marked by seizures and caused by abnormal electrical discharges in the brain.

Fluid intelligence: Mental efficiency, non-verbal abilities grounded in brain development.

Flynn effect: Because of better health, smaller families, increased complexity in the environment and more and better schooling, IQ test scores are steadily rising.

Generalised or tonic-clonic seizure: A seizure involving a large portion of the brain.

Gifted and talented learner: A very bright, creative and talented pupil.

Handicap: A disadvantage in a particular situation, sometimes caused by a disability.

Inclusion: The integration of all learners, including those with severe disabilities, into mainstream classes.

Individual Education Plan (IEP): This builds on the curriculum that a child with learning difficulties or disabilities is following and is designed to set out the strategies being used to meet each child's identified needs.

Insight: The ability to deal effectively with novel situations.

Intellectual disabilities: Significantly below-average intellectual and adaptive social behaviour, evident before age 18.

Intelligence: Ability or abilities to acquire and use knowledge for solving problems and adapting to the world.

Intelligence quotient (IQ): Score comparing mental and chronological ages.

Language disorders: A marked deficit in the ability to understand and express language.

Learned helplessness: The expectation, based on previous experiences with a lack of control, that all one's efforts will lead to failure.

Learning difficulty disability: Problem with acquisition and use of language; may show up as difficulty with reading, writing, reasoning and mathematics.

Learning preferences: Preferred ways of studying and learning, such as using pictures instead of text, working with other people versus alone, learning in structured or in unstructured situations, and so on.

Learning styles: Characteristic approaches to learning and studying.

Mental age: In intelligence testing, a score based on average abilities for that age group.

Spasticity: Overly tight or tense muscles, characteristic of some forms of cerebral palsy.

Speech disorder: Inability to produce sounds effectively for speaking.

Streaming or between-class ability grouping: System of grouping in which learners are assigned to classes based on their measured ability or their achievements.

Tacit knowledge: Knowing how rather than knowing that – knowledge that is more likely to be learned during everyday life than through formal schooling.

Theory of multiple intelligences: In Gardner's theory of intelligence, a person's eight separate abilities: logical-mathematical, linguistic, musical, spatial, bodily-kinesthetic, interpersonal, intrapersonal and naturalist.

Triarchic theory of successful intelligence: A three-part description of the mental abilities (thinking processes, coping with new experiences and adapting to context) that lead to more or less intelligent behaviour.

Voicing problems: Inappropriate pitch, quality, loudness and intonation.

Within-class ability grouping: System of grouping in which learners in a class are divided into two or three groups based on ability in an attempt to accommodate individual differences.

CHECK YOUR LEARNING!

WEB

In the Classroom: What Would They Do?

This chapter opens with a situation involving a teacher working with a class (including a child with impaired hearing, two pupils who speak very little English and a pupil with severe learning difficulties) that would challenge even the most seasoned teacher.

Here are some comments from two women working with children about ways in which such challenges are met within UK schools.

Maxine, teaching assistant in a rural primary school, Northern England, Year 1 (five- and six-year-olds)

I work with the children who have been found to have the poorest literacy scores as a result of their assessments when they entered Year 1 (aged five).

Every day I spend 20 minutes working with groups of six children, giving them literacy support. These children do not have SEN statements but they are not secure in reading and writing strategies. We spend time sounding out phonics, looking at cvc (consonant, vowel, consonant) words like 'cat' 'boy' 'dog' and so on and we also look at words with difficult sounds like 'said'. I use practical games to help them learn, such as holding up picture cards and identifying which words have the 'o' sounds – then we put the words that have the 'o' in the treasure chest and those that don't in the bin.

I find that their confidence increases as a result of small group work and they are usually ready to return to class literacy lessons after 12 weeks (one term). If not they stay longer – we don't force them back before they are ready.

Elizabeth, SENCO in suburban primary school, East Midlands

As a SENCO (Special Educational Needs Co-ordinator) I work with class teachers and advise on the provision for children with SEN state-ments. This year, at Easter, a seven-year-old girl, Tara, entered Year 2 at our school. She had a SEN statement and had been classified as displaying 'selective mutism'.

Her assessment had included a range of professionals (such as an educational psychologist and an occupational therapist) and she had been found to have no physical reason for her not speaking but she seemed unable to do so outside of her home.

When she first came to us she was not toilet trained, not eating well and of course, not talking. We were told that she had undergone major heart surgery as an infant and it seemed that her parents had 'babied' her since then. This explained her immature behaviour to some extent and you could see that her parents had overprotected her because they were afraid of her becoming ill again.

Despite her lack of physical skills, Tara was very bright (we found out that both of her parents were teachers) and had an appropriate reading age. It was her lack of gross and fine motor skills which stopped her being able to write. We worked on an IEP for Tara and she had lots of one-to-one work with three TAs including a link TA from the Nursery class. She has come on well and has started to talk to this TA but we are worried about her transfer to a different Junior school in September. Her parents have taken this decision although we have advised against it.

Overview

The cultural composition of classrooms is changing. This change is not confined to one country but a phenomenon replicated throughout much of the developed world. Nigel Grant in his comparative examination of multicultural education asserted that:

Europe is a multicultural entity by definition. Unless we can educate children and adults to value their own cultures and those of others and sensitise them to the unavoidable pluralism that we all live in now, a fearsomely difficult task, the alternative is terrifying to contemplate. (1997: 11)

Multicultural issues, therefore, have profound implications for the schooling of majority as well as minority groups. (1997: 21)

In this chapter, we examine something of the many cultures that form the fabric of our society. We begin by tracing schools' responses to different ethnic and cultural groups and consider the concept of multicultural education. With a broad conception of culture as a basis, we then examine three important dimensions of every pupil's identity: social class, ethnicity and gender. Then, we turn to a consideration of language and bilingual education. The last section of the chapter presents three general principles for teaching every student.

By the time you have completed this chapter, you should be able to answer the following questions:

- **What is the difference between assimilation, integration and multiculturalism?**
- **What is culture and what groups make up your own cultural identity?**
- **Why does the school achievement of low-income pupils often fall below that of middle- and upper-income pupils?**
- **What are some examples of conflicts and compatibilities between home and school cultures?**
- **What is the school's role in the development of gender differences?**
- **What is effective teaching in bilingual or multilingual classrooms?**
- **What are examples of culturally relevant pedagogy that fit the classes and subjects you teach?**
- **How can teachers create a 'resilient classroom'?**

In the Classroom

Classes in a local school include pupils from a wide variety of cultural and ethnic backgrounds. However, civil unrest in another country has provoked an influx of 'asylum seekers' to the school's catchment area. These new pupils seem to stick together and rarely make friends with others. Indeed pupils in classes are not mixing together as well as they did. When teachers ask people to select partners for projects, the divisions are usually on ethnic lines. Sometimes, insults are exchanged between the groups and the atmosphere in the classrooms is getting tense. Often pupils communicate in a native language – one teachers don't understand – and some staff assume that the joke is on them because of the looks and laughs directed their way.

What is the real problem here? How should the teachers handle the situation? How would staff teach classes to help the pupils feel more comfortable with each other? What are the first goals in working on this problem? How relevant is the age of the pupils in the class?

Group Activity

With four or five other members of your group, brainstorm as many reasonable ways as you can to address this situation. Come to a consensus on the two best solutions and present them to the group, with your rationale for why these are good choices.

Today's Diverse Classrooms

Who are the pupils in our classrooms today? Here are a few statistics about child poverty drawn from leading UK charities working with children, for example the End Child Poverty campaign (http://www.ecpc.org.uk/keyfacts.asp), the UK national statistics office and the European Commission Eurostat website:

- 3.5 million (28%) children are living in poverty in the UK – people living on or below 60% median income after housing costs.

- The UK has one of the worst rates of child poverty in the industrialised world. Figures for 2004 show 20% of children under 16 years of age in the European Union (25 countries) lived in poverty.

- In 2006, 9.5% of children living in the European Union (25 countries) lived in households where no-one works. The figure for the UK is 16.2%, the highest of all the European countries.

- One in three poor children in the UK do not have three meals a day; miss out on toys, school trips and out of school activities; and lack adequate clothing, particularly shoes and winter coats.

- Children aged up to 14 from unskilled UK families are five times more likely to die in an accident than children from professional families, and 15 times more likely to die in a fire at home.

- In 2004/5, 13.7% of pupils in state nursery and primary schools and 14.4% in secondary schools were eligible for free school meals (a common indicator in Britain of low-income families).

- Over the past decade, the number of ethnic minorities in Denmark has increased rapidly, now accounting for over 8% of the total population (Colding, Hummelgaard and Husted, 2005).

- 'In 2006, 21% of the maintained primary school population and 17% of the maintained secondary school population in England were classified as belonging to a minority ethnic group.' (DfES, 2006: 5)

- 'Minority ethnic pupils are more likely to experience deprivation than White British pupils, especially Pakistani, Bangladeshi, Black African and Black Caribbean pupils. For example, 70% of Bangladeshi pupils and almost 60% of Pakistani and Black African pupils live in the 20% most deprived postcode areas, compared to less than 20% of White British pupils.' (DfES, 2006: 5)

In this chapter there are many references to families and children living in poverty. We recognise the differences between characteristics of poverty in the developed world and developing world, and that the term 'poverty' is relative to the geographical context. Over a third of all children in developing countries – 674 million children – live in absolute poverty. Around 23% of the global population currently live in extreme poverty (Flaherty *et al.*, 2004). Furthermore, we recognise that contrasts in the use of relative terms of poverty are the differences between poor nutrition and a daily battle with starvation, between little disposable income and survival, between socio-economic aspiration and hopelessness. We will continue to accept the definition of poverty as income below 60% of the median family income after housing costs but only in the context of the developed world.

Connect and Extend

To discover to what extent the levels of Dutch language and literacy of minority children in The Netherlands differ from that of native Dutch children upon entrance to primary school, read Stoep, J. and Verhoeven, L. (2000), 'Family and classroom predictors of children's early language and literacy development', *National Reading Conference Yearbook*, 49, pp. 209–221.

Pupils in UK classrooms are increasingly diverse in race, ethnicity, language and economic level, and teachers too are more diverse. In January 2005, 9% of teachers in England were recorded in minority ethnic (non-white) groups (DfES, 2005a and DfES, 2005b). In the London region 40% of teachers were from minority ethnic groups (DfES, 2006) teaching pupil population proportions of 50–70% and over, from minority ethnic groups. No case is made here that white teachers cannot effectively teach diverse groups of pupils, rather that it is important for all teachers to better understand and work effectively with all their pupils.

Individuals, groups and society

Since the beginning of the 20th century, a flow of immigrants has entered the UK, Western Europe, Canada, Australia, the US, and many other developed countries. Many immigrants left their homelands to escape famine and abject poverty, or to seek safety from war, disaster and oppression. These new immigrants were expected to assimilate – that is, to enter the cultural melting pot and become like those who had arrived earlier. For years, the goal of schools was to be the fire under the melting pot. New immigrant children who spoke different languages and had diverse religious and cultural heritages were expected to come to the schools, to master English and learn to become mainstream citizens. Of course, schooling was designed to prepare all children to contribute to a developing technological society and specifically to prepare children from middle and higher income families for entry to the professions through an expansion in higher education. Immigrant children rather than the schools were expected to do the adapting and changing, and so gain access to mainstream citizenship.

Tariq Modood in his response to the London bombings of 7 July 2005, and in defence of a developing 'multicultural Britishness', makes a useful distinction between:

- 'assimilation' where the preferred result is one where newcomers 'become as much like their new compatriots as possible';

- 'integration' where members of the majority community as well as immigrants and ethnic minorities are required to become more like each other; and

- multiculturalism where processes of integration work differently for different groups.

In the 1960s and 1970s, some educators suggested that coloured children and children from low-income backgrounds had problems in school because they were 'culturally disadvantaged' or 'culturally handicapped'. From these suggestions developed a cultural deficit model, a model which attempts to explain the school achievement problems of ethnic minority pupils. Indeed, some writers have explored the notion of cultural disadvantage to readiness for schooling (Brooker, 2003; Grimley and Bennett, 2000).

The assumption of this cultural deficit model is that the children's home culture is inferior because it had not prepared them to fit into the schools. Today, educational psychologists and social psychologists reject the idea of cultural deficits. They believe that no culture is deficient, but rather that they wish to explore incompatibilities between the pupil's home culture and the expectations of the school (Lemmer, 2002; Gregory *et al.*, 2001; Blackledge, 1993).

We also begin to explore how the parents' traditions, cultures and values correspond to or conflict with the expectations of their children's schools particularly in relation to home-school relations. (Crozier, 2003: 1)

Melting pot

A metaphor for the absorption and assimilation of immigrants into the mainstream of society so that ethnic differences vanish.

Connect and Extend

'Multiculturalism can be defined as the challenging, the dismantling, the remaking of public identities in order to achieve an equality of citizenship' Tariq Modood (2005) in 'Remaking multiculturalism after 7/7' accessed at www.openDemocracy.net. Web-search for ways in which global writers have sought to frame ideas of multiculturalism in response to current serious national and international events.

Cultural deficit model

A model that explains the school achievement problems of ethnic minority pupils by assuming that their culture is inadequate and does not prepare them to succeed in school.

↹ Connect and Extend

Read Iris Andriessen, Karen Phalet, Willy Lens, 'Future goal setting, task motivation and learning of minority and non-minority students in Dutch schools', *British Journal of Educational Psychology, 76*(4), (December 2006), pp. 827–850.

Also during the 1960s and 1970s, there was growing concern for civil and human rights in Western developed nation states and an increasing sense among many ethnic groups in those countries that they did not want to assimilate completely into mainstream society. Rather, members of ethnic groups wanted to maintain their culture and identity while still being a respected part of the larger society. Multiculturalism was the goal.

Multicultural education

Multicultural education is:

the transferring of the recognition of our culturally pluralistic society into our educational system. Furthermore, multicultural education is the operationalisation of the education system in such a fashion that it appropriately and in a rightful manner includes all racial and cultural groups in a process which guides the total education enterprise. (Lemmer and Squelch, 1993: 3)

Multicultural education

Education that promotes equity in the schooling of all pupils.

It is also one response to the increasing diversity of the school population as well as to the growing demand for equity for all groups. An examination of the alternative approaches to multicultural education is beyond the scope of an educational psychology text, but be aware that there is no general agreement about the 'best' approach.

James Banks (2002) suggests that multicultural education has five dimensions, as shown in Figure 5.1. Many people are familiar only with the dimension of *content*

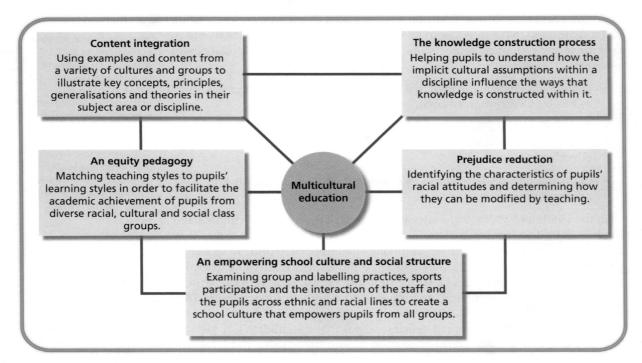

Figure 5.1
Banks's dimensions of multicultural education

Multicultural education is more than a change in curriculum. To make education appropriate for all pupils, we must consider other dimensions as well. The way the athletics and counselling programmes are structured, the teaching method used, lessons about prejudice, perspectives on knowledge – these and many more elements contribute to true multicultural education.

Source: From *Cultural Diversity and Education: Foundations, Curriculum, and Teaching* (5th ed.) by J. A. Banks. Published by Allyn and Bacon, Boston, MA. Copyright © 2006 by Pearson Education.

integration, using examples and content from a variety of cultures when teaching a subject. Because they believe that multicultural education is simply a change in curriculum, some teachers assume that it is irrelevant for subjects such as science and mathematics. But if you consider the other four dimensions – helping pupils understand how knowledge is influenced by beliefs, reducing prejudice, creating social structures in schools that support learning and development for all pupils, and using teaching methods that reach all pupils – then you will see that this view of multicultural education is relevant to all subjects and all pupils.

Multicultural education rejects the idea of the melting pot and supports a society that values diversity – more a salad bowl of many contributions. Investigate a range of international contexts and writers, including Burtonwood, 2002; Blackledge, 2001a; Chitty, 1995; Garcia-Lopez and Sales-Ciges, 1998; Savickiené and Kalédaité, 2005; Lenga and Short, 2002; Haan and Elbers, 2004; Joshee, 2003; Jackson, 2002. Then, let's take a closer look at the differences that make up the mosaic of cultural diversity.

Cultural diversity

> ### STOP AND THINK
>
> Take a quick break from reading and turn on the television or radio. (Don't do this if you won't come back to reading until next week!) Find a channel with commercial advertisements and listen to five or ten commercials. For each one, is the voice or the character in the advert a male or a female, old or young, economically privileged or poor? Can you tell the character's ethnicity or race? Do a quick tally of how many instances you observe in each category. What does this 'snapshot' of evidence tell you about the mosaic of cultural diversity in your society.

In this text, as we take a broad interpretation of culture and multicultural education, so we will examine social class, race, ethnicity and gender as aspects of diversity. We begin with a look at the meaning of culture. Many people associate this concept with the 'cultural events' section of the newspaper – art galleries, museums, theatre, music, and so on. However, culture has a much broader meaning; it embraces the whole way of life of a group of people.

Culture and group membership

There are many definitions of culture. Most include the knowledge, skills, rules, traditions, beliefs and values that guide behaviour in a particular group of people as well as the art and artifacts produced and passed down to the next generation (Craig, 2003; Segall, 1984; Brown, 1953). The group creates a culture – a programme for living – and communicates the programme to new members. Groups can be defined along regional, ethnic, religious, racial, gender, social class or other lines. Each of us is a member of many groups, so we all are influenced by many different cultures. Sometimes, the influences are incompatible or even contradictory. For example, if you are a feminist but also a Roman Catholic, you may have trouble reconciling the two different cultures' beliefs about the ordination of women as priests. Your personal belief will be based, in part, on how strongly you identify with each group (Rivière, 2005; Bryant, 1997; Grant, 1997; Gupta and O'Brien-Friederichs, 1995).

There are many different cultures within every modern country. In the UK, children growing up in a small rural town in central Scotland are part of a cultural group that is very different from that of children in a large urban centre like Liverpool or Leeds. In

Culture

The knowledge, values, attitudes and traditions that guide the behaviour of a group of people and allow them to solve the problems of living in their environment.

Connect and Extend

Read the *Review of Educational Research*, Spring 2000, for a whole issue on cultural competence and teaching, and *Educational Leadership*, 60(4) (2003) for an entire issue on 'Equity and Opportunity'.

The Netherlands, pupils living in the leafy suburbs of The Hague certainly differ in a number of ways from pupils growing up in a Rotterdam apartment block or on a farm in Dokkum. Within the small towns in northern Netherlands, the son or daughter of a *kleine winkel* (small shop) owner grows up in a different culture from the child of a city doctor or dentist. Individuals of African, Asian, Hispanic, Arabic or European descents have distinctive histories and traditions. The experiences of males and females are different in most ethnic and economic groups yet everyone living within a particular country shares many common experiences and values, especially because of the influence of the mass media whilst other aspects of their lives are shaped by differing cultural backgrounds.

Cautions in interpreting cultural differences

Before we examine the bases for cultural differences, two notes of caution are necessary. First, we will consider social class, ethnicity and gender separately, because much of the available research focuses on just one of these variables. Of course, real children are not just Asian British, or middle class, or female; they are complex beings and members of many groups.

The second caution comes from James Banks (1993), who has written several books on multicultural education:

> *Although membership in a gender, racial, ethnic, social-class, or religious group can provide us with important clues about an individual's behavior, it cannot enable us to predict behavior. Membership in a particular group does not determine behavior but makes certain types of behavior more probable. (1993: 13–14)*

It is an understandable fault of many practitioners to consider the social roots of the learner as an indicator of future academic performance – 'That's all we can expect; just look at her home life!' – but there is a rich fund of thinking and writing that would challenge similar assumptions (Maqsud, 1993; Prosser *et al.*, 1979; Webster and Feiler, 1999; Hodkinson, 2004).

Keep this in mind as you read about characteristics of economically disadvantaged pupils, of Black British pupils or male pupils. The information we will examine reflects tendencies and probabilities. It does not tell you about specific pupils you will teach. For example, suppose a pupil consistently arrives late. It may be that they have a job before school or is part of a micro-society that sees no value in schooling. Perhaps they are responsible for getting younger siblings to school or care for a disabled parent, or even dread school because of bullying.

Economic and Social Class Differences

Even though most researchers would agree that social class is one of the most meaningful cultural dimensions in people's lives, those same researchers have great difficulty defining social class (Liu *et al.*, 2004; Heemskerk, 2005; Van-Galen, 2004; Rassool, 2004; Savage, 2003). Different terms are used – social class, socioeconomic status (SES), economic background, wealth, poverty or privilege. Some people consider only economic differences; others add considerations of power, influence, mobility, control over resources and prestige.

Social class and SES

In modern societies, levels of wealth, power and prestige are not always consistent. Some people – for instance, university professors – are members of professions that are reasonably high in terms of social status, but provide little wealth or power. Other people have political power even though they are not wealthy, or they may be members of the higher social set in a town, even though their family money is long gone. Most people are generally aware of their social class – that is, they perceive that some groups are above them in social class and some are below. They may even show a kind of 'classism' (like racism or sexism), believing that they are 'better' than members of lower social classes and avoiding association with them.

There is another way of thinking about class differences that is commonly used in research. Sociologists and psychologists combine variations in wealth, power, control over resources, and prestige into an index called socioeconomic status (SES). In contrast to social class, most people are not conscious of their SES designation as the SES index is usually ascribed to people by researchers. Using different formulas might lead to different results (Liu *et al.*, 2004) and no single variable, not even income, is an effective measure of SES. Whatever the process of ascribing a status to groups or individuals, most researchers identify four general levels of SES: upper, middle, working and lower classes. As you watched or listened to the commercials earlier in this chapter, how many people did you see who appeared to be lower SES? If you did spot any, what role did the person play? If you did not hear or see somebody from the lower class, would a fair assertion be that the lower class is also the 'hidden' class?

Demographic and social grade definitions enable the classification of people of different lifestyles for the purposes of market research and social commentary. One useful set of grade definitions in a UK context are provided by the National Readership Survey (UK) social grade definitions. The main characteristics of the social grade definitions are summarised in Table 5.1.

Socioeconomic status (SES)

Relative standing in the society based on income, power, background and prestige.

Table 5.1 Selected characteristics of different socioeconomic classes

	A Upper middle class	B Middle class	C1 Lower middle class	C2 Skilled working class	D Working class
% of residents in England and Wales (1)	8.4	18.6	9.4	14.1	20.8
Estimate of income (2)	over £50K	£30K–£50K	£20K–£30K	£15K–£30K	£7K–£15K
Occupation (3)	Higher managerial and professional occupations	Lower managerial and professional occupations	Own account workers, lower supervisory and technical occupations	Own account workers, skilled manual workers	Semi-routine and routine occupations

1. Percentage of residents aged 16–74 by national statistic socioeconomic classification for England and Wales 2003.
Source: Office for National Statistics, Clairmant Count, Nomis, www.nomisweb.co.uk, Crown Copyright 2003.
2. Based on Levels of pay by occupational major groups; United Kingdom; April 2006. Sources: Office for National Statistics, Patterns of Pay: results of the annual survey of hours and earnings 1997–2005 and *Economic and Labour Market Review, 1*(2), February 2007, Patterns of pay: results of ASHE, 1997 to 2006.
3. Based on Office for National Statistics, 'Standard Occupation Classification 2000'.
Notes: The table does not include upper class (family money or corporate/professional leaders), media/sports personalities, the homeless, destitute, state pensioners or full-time students. Some C2s earn £50K or more, e.g. self-employed plumbers; some C1s earn £100K, e.g. top performing sales people; some Bs earn £100K+, e.g. enterprising 'portfolio' workers who generate a number of sources of income.

Poverty and school achievement

Table 5.1 also shows the link between low-status employment and very low family incomes. About one in three Britons under the age of 18 lives in poverty, defined in 2004 by the British government Department of Work and Pensions as a weekly income of £253 for a couple with two children aged five and 11. That means about four million children. Poverty shapes children's development. The End Childhood Poverty Group key facts sheet published on the campaign website asserts:

> *Before reaching his or her second birthday, a child from a poorer family is already more likely to show a lower level of attainment than a child from a better-off family. By the age of six a less able child from a rich family is likely to have overtaken an able child born into a poor family. (ECPC, 2006: 2)*

The Programme for International Student Assessment (PISA)

PISA is a three-yearly survey of the knowledge and skills of 15-year-olds in the principal industrialised countries. It is the product of a collaboration between participating governments through the Organization for Economic Co-operation and Development (OECD).

According to the PISA report (UK), 2000 (nothing in PISA 2003 contradicts these findings) which relates to more than 82% of the pupil population in the UK, proficiency in reading, mathematics and science literacies is most closely associated with the following characteristics, in descending order of importance:

- having parents with high socioeconomic status occupations;
- attending an independent (private, fee-paying) school;
- attending a single-sex school;

Poor children are far more likely to under-perform at school and poverty during pre-school years appears to have the greatest negative impact

- speaking English at home;

- having parents with qualifications at upper secondary level or higher;

- being an only child or having only one sibling;

- being a girl;

- living with both natural parents.

So what, conversely, are the effects of low socioeconomic status that might explain the lower school achievement of pupils whose parents do not have these high socio-economic status occupations, cannot afford to send their children to private, single-sex schools and who do not speak English at home? Many factors maintain a cycle of poverty and low achievement – no one cause is to blame (Deacon, 2003). It is clear, however, that education is at the heart of what in 1999 the British government called the 'cycle of inequality'.

Childhood disadvantage frequently leads to low educational attainment, low educational attainment leads to low pay and low employment, which in turn leads to low income and denial of opportunity for the next generation (HM Treasury, 1999: 27).

So what part is played by poor healthcare for mother and child, dangerous or unhealthy environments, limited resources, family stress, interruptions in schooling, exposure to violence, overcrowding, homelessness, discrimination and low-paying jobs, to another generation born in poverty? Garcia (1991), Evans (2004), and McLoyd (1998) describe other possible explanations. Some of these scholars and commentators are American. This reflects the proper attention paid to generational continuities within American welfare debate and a revival of interest in the 'cycle of disadvantage' as one aspect of what Robert Walker has called the 'Americanisation' of the British welfare debate (1998: 32). Let's take a closer look at some other contributory causes of the cycle of poverty, deprivation and disadvantage.

Connect and Extend

Read Gena Merrett's article 'Higher standards, better schools for all – a critique: can market forces close the social and achievement gap?', *Improving Schools, 9*(2) (July 2006), pp. 93–97.

Health, environment and stress

Poor children breathe more polluted air and drink more contaminated water (Evans, 2004). Children who live in older houses with lead paint and lead-soldered pipes, which exist in many inner-city areas, have greater concentrations of lead in their blood. Poor children are at least twice as likely as non-poor children to suffer lead poisoning, which is associated with lower school achievement and long-term neurological impairment (McLoyd, 1998). Poor people experience serious deprivations and stress: lack of food; electricity, gas and water disconnections due to unpaid bills; crowded or substandard housing, or lack of a cooker or refrigerator. Stress creates violence and violence has serious physical and psychological effects (Madela and Poggenpoel, 1993). Families in poverty have less access to good prenatal and infant health care and nutrition. Girls who grow up in poverty are more likely to become mothers at a younger age (ECPC, 2006: 2). Over half of all adolescent mothers receive no prenatal care at all. Poor mothers and adolescent mothers are more likely to have premature babies, and prematurity is associated with many cognitive and learning problems. Children in poverty are more likely to be exposed to both legal drugs (nicotine, alcohol) and illegal drugs (cocaine, heroin) before birth. Children whose mothers take drugs during pregnancy can have problems with organisation, attention and language skills.

Connect and Extend

Read Madela and Poggenpoel (1993), 'The experience of a community characterised by violence: implications for nursing', *Journal of Advanced Nursing, 18*(5) (May), pp. 691–700 which explores the interrelation of poverty, stress and violence in South African townships. Explore this interrelation and the implications for pupils in an internet journal search defined by your own context.

Low expectations – low academic self-image

Because poor pupils may wear different clothes, speak in a dialect or be less familiar with books and school activities, teachers and other pupils may assume that these pupils are not as bright. Teachers may avoid asking poor pupils to answer questions or give ideas in whole-class interactive teaching to protect them from the embarrassment of giving answers from a different perspective or answers which 'show up' their lack of familiarity with 'middle-class' norms of behaviour. Thus, low expectations become institutionalised and the educational resources provided are inadequate (Timperley and Phillips, 2003). Ultimately, the children come to believe that they aren't very good at schoolwork (Elrich, 1994).

Low expectations, along with a lower-quality educational experience, can lead to a sense of helplessness, described in the previous chapter. That is, economically disadvantaged pupils (or any pupils who fail continually) may come to believe that doing well in school is impossible. Studies have indicated that dropout rates are higher for pupils from families of low socioeconomic status (Cooper *et al.*, 2003; Macrae *et al.*, 2003). Lamb (1994) reported the association of particular family backgrounds with school dropouts; for example, manual occupations, parents having no qualifications and low family income.

The children who drop out or are forced out of schooling lose out because they stop learning. This is true for both truants (those who absent themselves from school) and for excluded pupils (those who are temporarily or permanently excluded from the school by the head teacher or principal). Excluded pupils may receive three or four hours of home tuition each week, some may be able to attend a special centre (Meo and Parker, 2004) and some get nothing. Both truancy and exclusion are associated with a significantly higher likelihood of becoming a teenage parent, of being unemployed or homeless later in life, or of ending up in prison (Social Exclusion Unit, 1998).

Without qualifications, these pupils find few rewards awaiting them in the world of work. Many available jobs for those without qualifications barely pay a living wage. For example, if the head of a family of three works full time (37.5 hours a week) at the minimum wage, the family's income will still be below the poverty line. Parents of low SES are less likely to believe that school offers real opportunities for social and economic advancement for their children (Dandy and Nettelbeck, 2002). Low-SES children, particularly those who also encounter racial discrimination, become convinced that attending school is a waste of time and effort, and that any investment of time and effort should be made elsewhere (Cullingford, 1999).

Peer influences and resistance cultures

Some researchers have suggested that low-SES pupils may become part of a resistance culture. To members of this culture, success in school means selling out and trying to act 'middle class'. In order to maintain their identity and their status within the group, low-SES pupils must reject the behaviours that would make them successful in school: studying, cooperating with teachers and regular attendance (Vitaro *et al.*, 2001). Similar reactions have been noted for high-school pupils in Papua New Guinea (Woolfolk Hoy, Demerath and Pape, 2002). This is not to say that all low-SES pupils resist achievement. Adolescents whose parents value academic achievement tend to select friends who also share those values (Berndt and Keefe, 1995). We should not forget that some aspects of schooling – competitive grading, public reprimands, stressful testing and assignments, and repetitive work that is too hard or too easy – can encourage resistance in all pupils (Okagaki, 2001).

Connect and Extend

The concepts of teacher expectation effects and self-fulfilling prophecies are very important in a consideration of cultural differences in the classroom. These concepts are discussed fully in Chapter 13 (p. 601).

Connect and Extend

The concept of learned helplessness was discussed in Chapter 4 (pp. 154–155) as one explanation for the lower achievement of pupils with learning disabilities and will be discussed again in Chapter 10 (p. 464) as a factor influencing motivation.

Resistance culture

Group values and beliefs about refusing to adopt the behaviours and attitudes of the majority culture.

Streaming

Another explanation for the lower achievement of many low-SES pupils is that these pupils experience streaming in low-ability groups and therefore have a different academic experience; that is, they are actually taught differently (Venkatakrishnan and Dylan, 2003). Streaming is different from setting for particular lessons because in streaming the pupil is placed in the same (low) ability group for all subjects, irrespective of particular gifts, talents or needs.

A substantial literature (e.g. Gamoran, 1986 and 1987; Hargreaves,1967; Schwartz, 1981; Burgess, 1983; Page, 1984; Anyon, 1980) shows a tendency for teaching in lower-ability groups to be different to that provided for high-ability groups. Some differences are to be expected, such as a slower pace and smaller steps, but our concern is that instruction in low-ability groups is over simplified with more highly-structured written work. Tasks for higher-ability classes tend to include more critical thinking tasks and high-ability groups are also allowed more independence and choice, more opportunities are provided for discussion and pupils are allowed to take responsibility for their own work. Low streams tend to undertake work that is more tightly structured. There is a concentration on basic skills, work sheets and repetition with fewer opportunities for independent learning, discussion and activities that promote critique and creativity. Schwartz (1981) also found that when high-stream pupils gave incorrect answers, teachers required correct answers, while low-stream pupils' incorrect responses were ignored. Page (1984) suggested that streaming sets in motion a 'vicious cycle'. Based on past experience and a 'proven' set of stereotypes, teachers held low expectations for low-ability pupils. Perceiving these teachers' views in the learning tasks they were offered, the pupils lowered their self-image, in turn confirming the low teacher expectations.

Home environment and resources

Families in poverty seldom have access to high-quality preschool care for their young children. Research has shown that high quality preschool care enhances cognitive and social development (Duncan and Brooks-Gunn, 2000). Poor children are thought to read less (Feiler and Webster, 1999) and spend more time watching television (Tubbs *et al.*, 2005); they have less access to books (Picaroni, 2004), computers (Attewell and Battle, 1999) libraries, trips and museums (Evans, 2004). These home and neighbourhood resources seem to have the greatest impact on children's achievement when school is not in session – during the summer or before pupils enter school. For example, Davies and Kerry (1999) found that low-SES pupils lost ground during summer while the high-SES pupils continued to improve academically.

Again, not all low-income families lack resources. Many of these families provide rich learning environments for their children. When parents of any SES level support and encourage their children – by reading to them, providing books and educational toys, taking the children to the library, making time and space for learning – the children tend to become better, more enthusiastic readers (Morrow, 1983; Stainthorp and Hughes, 2000).

Ethnic and Racial Differences

Ethnicity is used to refer to groups that identify with each other culturally, with respect to religion, language, food, music, and so on. One might call this 'cultural ethnicity' (Cole, 2003: 964). We all have some mix of cultural ethnic heritage, whether our background is Italian, Jewish, Ukrainian, Chinese, Japanese, Pakistani, West Indian,

Streaming

Ability grouping for the whole school timetable and therefore to different academic experiences based on achievement.

Setting

Ability grouping for part of the school timetable or for a particular activity and therefore to different academic experiences based on achievement.

Connect and Extend

Related information on the effects of ability grouping and streaming appears in Chapter 4 (pp. 145–6).

Ethnicity

A cultural heritage shared by a group of people.

Race

A group of people who share common biological traits that are seen as self-defining by the people of the group.

Hungarian, German, African or Irish – to name only a few. Race, on the other hand, is a term with a long history in social discourse and subject to a good deal of definitional diversity. The word also forms the root of pejorative terms such as racism and racialist and so attempts at definitions of race have often proved to be controversial. Early racial theorising divided humans into three (white, black, yellow) or five (Caucasian, African, Australasian, American and Asian) biological races, supposedly differing in intellect and personality. In an attempt to place human racial traits within a more general evolutionary framework, Theodosius Dobzhansky (1937) applied the term race to a particular inbred population with specific genetic characteristics within a species, resulting from some form of separation that limited interbreeding.

However, when in the 1970s the study of genetics advanced to the point at which it was possible to quantify genetic differences between individuals and groups, it became increasingly clear that these so-called races were far from genetically homogeneous. Indeed, in 1972, the evolutionary geneticist Richard Lewontin pointed out that 85% of human genetic diversity occurred within rather than between populations, and only 6%–10% of diversity is associated with broadly defined races. What is clear is that the term race needs to be used with some care and Lewontin's conclusions are not without their critics, particularly amongst those with strongly held socio-political beliefs.

Minority group

A group of people who have been socially disadvantaged – not always a minority in actual numbers.

Sociologists sometimes use another term, minority group, to label a group of people that receives unequal or discriminatory treatment. Strictly speaking, however, the term refers to a numerical minority compared to the total population. Referring to particular racial or ethnic groups as 'minorities' is technically incorrect in some situations, because in certain places, such as some areas of inner London, Leeds, Birmingham, Bradford and Manchester where the 'minority' group – British Blacks, British Indians or Pakistanis or British Chinese – is actually the majority. This practice of referring to people as 'minorities' because of their racial or ethnic heritage has been criticised because it can be misleading.

Connect and Extend

See *Educational Psychologist*, Winter 2001. This entire issue is devoted to 'Schooling of Ethnic Minority Children and Youth'.

The changing demographics: cultural differences

In 2001, 4.9 million (8.3%) of the total population of the UK were born overseas. This is more than double the 2.1 million (4.2%) in 1951. Compared with the UK-born population, the foreign-born population has a greater mix of ethnic groups. While 92% of people born in the UK identified themselves as white in 2001, 53% (2.6 million) of the foreign-born population was white. The next largest ethnic groups for people born overseas were Indian (569,800) and Pakistani (336,400). (Census, April 1951, 1971, 1981, 1991 and 2001, Office for National Statistics.) Many cultures are represented in Britain and the range and variety of those cultures continues to increase as the enlarged European Union provides for rights of economic migration across much of the continent.

Ricardo Garcia (1991) compares culture to an iceberg. One-third of the iceberg is visible; the rest is hidden and unknown. The visible signs of culture, such as costumes and marriage traditions, reflect only a small portion of the differences among cultures. Many of the differences are 'below the surface'. They are implicit, unstated, even unconscious biases and beliefs (Slater, 2001; Noble and Watkins, 2003). Cultures differ in rules for conducting interpersonal relationships. For example, in some groups, listeners give a slight affirmative nod of the head and perhaps an occasional 'uh huh' to indicate they are listening carefully. Whereas members of other cultures listen without giving acknowledgment, or with eyes downcast, as a sign of respect. In some cultures, high-status individuals initiate conversations and ask the

Many cultures, races and ethnicities are represented in British classrooms and demographic changes are predicted to continue for many years to come

questions, and low-status individuals only respond. In other cultures, the pattern is reversed.

Cultural influences are widespread and pervasive. Some psychologists even suggest that culture defines intelligence. For example, physical grace is essential in Balinese social life, so the ability to master physical movements is a mark of intelligence in that culture. Manipulating words and numbers is important in Western societies, so in these cultures such skills are indicators of intelligence (Gardner and Hatch 1989, Gardner, 1983). But it would be wrong to assume that every member of a cultural group is identical in beliefs, actions or values. In the context of conflict and terrorism in the Iberian Peninsula, Flynn questions:

an assumption, central to the longevity of ethnic discord, that membership of one collective entity is uncompromisingly exclusive and unvariegated (2001: 704).

Cultural conflicts

The differences between cultures may be very obvious, such as holiday customs, or they may be very subtle, such as how to get your turn in conversations. The more subtle and unconscious the difference, the more difficult it is to change or even recognise (Holliday, 1999; Alleyne, 2002). Cultural conflicts are usually about below-the-surface differences, because when subtle cultural differences meet, misunderstandings are common. These conflicts can happen when the values and competencies of the dominant, mainstream culture are used to determine what is considered 'normal' or appropriate behaviour in schools. In these cases, children who have been socialised in a different culture may be perceived as acting inappropriately, not following the rules, or being rude and disrespectful.

In 1997, the Department of Education for Northern Ireland made the decision to mainstream Traveller children into secondary schools. Before then, Traveller children over 11 years of age were taught in a dedicated school for all Traveller children of school age. Reynolds, McCartan and Knipe (2003) report that cultural and lifestyle differences (14–16-year-olds were often married or engaged, and were expected to make significant economic contribution to the family) acted as a deterrent to consistent attendance at school:

> *there were significant linguistic and dialect differences between Traveller children and their settled counterparts. These became very obvious when Traveller children entered mainstream schools. The effect was to set Traveller children apart from others, making them appear as somehow different and in doing so making them targets of unwarranted teasing or verbal abuse. Furthermore, many of the parents and children cited this clash of cultures as a deterrent to consistent attendance accompanied as it often was by stereotypical attitudes, bullying of Traveller children and physical assaults (2003: 412).*

Cultural compatibility

Not all cultural differences lead to clashes in school, however. A study comparing mothers in the People's Republic of China, Chinese American mothers and Caucasian American mothers found dramatic differences in beliefs about motivation and the value of education (Hess, Chih-Mei and McDevitt, 1987). For example, the mothers from the Republic of China attributed school failure to lack of effort more often than the Caucasian American mothers. The Chinese American mothers were in the middle, attributing failure to lack of effort more often than the Caucasian American mothers, but less often than the Republic of China mothers.

This does not mean that all Chinese children are perfectly equipped for school, however. Children may perform well on tests and assignments, but feel uncomfortable in collaborative social learning situations, where subtle rules for interacting are not second nature to them (Yee, 1992). Later in this chapter, we will explore other ways to make classrooms compatible with the home cultures of pupils. First, however, we need to examine some of the effects of cultural conflicts and discrimination on student achievement.

Ethnic and racial differences in school achievement

A major concern in schools is that some ethnic groups consistently achieve below the average for all pupils (Uline and Johnson, 2005). This pattern of results tends to hold for all standardised achievement tests, but the gaps have been narrowing over the past two to three decades and in some cases have been turned around as you can see in Figure 5.2. The General Certificate of Secondary Education (GCSE) is taken by pupils in England and Wales at the academic age of 15 (the year in which they become 16). Opportunities for continuing formal schooling after this age is associated with gaining at least five passes at grades A* to C.

Figure 5.2 shows that Black Caribbean and Black Other boys are two of the lowest attaining groups at GCSE. Only a third of boys in these groups achieved 5 or more A* to C grades at GCSE and equivalent in 2005, compared to 50% of White British boys.

Although there are consistent differences among ethnic groups on tests of cognitive abilities, we would assert that these differences are mainly the legacy of discrimination, the product of cultural mismatches or a result of growing up in a low-SES environment. Because many pupils from minority groups are also economically disadvantaged, it is important to separate the effects of these two sets of influences on school achievement. When we compare pupils from different ethnic and racial groups who are all at the same SES level, then their achievement differences diminish (Andriessen and Phalet, 2002). For example, in an analysis of National Assessment of Educational Progress (NAEP) mathematics test results, James Byrnes (2003) found that less than 5% of the variance in maths test scores was associated with race, but about 50% of the variance

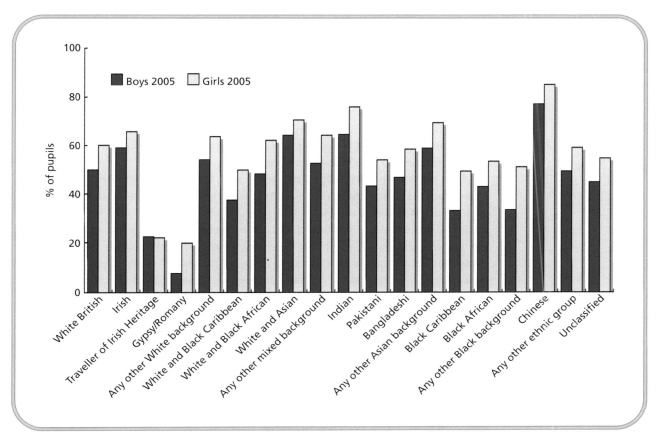

Figure 5.2
Proportion of pupils by ethnic group and gender achieving 5 or more A* to C GCSEs (and equivalent) in 2005.

Source: Department for Education and Skills (2006). Ethnicity and Education: the Evidence on Minority Ethnic Pupils aged 5–16. Research topic paper 0208-2006DOM-EN.

came from differences in SES, motivation and exposure to learning opportunities (coursework, calculator use, homework, etc.). Zsolnai (2002) concluded that parental motivation explained only 8% of the variance in subject grades, while the effect of teacher and peer motivation accounted only for 2%. Remarkably, 44% of the variance of intrinsic motivation (the key to success at school) is explained by importance of social factors of the personality in relation to learning motivation (e.g. self-image, conscientiousness and friendliness).

The legacy of discrimination

When we considered explanations for why low-SES pupils have trouble in school, we listed the low expectations and biases of teachers and fellow pupils. This has been the experience of many ethnic minority pupils as well. Imagine that the following (reported in a number of UK national newspapers in September 2004) is your story. How well would you have done at school?

Zoe's Story

My smart school still failed me: Zoe reveals the reality of education when your face doesn't fit

. . . It wasn't exactly racism. No one called me 'nigger'. But I can't remember anything we did about black history. The only black people we came across were in English Literature and they were slaves. No one taught me about Marcus Garvey. No one said 'you'll do great things'.

I don't come from a disadvantaged background. Nor do I fit any of the other stereotypes that commentators cite as the reasons for black children under-performing. My parents were keen to take an active role in my education. However, in the Eighties mentioning phrases such as 'positive racial identity' and the 'self-confidence of black children' was not welcomed by the staff at my school.

My mother soon earned a reputation as being 'difficult'. Talking with my parents now, we laugh about my early experiences. When it came to school plays, Nativity or otherwise, black children were either donkeys or devils. When my sister, who went to the school four years later, got to play a wise man in the Christmas play, it was considered ground-breaking by black parents at the school.

At secondary school I remember being made to stand in front of my English Literature class while an irate teacher shouted: 'Who do you think you are? You'll never amount to anything!' Those were pretty harsh words for a 13-year-old whose only crime was to forget her dictionary.

At 13, I was preparing to sit exams that would be used to decide which set I would be in for my GCSEs. I was predicted a very low grade for maths. My father, a former maths lecturer, was convinced that I could do much better and subjected me to hours of extra tuition after school.

When I received my results, my maths teacher told me I had got the highest mark possible. Yet she looked at me as if I had cheated.

When I was 14, my headmistress recommended to my parents that I repeat the year. Since primary school, I had been a year ahead, but my teachers at my secondary school seemed to think this was a mistake. They believed I wouldn't achieve five GCSE passes. The option of encouraging me to work harder or giving me extra help was never offered. Instead that role fell to my parents, who were adamant that I was more than capable of passing my exams without repeating the year.

With extra tuition from my father and family friends who were teachers, I achieved 10 GCSE passes all grade A* to C. While I was pleased to have done well, what gave me the greatest satisfaction was proving my teachers wrong.

The general lesson I learnt from my school years was that people's expectation of me were going to be zero and that I would have to prove myself and dispel their stereotyped views. Race is a problem in education as much as it is in any other part of life. Unfortunately, because school is an environment where children are subjected to the power of adults, the impact of any prejudice is much more intense.

Source: Extracts from 'My smart school still failed me' by Zoe Smith from *The Observer,* 12 September 2004, p. 18.

What is prejudice?

The word *prejudice* is closely related to the word *prejudge*. Prejudice is a rigid and irrational generalisation – a prejudgment – about an entire category of people. Prejudice is made up of beliefs, emotions and tendencies towards particular actions. For example, you are prejudiced against people who are overweight if you believe, amongst other things, that people are fat 'because they have no will power' or 'it's their own fault'. If you see fatness and the person as a single thing then for you, weight becomes an outward symbol of inner value (Crandall *et al.*, 2001).

Prejudice can be positive or negative; that is, you can have positive as well as negative irrational beliefs about a group, but the word usually refers to negative attitudes. Targets of prejudice can be based on race, ethnicity, religion, politics, geographic location, language, sexual orientation, gender or appearance.

Racial prejudice is pervasive and exists in Britain, in Europe, in the US and in the developed Southern Hemisphere nation states. We are not talking about a vulgar and antiquated racism, a belief that an 'out-group' is inferior, but rather a much more 'reasonable' yet insidious sentiment that newcomers or ethnic minority groups are different. In 2000, Colin Leach, Tim Peng and Julie Volckens reported on a survey of attitudes to different ethnic out-groups in France, the Netherlands, Western Germany and Britain. Results strongly confirmed that 'old racism' is alive and well in Western Europe despite the fact that respondents to the survey tended not to endorse such beliefs explicitly.

The development of prejudice

Two popular beliefs exist that young children are innocently colour-blind and that they will not develop biases unless their parents teach them to be prejudiced. Although these beliefs are appealing, they are not supported by research. Indeed, prejudice starts early. Drew Nesdale concludes (2001) that children's ethnic preferences are well established by six years of age and children may express racist statements towards ethnic out-groups by five years of age (Nesdale *et al.*, 2005).

One source of prejudice is the human tendency to divide the social world into two categories – *us* and *them*, or the *in-group* and the *out-group*. These divisions may be made on the basis of race, religion, sex, age, ethnicity or even sports team membership. We tend to see members of the out-group as inferior and different from us, but similar to each other – 'they all look alike' (Aboud, 2003; Lambert, 1995). Also, those who have more (more money, more social status, more prestige) may justify their privilege by assuming that they deserve to 'have' because they are superior to the 'have-nots'. This can lead to blaming the victims. People who live in poverty or women who are raped are seen as causing their problems by their behaviour – 'they got what they deserved'. Emotions play a part as well. When things go wrong, we look for someone or some whole group to blame. For example, after the tragic events of 9/11 in New York, some people vented their anger by attacking innocent Arab Americans (Myers, 2005), and after the London bombings there were 269 religious hate crimes in London during the three weeks following 7 July, compared with 40 in the same period of 2004 (BBC News, 2005).

But prejudice is more than a tendency to form in-groups, a self-justification or an emotional reaction – it is also a set of cultural values. Children learn about valued traits and characteristics from their families, friends, teachers and the world around them. Think back to your analysis of commercials – did you observe or hear many women or people of colour? For years, most of the models presented in books, films, television and advertising were middle-class and upper-class Europeans and European Americans. People of other ethnic and racial backgrounds were seldom the 'heroes' (Ward, 2004).

Prejudice

Prejudgment or irrational generalisation about an entire category of people.

STOP AND THINK

Have a break from reading and list three characteristics of first-year undergraduates, politicians, Buddhists, footballers' wives and members of a gun club. Compare your lists with others in your study group or on-line discussion forum. How do you explain the similarities in your lists and do they suggest some underlying prejudices in the social and professional groups to which you belong.

Prejudice is difficult to combat because it can be part of our thinking processes. You saw in Chapter 2 (p. 37) (if not then take a moment or two to consult the relevant section) that children develop *schemas* – organised bodies of knowledge – about objects, events and actions. We have schemas that organise our knowledge about people we know, the meaning of words, how to drink from a straw and all our daily activities. We can also form schemas about groups of people. When we asked you to list the traits most characteristic of first-year undergraduates, politicians, Buddhists, footballers' wives and members of a gun club you probably could generate a list. That list would show that you have a stereotype – a schema – that organises what you know (and believe) about the group (Vonk, 2002).

As with any schema, we use our stereotypes to make sense of the world. You will see in Chapter 7 (p. 310) that having a schema allows you to process information more quickly and efficiently, but it also allows you to distort information to make it fit your schema better (Macrae, Milne and Bodenhausen, 1994). This is the danger in racial and ethnic stereotypes. We notice information that confirms or agrees with our stereotype – our schema – and miss or dismiss information that does not fit. For example, if a juror has a negative stereotype of British Asians and is listening to evidence in the trial of a British Asian, the juror may interpret the evidence more negatively. The juror may actually forget testimony in favour of the defendant, and remember more damaging testimony instead. Information that fits the stereotype is even processed more quickly (Anderson, Klatzky and Murray, 1990).

Continuing discrimination

If prejudice consists of beliefs and feelings (usually negative) about an entire category of people, then a third element of prejudice is a tendency to act, called discrimination. Discrimination is unequal treatment of particular categories of people. Clearly, many people face prejudice and discrimination in subtle or blatant ways every day. One of the most discouraging findings we encountered whilst researching this chapter at the Office for National Statistics is that only 1.75% of the 3,941 existing top civil servants were British Blacks and Asians, only 3.3% of London's police officers are British Blacks and Asians; fewer than 1% of National Health Service organisations were led by Black or ethnic minority people, and that a lack of positive role models and entrenched stereotypes within the education system mean that British Black youths do not feel that science, technology and engineering offer a career option for them.

Stereotype

Schema that organises knowledge or perceptions about a category.

Discrimination

Treating or acting unfairly towards particular categories of people.

STOP AND THINK

Describe the possible effects of racial discrimination and bias on minority pupils. What can teachers and schools do to address the lingering effects of this discrimination?

Only 8% of Black British have university degrees and only 7% of British Pakistani/ Bangladeshis have degrees. Although some ethnic groups were more likely than the white population to have degrees, they were also more likely to have no qualifications at all. In particular, British Pakistani and Bangladeshis were most likely to be unqualified. Nearly half (48%) of British Bangladeshi women and 40% of British Bangladeshi men had no qualifications. Among British Pakistanis, 40% of women and 27% of men had no qualifications (Office for National Statistics, 2001/2) and unemployment rates for ethnic minority groups were up to five times higher than for White British.

In school, children from ethnic minorities are chosen less often for gifted classes and acceleration or enrichment programmes. They are more likely to be streamed into 'basic skills' classes. As they progress through secondary school or college their paths take them farther and farther out of the 'academic pipeline' that produces our scientists, mathematicians and engineers. If they do persist and become scientists or engineers, they, along with women, will still be paid less than white male employees for the same work (TUC, 2002).

There is another problem caused by stereotypes and prejudice that can undermine academic achievement – stereotype threat.

Stereotype threat

Stereotype threat 'is defined as the risk of confirming a negative stereotypic expectation about one's group' (Keller and Dauenheimer, 2003: 371). The basic idea is that when individuals are in situations in which a stereotype applies, they bear an extra emotional and cognitive burden. The burden is the possibility of confirming a stereotype of their own group, either in the eyes of others or in their own eyes. Thus, when girls are asked to solve complicated mathematics problems, for example, they are at risk of confirming widely held stereotypes that girls are inferior to boys in mathematics. Laurie O'Brien and Christian Crandall say it is not necessary that the individual even believes the stereotype. They continue:

> *For a person to experience stereotype threat, she or he need only to have knowledge that some people hold a negative stereotype about their group. This knowledge can make a person worried about being viewed stereotypically, even when she or he does not endorse the stereotype (2003: 782).*

What are the results of stereotype threat? Recent research provides answers that should interest all teachers.

Short-term effects: test performance

In the short run, the fear that you might confirm a negative stereotype can induce test anxiety and undermine performance. Jean-Claude Croizet and Gérard Després (at the Université Blaise Pascal, Clermont-Ferrand) tested a group of healthy science and psychology students using computer-mediated exercises of analytical intelligence. It was a widely held view amongst the students that the science students were more academically able than the students of psychology. (An idea at total variance to our observations over many years!) Half the students were told this was a test of their intellectual ability and the other half that it was a laboratory test not diagnostic of their ability. Results of the tests led Croizet *et al.* to observe:

> *Evidence is accumulating that stereotypic reputations of intellectual inferiority, which usually target ethnic group members and people from lower social classes, can undermine performance on intellectual testing beyond any actual differences in cognitive ability (2004: 721).*

Stereotype threat

The extra emotional and cognitive burden that your performance in an academic situation might confirm a stereotype that others hold about you.

Increases in mental load (and therefore undermined intellectual performance) were measured by monitoring heart rate variability. The results showed that the relevance to intellectual ability attached to the tests selectively affected group performance on standardised tests. Test instructions that mentioned intellectual ability had a disruptive effect on the performance of people targeted by a reputation of lower intelligence (the psychologists!). Under these conditions, their performance dropped and they underachieved in comparison to their peers. However, when the instructions accompanying an identical test did not mention ability evaluation, people who were reputed to be intellectually inferior showed improved performance.

All groups, not just minority-group pupils, can be susceptible to stereotype threat. The work of Croizet and his colleagues draws heavily upon other studies by other psychologists, particularly Joshua Aronson. In one study by Aronson, the subjects were white male college students who were very strong in mathematics. One group was told that the test they were taking would help experimenters determine why Asian students performed so much better than white students on that particular test. Another group just took the test. The group that faced the stereotype threat of confirming that 'Asians are better in maths' scored significantly lower on the test (Aronson *et al.*, 1999).

Why does stereotype threat affect test performance? One link is anxiety. Thomas Ford and his colleagues (2004) provide evidence in two studies that a coping sense of humour buffers women against the effects of stereotype threat on maths performance. Under stressful conditions of stereotype threat, women experienced less performance impairment to the extent that they were high in coping sense of humour. Furthermore, they suggested that a coping sense of humour buffers women from the effects of stereotype threat by predisposing them to experience less anxiety while taking a maths test. A good sense of humour meant less anxiety and less impairment to performance.

Long-term effects: dis-identification

As we will see in Chapter 10 (p. 465), pupils often develop self-defeating strategies to protect their self-esteem about academics. They withdraw, claim to not care, exert little effort, or even drop out of school – they psychologically disengage from success in the domain and claim 'maths is for nerds' or 'school is for losers'. Once pupils define academic attainment as 'uncool', it is unlikely they will exert the effort needed for real learning. There is some evidence that black male pupils are more likely than black female pupils and white pupils to *disidentify* with academic attainment – that is, to separate their sense of self-esteem from their academic achievement (Cokley, 2002). Other studies have questioned any straightforward connection between dis-identification and British ethnic communities.

Singh Ghuman (2002) makes it quite clear that South Asian young people in the UK (with the exception of Bangladeshis) are achieving as well as their white counterparts. Indeed, the rate of entry (particularly amongst girls) to universities is higher than that of whites. However, what emerges from the analysis is that there remain two main areas for concern; namely, the teaching of the mother tongue within the school curriculum and the entrenched negative attitudes (prejudice) of some teachers against South Asians. Another study found that African American adolescents who had strong Afrocentric beliefs also had higher achievement goals and self-esteem than adolescents who identified with the larger white culture (Spencer *et al.*, 2001). The message for teachers is to help all pupils see academic achievement as part of their ethnic, racial and gender identity.

Combating stereotype threat

Stereotypes are pervasive and difficult to change. Rather than wait for changes, it may be better to acknowledge that these images exist, at least in the eyes of many, and give pupils ways of coping (perhaps by appealing to their sense of humour!) with the stereotypes. In Chapter 10, we will further discuss test anxiety and how to overcome the negative effects of anxiety. Many of those strategies are also appropriate for helping pupils resist stereotype threat.

Self-belief is an important factor in pupils' achievement. Lucia Mason (2003) showed that pupils' self-belief in mathematics affected their performance disproportional to their abilities, that targeted interventions make a difference to personal attitudes and achievement, and that teachers have a remarkable influence on pupils' construction and deconstruction of their beliefs.

There is also evidence that self-suggestion can play an important role if targeted interventions are persuasive and authentic. Aronson (2002) demonstrated the powerful effects of changing beliefs about intelligence. African American and white undergraduates were asked to write letters to 'at-risk' middle-school pupils to encourage them to persist in school. Some of the undergraduates were given evidence that intelligence is *improvable* and encouraged to communicate this information to their pen pals. Others were given information about multiple intelligences, but not told that these multiple abilities can be improved. The middle-school pupils were not real, but the process of writing persuasive letters about improving intelligence proved powerful. The African American college pupils, and the white pupils to a lesser extent, who were encouraged to believe that intelligence can be improved had higher grade-point averages and reported greater enjoyment of and engagement in school when contacted at the end of the next school quarter. Thus, believing that intelligence can be improved might inoculate pupils against stereotype threat.

Girls and Boys: Differences in the Classroom

STOP AND THINK

Do you believe that boys and girls learn differently? What effect might this have upon different attainment, and what subjects pupils choose to study in school?

Whilst Anita Woolfolk (co-author of this book) was on a train journey, she was proof-reading this very page for a previous edition. The ticket inspector stopped beside her seat and said, 'I'm sorry, dear, for interrupting your homework, but do you have a ticket?' She had to smile at his (she is sure unintended) sexism. We doubt that he made the same comment to the man across the aisle who was writing on his legal pad. Like racial discrimination, messages of sexism can be subtle.

In this section, we examine the development of two related identities that can be the basis for discrimination – sexual identity and gender-role identity. We particularly focus on how men and women are socialised and the role of teachers in providing an equitable education for both sexes.

Sexual identity

The word *gender* usually refers to traits and behaviours that a particular culture judges to be appropriate for men and for women. In contrast, *sex* refers to biological differences (Deaux, 1993). Sexual identity includes gender identity, gender-role behaviours and sexual orientation (Patterson, 1995). *Gender identity* is a person's self-identification as male or female. *Gender-role behaviours* are those behaviours and characteristics that the culture associates with each gender, and *sexual orientation* involves the person's choice of a sexual partner. Relations among these three elements are complex. For example, a woman may identify herself as a female (gender-identity), but behave in ways that are not consistent with the gender role (play football), and may be heterosexual, bisexual or homosexual in her orientation. So sexual identity is a complicated construction of beliefs, attitudes and behaviours.

Sexual identity

A complex combination of beliefs and orientations about gender roles and sexual orientation.

Connect and Extend

Read Nicholas Addison (2005), 'Expressing the not-said: Art and design and the formation of sexual identities', *International Journal of Art and Design Education, 24*(1) (February), pp. 20–30.

Sexual orientation

During adolescence, about 8% of boys and 6% of girls report engaging in some same-sex activity or feeling strong attractions to same-sex individuals. Males are more likely than females to experiment with same-sex partners as adolescents, but females are more likely to experiment later, often in college. Fewer adolescents actually have a homosexual or bisexual orientation – about 4% of adolescents identify themselves as gay (males who chose male partners), lesbian (females who chose female partners) or bisexual (people who have partners of both sexes). This number increases to about 5% for adults (Johnson *et al.*, 2001).

Scientists debate the origins of homosexuality. Most of the research has been with men, so less is known about women. Evidence so far suggests that both biological and social factors are involved. For example, sexual orientation is more similar for identical twins than for fraternal twins, but not all identical twins have the same sexual orientation (Bailey and Pillard, 1991). They found that the concordance rate of homosexuality for genetically unrelated adoptive brothers was 11%, for non-twin biologic brothers about 9%, the rate for fraternal twins was 22% and for identical twins it was 52%.

There are quite a few models describing the development of sexual orientation. Most focus on how adolescents develop an identity as gay, lesbian or bisexual. Generally, the models include the following or similar stages (Yarhouse, 2001):

- *Feeling different* – Beginning around age six, the child may be less interested in the activities of other children who are the same sex. Some children may find this difference troubling and fear being 'found out'. Others do not experience these anxieties.

- *Feeling confused* – In adolescence, as they feel attractions for the same sex, pupils may be confused, upset, lonely, unsure of what to do. They may lack role models and try to change to activities and dating patterns that fit heterosexual stereotypes.

- *Acceptance* – As young adults, many of these youth sort through sexual orientation issues and identify themselves as gay, lesbian or bisexual. They may or may not make their sexual orientation public, but might share the information with a few friends.

The problem with phase models of identity development is that the identity achieved is assumed to be final. Actually, newer models emphasise that sexual orientation can be flexible, complex and multifaceted; it can change over the lifetime. For example, people

Table 5.2 Reaching out to help pupils struggling with sexual identity

These ideas come from the *Attic Speakers Bureau,* a programme of The Attic Youth Center, where trained peer educators reach out to youth and youth-service providers in schools, organisations and healthcare facilities.

Reaching out

If a lesbian, gay, bisexual or transgender youth or a youth questioning his or her own sexual orientation should come to you directly for assistance, remember the following simple, five-point plan:

- **LISTEN** It seems obvious, but the best thing that you can do in the beginning is allow that individual to vent and express what is going on in his or her life.
- **AFFIRM** Tell them, 'You are not alone.' This is crucial. A lot of l/g/b/t/q youth feel isolated and lack peers with whom they can discuss issues around sexual orientation. Letting them know that there are others dealing with the same issues is invaluable. This statement is also important because it does not involve a judgement call on your part.
- **REFER** You do not have to be the expert. A referral to someone who is trained to deal with these issues is a gift you are giving to that pupil, not a dismissal of responsibility.
- **ADDRESS** Deal with harassers – do not overlook issues of verbal or physical harassment around sexual orientation. It is important to create and maintain an environment where all youth feel comfortable and welcome.
- **FOLLOW-UP** Be sure to check with the individual to see if the situation has improved and if there is anything further you may be able to do.

There are also some things that you as an individual can do to better serve l/g/b/t/q youth and youth dealing with issues around sexual orientation:

- Work on your own personal comfort around issues of sexual orientation and sexuality.
- Get training on how to present information on sexual orientation effectively.
- Dispel myths around sexual orientation by knowing facts and sharing that information.
- Work on setting aside your own personal biases to better serve pupils dealing with issues around sexual orientation and sexuality.

Source: Adapted from Figure 3. Copyright © The Attic Youth Center and Carrie Jacobs, Ph.D. Reprinted with permission.

may have dated or married opposite-sex partners at one point in their lives, but have same-sex attractions or partners later in their lives, or vice versa (Garnets, 2002).

Table 5.2 provides advice on helping pupils struggling with their sexual identity.

Gender-role identity

Gender-role identity is the image each individual has of himself or herself as masculine or feminine in characteristics – a part of self-concept. Erikson and many other earlier psychologists thought that identifying your gender and accepting gender roles were straightforward; you simply realised that you were male or female and acted accordingly. But today, we know that some people experience conflicts about their gender identity. For example, transsexuals often report feeling trapped in the wrong body; they experience themselves as female, but their biological sex is male or vice versa (Yarhouse, 2001).

How do gender-role identities develop? As early as age two, children are aware of gender differences – they know whether they are girls or boys and that mummies

Gender-role identity

Beliefs about characteristics and behaviours associated with one sex as opposed to the other.

are girls and daddies are boys. It is likely that biology plays a role. Very early, hormones affect activity level and aggression, with boys tending to prefer active, rough, noisy play. By age four, children have a beginning sense of gender roles – they believe that some toys are for boys (trucks, for example) and some are for girls (dolls) and that some jobs are for girls (nurses) and others are for boys (police officers). The sense of gender roles is well established by the age of six (Skelton and Hall, 2001). Play styles lead young children to prefer same-sex play partners with similar styles, so by age four, children spend three times as much play time with same-sex playmates as with opposite-sex playmates; by age six, the ratio is 11 to one (Benenson, 1993; Maccoby, 1998). Of course, these are mean averages and individuals do not always fit the average. In addition, many other factors – social and cognitive – affect gender-role identity.

Parents and practitioners in early years settings are more likely to react positively to assertive behaviour on the part of their sons and emotional sensitivity in their daughters (Skelton and Hall, 2001; Fagot and Hagan, 1991). Through their interactions with family, peers, teachers and the environment in general, children begin to form gender schemas, or organised networks of knowledge about what it means to be male or female. Gender schemas help children make sense of the world and guide their behaviour (see Figure 5.3). So a young girl whose schema for 'girls' includes 'girls play with dolls and not with trucks' or 'girls can't be scientists' will pay attention to, remember and interact more with dolls than trucks, and she may avoid science activities (Liben and Signorella, 1993).

Gender schemas

Organised networks of knowledge about what it means to be male or female.

> ⬅➡ **Connect and Extend**
>
> For a lively debate on the terminology of gender and sex, see the March 1993 issue of *Psychological Science.*

Gender-role stereotyping in the early years settings

Different treatment of the sexes and gender-role stereotyping continue in early childhood. Researchers have found that boys are given more freedom to roam the neighbourhood, and they are not protected for as long a time as girls from potentially dangerous activities such as playing with sharp scissors or crossing the street alone. Parents quickly come to the aid of their daughters, but are more likely to insist that their sons handle problems themselves. Thus, independence and initiative seem to be encouraged more in boys than in girls (Soori and Bhopal, 2002; Fagot *et al.*, 1985).

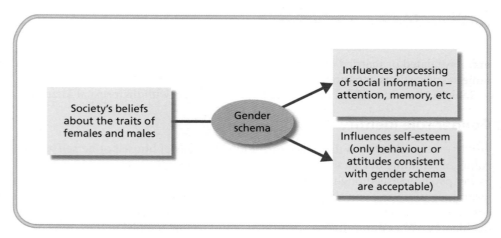

Figure 5.3
Gender schema theory

According to *gender schema theory,* children and adolescents use gender as an organising theme to classify and understand their perceptions about the world.

And then there are the toys! Walk through any store's toy section and see what is offered to girls and boys. Dolls and kitchen sets for girls and toy weapons for boys have been with us for decades, but what about even more subtle messages? Margot Mifflin went shopping for a toy for her four-year-old that was not gender-typed and found a farm set. Then she discovered that 'the farmer plugged into a round hole in the driver's seat of the tractor, but the mother – literally a square peg in a round hole – didn't' (Mifflin, 1999: 1). However, we cannot blame the toy makers alone because adults buying for children favour gender-typed toys and fathers tend to discourage young sons from playing with 'girls' toys (Brannon, 2002).

By age four or five, children have developed a gender schema that describes what clothes, games, toys, behaviours and careers are 'right' for boys and girls – and these ideas can be quite rigid (Skelton and Hall, 2001). Many of our student teachers are surprised when they hear young children talk about gender roles. Even in this era of great progress towards equal opportunity, an early years girl is more likely to tell you she wants to become a nurse than to say she wants to be an engineer. Early years children tend to have more stereotyped notions of sex roles than older children, and all ages seem to have more rigid and traditional ideas about male occupations than about what females do (Skelton and Hall, 2001).

Recognising gender schemas as potential barriers to success may allow children's choices to become less gender driven. For example, the 2002 film, *Bend it Like Beckham*, in which a teenage girl from a traditional Indian family aspires to succeed as a professional footballer, explores how society and different cultures define appropriate activities for girls and boys

Gender biases

Different views of males and females, often favouring one gender over the other.

Gender bias in the curriculum

During the primary school years children continue to learn about what it means to be male or female. Unfortunately, schools often foster these gender biases in a number of ways. Most of the textbooks produced for five- to eight-year-olds before 1970 portrayed both males and females in stereotyped roles. Publishers have now established guidelines to prevent these problems, but it still makes sense to check teaching materials for stereotypes. For example, even though children's books now have an equal number of males and females as central characters, there still are more males in the titles and the illustrations, and the characters (especially the boys) continue to behave in stereotypical ways. Boys are more aggressive and argumentative, and girls are more expressive and affectionate. Girl characters sometimes cross gender roles to be more active, but boy characters seldom show 'feminine' expressive traits (Evans and Davies, 2000). Videos, computer programs and testing materials also often feature boys more than girls (Schleiner, 2001).

Another 'text' that pupils read long before they arrive in your classroom is television. Remember the commercial count break we asked you to take earlier? (No – you can't take another one here.) A content analysis of television commercials found that white male characters were more prominent than any other group. Even when only the actor's voice could be heard, men were ten times more likely to narrate commercials. And the same pattern of men as the 'voice of authority' on television occurred in the UK, Europe, Australia and Asia. Women were more likely than men to be shown as dependent on men and often were depicted at home (Brannon, 2002). So, before and after going to school, pupils are likely to encounter texts that over-represent males.

STOP AND THINK

There has been much debate in the news media over possible gender bias in schools. What can a teacher do to reduce or eliminate gender bias and its effects?

Sex discrimination in classrooms

There has been quite a lot of research on teachers' treatment of male and female pupils. You should know, however, that most of these studies have focused on white pupils, so the results reported in this section hold mostly for white male and female pupils. One of the best-documented findings of the past 25 years is that teachers have more overall interactions and more negative interactions, but not more positive interactions with boys than with girls (Jones and Dindia, 2004). This is true from early years to post-18 education. Teachers ask more questions of males, give males more feedback (praise, criticism and correction), and give more specific and valuable comments to boys. As girls move through school, they have less and less to say. By the time pupils reach university, men are twice as likely to initiate comments as women (Sadker and Sadker, 1994). The effect of these differences is that from early years' settings to university, girls, on average, receive 1,800 fewer hours of attention and instruction than boys (Sadker, Sadker and Klein, 1991). Of course, these differences are not evenly distributed. Some boys, generally high-achieving white pupils, receive more than their share, whereas high-achieving girls receive the least teacher attention.

The imbalances of teacher attention given to boys and girls are particularly dramatic in maths and science classes. In one study, boys were questioned in science class 80% more often than girls (Baker, 1986). Teachers wait longer for boys to answer and give more detailed feedback to the boys (Bell, 2001; Sadker and Sadker, 1994). Boys also dominate the use of equipment in science labs, often dismantling the apparatus before the girls in the class have a chance to perform the experiments (Rennie and Parker, 1987).

Stereotypes are perpetuated in many ways, some obvious, some subtle. Boys with high scores on standardised maths tests are more likely to be put in a high-ability maths group than girls with the same scores. Parents, and teachers, often do not protest at all when a bright girl says she doesn't want to take any more maths or science courses, but will object when a boy of the same ability wants to forget about maths or science. More women than men are teachers, but men tend to be the senior school managers and teachers of advanced level maths and science. In these subtle ways, pupils' stereotyped expectations for themselves are reinforced (She, 2000; Renold, 2001).

Sex differences in mental abilities

Connect and Extend

See Latham, A. S. (1998), 'Gender differences on assessments', *Educational Leadership, 55*(4), pp. 88–89.

International comparisons in reading literacy for eight- and nine-year-olds (Mullis *et al.*, 2003) revealed that in 34 countries, boys scored below girls in reading literacy. Are these differences due to ability, interest, culture, social pressure, discrimination or something else? Let's see if we can make sense of this issue.

From infancy through the early years, most studies find few differences between boys and girls in overall mental and motor development or in specific abilities. During the school years and beyond, psychologists find no differences in general intelligence on the standard measures where tests have been designed and standardised to minimise sex differences. However, scores on some tests of specific abilities show sex differences. For example, throughout the years of compulsory schooling, girls score higher than boys on tests of reading and writing, and fewer girls require reading recovery programmes (Halpern, 2000; Fawcett *et al.*, 2001). However, academically gifted boys perform better than girls on mathematics tests. There also are more boys diagnosed with learning disabilities, ADHD and autism (Vardill and Calvert, 2000).

Data from a large sample of English 13- and 14-year-old pupils taking the national science tests in England and Wales were used to explore gender differences in science achievement (Preece *et al.*, 1999). The most pronounced gender differences, which were in favour of males, were found in the higher level papers taken by more able students, with the largest gender gaps occurring in physics questions and in 'more discriminating' questions.

In general, gender is the factor most directly associated with achievement regardless of ethnic background and findings of Feyisa Demie's (2001) study indicate that English girls outperform boys at seven, 11 and 16 across the school curriculum.

Diane Halpern summarises much of the current research:

Females and males show different average patterns of academic achievement and scores on cognitive ability tests. Females obtain higher grades in school, score much higher on tests of writing and content-area tests on which the questions are similar to material that was learned in school, attain a majority of college degrees, and are closing the gap in many careers that were traditionally male. By contrast, males score higher on standardised tests of mathematics and science that are not directly tied to their school curriculum, show a large advantage on visual spatial tests (especially those that involve judgments of velocity and navigation through three-dimensional space), and are much more knowledgeable about geography and politics (2004: 135).

In most studies of sex differences, race and socioeconomic status are not taken into account. In the Australian context 'underachieving' boys have tended to come from working class and/or indigenous backgrounds (Mills, 2000). British Black females (35%) outperform British Black males (23%) in gaining five or more A* to C grades at the General Certificate of Secondary Education (Demie, 2001). However, the results for British Indian females and males are almost identical (58.5% and 58.7% respectively), as are the results for British White pupils (40.2% and 40.5%). There is little or no difference in the performance of Asian American girls and boys in maths or science (Yee, 1992) but girls in general tend to get higher grades than boys in mathematics classes (Halpern, 2004).

Also, the 2003 'Programme for International Assessment of Students' (PISA) a comparative assessment of 15-year-olds in 41 countries, shows little sex differences in mathematics for half of the countries tested. In fact, in Iceland, girls significantly outperformed boys on all the maths tests, just as they usually do on their national maths exams (OECD, 2004).

What is the basis for the differences? The answers are complex. For example, males on average are better on tests that require mental rotation of a figure in space, prediction of the trajectories of moving objects, and navigating (there is a good deal of disagreement about the last of these amongst the authors of this book). Some researchers argue that evolution has favoured these skills in males (Geary, 1995 and 1999), but others relate these skills to males' more active play styles and to their participation in sports (Linn and Hyde, 1989; Newcombe and Baenninger, 1990; Stumpf, 1995). The cross-cultural comparisons suggest that much of the difference in mathematics scores comes from learning, not biology. Some studies reject the focus on male underperformance and suggest a systemic bias towards boys in our schools. Pertinently, Molly Warrington and Michael Younger contend:

that boys still dominate the classroom environment, that boys' laddish behaviour can have a negative effect on girls' learning, and that some teachers have lower expectations of girls and find boys more stimulating to teach. In short, the gender debate has been captured by those concerned predominantly with male underachievement, leaving girls to make the best they can in what often continues to be a male-dominated environment (2000: 493).

STOP AND THINK

What are the sources of possible miscommunication between pupils and teachers in the classroom because of cultural or gender differences? Identify steps a teacher can take to minimise such problems.

Eliminating gender bias

There is some evidence that teachers treat girls and boys differently in mathematics classes. For example, some primary school teachers spend more academic time with boys in maths and with girls in reading. In one study, high-school geometry teachers directed most of their questions to boys, even though the girls asked questions and volunteered answers more often. Several researchers have found that some teachers tend to accept wrong answers from girls, saying, in effect, 'Well, at least you tried.' But when boys give the wrong answer, the teachers are more likely to say, 'Try harder! You can figure this out.' It is female maths teachers who most consistently commit this blatant gender bias in favour of male pupils. These messages, repeated time and again, can convince girls that they just aren't cut out for mathematics (Horgan, 1995). Those of you with a particular interest in the experience of girls in mathematics classrooms should review the work of Jo Boaler (1994, 1997a, 1997b, 1997c, 1998; Boaler, William and Brown, 2000) and if you are like a few of the student teachers we have taught who 'really hate maths', please don't pass this attitude on to pupils. You may have been the victim of sex discrimination yourself. The Focus on Practice below provides additional ideas about avoiding sexism in teaching. Some are taken from Rop (1997/1998).

Connect and Extend

Read Sadker, D. (1998), 'Gender equity: Still knocking at the classroom door', *Educational Leadership, 56*(7), pp. 22–27.

FOCUS ON PRACTICE

Avoiding sexism in teaching

Textbooks and other materials used in schools should present an honest view of the options open to both males and females

Examples

1. Are both males and females portrayed in traditional and non-traditional roles at work, at leisure and at home?
2. School pupils are also subject to sex-role biases in other materials, for example magazine advertising, TV programmes, news reporting.

Unintended biases in classroom practices

Examples

1. Are pupils grouped by sex for certain activities? Is the grouping appropriate?
2. Is one sex or the other called on for certain answers, for example boys for maths and girls for poetry?

Schools sometimes limit the options open to male or female pupils

Examples

1. What advice is given to pupils in decisions about what subjects to take and future career directions?
2. Is there an appropriate sports programme available for both girls and boys?
3. Are girls encouraged to take advanced level courses in science and mathematics and boys in English and foreign languages?

Use gender-free language as much as possible

Examples
1. Do you speak of 'police officer' and 'postal worker' instead of 'policeman' and 'postman'?
2. Do you use the term 'chair' to head up a committee, instead of 'chairman'?

Provide role models

Examples
1. Recommend articles in professional journals written by female research scientists or mathematicians.
2. Have recent female graduates in science, maths, engineering or other technical fields come to class to talk about higher education.
3. Create electronic mentoring programmes for both male and female pupils to connect them with adults working in areas of interest to the pupils.

Make sure all pupils have a chance to do complex, technical work

Examples
1. Experiment with same-sex science groups so girls do not always end up as the secretaries and boys as the technicians.
2. Rotate jobs in groups or randomly allocate responsibilities.

Some authors have argued that boys and girls learn differently and that schools tend to reward the passive, cooperative behaviours of girls (Whitelaw *et al.*, 2000). For example, Maria Tsouroufli reports the comments of a teacher of English in a Greek secondary school.

> . . . *on a few occasions the English teacher seemed to be more lenient and helpful with girls because she believed that girls, being quieter than boys, should in a way be rewarded for their obedience.*
>
> *Margarita and Katerina do not participate in the lessons at all. But they are such quiet girls that I feel sorry for them. What am I going to do? I'm going to help them, give them better marks so that they can continue in the next year. [In Greek secondary schools, students who do not perform well have to repeat the year.] (2002: 142)*

Other people believe that schools shortchange girls and fail to be fair. Mills (2003) examines these issues.

In a review of the foregoing argument and research (for a further discussion check Salisbury *et al.*, 1999) there are, as yet, no totally convincing explanations of the phenomenon of gender bias, and therefore little hope of a universally effective strategy to deal with it. Yet we must make a better fist of dealing with gender bias in our schools and classrooms. Anything else is an affirmation of an unacceptable status quo, and teachers are rarely comfortable with that way of working.

DISCUSSION POINT

Do boys and girls learn differently?

As we have seen, there are a number of documented sex differences in mental abilities. Do these translate into different ways of learning and thus different needs in the classroom?

Agree: Yes, boys and girls learn differently

Since at least the 1960s, there have been questions about whether schools serve boys well. Accusations that schools were trying to destroy 'boys culture' and forcing 'feminine, frilly content' on boys caused some public concern (Connell, 1996). More recently, according to Connell:

> *Discrimination against girls has ended, the argument runs. Indeed, thanks to feminism, girls have special treatment and special programs. Now, what about the boys? It is boys who are slower to learn to read, more likely to drop out of school, more likely to be disciplined, more likely to be in programs for children with special needs. In school it is girls who are doing better, boys who are in trouble – and special programs for boys that are needed (1996: 207).*

In their book, *Boys and Girls Learn Differently*, Michael Gurian and Patricia Henley (2001) make a similar argument that boys and girls need different teaching approaches. Reviewing the book for The Men's Resource Network, J. Steven Svoboda (2001) writes:

> *Our schools seem to be creating overt depression in girls and covert depression in boys. Through violence, male hormones and brains cry out for a different school promoting closer bonding, smaller classes, more verbalisation, less male isolation, better discipline, and more attention to male learning styles. Most of all, boys need men in their schools (90% of primary school teachers are female). They need male teachers, male teaching assistants, male volunteers from the parents or grandparents, and older male pupils. Peer mentoring across age groups helps everybody involved.*

For girls, Gurian and Henley recommend developing their leadership abilities, encouraging girls to enjoy healthy competition, providing extra access to technology and helping them understand the impact of the media on their self-images.

Disagree: No, differences are too small or inconsistent to have educational implications

Many of Gurian and Henley's claims about sex differences in learning are based on sex differences in the brain. But John Bruer (1999) cautions that:

> *Although males are superior to females at mentally rotating objects, this seems to be the only spatial task for which psychologists have found such a difference.*

Moreover, when they do find gender differences, these differences tend to be very small. The scientific consensus among psychologists and neuroscientists who conduct these studies is that whatever gender differences exist may have interesting consequences for the scientific study of the brain, but they have no practical or instructional consequences (1999: 653–54).

In fact, there are boys who thrive in schools and boys who do not; girls who are strong in mathematics and girls who have difficulties; boys who excel in languages and those who do not. There is some evidence that the activities used to teach maths may make a difference for girls. Primary school-age girls may do better in maths if they learn in cooperative as opposed to competitive activities. Certainly, it makes sense to balance both cooperative and competitive approaches so that pupils who learn better each way have equal opportunities (Fennema and Peterson, 1988).

WHAT DO YOU THINK?
Agree or Disagree? Vote online at www.pearsoned.co.uk/woolfolkeuro.

Language Differences in the Classroom

Communication is at the heart of teaching and learning, but as we have seen in this chapter, culture and language differences affect communication within the classroom. In this section, we will examine two kinds of language differences – dialect differences and bilingualism (including host tongue as an additional language).

Dialects

A dialect is any variety of a language spoken by a particular group. Eugene Garcia defines a dialect as 'a regional variation of language characterised by distinct grammar, vocabulary, and pronunciation' (2002: 218). The dialect is part of the group's collective identity. Actually, every person reading this book speaks at least one dialect, maybe more, because there is no one absolute standard English. The English language has hundreds of different dialects and within each of these dialects are variations. Examples of dialects found in Britain can be heard at http://www.bbc.co.uk/voices.

Dialect
Rule-governed variation of a language spoken by a particular group.

A dialect continuum

Dialects differ in their rules about pronunciation, grammar and vocabulary, but it is important to remember that these differences are not errors. Each dialect is logical, complex, rule-governed and can be placed somewhere along a continuum of difference from the formal root language. In the case of English (for historical reasons the root language for many dialects around the world) one end of the continuum might included a group of 'languages' of the Caribbean, such as Jamaican Creole. Jamaican

Creole (JC) developed out of domination (English) and conquest (West African languages), under the requirements of European expansionism and the abominable trade of slavery. Studies of the use of a patois based on JC in urban communities (Bryan, 2004) show the use of dialect as a way of establishing and developing ethnic identities and dis-identification when young whites learn the patois of their friends.

Dis-identification

Recognition of a sub-persona of self-image, which may or may not be used according to social context.

At the other end of the dialect continuum is a variety of dialects that owe more to peculiar aspects of accent and a limited range of different construction than to significant differences to the root language. A good example is the kind of Liverpool 'Scouse' spoken by The Beatles. They certainly spoke with a different accent but there is also a different vocabulary and a variety of linguistic constructions in Scouse (Hughes and Trudgill, 1987). John Lennon's language was very recognisable as English but the differences with standard English went beyond pronunciation.

Another example of small changes to standard English is the use of the double negative. In many versions of English, the double negative construction, such as 'I don't know no difference,' is incorrect. But in many dialects such as some varieties of African Vernacular English, rural England English and in other languages (for instance, Russian, French, Spanish and Hungarian), the double negative is part of the grammatical rules. To say 'I don't want anything' in Spanish, you must literally say, 'I don't want nothing,' or 'No quiero nada.' Dialect is different to accent by itself. Accent uses the same grammar and vocabulary but pronounces parts of the words, particularly the vowels, in a markedly different manner. Dialect is different to accent but the line of difference is very blurred.

Dialects and pronunciation

Differences in pronunciation can lead to spelling problems. In some varieties of African Vernacular English and in South-Eastern British dialects, for instance, there is less attention paid to pronouncing final consonants, such as t. When endings are not pronounced, there are more *homonyms* (words that sound alike but have different meanings) in the pupil's speech than the unknowing teacher may expect; *spent* and *spend* might sound alike, for example. Even without the confusions caused by dialect differences, there are many homonyms in English (e.g. there, their and they're). Usually, special attention is given to words such as these when they come up in spelling lessons. If teachers are aware of the special homonyms in pupil dialects, they can teach these differences directly.

Dialects and teaching

Connect and Extend

Read Tim Parke and Rose Drury (2001), 'Language development at home and school: gains and losses in young bilinguals', *Early Years: An International Journal of Research and Development,* 21(2) (June), pp. 117–127.

What does all this mean for teachers? How can they cope with linguistic diversity in the classroom? First, they can be sensitive to their own possible negative stereotypes about children who speak a different dialect. Second, teachers can ensure comprehension by repeating instructions using different words and by asking pupils to paraphrase instructions or give examples.

What about the use of home dialect or 'language' in the classroom? The best teaching approach seems to be to focus on understanding the children and to accept their home dialect as a valid and correct system, but to teach the alternative forms of English (or whatever the dominant language is in your country) that are used in more formal work settings and writing, so that pupils will have access to a range of opportunities.

Code-switching

Successful switching between cultures in language, dialect or non-verbal behaviours to fit the situation.

Moving between two speech forms is called code-switching – something we all have learned to do. Sometimes, the code is formal speech for educational or professional communication and sometimes the code is informal for talk among friends and family or the codes are different dialects. An excellent example of what we are talking about is described by Lisa Delpit (1995). Martha Demientieff is a Native

Alaskan teacher of Athabaskan children in a small village. The teacher's goal is for her pupils to become fluent in both their dialects, which she calls 'Heritage English' and the 'Formal English' of employers and others outside the village. She explains to her pupils that people outside the village will judge them by the way they talk and write. She goes on to explain:

> We have to feel sorry for them because they have only one way to talk. We're going to learn two ways to say things. One will be our Heritage way. The other will be Formal English. Then when we go to get jobs, we'll be able to talk like those people who only know and can only listen to one way. Maybe after we get the jobs we can help them to learn how it feels to have another language, like ours, that feels so good. We'll talk like them when we have to, but we'll always know our way is best (Delpit, 1995: 41).

Learning the alternative versions of a language is easy for most children, as long as they have good models, clear instruction and opportunities for authentic practice.

Bilingualism

What does bilingualism mean?

There are disagreements about the meaning of *bilingualism*. Some definitions focus exclusively on a language-based meaning: bilingual people, or bilinguals, speak two languages. But this limited definition minimises the significant problems that bilingual pupils face. There is more to being bilingual than just speaking two languages. You must also be able to move back and forth between two cultures while still maintaining a sense of your own identity (Chawla, 2003; Blackledge, 2001b). Being bilingual and bicultural means mastering the knowledge necessary to communicate in two cultures as well as dealing with potential discrimination and as a teacher, you will have to help your pupils to learn all these skills. There are a number of misconceptions about becoming bilingual and Table 5.3 summarises a few of these taken from Brice (2002).

Bilingualism is a topic that sparks heated debates and touches many emotions. One reason is the changing demographics discussed earlier in this chapter. There is no official source giving a detailed breakdown of how many people in the UK have English as a second language or the ranking of community languages spoken in the UK. However, at least three million people living in the UK were born in countries where English is not the national language (CILT, 2006) and more than 30% of all London schoolchildren speak a language other than English at home (Baker and Eversley, 2000).

Three terms that you will see associated with bilingualism are English language learners (ELL), describing pupils whose primary or heritage language is not English, English as a Second Language (ESL classrooms, for example) and more recently, English as an Additional Language (EAL).

Becoming bilingual

Proficiency in a second language has two separate aspects: face-to-face communication (known as basic or contextualised language skills) and academic uses of language such as reading and doing grammar exercises (known as academic English) (Fillmore and Snow, 2000; Garcia, 2002). It takes pupils about two to three years in a good-quality teaching programme to be able to communicate face-to-face in a second language, but mastering academic language skills in the new language takes five to seven years (Collier, 1987). So pupils who seem in conversation to 'know' a second language may still have great difficulty with complex schoolwork in that language (Sowdon, 2003;

Bilingualism

Speaking two languages fluently.

English language learners (ELL)

Pupils whose primary or heritage language is not English.

English as a second language (ESL)

Designation for programmes and classes to teach English to pupils who are not native speakers of English.

Connect and Extend

Read Hedgcock, J. (2001), *Studies in Second Language Acquisition, 23*(1) (March), pp. 125–126.

English as an additional language (EAL)

Designation for programmes and classes to teach English to pupils who are not native speakers of English and may have other additional languages.

Table 5.3 Myths about bilingual pupils

In the following table, L1 means the original language and L2 means the second language.

Myth	Truth
Learning a second language (L2) takes little time and effort.	Learning English as a second language takes 2–3 years for oral and 5–7 years for academic language use.
All language skills (listening, speaking, reading, writing) transfer from L1 to L2.	Reading is the skill that transfers most readily.
Code-switching is an indication of a language disorder.	Code-switching indicates high-level language skills in both L1 and L2.
All bilinguals easily maintain both languages.	It takes great effort and attention to maintain high-level skills in both languages.
Children do not lose their first language.	Loss of L1 and underdevelopment of L2 are problems for second language learners (semilingual in L1 and L2).
Exposure to English is sufficient for L2 learning.	To learn L2, pupils need to have a reason to communicate, access to English speakers, interaction, support, feedback and time.
To learn English, pupils' parents need to speak only English at home.	Children need to use both languages in many contexts.
Reading in L1 is detrimental to learning English.	Literacy-rich environments in either L1 or L2 support development of necessary prereading skills.
Language disorders must be identified by tests in English.	Children must be tested in both L1 and L2 to determine language disorders.

Source: From *The Hispanic Child: Speech, Language, Culture and Education* by Alejandro E. Brice. Published by Allyn and Bacon, Boston, MA. Copyright © 2002 by Pearson Education.

Ovando, 1989). Here is how one international student, who went on to earn a doctoral degree and teach at a university, described her struggles with texts:

> I could not understand why I was doing so poorly. After all, my grammar and spelling were excellent. It took me a long time to realise that the way text is organised in English is considerably different from the way text is organised in a romance language, Spanish. The process involved a different set of rhetorical rules which were grounded in cultural ways of being. I had never heard of the thesis statement, organisational rules, cohesion, coherence, or other features of discourse (Sotillo, 2002: 280).

Because they may be struggling with academic English, even though they are very knowledgeable, bilingual pupils may be overlooked for gifted and talented programmes. The next section tells you how to avoid this situation.

Reaching every pupil: recognising giftedness in bilingual pupils

To identify gifted bilingual pupils, you can use a case study or portfolio approach in order to collect a variety of evidence, including interviews with parents and peers. You could also make use of informal assessments, samples of pupils' work and performances, pupil self-assessments and formal dynamic testing that takes account of cultural dissonance (Lidz and Macrine, 2001). This checklist from Castellano and Diaz (2002) is a useful guide and is not dissimilar to a number of other checklists for helping to identify gifted monolingual pupils. Watch for pupils who:

- learn English quickly;
- take risks in trying to communicate in English;
- practise English skills by themselves;
- initiate conversations with native English speakers;
- do not frustrate easily;
- are curious about new words or phrases and practise them;
- question word meanings. For example, 'How can a bat be an animal and also something you use to hit a ball?';
- look for similarities between words in their native language and English;
- are able to modify their language for less capable English speakers;
- use English to demonstrate leadership skills. For example, use English to resolve disagreements and to facilitate cooperative learning groups;
- prefer to work independently or with pupils whose level of English proficiency is higher than theirs;
- are able to express abstract verbal concepts with a limited English vocabulary;
- are able to use English in a creative way. For example, can make puns, poems, jokes, or tell original stories in English;
- become easily bored with routine tasks or drill work;
- have a great deal of curiosity;
- are persistent; stick to a task;
- are independent and self-sufficient;
- have a long attention span;
- become absorbed with self-selected problems, topics and issues;
- retain, easily recall and use new information;
- demonstrate social maturity, especially in the home or community.

Bilingual education

Virtually everyone agrees that all citizens should learn the official language of their country but when and how should instruction in that language begin? Here, the debate is bitter at times, but it is clear we have not solved the problem. For example, 'Spanish-speaking pupils – even when taught and tested in Spanish – still score at the [bottom] 32nd percentile in relation to a national comparison group (taught and tested in English)' (Goldenberg, 1996: 353).

Is it better to teach English language learners (ELL) to read first in their native language or should they begin reading instruction in English? Do ELL need some oral lessons in English before reading instruction can be effective? Should other subjects, such as mathematics and social studies, be taught in the primary (home) language until the children are fluent in English? Around these questions there forms two basic positions, which have given rise to two contrasting teaching approaches. The first focuses on making the *transition* to English as quickly as possible and the second attempts to *maintain* or improve the native language, and use the native language as the primary teaching language until English skills are more fully developed.

Proponents of the *transition* approach believe that English ought to be introduced as early as possible; they argue that valuable learning time is lost if pupils are taught in their native language. Most bilingual programmes today follow this line of thinking. Proponents of *native-language maintenance instruction*, however, raise four important issues (Armand *et al.*, 2004; Goldenberg, 1996). First, children who are forced to try to learn maths or science in an unfamiliar language are bound to have trouble. What if you had been forced to learn fractions or biology in a second language that you had studied for only a year or so? Some psychologists believe pupils taught by this approach may become semilingual; that is, they are not proficient in either language. Being semi-lingual may be one reason the dropout rate is so high for low-SES ethnic minority pupils (Halmari, 2005, Dostert, 2004).

Second, pupils may get the message that their home languages (and therefore, their families and cultures) are second class (Blackledge, 2001b; Heller, 1992). Third, the academic content (maths, science, history, etc.) that pupils are taught in their native language is learned – they do not forget the knowledge and skills when they are able to speak English.

Lastly is what Kenji Hakuta calls a 'paradoxical attitude of admiration and pride for school-attained bilingualism on the one hand and scorn and shame for home-brewed immigrant bilingualism on the other' (1986: 229). Ironically, by the time pupils have mastered academic English and let their home language deteriorate, they reach secondary school and are encouraged to learn a second language. A number of writers provide persuasive arguments that one goal of an educational system could be the development of *all pupils* as functional bilinguals (Errasti, 2003). In the UK, second language learning in schools is failing, with poor results at 16 and 18, and university language departments closing due to lack of student numbers. We suggest that many people in the developed English-speaking nation states are complacent about second language learning because English is commonly known to be the most widely spoken first or second global language. 'Surely somebody here must speak English!' is the mantra of mother tongue English speakers the world over. In this context, attempts to secure the 'development of all pupils as functional bilinguals' looks unlikely.

One approach to reaching this goal is to create classes that mix pupils who are learning a second language with pupils who are native speakers. The objective is for both groups to become fluent in both languages (Sheets, 2005). For truly effective bilingual education however, we will need many bilingual teachers. If you have any competence in another language, you might want to develop it fully for teaching.

Research on bilingual programmes

It is difficult to separate politics from practice in the debate about bilingual education. It is clear that high-quality bilingual education programmes can have positive results. Pupils improve in the subjects that were taught in their native language, in their mastery of English and in self-esteem as well (Hakuta and Gould, 1987; Wright and Taylor, 1995). English as a second language (ESL) programmes seem to have positive effects on reading comprehension (Koda, 1998). However, attention today is shifting

---

Semilingual

Not proficient in any language; speaking one or more languages inadequately.

Connect and Extend

Read Thomas, W. P. and Collier, V. P. (1998), 'Two languages are better than one', *Educational Leadership, 55*(4), pp. 23–27. This article makes the case that native and non-native speakers of English benefit greatly from learning together in two languages.

from debate about general approaches to a focus on effective teaching strategies. As you will see many times in this book effective teaching strategies include:

- a combination of clarity of learning goals and direct instruction in needed skills – including learning strategies and tactics;

- teacher- or peer-guided practice leading to independent practice;

- authentic and engaging tasks (including ICT);

- opportunities for interaction and conversation that are story focused; and

- warm encouragement from the teacher.

Refer to Chisholm, 1998; Robinson, 2001; Gersten, 1996; Ghson, 2002 for more detail about these strategies. Table 5.4 provides a set of constructs for promoting learning and language acquisition that capture many of these methods for effective teaching.

Table 5.4 Ideas for promoting learning and language acquisition

Effective teaching for pupils in bilingual and ESL classrooms combines many strategies – direct instruction, mediation, coaching, feedback, modelling, encouragement, challenge and authentic activities.

1. Structures, frameworks, scaffolds and strategies
   - Provide support to pupils by 'thinking aloud', building on and clarifying input of pupils
   - Use visual organisers, story maps or other aids to help pupils organise and relate information

2. Relevant background knowledge and key vocabulary concepts
   - Provide adequate background knowledge to pupils and informally assess whether pupils have background knowledge
   - Focus on key vocabulary words and use consistent language
   - Incorporate pupils primary language meaningfully

3. Mediation/feedback
   - Give feedback that focuses on meaning, not grammar, syntax or pronunciation
   - Give frequent and comprehensible feedback
   - Provide pupils with prompts or strategies
   - Ask questions that press pupils to clarify or expand on initial statements
   - Provide activities and tasks that pupils can complete

- Indicate to pupils when they are successful
- Assign activities that are reasonable, avoiding undue frustration
- Allow use of native language responses (when context is appropriate)
- Be sensitive to common problems in second language acquisition

4. Involvement
   - Ensure active involvement of all pupils, including low-performing pupils
   - Foster extended discourse

5. Challenge
   - Implicit (cognitive challenge, use of higher-order questions)
   - Explicit (high but reasonable expectations)

6. Respect for – and responsiveness to – cultural and personal diversity
   - Show respect for pupils as individuals, respond to things pupils say, show respect for culture and family, and possess knowledge of cultural diversity
   - Incorporate pupils' experiences into writing and language arts activities
   - Link content to pupils' lives and experiences to enhance understanding
   - View diversity as an asset, reject cultural deficit notions

---

Source: From 'Literacy instruction for language-minority students: The transition years' by R. Gersten, 1996, *The Elementary School Journal*, *96*, pp. 241–242. Copyright © 1996 by the University of Chicago Press. Adapted with permission.

We have dealt with a wide range of differences in this chapter. How can teachers provide an appropriate education for all their pupils? One answer is culturally responsive schools.

STOP AND THINK

Identify the major issues relating to the debate over bilingual education. Explain the major approaches to bilingual education, and describe steps that a teacher can take to promote the learning and language acquisition of non-English-speaking pupils.

Culturally responsive schools

Schools that provide culturally diverse pupils equitable access to the teaching-learning process.

Connect and Extend

Read Andrea Allard (2006), 'A bit of a chameleon act': a case study of one teacher's understandings of diversity', *European Journal of Teacher Education, 29*(3) (August), pp. 319–340.

Connect and Extend

Read Menkart, D. J. (1999). 'Deepening the meaning of heritage months', *Educational Leadership, 56*(7), pp. 19–21.

Culturally relevant pedagogy

Excellent teaching for pupils from ethnic minorities that includes academic success, developing/maintaining cultural competence, and developing a critical consciousness to challenge the status quo.

Creating Culturally Responsive Schools

Laurie Johnson (2003) uses the term 'culturally responsive' to describe schools that provide culturally diverse pupils with equitable access to the teaching–learning process. The goal of creating culturally responsive schools is to eliminate racism, sexism, classism and prejudice while adapting the content and methods of teaching to meet the needs of all pupils. In the past, discussions of teaching low-income pupils from racial, ethnic or language minority groups have focused on remedying problems or overcoming perceived deficits. However, thinking today emphasises teaching to the strengths and the 'resilience' of pupils. In the next section, we look at two approaches – culturally relevant pedagogy and fostering resilience.

Culturally relevant pedagogy

According to Geneva Gay, culturally relevant pedagogy is using 'the cultural knowledge, prior experiences, frames of references, and learning styles of ethnically diverse pupils to make learning encounters more relevant and effective for them. It teaches *to and through* the strengths of these pupils. It is culturally *validating and affirming*' (2000: 29). Smita Guha cautions us that 'Culturally responsive or culturally relevant teaching requires that teachers incorporate elements of students' culture in instruction, moving beyond cursory examples of food, festivals, and holidays' (2000: 16).

Several researchers have focused on teachers and teaching methods considered especially successful with pupils of colour and pupils in poverty (Stuart and Volk, 2002; Ladson-Billings, 1995; Le Roux, 2001, 2002; Johnson, 2003; Cairney, 2000). The work of Gloria Ladson-Billings (1990, 1992, 1995) is a good example. For three years, she studied excellent teachers in an African American community. In order to select the teachers, she asked parents and schools for nominations. Parents nominated teachers who respected them, created enthusiasm for learning in their children, and understood their children's need to operate successfully in two different worlds – the home community and the white world beyond. Schools nominated teachers who had few discipline problems, high attendance rates and high standardised test scores.

Based on her research, Ladson-Billings developed a conception of teaching excellence that encompasses, but also goes beyond, considerations of sociolinguistics or social organisations. She uses the term culturally relevant pedagogy to describe teaching that rests on three propositions. Pupils must:

1. **Experience academic success.** 'Despite the current social inequities and hostile classroom environments, pupils must develop their academic skills. The ways those skills are developed may vary, but all pupils need literacy, numeracy, technological, social, and political skills in order to be active participants in a democracy' (Ladson-Billings, 1995: 160).

2. **Develop/maintain their cultural competence.** As they become more academically skilled, pupils still retain their cultural competence. 'Culturally relevant teachers utilise pupils' culture as a vehicle for learning' (Ladson-Billings, 1995: 161). For example, one teacher used rap music to teach about literal and figurative meaning, rhyme, alliteration and onomatopoeia in poetry. Another brought in a community expert known for her sweet potato pies to work with pupils. Follow-up lessons included investigations of George Washington Carver's sweet potato research, numerical analyses of taste tests, marketing plans for selling pies and research on the educational preparation needed to become a chef. This approach goes far beyond cross-curricular opportunities but rather, espouses a celebration of cultures.

3. **Develop a critical consciousness to challenge the status quo.** In addition to developing academic skills while retaining cultural competence, excellent teachers help pupils 'develop a broader sociopolitical consciousness that allows them to critique the social norms, values, mores, and institutions that produce and maintain social inequities' (Ladson-Billings, 1995: 162). For example, in one school, pupils were upset that their textbooks were out of date. They mobilised to investigate the funding formulas that allowed middle-class pupils to have newer books, wrote letters to the newspaper editor to challenge these inequities and updated their texts with current information from other sources.

Connect and Extend

Read Midobuche, E. (1999), 'Respect in the classroom', *Educational Leadership, 56*(7), pp. 80–83. The story of the early school experiences of a Spanish-speaking child in an all-English world.

Johann Le Roux uses a South African context to explore what culturally responsive teaching entails. He argues it is a pro-active process that shows teachers appreciate the powerful variables (e.g. culture, ethnicity, gender, religion, SES and giftedness) in learning processes and that to empower learners, teachers must become culturally competent (Le Roux, 2001, 2002). Teachers who fail to appreciate and fail to be guided by different cultural habitual modes and norms are likened by Tamsyn Imison to 'seeing with one eye only' (DfEE, 1999: 50) and are, therefore, more likely to simply (and badly) transmit school knowledge rather than exploit diverse cultural resources in positive ways (Cairney, 2000).

Lisa Delpit (2003) describes three steps for teaching pupils of colour that are consistent with culturally relevant pedagogy:

1. Teachers must be convinced of the inherent intellectual capability, humanity and spiritual character of their pupils – they must believe in the children. There are many examples around of schools where low-income pupils are reading well above age levels and doing advanced maths. When results are poor, the fault is not in the pupils but in their education.

2. Teachers must fight the foolishness that high test scores or scripted lessons are evidence of good learning and good teaching. Delpit says that successful instruction is 'constant, rigorous, integrated across disciplines, connected to pupils' lived cultures, connected to their intellectual legacies, engaging, and designed for critical thinking and problem solving that is useful beyond the classroom' (2003: 18).

3. Teachers must learn who their pupils are and the legacies they bring. Pupils can then explore their own intellectual legacies and understand the important reasons for academic, social, physical and moral excellence – not just to 'get a job' but also 'for our community, for your ancestors, for your descendants' (2003: 19).

Fostering resilience

How many school-age children who have urgent needs for social and emotional support do not get help? Community and mental health services often don't reach the pupils who are at the highest risk. Yet many children at risk of academic failure not only survive – they thrive. They are resilient pupils. What can we learn from these pupils? What can teachers and schools do to encourage resilience?

Resilience

The ability to adapt successfully in spite of difficult circumstances and threats to development.

Resilient pupils

Some pupils who seem able to thrive in spite of serious challenges are actively engaged in school (Jackson and Martin, 1998). They have good interpersonal skills, confidence in their own ability to learn, positive attitudes towards school, pride in their ethnicity and high expectations (Borman and Overman, 2004; Lee, 2005). Also, pupils who have high intelligence or valued talents are more protected from risks. Being easy-going and optimistic is associated with resilience as well. It helps to have a warm relationship with a parent who has high expectations and supports learning by organising space and time at home for study. Even without such a parent, a strong bond with someone competent – a grandparent, aunt, uncle, teacher, mentor or other caring adult – can serve the same supportive function (Parry, 1997). Involvement in school, community or religious activities provides more connections to concerned adults and also teach lessons in social skills and leadership (Vitaro *et al.*, 1996; Berk, 2005).

In a study of two contrasting samples of 25-year-olds who had been brought up in care Jackson and Martin (1998) noted that there were more similarities than differences between their 'high achievers' group and a group 'who had not reached the threshold for inclusion in the study'. There were, however, a small number of variables that seemed to contribute to educational success and psychological well-being, including:

- receiving stability and continuity in care;
- learning to read early and fluently (one-third of the 'high achievers' group had learned to read by the age of four);
- receiving encouragement from parent/foster carer or other significant adult to go into further education;
- having friends outside care who did well at school;
- possessing high levels of internal locus of control and intrinsic motivation;
- meeting a significant adult who acted as a mentor and who offered consistent support and encouragement; and
- attending school regularly.

The convincing conclusion of Jackson and Martin was that 'educational success is a crucial factor in determining adult lifestyles and ensuring social inclusion for this most disadvantaged group of children. Instead of being a subsidiary consideration during placement decisions and case reviews, education should be clearly seen as a top priority' (1998: 581).

Resilient classrooms

You can't choose personalities for your pupils or choose parents for your pupils. Even if you could, problems happen for the most well-adjusted or even the most resilient pupils. Beth Doll and her colleagues suggest that we are in the business of changing classrooms instead of changing pupils because 'alternative strategies will be more enduring and most successful when they are integrated into naturally occurring systems of support [like schools] that surround children' (2005: 3). In addition, there is some evidence that changes in classrooms – such as reducing class size (Blatchford *et al.*, 2003) and forming supportive relationships with teachers (Pomeroy, 1999) have a greater impact on the academic achievement of pupils who are most at risk of disaffection and disassociation. So how can you create a classroom that supports resilience?

There are two strands of elements that bind pupils to their classroom community (see Figure 5.4). One strand emphasises the self-esteem (Stone, 2003), self-agency (Doll *et al.*, 2005) or self-evaluation (Sommer and Baumeister, 2002) of pupils – their capacity to set and pursue goals; the second strand emphasises caring and connected relationships in the classroom and the school (Marlowe, 2006; Forrester, 2005; Barber, 2002).

Self-Esteem/Self-Agency/Evaluation Strand

Academic self-efficacy, a belief in your own ability to learn, is one of the most consistent predictors of academic achievement. As you will see in Chapters 9 and 10, self-efficacy emerges when pupils tackle challenging, meaningful tasks with the support needed to be successful and observe other pupils doing the same thing. Accurate, timely and encouraging feedback from teachers also helps.

Behavioural self-control, or student self-regulation, is essential for a safe and orderly learning environment. Chapters 6, 9, and 12 will give you ideas for helping pupils develop self-regulation knowledge and skills.

Academic self-determination, making choices, setting goals and following through, is the third element in the self-agency strand. As you will see in Chapter 10, pupils who are self-determined are more motivated and committed to learning.

Relationship Strand

Caring teacher–pupil relationships are consistently associated with better school performance, especially for pupils who face serious challenges. We saw the power of caring teachers in Chapter 3 and will return to this theme in Chapter 11.

Effective peer relations, as we saw in Chapter 3, are also critical in connecting pupils to school.

Effective home–school relationships are the final element in building a caring, connected network for pupils. Actually these are about effective parent/ carer–teacher relationships as such associations form the nucleus of the partnership. Results reported by investigators (Stevenson and Baker, 1987; Song and Hattie, 1984; Campbell and Mandell, 1990; Georgiou, 1997) show significant correlation between parental involvement and child achievement. However, Stelios Georgiou (Ibid.) cautions us that only parental activities that are interpreted as supportive by the child are positively correlated to the child's performance. Activities, for example unsolicited homework (Solomon et al., 2002) that are perceived by the child as being 'undermining' help have the opposite effect.

Figure 5.4
The strands that bind pupils to the classroom community

FOCUS ON PRACTICE

Building learning communities

Joyce Epstein (1995) describes six types of family/school/community partnerships. The following guidelines are based on her six categories:

Parenting partnerships: help all families establish home environments to support children as pupils

Examples

1. Offer workshops, videos, courses, family literacy events and other information to help parents cope with parenting situations that they identify as important.
2. Establish family support programmes to assist with nutrition, health and social services.
3. Find ways to help families share information with the school about the child's cultural background, talents and needs – learn from the families.

Communication: design effective forms for school-to-home and home-to-school communication

Examples

1. Make sure communications fit the needs of families. Provide translations, visual support, large print – whatever is needed to make communication effective.
2. Visit families in their territory after gaining their permission. Don't expect family members to come to school until a trusting relationship is established.
3. Balance messages about problems with communications of accomplishments and positive information.

Volunteering: recruit and organise parent help and support

Examples

1. Do an annual survey to identify family talents, interests, times available and suggestions for improvements.
2. Establish a structure (telephone tree, e-mail, etc.) to keep all families informed. Make sure families without access to the internet are included.
3. If possible, set aside a room for volunteer meetings and projects.

Learning at home: provide information and ideas for families about how to help children with homework.

Examples

1. Provide a homework diary, homework policies and tips on how to help with schoolwork without 'doing' the work.
2. Get family input into choosing classroom resources.
3. Send home activity folders full of enjoyable learning activities, especially over school holidays.

Decision-making partnerships: include families in school decisions, developing family and community leaders and representatives

Examples

1. Create family advisory committees for the school with parent representatives, including parent governors.
2. Make sure all families are in a network with their parent governor representative.

Community partnerships: Identify and integrate resources and services from the community to strengthen school programmes, family practices and pupil learning and development

Examples

1. Have pupils and parents research existing resources – build a database.
2. Identify voluntary service projects for pupils.
3. Identify community members who are past pupils and get them involved in school activities.

For more ideas on partnerships with parents, see: Teachernet: Working with Parents http://www.teachernet.gov.uk/wholeschool/familyandcommunity/workingwithparents/

Source: Adapted extract from pp. 704–705, 'School/family/community partnerships: caring for children we share' by J. L. Epstein, *Phi Delta Kappan, 76*, pp. 701–712. Copyright © 1995 by Phi Delta Kappan. Reprinted with permission of Phi Delta Kappan and the author.

Diversity in Learning

This entire chapter has been about diversity, so here we want to focus on four areas where diversity among pupils can affect their learning in classrooms: social organisation, cultural values and learning preferences, sociolinguistics and the digital divide. The chapter will conclude with ideas that apply to all pupils.

Roland Tharp (1989) outlines several dimensions of classrooms that reflect the diversity of the pupils. The dimensions – social organisation, cultural values and learning styles and sociolinguistics – can be tailored to better fit the background of pupils.

Social organisation

Tharp states that 'a central task of educational design is to make the organisation of teaching, learning, and performance compatible with the social structures in which pupils are most productive, engaged, and likely to learn' (1989: 350). Social structure or social organisation in this context means the ways people interact to accomplish a particular goal. For example, the social organisation of Hawaiian society depends heavily on collaboration and cooperation. Children play together in groups of friends and siblings, with older children often caring for the younger ones. When cooperative work groups of four or five boys and girls were established in Hawaiian classrooms, pupil learning and participation improved (Okagaki, 2001). The teacher worked

Connect and Extend

Read O'Neil, J. (1990), 'Link between style, culture proves divisive', *Educational Leadership*, 48(2), p. 8. Focus Question: Why do some educationalists argue against linking learning styles to cultural differences?

intensively with one group while the children in the remaining groups helped each other. However, when the same structure was tried in a Navajo classroom, pupils would not work together. These pupils are socialised to be more solitary and not to play with the opposite sex. By setting up same-sex working groups of only two or three Navajo pupils, teachers encouraged them to help each other. If you have pupils from several cultures, you may need to provide choices and variety in grouping structures.

Cultural values and learning preferences

Rosa Sheets (2005) describes three characteristics of teachers who design culturally inclusive classrooms. The teachers (1) recognise the various ways all their pupils display their capabilities; (2) respond to pupils' preferred ways of learning; and (3) understand that a particular group's cultural practices, values and learning preferences may not apply to everyone in that group.

Results of some research suggest that British Asian pupils (girls in particular) are more oriented towards family and group loyalty. This may mean that these pupils prefer cooperative activities and dislike being made to compete with fellow pupils (Hennink *et al.*, 1999). Four values shared by many British Asian pupils (not all – remember Sheets's third characteristic cited above) are:

1. **Family loyalty** – tightly knit families with respect for elders within the extended family setting. Discussing family problems or business outside of the family may be seen as disloyal.

2. **Religious obligation** – value of interpersonal and spiritual harmony. Assertively voicing personal opinions or questioning/arguing may be seen as inappropriate.

3. **Community expectation** – members of community more willing to comment on the behaviour appearance or reaction of young people to other communities, for example respect for (older) people in authority (e.g. teachers, police and government officials).

4. **Cultural traditions** – valuing of traditions of dress, food and the traditional gender roles.

Those of you with specific interests in this context might wish to engage more accurately with the heterogeneous nature of the Asian community because as Jo Goodey cautions us:

> *As with Britain's white population, Asians are diverse in their social, cultural, economic, political and religious backgrounds, and bring with them the history of their countries of origin when settling in Britain (2001: 430).*

The learning styles of African/Black British boys may be inconsistent with teaching approaches in most schools. Some of the characteristics of this learning style are:

- a visual/global approach rather than a verbal/analytic approach;

- a preference for reasoning by inference rather than by formal logic;

- a focus on people and relationships;

- a preference for energetic involvement in several activities simultaneously rather than routine, step-by-step learning;

- a tendency to approximate numbers, space and time; and

- a greater dependence on non-verbal communication.

Pupils of colour who identify with their traditional cultures tend to respond better to open-ended questions with more than one answer, as opposed to single, right-answer questions. Questions that focus on meaning or the 'big picture' may be more productive than questions that focus on details (Archer and Yamashita, 2003; Starkey and Osler, 2001; Blair, 2002; Cross, 2003). British Black boys also adopt a number of strategies for dealing with classroom demands: to innovate new roles, to conform to, retreat from or rebel against the positioning they experience from teaching staff and peer group (Sewell, 1997). Understanding group and individual reactions in these ways can help us to adjust our teaching approaches.

Native Americans also appear to have a more global, visual style of learning. For example, Navajo pupils prefer hearing a story all the way through to the end before discussing the parts of the story. Teachers who stop to ask questions seem odd to these pupils and interrupt the learning process (Tharp, 1989). Also, these pupils sometimes show strong preferences for learning privately, through trial and error, rather than having their mistakes made public (Vasquez, 1990).

However, there are dangers in stereotyping both Asian and British Asian pupils as quiet, hardworking and passive, and British Black boys as being challenging 'phallo-centric underachievers' (Dore, 1995; Sewell, 1998). Suzuki (1983) suggests (when talking in an American context) that this practice of stereotyping 'tends to reinforce conformity and stifle creativity. Asian and Pacific American pupils, therefore, frequently do not develop the ability to assert and express themselves verbally and are channelled in disproportionate numbers into the technical/scientific fields. As a result, many Asian and Pacific American pupils are overly conforming, and have their academic and social development narrowly circumscribed' (1983: 9).

Suzuki's cautions are echoed by many critics of the research on ethnic differences in learning styles (Yee, 1992).

Cautions about learning styles research

In considering this research on learning styles, you should keep two points in mind. First, the validity of some of the learning styles research has been strongly questioned, as we saw in the previous chapter. Second, there is a heated debate today about whether identifying ethnic group differences in learning styles and preferences is a dangerous, racist sexist exercise. In our society, we are quick to move from the notion of 'difference' to the idea of 'deficits' and stereotypes (Gordon, 1991; Colley and Hodkinson, 2001). We have included the information about learning style differences because we believe that, used sensibly, this information can help you better understand your pupils.

It is dangerous and incorrect, however, to assume that every individual in a group shares the same learning style. The best advice for teachers is to be sensitive to individual differences in all your pupils and to make available alternative paths to learning. Never prejudge how a pupil will learn best on the basis of assumptions about the pupil's ethnicity or race. Get to know the individual.

Sociolinguistics

Sociolinguistics is the study of language and linguistic behaviour as influenced by social and cultural factors (e.g. gender, age, SES, ethnicity). A knowledge of sociolinguistics will help you understand why communication sometimes breaks down in classrooms. The classroom is a special setting for communicating; it has its own set of rules for when, how, to whom, about what subject, and in what manner to use language. Sometimes, the sociolinguistic skills of pupils do not fit the expectations of teachers as we saw earlier.

Sociolinguistics
The study of the formal and informal rules for how, when, about what, to whom, and how long to speak in conversations within cultural groups.

Pragmatics

The rules for when and how to use language to be an effective communicator in a particular culture.

Participation structures

The formal and informal rules for how to take part in a given activity.

In order to be successful, pupils must know the communication rules; that is, they must understand the pragmatics of the classroom – when, where and how to communicate. This is not such an easy task. As class activities change, rules change. Sometimes you have to raise your hand (during whole-class teaching), but sometimes you don't (during story time on the carpet). Sometimes it is good to ask a question (during discussion), but other times it isn't so good (when the teacher is reprimanding you). These differing activity rules are called participation structures, and they define appropriate participation for each class activity. Most classrooms have many different participation structures. To be competent communicators in the classroom, pupils sometimes have to read very subtle, non-verbal cues telling them which participation structures are currently in effect. It is common practice in English primary school classrooms for the teacher to hold one hand in the air as a single for silent attention. As children observe the signal by the teacher or another pupil, they signal they have seen this by holding up their hand, which in turn is a signal to other children working nearby. It is a kind of non-verbal 'Chinese whispers'.

Sources of misunderstandings

Connect and Extend

Read Leslie Irwin and Christine Nucci (2004), 'Perceptions of students' locus of control of discipline among pre-service and in-service teachers in multicultural classrooms', *Intercultural Education*, 15(1) (March), pp. 59–71.

Some children are simply better than others at reading the classroom situation because the participation structures of the school match the structures they have learned at home. The communication rules for most school situations are similar to those in middle-class homes, so children from these homes often appear to be more competent communicators. They know the unwritten rules. Pupils from different cultural backgrounds may have learned participation structures that conflict with the behaviours expected in school. For example, one study found that the home conversation style of Hawaiian children is to chime in with contributions to a story. In school, however, this overlapping style is viewed as 'interrupting'. When the teachers in one school learned about these differences and made their reading groups more like their pupils' home conversation groups, the young Hawaiian children in their classes improved in reading (Au, 1980).

The source of misunderstanding can be a subtle sociolinguistic difference, such as how long the teacher waits to react to pupils' responses. There is some evidence from American studies about differences between boys and girls and between different ethnic groups in the amount of time pupils need to formulate and deliver their entire answers but much of this is inconclusive and contradictory. See the Connect and Extend below.

Meanwhile, it seems that even pupils who speak the same language as their teachers may still have trouble communicating, and thus learning 'school', if the pupils' knowledge of pragmatics does not fit the school situation. What can teachers do? Especially in the early years, you should make communication rules for activities clear and explicit. Do not assume pupils know what to do. Use cues to signal pupils when changes occur.

Connect and Extend

For a concise discussion of cultural styles and the possible clashes of styles in classrooms, see Hilliard, A. G., III (1989), 'Teachers and cultural styles in a pluralistic society', *NEA Today*, 7(6), pp. 65–69.

Explain and demonstrate appropriate behaviour. We have seen teachers show young children how to use their 'special voice' or 'whisper voice'. One teacher said and then demonstrated, 'If you have to interrupt me while I'm working with other children, stand quietly beside me until I can help you.' The most important thing is to be consistent in responding to pupils. If pupils are supposed to raise their hands, don't call on those who break the rules. In these ways you teach pupils how to learn in school.

Sources of misunderstanding can be very subtle. The families of racial and ethnic minority pupils often have to be vigilant about discrimination to protect their children. They may teach their children to notice and resist possible discrimination. Teachers and schools may unintentionally offend these families if they

1. **All children who are fasting must bring a note at the beginning of the week** to let us know which days are involved. Failure to do this has previously resulted in the wastage of a lot of food.

2. **Children who are fasting must go home at lunchtime.** The only place the school could possibly supervise them is in the playground, which would be totally inappropriate at this time of year.

3. **We do NOT expect our young children to be fasting.** This means children below Years 5 and 6. (Those aged 10 and 11 years.) Remember, children have a very active day at school.

By keeping to these simple guidelines, we should be able to ensure the safety and well-being of your children. It also allows them to take full advantage of the educational opportunities offered at *Mayfield (anonomised)* and yet follow your example and lead in the observance of Ramadan.

Figure 5.5
A letter to the parents of Muslim children

Source: Gilbert, D. (2004). 'Racial and religious discrimination: the inexorable relationship between schools and the individual.' *Intercultural Education, 15*(3) (September), pp. 253–266.

are not sensitive to possible messages of discrimination. Figure 5.5 shows the transcript of a letter sent from a school in the North of England to parents of Muslim children attending the school. Okay, this source of misunderstanding isn't very subtle despite the letter making a reasonable request about the school being informed about who was fasting. Nevertheless, the letter generated enormous criticism because of the underlying tone and attitude it conveyed.

The digital divide

One area of teaching that often places pupils at risk of under-performance at school is the use of technology. Many pupils have limited access to technology at home or in their communities. Have a look at Table 5.5 which shows access to the internet by household in London.

STOP AND THINK

What benefits do pupils have who are on the 'right side' of the digital divide?

   This split in access to technology has been called the digital divide. Without seeking a precise definition of the digital divide at this point it is worth considering the short- and long-term effects of families and learners not having access to the emergent technological platforms of information and communication technologies (ICT). ICT and the information revolution has determined the unprecedented changes to many aspects of our social and economic lives. ICT is a critical resource for learning because of the way information is now organised, processed and distributed. Despite the prevalence of some communication technologies in many developed and developing nation states, being the wrong side of the digital divide can isolate children and their families from the means of fully participating in modern multicultural societies.

Digital divide

The disparities in access to technology between poor and more affluent pupils and families.

Table 5.5 Percentages by ethnicity of levels of home internet access amongst London households with children

In answer to the question of whether they had access to the internet at home the following responses occurred.

	Yes	No, can't afford	No, don't want
White British	61	18	21
White Irish	60	22	18
Mixed	51	31	18
Asian (incl. Chinese)	54	19	27
Black (incl. Caribbean)	53	27	20
Black African	44	31	25
Other (and as a postscript)	48	13	39
Those in London to ask for asylum	29	44	27

Source: Adapted from Londoners on-line: An analysis of levels of home internet access from the London Household Survey 2002, Table 12 and Table 13, p. 10. http://www.london.gov.uk/approot/gla/publications/e-london/londoners-online2.pdf. accessed April 2006.

Teaching every pupil

The goal of this chapter is to give you a sense of the diversity in today's and tomorrow's schools and to help teachers meet the challenges of teaching in a multicultural classroom. How should they understand and build on all the cultures of your pupils? How can they deal with many different languages? Here are three general principles to help find answers to these questions.

1. Know the pupils

We must learn who the pupils are and the legacies they bring (Delpit, 2003). Nothing you read in a chapter on cultural differences will teach anybody enough to understand the lives of all pupils. Reading about and studying other cultures are not enough as teachers need to know their pupils' families and communities. This includes taking time to talk to pupils, their parents and the school governors who represent parents and the community. Effective teachers know the community they serve: the shops and services; the social problems and celebrations; the special customs and events that shape the lives and experiences of the children. Teachers have a privileged position in the community and should strive to know and engage with the people who place their trust in them and in the work they do.

Effective teachers spend time with pupils and parents on projects outside of school. They ask parents to help in class or to talk about their jobs, their hobbies, or the history and heritage of their ethnic group. Many schools organise class meetings for parents and others in the family and show them videos of what is happening in the classroom. Parents share information about what is happening at home, about birthdays and other special events. Practitioners watch and listen to the ways that pupils interact in large and small groups, regularly eat lunch with different groups of pupils, and spend some non-teaching time with them.

2. Respect the pupils

From knowledge ought to come respect for pupils' learning strengths – for the struggles they face and the obstacles they have to overcome. We must believe in pupils (Delpit, 2003). For a child, genuine acceptance is a necessary condition for developing self-esteem. Sometimes the self-image and occupational aspirations of minority children actually decline in their early years in school, probably because of the emphasis on majority culture values, accomplishments and history. By presenting the accomplishments of particular members of an ethnic group or by bringing that group's culture into the classroom (in the form of literature, art, music or any cultural knowledge), teachers can help pupils maintain a sense of pride in their cultural group. This integration of culture must be more than the 'tokenism' of sampling ethnic foods or wearing costumes. Pupils should learn about the socially and intellectually important contributions of the various groups. There are many excellent references that provide background information, history and teaching strategies for different groups of pupils but fostering mutual confidence, and respect is the key to ensuring educational advantage for pupils and the establishment of a truly successful multicultural enterprise.

3. Teach the pupils

The most important thing that teachers can do for pupils is teach them to read, write, speak, compute, think and create – through consistent, rigorous and culturally connected teaching (Delpit, 2003). Too often, learning objectives for low-SES or minority group pupils have focused exclusively on basic skills. Pupils are taught words and sounds, but the meaning of the story is supposed to come later. Knapp, Turnbull and Shields (1990: 5) make these suggestions:

- Focus on meaning and understanding from beginning to end – for example, by orienting instruction towards comprehending reading passages, communicating important ideas in written text, or understanding the concepts underlying number facts.

- Balance routine skill learning with novel and complex tasks from the earliest stages of learning.

- Provide context for skills learning that establishes clear reasons for needing to learn the skills.

- Influence attitudes and beliefs about the academic content areas as well as skills and knowledge.

- Eliminate unnecessary redundancy in the curriculum (e.g. repeating instruction in the same mathematics skills year after year).

Finally, pupils need to be taught explicitly how to be expert pupils (refer to Chapter 8, pp. 372–384). In the early years, this could mean directly teaching the courtesies and conventions of the classroom: how to get a turn to speak, how and when to interrupt the teacher, how to whisper, how to get help in a small group, how to give an explanation that is helpful. In the later years, it may mean teaching the study skills that fit the subject. Pupils need to learn 'how we do it in school' without violating principle number two above – Respect the Pupils. Ways of asking questions around the kitchen table at home may be different from ways of asking questions in school, but pupils can learn both ways, without deciding that either way is superior and teachers can expand ways of doing it in school to include more possibilities. The Focus on Practice below gives more ideas.

Connect and Extend

Read Christine M. Rubie, Michael A. R. Townsend, Dennis W. Moore (2004), 'Motivational and academic effects of cultural experiences for indigenous minority students in New Zealand', *Educational Psychology, 24*(2) (2004), pp. 143–160.

FOCUS ON PRACTICE

Culturally relevant teaching

Experiment with different grouping arrangements to encourage social harmony and cooperation

Examples

1. Try 'study buddies' but remember to regularly rotate the pairs.
2. Organise heterogeneous groups of four or five.
3. Establish larger teams for older pupils.

Provide a range of ways to learn material to accommodate a range of learning styles

Examples

1. Give pupils materials at different reading levels.
2. Offer visual materials – charts, diagrams, models.
3. Provide tapes for listening and viewing.
4. Set up hands-on activities and projects.

Teach classroom procedures directly, even ways of doing things that you thought everyone would know

Examples

1. Tell pupils how to get the teacher's attention.
2. Explain when and how to interrupt the teacher if pupils need help.
3. Show which materials pupils can take and which require permission.
4. Demonstrate acceptable ways to disagree with or challenge another pupil.

Learn the meaning of different behaviours for your pupils

Examples

1. Ask pupils how they feel when you correct or praise them.
2. Talk to family and community members and other teachers to discover the meaning of expressions, gestures, or other responses that are unfamiliar to you.

Emphasise meaning in teaching

Examples

1. Make sure pupils understand what they read.
2. Try storytelling and other modes that do not require written materials.
3. Use examples that relate abstract concepts to everyday experiences; for instance, relate negative numbers to being overdrawn in your bank account.

Get to know the customs, traditions and values of your pupils

Examples

1. Use holidays as a chance to discuss the origins and meaning of traditions.
2. Analyse different traditions for common themes.
3. Attend community fairs and festivals.

Help pupils detect racist and sexist messages

Examples
1. Analyse curriculum materials for biases.
2. Make pupils 'bias detectives', reporting comments from the media.
3. Discuss the ways that pupils communicate biased messages about each other and what should be done when this happens.
4. Discuss expressions of prejudice such as anti-Semitism.

For ways to use technology for culturally relevant teaching, see
http://preservicetech.edreform.net/techindicator/culturallyrelevantpedagogy

SUMMARY TABLE

Today's Diverse Classrooms (pp. 186–190)

Distinguish between the 'melting pot' and multiculturalism

Statistics point to increasing cultural diversity in society. Old views – that minority group members and immigrants should lose their cultural distinctiveness and assimilate completely in the 'melting pot' or be regarded as culturally deficient – are being replaced by new emphases on multiculturalism, equal educational opportunity and the celebration of cultural diversity.

What is multicultural education?

Multicultural education is a field of study designed to increase educational equity for all pupils. According to the multicultural ideal, Europe should be transformed into a society that values diversity. James Banks suggests that multicultural education has five dimensions: integrating content, helping pupils understand how knowledge is influenced by beliefs, reducing prejudice, creating social structures in schools that support learning and development for all pupils and using teaching methods that reach all pupils.

What is culture?

There are many conceptions of culture, but most include the knowledge, skills, rules, traditions, beliefs and values that guide behaviour in a particular group of people: culture is a programme for living. Everyone is a member of many cultural groups, defined in terms of geographic region, nationality, ethnicity, race, gender, social class and religion. Membership in a particular group does not determine behaviour or values, but makes certain values and kinds of behaviour more likely. Wide variations exist within each group.

Economic and Social Class Differences (pp. 190–195)

What is SES and how does it differ from social class?

Social class reflects a group's prestige and power in a society. Most people are aware of the social class that they share with similar peers. Socioeconomic status (SES) is a term used by sociologists for variations in wealth, power, control over resources and prestige. Socioeconomic status is determined by several factors – not just income – and often overpowers other cultural differences. No single variable is an effective measure of SES, but many researchers identify six social grade definitions of SES: upper middle class, middle class, lower middle class, skilled working class, working class, and those at the lowest level of subsistence. The main characteristics of five of these six levels are summarised in Table 5.1.

What is the relationship between SES and school achievement?

Socioeconomic status and academic achievement are closely related. High-SES pupils of all ethnic groups show higher average levels of achievement on test scores and stay in school longer than low-SES pupils. Poverty during a child's pre-school years appears to have the greatest negative impact and the longer the child is in poverty, the stronger the impact is on achievement. Why is there a correlation between SES and school achievement? Low-SES pupils may suffer from inadequate health care, teachers' lowered expectations of them, low self-esteem, learned helplessness, participation in resistance cultures, school streaming and under-stimulating parenting styles and home environments. A striking finding is that low-SES children lose academic ground outside school over the summer, while higher-SES children continue to advance.

Ethnic and Racial Differences (pp. 195–205)

Distinguish between ethnicity and race

Ethnicity (culturally transmitted behaviour) and race (biologically transmitted physical traits) are socially significant categories people use to describe themselves and others. Minority groups (either numerically or historically unempowered) are rapidly increasing in population.

How can differences in ethnicity of teachers and pupils affect school performance?

Conflicts can arise from differences between teachers and pupils in culture-based beliefs, values and expectations. Cultural conflicts are usually about below-the-surface differences, because when subtle cultural differences meet, misunderstandings are common. Pupils in some cultures learn attitudes and behaviours that are more consistent with school expectations. Differences among ethnic groups in cognitive and academic abilities are largely the legacy of racial segregation and continuing prejudice and discrimination.

Distinguish among prejudice, discrimination and stereotype threat

Prejudice is a rigid and irrational generalisation – a prejudgement or attitude – about an entire category of people. Prejudice may target people in particular racial, ethnic, religious, political, geographic or language groups, or it may be directed towards the gender or sexual orientation of the individual. Discrimination is unequal and unfair treatment of or actions towards particular categories of people. Stereotype threat is the extra emotional and cognitive burden that performance in an academic situation might confirm a stereotype that others hold. It is not necessary that the individual even believe the stereotype. All that matters is that the person is *aware* of the stereotype and *cares about performing* well enough to disprove its unflattering implications. In the short run, the fear that might confirm a negative stereotype can induce test anxiety and undermine performance. Over time, experiencing stereotype threat may lead to dis-identification with schooling and academic achievement.

Girls and Boys: Differences in the Classroom (pp. 205–215)

What are the stages for achieving a sexual orientation for gay and lesbian pupils?

Stages of achieving a sexual orientation for gay and lesbian pupils can also follow a pattern from discomfort to confusion to acceptance. Some researchers contend that sexual identity is not always permanent and can change over the years.

What is gender-role identity and how do gender-role identities develop?

Gender-role identity is the image each individual has of himself or herself as masculine or feminine in characteristics – a part of self-concept. Biology (hormones) plays a role, as does the differential behaviour of parents and teachers towards male and female children. Through their interactions with family, peers, teachers and the environment in general, children begin to form gender schemas, or organised networks of knowledge about what it means to be male or female. Research shows that gender-role stereotyping begins in the pre-school years and continues through gender bias in the school curriculum and sex discrimination in the classroom. Teachers often unintentionally perpetuate these problems.

Are there sex differences in cognitive abilities?

Some measures of achievement and tests have shown sex-linked differences, especially in verbal and spatial abilities and mathematics. Males seem to be superior on tasks that require mental rotation of objects and females are better on tasks that require acquisition and use of verbal information. Research on the causes of these differences has been inconclusive, except to indicate that academic socialisation and teachers' treatment of male and female pupils in mathematics classes do play a role. Teachers can use many strategies for reducing gender bias.

Language Differences in the Classroom (pp. 215–222)

What are the origins of language differences in the classroom?

Language differences among pupils include dialects, bilingualism and culture-based communication styles. Dialects are not inferior languages and should be respected, but 'Standard English' should be taught for academic contexts. Dialects often affect the pronunciation of words, so teachers have to be able to distinguish a mistake from a dialect difference in oral language. Pupils who speak in dialect and pupils who are bilingual often use code-switching to communicate in different groups.

What is bilingual education?

Bilingual pupils speak a first language other than English, learn English as an additional language, may have some degree of limitation in English proficiency, and also must often struggle with social adjustment problems relating to biculturalism. Although there is much debate about the best way to help bilingual or multilingual pupils master English, studies show it is best if they are not forced to abandon their first language. The more proficient pupils are in their first language, the faster they will master the second or third. Mastering academic language skills in any new language takes five to seven years.

Creating Culturally Responsive Schools (pp. 222–227)

What is culturally relevant pedagogy?

'Culturally relevant pedagogy is an approach to teaching that uses the cultural knowledge, prior experiences, frames of references and learning styles of ethnically diverse pupils to make learning encounters more relevant and effective for them. It teaches *to and through* the strengths of these pupils' (Gay, 2000). Gloria Ladson-Billings describes culturally relevant teaching that rests on three propositions: pupils must experience academic success, develop/maintain their cultural competence, and develop a critical consciousness to challenge the status quo.

What are the elements of a resilient classroom?

There are two strands of elements that bind pupils to their classroom community. One strand emphasises the self-agency of pupils – their capacity to set and pursue goals. This includes academic self-efficacy, self-control and self-determination. The second strand emphasises caring and connected relationships with the teacher, peers and the home.

Diversity in Learning (pp. 227–235)

Teaching every pupil

There are three principles which can help teachers meet the challenges of teaching in a multicultural classroom. First, teachers must know their pupils and learn about the cultural legacies that they bring to the classroom. Second, they must have respect for pupils' learning strengths, for the personal struggles they face and the obstacles they overcome. Lastly, the most important thing that a teacher can do for their pupils is to teach them to read, write, speak, compute, think and create – through consistent, rigorous and culturally connected teaching (Delpit, 2003).

Glossary

Bilingualism: Speaking two languages fluently.

Code-switching: Successful switching between cultures in language, dialect or non-verbal behaviours to fit the situation.

Culture: The knowledge, values, attitudes and traditions that guide the behaviour of a group of people and allow them to solve the problems of living in their environment.

Cultural deficit model: A model that explains the school achievement problems of ethnic minority

pupils by assuming that their culture is inadequate and does not prepare them to succeed in school.

Culturally relevant pedagogy: Excellent teaching for pupils from ethnic minorities that includes academic success, developing/maintaining cultural competence, and developing a critical consciousness to challenge the status quo.

Culturally responsive school: Schools that provide culturally diverse pupils equitable access to the teaching-learning process.

Dialect: Rule-governed variation of a language spoken by a particular group.

Digital divide: The disparities in access to technology between poor and more affluent pupils and families.

Dis-identification: Recognition of a sub-persona of self-image, which may or may not be used according to social context.

Discrimination: Treating or acting unfairly towards particular categories of people.

English as a second language (ESL): Designation for programmes and classes to teach English to pupils who are not native speakers of English.

English as an additional language (EAL): Designation for programmes and classes to teach English to pupils who are not native speakers of English and may have other additional languages.

English language learners (ELL): Pupils whose primary or heritage language is not English.

Ethnicity: A cultural heritage shared by a group of people.

Gender biases: Different views of males and females, often favouring one gender over the other.

Gender-role identity: Beliefs about characteristics and behaviours associated with one sex as opposed to the other.

Gender schemas: Organised networks of knowledge about what it means to be male or female.

Melting Pot: A metaphor for the absorption and assimilation of immigrants into the mainstream of society so that ethnic differences vanish.

Minority group: A group of people who have been socially disadvantaged – not always a minority in actual numbers.

Multicultural education: Education that promotes equity in the schooling of all pupils.

Participation structures: The formal and informal rules for how to take part in a given activity.

Pragmatics: The rules for when and how to use language to be an effective communicator in a particular culture.

Prejudice: Prejudgment or irrational generalisation about an entire category of people.

Race: A group of people who share common biological traits that are seen as self-defining by the people of the group.

Resilience: The ability to adapt successfully in spite of difficult circumstances and threats to development.

Resistance culture: Group values and beliefs about refusing to adopt the behaviours and attitudes of the majority culture.

Semilingual: Not proficient in any language; speaking one or more languages inadequately.

Setting: Ability grouping for part of the school timetable or for a particular activity and therefore to different academic experiences based on achievement.

Sexual identity: A complex combination of beliefs and orientations about gender roles and sexual orientation.

Socioeconomic status (SES): Relative standing in the society based on income, power, background and prestige.

Sociolinguistics: The study of the formal and informal rules for how, when, about what, to whom, and how long to speak in conversations within cultural groups.

Stereotype: Schema that organises knowledge or perceptions about a category.

Stereotype threat: The extra emotional and cognitive burden that your performance in an academic situation might confirm a stereotype that others hold about you.

Streaming: Ability grouping for the whole school timetable and therefore to different academic experiences based on achievement.

CHECK YOUR LEARNING! WEB

In the Classroom: What Would They Do?

Here is how some teachers responded to the teaching situation presented at the beginning of this chapter about bringing together a class that was becoming divided along ethnic lines.

Lisbeth Jonsson, primary school teacher, Sotenäs Kompetenscentrum, Kungshamn, Sweden

Yes, we have the same situation! In lower classes they mix very well, I think. The younger children find the newcomers exciting and the Swedes are nice and helpful. In higher grades (teenagers) it is a very tricky situation. The Swedish teenagers are insecure and have little self-esteem and the same goes for the newcomers. I think the best thing to do, is to let them be separated if possible. Let the immigrants stay together until they know a language they can communicate in. Let them make friends within the group and let them 'struggle' together with the situation they didn't choose for themselves. No wonder they feel frustrated! And frustration leads to anger and violence.

Lizzie Meadows, primary school deputy head teacher, The Park Primary School, Kingswood, Bristol

The age of the pupils in this situation does have some relevance as, in general, primary age pupils are more accepting of others and have less preconceptions and negative attitudes, and stereotypes have had less time to embed. The teachers and school management need to tackle the problem and issues in a very proactive and up-front way by promoting cultural understanding and differences. If comfortable, the children could be asked to share their experiences and information about their country. Children could undertake a research project on the country involved. Local community groups could be asked to visit school to promote cultural awareness. In the classrooms, teachers need to ensure that they consider the seating arrangements to avoid any form of apartheid and engineer who works with whom on projects. They could also establish some ground rules for languages spoken in the classroom, allowing specific times for pupils to use their native language.

Tessa Herbert, English teacher, John Masefield High School, Ledbury

The problem is ignorance and fear (cliché, but quite possibly true). Language is the 'key'. There is a need for excellent specialised teaching of English, often not present in secondary schools at the moment. The ethos of the school should be nurturing, acknowledging and exploiting common interests, rather than differences. The work should start from the tutor groups in the first instance, and give pupils a sense of responsibility for the newcomers. Grouping in lessons needs to be done sensitively, just throwing people together rarely works. The 'new' group could be encouraged to talk about their culture, looking for similarities as well as acknowledging differences. Texts in English classes could be chosen to explore literary parallels to the current situation.

Lee Card, primary school teacher, Bosbury Church of England Primary School

The influx in such a short time is arguably the biggest problem in this situation. The children have all been thrown in at once, an occurrence that would never usually happen, affecting the dynamic of the entire school instantly. It is only natural that they would initially stick together and this obvious 'ethnic division' is reverberating around the school changing other attitudes and behaviours. The communication barrier must be broken down as a priority. The school should seek to bring in a translator for each classroom as quickly as possible to give these new children 'a voice' in the school.

Teachers in the school need to attempt to bring their classes 'together' using a means other than spoken language. Sport and music could be very powerful tools to encourage the joining of forces in their classrooms, something that ends in a group collaborative achievement. If this means throwing the curriculum out of the window for a couple of weeks then so be it. The group dynamic must be regained as another short-term priority and group achievement may well be a tangible solution. I would personally be inclined to use the current mixture of nationalities in English Football Premier League teams as a good example of groups of diverse people working together for a common goal.

I would be inclined to suggest that younger children find accepting and embracing differences easier than, for example, secondary age children. However, in this context of immediate school unrest, I fear age may be irrelevant.

Jackie Day, special educational needs co-ordinator, The Ridge Primary School, Yate

The real problem here is probably the attitude of the local community to asylum seekers. The new pupils may be acting defensively because they are aware of prejudice against their families. Children's behaviour often reflects values assimilated from home.

The school already has a wide variety of cultural and ethnic backgrounds, so presumably there is usually respect for racial difference. Opportunities will need to be engineered for pupils, parents (and staff) to express their feelings in controlled situations to promote better understanding. The first goals are to help pupils identify the cause of the unpleasant atmosphere in the school, and to encourage them to find ways of solving the problem themselves. Help from external agencies in setting up such groups might well be needed. I would think this would be easier with younger children than with teenagers.

Visit the website www.pearsoned.co.uk/woolfolkeuro for more responses.

Overview

We begin this chapter with a general definition of learning that takes into account the opposing views of different theoretical groups. Learning is at the centre of education but as we discussed in the section above the type of learning which takes place is affected by the class environment. So it may be that many children within 'difficult' classes are learning about how to get away with not working, how to be amusing and resist authority, or how to be bored and frustrated because others are disrupting lesson, but they are not learning the subjects they are required to know. We will highlight one theoretical group, the behavioural theorists, in this chapter; another major group, the cognitive theorists, in Chapters 7 and 8; and then look at current social cognitive views and constructivism in Chapter 9.

Our discussion in this chapter will focus on three behavioural learning processes: *contiguity, classical conditioning* and *operant conditioning* (explained later) with the greatest emphasis on the last process as this is most relevant to the learning situation in schools. After examining the implications of applying behavioural concepts to the learning situation, we look at two recent directions in behavioural approaches to learning – self-management and cognitive behaviour modification.

By the time you have completed this chapter, you should be able to answer the following questions:

- **What is learning?**
- **What are the similarities and differences among contiguity, classical conditioning and operant conditioning?**
- **What are examples of four different kinds of consequences that can follow any behaviour and what effect is each likely to have on future behaviour?**
- **How could you use applied behaviour analysis (group consequences, token economies, contingency contracts) to solve common academic or behaviour problems?**
- **What and how can children and young people learn through observation?**
- **What is cognitive behaviour modification and how does it apply to teaching?**

In the Classroom

Were you ever part of an 'unruly' class during your school or college years? Perhaps there were people in this class who walked round the room for a chat with their friends or talked while the teacher was talking. There might have been squabbles taking place during group work and people eating snacks as they wished. It is likely that there was a charismatic ringleader within the class who defied the authority of the teacher and entertained his or her admirers with defiance and backchat. The teacher probably seemed ineffective and unable to cope with the noise, constant interruptions and demands of some of the class. Whilst it may have been fun for some individuals there was little academic learning taking place and it certainly was not fun for the teacher who was probably exhausted and demoralised by the constant battle to be heard and regain control. It seems that the behaviour of the pupils is making it impossible for the teacher to teach effectively and impossible for the class to do the very thing that school is there for: to learn.

Think about the following:
- If you were taking charge of a class like this how would you approach the situation?
- Which problem behaviours might be tackled first?
- Would giving rewards or administering punishment be useful in this situation? Why or why not?

Group Activity

With two other members of your group discuss your own experiences as a learner of being part of a disruptive class. Consider questions such as:
- **How did the teacher try to manage your behaviour?**
- **Why do you think the strategies used failed to work?**
- **Identify any strategies that were used by effective teachers and discuss possible reasons for their effectiveness.**

Keep these points in mind as you read this chapter.

Understanding Learning

When we hear the word *learning*, most of us think of studying and school. We think about subjects or skills we intend to master, such as algebra, French, chemistry or football/netball. However, learning is not limited to school. We learn every day of our lives. Babies learn to kick their legs to make the mobile above their cribs move, teenagers learn the lyrics to all their favourite songs, middle-aged people learn to change their diet and exercise patterns, and every few years we all learn to find a new style of dress attractive when the old styles (the styles we once loved) go out of fashion. This last example shows that learning is not always intentional. We don't try to like new styles and dislike old ones; it just seems to happen. We don't intend to become nervous when we hear the sound of a dentist's drill or when we step onto a stage, yet many of us do. So what is this powerful phenomenon called learning? The next section will supply us with some answers.

Learning: a definition

Learning

Process through which experience causes permanent change in knowledge or behaviour.

In the broadest sense, learning occurs when experience causes a relatively permanent change in an individual's knowledge or behaviour. The change may be deliberate or unintentional, for better or for worse, correct or incorrect, and conscious or unconscious (Hill, 2002). Let us first be clear about what is and is not defined as learning. To qualify as learning, the change in knowledge or behaviour must be brought about by experience – by the interaction of a person with his or her environment. On the other hand, changes simply caused by maturation, such as acquiring teeth, growing taller or turning grey, do not qualify as learning. Temporary changes resulting from illness, fatigue or hunger are also excluded from a general definition of learning. A person who has gone without food for two days does not learn to be hungry, and a person who is ill does not learn to run more slowly. Of course, learning does play a part in how we respond to hunger or illness depending on what has happened on previous occasions. For example, if we have learned that being ill means that we miss a dreaded test at school or results in more love and attention from our family, we might be more likely to see illness more positively.

However, our definition specifies that the changes resulting from learning are in the individual's knowledge or behaviour. Most psychologists would agree with this statement, but some tend to emphasise the change in knowledge, others the change in behaviour. Cognitive psychologists, who focus on changes in knowledge, believe learning is an internal mental activity that cannot be observed directly. As you will see in the next chapter, cognitive psychologists studying learning are interested in unobservable mental activities such as thinking, remembering and solving problems (Schwartz, Wasserman and Robbins, 2002).

Behavioural learning theories

Explanations of learning that focus on external events as the cause of changes in observable behaviours.

The psychologists discussed in this chapter, on the other hand, favour behavioural learning theories. The behavioural view generally assumes that the outcome of learning is change in behaviour, and it emphasises the effects of external events on the individual. For example, if we have learnt about crossing roads safely then our future behaviour when crossing the road will change to take account of this. Some early behaviourists such as J. B. Watson took the radical position that because thinking, intentions and other internal mental events could not be seen or studied rigorously and scientifically, these 'mentalisms', as he called them, should not even be included in an explanation of learning. Before we look in depth at behavioural explanations of learning, let's look at an example taken from an actual classroom and note the possible results of learning.

Learning is not always what it seems

After weeks of working with her mentor, Elizabeth was ready to take over on her own. She was ready to teach a Personal, Social and Health Education (PSHE)/Citizenship session with Year 8 (12–13-year-old) pupils. As she moved from behind the desk to the front of the room, she saw another adult approach the classroom door. It was Mr Ross, her supervisor from college. Elizabeth's neck and facial muscles suddenly became very tense and her hands trembled.

'I've stopped by to observe your teaching,' Mr Ross said. 'This will be my first of six visits. I couldn't contact you last night to tell you.'

Elizabeth tried to hide her reaction, but her hands trembled as she gathered the notes for the lesson. She began: 'Let's start today with a kind of game. I will say some words, and then I want you to tell me the first words you can think of. Don't bother to raise your hands. Just say the words out loud, and I will write them on the board. Don't all speak at once, though. Wait until someone else has finished before you say your word. Okay, here is the first one: "Being healthy".'

'Eating proper food', 'Exercise', 'Getting enough sleep', 'Not smoking and drinking'. The answers came very quickly, and Elizabeth was relieved to see that the class understood the game.

'All right, very good,' she said. 'Now try another one: "mobile".'

'Mobile phones', 'Pay as you go', 'Over baby's cots', 'Being able to move about alright', 'Ronaldinho'. With this last answer, a ripple of laughter moved across the room.

'Ronaldinho?' Elizabeth exclaimed, 'how did we get to him?' Then she laughed too. Soon all the children were laughing. 'Alright, settle down,' Elizabeth said. 'Here is another word: "Accessibility".'

'Credit card.' The class continued to laugh. 'Hole in the wall', 'Wall paper', 'Paper underwear.' More laughter and a few appropriate gestures.

'Just a minute,' Elizabeth pleaded. 'These ideas are getting a bit off target!'

'Off target? Missed penalty,' shouted the boy who had first mentioned Ronaldinho. He stood up and started kicking balls of paper to a friend in the back of the room.

'England.' 'No, Brazil.' 'Ball games.' 'The World Cup.' 'Hot dogs.' 'Films.' 'DVDs.' 'Ronaldinho.' The responses now came too fast for Elizabeth to stop them. For some reason, the Ronaldinho line got an even bigger laugh the second time around, and Elizabeth suddenly realised she had lost the class.

'Alright then, because you know so much about access to healthy living, close your books and take out a pen,' Elizabeth said, obviously angry. She passed out the worksheet that she had planned as a group, open-book activity. 'You have 20 minutes to finish this test!'

'You didn't tell us we were having a test!' 'That's not fair!' 'We haven't even covered this yet!' 'I didn't do anything wrong!' There were moans and disgusted looks, even from the quietest members of the group. 'I'm reporting you to the head teacher; we do have our rights you know!'

This last comment really hit home. The class had just finished discussing human rights as preparation for the work on inclusion. As she listened to the protests, Elizabeth felt terrible. How was she going to mark these 'tests'? The first section of the worksheet involved facts which they had not been given and the second section asked pupils to create a news-style programme interviewing ordinary people affected by being excluded from everyday facilities such as gymnasiums.

'All right, all right, it won't be a test. But you do have to complete this worksheet for a coursework mark. I was going to let you work together, but your behaviour this morning tells me that you are not ready for group work. If you can complete the first section of the

*sheet working quietly and seriously, you can work together on the second section.'
Elizabeth knew that her pupils would like to work together on writing the script for the
news interview programme.*

*Elizabeth was afraid to look back at her supervisor. What was he writing on his
observation form?*

It appears, on the surface at least, that very little learning of any sort was taking
place in Elizabeth's classroom. In fact, Elizabeth had some good ideas, but she also
made some mistakes in her application of learning principles. We will return to this
episode several times in the chapter to analyse various aspects of what took place. To
get us started, four events can be singled out, each possibly related to a different learning process.

First, the students were able to associate the word *phone* with the word *mobile*. Second, Elizabeth's hands trembled when her college supervisor entered the room. Third,
one learner continued to disrupt the class with inappropriate responses and fourth,
after Elizabeth laughed at a pupil's comment, the class joined in her laughter. The four
learning processes represented are contiguity, classical conditioning, operant conditioning and observational learning. In the following pages we will examine these four
kinds of learning, starting with contiguity and classical conditioning.

Early Explanations of Learning: Contiguity and Classical Conditioning

Contiguity

Association of two events
because of repeated pairing.

Stimulus

Event that activates
behaviour.

Response

Observable reaction to
a stimulus.

One of the earliest explanations of learning came from Aristotle (384–322 BC). He said
that we remember things together (1) when they are similar, (2) when they contrast and
(3) when they are *contiguous* (presented together). This last principle is the most important, because it is included in all explanations of *learning by association*. The principle of
contiguity states that whenever two or more sensations occur together often enough,
they will become associated. Later, when only one of these sensations (a stimulus)
occurs, the other will be remembered too (a response) (Rachlin, 1991; Wasserman and
Miller, 1997). For example, when Elizabeth said 'mobile', the class associated the word
'phone' because they had heard these words together many times. Other learning processes may also be involved when children learn these phrases, but contiguity is a factor.

Contiguity also plays a major role in another learning process best known as *classical conditioning*.

STOP AND THINK

Close your eyes and focus on a vivid image of the following:

- the smell of bread baking,
- a time you were really embarrassed at school,
- the taste of chocolate fudge,
- the sound of a dentist's drill.

What did you notice as you formed these images? What were you feeling as you
thought about them?

Clearly these responses are involuntary and involve physical reactions over which we have little control. Classical conditioning helps to explain the way in which we have learned these responses and focuses on the learning of *involuntary* emotional or physiological responses such as fear, increased muscle tension, salivation or sweating. These sometimes are called respondents because they are automatic responses to stimuli. Through the process of classical conditioning, humans and animals can be trained to react involuntarily to a stimulus that previously had no effect – or a very different effect – on them. The stimulus comes to *elicit*, or bring forth, the response automatically. So muscular tenseness on hearing a dentist's drill has been conditioned by one's experiences of painful dental work.

Classical conditioning was identified in the 1920s by Ivan Pavlov, a Russian physiologist trying to determine how long it took a dog to secrete digestive juices after it had been fed. But the intervals of time kept changing (Pavlov, 1927). At first, the dogs salivated as expected while they were being fed. Then the dogs began to salivate as soon as they saw the food and then as soon as they heard the scientists walking towards the lab. Pavlov decided to move away from his original experiments and examine these unexpected interferences in his work.

In one of his first experiments, Pavlov began by sounding a tuning fork and recording a dog's response. As expected, there was no salivation. At this point, the sound of the tuning fork was a neutral stimulus because it brought forth no salivation. Then Pavlov fed the dog. The response was salivation. The food was an unconditioned stimulus (US) because no prior training or 'conditioning' was needed to establish the natural connection between food and salivation. The salivation was an unconditioned response (UR), again because it was elicited automatically – no conditioning required.

Using these three elements – the food, the salivation and the tuning fork – Pavlov demonstrated that a dog could be conditioned to salivate after hearing the tuning fork. He did this by contiguous pairing of the sound with food. At the beginning of the experiment, he sounded the fork and then quickly fed the dog. After Pavlov repeated this several times, the dog began to salivate after hearing the sound, but before receiving the food. Now the sound had become a conditioned stimulus (CS) that could bring forth salivation by itself. The response of salivating after the tone was now a conditioned response (CR).

This is quite amazing if you pause to think about it because a reflex action (salivating) which we assume is a 'natural' reaction has been evoked in response to an 'unnatural' stimulus (tuning fork). We might assume that this is limited to less complex creatures such as dogs but research suggests that it works with humans too.

Work on humans was carried out in 1937 using the natural response of vasoconstriction (constriction of blood vessels making the skin look pale). Every time a participant heard a buzzer, he placed his hand in a bucket of ice-cold water. When he became conditioned to this, whenever he heard the buzzer the vasoconstriction took place without putting his hands in the water (Menzies, 1937). Again this is surprising as we normally assume that these responses are 'natural' and outside of our control. However, this and other evidence suggests that humans can be classically conditioned to respond with reflex actions such as eye blinking (Lavond *et al.*, 1993; Woodruff-Pak and Steinmetz, 2000). More recently, Canadian research indicated that implicit self-esteem (the automatic, unconscious aspect of self-esteem) was increased by classical conditioning. Psychologists used a computer game which repeatedly paired information about the player with smiling faces and found significant increases in self-esteem (Baccus, Baldwin and Packer, 2004).

This links with notions that our emotional reactions to various situations are learned in part through classical conditioning. The medical profession have a term,

Classical conditioning
Association of automatic responses with new stimuli.

Respondents
Responses (generally automatic or involuntary) elicited by specific stimuli.

Neutral stimulus
Stimulus not connected to a response.

Unconditioned stimulus (US)
Stimulus that automatically produces an emotional or physiological response.

Unconditioned response (UR)
Naturally occurring emotional or physiological response.

Conditioned stimulus (CS)
Stimulus that evokes an emotional or physiological response after conditioning.

Conditioned response (CR)
Learned response to a previously neutral stimulus.

'white coat syndrome,' that describes people whose blood pressure (an involuntary response) goes up when tested in the doctor's office, usually by someone in a white coat. Another example, Elizabeth's trembling hands when she saw her teaching supervisor, might be traced to previous unpleasant experiences. Perhaps she had been embarrassed or scared during past evaluations of her performance, and now just the thought of being observed elicits a pounding heart and sweaty palms. Classical conditioning has implications for teachers as well as those working in advertising. You have only to look at TV or magazine adverts to see how marketing managers are hoping to form conditioned responses to their products (e.g. happy, smiling faces and certain brands of breakfast cereals; voluptuous models and certain types of cars, and so on). Remember that emotions and attitudes as well as facts and ideas are learned in classrooms. This emotional learning can sometimes interfere with academic learning. Procedures based on classical conditioning also can be used to help people learn more adaptive emotional responses, as the following Focus on Practice suggests. However, critics of classical conditioning argue that it assumes humans to be simple, machine-like creatures who simply respond to stimuli without thinking.

FOCUS ON PRACTICE

Applying classsical conditioning

Associate positive, pleasant events with learning tasks

Examples

1. Emphasise group competition and cooperation over individual competition. Many learners have negative emotional responses to individual competition because they may have repeatedly lost or been embarrassed and that may generalise to other learning.
2. Make mathematics tasks, such as division, fun by having children decide how to divide refreshments equally, then letting them eat the results.
3. Make voluntary reading appealing by creating a comfortable reading corner with pillows, colourful displays of books which are kept in a good state of repair and reading props such as puppets (especially for children still at the real objects/concrete-operational stage – see the section on Piaget in Chapter 2).

Help learners to risk anxiety-producing situations voluntarily and successfully

Examples

1. Ask a shy member of the class who knows the procedures to take on the responsibility of teaching two other children how to distribute materials for a painting session.
2. Devise small steps towards a larger goal. For example, give practice tests daily, and then weekly, to learners who tend to 'freeze' in test situations.

3. If a learner is afraid of speaking in front of the class, let them read a report to a small group while seated, then read it while standing, then give the report from notes instead of reading it verbatim. Next, move in stages towards having the learner give a report to the whole class.

Help learners recognise differences and similarities among situations so they can discriminate and generalise appropriately

Examples

1. Explain that it is appropriate to avoid strangers who offer gifts or rides, but safe to accept treats from adults when parents are present.
2. Assure learners who are anxious about taking important tests (such as SATs or GCSEs) that this test is like all the other achievement tests they have taken.

Operant Conditioning: Trying New Responses

So far, we have concentrated on the automatic conditioning of involuntary responses such as salivation and fear. Clearly, not all human learning is so automatic and unintentional. Most behaviours are not involuntary responses. People act or 'operate' on their environment to produce different kinds of consequences. So you might be reading this page in order to understand operant conditioning and this deliberate action is an example of an operant. The learning process involved in operant behaviour is called operant conditioning because we learn to behave in certain ways (become conditioned) as we operate on the environment. So if you understand what you are reading and find it helpful you might be more likely to read further or on another occasion.

The person generally thought to be responsible for developing the concept of operant conditioning is B.F. Skinner (1953). Skinner began with the belief that the principles of classical conditioning account for only a small portion of learned behaviours. Many human behaviours are operants, not respondents. Classical conditioning describes only how existing behaviours might be paired with new stimuli; it does not explain how new operant behaviours are acquired.

Behaviour, like response or action, is simply a word for what a person does in a particular situation. Conceptually, we may think of a behaviour as sandwiched between two sets of environmental influences: those that precede it (its antecedents) and those that follow it (its consequences) (Skinner, 1950). This relationship can be shown very simply as antecedent–behaviour–consequence, or A–B–C. As behaviour is ongoing, a given consequence becomes an antecedent for the next ABC sequence. So if, for example, you are feeling worried or stressed, eat a piece of chocolate cake and feel comforted or more relaxed you are more likely to eat chocolate cake the next time you are feeling stressed. So the Antecedent (A) might be the sight of or smell of chocolate cake, the behaviour (B) would be eating it and the consequences (C) would be feeling better as a result. Research in operant conditioning shows that operant behaviour can be altered by changes in the antecedents, the consequences, or both. So if, for example, you felt nauseous after the chocolate cake you might not eat it the next time you felt stressed. Let us look now at some types of consequences within the learning situation.

Operants

Voluntary (and generally goal-directed) behaviours emitted by a person or an animal.

Operant conditioning

Learning in which voluntary behaviour is strengthened or weakened by consequences or antecedents.

Antecedents

Events that precede an action.

Consequences

Events that follow an action.

Types of consequences

STOP AND THINK

Think back to the consequences that followed your behaviour when in the learning situation. Did those working with you use rewards or punishments?
Try to remember different types of rewards:

- Concrete rewards (stickers, food, prizes, certificates)
- Activity rewards (free time, class games, free reading)
- 'Exemption' rewards (no homework, no weekly test)
- Social rewards (praise, recognition).

What about punishments?

- Loss of privileges (cannot sit where you want, cannot work with friends)
- Fines (lost team points, grades, money)
- Extra work (homework, lines, laps, push-ups).

According to the behavioural view, consequences determine to a great extent whether a person will repeat the behaviour that led to the consequences. The type and timing of consequences can either strengthen or weaken behaviours (as with eating the chocolate cake discussed earlier). We will look first at consequences that strengthen behaviour.

Reinforcement

Reinforcement

Use of consequences to strengthen behaviour.

Reinforcer

Any event that follows a behaviour and increases the chances that the behaviour will occur again.

Although reinforcement is commonly understood to mean 'reward', this term has a particular meaning in psychology. A reinforcer is any consequence that strengthens the behaviour it follows. So, by definition, *reinforced behaviours increase in frequency or duration*. Whenever you see a behaviour persisting or increasing over time, you can assume the consequences of that behaviour are reinforcers for the individual involved (Landrum and Kauffman, 2006). The reinforcement process can be shown as follows:

$$\text{Behaviour} \longrightarrow \overset{\textbf{Consequence}}{\text{Reinforcer}} \longrightarrow \overset{\textbf{Effect}}{\text{Strengthened or repeated behaviour}}$$

We can be fairly certain that food will be a reinforcer for a hungry animal, but what about people? It is not clear why a particular event acts as a reinforcer for an individual, but there are many theories about why reinforcement works. For example, some psychologists suggest that reinforcers satisfy needs, while other psychologists believe that reinforcers reduce tension or stimulate a part of the brain (Rachlin, 1991). This is sometimes informally referred to as 'getting something out of it'. Whether the consequences of any action are reinforcing probably depends on the individual's perception of the event and the meaning it holds for him or her. For example, learners who repeatedly get themselves sent to the head teacher's office for misbehaving may be indicating that something about this consequence is reinforcing for them, even if it doesn't seem desirable to you. Perhaps, for example, they are rewarded by the special attention or 'singling out' that it involves for them. By the way, Skinner did not speculate about why reinforcers increase behaviour. He believed that it was useless to talk about 'imaginary constructs' such as meaning, expectations, needs or tensions. Skinner simply described the tendency for a given operant to increase after certain consequences (Hill, 2002; Skinner, 1953, 1989).

There are two types of reinforcement. The first, called positive reinforcement, occurs when the behaviour produces a new stimulus. Examples include pecking on the red key producing food for a pigeon, wearing a new outfit producing many compliments, or falling out of your chair producing cheers and laughter from classmates. This co-author's 13-year-old daughter instructs her not to crease new bags from clothes shops. Certain of these are selected and used to carry such things as PE kit to school. Clearly she is receiving positive reinforcement from her friends such as, 'More new clothes then – cool!' which means that this behaviour is continued.

Notice that positive reinforcement can occur even when the behaviour which is being reinforced (falling out of a chair) is not 'positive' from the teacher's point of view. In fact, positive reinforcement of inappropriate behaviours occurs unintentionally in many classrooms. Teachers help maintain problem behaviours by inadvertently reinforcing them. For example, Elizabeth may have unintentionally reinforced problem behaviour in her class by laughing the first time the boy answered, 'Ronaldinho'. The problem behaviour may have persisted for other reasons, but the consequence of Elizabeth's laughter could have played a role.

When the consequence that strengthens a behaviour is the *appearance* (*addition*) of a new stimulus, the situation is defined as *positive* reinforcement so the boy who said 'Ronaldinho' was positively reinforced by the laughter of the class and Elizabeth. In contrast, when the consequence that strengthens a behaviour is the *disappearance* (*subtraction*) of a stimulus, the process is called negative reinforcement. If a particular action leads to avoiding or escaping an aversive (unpleasant) situation, the action is likely to be repeated in a similar situation. A common example is the car seatbelt buzzer. As soon as you put on your seatbelt, the irritating buzzer stops. You are likely to repeat this behaviour (putting on the seatbelt) in the future because the action made an aversive stimulus (buzzer) disappear. Consider learners who continually 'feel sick' just before a test and are sent to see the nurse. The behaviour allows the learners to escape aversive situations – a test – so 'feeling sick' is being maintained, in part, through negative reinforcement. It is negative because the stimulus (the test) disappears; it is reinforcement because the behaviour that caused the stimulus to disappear ('feeling sick') increases or repeats. It is also possible that classical conditioning plays a role. The pupils may have been conditioned to experience unpleasant physiological reactions to tests. Let us now move on to *punishment*.

Punishment

Negative reinforcement is often confused with punishment. The process of reinforcement (positive or negative) always involves strengthening behaviour. Punishment, on the other hand, involves *decreasing or suppressing behaviour*. A behaviour followed by a punisher is *less* likely to be repeated in similar situations in the future. Again, it is the effect that defines a consequence as punishment, and different people have different perceptions of what is punishing. One learner may find suspension from school punishing, while another wouldn't mind at all. The process of punishment is shown as follows:

Behaviour ⟶ **Consequence** Punisher ⟶ **Effect** Weakened or decreased behaviour

Like reinforcement, punishment may take one of two forms. The first type is presentation (or positive) punishment (sometimes called Type I punishment). This occurs when the appearance of a stimulus following the behaviour suppresses or decreases the behaviour. When teachers give out extra work, running laps, detentions, and so on, they are using presentation punishment. The other type of punishment is

---

Positive reinforcement

Strengthening behaviour by presenting a desired stimulus after the behaviour.

Negative reinforcement

Strengthening behaviour by removing an aversive stimulus when the behaviour occurs.

Aversive

Irritating or unpleasant.

Punishment

Process that weakens or suppresses behaviour.

Presentation (or positive) punishment

Decreasing the chances that a behaviour will occur again by presenting an aversive stimulus following the behaviour; also called Type I punishment.

Figure 6.1
Kinds of reinforcement and punishment

Negative reinforcement and punishment are often confused. It might help to remember that reinforcement always involves **increases** in behaviours and punishment always involves **decreasing** or suppressing behaviours.

REINFORCEMENT
Behaviour encouraged

POSITIVE REINFORCEMENT
('Reward')
e.g. work rewarded with a high grade

PUNISHMENT
Behaviour suppressed

PRESENTATION PUNISHMENT
('Type I' punishment)
e.g. detention after school

NEGATIVE REINFORCEMENT
('Escape')
e.g. excused from homework

REMOVAL PUNISHMENT
('Type II' punishment)
e.g. no pocket money for a week

Removal (or negative) punishment

Decreasing the chances that a behaviour will occur again by removing a pleasant stimulus following the behaviour; also called Type II punishment.

Continuous reinforcement schedule

Presenting a reinforcer after every appropriate response.

Intermittent reinforcement schedule

Presenting a reinforcer after some but not all responses.

removal (or negative) punishment (Type II punishment). This involves removing a stimulus. When teachers or parents take away privileges after a young person has behaved inappropriately, they are applying removal punishment perhaps by withholding pocket money or keeping the person from going to a party or on a planned outing or by denying them their usual TV viewing. With both types, the effect is to decrease the behaviour that led to the punishment. Figure 6.1 summarises the processes of reinforcement and punishment.

Let us now look at the frequency and regularity of reinforcement to see how they impact upon behaviour.

Reinforcement schedules

When people are learning a new behaviour, they will learn it faster if they are reinforced for every correct response. This is a continuous reinforcement schedule. Then, when the new behaviour has been mastered, they will maintain it best if they are reinforced intermittently rather than every time. An intermittent reinforcement schedule helps learners to maintain skills without expecting constant reinforcement.

There are two basic types of intermittent reinforcement schedules. One – called an interval schedule – is based on the amount of time that passes between reinforcers. The other – a ratio schedule – is based on the number of responses learners give between reinforcers. Interval and ratio schedules may be either *fixed* (predictable) or *variable* (unpredictable). Table 6.1 summarises the five possible reinforcement schedules (the continuous schedule and the four kinds of intermittent schedules).

What are the effects of different schedules? Speed of performance depends on control. If reinforcement is based on the number of responses you give, then you have more control over the reinforcement: the faster you accumulate the correct number of responses, the faster the reinforcement will come. A teacher who says, 'As soon as you complete these ten problems correctly, you can go for a break,' can expect higher rates of performance than a teacher who says, 'Work on these ten problems for the next 20 minutes. Then I will check your work and those with ten correct can have their break.'

It seems that persistence in performance depends on unpredictability. Continuous reinforcement and both kinds of fixed reinforcement (ratio and interval) are quite predictable. We come to expect reinforcement at certain points and are generally quick to give up when the reinforcement does not meet our expectations. So, if a teacher always

Interval schedule
Length of time between reinforcers.

Ratio schedule
Reinforcement based on the number of responses between reinforcers.

Table 6.1 Reinforcement schedules

Schedule	Definition	Example	Response pattern	Reaction when reinforcement stops
Continuous	Every single response reinforced	1. Receiving A grade for every piece of work 2. Turning on the TV	Rapid learning of response	Very little persistence – disappears rapidly
Fixed interval	Reinforcement after set period of time	Giving yourself a 15-minute break after every hour of studying	Response rate speeds up as next reinforcement approaches but drops afterwards	Little persistence
Variable interval	Reinforcement after varying length of time	1. Searching through a range of books before finding relevant information 2. Finally receiving an answer after dialling a busy line	Slow, steady rate of response	Greater persistence – slow decline in response rate
Fixed ratio	Reinforcement after set number of responses	Credits/grades awarded for completion of set number of assignments	Rapid response rate-pause after reinforcement	Little persistence-rapid drop in response rate when expected number of responses given but no reinforcement occurs
Variable ratio	Reinforcement after varying number of responses	1. Receiving an A grade after a number of Cs 2. Slot machines	Very high response rate – little pause after reinforcement	Highest persistence-response rate stays high and gradually drops off

Slot machines are a good example of the effectiveness of intermittent reinforcement. People 'learn' to continue losing their money because it 'might' result in them winning the jackpot

praises a class for sitting quietly they may stop behaving in this way after a while because it is predictable and the praise loses its value. To encourage persistence of response, variable schedules are most appropriate. In fact, if the schedule is gradually changed until it becomes very 'lean' – meaning that reinforcement occurs only after many responses or a long time interval – then people can learn to work for extended periods without any reinforcement at all. Just watch gamblers playing slot machines to see how powerful a lean reinforcement schedule can be.

Reinforcement schedules influence how persistently we will respond when reinforcement is withheld. What happens then when reinforcement is completely withdrawn?

Extinction

In classical conditioning, the conditioned response is extinguished (disappears) when the conditioned stimulus appeared, but the unconditioned stimulus did not follow (tone, but no food) perhaps because the food container is empty. In operant conditioning, a person or an animal will not persist in a certain behaviour if the usual reinforcer is withheld long enough. The behaviour will eventually be extinguished (stop). For example, if you repeatedly e-mail someone but never get a reply, you may give up. Removal of reinforcement altogether leads to extinction. The process may take a while, however, as you know if you have tried to extinguish a child's tantrums by withholding your attention. Often the child wins – you give up ignoring and instead of extinction, intermittent reinforcement occurs. This, of course, may encourage even more persistent tantrums in the future which is the opposite of your intention so let's look at the *antecedents* or what happened before the tantrum.

Extinction

The disappearance of a learned response.

Antecedents and behaviour change

In operant conditioning, antecedents – the events preceding behaviours – provide information about which behaviours will lead to positive consequences and which will lead to unpleasant ones. When formulating his ideas on operant conditioning (which suggest that humans learn to behave in certain ways in response to the events which occurred before and after a certain behaviour). Skinner conditioned pigeons to peck for food when a light was on, but not to bother when the light was off, because no food followed pecking when the light was off. In other words, they learned to use the antecedent light as a cue to discriminate the likely consequence of pecking. The pigeons' pecking was under stimulus control, controlled by the discriminative stimulus of the light. This idea is related to discrimination in classical conditioning but here we are talking about *voluntary* behaviours such as pecking, not *reflex actions* such as salivating.

We all learn to discriminate – to read situations. When should you ask to borrow your friend's car – after a major disagreement or after you both have had a good time at a party? The antecedent cue of a school head teacher standing in the corridor helps learners discriminate the probable consequences of running or throwing litter around. We often respond to such antecedent cues without fully realising that they are influencing our behaviour. Teachers, however, can use cues deliberately in the classroom to encourage the desired behaviour, as we shall now see.

Stimulus control

Capacity for the presence or absence of antecedents to cause behaviours.

Cueing

By definition, cueing is the act of providing an antecedent stimulus just before a particular behaviour is supposed to take place. Cueing is particularly useful in setting the stage for behaviours that must occur at a specific time, but are easily forgotten. In working with young people, teachers often find themselves correcting behaviours after the fact. For example, they may ask the class, 'When are you going to start remembering to have your books out ready to start the lesson?' Such reminders often lead to irritation. The mistake is already made, and the young person is left with only two choices: to promise to try harder or to say, 'Why don't you leave me alone?' Neither response is very satisfying. Presenting a nonjudgmental cue, such as putting your own books out or standing quietly waiting at the front of the class, can help prevent these negative confrontations. When a learner performs the appropriate behaviour after a cue (opens bag and places books on the table) the teacher can reinforce the accomplishment instead of punishing the failure ('Good, I'm glad to see that you are ready to start. Well done.')

Cueing

Providing a stimulus that 'sets up' a desired behaviour.

Prompting

Sometimes learners need help learning to respond to a cue in an appropriate way so the cue becomes a discriminative stimulus and tells them how to behave in a certain situation. Many parents and caregivers will place a finger over their lips to tell children to be quiet perhaps when entering a library or when the show is about to begin in a theatre or cinema. One approach is to provide an additional cue, called a prompt, following the first cue. There are two principles for using a cue and a prompt to teach a new behaviour. First, make sure the environmental stimulus that you want to become a cue (perhaps standing at the front of the class and clapping your hands once or standing up before leaving a party or meeting) occurs immediately before the prompt you are using (asking the class to listen in silence or telling people that you are about to leave) so that children and young people will learn to respond to the cue and not rely only on the prompt. Second, gradually stop using the prompt as soon as possible so that learners do not become dependent on it (Alberto and Troutman, 2006). Let us now move to applied behaviour analysis which takes these principles a stage further.

Prompt

A reminder that follows a cue to make sure the person reacts to the cue.

Applied Behaviour Analysis

Although behaviourism was 'born' in the US and remains the driving force behind many of the applied educational techniques described here, behavioural management models are currently increasingly accepted within UK education and some parts of

Europe particularly when working with children who have behavioural or emotional problems. There are rising numbers of texts by writers such as Bill Rogers (2000, 2002, 2004 and 2006) and Sue Cowley (2003a, 2003b, 2006) that are used by those working within teacher education and by the teachers themselves. There is also currently a plethora of television programmes in the UK aimed at helping parents manage their children's behaviour, which is an indication of the popularity of this approach.

Applied behaviour analysis is the application of behavioural learning principles to change behaviour. The method is sometimes called behaviour modification, but this term has negative connotations for many people, and is often misunderstood (Alberto and Troutman, 2006; Kazdin, 2001). Ideally, applied behaviour analysis requires clear specification of the behaviour to be changed, careful measurement of the behaviour, analysis of the antecedents and reinforcers that might be maintaining inappropriate or undesirable behaviour, interventions based on behavioural principles to change the behaviour, and careful measurement of changes. In research on applied behaviour analysis, an ABAB design (described in Chapter 1) is common. That is, researchers take a baseline measurement of the behaviour (A), then apply the intervention (B), then stop the intervention to see if the behaviour goes back to the baseline level (A), and then reintroduce the intervention (B) as shown in the following diagram:

Applied behaviour analysis

The application of behavioural learning principles to understand and change behaviour.

Behaviour modification

Systematic application of antecedents and consequences to change behaviour.

| **A**
Measure
behaviour | → | **B**
Apply
intervention | → | **A**
Stop
intervention | → | **B**
Reintroduce
intervention |

Below in the Focus on Practice are some suggestions for those working with children in classrooms. Let us now consider some specific methods for accomplishing step 2 – the *intervention*.

Methods for encouraging behaviours

As we discussed earlier, to encourage behaviour is to reinforce it. There are several specific ways to encourage existing behaviours or teach new ones. These include praise, the Premack principle, shaping and positive practice, which we will now consider.

FOCUS ON PRACTICE

ABAB steps

In classrooms, teachers may be unable to follow all the ABAB steps, but they can do the following:

1. Clearly specify the behaviour to be changed and note the current level. For example, if a learner is 'careless,' does this mean 2, 3, 4 or more calculation errors for every ten maths problems?
2. Plan a specific intervention using antecedents, consequences, or both.
   For example, offer the learner one extra minute of computer time for every problem completed with no errors.
3. Keep a record of the results, and modify the plan if necessary.

Reinforcing with teacher attention

Many psychologists advise teachers to 'accentuate the positive' – praise learners for good behaviour, while ignoring misbehaviour. In fact, some researchers believe that 'the systematic application of praise and attention may be the most powerful motivational and classroom management tool available to teachers' (Alber and Heward, 1997, p. 277; Alber and Heward, 2000). In the UK both behaviour enhancement and reduction techniques have been applied in classrooms across all age groups (Wheldall and Merret, 1992; Houghton *et al.*, 1990) but research in Greece suggested that those working in nursery settings are most likely to use positive ways of encouraging appropriate behaviour (Papatheodorou, 2000).

A related strategy is *differential reinforcement*, or ignoring inappropriate behaviours, while being sure to reinforce appropriate behaviours as soon as they occur. For example, if a learner is prone to making irrelevant comments ('when do we break up for summer?'), teachers should ignore the off-task comment, but recognise a task-related contribution as soon as it occurs (Landrum and Kauffman, 2006).

However, this *praise-and-ignore approach* can be helpful, but it does not solve all classroom management problems. Several studies have shown that disruptive behaviours persist when teachers use positive consequences (mostly praise) as their only classroom management strategy (Pfiffner and O'Leary, 1987; Sullivan and O'Leary, 1990) and that other strategies (such as removing tokens when undesired behaviour occurs and then rewarding those with a required number of tokens left) may be more effective (McGoey and DuPaul, 2000). Also, if peer attention is maintaining the problem behaviours, the teacher's ignoring them won't do much to help as the learner is gaining positive reinforcement from this.

There is a second consideration when using praise. The positive results found in research occur when teachers carefully and systematically praise their students (Landrum and Kauffman, 2006). Merely 'handing out compliments' will not improve behaviour. To be effective, praise must (1) be contingent on the behaviour to be reinforced, (2) specify clearly the behaviour being reinforced, and (3) be believable. In other words, the praise should be sincere recognition of a well-defined behaviour so that learners understand what they did to warrant the recognition. It is important that teachers and others working with children receive adequate training as this increases the effectiveness of their management skills (Slider, Noell and Williams, 2006). Teachers who have not received special training often fail to do this effectively (Brophy, 1981). Ideas for using praise effectively, based on Brophy's extensive review of the subject, are presented in the following Focus on Practice.

Connect and Extend

See Infantino, J. and Little, E. (2005), 'Students' perceptions of classroom behaviour problems and the effectiveness of different disciplinary methods', *Educational Psychology*, 5, pp. 491–508 for an account of Australian research involving 350 secondary school learners and their views of interventions for disruptive behaviour.

FOCUS ON PRACTICE

Using praise appropriately

Be clear and systematic in giving praise

Examples
1. Make sure praise is tied directly to appropriate behaviour.
2. Make sure the learner understands the specific action or accomplishment that is being praised. Say, 'You returned this book on time and in good condition,' not, 'You were very responsible.'

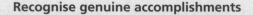

Recognise genuine accomplishments

Examples

1. Reward the attainment of specified goals, not just participation.
2. Do not reward uninvolved learners just for being quiet and not disrupting the class.
3. Tie praise to learners' improving competence or to the value of their accomplishment. Say, 'I noticed that you had checked all of your answers carefully. Your mark shows the care you have taken.'

Set standards for praise based on individual abilities and limitations

Examples

1. Praise progress or accomplishment in relation to the individual learner's past efforts.
2. Focus the learner's attention on his or her own progress, not on comparisons with others.

Attribute the learner's success to effort and ability so that he or she will gain confidence and believe that success is possible again

Examples

1. Don't imply that the success may be based on luck, extra help or easy questions.
2. Ask learners to describe the problems they encountered and how they solved them.

Make praise really reinforcing

Examples

1. Don't attempt to influence the rest of the class by singling out some learners for praise. This tactic frequently backfires, because learners know what's really going on. In addition, you risk embarrassing the person you have chosen to praise.
2. Don't give undeserved praise to learners simply to balance failures. It is seldom consoling and calls attention to the learner's inability to earn genuine recognition.

For more information on teacher praise, see http://moodle.ed.uiuc.edu/wiked/index.php/Praise. To assess your learners' preferences for praise, see http://www.csu.edu.au/research/staff/burnett/PraisePercScale.htm

Some psychologists have suggested that teachers' use of praise tends to focus learners on learning to win approval rather than on learning for its own sake. Perhaps the best advice for those managing behaviour is to be aware of the potential dangers of the overuse or misuse of praise and to navigate accordingly.

Selecting reinforcers: the Premack principle

In most classrooms, there are many readily available reinforcers other than teacher attention, such as the chance to talk to classmates or feed the class animals. However, teachers tend to offer these opportunities in a rather haphazard way. Just as with praise, by making privileges and rewards directly contingent on learning and positive behaviour, the teacher can greatly increase both learning and desired behaviour.

A helpful guide for choosing the most effective reinforcers is the Premack principle, named for the ground-breaking psychologist David Premack (1965). According to the Premack principle, a high-frequency behaviour (a preferred activity) can be an effective reinforcer for a low-frequency behaviour (a less-preferred activity). This is sometimes referred to as 'Grandma's rule': first, do what I want you to do, then you may do what you want to do. For example, 'Eat up your vegetables and then you can have some ice-cream.' Elizabeth used this principle in her class when she told them they could work together on the second section of the work sheet if they complete the first section quietly alone.

If learners didn't have to study, what would they do? The answers to this question may suggest many possible reinforcers. For most children and young people, talking, moving around the room, sitting near a friend, being exempt from homework or tests, reading magazines, using the computer or playing games are preferred activities. The best way to determine appropriate reinforcers for learners may be to watch what they do in their free time and use these if suitable.

For the Premack principle to be effective, the low-frequency (less preferred) behaviour must happen first. In the following dialogue, notice how the teacher loses a perfect opportunity to use the Premack principle:

Class: Oh, no! Do we have to work on grammar again today? The other classes had a discussion about the film we saw in the hall this morning.

Teacher: But the other classes finished the lesson on sentences yesterday. We're almost finished too. If we don't finish the lesson, I'm afraid you'll forget the rules we were learning yesterday.

Class: Why don't we finish the sentences at the end of the period and talk about the film now?

Teacher: Alright, if you promise to complete the sentences later.

Discussing the film could have served as a reinforcer for completing the lesson. As it is, the class may well spend the entire period discussing the film. Just as the discussion becomes fascinating, the teacher will have to end it and insist that the class return to the grammar lesson.

Let us now move on to consider 'shaping' techniques to encourage desired behaviour, the second approach identified at the beginning of this chapter.

Shaping

What happens when learners continually fail to gain reinforcement because they simply cannot perform a skill in the first place? Consider these examples:

- A nine-year-old child looks at the results of the latest mathematics test. 'I got nearly half of these marked wrong because I made one simple mistake in each problem. I hate maths!'

- A 15-year-old learner tries each week to find some excuse for avoiding the cricket game in PE. The learner cannot catch a ball and now refuses to try.

In both situations, the learners are receiving no reinforcement for their work because the end product of their efforts is not good enough. A safe prediction is that the learners will soon learn to dislike the class, the subject, and perhaps the teacher and school in general. One way to prevent this problem is the strategy of shaping, also called successive approximations. Shaping involves reinforcing progress instead of waiting for perfection.

Premack principle

Principle stating that a more-preferred activity can serve as a reinforcer for a less-preferred activity.

Shaping

Reinforcing each small step of progress towards a desired goal or behaviour.

Successive approximations

Small components that make up a complex behaviour.

Task analysis

System for breaking down a task hierarchically into basic skills and sub-skills.

In order to use shaping, the teacher must take the final complex behaviour the learner is expected to master and break it down into a number of small steps. One approach that identifies the small steps is task analysis, originally developed by R. B. Miller (1962) to help the armed services train personnel. Miller's system begins with a definition of the final performance requirement, what the trainee (or learner) must be able to do at the end of the programme or unit. Then, the steps that will lead to the final goal are specified. The procedure simply breaks skills and processes down into sub-skills and sub-processes.

Consider an example of task analysis in which learners must write a report based on library research. If the teacher gave out the report task without analysing it in this way, what could happen? Some of the class might not know how to do computer research. They might search through one or two encyclopedias, then write a summary of the issues based only on the encyclopedia entries. Another group of learners might know how to use computers, tables of contents and indexes, but have difficulty reaching conclusions. They might hand in lengthy reports listing summaries of different ideas. Another group of learners might be able to draw conclusions, but their written presentations might be so confusing and grammatically incorrect that the teacher could not understand what they were trying to say. Each of the groups would have failed in fulfilling the assigned task, but for different reasons.

A task analysis gives a picture of the logical sequence of steps leading towards the final goal. An awareness of this sequence can help teachers make sure that learners have the necessary skills before they move to the next step. In addition, when learners have difficulty, the teacher can pinpoint problem areas. Many behaviours can be improved through shaping, especially skills that involve persistence, endurance, increased accuracy, greater speed, or extensive practice to master. Because shaping is a time-consuming process, however, it should not be used if success can be attained through simpler methods such as cueing. Let us move on to positive practice to examine how useful this might be when working with children and young people.

Positive practice

Positive practice

Practising correct responses immediately after errors.

In positive practice, learners replace one behaviour with another. This approach is especially appropriate for dealing with academic errors. When learners make a mistake, they must correct it as soon as possible and practise the correct response (Gibbs and Luyben, 1985; Kazdin, 1984). The same principle can be applied when learners break classroom rules. Instead of being punished, the learner might be required to practise the correct alternative action.

The Focus on Practice below summarises approaches for encouraging positive behaviour.

FOCUS ON PRACTICE

Encouraging positive behaviours

Teachers should make sure that they recognise positive behaviour in ways that are valued by learners

Examples

1. When presenting class rules, set up positive consequences for following rules as well as negative consequences for breaking rules.

2. Recognise honest admissions of mistakes by giving a second chance: 'Because you admitted that you copied your answer from a book, I'm giving you a chance to rewrite it.'
3. Offer desired rewards for academic efforts, such as extra break time, exemptions from homework or tests, or team points which lead to a prize at the end of the week.

When learners are tackling new material or trying new skills, give plenty of reinforcement

Examples
1. Find and comment on something right in every learner's first life drawing or map of the school.
2. Reinforce pupils for encouraging each other. 'French pronunciation is difficult and awkward at first. Let's help each other by not allowing giggles when someone is brave enough to attempt a new word.'

After new behaviours are established, give reinforcement on an unpredictable schedule to encourage persistence

Examples
1. Offer surprise rewards for good participation in class.
2. Start classes with a short, written extra piece of work. Learners don't have to answer, but a good answer will add points to their total for the term.
3. Make sure the good learners get compliments for their work from time to time. Don't take them for granted.

Use cueing to help establish new behaviours

Examples
1. Put up humorous signs in the classroom to remind learners of rules.
2. At the beginning of the year, as learners enter class, call their attention to a list on the board of the materials they should have with them when they come to class.

Make sure all learners, even those who often cause problems, receive some praise, privileges or other rewards when they do something well

Examples
1. Review your class list occasionally to make sure all learners are receiving some reinforcement.
2. Set standards for reinforcement so that all learners will have a chance to be rewarded.
3. Make sure of your own biases. Are boys getting more opportunities for reinforcement than girls, or vice versa? How about learners of different ethnic cultures?

Establish a variety of reinforcers

Examples
1. Let learners suggest their own reinforcers or choose from a 'menu' of reinforcers with 'weekly specials'.
2. Talk to other teachers or parents about ideas for reinforcers.

Use the Premack principle to identify effective reinforcers

Examples
1. Watch what learners do with their free time.
2. Notice which learners like to work together. The chance to work with friends is often a good reinforcer.

For more ideas about building positive behaviours, see these sites: http://www.afcec.org/tipsforteachers/tips_c4.html and http://www.afcec.org/tipsforteachers/tips_c4.html

Coping with undesirable behaviour

No matter how successful teachers are at accentuating the positive, there are times when they must cope with undesirable behaviour, either because other methods fail or because the behaviour itself is dangerous and calls for direct action. For this purpose, negative reinforcement, satiation, reprimands and response cost, and social isolation all offer possible solutions. Let us look at each of these:

Negative reinforcement

Recall the basic principle of negative reinforcement: If an action stops or avoids something unpleasant, then the action is likely to occur again in similar situations. Negative reinforcement was operating in Elizabeth's classroom. When they moaned and complained, her class escaped the test, so they may have learned to complain more in the future through negative reinforcement.

Negative reinforcement can also be used to enhance learning. To do this, you place learners in mildly unpleasant situations so they can 'escape' when their behaviour improves. Consider these examples:

- *Teacher to a class of seven- and eight-year-olds:* 'When the coloured pencils are put back in the container and each of you is sitting quietly, we will go outside. Until then, we will miss our break.'

- *Secondary school teacher to a learner who seldom finishes work in-class:* 'As soon as you complete the work, you may join the class to watch the programme in the hall. But until you finish, you have to work in the library.'

You may wonder why the examples above are not considered punishment. Surely staying in during break or not accompanying the class to a special programme is punishing. However, the focus in each case is on strengthening specific behaviours (putting away pencils or finishing classwork). The teacher strengthens (reinforces) the behaviours by removing something aversive *as soon as the desired behaviours occur*. Because the consequence involves removing or 'subtracting' a stimulus, the reinforcement is negative.

Actually, a true behaviourist might object to identifying these situations as examples of negative reinforcement because too much learner thinking and understanding is required to make them work. Teachers cannot treat children and young people in the way that laboratory animals were once treated, delivering a mild shock to their feet until they give a right answer, then turning off the shock briefly. However, teachers can make sure that unpleasant situations improve when learners' behaviour improves.

Negative reinforcement gives learners a chance to exercise control. Missing break and staying behind in the library are unpleasant situations, but in each case, the learners retain control. As soon as they perform the appropriate behaviour, the unpleasant situation ends. In contrast, punishment occurs *after* the fact, and a learner cannot so easily control or terminate it.

There are several rules for negative reinforcement which are described in the Focus on Practice below.

Satiation

Another way to stop problem behaviour is to insist that learners continue the behaviour until they are tired of doing it. An example of this might be if learners are laughing in an exaggerated or inappropriate manner they might be encouraged to continue in order that they become tired of this behaviour. This procedure, called satiation, should be applied with care, however. Forcing learners to continue some behaviours may be physically or emotionally harmful, or even dangerous.

Teachers or others working with children and young people also can allow learners to continue some action until they stop by themselves, if the behaviour is not interfering with the rest of the class. A teacher can do this by simply ignoring the behaviour. Remember that responding to an ignorable behaviour may actually reinforce it.

In using satiation, a teacher must take care not to give in before the learners do. It is also important that the repeated behaviour be the one you are trying to end.

Satiation

Requiring a person to repeat a problem behaviour past the point of interest or motivation.

Reprimands

Soft, calm, private reprimands are more effective than loud, public reprimands in decreasing disruptive behaviour (Landrum and Kauffman, 2006). Research has shown that when reprimands are loud enough for the entire class to hear, disruptions increase or continue at a constant level. Some learners enjoy public recognition for misbehaviour, or they don't want classmates to see them 'lose' in a confrontation with the teacher. If they are not used too often, and if the classroom is generally a positive, warm environment, then learners usually respond quickly to private reprimands (Kaplan, 1991; Van Houten and Doleys, 1983).

Reprimands

Criticisms for misbehaviour; rebukes.

FOCUS ON PRACTICE

Applying negative reinforcement

- Describe the desired change in a positive way.
- Don't bluff by threatening consequences which are not possible.
- Make sure you can enforce your unpleasant situation.
- Follow through despite complaints.
- Insist on action, not promises.
- If the unpleasant situation terminates when learners promise to be better next time, you have reinforced making promises, not making changes (Alberto and Troutman, 2006; O'Leary, 1995).

Response cost

The concept of response cost is familiar to anyone who has ever paid a fine such as a parking ticket or library fine. For certain infractions of the rules, people must lose some reinforcer – money, time, privileges (Walker, Shea and Bauer, 2004). In a class, the concept of response cost can be applied in a number of ways. The first time a learner breaks a class rule, the teacher gives a warning. The second time, the teacher makes a mark beside the learner's name on the class list. The learner loses two minutes of break for each mark accumulated. For older children and young people, a certain number of marks might mean losing the privilege of leaving whole-school assemblies ahead of younger children.

Social isolation

One of the most controversial behavioural methods for decreasing undesirable behaviour is the strategy of social isolation, often called time out from reinforcement. The process involves removing a highly disruptive learner from the classroom for five to ten minutes. The learner is placed in an empty, uninteresting room alone – the punishment is brief isolation from other people. A trip to the head teacher's office or confinement to a chair in the corner of the regular classroom does not have the same effect as sitting alone in an empty room.

Some cautions

Punishment in and of itself, however, does not lead to any positive behaviour. Harsh punishment communicates to learners that 'might makes right' or that those with the power are the people who decide upon and dish out the punishment. This may encourage retaliation (Alberto and Troutman, 2006; Walker, Shea and Bauer, 2004) and for younger children, who are often unsure about what to do or how something should be done it may result in fear and anxiety, so increasing the undesired behaviour (Mayhew, 1997). Thus, whenever teachers consider the use of punishment, it should be part of a two-pronged attack. The first goal is to carry out the punishment and suppress the undesirable behaviour. The second goal is to make clear what the learner should be doing instead and to provide reinforcement for those desirable actions. Thus, while the problem behaviours are being suppressed, positive alternative responses are being strengthened. As you will see next, recent approaches really emphasise supporting positive behaviours. The following Focus on Practice gives ideas for using punishment for positive purposes.

FOCUS ON PRACTICE

Using punishment

Teachers and people working with children and young people should try to structure the situation so that they can use negative reinforcement rather than punishment

Examples
1. Allow learners to escape unpleasant situations (completing additional work, weekly maths tests) when they reach a level of competence.

2. Insist on actions, not promises. Do not allow learners to convince you to change the terms of the agreement.

Be consistent in your application of punishment

Examples
1. Avoid inadvertently reinforcing the behaviour you are trying to punish. Keep confrontations private, so that learners don't become heroes for standing up to the teacher in a public argument.
2. Let learners know in advance the consequences of breaking the rules by putting class rules on the walls for younger learners or outlining rules and consequences in a course syllabus for older learners.
3. Tell learners they will receive only one warning before punishment is given. Give the warning in a calm way, then follow it through.
4. Make punishment as unavoidable and immediate as is reasonably possible.

Focus on the learners' actions, not on their personal qualities

Examples
1. Reprimand in a calm but firm voice.
2. Avoid vindictive or sarcastic words or tones of voice. You might hear your own angry words later when learners imitate your sarcasm.
3. Stress the need to end the problem behaviour instead of expressing any dislike you might feel for the learner.
4. Be aware that learners from ethnic minority groups may be disproportionately punished, sent to detention and excluded from school – are your policies fair?

Adapt the punishment to the rule breaking

Example
1. Ignore minor misbehaviours that do not disrupt the class, or stop these misbehaviours with a disapproving glance or a move towards the learner.
2. Make sure the punishment fits the crime – don't take away all the free time a learner has earned for one infraction of the rules, for example (Landrum and Kauffman, 2006).
3. Don't use homework as a punishment for misbehaviours such as talking in class.
4. When a learner misbehaves to gain peer acceptance, removal from the group of friends can be effective, because this is really 'time out' from a reinforcing situation.
5. If the problem behaviours continue, analyse the situation and try a new approach. Your punishment may not be very punishing, or you may be inadvertently reinforcing the misbehaviour.

For more information on punishment, see http://www.ext.vt.edu/pubs/family/350-111/350-111.html

Let us now look at a currently effective approach to managing behaviour.

Reaching every learner: functional behavioural assessment and positive behaviour support

Teachers in both mainstream schools and special schools have had success with a new way of dealing with problem behaviours which begins by asking, 'What are learners getting out of their problem behaviours – what functions do these behaviours serve?' The focus is on the *why* of the behaviour, not on the *what* (Lane, Falk and Wehby, 2006). The reasons for problem behaviours generally fall into four categories (Barnhill, 2005; Maag and Kemp, 2003). Learners act in this way to:

1. Receive attention from others – teachers, parent or peers.
2. Escape from some unpleasant situation – an academic or social demand.
3. Obtain a desired item or activity.
4. Meet sensory needs, such as stimulation from rocking or flapping arms for some children with autism.

If the reason for the behaviour is known, then the teacher can devise ways of supporting positive behaviours that will serve the same 'why' function. For example, a child who always misbehaves and disrupts PE lessons is sent in to the library. It is easy to spot the function of the disruptions – they always led to (1) escape from PE lessons which the child hated because he was never picked for teams (negative reinforcement) and (2) time in the library to read which the boy enjoyed (positive reinforcement). Perhaps a way of changing this would be to allow some extra-curricular football practice in a small group and allowing him time in the library after taking part in the PE lesson appropriately. The new positive behaviours would serve many of the same functions as the old problem behaviours.

Positive behavioural supports

Positive behavioural supports (PBS)

Interventions designed to replace problem behaviours with new actions that serve the same purpose for the learner.

Functional behavioural assessment (FBA)

Procedures used to obtain information about antecedents, behaviours and consequences to determine the reason or function of the behaviour.

Positive behavioural supports are interventions designed to replace problem behaviours with new actions that serve the same purpose for the learner. The process of understanding the problem behaviour is known as a functional behavioural assessment (FBA) – 'a collection of methods or procedures used to obtain information about antecedents, behaviours, and consequences to determine the reason or function of the behaviour' (Barnhill, 2005, p. 132). With information from this assessment, teachers can develop an intervention package, as in the above example with the pupil who disrupted PE lessons which will ensure consistency and effectiveness of the strategies used.

Positive behaviour supports based on functional behavioural assessments can help learners with special educational needs succeed in mainstream classrooms. These can include an initial assessment conducted by the regular teaching staff followed by planned interventions such as making sure that work is at right difficulty level, providing assistance with set tasks, teaching the learners how to ask for help and for a break from assigned work (Soodak and McCarthy, 2006; Umbreit, 1995). However, these approaches are not only for learners with special educational needs. Research in Australia shows that disciplinary referrals decrease when the whole school uses these approaches for all pupils (Lewis, Sugai and Colvin, 1998). American research found that about 5% of pupils account for half of the discipline referrals so therefore it makes sense to develop interventions for those learners. Positive behaviour interventions based on functional assessments can reduce these behaviour problems by 80% (Crone and Horner, 2003).

Doing functional behavioural assessments

Many different procedures might help to determine the functions of a behaviour. You can simply talk with learners about their behaviours. In one study, learners were asked to describe what they did that got them into trouble at school, what happened just before, and what happened just after they misbehaved. Even though the learners were not always sure why they misbehaved, they seemed to benefit from talking to a concerned adult who was trying to understand their situation, not just reprimand them (Murdock, O'Neill and Cunningham, 2005). Teachers also can observe learners with these questions in mind:

- When and where does the problem behaviour occur?

- What people or activities are involved?

- What happens just before – what do others do or say and what did the learner in question do or say?

- What happens immediately after the behaviour – what did the teacher, other learners or the learner in question do or say?

- What does this learner gain or escape from – what changes after the learner misbehaves?

The answers to this question often shed new light upon the learner's behaviour and provide the teacher with different options for dealing with him or her.

STOP AND THINK

Think for a moment about your own 'problem' behaviour. For example, do you find it difficult to actually get on with a task that you know has to be done but you do not enjoy? Perhaps you find that you are doing all sorts of unnecessary things (tidying up, making coffee, visiting the loo) rather than begin the task? Does this occur most when you are at work/college/university or when you are at home? Are other people involved? What do you gain/escape from by not doing the work? What changes after you have delayed?

You may find that you have learned something about your own behaviour by doing this exercise and are then able to apply it to other situations and people. You may also be able to plan changes for your future behaviour based upon this information.

Behavioural Approaches to Teaching and Management

The behavioural approach to learning has made several important contributions to instruction, including systems for specifying learning objectives, mastery learning and direct instruction (we will look at these topics in Chapter 13 when we discuss teaching) and class management systems such as group consequences, token economies and contingency contracts (Landrum and Kauffman, 2006). These approaches are useful when the goal is to learn *explicit information* or change *behaviours* and when the material is *sequential* and *factual*.

Posters listing rules, consequences and rewards are useful reminders about appropriate behaviours

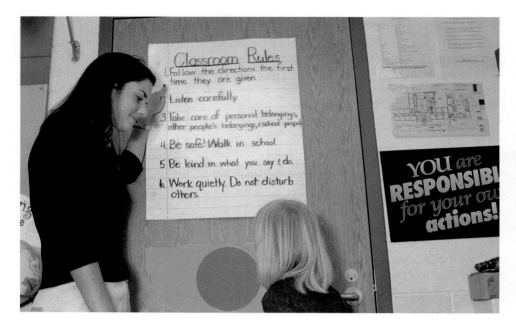

First, let's consider one element that is part of every behavioural learning programme – specific practice of correct behaviours. Contrary to popular wisdom, practice does not make *perfect*. Instead, practice makes *permanent* the behaviours practised, so practising accurate behaviours is important. None of the world famous gymnasts and sportsmen/women gained their expertise without extensive practice. As an example of a behavioural approach let us examine group consequences.

Group consequences

A teacher can base reinforcement for the class on the cumulative behaviour of all members of the class, usually by adding each class member's points to a class or a team total. The good behaviour game is an example of this approach. Teachers and learners discuss what would make the classroom a better place. Then, they identify behaviours that get in the way of learning. Based on this discussion, class rules are developed and the class is divided into two teams. Each time a learner breaks one of the rules, that person's team is given a mark. The team with the fewest marks at the end of the lesson receives a special reward or privilege (longer break, first to lunch, and so on). If both teams earn fewer than a pre-established number of marks, both teams receive the reward. Most studies indicate that even though the game generates only small improvements in academic achievement, it can produce definite improvements in the behaviours listed in the good behaviour rules and it can prevent many behaviour problems (Embry, 2002).

Group consequences may also be used without dividing the class into teams; that is, you can base reinforcement on the behaviour of the whole class. Wilson and Hopkins (1973) conducted a study using group consequences to reduce classroom noise levels. Radio music served effectively as the reinforcer for learners in a class. Whenever noise in the class was below a predetermined level, learners could listen to the radio; when the noise exceeded the level, the radio was turned off. Given the success of this simple method, such a procedure might be considered in any class where music does not interfere with the task at hand.

However, caution is needed using group approaches. The whole group should not suffer for the misbehaviour or mistakes of one individual if the group has no real

Good behaviour game

Arrangement where a class is divided into teams and each team receives a black mark or demerit points for breaking agreed-upon rules of good behaviour.

Group consequences

Rewards or punishments given to a class as a whole for adhering to or violating rules of conduct.

influence over that person (Epanchin, Townsend and Stoddard, 1994). This might lead to a person becoming extremely unpopular and increasingly isolated within a class which is being consistently penalised (perhaps by losing break time) for the misbehaviour of that person.

Peer pressure in the form of support and encouragement, however, can be a positive influence. Group consequences are recommended for situations in which learners care about the approval of their peers (Theodore *et al.*, 2001). If a few members of the class seem to enjoy sabotaging the system, then they may need separate arrangements. If the misbehaviour of several learners seems to be encouraged by the attention and laughter of other classmates, then group consequences could be helpful.

Token reinforcement programmes

> ### STOP AND THINK
>
> Have you ever participated in a programme where you earned points or credits that you could exchange for a reward? Do you have a loyalty card for spending money at a particular supermarket or store? Do you get one free DVD for every ten rentals? Does being a part of such a scheme affect your buying habits? How?

However, it is often difficult to provide positive consequences for all the learners who deserve them. A token reinforcement system can help solve this problem by allowing all learners to earn tokens for both academic work and positive classroom behaviour. The tokens may be points, stickers, holes punched in a card, play money, or anything else that is easily identified as the learner's property. Periodically, the learners exchange the tokens they have earned for some desired reward (Capstick, 2005; Kazdin, 2001; Alberto and Troutman, 2006).

Depending on the age of the learner, the rewards could be small toys, school supplies, free time, special class jobs, money or other privileges. When a 'token economy,' as this kind of system is called, is first established, the tokens should be given out on a fairly continuous schedule, with chances to exchange the tokens for rewards often available. Once the system is working well, however, tokens should be distributed on an intermittent schedule and saved for longer periods of time before they are exchanged for rewards. This will ensure that they will operate most effectively as we saw in the reinforcement schedule section earlier (Table 6.1).

Another variation is to allow learners to earn tokens in the classroom and then exchange them for rewards at home. These plans are very successful when parents are willing to cooperate. Usually a note or report form is sent home daily or twice a week. The note indicates the number of points earned in the preceding time period. The points may be exchanged for minutes of television viewing, access to special toys, or private time with parents. Points can also be saved up for larger rewards such as trips. It is not advisable to use this procedure, however, if you think that parents will not cooperate or suspect that the child might be severely punished for poor reports.

Token reinforcement systems are complicated and time-consuming. Generally, they should be used in only three situations: (1) to motivate learners who are completely uninterested in their work and have not responded to other approaches; (2) to encourage learners who have consistently failed to make academic progress; and (3) to deal with a class that is out of control. Some groups of learners seem to benefit from token economies more than others. Learners with special educational needs, children

Token reinforcement system

System in which tokens earned for academic work and positive classroom behaviour can be exchanged for some desired reward.

who have failed often, pupils with few academic skills, and learners with behaviour problems all seem to respond to the concrete, direct nature of token reinforcement.

Before trying a token system, teachers should be sure that teaching methods and materials are right for the learners. Sometimes, class disruptions or lack of motivation indicate that teaching practices need to be changed. Perhaps the class rules are unclear or are enforced inconsistently. It could be that the work is too easy or too hard. Perhaps the pace is wrong. If these problems exist, a token system may improve the situation temporarily, but the learners will still have trouble learning the academic material. Let us look at contingency contract programmes to see how they work and how they might help.

Contingency contract programmes

Contingency contract

A contract between the teacher and a learner specifying what the learner must do to earn a particular reward or privilege.

In a contingency contract programme, the teacher draws up an individual contract with each learner, describing exactly what the person must do to earn a particular privilege or reward. In some programmes, learners suggest behaviours to be reinforced and the rewards that can be gained. The negotiating process can be an educational experience itself, as pupils learn to set reasonable goals and abide by the terms of a contract. It is also true that if learners participate in setting the goals, they often are more committed to reaching them (Locke and Latham, 1990; Pintrich and Schunk, 2002). If, for example, a learner has difficulty in completing homework on time a contingency contract for completing homework could be compiled. First the teacher and learner would agree dates for giving in the work and these would be put onto a chart (perhaps in red). Whenever the learner submits the work on time the date is entered (in blue perhaps) on the chart. Each time a 'blue' date appears the learner is given free time or other negotiated rewards.

The positive aspects of using these is that this chart serves as a contract, assignment sheet and progress record which allows tracking of a learner. Information about progress can also support learner motivation (Schunk, 2004) as there is an observable record of this available.

The few pages devoted here to token reinforcement and contingency contracts can offer only an introduction to these programmes. If a large-scale reward programme is used in a classroom, it is wise to seek professional advice.

Many of the systematic applications of behavioural principles focus on classroom management. The next section describes two examples that successfully applied behavioural principles to improve behaviours of pupils with special needs.

Learners with severe behaviour problems

Learners with severe behaviour problems provide some of the most difficult challenges for teachers. Two studies show how behavioural principles can be useful in helping these learners.

Lea Theodore and her colleagues (2001) worked with the teacher of five adolescent males who were diagnosed as having severe emotional disorders. A short list of clear rules was established (e.g. no obscene words, comply with teacher's requests within five seconds, no verbal insults). The rules were written on index cards taped to each learner's desk. The teacher had a checklist on his desk with each boy's name to note any rule-breaking. This checklist was easily observable, so learners could monitor their own and each others' performance. At the end of the 45-minute period, a learner chose from various options in a jar which included performance of the whole group, person with the highest score, person with the lowest score, the average of all learners, or a random single learner. If the learner or learners picked from the jar had five marks

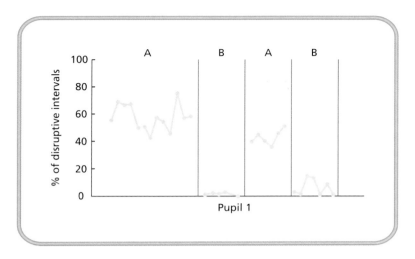

Figure 6.2
Using an ABAB design to evaluate an improvement strategy with a pupil who had severe behaviour problems

Source: For details of both of these approaches see: 'Randomization of group contingencies and reinforcers to reduce classroom disruptive behavior' by L. A. Theodore, M. A. Bray, T. J. Kehle and W. R. Jenson, 2001, *Journal of School Psychology, 39*, 267–277 and 'Token reinforcement and response cost procedures: reducing disruptive behavior of preschool children with attention-deficit/hyperactivity disorder' by K. E. McGoey and G. J. DuPaul, 2000, *School Psychology Quarterly, 15*, 330–343.

on the checklist or fewer for rule-breaking, then the whole class got a reward, also chosen randomly from a jar. The possible rewards were things like a fizzy drink, a bag of crisps, a bar of chocolate, or a pass allowing a late start to lessons. An ABAB design was used – baseline, two-week intervention, two-week withdrawal of intervention, and two-week return to group consequences. All learners showed clear improvement in following the rules when the reward system was in place, as you can see in Figure 6.2, a chart for one of the pupils. Pupils liked the approach and the teacher found it easy to implement.

In the second study, Kara McGoey and George DuPaul (2000) worked with teachers in three preschool classrooms to address problem behaviours of four children diagnosed as having attention-deficit hyperactive disorder (ADHD). The teachers tried both a token reinforcement programme (children earned small and large buttons on a chart for following class rules), and a response cost system (children began with five small buttons and one large button per activity each day and lost buttons for not following rules). Both procedures were effective in lowering rule-breaking, but the teachers found the response cost system easier to implement.

As behavioural approaches to learning developed, some researchers added a new element – thinking about behaviour.

Observational Learning and Cognitive Behaviour Modification: Thinking about Behaviour

In recent years, most behavioural psychologists have found that operant conditioning offers too limited an explanation of learning. Many have expanded their view of learning to include the study of cognitive processes that cannot be directly observed, such as expectations, thoughts, mental maps and beliefs. Three examples of this expanded view are observational learning, self-management and cognitive behaviour modification which we shall look at in this section.

Observational learning

Over 30 years ago, Albert Bandura noted that the traditional behavioural views of learning were accurate – but incomplete – because they gave only a partial explanation of learning and overlooked important elements, particularly social influences. His early work on learning was grounded in the behavioural principles of reinforcement and punishment, but he added a focus on *learning from observing others*. This expanded view was labelled social learning theory; it was considered a *neobehavioural* approach (Bandura, 1977; Hill, 2002; Zimmerman and Schunk, 2003).

To explain some limitations of the behavioural model, Bandura distinguished between the *acquisition of knowledge* (learning) and the *observable performance based on that knowledge* (behaviour). In other words, Bandura suggested that we all may know more than we show in our behaviour. An example is found in one of Bandura's early studies (1965). Preschool children saw a film of a model kicking and punching an inflatable 'Bobo' doll. One group saw the model rewarded for the aggression, another group saw the model punished, and a third group saw no consequences. When they were moved to a room with the Bobo doll, the children who had seen the punching and kicking reinforced on the film were the most aggressive towards the doll. Those who had seen the attacks punished were the least aggressive. However, when the children were promised rewards for imitating the model's aggression, all of them demonstrated that they had learned the behaviour.

Thus, we can see that incentives can affect performance. Even though learning might have occurred, it may not be demonstrated until the situation is appropriate or there are incentives to perform. This might explain why some learners don't perform 'bad behaviours' such as swearing or smoking that they all see modelled by adults, peers and the media. Personal consequences may discourage them from performing the behaviours. In other examples, children may have learned how to write the alphabet, but perform badly because their fine motor coordination (involving small hand movements coordinated with the eyes) is limited, or they may have learned how to calculate fractions, but perform badly on a test because they are anxious. In these cases, their performance is not an indication of their learning.

Recently, Bandura has focused on cognitive factors such as beliefs, self-perceptions and expectations, so his theory is now called a social cognitive theory (Hill, 2002). Social cognitive theory (discussed more thoroughly in Chapters 9 and 10) distinguishes between enactive and vicarious learning. *Enactive learning* is learning by doing and experiencing the consequences of your actions. This may sound like operant conditioning all over again, but it is not, and the difference has to do with the role of consequences. Proponents of operant conditioning believe that consequences strengthen or weaken behaviour. In enactive learning, however, consequences are seen as providing information. Our interpretations of the consequences create expectations, influence motivation and shape beliefs (Schunk, 2004). We will see many examples of enactive learning – learning by doing – throughout this book.

Vicarious learning is learning by observing others. People and animals can learn merely by observing another person or animal learn, and this fact challenges the behaviourist idea that cognitive factors are unnecessary in an explanation of learning. If people can learn by watching, they must be focusing their attention, constructing images, remembering, analysing and making decisions that affect learning. Thus, much is going on mentally before performance and reinforcement can even take place. Cognitive apprenticeships, discussed in Chapter 9, are examples of vicarious learning – learning by observing others.

Social learning theory

Theory that emphasises learning through observation of others.

Children learn to behave aggressively to the 'Bobo' doll having observed adults doing this

Social cognitive theory

Theory that adds concern with cognitive factors such as beliefs, self-perceptions and expectations to social learning theory.

Elements of observational learning

> ### STOP AND THINK
>
> Think about the people in your own life who have acted as role models for you. Are there elements of their behaviour which you have taken on as part of your own? Are you aware, for example, that you hear yourself saying or see yourself doing things that your parents or teachers have done?

Through observational learning, we learn not only how to perform a behaviour but also what will happen to us in specific situations if we do perform it. Observation can be a very efficient learning process. The first time children hold hairbrushes, cups or tennis rackets, they usually brush, drink or swing as well as they can, given their current muscle development and coordination. They do this because they have seen others doing or modelling this. Let's take a closer look at how observational learning occurs. Bandura (1986) notes that observational learning includes four elements: *paying attention, retaining information or impressions, producing behaviours* and *being motivated* to repeat the behaviours.

Observational learning

Learning by observation and imitation of others.

Attention

In order to learn through observation, we have to pay attention; otherwise we are simply not observing. In learning environments teachers will have to ensure learners' attention to the critical features of the lesson by making clear presentations and highlighting important points. In demonstrating a skill (e.g. threading a sewing machine or operating a lathe), learners may need to look over the teacher's shoulder as they work. Seeing the teacher's hands from the same perspective as they see their own directs their attention to the right features of the situation and makes observational learning easier. Similar factors apply in PE lessons where perhaps a shooting position is being modelled in football or netball or a dance step demonstrated.

Retention

In order to imitate the behaviour of a model, you have to remember it. This involves mentally representing the model's actions in some way, probably as verbal steps (step on left foot then kick right, half turn, jump onto right foot, etc.), or as visual images, or both. Retention can be improved by mental rehearsal (imagining imitating the behaviour) or by actual practice. In the retention phase of observational learning, practice helps us remember the elements of the desired behaviour, such as the sequence of steps.

Production

Once we 'know' how a behaviour should look and remember the elements or steps we have seen modelled we still may not perform it smoothly. Sometimes, we need a great deal of practice, feedback and coaching about subtle points before we can reproduce the behaviour of the model. In the production phase, practice makes the behaviour smoother and more expert.

Motivation and reinforcement

As mentioned earlier, social learning theory distinguishes between acquisition and performance. We may acquire a new skill or behaviour through observation, but we may not perform that behaviour until there is some motivation or incentive to do so. Reinforcement can play several roles in observational learning. If we anticipate being reinforced for imitating the actions of a model, we may be more motivated to pay attention, remember and reproduce the behaviours. In addition, reinforcement is important in maintaining learning. A person who tries a new behaviour is unlikely to persist without reinforcement (Ollendick, Dailey and Shapiro, 1983; Schunk, 2004). For example, if an unpopular member of the class adopted the dress of the 'in' group, but was ignored or ridiculed, it is unlikely that the imitation would continue.

Bandura identifies three forms of reinforcement (direct, vicarious and self) that can encourage observational learning. First, of course, the observer may reproduce the behaviours of the model and receive *direct reinforcement*, as when a gymnast successfully executes a front flip/round-off combination and the coach says, 'Excellent!'

However, the reinforcement need not be direct – it may be vicarious reinforcement. The observer may simply see others reinforced for a particular behaviour and then increase his or her production of that behaviour. For example, if you compliment two learners on the clear diagrams in their science homework, several other class members who observe your compliments may hand in clear diagrams next time. Most TV advertisements hope for this kind of effect. People in commercials become deliriously happy when they drive a particular car or drink a specific juice, and the viewer is supposed to do the same; the viewer's behaviour is reinforced vicariously by the actors' obvious pleasure. Punishment can also be vicarious: you may slow down on a particular stretch of road after seeing several people get speeding tickets there.

The final form of reinforcement is self-reinforcement, or controlling your own reinforcers. This sort of reinforcement is important for both learners and teachers. We want learners to improve not because it leads to external rewards, but because they themselves value and enjoy their growing competence. It is also important for teachers particularly when demands are high and rewards low; self-reinforcement may be all that keeps them going. Let us consider some of the factors which influence whether we learn from others.

Factors that influence observational learning

What causes an individual to learn and perform modelled behaviours and skills? Several factors play a role, as shown in Table 6.2. The developmental level of the observer makes a difference in learning. As children grow older, they are able to focus attention for longer periods of time, use memory strategies to retain information and motivate themselves to practice (see Chapter 7 for more on this). A second influence is the status of the model. Children are more likely to imitate the actions of others who seem competent, powerful, prestigious and enthusiastic: so parents, teachers, older siblings, athletes, action heroes, rock stars, film personalities and people belonging to the 'celebrity' culture in general may serve as models, depending on the age and interests of the child. Third, by watching others, we learn about what behaviours are appropriate for people like ourselves, so models who are seen as similar are more readily imitated (Pintrich and Schunk, 2002). Unfortunately it is also possible for children and

Vicarious reinforcement

Increasing the chances that we will repeat a behaviour by observing another person being reinforced for that behaviour.

Self-reinforcement

Controlling your own reinforcers.

Table 6.2 Factors that affect observational learning

Characteristic effects of modelling

Developmental status	Improvements with development include longer attention and increased capacity to process information, use strategies, compare performances with memorial representations and adopt intrinsic motivators.
Model prestige and competence	Observers pay greater attention to competent, high-status models. Consequences of modelled behaviours convey information about functional value. Observers attempt to learn actions they believe they will need to perform.
Vicarious consequences	Consequences to models convey information about behavioural-appropriateness and likely outcomes of actions. Valued consequences motivate observers. Similarity in attributes or competence signals appropriateness and heightens motivation.
Outcome expectations	Observers are more likely to perform modelled actions they believe are appropriate and will result in rewarding outcomes.
Goal setting	Observers are likely to attend to models who demonstrate behaviours that help observers attain goals.
Self-efficacy	Observers attend to models when they believe they are capable of learning or performing the modelled behaviour. Observation of similar models affects self-efficacy ('If they can do it, I can too').

Source: From Schunk, Dale H., *Learning Theories: An Educational Perspective*, 4th Edition, © 2004, p. 92. Reprinted by permission of Pearson Education, Inc., Upper Saddle River, NJ.

young/people to learn from 'bad' role models whom they identify with. The current trend for some preadolescent girls to present themselves in sexually inappropriate ways might be learned from role models such as Britney Spears and Christina Aguilera (Siasoco, 2006). All learners need to see successful, capable models who look and sound like them, no matter what their ethnicity, socioeconomic status or gender. This means that teaching cohorts should reflect this in order for successful modelling to take place.

Look at Table 6.2. The last three influences involve goals and expectations. If observers expect that certain actions of models will lead to particular outcomes (such as particular practice schedules leading to improved athletic performance) and the observers value those outcomes or goals, then the observers are more likely to pay attention to the models and try to reproduce their behaviours. Finally, observers are more likely to learn from models if the observers have a high level of self-efficacy – that is, if they believe they are capable of doing the actions needed to reach the goals, or at least of learning how to do so (Bandura, 1997; Pintrich and Schunk, 2002). We will discuss goals, expectations and self-efficacy in greater depth in Chapter 10 on motivation.

Self-efficacy

A person's sense of being able to deal effectively with a particular task.

Observational learning in teaching

STOP AND THINK

How might teachers incorporate observational learning into their teaching? What are the skills, attitudes and strategies that might be modelled in teaching PSHE (personal, social and health education)?

There are five possible outcomes of observational learning: directing attention, encouraging existing behaviours, changing inhibitions, teaching new behaviours and attitudes and arousing emotions. Let's look at each of these as they occur in classrooms.

Directing attention

By observing others, we not only learn about actions but also notice the objects involved in the actions. For example, in a preschool class, when one child plays enthusiastically with a toy that has been ignored for days, many other children may want to have the toy, even if they play with it in different ways or simply carry it around. This happens, in part, because the children's attention has been drawn to that particular toy.

Fine-tuning already-learned behaviours

All of us have had the experience of looking for cues from other people when we find ourselves in unfamiliar situations. Observing the behaviour of others tells us which of our already-learned behaviours to use: when to start eating at a formal dinner, when to leave a meeting or party, what kind of language is appropriate, and so on. Adopting the dress, grooming styles and ways of speaking which TV or music 'celebrities' use is another example of this kind of effect.

Strengthening or weakening inhibitions

If class members witness one learner breaking a class rule and getting away with it, they may learn that undesirable consequences do not always follow rule breaking. If the rule breaker is a well-liked, high-status class member, the effect of the modelling may be even more pronounced, as we saw in the case at the beginning of this chapter. However, it is possible for teachers to take advantage of the 'ripple effect' (Kounin, 1970) which can work for the teacher's benefit. When the teacher deals effectively with a rule breaker, especially a class leader, the idea of breaking this rule may be inhibited for the other learners viewing the interaction. This does not mean that teachers must reprimand each learner who breaks a rule, but once a teacher has called for a particular action, following through is an important part of capitalising on the ripple effect.

Ripple effect
'Contagious' spreading of behaviours through imitation.

Teaching new behaviours

Modelling has long been used, of course, to teach dance, sports and crafts, as well as skills in subjects such as food technology, chemistry and welding. Modelling can also be applied deliberately in the classroom to teach mental skills and to broaden horizons – to teach new ways of thinking. Teachers serve as models for a vast range of

Modelling
Changes in behaviour, thinking or emotions that occur through observing another person – a model.

behaviours, from pronouncing vocabulary words, to reacting to the seizure of a pupil with epilepsy, to being enthusiastic about learning. For example, a teacher might model sound critical thinking skills by thinking 'out loud' about a learner's question. Or a secondary-school teacher concerned about girls who seem to have stereotyped ideas about careers might invite women with non-traditional jobs to speak to the class. Studies indicate that modelling can be most effective when the teacher makes use of all the elements of observational learning described in the previous section, especially reinforcement and practice.

Models who are the same age as the learners may be particularly effective. For example, Schunk and Hanson (1985) compared two methods for teaching subtraction to seven- and eight-year-olds who had difficulties learning this skill. One group of children observed other seven- and eight-year-olds learning the procedures, while another group watched a teacher's demonstration. Then both groups participated in the same instructional programme. The pupils who observed peer models learning not only scored higher on tests of subtraction after instruction but also gained more confidence in their own ability to learn. For pupils who doubt their own abilities, a good model is a low-achieving pupil who keeps trying and finally masters the material (Schunk, 2004).

Arousing emotion

Finally, through observational learning, people may develop emotional reactions to situations they have never experienced personally, such as flying or driving. A child who watches a friend fall from a swing and break an arm may become fearful of swings. After news of children being abducted and/or murdered other children may become more anxious about talking to strangers. News reports of dog attacks upon children have a similar effect. Even the threatened outbreak of bird flu recently had people becoming afraid of contact with birds. Note that hearing and reading about a situation are also forms of observation. When frightening things happen to people who are similar in age or circumstances to your learners, they may need to talk about their emotions.

The following Focus on Practice will give you some ideas about the use of observational learning in the classroom.

FOCUS ON PRACTICE

Using observational learning

Model behaviours and attitudes you want children to learn

Examples

1. Show enthusiasm for the subject you teach.
2. Be willing to demonstrate both the mental and the physical tasks you expect the learners to perform. A teacher was observed sitting down in the sandbox while her class of four-year-olds watched her demonstrate the difference between 'playing with sand' and 'throwing sand'.

3. When reading to children, model good problem solving. Stop and say, 'Now let me see if I remember what happened so far,' or 'That was a hard sentence. I'm going to read it again.'
4. Model good problem solving – think out loud as you work through a difficult problem.

Use peers as models

Examples

1. In group work, pair learners who do well with those who are having difficulties.
2. Ask children to demonstrate the difference between 'whispering' and 'silence – no talking.'

Make sure learners see that positive behaviours lead to reinforcement for others

Examples

1. Point out the connections between positive behaviour and positive consequences in stories.
2. Be fair and consistent in giving reinforcement. The same rules for rewards should apply to the problem learners as to the good learners.

Examples

1. Ask a well-liked learner to be friendly to an isolated, fearful member of the class.
2. Let popular/high-achieving learners lead an activity when you need class cooperation or when children are likely to be reluctant at first. Perhaps this might apply when initiating drama activities or children presenting a talk to the class.

For more information on observational learning, see http://mentalhelp.net/psyhelp/chap4/chap4g.htm

Let us now move from our discussion of encouraging desired behaviours in others to a consideration of how we 'manage' or discipline ourselves.

Self-management

If one goal of education is to produce people who are capable of educating themselves, then people must learn to manage their own lives, set their own goals and provide their own reinforcement. In adult life, rewards are sometimes vague and goals often take a long time to reach. Think about how many small steps are required to complete an education and find your first job. Life is filled with tasks that call for this sort of self-management (Rachlin, 2000).

Learners may be involved in any or all of the steps in implementing a basic behaviour change programme. They may help set goals, observe their own work, keep records of it and evaluate their own performance. Finally, they can select and deliver reinforcement.

Self-management

Use of behavioural learning principles to change your own behaviour.

Goal setting

It appears that the goal-setting phase is very important in self-management (Pintrich and Schunk, 2002; Reeve, 1996). In fact, some research suggests that setting specific goals and making them public may be the critical elements of self-management pro-grammes. For example, S. C. Hayes and his colleagues identified college students who had serious problems with studying and taught them how to set specific study goals. Learners who set goals and announced them to the experimenters performed signifi-cantly better on tests covering the material they were studying than students who set goals privately and never revealed them to anyone (Hayes *et al.*, 1985). More recently it has been found that higher standards tend to lead to higher performance (Locke and Latham, 2002) but unfortunately, learner-set goals have a tendency to reflect lower and lower expectations. Teachers, then, can help learners maintain high standards by monitoring the goals set and reinforcing high standards.

Monitoring and evaluating progress

Learners may also participate in the monitoring and evaluation phases of a behaviour change programme (Mace, Belfiore and Hutchinson, 2001). Some examples of behav-iours that are appropriate for self-monitoring are the number of assignments completed, time spent practising a skill, number of books read, number of problems answered correctly and time taken to run a mile. Tasks that must be accomplished without teacher supervision, such as homework or private study, are also good candidates for self-monitoring. Learners keep a chart, diary or checklist that records the frequency or duration of the behaviours in question. A progress record card can help older learners break down assignments into small steps, determine the best sequence for completing the steps, and keep track of daily progress by setting goals for each day. The record card itself serves as a prompt that can be faded out.

Self-evaluation is somewhat more difficult than simple self-recording because it in-volves making a judgement about quality. Learners can evaluate their behaviour with reasonable accuracy, especially if they learn standards for judging a good performance or product. For example, Sweeney *et al.* (1993) taught secondary school pupils how to evaluate their handwriting for size, slant, shape and spacing. One key to accurate self-evaluation seems to be for the teacher to periodically check learners' assessments and give reinforcement for accurate judgements. Older learners may learn accurate self-evaluation more readily than younger children. Again, bonus points can be awarded when the teachers' and learners' evaluations match (Kaplan, 1991). Self-correction can accompany self-evaluation. Learners first evaluate, then alter and improve their work, and finally, compare the improvements to the standards again (Mace, Belfiore and Hutchinson, 2001).

Self-reinforcement

The last step in self-management is self-reinforcement. There is some disagreement, however, as to whether this step is actually necessary. Some psychologists believe that setting goals and monitoring progress alone are sufficient and that self-reinforcement adds nothing to the effects (Hayes *et al.*, 1985). Others believe that rewarding your-self for a job well done can lead to higher levels of performance than simply setting goals and keeping track of progress (Bandura, 1986). If you are willing to be tough and really deny yourself something you want until your goals are reached, then per-haps the promise of the reward can provide extra incentive for work. With that in mind, you may want to think of some way to reinforce yourself when you finish read-ing this chapter. A similar approach helped me write this chapter in the first place.

Connect and Reflect

See O'Reilly, M. *et al.* (2005), 'Evaluation of video feedback and self-management to decrease schoolyard aggression and increase pro-social behaviour in two students with behavioural disorders', *Educational Psychology*, 25(2–3), pp. 199–206 for an account of research combining video feedback with self-management strategies.

At times, families can be enlisted to help their children develop self-management abilities. Working together, teachers and parents can focus on a few goals and, at the same time, support the growing independence of the learners. Sometimes, teaching children self-management can solve a problem for teachers and provide fringe benefits as well. For example, the trainers of a competitive swim team with members aged nine to 16 were having difficulty persuading swimmers to maintain high work rates. Then the trainers drew up four charts indicating the training programme to be followed by each member and displayed the charts near the pool. The swimmers were given the responsibility of recording both their numbers of laps and their completion of each training unit. Because the recording was public, swimmers could see their own and their teammates progress and keep accurate track of the work units completed. Work output increased by 27%. The trainers also liked the system because swimmers could begin to work immediately without waiting for instructions (McKenzie and Rushall, 1974).

Cognitive behaviour modification and self-instruction

Cognitive behaviour modification

Procedures based on both behavioural and cognitive learning principles for changing your own behaviour by using self-talk and self-instruction.

Self-management generally means getting learners involved in the basic steps of a behaviour change programme. Cognitive behaviour modification adds an emphasis on thinking and self-talk. For this reason, many psychologists consider cognitive behaviour modification more a cognitive approach than a behavioural one. It is presented here because it serves as a bridge to Chapters 7 and 8 on cognitive learning.

As noted in Chapter 2, there is a stage in cognitive development when young children seem to guide themselves through a task using private speech (see Vygotsky, Chapter 2). They talk to themselves, often repeating the words of a parent or teacher. In cognitive behaviour modification, learners are taught directly how to use self-instruction. Meichenbaum outlined the steps:

Self-instruction

Talking oneself through the steps of a task.

1. An adult model performs a task while talking to him or herself out loud (cognitive modelling).

2. The child performs the same task under the direction of the model's instructions (overt, external guidance).

3. The child performs the task while instructing him or herself aloud (overt, self-guidance).

4. The child whispers the instructions to him or herself as he or she goes through the task (faded, overt self-guidance).

5. The child performs the task while guiding his or her performance via private speech (covert self-instruction) (1977: 32).

This relates to Brenda Manning and Beverly Payne's (1996) list of four skills that can increase pupil learning: *listening, planning, working* and *checking*. How might cognitive self-instruction help learners develop these skills? One possibility is to use personal booklets or class posters that prompt learners to 'talk to themselves' about these skills. For example, one class of ten- and 11-year-olds designed a set of prompts for each of the four skills and displayed these around the classroom. The prompts for listening included 'Does this make sense?' 'Do I understand this?' 'I need to ask a question now before I forget.' 'Pay attention!' 'Can I do what he's telling us to do?' Planning prompts were 'Do I have everything together that I need?' 'Am I paying attention to this and not my friends?' 'Let me get organised first.' 'What order will I do this in?' 'I know this already.'

Actually, cognitive behaviour modification as it is practised by Meichenbaum and others has many more components than just teaching learners to use self-instruction. Meichenbaum's methods also include dialogue and interaction between teacher and learner, modelling , guided discovery, motivational strategies, feedback, careful matching of the task with the learner's developmental level, and other principles of good teaching. The learner is even involved in designing the programme (Harris, 1990; Harris and Pressley, 1991). Given all this, it is no surprise that learners seem to be able to generalise the skills developed with cognitive behaviour modification to new learning situations (Harris, Graham and Pressley, 1991).

Problems and Issues

The preceding sections provide an overview of several strategies for changing classroom behaviour. However, you should be aware that these strategies are tools that can be used both responsibly and irresponsibly. What, then, are some issues you should keep in mind?

Criticisms of behavioural methods

STOP AND THINK

A teacher last year got into trouble for bribing his class with homework exemptions to get them to behave in class. What do you think about using rewards and punishments in teaching?

While you think about your answer to this question, look at the Discussion Point below to see two different perspectives.

DISCUSSION POINT

Should learners be rewarded for learning?

For years, educators and psychologists have debated whether learners should be rewarded for school work and academic accomplishments. In the early 1990s, Paul Chance and Alfie Kohn exchanged opinions in several issues of *Phi Delta Kappan* (March 1991; November 1992; June 1993). Then, Judy Cameron and W. David Pierce (1994) published an article on reinforcement in the *Review of Educational Research* that precipitated extensive criticisms and rebuttals in the same journal from Mark Lepper, Mark Keavney, Michael Drake, Alfie Kohn, Richard Ryan and Edward Deci. Many of the same people exchanged opinions in the November 1999 issue of *Psychological Bulletin*. What are the arguments?

Agree: Yes, rewards help to increase motivation to learn

According to Paul Chance:

Behavioural psychologists in particular emphasize that we learn by acting on our environment. As B. F. Skinner put it: '[People] act on the world, and change it, and are changed in turn by the consequences of their actions.' Skinner, unlike Kohn, understood that people learn best in a responsive environment. Teachers who praise or otherwise reward student performance provide such an environment. If it is immoral to let students know they have answered questions correctly, to pat students on the back for a good effort, to show joy at a student's understanding of a concept, or to recognize the achievement of a goal by providing a gold star or a certificate – if this is immoral, then count me a sinner (1993: 788).

Do rewards undermine interest? In their review of research, Cameron and Pierce concluded, 'When tangible rewards (e.g. gold star, money) are offered contingent on performance on a task [not just on participation] or are delivered unexpectedly, intrinsic motivation is maintained' (1994: 49). In a later review of research, Eisenberg, Pierce and Cameron added that 'Reward procedures requiring specific high task performance convey a task's personal or social significance, increasing intrinsic motivation' (1999: 677). Even psychologists such as Edward Deci and Mark Lepper who suggest that rewards might undermine intrinsic motivation agree that rewards can also be used positively. When rewards provide learners with information about their growing mastery of a subject or when the rewards show appreciation for a job well done, then the rewards bolster confidence and make the task more interesting to the learners, especially those who lacked ability or interest in the task initially. Nothing succeeds like success. As Chance points out, if learners master reading or mathematics with the support of rewards, they will not forget what they have learned when the praise stops. Would they have learned without the rewards? Some would, but some might not. Would you continue working for a company that didn't pay you, even though you liked the work? Will freelance writer Alfie Kohn, for that matter, lose interest in writing because he gets paid fees and royalties?

Disagree: No, rewards may decrease interest in learning

Alfie Kohn argues that 'Applied behaviourism, which amounts to saying, "do this and you'll get that," is essentially a technique for controlling people. In the classroom it is a way of doing things *to* children rather than working *with* them' (1993: 784). He contends that rewards are ineffective because when the praise and prizes stop, the behaviours stop too. After analysing 128 studies of extrinsic rewards, Edward Deci, Richard Koestner and Richard Ryan concluded that 'tangible rewards tend to have a substantial effect on intrinsic motivation, with the limiting conditions we have specified. Even when tangible rewards are offered as indicators of good performance, they typically decrease intrinsic motivation for interesting activities' (1999: 658–659).

The problem with rewards does not stop here. According to Kohn, rewarding children and young people for learning actually makes them less interested in the material:

All of this means that getting children to think about learning as a way to receive a sticker, a gold star, or a grade – or even worse, to get money or a toy for a grade, which amounts to an extrinsic motivator for an extrinsic motivator – is likely to turn learning from an end into a means. Learning becomes something that must be gotten through in order to receive the reward. Take the depressingly pervasive program by which children receive certificates for pizzas when they have read a certain number of books. John Nicholls of the University of Illinois comments, only half in jest, that the likely consequence of this program is 'a lot of fat kids who don't like to read' (1993: 785).

Source: From 'Sticking up for rewards' by P. Chance, June 1993, *Phi Delta Kappan, 74*, pp. 787–790. Copyright © 1993 by Phi Delta Kappan. Reprinted with permission of Phi Delta Kappan and the author. From 'Rewards versus learning: A response to Paul Chance' by A. Kohn, June 1993, *Phi Delta Kappan*, p. 783 and p. 785. Copyright © 1993 by Alfie Kohn. Reprinted from Phi Delta Kappan with the author's permission.

WHAT DO YOU THINK?

Agree or Disagree? Vote online at www.pearsoned.co.uk/woolfolkeuro.

Limitations

Properly used, the strategies in this chapter can be effective tools to help children and young people learn academically and grow in self-sufficiency. Effective tools, however, do not automatically produce excellent work, and behavioural strategies are often implemented haphazardly, inconsistently, incorrectly, or superficially (Landrum and Kauffman, 2006). The indiscriminate use of even the best tools can lead to difficulties.

Some psychologists fear that rewarding children and young people for all learning will cause them to lose interest in learning for its own sake (Deci, 1975; Deci and Ryan, 1985; Kohn, 1993, 1996; Lepper and Greene, 1978; Lepper, Keavney and Drake, 1996; Ryan and Deci, 1996). Studies have suggested that using reward programmes with learners who are already interested in the subject matter may, in fact, cause them to be less interested in the subject when the reward programme ends, as you can see in the previous Discussion Point. In addition, there is some evidence that praising learners for being intelligent when they succeed can undermine their motivation if they do not perform as well the next time. After they fail, learners who had been praised for being bright or clever may be less persistent and enjoy the task less compared with learners who had been praised earlier for working hard (Mueller and Dweck, 1998).

Just as you must take into account the effects of a reward system on the individual, you must also consider its impact on other members of the class. Using a reward programme or giving one person increased attention may have a detrimental effect on the

Connect and Extend

See Smith, D. *et al.* (2004) 'You, me and us: How a project set up by an LEA educational psychology service helped a school to support the inclusion of pupils with EBD', *Emotional and Behavioural Difficulties*, *9*(3), pp. 171–180, for an account of a two-year project in central England which built a whole school approach to positive behaviour management.

other learners in the classroom. Is it possible perhaps that other people in the class will learn to be 'bad' in order to be included in the reward programme? Most of the evidence on this question suggests that using individual adaptations such as reward programmes does not have any adverse effects on learners who are not participating as long as the teacher believes in the programme and explains the reasons for using it to the non-participating learners. After interviewing 98 primary school pupils (six to 11 year olds) Cindy Fulk and Paula Smith concluded that 'Teachers may be more concerned about equal treatment of students than students are' (1995: 416). If the conduct of some learners does seem to deteriorate when their peers are involved in special programmes, many of the same procedures discussed in this chapter should help them return to previous levels of appropriate behaviour (Chance, 1992, 1993).

Ethical issues

The ethical questions related to the use of the strategies described in this chapter are similar to those raised by any process that seeks to influence people. What are the goals? How do these goals fit with those of the school as a whole? What effect will a strategy have on the individuals involved? Is too much control being given to the teacher, or to a majority?

Goals

The strategies described in this chapter could be applied exclusively to teaching learners to sit still, raise their hands before speaking, and remain silent at all other times (Winett and Winkler, 1972). This certainly would be an unethical use of the techniques. It is true that a teacher may need to establish some organisation and order, but stopping with improvements in conduct will not ensure academic learning. On the other hand, in some situations, reinforcing academic skills may lead to improvements in conduct. Whenever possible, emphasis should be placed on academic learning. Academic improvements generalise to other situations more successfully than do changes in classroom conduct.

Strategies

Punishment can have negative side effects: It can serve as a model for aggressive responses, and it can encourage negative emotional reactions. Punishment is unnecessary and even unethical when positive approaches, which have fewer potential dangers, might work as well. When simpler, less-restrictive procedures fail, then more complicated procedures should be tried.

A second consideration in the selection of a strategy is the impact of the strategy on the individual learner. For example, some teachers might arrange for children to be rewarded at home with a gift or special activities based on good work in school. But if a learner has a history of being severely punished at home for bad reports from school, a home-based reinforcement programme might be very harmful to that learner. Reports of unsatisfactory progress at school could lead to increased abuse at home.

Diversity and Convergence in Behavioural Learning

There is great *diversity* in the learning histories of people. Every learner in a class will come to you with different fears and anxieties. Some members of the class may be terrified of speaking in public or of failing in competitive sports. Others will be anxious around various animals. Different activities or objects will serve as reinforcers for some learners, but not others. Some learners will work for the promise of good grades – others could not care less. All class members will have learned from different models in their homes, neighbourhoods or communities.

The research and theories presented in this chapter should help you understand how the learning histories of children and young peoples might have taught them to respond automatically to tests with sweaty palms and racing hearts – possible classical conditioning at work. Their learning histories might have included being reinforced for persistence or for whining – operant conditioning at work. The chance to work in a group may be a reinforcer for some pupils and a punisher for others. Remember, what works for one person may not be right for another and learners can get 'too much of a good thing'; reinforcers can lose their potency if they are overused.

In addition to providing a diversity of reinforcers, teachers, classrooms and schools should provide a diversity of models because individuals learn though observation. Do learners see themselves in the literacy and science texts? Are there characters and authors in literature that reflect the background and values of the learners and the community? Whose work is displayed in the classroom? Who gets the privileges and responsibilities?

Even though a classroom may be filled with many different learning histories, there are some principles that apply to all people:

1. No one eagerly repeats behaviours that have been punished or ignored. Without some sense of progress, it is difficult to persist.

2. When actions lead to consequences that are positive for the person involved, those actions are likely to be repeated.

3. Teachers often fail to use reinforcement to recognise appropriate behaviour; they respond instead to inappropriate behaviours, sometimes providing reinforcing attention in the process.

4. To be effective, praise must be a sincere recognition of a real accomplishment.

5. Whatever their current level of functioning, people can learn to be more self-managing.

SUMMARY TABLE

Understanding Learning (pp. 244–246)

What is learning?

Although theorists disagree about the definition of learning, most would agree that learning occurs when experience causes a change in a person's knowledge or behaviour. Changes simply caused by maturation, illness, fatigue or hunger are excluded from a general definition of learning. Behavioural theorists emphasise the role of environmental stimuli in learning and focus on behaviour or observable responses. Behavioural learning processes include contiguity learning, classical conditioning, operant conditioning and observational learning.

Early Explanations of Learning: Contiguity and Classical Conditioning (pp. 246–249)

How does a neutral stimulus become a conditioned stimulus?

In classical conditioning, which was identified by Pavlov, a previously neutral stimulus is repeatedly paired with a stimulus that evokes an emotional or physiological response. Later, the previously neutral stimulus alone evokes the response – that is, the neutral stimulus is conditioned to bring forth a conditioned response. The neutral stimulus has become a conditioned stimulus.

What are some everyday examples of classical conditioning?

Here are a few; add your own. Salivating when you smell your favourite foods, tension when you hear a dentist's drill, nervousness when you step on stage.

Operant Conditioning: Trying New Responses (pp. 249–255)

What defines a consequence as a reinforcer? As a punisher?

According to Skinner's concept of operant conditioning, people learn through the effects of their deliberate responses. For an individual, the effects of consequences following an action may serve as either reinforcers or punishers. A consequence is defined as a reinforcer if it strengthens or maintains the response that brought it about, whereas a consequence is defined as a punishment if it decreases or suppresses the response that brought it about.

Negative reinforcement is often confused with punishment. How are they different?

The process of reinforcement (positive or negative) always involves *strengthening behaviour*. The teacher strengthens (reinforces) desired behaviours by removing something

aversive *as soon as the desired behaviours occur.* Because the consequence involves removing or 'subtracting' a stimulus, the reinforcement is negative. Punishment, on the other hand, involves *decreasing or suppressing behaviour.* A behaviour followed by a 'punisher' is *less* likely to be repeated in similar situations in the future.

How can you encourage persistence in a behaviour?

Ratio schedules (based on the number of responses) encourage higher rates of response, and variable schedules (based on varying numbers of responses or varying time intervals) encourage persistence of responses.

What is the difference between a prompt and a cue?

A cue is an antecedent stimulus just before a particular behaviour is to take place. A prompt is an additional cue following the first cue. Make sure the environmental stimulus that you want to become a cue occurs immediately before the prompt you are using, so that learners will learn to respond to the cue and not rely only on the prompt. Then, allow the prompt to disappear as soon as possible so people do not become dependent on it.

Applied Behaviour Analysis (pp. 255–267)

What are the steps in applied behaviour analysis?

The steps are: (1) Clearly specify the behaviour to be changed and note the current level. (2) Plan a specific intervention using antecedents, consequences or both. (3) Keep a record of the results and modify the plan if necessary.

How can the Premack principle help identify reinforcers?

The Premack principle states that a high-frequency behaviour (a preferred activity) can be an effective reinforcer for a low-frequency behaviour (a less-preferred activity). The best way to determine appropriate reinforcers for learners may be to watch what they do in their free time. For most children and young people, talking, moving around the room, sitting near a friend, being 'let off' assignments or tests, reading magazines or playing games are preferred activities.

When is shaping an appropriate approach?

Shaping helps learners develop new responses a little at a time, so it is useful for building complex skills, working towards difficult goals, and increasing persistence, endurance, accuracy, or speed. Because shaping is a time-consuming process, however, it should not be used if success can be attained through simpler methods such as cueing.

What are some cautions in using punishment?

Punishment in and of itself does not lead to any positive behaviour. Thus, whenever you consider the use of punishment, make it part of a two-pronged attack. First, carry out the punishment and suppress the undesirable behaviour. Second, make clear what the pupil *should* be doing instead and provide reinforcement for those desirable actions. Thus, while the problem behaviours are being suppressed, positive alternative responses are being strengthened.

How can functional behavioural assessment and positive behavioural supports be used to improve learner behaviours?

In doing a functional behavioural assessment, a teacher studies the antecedents and consequences of problem behaviours to determine the reason or function of the behaviour. Then, positive behavioural supports are designed to replace problem behaviours with new actions that serve the same purpose for the person, but do not have the same problems.

Behavioural Approaches to Teaching and Management (pp. 267–271)

Describe the managerial strategies of group consequences, token programmes and contracts

Using group consequences involves basing reinforcement for the whole class on the behaviour of the whole class. In token programmes, individuals earn tokens (points, vouchers, play money, holes punched in a card, etc.) for both academic work and positive classroom behaviour. Periodically, the learners exchange the tokens they have earned for some desired reward. In a contingency contract programme, the teacher draws up an individual contract with each person in the class, describing exactly what they must do to earn a particular privilege or reward. A teacher must use these programmes with caution, emphasising learning and not just 'good' behaviour.

Observational Learning and Cognitive Behaviour Modification: Thinking about Behaviour (pp. 271–281)

Distinguish between social learning and social cognitive theories

Social learning theory was an early neo-behavioural theory that expanded behavioural views of reinforcement and punishment. In behavioural views, reinforcement and punishment directly affect behaviour. In social learning theory, seeing another person, a model, reinforced or punished can have similar effects on the observer's behaviour. Social cognitive theory expands social learning theory to include cognitive factors such as beliefs, expectations and perceptions of self.

Distinguish between enactive and vicarious learning

Enactive learning is learning by doing and experiencing the consequences of your actions. *Vicarious learning* is learning by observing, which challenges the behaviourist idea that cognitive factors are unnecessary in an explanation of learning. Much is going on mentally before performance and reinforcement can even take place.

What are the elements of observational learning?

In order to learn through observation, we have to pay attention to aspects of the situation that will help us learn. In order to imitate the behaviour of a model, you have to retain the information. This involves mentally representing the model's actions in some way, probably as verbal steps. In the production phase, practice makes the behaviour smoother and more expert. Sometimes, we need a great deal of practice, feedback and coaching about subtle points before we can reproduce the behaviour of the model. Finally, motivation shapes observational learning through incentives and reinforcement. We may not perform a learned behaviour until there is some motivation or incentive to do so. Reinforcement can focus attention, encourage reproduction or practice and maintain the new learning.

What are the steps in self-management?

Learner can apply behaviour analysis on their own to manage their own behaviour. Teachers can encourage the development of self-management skills by allowing individuals to participate in setting goals, keeping track of progress, evaluating accomplishments and selecting and giving their own reinforcers. Teachers can also use cognitive behaviour modification, a behaviour change programme described by Meichenbaum in which learners are directly taught how to use self-instruction.

Problems and Issues (pp. 281–284)

What are the main criticisms of behavioural approaches?

The misuse or abuse of behavioural learning methods is unethical. Critics of behavioural methods also point out the danger that reinforcement could decrease interest in learning by overemphasising rewards and could have a negative impact on other learners. Teachers can use behavioural learning principles appropriately and ethically.

Glossary

Antecedents: Events that precede an action.

Applied behaviour analysis: The application of behavioural learning principles to understand and change behaviour.

Aversive: Irritating or unpleasant.

Behavioural learning theories: Explanations of learning that focus on external events as the cause of changes in observable behaviours.

Behaviour modification: Systematic application of antecedents and consequences to change behaviour.

Classical conditioning: Association of automatic responses with new stimuli.

Cognitive behaviour modification: Procedures based on both behavioural and cognitive learning principles for changing your own behaviour by using self-talk and self-instruction.

Conditioned response (CR): Learned response to a previously neutral stimulus.

Conditioned stimulus (CS): Stimulus that evokes an emotional or physiological response after conditioning.

Consequences: Events that follow an action.

Contiguity: Association of two events because of repeated pairing.

Contingency contract: A contract between the teacher and a learner specifying what the learner must do to earn a particular reward or privilege.

Continuous reinforcement schedule: Presenting a reinforcer after every appropriate response.

Cueing: Providing a stimulus that 'sets up' a desired behaviour.

Extinction: The disappearance of a learned response.

Functional behavioural assessment (FBA): Procedures used to obtain information about antecedents, behaviours and consequences to determine the reason or function of the behaviour.

Good behaviour game: Arrangement where a class is divided into teams and each team receives a black mark or demerit points for breaking agreed-upon rules of good behaviour.

Group consequences: Rewards or punishments given to a class as a whole for adhering to or violating rules of conduct.

Intermittent reinforcement schedule: Presenting a reinforcer after some but not all responses.

Interval schedule: Length of time between reinforcers.

Learning: Process through which experience causes permanent change in knowledge or behaviour.

Modelling: Changes in behaviour, thinking or emotions that occur through observing another person – a model.

Negative reinforcement: Strengthening behaviour by removing an aversive stimulus when the behaviour occurs.

Neutral stimulus: Stimulus not connected to a response.

Observational learning: Learning by observation and imitation of others.

Operant conditioning: Learning in which voluntary behaviour is strengthened or weakened by consequences or antecedents.

Operants: Voluntary (and generally goal-directed) behaviours emitted by a person or an animal.

Positive behavioural supports (PBS): Interventions designed to replace problem behaviours with new actions that serve the same purpose for the learner.

Positive practice: Practising correct responses immediately after errors.

Positive reinforcement: Strengthening behaviour by presenting a desired stimulus after the behaviour.

Premack principle: Principle stating that a more-preferred activity can serve as a reinforcer for a less-preferred activity.

Presentation punishment: Decreasing the chances that a behaviour will occur again by presenting an aversive stimulus following the behaviour; also called Type I punishment.

Prompt: A reminder that follows a cue to make sure the person reacts to the cue.

Punishment: Process that weakens or suppresses behaviour.

Ratio schedule: Reinforcement based on the number of responses between reinforcers.

Reinforcer: Any event that follows a behaviour and increases the chances that the behaviour will occur again.

Reinforcement: Use of consequences to strengthen behaviour.

Removal punishment: Decreasing the chances that a behaviour will occur again by removing a pleasant stimulus following the behaviour; also called Type II punishment.

Reprimands: Criticisms for misbehaviour; rebukes.

Respondents: Responses (generally automatic or involuntary) elicited by specific stimuli.

Response: Observable reaction to a stimulus.

Response cost: Punishment by loss of reinforcers.

Ripple effect: 'Contagious' spreading of behaviours through imitation.

Satiation: Requiring a person to repeat a problem behaviour past the point of interest or motivation.

Self-efficacy: A person's sense of being able to deal effectively with a particular task.

Self-instruction: Talking oneself through the steps of a task.

Self-management: Use of behavioural learning principles to change your own behaviour.

Self-reinforcement: Controlling your own reinforcers.

Shaping: Reinforcing each small step of progress towards a desired goal or behaviour.

Social cognitive theory: Theory that adds concern with cognitive factors such as beliefs, self-perceptions and expectations to social learning theory.

Social isolation: Removal of a disruptive member of the class for five to ten minutes.

Social learning theory: Theory that emphasises learning through observation of others.

Stimulus: Event that activates behaviour.

Stimulus control: Capacity for the presence or absence of antecedents to cause behaviours.

Successive approximations: Small components that make up a complex behaviour.

Task analysis: System for breaking down a task hierarchically into basic skills and sub-skills.

Time out: Technically, the removal of all reinforcement. In practice, isolation of a learner from the rest of the class for a brief time.

Token reinforcement system: System in which tokens earned for academic work and positive classroom behaviour can be exchanged for some desired reward.

Unconditioned response (UR): Naturally occurring emotional or physiological response.

Unconditioned stimulus (US): Stimulus that automatically produces an emotional or physiological response.

Vicarious reinforcement: Increasing the chances that we will repeat a behaviour by observing another person being reinforced for that behaviour.

CHECK YOUR LEARNING!   WEB

In the Classroom: What Would They Do?

Below are some comments from practitioners who responded to the teaching situation involving Elizabeth, a student teacher, presented at the start of the chapter. Elizabeth was struggling to retain control with the class and inadvertently encouraging inappropriate behaviour. The comments are also generally applicable to In the Classroom at the beginning of the chapter:

Experienced school practice supervisor

Elizabeth should have begun the lesson with an outline of the objectives for the lesson so that everyone was clear. She should also have had a copy of her lesson plan available to hand to her supervisor. It wasn't clear whether she actually did

write the class responses on the board but she should have done so. OFSTED would expect her to refer to the task as 'brainstorming' rather than a game to fit with their requirements.

In terms of the problem behaviour that occurred, the class should have been reminded of the ground rules by Elizabeth in order to establish clear understanding and allow action to be taken on the basis of these. Otherwise she did the right thing.

Ann, Deputy Head Teacher of large primary school in central UK

Elizabeth should have avoided the situation in the first place by taking the responses in an orderly way with children using their hand as an indication they wished to say something. If a child responded in a 'cheeky' way she should try to bring them in line by referring to something positive that another might say or take the attention away from them somehow.

Sarah, newly qualified secondary school teacher

There should be a statement of objectives at the beginning of the lesson and a proper explanation of what the lesson was about. Because the class were not asked to put their hands up she could not respond to let them know whether they were right or wrong. Elizabeth would have had the chance to say 'Stop' then, when they gave inappropriate answers. When she laughed it reinforced that is was OK to laugh and so she modelled that to them and they laughed more and it escalated. By losing her temper and then reverting to her earlier plan she was not putting firm boundaries in place and they lost respect for her. There was no behaviour management plan or clear rules in the class.

Overview

In this chapter, we turn from behavioural theories of learning to the cognitive perspective. This means a shift from ' viewing the learners and their behaviours as products of incoming environmental stimuli' to seeing the learners as 'sources of plans, intentions, goals, ideas, memories, and emotions actively used to attend to, select, and construct meaning from stimuli and knowledge from experience' (Wittrock, 1982: 1–2). In other words the learner is seen as central in constructing her own learning rather than responding to the rewards and punishments around her. So the source of control (over what is learned) moves from the teacher to the learner.

We will begin with a discussion of the general cognitive approach to learning and memory and the importance of knowledge in learning. To understand memory, we will consider a widely accepted cognitive model, information processing, which suggests that information is manipulated in different storage systems. Next, we will explore metacognition, a field of study that may provide insights into individual and developmental differences in learning. Then, we turn to ideas about how teachers can help their learners become more knowledgeable.

By the time you have completed this chapter, you should be able to answer the following questions:

- **What is the role of knowledge in learning?**
- **What is the human information processing model of memory?**
- **How do perception, attention, schemas and scripts influence learning and remembering?**
- **What are declarative, procedural and conditional knowledge?**
- **Why do learners forget what they have learned?**
- **What is the role of metacognition in learning and remembering?**
- **What are the stages in the development of cognitive skills?**

In the Classroom

The 15–16-year-old learners, who are due to take their exams at the end of the school year, seem to equate understanding with memorising. They prepare for each test by memorising the exact words of the textbook. Even the best pupils seem to think that this is the only learning strategy possible. In fact, when their teacher tries to get them to think about history by reading some original sources, debating issues in class or examining art and music from the time period they are studying, they rebel. 'Will this be on the exam paper?' 'Why are we looking at these pictures – will we have to know who painted them and when?' 'What's this got to do with history?' Even the learners who participate in the debates seem to use words and phrases straight from the textbook without knowing what they are saying.

What are these learners' beliefs and expectations, and how do these affect their learning? Why do you think they insist on using the rote memory approach? How might the teacher use what the learners already know to help them learn in better, more meaningful ways? How might these issues affect the learners' results?

Group Activity

With two or three other people in your group, talk about teachers you've had who helped you develop 'deep' knowledge about a topic. How did they guide your thinking to move past memorising to a more complete understanding?

Elements of the Cognitive Perspective

Let us think for a moment about the cognitive perspective and its place within theoretical perspectives of learning. The cognitive perspective is both the oldest and one of the youngest members of the psychological community. It is old because discussions of the nature of knowledge, the value of reason, and the contents of the mind date back at least to the ancient Greek philosophers (Hernshaw, 1987). From the late 1800s until several decades ago, however, cognitive studies fell from favour as academics placed increased emphasis upon science and measurement and behaviourism thrived. Then, research during World War Two on the development of complex human skills, the computer revolution and breakthroughs in understanding language development all stimulated a resurgence in cognitive research. Evidence accumulated indicating that people plan their responses, use strategies to help themselves remember and organise the material they are learning in their own unique ways (Miller, Galanter and Pribram, 1960; Shuell, 1986). Educational psychologists became interested in how people think, learn concepts and solve problems (e.g. Ausubel, 1963; Bruner, Goodnow and Austin, 1956). Two different models of instruction based upon the principles of cognitive learning – Bruner's discovery learning and Ausubel's expository teaching – are described in Chapter 8.

Interest in concept learning and problem solving soon gave way, however, to interest in how knowledge is represented in the mind and particularly how it is remembered. Remembering and forgetting, as key elements of human thinking, became major topics for investigation in cognitive psychology in the 1970s and 1980s, and the information processing model of memory dominated research.

Today, there is renewed interest in learning, thinking and problem solving. The cognitive view of learning can be described as a generally agreed-upon philosophical orientation. This means that cognitive theorists share basic notions about learning and memory. Most importantly, cognitive psychologists assume that mental processes exist, that they can be studied scientifically and that humans are active participants in their own acts of cognition (Ashcraft, 2006). Let us see how cognitive and behavioural views compare.

Cognitive view of learning

A general approach that views learning as an active mental process of acquiring, remembering and using knowledge.

Comparing cognitive and behavioural views

The cognitive and behavioural views differ in their assumptions about what is learned. In the behavioural view, new behaviours themselves are learned (Shuell, 1986) whereas according to the cognitive view, knowledge is learned, and changes in knowledge make changes in behaviour possible. Both behavioural and cognitive theorists believe reinforcement is important in learning, but for different reasons. The strict behaviourist maintains that reinforcement strengthens responses; cognitive theorists see reinforcement as a source of information that provides feedback about what is likely to happen if behaviours are repeated or changed.

The cognitive view sees learning as extending and transforming the understanding we already have, not simply writing associations on the 'tabula rasa' (Locke, 1690) or blank slates of our brains (Greeno, Collins and Resnick, 1996). Instead of being passively influenced by environmental events, people actively choose, practice, pay attention, ignore, reflect and make many other decisions as they pursue goals. Newer cognitive approaches reflect this active view of learning and stress the *construction* of knowledge (Anderson, Reder and Simon, 1996; Greeno, Collins and Resnick, 1996; Mayer, 1996).

The methods of cognitive and behavioural researchers also differ. Much of the work on behavioural learning principles has been with animals in controlled laboratory settings. The goal is to identify a few general laws of learning that apply to all higher organisms – including humans, regardless of age, intelligence, or other individual differences. Cognitive psychologists, on the other hand, study a wide range of learning situations. Because of their focus on individual and developmental differences in cognition, they have not been as concerned with general laws of learning. This is one of the reasons that there is no single cognitive model or theory of learning that is representative of the entire field.

The importance of knowledge in learning

> ### STOP AND THINK
>
> Quickly, list ten terms that relate to educational psychology. Now list ten terms that relate to electronic engineering.

Unless you are studying electronic engineering, it probably took you longer to list ten terms from that field than from educational psychology. Some of you may still be asking, 'What is electronic engineering anyway?' Your answers depend on your knowledge of electronic engineering (e.g. you could have included electricity and electromagnetism, imaging and display systems, optical principles, power, telecommunications, the interaction of light with semiconductors and insulators, visual requirements of displays, the operational principles of 2D and 3D capture and display systems).

Knowledge and knowing are the outcomes of learning. When we learn the history of cognitive psychology, the products of electronic engineering, or the rules of tennis, we know something new. However, knowing is more than the end product of previous learning; it also guides new learning. The cognitive approach suggests that one of the most important elements in the learning process is what the individual brings to new learning situations. What we already know is the foundation and frame for constructing all future learning. Knowledge determines to a great extent what we will pay attention to, perceive, learn, remember and forget (Alexander, 1996; Bransford, Brown and Cocking, 2000). In other words if we have no knowledge about something we tend to ignore it. I wonder how many of you bothered to pay attention to the examples of electronic engineering terms provided above?

An example study

A study by Masoura and Gathercole (2005) shows the importance of existing knowledge in learning new words in a second language. A group of 80 Greek children (8–13-year-olds) with an average of three years of studying English as a foreign language in Greek schools were placed into four groups depending upon their scores in English vocabulary and short-term memory tests. They were then presented with a paired-associative learning task with English picture-word pairs depicting objects or animals they were unlikely to have encountered in their studies of English so far. The results of the study showed that the speed of learning these new words was strongly related to the child's current knowledge of the English language rather than their short-term memory abilities. Those children placed in the high English vocabulary group made more correct responses on the learning task (70.5% correct) than the low English vocabulary group (40.3% correct) but there was little difference between those scoring high on the short-term memory task (high repetition group) namely 61.5% and those scoring low on the short-term memory task (low repetition group)

64.0%. It seems then that previous knowledge of the language was the key factor regardless of how good a short-term memory the children had. This allowed them to learn the new words more easily because they were familiar with the phonological structures (sound systems) of the language and the results demonstrated the power of knowledge.

General and specific knowledge

Knowledge in the cognitive perspective includes both subject-specific understandings (maths, history, sport, etc.) and general cognitive abilities, such as planning, solving problems and comprehending language (Greeno, Collins and Resnick, 1996). So, there are different kinds of knowledge. Some is domain-specific knowledge that relates to a particular task or subject. For example, knowing that the wicket-keeper stands behind the batsman is specific to the domain of cricket. Some knowledge, on the other hand, is general – it applies to many different situations. For example, general knowledge about how to read or write or use a computer is useful both in and out of school. Of course, there is no absolute line between general and domain-specific knowledge. When you were first learning to read, you may have studied specific facts about the sounds of letters. At that time, knowledge about letter sounds was specific to the domain of reading. But now you can use both knowledge about sounds and the ability to read in more general ways (Alexander, 1992; Schunk, 2004).

What we know exists in our memory. To know something is to remember it over time and be able to find it when you need it. Psychologists have studied memory extensively. Let's see what they have learned.

Domain-specific knowledge

Information that is useful in a particular situation or that applies mainly to one specific topic.

General knowledge

Information that is useful in many different kinds of tasks; information that applies to many situations.

The Information Processing Model of Memory

There are a number of theories of memory, but the most common are the information processing explanations (Ashcraft, 2006; Hunt and Ellis, 1999; Sternberg, 1999). We will use this well-researched framework for examining learning and memory.

Early information processing views of memory used the computer as a model. Like the computer, the human mind takes in information, performs operations on it to change its form and content, stores the information, retrieves it when needed, and generates responses to it. Thus, processing involves gathering information and organising it in relation to what you already know, or *encoding*; holding information, or *storage*; and getting at the information when needed, or *retrieval*. The whole system is guided by *control processes* (brain processes which guide thought and behaviour) that determine how and when information will flow through the system.

For most cognitive psychologists, the computer model is only a metaphor for human mental activity. However, other cognitive scientists, particularly those studying artificial intelligence, try to design and program computers to 'think' and solve problems like human beings (Anderson, 2005; Schunk, 2000). Some theorists suggest that the operation of the brain resembles a large number of very slow computers, all operating in parallel (at the same time) with each computer dedicated to a different, specific task (Ashcraft, 2006).

Figure 7.1 is a schematic representation of a typical information processing model of memory, derived from the ideas of several theorists (Atkinson and Shiffrin, 1968; Gagne, 1985; Neisser, 1976). In order to understand this model, let's examine each element.

Information processing

The human mind's activity of taking in, storing and using information.

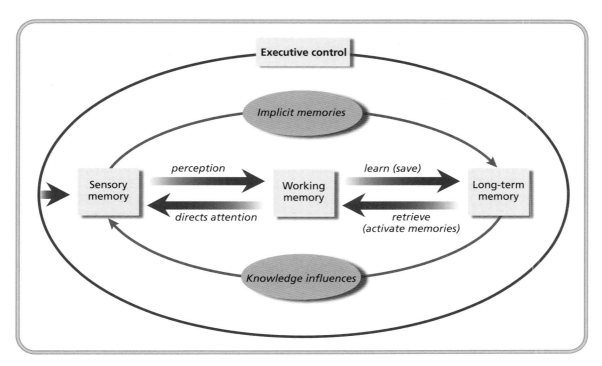

Figure 7.1
The information processing system

Information is encoded in sensory memory where perception and attention determine what will be held in working memory for further use. In working memory, new information connects with knowledge from long-term memory. Thoroughly processed and connected information becomes part of long-term memory, and can be activated to return to working memory. Implicit memories are formed without conscious effort.

Sensory memory

Stimuli from the environment (sights, sounds, smells, etc.) constantly bombard our body's mechanisms for seeing, hearing, tasting, smelling and feeling. Sensory memory is the initial processing that transforms these incoming stimuli into information so we can make sense of them. Even though sights and sounds may last only fractions of a second, the transformations (information) that represent these sensations are briefly held in the *sensory register* or *sensory information store* (a unit for storing environmental information) so that this initial processing can take place (Driscoll, 2005; Sperling, 1960).

Sensory memory
System that holds sensory information very briefly.

Capacity, duration and contents of sensory memory

The *capacity* of sensory memory is very large, and can take in more information than we can possibly handle at once. But this vast amount of sensory information is fragile in *duration*. It lasts between one and three seconds.

The information *content* of sensory memory resembles the sensations from the original stimulus. Visual sensations are coded briefly by the sensory register as images, almost like photographs. Auditory sensations are coded as sound patterns, similar to echoes. It may be that the other senses also have their own codes. Thus, for a second or so, a wealth of data from sensory experience remains intact. In these moments, we have a brief chance to select and organise information for further processing. Failure to process the information will mean that it is lost so perception and attention are critical at this stage to make sure that important aspects are registered.

Perception

Perception
Interpretation of sensory information.

The process of detecting a stimulus and assigning meaning to it is called perception. This meaning is constructed based on both physical representations from the world and our existing knowledge. For example, consider these marks: I3. If asked what the letter is, you would say 'B'. If asked what the number is, you would say '13'. The actual marks remain the same; their meaning changes in keeping with your expectation to recognise a letter or a number. To a child without appropriate knowledge to perceive either a letter or a number, the marks would probably be meaningless (Smith, 1975).

Gestalt
German for *pattern* or *whole*. Gestalt theorists hold that people organise their perceptions into coherent wholes.

Some of our present-day understanding of perception is based on studies conducted in Germany early in this century (and later in the US) by psychologists called *Gestalt theorists*. Gestalt, which means 'pattern' or 'configuration' in German, refers to people's tendency to organise sensory information into figures and whole forms. Instead of perceiving bits and pieces of unrelated information, we usually try to make sense of objects or events by seeing them as whole. So humans have a tendency to 'finish off' or complete aspects of their environment based upon the parts of it that they can see. If, for example, you drew the diagram below and showed it to a class of six-year-olds and asked them what it was they would probably reply without hesitation 'Cat's ears' or something similar because they would automatically make sense of what they are seeing on the basis of what they have previously seen.

Bottom-up processing
Perceiving based on noticing separate defining features and assembling them into a recognisable pattern.

Figure 7.2 presents a few Gestalt principles. These principles are reasonable explanations of certain aspects of perception, but they do not provide the whole story. There are two other kinds of explanations in information processing theory for how we recognise patterns and give meaning to sensory events. The first is called *feature analysis*, or bottom-up processing because the stimulus must be analysed into features or components and assembled into a meaningful pattern 'from the bottom up'. For example, a capital letter A consists of two relatively straight lines joined at a 45-degree angle and a horizontal line through the middle. Whenever we see these features, or anything close enough, including, A, *A*, **A**, A, **A** and A, we recognise an A (Anderson, 2005). This explains how we are able to read words written in other people's handwriting. We also have a prototype (a best example or classic case) of an A stored in memory to use along with features to help us detecting the letter A (Driscoll, 2005).

Prototype
A best example or best representative of a category.

a. Figure-ground
What do you see?
Faces or a vase? Make
one figure – the other
ground.

b. Proximity
You see these lines as
three groups because
of the proximity of
the lines.

c. Similarity
You see these lines as
an alternating pattern
because of the similarity
in height of lines.

d. Closure
You perceive a
circle instead of
dotted curved lines.

Figure 7.2
Examples of Gestalt principles

Gestalt principles of perception explain how we 'see' patterns in the world around us.

Source: Schunk, Dale H., *Learning Theories: An Educational Perspective*, 4th Edition, © 2004, p. 56. Reprinted by permission of Pearson Education, Inc., Upper Saddle River, NJ.

If all perception relied only on feature analysis and prototypes, learning would be very slow. Luckily, humans are capable of another type of perception based on knowledge and expectation often called top-down processing. To recognise patterns rapidly, in addition to noting features, we use what we already know about the situation – what we know about words or pictures or the way the world generally operates. For example, you would not have seen the marks above as the letter A if you had no knowledge of the Roman alphabet. So, what you know also affects what you are able to perceive. The role of knowledge in perception is represented by the arrows pointing left in Figure 7.1 from long-term memory (stored knowledge) to working memory and then to sensory memory.

Top-down processing

Perceiving based on the context and the patterns you expect to occur in that situation.

The role of attention

If every variation in colour, movement, sound, smell, temperature, and so on ended up in working memory, life would be impossible. However, attention is selective. By paying attention to selected stimuli and ignoring others, we limit the possibilities that we will perceive and process. What we pay attention to is guided to a certain extent by what we already know, what we need to know and what we would like to know so attention is involved in and influenced by all three memory processes in Figure 7.1. Attention is also affected by what else is happening at the time, by the complexity of the task, and by your ability to control or focus your attention (Driscoll, 2005). Before children reach approximately five years of age they exhibit 'spontaneous' attention which means that their attention span changes rapidly from one object to another. The school-aged child is able to concentrate for longer periods and is usually able to do this when necessary and thus exhibits 'selective' attention. However, some learners with attention-deficit disorder have great difficulty focusing attention or ignoring competing stimuli.

Attention

Focus on a stimulus.

As we know, attention takes effort and is a limited resource. I expect you have to work a bit to pay attention to these words about attention (depending upon how you feel, how motivated you are, what is happening around you and so on). We can pay attention to only one cognitively demanding task at a time (Anderson, 2005). For example, when this co-author was learning to drive, she couldn't listen to the radio and drive at the same time. After some practice, she could listen, but had to turn the radio

Automaticity

The ability to perform thoroughly learned tasks without much mental effort.

off when traffic was heavy. After years of practice, she can plan a lecture in her head, listen to the radio, and carry on a conversation as she drives. This is possible because many processes that initially require attention and concentration become automatic with practice. Actually, automaticity is a matter of degree; we are not completely automatic, but rather more or less automatic in our performances depending on how much practice we have had and the situation. For example, even experienced drivers might become very attentive and focused during a blinding blizzard (Anderson, 2005) and this co-author certainly become very focused when driving on icy roads.

Attention and teaching

The first step in learning is paying attention. Learners cannot process information that they do not acknowledge, recognise or perceive (Lachter, Forster and Ruthruff, 2004). Many factors in the classroom influence people's attention. Eye-catching or startling displays or actions can draw attention at the beginning of a lesson. A teacher might begin a science lesson on air pressure by blowing up a balloon until it pops. This co-author remembers vividly a visiting lecturer arriving to talk about teaching methods to the large group of second-year teaching students to which she belonged. The lecturer placed his black case on the lectern, opened it and began taking out and screwing together the various sections of a trumpet. The usual buzz of conversation slowly faded as we realised what he was doing. When it was finished he raised the instrument to his lips and played 'Reveille'. He then put the trumpet down and looked slowly round the silent room. 'That was your first lesson in how to gain spontaneous attention,' he said. It worked and it is still fresh in my memory 30 years later.

Less dramatic but also effective are bright colours, underlining, highlighting of written or spoken words, calling individuals by name, surprise events, intriguing questions, variety in tasks and teaching methods, and changes in voice level, lighting or pacing. These can all be used to gain attention. If people are to learn they have to maintain attention – they have to stay focused on the important features of the learning situation. The Focus on Practice below offers additional ideas for capturing and maintaining learners' attention.

FOCUS ON PRACTICE

Gaining and maintaining attention

Use signals

Examples
1. Develop a signal that tells learners to stop what they are doing and focus on you. Some teachers move to a particular spot in the room, flick the lights, blow a whistle, tap the table, or play a chord on the class piano. Mix visual and auditory signals.
2. Avoid distracting behaviours, such as tapping a pencil while talking, that interfere with both signals and attention to learning.
3. Give short, clear directions before, not during, transitions.

Make sure the purpose of the lesson or assignment is clear to the class

Examples

1. Write the goals or objectives on the board and discuss them with learners before starting. Ask them to summarise or restate the goals.
2. Explain the reasons for learning, and ask individuals for examples of how they will apply their understanding of the material.
3. Tie the new material to previous lessons – show an outline or map of how the new topic fits with previous and upcoming material.

Incorporate variety, curiosity and surprise

Examples

1. Arouse curiosity with questions such as ' What would happen if?'
2. Create shock by staging an unexpected event such as a loud argument (or a trumpet call!) just before a lesson on communication.
3. Alter the physical environment by changing the arrangement of the room or moving to a different setting.
4. Encourage the use of different sensory channels by giving a lesson that requires students to touch, smell or taste.
5. Use movements, gestures and voice inflection – walk around the room, point, and speak softly and then more emphatically.

Ask questions and provide frames for answering

Examples

1. Ask learners why the material is important, how they intend to study and what strategies they will use.
2. Give learners self-checking or self-editing guides that focus on common mistakes or have them work in pairs to proofread and improve each other's work – sometimes it is difficult to pay attention to your own errors.

For more ideas about gaining learners' attention, see
http://www.inspiringteachers.com/tips/management/attention.html

Working memory

Having considered the critical role of attention in the learning process, let us now think about the next part of the process. The information gathered when we pay attention to something is in our sensory memory and is available for further processing as soon as it is noticed and transformed into patterns of images or sounds (or perhaps other types of sensory codes). Working memory is the 'workbench' of the memory

Working memory

The information that you are focusing on at a given moment.

system, the interface where new information is held temporarily and combined with knowledge from long-term memory, to solve problems or comprehend a lecture, for example. Working memory 'contains' what you are thinking about at the moment. For this reason, some psychologists consider the working memory to be synonymous with 'consciousness' (Sweller, van Merrienboer and Paas, 1998). Unlike sensory memory or long-term memory, working memory capacity is very limited – something many lecturers within higher education seem to forget as they race through a lecture while students work to hold and process the information.

Short-term memory

Component of memory system that holds information for about 20 seconds.

You may have heard the term short-term memory. This was an earlier name for the brief memory component of the information processing system. Short-term memory is not exactly the same as working memory. Working memory includes both temporary storage and active processing – the workbench of memory – where active mental effort is applied to both new and old information. But short-term memory usually means just storage, the immediate memory for new information that can be held about 15 to 20 seconds (Baddeley, 2001). Early experiments suggested that the capacity of short-term memory was only about five to nine separate new items at once (Miller, 1956). This is sometimes known as 'Miller's magic seven' as most people are able to store approximately seven items at a time. Later, we will see that this limitation can be overcome using strategies such as chunking or grouping, but the five to nine limit generally holds true in everyday life. It is quite common to remember a new phone number after looking it up, as you walk across the room to make the call. But what if you have two phone calls to make in succession? Two new phone numbers (14 digits) probably cannot be stored simultaneously. Similar problems apply for many of us with mobile phone numbers which are usually 11 digits long so it is probably just as well that we can store them in the phone's 'memory'.

A current view of working memory is that it is composed of at least three elements: the central executive that controls attention and other mental resources (the 'worker' of working memory), the phonological loop (or store) that holds verbal and acoustical (sound) information, and the visuospatial sketchpad (which holds an image temporarily) for visual and spatial information (Gathercole *et al.*, 2004).

STOP AND THINK

Solve this problem from Ashcraft (2002: 186) and pay attention to how you go about the process:

$$\frac{(4 + 5) \times 2}{3 + (12/4)}$$

The central executive

Central executive

The part of working memory that is responsible for monitoring and directing attention and other mental resources.

As you solved the problem above, the central executive of your working memory focused your attention on the facts that you needed (what is $4 + 5$? 9×2?), retrieved rules for which operations to do first, and recalled how to divide. The central executive supervises attention, makes plans, retrieves and integrates information. It also deals with language comprehension, reasoning, rehearsing information to transfer to long-term memory as well as other activities as you can see in Figure 7.3. Two systems help out and support the central executive – the phonological loop and the visuospatial sketchpad.

WORKING MEMORY

Central executive
(Pool of mental resources)

Activities:
Initiate control and decision processes
Reasoning, language comprehension
Transfer information to long-term
memory via rehearsal, recoding

Phonological loop
(Short-term buffer)

Activities:
Recycling items for immediate recall
Articulatory processes
(Executive's resources are drained if
articulation task is difficult)

Visuospatial sketchpad

Activities:
Visual imagery tasks
Spatial, visual search tasks
(Executive's resources are drained if
imagery or spatial task is difficult)

Figure 7.3
Three parts of working memory

The central executive system is the pool of mental resources for such cognitive activities as focusing attention, reasoning and comprehension. The phonological loop holds verbal and sound information, and the visuospatial sketchpad holds visual and spatial information. The system is limited and can be overwhelmed if information is too much or too difficult.

Source: Ashcraft, Mark H. *Cognition*, 3rd Edition, © 2002, p. 187. Reprinted by permission of Pearson Education, Inc., Upper Saddle River, NJ.

The phonological loop

The phonological loop is a system for rehearsing words and sounds for short-term memory. It is the place you put the '18' $(4 + 5 = 9 \times 2 = 18)$ from the top line of the problem above while you calculated the $3 + (12/4)$ on the bottom of the problem. Baddeley (1986, 2001) suggests that we can hold as much in the phonological loop as we can rehearse (say to ourselves) in 1.5 to 2 seconds. The seven-digit telephone number fits this limitation. But what if you tried to hold these seven words in mind: *disentangle appropriation gossamer anti-intellectual preventative foreclosure documentation* (Gray, 2002). Besides being a mouthful, these words take longer than two seconds to rehearse and are more difficult to hold in working memory than seven single digits or seven short words.

Remember – put in your working memory (which contains the phonological loop) – that we are discussing temporarily holding *new information*. In daily life we certainly can hold more than five to nine bits or 1.5 seconds of information at once. While you are dialling that seven-digit phone number you just looked up, you are bound to have other things 'on your mind' – in your memory – such as how to use a telephone, who you are calling and why. You don't have to pay attention to these things; they are not new knowledge. Some of the processes, such as dialling the phone, have become automatic. However, because of the working

Phonological loop

Part of working memory. A memory rehearsal system for verbal and sound information of about 1.5 to two seconds.

Connect and Extend

See Alloway, T. *et al.* (2004), 'A structured analysis of working memory and related cognitive skills in young children', *Journal of Experimental Child Psychology*, *87*, pp. 85–106, for an account of research that links working memory to literacy and subsequent academic development.

memory's limitations, if you were in a foreign country and were attempting to use an unfamiliar telephone system, you might very well have trouble remembering the phone number because your central executive was trying to figure out the phone system at the same time. Even a few bits of new information can be too much to remember if the new information is very complex or unfamiliar or if you have to integrate several elements to make sense of a situation (Sweller, van Merrienboer and Paas, 1998).

The visuospatial sketchpad

STOP AND THINK

If you rotate a *p* 180 degrees, do you get a *b* or a *d*?
Now try this problem from Gray (2002):

Visuospatial sketchpad

Part of working memory. A holding system for visual and spatial information.

Most people answer the question above by creating a visual image of a 'p' and rotating it. The visuospatial sketchpad is the place where you manipulated the image (after your central executive retrieved the meaning of '180 degrees,' of course). Working in the visuospatial sketchpad has some of the same aspects as actually looking at a picture or object. If you have to solve the 'p' problem and also pay attention to an image on a screen, you will be slowed down just like you would be if you had to look back and forth between two different objects because you are trying to hold too much visual information. However, if you had to solve the 'p' problem while repeating digits, there is little slow down because you would be using your phonological loop to access verbal information. You can use your phonological loop and your visuospatial sketchpad at the same time, but each is quickly filled and easily overburdened. In fact, each kind of task – verbal and visual – appears to happen in different areas of the brain. As we will see later, there are some individual differences in the capacities of these systems, too (Ashcraft, 2006; Gray, 2002).

Duration and contents of working memory

It is clear that the *duration* of information in the working memory system is short, about five to 20 seconds, unless you keep rehearsing the information or process it some other way. It may seem to you that a memory system with a 20-second time limit is not very useful (slightly better than the traditional perception of a goldfish!) but, without this system, you would have already forgotten what you read in the first part of this sentence before you came to these last few words. This would clearly make understanding sentences difficult.

The *contents* of information in working memory may be in the form of sounds and images that resemble the representations in sensory memory, or the information may be structured more abstractly, based on meaning.

Retaining information in working memory

Because information in working memory is fragile and easily lost, it must be kept activated to be retained. Activation is high as long as you are focusing on information, but activation decays or fades quickly when attention shifts away. Holding information in working memory is like keeping a series of plates spinning on top of poles in a circus act. The performer gets one plate spinning, moves to the next plate, and the next, but has to return to the first plate before it slows down too much and falls off its pole. If we don't keep the information 'spinning' in working memory – keep it activated – it will

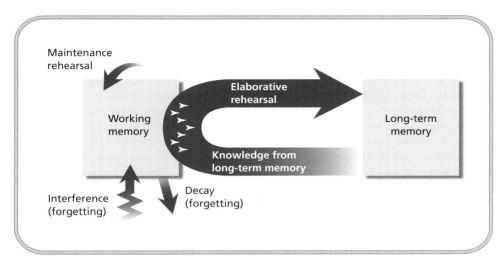

Figure 7.4
Working memory

Information in working memory can be kept activated through maintenance rehearsal or transferred into long-term memory by being connected with information in long-term memory (elaborative rehearsal).

'fall off' (Anderson, 2005, 1995b). When activation fades, forgetting follows, as shown in Figure 7.4. To keep information activated in working memory for longer than 20 seconds, most people keep rehearsing the information mentally. I certainly do this when I have looked up a phone number and then have to move to the phone to dial it.

There are two types of rehearsal (Craik and Lockhart, 1972). Maintenance rehearsal involves repeating the information in your mind. As long as you repeat the information, it can be maintained in working memory indefinitely. Maintenance rehearsal is useful for retaining something you plan to use and then forget, such as a phone number or a location on a map.

Elaborative rehearsal involves connecting the information you are trying to remember with something you already know, with knowledge from long-term memory. For example, if you meet someone at a party whose name is the same as your brother's, you don't have to repeat the name to keep it in memory; you just have to make the association. This kind of rehearsal not only retains information in working memory but also helps move information to long-term memory. Rehearsal is a process the central executive controls to manage the flow of information through the information processing system.

The limited capacity of working memory can also be somewhat circumvented by the process of chunking. Because the number of bits of information, not the size of each bit, is a limitation for working memory, you can retain more information if you can group individual bits of information. For example, if you have to remember the six digits 3, 5, 4, 8, 7 and 0, it is easier to put them together into three chunks of two digits each (35, 48, 70) or two chunks of three digits each (354, 870). With these changes, there are only two or three bits of information rather than six to hold at one time so chunking helps you remember information such as a telephone number (Driscoll, 2005).

Forgetting

Information may be lost from working memory through interference or decay (see Figure 7.4). Interference is fairly straightforward and means that processing new information interferes or gets confused with old information. Visualise for a moment yourself rehearsing your bank account number (usually eight or nine digits) in order to write it onto a form you are filling in and the phone rings. You answer it to find it is only someone trying to sell you something but on returning to the form you find that you have forgotten your bank account number and have to go through the process again.

Maintenance
rehearsal

Keeping information in working memory by repeating it to yourself.

Elaborative
rehearsal

Keeping information in working memory by associating it with something else you already know.

Chunking

Grouping individual bits of data into meaningful larger units.

Decay

The weakening and fading of memories with the passage of time.

Answering the phone and thinking about something else (even briefly) has 'interfered' with your working memory. As new thoughts accumulate, old information is lost from working memory. Information is also lost by time decay. If you don't continue to pay attention to information, the activation level decays (weakens) and finally drops so low that the information cannot be reactivated – it disappears altogether.

Actually, forgetting is very useful. Without forgetting, people would quickly overload their working memories and learning would cease. Also, it would be a problem if you remembered permanently every sentence you ever read, every sound you ever heard and every picture you ever saw. Finding a particular bit of information in all that sea of knowledge would be impossible. It is helpful to have a system that provides temporary storage and that 'weeds out' some information from everything you experience.

We turn next to long-term memory. Because this is such an important topic, we will spend quite a bit of time on it. We do hope you find some of it memorable!

Long-Term Memory: The Goal of Teaching

Long-term memory

Permanent store of knowledge.

Working memory holds the information that is currently activated, such as a telephone number you have just found and are about to dial. Long-term memory holds the information that is well learned, such as all the other telephone numbers you know.

Capacity, duration and contents of long-term memory

There are a number of differences between working and long-term memory, as you can see in Table 7.1.

Information enters working memory very quickly. To move information into long-term storage requires more time and a bit of effort as we shall see. Whereas the capacity of working memory is limited, the capacity of long-term memory appears to be, for all practical purposes, unlimited. In addition, once information is securely stored in long-term memory, it can remain there permanently. Our access to information in working memory is immediate because we are thinking about the information at that very moment but access to information in long-term memory requires time and effort. Recently, some psychologists have suggested that there are not two separate memory stores (working and long-term). Rather, working memory is the part of long-term

Table 7.1 Working and long-term memory

Type of memory	Input	Capacity	Duration	Contents	Retrieval
Working	Very fast	Limited	Very brief: 5–20 sec.	Words, images, ideas, sentences	Immediate
Long-term	Relatively slow	Practically unlimited	Practically unlimited	Propositional networks, schemata, productions, episodes, perhaps images	Depends on representation and organisation

Source: From *Comprehension and Learning: A Conceptual Framework for Teachers* by F. Smith, 1975, New York: Holt, Rinehart, and Winston.

memory that works on (processes) currently activated information – so working memory is more about processing than storage (Wilson, 2001). Another view on the information processing model is the notion of long-term working memory (Kintsch, 1998). Long-term working memory holds the retrieval structures and strategies that pull from long-term memory the information needed at the moment. As you develop knowledge and expertise in an area, you create efficient long-term working memory structures for solving problems in that area. So long-term working memory involves a set of domain-specific access tools that improve as you gain expertise in that domain. For example, an individual reading a sentence in a novel or story book must have access to previously mentioned characters and objects to understand references to pronouns (Ericsson and Kintsch, 1994) and the children in the Greek study by Masoura and Gathercole (2005) mentioned earlier were able to apply their language strategies for English to the new words they were required to learn.

> **Long-term working memory**
>
> Holds the strategies for pulling information from long-term memory into working memory.

Contents of long-term memory: declarative, procedural and conditional knowledge

What we know is stored in long-term memory. Earlier, we talked about general and specific knowledge. Another way to categorise knowledge is as declarative, procedural or conditional (Paris and Cunningham, 1996; Paris, Lipson and Wixson, 1983). Declarative knowledge is knowledge that can be declared or stated through words and symbol systems of all kinds including spoken and written language, Braille, sign language, dance or musical notation, mathematical symbols, and so on (Farnham-Diggory, 1994). Declarative knowledge is 'knowing that' something is the case. The history class in the opening 'In the Classroom' situation was focusing exclusively on declarative knowledge about history. The range of declarative knowledge is tremendous. You can know very specific facts (the atomic weight of gold is 196.967), or generalities (leaves of some trees change colour in autumn), or personal preferences (I don't like broad beans), or rules (to divide fractions, invert the divisor and multiply). Small units of declarative knowledge can be organised into larger units; for example, principles of reinforcement and punishment can be organised in your thinking into a theory of behavioural learning (Gagne, Yekovich and Yekovich, 1993).

> **Declarative knowledge**
>
> Verbal information; facts; 'knowing that' something is the case.

Procedural knowledge is 'knowing how' to do something such as divide fractions or check the oil in a car engine – it is knowledge in action. Procedural knowledge must be demonstrated. Notice that repeating the rule 'to divide fractions, invert the divisor and multiply' shows *declarative* knowledge – the learner can state the rule. However, to show *procedural* knowledge, the learner must act. When faced with a fraction to divide, the person must divide correctly. Learners demonstrate procedural knowledge when they translate a passage into French or German, correctly categorise a geometric shape or construct a coherent paragraph.

> **Procedural knowledge**
>
> Knowledge that is demonstrated when we perform a task; 'knowing how'.

Conditional knowledge is 'knowing when and why' to apply your declarative and procedural knowledge. Given the many kinds of maths problems, it takes conditional knowledge to know when to apply one procedure and when to apply another to solve each problem. It takes conditional knowledge to know when to read every word in a text and when to skim. For many learners, conditional knowledge is a stumbling block. They have the facts and can do the procedures, but they don't seem to understand how to apply what they know at the appropriate time.

> **Conditional knowledge**
>
> 'Knowing when and why' to use declarative and procedural knowledge.

Table 7.2 illustrates how declarative, procedural and conditional knowledge can be either general or domain-specific.

Contents of long-term memory: words and images

Allan Paivio, a psychologist who made key contributions in this area (1971, 1986; Clark and Paivio, 1991), suggested that information is stored in long-term memory as either

Table 7.2 Kinds of knowledge

	General knowledge	**Domain-specific knowledge**
Declarative	Hours the library is open Rules of grammar	Definition of 'hypotenuse' The lines of the poem 'Daffodils'
Procedural	How to use your word processor How to drive	How to solve a simultaneous equation How to tie a shoelace
Conditional	When to give up and try another approach When to skim and when to read carefully	When to volley in tennis When to use Pythagoras's theorem

visual images or verbal units, or both. Psychologists who agree with this point of view believe that information coded both visually and verbally is easiest to learn (Mayer and Sims, 1994). This may be one reason why explaining an idea with words and representing it visually in a diagram or figure, as we do in textbooks, has proved helpful to readers. For example, Richard Mayer and his colleagues (Mayer, 1999, 2001; Mautone and Mayer, 2001) have found that illustrations like the one in Figure 7.8 (later in this chapter) are helpful in improving learners' understanding of science concepts. Paivio's ideas have support, but critics contend that many images are actually stored as verbal codes and then translated into visual information when an image is needed (Driscoll, 2005).

Most cognitive psychologists distinguish two categories of long-term memory, explicit and implicit, with subdivisions under each category, as shown in Figure 7.5.

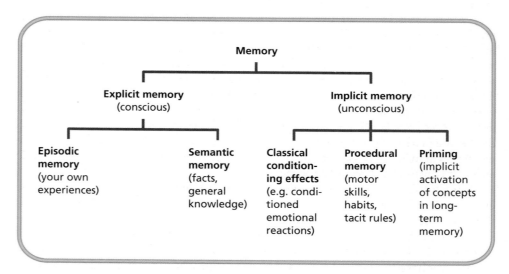

Figure 7.5
Long-term memory: explicit and implicit

Explicit and implicit memory systems follow different rules and involve different neural systems of the brain. The sub-divisions of each kind of memory also may involve different neural systems.

Source: From *Psychology* 4E by Peter Gray, Fig. 9.11, p. 344. Published by Worth Publishers. Copyright © 1991, 1994, 1999, 2002 by Worth Publishers. Adapted with permission of the publisher.

Explicit memory is knowledge from long-term memory that can be recalled and consciously considered. We are aware of these memories – we know we have remembered them. So if I asked you to state your date of birth you would know that you could provide this information easily because you would know that you know. Implicit memory, on the other hand, is knowledge that we are not conscious of recalling, but that influences behaviour or thought without our awareness. For example someone with a phobia about confined spaces (claustrophobia) might have no idea of why they experience such an extreme fear response but they would know that they feel it. However, their implicit memory clearly holds a relevant memory. These different kinds of memory are associated with different parts of the brain (Ashcraft, 2006). The behavioural approach (Chapter 6) would perhaps explain this as a result of classical conditioning. Let us now explore the idea of explicit memory.

Explicit memories: semantic and episodic

In Figure 7.5, you will see that explicit memories can be either semantic or episodic. Semantic memory, very important in schools, is memory for meaning, including words, facts, theories and concepts – declarative knowledge. These memories are not tied to particular experiences and are stored as *propositions, images* and *schemas*.

Propositions and propositional networks

A *proposition* is the smallest unit of knowledge that can be judged true or false. The statement, 'Alice borrowed the crystal wine glasses' has two propositions:

1. Alice borrowed the wine glasses.

2. The wine glasses are made of crystal.

Propositions that share information, such as the two above that share information about the wine glasses, are linked in what cognitive psychologists call propositional networks. It is the meaning, not the exact words or word order that is stored in the network. The same propositional network would apply to the sentence: 'The crystal wine glasses were borrowed by Alice.' The meaning is the same, and it is this *meaning* that is stored in memory as a set of relationships.

It is possible that most information is stored and represented in propositional networks. When we want to recall a bit of information, we can translate its meaning (as represented in the propositional network) into familiar phrases and sentences, or mental pictures. Also, because propositions are networked, recall of one bit of information can trigger or *activate* recall of another. We are not aware of these networks, for they are not part of our conscious memory (Anderson, 1995a). In much the same way, we are not aware of underlying grammatical structure when we form a sentence in our own language; we don't have to diagram a sentence in order to say it.

Images

Images are representations based on the structure or appearance of the information (Anderson, 1995a). As we form images (like you did in the 'p' problem), we try to remember or recreate the physical attributes and spatial structure of information. For example, when asked how many windowpanes are in their living room, most people conjure up an image of the windows 'in their mind's eye' and count the panes – the more panes, the longer it takes to respond. If the information were represented only in a proposition such as ' my living room has seven window panes,' then everyone would take about the same time to answer, whether the number was one or 24 (Mendell, 1971). However, as we saw earlier, researchers don't agree on exactly how images are stored in memory. Some psychologists believe that images are stored as pictures;

Explicit memory

Long-term memories that involve deliberate or conscious recall.

Implicit memory

Knowledge that we are not conscious of recalling, but influences behaviour or thought without our awareness.

Semantic memory

Memory for meaning.

Propositional network

Set of interconnected concepts and relationships in which long-term knowledge is held.

Images

Representations based on the physical attributes – the appearance – of information.

others believe we store propositions in long-term memory and convert to pictures in working memory when necessary.

There probably are features of each process involved – some memory for images and some verbal or propositional descriptions of the image. Seeing images 'in your mind's eye' is not exactly the same as seeing the actual image. It is more difficult to perform complicated transformations on mental images than on real images (Driscoll, 2005; Matlin and Foley, 1997). For example, if you had a plastic 'p' you could very quickly rotate it. Rotating mentally takes more time for most people. Nevertheless, images are useful in making many practical decisions such as how a sofa might look in your living room or how to line up a golf or snooker shot. Images may also be helpful in abstract reasoning. Physicists, such as Faraday and Einstein, report creating images to reason about complex new problems. Einstein claimed that he was visualising chasing a beam of light and catching up to it when the concept of relativity came to him (Kosslyn and Koenig, 1992).

Schemas

Schemas

(singular, schema)
Basic structures for organising information; concepts.

Propositions and single images are appropriate for representing single ideas and relationships, but often our knowledge about a topic combines images and propositions. To explain this kind of complex knowledge, psychologists developed the idea of a schema (Gagne, Yekovich and Yekovich, 1993). Schemas (sometimes called *schemata*) are abstract knowledge structures that organise vast amounts of information. A schema (the singular form) is a pattern or guide for representing an event, concept or skill. For example, Figure 7.6 is a partial representation of a schema for knowledge about 'reinforcement'.

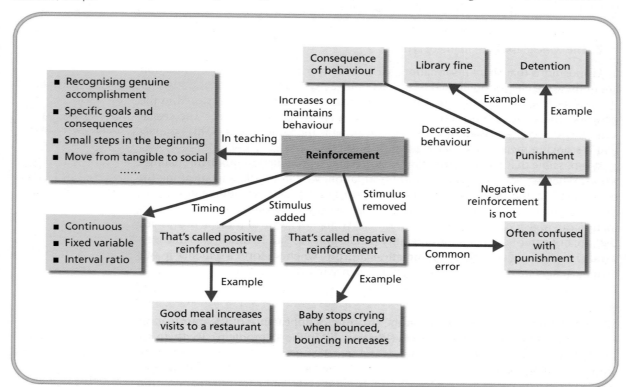

Figure 7.6
A partial schema for 'reinforcement'

The concept of 'reinforcement' is under the general category of 'consequence'. It is related to other concepts such as eating in restaurants or bouncing babies, depending on the individual's experiences.

The schema tells you what features are typical of a category, what to expect about an object or situation. The pattern has 'slots' that are filled with specific information as we apply the schema in a particular situation. And schemas are personal. For example, my schema of reinforcement is less richly developed than Skinner's schema must have been. You encountered a very similar concept of scheme in the discussion of Piaget's theory of cognitive development in Chapter 2.

When you hear the sentence, ' Alice borrowed the crystal wine glasses,' you know even more about it than the two propositions because you have schemas about borrowing, wine glasses, crystal, and maybe even Alice herself. You know without being told, for example, that the lender does not have the wine glasses now, because they are in Alice's possession, and that Alice has an obligation to return the wine glasses to the lender (Gentner, 1975). None of this information is explicitly stated, but it is part of our schema for the meaning of ' borrow'. Other schemas allow you to infer that the glasses are not plastic (if they are real crystal) and that Alice has probably invited guests for a meal. If you actually knew Alice your schema about her may even allow you to predict how promptly the glasses will be returned and in what condition.

Another type of schema, a story grammar (sometimes called a schema for text or story structure) helps learners to understand and remember stories (Gagne, Yekovich and Yekovich, 1993; Rumelhart and Ortony, 1977). A story grammar could be something like this: murder discovered, search for clues, murderer's fatal mistake identified, trap set to trick suspect into confessing, murderer takes bait . . . mystery solved! In other words, a story grammar is a typical general structure that could fit many specific stories. To comprehend a story, we select a schema that seems appropriate. Then, we use this framework to decide which details are important, what information to seek, and what to remember. It is as though the schema is a theory about what should occur in the story. The schema guides us in 'interrogating' the text, pointing to the specific information we expect to find so that the story makes sense. If we activate our 'murder mystery schema', we may be alert for clues or a murderer's fatal mistake. Without an appropriate schema, trying to understand a story, textbook or classroom lesson is a very slow, difficult process, something like finding your way through a new town without a map. A schema representing the typical sequence of events in an everyday situation is called a script or an *event schema*. Children as young as age three have basic scripts for the familiar events in their lives (Nelson, 1986). So they quickly learn scripts for going to the supermarket or visiting friends for tea and this seems to help them develop their memory skills because it provides them with a structure for their memories. Parents and teachers are often amused or perplexed when young children write or narrate brief accounts of exciting events like a camping holiday which focus on everyday aspects such as ' then we had tea and went to bed'. It is likely that they have not yet developed the appropriate schema for this event and so use a well-tried one instead.

Storing knowledge of the world in schemas and scripts has both advantages and disadvantages. A schema can be applied in many contexts, depending on what part of the schema is relevant. You can use what you know about reinforcement, for example, to take a test in educational psychology, to analyse why a learner continues to be sent to the head teacher's office, or to design an incentive scheme for your employees. Having a well-developed schema about Alice lets you recognise her (even as her appearance changes), remember many of her characteristics, and make predictions about her behaviour. However, it also allows you to be wrong. You may have incorporated incorrect or biased information into your schema of Alice. For example, if Alice is a member of an ethnic group different from yours and if you believe that group is dishonest because you are influenced by social sources, you may assume that Alice will keep the wine glasses. In this way, racial and ethnic stereotypes can function as schemas for

Story grammar

Typical structure or organisation for a category of stories.

Script

Schema or expected plan for the sequence of steps in a common event such as buying groceries or ordering take-away pizza.

misunderstanding individuals and for racial discrimination (Sherman and Bessenoff, 1999).

The second kind of explicit memory is episodic. We turn to that now.

Episodic memory

Memory for information tied to a particular place and time, especially information about the events or episodes of your own life, is called episodic memory. Episodic memory is about events we have experienced, so we often can explain *when* the event happened. In contrast, we usually can't describe when we acquired a semantic memory. For example, you may have a difficult time remembering when you developed semantic memories for the meaning of the word 'injustice', but you can easily remember a time that you felt unjustly treated. Episodic memory also keeps track of the order of things, so it is a good place to store jokes, gossip, or plots from films.

Memories for dramatic or emotional moments in your life are called flashbulb memories. These memories are vivid and complete, as if your brain demanded that you 'record this moment'. Under stress, more glucose energy goes to fuel brain activity, while stress-induced hormones signal the brain that something important is happening (Myers, 2005). So when we have strong emotional reactions, memories are stronger and more lasting. Many people have vivid memories of very positive or very negative events in school, winning a prize or being humiliated, for example. You probably know just where you were and what you were doing when you first heard or saw reports of the planes crashing into the Twin Towers.

Implicit memories

Look back at Figure 7.5. You see that there are three kinds of implicit or out-of-awareness memories: classical conditioning, procedural memory and priming effects. In classical conditioning, as we saw in Chapter 6, some out-of-awareness memories

Episodic memory

Long-term memory for information tied to a particular time and place, especially memory of the events in a person's life.

Flashbulb memories

Clear, vivid memories of an emotionally important event in your life.

Implicit memory includes the knowledge of skills that may have taken a while to learn but then tend to be remembered for a long time and performed without intense concentration

may cause you to feel anxious as you take a test or make your heart rate increase when you hear a dentist's drill.

The second type of implicit memory is procedural memory for skills, habits and how to do things – in other words, memory for procedural knowledge. It may take a while to learn a procedure – such as how to ride a bicycle, serve a tennis ball or work out an equation, but once learned, this knowledge tends to be remembered for a long time. Procedural memories are represented as *condition-action rules*, sometimes called productions. Productions specify what to do under certain conditions: if A occurs, then so does B. A production might be something like, 'If you want to cycle uphill lean forward and stand up on the pedals,' or 'If your goal is to increase learner attention and a learner has been paying attention a bit longer than usual, then praise the learner.' People can't necessarily state all their condition-action rules, and don't even know that they are following these rules, but they act on them nevertheless. The more practised the procedure, the more automatic the action and the more implicit the memory (Anderson, 1995a).

> **Procedural memory**
>
> Long-term memory for how to do things.
>
> **Productions**
>
> The contents of procedural memory; rules about what actions to take, given certain conditions.

STOP AND THINK

Fill in these blanks: ME _ _ _ _

The final type of implicit memory involves priming, or activating information that already is in long-term memory through some out-of-awareness process. You might have seen an example of priming in the fill-in-the-blank question above. Priming may be the fundamental process for retrieval as associations are activated and spread through the memory system (Ashcraft, 2006). If you wrote MEMORY instead of MENTOR or MEMBER, or METEOR or other ME words, then priming may have played a role because the word 'memory' has occurred many times in this chapter. Let us now look at how information is stored in and retrieved from long-term memory.

> **Priming**
>
> Activating a concept in memory or the spread of activation from one concept to another.

Storing and retrieving information in long-term memory

Just what is done to 'save' information permanently – to create explicit (those we are aware of) and implicit (those we are not aware of) memories? How can we make the most effective use of our practically unlimited capacity to learn and remember? *The way you learn information in the first place* – the way you process it in working memory at the outset – strongly affects its recall later. It seems that one important requirement for learning is that you integrate new information with knowledge already stored in long-term memory as you construct an understanding. What you are doing is making connections with or building upon what you already know. Here, *elaboration, organisation* and *context* play a role.

Elaboration is adding meaning to new information by connecting the information with already existing knowledge. We apply our schemas and draw on already existing knowledge to construct an understanding. Frequently, we change our existing knowledge in the process. We often elaborate automatically. For example, a paragraph about an historic figure in ancient Rome tends to activate our existing knowledge about that period or if we encounter an old friend after a gap of time we try to bring to mind all our existing knowledge about him and then 'catch up' in the course of conversation. We use the old knowledge as a basis for understanding the new.

> **Elaboration**
>
> Adding and extending meaning by connecting new information to existing knowledge.

Material that is elaborated when first learned will be easier to recall later. First, as we saw earlier, elaboration is a form of rehearsal. It keeps the information activated in working memory long enough to have a chance for the new information to be linked with knowledge in long-term memory. Second, elaboration builds extra links to existing knowledge. The more one bit of information or knowledge is associated with other bits, the more routes there are to follow to get to the original bit. To put it another way, you have several 'handles' or priming/retrieval cues to 'pick up' or recognise the information you might be seeking (Schunk, 2004). For example, if your friend's birthday is on the same day as your father's, which you know is at the beginning of September when you return to school/college, you are more likely to remember both because of the number of connections made. So planning to return to school/college would serve as a retrieval cue to remind you of your father's birthday and that would remind you of your friend's birthday.

The more learners elaborate new ideas, the more they 'make them their own,' the deeper their understanding and the better their memory for the knowledge will be. We help learners to elaborate when we ask them to translate information into their own words, create examples, explain to a peer, draw or act out the relationships, or apply the information to solve new problems. Of course, if learners elaborate new information by developing misguided explanations, these misconceptions will be remembered too so it is important for teachers to monitor their understanding through discussions and tests.

Organisation

Ordered and logical network of relations.

Organisation is a second element of processing that improves learning. Material that is well organised is easier to learn and to remember than bits and pieces of information, especially if the information is complex or extensive. Placing a concept in a structure will help you learn and remember both general definitions and specific examples. The structure serves as a guide back to the information when you need it. For example, Table 7.1 gives an organised view of the capacity, duration, contents and retrieval of information from working and long-term memory; Table 7.2 organises information about types of knowledge; and Figure 7.6 organises my knowledge about reinforcement. If material is not organised it can become confused with other material, therefore harder to retrieve or lost.

Context

The physical or emotional backdrop associated with an event.

Context is a third element of processing that influences learning. Aspects of physical and emotional context – places, rooms, moods, who is with us – are learned along with other information. Later, if you try to remember the information, it will be easier if the current context is similar to the original one. Context is a kind of priming that activates the information. This has been demonstrated in the laboratory. Learners who learned material in one type of room performed better on tests taken in a similar room than they did on comparable tests taken in a very different-looking room (Smith, Glenberg and Bjork, 1978). So, studying for a test under 'test-like' conditions may result in improved performance. Of course, you can't always go back to the same place or a similar one in order to recall something but if you can picture the setting, the time of day, and your companions, you may eventually reach the information you seek. A colleague had misplaced his contact lenses following a party. He was mystified because he had searched all the usual places but there was no sign of them. It wasn't until he was making tea in his kitchen and warming the teapot that he remembered. There, positioned carefully either side of the spout were the lenses and with them his thinking at the time came flooding back which was that they made the teapot look like an elephant with eyes either side of the trunk and that it would be a really safe place to leave them. A few too many glasses of wine perhaps had influenced his thinking.

Now that we have looked at the part elaboration, organisation and context play when storing information, let us look at Craik and Lockhart's notion of levels of processing information.

Levels of processing theories

Craik and Lockhart (1972) first proposed their levels of processing theory as an alternative to short-/long-term memory models, but levels of processing is particularly related to the notion of elaboration described above. Craik and Lockhart suggested that what determines how long information is remembered is *how extensively* the information is analysed and connected with other information. The more completely information is processed, the better are our chances of remembering it. For example, according to the levels of processing theory, if you were asked to sort pictures of dogs based on the colour of their coats, you might not remember many of the pictures later. But if you were asked to rate each dog on how likely it is to chase you as you walk past, you probably would remember more of the pictures. To rate the dogs, you must pay attention to details in the pictures, relate features of the dogs to characteristics associated with danger, and so on. This rating procedure requires 'deeper' processing and more focus on the *meaning* of the features in the photos.

Levels of processing theory

Theory that recall of information is based on how deeply it is processed.

Retrieving information from long-term memory

When we need to use information from long-term memory, we search for it. Sometimes, the search is conscious, as when you see a friend approaching and search for her name. At other times, locating and using information from long-term memory is automatic, as when you dial a telephone or solve a maths problem without having to search for each step, or the word 'memory' pops to mind when you see ME _ _ _ _. Think of long-term memory as a huge shelf full of tools (skills, procedures) and supplies (knowledge, schemas) ready to be brought to the workbench of working memory to accomplish a task. The shelf (long-term memory) stores an incredible amount, but it may be hard to find what you are looking for quickly. The workbench (working memory) is small, but anything on it is immediately available. Because it is small, however, supplies (bits of information) sometimes are lost when the workbench overflows or when one bit of information covers (interferes with) another (Gagne, 1985).

Spreading activation

As we have seen, then, the size of the network in long-term memory is huge, but only small parts from it are activated at any one time. Only the information we are currently thinking about is in working memory. Information is retrieved in this network through spreading activation. When a particular proposition or image is active – when we are thinking about it – other closely associated knowledge can be *primed* or triggered as well, and activation can spread through the network (Anderson, 2005; Gagne, Yekovich and Yekovich, 1993). Thus, as one focuses on the propositions, 'I'd like to go for a drive in the country to see the autumn leaves,' related ideas such as, 'I should rake the leaves from the lawn,' and 'I need to check the oil in the car engine,' come to mind. As activation spreads from the 'car trip' to the 'oil check,' the original thought, or active memory, disappears from working memory because of the limited space. Thus, retrieval from long-term memory occurs partly through the spreading of activation from one bit of knowledge to related ideas in the network. We often use this spreading in reverse to retrace our steps in a conversation, as in, 'Before we got onto the topic of where the oil can is, what were we talking about? Oh yes, looking at the leaves.' The learning and retrieving processes of long-term memory are shown in Figure 7.7.

Spreading activation

Retrieval of pieces of information based on their relatedness to one another. Remembering one bit of information activates (stimulates) recall of associated information.

Retrieval

Process of searching for and finding information in long-term memory.

Reconstruction

In long-term memory, the information is still available, even when it is not activated, even when you are not thinking about it at the moment. If spreading activation does

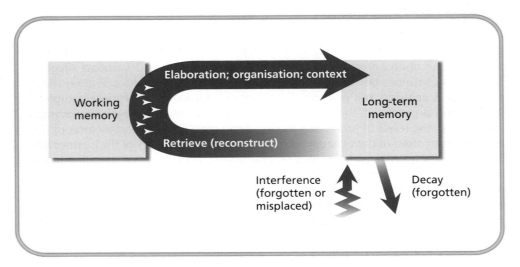

Figure 7.7
Long-term memory

We activate information from long-term memory to help us understand new information in working memory. With mental work and processing (elaboration, organisation, context) the new information can be stored permanently in long-term memory. Forgetting is caused by interference and time decay.

Reconstruction

Recreating information by using memories, expectations, logic and existing knowledge.

not 'find' the information we seek, then we might still come up with an answer through reconstruction, a cognitive tool or problem-solving process that makes use of logic, cues and other knowledge to *construct* a reasonable answer by filling in any missing parts (Koriat, Goldsmith and Pansky, 2000). Sometimes reconstructed recollections are incorrect. For example, in 1932, F. C. Bartlett conducted a series of famous studies on remembering stories. He read a complex, unfamiliar Native American tale to students at Cambridge University and, after various lengths of time, asked the students to recall the story. Stories the students recalled were generally shorter than the original and were translated into the concepts and language of the Cambridge student culture. The story told of a seal hunt, for instance, but many students remembered (reconstructed) a 'fishing trip', an activity closer to their experiences and more consistent with their schemas.

One area where reconstructed memory can play a major role is eyewitness testimony. Elizabeth Loftus and her colleagues have conducted a number of studies showing that misleading questions or other information during questioning can affect memory. For example, in a classic study, Loftus and Palmer (1974) showed subjects slides of a car crash. Later, the experimenters asked some subjects, 'How fast were the cars going when they *hit* each other?' while other subjects who saw the same slides were asked, 'How fast were the cars going when they *smashed* into each other?' The difference in verbs was enough to bias the subjects' memories – the 'hit' subjects estimated the cars were travelling an average of 34 miles per hour, but the 'smashed' subjects estimated almost 41 miles per hour. And one week later, 32% of the 'smashed' subjects remembered seeing broken glass at the scene of the wreck, while only 14% of the 'hit' subjects remembered glass. (There was no broken glass visible in any of the slides.) This has important implications for people giving evidence in court where they might be 'led' by the questions asked. The effect seems most pronounced in young children. Warren, Hulse-Trotter and Tubbs (1991) used the Gudjonsson Suggestibility Scale (GSS), a research and clinical tool to assess responses to 'misleading questions' and 'negative feedback' in the context of recalling a particular event with seven-year-olds, 12-year-olds and adults. They found that seven-year-olds showed greater vulnerability to suggestion than the older children and adults. Further work by Danielsdottir *et al.*, (1993) obtained similar data in a study using Icelandic children.

Forgetting and long-term memory

Information in working memory that is lost before it has a chance to integrate into the network of long-term memory truly disappears. No amount of effort or searching will bring it back but information stored in long-term memory may be available, given the right cues. Some people believe that nothing is ever lost from long-term memory; however, research casts doubts on this assertion (Schwartz, Wasserman and Robbins, 2002).

Information appears to be lost from long-term memory through time decay and interference. One explanation for this decline is that neural connections, like muscles, grow weak without use. After 25 years, it may be that the memories are still somewhere in the brain, but they are too weak to be reactivated (Anderson, 2005, 1995b) and some neurons simply die. Finally, newer memories may interfere with or obscure older memories, and older memories may interfere with memory for new material. It seems that memory is not like a DVD/video recording which can be played as many times as you like but remains unchanged. Rather, memory is constructed from where we are in the present and the events, experiences and memories which have occurred since the remembered event influence and inform that memory as we saw with the car crash/hit example.

Interference

The process that occurs when remembering certain information is hampered by the presence of other information.

Even with decay and interference, long-term memory is remarkable. In a review of almost 100 studies of memory for knowledge taught in school, George Semb and John Ellis concluded that, 'contrary to popular belief, students retain much of the knowledge taught in the classroom' (1994: 279). It appears that teaching strategies that encourage learner engagement and lead to higher levels of *initial* learning (such as frequent reviews and tests, elaborated feedback, high standards, mastery learning and active involvement in learning projects) are associated with longer retention. An Australian study of university students confirmed the importance of distinctive features within learning materials (Herbert and Burt, 2004). These features enriched the learning experience and seemed to serve as memory cues, enabling learners to remember for longer and in more detail. The Focus on Practice below gives applications of information processing for teaching.

FOCUS ON PRACTICE

Using information processing ideas in the classroom

Make sure the learners' attention is engaged

Examples
1. Develop a signal that tells learners to stop what they are doing and focus on you. Make sure learners respond to the signal – don't let them ignore it. Practice using the signal.
2. Move around the room, use gestures and avoid speaking in a monotone.
3. Begin a lesson by asking a question that stimulates interest in the topic.

4. Regain the attention of individual learners by walking closer to them, using their names or asking them a question.

Help learners separate essential from non-essential details and focus on the most important information

Examples
1. Summarise instructional objectives to indicate what the class should be learning. Relate the material you are presenting to the objectives as you teach: 'Now I'm going to explain exactly how you can find the information you need to answer the first question on the board – determining the tone of the story.'
2. When you make an important point, pause, repeat, ask a learner to paraphrase, note the information on the board in coloured chalk, or tell learners to highlight the point in their notes or readings.

Help learners make connections between new information and what they already know

Examples
1. Review prerequisites to help learners bring to mind the information they will need to understand new material: 'Who can tell us the definition of a quadrilateral? Now, what is a rhombus? Is a square a quadrilateral? Is a square a rhombus? What did we say yesterday about how you can tell? Today we are going to look at some other quadrilaterals.'
2. Use an outline or diagram to show how new information fits with the framework you have been developing. For example, 'Now that you know the duties of the Minister of Education, where would you expect to find him or her in this diagram of the branches of the UK government?'
3. Give an assignment that specifically calls for the use of new information along with information already learned.

Provide for repetition and review of information

Examples
1. Begin the class with a quick review of the homework task.
2. Give frequent, short tests.
3. Build practice and repetition into games, or have learners work with partners to test each other.

Present material in a clear, organised way

Examples
1. Make the purpose of the lesson very clear.
2. Give learners a brief outline to follow. Put the same outline on an overhead transparency or powerpoint so you can keep yourself on task. When learners

ask questions or make comments, relate these to the appropriate section of the outline.

3. Use summaries in the middle and at the end of the lesson.

Focus on meaning, not memorisation

Examples

1. In teaching new words, help learners associate the new word to a related word they already understand: 'Enmity is from the same root as *enemy*.'
2. In teaching about remainders, have learners group 12 objects into sets of 2, 3, 4, 5, 6, and ask them to count the 'leftovers' in each case.

For more information on information processing, see http://chiron.valdosta.edu/whuitt/col/cogsys/infoproc.html

One question that intrigues many cognitive psychologists is why some people learn and remember more than others. For those who hold an information processing view, part of the answer lies in the concept of metacognition.

Metacognition

The executive control processes shown in Figure 7.1 guide the flow of information through the information processing system. We have already discussed a number of control processes, including attention, maintenance rehearsal, elaborative rehearsal, organisation and elaboration. These executive control processes are sometimes called *metacognitive skills*, because they can be intentionally used to regulate cognition.

Metacognitive knowledge and regulation

Donald Meichenbaum and his colleagues described metacognition as people's 'awareness of their own cognitive machinery and how the machinery works' (Meichenbaum *et al.*, 1985: 5). Metacognition literally means cognition about cognition – or knowledge about knowing and learning. This metacognitive knowledge is higher-order cognition used to monitor and regulate cognitive processes such as reasoning, comprehension, problem solving, learning, and so on (Metcalfe and Shimamura, 1994). Because people differ in their metacognitive knowledge and skills, they differ in how well and how quickly they learn (Brown *et al.*, 1983; Morris, 1990).

Metacognition involves the three kinds of knowledge we discussed earlier: (1) *declarative knowledge* about yourself as a learner, the factors that influence your learning and memory, and the skills, strategies and resources needed to perform a task – knowing *what* to do; (2) *procedural knowledge* or knowing *how* to use the strategies; and (3) *conditional knowledge* to ensure the completion of the task – knowing *when* and *why* to apply the procedures and strategies (Bruning *et al.*, 2004). Metacognition is the strategic application of this declarative, procedural and conditional knowledge to accomplish goals and solve problems (Schunk, 2004).

Executive control processes

Processes such as selective attention, rehearsal, elaboration and organisation that influence encoding, storage and retrieval of information in memory.

Metacognition

Knowledge about our own thinking processes.

Metacognition involves choosing the best way to approach a learning task

Metacognitive knowledge is used to regulate thinking and learning (Brown, 1987; Nelson, 1996). There are three essential skills that allow us to do this: planning, monitoring and evaluating. *Planning* involves deciding how much time to give to a task, which strategies to use, how to start, what resources to gather, what order to follow, what to skim and what to pay close attention to, and so on. *Monitoring* is the real-time awareness of 'How I'm doing.' Monitoring entails asking, 'Is this making sense? Am I trying to go too fast? Have I studied enough?' *Evaluating* involves making judgements about the processes and outcomes of thinking and learning. 'Should I change strategies? Get help? Give up for now? Is this essay (painting, model, poem, plan, etc.) finished?'

Of course, we don't have to be metacognitive all the time. Some actions become routine. Metacognition is most useful when tasks are challenging, but not too difficult. Then planning, monitoring and evaluating can be helpful and even when we are planning, monitoring and evaluating, these processes are not necessarily conscious, especially in adults. We may use them automatically without being aware of our efforts (Perner, 2000). Experts in a field plan, monitor and evaluate as second nature; they have difficulty describing their metacognitive knowledge and skills (Bargh and Chartrand, 1999; Reder, 1996).

Connect and Extend

See Desoete, A. *et al.* (2006), 'Metacognitive skills in Belgian third grade children (age 8–9) with and without mathematical learning disabilities', *Metacognition and Learning*, *1*(2), pp. 119–135, for an account of mathematical problem solving and metacognition.

Metacognitive strategies for learners with learning difficulties

For learners with learning dificulties, executive control processes (that is, metacognitive strategies) such as planning, organising, monitoring progress and making adaptations are especially important, but often underdeveloped (Kirk *et al.*, 2006). It makes sense to teach these strategies directly. Some approaches make use of mnemonics such as the SelfSpell and SpellMaster instructional programmes for learners with dyslexia. Research by Nicolson and Fawcett (1994) at the University of Sheffield found that the combination of mnemonic and mastery techniques (to help with letter identification, sounds and so on) was highly effective at addressing the spelling problems of 10–12-year-old children with extreme spelling difficulties.

Table 7.3 Teaching strategies for improving learners' metacognitive knowledge and skills

These eight guidelines from Pressley and Woloshyn (1995) may be useful when teaching metacognitive strategy.

1. Teach a few strategies at a time, intensively and extensively as part of the ongoing curriculum.
2. Model and explain new strategies.
3. If parts of the strategy were not understood, model again and re-explain strategies in ways that are sensitive to those confusing or misunderstanding aspects of strategy use.
4. Explain to learners where and when to use the strategy.
5. Provide plenty of practice, using strategies for as many appropriate tasks as possible.
6. Encourage learners to monitor what they are doing when they are using strategies.
7. Increase learners' motivation to use strategies by heightening their awareness that they are acquiring valuable skills – skills that are at the heart of competent functioning.
8. Emphasise reflective processing rather than speedy processing; do all possible to eliminate high anxiety in learners; encourage learners to shield themselves from distractions so they can attend to academic tasks.

Source: Adapted from Pressley, M. and Woloshyn, V. (1995) *Cognitive Strategy Instruction that Really Improves Children's Academic Performance,* 2nd Edition, p. 18. Copyright © by Brookline Books.

Michael Pressley (a professor of education and psychology in Indiana, US) and his colleagues (1995) developed the *Cognitive Strategies Model* as a guide for teaching learners, to improve their metacognitive strategies. Table 7.3 describes the steps in teaching these strategies.

Now that we have examined the information processing explanation of how knowledge is represented and remembered, let's turn to the really important question: How can teachers support the development of knowledge?

Becoming Knowledgeable: Some Basic Principles

Understanding a concept such as 'crystal' involves *declarative knowledge* about characteristics and images as well as *procedural knowledge* about how to apply rules to categorise specific types of crystal. We will discuss the development of declarative and procedural knowledge separately, but keep in mind that real learning is a combination and integration of these elements.

Development of declarative knowledge

Within the information processing perspective, to learn declarative knowledge is really to integrate new ideas with existing knowledge and construct an understanding. As you have seen, people learn best when they have a good base of knowledge in the area they are studying. With many well-elaborated schemas and scripts to guide them, new material makes more sense, and there are many possible spots in the long-term memory network for connecting new information with old. However, learners don't always have a good base of knowledge. In the early phases of learning, learners of any age must grope around the landscape a bit, searching for landmarks and direction. Even experts in an area must use some learning strategies when they encounter unfamiliar material or new problems (Alexander, 1996, 1997; Garner, 1990; Perkins and Salomon, 1989; Shuell, 1990).

What are some possible strategies? Perhaps the best single method for helping learners learn is to make each lesson as meaningful as possible.

Making it meaningful

Meaningful lessons are presented in vocabulary that makes sense to the learners. New terms are clarified through ties with more familiar words and ideas. Meaningful lessons are well organised, with clear connections between the different elements of the lesson. Finally, meaningful lessons make natural use of old information to help learners understand new information through examples or analogies.

The importance of meaningful lessons is emphasised in the Stop and Think below.

STOP AND THINK

Look at the three lines below. Begin by covering all but the first line. Look at it for a second, close the book, and write down all the letters you remember. Then repeat this procedure with the second and third lines.

1. KBVODUWGPJMSQTXNOGMCTRSO
2. READ JUMP WHEAT POOR BUT SEEK
3. KNIGHTS RODE HORSES INTO WAR

Source: Smith (1975).

Each line has the same number of letters, but the chances are great that you remembered all the letters in the third line, a good number of letters in the second line, and very few in the first line. The first line makes no sense. There is no way to organise it in a brief glance. Working memory is simply not able to hold and process all that information quickly. The second line is more meaningful. You do not have to see each letter because your long-term memory brings prior knowledge of spelling rules and vocabulary to the task. The third line is the most meaningful. Just a glance and you can probably remember all of it because you bring to this task prior knowledge not only of spelling and vocabulary but also of rules about syntax and probably some historical information about knights (they didn't ride in tanks). This sentence is meaningful because you have existing schemas for assimilating it. It is relatively easy to associate the words and meaning with other information already in long-term memory (Sweller, van Merrienboer and Paas, 1998).

The challenge, for teachers and those working with learners, is to make lessons less like learning the first line and more like learning the third line. Although this may seem obvious, think about the times when *you* have read a sentence in a text or heard an explanation from a teacher/lecturer that might just as well have been KBVODUWG-PJMSQTXNOGMCTRSO. However, remember, attempts to change the ways that individuals are used to learning – moving from memorising to meaningful activities as in the opening 'In the Classroom' situation – are not always greeted with learner enthusiasm. Learners may be concerned about their grades; at least when memorisation gains an A, they know what is expected. Meaningful learning can be riskier and more challenging. In Chapters 8, 9 and 13 we will examine a variety of ways in which teachers can support meaningful learning and understanding.

Visual images and illustrations

Is a picture worth 1000 words in teaching? Richard Mayer (1999, 2001) has studied this question for several years and found that the right combination of pictures and words can make a significant difference in people's learning. Mayer's cognitive theory of multimedia learning includes three ideas:

1. *Dual coding*: Visual and verbal materials are processed in different systems (Clark and Paivio, 1991).
2. *Limited capacity*: Working memory for verbal and visual material is severely limited (Baddeley, 2001).
3. *Generative learning*: Meaningful learning happens when learners focus on relevant information and generate or build connections (Mayer, 1999).

The problem: How to build complex understandings that integrate information from visual (pictures, diagrams, graphs, films) and verbal (text, lecture) sources, given the limitations of working memory? The answer: Make sure the information is available at the same time or in focused small bites. Mayer and Gallini (1990) provide an example. They used three kinds of texts to explain how a bicycle pump works. One text used only words, the second had pictures that just showed the parts of the brake system and the steps, and the third (this one improved student learning and recall) showed both the 'on' and the 'off' states of the pumps with labels for each step, as in Figure 7.8.

The moral of the story? Give learners multiple ways to understand – pictures *and* explanations. But don't overload working memory – 'package' the visual and verbal information together in bite-size (or memory-size) pieces.

Another memory strategy that often makes use of images is mnemonics.

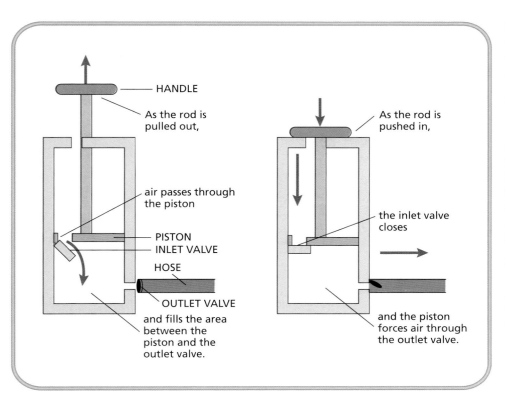

Figure 7.8
Images and words that help pupils understand

Is a picture worth a thousand words in teaching? The right combination of pictures and words, like the labelled illustrations here, can make a significant difference in pupils' learning.

Source: Adapted from *The World Book Encyclopedia*. Copyright © 2003 World Book, Inc. www.worldbook.com

Mnemonics

Mnemonics

Techniques for remembering; also, the art of memory.

Mnemonics are systematic procedures for improving memory (Atkinson *et al.*, 1999; Levin, 1994; Rummel, Levin and Woodward, 2003). When information has little inherent meaning, mnemonic strategies build in meaning by connecting what is to be learned with established words or images. One mnemonic strategy is known as the *loci* method.

Loci method

Technique of associating items with specific places.

The loci method derives its name from the plural of the Latin word *locus,* meaning 'place'. To use loci, you must first imagine a very familiar place, such as your own house or flat, and pick out particular locations. Every time you have a list to remember, the same locations serve as 'pegs' to 'hang' memories. Simply place each item from your list in one of these locations. For instance, let's say you want to remember to buy milk, bread, butter and cereal at the store. Imagine a giant bottle of milk blocking the entry hall, a lazy loaf of bread sleeping on the living room sofa, a stick of butter melting all over the dining room table and cereal covering the kitchen floor. When you want to remember the items, all you have to do is take an imaginary walk through your house. Other peg-type mnemonics use a standard list of words (one is bun, two is shoe) as pegs. Then, the items to be remembered are linked to the pegs through images or stories. The rhyming primes the list of pegs.

Peg-type mnemonics

Systems of associating items with cue words.

If you need to remember information for long periods of time, an acronym may be the answer. An acronym is a form of abbreviation – a word formed from the first letter of each word in a phrase, for example a particularly appropriate one for teachers to remember the various elements of the Independent Educational Programme (IEP) is SMART which stands for Specific, Measurable, Appropriate, Recorded and Time-framed (Ofsted, 2006). This one works on two levels because it not only provides the first letter to serve as a mnemonic but it also reminds us that the aim of this

Acronym

Technique for remembering names, phrases or steps by using the first letter of each word to form a new, memorable word.

"How many times must I tell you—it's 'cat' before 'temple' except after 'slave.'"

Source: From *Phi Delta Kappan*.

initiative is to enable children to become 'smart'. Another method forms phrases or sentences out of the first letter of each word or item in a list, for example, Richard Of York Gave Battle in Vain for the colours in the spectrum (red, orange, yellow, blue, indigo and violet) or Every Good Boy Deserves Fruit to remember the lines on the G clef – E, G, B, D, F. Because the words must make sense as a sentence, this approach also has some characteristics of chain mnemonics, methods that connect the first item to be memorised with the second, the second item with the third, and so on. In one type of chain method, each item on a list is linked to the next through some visual association or story. Another chain-method approach is to incorporate all the items to be memorised into a jingle such as 'i before e except after c'.

The mnemonic system that has been most extensively researched in teaching is the keyword method. Joel Levin and his colleagues use a mnemonic (the *3 Rs*) to teach the keyword mnemonic method:

- *Recode* the to-be-learned vocabulary item as a more familiar, concrete keyword – this is the keyword.

- *Relate* the keyword clue to the vocabulary item's definition through a sentence.

- *Retrieve* the desired definition.

This has proved useful for aspects such as remembering the gender of nouns when learning a foreign language by incorporating a gender tag in the image. This may be as simple as including a man or a woman (or some particular object, when the language also contains a neutral gender), or you could use some other code – for example, if learning German, you could use the image of a deer for the masculine gender (Jones *et al.*, 2000).

A similar approach has been used to help learners connect artists with particular aspects of their paintings. For example, individuals are told to imagine that the heavy dark lines of paintings by Rouault are made with a *ruler* (*rouault*) dipped in black paint (Carney and Levin, 2000).

The keyword method does not work well if it is difficult to identify a keyword for a particular item. Many words and ideas that learners need to remember are quite a challenge to associate with keywords (Hall, 1991; Pressley, 1991). Also, vocabulary learned with keywords can be easily forgotten if learners are given keywords and images instead of being asked to supply words and images that are relevant to them. When the teacher provides the memory links, these associations may not fit the learners' existing knowledge and may be forgotten or confused later; as a result, remembering suffers (Wang and Thomas, 1995; Wang, Thomas and Ouelette, 1992). Younger learners have some difficulty forming their own images. For them, memory aids that rely on auditory cues – rhymes such as 'Thirty days hath September' seem to work better (Willoughby *et al.*, 1999).

Many teachers use a mnemonic system to quickly learn their pupils' names. Until we have some knowledge to guide learning, it may help to use some mnemonic approaches to build vocabulary and facts. Not all educators agree, however, as you will see in the Discussion Point below.

Rote memorisation

Very few things need to be learned by rote. The greatest challenge teachers face is to help learners think and understand, not just memorise. Unfortunately, many learners, including those in the scenario opening this chapter, see rote memorising and learning as the same thing (Iran-Nejad, 1990).

Chain mnemonics

Memory strategies that associate one element in a series with the next element.

Keyword method

System of associating new words or concepts with similar-sounding cue words and images.

Rote memorisation

Remembering information by repetition without necessarily understanding the meaning of the information.

DISCUSSION POINT

Should pupils memorise information to assist their learning?

For years, learners have relied on memorisation to learn vocabulary, procedures, steps, names and facts. Is this a bad idea? Let us look at views for and against this approach.

Agree: Yes, memorising helps to learn new information

Memorisation may not be such a bad way to learn new information that has little inherent meaning, such as foreign language vocabulary. Alvin Wang, Margaret Thomas and Judith Ouellette (1992) compared learning Tagalog (the national language of the Philippines) using either rote memorisation or the keyword approach. The keyword method is a way of creating connections and meaning for associating new words with existing words and images. In their study, even though the keyword method led to faster and better learning initially, long-term forgetting was *greater* for individuals who had used the keyword method than for learners who had learned by rote memorisation.

There are times when learners must memorise and we do them a disservice if we don't teach them how. Every discipline has its own terms, names, facts and rules. As adults, we want to work with physicians who have memorised the correct names for the bones and organs of the body or the drugs needed to combat particular infections. Of course, they can look up some information or research certain conditions, but they have to know where to start. We want to work with accountants who give us accurate information about the new tax codes, information they probably had to memorise because it changes from year to year in ways that are not necessarily rational or meaningful. We want to deal with computer salespeople who have memorised their stock and know exactly which printers will work with our computer. Just because something was learned through memorisation does not mean it is inert knowledge. The real question is whether you can *use* the information flexibly and effectively to solve new problems.

Disagree: No, memorisation does not help learning

Years ago William James described the limitations of rote learning by telling a story about what can happen when people memorise but do not understand:

> *A friend of mine, visiting a school, was asked to examine a young class in geography. Glancing at the book, she said: 'Suppose you should dig a hole in the ground, hundreds of feet deep, how should you find it at the bottom – warmer or colder than on top?' None of the class replying, the teacher said: 'I'm sure they know, but I think you don't ask the question quite rightly. Let me try.' So, taking the book, she asked: 'In what condition is the interior of the globe?'*

And received the immediate answer from half the class at once. 'The interior of the globe is in a condition of igneous fusion' (1912: 150).

The class had memorised the answer, but they had no idea what it meant. Perhaps they didn't understand the meaning of 'interior', 'globe' or 'igneous fusion'. At any rate, the knowledge was useful to them only when they were answering test questions, and only then when the questions were phrased exactly as they had been memorised. Learners often resort to memorising the exact words of definitions when they have no hope of actually understanding the terms or when teachers deduct marks for definitions that are not exact.

More recently Paul Black and Dylan Wiliam of King's College, London carried out an extensive review of research literature related to assessments and raising standards in school education (Black and Wiliam, 1998). They concluded that one of the most important difficulties found in the UK and elsewhere (Australia, France, Hong Kong, South Africa and the US) is concerned with effective learning:

Teachers' tests encourage rote learning; this is seen even where teachers say they want to develop understanding – and many seem unaware of the inconsistency (Black and Wiliam, 2002: 4).

They argue that since the 1988 Education Reform Act teachers have become focused upon summative (total scores) rather than formative (ongoing) assessments because of concentration upon tests at the end of Key Stages which has encouraged rote learning.

On the other hand, some academics take a different view.

WHAT DO YOU THINK?
Agree or Disagree? Vote online at www.pearsoned.co.uk/woolfolkeuro.

However, on rare occasions we have to memorise something word-for-word, such as lines in a song, poem or play. How would you do it? If you have tried to memorise a list of items that are all similar to one another, you may have found that you tended to remember items at the beginning and at the end of the list, but forgot those in the middle. This is called the serial-position effect and works on the principle that the latest items are likely to be still in your working memory (recency effect) whilst the first have been rehearsed and transferred to your long-term memory (primacy effect). The words in the middle, therefore, are neglected and so not remembered unless they contain words which are familiar and meaningful to us. For example, you might remember the word 'butter' even though it is in the middle of a list because it is the name of your pet cat. This is known as the Von Restorff or 'distinctive coding' effect (Von Restorff, 1933). Part learning, breaking the list into smaller segments, can help prevent this effect, because breaking a list into several shorter lists means there will be fewer middle items to forget.

Another strategy for memorising a long selection or list is the use of distributed practice. A person who studies Hamlet's soliloquy intermittently throughout the weekend will probably do much better than a learner who tries to memorise the entire speech on Sunday night. Studying for an extended period is called massed practice.

Serial-position effect

The tendency to remember the beginning and the end but not the middle of a list.

Part learning

Breaking a list of rote learning items into shorter lists.

Distributed practice

Practice in brief periods with rest intervals.

Massed practice

Practice for a single extended period.

Massed practice leads to fatigue and flagging motivation. Distributed practice gives time for deeper processing and the chance to move information into long-term memory (Mumford *et al.*, 1994). What is forgotten after one session can be relearned in the next with distributed practice.

Becoming an expert: development of procedural and conditional knowledge

Experts in a particular field have a wealth of domain-specific knowledge, that is, knowledge that applies specifically to their area or domain. This includes *declarative knowledge* (facts and verbal information), *procedural knowledge* (how to perform various cognitive activities) and *conditional knowledge* (knowing when and why to apply what they know). In addition, it appears that experts have developed their *long-term working memories* in the domain and can quickly access relevant knowledge and strategies for solving problems in that domain.

Another characteristic distinguishes experts from novices. Much of the expert's declarative knowledge has become 'proceduralised', that is, incorporated into routines they can apply automatically without making many demands on working memory. Explicit memories have become implicit and the expert is no longer aware of them. Skills that are applied without conscious thought are called automated basic skills. An example is changing gear in a car with a manual gear-box. At first you had to think about every step, but as you became more expert (if you did), the procedure became automatic. However, not all procedures can be automatic, even for experts in a particular domain. For example, no matter how expert you are in driving, you still have to consciously watch the traffic around you. This kind of conscious procedure is called a *domain-specific strategy*. Automated basic skills and domain-specific strategies are learned in different ways (Gagne, Yekovich and Yekovich, 1993).

Automated basic skills

Skills that are applied without conscious thought.

Driving a car uses both automated basic skills and domain-specific strategies

Automated basic skills

Most psychologists identify three stages in the development of an automated skill: *cognitive, associative* and *autonomous* (Anderson, 1995b; Fitts and Posner, 1967). At the *cognitive stage,* when we are first learning, we rely on declarative knowledge and general problem-solving strategies to accomplish our goal. For example, to learn to assemble a bookshelf, we might try to follow steps in the instruction manual, putting a tick beside each step as we complete it to keep track of our progress. At this stage, we have to 'think about' every step and perhaps refer back to the pictures of parts to see what a 'four-inch metal bolt with lock nut' looks like. The load on working memory is heavy. There can be quite a bit of trial-and-error learning at this stage when, for example, the bolt we chose doesn't fit. This co-author has painful memories of trying to assemble a wardrobe in this way and it took 24 hours, not the 'within an hour' estimated on the packaging.

At the *associative stage,* individual steps of a procedure are combined or 'chunked' into larger units. We reach for the right bolt and put it into the right hole. One step smoothly cues the next. With practice, the associative stage moves to the *autonomous stage,* where the whole procedure can be accomplished without much attention. So if you assemble enough bookshelves, you can have a lively conversation as you do, paying little attention to the assembly task. This movement from the cognitive to the associative to the autonomous stage holds for the development of basic cognitive skills in any area, but science, medicine, chess and mathematics have been most heavily researched.

What can teachers do to help their pupils pass through these three stages and become more expert learners? In general, it appears that two factors are critical: *prerequisite knowledge* and *practice with feedback.* First, if learners don't have the essential prior knowledge (schemas, skills, etc.), the load on working memory will be too great. In order to compose a poem in a foreign language, for example, you must know some of the vocabulary and grammar of that language, and you must have some understanding of poetry forms. To learn the vocabulary, grammar *and* forms as you also try to compose the poem would be too much. Similarly, children learning to read must first have the ability to recognise shapes in order to differentiate the letters involved in words.

Second, practice with feedback allows you to form associations, recognise cues automatically, and combine small steps into larger condition-action rules or *productions.* Even from the earliest stage, some of this practice should include a simplified version of the whole process in a real context. Practice in real contexts helps children learn not only *how* to do a skill but also *why* and *when* (Collins, Brown and Newman, 1989; Gagne, Yekovich and Yekovich, 1993). Of course, as every PE/sports teacher knows, if a particular step, component or process is causing trouble, that element needs to be practised alone until it is more automatic, and then put back into the whole sequence, to lower the demands on working memory (Anderson, Reder and Simon, 1996). This co-author is currently watching Wimbledon between writing sections of this chapter and hears plenty of comments about a particular player having 'worked on his serve' or another who has 'developed a new backhand' which are indicative of the fact that exactly this process of practice with feedback has taken place presumably because it was not working effectively even for an expert tennis player.

Domain-specific strategies

As we saw earlier, some procedural knowledge, such as monitoring the traffic while you drive, is not automatic because conditions are constantly changing. Once you decide to change lanes, the manoeuvre may be fairly automatic, but the decision to change lanes was conscious, based on the traffic conditions around you. Domain-specific strategies are consciously applied skills that organise thoughts and actions to reach a goal. To support this kind of learning, teachers need to provide opportunities for practice in many different situations – for example, practise reading with newspapers, package labels, magazines, books, letters, operating manuals, and so on. In the next chapter's discussion of problem-solving and study strategies, we will examine other ways to help learners develop domain-specific strategies.

Domain-specific strategies

Consciously applied skills to reach goals in a particular subject or problem area.

SUMMARY TABLE

Elements of the Cognitive Perspective (pp. 294–296)

Contrast cognitive and behavioural views of learning in terms of what is learned and the role of reinforcement

Cognitive learning theorists focus on the human mind's active attempts to make sense of the world. In the cognitive view, knowledge is learned, and changes in knowledge make changes in behaviour possible. In the behavioural view, the new behaviours themselves are learned. Both behavioural and cognitive theorists believe reinforcement is important in learning, but for different reasons. The strict behaviourist maintains that reinforcement strengthens responses; cognitive theorists see reinforcement as a source of feedback about what is likely to happen if behaviours are repeated or changed – as a source of information.

How does knowledge affect learning?

The cognitive approach suggests that one of the most important elements in the learning process is knowledge the individual brings to the learning situation. Knowledge is the outcome of learning and a guide that shapes new learning. What we already know determines to a great extent what we will pay attention to, perceive, learn, remember and forget.

The Information Processing Model of Memory (pp. 296–306)

Give two explanations for perception

The Gestalt principles are valid explanations of certain aspects of perception, but there are two other kinds of explanations in information processing theory for how we recognise patterns and give meaning to sensory events. The first is called *feature analysis,* or *bottom-up processing,* because the stimulus must be analysed into features or components and assembled into a meaningful pattern. The second type of perception, *top-down processing,* is based on knowledge and expectation. To recognise patterns rapidly, in addition to noting features, we use what we already know about the situation.

What is working memory?

Working memory is both short-term storage in the phonological loop and visuospatial sketchpad and processing guided by the central executive – it is the workbench of conscious thought. To keep information activated in working memory for longer than 20 seconds, people use maintenance rehearsal (mentally repeating) and elaborative rehearsal (making connections with knowledge from long-term memory). This kind of rehearsal also helps move new information to long-term memory. The limited capacity of working memory can also be somewhat circumvented by the control process of chunking.

Long-Term Memory: The Goal of Teaching (pp. 306–319)

Compare declarative, procedural and conditional knowledge

Declarative knowledge is knowledge that can be declared, usually in words or other symbols. Declarative knowledge is 'knowing that' something is the case. Procedural knowledge is 'knowing how' to do something; it must be demonstrated. Conditional knowledge is 'knowing when and why' to apply your declarative and procedural knowledge.

How is information represented in long-term memory, and what role do schemas play?

Long-term memory seems to hold an unlimited amount of information for a very long time. Memories may be explicit (semantic or episodic) or implicit (procedural, classical conditioning or priming). In long-term memory, bits of information may be stored and interrelated in terms of propositional networks or images and in schemas that are data structures that allow us to represent large amounts of complex information, make inferences and understand new information.

What learning processes improve long-term memory?

The way you learn information in the first place affects its recall later. One important requirement is to integrate new material with knowledge already stored in long-term memory using elaboration, organisation and context. Another view of memory is the levels of processing theory, in which recall of information is determined by how completely it is processed.

Why do we forget?

Information lost from working memory truly disappears, but information stored in long-term memory may be available, given the right cues. Information appears to be lost from long-term memory through time decay (neural connections, like muscles, grow weak without use) and interference (newer memories may interfere with or obscure older memories, and older memories may interfere with memory for new material).

Metacognition (pp. 319–321)

What are the three metacognitive skills?

The three metacognitive skills used to regulate thinking and learning are planning, monitoring and evaluating. Planning involves deciding how much time to give to a task, which strategies to use, how to start, and so on. Monitoring is the awareness of 'how I'm doing'. Evaluating involves making judgements about the processes and outcomes of thinking and learning and acting on those judgements.

How can using better metacognitive strategies improve children's working and long-term memories?

Younger children can be taught to use organisation to improve memory, but they probably won't apply the strategy unless they are reminded. Children also become more able to use elaboration as they mature, but this strategy is developed late in childhood. Creating images or stories to remember ideas is more likely for older elementary school students and adolescents.

Becoming Knowledgeable: Some Basic Principles (pp. 321–330)

Describe three ways to develop declarative knowledge

Declarative knowledge develops as we integrate new information with our existing understanding. The most useful and effective way to learn and remember is to understand and use new information. Making the information to be remembered meaningful is important and often is the greatest challenge for teachers. Mnemonics are memorisation aids: They include peg-type approaches such as the loci method, acronyms, chain mnemonics and the keyword method. A powerful but limiting way to accomplish this is rote memorisation, which can best be supported by part learning and distributed practice.

Describe some methods for developing procedural knowledge

Automated basic skills and domain-specific strategies – two types of procedural knowledge – are learned in different ways. There are three stages in the development of an automated skill: cognitive (following steps or directions guided by declarative knowledge), associative (combining individual steps into larger units) and autonomous (where the whole procedure can be accomplished without much attention). Prerequisite knowledge and practice with feedback help students move through these stages. Domain-specific strategies are consciously applied skills of organising thoughts and actions to reach a goal. To support this kind of learning, teachers need to provide opportunities for practice and application in many different situations.

Glossary

Acronym: Technique for remembering names, phrases or steps by using the first letter of each word to form a new, memorable word.

Attention: Focus on a stimulus.

Automated basic skills: Skills that are applied without conscious thought.

Automaticity: The ability to perform thoroughly learned tasks without much mental effort.

Bottom-up processing: Perceiving based on noticing separate defining features and assembling them into a recognisable pattern.

Central executive: The part of working memory that is responsible for monitoring and directing attention and other mental resources.

Chain mnemonics: Memory strategies that associate one element in a series with the next element.

Chunking: Grouping individual bits of data into meaningful larger units.

Cognitive view of learning: A general approach that views learning as an active mental process of acquiring, remembering and using knowledge.

Conditional knowledge: 'Knowing when and why' to use declarative and procedural knowledge.

Context: The physical or emotional backdrop associated with an event.

Decay: The weakening and fading of memories with the passage of time.

Declarative knowledge: Verbal information; facts; 'knowing that' something is the case.

Distributed practice: Practice in brief periods with rest intervals.

Domain-specific knowledge: Information that is useful in a particular situation or that applies mainly to one specific topic.

Domain-specific strategies: Consciously applied skills to reach goals in a particular subject or problem area.

Elaboration: Adding and extending meaning by connecting new information to existing knowledge.

Elaborative rehearsal: Keeping information in working memory by associating it with something else you already know.

Episodic memory: Long-term memory for information tied to a particular time and place, especially memory of the events in a person's life.

Executive control processes: Processes such as selective attention, rehearsal, elaboration and organisation that influence encoding, storage and retrieval of information in memory.

Explicit memory: Long-term memories that involve deliberate or conscious recall.

Flashbulb memories: Clear, vivid memories of an emotionally important event in your life.

General knowledge: Information that is useful in many different kinds of tasks; information that applies to many situations.

Gestalt: German for *pattern* or *whole*. Gestalt theorists hold that people organise their perceptions into coherent wholes.

Images: Representations based on the physical attributes – the appearance – of information.

Implicit memory: Knowledge that we are not conscious of recalling, but influences behaviour or thought without our awareness.

Information processing: The human mind's activity of taking in, storing and using information.

Interference: The process that occurs when remembering certain information is hampered by the presence of other information.

Keyword method: System of associating new words or concepts with similar-sounding cue words and images.

Levels of processing theory: Theory that recall of information is based on how deeply it is processed.

Loci method: Technique of associating items with specific places.

Long-term memory: Permanent store of knowledge.

Long-term working memory: Holds the strategies for pulling information from long-term memory into working memory.

Maintenance rehearsal: Keeping information in working memory by repeating it to yourself.

Massed practice: Practice for a single extended period.

Metacognition: Knowledge about our own thinking processes.

Mnemonics: Techniques for remembering; also, the art of memory.

Organisation: Ordered and logical network of relations.

Part learning: Breaking a list of rote learning items into shorter lists.

Peg-type mnemonics: Systems of associating items with cue words.

Perception: Interpretation of sensory information.

Phonological loop: Part of working memory. A memory rehearsal system for verbal and sound information of about 1.5 to two seconds.

Priming: Activating a concept in memory or the spread of activation from one concept to another.

Procedural knowledge: Knowledge that is demonstrated when we perform a task; 'knowing how'.

Procedural memory: Long-term memory for how to do things.

Productions: The contents of procedural memory; rules about what actions to take, given certain conditions.

Propositional network: Set of interconnected concepts and relationships in which long-term knowledge is held.

Prototype: A best example or best representative of a category.

Reconstruction: Recreating information by using memories, expectations, logic and existing knowledge.

Retrieval: Process of searching for and finding information in long-term memory.

Rote memorisation: Remembering information by repetition without necessarily understanding the meaning of the information.

Schemas (singular, schema): Basic structures for organising information; concepts.

Script: Schema or expected plan for the sequence of steps in a common event such as buying groceries or ordering take-away pizza.

Semantic memory: Memory for meaning.

Sensory memory: System that holds sensory information very briefly.

Serial-position effect: The tendency to remember the beginning and the end but not the middle of a list.

Short-term memory: Component of memory system that holds information for about 20 seconds.

Spreading activation: Retrieval of pieces of information based on their relatedness to one another. Remembering one bit of information activates (stimulates) recall of associated information.

Story grammar: Typical structure or organisation for a category of stories.

Top-down processing: Perceiving based on the context and the patterns you expect to occur in that situation.

Visuospatial sketchpad: Part of working memory. A holding system for visual and spatial information.

Working memory: The information that you are focusing on at a given moment.

CHECK YOUR LEARNING! WEB

In the Classroom: What Would They Do?

Here is how some practising teachers responded to the teaching situation presented at the beginning of this chapter about the history class who were intent on memorising information.

Experienced history teacher from large comprehensive school in Leeds (Northern England)

It is clear that the young people in this class come from a background where assessments and grades are seen as the learning which has any purpose. This is regrettable and unlikely to be helpful for them in learning about history in any meaningful way. Understanding causes and experiences of past events is what history is about and the only way that they can learn is through the process of wide-based enquiry which uses source materials. They need to realise that the historical skills they will learn can be transferred to other areas of historical

study and will allow them to do better within an exam situation. To see the questions in a narrow, factual way is wrong because they should be asking themselves the question: 'Is this teaching me things that will help me to deal with any question about the historical past?'

Primary school teacher from rural area in Staffordshire (Central England)

We always start from where the children are and what they know so when we do history we begin with them. For example, when looking at the Second World War (WW2) we find out whether any of the children have relatives who were in the war. This means they have to ask their parents, grandparents and other family members about this and we encourage them to bring in articles such as photographs, medals, gas-masks or any other artefacts. We would have class talks about the things they have brought and perhaps include it in Circle-time/ PSHE (personal, social and health education) discussion. Last year we asked children to dress up in costumes from WW2 – that was great fun for the children but a nightmare for some of the parents. The younger parents had little idea themselves of the clothes/uniforms that were worn so they had to do a bit of historical research as well. By doing things like this history is brought to life for the children and they start to see it as relevant to them. That is the essential thing if it is going to be real and meaningful for their learning.

Adult education history tutor (Access programme) at a further education college in Kent (SE England)

When people are returning to learning as adults, often after a failed attempt within statutory education, they have their own life-history. So that's what I try to tap into right from the beginning.

There is no way they would stay if I started talking facts, figures, policies and textbooks because that would take them straight back to the first time they did history as a subject, at secondary school. What I do is begin with their personal 'story' and then point out that this is a form of history. We spend a while talking this through and establishing what history actually is and why it is relevant. Then I help them to begin to research their own family history so that their first piece of coursework is a family tree. I provide them with lists of places to go and links which they can use to help them find out more about their families but they are developing a whole range of skills in the process of discovering and structuring the information they gather. They really love it. Every year I feel a glow of satisfaction when I see people develop through their engagement with the course, their own sense of value and personal identity. History is about learning to learn about history – if they can do that they can apply it to any topic.

Overview

8 Complex Cognitive Processes

In the previous chapter, we focused on the development of knowledge – how people make sense of and remember information and ideas. In this chapter, we consider complex cognitive processes that lead to understanding. Understanding is more than memorising. It is more than retelling in your own words. Understanding involves appropriately *transforming* and *using* knowledge, skills and ideas. These understandings are considered 'higher-level cognitive objectives' in a commonly used system of educational objectives (Krathwohl, 2002; Bloom *et al.,* 1956). We will focus on the implications of cognitive theories for the day-to-day practice of teaching.

Because the cognitive perspective is a philosophical orientation and not a unified theoretical model, teaching methods derived from it are varied. In this chapter, we will first examine four important areas in which cognitive theorists have made suggestions for learning and teaching: concept learning, problem solving, creativity and learning strategies and tactics.

Finally, we will explore the question of how to encourage the transfer of learning from one situation to another to make learning more useful.

By the time you have completed this chapter, you should be able to answer the following questions:

- **What are the characteristics of a good lesson for teaching a key concept?**
- **What are the steps in solving complex problems?**
- **What are the roles of problem representation, algorithms and heuristics in problem solving?**
- **How can teachers encourage creativity in their pupils?**
- **How could you apply new learning strategies and tactics to prepare for tests and assignments in your current courses?**
- **What are three ways a teacher might encourage positive transfer of learning?**

In the Classroom

'My pupils need good study skills to do well in both their current and future classes but many of them just don't seem to know how to study. They can't seem to read a longer text, make sense of it or remember what they read. They have trouble completing larger projects – many wait until the last minute. They can't organise their work or decide what is most important.' This teacher is concerned because the pupils will need good study skills and strategies as they progress through their education. Also, there is so much curriculum material to cover that many of the pupils never finish anything and are just drowning in the amount of work. What study skills do pupils need for different subjects or age groups?

What could a teacher do to teach these skills, while still covering all the curriculum material needed for yearly assessments? What would you advise?

Group Activity

With three or four members of your group, identify learning skills and study strategies that pupils will need for a preferred age range or subject. Then, analyse the skills and strategies you have identified and consider how they are best taught.

Learning and Teaching about Concepts

STOP AND THINK

According to Piaget, a person cannot think in abstract terms until the stage of formal operations is reached. How then can a child learn abstract concepts such as 'yesterday' and 'happy'?

What makes a cup a cup? List the characteristics of *cupness*. What is a fruit? Is a banana a fruit? Is a tomato a fruit? How about a squash? A watermelon? A sweet potato? An olive? How did you learn what makes a fruit a fruit?

Most of what we know about cups and fruits involves concepts and connections among and between concepts (Koschmann, 2005). But what exactly is a concept? A concept is a category used to group similar events, ideas, objects or people. When we talk about a particular concept such as *student,* we refer to a category of people who are similar to one another – they all study a subject. Students may be old or young, in university or not; they may be studying medicine or Mozart, but they all can be categorised as students. Concepts are abstractions. They do not exist in the real world. Only individual examples of concepts exist. Concepts help us organise vast amounts of information into manageable units. For instance, there are about 7.5 million distinguishable differences in colours. By categorising these colours into some dozen or so groups, we manage to deal with this diversity quite well (Bruner, 1973).

Concept

A general category of ideas, objects, people or experiences whose members share certain properties.

Views of concept learning

In early research, psychologists assumed that concepts share a set of defining attributes or distinctive features. For example, books all contain pages that are bound together in some way. The defining attributes theory of concepts suggests that we recognise specific examples by noting key required features, in the case of books, bound pages.

Defining attributes

Distinctive features shared by members of a category.

Since the 1930s, however, these straightforward views about the nature of concepts have been challenged (Mller-Freienfels, 1935). Although some concepts, such as equilateral triangle, have clear-cut defining attributes, most concepts do not. Take the concept of *party.* What are the defining attributes? You might have difficulty listing these attributes, but you probably recognise a party when you see or hear one (unless, of course, we are talking about political parties, or the other party in a court case, where the sound might not help you recognise the 'party'). What about the concept of *bird*? Your first thought might be that birds are animals that fly but is an ostrich a bird? What about a penguin or a bat? Earlier we talked about the concept of book, whose defining attributes were pages that are bound together in some way. But what about *electronic books*? They do not conform to the defining attributes of *book* but rather those of *electronic book*.

Prototypes and exemplars

Current views of concept learning suggest that we have in our minds a prototype of a party and a bird – an image that captures the essence of each concept. A prototype is the best representative of its category. For instance, the best representative of the 'birds' category for many people might be a robin as it is a common garden bird, easily

Prototype

Best representative of a category.

Concepts have many attributes and may not remain constant. For example, recent technological applications such as Instant Messenging may have changed the concept of 'conversation'

recognised and often depicted on Christmas cards. Other members of the category may be very similar to the prototype (sparrow) or similar in some ways but different in others (chicken, ostrich). At the boundaries of a category, it may be difficult to determine if a particular instance really belongs. For example, is a telephone 'furniture'? Is a lift a 'vehicle'? Is an olive a 'fruit'? Whether something fits into a category is a matter of degree. Thus, categories have fuzzy boundaries. Some events, objects or ideas are simply better examples of a concept than others (Goldstone, Steyvers and Rogosky, 2003).

Another explanation of concept learning suggests that we identify members of a category by referring to exemplars. Exemplars are our actual memories of specific birds, parties, furniture, and so on that we use to compare with an item in question to see if that item belongs in the same category as our exemplar. For example, if you see a strange steel-and-stone construction in a shopping centre, you may compare it to the sofa in your living room to decide if the uncomfortable-looking creation is still for sitting or if it has crossed a fuzzy boundary into 'sculpture'.

Prototypes probably are built from experiences with many exemplars. This happens naturally because episodic memories of particular events tend to blur together over time, creating an average or typical sofa prototype from all the sofa exemplars you have experienced (Hampton and Cannon, 2004).

Concepts and schemas

In addition to prototypes and exemplars, there is a third element involved when we recognise a concept – our schematic knowledge related to the concept. How do we know that counterfeit money is not 'real' money, even though it perfectly fits our 'money' prototype and exemplars? We know because of its history. The 'wrong' people printed the money. So our understanding of the concept of money is connected with concepts of crime, forgery, the treasury and many others.

Jacob Feldman (2003) – a psychologist working in the field of cognitive science – suggests a final aspect of concept learning: the simplicity principle. Feldman says that

Exemplar

A specific example of a given category that is used to classify an item.

when humans are confronted with examples, they induce the simplest category or rule that would cover all the examples. Sometimes, it is easy to come up with a simple rule (triangles) and sometimes it is more difficult (fruit), but humans seek a simple hypothesis for collecting all the examples they perceive under one concept. Feldman suggests that this simplicity principle is one of the oldest ideas in cognitive psychology: 'organisms seek to understand their environment by reducing incoming information to a simpler, more coherent, and more useful form' (2003: 231). Does this remind you of the Gestalt principles of perception in Chapter 7 (pp. 298–299) where the organised whole is perceived as more than the sum of its parts?

> ## STOP AND THINK
>
> Teachers devote much effort to the development of concepts that are vital in learning subject knowledge, understanding and skills. What are the major approaches to teaching concepts? Describe their strengths and limitations.

Strategies for teaching concepts

Both prototypes and defining attributes are important in learning. Children first learn many concepts in the real world from the best examples or prototypes, pointed out by adults sometimes using visual representations (Keogh, 1999). However, when examples are ambiguous (is an olive a fruit?), we may consult the defining attributes to make a decision. Olives are foods with seeds in the edible parts, which matches the defining attributes for fruits, so they must be fruits, even though olives are not typical or prototypic fruits.

Like the learning of concepts, the teaching of concepts can combine both defining attributes and prototypes. One approach to teaching about concepts is called *concept attainment* – a way of helping pupils construct an understanding of specific concepts and practise thinking skills such as hypothesis testing (Betres *et al.*, 1984; Klausmeier, 1992).

An example concept-attainment lesson

Here is how a teacher helped his pupils aged nine and ten learn about a familiar concept and practise thinking skills at the same time (Eggen and Kauchak, 2001: 148–151). The teacher began a lesson by saying that he had an idea in mind and wanted pupils to work out 'what it is'. He placed two signs on a table – 'examples' and 'non-examples'. Then he placed an apple in front of the 'examples' sign and a rock in front of the 'non-examples' sign. He asked his pupils, 'What do you think the idea might be?' 'Things we eat!' was the first suggestion. The teacher wrote 'hypotheses' on the board and, after a brief discussion of the meaning of 'hypotheses', listed 'things we eat' under this heading. Next he asked for other hypotheses – 'living things' and 'things that grow on plants' came next. After some discussion about plants and living things, the teacher brought out a tomato for the 'examples' side and a carrot for the 'non-examples'. Animated reconsideration of all the hypotheses followed these additions and a new hypothesis – 'red things' – was suggested. Through discussion of more examples (peach, squash, orange) and non-examples (lettuce, artichoke, potato), the pupils narrowed their hypothesis to 'things with seeds in the parts you eat'. The pupils had 'constructed' the concept of 'fruit' – foods with seeds in the edible parts (or, a more advanced definition, any engorged ovary, such as a pea pod, nut, tomato, pineapple, or the edible part of a plant developed from a flower).

Lesson components

Whatever strategy you use for teaching concepts, you will need four components in any lesson: examples and non-examples, relevant and irrelevant attributes, the name of the concept and a definition (Joyce *et al.*, 2006). In addition, visual aids such as pictures, diagrams or maps can improve learning of many concepts (Ellis and Whitehill, 1996; Reid and Beveridge, 1986).

Examples

More examples are needed in teaching complicated concepts and in working with younger or less knowledgeable pupils. Both examples and non-examples (sometimes called positive and negative instances) are necessary to make the boundaries of the category clear. A discussion of why a bat (non-example) is not a bird will help pupils define the boundaries of the bird concept.

Relevant and irrelevant attributes

The ability to fly, as we've seen, is not a directly relevant attribute for classifying animals as birds. Even though many birds fly, some birds do not (ostrich, penguin), and some non-birds do (bats, bees). The ability to fly would have to be included in a discussion of the bird concept, but pupils should understand that flying alone does not define an animal as a bird. Relevant attributes can be more or less directly relevant rather like an example of a concept can be deemed 'better' than another, some attributes are not helpful in defining the concept. For example, the attribute of having a head, though essential for a complete bird, does not contribute anything to defining the bird-ness of a bird.

Name   Simply learning a label does not mean the person understands the concept, although the label is necessary for sharing understanding. In the example above, pupils probably already used the 'fruit' name, but may not have understood that tomatoes, peas and avocados are fruits.

Definition   A good definition has two elements: a reference to any more general category for the new concept, and a statement of the new concept's defining attributes (Adeyemi, 2002). For example, a fruit is food (general category) with seeds in the edible parts (defining attributes). An equilateral triangle is a plane, a simple, closed figure (general category), with three equal sides and three equal angles (defining attributes). This kind of definition helps place the concept in a schema of related knowledge.

STOP AND THINK

What would be the defining attributes of 'democracy'?

In teaching some concepts, 'a picture is worth a thousand words' – or at least a few hundred, as we saw in the 'Development of declarative knowledge' Chapter 7 (p. 307). Handling specific examples, or pictures of examples, helps young children learn concepts. For pupils of all ages, the complex concepts in history, science and mathematics can often be illustrated in diagrams or graphs. For example, pupils often work with diagrams such as the one in Figure 8.1 to understand the penetrative powers of different radiations.

Figure 8.1
Understanding
complex concepts

Illustrations can help
pupils grasp difficult
concepts

Source:
http://www.bbc.co.uk/
schools/gcsebitesize/
physics/radioactivity/
characteristics_of_
radiationrev2.shtml

3. Gamma radiation

Gamma radiation is the most penetrating. It can penetrate air, paper or thin metal. It can only be stopped by many centimetres of lead or many metres of concrete.

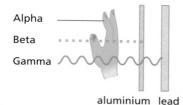

aluminium   lead

Check your understanding by having a go at this animation. Click on each image of the rock to discover the reading on the radiation meter. Use the readings to confirm that the rock gives out beta radiation.

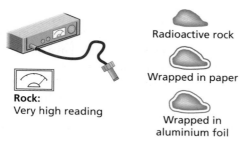

Radioactive rock

Wrapped in paper

Rock:
Very high reading

Wrapped in
aluminium foil

Lesson structure

The fruit lesson above is an example of good concept teaching for several reasons. First, it is more effective to examine examples and non-examples before discussing attributes or definitions. Start your concept lesson with prototypes, or best examples, to help the pupils establish the category. In the fruit lesson, the teacher began with the classic fruit example, an apple, then moved to less typical examples such as tomatoes and squash. These examples show the wide range of possibilities the category includes and the variety of irrelevant attributes within a category. Including fruits that have one seed or many, have a sweet taste or not, are different colours, and have thick or thin skin, will prevent undergeneralisation, or the exclusion of some foods, such as squash, from their rightful place in the category fruit.

Non-examples should be very close to the concept, but miss by one or just a few critical attributes. For instance, sweet potatoes and rhubarb are *not* fruits, even though sweet potatoes are sweet and rhubarb is used to make pies. Including non-examples will prevent overgeneralisation, or the inclusion of substances that are not fruits.

After the pupils seem to have grasped the concept under consideration, it is useful to ask them to think about the ways that they formed and tested their hypotheses. Thinking back helps pupils develop their metacognitive skills and shows them that different people approach problems in different ways. Figure 8.2 summarises the stages of concept teaching.

Extending and connecting concepts

Once pupils have a good sense of a concept, they should use it. This might mean completing tasks, solving problems, explaining, teaching or any other activity that requires

**Under-
generalisation**

Exclusion of some true members from a category; limiting a concept.

**Over-
generalisation**

Inclusion of non-members in a category; overextending a concept.

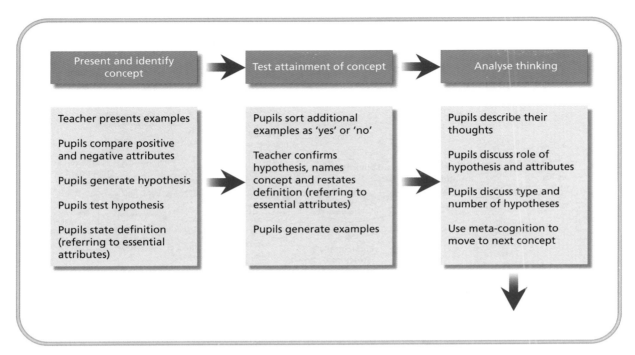

Figure 8.2
The stages of concept teaching

them to apply their new understanding. This will connect the concept into the pupils' web of related schematic knowledge. One approach that you may see in some texts and workbooks for pupils is concept mapping (Novak and Gowin, 1984). Pupils 'diagram' their understanding of a new or unfamiliar concept, by showing links to their current schema. An example of a concept map is given in Figure 8.3. This is a concept map of the concept of concept mapping! Later on in this chapter in the section on 'Visual tools for organising' we will have more to say about how pupils can diagram their understanding of a new concept.

Teaching concepts through discovery

Early researches on thinking by Jerome Bruner, a key 20th-century theorist in educational psychology (Bruner, Goodnow and Austin, 1956), inspired his interest in educational approaches that encourage concept learning and the development of thinking. Bruner's work emphasised the importance of understanding the structure of a subject being studied; the need for active learning as the basis for true understanding; and the value of inductive reasoning in learning.

Structure and discovery

Subject structure refers to the fundamental ideas, relationships or patterns of the field of enquiry – the essential information. As structure does not depend upon the inclusion of specific facts or details, the essential structure of an idea can be represented as a diagram, a set of principles or a formula. According to Bruner it follows that learning will be more meaningful, useful and memorable for pupils if they focus on understanding the structure of the subject being studied.

In order to grasp the structure of information, Bruner believes, pupils must be active – they must identify key principles for themselves rather than simply accepting

Connect and Extend

There are a number of variations on the original approach of concept mapping (Ahlberg, 2004) worth investigating and it is also worth thinking about how teachers can and do respond to the concept maps created by pupils (Conlon, 2004). See the Companion Website (Web Link 8.1) for more on concept maps.

Concept mapping

Pupil's diagram of his or her understanding of a concept.

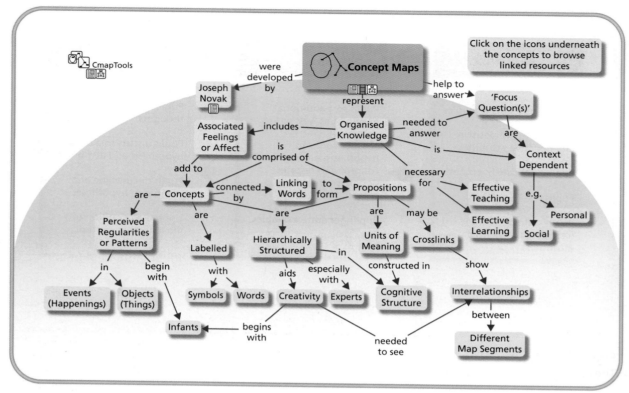

Figure 8.3
A concept map of concept mapping

Source: From http://cmapskm.ihmc.us/servlet/SBReadResourceServlet?rid=1064009710027_1483270340_27090&partName=htmltext at http://cmap.ihmc.us/

Discovery learning

Bruner's approach, in which pupils work on their own to discover basic principles.

Inductive reasoning

Formulating general principles based on knowledge of examples and details.

Intuitive thinking

Making imaginative leaps to correct perceptions or workable solutions.

teachers' explanations. This process has been called discovery learning. In discovery learning, the teacher presents examples and the pupils work with the examples until they discover the interrelationships, the patterns – the subject's structure. Thus, Bruner believes that classroom learning should take place through inductive reasoning, that is, by using specific examples to formulate a general principle. The concept attainment lesson on fruit above used this approach.

Discovery in action

An inductive approach requires intuitive thinking on the part of pupils. Bruner suggests that teachers can nurture this intuitive thinking by encouraging pupils to make guesses based on incomplete evidence and then to confirm or disprove the guesses systematically (Bruner, 1960). After learning about ocean currents and the shipping industry, for example, pupils might be shown old maps of three harbours and asked to guess which one became a major port. Then, they could check their guesses through systematic research. Unfortunately, it could be argued that educational practices often discourage intuitive thinking by punishing wrong guesses and rewarding safe, but uncreative answers. Furthermore, children learn to associate wrong guesses with failure rather than an essential part of learning.

The learning zone

Incorrect or partially correct guesses, puzzlement, muddle, turmoil and cognitive untidiness are all part of classrooms that engage pupils in discovery learning. In *Promoting Positive Behaviour* (1998) – a book we also refer to in Chapter 12 (p. 536) – Tim O'Brien, whilst talking about differentiation – check out Chapter 4 (p. 176) – likens learning to a style of painting:

> *If we were able to spend some time inside a child's head I am sure that we would find learning to be a very noisy and colourful process. For most children there are few occasions when learning is smooth, balanced, compartmentalised and rhythmical – like a Mondrian paining. The reality is that learning is more likely to be loud, chaotic, syncopated and explosive – less like Mondrian, more like Kandinsky. Learning is a noisy and risky business and differentiation should aim to reduce the sound of cognitive dissonance (1998: 46).*

Teachers who understand this will nurture an appreciation in their pupils that it is not just okay to make a wrong guess; it is a requirement so pupils can enter their learning zone. Learning can only take place where there is temporary misunderstanding or a new piece of knowledge is being experienced. We know of classrooms where if somebody says 'I don't understand!' everybody else applauds and the teacher announces that the 'learning zone is open for business'.

A distinction is usually made between pure discovery learning, in which the pupils work on their own to a very great extent, and guided discovery, in which the teacher provides direction. In 2005, Keith Taber wrote:

> *Some decades ago there was an idea that we could set up school students to discover the great ideas of physics and other sciences by putting them in an environment where they had the opportunity to find out in an hour what Galileo, Newton, Curie or Meitner spent months struggling with. However, the accepted principles of physics were seldom rediscovered. What* was *discovered is that learning physics is a lot quicker when novices learn from experts, through a combination of exposition and structured experience (2005: 497).*

Unguided or pure discovery may be appropriate for early years pupils, but in a typical primary or secondary classroom, unguided activities usually prove unmanageable and unproductive. For these situations, guided discovery is preferable. Pupils are presented with intriguing questions, baffling situations or interesting problems: Why does the flame go out when we cover it with a jar? Why does this pencil seem to bend when you put it in water? What is the rule for grouping these words together? Instead of explaining how to solve the problem, the teacher provides the appropriate materials and encourages pupils to make observations, form hypotheses and test solutions. The Focus on Practice below should help teachers apply Bruner's suggestions.

Learning zone

A part of a lesson or activity where a pupil is open to new learning. It is usually signalled by the pupil acknowledging that he or she doesn't know or understand something.

Guided discovery

An adaptation of discovery learning, in which the teacher provides some direction.

Connect and Extend

Many teachers, especially in mathematics and science, believe that meaningful learning in their areas is best supported by discovery learning. For a further discussion see the Winter 2004 special issue of the *Educational Psychologist* on 'Personal Epistemology: Paradigmatic Approaches to Understanding Students' Beliefs about Knowledge and Knowing', *39*(1).

FOCUS ON PRACTICE

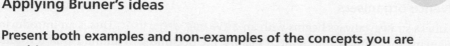

Applying Bruner's ideas

Present both examples and non-examples of the concepts you are teaching

Examples

1. In teaching about mammals, include people, kangaroos, whales, cats, dolphins and camels as examples, and chickens, fish, alligators, frogs and penguins as non-examples.
2. Ask pupils for additional examples and non-examples.

Help pupils see connections among concepts

Examples

1. Ask questions such as these: What else could you call this apple? (Fruit) What do we do with fruit? (Eat) What do we call things we eat? (Food)
2. Use diagrams, outlines and summaries to point out connections.

Pose a question and let pupils try to find the answer

Examples

1. How could the human hand be improved?
2. What is the relation between the area of one tile and the area of the whole floor?

Encourage pupils to make intuitive guesses

Examples

1. Instead of giving a word's definition, say, 'Let's guess what it might mean by looking at the words around it.'
2. Give pupils a map of ancient Greece and ask where they think the major cities were.
3. Don't comment after the first few guesses. Wait for several ideas before giving the answer.
4. Use guiding questions to focus pupils when their discovery has led them too far astray.

For more information on Bruner and discovery learning, see http://evolution.massey. ac.nz/assign2/HB/jbruner.html

---

Deductive reasoning

Drawing conclusions by applying rules or principles; logically moving from a general rule or principle to a specific solution.

Expository teaching

Ausubel's method – teachers present material in complete, organised form, moving from broadest to more specific concepts.

Meaningful verbal learning

Focused and organised relationships among ideas and verbal information.

Advance organiser

Statement of inclusive concepts to introduce and sum up material that follows.

Teaching concepts through exposition

In contrast to Bruner, David Ausubel (1963, 1977, 1982) believed that people acquire knowledge primarily through reception, not discovery. Concepts, principles and ideas are presented and understood using deductive reasoning – from general ideas to specific cases, not discovered from specific cases leading to general concepts. Ausubel's expository teaching model stresses what is known as meaningful verbal learning – verbal information, ideas and relationships among ideas, taken together. Therefore, learning off by heart by repetition (rote memorisation) is not meaningful learning, because material learned by rote is not *connected* with existing knowledge.

Advance organisers

Ausubel's strategy always begins with an advance organiser. This is an introductory statement (for example, 'In modern history, the beginning of an industrial revolution is often associated with a military uprising') broad enough to encompass all the information that will follow. The organisers can serve three purposes: they direct your attention to what is important in the coming material, they highlight relationships among ideas that will be presented, and they remind you of relevant information you already have.

In general, advance organisers fall into one of two categories, *comparative* and *expository* (Mayer, 1984). Comparative organisers *activate* or *reactivate* (bring into working memory) already existing schemas. They remind you of what you already know, but

Expository teaching methods present information to learners in an organised, 'finished' form, rather than having them discover it for themselves

may not realise is relevant. A comparative advance organiser for a history lesson on revolutions might be a statement that contrasts military uprisings with the physical and social changes involved in a industrial revolution; you could also compare the common aspects of the French, English, Mexican, Russian, Iranian and American revolutions (Salomon and Perkins, 1989).

In contrast, *expository organisers* provide *new* knowledge that pupils will need to understand the upcoming information. In an English class, you might begin a large thematic unit on rites of passage in literature with a very broad statement of the theme and why it has been so important. For example, you might say: 'A character coming of age must learn to know himself or herself, often makes some kind of journey of self-discovery, and must decide what in the society they wish to accept and what to reject.'

The general conclusion of research on advance organisers (Corkill, 1992; Langan-Fox, Waycott and Albert, 2000; Morin and Miller, 1998) is that they do help pupils learn (especially when the material to be learned is quite unfamiliar, complex or difficult) if two conditions are met. First, to be effective, the organiser must be understood by the pupils. This was demonstrated dramatically in a study by Dinnel and Glover (1985). They found that instructing pupils to paraphrase an advance organiser – which, of course, requires them to understand its meaning – increased the effectiveness of the organiser. Second, the organiser must really be an organiser: it must indicate relations among the basic concepts and terms that will be used. Concrete models, diagrams or analogies seem to be especially good organisers (Robinson, 1998; Robinson and Kiewra, 1995).

Steps in an exposition

After the advance organiser, the next step is to present content in terms of similarities and differences using specific examples, perhaps provided by the pupils themselves. Imagine a lesson on the coming-of-age theme in literature, using *The Diary of Anne Frank* and *The*

Connect and Extend

Explanatory analogies can help children acquire information from expository text. For example, 'an infection is like a war', 'a stomach is like a blender'. (Vosniadou and Schommer, 1988). See the Companion Website (Web Link 8.2).

Figure 8.4
Phases of expository teaching

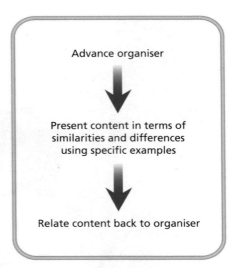

Advance organiser

↓

Present content in terms of
similarities and differences
using specific examples

↓

Relate content back to organiser

Adventures of Huckleberry Finn. As the pupils read, the teacher might ask them to compare the central character's growth, state of mind and position in society with characters from other novels, plays and films (connect to pupils' prior knowledge). Then pupils can compare Anne Frank's inner journey with Huck Finn's trip down the Mississippi. As comparisons are made, the teacher should underscore the learning intentions of the lesson and elaborate the advance organiser.

The best way to point out similarities and differences is with examples. Huck Finn's and Anne Frank's dilemmas must be clear. Finally, when all the material has been presented, the pupils are asked to discuss how the examples can be used to expand on the original advance organiser. The phases of exposition are summarised in Figure 8.4.

Exposition is more developmentally appropriate for pupils of ten or 11 years (Luiten, Ames and Ackerson, 1980). The Focus on Practice below should help you follow the main steps in exposition. Spend some time thinking through examples of lessons where your teachers have used exposition. To what extent have they applied Ausubel's ideas and provided *comparative* and *expository* advance organisers, and focused on similarities and differences using a number of examples?

FOCUS ON PRACTICE

Applying Ausubel's ideas

Use advance organisers

Examples

1. *English:* Shakespeare used the social ideas of his time as a framework for his plays – *Julius Caesar, Hamlet* and *Macbeth* dealt with concepts of natural order, a nation as the human body, etc.
2. *Social studies:* geography dictates economy in pre-industrialised regions or nations.
3. *History:* important concepts during the Renaissance were symmetry, admiration of the classical world, the centrality of the human mind.

Use a number of examples

Examples

1. In mathematics class, ask pupils to point out all the examples of right angles that they can find in the room.
2. In teaching about islands and peninsulas, use maps, slides, models, postcards.

Focus on both similarities and differences

Examples

1. In a history class, ask pupils to list the ways in which the Royalists and Parliamentarians were alike and different before the English Civil War.
2. In a biology class, ask pupils how they would transform spiders into insects or an amphibian into a reptile.

For more information on advance organisers, see http://www.learningandteaching.info/teaching/advance_organisers.htm

Reaching every pupil: learning disabilities and concept teaching

A recent approach to teaching concepts that also emphasises connections with prior knowledge is called analogical instruction (Bulgren *et al.*, 2000). This approach has proved helpful for teaching scientific or cultural knowledge in heterogeneous secondary classes that include pupils who are less academically prepared and pupils with learning disabilities. In secondary classrooms, as the amount and complexity of content increases, these pupils are especially at risk of failure. The goal of analogical instruction is to identify knowledge that these pupils already have in memory that can be used as a starting point for learning the new, complex material. Analogies have long been used in problem solving, but until recently studies of analogies in teaching content have been rare, whereas the importance of problem solving as a complex cognitive process is widely accepted to underpin the construction of new knowledge and understandings. Therefore, in the next section we are going to spend a significant amount of time explaining the importance of problems and problem solving to cognitive development.

Analogical instruction

Teaching new concepts by making connections (analogies) with information that the pupil already understands.

Problem Solving

Anita Woolfolk, co-author of this text, was being interviewed for a position as a school psychologist. The interviewer was known for asking unorthodox interview questions. He handed her a pad of paper and a ruler and says, 'Tell me, what is the exact thickness of a single sheet of paper?'

A good method (of course) was to measure the thickness of the entire pad and divide by the number of pages in the pad. Anita got the answer and the job, but what a tense moment that was. We suppose the interviewer was interested in her ability to solve problems – under pressure! Next, we discuss problems and how to solve them.

A problem has an initial state (the current situation), a goal (the desired outcome) and a path for reaching the goal (including operations or activities that move you towards

Problem

Any situation in which you are trying to reach some goal and must find a means to do so.

the goal). Problem solvers often have to set and reach sub-goals as they move towards the final solution. For example, if your goal is to drive to the beach, but along the way the engine dies and will not restart, you are faced with a new problem of what is wrong with the car? The first operation that moves you towards the new goal of restarting the engine is to check the fuel gauge, which shows empty, and so you now have to reach a sub-goal of refuelling before you can continue towards the original goal. Problems can range from *well-structured* to *ill-structured*, depending on how clear-cut the goal is and how much structure is provided for solving the problem. Most arithmetic problems are well-structured, but finding the right university course is ill-structured – many different solutions and paths to solutions are possible. Life presents many ill-structured problems.

Problem solving

Creating new solutions for problems.

Problem solving is usually defined as formulating new answers, going beyond the simple application of previously learned rules to achieve a goal. Problem solving is what happens when no solution is obvious (Mayer and Wittrock, 1996) – when, to return to the example of breaking down on the way to the beach, you have no spare fuel in the emergency can, no money, no mobile phone and no idea of the whereabouts of the nearest petrol station. Some psychologists suggest that most human learning involves problem solving (Tan, 2002).

However, there is a debate about problem solving. Some psychologists believe that effective problem-solving skills are specific to the problem area. That is, the problem-solving skills in mathematics are unique to maths; the skills in art are unique to art, and so on. The other side of the debate claims that there are some general problem-solving skills that can be useful in many areas. Actually, there is evidence for both sides of the argument. In their research with eight- to 12-year-olds, Robert Kail and Lynda Hall (1999) found that both domain-specific and general factors affected performance on arithmetic word problems. The influences were *arithmetic knowledge* – assessed by the time needed and errors produced in solving simple addition and subtraction problems – and *general information-processing skills*, including reading comprehension, information processing time and, to a lesser extent, memory span.

It appears that people move between general and specific skills, depending on the situation and their level of expertise. Early on, when we know little about a problem area or domain, we can rely on general learning and problem-solving skills to make sense of the situation. As we gain more domain-specific knowledge (particularly procedural knowledge about how to do things in the domain), we consciously apply the general skills less and less; our problem solving becomes more automatic. However, if we encounter a problem outside our current knowledge, we may return to relying on general skills to attack the problem (Alexander, 1992, 1996; Perkins and Salomon, 1989; Shuell, 1990).

Let's consider general problem-solving strategies first. Think of a general problem-solving strategy as a beginning point, a broad outline. Such strategies usually have five stages (Gick, 1986). John Bransford and Barry Stein (1993) use the acronym IDEAL to identify the five steps:

I *Identify* problems and opportunities.

D *Define* goals and represent the problem.

E *Explore* possible strategies.

A *Anticipate* outcomes and *Act*.

L *Look* back and *Learn*.

We will examine each of these steps because they are found in many approaches to problem solving.

Connect and Extend

Many of the early ideas of John Dewey are consistent with a recent emphasis on teaching pupils to be effective problem solvers. See Gregory *et al.* (2001), 'From ivory tower to urban street: using the classroom as a community research and development tool', in *PS: Political Science and Politics, 34*(1) (March), pp. 119–124.

Connect and Extend

It is important to identify the steps in the general problem-solving process. In order to describe the techniques that pupils can employ to build useful representations of problems in a mathematics context see Dixon, J. A. *et al.* (2001), 'The representations of the arithmetic operations include functional relationships' in *Memory and Cognition, 29*(3) (April), pp. 462–477.

Identifying: problem finding

The first step, identifying that a problem exists and treating the problem as an opportunity begins the process. This is not always straightforward. There is a story about tenants who were angry because the lifts in their building were slow. Consultants hired to 'fix the problem' reported that they were no worse than average and that improvements would be very expensive. One day, as the building caretaker watched people waiting impatiently for a lift, he realised that the problem was not slow lifts, but the fact that people were bored; they had nothing to do while they waited. When the boredom problem was identified and seen as an opportunity to improve the 'waiting experience', the simple solution of installing a mirror by the lift doors on each floor eliminated complaints.

Identifying the problem is a critical first step. Research indicates that people often hurry through this important step and 'leap' to naming the first problem that comes to mind ('the lifts are too slow!'). Experts in a field are more likely to spend time carefully considering the nature of the problem (Mirel and Allmendinger, 2004). Finding a solvable problem and turning it into an opportunity is the process behind many successful inventions, such as the ballpoint pen, rubbish disposal, appliance timer, alarm clock, self-cleaning oven, and thousands of others.

Once a *solvable* problem is identified, what next?

Defining goals and representing the problem

Let's take a real problem: The machines designed to pick tomatoes are damaging the tomatoes. What should we do? If we represent the problem as a faulty machine design, then the goal is to improve the machine. But if we represent the problem as faulty tomatoes, then the goal is to develop a tougher tomato. The problem-solving process follows two entirely different paths, depending on which representation and goal are chosen. To represent the problem and set a goal, you have to *focus attention* on relevant information, *understand* the words of the problem, and *activate the right schema* to understand the whole problem.

> ### STOP AND THINK
>
> 'Roll up! Roll up, to play for this brand new Jaguar XJ6. For just ten euro you get the chance to own this superb new limousine. Roll six dice, get six sixes and the car is yours to drive away today. You must roll them all at the same time to win the prize.'
> What chance do you have of winning at each attempt if you spend €50 at the stall?

Focusing attention

Representing the problem often requires finding the relevant information and ignoring the irrelevant details. For example, what information was relevant in solving the above dice problem? Did you realise that the information about rolling all the dice together is irrelevant? As is the number of attempts you make if you are calculating the probability of getting six sixes at each attempt; 6 raised to the power of 6 (6^6) gives you the total number of possible outcomes, of which only one will give you the six sixes you need.

Understanding the words

The second task in representing a story problem is understanding the meaning of the words and sentences (Moreau and Coquin-Viennot, 2003). For example, the main stumbling block in representing many word problems is the pupils' understanding of part-whole relations (Cummins, 1991). Pupils have trouble working out what is part of what, as is evident in this dialogue between a teacher and a six-year-old:

Teacher: Peter has three apples. Ann also has some apples. Peter and Ann have nine apples altogether. How many apples does Ann have?

Pupil: Nine.

Teacher: Why?

Pupil: Because you just said so.

Teacher: Can you retell the story?

Pupil: Peter had three apples. Ann also had some apples. Ann had nine apples. Peter also has nine apples.

Adapted from De Corte and Verschaffel (1985: 19).

Connect and Extend

Piaget (Chapter 2, pp. 38–52) identified children's difficulties with part–whole relations years ago when he asked questions such as, 'There are six daisies and two daffodils; are there more daisies or flowers?' Young children usually answer, 'Daisies!'

The pupil interprets 'altogether' (the whole) as 'each' (the parts). Sometimes, pupils have been taught to search for key words (more, less, greater, etc.) and to pick a strategy or formula based on the key words (more means 'add'), and apply the formula. However, this actually (and usually) gets in the way of forming a conceptual understanding of the whole problem.

Understanding the whole problem

The third task in representing a problem is to assemble all the relevant information and sentences into an accurate understanding or translation of the total problem. This means that pupils needs to form a conceptual model of the problem – they have to understand what the problem is really asking (Jonassen, 2003). Consider the example shown in Figure 8.5.

STOP AND THINK

Two train stations are 50 kilometres apart. At 2 p.m. one Saturday afternoon, two trains start towards each other, one from each station. Just as the trains pull out of the stations, a bird springs into the air in front of the first train and flies ahead to the front of the second train. When the bird reaches the second train it turns back and flies towards the first train. The bird continues to do this until the trains meet. If both trains travel at the rate of 25 kilometres per hour and the bird flies at 100 kilometres per hour, how many miles will the bird have flown before the trains meet? (Posner, 1973)

Your interpretation of the problem is called a translation because you translate the problem into a schema that you understand. If you translate this as a distance problem and set a goal ('I have to calculate how far the bird travels before it meets the oncoming train and turns around, then how far it travels before it has to turn again, and finally add up all the trips back and forth'), then you have a very complicated task to perform!

I once asked two six-year-olds to show, in their own way, the game they were playing about finding the differences between two lots of counters, determined by a die [see Figure 1 below]. Tania's record is rich in mathematically superfluous detail, clearly showing her interpretation of my request as referring to the whole context. Melanie, however, homed in on the counters, indicating the difference by colouring in (as her Fletcher – a widely used maths scheme at the time – maths book did). When asked if she could show the difference in a quicker way, she put a line between the 7 and 8, which might be seen either as a separator, or as an invented symbol for difference, like a minus sign on its side. She read what she had done as 'the difference between 7 and 8 is 1'.

A similar symbol is used by Karen and read as 'You need 4 to get from 2 up to 6' [see Figure 2 below]. Karen also circles the difference number: this common device clearly seems to serve a punctuating function, of emphasising the result of the calculation.

Figure 1 Melanie and Tania

Figure 2 Karen

Figure 8.5
Three different ways to represent a problem

Source: Atkinson, S. (ed.) (1992). *Mathematics with Reason: The Emergent Approach to Primary Maths.* Hodder and Stoughton, pp. 70–71.

There is a better way to structure the problem. You can represent it as a question of time and focus on the time the bird is in the air. The solution could be stated like this:

The trains are going the same speed so they will meet in the middle, 25 kilometres from each station. This will take one hour *because they are travelling 25 km/h. In an hour, the bird will cover 100 kilometres because it is flying at 100 kilometres per hour. Easy!*

Research shows that pupils can be too quick to decide what a problem is asking. Once a problem is categorised – 'Aha, it's a distance problem!' – a particular schema is activated. The schema directs attention to relevant information and sets up expectations for what the right answer should look like (Kalyuga *et al.*, 2001).

When pupils lack the necessary schemas to represent problems, they often rely on surface features of the situation and represent the problem incorrectly, like the pupil who wrote '15 + 24 = 39' as the answer to, 'Joan has 15 bonus points and Louise has 24. How many more does Louise have?' This pupil saw two numbers and the word 'more', so he applied the *add to get more* procedure. When pupils use the wrong schema, they overlook critical information, use irrelevant information, and may even misread or misremember critical information so that it fits the schema. But when pupils use the proper schema to represent a problem, they are less likely to be confused by irrelevant information or tricky wording, such as *more* in a problem that really requires *subtraction* (Resnick, 1981). Figure 8.5 gives examples of different ways pupils might represent a simple mathematics problem.

Translation and schema training

How can pupils improve translation and schema selection? To answer this question, we often have to move from general to area-specific problem-solving strategies because schemas are specific to content areas. In mathematics, for example, it appears that pupils benefit from seeing and exploring many different kinds of example problems worked out correctly for them. The common practice of showing pupils a solution to a few examples, then having pupils work many problems on their own, is less effective. Worked-out examples are helpful especially when problems are unfamiliar or difficult and when pupils have less knowledge (Cooper and Sweller, 1987). Ask pupils to compare examples. What is the same about each solution? What is different? Why?

The same procedures may be effective in areas other than mathematics. Adrienne Lee and Laura Hutchinson (1998) found that undergraduate students learned more when they had examples of chemistry problem solutions that were annotated to show an expert problem solver's thinking at critical steps. In Australia, Slava Kalyuga and colleagues (2001) found that worked-out examples helped apprentices to learn about electrical circuits when the apprentices had less experience in the area. Asking pupils to reflect on the examples helped too, so both explanation and reflection can make worked-out examples more effective. Some of the benefit from worked-out examples comes when pupils use the examples to explain to themselves what is happening at each step or to check their understanding by anticipating the next step. In this way, pupils have to be mentally engaged in making sense of the examples (Atkinson, Renkl and Merrill, 2003).

Familiar examples can serve as analogies or models for solving new problems. However, novices are likely to remember the surface features of an example or case instead of the deeper meaning or the structure. It is the meaning or structure, not the surface similarities that help in solving new, analogous problems. We have heard pupils complain that the problems in their maths lessons were about river currents, but in end of topic tests they were asked about wind speed. They protested, 'There were no problems about boats on the test!' Of course, the problems on the test about wind could be solved in similar ways as the 'boat' problems but the pupils were focusing only on the surface features. Problems of speed are solved in similar ways because speed is always a function of time and distance. One way to overcome this tendency to focus on surface features is to have pupils compare examples or cases so they can develop a general problem-solving schema that captures the common structure, not the surface features of the cases (Gentner *et al.*, 2003).

How else might pupils develop the schemas they will need to represent problems in a particular subject area? Mayer (1983) has recommended giving pupils practice in the following: (1) recognising and categorising a variety of problem types; (2) representing problems – either concretely in pictures, symbols or graphs, or in words; and (3) selecting relevant and irrelevant information in problems.

The results of problem representation

There are two main outcomes of the problem representation stage of problem solving, as shown in Figure 8.6. If your representation of the problem suggests an immediate solution, your task is done. In one sense, you haven't really solved a new problem; you have simply recognised the new problem as a 'disguised' version of an old problem that you already know how to solve. This has been called schema-driven problem solving. In terms of Figure 8.6, you have taken the *schema-activated route* and have proceeded directly to a solution. What if you have no existing way of solving the problem or if your activated schema fails? Then it is time to search for a solution!

Exploring possible solution strategies

If you do not have existing schemas that suggest an immediate solution, then you must take the *search-based route* indicated in Figure 8.6. Obviously, this path is not as efficient as activating the right schema, but sometimes it is the only way. In conducting your search for a solution, you have available two general kinds of procedures: algorithmic and heuristic.

Schema-driven problem solving

Recognising a problem as a 'disguised' version of an old problem for which one already has a solution.

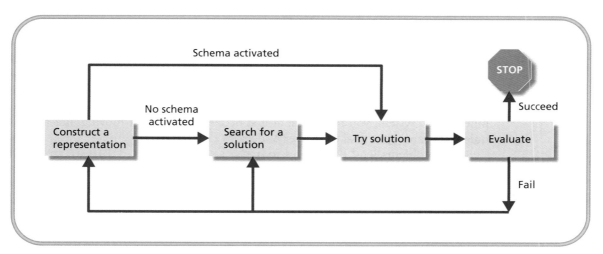

Figure 8.6
Diagram of the problem-solving process

There are two paths to a solution. In the first, the correct schema is activated and the solution is apparent. But if no schema is available, searching and testing may become the path to a solution.

Source: From *Educational Psychologist* by M. L. Gick. Copyright 1986 by Lawrence Erlbaum Associates, Inc.–Journals. Reproduced with permission of Lawrence Erlbaum Associates Inc.–Journals in the format Textbook via Copyright Clearance Center.

Algorithms

Algorithm

Step-by-step procedure for solving a problem; a prescription for solutions.

An algorithm is a step-by-step prescription for achieving a goal. It usually is domain-specific; that is, it is tied to a particular subject area. In solving a problem, if you choose an appropriate algorithm and implement it properly, a correct answer is guaranteed. Unfortunately, pupils often apply algorithms unsystematically. They try first this, then that. They may even happen on the right answer, but not understand how they found it. For some pupils, applying algorithms haphazardly could be an indication that formal operational thinking and the ability to work through a set of possibilities systematically, as described by Piaget, is not yet developed.

Even when applied appropriately and correctly many problems cannot be solved by algorithms, because there is no obvious step-by-step procedure for achieving the goal. What then?

Heuristics

Heuristic

General strategy used in attempting to solve problems.

A heuristic is a general strategy that might lead to the right answer. As many of life's problems (careers, relationships, etc.) are not straightforward, have ill-defined problem statements and no apparent algorithms, the discovery or development of effective heuristics is important (Korf, 1999). So let's examine a few.

Means-ends analysis

Heuristic in which a goal is divided into sub-goals.

In means-ends analysis, the problem is divided into a number of intermediate goals or sub-goals, and then a means of solving each intermediate sub-goal is figured out. For example, writing an 8,000-word assignment can loom as an insurmountable problem for some students. They would be better off breaking this task into several intermediate goals, such as selecting a topic, locating sources of information, reading and organising the information, making an outline, and so on. As they attack a particular intermediate goal, they may find that other goals arise. For example, locating information may require that they find someone to refresh their memory about using the library computer search system. Please keep in mind that psychologists have yet to discover an effective heuristic for students who are just starting their assignment the night before it is due to be handed in.

A second aspect of means-ends analysis is *distance reduction*, or pursuing a path that moves directly towards the final goal. People tend to look for the biggest difference between the current state of affairs and the goal and then search for a strategy that reduces the difference. We resist taking detours or making moves that are indirect as we search for the quickest way to reach the goal. So when you realise that reaching the goal of completing an assignment may require a detour of relearning the library computer search system, you may resist at first because you are not moving directly and quickly towards your final objective (Anderson, 1993).

Working-backward strategy

Heuristic in which one starts with the goal and moves backward to solve the problem.

Some problems lend themselves to a working-backward strategy, in which you begin at the goal and move back to the unsolved initial problem. Working backward is sometimes an effective heuristic for solving geometry proofs. It can also be a good way to set intermediate deadlines ('Let's see, if I have to submit this chapter in three weeks, then it has to be in the post by the 28th, so I should have a first draft finished by the 11th').

Analogical thinking

Heuristic in which one limits the search for solutions to situations that are similar to the one at hand.

Another useful heuristic is analogical thinking (Gentner *et al.*, 2003), which limits your search for solutions to situations that have something in common with the one you currently face. For example, when submarines were first used engineers had to figure out how battleships could determine the presence and location of vessels hidden in the depths of the sea. Studying how bats solve an analogous problem of navigating in the dark led to the invention of Sound Navigation and Ranging systems (SONAR).

One of the advantages of having pupils working in groups in problem-solving situations is that they are expected to explain their proposed solutions to one another. Putting solutions into words usually improves problem solving

Analogical reasoning can lead to faulty problem solving, too. When word processors first came out, some people used the analogy of the typewriter and failed to take advantage of the computer's features. They were focusing on the surface similarities. It seems that people need knowledge in both the problem domain and the analogy domain in order to use an analogy effectively (Gagné, Yekovich and Yekovich, 1993). In addition, they must focus on meaning, and not surface similarities when forming the analogies.

Putting your problem-solving plan into words and giving reasons for selecting it can lead to successful problem solving (Lee and Hutchinson, 1998). You may have discovered the effectiveness of this verbalisation process accidentally, when a solution 'popped into your head' as you were explaining a problem to someone else. After representing the problem and exploring possible solutions, the next step is to select a solution and *anticipate the consequences*. For example, if you decide to solve the damaged tomato problem by developing a tougher tomato, how will consumers react? If you take time to learn a new graphics program to enhance your assignment (and improve your mark), will you still have enough time to finish the project? Furthermore, will the solution stand up to scrutiny?

Verbalisation
Putting your problem-solving plan and its logic into words.

Anticipating acting, and looking back

STOP AND THINK

What do you think about letting pupils use calculators and spell checkers? Do you think this is making learning too easy? How are these questions relevant to evaluating solutions to problems?

After you choose a solution strategy and implement it, evaluate the results by checking for evidence that confirms or contradicts your solution. Many people tend to stop working before reaching the best solution and simply accept an answer that works in some cases. In mathematical problems, evaluating the answer might mean applying a checking routine, such as adding to check the result of a subtraction problem or, in a long addition algorithm, adding the column from bottom to top instead of top to bottom. Another possibility is estimating the answer. For example, if the computation was 11×21, the answer should be around 200, because 10×20 is 200. A pupil who reaches an answer of 2,311 or 23 or 562 should quickly realise these answers cannot be correct. Estimating an answer is particularly important when pupils rely on calculators or computers because without an estimate pupils are less likely to spot an error in their solution.

DISCUSSION POINT

Should pupils be discouraged from using spell checkers and calculators?

Not all educators believe that teachers should allow pupils to use calculators and other technical tools for performing operations and checking their work.

Agree: Yes, calculators and spell checkers are 'crutches' that can prevent the acquisition of skills and knowledge

One feature of the National Numeracy Strategy introduced into English Primary Schools in September 1999 was a 'ban' for pupils under eight years old on the use of calculators for purposes of calculating and checking work. The Strategy emphasises the importance of mental methods and any reliance on calculators was seen to be counter to the development of understanding and competence in mental calculation and formal written methods. The Final Report of the Numeracy Task Force (1998) concluded:

> There is no place in primary school mathematics lessons for using calculators as a prop for simple arithmetic, since children are still learning the mental calculation skills and written methods that they will need throughout their lives' (paragraph 113). http://www.dfes.gov.uk/numeracy/chapter3.shtml

I've watched pupils at 15 and 16 going straight for their calculators when having to calculate the most straightforward product of two values. These pupils' ability to solve problems or handle data was dependent upon access to a calculator and their 'train of thought' was disturbed by the need to push the right buttons to find the product of seven eights or to discover how many fives in one hundred and twenty. What is worse is that they accept the displayed answer without any question even if it makes no sense at all.

Also I don't see how a red squiggly line under 'accomodation' helps when applied to there, they're or their. What research points to any improvement in spelling for pupils who use electronic spell checkers, I don't think it exists. What's wrong with a dictionary? Word processing is just a very expensive way of getting teachers out of checking and correcting pupils' spelling and grammar mistakes.

Disagree: No, calculators and spell checkers can support the acquisition of skills and knowledge

Just because pupils learned mathematics in the past with paper-and-pencil procedures and abundant practice does not mean that this is the best way to learn. Today, we have to consider each teaching situation on a case-by-case basis to determine if paper-and-pencil procedures or technology or some combination provides the best way to learn (Waits and Demana, 2000). For example, in the Third International Mathematics and Science Study (TIMSS, 1998), on every test at the advanced level, students who said that they used calculators in their daily maths coursework performed much better than students who rarely or never used calculators. In fact, rather than eroding basic skills, the research on calculators over the past decade has found that using calculators has positive effects on students' problem-solving skills and attitudes towards maths (Waits and Demana, 2000).

In an account of the work of the UK 'Calculator-aware' Number curriculum project (known as CAN) which ran from 1986–92, Hilary Shuard and her colleagues (1991) claimed that children with free access to calculators developed good numeracy skills. Furthermore, by Key Stage 2 the 'CAN children' were found to be more liable to compute mentally and adopt powerful mental strategies (Ruthven, 1998). The findings of this project, which allowed young children access to calculators at all times, appear to suggest that free calculator use helps rather than hinders the mathematical thinking strategies and number awareness of young children.

What about word processors and spelling checkers? Pricilla Norton and Debra Sprague suggest that 'no other technology resource has had as great an impact on education as word processing' (2001: 78). They list the following effects: word processing enhances learners' perceptions of themselves as 'real' writers, lets pupils reflect on the thinking that goes on behind the writing, facilitates collaborative writing, and helps pupils be more critical and creative in their writing.

WHAT DO YOU THINK?
Agree or Disagree? Vote online at www.pearsoned.co.uk/woolfolkeuro.

Factors that hinder problem solving

STOP AND THINK

You enter a room. There are two ropes suspended from the ceiling. You are asked by the experimenter to tie the two ends of the ropes together and are assured that the task is possible. On a nearby table are a few tools, including a hammer and pliers. You grab the end of one of the ropes and walk towards the other rope. You immediately realise that you cannot possibly reach the end of the other rope. You try to extend your reach using the pliers but still cannot grasp the other rope. What can you do? (Maier, 1933)

Fixation

Problem solving requires seeing things in new ways. The rope problem can be solved if you tie the hammer or the pliers to the end of one rope and start swinging it like a pendulum. Then you will be able to catch it while you are standing across the room holding the other rope. You can use the weight of the tool to make the rope come to you instead of trying to stretch the rope. People often fail to solve this problem, because they fixate on conventional uses for materials. This difficulty is called functional fixedness (Duncker, 1945). In your everyday life, you may often exhibit functional fixedness. Suppose a screw on a dresser-drawer handle is loose. Will you spend 10 minutes searching for a screwdriver or will you fix it with a ruler edge or a coin?

Another kind of fixation that blocks effective problem solving is response set, getting stuck on one way of representing a problem. Try this:

Functional fixedness

Inability to use objects or tools in a new way.

Response set

Rigidity; tendency to respond in the most familiar way.

STOP AND THINK

In each of the four matchstick arrangements below, move only one stick to change the equation so that it represents a true equality such as V = V.

V = VII   VI = XI   XII = VII   VI = II

You probably figured out how to solve the first example quite quickly. You simply move one matchstick from the right side over to the left to make VI = VI. Examples two and three can also be solved without too much difficulty by moving one stick to change the V to an X or vice versa. But the fourth example (taken from Raudsepp and Haugh, 1977) probably has you stumped. To solve this problem, you must change your response set or switch schemas, because what has worked for the first three problems will not work this time. The answer here lies in changing from Roman numerals to Arabic numbers and using the concept of square root. By overcoming response set, you can move one matchstick from the right to the left to form the symbol for square root; the solution reads $\sqrt{1} = 1$, which is simply the symbolic way of saying that the square root of 1 equals 1. Recently, a creative reader of an earlier US edition of this text e-mailed some other solutions. Jamaal Allan, then a masters' student at Pacific University, pointed out that you could use any of the matchsticks to change the = sign to ≠ Then, the last example would be V ≠ II or 5 does not equal 2, an accurate statement. He suggested that you also might move one matchstick to change = to < or >, and the statements would still be true (but not equalities as specified in the problem above). Can you come up with any other solutions?

Some problems with heuristics

We often apply heuristics automatically to make quick judgements; that saves us time in everyday problem solving. The mind can react automatically and instantaneously, but the price we often pay for this efficiency may be bad problem solving, which can be costly. Making judgements by invoking your stereotypes leads even clever people to make wrong decisions. For example, we might use representativeness heuristics to make judgements about possibilities based on prototypes – what we think is representative of a category.

For example, at a recent conference Malcolm Hughes, co-author of this text, was invited by his co-organiser to find his host's PA in the next room. 'Blue business

Representativeness heuristic

Judging the likelihood of an event based on how well the events match your prototypes – what you think is representative of the category.

suit and ponytail' was the description. The problem was to find the PA in a large room packed with delegates. Of course our asinine co-author went looking for a ponytail only to find that all the women in the room had short hair or were wearing their hair down or clipped back (and almost everybody was wearing a blue suit!). Finally the penny dropped that it just might be a man with a ponytail. Malcolm's prototype was of a woman PA and to some extent was an understandable if reprehensible stereotype. Women PAs in the UK numbered 358,000 and men just 7,000 meaning women PAs outnumbered men by 51 to 1 (UK Labour Force Survey, 2005). No statistics are available about the number of men and women PAs who have ponytails.

Teachers and pupils are busy people, and they often base their decisions on what they have in their minds at the time. When judgements are based on the availability of information in our memories, we are using the availability heuristic. If instances of events come to mind easily, we think they are common occurrences, but that is not necessarily the case; in fact, it is often wrong. People remember vivid stories and quickly come to believe that such events are the norm, but often they are wrong. For example, you may have been surprised to read in Chapter 5 that if the head of a family of three works full time (37.5 hours a week) at the minimum wage, the family's income will still be below the poverty line. You would likely be more surprised if you first believed that the introduction of a statutory minimum wage would raise families out of poverty. Again for you, data do not support that judgement. But belief perseverance, or the tendency to hold on to our beliefs, even in the face of contradictory evidence, may make us resist change.

The confirmation bias is the tendency to search for information that confirms our ideas and beliefs: this arises from our eagerness to get a good solution. You have often heard the saying 'Don't confuse me with the facts'. This aphorism captures the essence of the confirmation bias. Most people seek evidence that supports their ideas more readily than they search for facts that might refute them (Myers, 2005). For example, once you decide to buy a certain car, you are more likely to notice reports about the good features of the car you chose, not any good news about the cars that you rejected. Our automatic use of heuristics to make judgements, our eagerness to confirm what we like to believe, and our tendency to explain away failure combine to generate *overconfidence*. University students usually are overconfident about how fast they can get their assignments written; it typically takes twice a long as they estimate (Buehler, Griffin and Ross, 1994). In spite of their underestimation of their completion time, they remain overly confident of their next prediction.

The importance of flexibility

Functional fixedness, response set, the confirmation bias and belief perseverance point to the importance of flexibility in understanding problems. If you get started with an inaccurate or inefficient representation of the true problem, it will be difficult – or at least very time-consuming – to reach a solution. Sometimes, it is helpful to 'play' with the problem. Ask yourself: 'What do I know? What do I need to know to answer this question? Can I look at this problem in other ways?' Try to think conditionally rather than rigidly, and divergently rather than convergently. Ask 'What could this be?' instead of 'What is it?' (Benjafield, 1992).

If you open your mind to multiple possibilities, you may have what the Gestalt psychologists called an insight. Insight is the sudden reorganisation or reconceptualisation of a problem that clarifies the problem and suggests a feasible solution. The caretaker described earlier, who suddenly realised that the problem in his building was not slow lifts but impatient, bored tenants, had an insight that allowed him to reach

Availability heuristic

Judging the likelihood of an event based on what is available in your memory, assuming those easily remembered events are common.

Belief perseverance

The tendency to hold on to beliefs, even in the face of contradictory evidence.

Confirmation bias

Seeking information that confirms our choices and beliefs, while disconfirming evidence.

Insight

Sudden realisation of a solution.

the solution of installing mirrors by the lifts. In this case the caretaker was an effective, perhaps expert, problem solver.

Effective problem solving: what do the experts do?

Most psychologists agree that effective problem solving is based on an ample store of knowledge about the problem area. In order to solve the matchstick problem, for example, you had to understand Roman and Arabic numbers as well as the concept of square root. You also had to know that the square root of 1 is 1. Let's take a moment to examine this expert knowledge.

Expert knowledge

The modern study of expertise began with investigations of chess masters (Simon and Chase, 1973). Results indicated that chess masters can quickly recognise about 50,000 different arrangements of chess pieces. They can look at one of these patterns for a few seconds and remember where every piece on the board was placed. It is as though they have a 'vocabulary' of 50,000 patterns. Michelene Chi (1978) demonstrated that seven- to 13-year-old chess experts had a similar ability to remember chess piece arrangements. For all the masters, patterns of pieces are like words. If you were shown any word from your vocabulary store for just a few seconds, you would be able to remember every letter in the word in the right order (assuming you could spell the word).

But a series of letters arranged randomly is hard to remember, as you saw in Chapter 7. An analogous situation holds for chess masters. When chess pieces are placed on a board randomly, masters are no better than average players at remembering the positions of the pieces. The master's memory is for patterns that make sense or could occur in a game.

A similar phenomenon occurs in other fields. There may be an intuition about how to solve a problem based on recognising patterns and knowing the 'right moves' for those patterns. Experts in physics, for example, organise their knowledge around central principles, whereas beginners organise their smaller amounts of physics knowledge around the specific details stated in the problems (Ericsson, 1999). For instance, when asked to sort physics problems from a textbook in any way they wanted, novices sorted based on superficial features such as the kind of apparatus mentioned – a lever or a pulley – whereas the experts grouped problems according to the underlying physics principle needed to solve the problem, such as Boyle's or Newton's laws (Hardiman, Dufresne and Mestre, 1989).

In addition to representing a problem very quickly, experts know what to do next. They have a large store of productions or *condition-action schemas* about what action to take in various situations. An expert and experienced plumber or electrician knows just what to do when something goes wrong, unlike the rest of us that panic or get a nasty shock! Thus, the steps of understanding the problem and choosing a solution happen simultaneously and fairly automatically (Ericsson and Charness, 1999). Of course, this means that they must have many, many schemas available. A large part of becoming an expert is simply acquiring a great store of *domain knowledge* or knowledge that is particular to a field (Alexander, 1992). To do this, you must encounter many different kinds of problems in that field, study or observe problems solved by others, and practise solving many yourself. Some estimates are that it takes ten years or 10,000 hours of study to become an expert in most fields (Simon, 1995).

Experts' rich store of knowledge is *elaborated* and *well practised,* so that it is easy to retrieve from long-term memory when needed (Anderson, 1993). Experts can use their extensive knowledge to *organise* information for easier learning and retrieval.

Compared to eight-year-olds with little knowledge of soccer, eight-year-olds who were soccer experts learned and remembered far more new soccer terms, even though the abilities of the two groups to learn and remember non-soccer terms were the same. The soccer experts organised and clustered the soccer terms to aid in recall (Schneider and Bjorklund, 1992). Even very young children who are experts on a topic can use strategies to organise their knowledge. To get an example of the use of category knowledge about dinosaurs, Anita called her nephews, Lucas and Geoffrey (four and three years old at the time). They promptly ran down the list of large and small plant- and meat-eating dinosaurs (their organising categories), from the well-known stegosaurus (large, plant eater) to the less familiar ceolophysis (small, meat eater).

With organisation comes planning and monitoring. Experts spend more time analysing problems, drawing diagrams, breaking large problems down into sub-problems and making plans. Whereas a novice might begin immediately perhaps by writing equations for a physics problem or drafting the first paragraph of a conference paper. Experts plan out the whole solution and often make the task simpler in the process. As they work, experts monitor progress, so time is not lost pursuing dead ends or weak ideas (Schunk, 2004).

Chi, Glaser and Farr (1988) summarise the superior capabilities of experts. Experts:

- perceive large, meaningful patterns in given information;
- perform tasks quickly and with few errors;
- deal with problems at a deeper level;
- hold more information in working and long-term memories;
- take a great deal of time to analyse a given problem; and
- are better at monitoring their performance.

When the area of problem solving is fairly well defined, such as chess, physics or computer programming, then these skills of expert problem solvers hold fairly consistently. But when the problem-solving area is less well defined and has fewer clear underlying principles, such as problem solving in economics or psychology, then the differences between experts and novices are not as clear-cut (Alexander, 1992).

Novice knowledge

Studies of the differences between experts and novices in particular areas have revealed some surprising things about how novices understand and misunderstand a subject. Physics again provides many examples. Most beginners approach physics with a great deal of misinformation, partly because many of their intuitive ideas about the physical world are wrong. Most primary school children believe that light helps us see by brightening the area around objects. They do not realise that we see an object because the light is reflected by the object to our eyes. This concept does not fit with the everyday experience of turning on a light and 'brightening' the dark area. Peter Cheng and David Shipstone (2003) from the School of Psychology, University of Nottingham, UK developed a new approach to the teaching of electricity that used box and AVOW diagrams, novel representations of the properties of the electric circuit which portray current, voltage, resistance and power. The diagrams were developed as aids to learning, understanding and problem solving. They also promoted conceptual change by challenging a number of commonly held misconceptions, for example that batteries create electricity.

It seems quite important for science teachers to understand their pupils' intuitive models of basic concepts. If the pupils' intuitive model includes misconceptions and inaccuracies, then the pupils are likely to develop inadequate or misleading representations of a problem. (You should note that some researchers don't use the term 'misconception,' but refer to *naïve* or *intuitive conceptions* to describe pupils' beginning knowledge in an area.) In order to learn new information and solve problems, pupils must sometimes 'unlearn' commonsense ideas. Changing your intuitive ideas about concepts involves motivation, too.

Pintrich, Marx and Boyle (1993) suggest that four conditions are necessary for people to change basic concepts:

1. Pupils have to be dissatisfied with the current concept; that is, their existing concept must be seen as inaccurate, incomplete or not useful.

2. Pupils must understand the new concept.

3. The new concept must be plausible – it must fit in with what the pupils already know.

4. The new concept must be fruitful – it must be seen as useful in solving problems or answering questions.

The Focus on Practice below gives some ideas for helping pupils become expert problem solvers.

FOCUS ON PRACTICE

Problem solving

Ask pupils if they are sure they understand the problem

Examples
1. Can they separate relevant from irrelevant information?
2. Are they aware of the assumptions they are making?
3. Encourage them to visualise the problem by diagramming or drawing it.
4. Ask them to explain the problem to someone else. What would a good solution look like?

Encourage attempts to see the problem from different angles

Examples
1. Suggest several different possibilities yourself, and then ask pupils to offer some.
2. Give pupils practice in taking and defending different points of view on an issue.

Help pupils develop systematic ways of considering alternatives

Examples
1. Think out loud as you solve problems.
2. Ask, 'What would happen if?'
3. Keep a list of suggestions.

Teach heuristics

Examples

1. Ask pupils to explain the steps they take as they solve problems.
2. Use analogies to solve the problem of limited parking in the shopping area of town. How are other 'storage' problems solved?
3. Use the working backward strategy to plan a party.

Let pupils do the thinking; don't just hand them solutions

Examples

1. Offer individual problems as well as group problems, so that each pupil has the chance to practise.
2. Give partial credit if pupils have good reasons for 'wrong' solutions to problems.
3. If pupils are stuck, resist the temptation to give too many clues. Let them think about the problem overnight.

For more resources and links on problem solving, see http://en.wikipedia.org/wiki/Problem_solving

Creativity and Creative Problem Solving

Consider the story of this pupil.

In my third week [at a new school] I was summoned to the headmaster's study and told that I had broken some rule; I think I had walked on to a patch of hallowed grass to retrieve a football. I had to bend down and I was caned across my bottom six times. I was trouble – and always in trouble. Aged eight I still couldn't read. In fact, I was dyslexic and short-sighted. Despite sitting at the front of the class, I couldn't read the blackboard. Only after a couple of terms did anyone think to have my eyes tested. Even when I could see, the letters and numbers made no sense at all. Dyslexia wasn't deemed a problem in those days, or, put more accurately, it was only a problem if you were dyslexic yourself. Since nobody had ever heard of dyslexia, being unable to read, write or spell just meant to the rest of the class and the teachers that you were either stupid or lazy. And at prep school you were beaten for both. I was soon being beaten once or twice a week for doing poor classwork or confusing the date of the Battle of Hastings.

From Chapter 1 of Losing My Virginity *by . . . Guess who?*

Do you think this pupil is likely to be creative, or to become a creative problem solver? Well, this 'beaten' pupil was Richard Branson, who has become one of the world's best known and richest entrepreneurs. More information and the story of Richard Branson can be found at http://www.virgin.com/aboutvirgin/allaboutvirgin/richardsautobiography/.

There are many such examples of people who have overcome dyslexia to become amazingly creative people. Examples include John Irving, Albert Einstein, Walt Disney, Alexander Graham Bell, Leonardo DeVinci, Henry Ford, Hans Christian Anderson, Pablo Picasso, Enrico Caruso, Auguste Rodin and Michael Faraday. How do we explain their amazing creativity? What is creativity? The choice of Richard Branson as our exemplar is not accidental as there is a danger in thinking of creativity and creative problem solving as relating only to the arts or sciences, but we know differently.

Defining creativity

Let's start with what creativity is not. Here are four myths about creativity (Plucker *et al.*, 2004):

1. **People are born creative.** Actually, years of research show that creativity can be developed, enhanced and supported by the individual's or group's environment.

2. **Creativity is intertwined with negative qualities.** It is true that some creative people are non-conforming or some may have mental or emotional problems, but many non-creative people do, too. The danger with this myth is that teachers may expect creative pupils to be troublemakers and treat these pupils in a biased way (Scott, 1999).

3. **Creativity is a fuzzy, soft construct.** In contrast to seeing a creative person as mentally unbalanced, some people think creative individuals are New Age hippies. Actually, even though creative people may be open to new experiences and be generally non-conforming, they also may be focused, organised and flexible.

4. **Creativity is enhanced within a group.** It is true that brainstorming in a group can lead to creative ideas, but these group efforts tend to be more creative if individuals brainstorm on their own first.

Creativity

Imaginative, original thinking or problem solving.

So what is creativity? Creativity is the ability to produce work that is original, but still appropriate and useful (Berk, 2005). Most psychologists agree that there is no such thing as 'all-purpose creativity'; people are creative *in a particular area,* as, for example, John Irving was in writing fiction. However, to be creative, the 'invention' must be intended. An accidental spilling of paint that produces a novel design is not creative unless the artist recognises the potential of the 'accident' or uses the spilling technique intentionally to create new works (Weisberg, 1993). As we have mentioned before, although we frequently associate the arts with creativity, any subject can be approached in a creative manner.

A definition that combines many aspects of creativity (Plucker *et al.*, 2004) highlights that creativity:

- often involves more than one person;

- happens when people apply their abilities as part of a helpful process in a supportive environment; and

- results in an identifiable product that is new and useful in a particular culture or situation.

What are the sources of creativity?

Researchers have studied cognitive processes, personality factors, motivational patterns and background experiences to explain creativity but to truly understand creativity, we must include the social environment too. Both intrapersonal (cognition, personality) and social factors support creativity (Simonton, 2000). Teresa Amabile (1996) proposes a three-component model of creativity. Creative individuals or groups must have:

1. *Domain-relevant skills* including talents and competencies that are valuable for working in the domain. An example would be Michelangelo's skills in shaping stone, developed when he lived with a stonecutter's family as a child.

2. *Creativity-relevant processes* including work habits and personality traits such as Richard Branson who regularly starts his working day at 04.30 and sees no

difference between work and play and John Irving's habit of working ten-hour days to write and rewrite and rewrite until he perfected his stories.

3. *Intrinsic task motivation* or a deep curiosity and fascination with the task. This aspect of creativity can be greatly influenced by the social environment (as we will see in Chapter 10), and by supporting autonomy, stimulating curiosity, encouraging fantasy and providing challenge.

Another social factor that influences creativity is whether the field is ready and willing to acknowledge the creative contribution (Nakamura and Csikszentmihalyi, 2001). History is filled with examples of creative breakthroughs rejected at the time (e.g. Galileo's theory of the sun at the center of the solar system) and of rivalries between creators that led each to push the edges of creativity (the friendly and productive rivalry between Picasso and Matisse).

Creativity and cognition

Having a rich store of knowledge in an area is the basis for creativity, but something more is needed. For many problems, that 'something more' is the ability to break up the normal set – restructuring the problem to see things in a new way, which leads to a sudden insight. Often this happens when a person has struggled with a problem or project, then sets it aside for a while. Some psychologists believe that time away from the problem allows for *incubation,* a kind of unconscious working through the problem. It is more likely that leaving the problem for a time interrupts rigid ways of thinking so you can restructure your view of the situation (Gleitman *et al.,* 1999). So it seems that creativity requires extensive knowledge, flexibility and the continual reorganising of ideas. Also, we saw that motivation, persistence and social support play important roles in the creative process as well.

> **Restructuring**
> Conceiving of a problem in a new or different way.

Assessing creativity

> ### STOP AND THINK
>
> How many uses can you list for a brick? Take a moment and brainstorm – write down as many as you can.

Like many of our examples of creative people named earlier, Paul Torrance also had a learning disability; he became interested in educational psychology when he was a high school English teacher and later became known as the 'Father of Creativity'. He developed two types of creativity tests: verbal and graphic (Torrance, 1972; Torrance and Hall, 1980). In the verbal test, you might be instructed to think up as many uses as possible for a brick (as you did above) or asked how a particular toy might be changed to make it more fun. For the graphic test, you might be given 30 circles and asked to create 30 different drawings, with each drawing including at least one circle. Figure 8.7 shows the creativity of an eight-year-old girl in completing this task.

These tests require divergent thinking, an important component of many conceptions of creativity. Divergent thinking is the ability to propose many different ideas or answers. Convergent thinking is the more common ability to identify only one answer. Responses to all Torrance's creativity tasks are scored for originality, fluency and flexibility, three aspects of divergent thinking. *Originality* can be determined statistically. In Torrance's tests, any response in order to be deemed original, must be given

> **Divergent thinking**
> Coming up with many possible solutions.

> **Convergent thinking**
> Narrowing possibilities to a single answer.

Figure 8.7
A graphic assessment of the creativity of an eight-year-old

The titles she gave her drawings, from left to right, are as follows: 'Dracula', 'one-eyed monster', 'pumpkin', 'Hula-Hoop', 'poster', 'wheelchair', 'earth', 'moon', 'planet', 'movie camera', 'sad face', 'picture', 'stoplight', 'beach ball', 'the letter O', 'car', 'glasses'.

Source: 'A Graphic Assessment of the Creativity of an Eight-Year-Old Girl . . .' from *Torrance Tests of Creative Thinking* by E. P. Torrance, 1966, 2000. Reprinted with permission of Scholastic Testing Service, Inc., Bensenville, IL 60106, USA.

by fewer than five (or ten depending on the test) people out of every 100 who take the test. *Fluency* is the number of different responses. *Flexibility* is generally measured by the number of different categories of responses. For instance, if you listed 20 uses of a brick, but each was to build something, your fluency score might be high, but your flexibility score would be low. Of the three measures, fluency – the number of responses – is the best predictor of divergent thinking, but there is more to real-life creativity than divergent thinking (Plucker *et al.*, 2004).

Teachers are not always the best judges of creativity. In fact, Paul Torrance (1972) reports data from a 12-year follow-up study indicating no relationship between teachers' judgements of their pupils' creative abilities and the actual creativity these pupils revealed in their adult lives. However, there are studies, for example that of John Ruscio and his colleagues in 1998, which set out to identify specific task behaviours that predict observable product creativity and to identify which of those behaviours mediate the well-established link between intrinsic motivation and creativity. Other predictors reflect domain-relevant skills and creativity-relevant processes, lending support to the componential model of creativity.

More generally, a few possible indicators of creativity in your pupils are curiosity, concentration, adaptability, high energy, humour (sometimes bizarre), independence, playfulness, non-conformity, risk taking, attraction to the complex and mysterious, willingness to fantasise and daydream, intolerance for boredom and inventiveness (Sattler, 1992). However, these indicators are also those that might be used for identifying children who are gifted or talented in a particular field or more generally. Indeed, there is some definitional diversity amongst educators when moving freely between talking about giftedness and talking about creativity and you should look out for muddled thinking in this context.

Creativity in the classroom

Today's and tomorrow's complex problems require creative solutions and creativity is important for an individual's psychological, physical, social and career success (Plucker *et al.*, 2004). How can teachers promote creative thinking? All too often, in the crush of day-to-day classroom life, national curricula and prescriptive norms of teaching methods, teachers stifle creative ideas without realising what they are doing. Yet, they are in a unique position to encourage or discourage creativity through their acceptance or rejection of the unusual and imaginative. The Focus on Practice below, adapted from Fleith (2000) and Sattler (1992), describe other possibilities for encouraging creativity.

FOCUS ON PRACTICE

Encouraging creativity

Accept and encourage divergent thinking

Examples
1. During class discussion, ask: 'Can anyone suggest a different way of looking at this question?'
2. Reinforce attempts at unusual solutions to problems, even if the final product is not perfect.
3. Offer choices in topics for projects or modes of presentation (written, oral, visual or graphic, using technology).

Tolerate dissent

Examples
1. Ask pupils to support dissenting opinions.
2. Make sure non-conforming pupils receive an equal share of classroom privileges and rewards.

Encourage pupils to trust their own judgement

Examples
1. When pupils ask questions you think they can answer, rephrase or clarify the questions and direct them back to the pupils.
2. Set assignments with no obvious right or wrong answers or outcomes.

Emphasise that everyone is capable of creativity in some form

Examples
1. Avoid describing the feats of great artists or inventors as if they were superhuman accomplishments.
2. Recognise creative efforts in each pupil's work. Make a separate comment for originality on assignment feedbacks.

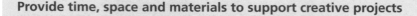

Provide time, space and materials to support creative projects

Examples

1. Collect 'found' materials for collages and creations – buttons, stones, shells, paper, fabric, beads, seeds, drawing tools, clay – try flea markets and friends for donations. Have mirrors and pictures for drawing faces.
2. Make a well-lit space available where children can work on projects, and leave them be.
3. Follow up on memorable occasions (field trips, news events, holidays) with opportunities to draw, write or make music.

Be a stimulus for creative thinking

Examples

1. Use a class brainstorming session whenever possible.
2. Model creative problem solving by suggesting unusual solutions for class problems.
3. Encourage pupils to delay judging a particular suggestion for solving a problem until all the possibilities have been considered.

See www.ncaction.org.uk/creativity/about.htm for more ideas.

Connect and Extend

Research the integrated approach to the principles and actual practice of Steiner Waldorf Education. How is creativity developed in the Steiner Waldorf schools?

Brainstorming

Generating ideas without stopping to evaluate them.

Connect and Extend

For recent research on brainstorming, see Brown, V. R. and Paulus, P. B. (2002), 'Making group brainstorming more effective: Recommendations from an associative memory perspective', *Current Directions in Psychological Science, 11,* pp. 208–212.

Brainstorming

In addition to encouraging creativity through everyday interactions with pupils, teachers can try brainstorming. The basic tenet of brainstorming is to separate the process of creating ideas from the process of evaluating them because evaluation often inhibits fluency and flexibility (Osborn, 1963). Evaluation, discussion and criticism are postponed until all possible suggestions have been made. In this way, one idea inspires others; people do not withhold potentially creative solutions out of fear of criticism. John Baer (1997: 43) gives these rules for brainstorming:

1. Defer judgement.
2. Avoid ownership of ideas. When people feel that an idea is 'theirs', egos sometimes get in the way of creative thinking. They are likely to be more defensive later when ideas are critiqued, and they are less willing to allow their ideas to be modified.
3. Feel free to 'hitchhike' on other ideas. This means that it's okay to borrow elements from ideas already on the table, or to make slight modifications of ideas already suggested.
4. Encourage wild ideas. Impossible, totally unworkable ideas may lead someone to think of other, more possible, more workable ideas. It's easier to take a wildly imaginative bad idea and tone it down to fit the constraints of reality than to take a boring bad idea and make it interesting enough to be worth thinking about.

Individuals as well as groups may benefit from brainstorming. For example, in writing this book we have sometimes found it helpful to list all the different topics that could be covered in a chapter, then leave the list and return to it later to evaluate the ideas. Brainstorming can be a very enjoyable activity as in many senses there is no right or wrong. It's a bit like 'playing' with all the possible ideas, selecting, rejecting and moving ideas around – until the organised whole seems to be more than the sum of its parts. Playing with ideas can be a very creative experience.

Take your time – and play!

Years ago, Sigmund Freud linked creativity and play:

> Might we not say that every child at play behaves like a creative writer, in that he creates a world of his own, or, rather, rearranges the things of his world in a new way which pleases him? The creative writer does the same as the child at play. He creates a world of fantasy which he takes very seriously – that is, which he invests with large amounts of emotion (1959: 143–144).

There is some evidence that early-years children who spend more time in fantasy and pretend play are more creative. In fact, playing before taking a creativity test results in higher scores on the test for the young pupils (Berk, 2001; Bjorklund, 1989). Teachers can encourage pupils of all ages to be more reflective – to take time for ideas to grow, develop and be restructured.

The big C: revolutionary innovation

Ellen Winner (2000) describes the 'big-C creativity' or innovation that establishes a new field or revolutionises an old one. Even child prodigies do not necessarily become adult innovators. Prodigies have mastered well-established domains, such as reading and mathematics, very early, but innovators change the entire domain. 'Individuals who ultimately make creative breakthroughs tend from their earliest days to be explorers, innovators, and tinkerers. Often this adventurousness is interpreted as insubordination, though more fortunate tinkerers receive from teachers or peers some form of encouragement for their experimentation' (Gardner, 1993a: 32–33). Howard Gardner (1993b) helps to clarify the differences between and convergences of creativity and giftedness by placing emphasis on the creators ability to change and not (just!) master. So, what are the pitfalls for parents and teachers in trying to encourage these potential creators? Winner (2000) lists four dangers to avoid:

1. Avoid pushing so hard that the child's intrinsic passion to master a field becomes a craving for extrinsic rewards.
2. Avoid pushing so hard that the child later looks back on a missed childhood.
3. Avoid freezing the child into a safe, technically perfect way of performing that has led to lavish rewards.
4. Be aware of the psychological wounds that can follow when the child who can perform perfectly becomes the forgotten adult who can do nothing more than continue to perform perfectly – without ever creating something new.

Finally, teachers and parents can encourage pupils with outstanding abilities and creative talents to give back to the society that has provided them with the extra support and resources that they needed. Service learning, discussed in Chapter 11, is one opportunity.

We may not all be revolutionary in our creativity, but we all can be experts in one area – learning.

Developing Expert Pupils: Learning Strategies and Study Skills

Connect and Extend

Dahl, T. I. *et al.* (2005), 'Are students' beliefs about knowledge and learning associated with their reported use of learning strategies?' *British Journal of Educational Psychology*, 75(2) (June), pp. 257–273.

This study looks at the beliefs about how thoroughly knowledge is integrated in networks and how rehearsal and organisational strategies are linked to elaboration and critical thinking strategies.

Rote learning

A type of memorisation by repetition to facilitate automatic and accurate recall of, for example, number facts, historical dates or lines from a Shakespeare sonnet.

Learning strategies

General plans for approaching learning tasks.

Learning tactics

Specific techniques for learning, such as using mnemonics or outlining a passage.

Connect and Extend

For suggestions about the effective use of learning strategies see the Companion Website (Web Link 8.3).

Most teachers will tell you that they want their pupils to 'learn how to learn'. Years of research indicate that using good learning strategies helps pupils learn and that these strategies can be taught (Hamman *et al.*, 2000). However, think back on your time in school. Were you taught 'how to learn'? Powerful and sophisticated learning strategies and study skills are seldom taught directly until secondary or higher education, so younger pupils have little practice with these powerful strategies. Furthermore, younger pupils are usually encouraged to use repetition and rote learning. They have extensive practice with these strategies because, unfortunately, some teachers think that memorising is learning (Hofer and Pintrich, 1997). This may explain why many older pupils cling to flash cards and memorising tactics like 'look-cover-write-check' – they don't know what else to do (Willoughby *et al.*, 1999).

As we saw in Chapter 7, the way something is learned in the first place greatly influences how readily we remember and how appropriately we can apply the knowledge later. First, pupils must be *cognitively engaged* in order to learn – they have to focus attention on the relevant or important aspects of the material. Second, they have to *invest effort*, make connections, elaborate, translate, organise and reorganise in order to *think and process deeply* – the greater the practice and processing, the stronger the learning. Finally, pupils must *regulate and monitor* their own learning – keep track of what is making sense and notice when a new approach is needed. The emphasis today is on helping pupils develop effective learning strategies and tactics that *focus attention and effort, process information deeply*, and *monitor understanding*.

Learning strategies and tactics

Learning strategies are ideas for accomplishing learning goals, a kind of overall plan of attack. Learning tactics are the specific techniques that make up the plan (Derry, 1989). Your strategy for learning the material in this chapter might include the tactics of using mnemonics to remember key terms, skimming the chapter to identify the organisation, using a mind map to explore the connections and then writing outline answers to possible essay questions. Your use of strategies and tactics reflects metacognitive knowledge: that is knowing about knowing; learning about learning. Using learning strategies and study skills is associated with better examination success in school and higher student retention rates in higher education (Robbins *et al.*, 2004).

Researchers have identified several important principles of using learning strategies:

1. Pupils must be exposed to a number of *different strategies,* not only general learning strategies but also very specific tactics, such as the graphic strategies described later in this section.

2. Pupils should be taught *conditional knowledge* about when, where and why to use various strategies. Although this may seem obvious, teachers often neglect this step. A strategy is more likely to be maintained and employed if pupils know when, where and why to use it.

3. Pupils may know when and how to use a strategy, but unless they also *develop the desire to employ these skills,* general learning ability will not improve. Several learning strategy programmes include a motivational

training component. In Chapter 10 we look more closely at this important issue of motivation.

4. Pupils should receive *direct instruction in schematic knowledge;* this is often an important component of strategy training. In order to identify main ideas – a critical skill for a number of learning strategies – you must have an appropriate schema for making sense of the material. It will be difficult to summarise a paragraph about ichthyology, for example, if you don't know much about fish.

Table 8.1 summarises several tactics for learning declarative (verbal) knowledge and procedural skills (Derry, 1989). See also http://www.uwe.ac.uk/library/for more ideas to help you with your own study strategies.

Deciding what is important

You can see from the first entry in Table 8.1, that learning begins with focusing attention – deciding what is important. However, distinguishing the main idea from less important information is not always easy. Often pupils focus on the 'seductive details' or the concrete examples, perhaps because they are more interesting (Gardner *et al.*, 1992). You

---

Table 8.1 Examples of learning tactics

	Examples	Use when?
Tactics for learning verbal information	1. Attention focusing	
	• Making outlines, underlining	With easy, structured materials; for good readers
	• Looking for headings and topic sentences	For poorer readers; with more difficult materials
	2. Schema building	
	• Story grammars	With poor text structure, goal is to encourage active comprehension
	• Theory schemas	
	• Networking and mapping	
	3. Idea elaboration	
	• Self-questioning	To understand and remember specific ideas
	• Imagery	
Tactics for learning procedural information	1. Pattern learning	
	• Hypothesising	To learn attributes of concepts
	• Identifying reasons for actions	To match procedures to situations
	2. Self-instruction	
	• Comparing own performance to expert model	To tune, improve complex skills
	3. Practice	
	• Part practice	When few specific aspects of a performance need attention
	• Whole practice	To maintain and improve skill

Source: Based on 'Putting learning strategies to work' by S. Derry, 1989, *Educational Leadership, 47*(5), pp. 5–6.

may have had the experience of remembering a joke or an intriguing aside from a lecture, but not being clear about the larger point the lecturer was trying to make. Finding the central idea is especially difficult if you lack prior knowledge in an area and the amount of new information provided is extensive. Teachers can give pupils practice using signals in texts such as headings, bold words, outlines or other indicators to identify key concepts and main ideas. Teaching pupils how to summarise material can be helpful, too (Lorch *et al.*, 2001).

Summaries

Creating summaries can help pupils learn, but pupils have to be taught how to summarise (Byrnes, 1996; Palincsar and Brown, 1984). Jeanne Ormrod (2004) summarises these suggestions for helping pupils create summaries. For each summary, ask pupils to:

- find or write a *topic sentence* for each paragraph or section;
- identify *big ideas* that cover several specific points;
- find some *supporting information* for each big idea; and
- delete any *redundant information* or unnecessary details.

> **Connect and Extend**
>
> Direct instruction in learning strategies is especially important for pupils with learning disabilities, as described in Chapter 4 (p. 153).

Begin doing summaries of short, easy, well-organised readings. Introduce longer, less organised and more difficult passages gradually. Ask pupils to compare their summaries and discuss what ideas they thought were important and why – what's their evidence? In the next section we explore the idea that 'selection' as one spur to engagement with the subject knowledge, particularly where enormous amounts of information is available on the internet.

Engaging with knowledge – engaging with learning

A fictitious teacher's tale

I set my class of 13-year-olds the task of searching the internet for information to include in their coursework about Stalin's rule of Russia. Most of them are really happy about using search engines and many have access to the internet at home. They came back with an abundance of materials: excellent narratives, copies of archives and other primary sources including maps, photographs, newsreel and newspaper reports. The collection of sources was stunning but their selection was less impressive. My pupils clearly recognised the kind of sources they needed but didn't know how to interpret or synthesise meanings from the miscellany they had accumulated. We then had to set about trying to make sense of it all. It took so long, I couldn't help wondering if the internet had been a hindrance or a boon.

One fundamental idea drawn from the story above is that pupils are not always engaged in powerful cognitive processes whilst engaged in searching, gathering and selection activities. Yet, they should understand in what cognitive processes they are engaged, should recognise when they cease to be engaged with their own learning and should be able to apply strategies to re-engage with the materials. Teaching should recognise the impact of the processes of metacognition on developing understanding and knowledge.

Pupils' understanding of how they are learning

As the definition of learning has shifted from a historical view of a collection of facts to a *gestalt* process of interrelated skills and strategies, teachers' interest has turned to the pupils' active role during learning. Good learners keep track of their understanding of text and take measures (fix-it strategies) to deal with any difficulties that arise. Rather than constructing meaning randomly, good learners use conscious and sub-conscious strategies to derive meaning from text (Vygotsky, 1962; Lye, 1997). As individuals become increasingly aware of the processes involved in understanding text, they begin to exercise a degree of control over their own learning (Levine, 1985; BEA, 1997; Nelson and Narens, 1996). This metacognitive awareness and problem solving approach should be taught to beginning and unskilled learners and reinforced during the learning experience.

Current researchers and writers have attempted to devise models to describe metacognitive problem solving (Nelson and Narens, 1996; Flavell, 1976; Brown and DeLoache, 1978); perhaps the best known is Flavell's in which there are three broad components:

1. Cognitive mindfulness: a learner's perception about his or her own cognitive resources and an evaluation of the learning task to be accomplished.

2. Self-regulatory measures (cognitive scrutinising): a person's ability to actively regulate what they know during learning (comprehension monitoring) and when problem solving.

3. Compensatory strategies: a person's use of fix-it strategies during the actual 'information-in' process.

When applied to our story of non-learning in history, theories of metacognitive problem solving provide useful insights into the process of gaining understanding. In comparison to straightforward comprehension, which might be defined as understanding content, metacognition goes a step further. Brown and DeLoache (1978) contrast this further step as a distinction between knowledge that one has, and the understanding of that knowledge in terms of awareness and appropriate use.

Despite these insights and the powerful arguments of learning theorists, perhaps most notably Vygotsky and Bruner, there remains a deeply entrenched view in schools and universities that regards students as curriculum consumers, in the same way as they are consumers (hopefully) of teacher's textbooks. Such a view can be traced back to the 'Nurnberg funnel' model of education, the shortcomings of which are expertly laid bare by Jack Carroll in his book of this title (Carroll, 1990). The Nurnberg funnel was used to pour learning into the flip-top heads of learners.

There appears to be little evidence that the wholesale introduction of computers into classrooms has changed the predominance of the 'Nurnberg funnel' view of learning, despite general acceptance that learning cannot be delivered and is not a passive process of absorption. Teachers who attempt to use computers and other related technologies as part of historical enquiry should also be teaching pupils the rationale for and facility of metacognition in both explicit ways and by the structuring of learning experiences. Despite teachers' best intentions, we suggest that too much time continues to be used up in assembling text and graphics on screen, the modern equivalent of colouring titles, maps and diagrams, and pupils find it difficult to maintain interest in such low-level tasks.

Our concerns are reflected in criticism from writers such as Terry Haydn (1997), who identified colouring and labelling as a prevalent form of activity in history lessons. In his article 'Why and how we teach history in schools: the case of the Roman soldier' Haydn recalls drawing a Roman soldier and labelling the weapons and armour in Latin, a task which he considers 'low level' and contributing little to his ability to make sense of historical data.

The experience leads him to ask:

Do we have to wrestle with the knowledge in some way for it to be fully assimilated or usable, or is (historical) knowledge for its own sake both necessary and sufficient? Whether they have read it on screen, heard it from the teacher or read it in a book, the question is, do children have to do anything further with the information they have received in order to transform it into 'usable' and 'integrated' knowledge?
(Haydn, 1997: 27)

Have colouring and copying been replaced by Copy and Paste or the 'Encarta syndrome' (Walsh in Haughton, 1999)? The 'Encarta syndrome' is a common pupil response to a request to find out about a given topic. Pupils search the Encarta CD-ROM encyclopaedia and print out many pages of information.

In his article 'Why Gerry likes history now: The power of the word processor', historian and author Ben Walsh (1998) describes the problem of unstructured collection of information. He goes on to suggest ways to combat the problem, for example, asking pupils to find out the five most important things about Lenin. Selecting five things about Lenin may not structure the learning experience sufficiently to answer concerns about a lack of cognitive engagement when pupils gain access to huge amounts of information. However, the way teachers structure their questions does go some way to preventing pupils merely gathering, listing and printing information indiscriminately.

We believe that the way in which a key question is framed (Counsell, 2000) will have a powerful influence on the ways in which pupils use ICT to pursue a historical enquiry. Questions are usually one of three types:

1. **Open questions:** 'What can you find out about castles?' is a very open question that gives enormous scope for pupils to gather huge amounts of information. ICT can make that gathering exercise very fast and can also produce large quantities of beautifully presented 'work'. However, we have already shown that this is not historical 'work' at all. The information has not been worked in any way to provoke and allow learning to take place.

2. **Closed questions:** 'Name the five largest castles in Wales' is a closed question with a correct set of responses. The answers can be found quickly using a database of castles containing a field relevant to the area within the walls (or some similar dimension). Pupils can show their ability to search for and interrogate a database, but not much else.

3. **Structured questions:** Questions requiring the pupils to engage in one or more of the activities contained in our 'Information Processing' box (see Figure 8.8) are much more likely to engage the pupil in their own learning and to structure the experience. For example, we might ask the question 'Why do spiral stairs in castle towers often ascend in an anti-clockwise direction?' We can then plan to use ICT to make the learning focus on making causal connections between observed phenomena.

The first element of the model includes the typical activities of searching and selecting from CD-ROMs and the internet, notes from local fieldwork and whole-class interactive teaching, and responding to original source materials and historical accounts. The third element might include individual presentation, extended writing, creating an artefact, simulation and role-play. We suggest that the use of ICT is able to support all three elements of activity, but it is the middle set of activities, defining 'wrestling with historical knowledge', that are important in engaging pupils with the subject knowledge.

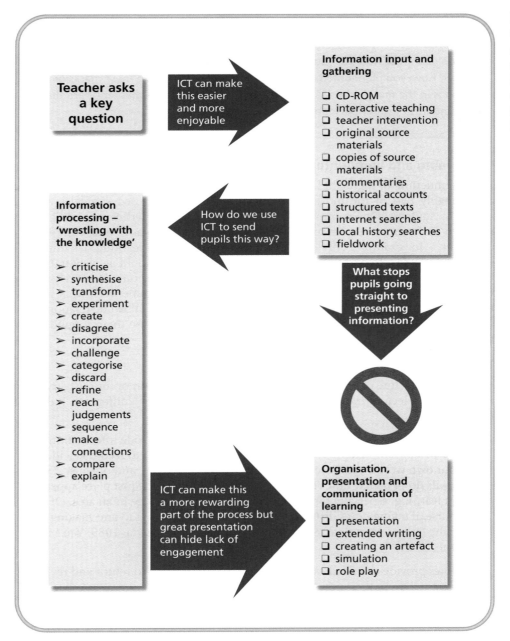

Figure 8.8
Careful questioning encourages learners to engage with the subject knowledge

The kinds of activities we consider as processing activities are to interpret, extrapolate, react, empathise with, criticise, synthesise, transform, experiment, create, incorporate, challenge, categorise, discard, refine, reach judgements, create logical sequences, consider relationships and make comparisons. This is not an exhaustive list but seeks to characterise the kinds of learning activities during which pupils process and 'wrestle' with the knowledge and are key to effective teaching not only in history but many other areas of learning.

Two other study strategies that are based on identifying key ideas are *underlining* texts and *taking notes*.

Processing activities

Types of activities that encourage children to process the information in same way rather than re-present subject knowledge they have found.

> ## STOP AND THINK
>
> How do you make notes as you read? Look back over the past several pages of this chapter. Have you highlighted any words in yellow or pink? Are there marks or drawings in the margins and if so, do the notes pertain to the chapter or are they shopping lists or other personal memos?

Underlining and highlighting

Do you underline or highlight key phrases in textbooks? Underlining and note taking are probably two of the most commonly but ineffectively used strategies among university students. One common problem is that pupils underline or highlight too much. It is far better to be selective. In studies that limit how much pupils can underline – for example, only one sentence per paragraph – learning has improved (Snowman, 1984). In addition to being selective, you also should actively transform the information into your own words as you underline or take notes. Don't rely on the words of the book. Make notes about connections you think of between what you are reading and other things you already know. Draw diagrams to illustrate relationships. Finally, look for organisational patterns in the material and use them to guide your underlining or note taking (Irwin, 1991; Kiewra, 1988).

Taking notes

As you sit in a lecture or seminar, filling your notepad with words or furiously trying to keep up with a lecturer, you may wonder if taking notes makes a difference. It does, if used well:

- Taking notes focuses attention during class and helps encode information so it has a chance of making it to long-term memory. In order to record key ideas in your own words, you have to translate, connect, elaborate and organise. Even if pupils don't review notes before a test, taking them in the first place appears to aid learning, especially for those who lack prior knowledge in an area. Of course, if taking notes distracts you from actually listening to and making sense of the lecture, then note taking may not be effective (Kiewra, 1989; Van Meter *et al.*, 1994).

- Notes provide extended external storage that allows you to return and review. Pupils who use their notes to study tend to perform better on tests, especially if they take many high-quality notes – more is better as long as you are capturing key ideas, concepts and relationships, not just intriguing details (Kiewra, 1985, 1989; Peverly *et al.*, 2003).

- Expert pupils match notes to their anticipated use and modify strategies after tests or assignments; use personal codes to flag material that is unfamiliar or difficult; fill in holes by consulting relevant sources (including other pupils in the class); record information verbatim (word-for-word) only when a verbatim response will be required. In other words, they are *strategic* about taking and using notes (Van Meter *et al.*, 1994).

- To help pupils organise their note taking, some teachers provide matrices or maps. When pupils are first learning to use these maps, you might fill in some of the spaces for them. If you use maps and matrices with your pupils, encourage them to exchange their filled-in maps and explain their thinking to each other.

Visual tools for organising

To use underlining and note taking effectively, you must identify main ideas. In addition, you must understand the organisation of the text or lecture – the connections and relationships among ideas. Some visual strategies have been developed to help pupils with this key element (Van Meter, 2001). There is some evidence that creating graphic organisers such as maps or charts is more effective than outlining in learning from texts (Robinson, 1998; Robinson and Kiewra, 1995). This relates to our earlier point about learning through visual representation in 'Strategies for teaching concepts' (pp. 340–343). 'Mapping' relationships by noting causal connections, comparison/contrast connections and examples improved recall. Pupils should compare 'maps' and discuss the differences. The concept map of concept mapping shown in Figure 8.3 is a hierarchical graphic depiction of the relationships among concepts. There are other ways to visualise organisation, such as Venn diagrams, which show how ideas or concepts overlap, and tree diagrams, which show how ideas branch off each other. Time lines organise information in sequence and are useful in classes such as history or geology.

One exciting possibility is Cmaps, which is Joseph Novak's term for concept maps created on a computer screen. The good news is that this software is available for downloading at no cost. Computer Cmaps can be linked to the internet and pupils in different classrooms and schools all over the world can collaborate on them. The home page of the Cmap tools is shown in Figure 8.9.

Cmaps

Tools for concept mapping developed by the Institute for Human Machine Cognition that are connected to many knowledge maps and other resources on the internet.

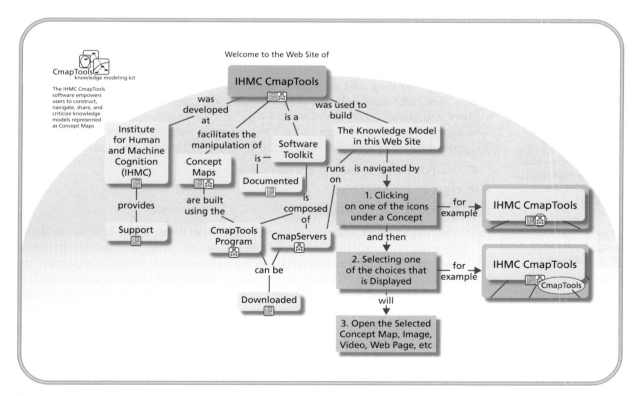

Figure 8.9
The website for the Institute for Human Machine Cognition Cmap tools

At this site, you can download concept mapping tools to construct, share and criticise knowledge on any subject.

Source: Institute for Human Machine Cognition Cmap tools home page http://cmap.ihmc.us/. Reprinted with permission from the IHMC.

Reading strategies

As we saw above, effective learning strategies and tactics should help pupils focus attention, invest effort (elaborate, organise, summarise, connect, translate) so they process information deeply, and monitor their understanding. There are a number of strategies that support these processes in reading. Many use mnemonics to help pupils remember the steps involved. For example, one strategy designed for older pupils is READS:

R *Review* headings and subheadings.

E *Examine* boldface words.

A *Ask,* 'What do I expect to learn?'

D *Do* it – Read!

S *Summarise* in your own words. (Friend and Bursuck, 1996).

A strategy that can be used in reading literature is CAPS:

C Who are the *characters*?

A What is the *aim* of the story?

P What *problem* happens?

S How is the problem *solved*?

Anderson (1995) suggests several reasons why strategies such as CAPS or READS are effective. First, following the steps makes pupils more aware of the organisation of a given chapter. How often have you ignored reading headings entirely and thus missed major clues about the way the information is organised? Next, these steps require pupils to study the chapter in sections instead of trying to learn all the information at once. Creating and answering questions about the material forces pupils to process the information more deeply and with greater elaboration (Doctorow, Wittrock and Marks, 1978; Hamilton, 1985).

Many teachers use a strategy called KWL to guide reading and inquiry in general. This general frame can be used with most age groups. The steps are:

K What do I already *know* about this subject?

W What do I *want* to know?

L At the end of the reading or inquiry, what have I *learned*?

No matter what strategies you use, pupils have to be taught how to use them. Direct teaching, explanation, modelling and practice with feedback are necessary. Direct teaching of learning and reading strategies is especially important for pupils with learning challenges and pupils whose first language is not English. Case study materials linking literacy and science from a national literacy strategy describe how one teacher used modelling and discussion to teach the KWL strategy (see Figure 8.10). After reviewing the steps, the teacher models an example of using KWL to learn about 'The Earth in Space'. The pupils then completed their own KWL frame and then created complex sentences using a planning frame to scaffold their report writing.

READS

A five-step reading strategy: *Review* headings; *Examine* boldface words; *Ask,* 'What do I expect to learn?'; *Do* it – Read; *Summarise* in your own words.

CAPS

A strategy that can be used in reading literature: *Characters, Aim* of story, *Problem, Solution.*

KWL

A strategy to guide reading and inquiry: Before – What do I already *know?* What do I *want* to know? After – What have I *learned?*

Connect and Extend

See Leppänen, U., Aunola, K. and Nurmi, J-E. (2005), 'Beginning readers' reading performance and reading habits', *Journal of Research in Reading, 28*(4) pp. 383–399.

KWL Grid
Name:
Topic: The Earth in Space

What do I know already	What do I want to find out? (Who, where, when, why, what, how?)	What have I learnt? (and where did I find it?)
• Only planet with water, Earth has oxygen, • Earth has life. • 3rd closest to sun, Earth orbits Sun. • Milkyway, Solar System has 9 planets. • Moon orbits Earth, Earth has one moon.	• What is space? • How many planets have water? • What makes the planets orbit the Sun? • How was the Earth formed? • Why do we have day and night? • When will the Earth die? • How far is the moon from Earth? • What is Earth made of? • What is our nearest galaxy? • How far is the Earth from the Sun?	• Earth, Mars had water • Oort cloud of comets left over when Sun + planets formed – Robert Sneddon • because the moon is always orbiting Earth – Jessicar Tessar • 348,294 km • Gas, rock – Robert Sneddon • Milkyway • 158 million km – Jessicar Tessar • 100,000,000,000 km (Galaxy)

Figure 8.10
KWL grid

This is an example of pupils' work using the KWL strategy

Source: DFeS (2001) *Non-fiction Case Studies: Y5 Non-chronological report writing*, p. 6. http://www. standards.dfes.gov.uk/ primary/casestudies/literacy/ 403685/624501/nls_cs_ nfy5report.pdf

FOCUS ON PRACTICE

Developing expert pupils

Make sure pupils have the necessary declarative knowledge (facts, concepts, ideas) to understand new information

Examples
1. Make definitions of key vocabulary available as they study.
2. Encourage pupils to review required facts and concepts before attempting new material.

Make clear what type of test will be given (essay, short answer, multiple choice answers) and structure the material with that in mind

Examples
1. For a test with detailed questions, provide time to practise writing answers to possible questions.
2. For a multiple-choice test, teach mnemonics to help pupils recall definitions of key terms.

Make sure pupils are familiar with the organisation of the materials to be learned

Examples

1. Teach pupils to preview the headings, introductions, topic sentences and summaries of the text.
2. Alert pupils to words and phrases that signal relationships, such as *on the other hand, because, first, second, however, since.*

Teaching explicitly about cognitive skills and how to use them deliberately

Examples

1. Use examples and analogies to relate new material to something pupils care about and understand well, such as sports, hobbies or films.
2. Explain that if one study technique does not work, then try another – the goal is to stay involved, not to use any one particular strategy.

Study the right information in the right way

Examples

1. Be sure pupils know exactly what topics and readings the exam will cover.
2. Make sure pupils spend more time on the important, difficult and unfamiliar material that will be required for the exam or assignment.
3. Encourage pupils to list any parts of the text that give them trouble and to spend more time on these pages.
4. Teach pupils how to process the important information thoroughly by using mnemonics, forming images, creating examples, answering questions, making notes in their own words and elaborating on the text. Dissuade pupils from trying to memorise the author's words – encourage them to use their own.

Monitor comprehension

Examples

1. Teach 'reciprocal questioning' (Chapter 11, pp. 493–496) to check their understanding.
2. Suggest that if reading speed slows down, pupils should decide if the information in the passage is important. If it is, they should note the problem so they can re-read or get help to understand. If it is not important, they should ignore it.

For ideas on becoming an expert university student, see Cottrell, S. (1999), *The Study Skills Handbook,* Basingstoke: Macmillan; and Holmes, A. (2005). *Pass Your Exams: Study Skills for Success.* Oxford: Infinite Ideas.

Source: Adapted extract from Armbruster, B. B. and Anderson, T. H. (1981) Research Synthesis on Study Skills, *Educational Leadership,* **39**(2), p. 154. Reprinted with permission. The Association for Supervision and Curriculum Development is a worldwide community of educators advocating sound policies and sharing best practices to achieve the success of each learner. To learn more, visit ASCD at www.ascd.org.

Applying learning strategies

Assuming pupils have developed a repertoire of powerful learning strategies, exemplified in the Focus on Practice above, how will they use them? Several conditions must be met (Ormrod, 2004). First, of course, the learning task must be appropriate. With appropriate tasks, memorising will be rewarded and the best strategies involve distributed practice and perhaps mnemonics (described in Chapter 7). Why would pupils use more complex learning strategies when the task set by the teacher is to 'learn and return' the exact words of the text or lesson? Of course, we hope that there are few of these kinds of tasks in contemporary teaching. So if the task is to understand, not simply to memorise, what else is necessary?

Connect and Extend

The *Focus on Practice: Developing expert pupils* involves the metacognitive abilities and executive control processes discussed in Chapter 7. See pp. 307–309 for a discussion of declarative, procedural and conditional knowledge.

Valuing learning

The second condition for pupils using sophisticated strategies is that they must care about learning and understanding and that goals are set that can be reached using effective strategies (Zimmerman and Schunk, 2001). Many of our colleagues in university departments complain that our students in education and psychology classes are focused on passing the assignments related to particular courses and often fail to show any enthusiasm for wider reading or any activities that are not ostensibly and obviously related to passing the course. Even the best of students tend to a performance goal rather than a learning goal (learning for learning's sake) – indeed, current achievement goal models assume that individuals with a learning goal use deeper strategies than those with a performance goal (Escribe and Huet, 2005). By reading this text you obviously show yourself to be one of the 'best of students'! So are you studying this text to learn about making classrooms better arenas of learning or to pass the course? Such motives are not mutually exclusive.

Effort and efficacy

Our pupils are also concerned about effort. The third condition for applying learning strategies is that pupils must believe the effort and investment required to apply the strategies are *reasonable,* given the likely return. Of course, pupils must believe that they are capable of using the strategies; that is, they must have self-efficacy for using the strategies to learn the material in question (Seegers *et al.,* 2002). This is related to another condition. Pupils must have a base of knowledge and/or experience in the area. No learning strategies will help pupils accomplish tasks that are completely beyond their current understandings.

Connect and Extend

See the Winter 2004 special issue of the *Educational Psychologist* on 'Personal Epistemology: Paradigmatic Approaches to Understanding Students' Beliefs about Knowledge and Knowing' *39*(1).

Epistemological beliefs

Finally, what pupils believe about knowledge and learning (their epistemological beliefs) will influence the kinds of strategies that they use.

Using questions like those in the Stop and Think below, researchers have identified several dimensions of epistemological beliefs (Chan and Sachs, 2001; Schommer, 1997; Schraw and Olafson, 2002).

For example:

- **Structure of knowledge:** Is knowledge in a field a simple set of facts or a complex structure of concepts and relationships?

- **Stability/certainty of knowledge:** Is knowledge fixed or evolving over time?

- **Ability to learn:** Is the ability to learn fixed (based on innate ability) or changeable?

Epistemological beliefs

Beliefs about the structure, stability and certainty of knowledge and how knowledge is best learned.

STOP AND THINK

How would you answer these questions taken from Chan and Sachs (2001)?

1. The most important thing in learning maths is to: (a) remember what the teacher has taught you, (b) practise lots of problems, (c) understand the problems you work on.
2. The most important thing you can do when trying to do science is (a) faithfully do the work the teacher tells you, (b) try to see how the explanation makes sense, (c) try to remember everything you are supposed to know.
3. If you wanted to know everything there is about something, say animals, how long would you have to study it? (a) less than a year if you study hard, (b) about one or two years, (c) forever.
4. As you learn more and more about something (a) the questions get more and more complex, (b) the questions get easier and easier, (c) the questions all get answered.

- **Speed of learning:** Can we gain knowledge quickly or does it take time to develop knowledge?

- **Nature of learning:** Does learning mean memorising facts passed down from or developing your own integrated understandings?

Pupils' beliefs about knowing and learning affect their use of learning strategies. For example, if you believe that knowledge should be gained quickly, you are likely to try one or two quick strategies (read the text once, spend two minutes trying to solve the word problem) and then stop. If you believe that learning means developing integrated understandings, you will process the material more deeply, connect to existing knowledge, create your own examples, or draw diagrams, and generally elaborate the information to make it your own (Hofer and Pintrich, 1997; Kardash and Howell, 2000). In one study, nine- and 11-year-olds who believed that learning is understanding, processed science texts more deeply than pupils who believed that learning is reproducing facts (Chan and Sachs, 2001). The earlier questions about learning above were used in that study to assess the pupils' beliefs. The answers associated with a belief in complex, evolving, knowledge that takes time to understand and grows from active learning are 1c, 2b, 3c and 4a.

Here is an important question: What is the purpose of all that studying if you never use the knowledge – if you never transfer it to new situations?

Teaching for Transfer

STOP AND THINK

Think back for a moment to one of your school subjects that you dropped at 14 or 16. Imagine the teacher, the room and the textbook you used. Now remember what you actually learned in class.

Like most of us, you may remember that you learned things like formulas and laws (such as Boyle's Law), but by now you may not be quite sure exactly what you learned. Were those hours wasted? These questions are about the transfer of learning and we turn to that important topic next. Let's begin with a definition of transfer.

Whenever something previously learned influences current learning or when solving an earlier problem affects how you solve a new problem, transfer has occurred (Mayer and Wittrock, 1996). Erik De Corte calls transfer 'the productive use of cognitive tools and motivations' (2003: 142). This meaning of transfer emphasises doing something new (something productive) not just reproducing a previous application of the tools. If pupils learn a mathematical principle in one lesson and use it to solve a physics problem days or weeks later in another lesson, then transfer has taken place. However, the effect of past learning on present learning is not always positive. Functional fixedness and response set (described earlier in this chapter; pp. 359–360) are examples of negative transfer because they are attempts to apply familiar but inappropriate strategies to a new situation.

The many views of transfer

It is because transfer of learning is considered so important that is has been a focus of research in educational psychology for over 100 years. After all, the productive use of knowledge, skills and motivations across a lifetime is a fundamental goal of education (De Corte, 2003). Early work focused on specific transfer of skills and the general transfer of mental discipline gained from studying rigorous subjects such as Latin or mathematics. But in 1924, E. L. Thorndike demonstrated that there was no mental discipline benefit from learning Latin. Learning Latin just helped you learn more Latin. So, thanks in part to Thorndike, you were probably not required to learn Latin at school! Other researchers looked at positive and negative transfer, such as the appropriate and inappropriate uses of heuristics in solving problems (e.g. analogical thinking which limits a search to situations that have something in common with the current problem).

More recently, researchers distinguish between the automatic, direct use of skills such as reading or writing in everyday applications versus the extraordinary transfer of knowledge and strategies to arrive at innovative solutions to complex problems (Tsai and Tsai, 2005; Leat and Lin, 2003; Salomon and Perkins, 1989).

Gabriel Salomon and David Perkins (1989) describe these two kinds of transfer, termed low-road and high-road transfer. Low-road transfer 'involves the spontaneous, automatic transfer of highly practised skills, with little need for reflective thinking' (1989: 118). The key to low-road transfer is practising a skill often, in a variety of situations, until your performance becomes automatic. So if you worked one summer for a temporary secretarial service and were sent to many different offices to work on all kinds of computers, by the end of the summer you probably would be able to handle most machines easily. Your practice with many machines would let you transfer your skill automatically to a new situation. Bransford and Schwartz (1999) refer to this kind of transfer as direct-application transfer.

High-road transfer, on the other hand, involves consciously applying abstract knowledge or strategies learned in one situation to a different situation. This can happen in one of two ways. First, you may learn a principle or a strategy, intending to use it in the future – *forward-reaching* transfer. For example, if you plan to apply what you learn in human biology to later work in a life-drawing course, you may search for principles about human proportions, muscle definition, and so on. Second, when you are faced with a problem, you may look back on what you have learned in other situations

Transfer

Influence of previously learned material on new material.

Low-road transfer

Spontaneous and automatic transfer of highly practised skills.

High-road transfer

Application of abstract knowledge learned in one situation to a different situation.

Table 8.2 Kinds of transfer

	Low-road transfer (direct-application)	High-road transfer (preparation for future learning)
Definition	Automatic transfer of highly practised skill	Conscious application of abstract knowledge to a new situation Productive use of cognitive tools and motivations
Key conditions	Extensive practice Variety of settings and conditions Overlearning to automaticity	Mindful focus on abstracting a principle, main idea or procedure that can be used in many situations Learning in powerful teaching-learning environments
Examples	Driving many different cars Finding your gate in an airport	Applying KWL or READS strategies Applying procedures from maths in designing a page layout for the school newspaper

to help you in this new one – *backward-reaching* transfer. Analogical thinking is an example of this kind of transfer. You search for other related situations that might provide clues to the current problem. Bransford and Schwartz (1999) consider this kind of high-road transfer to be *preparation for future learning*.

The key to high-road transfer is *mindful abstraction*, or the deliberate identification of a principle, main idea, strategy or procedure that is not tied to one specific problem or situation, but could apply to many. Such an abstraction becomes part of your metacognitive knowledge, available to guide future learning and problem solving. Bransford and Schwartz (1999) add another key – a resource-rich environment that supports productive, appropriate transfer. Table 8.2 summarises the types of transfer.

Teaching for positive transfer

Years of research and experience show that pupils will master new knowledge, problem-solving procedures and learning strategies, but usually they will not use them unless prompted or guided. For example, studies of real-world mathematics show that people do not always apply maths procedures learned in school to solve practical problems in their homes or when shopping (Bonotto and Basso, 2001). This happens because learning is situated; that is, learning happens in specific situations. We learn solutions to particular problems, not general, all-purpose solutions that can fit any problem. We may not realise that the knowledge is relevant when we encounter a problem that seems different, at least on the surface, because we believe knowledge is learned as a tool to solve particular problems (Volman and Ten Dam, 2000; Bridges, 1993; Singley and Anderson, 1989). How can you make sure your pupils will use what they learn, even when situations change?

What is worth learning?

First, you must answer the question 'What is worth learning?' The learning of basic skills such as reading, writing, computing, cooperating and speaking will definitely transfer to other situations, because these skills are necessary for later work both in and out of school: writing job applications, reading novels, paying bills, working in a team, locating and evaluating healthcare services. All later learning depends on positive transfer of basics skills to new situations.

Teachers must also be aware of what the future is likely to hold for their pupils, both as a group and as individuals. What will society require of them as adults? As a child growing up in the 1950s and 1960s, I studied nothing about computers, yet now I spend hours at my desktop PC or my notebook. Computer programming and word processing were not part of my school curriculum, but I learned to use a slide rule. Now, calculators and computers have made this skill obsolete. My teachers encouraged me to take advanced level examinations in maths and geography instead of typing or graphic design. Maths and geography were great subjects, but I struggle with typing and graphics every day at my computer – so who knew best? Undoubtedly, changes as extreme and unpredictable as these await the pupils you will teach. For this reason, the general transfer of principles, attitudes, learning strategies, motivations and problem solving will be just as important for your pupils as the specific transfer of basic skills.

How can teachers help?

For basic skills, greater transfer can also be ensured by over-learning, practising a skill past the point of mastery. Many of the basic facts pupils learn in primary school, such as the multiplication tables, are traditionally over-learned. Over-learning helps pupils retrieve the information quickly and automatically when it is needed. For higher-level transfer, pupils must first learn and understand. Pupils will be more likely to transfer knowledge to new situations if they have been actively involved in the learning process. They must be encouraged to form abstractions that they will apply later. Erik De Corte (2003) believes that teachers support transfer, the productive use of cognitive tools and motivations, when they create powerful teaching-learning environments using these design principles:

Overlearning

Practising a skill past the point of mastery.

- The environments should support constructive learning processes in all pupils.

- The environments should encourage the development of pupil self-regulation, so that teachers gradually give over more and more responsibilities to the pupils.

- Learning should involve interaction and collaboration.

- Learners should deal with problems that have personal meaning for them, problems like they will face in the future.

- The classroom culture should encourage pupils to become aware of and develop their cognitive and motivational processes. In order to be productive users of these tools, pupils must know about and value them.

Connect and Extend

'The greatest enemy of understanding is coverage. As long as you are determined to cover everything, you actually ensure that most kids are not going to understand.' Read more of what Howard Gardner says in Brandt, R. (1993), 'On teaching for understanding: A conversation with Howard Gardner', *Educational Leadership, 50*(7), p. 7.

There is one last kind of transfer that is especially important for pupils – the transfer of the learning strategies we encountered in the previous section. Learning strategies and tactics are meant to be applied across a wide range of situations, but this often does not happen, as you will see below.

Stages of transfer for strategies

Sometimes learners simply don't understand that a particular strategy applies in new situations or they don't know how to adapt it to fit. As we saw above, they may think the strategy takes too much time (Campbell and Austin, 2002).

Gary Phye (1992, 2001; Phye and Sanders, 1994) suggests we think of the transfer of learning strategies as a tool to be used in a 'mindful' way to solve academic problems. He describes three stages in developing strategic transfer. In the *acquisition phase,* pupils should not only receive instruction about a strategy and how to use it, but they should also rehearse the strategy and practise being aware of when and how they are using it. In the *retention phase,* more practice with feedback helps pupils hone their strategy use. In the *transfer phase,* the teacher should provide new problems that can be solved with the same strategy, even though the problems appear different on the surface. To enhance motivation, point out to pupils how using the strategy will help them solve many problems and accomplish different tasks. These steps help build both procedural and conditional knowledge – how to use the strategy as well as when and why.

This chapter has covered quite a bit of territory, partly because the cognitive perspective has so many implications for teaching. Although they are varied, you can see that most of the cognitive ideas for teaching concepts, creative problem-solving skills

FOCUS ON PRACTICE

Promoting transfer

Keep families informed about their child's curriculum so they can support learning

Examples

1. At the beginning of a learning unit or major project, send a letter home summarising the key learning objectives, the titles of a few of the major assignments, and some common problems pupils have in learning the material for that unit.
2. Ask parents for suggestions about how their child's home interests could be connected to the curriculum topics.
3. Invite parents to school for an evening of 'learning about learning'. Have the pupils teach their family members one of the strategies they have learned in school.

Give families ideas for how they might encourage their children to practise, extend or apply learning from school

Examples

1. To extend writing, ask parents to encourage their children to write letters or to e-mail companies or civic organisations asking for information or free products.

Provide an outline letter frame for structure and ideas and include addresses of companies that provide free samples or information.

2. Ask family members to include their children in some projects that require measurement, halving or doubling recipes or estimating costs.

3. Suggest that pupils work with grandparents to create a family memory book. Combine historical research and writing.

Show connections between learning in school and life outside school

Examples

1. Ask families to talk about and show how they use the skills their children are learning in their jobs, hobbies or community involvement projects.

2. Ask family members to come to class to demonstrate how they use reading, writing, science, maths or other knowledge in their work.

Make families partners in practising learning strategies

Examples

1. Focus on one learning tactic at a time – ask families to remind their children to use a particular tactic with homework that week.

2. Develop a lending library of books and videotapes/dvds to teach families about learning strategies.

For more information on promoting transfer see http://www.nottingham.ac.uk/ education/centres/cdell/LearnersPaper.doc

and learning strategies emphasise the role of the pupil's prior knowledge and the need for active, mindful learning.

As you have seen throughout this chapter, in the beginning, as pupils learn problem solving or try to transfer cognitive tools to new situations, there is a tendency to focus on surface features. For all novices, their challenge is to grasp the abstractions: underlying principles, structures, strategies or big ideas. It is those larger ideas that lead to understanding and serve as a foundation for future learning (Chen and Mo, 2004).

Second, with all pupils there is a positive relationship between using learning strategies and academic gains in pupil performance in public examinations and student retention at university (Robbins, Le and Lauver, 2005). Some pupils will learn productive strategies on their own, but all pupils can benefit from direct teaching, modelling and practice of learning strategies and study skills. This is one important way to prepare all your pupils for their futures. Newly mastered concepts, principles and strategies must be applied in a wide variety of situations and problems (Chen and Mo, 2004). Positive transfer is encouraged when skills are practised under authentic conditions, similar to those that will exist when the skills are needed later. Pupils can learn to write by corresponding with e-mail pen pals in other countries. They can learn historical research methods by researching their own families. Some of these applications should involve complex, ill-defined, unstructured problems, because many of the problems to be faced in later life, both in school and out, will not come to pupils complete with instructions.

SUMMARY TABLE

Learning and Teaching about Concepts (pp. 338–349)

Distinguish between prototypes and exemplars

Concepts are categories used to group similar events, ideas, people or objects. A prototype is the best representative of its category. For instance, the best representative of the 'birds' category for many people might be a robin or a sparrow. Exemplars are our actual memories of specific birds and so on that we use to compare with an item in question to see if that item belongs in the same category as our exemplar. We probably learn concepts from prototypes or exemplars of the category, understand in terms of our schematic knowledge, and then refine concepts through our additional experience of relevant and irrelevant features.

What are the four elements needed in concept teaching?

Lessons about concepts include four basic components: concept examples (along with non-examples), relevant and irrelevant attributes, name and definition. The concept attainment model is one approach to teaching concepts that asks pupils to form hypotheses about why particular examples are members of a category and what that category (concept) might be.

What are the key characteristics of Bruner's discovery learning?

In discovery learning, the teacher presents examples and the pupils work with the examples until they discover the interrelationships – the subject's structure. Bruner believes that classroom learning should take place through inductive reasoning, that is, by using specific examples to formulate a general principle.

What are the stages of Ausubel's expository teaching?

Ausubel believes that learning should progress deductively: from the general to the specific, or from the rule or principle to examples. After presenting an advance organiser, the next step in a lesson using Ausubel's approach is to present content in terms of basic similarities and differences, using specific examples. Finally, when all the material has been presented, ask pupils to discuss how the examples can be used to expand on the original advance organiser.

How can you teach concepts through analogies?

By identifying known information that relates to a new concept, teachers and pupils can map the analogies between the known and the new, then summarise an understanding of the new concept by explaining the similarities and differences between the known and the new concepts.

Problem Solving (pp. 349–365)

What are the steps in the general problem-solving process?

Problem solving is both general and domain-specific. The five stages of problem solving are contained in the acronym IDEAL: *I*dentify problems and opportunities; *D*efine goals and represent the problem; *E*xplore possible strategies; *A*nticipate outcomes and *A*ct; *L*ook back and *L*earn.

Why is the representation stage of problem solving so important?

To represent the problem accurately, you must understand both the whole problem and its discrete elements. Schema training may improve this ability. The problem-solving process follows entirely different paths, depending on what representation and goal are chosen. If your representation of the problem suggests an immediate solution, the task is done; the new problem is recognised as a 'disguised' version of an old problem with a clear solution. But if there is no existing way of solving the problem or if the activated schema fails, then pupils must search for a solution. The application of algorithms and heuristics – such as means-ends analysis, analogical thinking, working backwards and verbalisation – may help pupils solve problems.

Describe factors that can interfere with problem solving

Factors that hinder problem solving include functional fixedness or rigidity (response set). These disallow the flexibility needed to represent problems accurately and to have insight into solutions. As we make decisions and judgements, we may overlook important information because we base judgements on what seems representative of a category (representativeness heuristic) or what is available in memory (availability heuristic). We then pay attention only to information that confirms our choices (confirmation bias) so that we hold onto beliefs, even in the face of contradictory evidence (belief perseverance).

What are the differences between expert and novice knowledge in a given area?

Expert problem solvers have a rich store of declarative, procedural and conditional knowledge. They organise this knowledge around general principles or patterns that apply to large classes of problems. They work faster, remember relevant information and monitor their progress better than novices.

How do misconceptions interfere with learning?

If the pupils' intuitive model includes misconceptions and inaccuracies, then the pupils are likely to develop inadequate or misleading representations of a problem. In order to learn new information and solve problems, pupils must sometimes 'unlearn' commonsense ideas.

Creativity and Creative Problem Solving (pp. 365–371)

What are some myths about creativity?

These four statements are completely or partly wrong. Creativity is determined at birth. Creativity comes with negative personality traits. Creative people are disorganised hippie types. Working in a group enhances creativity. The facts are: creativity can be developed; a few but not all creative people are nonconforming or have emotional problems; many creative people are focused, organised and part of the mainstream; finally, groups can limit as well as enhance creativity.

What is creativity and how is it assessed?

Creativity is a process that involves independently restructuring problems to see things in new, imaginative ways. Creativity is difficult to measure, but tests of divergent thinking can assess originality, fluency and flexibility. Originality is usually determined statistically. To be original, a response must be given by fewer than five (or ten) people out of every 100 who take the test. Fluency is the number of different responses. The number of different categories of responses measures flexibility. Teachers can encourage creativity by providing opportunities for play, using brainstorming techniques and accepting divergent ideas.

What can teachers do to support creativity in the classroom?

Teachers can encourage creativity in their interactions with pupils by accepting unusual, imaginative answers, modelling divergent thinking, using brainstorming and tolerating dissent.

Developing Expert Pupils: Learning Strategies and Study Skills (pp. 372–384)

Distinguish between learning strategies and tactics

Learning strategies are ideas for accomplishing learning goals, a kind of overall plan of attack. Learning tactics are the specific techniques that make up the plan. A strategy for learning might include several tactics such as mnemonics to remember key terms, skimming to identify the organisation, and then writing answers to possible essay questions. Use of strategies and tactics reflects metacognitive knowledge.

What key functions do learning strategies play?

Learning strategies help pupils *become cognitively engaged* – focus attention on the relevant or important aspects of the material. Second, they encourage pupils to *invest effort,* make connections, elaborate, translate, organise and reorganise in order to *think and process deeply* – the greater the practice and processing, the stronger the learning. Finally, strategies help pupils *regulate and monitor* their own learning – keep track of what is making sense and notice when a new approach is needed.

Describe some procedures for developing learning strategies

Expose pupils to a number of different strategies, not only general learning strategies but also very specific tactics, such as the graphic strategies. Teach conditional knowledge about when, where and why to use various strategies. Develop motivation to use the strategies and tactics by showing pupils how their learning and performance can be improved. Provide direct instruction in content knowledge needed to use the strategies.

When will pupils apply learning strategies?

If they have appropriate strategies, pupils will apply them if they are faced with a task that requires good strategies, value doing well on that task, think the effort to apply the strategies will be worthwhile, and believe that they can succeed using the strategies. Also, to apply deep processing strategies, pupils must assume that knowledge is complex and takes time to learn and that learning requires their own active efforts.

Teaching for Transfer (pp. 384–389)

What is transfer?

Transfer occurs when a rule, fact, or skill learned in one situation is applied in another situation; for example, applying rules of punctuation to write a job application letter. Transfer also involves applying to new problems the principles learned in other, often dissimilar situations.

Distinguish between low-road and high-road transfer

Transfer involving spontaneity and automaticity in familiar situations has been called *low-road transfer. High-road transfer* involves reflection and conscious application of abstract knowledge to new situations. Learning environments should support active constructive learning, self-regulation, collaboration and awareness of cognitive tools and motivational processes. In addition, pupils should deal with problems that have meaning in their lives. Teachers can help pupils transfer learning strategies by teaching strategies directly, providing practice with feedback and then expanding the application of the strategies to new and unfamiliar situations.

Glossary

Advance organiser: Statement of inclusive concepts to introduce and sum up material that follows.

Algorithm: Step-by-step procedure for solving a problem; a prescription for solutions.

Analogical instruction: Teaching new concepts by making connections (analogies) with information that the pupil already understands.

Analogical thinking: Heuristic in which one limits the search for solutions to situations that are similar to the one at hand.

Availability heuristic: Judging the likelihood of an event based on what is available in your memory, assuming those easily remembered events are common.

Belief perseverance: The tendency to hold on to beliefs, even in the face of contradictory evidence.

Brainstorming: Generating ideas without stopping to evaluate them.

CAPS: A strategy that can be used in reading literature: *Characters, Aim* of story, *Problem, Solution.*

Cmaps: Tools for concept mapping developed by the Institute for Human Machine Cognition that are connected to many knowledge maps and other resources on the internet.

Concept: A general category of ideas, objects, people or experiences whose members share certain properties.

Concept mapping: Pupil's diagram of his or her understanding of a concept.

Confirmation bias: Seeking information that confirms our choices and beliefs, while disconfirming evidence.

Convergent thinking: Narrowing possibilities to a single answer.

Creativity: Imaginative, original thinking or problem solving.

Deductive reasoning: Drawing conclusions by applying rules or principles; logically moving from a general rule or principle to a specific solution.

Defining attributes: Distinctive features shared by members of a category.

Discovery learning: Bruner's approach, in which pupils work on their own to discover basic principles.

Divergent thinking: Coming up with many possible solutions.

Epistemological beliefs: Beliefs about the structure, stability and certainty of knowledge and how knowledge is best learned.

Exemplar: A specific example of a given category that is used to classify an item.

Expository teaching: Ausubel's method – teachers present material in complete, organised form, moving from broadest to more specific concepts.

Functional fixedness: Inability to use objects or tools in a new way.

Guided discovery: An adaptation of discovery learning, in which the teacher provides some direction.

Heuristic: General strategy used in attempting to solve problems.

High-road transfer: Application of abstract knowledge learned in one situation to a different situation.

Inductive reasoning: Formulating general principles based on knowledge of examples and details.

Insight: Sudden realisation of a solution.

Intuitive thinking: Making imaginative leaps to correct perceptions or workable solutions.

KWL: A strategy to guide reading and inquiry: Before – What do I already *know?* What do I *want* to know? After – What have I *learned?*

Learning strategies: General plans for approaching learning tasks.

Learning tactics: Specific techniques for learning, such as using mnemonics or outlining a passage.

Learning zone: A part of a lesson or activity where a pupil is open to new learning. It is usually signalled by the pupil acknowledging that he or she doesn't know or understand something.

Low-road transfer: Spontaneous and automatic transfer of highly practised skills.

Meaningful verbal learning: Focused and organised relationships among ideas and verbal information.

Means-ends analysis: Heuristic in which a goal is divided into subgoals.

Overgeneralisation: Inclusion of non-members in a category; overextending a concept.

Overlearning: Practising a skill past the point of mastery.

Problem: Any situation in which you are trying to reach some goal and must find a means to do so.

Problem solving: Creating new solutions for problems.

Processing activities: Types of activities that encourage children to process the information in same way rather than re-present subject knowledge they have found.

Prototype: Best representative of a category.

READS: A five-step reading strategy: *Review* headings; *Examine* boldface words; *Ask,* 'What do I expect to learn?'; *Do* it – Read; *Summarise* in your own words.

Representativeness heuristic: Judging the likelihood of an event based on how well the events match your prototypes – what you think is representative of the category.

Response set: Rigidity; tendency to respond in the most familiar way.

Restructuring: Conceiving of a problem in a new or different way.

Rote learning: A type of memorisation by repetition to facilitate automatic and accurate recall of, for example, number facts, historical dates or lines from a Shakespeare sonnet.

Schema-driven problem solving: Recognising a problem as a 'disguised' version of an old problem for which one already has a solution.

Transfer: Influence of previously learned material on new material.

Undergeneralisation: Exclusion of some true members from a category; limiting a concept.

Verbalisation: Putting your problem-solving plan and its logic into words.

Working-backward strategy: Heuristic in which one starts with the goal and moves backward to solve the problem.

CHECK YOUR LEARNING!   WEB

In the Classroom: What Would They Do?

You may remember that a teacher was concerned because pupils will need good study skills and strategies as they progress through their education and there was so much curriculum material to cover that many of the pupils never finished anything. They were just drowning in the amount of work. What study skills do pupils need for different subjects or age groups? What could a teacher do to teach these skills, while still covering all the curriculum material needed for yearly assessments?

Here is how some practising teachers responded to these questions:

Jackie Day, special needs co-ordinator, The Ridge Primary School, Yate

Before specific study skills can be taught, children must have acquired mastery of the basics. If a child is unable to read fluently, write confidently or use basic mathematical operations, he will be unable to tackle independent study. Therefore, all young children need access to structured multi-sensory programmes. The Rose Report (2006) recommends the use of synthetic phonics for literacy. Many children need a similar approach to learn number concepts and facts. Also, a growing number of children are being identified with speech and language difficulties. These problems will impact their ability to follow instructions or understand what they have read, and will need addressing. Having secured the basic skills, older children need explicit teaching in how to approach different tasks. Many children fail to monitor their own reading, and 'skip over' words they cannot read or do not understand. 'Getting the gist' of a text is a skill which needs teaching as much as scanning text to find answers to questions. Further skills to be taught include mind mapping, research skills, notetaking, time management and structuring written work. All these must be incorporated whilst covering the curriculum so that the skills become automatic, and children take control of their own learning.

Lisbeth Jonsson, primary school teacher, Sotenäs Kompetenscentrum, Kungshamn, Sweden

I think, that the problem lies in the reading skill. Many children nowadays seem to watch TV and play computer games instead of reading. Anyway, these children must be taught to concentrate on texts by making notes on the context. This must be done in the early school years. Once they have fallen behind there's too much to catch up with. A good way of learning (in the beginning) is to let them watch films and retell the stories in as few words as possible. Questions on texts is good exercise and I myself exercise this every week with my special pupils (i.e. the ones who can't attend regular education). Another exercise is mind mapping. I would suggest extra lessons for these pupils and not only concerning study skills.

Lee Card, primary school teacher, Bosbury Church of England Primary School, Herefordshire

If the children are not completing anything then the work is not being given adequate time and the teacher is at fault. How can we possibly expect children to develop 'study skills' and enjoy learning when they never get an end product? In not allowing time for completion and achievement, any attempt to build upon study skills is futile, as the learners are unmotivated and unwilling to start a losing battle. The first step, therefore, is to structure the curriculum into

blocks of meaningful learning. There is nothing new about cross-curricular or themed work and the New Primary Framework lends itself to this, even compacting and connecting units together that make sense (Authors and Letters – Year 3, for example). If it takes an extra few days to complete re-drafting that brilliant letter into best, or typing it up on the PC to look professional, DO IT!! It would be naïve to suggest that study skills just 'happen' as a result of administering manageable tasks or allowing children to finish a bit of work. What that will do, however, is give them the motivation to want to complete the next task, making the teaching of such skills rather more achievable.

Tessa Herbert, English teacher, John Masefield High School, Ledbury

In the secondary sector it is a good investment to dedicate time to study skills in Year 7, to equip them for the styles of work they will face. Within the secondary curriculum, units should be clearly structured in a logical way so that pupils are supported throughout. Tasks within each unit should be discrete and build to the bigger picture. Within the English curriculum pupils need to read actively (questioning, predicting, understanding inference); learn to read for information; synthesise; and, when writing, make the purpose and audience clear. These skills can be built into all units with guided reading, modelled writing and frameworks to support the lower ability pupils.

Lizzie Meadows, deputy head teacher, The Park Primary School, Kingswood, Bristol

As an immediate response to the study skills issue I would suspend the curriculum for a day or two and concentrate solely on activities that directly taught and reinforced a range of study skills. Depending on the age of the children a range of activities could be used. For example, if there are problems organising thoughts then using a mind mapping technique and associated software may be useful. It may also be helpful to model how to organise a longer project and practise looking and picking information that is relevant to the question. I would also reinforce these skills at every possible opportunity.

In the longer term the school maybe needs to look at slimming some of the curriculum content in favour of explicitly taught study skills or dedicating significant periods of time to learning to learn.

Overview

For the past three chapters, we have analysed different aspects of learning. We considered behavioural and information processing explanations of what and how people learn. We have examined complex cognitive processes such as concept learning and problem solving. These explanations of learning focus on the individual and what is happening in his or her 'head'. Recent perspectives have called attention to two other aspects of learning that are critical – social and cultural factors. In this chapter, we look at the role of other people and the cultural context in learning.

Two general theoretical frames include social and cultural factors as major elements. The first, social cognitive theory, has its roots in Albert Bandura's early social learning theories of observational learning and vicarious reinforcement. You will remember reading about these early versions in Chapter 6. The second, sociocultural constructivist theories, have roots in cognitive perspectives, but have moved well beyond these early explanations. Rather than debating the merits of each approach, we will consider the contributions of these different models of instruction, grounded in different theories of learning.

Don't feel that you must choose the 'best' approach – there is no such thing. Even though theorists argue about which model is best, those applying the approaches successfully select from all the approaches as appropriate.

By the time you have completed this chapter, you should be able to answer the following questions:

- **What is reciprocal determinism and what role does it play in social cognitive theory?**
- **What is self-efficacy, and how does it affect learning in school?**
- **What is a teacher's sense of efficacy?**
- **How can teachers support the development of self-efficacy and self-regulated learning?**
- **What are three constructivist perspectives on learning?**
- **How might enquiry, problem-based learning, instructional conversations and cognitive apprenticeships be incorporated within the learning situation?**
- **What dilemmas do constructivist teachers face?**

In the Classroom

Simon, a recently qualified teacher, begins working in a secondary school teaching English. In order to get a sense of the interests of the class he asks them to write a 'review' of the last book they read, as if they were on TV doing a 'book review' slot. After a bit of grumbling the class seem to be writing and that night Simon looks over the 'book reviews'. Either the pupils are testing him out, or few of them have read anything lately. Several pupils mention a text from another class, but their reviews are one-sentence evaluations – usually containing the words 'boring' or 'useless' (often misspelled). In stark contrast are the reviews of three pupils – they are a pleasure to read and they reflect a fairly sophisticated understanding of some good literature.

How could Simon adapt his plans for this group? What might he do the next day? Which teaching approaches do you think will work with this class? How will Simon work with the three pupils who are more advanced?

Group Activity

With two or three other members of your group, redesign the assignment to get pupils more engaged. How could you prepare them to use what they know in order to succeed with this task?

Social Cognitive Theory

Social learning theory

Theory that emphasises learning through observation of others.

Social cognitive theory

Theory that adds concern with cognitive factors such as beliefs, self-perceptions and expectations to social learning theory.

As we saw in Chapter 6, in the early 1960s, Albert Bandura, who expanded behavioural explanations of learning to include social influences, demonstrated that people can learn by observing the actions and consequences of others. Bandura's social learning theory emphasised observation, modelling and vicarious reinforcement. Over time, Bandura's explanations of learning included more attention to cognitive factors such as expectations and beliefs in addition to the social influences of models. His current perspective is called social cognitive theory.

Reciprocal determinism

In social cognitive theory, both internal and external factors are important. Environmental events, personal factors, and behaviours are seen as interacting in the process of learning:

- personal factors (beliefs, expectations, attitudes, and knowledge),
- physical and social environment (resources, consequences of actions, other people, and physical settings), and
- behaviour (individual actions, choices, and verbal statements)

All of these influence and are influenced by each other. Bandura calls this interaction of forces reciprocal determinism.

Reciprocal determinism

An explanation of behaviour that emphasises the mutual effects of the individual and the environment upon each other.

Figure 9.1 shows the interaction of person, environment and behaviours in learning settings (Schunk, 2004). Social factors such as models (those around us that we observe and imitate) instructional strategies or feedback (the ways in which we are taught and responded to) are all elements of the *environment* for learners. These can affect learners' *personal* factors such as goals, sense of efficacy for the task (described in the next section), attributions (beliefs about causes for success and failure), and

These children are clearly engaged in learning. What web of social engagement might support their engagement?

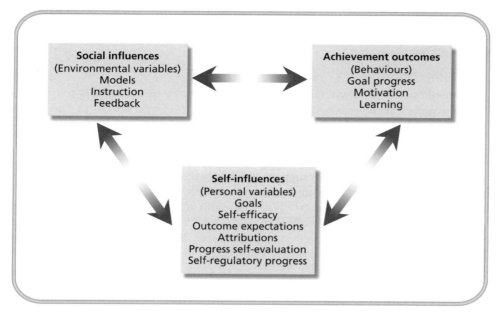

Figure 9.1
Reciprocal influences

All three forces – personal, social/environmental and behavioural – are in constant interaction. They influence and are influenced by each other.

Source: From *Educational Psychologist* by D. H. Schunk. Copyright 1999 by Lawrence Erlbaum Associates, Inc – Journals. Reproduced with permission of Lawrence Erlbaum Associates Inc – Journals in the format Textbook via Copyright Clearance Center.

processes of self-regulation such as planning, monitoring and controlling distractions. For example, teacher feedback can lead learners to set higher goals. Social influences in the environment and personal factors encourage the *behaviours* that lead to achievement such as persistence and effort (motivation) and learning. However, these behaviours also reciprocally impact upon personal factors. As learners achieve, their confidence and interest increase, for example and behaviours also affect the social environment. For example, if learners do not persist or if they seem to misunderstand, teachers may change instructional strategies or feedback. So the process of reciprocal determinism is dynamic and ongoing.

Think for a minute about the power of reciprocal determinism in classrooms. If personal factors, behaviours and the environment are in constant interaction, then cycles of events are progressive and self-perpetuating. Suppose a pupil who is new to the school walks into class late because he was lost in the unfamiliar building. The pupil has a tattoo and several visible pierced body parts. The pupil actually is anxious about his first day and hopes to do better at this new school, but the teacher's initial reaction to the late entry and dramatic appearance is a bit hostile. The pupil feels insulted and responds in kind, so the teacher begins to form expectations about the pupil and becomes more vigilant, less trusting. The pupil senses the distrust and feels that the teacher is 'on his case' so he decides that this school will be just as worthless as his previous one – and wonders why he should bother to try. The teacher sees the pupil's disengagement, invests less effort in teaching him, and the cycle continues.

Of course this complex interplay of forces may work positively to affect the experiences of learners within schools and their lives as when people respond positively to a teacher's beliefs and expectations.

Self-efficacy

Albert Bandura (1986, 1997) suggests that predictions about possible outcomes of behaviour are critical for learning because they affect motivation. 'Will I succeed or fail? Will I be liked or laughed at?' 'Will I be more accepted by teachers in this new school?' These predictions are affected by self-efficacy – our beliefs about our personal competence or effectiveness *in a given area*. Bandura defines self-efficacy as 'beliefs in one's capabilities to organise and execute the courses of action required to produce given attainments' (1997: 3).

Self-efficacy

A person's sense of being able to deal effectively with a particular task.

Self-efficacy, self-concept and self-esteem

Most people assume self-efficacy is the same as self-concept or self-esteem, but it isn't. Self-concept is a more global construct that contains many perceptions about the self, including self-efficacy. Self-concept is developed as a result of external and internal comparisons, using other people or other aspects of the self as frames of reference. Self-efficacy is future-oriented, 'a context-specific assessment of competence to perform a specific task' (Pajares, 1997: 15). But self-efficacy focuses on *your* ability to successfully accomplish a particular task with no need for comparisons – the question is whether *you* can do it, not whether others would be successful. Also, self-efficacy beliefs are strong predictors of behaviour but self-concept has weaker predictive power (Bandura, 1997).

Self-efficacy refers to the knowledge of one's own ability to successfully accomplish a particular task with no need for comparison – the question is 'Can I do it?' not 'Are others better than I am?'

Compared to self-esteem, self-efficacy is concerned with judgements of personal capabilities; self-esteem is concerned with judgements of self-worth. There is no direct relationship between self-esteem and self-efficacy. It is possible to feel highly efficacious in one area and still not have a high level of self-esteem, or vice versa (Valentine, DuBois and Cooper, 2004). However, this is likely to be related to how important this area is in your life. For example, I have very low self-efficacy for playing computer games, but my self-esteem is not affected, probably because my life does not require me to play computer games. However, if my self-efficacy for teaching a particular topic started dropping after several bad experiences, I know my self-esteem would suffer.

Sources of self-efficacy

Bandura identified four sources of self-efficacy expectations: mastery experiences, physiological and emotional arousal, vicarious experiences and social persuasion. Mastery experiences are our own direct experiences – the most powerful source of efficacy information. Successes raise efficacy beliefs, while failures lower efficacy. Level of arousal affects self-efficacy, depending on how the arousal is interpreted. As you face the task, are you anxious and worried (lowers efficacy) or excited and 'psyched up' (raises efficacy) (Bandura, 1997; Pintrich and Schunk, 2002)?

In vicarious experiences, someone else models accomplishments. The more closely the learner identifies with the model, the greater the impact on self-efficacy will be. When the model performs well, the learner's efficacy is enhanced, but when the model performs poorly, efficacy expectations decrease. Although mastery experiences generally are acknowledged as the most influential source of efficacy beliefs in adults, Keyser and Barling (1981) found that children (11–12-year-olds in this study) rely more on modelling as a source of self-efficacy information.

Social persuasion can be a 'pep talk' or specific performance feedback. Social persuasion alone can't create enduring increases in self-efficacy, but a persuasive boost in self-efficacy can lead a learner to make an effort, attempt new strategies, or try hard enough to succeed (Bandura, 1982). Social persuasion can counter occasional setbacks that might have instilled self-doubt and interrupted persistence. The potency of persuasion depends on the credibility, trustworthiness and expertise of the persuader (Bandura, 1997). Let us now look at the importance of self-efficacy when applying social cognitive theory to learning and teaching before moving on to self-regulated learning.

Mastery experiences

Our own direct experiences – the most powerful source of efficacy information.

Arousal

Physical and psychological reactions causing a person to feel alert, excited or tense.

Vicarious experiences

Accomplishments that are modelled by someone else.

Modelling

Changes in behaviour, thinking or emotions that happen through observing another person – a model.

Social persuasion

A 'pep talk' or specific performance feedback – one source of self-efficacy.

Applying Social Cognitive Theory

Self-efficacy and self-regulated learning are two key elements of social cognitive theory that are especially important in learning and teaching. They are discussed in the section which follows.

STOP AND THINK

On a scale from 1 to 100, how confident are you that you will finish reading this chapter today?

Self-efficacy and motivation

Let's assume your sense of efficacy is around 90 for completing this chapter. Greater efficacy leads to greater effort and persistence in the face of setbacks, so even if you are interrupted in your reading, you are likely to return to the task. This co-author believes she can finish writing this section tonight, so she has returned to working on it after stopping to pick up her daughter from school and preparing tea. Of course, that could mean a late night, because she has to teach two groups of learners tomorrow as well. Self-efficacy also influences motivation through goal setting. If we have a high sense of efficacy in a given area, we will set higher goals, be less afraid of failure and find new strategies when old ones fail. If your sense of efficacy for reading this chapter is high, you are likely to set high goals for completing the chapter – maybe you will take some notes, too. If your sense of efficacy is low, however, you may avoid the reading altogether or give up easily when problems arise (Bandura, 1993, 1997; Zimmerman, 2002).

What is the most motivating level of efficacy? Should learners be accurate, optimistic or pessimistic in their predictions? There is evidence that a higher sense of self-efficacy supports motivation, even when the efficacy is an overestimation. Children and adults who are optimistic about the future are more mentally and physically healthy, less depressed and more motivated to achieve (Flammer, 1995).

As you might expect, there are dangers in underestimating abilities because then learners are more likely to make a weak effort and give up easily, but there are dangers in continually overestimating performance as well. Learners who think that they are better readers than they actually are may not be motivated to go back and repair misunderstandings as they read. Thus they do not discover that they did not really understand the material until it is too late (Pintrich and Zusho, 2002).

Research indicates that performance in school is improved and self-efficacy is increased when learners (a) adopt short-term goals so it is easier to judge progress; (b) are taught to use specific learning strategies such as outlining or summarising that help them focus attention; and (c) receive rewards based on achievement, not just engagement, because achievement rewards signal increasing competence (Graham and Weiner, 1996). Recent research in the UK found significant improvements in the reading scores of a group of primary school pupils who had experienced an integrated approach in literacy lessons, including techniques to focus upon and find answers to their relevant questions to increase their self-efficacy (Galbraith and Alexander, 2005). Let us now consider the role which self-efficacy plays within teachers.

Teachers' sense of efficacy

Teachers' sense of efficacy

A teacher's belief that he or she can reach even the most difficult learners and help them learn.

An interesting area of research has focused on a particular kind of self-efficacy – teachers' sense of efficacy (Tschannen-Moran and Woolfolk Hoy, 2001; Woolfolk Hoy and Burke-Spero, 2005). A teacher's sense of efficacy, or a teacher's belief that he or she can reach even difficult pupils to help them learn, appears to be one of the few personal characteristics of teachers that is correlated with learner achievement. Self-efficacy theory predicts that teachers with a high sense of efficacy work harder and persist longer even when learners are difficult to teach, in part because these teachers believe in themselves and in their learners. A longitudinal study of ten German schools found that teachers' personal self-efficacy related to successful teaching and seemed to make them more resilient (Schwarzer and Schmitz, 2005). They are also less likely to experience exhaustion or 'burn-out' (Fives, Hamman and Olivarez, 2005).

We have found that prospective teachers tend to increase in their personal sense of efficacy as a consequence of completing pupil teaching but sense of efficacy may go down after the first year as a teacher, perhaps because the support that was there for the first year is gone (Woolfolk, Hoy and Burke-Spero, 2005). Teachers' sense of efficacy is higher in schools where the other teachers and administrators have high expectations for learners and where teachers receive help from their managers in solving instructional and management problems (Capa, 2005; Hoy and Woolfolk, 1993). Another important conclusion from research is that efficacy grows from real success with learners, not just from the moral support or 'cheerleading' by mentors and colleagues. Any experience or training that helps people succeed in the day-to-day tasks of teaching will provide a foundation for developing a sense of efficacy in your career.

As with any kind of efficacy, there may be both benefits and dangers in overestimating abilities. Optimistic teachers probably set higher goals, work harder, reteach when necessary and persist in the face of problems. However, there may be some benefits which might follow from people having doubts about their efficacy. Doubts might foster reflection, motivation to learn, greater responsiveness to diversity, productive collaboration, and the kind of disequilibrium described by Piaget that motivates change (Wheatley, 2002). It seems that a sense of efficacy for learning to teach would be necessary to respond to doubts in these positive ways, but it is true that persistent high efficacy perceptions in the face of poor performance can produce avoidance rather than action.

STOP AND THINK

How are you studying at the moment? What goals have you set for your reading today? What is your plan for learning, and what strategies are you using right now to learn? How did you learn those strategies?

Self-regulated learning

Self-regulated learning (SRL) has emerged within the last decade as an important new construct within education. Monique Boekaerts (1999), who has carried out considerable research into self-regulation and learning in the Netherlands, suggests that governments and educationalists have welcomed this partly because of dissatisfactions with educational provision which have been building in all countries in Europe and North America. Barry Zimmerman (2002) defines self-regulation as the process we use to activate and sustain our thoughts, behaviours and emotions in order to reach our goals. When the goals involve learning, we talk about self-regulated learning.

Today, people change jobs an average of seven times before they retire. Many of these career changes require new learning that must be self-initiated and self-directed (Martinez-Pons, 2002; Weinstein, 1994). Thus, one goal of teaching should be to free learners from the need for teachers, so the learners can continue to learn independently throughout their lives. To continue learning independently throughout life, you must be a self-regulated learner. Self-regulated learners have a combination of academic learning skills and self-control that makes learning easier, so they are more motivated; in other words, they have the *skill* and the *will* to learn (McCombs and Marzano, 1990; Murphy and Alexander, 2000). Self-regulated learners transform their mental abilities, whatever they are, into academic skills and strategies (Zimmerman, 2002). Many studies link strategy use to different measures of academic achievement, especially for older children and young people (Fredricks *et al.*, 2004).

What influences self-regulation?

The concept of self-regulated learning integrates much of what is known about effective learning and motivation. As you can see from the models and processes described

Self-regulation

Process of activating and sustaining thoughts, behaviours and emotions in order to reach goals.

above, three factors influence self-regulated learners: knowledge, motivation and self-discipline or volition.

To be self-regulated learners, people need *knowledge* about themselves, the subject, the task, strategies for learning, and the contexts in which they will apply their learning. 'Expert' learners know about *themselves* and how they learn best. For example, they know their preferred learning styles; what is easy and what is hard for them; how to cope with the difficult parts; what their interests and talents are; and how to use their strengths (see Chapter 4 of this book). They might, for example, if they find it easier to process visual information, turn to the diagrams in this book first to help them digest the text. These experts also know quite a bit about the *subject* being studied – and the more they know, the easier it is to learn more (Alexander, 2006). They probably understand that different *learning tasks* require different approaches on their part. A simple memory task, for example, might require a mnemonic strategy (see Chapter 7); whereas a complex comprehension task might be approached by means of concept maps (a visualisation technique to plot the relationship between concepts) of the key ideas (see Chapter 8). Also, these self-regulated learners know that learning is often difficult and knowledge is seldom absolute; there usually are different ways of looking at problems as well as different solutions (Pressley, 1995; Winne, 1995).

These expert learners not only know what each task requires but they also can apply the *strategy* needed. They can skim or read carefully. They can use memory strategies (such as mnemonics) or reorganise the material. As they become more knowledgeable in a field, they apply many of these strategies automatically. In short, they have mastered a large, flexible repertoire of learning strategies and tactics (see Chapter 8).

Finally, expert learners think about the *contexts* in which they will apply their knowledge – when and where they will use their learning – so they can set motivating goals and connect present work to future accomplishments (Wang and Palincsar, 1989; Weinstein, 1994; Winne, 1995).

Self-regulated learners are *motivated* to learn (see Chapter 10). They find many tasks in school interesting because they value learning, not just performing well in the eyes of others. But even if they are not intrinsically motivated by a particular task, they are serious about getting the intended benefit from it. They know *why* they are studying, so their actions and choices are self-determined and not controlled by others. However, knowledge and motivation are not always enough. Self-regulated learners need volition or self-discipline. 'Where motivation denotes commitment, volition denotes follow-through' (Corno, 1992: 72). Let us look at this now.

It is late summer and this co-author's family is deciding where they want to go today. She wants to join them but is back at work next week and wants to keep writing because the deadline for this chapter is very near. She has knowledge and motivation, but to keep going needs a good dose of *volition*. Volition is an old-fashioned word for willpower. The technical definition for volition is *protecting opportunities to reach goals by applying self-regulated learning*. Self-regulated learners know how to protect themselves from distractions – where to study, for example, so they are not interrupted. They know how to cope when they feel anxious, drowsy or lazy (Corno, 1992, 1995; Snow, Corno and Jackson, 1996). They know what to do when tempted to stop working and have (another) cup of tea – the temptation the author is facing now – that, and a beautiful sunny day that beckons her to the countryside.

Obviously, not all learners will be expert self-regulated learners when it comes to academics. In fact, some psychologists suggest that you think of this capacity as one of many characteristics that distinguish individuals (Snow, Corno and Jackson, 1996). Some learners are much better at it than others. How can more children and young

Volition

Willpower; self-discipline; work styles that protect opportunities to reach goals by applying self-regulated learning.

people be encouraged to become self-regulated learners in school? What is involved in being self-regulated?

Models of self-regulated learning and agency

Models of self-regulated learning describe how learners make choices among the skills they use to learn and how they manage factors that affect learning. There are several models (Puustinen and Pulkkinen, 2001). Let's look at one developed by Phil Winne and Allyson Hadwin (1998), depicted in Figure 9.2. It has many facets, as it should when the topic at hand is how you manage your academic life.

The model of self-regulated learning in Figure 9.2 is based on a position that learners are agents. Agency is the capacity to coordinate learning skills, motivation and emotions to reach your goals. Agents are not puppets on strings held by teachers, textbook authors or web page designers. Instead, agents control many factors that influence how they learn. Self-regulating learners exercise agency as they engage in a cycle of four main stages: *analysing* the task, setting goals and *designing* plans, *engaging* in learning and *adjusting* their approach to learning.

Self-regulated learning

A view of learning as a combination of academic learning skills and self-control.

Agency

The capacity to coordinate learning skills, motivation and emotions to reach your goals.

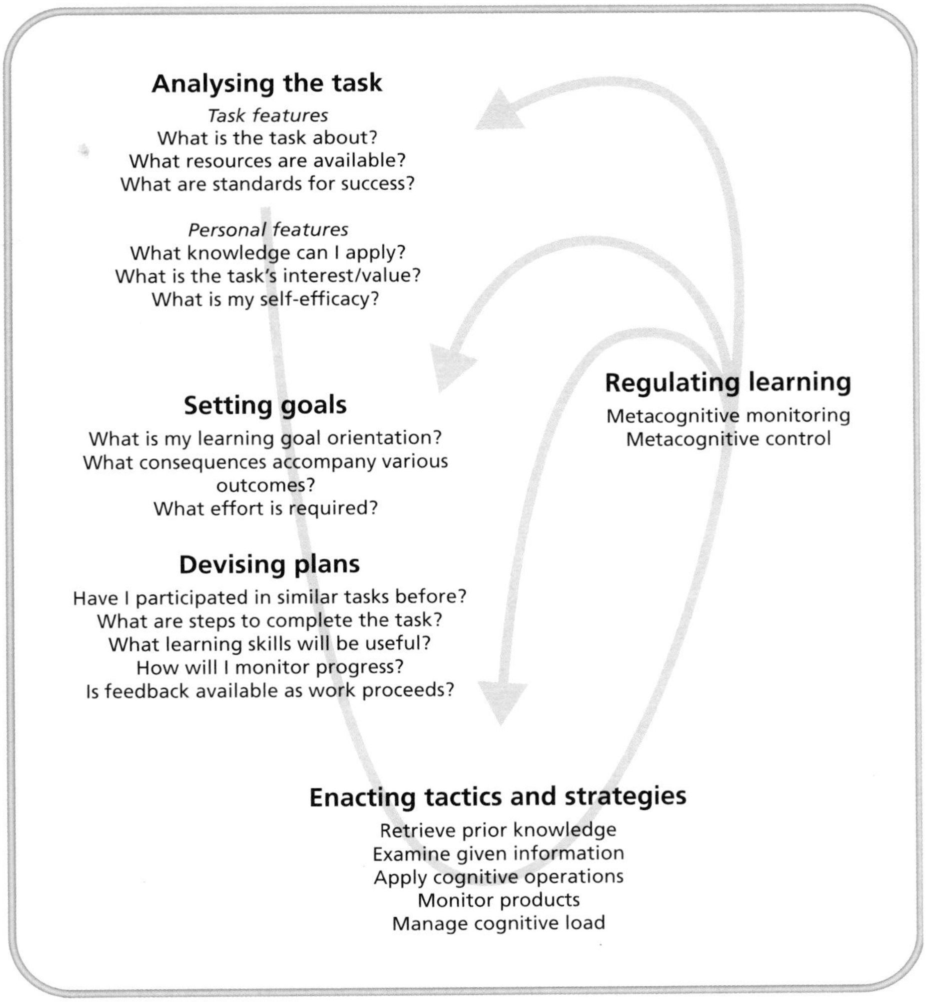

Figure 9.2
The cycle of self-regulated learning

Source: 'The cycle of self-regulated learning' adapted from *Educational Psychology* (3rd Canadian ed.) by A. E. Woolfolk, P. H. Winne and N. E. Perry. Toronto: Pearson, 2006, p. 307, Fig. 8.9. Reprinted with permission by Pearson Education Canada Inc. and Philip Winne.

1. **Analysing the learning task.** You are probably familiar with this stage of self-regulated learning. What do learners do when a teacher announces there will be at test? They ask about conditions they believe will influence how they will study. Is it in essay form or multiple-choice? Is my best friend more up-to-date than I? In general, learners examine whatever information they think is relevant in order to construct a sense of what the task is about, what resources to bring to bear, and how they feel about the work to be done.

2. **Setting goals and devising plans.** Knowing conditions that influence work on tasks provides information that learners use to create goals for learning. Then, plans can be developed about how to reach those goals. What goals for studying might you set if you were given a test covering only one chapter that is worth only 3% of the final grade? Would your goals change if the test covered the last six chapters and counted as 30% towards the final grade? What targets are identified in these goals – repeating definitions, being able to discuss how a teacher could apply findings from key research studies described in the textbook, or critiquing theoretical positions? Choosing goals affects the shape of a learner's plans for how to study. Is cramming or revising all of the information shortly before the test/exam (known as massed practice) the best approach? Is a better plan to study a half-hour each day, overlapping content a bit from one day to the next (distributed practice)?

3. **Enacting tactics and strategies to accomplish the task.** Self-regulated learners are especially alert during this stage as they monitor how well the plan is working. This is metacognitive monitoring (see Chapter 7). The question might be are you reaching your goals? Is the approach you take to learning too much effort for the results you are achieving? Is your progress rate fast enough to be ready in time for the test?

4. **Regulating learning.** In this stage of self-regulated learning, learners make decisions about whether changes are needed in any of the three preceding stages. For example, if learning is slow: should you study with your best friend? Do you need to review some prior material that provides foundations for the content you are now studying?

An individual example

Learners today are faced with constant distractions.

An important exam (mock GCSE) is two weeks away, and Patrick has begun to study while listening to dance music in order to 'get himself going' or motivated for learning. Patrick has not set any study goals for himself – instead he simply tells himself there is still time left to learn before the exam. He uses no specific learning strategies for condensing and memorising important material and does not plan out his study time but only uses class time spent working on past exam papers to prepare him. He ends up cramming for a few hours before the exam using a revision guide. He has some self-evaluative standards and some idea of how to gauge his academic preparation accurately. Patrick attributes his learning difficulties to an inherent lack of mathematical ability and is very defensive about his poor study methods. However, he does not ask for help from others because he thinks it will have no effect. Nor does he seek out supplementary materials from the library because he feels that he will not be able to understand it. He finds studying to be boring and is not motivated, seeing little intrinsic value in acquiring mathematical skill.

Clearly, Patrick is unlikely to do well in the exam. What would help? For an answer, let's consider the Winne and Hadwin model described above. If we look at Winne and Hadwin's steps 1 and 2 of analysing the task and setting goals, Patrick needs to set clear, reasonable goals and plan a few strategies for accomplishing those goals and Patrick's beliefs about motivation make a difference at this point too. If Patrick had a sense of self-efficacy for applying the strategies that he planned, if he believed that using those strategies would lead to mathematical learning and success on the exam, if he saw some connections between his own interests and the mathematical learning, and if he were trying to master the material – not just look good or avoid looking bad – then he would be on the road to self-regulated learning.

Moving to Winne and Hadwin's step 3 of enacting the strategies brings new challenges. Now Patrick must have a repertoire of self-control (volitional) and learning strategies, including using imagery, mnemonics, attention focusing and other techniques such as those described in Chapters 7 and 8 (Kiewra, 2002). He also will need to self-observe, that is, monitor how things are going so he can change strategies if needed. Actual recording of time spent, problems solved or pages written may provide clues about when or how to make the best use of study time.

Finally, Patrick needs to move to Winne and Hadwin's step 4 of regulating learning, by looking back on his performance and *reflecting* on what happened. It will help him develop a sense of efficacy if he attributes successes to effort and good strategy use and avoids self-defeating actions such as making weak efforts or pretending not to care.

Both Winne and Hadwin's and other models, such as Zimmerman's (2002) cycle of self-regulated learning, emphasise the cyclical nature of self-regulated learning: each phase flows into the next, and the cycle continues as learners encounter new learning challenges. Both models begin with being informed about the task so you can set good goals. Having a repertoire of learning strategies and tactics also is necessary in both models and self-monitoring of progress followed by modifying plans if needed are critical to both. Notice also that the way learners think about the task and their ability to do it – their sense of efficacy for self-regulation – is a key factor as well.

Within the classrooms

Learners differ in their self-regulation knowledge and skills but teachers must work with an entire classroom, and still manage to connect with them all. Here is an example of a real situation where teachers did just that.

Mathematical problem solving

Lynn Fuchs and her colleagues (2003) assessed the value of incorporating self-regulated learning strategies into mathematics problem-solving lessons in real classrooms. The researchers worked with 24 teachers. All of the teachers taught the same content in their classes of eight- and nine-year-olds. Some of these teachers (randomly chosen) taught in their usual way. Another randomly chosen group incorporated strategies to encourage problem-solving *transfer* – using skills and knowledge learned in the lessons to solve problems in other situations and classes. The third group of teachers added transfers and self-regulated learning strategies to their units on mathematical problem solving. Here are a few of the transfer and self-regulated learning strategies taught:

- Using a key, children scored their homework and gave it to a homework collector (a peer).

- Children recorded their completion of homework as a graph on a class report.

- Children used individual thermometer graphs that were kept in folders to chart their daily scores on individual problems.

- At the beginning of each session, children inspected their previous charts and set goals to beat their previous scores.

- Children discussed with partners how they might apply problem-solving strategies outside class.

- Before some lessons, children reported to the group about how they had applied problem-solving skills outside class.

Connect and Extend

See the Companion Website (Web Link 9.1) for an account of research in Cyprus which indicates that the use of a SRL mathematical problem-solving model can have a positive impact upon performance.

Both transfer and self-regulated learning strategies helped children learn mathematical problem solving and apply this knowledge to new problems. The addition of self-regulated learning strategies was especially effective when children were asked to solve problems that were very different from those they encountered in the lessons. Children at every achievement level as well as those with learning disabilities benefited from learning the strategies.

Families and self-regulated learning

Children begin to learn self-regulation in their homes. Parents can teach and support self-regulated learning through modelling, encouragement, facilitation, rewarding of goal setting, good strategy use and other processes described in the next section (Martinez-Pons, 2002).

Teaching towards self-efficacy and self-regulated learning

Most teachers agree that learners need to develop skills and attitudes for independent, life-long learning (self-regulated learning and a sense of efficacy for learning). Fortunately, there is a growing body of research that offers guidance about how to design tasks and structure classroom interactions to support learners' development of and engagement in self-regulated learning (Neuman and Roskos, 1997; Woolfolk, Winne and Perry, 2006; Zimmerman, 2002). This research indicates that learners develop academically effective forms of self-regulated learning (SRL) and a sense of efficacy for learning when teachers involve them in complex meaningful tasks that extend over long periods of time, much like the constructivist activities described later in this chapter. Also, to develop self-regulated learning and self-efficacy for learning, pupils need to have some control over their learning processes and work they produce – they need to make choices. It follows then that because self-monitoring and self-evaluation are key to effective SRL and a sense of efficacy, teachers can help learners develop SRL by involving them in setting criteria for evaluating their learning processes and outcomes, then giving them opportunities to make judgements about their progress using those standards. Finally, it helps to work collaboratively with peers and seek feedback from them.

Complex tasks

Teachers do not want to assign learners tasks that are too difficult and that lead to frustration. This is especially true when children and young people have learning difficulties or disabilities. In fact, research indicates that the most motivating and academically beneficial tasks for learners are those that challenge, but don't overwhelm them (Rohrkemper and Corno, 1988; Turner, 1997); complex tasks need not be overly difficult for learners.

The term *complex* refers to the design of tasks, not their level of difficulty. From a design point of view, tasks are complex when they address multiple goals and involve large chunks of meaning, such as projects and thematic units. Furthermore, complex tasks extend over long periods of time, engage learners in a variety of cognitive and metacognitive processes and allow for the production of a wide range of products (Perry *et al.*, 2002; Wharton-McDonald *et al.*, 1997). For example, a study of Egyptian pyramids might result in the production of written reports, maps, diagrams and models.

Even more important, complex tasks provide learners with information about their learning progress. These tasks require them to engage in deep, elaborative thinking and problem solving. In the process, learners develop and refine their cognitive and metacognitive strategies. Furthermore, succeeding at such tasks increases learners' self-efficacy and intrinsic motivation (McCaslin and Good, 1996; Turner, 1997). Rohrkemper and Corno (1988) advised teachers to design complex tasks that provide opportunities for learners to modify the learning conditions in order to cope with challenging problems. Learning to cope with stressful situations and make adaptations is an important educational goal. Remember from Chapter 4, that according to Sternberg, one aspect of intelligence is choosing or adapting environments so that you can succeed.

Control

Teachers can share control with learners by giving them choices. When learners have choices (e.g. about what to produce, how to produce it, where to work, who to work with), they are more likely to anticipate a successful outcome (increased self-efficacy) and consequently increase effort and persist when difficulty arises (Turner and Paris, 1995). Also, by involving learners in making decisions, teachers invite them to take responsibility for learning by planning, setting goals, monitoring progress and evaluating outcomes (Turner, 1997). These are qualities of highly effective, self-regulating learners.

Giving learners choices creates opportunities for them to adjust the level of challenge particular tasks present (e.g. they can choose easy or more challenging reading materials, determine the nature and amount of writing in a report, supplement writing with other expressions of learning). However, what if learners make poor academic choices? Highly effective, high-SRL teachers carefully consider the choices they give to learners. They make sure learners have the knowledge and skills they need to operate independently and make good decisions (Perry and Drummond, 2002). For example, when children or young people are learning new skills or routines, teachers can offer choices with constraints (e.g. learners must write a minimum of four sentences/paragraphs/pages, but they can choose to write more; they must demonstrate their understanding of an animal's habitat, food and young, but they can write, draw or speak their responses).

Highly effective teachers also teach and model good decision making. For example, when learners are choosing partners, they ask them to consider what they need from their partner (e.g. shared interest and commitment, perhaps knowledge or skills that they need to develop). When learners are making choices about how best to use their time, these teachers ask, 'What can you do when you're finished? What can you do if you are waiting for my help?' Often, lists are generated and displayed, so that learners can refer to them while they work. Finally, highly effective teachers give learners feedback about the choices they make and tailor the choices they give to suit the unique characteristics of particular learners. For example, they might encourage some of the class to select research topics for which resources are readily available and written at a level that is accessible to the learner. Alternatively, they might encourage some learners to work collaboratively versus independently to ensure they have the support they need to be successful.

> **⇄ Connect and Extend**
>
> See Little, D. *et al.* (2003), *Learner Autonomy in the Foreign Language Classroom: Teacher, Learner, Curriculum and Assessment*, Authentik Language Learning Resources Limited, for a discussion of independent learning and foreign language learning.

Self-evaluation

Evaluation practices that support SRL are non-threatening. They are embedded in ongoing activities, emphasise process as well as products, focus on personal progress and help learners to interpret errors as opportunities for learning to occur. In these contexts, learners enjoy and actually seek challenging tasks because the cost of participation is low (Paris and Ayres, 1994). Involving learners in generating evaluation criteria and evaluating their own work also reduces the anxiety that often accompanies assessment by giving people a sense of control over the outcome. Learners can judge their work in relation to a set of qualities both they and their teachers identify as 'good' work. They can consider the effectiveness of their approaches to learning and alter their behaviours in ways that enhance it (Winne and Perry, 2000).

In high-SRL (self-regulated learning) classrooms, there are both formal and informal opportunities for learners to evaluate their learning. For example, one teacher asked nine- and ten-year-old pupils to submit reflective journals describing the games they designed with a partner or small group of collaborators in a probability and statistics unit (Perry, Phillips and Dowler, 2004). Their journals explained their contribution to the group's process and product, and described what they learned from participating. The teacher took these reflections into account when she evaluated the games. More informally, teachers ask learners: 'What have you learned about yourself as a writer today?', 'What do good researchers and writers do?', 'What can we do that we couldn't do before?' Questions like these, posed to individuals or embedded in class discussions, prompt learners' metacognition, motivation and strategic action – the components of SRL.

Collaboration

Collaborative learning is concerned with constructing meaning through interactions with others and is an effective teaching and learning strategy for encouraging the sharing of ideas and discussion. Current research in the UK suggests that the use of ICT (information and computer technology) can be particularly effective in supporting and encouraging collaborative learning and this is being encouraged by the Department for Education and Skills (DfES, 2005). Further, there is evidence that collaborative learning is particularly helpful for enhancing the language skills of bilingual pupils (Gibbons, 2002). The National Association for Language Development in the Curriculum gives an example of teaching Macbeth to a group of nine- and ten-year-old children in a city primary school where 80% of the children were from a range of ethnic minority communities and most were bilingual. Group work as well as other teaching strategies is used to stimulate dialogue and support the development of language skills (NALDIC, 2006). (See the NALDIC website for details of this at http://www.naldic.org.uk/ITTSEAL2/teaching/SupportingLanguageandCognitivedevelopment.cf)

The most effective uses of cooperative/collaborative relationships are those that reflect a climate of community and shared problem solving (Perry and Drummond, 2003; Perry et al., 2002). In these contexts, teachers and learners actually co-regulate one another's learning (McCaslin and Good, 1996), offering support, whether working alone, in pairs or small groups. This support is instrumental to individuals' development and uses metacognition, intrinsic motivation (internal drive to achieve) and strategic action (e.g. sharing ideas, comparing strategies for solving problems, identifying *everyone's* area of expertise). As you will see in Chapter 12, developing useful management and learning procedures and routines takes time in the beginning of the year, but it is time well spent. Once routines and patterns of interaction are established, learners can focus on learning and teachers can attend to teaching academic skills and the curriculum.

The last element of teaching for self-regulation, collaboration, is an important ingredient in constructivist (learner directed) learning. We will spend the rest of the chapter exploring more closely this important and very current perspective.

Cognitive and Social Constructivism

Consider this situation:

A young child who has never been to the hospital is in her bed in the children's ward. The nurse at her desk further down the ward calls over the intercom above the bed, 'Hello Chelsea, how are you feeling? Is there anything you need?' The girl looks puzzled and does not answer. The nurse repeats the question with the same result. Finally, the nurse says emphatically, 'Chelsea, are you there? Can you say something, please?' The little girl responds tentatively, 'Hello wall – I'm here.'

Chelsea encountered a new situation – a talking wall. The wall is persistent. It sounds like a grown-up wall. She shouldn't talk to strangers, but she is not sure about walls. She uses what she knows and what the situation provides to *construct* meaning and to act.

Constructivist theories of learning focus on how people make meaning, both on their own like Chelsea and in interaction with others.

Constructivist views of learning

Constructivism is a broad term used by philosophers, curriculum designers, psychologists, educators and others. Constructivist perspectives are grounded in the research of Piaget, Vygotsky, the *Gestalt* psychologists, Bartlett and Bruner, as well as the philosophy of John Dewey, to mention just a few intellectual roots.

There is no one constructivist theory of learning, but 'most constructivists share two main ideas: that learners are active in constructing their own knowledge and that social interactions are important to knowledge construction' (Bruning *et al.*, 2004: 195).

Constructivism

View that emphasises the active role of the learner in building understanding and making sense of information.

Social constructivists see learning as actively participating with others within cultural contexts

Constructivism views learning as more than receiving and processing information transmitted by teachers or texts. Rather, learning is the active and personal construction of knowledge (De Kock, Sleegers and Voeten, 2004). Thus, many theories in cognitive science include some kind of constructivism because these theories assume that individuals construct their own cognitive structures as they learn (Palincsar, 1998). There are constructivist approaches in science and mathematics education, in educational psychology and anthropology, and in computer-based education. Thus, even though many psychologists and educators use the term *constructivism,* they often mean very different things (Driscoll, 2005; McCaslin and Hickey, 2001; Phillips, 1997).

One way to organise constructivist views is to talk about two forms of constructivism: psychological and social construction (Palincsar, 1998; Phillips, 1997). We could oversimplify a bit and say that psychological constructivists focus on how individuals use information, resources and even help from others to build and improve their mental models and problem-solving strategies. In contrast, social constructivists see learning as increasing our abilities to participate with others in activities that are meaningful in the culture (Windschitl, 2002). Let us look a little more closely at each type of constructivism.

Psychological/individual constructivism

Psychological constructivists 'are concerned with how *individuals* build up certain elements of their cognitive or emotional apparatus' (Phillips, 1997: 153). These constructivists are interested in individual knowledge, beliefs, self-concept or identity, so they are sometimes called *individual* constructivists or *cognitive* constructivists; they all focus on the inner psychological life of people. When Chelsea talked to the wall in the previous section, she was making meaning using her own individual knowledge and beliefs about how to respond when someone (or something) talks to you. She was using what she knew to impose intellectual structure on her world (Piaget, 1971; Windschitl, 2002).

The most recent information processing theories are constructivist (Mayer, 1996). Information processing approaches to learning regard the human mind as a symbol processing system. This system converts sensory input into symbol structures (propositions, images or schemas), and then processes (rehearses or elaborates) those symbol structures so knowledge can be held in memory and retrieved. The outside world is seen as a source of input, but once the sensations are perceived and enter working memory, the important work is assumed to be happening 'inside the head' of the individual (Schunk, 2000; Vera and Simon, 1993). Some psychologists, however, believe that information processing is 'trivial' or 'weak' constructivism because the individual's only constructive contribution is to build accurate representations of the outside world (Derry, 1992; Garrison, 1995; Marshall, 1996; Windschitl, 2002).

In contrast with information processing approaches, Piaget's psychological (cognitive) constructivist perspective is less concerned with 'correct' representations and more interested in meaning as constructed by the individual. As we saw in Chapter 2, Piaget proposed a sequence of cognitive stages that all humans pass through. Thinking at each stage builds on and incorporates previous stages as it becomes more organised and adaptive, and less tied to concrete events. Piaget's special concern was with logic and the construction of universal knowledge that cannot be learned directly from the environment – knowledge such as conservation or reversibility (Miller, 2002). Such knowledge comes from reflecting on and coordinating our own cognitions or thoughts, not from mapping external reality. Piaget saw the social environment as an important factor in development, but did not believe that social interaction was the main mechanism for changing thinking (Moshman, 1997). Some educational and developmental psychologists have referred to Piaget's kind of constructivism as 'first wave constructivism' or

First wave constructivism

A focus on the individual and psychological sources of knowing, as in Piaget's theory.

'solo' constructivism, with its emphasis on individual meaning making (De Corte, Greer and Verschaffel, 1996; Paris, Byrnes and Paris, 2001).

At the extreme end of individual constructivism is the notion of radical constructivism. This perspective holds that there is no reality or truth in the world, only the individual's perceptions and beliefs. Each of us constructs meaning from our own experiences, but we have no way of understanding or 'knowing' the reality of others (Woods and Murphy, 2002). A difficulty with this position is that, when pushed to the extreme of relativism, all knowledge and all beliefs are equal because they are all valid individual perceptions. There are problems with this thinking for educators. First, teachers have a professional responsibility to emphasise some values, such as honesty or justice, over others such as bigotry and deception. All perceptions and beliefs are not equal. Teachers ask learners to work hard to learn. If learning cannot advance understanding because all understandings are equally good then teaching becomes pointless (Moshman, 1997). Also, it appears that some knowledge, such as counting and one-to-one correspondence, is not constructed, but universal.

Radical constructivism

Knowledge is assumed to be the individual's construction; it cannot be judged right or wrong.

Vygotsky's social constructivism

As you also saw in Chapter 2, Vygotsky believed that social interaction, cultural tools and activity shape individual development and learning. By participating in a broad range of activities with others, learners appropriate (internalise or take for themselves) the outcomes produced by working together; these outcomes could include both new strategies and knowledge. Putting learning in social and cultural context is 'second wave' constructivism (Paris, Byrnes and Paris, 2001).

Appropriate

Internalise or take for yourself knowledge and skills developed in interaction with others or with cultural tools.

Because his theory relies heavily on social interactions and the cultural context to explain learning, most psychologists classify Vygotsky as a social constructivist (Palincsar, 1998; Prawat, 1996). However, some theorists categorise him as a psychological constructivist because he was primarily interested in development within the individual (Moshman, 1997; Phillips, 1997). In a sense, Vygotsky was both. One advantage of his theory of learning is that it gives us a way to consider both the psychological and the social: he bridges both camps. For example, Vygotsky's concept of the zone of proximal development – the area where a child can solve a problem with the help (scaffolding) of an adult or more able peer – has been called a place where culture and cognition create each other (Cole, 1985). Culture creates cognition when the adult uses tools and practices from the culture (language, maps, computers, looms or music) to steer the child towards goals the culture values (reading, writing, weaving, dance). Cognition creates culture as the adult and child together generate new practices and problem solutions to add to the cultural group's repertoire (Serpell, 1993). One way of integrating individual and social constructivism is to think of knowledge as individually constructed and socially mediated (Windschitl, 2002).

Second wave constructivism

A focus on the social and cultural sources of knowing, as in Vygotsky's theory.

The term constructionism is sometimes used to talk about how public knowledge is created. Although this is not our main concern in educational psychology, it is worth a quick look.

Constructionism or sociological constructivism

Sociological constructivists (sometimes called construc*tionists*) do not focus on individual learning. Their concern is how public knowledge in disciplines such as science, mathematics, economics or history is constructed. Beyond this kind of academic knowledge, constructionists also are interested in how common-sense ideas, everyday beliefs and commonly held understandings about people and the world are communicated to new members of a sociocultural group (Gergen, 1997; Phillips, 1997). Questions raised might include who determines what constitutes history, what is the appropriate way to behave in public, or how to get chosen for a sports team. All knowledge is socially constructed, and, more important, some people have more power than others to define what constitutes such knowledge. Relationships between and among teachers, learners, families and the community are the central issues. Collaboration to understand diverse viewpoints is encouraged, and traditional bodies of knowledge often are challenged (Gergen, 1997). The philosophies of Jacques Dierrida and Michel Foucault are important sources for constructionists. Vygotsky's theory, with its attention to how cognition creates culture, has some elements in common with sociological constructivism or constructionism.

These different perspectives on constructivism raise some general questions, and disagree on the answers. These questions can never be fully resolved, but different theories tend to favour different positions. Let's consider the questions.

How is knowledge constructed?

One tension among different approaches to constructivism is based on *how* knowledge is constructed. Moshman (1982) describes three explanations.

1. *The realities and truths of the external world direct knowledge construction.* Individuals *reconstruct* outside reality by building accurate mental representations such as propositional networks, concepts, cause-and-effect patterns and condition-action production rules that reflect 'the way things really are'. The more the person learns, the deeper and broader his or her experience is, then the closer that person's knowledge will reflect objective reality. Information processing holds this view of knowledge (Cobb and Bowers, 1999).

2. *Internal processes such as Piaget's organisation, assimilation and accommodation direct knowledge construction.* New knowledge is abstracted from old knowledge. Knowledge is not a mirror of reality, but rather an abstraction that grows and develops with cognitive activity. Knowledge is not true or false; it just grows more internally consistent and organised with development.

3. *Both external and internal factors direct knowledge construction.* Knowledge grows through the *interactions* of internal (cognitive) and external (environmental and social) factors. Vygotsky's description of cognitive development through the appropriation and use of cultural tools such as language is consistent with this view (Bruning *et al.*, 2004). Another example is Bandura's theory of reciprocal interactions among people, behaviours and environments (Schunk, 2000). Table 9.1 summarises the three general explanations about how knowledge is constructed.

Knowledge: situated or general?

A second question that cuts across many constructivist perspectives is whether knowledge is internal, general and transferable, or bound to the time and place in which it is constructed. Psychologists who emphasise the social construction of knowledge and situated learning affirm Vygotsky's notion that learning is inherently social and embedded in a particular cultural setting (Cobb and Bowers, 1999). What is true in one time and place – such as the 'fact' before Columbus's time that the earth was flat – becomes false in another time and place. Particular ideas may be useful within a specific community of practice, such as 15th-century navigation, but useless outside that community. What counts as new knowledge is determined in part by how well the new idea fits with current accepted practice. Over time, the current practice may be questioned and even overthrown, but until such major shifts occur, current practice will shape what is considered valuable.

Situated learning emphasises that learning in the real world is not like studying in school. It is more like an apprenticeship where novices, with the support of an

Community of practice

Social situation or context in which ideas are judged useful or true.

Situated learning

The idea that skills and knowledge are tied to the situation in which they were learned and difficult to apply in new settings.

Table 9.1 How knowledge is constructed

Type	Assumptions about learning and knowledge	Example theories
External direction	Knowledge is acquired by constructing a representation of the outside world. Direct teaching, feedback and explanation affect learning. Knowledge is accurate to the extent that it reflects the 'way things really are' in the outside world.	Information processing
Internal direction	Knowledge is constructed by transforming, organising and reorganising previous knowledge. Knowledge is not a mirror of the external world, even though experience influences thinking and thinking influences knowledge. Exploration and discovery are more important than teaching.	Piaget
Both external and internal direction	Knowledge is constructed based on social interactions and experience. Knowledge reflects the outside world as filtered through and influenced by culture, language, beliefs, interactions with others, direct teaching and modelling. Guided discovery, teaching, models and coaching as well as the individual's prior knowledge, beliefs and thinking affect learning.	Vygotsky

expert guide and model, take on more and more responsibility until they are able to function independently. Proponents of this view believe situated learning explains learning in factories, around the dinner table, in secondary schools halls, in street gangs, in the business office and in the playground.

Situated learning is often described as 'enculturation' or adopting the norms, behaviours, skills, beliefs, language and attitudes of a particular community. The community might be mathematicians or gang members or writers or learners in a Year 7 class (11–12-year-olds) or football players – any group that has particular ways of thinking and doing. Knowledge is seen *not* as individual cognitive structures but as a creation of the community over time. The practices of the community – the ways of interacting and getting things done, as well as the tools the community has created – constitute the knowledge of that community. Learning means becoming more able to participate in those practices, use the tools, and take on the identity of a member of the community (Derry, 1992; Garrison, 1995; Greeno, Collins and Resnick, 1996; Rogoff, 1998).

At the most basic level, 'situated learning emphasises the idea that much of what is learned is specific to the situation in which it is learned' (Anderson, Reder and Simon, 1996: 5). Thus, some would argue, learning to do mathematics at school may help pupils do more school mathematics, but it may not help them balance a chequebook, because the skills can be applied only in the context in which they were learned, namely school (Lave, 1997; Lave and Wenger, 1991). However, it also appears that knowledge and skills can be applied across contexts that were not part of the initial learning situation, as when you use your ability to read and calculate to do your income taxes, even though income tax forms were not part of your school curriculum (Anderson, Reder and Simon, 1996).

Learning that is situated in school then does not have to be doomed or irrelevant (Bereiter, 1997). As you saw in Chapter 8, a major question in educational psychology and education in general concerns the *transfer* of knowledge from one situation to another. How can this transfer be encouraged? The next section addresses this question.

Common elements of constructivist perspectives

> ### STOP AND THINK
>
> What makes a lesson pupil-centred? List the characteristics and features that put the learner in the centre of learning.

We have looked at some areas of disagreement among the constructivist perspectives, but what about areas of agreement? All constructivist theories assume that knowing develops as learners, like Chelsea, try to make sense of their experiences. 'Learners, therefore, are not empty vessels waiting to be filled, but rather active organisms seeking meaning' (Driscoll, 2005: 487). These learners construct mental models or schemas and continue to revise them to make better sense of their experiences. Their constructions do not necessarily resemble external reality; rather, they are the unique interpretations of the learner, like Chelsea's friendly, persistent wall. This doesn't mean that all constructions are equally useful or viable. Learners test their understandings against experience and the understandings of other people – they negotiate and co-construct meanings.

Constructivists share similar goals for learning. They emphasise knowledge in use rather than the storing of inert facts, concepts and skills. Learning goals include developing abilities to find and solve ill-structured problems, critical thinking, enquiry, self-determination and openness to multiple perspectives (Driscoll, 2005).

Even though there is no single constructivist theory, many constructivist approaches recommend the following conditions for learning:

1. Embed learning in complex, realistic and relevant learning environments.
2. Provide for social negotiation and shared responsibility as a part of learning.
3. Support multiple perspectives and use multiple representations of content.
4. Nurture self-awareness and an understanding that knowledge is constructed.
5. Encourage ownership in learning (Driscoll, 2005; Marshall, 1992).

Before we discuss particular teaching approaches, let us look more closely at these dimensions of constructivist teaching.

Complex learning environments and authentic tasks

Complex learning environments

Problems and learning situations that mimic the ill-structured nature of real life.

Constructivists believe that learners should not be given stripped-down, simplified problems and basic skills exercises, but instead should encounter complex learning environments that deal with 'fuzzy', ill-structured problems. The world beyond school presents few simple problems or step-by-step directions, so schools should be sure that *every* learner has experience of solving complex problems. Complex problems are not simply difficult ones; they have many parts. There are multiple, interacting elements in complex problems and multiple solutions are possible. There is no one right way to reach a conclusion, and each solution may bring a new set of problems. These complex problems should be embedded in authentic tasks and activities, the kinds of situations that learners will face as they apply what they are learning to the real world (Needles and Knapp, 1994). Pupils may need support as they work on these complex problems, with teachers helping them find resources, keeping track of their progress, breaking larger problems down into smaller ones, and so on. This aspect of constructivist approaches is consistent with situated learning in emphasising learning in *situations* where the learning will be applied.

Social negotiation

Many constructivists share Vygotsky's belief that higher mental processes develop through social negotiation and interaction, so collaboration in learning is valued. From this perspective a major goal of teaching is to develop learners' abilities to establish and defend their own positions while respecting the positions of others and working together to negotiate or co-construct meaning. To accomplish this exchange, learners must talk and listen to each other. It is a challenge for children in cultures that are individualistic and competitive, such as the US, to adopt what has been called an intersubjective attitude – a commitment to build shared meaning by finding common ground and exchanging interpretations.

Multiple perspectives and representations of content

When learners encounter only one model, one analogy, one way of understanding complex content, they often oversimplify as they try to apply that one approach to every situation. So if learners are only given one example of how to perform a certain activity they may copy this and perhaps fail to understand the content properly. Therefore it is better to provide multiple representations of content using different analogies, examples and metaphors.

Rand Spiro and his colleagues suggest that 'revisiting the same material, at different times, in rearranged contexts, for different purposes, and from different conceptual perspectives is essential for attaining the goals of advanced knowledge acquisition' (1991: 28). This idea is consistent with Jerome Bruner's (1966) spiral curriculum, a structure for teaching that introduces the fundamental structure of all subjects – the 'big ideas' – early in the school years, then revisits the subjects in more and more complex forms over time.

Understanding the knowledge construction process

Constructivist approaches emphasise making learners aware of their own role in constructing knowledge (Cunningham, 1992). The assumptions we make, our beliefs and our experiences shape what each of us comes to 'know' about the world. Different assumptions and different experiences lead to different knowledge. If learners are aware of the influences that shape their thinking, they will be more able to choose, develop and defend positions in a self-critical way while respecting the positions of others.

Ownership of learning

'While there are several interpretations of what [constructivist] theory means, most agree that it involves a dramatic change in the focus of teaching, putting the learners' own efforts to understand at the centre of the educational enterprise' (Prawat, 1992: 357). Learner ownership does not mean that the teacher abandons responsibility for instruction, however. The section that follows discusses examples of this.

Applying Constructivist Perspectives

Even though there are many applications of constructivist views of learning, we can recognise constructivist approaches by the activities of the teacher and the learners. The Focus on Practice below suggests ways to encourage meaningful learning.

In this section, we will examine three specific teaching approaches that put the learner at the centre: enquiry and problem-based learning, dialogue and instructional

---

Social negotiation

Aspect of learning process that relies on collaboration with others and respect for different perspectives.

Intersubjective attitude

A commitment to build shared meaning with others by finding common ground and exchanging interpretations.

Multiple representations of content

Considering problems using various analogies, examples and metaphors.

Spiral curriculum

Bruner's structure for teaching that introduces the fundamental structure of all subjects early in the school years, then revisits the subjects in more and more complex forms over time.

FOCUS ON PRACTICE

Applying constructivist principles

Mark Windschitl (2002) suggests that the following activities encourage meaningful learning:

- Teachers elicit learners' ideas and experiences in relation to key topics and then fashion learning situations that help learners elaborate on or restructure their current knowledge.
- Learners are given frequent opportunities to engage in complex, meaningful, problem-based activities.
- Teachers provide learners with a variety of information resources as well as the tools (technological and conceptual) necessary to mediate learning.
- Learners work collaboratively and are given support to engage in task-oriented dialogue with one another.
- Teachers make their own thinking processes explicit to learners and encourage pupils to do the same through dialogue, writing, drawings or other representations.
- Learners are routinely asked to apply knowledge in diverse and authentic contexts, to explain ideas, interpret texts, predict phenomena and construct arguments based on evidence, rather than to focus exclusively on the acquisition of predetermined 'right answers'.
- Teachers encourage learners' reflective and autonomous thinking in conjunction with the conditions listed above.
- Teachers employ a variety of assessment strategies to understand how learners' ideas are evolving and to give feedback on the processes as well as the products of their thinking.

Source: Adapted from Windschitl, M. (2002). 'Framing constructivism in practice as the negotiation of dilemmas; An analysis of the conceptual, pedagogical, cultural, and political challenges facing teachers', *Review of Educational Research, 72,* pp. 131–175, copyright 2002 by Sage Publications. Reprinted by permission of Sage Publications, Inc.

conversations, and cognitive apprenticeships. Whilst it could be legitimately argued that every effective teacher uses all these approaches at some point in their teaching it is worth examining them in order to understand these different forms of teaching. Two other approaches consistent with constructivism are cooperative learning, discussed in Chapter 11, and conceptual change, discussed in Chapter 13.

Enquiry and problem-based learning

Enquiry learning

Approach in which the teacher presents a puzzling situation and pupils solve the problem by gathering data and testing their conclusions.

John Dewey, an influential American psychologist and philosopher, described the basic enquiry learning format in 1910. There have been many adaptations of this strategy, but the form usually includes the following elements (Echevarria, 2003; Lashley, Matczynski and Rowley, 2002). The teacher presents a puzzling event, question or problem. The learners:

- formulate hypotheses to explain the event or solve the problem;
- collect data to test the hypotheses;

- draw conclusions; and

- reflect on the original problem and the thinking processes needed to solve it.

Examples of enquiry

In one kind of enquiry, teachers present a problem and learners ask yes/no questions to gather data and test hypotheses. This allows the teacher to monitor pupils' thinking and guide the process. Here is an example:

1. *Teacher presents discrepant (unexpected) event* (after clarifying ground rules). The teacher blows softly across the top of an A4 sheet of paper, and the paper rises. She tells the class to work out why it rises.

2. *Learners ask questions* to gather more information and to isolate relevant variables. Teacher answers only 'yes' or 'no'. Learners ask if temperature is important (no). They ask if the paper is of a special kind (no). They ask if air pressure has anything to do with the paper rising (yes). Questions continue.

3. *Learners test causal relationships.* In this case, they ask if the nature of the air on top causes the paper to rise (yes). They ask if the fast movement of the air results in less pressure on the top (yes). Then they test out the rule with other materials – for example, thin plastic.

4. *Learners form a generalisation* (principle): 'If the air on the top moves faster than the air on the bottom of a surface, then the air pressure on top is lessened, and the object rises.' Later lessons expand learners' understanding of the principles and physical laws through further experiments.

5. *The teacher leads learners in a discussion of their thinking processes.* What were the important variables? How did you put the causes and effects together? and so on (Pasch *et al.*, 1991: 188–189).

Shirley Magnusson and Annemarie Palincsar have developed a teachers' guide for planning, implementing and assessing different phases of enquiry science units (Palincsar *et al.*, 1998). The model, called *Guided Enquiry Supporting Multiple Literacies* or GIsML, is shown in Figure 9.3.

The idea is based around the teacher first identifying a curriculum area and some general guiding questions, puzzles or problems. For example, a primary school teacher chooses communication as the area and asks this general question: 'How and why do humans and animals communicate?' Next, several specific focus questions are posed: 'How do whales communicate?', 'How do gorillas communicate?' The focus questions have to be carefully chosen to guide learners towards important understandings. One key idea in understanding animal communication is the relationship among the animal's structures, survival functions and habitat. Animals have specific *structures* such as large ears or echo-locators, which *function* to find food or attract mates or identify predators, and these structures and functions are related to the animals' *habitats*. Thus, focus questions must ask about animals with different structures for communication, different functional needs for survival and different habitats. Questions about animals with the same kinds of structures or the same habitats would not be good focus points for enquiry (Magnusson and Palincsar, 1995).

The next phase is to engage learners in the enquiry, perhaps by playing different animal sounds, having the class make guesses and claims about communication, and asking the learners questions about their guesses and claims. Then, the class conducts both first-hand and second-hand investigations. *First-hand investigations* are direct experiences and experiments, for example, measuring the size of bats' eyes and ears in relation to their bodies (using pictures or videos). In *second-hand investigations,* learners

Figure 9.3
A model to guide teacher thinking about inquiry-based science instruction

The straight lines show the sequence of phases in instruction and the curved lines show cycles that might be repeated during instruction.

Source: From 'Designing a community of practice: principles and practices of the GisML community' by A. S. Palincsar, S. J. Magnusson, N. Marano, D. Ford and N. Brown, 1998, *Teaching and Teacher Education, 14,* p. 12.

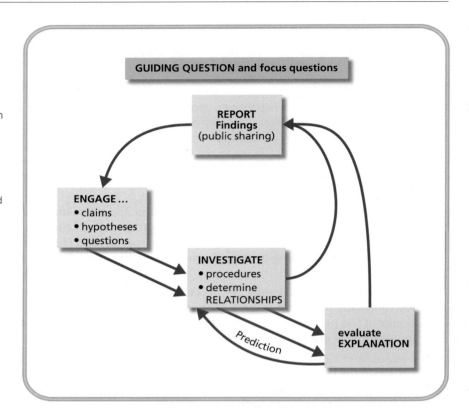

consult books, the internet, interviews with experts and other resources to find specific information or get new ideas. As part of their investigating, the learners begin to identify patterns. The curved line in Figure 9.3 shows that cycles can be repeated. In fact, learners might go through several cycles of investigating, identifying patterns and reporting results before moving on to constructing explanations and making final reports. Another possible cycle is to evaluate explanations before reporting by making and then checking predictions, applying the explanation to new situations.

Enquiry teaching allows learners to discover content and process at the same time. In the examples above, pupils learned about the effects of air pressure, how aeroplanes fly, how animals communicate and how structures are related to habitats. In addition, they learned the enquiry process itself – how to solve problems, evaluate solutions and think critically. Let us now look at problem-based learning.

Problem-based learning

Problem-based learning

Methods that provide pupils with realistic problems that don't necessarily have 'right' answers.

The goals of problem-based learning are to help learners develop *flexible* knowledge that can be applied in many situations in contrast to *inert* knowledge (information which is memorised but rarely used) which invites passivity in learners and low-level learning (Brown and Askew, 1997). Other goals of problem-based learning are to enhance intrinsic motivation and skills in problem solving, collaboration and self-directed lifelong learning. In problem-based learning, pupils are confronted with a problem that launches their enquiry as they collaborate to find solutions. The process of problem-based learning is similar to the GIsML (Guided Enquiry Supporting Multiple Literacies) shown in Figure 9.3. The learners are confronted with a problem scenario, they identify and analyse the problem based on the facts from the scenario and then they begin to generate hypotheses about solutions. As they suggest hypotheses, they identify missing information – what do they need to know to test their solutions? This launches a phase of self-directed learning and research. Then, learners apply their new knowledge, evaluate their problem solutions, reapply to re-search again if necessary, and finally reflect on the knowledge and skills they have gained (Hmelo-Silver, 2004).

James Atherton, an experienced educational practitioner and teaching fellow in the UK, provides a useful on-line discussion of problem-based learning. He suggests that there are various forms of problem-based learning, ranging from its *weakest* form to real-thing PBL (Atherton, 2003). Below are some examples of how this might work within the learning situation:

Weakest PBL might be simplified 'real-world' mathematical problems, such as:

- If I buy three bottles of juice costing 80 pence each, how much change will I get from my five pound pocket money?

Weak form of PBL which includes other information outside of the problem but necessary to solve it, such as:

- Using the timetables and price-lists provided work out the cheapest form of travel from central England to Amsterdam for two people travelling mid-week.

A *stronger* form of PBL involves finding out the additional information with some/little guidance which means working out what you need to know, finding this and applying it perhaps in a group:

- The school has been asked to put on a pantomime at the local community centre. Draw up plans for this production including details of auditions, rehearsals, costumes and costing.

The '*real thing*' would be the truest from of PBL where the project (such as putting on a pantomime) actually happens and forms part of the curriculum. This is fairly far-reaching because the conventional subject or curriculum areas are subsumed within the 'problem' or project, challenging traditional modes of assessment and teaching.

Source: Atherton, J. S. (2003) *Learning and Teaching: Problem-Based Learning* [Online] UK: Available http://146.227.1.20~jamesa//teaching/pbl.htm. Accessed: 31 May 2007.

Other authentic problems that might be the focus for learning projects are reducing pollution in local rivers, resolving pupil conflicts in school, raising money for tsunami or hurricane relief, or building a playground for young children. The teacher's role in problem-based learning is summarised in Table 9.2.

Research on enquiry and problem-based learning

Enquiry methods are similar to discovery learning and share some of the same problems, so enquiry must be carefully planned and organised, especially for less-prepared learners who may lack the background knowledge and problem-solving skills needed to benefit. Some research has shown that discovery methods are ineffective and even detrimental for lower-ability learners (Corno and Snow, 1986; Mayer, 2004). In 1993, a comparison was made of problem-based instruction in medical school. Individuals learning through problem-based instruction were better at clinical skills such as problem formation and

Table 9.2 The teacher's role in problem-based learning

Phase	Teacher behaviour
Phase 1 Orient pupils to the problem	Teacher goes over the objectives of the lesson, describes important logistical requirements and motivates pupils to engage in self-selected problem-solving activity.
Phase 2 Organise pupils for study	Teacher helps pupils define and organise study tasks related to the problem.
Phase 3 Assist independent and group investigation	Teacher encourages pupils to gather appropriate information, conduct experiments and search for explanations and solutions.
Phase 4 Develop and present artifacts and exhibits	Teacher assists pupils in planning and preparing appropriate artifacts such as reports, videos and models and helps them share their work with others.
Phase 5 Analyse and evaluate the problem-solving process	Teacher helps pupils to reflect on their investigations and the processes they used.

Source: Adapted from *Classroom Instruction and Management* (p. 161) by R. I. Arends. Published by McGraw-Hill. Copyright © 1997 by McGraw-Hill. Reprinted with permission of The McGraw-Hill Companies.

reasoning, but they were worse in their basic knowledge of science and felt less prepared in science (Albanese and Mitchell, 1993). In another study, undergraduates who learned a concept using problem-based methods were better at explaining the concept than those who had learned the concept from lecture and discussion (Capon and Kuhn, 2004). Learners who are better at self-regulation may benefit more from problem-based methods (Evensen, Salisbury-Glennon and Glenn, 2001), but using problem-based methods over time can help learners to develop self-directed learning skills.

In terms of the goals of problem-based learning listed earlier, Cindy Hmelo-Silver (2004) reviewed the research and found good evidence that problem-based learning supports the construction of flexible knowledge and the development of problem-solving and self-directed learning skills, but there is less evidence that participating in problem-based learning is intrinsically motivating or that it teaches learners to collaborate. In addition, most of the research has been done in higher education, especially medical schools.

The best approach in primary and secondary schools may be a balance of content-focused and enquiry or problem-based methods (Arends, 2004). For example, Eva Toth, David Klahr and Zhe Chen (2000) tested a balanced approach for teaching nine-year-olds how to use the controlled variable strategy (maintaining consistency) in science to design good experiments. The method had three phases: (1) in small groups, learners conducted exploratory experiments to identify variables that made a ball roll farther down a ramp; (2) the teacher led a discussion, explained the controlled variable strategy, and modelled good thinking about experiment design; and (3) the learners designed and conducted application experiments to isolate which variables caused the ball to roll farther. The combination of enquiry, discussion, explanation and modelling was successful in helping the learners understand the concepts.

Another constructivist approach that relies heavily on interaction is instructional conversations.

Dialogue and instructional conversations

One implication of Vygotsky's theory of cognitive development is that important learning and understanding require interaction and conversation. Learners need to grapple with problems in their zone of proximal development (learning which is within their grasp) and they need the scaffolding provided by interaction with a teacher or other learners. Here is a good definition of scaffolding that emphasises the knowledge that both teacher and learner bring – both are experts on something: 'Scaffolding is a powerful conception of teaching and learning in which teachers and learners create meaningful connections between teachers' cultural knowledge and the everyday experience and knowledge of the students' (McCaslin and Hickey, 2001: 137).

Instructional conversations are *instructional* because they are designed to promote learning, but they are *conversations*, not lectures or traditional discussions. These often take place within small group or one-to-one discussions and form part of the most successful teaching strategies. A recent review of effective literacy teaching in the 4–14 age range in mainstream UK schools suggests that a teaching style where teachers talk to children in conversational rather than interrogational ways is most beneficial for learning (Hall and Harding, 2003).

In instructional conversations, the teacher's goal is to keep everyone cognitively engaged in a substantive discussion. In the above conversation, the teacher takes almost every other turn. As the learners become more familiar with this learning approach, we would expect them to talk more among themselves with less teacher talk. These conversations do not have to be long. Even collecting dinner money can be an opportunity for an instructional conversation:

> *During the first few minutes of the day, Ms White asked how many children wanted hot lunches that day. Eighteen children raised their hands. Six children were going to eat cold lunches. Ms White asked, 'How many children are going to eat lunch here today?'*
>
> *By starting with 18 and counting on, several children got to the answer of 24. One child got out counters and counted out a set of 18 and another set of 6. He then counted all of them and said '24'.*
>
> *Ms White then asked, 'How many more children are eating hot lunch than are eating cold lunch?'*
>
> *Several children counted back from 18 to 12. The child with the blocks matched 18 blocks with 6 blocks and counted the blocks left over.*
>
> *Ms White asked the children who volunteered to tell the rest of the class how they got the answer. Ms White continued asking for different solutions until no one could think of a new way to solve the problem (Peterson, Fennema and Carpenter, 1989: 45).*

Ms White created an environment in which learners can make sense of mathematics and use mathematics to make sense of the world. To accomplish these goals, teaching begins with the learner's current understanding. Teachers can capitalise on the natural use of counting strategies to see how many different ways learners can solve a problem. The emphasis is on mathematical thinking, not on mathematical 'facts' or on learning the one best (teacher's) way to solve the problem. The teacher is a guide, helping learners construct their own understandings through dialogue (Putnam and Borko, 1997).

Table 9.3 summarises the elements of productive instructional conversations.

Connect and Extend

See the Companion Website (Web Link 9.2) for an exploration of why people fail to learn and the need to 'un-learn' in order to change this.

WEB

Instructional conversation

Situation in which individuals learn through interactions with teachers and/or peers.

Table 9.3 Elements of the instructional conversation

Good instructional conversations must have elements of both instruction and conversation.

Instruction

1. *Thematic focus.* Teacher selects a theme on which to focus the discussion and has a general plan for how the theme will unfold, including how to 'chunk' the text to permit optimal exploration of the theme.

2. *Activation and use of background knowledge.* Teacher either 'hooks into' or provides pupils with pertinent background knowledge necessary for understanding a text, weaving the information into the discussion.

3. *Direct teaching.* When necessary, teacher provides direct teaching of a skill or concept.

4. *Promotion of more complex language and expression.* Teacher elicits more extended student contributions by using a variety of elicitation techniques: invitation to expand, questions, restatements and pauses.

5. *Promotion of bases for statements or positions.* Teacher promotes pupils' use of text, pictures and reasoning to support an argument or position, by gently probing: 'What makes you think that?' or 'Show us where it says ____.'

Conversation

6. *Fewer 'known-answer' questions.* Much of the discussion centres on questions for which there might be more than one correct answer.

7. *Responsiveness to student contributions.* While having an initial plan and maintaining the focus and coherence of the discussion, teacher is also responsive to pupils' statements and the opportunities they provide.

8. *Connected discourse.* The discussion is characterised by multiple, interactive, connected turns; succeeding utterances build on and extend previous ones.

9. *Challenging, but non-threatening, atmosphere.* Teacher creates a challenging atmosphere that is balanced by a positive affective climate. Teacher is more collaborator than evaluator and pupils are challenged to negotiate and construct the meaning of the text.

10. *General participation, including self-selected turns.* Teacher does not hold exclusive right to determine who talks; pupils are encouraged to volunteer or otherwise influence the selection of speaking turns.

Source: Adapted from *Instructional Conversations and Their Classroom Application* (p. 7) by Claude Goldenberg, 1991, Santa Cruz, CA and Washington, DC: National Center for Research on Cultural Diversity and Second Language Learning. Copyright © 1991 by National Center for Research on Cultural Diversity and Second Language Learning. Reprinted with permission from CREDE.

Cognitive apprenticeships

Over the centuries, apprenticeships have proved to be an effective form of education. By working alongside a master and perhaps other apprentices, young people have learned many skills, trades and crafts. Knowledgeable guides provide models, demonstrations and corrections, as well as a personal bond that is motivating. The performances required of the learner are real and important and grow more complex as the learner becomes more competent (Collins, Brown and Holum, 1991; Collins, Brown and Newman, 1989; Hung, 1999).

With *guided participation* in real tasks comes *participatory appropriation* – learners appropriate the knowledge, skills and values involved in doing the tasks (Rogoff, 1995, 1998). In addition, both the newcomers to learning and the well-practised contribute to the community of practice by mastering and remastering skills – and sometimes improving these skills in the process (Lave and Wenger, 1991).

Allan Collins and his colleagues (1989) suggest that knowledge and skills learned in school have become too separated from their use in the world beyond school. To correct this imbalance, some educators recommend that schools adopt many of the features of apprenticeships. However, rather than learning to sculpt or dance or build a cabinet, apprenticeships in school would focus on cognitive objectives such as reading comprehension, writing or mathematical problem solving. There are many cognitive apprenticeship models, but most share six features:

1. Learners observe an expert (usually the teacher) *model* the performance.

2. Learners get external support through *coaching* or tutoring (including hints, feedback, models and reminders).

3. Learners receive conceptual *scaffolding*, which is then gradually faded as the learner becomes more competent and proficient.

4. Learners continually *articulate* their knowledge – putting into words their understanding of the processes and content being learned.

5. Learners *reflect* on their progress, comparing their problem solving to an expert's performance and to their own earlier performances.

6. Learners are required to *explore* new ways to apply what they are learning – ways that they have not practised at the master's side.

Cognitive apprenticeship

A relationship in which a less experienced learner acquires knowledge and skills under the guidance of an expert.

As novices learn, they are challenged to master more complex concepts and skills and to perform them in many different settings (Roth and Bowen, 1995; Shuell, 1996).

How can teaching provide cognitive apprenticeships? Increasingly the use of ICT (which supports communication) in schools invites the use of constructivist methods including the notion of cognitive apprenticeship (Tangney *et al.*, 2001, Lajoie and Greer, 1995). The English government includes particular elements of cognitive apprenticeships such as demonstrations and modelling as a key element for the improvement of teaching 11–14-year-olds. From 1997 the Nuffield Primary History Project implemented a programme for teachers' professional development, based around Collins *et al.*'s model. This was monitored and suggested that cognitive apprenticeship underpinned a wide range of expert practice (Nichol and Turner-Bisset, 2006). Holmes and Greik (1998) compared the experiences of children in one-teacher, rural primary schools in Ireland with that of Japanese learners who use a *han* system. A *han* is a group of three or four learners within a class who have group responsibility for ensuring that all group members progress through the learning materials appropriately. This is fundamentally different from the Western system which focuses upon individual progress and achievement and suggests that more use could be made of cognitive apprenticeships within Western educational systems. The quote below (taken from an interview with a Japanese teacher) illustrates this:

> *It looks like in the UK that students should not disturb other students; but in Japan, in such a class, it is encouraged. One plus one is usually more than two. Partly because of this, students turn to each other for help before turning to the teacher. Since the class moves at the same pace they will help each other to move forward, students rarely compete with each other in class (Holmes and Griek, 1998).*

Another successful example of cognitive apprenticeships, the reciprocal teaching approach for reading comprehension, is discussed in Chapter 12.

A cognitive apprenticeship in learning mathematics

Schoenfeld's (1989, 1994) teaching of mathematical problem solving is another example of the cognitive apprenticeship instructional model. Schoenfeld found that novice problem solvers began ineffective solution paths and continued on these paths even though they were not leading towards a solution. In comparison, expert problem solvers moved towards solutions using various cognitive processes such as planning, implementing and verifying, altering their behaviour based on judgements of the validity of their solution processes.

To help learners become more expert problem solvers, Schoenfeld asks three important questions: What are you doing? Why are you doing it? and How will success in what you are doing help you find a solution to the problem? These questions help learners control the processes they use and build their metacognitive awareness. Here is an example:

> Problem sessions begin when I hand out a list of questions . . . Often one has an 'inspiration' . . . My task is not to say yes or no, or even to evaluate the suggestion. Rather it is to raise the issue for discussion . . . Typically a number of students respond [that they haven't made sense of the problem]. When we have made sense of the problem, the suggestion [X] simply doesn't make sense . . . When this happens, I step out of my role as moderator to make the point to the whole class: If you make sure you understand the problem before you jump into a solution, you are less likely to go off on a wild goose chase (Schoenfeld, 1987: 201).

This monitoring of the understanding of a problem and the problem-solving process helps learners begin to think and act as mathematicians. Throughout this process, Schoenfeld repeats his three questions (What are you doing? Why? How will this help?). Each of these components is essential in helping learners to be aware of and to regulate their behaviours. Let us now look at apprenticeships in thinking.

Apprenticeships in thinking

Many educational psychologists believe that good thinking can and should be developed in school but clearly, teaching thinking entails much more than the standard classroom practices of answering 'thought' questions at the end of the chapter or participating in teacher-led discussions. What else is needed? One approach has been to focus on the development of *thinking skills*, either through stand-alone programmes that teach skills directly, or through indirect methods that embed development of thinking in the regular curriculum. The advantage of stand-alone thinking skills programmes is that learners do not need extensive subject matter knowledge to master the skills. Learners who have had trouble with the traditional curriculum may achieve success – and perhaps an enhanced sense of self-efficacy – through these programmes. The disadvantage is that the general skills often are not used outside the programme unless teachers make a concerted effort to show learners how to apply the skills in specific subjects, as you can see in the Discussion Point below (Mayer and Wittrock, 1996; Prawat, 1991).

Developing thinking in every class

Another way to develop learners' thinking is to provide cognitive apprenticeships in analysis, problem solving and reasoning through the regular lessons of the curriculum. David Perkins and his colleagues (Perkins, Jay and Tishman, 1993) propose that teachers do this by creating a culture of thinking in their classrooms. This means that there is a spirit of inquisitiveness and critical thinking, a respect for reasoning and creativity, and an expectation that learners will learn and understand. In such a classroom, education is seen as *enculturation*, a broad and complex process of acquiring knowledge and understanding consistent with Vygotsky's theory of mediated learning. Just as our home culture taught us lessons about the use of language, the culture of a classroom can teach lessons about thinking by giving us models of good thinking;

Stand-alone thinking skills programmes

Programmes that teach thinking skills directly without need for extensive subject matter knowledge.

providing direct instruction in thinking processes; and encouraging practice of those thinking processes through interactions with others.

Critical thinking

Critical thinking skills are useful in almost every life situation – even in evaluating the media advertisements that constantly bombard us. When you see a group of 'beautiful' people extolling the virtues of a particular brand of orange juice as they frolic in skimpy bathing suits, you must decide if sex appeal is a relevant factor in choosing a fruit drink (remember Pavlovian advertising from Chapter 6 where classical conditioning was used to link a response with a product). As you can see in the Discussion Point below educators do not always agree about the best way to encourage critical thinking in schools.

Critical thinking
Evaluating conclusions by logically and systematically examining the problem, the evidence and the solution.

DISCUSSION POINT

Should schools teach critical thinking and problem solving?

The question of whether schools should focus on process or content, problem-solving skills or core knowledge, higher-order thinking skills or academic information has been debated for years. Some educators suggest that learners must be taught how to think and solve problems, while other educators assert that learners cannot learn to 'think' in the abstract. They must be thinking about something – some content. Should teachers focus on knowledge or thinking?

Agree: Yes, problem solving and higher-order thinking can and should be taught

Research findings tend to support claims that children can be taught to think critically using various programmes aimed at encouraging thinking skills (Romney and Samuels, 2001). Large gains have been found in mathematics, English, reasoning and the results for some projects have been replicated in countries other than the US such as Iceland (Sigurborsdottir, 1998) as well as in other subject areas such as science (Sprod, 1998).

Within the UK there are a wide range of programmes, such as TASC (*Thinking Actively in a Social Context:* Wallace and Adams, 1993) or ACTS (*Activating Children's Thinking Skills:* McGuinness, 1999) drawing on the work of Schwartz and Parks in the US; as well as approaches in specific subjects such as *Thinking Through Geography:* Leat, 1998; *Thinking Through Primary Teaching:* Higgins, 2001; *Thinking Through History:* Fisher, 2002. Most programmes and approaches acknowledge the importance of language, articulation and discussion as a key element, e.g. *Thinking Together* (Dawes *et al.,* 2000).

Disagree: No, thinking and problem-solving skills do not transfer

The CoRT (Cognitive Research Trust) programme has been used in over 5,000 classrooms in ten nations but Polson and Jeffries report that 'after 10 years of widespread use we have no adequate evidence concerning the effectiveness of the program' (1985: 445). In addition, Mayer and Wittrock (1996) note that field studies of problem solving in real situations show that people often fail to apply the mathematical problem-solving approaches they learn in school to actual problems encountered in the supermarket or at home.

Even though educators have been more successful in teaching metacognitive skills, critics still caution that there are times when such teaching hinders rather than helps learning. Robert Siegler (1993) suggests that teaching self-monitoring strategies to low-achieving learners can interfere with the development of adaptive strategies. Forcing learners to use the strategies of experts may put too much burden on working memory as the learners struggle to use an unfamiliar strategy and miss the meaning or content of the lesson. For example, rather than teach strategies for figuring out words from context, it may be helpful for learners to focus on learning more vocabulary words.

WHAT DO YOU THINK?

Agree or Disagree? Vote online at www.pearsoned.co.uk/woolfolkeuro.

No matter which approach is used to develop critical thinking, it is important to follow up with additional practice. One lesson is not enough. For example, if a class examined a particular historical document to determine if it reflected bias or propaganda, it should be followed up by analysing other written historical documents, contemporary advertisements or news stories. Until thinking skills become overlearned and relatively automatic, they are not likely to be transferred to new situations. Instead, learners will use these skills only to complete the lesson in history, not to evaluate the claims made by friends, politicians, toy manufacturers or diet plans. Table 9.4 provides a representative list of critical thinking skills.

Table 9.4 Examples of critical thinking skills

Defining and clarifying the problem

1. Identify central issues of problems.
2. Compare similarities and differences.
3. Determine which information is relevant.
4. Formulate appropriate questions.

Judging information related to the problem

5. Distinguish among fact, opinion and reasoned judgement.
6. Check consistency.

7. Identify unstated assumptions.
8. Recognise stereotypes and clichés.
9. Recognise bias, emotional factors, propaganda and semantic slanting.
10. Recognise different value systems and ideologies.

Solving problems/drawing conclusions

11. Recognise the adequacy of data.
12. Predict probable consequences.

Source: From 'California assesses critical thinking' by P. Kneedler (1985). In A. Costa (ed.), *Developing Minds: A Resource Book for Teaching Thinking,* p. 277. Alexandria, Virginia: ASCD. Reprinted with permission.

STOP AND THINK

How many different words can you list that describe aspects of thinking? Try to 'think' of at least 20.

The language of thinking

The language of thinking consists of natural language terms that refer to mental processes and mental products – 'words like think, believe, guess, conjecture, hypothesis, evidence, reasons, estimate, calculate, suspect, doubt and theorise – to name just a few' (Tishman, Perkins and Jay, 1995: 8). The learning situation should be filled with a clear, precise and rich vocabulary of thinking. Rather than saying, 'What do you think about Jamie's answer?' the teacher might ask questions that expand thinking such as, 'What evidence can you give to refute or support Jamie's answer?', 'What assumptions is Jamie making?', 'What are some alternative explanations?' Learners surrounded by a rich language of thinking are more likely to think deeply about thinking. People learn more when they engage in talk that is interpretive and that analyses and gives explanations. Talk that just describes is less helpful in learning than talk that explains, give reasons, identifies parts, makes a case, defends a position or evaluates evidence (Palincsar, 1998). Thus for those working with learners it is important to encourage and model the use of these critical skills through choice of language in order to facilitate this. Let us finish this chapter by reviewing the different aspects of learning.

Looking Back at Learning

For the past four chapters, we have examined different aspects of learning. We considered behavioural, information processing, social cognitive, constructivist and situated learning explanations of what people learn and how they learn it. Table 9.5 presents a summary of several of these perspectives on learning.

Rather than debating the merits of each approach, consider their contributions to understanding learning and improving teaching. Don't feel that you must choose the 'best' approach – there is no such thing. Chemists, biologists and nutritionists rely on different theories to explain and improve health. Different views of learning can be used together to create productive learning environments for the diverse range of learners in teaching groups. Behavioural theory helps us understand the role of cues in setting the stage for behaviours and the role of consequences and practice in encouraging or discouraging behaviours. However, much of humans' lives and learning is more than behaviours. Language and higher-order thinking require complex information processing and memory – something the cognitive models of the thinker-as-computer have helped us understand and what about the person as a creator and constructor of knowledge, not just a processor of information? Here, constructivist perspectives have much to offer.

Table 9.5 Four views of learning

There are variations within each of these views of learning that differ in emphasis. There is also an overlap in constructivist views.

| | Cognitive | | Constructivist | |
	Behavioural	**Information processing**	**Psychological/ individual**	**Social/situated**
	Skinner	*J. Anderson*	*Piaget*	*Vygotsky*
Knowledge	Fixed body of knowledge to acquire	Fixed body of knowledge to acquire	Changing body of knowledge, individually constructed in social world	Socially constructed knowledge
	Stimulated from outside	Stimulated from outside	Built on what learner brings	Built on what participants contribute, construct together
		Prior knowledge influences how information is processed		
Learning	Acquisition of facts, skills, concepts	Acquisition of facts, skills, concepts and strategies	Active construction, restructuring prior knowledge	Collaborative construction of socially defined knowledge and values
	Occurs through drill, guided practice	Occurs through the effective application of strategies	Occurs through multiple opportunities and diverse processes to connect to what is already known	Occurs through socially constructed opportunities
Teaching	Transmission	Transmission	Challenge, guide thinking towards more complete understanding	Co-construct knowledge with pupils
	Presentation (Telling)	Guide pupils towards more 'accurate' and complete knowledge		
Role of teacher	Manager, supervisor	Teach and model effective strategies	Facilitator, guide	Facilitator, guide
	Correct wrong answers	Correct misconceptions	Listen for pupils' current conceptions, ideas, thinking	Co-participant
				Co-construct different interpretation of knowledge; listen to socially constructed conceptions
Role of peers	Not usually considered	Not necessary but can influence information processing	Not necessary but can stimulate thinking, raise questions	Ordinary part of process of knowledge construction
Role of pupil	Passive reception of information	Active processor of information, strategy user	Active construction (within mind)	Active co-construction with others and self
	Active listener, direction-follower	Organiser and reorganiser of information	Active thinker, explainer, interpreter, questioner	Active thinker, explainer, interpreter, questioner
		Rememberer		Active social participator

Source: From *Reconceptualizing Learning for Restructured Schools* by H. H. Marshall. Paper presented at the Annual Meeting of the American Educational Research Association, April 1992. Copyright © Hermine H. Marshall. Adapted with permission.

SUMMARY TABLE

Social Cognitive Theory (pp. 398–401)

Distinguish between social learning and social cognitive theories

Social learning theory expanded behavioural views of reinforcement and punishment. In behavioural views, reinforcement and punishment directly affect behaviour. In social learning theory, seeing another person, a model, reinforced or punished can have similar effects on the observer's behaviour. Social cognitive theory expands social learning theory to include cognitive factors such as beliefs, expectations and perceptions of self.

What is reciprocal determinism?

Personal factors (beliefs, expectations, attitudes and knowledge), the physical and social environment (resources, consequences of actions, other people and physical settings), and behaviour (individual actions, choices and verbal statements) all influence and are influenced by each other.

What is self-efficacy, and how is it different from other self-schemas?

Self-efficacy is distinct from other self-schemas in that it involves judgements of capabilities *specific to a particular task*. Self-concept is a more global construct that contains many perceptions about the self, including self-efficacy. Compared to self-esteem, self-efficacy is concerned with judgements of personal capabilities; self-esteem is concerned with judgements of self-worth.

What are the sources of self-efficacy?

Four sources are mastery experiences (direct experiences), level of arousal as you face the task, vicarious experiences (accomplishments are modelled by someone else) and social persuasion (a 'pep talk' or specific performance feedback).

Applying Social Cognitive Theory (pp. 401–410)

How does efficacy affect motivation?

Greater efficacy leads to greater effort, persistence in the face of setbacks, higher goals and finding new strategies when old ones fail. If sense of efficacy is low, however, people may avoid a task altogether or give up easily when problems arise.

What is a teacher's sense of efficacy?

One of the few personal characteristics of teachers related to learner achievement is a teacher's efficacy belief that he or she can reach even difficult pupils to help them learn. Teachers with a high sense of efficacy work harder, persist longer, and are less likely to experience stress and exhaustion. Teachers' sense of efficacy is higher in schools where the other teachers and administrators have high expectations for learners and where teachers receive help from their head teachers or principals in solving instructional and management problems. Efficacy grows from real success with learners, so any experience or training that helps you succeed in the day-to-day tasks of teaching will give you a foundation for developing a sense of efficacy in your career.

What factors are involved in self-regulated learning?

One important goal of teaching is to prepare people for lifelong learning. To reach this goal, individuals must be self-regulated learners; that is, they must have a combination of the knowledge, motivation to learn and volition that provides the skill and will to learn independently and effectively. Knowledge includes an understanding of self, subject, task, learning strategy and contexts for application. Motivation to learn provides the commitment, and volition is the follow-through that combats distraction and protects persistence.

What is the self-regulated learning cycle?

There are several models of self-regulated learning. Winne and Hadwin describe a four-phase model: analysing the task, setting goals and designing plans, enacting tactics to accomplish the task and regulating learning. Zimmerman notes three similar phases: forethought (which includes setting goals, making plans, self-efficacy and motivation); performance (which involves self-control and self-monitoring); and reflection (which includes self-evaluation and adaptations, leading to the forethought/planning phase again).

How can teachers support the development of self-efficacy and self-regulated learning?

Teachers should involve learners in complex meaningful tasks that extend over long periods of time; provide them control over their learning processes and products – they need to make choices. Involve learners in setting criteria for evaluating their learning processes and products, then give them opportunities to make judgements about their progress using those standards. Finally, encourage pupils to work collaboratively with and seek feedback from peers.

Cognitive and Social Constructivism (pp. 411–417)

Describe two kinds of constructivism. And distinguish these from constructionism

Psychological constructivists such as Piaget are concerned with how *individuals* make sense of their world, based on individual knowledge, beliefs, self-concept or identity – also called *first wave constructivism. Social* constructivists such as Vygotsky believe that social interaction, cultural tools and activity shape individual development and learning – also called *second wave constructivism.* By participating in a broad range of activities with others, learners appropriate the outcomes produced by working together; they acquire new strategies and knowledge of their world. Finally, constructionists are interested in how public knowledge in academic disciplines is constructed as well as how everyday beliefs about the world are communicated to new members of a sociocultural group.

In what ways do constructivist views differ about knowledge sources, accuracy and generality?

Constructivists debate whether knowledge is constructed by mapping external reality, by adapting and changing internal understandings, or by an interaction of external forces and internal understandings. Most psychologists posit a role for both internal and external factors, but differ in how much they emphasise one or the other. Also, there is discussion about whether knowledge can be constructed in one situation and applied to another or whether knowledge is situated, that is, specific and tied to the context in which it was learned.

What are some common elements in most constructivist views of learning?

Even though there is no single constructivist theory, many constructivist approaches recommend complex, challenging learning environments and authentic tasks; social negotiation and co-construction; multiple representations of content; understanding that knowledge is constructed; and ownership of learning.

Applying Constructivist Perspectives (pp. 417–429)

Distinguish between enquiry methods and problem-based learning

The enquiry strategy begins when the teacher presents a puzzling event, question or problem.

The pupils ask questions (only yes-no questions in some kinds of enquiry) and then formulate hypotheses to explain the event or solve the problem; collect data to test the hypotheses about casual relationships; form conclusions and generalisations; and reflect on the original problem and the thinking processes needed to solve it. Problem-based learning may follow a similar path, but the learning begins with an authentic problem – one that matters to the pupils. The goal is to learn maths or science or history or some other important subject while seeking a real solution to a real problem.

What are instructional conversations?

Instructional conversations are *instructional* because they are designed to promote learning, but they are *conversations,* not lectures or traditional discussions. They are responsive to pupils' contributions, challenging but not threatening, connected and interactive – involving all the pupils. The teacher's goal is to keep everyone cognitively engaged in a substantive discussion.

Describe six features that most cognitive apprenticeship approaches share

Learners observe an expert (usually the teacher) *model* the performance; get external support through *coaching* or tutoring; and receive conceptual *scaffolding,* which is then gradually faded as the learner becomes more competent and proficient. Learners continually *articulate* their knowledge – putting into words their understanding of the processes and content being learned. They *reflect* on their progress, comparing their problem solving to an expert's performance and to their own earlier performances. Finally, learners *explore* new ways to apply what they are learning – ways that they have not practised at the master's side.

What is meant by thinking as enculturation?

Enculturation is a broad and complex process of acquiring knowledge and understanding consistent with Vygotsky's theory of mediated

learning. Just as our home culture taught us lessons about the use of language, the culture of a classroom can teach lessons about thinking by giving us *models* of good thinking; providing *direct instruction* in thinking processes; and encouraging *practice* of those thinking processes through *interactions* with others.

What is critical thinking?

Critical thinking skills include defining and clarifying the problem, making judgements about the consistency and adequacy of the information related to a problem, and drawing conclusions. No matter what approach you use to develop critical thinking, it is important to follow up activities with additional practice. One lesson is not enough.

Glossary

Agency: The capacity to coordinate learning skills, motivation and emotions to reach your goals.

Appropriate: Internalise or take for yourself knowledge and skills developed in interaction with others or with cultural tools.

Arousal: Physical and psychological reactions causing a person to feel alert, excited or tense.

Cognitive apprenticeship: A relationship in which a less experienced learner acquires knowledge and skills under the guidance of an expert.

Community of practice: Social situation or context in which ideas are judged useful or true.

Complex learning environments: Problems and learning situations that mimic the ill-structured nature of real life.

Constructivism: View that emphasises the active role of the learner in building understanding and making sense of information.

Critical thinking: Evaluating conclusions by logically and systematically examining the problem, the evidence and the solution.

Enquiry learning: Approach in which the teacher presents a puzzling situation and pupils solve the problem by gathering data and testing their conclusions.

First wave constructivism: A focus on the individual and psychological sources of knowing, as in Piaget's theory.

Instructional conversation: Situation in which individuals learn through interactions with teachers and/or peers.

Intersubjective attitude: A commitment to build shared meaning with others by finding common ground and exchanging interpretations.

Mastery experiences: Our own direct experiences – the most powerful source of efficacy information.

Modelling: Changes in behaviour, thinking or emotions that happen through observing another person – a model.

Multiple representations of content: Considering problems using various analogies, examples and metaphors.

Problem-based learning: Methods that provide pupils with realistic problems that don't necessarily have 'right' answers.

Radical constructivism: Knowledge is assumed to be the individual's construction; it cannot be judged right or wrong.

Reciprocal determinism: An explanation of behaviour that emphasises the mutual effects of the individual and the environment upon each other.

Second wave constructivism: A focus on the social and cultural sources of knowing, as in Vygotsky's theory.

Self-efficacy: A person's sense of being able to deal effectively with a particular task.

Self-regulated learning: A view of learning as a combination of academic learning skills and self-control.

Self-regulation: Process of activating and sustaining thoughts, behaviours and emotions in order to reach goals.

Situated learning: The idea that skills and knowledge are tied to the situation in which they were learned and difficult to apply in new settings.

Social cognitive theory: Theory that adds concern with cognitive factors such as beliefs, self-perceptions and expectations to social learning theory.

Social learning theory: Theory that emphasises learning through observation of others.

Social negotiation: Aspect of learning process that relies on collaboration with others and respect for different perspectives.

Social persuasion: A 'pep talk' or specific performance feedback – one source of self-efficacy.

Spiral curriculum: Bruner's structure for teaching that introduces the fundamental structure of all subjects early in the school years, then revisits the subjects in more and more complex forms over time.

Stand-alone thinking skills programmes: Programmes that teach thinking skills directly without need for extensive subject matter knowledge.

Teachers' sense of efficacy: A teacher's belief that he or she can reach even the most difficult pupils and help them learn.

Vicarious experiences: Accomplishments that are modelled by someone else.

Volition: Willpower; self-discipline; work styles that protect opportunities to reach goals by applying self-regulated learning.

In the Classroom: What Would They Do?

Remember Simon, the secondary school English teacher at the beginning of the chapter? He had asked his pupils to write a review of their most recent reading but found that only three of the class really responded. Let us see how some current practitioners manage to engage their learners:

Ivan, a psychology teacher working with adults returning to education on an Access (to Higher Education) programme

The main problem at first is that they all feel scared that they won't be able to cope and they usually all think that they are more ignorant than the others. So the first thing I do is to try to put them at ease both in terms of me (as a teacher and a 'psychologist') and their peers. It is hard enough to get over the authority figure thing many people have about teachers but it's even harder if you happen to be a psychology teacher because they think that you are able to read their minds. I quickly disabuse them of this notion and talk to them about the fact that I am a psychology teacher which is different from a psychologist or psychiatrist. There are many confusions around these different terms and I use this as a starting point. I also give them some background about myself telling them that I was also an adult returner so they should think of me as a sign writer because that was my job for ten years.

I use a lot of group exercises so that they become more comfortable with talking in small groups to each other and then I visit the groups and have a chat with them about their conclusions before feeding back to the whole class. I tell them that we are less interested in a 'correct' answer than a range of different answers which reflect their different views. It is important to build upon their knowledge and experience and I invite them to apply the different concepts we look at to their own lives if they feel comfortable with this. I think this helps them to learn but also to gain self-esteem and respect. It is amazing how they grow in confidence and self-esteem over the course of the year and many of them go on to achieve honours degrees afterwards.

Veronica, an English teacher of 11–18-year-olds

It was very difficult when I started teaching because I had classes with perhaps 30 or more pupils of all ability levels so some of them were very competent users of the language both in terms of grammar, vocabulary and depth of understanding whereas others could barely read. I found that with the younger ones the most effective ways of engaging them was to provide a fairly short but meaningful stimulus and then getting them to talk and/or write about it. I remember one of the first successes I had. It was a crisp Autumn day but hot in the classroom, last lesson of the afternoon and the children (11-year-olds) were restless and noisy so we went for a walk in the school grounds and looked at the different trees and fallen leaves. I told each of them they had to collect a fallen leaf which they liked and to take back into the classroom. Then they worked in pairs to compare their leaves before writing as accurately as possible a description of their own leaf so that it was distinguishable from their partner's. Then we had some of the pairs reading these to the rest of the class and the other children had to identify the selected leaf. It was simple in one way but meant they were really using their observational, critical and vocabulary skills in a precise way. They loved it and worked really hard. I was amazed that some of those who had limited vocabularies were using words much more adventurously, imaginatively and accurately than I had thought possible. I remember one boy who had barely spoken before in class describing his leaf as 'tabby-cat striped' to convey the pattern on his leaf. I thought that here were poetical, creative possibilities that I had not dreamed of.

Overview

Most educators agree that motivating learners is one of the critical tasks of teaching. In order to learn, individuals must be cognitively, emotionally and behaviourally engaged in productive class activities. We begin with the question 'What is motivation?' and examine many of the answers that have been proposed, including a discussion of intrinsic and extrinsic motivation and four general theories of motivation: behavioural, humanistic, cognitive and sociocultural.

Next, we consider more closely several personal factors that frequently appear in discussions of motivation: needs and goal orientations; interests and emotions; and beliefs, including the important concept of self-efficacy.

How is all this information put together in teaching? How are environments, situations and relationships created that encourage motivation and engagement in learning? First, we consider how the personal influences on motivation come together to support motivation to learn. Then, we examine how motivation is influenced by the academic work of the class, the value of the work and the setting in which the work must be done. Finally, we discuss a number of strategies for developing motivation as a constant state in the classroom and as a permanent trait in learners.

By the time you have completed this chapter, you should be able to answer the following questions:

- **What are intrinsic and extrinsic motivation and motivation to learn?**
- **How is motivation conceptualised in the behavioural, humanistic, cognitive and sociocultural perspectives?**
- **What are the possible motivational effects of success and failure, and how do these effects relate to beliefs about ability?**
- **What are the roles of goals, interests, emotions and beliefs about the self in motivation?**
- **What external factors can teachers influence that will encourage individuals' motivation to learn?**

In the Classroom

Every day Michael faces learners who seem defeated about learning. Before even really looking at the work he sets they protest that they cannot do it because it is too hard, too long or too boring. Because the learners do not put much effort into their work, of course, they prove themselves right every time – they cannot do the work. Despite Michael setting up rewards and punishments these attitudes continue. Some of Michael's colleagues blame the learners' negative attitudes on social and economic challenges in their homes but this is not always the case as Michael has noticed that some learners from more advantaged backgrounds display similar attitudes.

Are these learners 'unmotivated'? Why might they be so pessimistic about learning? How might their attitudes be changed? In what ways does the learners' lack of motivation affect teachers?

Group Activity

With two or three other members of your group, brainstorm what could be done to motivate learners.

What is Motivation?

Motivation

An internal state that arouses, directs and maintains behaviour.

Motivation is usually defined as *an internal state that arouses, directs and maintains behaviour.* Psychologists studying motivation have focused on five basic questions:

1. *What choices do people make about their behaviour?* Why do some learners, for example, focus on their homework and others watch television?

2. *How long does it take to get started?* Why do some learners start their homework straight away, while others procrastinate?

3. *What is the intensity or level of involvement in the chosen activity?* Once the learner has begun a task is he or she absorbed and focused or just going through the motions?

4. *What causes a person to persist or to give up?* Will a learner read the entire Shakespeare assignment or just a few pages?

5. *What is the individual thinking and feeling whilst engaged in the activity?* Is the learner enjoying Shakespeare, feeling competent, or worrying about a forthcoming test (Graham and Weiner, 1996; Pintrich, Marx and Boyle, 1993)?

Answering these questions about real learners in classrooms is a challenge. As you will see in this chapter and the next, many factors influence motivation. Let us begin by looking at internal and external aspects of motivation.

Intrinsic and extrinsic motivation

We all know how it feels to be motivated, to move energetically towards a goal or to work hard, even if we are bored by the task. What energises and directs our behaviour? The explanation could be drives, needs, incentives, fears, goals, social pressure, self-confidence, interests, curiosity, beliefs, values, expectations and more. Some psychologists have explained motivation in terms of personal *traits* or individual characteristics. Certain people, so the theory goes, have a strong *need* to achieve, a *fear* of exams or an enduring *interest* in art, so they work hard to achieve, avoid exams or spend hours in art galleries. Other psychologists see motivation more as a *state*, a temporary situation. If, for example, you are reading this paragraph because you have a test tomorrow, you are motivated (at least for now) by the situation. Of course, the motivation we experience at any given time usually is a combination of trait and state. You may be studying because you value learning *and* because you are preparing for a test.

Intrinsic motivation

Motivation associated with activities that are their own reward.

As you can see, some explanations of motivation rely on internal, personal factors such as needs, interests and curiosity. Other explanations point to external, environmental factors – rewards, social pressure, punishment, and so on. A classic distinction in motivation is between intrinsic and extrinsic. Intrinsic motivation is the natural tendency to seek out and conquer challenges as we pursue personal interests and exercise capabilities (Deci and Ryan, 1985, 2002; Reeve, 1996). When we are intrinsically motivated, we do not need incentives or punishments, because *the activity itself is rewarding*. So we do something for the joy of doing it rather than the reward at the end.

Extrinsic motivation

Motivation created by external factors such as rewards and punishments.

In contrast, when we do something in order to earn a grade, avoid punishment, please the teacher, or for some other reason that has very little to do with the task itself, we experience extrinsic motivation. We are not really interested in the activity for its own sake; we care only about what we gain by doing it.

According to psychologists who adopt the intrinsic/extrinsic concept of motivation, it is impossible to tell just by looking if a behaviour is intrinsically or extrinsically motivated. The essential difference between the two types of motivation is the person's reason for acting, that is, whether the locus of causality for the action (the location of the cause) is internal or external – inside or outside the person. Learners who read or practise their backstroke or paint may be reading, swimming or painting because they freely chose the activity based on personal interests (*internal locus* of causality/ intrinsic motivation) or because someone or something else outside is influencing them (*external locus* of causality/extrinsic motivation) (Reeve, 1996).

As you think about your own motivation, you probably realise that the dichotomy between intrinsic and extrinsic motivation is too simple – too all-or-nothing. It may be that your motivation for reading this chapter contains elements of both intrinsic and extrinsic motivation in that you find it interesting in itself (we hope) and that you need to know about motivation for an essay you are writing. One explanation is that our activities fall along a continuum from fully *self-determined* (intrinsic motivation) to fully *determined by others* (extrinsic motivation). For example, learners may freely choose to work hard on activities that they don't find particularly enjoyable because they know the activities are important in reaching a valued goal – such as spending hours studying anatomy in order to become a physician. Is this intrinsic or extrinsic motivation? Actually, it is in between – the person is freely choosing to respond to out-side causes such as medical school requirements and then is trying to get the most benefit from the requirements. The person has *internalised an external cause*.

Recently, the notion of intrinsic and extrinsic motivation as two ends of a con-tinuum has been challenged. An alternative explanation is that just as motivation can include both trait and state factors, it also can include both intrinsic and extrinsic fac-tors. Intrinsic and extrinsic tendencies are two independent possibilities and, at any given time, we can be motivated by some of each (Covington and Mueller, 2001). Teaching can create intrinsic motivation by connecting to learners' interests and sup-porting growing competence but this won't work all the time. Did you find long divi-sion inherently interesting? Was your curiosity piqued by irregular verbs? If teachers count on intrinsic motivation to energise all their learners all of the time, they will be disappointed. There are situations where incentives and external supports are neces-sary. Teachers must encourage and nurture intrinsic motivation, while making sure that extrinsic motivation supports learning (Brophy, 1988, 2003; Deci, Koestner and Ryan, 1999; Ryan and Deci, 1996). To do this, they need to know about the factors that influence motivation.

Locus of causality

The location – internal or external – of the cause of behaviour.

General approaches to motivation

STOP AND THINK

Why are you reading this chapter? Are you curious about motivation and interested in the topic? Or are you reading for an assignment or test in the near future? Perhaps you believe that you will do well in this subject, and that belief keeps you working. Perhaps it is some combination of these reasons. What motivates you to study motivation?

Motivation is a vast and complicated subject encompassing many theories which reflect different approaches to understanding human thinking and behaviour. Our examination of the field will be selective otherwise we would never finish the topic. The following sections, therefore, consider the behavioural, humanistic, cognitive and socio-cultural approaches. Let us begin by looking at Freud's original ideas of motivation.

Psychoanalytic theory

Based upon the work of Sigmund Freud.

Freud, the 'father' of psychoanalysis and highly influential though controversial figure in psychology, suggested that all actions and behaviours are a result of internal, biological instincts which drive them (Freud, 1990). The concept of 'drive' within psychoanalytical theory corresponds with the notion of motivation. Thus the person responds to either the drive towards life (sexual) or death (aggression) but this is complicated by the fact that these drives become unconscious as children learn that overt sexual and aggressive behaviour are unacceptable. In other words, society does not allow these to be shown and so they are punished by parents and others in authority. Eventually, children repress or hide these feelings even from themselves. So Freud suggested that people are often unaware of their real reason for acting in a certain way (motivation) which results in internal conflicts. Whilst many of Freud's followers, such as Erikson and Jung, rejected this idea because it neglected other key areas (such as social relationships and disposition) the psychoanalytic approach to motivation does provide deep insights into human behaviour and was dominant within the field of psychology for the first part of the 20th century. However, the behavioural view of motivation rejected the notion of hidden, internal processes because they were impossible to observe or measure in a systematic way.

Behavioural approaches to motivation

Reward

An attractive object or event supplied as a consequence of a behaviour.

Incentive

An object or event that encourages or discourages behaviour.

According to the behavioural view, pioneered by theorists such as J.B. Watson, Skinner and Pavlov, an understanding of learner motivation begins with a careful analysis of the incentives and rewards present in the classroom (Chapter 6 includes a thorough exploration of behaviourist approaches to learning). A reward is an attractive object or event supplied as a consequence of a particular behaviour. For example, a biology teacher might believe that bonus points are rewards for pupils who submit neat, accurate diagrams. An incentive is an object or event that encourages or discourages behaviour. The promise of an A+ may be an incentive. Actually receiving the grade is a reward.

If we are consistently reinforced for certain behaviours, we may develop habits or tendencies to act in certain ways. For example, if a learner is repeatedly rewarded with

Providing sticker or star charts is an attempt to motivate learners by extrinsic means

affection, money, praise or privileges for gaining dance certificates, but receives little recognition for studying, the individual will probably work longer and harder on perfecting his or her pirouettes than on understanding geometry. Providing grades, stars, stickers and other reinforcers for learning – or demerits/black marks/unhappy faces for misbehaviour – is an attempt to motivate learners by extrinsic means of incentives, rewards and punishments. Of course, in any individual case, other factors may affect how a learner behaves because all individuals are complex, human beings. Let us look at an alternative way of explaining motivation which takes more account of internal factors.

Humanistic approaches to motivation

In the 1940s, proponents of humanistic psychology such as Carl Rogers argued that neither of the dominant schools of psychology, behavioural or Freudian, adequately explained why people act as they do. Humanistic interpretations of motivation emphasise such intrinsic sources of motivation as a person's needs for 'self-actualisation' (Maslow, 1968, 1970), the inborn 'actualising tendency' (Rogers and Freiberg, 1994), or the need for 'self-determination' (Deci *et al.*, 1991). So, from the humanistic perspective, to motivate means to encourage peoples' inner resources – their sense of competence, self-esteem, autonomy and self-actualisation (successful personal development). Maslow's theory has been an influential humanistic explanation of motivation.

Humanistic interpretation

Approach to motivation that emphasises personal freedom, choice, self-determination and striving for personal growth.

Maslow's hierarchy

Abraham Maslow (1970) suggested that humans have a hierarchy of needs ranging from lower-level needs for survival and safety to the top-level of self-actualisation. Self-actualisation is Maslow's term for self-fulfilment and the realisation of personal potential. Each of the lower needs must be met before the next higher need can be addressed.

Maslow (1968) called the four lower-level needs – for survival, then safety, followed by belonging and then self-esteem – deficiency needs. When these needs are satisfied, the motivation for fulfilling them decreases. He termed the top-level growth needs or being needs. When they are met, a person's motivation does not cease; instead, it increases to seek further fulfilment. Unlike the deficiency needs, these 'being needs' can never be completely filled. For example, the more successful you are in your efforts to develop as a teacher, the harder you are likely to strive for even greater improvement.

Maslow's theory has been criticised for the very obvious reason that people do not always appear to behave as the theory would predict. Most of us move back and forth among different types of needs and may even be motivated by many different needs at the same time. Some people, such as those dedicated to saving lives or discovering new things, deny themselves safety or friendship in order to achieve knowledge, understanding or greater self-esteem.

However, criticisms aside, Maslow's theory does give us a way of looking at the whole person, whose physical, emotional and intellectual needs are all interrelated. A child whose feelings of safety and sense of belonging are threatened by divorce may have little interest in learning how to divide fractions. If school is a fearful, unpredictable place where neither teachers nor pupils know where they stand, they are likely to be more concerned with security and less with learning or teaching. Belonging to a social group and maintaining self-esteem within that group, for example, are important to learners. If doing what the teacher says conflicts with group rules, learners may choose to ignore the teacher's wishes or even defy the teacher.

Hierarchy of needs

Maslow's model of levels of human needs, from basic physiological requirements to the need for self-actualisation.

Self-actualisation

Fulfilling one's potential.

Deficiency needs

Maslow's four lower-level needs, which must be satisfied first.

Being needs

Maslow's top-level needs, sometimes called growth needs.

Figure 10.1
Maslow's
hierarchy of needs

Source: Abraham
Maslow, *Motivation and
Personality* (2nd ed.),
Harper and Row, 1970.
Reprinted by permission
of Ann Kaplan.

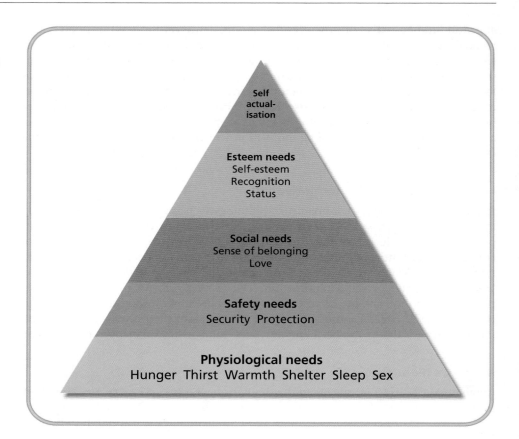

A more recent approach to motivation that focuses on human needs is self-determination theory (Deci and Ryan, 2002), discussed later in this chapter. The next general approach to motivation (cognitive and social-cognitive) focuses upon the way that individuals think about themselves and the world.

Cognitive and social cognitive approaches to motivation

In cognitive theories, people are viewed as active and curious, searching for information to solve personally relevant problems. Thus, cognitive theorists emphasise intrinsic motivation. In many ways, cognitive theories of motivation also developed as a reaction to the behavioural views. Cognitive theorists believe that behaviour is determined by our thinking, not simply by whether we have been rewarded or punished for the behaviour in the past (Stipek, 2002). Behaviour is initiated and regulated by plans (Miller, Galanter and Pribram, 1960), goals (Locke and Latham, 2002), schemas (Ortony, Clore and Collins, 1988), expectations (Vroom, 1964) and attributions (Weiner, 2000). We will look at goals and attributions later in this chapter.

Expectancy D7 value theories

Expectancy D7
value theories

Explanations of motivation
that emphasise individuals'
expectations for success
combined with their valuing
of the goal.

Theories that take into account both the behaviourists' concern with the effects or outcomes of behaviour and the cognitivists' interest in the impact of individual thinking can be characterised as expectancy D7 value theories. This means that motivation is seen as the product of two main forces: the individual's expectation of reaching a goal and the value of that goal to him or her. In other words, the important questions are, 'If I try hard, can I succeed?' and 'If I succeed, will the outcome be valuable or rewarding to me?' Motivation is a product of these two forces, because if either factor is zero, there is no motivation to work towards the goal. For example, if I believe I have a good chance of making the basketball team (high expectation), and if making the team is very important to me (high value), then my motivation should be strong. However, if either factor is zero (I believe I haven't a chance of making the team, or I couldn't care less about playing basketball), then my motivation will be zero, too (Tollefson, 2000).

The element of *cost* may also be added to the expectancy X value equation. Values have to be considered in relation to the cost of pursuing them. How much energy will be required? What could I be doing instead? What are the risks if I fail? Will I look or feel stupid (Eccles and Wigfield, 2001; Wigfield and Eccles, 2002)? Bandura's theory of self-efficacy, discussed later in this chapter, is a social cognitive expectancy X value approach to motivation (Feather, 1982; Pintrich and Schunk, 2002). Let us now look at an approach which focuses upon the importance of the social context within motivation.

Sociocultural conceptions of motivation

> **STOP AND THINK**
>
> Finish this sentence: I am a/an . . . . What is your identity? With what groups do you identify most strongly?

Sociocultural views of motivation emphasise participation in communities of practice. People engage in activities to maintain their identities and their interpersonal relations within the community. Thus, learners are motivated to learn if they are members of a classroom or school community that values learning. Just as we learn through socialisation to speak or dress or order food in restaurants – by watching and learning from more capable members of the culture – we also learn to be learners by watching and learning from members of our school/college community. In other words, we learn by the company we keep (Hickey, 2003; Rogoff, Turkanis and Bartlett, 2001).

The concept of identity is central in sociocultural views of motivation. When we see ourselves as tennis players, or sculptors, or engineers, or teachers or psychologists, we have an identity within a group. Part of our socialisation is moving from legitimate peripheral participation to central participation in that group. Legitimate peripheral participation means that beginners are genuinely involved in the work of the group, even if their abilities are undeveloped and their contributions are small. The novice weaver learns to dye wool before spinning and weaving, and the novice teacher learns to tutor one child before working with the whole group. Each task is a piece of the real work of the expert. The identities of both the novice and the expert are bound up in their participation in the community. They are motivated to learn the values and practices of the community to keep their identity as community members (Lave and Wenger, 1991; Wenger, 1998).

Some learning environments are intentionally structured as learning communities. For example, the first European learning community site, created in Ronneby, Sweden in 1997, used new computer technologies to strengthen communications between communities consisting of schools, universities, associations and companies. This European 5D project (based on the idea of the Fifth Dimension – local learning

Sociocultural views of motivation

Perspectives that emphasise participation, identities and interpersonal relations within communities of practice.

> **Connect and Extend**
>
> For an interesting report into the way that secondary school learners are motivated to learn a second language, see Williams, M. *et al.* (2002), '"French is the language of love and stuff": student perceptions of issues related to motivation in learning a foreign language', *British Educational Research Journal*, 28(4), pp. 503–528.

Legitimate peripheral participation

Genuine involvement in the work of the group, even if your abilities are undeveloped and contributions are small.

	Behavioural	**Humanistic**	**Cognitive**	**Sociocultural**
Source of motivation	Extrinsic	Intrinsic	Intrinsic	Intrinsic
Important influences	Reinforcers, rewards, incentives and punishers	Need for self-esteem, self-fulfilment and self-determination	Beliefs, attributions for success and failure, expectations	Engaged participation in learning communities; maintaining identity through participation in activities of group
Key theorists	Skinner	Maslow Deci	Weiner Graham	Lave Wenger

Table 10.1 Four views of motivation

communities in a global world which originated in California in the mid 1980s) was expanded to Barcelona, Spain (1998) and Copenhagen, Denmark (2000), and aims to develop and spread learning communities further in Europe (K2-E-Learning made in Europe, 2004).

The challenge in these approaches is to be sure that all learners are fully participating members of the community, because motivation comes from both identity and legitimate participation. Thus, engagement is 'meaningful participation in a context where to-be-learned knowledge is valued and used' (Hickey, 2003: 411).

The behavioural, humanistic, cognitive and sociocultural approaches to motivation are summarised in Table 10.1. These theories differ in their answers to the question, 'What is motivation?' but each contributes in its own way towards a comprehensive understanding.

To organise the many ideas about motivation in a way that is useful for those working with children and young people within a learning situation let us examine four broad areas. Most contemporary explanations of motivation include a discussion of needs, goals, interests and emotions, and self-perceptions (Murphy and Alexander, 2000).

Needs: Competence, Autonomy and Relatedness

We have already seen one motivation theory that focused on needs – Maslow's hierarchy of needs. Other early research in psychology conceived of motivation in terms of trait-like needs or consistent personal characteristics. Three of the main needs studied extensively were the needs for achievement, power and affiliation (Pintrich, 2003). We will look at one recent theory that emphasises similar needs through a focus on self-determination.

Self-determination

Self-determination theory suggests that we all need to feel competent and capable in our interactions in the world, to have some choices and a sense of control over our lives and to be connected to others – to belong to a social group. Notice that these are similar to earlier conceptions of basic needs: competence (achievement), autonomy and control (power), and relatedness (affiliation).

Need for autonomy is central to self-determination because it is the desire to have our own wishes, rather than external rewards or pressures, determine our actions (Deci and Ryan, 2002; Reeve, Deci and Ryan, 2004; Ryan and Deci, 2000). People strive to be in charge of their own behaviour. They constantly struggle against pressure from external controls such as the rules, schedules, deadlines, orders and limits imposed by others. Sometimes, even help is rejected so that the individual can remain in command (deCharms, 1983).

Need for autonomy

The desire to have our own wishes, rather than external rewards or pressures, determine our actions.

Self-determination in the classroom

Classroom environments that support learner self-determination and autonomy are associated with greater learner interest, sense of competence, creativity, conceptual learning and preference for challenge. These relationships appear to continue throughout education (Deci and Ryan, 2002; Williams *et al.*, 1993). When learners can make choices, they are more likely to believe that the work is important, even if it is not 'fun'. Thus, they tend to internalise educational goals and take them as their own.

In contrast to autonomy-supporting classrooms, controlling environments tend to improve performance only on rote recall tasks. When learners are pressured to perform, they often seek the quickest, easiest solution. One discomforting finding, however, is that both learners and parents seem to prefer more controlling teachers, even though the learners learn more when their teachers support autonomy (Flink, Boggiano and Barrett, 1990). It seems then that one answer is to focus on *information*, not *control*, in interactions with learners.

Information and control

Many things happen to learners throughout the school day. They are praised or criticised, reminded of deadlines, given grades, given choices, lectured about rules, and on and on. Cognitive evaluation theory (Deci and Ryan, 2002; Ryan and Deci, 2000) explains how these events can influence the learners' intrinsic motivation by affecting their sense of self-determination and competence. According to this theory, all events have two aspects, controlling and informational. If an event is highly controlling, that is, if it pressures learners to act or feel a certain way, then they will experience less control and their *intrinsic motivation* will be diminished. If, on the other hand, the event provides information that increases the learners' sense of competence, then intrinsic motivation will increase. Of course, if the information provided makes learners feel less competent, it is likely that motivation will decrease (Pintrich, 2003).

Cognitive evaluation theory

Suggests that events affect motivation through the individual's perception of the events as controlling behaviour or providing information.

For example, a teacher might praise a learner by saying, 'Good for you! You got an A because you finally followed my instructions correctly.' This is a highly controlling statement, giving the credit to the teacher and thus undermining the learner's sense of self-determination and intrinsic motivation. The teacher could praise the same work by saying, 'Good for you! Your understanding of the author's use of metaphors has improved tremendously. You got an A.' This statement provides information about the learner's growing competence and should increase intrinsic motivation.

What can teachers do to support learner needs for autonomy and competence? An obvious first step is to limit their controlling messages to their learners and make sure the information they provide highlights learners' growing competence. The Focus on Practice below gives some ideas.

FOCUS ON PRACTICE

Supporting self-determination and autonomy

Learners allowed and encouraged to make choices

Examples

1. Designing several different ways to meet a learning objective (e.g. an essay, a compilation of interviews, a test, news broadcast) and allowing learners to choose one. Encouraging them to explain the reasons for their choice.
2. Setting up class committees to make suggestions about streamlining procedures such as caring for class pets or distributing equipment.
3. Providing time for independent and extended projects.

Helping learners plan actions to accomplish self-selected goals

Examples

1. Experimenting with cards which record goals. Learners could list their short- and long-term goals and then record three or four specific actions that will move them towards the goals. Goal cards are personal to the individual.
2. Encouraging older learners to set goals in each subject area, recording them in a goal book or on a floppy disk, and checking progress towards the goals on a regular basis.

Holding learners accountable for the consequences of their choices

Examples

1. If learners choose to work with friends and do not finish a project because too much time was spent socialising, the project is graded appropriately and learners are helped to see the connection between lost time and poor performance.
2. When learners choose a topic that captures their imagination, the connections between their investment in the work and the quality of the products that follow are discussed.

Providing rationales for limits, rules and constraints

Examples

1. Explaining reasons for rules.
2. Respecting rules and constraints in own behaviour.

Acknowledging that negative emotions are valid reactions to teacher control

Examples

1. Communicating that it is okay (and normal) to feel bored waiting for a turn, for example.
2. Communicating that sometimes important learning involves frustration, confusion, weariness.

Using non-controlling, positive feedback

Examples

1. Seeing poor performance or behaviour as a problem to be solved, not a target of criticism.
2. Avoiding controlling language, 'should,' 'must,' 'have to'.

For more information on self-determination theory see http://www.psych. rochester.edu/SDT/.

Source: From *150 Ways to Increase Intrinsic Motivation in the Classroom* by James P. Raffini. Published by Allyn and Bacon, Boston, MA. Copyright © 1996 by Pearson Education. Adapted by permission of the publisher. And *Motivating Others: Nurturing Inner Motivational Resources* by J. Reeve. Published by Allyn and Bacon, Boston, MA. Copyright © 1996 by Pearson Education.

The need for relatedness

The need for relatedness is the desire to establish close emotional bonds and attachments with others. When teachers and parents are responsive and demonstrate that they care about the children's interests and well-being, the children show high intrinsic motivation. However, when children are denied the interpersonal involvement they seek from adults – when adults, for example, are unresponsive to their needs – the children lose intrinsic motivation (Solomon *et al.*, 2000). Learners who feel a sense of relatedness to teachers, parents and peers are more emotionally engaged in school (Furrer and Skinner, 2003). In addition, emotional and physical problems – ranging from eating disorders to suicide – are more common among people who lack social relationships (Baumeister and Leary, 1995). Relatedness is similar to a sense of belonging, discussed in Chapter 3. We will explore belonging and engaged learning in the next chapter (Osterman, 2000). Next we will look at how needs are involved in the learning situation.

Needs: lessons for teachers

From infancy to old age, people want to be both competent and connected. Learners are more likely to participate in activities that help them become more competent and less likely to engage in activities that cause them to fail. This means that the learners need appropriately challenging tasks – not too easy, but not impossible either. They also benefit from ways of watching their competence grow, perhaps through self-monitoring systems or portfolios. To be connected, learners need to feel that people in school care about them and can be trusted to help them learn.

What else matters in motivation? Many theories include goals as key elements.

Goal Orientations and Motivation

Goal

What an individual strives to accomplish.

A goal is an outcome or attainment an individual is striving to accomplish (Locke and Latham, 2002). When learners strive to read a chapter or complete an assignment, they are involved in *goal-directed behaviour*. In pursuing goals, learners are generally aware of some current condition (I haven't even opened my book), some ideal condition (I have understood every page), and the discrepancy between the current and ideal situations. Goals motivate people to act in order to reduce the discrepancy between 'where they are' and 'where they want to be'. Goal setting is usually effective for this co-author. In addition to the routine tasks, such as eating lunch, which will happen without much attention, she often sets goals for each day. For example, today she intends to finish this section, answer all emails, call at the supermarket and stock up with enough food for the next four days, and wash another load of clothes (not too exciting). Having decided to do these things, she will feel uncomfortable if she doesn't complete the list.

According to Locke and Latham (2002), there are four main reasons why goal setting improves performance. Goals:

1. *Direct our attention* to the task at hand and away from distractions. Every time my mind wanders from this chapter, my goal of finishing the section helps direct my attention back to the writing.

2. *Energise effort.* The more challenging the goal, to a point, the greater the effort.

3. *Increase persistence.* When we have a clear goal, we are less likely to give up until we reach the goal: hard goals demand effort and tight deadlines lead to faster work.

4. *Promote the development of new knowledge and strategies* when old strategies fall short. For example, if your goal is getting an A and you don't reach that goal on your first assignment, you might try a new approach for the next assignment, such as discussing the key points with a tutor.

Types of goals and goal orientations

The types of goals we set influence the amount of motivation we have to reach them. Goals that are specific, moderately difficult and likely to be reached in the near future tend to enhance motivation and persistence (Pintrich and Schunk, 2002; Stipek, 2002). Specific goals provide clear standards for judging performance. If performance falls short, we keep going. For example, this co-author has decided to 'finish this section' instead of deciding to 'work on the book'. Anything short of having the section ready to send means 'keep working' (not looking out of the window at the rain!). Moderate difficulty provides a challenge, but not an unreasonable one. She can finish this section if she sticks at it. Finally, goals that can be reached fairly soon are not likely to be pushed aside by more immediate concerns. Self-help groups such as Alcoholics Anonymous show they are aware of the motivating value of short-term goals when they encourage their members to stop drinking 'one day at a time'. Let us look at some goal orientations within the context of schools.

Four goal orientations in school

Goals are specific targets. Goal orientations are patterns of beliefs about goals related to achievement in school. Goal orientations include the reasons we pursue goals and the standards we use to evaluate progress towards those goals. There are four main goal orientations – mastery (learning), performance (looking good), work-avoidance and social (Murphy and Alexander, 2000; Pintrich and Schunk, 2002). In the Stop and Think exercise above, can you tell which goal orientations are reflected in the different answers? Most of the questions were adapted from a study on learners' theories about learning mathematics (Nicholls *et al.*, 1990).

The most common distinction in research on learners' goals is between mastery goals (also called *task goals* or *learning goals*) and performance goals (also called *ability goals* or *ego goals*) (Midgley, 2001). The point of a mastery goal is to improve, to learn, no matter how many mistakes you make or how awkward you appear. People who set mastery goals tend to seek challenges and persist when they encounter difficulties. Because they focus on the task at hand and are not worried about how their performance 'measures up' compared to others in the class, these learners have been called task-involved learners (Nicholls and Miller, 1984). We often say that these people 'get lost in their work'. In addition, they are more likely to seek appropriate help, use deeper cognitive processing strategies, apply better study strategies and generally approach academic tasks with confidence (Butler and Neuman, 1995; Midgley, 2001; Young, 1997).

The second kind of goal is a performance goal. Learners with performance goals care about demonstrating their ability to others. They may be focused on getting good exam and assignment grades, or they may be more concerned with winning and beating others (Wolters, Yu and Pintrich, 1996). Learners whose goal is outperforming others may do things to look clever, such as reading easy books in order to 'read the most books' (Young, 1997). The evaluation of their performance by others, not what they learn, is what matters. These learners have been called ego-involved learners because they are preoccupied with themselves. People with performance goals may act in ways that actually interfere with learning. For example, they may cheat or use shortcuts to get finished, work hard only on graded assignments, be upset and hide work with low grades, choose tasks that are easy, and be very uncomfortable with assignments that have unclear evaluation criteria (Stipek, 2002).

Are performance goals always bad?

Performance goals sound fairly dysfunctional, don't they? Earlier research indicated that performance goals generally were detrimental to learning, but like extrinsic motivation, a performance goal orientation may not be all bad all of the time. In fact, some research indicates that both mastery and performance goals are associated with using active learning strategies and high self-efficacy (Midgley, Kaplan and Middleton, 2001; Stipek, 2002). And, like intrinsic and extrinsic motivation, learners can, and often do pursue mastery and performance goals at the same time.

Goal orientations

Patterns of beliefs about goals related to achievement in school.

Mastery goal

A personal intention to improve abilities and learn, no matter how performance suffers.

Task-involved learners

Learners who focus on mastering the task or solving the problem.

Performance goal

A personal intention to seem competent or perform well in the eyes of others.

Ego-involved learners

Learners who focus on how well they are performing and how they are judged by others.

Table 10.2 Goal orientations

Pupils may have either an approach or an avoidance focus for mastery and performance goal orientations.

Goal orientation	Approach focus	Avoidance focus
Mastery	*Focus:* Mastering the task, learning, understanding	*Focus:* Avoiding misunderstanding or not mastering the task
	Standards used: Self-improvement, progress, deep understanding (task-involved)	*Standards used:* Just don't be wrong; perfectionists don't make mistakes
Performance	*Focus:* Being superior, winning, being the best	*Focus:* Avoiding looking stupid, avoid losing
	Standards used: Normative – getting the highest grade, winning the competition (ego-involved goal)	*Standards used:* Normative – don't be the worst, get the lowest grade, or be the slowest (ego-involved goal)

Source: Schunk, Dale H.; Pintrich, Paul R.; Meese, Judith, *Motivation in Education: Theory, Research, and Applications, 3rd Edition,* © 2008, p. 189.

To account for these recent findings, educational psychologists have added the distinction of approach/avoidance to the mastery/performance distinction. In other words, learners may be motivated to either approach mastery or avoid misunderstanding. They may approach performance or avoid looking stupid. Table 10.2 shows examples and the effects of each kind of goal orientation. Where do you see the most problems? Do you agree that the real problems are with avoidance? Learners who fear misunderstanding (mastery avoid) may be perfectionist – focused on getting it exactly right. Learners who avoid looking stupid (performance avoid) may adopt defensive, failure-avoiding strategies such as pretending not to care, making a show of 'not really trying', or cheating (Harackiewiz *et al.*, 2002).

Beyond mastery and performance

Some learners don't want to learn or to look clever; they just want to avoid work. These learners try to complete assignments and activities as quickly as possible without exerting much effort (Pintrich and Schunk, 2002). John Nicholls (1984) called these students work-avoidant learners – they feel successful when they don't have to try hard, when the work is easy, or when they can 'play around' instead of working.

A final category of goals becomes more important as people get older – social goals. As learners move into adolescence, their social networks change to include more peers and the learning goals set by schools may serve to frustrate learners' social goals (Boekaerts, 2002). Non-academic activities such as going out socially with friends, dating and 'chilling out' compete with schoolwork (Urdan and Maehr, 1995). Social goals include a wide variety of needs and motives that have different relationships to learning – some help, but some hinder learning. For example, adolescents' goal of maintaining friendly relations can get in the way of learning when cooperative learning group members don't challenge wrong answers or misconceptions because they are afraid to hurt each other's feelings (Anderson, Holland and Palincsar, 1997). Certainly, pursuing goals such as having fun with friends or avoiding being labelled a

Work-avoidant learners

Learners who don't want to learn or to look smart, but just want to avoid work.

Social goals

A wide variety of needs and motives to be connected to others or part of a group.

'geek' can get in the way of learning, but the goal of bringing honour to your family or team by working hard can also support learning (Urdan and Maehr, 1995). Social goals that include being a part of peer groups that value academics certainly can support learning (Pintrich, 2003; Ryan, 2001). It is worth remembering, also, that teachers impose social goals upon their learners by placing conditions around their learning experiences (e.g. 'you have to work in groups for this presentation task' or 'this work must be done on your own') which may conflict with other goals. Boekaerts (2002) suggests that many forms of misbehaviour in class can be seen in terms of goal conflict and that teachers should treat learners with respect and explain their reasons for imposing the demands that they do.

We talk about goals in separate categories, but learners have to coordinate their goals so they can make decisions about what to do and how to act. As noted above, sometimes social and academic goals are incompatible. For example, if learners do not see a connection between achievement in school and success in life, particularly because discrimination prevents them from succeeding, then those individuals are not likely to set academic achievement as a goal. Sometimes, succeeding in the peer group means not succeeding in school – and succeeding in the peer group is important. The need for social relationships is basic and strong for most people. Such anti-academic peer groups seem to exist in many American and English secondary schools (Elliott *et al.*, 2000) although Hufton *et al.* (2002) found differences in Russian secondary schools where peer influence was generally actively pro-learning and study. Clearly there are cultural differences here which are influencing the perceptions of learners about desirable goals.

Feedback and goal acceptance

Besides having specific goals and creating supportive social relationships, there are two additional factors that make goal-setting in the classroom effective. The first is *feedback*. In order to be motivated by a discrepancy between 'where you are' and 'where you want to be', you must have an accurate sense of both your current status and how far you have to go. There is evidence that feedback emphasising progress is the most effective. In one study, feedback to adults emphasised either that they had accomplished 75% of the standards set or that they had fallen short of the standards by 25%. When the feedback highlighted accomplishment, the participants' self-confidence, analytic thinking and performance were all enhanced (Bandura, 1997).

The second factor affecting motivation to pursue a goal is *goal acceptance*. If learners reject goals set by others or refuse to set their own goals, then motivation will suffer. Generally, individuals are more willing to commit to the goals of others if the goals seem realistic, reasonably difficult and meaningful – and if good reasons are given for the value of the goals (Grolnick *et al.*, 2002). Commitment matters – the relationship between higher goals and better performance is strongest when people are committed to the goals (Locke and Latham, 2002). Let us now consider ways in which goals impact upon the learning situation.

Goals: lessons for teachers

Learners are more likely to work towards goals that are clear, specific, reasonable, moderately challenging and attainable within a relatively short period of time. If teachers focus on learner performance, high grades and competition, they may encourage individuals to set performance goals. This could undermine the learners' ability to learn and become task-involved (Anderman and Maehr, 1994). Learners may not yet be expert at setting their own goals or keeping these goals in mind, so encouragement and accurate feedback are necessary. If teachers use any reward or incentive systems, they need to ensure that the goal set is to *learn and improve* in some area, not just to perform well or look clever. They also need to be sure that the goal is not too difficult. Children and young people, like adults, are unlikely to stick with tasks or respond well to teachers who make them feel insecure or incompetent.

What else do we know about motivation? We know that feelings matter.

Interests and Emotions

How do you feel about learning? Excited, bored, curious, fearful? Today, researchers emphasise that learning is not just about the *cold cognition* of reasoning and problem solving. Learning and information processing are also influenced by emotion, so *hot cognition,* or heightened responses to stimuli, plays a role in learning as well (Miller, 2002; Pintrich, 2003). Learners are more likely to pay attention to, learn about, and remember events, images and readings that provoke emotional responses (Alexander and Murphy, 1998; Cowley and Underwood, 1998; Reisberg and Heuer, 1992) or that are related to their interests (Renninger, Hidi and Krapp, 1992). Sometimes, emotions interfere with learning by taking up attention or working memory space that could be used for learning (Pekrun *et al.,* 2002). How can these findings be used then to support learning in school?

Tapping interests

There are two kinds of interests – personal (individual) and situational – the trait and state distinction again. *Personal* or *individual interests* are more enduring aspects of the person, such as an enduring tendency to be attracted to or to enjoy subjects such as languages, history or mathematics, or activities such as sports, music or films. Learners with individual interests in learning in general seek new information and have more positive attitudes towards schooling. *Situational interests* are more short-lived

Learners' interest in and excitement about what they are learning are the most important factors in education

aspects of the activity, text or materials that catch and keep the learner's attention. Both personal and situational interests are related to learning from texts – greater interest leads to more positive emotional responses to the material, then to greater persistence, deeper processing, better remembering of the material and higher achievement (Ainley, Hidi and Berndorf, 2002; Pintrich, 2003; Schraw and Lehman, 2001). Interests increase when learners feel competent, so even if individuals are not initially interested in a subject or activity, they may develop interests as they experience success (Stipek, 2002).

Catching and holding interests

Whenever possible, it helps to connect academic content to learners' enduring personal interests but given that the content of teaching is determined by standards in most classrooms today, it is difficult to tailor lessons to each learner's personal interests. Teachers have to rely more on situational interest. A case study into the teaching of English as a second language in Hungarian secondary schools found that introducing physical objects (such as souvenirs, cartoons, newspapers, stamps, tickets, receipts, etc.) to bring the target culture into the classroom increased awareness and interest in pupils (Sztefka, 2002). Learners were encouraged to compare and contrast these with those in their own culture leading to discussions using English to increase fluency. However, the challenge is to not only to *catch* but also to *hold* learners' interest (Pintrich, 2003). For example, a study in secondary schools in the US found that using computers, groups and puzzles caught learners' interest in secondary mathematics classes, but the interests did not hold (Mitchell, 1993). Lessons that held interests over time included maths activities that were related to real-life problems and active participation in laboratory activities and projects. However, there are cautions in responding to learners' interests, as you can see in the Discussion Point below.

DISCUSSION POINT

Does making learning fun result in good learning?

When many new teachers are asked about how to motivate learners, they often mention making learning fun. It is true that connecting to learners' interests, stimulating curiosity and using fantasy all encourage motivation and engagement. But is it necessary for learning to be fun? Let us look at both sides to this debate.

Agree: Yes, making learning fun encourages good learning

A search for 'making learning fun' on Google.com brings up almost 32,000,000 entries. Clearly, there is interest in making learning fun. In 1987, Thomas Malone and Mark Lepper wrote a chapter on 'Making Learning Fun: A Taxonomy of Intrinsic Motivations for Learning'. Research shows that passages in texts that are more interesting are remembered better (Pintrich and Schunk, 2002). For example, learners who read books that interested them spent more time reading, read more words in the books and felt more positively about reading (Guthrie and Alao, 1997). Games and simulations can make learning more fun, too. A highly motivating primary school teacher in another study had her class set up a post office for the whole school. Each classroom in the school had an address and zip (postal) code. Children had jobs in the post office, and everyone in the school used the post office to deliver letters to pupils and teachers. Children designed their own stamps and set postal rates. The teacher said that the system 'improves their creative writing without them knowing it' (Dolezal *et al.*, 2003: 254).

Disagree: No, making learning fun may get in the way of good learning

As far back as the early 1900s, educators warned about the dangers of focusing on fun in learning. None other than John Dewey, who wrote extensively about the role of interest in learning, cautioned that you can't make boring lessons interesting by mixing in fun like you can make bad chilli good by adding some spicy hot sauce. Dewey wrote, 'When things have to be made interesting, it is because interest itself is wanting. Moreover, the phrase itself is a misnomer. The thing, the object, is no more interesting than it was before' (Dewey, 1913: 11–12). There is a good deal of research now indicating that adding interest by adding fascinating but irrelevant details actually gets in the way of learning the important information. These 'seductive details', as they have been called, divert the readers' attention from the less interesting main ideas (Harp and Mayer, 1998). For example, learners who read biographies of historical figures remembered more very interesting but unimportant information compared to interesting main ideas (Wade *et al.*, 1993). Shannon Harp and Richard Mayer (1998) found similar results with secondary school science texts. These texts added emotional interest and seductive details about swimmers and golfers who are injured by lightning to a lesson on the process of lightning. They concluded that, 'in the case of emotional interest versus cognitive interest, the verdict is clear. Adjuncts aimed at increasing emotional interest failed to improve understanding of scientific explanations' (1998: 100). The seductive details may have disrupted learners' attempts to follow the logic of the explanations and thus interfered with comprehending the text. Harp and Mayer conclude that 'the best way to help students enjoy a passage is to help them understand it' (1998: 100).

WHAT DO YOU THINK?

Agree or Disagree? Vote online at www.pearsoned.co.uk/woolfolkeuro.

Another source of interest is fantasy. For example, Cordova and Lepper (1996) found that individuals learned more mathematical facts during a computer exercise when they were challenged, as captains of star ships, to navigate through space by solving maths problems. The learners named their ships, stocked the (imaginary) galley with their favourite snacks, and named all the crew members after their friends. The Focus on Practice below gives other ideas.

FOCUS ON PRACTICE

Building on interests

Relating content objectives to learner experiences

Examples
1. With a teacher in another school, establishing pen pals across the classes. Through writing letters, learners might exchange personal experiences, photos, drawings, written work and ask and answer questions ('Have you done joined up writing yet?' 'What are you doing in maths now?' 'What are you reading?'). Letters can be mailed in one large envelope to save stamps.
2. Identifying classroom experts for different assignments or tasks. Who knows how to use the computer for graphics? How to search the Net? How to cook? How to use an index?

Identifying learner interests, hobbies and extracurricular activities that can be incorporated into class lessons and discussions

Examples
1. Having learners design and conduct interviews and surveys to learn about each other's interests.
2. Keeping the class library stocked with books that connect to learners' interests and hobbies.

Supporting instruction with humour, personal experiences and anecdotes that show the human side of the content

Examples
1. Sharing your own hobbies, interests and favourites.
2. Telling learners there will be a surprise visitor; then dressing up as the author of a story and talking about 'yourself' and your writing.

Using original source material with interesting content or details

Examples
1. Letters and diaries in history.
2. Darwin's notes in biology.

Creating surprise and curiosity

Examples
1. Having learners predict what will happen in an experiment, then showing them that they are wrong.
2. Providing quotes from history and asking learners to guess who said it.

Allowing choices based on learner interests

Examples

1. Choice of novels or short stories.
2. Choice of project focus in science.

For more information on learners' interests and motivation, see http://mathforum.org/~sarah/Discussion.Sessions/biblio.motivation.html.

Source: From *150 Ways to Increase Intrinsic Motivation in the Classroom* by James P. Raffini. Published by Allyn and Bacon, Boston, MA. Copyright © 1996 by Pearson Education. Also Pintrich, Paul R.; Schunk, Dale H., *Motivation in Education: Theory, Research, and Applications, 2nd Edition*, © 2002, pp. 298–299. Reprinted by permission of Pearson Education, Inc., Upper Saddle River, NJ.

Arousal: excitement and anxiety in learning

Arousal

Physical and psychological reactions causing a person to be alert, attentive, wide awake.

Just as we all know how it feels to be motivated, we all know what it is like to be aroused. Arousal involves both psychological and physical reactions – changes in brain wave patterns, blood pressure, heart rate and breathing rate. We feel alert, wide awake, even excited. To understand the effects of arousal on motivation, think of two extremes. The first is late at night. You are trying for the third time to understand a required reading, but you are so sleepy. Your attention drifts as your eyes droop. You decide to go to bed and get up early to study (a plan that you know seldom works). At the other extreme, imagine that you have a critical test tomorrow – one that determines whether you will get into the college/university you want. You feel tremendous pressure from everyone to do well. You know that you need a good night's sleep, but you are wide awake. In the first case, arousal is too low and in the second, too high.

Psychologists have known for years that there is an optimum level of arousal for most activities (Yerkes and Dodson, 1908). Generally speaking, higher levels of arousal are helpful on simple tasks such as sorting clothes to be washed, but lower levels of arousal are better for complex tasks such as taking exams. Let's look for a moment at how to increase arousal by arousing curiosity.

Curiosity: novelty and complexity

Interest and curiosity are related. Curiosity could be defined as a tendency to be interested in a wide range of areas (Pintrich, 2003). Almost 40 years ago, psychologists suggested that individuals are naturally motivated to seek novelty, surprise and complexity (Berlyne, 1966). Research on teaching has found that variety in teaching approaches and tasks can support learning (Brophy and Good, 1986; Stipek, 2002). For younger learners, the chance to manipulate and explore objects relevant to what is being studied may be the most effective way to keep curiosity stimulated. For older learners, well-constructed questions, logical puzzles and paradoxes can have the same effect. However, teachers have to do more than catch learners' interest, they have to hold it, so the questions and puzzles should be related to meaningful learning.

Some research suggests that curiosity arises when attention is focused on a gap in knowledge. 'Such information gaps produce the feeling of deprivation labelled *curiosity*. The curious person is motivated to obtain the missing information to reduce or eliminate the feeling of deprivation' (Lowenstein, 1994: 87). This idea is similar to Piaget's concept of disequilibrium, discussed in Chapter 2, and has a number of implications for teaching. First, learners need some base of knowledge before they can experience gaps in knowledge leading to curiosity. Second, learners must be aware of the gaps in order for curiosity to result. Asking learners to make guesses and then providing feedback can be helpful and mistakes, properly handled, can stimulate curiosity by pointing to missing knowledge. Finally, the more we learn about a topic, the more curious we may become about that subject. As Maslow (1970) predicted, fulfilling the need to know increases, not decreases, the need to know more. Let us now move on to consider the role of anxiety in learning and motivation.

As we discussed earlier, sometimes arousal is too high, not too low. Because classrooms are places where learners are tested and graded, anxiety can become a factor in classroom motivation.

Anxiety in the classroom

At one time or another, everyone has experienced anxiety, or a general uneasiness, a feeling of self-doubt and sense of tension. The effects of anxiety on school achievement are clear. 'From the time of the earliest work on this problem, starting with the pioneering work of Yerkes and Dodson (1908), to the present day, researchers have consistently reported a negative correlation between virtually every aspect of school achievement and a wide range of anxiety measures' (Covington and Omelich, 1987: 393). Anxiety can be both a cause and an effect of school failure – learners do poorly because they are anxious, and their poor performance increases their anxiety. Anxiety probably is both a trait and a state. Some learners tend to be anxious in many situations as it is part of their personality (trait anxiety), but some situations, such as tests, are especially anxiety provoking (state anxiety) (Covington, 1992; Zeidner, 1998).

Anxiety seems to have both cognitive and affective components. The cognitive side includes worry and negative thoughts – thinking about how bad it would be to fail and worrying that you will, for example. The affective side involves physiological and emotional reactions such as sweaty palms, upset stomach, racing heartbeat or fear (Pintrich and Schunk, 2002; Zeidner, 1995, 1998). Whenever there are pressures to perform, severe consequences for failure and competitive comparisons among learners, anxiety may be encouraged (Wigfield and Eccles, 1989). Also, research with school-age children shows a relationship between the quality of sleep (how quickly and how well you sleep) and anxiety. Better-quality sleep is associated with positive arousal or an 'eagerness' to learn (Meijer and van den Wittenboer, 2004). Poor-quality sleep, on the other hand, was related to debilitating anxiety and decreased school performance. You may have discovered these relationships for yourself in your own school career or working life.

How does anxiety interfere with achievement?

Anxiety interferes with learning and test performance at three points: focusing attention, learning and testing. When learners are engaging with new material, they must pay attention to it. Highly anxious learners evidently divide their attention between the new material and their preoccupation with how worried and nervous they are feeling. Instead of concentrating, they keep noticing the tight feelings in their chest, thinking, 'I'm so tense, I'll never understand this stuff!' From the beginning, anxious learners may miss much of the information they are supposed to learn because their thoughts are focused on their own worries (Cassady and Johnson, 2002; Paulman and Kennelly, 1984).

Further, the problems do not end here. Even if they are paying attention, many anxious learners have trouble learning material that is somewhat disorganised and difficult – material that requires them to rely on their memory. Unfortunately, much material in school could be described this way. In addition, many highly anxious learners have poor study habits. Simply learning to be more relaxed will not automatically

Anxiety

General uneasiness, a feeling of tension.

improve these individuals' performance; their learning strategies and study skills must be improved as well (Naveh-Benjamin, 1991).

Finally, anxious learners often know more than they can demonstrate on a test. They may lack critical test-taking skills, or they may have learned the materials but 'freeze and forget' on tests (Naveh-Benjamin, McKeachie and Lin, 1987).

Coping with anxiety

Some individuals, particularly those with learning disabilities or emotional disorders, may be especially anxious in school. When learners face stressful situations such as tests, they can use three kinds of coping strategies: *problem solving, emotional management* and *avoidance.* Problem-focused strategies might include planning a study schedule, borrowing good notes or finding a protected place to study. Emotion-focused strategies are attempts to reduce the anxious feelings, for example, by using relaxation exercises or describing the feelings to a friend. Of course, the latter might become an avoidance strategy, along with going out for a pizza or suddenly launching an all-out desk-cleaning attack (can't study until you get organised!). Different strategies are helpful at different points – for example, problem solving before and emotion management during an exam. Different strategies fit different people and situations (Zeidner, 1995, 1998).

Teachers may help highly anxious learners to set realistic goals, because these individuals often have difficulty making wise choices. They tend to select either extremely difficult or extremely easy tasks. In the first case, they are likely to fail, which will increase their sense of hopelessness and anxiety about school. In the second case, they will probably succeed on the easy tasks, but they will miss the sense of satisfaction that could encourage greater effort and ease their fears about schoolwork. Goal cards, progress charts or goal-planning journals may be helpful here.

Interests and emotions: lessons for teachers

It is important for teachers to make efforts to keep the level of arousal right for the task at hand. If learners are going to sleep, they could be energised by the introduction of variety, stimuli to pique their curiosity, items which surprise them or perhaps a brief chance to be physically active. Learning about their interests and incorporating these interests into lessons and assignments would be helpful. The Focus on Practice below includes suggestions for dealing with anxiety.

FOCUS ON PRACTICE

Coping with anxiety

Using competition carefully

Examples
1. Teachers should monitor activities to make sure no learners are being put under undue pressure.

2. During competitive games, teachers should ensure that all learners involved have a reasonable chance of succeeding.
3. Experimenting with cooperative learning activities might be useful.

Avoiding situations in which highly anxious learners will have to perform in front of large groups

Examples
1. Teachers might ask anxious learners questions that can be answered with a simple yes or no, or some other brief reply.
2. Giving anxious learners practice in speaking before smaller groups can help to reduce anxiety.

Making sure all instructions are clear. Uncertainty can lead to anxiety

Examples
1. Writing test instructions on the board or on the test itself instead of giving them orally.
2. Checking with learners to make sure they understand. Asking several individuals how they would do the first question, exercise or sample question on a test. Correct any misconceptions.
3. If a new format is to be used or a new type of task started, giving learners examples or models to show how it is done.

Avoiding unnecessary time pressures

Examples
1. Giving occasional tests which can be completed at home.
2. Making sure all learners can complete classroom tests within the time period given.

Removing some of the pressures from major tests and exams

Examples
1. Teaching test-taking skills; giving practice tests; providing study guides.
2. Avoiding basing most of a report on one test result.
3. Making extra-credit work available to add points to course grades.
4. Using different types of items in testing because some learners have difficulty with particular formats.

Developing alternatives to written tests

Examples
1. Trying oral, open-book or group tests.
2. Having learners do projects, organise portfolios of their work, make oral presentations or create a finished product.

Teaching learners self-regulation strategies (Schutz and Davis, 2000)

Examples

1. Before the test: encouraging individuals to see the test as an important and challenging task that they have the capabilities to prepare for. Helping learners stay focused on the task of getting as much information as possible about the test.
2. During the test: reminding learners that the test is important (but not overly important). Encouraging task focus – picking out the main idea in the question, slowing down, staying relaxed.
3. After the test: thinking back on what went well and what could be improved. Focus on controllable attributions – study strategies, effort, careful reading of questions, relaxation strategies.

For more information about test anxiety, see http://www.couns.uiuc.edu/Brochures/testanx.htm.

Beliefs and Self-Schemas

Thus far, we have talked about needs, goals, interests and emotions, but there is another factor that must be considered in explaining motivation. What do learners believe about themselves – their competence and the causes for success or failure? Let's start with a basic question: what do they believe about ability?

Beliefs about ability

STOP AND THINK

Rate these statements taken from Dweck (2000) on a scale from 1 (strongly agree) to 6 (strongly disagree).

- ☐ You have a certain amount of intelligence and you really can't do much to change it.
- ☐ You can learn new things, but you can't really change your basic intelligence.
- ☐ No matter who you are, you can change your intelligence a lot.
- ☐ No matter how much intelligence you have, you can always change it quite a bit.

Entity view of ability

Belief that ability is a fixed characteristic that cannot be changed.

Some of the most powerful beliefs affecting motivation in school are about *ability*. By examining these beliefs and how they affect motivation, we will understand why some people set inappropriate, unmotivating goals; why some learners adopt self-defeating strategies; and why some people seem to give up altogether.

Adults use two basic concepts of ability (Dweck, 1999, 2002). An entity view of ability assumes that ability is a *stable, uncontrollable* trait – a characteristic of the individual that cannot be changed. According to this view, some people have more ability than others, but the amount each person has is set. An incremental view of ability, on the other hand, suggests that ability is unstable and controllable – 'an ever-expanding repertoire of skills and knowledge' (Dweck and Bempechat, 1983: 144). By hard work, study or practice, knowledge can be increased and thus ability can be improved. What is your view of ability? Look back at your answers in the Stop and Think box above to see.

Young children tend to hold an exclusively incremental view of ability. Through the early primary years, most children believe that effort is the same as intelligence. Clever people try hard, and trying hard makes you clever. If you fail, you aren't clever and you didn't try hard (Dweck, 2000; Stipek, 2002). Children are age 11 or 12 before they can differentiate among effort, ability and performance. About this time, they come to believe that someone who succeeds without working at all must be *really* clever. This is when beliefs about ability begin to influence motivation (Anderman and Maehr, 1994).

Learners who hold an entity (unchangeable) view of intelligence tend to set performance goals to avoid looking bad in the eyes of others. They seek situations where they can look clever and protect their self-esteem. These learners keep doing what they can do well without expending too much effort or risking failure, because either one – working hard or failing – indicates (to them) low ability. To work hard but still fail would be devastating. Learners with learning disabilities are more likely to hold an entity view. Teachers who hold entity views are quicker to form judgements about learners and slower to modify their opinions when confronted with contradictory evidence (Stipek, 2002).

Incremental theorists, in contrast, tend to set mastery goals and seek situations in which learners can improve their skills, because improvement means getting smarter. Failure is not devastating; it simply indicates more work is needed. Ability is not threatened. Incremental theorists tend to set moderately difficult goals, the kind we have seen are the most motivating.

Beliefs about ability are related to other beliefs about what you can and cannot control in learning.

Beliefs about causes and control: attribution theory

One well-known explanation of motivation begins with the assumption that we try to make sense of our own behaviour and the behaviour of others by searching for explanations and causes. To understand our own successes and failures, particularly unexpected ones, we all ask 'Why?' Learners ask themselves, 'Why did I fail the test?' or 'Why did I do so well this term?' They may attribute their successes and failures to ability, effort, mood, knowledge, luck, help, interest, clarity of instructions, the interference of others, unfair policies, and so on. To understand the successes and failures of others, we also make attributions – that the others are clever or lucky or work hard, for example. Attribution theories of motivation describe how the individual's explanations, justifications and excuses about self or others influence motivation.

Bernard Weiner is one of the main educational psychologists responsible for relating attribution theory to school learning (Weiner, 1979, 1986, 1992, 1994a, 1994b, 2000; Weiner and Graham, 1989). According to Weiner, most of the attributed causes for successes or failures can be characterised in terms of three dimensions:

1. *locus* (location of the cause – whether it is internal or external to the person);
2. *stability* (whether the cause is likely to stay the same in the near future or can change); and
3. *controllability* (whether the person can control the cause).

Incremental view of ability

Belief that ability is a set of skills that can be changed.

Attribution theories

Descriptions of how individuals' explanations, justifications and excuses influence their motivation and behaviour.

Table 10.3 Weiner's theory of causal attribution

There are many explanations pupils can give for why they fail a test. Below are eight reasons representing the eight combinations of locus, stability and responsibility in Weiner's model of attributions.

Dimension classification	Reason for failure
Internal–stable–uncontrollable	Low aptitude
Internal–stable–controllable	Never studies
Internal–unstable–uncontrollable	Sick the day of the exam
Internal–unstable–controllable	Did not study for this particular test
External–stable–uncontrollable	School has hard requirements
External–stable–controllable	Instructor is biased
External–unstable–uncontrollable	Bad luck
External–unstable–controllable	Friends failed to help

Source: *Human Motivation: Metaphors, Theories, and Research* by Weiner, Bernard. Copyright 2005 by Sage Publications Inc Books. Reproduced with permission of Sage Publications Inc Books in the Format Textbook via Copyright Clearance Center.

Every cause for success or failure can be categorised on these three dimensions. For example, luck is external (locus), unstable (stability) and uncontrollable (controllability). Table 10.3 shows some common attributions for success or failure on a test. Notice that ability is usually considered stable and uncontrollable, but incremental theorists (who see abilities as changeable) would argue that ability is unstable and controllable. Weiner's locus and controllability dimensions are closely related to Deci's concept of *locus of causality*.

Weiner believes that these three dimensions have important implications for motivation because they affect expectancy and value. The *stability* dimension, for example, seems to be closely related to expectations about the future. If learners attribute their failure to stable factors such as the difficulty of the subject, they will expect to fail in that subject in the future but if they attribute the outcome to unstable factors such as mood or luck, they can hope for better outcomes next time. The *internal/external locus* seems to be closely related to feelings of self-esteem (Weiner, 2000). If success or failure is attributed to internal factors, success will lead to pride and increased motivation, whereas failure will diminish self-esteem. The *controllability* dimension is related to emotions such as anger, pity, gratitude or shame. If we feel responsible for our failures, we may feel guilt; if we feel responsible for successes, we may feel proud. Failing at a task we cannot control can lead to shame or anger.

Also, feeling in control of your own learning seems to be related to choosing more difficult academic tasks, putting in more effort, using better strategies and persisting longer in school work (Schunk, 2000; Weiner, 1994a, 1994b). Factors such as continuing discrimination against women, people of other races and individuals with special needs can affect these individuals' perceptions of their ability to control their lives (Beane, 1991; van Laar, 2000).

Attributions in the classroom

When usually successful learners fail, they often make internal, controllable attributions: they misunderstood the directions, lacked the necessary knowledge or simply did not study hard enough, for example. As a consequence, they usually focus on strategies for succeeding next time. This response often leads to achievement, pride and a greater feeling of control (Ames, 1992; Stipek, 2002).

The greatest motivational problems arise when learners attribute failures to stable, uncontrollable causes. Such learners may seem resigned to failure, depressed, helpless – what we generally call 'unmotivated' (Weiner, 2000). These individuals respond to failure by focusing even more on their own inadequacy and their attitudes towards schoolwork may deteriorate even further (Ames, 1992). Apathy is a logical reaction to failure if learners believe the causes are stable, unlikely to change and beyond their control. In addition, individuals who view their failures in this light are less likely to seek help; they believe nothing and no one can help (Ames and Lau, 1982).

Teacher actions and learner attributions

How do learners determine the causes of their successes and failures? Remember, we also make attributions about the causes of other peoples' successes and failures. When teachers assume that learner failure is attributable to forces beyond the learners' control, the teachers tend to respond with sympathy and avoid giving punishments. If, however, the failures are attributed to a controllable factor such as lack of effort, the teacher's response is more likely to be irritation or anger, and reprimands may follow. These tendencies seem to be consistent across time and cultures (Weiner, 1986, 2000).

What do learners make of these reactions from their teachers? Sandra Graham (1991; Graham and Weiner, 1996) gives some surprising answers. There is evidence that when teachers respond to learners' mistakes with pity, praise for a 'good try' or unsolicited help, the learners are more likely to attribute their failure to an uncontrollable cause – usually lack of ability. For example, Graham and Barker (1990) asked subjects of various ages to rate the effort and ability of two boys viewed on a videotape. On the tape, a teacher circulated around the class while learners worked. The teacher stopped to look at the two boys' papers, did not make any comments to the first boy, but said to the second, 'Let me give you a hint. Don't forget to carry your tens.' The second boy had not asked for help and did not appear to be stumped by the problem. All the age groups watching the tapes, even the youngest, perceived the boy who received help as being lower in ability than the boy who did not get help. It is as if the subjects read the teacher's behaviour as saying, 'You poor child, you just don't have the ability to do this hard work, so I will help.'

Does this mean that teachers should be critical and withhold help? Of course not! However, it is a reminder that 'praise as a consolation prize' for failing (Brophy, 1985) or over-solicitous help can give unintended messages. Graham (1991) suggests that many minority-group learners could be the victims of well-meaning pity from teachers. Seeing the very real problems that the learners face, teachers may relax requirements so the learners will 'experience success'. However, a subtle communication may accompany the pity, praise and extra help: 'You don't have the ability to do this, so I will overlook your failure.' It may be that children of racial origins other than those of the dominant culture are 'more likely to be the targets of sympathetic feedback from teachers and thus the recipients of low-ability cues' (1991: 28). This kind of benevolent feedback, even if well-intended, can be a subtle form of racism.

Beliefs about self-efficacy

We have already examined one of the most important self beliefs affecting motivation: self-efficacy. Self-efficacy is our beliefs about our personal competence or effectiveness *in a given area*. Bandura defines self-efficacy as 'beliefs in one's capabilities to organise and execute the courses of action required to produce given attainments' (1997: 3). In schools, we are particularly interested in self-efficacy for learning mathematics, writing, history, science, sports and other subjects, as well as for using learning strategies and for the many other challenges that classrooms present. Because it is a key concept in social cognitive theory, we discussed self-efficacy in depth in Chapter 9.

Self-efficacy

Beliefs about personal competence in a particular situation.

Self-efficacy and attributions affect each other. If success is attributed to internal or controllable causes such as ability or effort, then self-efficacy is enhanced. However, if success is attributed to luck or to the intervention of others, then self-efficacy may not be strengthened and efficacy also affects attributions, too. People with a strong sense of self-efficacy for a given task ('I'm good at maths') tend to attribute their failures to lack of effort ('I should have double-checked my work'). However, people with a low sense of self-efficacy ('I'm really bad at maths') tend to attribute their failures to lack of ability ('I'm just stupid'). So having a strong sense of self-efficacy for a certain task encourages controllable attributions, and controllable attributions increase self-efficacy. You can see that if a learner held an entity view (ability cannot be changed) and a low sense of self-efficacy, motivation would be destroyed when failures were attributed to lack of ability ('I just can't do this and I'll never be able to learn') (Bandura, 1997; Pintrich and Schunk, 2002). Teachers often voice frustrations about pupils who make no effort at all to learn or improve their work. The application of attribution theory may well be helpful in understanding and hopefully improving their motivation.

Beliefs about learned helplessness

Whatever the label, most theorists agree that a sense of efficacy, control or self-determination is critical if people are to feel intrinsically motivated. When people come to believe that the events and outcomes in their lives are mostly uncontrollable, they have developed learned helplessness (Seligman, 1975). (We looked at this briefly in Chapter 4 when we were considering learners with disabilities and the effects this might have upon their learning.) To understand the power of learned helplessness, consider this experiment (Hiroto and Seligman, 1975). Subjects receive either solvable or unsolvable puzzles. In the next phase of the experiment, all subjects are given a series of solvable puzzles. The subjects who struggled with unsolvable problems in the first phase of the experiment usually solve significantly fewer puzzles in the second phase. They have learned that they cannot control the outcome, so why should they even try?

Learned helplessness appears to cause three types of deficits: motivational, cognitive and affective. Learners who feel hopeless will be unmotivated and reluctant to attempt work. They expect to fail, so why should they even try – thus motivation suffers. Because they are pessimistic about learning, these learners miss opportunities to practise and improve skills and abilities, so they develop cognitive deficits. Finally, they often suffer from affective problems such as depression, anxiety and listlessness (Alloy and Seligman, 1979). Once established, it is very difficult to reverse the effects of learned helplessness. As we saw in Chapters 4 and 5, learned helplessness is a particular danger for learners with disabilities and learners who are the victims of discrimination. This has links with what we believe about our own self-worth so let us move on to this now.

Beliefs about self-worth

What are the connections between attributions for success and failure, and beliefs about ability, self-efficacy and self-worth? Covington and his colleagues suggest that these factors come together in three kinds of motivational sets: *mastery-oriented, failure-avoiding* and *failure-accepting*, as shown in Table 10.4 (Covington, 1992; Covington and Mueller, 2001; Covington and Omelich, 1987).

Mastery-oriented learners tend to value achievement and see ability as improvable (an incremental view), so they focus on mastery goals in order to increase their skills and abilities. They are not fearful of failure, because failing does not threaten their sense of competence and self-worth. This allows them to set moderately difficult

---

Learned helplessness

The expectation, based on previous experiences with a lack of control, that all one's efforts will lead to failure.

Mastery-oriented learners

Learners who focus on learning goals because they value achievement and see ability as improvable.

Table 10.4 Mastery-oriented, failure-avoiding and failure-accepting pupils

	Attitude towards failure	Goals set	Attributions	View of ability	Strategies
Mastery-oriented	Low fear of failure	Learning goals: moderately difficult and challenging	Effort, use of right strategy, sufficient knowledge is cause of success	Incremental; improvable	Adaptive strategies; e.g. try another way, seek help, practise/study more
Failure-avoiding	High fear of failure	Performance goals; very hard or very easy	Lack of ability is cause of failure	Entity; set	Self-defeating strategies; e.g. make a feeble effort, pretend not to care
Failure-accepting	Expectation of failure; depression	Performance goals or no goals	Lack of ability is cause of failure	Entity; set	Learned helplessness; likely to give up

goals, take risks and cope with failure constructively. They generally attribute success to their own effort, and thus they assume responsibility for learning and have a strong sense of self-efficacy. They perform best in competitive situations, learn fast, have more self-confidence and energy, are more aroused, welcome concrete feedback (it does not threaten them) and are eager to learn 'the rules of the game' so that they can succeed. All of these factors make for persistent, successful learning (Covington and Mueller, 2001; McClelland, 1985).

Failure-avoiding learners tend to hold an entity view of ability, so they set performance goals. They lack a strong sense of their own competence and self-worth separate from their performance. In other words, they feel only as clever as their last assignment or test grade, so they never develop a solid sense of self-efficacy. In order to feel competent, they must protect themselves (and their self-images) from failure. If they have been generally successful, they may avoid failure by taking few risks and 'sticking with what they know'. If, on the other hand, they have experienced some successes but also a good bit of failure, then they may adopt self-defeating strategies such as feeble efforts, setting very low or ridiculously high goals, or claiming not to care. Just before a test, a learner might say, 'I didn't revise this at all!' or 'All I want to do is pass.' Then, any grade above passing is a success. Procrastination is another self-protective strategy. Low grades do not imply low ability if the learner can claim, 'I did okay considering I didn't start the work until last night.' Some evidence suggests that blaming anxiety for poor test performance can also be a self-protective strategy (Covington and Omelich, 1987). As we can see, very little learning is going on here as individuals seek to protect themselves from failure in ways which negatively impact upon their actual learning.

Unfortunately, failure-avoiding strategies generally lead to the very failure the learners were trying to avoid. If failures continue and excuses wear thin, the learners may finally decide that they are incompetent. Their sense of self-worth and self-efficacy deteriorate. They give up and thus become failure-accepting learners. They are

Failure-avoiding learners

Learners who avoid failure by sticking to what they know, by not taking risks, or by claiming not to care about their performance.

Failure-accepting learners

Learners who believe their failures are due to low ability and there is little they can do about it.

Mastery-oriented learners are eager to learn and welcome feedback.

convinced that their problems are due to low ability. As we saw earlier, those learners who attribute failure to low ability and believe ability is fixed are likely to become depressed, apathetic and helpless feeling that they have little hope for change.

Teachers may be able to prevent some failure-avoiding learners from becoming failure-accepting by helping them to find new and more realistic goals. Also, some learners may need support in aspiring to higher levels in the face of sexual, social or ethnic stereotypes about what they 'should' want or what they 'should not' be able to do well such as girls being unable to do maths. This kind of support could make all the difference. Instead of pitying or excusing these learners, teachers can teach them how to learn, provide examples of role models and hold individuals accountable for their learning. This will help the learners develop a sense of self-efficacy for learning and avoid learned helplessness.

Beliefs and self-schemas: lessons for teachers

If learners believe they lack the ability to deal with higher mathematics, they will probably act on this belief even if their actual abilities are well above average. These people are likely to have little motivation to tackle trigonometry or calculus, because they expect to do poorly in these areas. If learners believe that failing means they are stupid, they are likely to adopt many self-protective, but also self-defeating, strategies. Just telling learners to 'try harder' is not particularly effective. Individuals need real evidence that effort will pay off, that setting a higher goal will not lead to failure, that they can improve and that abilities can be changed. They need authentic mastery experiences. The Focus on Practice below provides ideas for encouraging self-efficacy and self-worth.

How can we put together all this information about motivation? How can teachers create environments, situations and relationships that encourage motivation? We address these questions next.

FOCUS ON PRACTICE

Encouraging self-efficacy and self-worth

Emphasise learners' progress in a particular area

Examples

1. Return to earlier material when reviewing progress and show how 'easy' it is now.
2. Encourage learners to improve projects when they have learned more.
3. Keep examples of particularly good work in portfolios.

Make specific suggestions for improvement and revise grades when improvements are made

Examples

1. Return work with comments noting what the pupils did right, what they did wrong, and why they might have made the mistakes.
2. Experiment with peer editing.
3. Show learners how their revised, higher grade reflects greater competence and raises their overall grades.

Stress connections between past efforts and past accomplishments

Examples

1. Have individual goal-setting and goal-review sessions with learners, in which to reflect on how they solved difficult problems.
2. Confront self-defeating, failure-avoiding strategies directly.

Set learning goals for learners and model a mastery orientation for them

Examples

1. Recognise progress and improvement.
2. Share examples of how you have developed your abilities in a given area and provide other models of achievement who are similar to learners – no supermen or superwomen whose accomplishments seem unattainable.
3. Read stories about people who overcame physical, mental or economic challenges.
4. Don't excuse failure because a learner has problems outside school. Help the person succeed inside school.

For more in formation on self-efficacy, see www.emory.edu/EDUCATION/mfp/self-efficacy.html.

Motivation to Learn in School

Motivation to learn

The tendency to find academic activities meaningful and worthwhile and to try to benefit from them.

Teachers are concerned about developing a particular kind of motivation in their learners – the motivation to learn. Jere Brophy, a professor of teacher education in the US, describes motivation to learn as 'a student tendency to find academic activities meaningful and worthwhile and to try to derive the intended academic benefits from them. Motivation to learn can be construed as both a general trait and a situation-specific state' (1998: 205–206). Motivation to learn involves more than wanting or intending to learn. It includes the quality of the learner's mental efforts. For example, reading the text ten times may indicate persistence, but motivation to learn implies more thoughtful, active study strategies, such as summarising, elaborating the basic ideas, outlining in your own words, drawing graphs of the key relationships, and so on (Brophy, 1988).

What makes learner motivation a challenge in classrooms? In an interview, Jere Brophy listed five obstacles:

First, school attendance is compulsory and curriculum content and learning activities are selected primarily on the basis of what society believes students need to learn, not on the basis of what students would choose to do if given the opportunity . . . Second, teachers usually work with classes of 20 or more students and therefore cannot always meet each individual's needs, so some students are often bored and others are often confused or frustrated. Third, classrooms are social settings in which much that occurs is public, so that failures often produce not only personal disappointment but public embarrassment. Fourth, students are graded, and periodic reports are sent home to their parents. Finally, teachers and students often settle into familiar routines that become the 'daily grind'. School reduces to covering content (for the teachers) and completing assignments (for the students) (Gaedke and Shaughnessy, 2003: 206–207).

Although this is contextualised within the US similar concerns are present within many European settings such as England, Wales, France and Germany (QCA, 2006). In this challenging context, it would be wonderful if all learners were filled with the motivation to learn, but they are not. Teachers have three major goals. The first is to get learners productively involved with the work of the class; in other words, to create a *state* of motivation to learn. The second and longer-term goal is to develop in learners the *trait* of being motivated to learn so they will be able 'to educate themselves throughout their lifetime' (Bandura, 1993: 136). Finally, it is desirable for learners to be cognitively engaged – to think deeply about what they study. In other words, we want them to be *thoughtful* (Blumenfeld, Puro and Mergendoller, 1992).

In this chapter we examined the roles of intrinsic and extrinsic motivation, attributions, goals, interests, emotions and self-schemas in motivation. Table 10.5 shows how each of these factors contributes to motivation to learn. The central questions for the remainder of the chapter are: What can teachers do to encourage and support motivation to learn? How can teachers use knowledge about attributions, goals, interests, beliefs and self-schemas to increase motivation to learn? Let us begin by looking at the sorts of tasks which teachers give to learners.

Academic tasks

The work the pupil must accomplish, including the content covered and the mental operations required.

Tasks for learning

To understand how an academic task can affect learners' motivation, we need to analyse the task. Tasks can be interesting or boring for children and young people and tasks have different values for learners.

Table 10.5 Building a concept of motivation to learn

Motivation to learn is encouraged when the following six elements come together:

Source of motivation	Optimum characteristics of motivation to learn	Characteristics that diminish motivation to learn
Type of goal set	INTRINSIC: Personal factors such as needs, interests, curiosity, enjoyment	EXTRINSIC: Environmental factors such as rewards, social pressure, punishment
	LEARNING GOAL: Personal satisfaction in meeting challenges and improving; tendency to choose moderately difficult and challenging goals	PERFORMANCE GOAL: Desire for approval for performance in others' eyes; tendency to choose very easy or very difficult goals
Type of involvement	TASK-INVOLVED: Concerned with mastering the task	EGO-INVOLVED: Concerned with self in others' eyes
Achievement motivation	Motivation to ACHIEVE: Mastery orientation	Motivation to AVOID FAILURE: Prone to anxiety
Likely attributions	Successes and failures attributed to CONTROLLABLE effort and ability	Success and failures attributed to UNCONTROLLABLE causes
Beliefs about ability	INCREMENTAL VIEW: Belief that ability can be improved through hard work and added knowledge and skills	ENTITY VIEW: Belief that ability is a stable, uncontrollable trait

Task value

As you probably recall, many theories suggest that the strength of our motivation in a particular situation is determined by both our *expectation* that we can succeed and the *value* of that success to us. Learners' beliefs about the value of a task seem to predict the choices they make, such as whether to enroll in advanced science classes or join a team. Efficacy expectations predict achievement in doing the task – how well the learners actually perform in the advance science class or on the team (Wigfield and Eccles, 2002).

We can think of a task value as having four components: importance, interest, utility and cost (Eccles and Wigfield, 2001; Eccles, Wigfield and Schiefele, 1998). Importance or attainment value is the significance of doing well on the task; this is closely tied to the needs of the individual (e.g. the need to be well-liked or athletic). For instance, if someone has a strong need to appear intelligent and believes that a high grade on a piece of work shows this, then the piece of work has high attainment value for that person. A second component is interest or intrinsic value. This is simply the enjoyment one gets from the activity itself. Some people like the experience of academic learning. Others enjoy the feeling of hard physical effort or the challenge of solving puzzles. Tasks also can have utility value; that is, they help us achieve a short-term or long-term goal such as gain a degree. Finally, tasks have costs – negative consequences that might follow from doing the task such as not having time to do other things or looking awkward as you perform the task.

Importance or attainment value
The importance of doing well on a task; how success on the task meets personal needs.

Intrinsic or interest value
The enjoyment a person gets from a task.

Utility value
The contribution of a task to meeting one's goals.

You see from our discussion of task value that personal and environmental influences on motivation interact constantly. The task that learners are asked to accomplish is an aspect of the environment; it is external to the individual but the value of accomplishing the task is bound up with the internal needs, beliefs and goals of the learner.

Authentic task

Tasks that have some connection to real-life problems the learners will face outside the classroom.

Problem-based learning

Methods that provide learners with realistic problems that don't necessarily have right answers.

Authentic tasks

Recently, there has been a great deal written about the use of authentic tasks in teaching. An authentic task is one that has some connection to the real-life problems and situations that learners will face outside the classroom, both now and in the future. If you ask individuals to memorise definitions they will never use, to learn the material only because it is for a test, or to repeat work they already understand, then there can be little motivation to learn. However, if the tasks are authentic, learners are more likely to see the genuine utility value of the work and are also more likely to find the tasks meaningful and interesting. Problem-based learning is one example of the use of authentic tasks in teaching.

An example problem presented to one group of 12- and 13-year-olds in Illinois was, 'What should be done about a nuclear waste dump site in our area?' The learners soon learned that this real problem was not a simple one. Scientists disagreed about the dangers. Environmental activists demanded that the materials be removed, even if this bankrupted the company involved – one that employed many local residents. Some members of the state assembly wanted the material taken out of state, even though no place in the country was licensed to receive the toxic materials. The company believed the safest solution was to leave the materials buried. The learners had to research the situation, interview parties involved, and develop recommendations to be presented to state experts and community groups. In problem-based learning individuals take on different roles of people who have a genuine stake in the issue. This increases their motivation because they become part of the problem (Stepien and Gallagher, 1993). Let us now look at the choice and autonomy allowed to learners and consider how this might affect their motivation.

Connect and Extend

For an example of how learners' motivation might be increased, see Sarnow, K. (2006) *German school among first in Europe to host web experiment.* See the Companion Website (Web Link 10.1).

Supporting autonomy and recognising accomplishment

The second area which is relevant for teachers and those working with children involves how much choice and autonomy learners are allowed. Choice in schools is not the norm within mainstream schools in many parts of Europe and the US (QCA, 2006). Children and adolescents spend literally thousands of hours in schools where other people decide what will happen. Yet we know that self-determination and a sense of internal locus of causality are critical to maintaining intrinsic motivation (Reeve, Nix and Hamm, 2003). What can teachers do to support choice without creating chaos?

Supporting choices

Like totally unguided discovery or aimless discussions, unstructured or unguided choices can be counterproductive for learning (Garner, 1998). For example, Dyson (1997) found that children become anxious and upset when directed by teachers to draw or write about anything they want in any way they want. Dyson says that learners see this *unbounded choice* as a 'scary void'. Some undergraduate students find it disconcerting when they approach their independent study (dissertation) in the final year. This allows them to select an educational topic which is interesting to them. They are confused by too much choice and need tutorial support and guidance in order to help them narrow their options and decide upon a focus for their research.

The alternative is *bounded choice* – giving learners a range of options that set valuable tasks for them, but also allow them to follow personal interests. The balance must be just right: 'too much autonomy is bewildering and too little is boring' (Guthrie *et al.*, 1998: 185). One study found that, compared to controlling teachers, autonomy-supporting teachers listened more, resisted giving solutions to problems, gave fewer directives and asked more questions about what learners wanted to do (Reeve, Bolt and Cai, 1999). Let us now look at the way in which learners' achievements are recognised by teachers and how this impacts upon their motivation.

Recognising accomplishment

Learners should be recognised for improving on their own personal best, for tackling difficult tasks, for persistence and for creativity – not just for performing better than others. In Chapter 6 we noted that giving learners rewards for activities that they already enjoy can undermine intrinsic motivation which indicates the complexity involved in teaching. At times, praise can have paradoxical effects. For example, if two learners succeed and the teacher praises only one of them, the message, to other children at least, may be that the praised person had less ability and had to work harder to succeed, thus earning praise. So pupils may use the teacher's praise or criticism as cues about capabilities – praise means I'm not very clever, so when I succeed, I deserve recognition. Criticism means my teacher thinks I'm clever and could do better (Stipek, 2002).

What sort of recognition leads to engagement? An inquiry into pupil motivation at the University of Glasgow (Smith, 2005) concluded that feedback should be specific and realistic in order to have a positive effect. The inquiry also commented upon the complexity of praise and the way its effectiveness is related to the credibility of the person giving the praise, as well as the timing and frequency of the praise. Another area which is relevant to teachers in terms of learner motivation is relationships with other people within the learning situation.

Grouping, evaluation and time

You may remember a teacher who made you want to work hard – someone who made a subject come alive. Or you may remember how many hours you spent practising as a member of a team, orchestra, choir or theatre group. If you do, then you know the motivational power of relationships with other people.

Grouping and goal structures

Motivation can be greatly influenced by the ways we relate to the other people who are also involved in accomplishing a particular goal. Johnson and Johnson (1999) have labelled this interpersonal factor the goal structure of the task. There are three such structures: cooperative (which involves team work and team achievements, e.g. a relay race), competitive (where individuals believe they can only achieve their goals if others do not, e.g. a singles tennis match) and individualistic (where learners believe their own progress is not related to that of others, e.g. learning a new language).

Goal structure

The way learners relate to others who are also working towards a particular goal.

When the task involves complex learning and problem-solving skills, cooperation leads to higher achievement than competition, especially for learners with lower abilities. Individuals learn to set attainable goals and negotiate. They become more altruistic. The interaction with peers that learners enjoy so much becomes a part of the learning process and is likely to result in the need for belonging described by Maslow being met and motivation increasing (Stipek, 2002; Webb and Palincsar, 1996). There are many approaches to peer learning or group learning. We will examine these approaches in depth in Chapter 11.

Evaluation

The greater the emphasis on competitive evaluation and grading, the more learners will focus on performance goals rather than mastery and low-achieving individuals who have little hope of either performing well or mastering the task may simply want to get it over with. One study of six-year-olds found that low-achieving learners made up answers, filled in the page with patterns, or copied from others, just to get through their work. As one child said when she finished a word/definition matching exercise, 'I don't know what it means, but I did it' (Anderson *et al.*, 1985: 132). On closer examination, the researchers found that the work was much too hard for these learners, so they connected words and definitions at random.

How can teachers prevent learners from simply focusing on the grade or doing the work 'just to get finished'? The most obvious answer is to de-emphasise grades and emphasise learning in the class. Pupils need to understand the value of the work. Instead of saying, 'You will need to know this for the test,' learners could be told how the information will be useful in solving problems they want to solve. Teachers might suggest that the lesson will answer some interesting questions and communicate that understanding is more important than finishing. Unfortunately, many teachers find it difficult to follow this advice, particularly when they are constrained by the prescribed curriculum. One way to emphasise learning rather than grades is to use self-evaluation so that pupils are encouraged to assess their own work or progress. This strategy also supports autonomy.

Time

Most experienced teachers know that there is too much work and not enough time in the school day. Even if they become engrossed in a project, classes must stop and turn their attention to another subject area when the bell rings or when the timetable indicates it's time to move on to a new subject. Furthermore, learners must progress as a group. If particular individuals can move faster or if they need more time, they may still have to follow the pace of the whole group. So scheduling often interferes with motivation by making individuals move faster or slower than would be appropriate or by interrupting their involvement. It is difficult to develop persistence and a sense of self-efficacy when learners are not allowed to stick with a challenging activity. It is often a challenge for teachers to be able to make time for engaged and persistent learning.

Research in the US involved observing and interviewing primary teachers in eight Catholic schools and determined whether learners were low, moderate or high in their level of motivation (Dolezal *et al.*, 2003). Children in the low-engagement classes were restless and chatty as they faced their easy, undemanding classwork. The classrooms were bare, unattractive and filled with management problems. Instruction was disorganised. The class atmosphere was generally negative. The moderately engaged classrooms were organised to be learner-friendly with reading areas, group work area, posters and children's art work. The teachers were warm and caring, and they connected lessons to learners' background knowledge. Management routines were smooth and organised, and the class atmosphere was positive. The teachers were good at catching children's attention and encouraging them to become more self-regulating, but they had trouble holding attention, probably because the tasks were too easy. Highly engaging teachers had all the positive qualities of learner-friendly classrooms – positive atmosphere, smooth management routines, support for learner self-regulation and effective instruction – but they added more challenging tasks along with the support to succeed at these tasks. These teachers did not rely on one or two approaches to motivate their class; they applied a large repertoire of strategies.

Connect and Extend

Visit the DfES Standards website at www.standards.dfes.gov.uk/ and type in 'motivation' to access a range of interesting resources and discussions relevant to the learning situation in the UK.

Conclusions: Strategies to Encourage Motivation and Thoughtful Learning

Until four basic conditions are met, no motivational strategies are likely to succeed. First the classroom or learning area must be fairly organised and free constant interruptions and disruptions (Chapter 11 gives more detailed information on this). Second, the teacher needs to be patient and supportive, avoiding embarrassing learners for mistakes. The class should be encouraged to see mistakes as learning opportunities (Clifford, 1990, 1991). Third, the work must be challenging but reasonable. If it is too easy or too difficult, learners will have less motivation to learn and are likely to focus upon finishing the work rather than learning. Finally, the learning tasks should be authentic (Stipek, 1993).

Once these four basic conditions are met, the influences which teachers might have upon learners' motivation to learn in a particular situation can be summarised in three questions:

1. *Can I succeed at this task?*

2. *Do I want to succeed?*

3. *What do I need to do to succeed?*

(Eccles and Wigfield, 1985)

Teachers will want to encourage confidence in learners so that they approach tasks with energy and enthusiasm. They want learners to see the value of the tasks and strive to learn not to just get a good grade or finish the work as quickly as possible. Teachers want learners to believe that they will succeed if they apply appropriate learning strategies instead of believing that their only option is to use self-defeating strategies which confirm their inability to learn. Table 10.6 summarises these basic requirements and strategies for encouraging learners' motivation.

Table 10.6 Strategies to encourage motivation to learn

This table refers to the entire motivation to learn in schools section of the text.

Fulfill basic requirements

- Provide an organised class environment
- Be a supportive teacher
- Assign challenging, but not too difficult, work
- Make tasks worthwhile

Build confidence and positive expectations

- Begin work at the pupils' level
- Make learning goals clear, specific and attainable
- Stress self-comparison, not competition
- Communicate that academic ability is improvable
- Model good problem solving

Show the value of learning

- Connect the learning task to the needs of the pupils

- Tie class activities to the pupils' interests
- Arouse curiosity
- Make the learning task fun
- Make use of novelty and familiarity
- Explain connections between present learning and later life
- Provide incentives and rewards, if needed

Help pupils stay focused on the task

- Give pupils frequent opportunities to respond
- Provide opportunities for pupils to create a finished product
- Avoid heavy emphasis on grading
- Reduce task risk without oversimplifying the task
- Model motivation to learn
- Teach learning tactics

SUMMARY TABLE

What is Motivation? (pp. 438–444)

Define motivation

Motivation is an internal state that arouses, directs and maintains behaviour. The study of motivation focuses on how and why people initiate actions directed towards specific goals, how long it takes them to get started in the activity, how intensively they are involved in the activity, how persistent they are in their attempts to reach these goals, and what they are thinking and feeling along the way.

What is the difference between intrinsic and extrinsic motivation?

Intrinsic motivation is the natural tendency to seek out and conquer challenges as we pursue personal interests and exercise capabilities – it is motivation to do something when we don't have to. Extrinsic motivation is based on factors not related to the activity itself. We are not really interested in the activity for its own sake; we care only about what it will gain us.

How does locus of causality apply to motivation?

The essential difference between intrinsic and extrinsic motivation is the person's reason for acting, that is, whether the locus of causality for the action is inside or outside the person. If the locus is internal, the motivation is intrinsic; if the locus is external, the motivation is extrinsic. Most motivation has elements of both. In fact, intrinsic and extrinsic motivation may be two separate tendencies – both can operate at the same time in a given situation.

What are the key factors in motivation according to a behavioural viewpoint? A humanistic viewpoint? A cognitive viewpoint? A sociocultural viewpoint?

Behaviourists tend to emphasise extrinsic motivation caused by incentives, rewards and punishment. Humanistic views stress the intrinsic motivation created by the need for personal growth, fulfilment and self-determination. Cognitive views stress a person's active search for meaning, understanding and competence and the power of the individual's attributions and interpretations. Sociocultural views emphasise legitimate engaged participation and identity within a community.

Distinguish between deficiency needs and being needs in Maslow's theory

Maslow called four lower-level needs – survival, safety, belonging and self-esteem – deficiency needs. When these needs are satisfied, the motivation for fulfilling them decreases. He labelled the top-level needs as being needs. When they are met, a person's motivation does not cease; instead, it increases to seek further fulfilment.

What are expectancy D7 value theories?

Expectancy D7 value theories suggest that motivation to reach a goal is the product of our expectations for success and the value of the goal to us. If either is zero, our motivation is zero also.

What is legitimate peripheral participation?

Legitimate peripheral participation means that beginners are genuinely involved in the work of the group, even if their abilities are undeveloped and their contributions are small. The identities of the novice and the expert are bound up in their participation in the community. They are motivated to learn the values and practices of the community to keep their identity as community members.

Needs: Competence, Autonomy and Relatedness (pp. 444–447)

What are the basic needs that affect motivation and how does self-determination affect motivation?

Self-determination theory suggests that motivation is affected by the need for competence, autonomy and control and relatedness. When learners experience self-determination, they are intrinsically motivated – they are more interested in their work, have a greater sense of self-esteem and learn more. Whether learners experience self-determination depends in part on whether the teacher's communications with learners provide information or seek to control them. In addition, teachers must acknowledge the learners' perspective, offer choices, provide rationales for limits and treat poor performance as a problem to be solved rather than a target for criticism.

Goal Orientations and Motivation (pp. 448–452)

What kinds of goals are the most motivating?

Goals increase motivation if they are specific, moderately difficult and able to be reached in the near future.

Describe mastery, performance, work-avoidant and social goals

A mastery goal is the intention to gain knowledge and master skills, leading learners to seek challenges and persist when they encounter difficulties. A performance goal is the intention to get good grades or to appear smarter or more capable than others, leading learners to be preoccupied with themselves and how they appear (ego-involved learners). Learners can approach or avoid these two kind of goals – the problems are greatest with avoidance. Another kind of avoidance is evident with work-avoidant learners, who simply want to find the easiest way to handle the situation. Learners with social goals can be supported or hindered in their learning, depending on the specific goal (i.e. have fun with friends or bring honour to the family).

What makes goal-setting effective in the classroom?

In order for goal-setting to be effective in the classroom, learners need accurate feedback about their progress towards goals and they must accept the goals set. Generally, learners are more willing to adopt goals that seem realistic, reasonably difficult and meaningful, and for which good reasons are given for the value of the goals.

Interests and Emotions (pp. 452–460)

How do interests and emotions affect learning?

Learning and information processing are influenced by emotion. Learners are more likely to pay attention to, learn and remember events, images and readings that provoke emotional responses or that are related to their personal interests. However, there are cautions in responding to learners' interests. 'Seductive details', interesting bits of information that are not central to the learning, can hinder learning.

What is the role of arousal in learning?

There appears to be an optimum level of arousal for most activities. Generally speaking, a higher level of arousal is helpful on simple tasks, but lower levels of arousal are better for complex tasks. When arousal is too low, teachers can stimulate curiosity by pointing out gaps in knowledge or using variety in activities. Severe anxiety is an example of arousal that is too high for optimal learning.

How does anxiety interfere with learning?

Anxiety can be the cause or the result of poor performance; it can interfere with attention to, learning of, and retrieval of information. Many anxious learners need help in developing effective test-taking and study skills.

Beliefs and Self-Schemas (pp. 460–467)

How do beliefs about ability affect motivation?

When people hold an entity theory of ability – that is, they believe that ability is fixed – they tend to set performance goals and strive to protect themselves from failure. When they believe ability is improvable (an incremental theory), however, they tend to set mastery goals and handle failure constructively.

What are the three dimensions of attributions in Weiner's theory?

According to Weiner, most of the attributed causes for successes or failures can be characterised in terms of three dimensions: *locus* (location of the cause internal or external to the person), *stability* (whether the cause stays the same or can change) and *responsibility* (whether the person can control the cause). The greatest motivational problems arise when learners attribute failures to stable, uncontrollable causes. These learners may seem resigned to failure, depressed, helpless – what we generally call 'unmotivated'.

What is self-efficacy, and how does it relate to learned helplessness?

Self-efficacy is a belief about personal competence in a particular situation such as learning or teaching fractions. A sense of efficacy, control or self-determination is critical if people are to feel intrinsically motivated. When people come to believe that the events and outcomes in their lives are mostly uncontrollable, they have developed learned helplessness, which is associated with three types of deficits: motivational, cognitive and affective. Learners who feel hopeless will be unmotivated and reluctant to attempt work. They miss opportunities to practise and improve skills and abilities, so they develop cognitive deficits and they often suffer from affective problems such as depression, anxiety and listlessness.

How does self-worth influence motivation?

Mastery-oriented learners tend to value achievement and see ability as improvable, so they focus on mastery goals, take risks and cope with failure constructively. A low sense of self-worth seems to be linked with the failure-avoiding and failure-accepting strategies intended to protect the individual from the consequences of failure. These strategies may seem to help in the short term, but are damaging to motivation and self-esteem in the long run.

Motivation to Learn in School (pp. 468–472)

Define motivation to learn

Teachers are interested in a particular kind of motivation – pupil motivation to learn. Pupil motivation to learn is both a trait and a state. It involves taking academic work seriously, trying to get the most from it, and applying appropriate learning strategies in the process.

What does TARGET stand for?

TARGET is an acronym for the six areas where teachers make decisions that can influence pupil motivation to learn: the nature of the *task* that learners are asked to do, the *autonomy* learners are allowed in working, how learners are *recognised* for their accomplishments, *grouping* practices, *evaluation* procedures and the scheduling of *time* in the classroom.

How do tasks affect motivation?

The tasks that teachers set affect motivation. When learners encounter tasks that are related to their interests, stimulate their curiosity, or are connected to real-life situations, the learners are more likely to be motivated to learn. Tasks can have attainment, intrinsic, or utility value for learners. Attainment value is the importance to the pupil of succeeding. Intrinsic value is the enjoyment the pupil gets from the task. Utility value is determined by how much the task contributes to reaching short-term or long-term goals.

Distinguish between bounded and unbounded choices

Like totally unguided discovery or aimless discussions, unstructured or unbounded choices can be counterproductive for learning. The alternative is bounded choice – giving learners a range of options that set out valuable tasks for them, but also allow them to follow personal interests. The balance must be just right so that learners are not bewildered by too much choice or bored by too little room to explore.

How can recognition undermine motivation and a sense of self-efficacy?

Recognition and reward in the classroom will support motivation to learn if the recognition is for personal progress rather than competitive victories. Praise and rewards should focus on learners' growing competence. At times, praise can have paradoxical effects when learners use the teacher's praise or criticism as cues about capabilities.

List three goal structures and distinguish among them

How learners relate to their peers in the classroom is influenced by the goal structure of the activities. Goal structures can be competitive, individualistic or cooperative. Cooperative goal structures can encourage motivation and increase learning, especially for low-achieving learners.

How does evaluative climate affect goal-setting?

The more competitive the grading, the more learners set performance goals and focus on 'looking competent', that is, the more they are ego-involved. When the focus is on performing rather than learning, learners often see the goal

of classroom tasks as simply finishing, especially if the work is difficult.

What are some effects of time on motivation?

In order to foster motivation to learn, teachers should be flexible in their use of time in the classroom. Learners who are forced to move faster or slower than they should or who are interrupted as they become involved in a project are not likely to develop persistence for learning.

Glossary

Academic tasks: The work the pupil must accomplish, including the content covered and the mental operations required.

Anxiety: General uneasiness, a feeling of tension.

Arousal: Physical and psychological reactions causing a person to be alert, attentive, wide awake.

Attribution theories: Descriptions of how individuals' explanations, justifications and excuses influence their motivation and behaviour.

Authentic task: Tasks that have some connection to real-life problems the learners will face outside the classroom.

Being needs: Maslow's top-level needs, sometimes called growth needs.

Cognitive evaluation theory: Suggests that events affect motivation through the individual's perception of the events as controlling behaviour or providing information.

Deficiency needs: Maslow's four lower-level needs, which must be satisfied first.

Ego-involved learners: Learners who focus on how well they are performing and how they are judged by others.

Entity view of ability: Belief that ability is a fixed characteristic that cannot be changed.

Expectancy D7 value theories: Explanations of motivation that emphasise individuals' expectations for success combined with their valuing of the goal.

Extrinsic motivation: Motivation created by external factors such as rewards and punishments.

Failure-accepting learners: Learners who believe their failures are due to low ability and there is little they can do about it.

Failure-avoiding learners: Learners who avoid failure by sticking to what they know, by not taking risks, or by claiming not to care about their performance.

Goal: What an individual strives to accomplish.

Goal orientations: Patterns of beliefs about goals related to achievement in school.

Goal structure: The way learners relate to others who are also working towards a particular goal.

Hierarchy of needs: Maslow's model of levels of human needs, from basic physiological requirements to the need for self-actualisation.

Humanistic interpretation: Approach to motivation that emphasises personal freedom, choice, self-determination and striving for personal growth.

Importance or attainment value: The importance of doing well on a task; how success on the task meets personal needs.

Incentive: An object or event that encourages or discourages behaviour.

Incremental view of ability: Belief that ability is a set of skills that can be changed.

Intrinsic motivation: Motivation associated with activities that are their own reward.

Intrinsic or interest value: The enjoyment a person gets from a task.

Learned helplessness: The expectation, based on previous experiences with a lack of control, that all one's efforts will lead to failure.

Legitimate peripheral participation: Genuine involvement in the work of the group, even if your abilities are undeveloped and contributions are small.

Locus of causality: The location – internal or external – of the cause of behaviour.

Mastery goal: A personal intention to improve abilities and learn, no matter how performance suffers.

Mastery-oriented learners: Learners who focus on learning goals because they value achievement and see ability as improvable.

Motivation: An internal state that arouses, directs and maintains behaviour.

Motivation to learn: The tendency to find academic activities meaningful and worthwhile and to try to benefit from them.

Need for autonomy: The desire to have our own wishes, rather than external rewards or pressures, determine our actions.

Performance goal: A personal intention to seem competent or perform well in the eyes of others.

Problem-based learning: Methods that provide learners with realistic problems that don't necessarily have right answers.

Psychoanalytic theory: Based upon the work of Sigmund Freud.

Reward: An attractive object or event supplied as a consequence of a behaviour.

Self-actualisation: Fulfilling one's potential.

Self-efficacy: Beliefs about personal competence in a particular situation.

Social goals: A wide variety of needs and motives to be connected to others or part of a group.

Sociocultural views of motivation: Perspectives that emphasise participation, identities and interpersonal relations within communities of practice.

Task-involved learners: Learners who focus on mastering the task or solving the problem.

Utility value: The contribution of a task to meeting one's goals.

Work-avoidant learners: Learners who don't want to learn or to look smart, but just want to avoid work.

CHECK YOUR LEARNING!

In the Classroom: What Would They Do?

At the beginning of the chapter we looked at a teacher confronted with pupils who lacked motivation and raised the following questions:

- Are these learners 'unmotivated'?
- Why might they be so pessimistic about learning?
- How might their attitudes be changed?
- In what ways does the learners' lack of motivation affect teachers?

Here is how some practising teachers responded to the challenge of motivating learners:

Janet, secondary school teacher in Edinburgh, Scotland

I would start off by finding ways for these demotivated children to succeed – even if it was only on small tasks, so that their subsequent 'I can't do it' comments can be challenged against their success. Everyone wants to succeed, even if they pretend otherwise, so it is about encouraging and allowing them to do this in their own ways, developing their own strengths.

I had a lad called Steven in my English Literature class who was a real rebel and did very little work – what he did do was of a poor standard and his grammar was awful. He had the reputation of being tough and his peers treated him with a sort of grudging respect but he didn't really have any friends. I gave them some creative writing to do which including dialogue (in a script format) about a 'family breakfast'. His was excellent. It had everything – realism, dialect, humour – I was amazed. I reflected that when he wasn't constrained by the limits of formal language, his use of it was creative and acutely observed. I read it aloud to the class (with regional accents) along with a selection of others (all anonymously) and asked the class to feedback and comment. They all thought Steven's was really good and wanted to know who had written it. One boy even said, 'Is it yours, Miss?'

There was no looking back after this as Steven had found a way to succeed and realised the genuineness of the feedback – it wasn't just to encourage him it was real. His formal English improved along with his motivation and he eventually got a high grade in the GCSE exams. I saw him years later and he told me he had succeeded in getting a place at university and how proud his family were. He just needed that self-belief to motivate him.

Mervyn, primary school teacher in West Midlands, England

The first class I was ever given was really hard because the children just didn't want to be there. They were ten- and 11-year-olds so they were in their last year of upper primary (or junior school) before going on to secondary school and three of the children had twice been excluded for bad behaviour. There was a feeling of real apathy in that class so that you could almost hear the yawns. The only time they sat up straight and paid attention was when the bell was due to ring. It didn't seem to matter how hard I tried to make the lessons interesting, they just didn't want to know. I found myself dreading every day and thinking that teaching was not for me. This made me give up in the same way that the class seemed to have given up. It was very depressing. Luckily the head teacher was aware enough to see what was happening and she arranged for me to teach another class for two afternoons each week. The difference was amazing – the new class actually seemed motivated to learn and were much more responsive to the work I had prepared. I began to believe that I could teach and started to be more creative and relaxed in my teaching. I was surprised to find that this rubbed off to some extent with my own class and some of them became more engaged as a result. I realised that teaching and motivation is a two-way process.

Overview

11 Engaged Learning: Cooperation and Community

In this chapter, we look at several important aspects of engagement that are critical for success both in and out of school. We begin with collaboration and cooperation – working with others to learn. Next, we examine the idea of the larger classroom community. Finally, we move to examine learning through engagement outside the classroom walls. Throughout the chapter, we focus on what teachers can do to support engagement in learning for all pupils.

By the time you have completed this chapter, you should be able to answer the following questions:

- **How do social relationships affect learning in school?**

- **How can cooperative learning strategies promote academic and social development?**

- **What are some of the problems that might occur with cooperative learning, and how can teachers avoid them?**

- **How can teachers create a learning community in the classroom?**

- **What can be done to prevent and respond to school violence?**

- **What are the possibilities and potential problems with community service learning?**

In the Classroom

Recently you noticed that some of the girls in your class have become increasingly reticent to answer questions or take part in group discussions and projects. One of them, Emily, is a bright girl who at the start of the year had a cheerful disposition and seemed quite popular. At parents' evening her mother complains that she expected her to change as she grew up 'but not like this! Emily has always been such a good girl, but now she won't go to bed, won't get up in the morning, won't eat the food we cook and is rude and moody. I almost have to drag her to school and all she does in the evenings is hang around in the local park.'

All this sounds pretty normal to you except there are rumours in the school that a group of older girls in another class have formed a gang called 'The Posse' and several girls and boys in the school have complained about bullying and intimidation. If the stories are to be believed, the posse 'picks off' targets – younger girls to be their spies in other classes and report anyone who answers questions, takes an active part in the lesson or shows any interest. Thinking back it has been increasingly hard to get the class going on group tasks or to get any response in question and answer sessions. It's not quite out-and-out rebellion but Emily isn't the only one in the class who might have been got at by 'The Posse'. In the staff room there is talk of other secret gangs in the school – based on neighbourhood gangs – which are becoming increasingly powerful and 'out of hand'. There's even been reports of pupils bringing knives into school but some spot checks have revealed none to date. What should you do? What is your immediate response to Emily's mother? How would you find out what is happening without making the situation worse? Over the next few weeks and months, how should the school to respond to parents' and teachers' concerns about gangs developing in the school?

Group Activity

With another member of your group, role-play what you would say to Emily's mother and to Emily when you next challenge her about her seeming lack of interest. With a larger group role-play a staff meeting discussion about what should be done.

Introduction

Connect and Extend

Review sections in Chapter 3, Encouraging Cooperation, Chapter 6, Observation Learning, Chapter 9, Self-efficacy and Chapter 10, Motivation, using page references from the Name Index for Albert Bandura. Bandura's *Principles of Behaviour Modification* (1969) is an excellent read for those seeking an in-depth approach to many of the themes in this present chapter.

Connect and Extend

Volume 39, nos 1–2, of the *International Journal of Educational Research* (2003) is entirely devoted to pupil groupings in classrooms and schools and the structuring of collaborative work.

The focus of this chapter is engaged learning. In some ways, the chapter is a culmination of what we have learned so far about individual differences, learning and motivation. Engagement includes behaviours such as attention, effort, persistence and resistance to distractions as well as emotions such as enthusiasm, pride, interest and enjoyment. Pupils can be engaged with their schools through friendships with their peers and teachers, participation in team sports and involvement in other extra-curricular activities: so engagement may incorporate social connections. Finally, engagement is cognitive because engaged pupils are investing their mental abilities in learning. They are using cognitive and metacognitive strategies, processing information, remembering and forming beliefs about themselves and others as learners.

Engaged learning is important for all pupils and schools because engaged pupils tend to be higher-achieving pupils; disengaged pupils are more likely to truant or drop out of school altogether (Fredricks, Blumenfeld and Paris, 2004). The consequences of disengagement are serious, especially for pupils placed at risk by poverty or discrimination. Pupils from privileged families seem better able to recover from dropping out of school, whether the dropping out is psychological or actual (Lee and Ip, 2003). However, pupils without social or financial advantages pay dearly in terms of life choices if they are disengaged (Vitaro *et al.*, 2001; Kalmijn and Kraaykamp, 2003; Jordan, 2001). Without educational credentials and skills, these pupils are at risk of poverty, unemployment, poor health and involvement in the criminal justice system. Yet many schools serving these pupils fail to engage them cognitively, emotionally or behaviorally (Leach, 2003; de Winter, Kroneman and Baerveldt, 1999; Brabant, Bourdon and Jutras 2003; Elliott *et al.*, 2001). What is needed? We say that attention to social processes is critical.

This girl is clearly engaged in learning. What web of social relations might support her engagement?

Social Processes in Learning

When you think about engagement in school, do you think about social and cultural influences on the pupils' learning? For example, do reading and books have different meanings for various pupils in classes. Have pupils seen different models of reading in their lives outside school. In the following pages, we will discuss how people learn through interactions with others and how social interaction, dialogue and culture affect learning – all are increasingly important topics in educational psychology. Two decades ago, Jerome Bruner, who pioneered the study of individual concept learning, said, 'I have come increasingly to recognize that learning in most settings is a communal activity, a sharing of culture' (1986: 27).

Let's consider three social influences on pupils – peers, parents and teachers.

Connect and Extend

See the entire issue of *Educational Leadership*, September 2002, *60*(1) for 14 articles on 'Do pupils care about learning?' These articles discuss how to create enthusiasm, excitement and investment in learning.

Peers

> **STOP AND THINK**
>
> Think back to secondary school – did you have friends in any of these groups: druggies, smokers, geeks, goths, bible bashers, trendies, normals, greebos, sporties, fakes, plastics, boffs? What were the main 'crowds' at your school? How did your friends influence you?

Over the past decade there have been any number of influential and informative studies into the effects of social groups, working groups, peer pressure, gender differences and social image on the attainment of pupils (e.g. Warrington *et al.*, 2000; Bevington and Wishart, 1999; Tinklin, 2003; Kutnick *et al.*, 2002). To understand the power of peers, we can also draw on our own experiences both as a pupil and a parent. In my 'former life' as a pupil, this co-author remembers the influence (not always good!) that 'friends' had on his attitude and behaviour in class. (He used to smoke on the back row of his maths class hiding the cigarettes in the desks and blowing the smoke out of an open window, and he still has trouble with logarithms.) He also remembers as a parent, watching his perfectly sweet and loveable son (who craved learning and doing new things) become a surly, ill-attentive, reluctant and disruptive ne'er-do-well at school, because (he argued) 'I'm not a geek or a boff!' All parents know just how expensive their children become once their peers discover branded fashion items (Elliott and Leonard, 2004).

Molly Warrington and colleagues at the University of Cambridge drew on a range of evidence from a three-year study in East Anglian schools pointing to different attitudes to General Certificate of Secondary Education (GCSE) work (public examinations taken at the age of 16). Their emphasis was on peer pressure, image and social groupings:

> *although these were relevant to both sexes, it was found to be more acceptable for girls to work hard and still be part of the 'in crowd', whilst boys were under greater pressure to conform to a 'cool', masculine image, and were more likely to be ridiculed for working hard (2000; 403).*

In particular they found that for boys acceptance by and into a group, usually entailed behaving in a laddish way: openly challenging authority, drawing attention to themselves, pretending not to care about work. This co-author often visits a wide

Connect and Extend

For Carolyn Jackson's article see the Companion Website (Web Link 11.1).

Connect and Extend

We saw in Chapter 5 that different SES groups and ethnic groups have different attitudes towards schooling and academic achievement. You might review some of those differences now.

range of secondary-school classrooms and cannot help but feel enormous sympathy for boys who privately see that such behaviour is not in their long-term interest but find it impossible to deviate from the accepted and expected group norm. Girls, too, are increasingly not protected from such peer group pressure.

Carolyn Jackson at Lancaster University explored whether some schoolgirls are adopting 'laddish' attitudes and behaviours (becoming 'ladettes'), and if they are, what the consequences might be in terms of educational experiences and outcomes. Overall, she made a strong case for arguing that 'laddish' behaviours are motivated in part by fears of academic failure, but that becoming laddettes can also be motivated by social goals; 'laddish' ways of performing are generally regarded as 'cool' and earn girls (and boys) 'popularity points' amongst peers. In other words, some girls may behave 'laddishly' in an attempt to be popular, or to avoid being unpopular. Social relationships constitute a crucial component of school life, and the consequences of social failure – frequently marginalisation and/or bullying – can be extremely distressing for all pupils. Fears of social failure motivate many pupils to try to 'fit in' because they are afraid of the consequences of becoming unpopular.

Parents and teachers

Does parental style affect how well pupils do at school? Well, if we compare the distribution of parental styles (e.g. degrees of acceptance, control, involvement and expectations) with various family characteristics (such as socioeconomic status, family structure, number of children, order of birth of the children) in a group of adolescents with normal academic achievement, parental style better predicts achievement. For pupils with low achievement, family variables play a more important role in predicting achievement (Casanova *et al.*, 2005).

So much for predicting achievement, but what about predicting problem behaviours. In 2005 Kaisa Aunola and Jari-Erik Nurmi (psychologists working at the University of Jyväskylä, Finland) investigated parenting styles (affection, behavioural control and psychological control) that would be most influential in predicting young children's problem behaviours. A total of 196 children (aged five and six years) were followed up six times to measure their problem behaviours. Mothers parenting styles dominated. The results showed that a high level of psychological control exercised by mothers combined with high affection predicted increases in the levels of problem behaviours among children. Behavioural control exercised by mothers decreased children's external problem behaviour but only when combined with a low level of psychological control.

It shouldn't really surprise us to find evidence going back many years that lack of parental love and approval in childhood result in a feeling of insecurity, low self-worth and of a difficulty in that most difficult arena for interpersonal relationships, the classroom (Bowlby, 1988). Loeber and Stouthamer-Loeber (1986), in considering the results of British, American and Scandinavian studies on family factors and behaviour, concluded that the primary influence was neglect of their children by parents, and the consequent lack of an active interest in them and a relationship with them. Also, poor parental control has been found in many studies to be related to problem behaviour and rejection of learning opportunities (e.g. McCord, 1979; Wilson, 1980; Riley and Shaw, 1985). What's needed is a clear, consistent system of rules and control based on a loving relationship. If the control structure is not applied, or if control is applied in an unloving way, then children lose the ability later on to rebuff negative peer pressure.

How about pupils who are a little older than those studied by Aunola and Nurmi? The class teachers of 109 nine- to 11-year-old primary school pupils (Riding and Fairhurst, 2001) were asked by Richard Riding and Pamela Fairhurst to rate the classroom conduct behaviour and home background of their pupils on five-point scales from very poor through to very good. This was done during the summer term and repeated by the new teachers of the classes during the following autumn term of the next school year. Unsurprisingly, the study confirmed that 'A child's behaviour will probably be greatly influenced by the quality of love and the stability of the home environment, and the control given' (Charlton and David, 1993: 32–36). Further-more, and again not surprisingly, they traced an interaction between gender and home background with girls behaving better than boys, and this being most pronounced when the home background was rated as poor.

In a couple of American studies pupils described their parents' styles and their peer-group orientation. Adolescents who characterised their parents as authori-tative (demanding but responsive, rational and democratic) were more likely to favour well-rounded crowds that rewarded both adult- and peer-supported norms such as 'normals' and 'boffs'. Pupils, especially girls, who characterised their parents as uninvolved were more likely to be oriented towards 'partyers' and 'druggies' who did not endorse adult values. Finally, boys with indulgent parents were more likely to be oriented towards fun-cultures such as 'partyers' (Durbin *et al.*, 1993). In fact, adolescents with authoritative parents are more likely to respond to peer pressure to do well in school and less likely to be swayed by peer pressure to use drugs or alcohol, especially when their friends also have authoritative parents (Collins *et al.*, 2000).

> **Connect and Extend**
>
> We saw in Chapter 3 (p. 103) that caring teachers are especially important for pupils who are placed at risk in schools.

When children do not have friends or have few friends, parents and teachers can play an important role in supporting school achievement. Kathryn Wentzel and her colleagues have found that perceived support from teachers is related to positive moti-vation for learning and adjustment in school for pupils (Wentzel and Battle, 2001). In addition, being liked by teachers can offset the negative effects of peer rejection in the middle years of schooling. Pupils who have few friends, but are not rejected – simply ignored by other pupils – can remain on-track academically and socially when they are liked and supported by teachers.

We can sum up the importance of social processes in supporting engaged learning by listening to the report of the Committee on Increasing High School Pupils' Engage-ment and Motivation to Learn:

> *Although learning involves cognitive processes that take place within each individual, motivation to learn also depends on the student's involvement in a web of social relationships that supports learning. The likelihood that pupils will be motivated and engaged is increased to the extent that their teachers, family, and friends effectively support their purposeful involvement in learning in school. Thus a focus on engagement calls attention to the connection between a learner and the social context in which learning takes place. Engaging schools promote a sense of belonging by personalizing instruction, showing an interest in pupils' lives, and creating a supportive, caring social environment (2004: 3).*

In order to explore how to create a supportive, caring social environment, we begin by examining collaboration and cooperation.

Collaboration and Cooperation

Even with all the concern about academic standards, performance on proficiency tests and international comparisons of student achievement (check out Chapter 14), schooling has always been about more than academic learning. Of course, academic learning is the prime directive, 'but schools have major responsibilities for other

Connect and Extend

The Winter 2002 issue of *Theory Into Practice* is devoted to 'Promoting thinking through peer learning'. The editor for this volume was Angela O'Donnell, one of the top researchers in the area of cooperative learning.

aspects of pupils' development as well, such as helping pupils develop the attitudes, skills, and orientations needed to lead humane lives and act effectively as citizens to sustain democratic institutions' (Battistich *et al.*, 1999). In addition, an education that prepares pupils to live humane lives has value in the wider society. The following is taken from the 'Aims' section of the National Curriculum for England & Wales (1999):

Foremost is a belief in education, at home and at school, as a route to the spiritual, moral, social, cultural, physical and mental development, and thus the well-being, of the individual. Education is also a route to equality of opportunity for all, a healthy and just democracy, a productive economy and sustainable development. Education should reflect the enduring values that contribute to these ends. These include valuing ourselves, our families and other relationships, the wider groups to which we belong, the diversity in our society and the environment in which we live. Education should also reaffirm our commitment to the virtues of truth, justice, honesty, trust and a sense of duty.

Source: http://www.nc.uk.net/nc/contents/aboutcurr.htm

For the past three decades, researchers have examined collaboration and cooperation in schools. Although there are some inconsistencies, the majority of the studies indicate that truly cooperative groups have positive effects on pupils' empathy, tolerance for differences, feelings of acceptance, friendships, self-confidence and even school attendance (Solomon, Watson and Battistich, 2001). It is even argued that cooperative learning experiences are crucial in preventing the social problems that plague children and adolescents (Gillies, 2003, 2004) and is preferable to the alternatives such as a preponderance of whole-class teaching (Abrami *et al.*, 2000).

Collaboration, group work and cooperative learning

The terms *collaboration, group work* and *cooperative learning* often are used as if they mean the same thing. Certainly there is some overlap, but there are differences as well.

Effectively used cooperative learning strategies enhance collaborative skills, positive inter-dependence and individual accountability

However, the distinctions between collaboration and cooperation are not always clear or indeed agreed between the co-authors of this text! In the face of such definitional diversities we can turn to others for help. Ted Panitz (1996) suggests the following differences. Collaboration is a philosophy about how to relate to others – how to learn and work. Collaboration is a way of dealing with people that respects differences, shares authority and builds on the knowledge that is distributed among other people. Cooperation, on the other hand, is a way of working with others to attain a shared goal (Gillies, 2003). Collaborative learning has roots in the work of teachers who wanted their pupils to respond in more active ways as they learned. Cooperative learning has roots in the work of psychologists John Dewey and Kurt Lewin. You could say that cooperative learning is one way to collaborate.

Another way of looking at the difference between the two is to view cooperation as a way of learning by working and talking together to share thinking, whilst collaboration is agreed behaviour contributing towards the achievement of a common goal. You cooperate together but you can collaborate apart for much of the time then bring together the fruit of joint and independent work to assemble the collaborative outcome. This co-author tends to prefer this last set of ideas as it describes two different types of activity that you might typically find in school settings (discussing together to solve a problem and working on a joint project) – and, of course, he did write them!

Group work, on the other hand, is simply several pupils working together – they may or may not be cooperating but they might be collaborating. Many activities can be completed in collaborative groups. For example, pupils can work together to conduct a local survey. How do people feel about the plan to build a new shopping precinct that will bring more shopping and more traffic? Would the community support or oppose the building of a nuclear power plant? If pupils must learn ten new definitions in a biology class, why not let pupils divide up the terms and definitions and teach one another? Be sure, however, that everyone in the group can handle the task because sometimes one or two pupils end up doing the work of the entire group.

Group work can be useful, but true cooperative learning requires much more than simply putting pupils in groups.

Beyond groups to cooperation

Cooperative learning has a long history in education. In the early 1900s, John Dewey criticised the use of competition in education and encouraged educators to structure schools as democratic learning communities. In the 1940s and 1950s these ideas fell from favour in part due to major world conflict and the aftermath, and characterised by a resurgence of competition. In the 1960s, there was a swing back to individualised and cooperative learning structures, stimulated in part by concern for human rights and inter-racial relations (Webb and Palincsar, 1996). Today, there are evolving 'communal constructivist' (Meehan *et al.*, 2001; Leask and Younie, 2001) perspectives on learning where learners cooperate to build knowledge not only with each other (social constructivism – see Chapter 2), but also for each other: making extensive use of ICT and peer tutoring. The roles of pupil and teacher are deliberately blurred, with the children tutoring not only their peers, but also their teachers.

Different learning theory approaches favour cooperative learning for different reasons (O'Donnell, 2002; O'Donnell and O'Kelly, 1994). For example, information processing theorists (e.g. Huitt, 2003) point to the value of group discussion in helping participants rehearse, elaborate and expand their knowledge. As group members question and explain, they have to organise their knowledge, make connections and review – all processes that support information processing and memory. Advocates of a Piagetian perspective (again check out Chapter 2, p. 38) suggest that the interactions in groups can create the cognitive conflict and disequilibrium that lead an individual to

Collaboration

Working together and in parallel with others to reach a shared goal.

Cooperation

A way of dealing with people that respects differences, shares authority and builds on the combined knowledge of self and others.

Cooperative learning

Arrangement in which pupils work in groups and make gains in learning on the basis of the success of the group.

Table 11.1 Different forms of cooperative learning for different purposes

Different forms of cooperative learning (Elaboration, Piagetian and Vygotskian) fit different purposes, need different structures, and have their own potential problems and possible solutions.

Considerations	Elaboration	Piagetian	Vygotskian
Group size	Small (2–4)	Small	Dyads
Group composition	Heterogeneous/homogeneous	Homogeneous	Heterogeneous
Tasks	Rehearsal/integrative	Exploratory	Skills
Teacher role	Facilitator	Facilitator	Model/guide
Potential problems	Poor help-giving Unequal participation	Inactive No cognitive conflict	Poor help-giving Providing adequate time/dialogue
Averting problems	Direct instruction in help-giving Modelling help-giving Scripting interaction	Structuring controversy	Direct instruction in help-giving Modelling help-giving

Source: From 'Learning from peers: Beyond the rhetoric of positive results' by A. M. O'Donnell and J. O'Kelly. *Educational Psychology Review, 6*, p. 327, Table 13.3. Copyright © 1994 by Plenum Publishing Corporation. Reprinted with kind permission from Springer Science and Business Media.

question his or her understanding and try out new ideas. Or, as Piaget (1985) said, 'to go beyond his current state and strike out in new directions' (p. 10). Those who favour Vygotsky's theory suggest that social interaction is important for learning because higher mental functions such as reasoning, comprehension and critical thinking originate in social interactions and are then internalised by individuals. The important idea for you to embrace is that children can accomplish cognitive tasks with social support before they can do them alone. Thus, cooperative learning provides the social support and scaffolding that pupils need to move learning forward. Table 11.1 summarises the functions of cooperative learning from different theoretical perspectives, and describes some of the elements of each kind of group.

To benefit from the dimensions of cooperative learning listed in Table 11.1, groups must be cooperative – all members must participate. However, as any teacher or parent knows, cooperation is not automatic just because we put pupils into groups.

What can go wrong: misuses of group learning

Without careful planning and monitoring by the teacher, off-task group interactions can hinder learning and reduce rather than improve social relations in classes. For example, if there is pressure in a group for conformity – perhaps because rewards are being misused or one student dominates the others – interactions can be unproductive and unreflective. Misconceptions might be reinforced, or the worst not the best ideas may be combined to construct a superficial understanding (Battistich, Solomon and Delucci, 1993). Pupils who work in groups but arrive at wrong answers may be more confident that they are right – a case of 'two heads are worse than one' (Puncochar and Fox, 2004). Also, the ideas of unpopular pupils may be ignored or even ridiculed while the contributions of popular pupils are accepted and reinforced, regardless of the merit of either set of ideas (Cohen, 1986). Mary McCaslin and Tom Good (1996) list several other potential disadvantages of group learning:

- Pupils often value the process or procedures over the learning. Speed and finishing early take precedence over thoughtfulness and learning.

- Rather than challenging and correcting misconceptions, pupils support and reinforce misunderstandings.

- Socialising and interpersonal relationships may take precedence over learning.

- Pupils may simply shift dependency from the teacher to the 'expert' in the group – learning is still passive and what is 'learned' can be wrong.

- Status differences may be increased rather than decreased. Some pupils learn to 'free-wheel' because the group progresses with or without their contributions. Others become even more convinced that they are unable to understand without the support of the group.

Simon Veenman, Brenda Kenter and Kiki Post at the University of Nijmegen examined the teachers' use of cooperative grouping in a sample of Dutch primary schools (Veenman *et al.*, 2000). This thorough and fascinating study shows that without careful planning and monitoring the implementation of cooperative grouping will continue to reinforce a predominance of individualistic learning at school. It's worth finding the paper, perhaps using an on-line electronic journals database, before moving on to the next sections where we examine how teachers can avoid these problems and encourage true cooperation.

Connect and Extend

Maroussia Raveaud provides an interesting example of comparative classroom research into grouping in a sample of English and French primary schools. Raveaud, M. (2005). 'Hares, tortoises and the social construction of the pupil: differentiated learning in French and English primary schools', *British Educational Research Journal, 31*(4) (August), pp. 459–479.

Tasks for cooperative learning

Like so many other decisions in teaching, plans for using cooperative groups begin with a goal. What are pupils supposed to accomplish? What is the task? Tasks for cooperative groups may be more or less structured. Highly-structured tasks include work that has right answers – drill and practice, applying routines or procedures, answering questions from readings, calculations in mathematics, and so on. Gently-structured complex tasks have multiple answers and unclear procedures, requiring problem finding and higher-order thinking. These gently-structured complex tasks are true group tasks; that is, they are likely to require the resources (knowledge, skills, problem-solving strategies, creativity) of all the group members to accomplish, whereas highly-structured tasks often can be accomplished just as effectively by individuals. These distinctions are important because gently-structured, complex, true group tasks appear to require more and higher-quality interventions than routine tasks, if learning and problem solving are to occur (Cohen, 1994; Gillies, 2004).

Highly structured, review and skill-building tasks

A relatively structured task such as reviewing previously learned material for an exam might be well served by a structured technique such as STAD (Student Teams Achievement Divisions). In the STAD technique, teams of four pupils compete to determine which team's members can amass the greatest improvement over previous achievement levels (Slavin, 1995). Praise, recognition or extrinsic rewards can enhance motivation, effort and persistence under these conditions, and thus increase learning. Focusing the dialogue by assigning narrow roles also may help pupils stay engaged when tasks are routine or practice-based, or to review previous learning.

Gently-structured, conceptual and problem-solving tasks

If the task is gently-structured and more cognitive in nature, then an open exchange and elaborated discussion will be more helpful (Ross and Raphael, 1990). Thus, strategies that encourage extended and productive interactions are appropriate when the goal is to develop higher-order thinking and problem solving. In these situations, a tightly structured process, competition among groups for rewards and rigid assignment of roles is likely to inhibit the richness of the pupils' interactions and interfere with progress towards the goal. Strategies that encourage interaction include open-ended techniques such as:

- reciprocal questioning (where teachers and pupils exchange questions and answers, see King, 1994);

- reciprocal teaching (where teachers and pupils exchange summaries, explanations and predictions, see Palincsar and Brown, 1984; Rosenshine and Meister, 1994);

- pair-share (where pairs of learners share their initial understanding of a question or idea posed or presented by the teacher, see Kagan, 1994); or

- Jigsaw (where one member of a group swaps into another classroom group to share thinking or conclusions, see http://www.jigsaw.org).

Further discussion of some of these techniques is provided in the 'Designs for cooperation' section later in this chapter.

When used appropriately, reciprocal questioning, reciprocal teaching, pair-share and Jigsaw encourage more extensive interaction and elaborate thought in situations where pupils are being exposed to complex materials. In these instances, the use of rewards may well divert the group away from the goal of in-depth cognitive processing. When rewards are offered, the goal often becomes achieving the reward as efficiently as possible (Webb and Palincsar, 1996).

Social skills and communication tasks

When the goal of peer learning is enhanced social skills or increased inter-group understanding and appreciation of diversity, the assignment of specific roles and functions within the group might support communication (Cohen, 1994; Kagan, 1994). In these situations, it can be helpful to rotate leadership roles so that minority group pupils and females have the opportunity to demonstrate and develop leadership skills; in addition, all group members can experience the leadership capabilities of each individual (Miller and Harrington, 1993). Rewards probably are not necessary, and they may actually get in the way because the goal is to build community, a sense of respect and responsibility for all team members.

Connect and Extend

How would you defend the use of cooperative learning groups in classrooms by making reference to David and Roger Johnson's (1999) five elements that define true cooperative learning groups: face-to-face interaction; positive interdependence; individual accountability; collaborative skills; group processing?

Preparing pupils for cooperative learning

In 1999, David and Roger Johnson (researchers into cooperative learning) attempted to define true cooperative learning groups by looking at elements of cooperation in the classroom. Pupils *interact face-to-face* and close together, not across the room. Group members experience *positive interdependence* – they need each other for support, explanations and guidance. Even though they work together and help each other, members of the group must ultimately demonstrate learning on their own; they are held *individually accountable* for learning, often through individual tests or other assessments. *Collaborative skills* are necessary for effective group functioning. Often, these skills, such as giving constructive feedback, reaching consensus and involving every member, must be taught and practised before the groups tackle a learning task. Finally, members monitor *group processes* and relationships to make sure the group is working effectively and to learn about the dynamics of groups. They take time to ask, 'How are we doing as a group? Is everyone working together?'

Research in learning by 13- to 17-year-olds in Australia found that pupils in cooperative groups structured to require positive interdependence and mutual helping learned more in maths, science and English than pupils in unstructured learning groups (Gillies, 2003). In addition, compared to pupils in the unstructured groups, pupils in the structured groups also said learning was more fun!

Setting up cooperative groups

How large should a cooperative group be? Again, the answer depends on your learning goals. If the purpose is for the group members to review, rehearse information or practice, four to five or six pupils is about the right size. But if the goal is to encourage each pupil to participate in discussions, problem solving or computer learning, then groups of two to four members work best. Also, when setting up cooperative groups, it often makes sense to balance the number of boys and girls. Some research indicates that when there are just a few girls in a group, they tend to be left out of the discussions unless they are the most able or assertive members. By contrast, when there are only one or two boys in the group, they tend to dominate and be 'interviewed' by the girls unless these boys are less able than the girls or are very shy. In general, for very shy and introverted pupils, cooperative learning using connected technologies may be a better approach (O'Donnell and O'Kelly, 1994; Webb, 1985; Webb and Palincsar, 1996). Whatever the case, teachers must monitor groups to make sure everyone is contributing and learning.

Giving and receiving explanations

In practice, the effects of learning in a group vary, depending on what actually happens in the group and who is in it. If only a few people take responsibility for the work, these people will probably learn, but the non-participating members probably will not. Pupils who ask questions, get answers and attempt explanations are more likely to learn than pupils whose questions go unasked or unanswered. In fact, there is evidence that the more a pupil provides elaborated, thoughtful explanations to other pupils in a group, the more the *explainer* learns. Giving good explanations appears to be even more important for learning than receiving explanations (Webb *et al.*, 2002; Webb and Palincsar, 1996). In order to explain, you have to organise the information, put it into your own words, think of examples and analogies (which connect the information to things you already know), and test your understanding by answering questions. These are excellent learning strategies (O'Donnell and O'Kelly, 1994).

Good explanations are relevant, timely, correct and elaborated enough to help the listener correct misunderstandings; the best explanations tell why (Webb *et al.*, 2002; Webb and Mastergeorge, 2003).

Anna de Carvalho from the University of Sao Paulo studied how pupils in the first years of primary school (children from seven to ten years of age) are initiated into the construction of explanations of physical phenomena in the teaching of science. A series of classes were video-taped where children, working in groups, solved 15 different investigative problems by raising and testing their own hypotheses. In case of the pendulum experiment in Figure 11.1, the experimentation phase lasted about 20 minutes.

The teacher presented the problem to the pupils as follows:

Teacher: Now, here's what I want you to do: each group is going to get two of these little balls, one black and one rusty. You're going to roll one ball at a time down

Figure 11.1
Experimental set for the pendulum problem: a ramp, two little balls of the same size but of different mass, and a pendulum

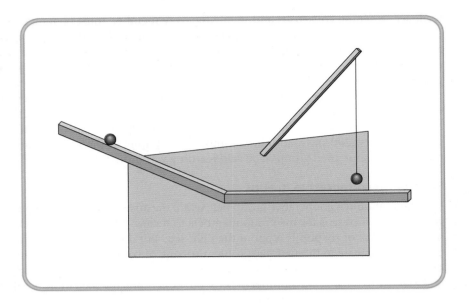

the track and find some way for them to raise the little white ball the same distance. I want you to make the black ball and the rusty ball each move the hanging ball the same amount, OK? Now I'm going to distribute the balls and I'll go from group to group to make sure you all understood.

Teacher: What did you do to get those two little balls to raise the white or yellow ball to the same height? Can anyone explain it to us?

Children then attempted, by means of discussion provoked by the teacher, to explain how each problem was solved and why it worked. Pupils constructed their own causal explanations by following a sequence of 'levels of construction of causal explanations' shown in Figure 11.2.

The level of explanations offered and received was found to be significantly related to learning; the further along the level, the more learning. So, asking appropriate questions and giving clear explanations are critical, and usually these skills must be taught and modelled.

Assigning roles

Some teachers assign roles to pupils to encourage cooperation and full participation. Several roles are described in Table 11.2. If you use roles, be sure that the roles support learning. In groups that focus on social skills, roles should support listening, encouragement and respect for differences. In groups that focus on practice, review or mastery of basic skills, roles should support persistence, encouragement and participation. In groups that focus on higher-order problem solving or complex learning, roles should encourage thoughtful discussion, sharing of explanations and insights, probing, brainstorming and creativity. Make sure that you don't communicate to pupils that the major purpose of the groups is simply to do the procedures – the roles. Roles are supports for learning, not ends in themselves (Woolfolk Hoy and Tschannen-Moran, 1999).

Often, cooperative learning strategies include group reports to the entire class. If you have been on the receiving end of these class reports, you know that they can be deadly dull. To make the process more useful for the audience as well as the reporters, Annemarie Palincsar and Leslie Herrenkohl (2002) taught the class members to use

Levels of construction of causal explanations	Behavioural objective and action	Type of prompt modelled by teacher
Arousal of awareness	Reconstruct actions and observations	Questions of 'What . . . ?' or 'When . . .' to establish a common memory
Making connections	Establish links between personal or other pupils' actions and the reactions of apparatus (or spreadsheet or visual model)	Questions of 'Why . . . ?' or 'How . . . ?' to establish a common interpretation
Disassociation	Relate connections or links made to objects' physical attributes and respective results	Direct attention to object by asking 'What if . . . ?' to establish a common explanation
Conceptualisation	Elaborate links to old 'learnings' and 'knowings' including accounting for novelties in the observed phenomena	Change the context by asking 'Would this . . . ?' questions to establish a common understanding

Figure 11.2
The construction of causal explanation and conceptual learning

Source: Structured and adapted from the conclusions and discussion of Anna Maria Pessoa de Carvalho (2004). 'Building up explanations in physics teaching', *International Journal of Science Education, 26*(2) (February), pp. 225–237.

intellectual roles as they listened to reports. These roles were based on the scientific strategies of predicting and theorising, summarising results, and relating predictions and theories to results. Some audience members were assigned the role of checking the reports for clear relationships between predictions and theories. Other pupils in the audience listened for clarity in the findings. The rest of the pupils were responsible for evaluating how well the group reports linked prediction, theories and findings. Research shows that using these roles promotes class dialogue, thinking and problem solving, and conceptual understanding (Palincsar and Herrenkohl, 2002). Table 11.3 summarises the considerations in designing cooperative learning, based on the goals of the group.

Designs for cooperation

We now turn to different strategies that build in structures to support both social and cognitive learning.

Reciprocal questioning

Reciprocal questioning requires no special materials or testing procedures and can be used with a wide range of ages. After a lesson or presentation by the teacher, pupils in pairs or threes ask and answer questions about the material (King, 2002; Mason, 2004; Pallante and Lindsey, 1991; Feldman, 1986). The teacher provides question stems (see Table 11.4), then pupils are taught how to develop specific questions on the lesson material using the generic question stems. The pupils create questions, then take turns asking and answering. This process has proved more effective than

Reciprocal questioning

Approach where groups of two or three pupils ask and answer each other's questions after a lesson or presentation.

Table 11.2 Possible pupil roles in cooperative learning groups

Depending on the purpose of the group and the age of the participants, having these assigned roles might help pupils cooperate and learn. Of course, pupils may have to be taught how to enact each role effectively, and roles should be rotated so pupils can participate in different aspects of group learning.

Role	Description
Encourager	Encourages reluctant or shy pupils to participate
Praiser/Cheerleader	Shows appreciation of other's contributions and recognises accomplishments
Gate Keeper	Equalises participation and makes sure no one dominates
Coach	Helps with the academic content, explains concepts
Question Commander	Makes sure all pupils' questions are asked and answered
Checker	Checks the group's understanding
Taskmaster	Keeps the group on task
Recorder	Writes down ideas, decisions and plans
Reflector	Keeps group aware of progress (or lack of progress)
Quiet Captain	Monitors noise level
Materials Monitor	Picks up and returns materials

Source: Copied and adapted with permission from Kagan Publishing. Kagan, Spencer – *Cooperative Learning* © 1994, Kagan Publishing, San Clemente, CA. 1 (800) 933-2667, www.KaganOnline.com.

traditional discussion groups because it seems to encourage deeper thinking about the material. Questions such as those in Table 11.4, which encourage pupils to make connections between the lesson and previous knowledge or experience, seem to be the most helpful.

For example, using the question stems in Table 11.4, Sally, Jim and Barry, a small group in Mr Garcia's class of 14-year-olds had the following discussion about the concept of 'culture':

Sally: In your own words, what does *culture* mean?

Jim: Well, Mr Garcia said in the lesson that a culture is the knowledge and understandings shared by the members of a society. I guess it's all the things and beliefs and activities that people in a society have in common. It includes things like religion, laws, music, medical practices, stuff like that.

Sally: And dance, art, family roles.

Barry: Knowledge includes language. So, I guess culture includes language, too.

Jim: Actually, I have a question about that: How does a culture influence the language of a society?

Barry: Well, for one thing, the language is made up of words that are important to the people of that culture. Like, the words name things that the people care about,

Table 11.3 What should you consider in planning and doing cooperative learning?

Considerations	Social skills tasks: team building, cooperation skills	Structured tasks: review, practise facts and skills	Unstructured tasks: conceptual, problem solving, thinking and reasoning
Group size and composition	groups of 2–5, common interest groups, mixed groups, random groups	groups of 2–4, mixed ability, high medium/medium-low or high low/medium-medium	groups of 2–4, select members to encourage interaction
Why assign roles?	to monitor participation and conflict, rotate leadership	to monitor engagement and ensure low-status pupils have resources to offer, i.e. Jigsaw	only to encourage interaction, divergent thinking and extended, connected discourse, i.e. debate sides, group facilitator
Extrinsic rewards/incentives	not necessary, may be helpful	to support motivation, effort, persistence	not necessary
Teacher's role	model, encourager	model, director, coach	model facilitator
Pupil skills needed	listening, turn-taking, encouraging, managing conflict	questioning, explaining, encouraging, content knowledge, learning strategies	questioning, explaining, elaborating, probing, divergent thinking, providing rationales, synthesising
What supports learning? Watch and listen for . . .	modelling and practice	giving multiple, elaborated explanations, attention and practice	quantity and quality of interactions, using and connecting knowledge resources, probing and elaboration
Potential problems	unproductive conflict, non-participation	poor help-giving skills, disengaged or excluded pupils	disengaged or excluded pupils cognitive loafing, superficial thinking, avoiding controversy
Averting problems	simpler task, direct teaching of social skills, team building, conflict resolution skills, discuss group process	structure interdependence and individual accountability, teach helping and explaining	structure controversy, assign 'thinking roles', allow adequate time
Small start	one or two skills, i.e. listening and paraphrasing	pairs of pupils quizzing each other	numbered heads together

Source: *Cognitive Perspectives on Peer Learning* by A. Woolfolk Hoy and M. Tschannen-Moran. Copyright 1999 by Lawrence Erlbaum Associates Inc–Books [T]. Reprinted with permission of Lawrence Erlbaum Associates Inc–Books [T] in the Format Textbook via Copyright Clearance Centre.

Table 11.4 Question stems to encourage dialogue in reciprocal questioning

After studying materials or participating in a lesson, pupils use these stems to develop questions and share answers.

What is a new example of . . . ?

How would you use . . . to . . . ?

What would happen if . . . ?

What are the strengths and weaknesses of . . . ?

How does . . . tie in with what we learned before?

Explain why . . . Explain how . . .

How does . . . affect . . . ?

What is the meaning of . . . ?

Why is . . . important?

How are . . . and . . . similar? How are . . . and . . . different?

What is the best . . . and why?

Compare . . . and . . . with regard to . . .

What do you think causes . . . ?

What conclusions can you draw about . . . ?

Do you agree or disagree with this statement . . . ? Support your answer.

Connect and Extend

Read Mason, L. H. (2004), 'Explicit self-regulated strategy development versus reciprocal questioning: Effects on expository reading comprehension among struggling readers', *Journal of Educational Psychology, 96* (2), pp. 283–296.

or need, or use. And so, different cultures would have different vocabularies. Some cultures may not even have a word for *telephone*, because they don't have any. But, phones are important in our culture, so we have lots of different words for phones, like *cell phone, digital phone, desk phone, cordless phone, phone machine*, and . . .

Jim (laughing): I'll bet desert cultures don't have any words for *snow* or *skiing*.

Sally (turning to Barry): What's your question?

Barry: I've got a great question! You'll never be able to answer it. What would happen if there was a group somewhere without any spoken language? Maybe they were all born not being able to speak, or something like that. How would that affect their culture, or could there even *be* a culture?

Sally: Well, it would mean they couldn't communicate with each other.

Jim: And they wouldn't have any music because they wouldn't be able to sing!

Barry: But wait! Why couldn't they communicate? Maybe they would develop a non-verbal language system, you know, the way people use hand signals, or the way deaf people use sign language (King, 2002: 34–35).

Scripted cooperation

A learning strategy in which two pupils take turns summarising material and critiquing the summaries.

Scripted cooperation

Donald Dansereau and his colleagues have developed a method for learning in pairs called scripted cooperation. Pupils work together on almost any task, including reading a selection of text, solving maths problems or editing writing drafts. In reading, for example, both partners read a passage, then one student gives an oral summary. The other partner comments on the summary, noting omissions or errors. Next, the partners work together to elaborate on the information – create associations, images, mnemonics, ties to previous work, examples, analogies, and so on. The partners switch roles of summariser and listener for the next section of the reading, and then continue to take turns until they finish the assignment (Dansereau, 1985; O'Donnell and O'Kelly, 1994).

In addition to these approaches, Spencer Kagan (1994) has developed many cooperative learning structures designed to accomplish different kinds of academic and social tasks. The Focus on Practice below gives you ideas for integrating cooperative learning into your teaching.

Connect and Extend

STAD and Jigsaw are just two of many cooperative learning techniques, each designed for different teaching purposes. See the Companion Website (Web Link 11.2).

FOCUS ON PRACTICE

Using cooperative learning

Fit group size and composition to your learning intentions

Examples

1. For social skills and team-building goals, use groups of 2–5, common interest groups, mixed groups or random groups.
2. For structured fact and skill-based practice and review tasks, use groups of 2–4, mixed ability such as high-middle and middle-low or high-low and middle-middle group compositions.
3. For higher-level conceptual and thinking tasks, use groups of 2–4; select members to encourage interaction.

Assign appropriate roles

Examples

1. For social skills and team-building goals, assign roles to monitor participation and conflict and rotate leadership of the group.
2. For structured fact and skill-based practice and review tasks, assign roles to monitor engagement and ensure less popular pupils have resources to offer, as in 'Jigsaw'.
3. For higher-level conceptual and thinking tasks, assign roles only to encourage interaction, divergent thinking and extended, connected discourse, for example, debate teams. Don't let roles get in the way of learning.

Make sure you assume a supporting role as the teacher

Examples

1. For social skills and team-building goals, be a model and encourager.
2. For structured fact and skill-based practice and review tasks, be a model, director or coach.
3. For higher-level conceptual and thinking tasks, be a model and facilitator.

Move around the room and monitor the groups

Examples
1. For social skills and team-building goals, watch for listening, turn-taking, encouraging and managing conflict.
2. For structured fact and skill-based practice and review tasks, watch for questioning, giving multiple elaborated explanations, attention and practice.
3. For higher-level conceptual and thinking tasks, watch for questioning, explaining, elaborating, probing, divergent thinking, providing rationales, synthesising, using and connecting knowledge sources.

Start small and simple until you and the pupils know how to use cooperative methods

Examples
1. For social skills and team-building goals, try one or two skills, such as listening and paraphrasing.
2. For structured fact and skill-based practice and review tasks, try pairs of pupils quizzing each other.
3. For higher-level conceptual and thinking tasks, try reciprocal questioning using pairs and just a few question stems.

Source: Based on 'Implications of cognitive approaches to peer learning for teacher education' by A. Woolfolk Hoy and M. Tschannen-Moran, 1999. In A. O'Donnell and A. King (eds), *Cognitive Perspectives on Peer Learning* (pp. 257–284). Mahwah, NJ: Lawrence Erlbaum.

Reaching every pupil: using cooperative learning wisely

Cooperative learning always benefits from careful planning, but sometimes including pupils with special needs requires extra attention to planning and preparation. For example, cooperative structures such as scripted questioning and peer tutoring depend on a balanced interaction between the person taking the role of questioner or explainer and the pupil who is answering or being taught. In these interactions, you want to see and hear explaining and teaching, not just telling or giving right answers. However, many pupils with learning disabilities have difficulties understanding new concepts, so both the explainer and the pupil can get frustrated, and social rejection for the pupil with learning disabilities can follow. As pupils with learning disabilities often have problems with social relations, it is not a good idea to put them in situations where more rejection is likely. So when pupils are learning new or difficult-to-grasp concepts, cooperative learning might not be the best choice for pupils with learning disabilities (Kirk *et al.*, 2006). In fact, research has found that cooperative learning in general is not always effective for pupils with learning disabilities (Smith, 2006) and the influence of classroom peers on cognitive performance in children with behavioural problems is usually detrimental (Bevington and Wishart, 1999).

Gifted pupils also may not benefit from cooperative learning when groups are mixed in ability. The pace often is too slow, the tasks too simple, and there is too much repetition. Also, gifted pupils often fall into the role of teacher or end up just doing the work quickly for the whole group. If you use mixed-ability groups and include gifted pupils, the challenges are to use complex tasks that allow work at different levels and to keep gifted pupils engaged without losing the rest of the class (Smith, 2006).

Cooperative learning may be an excellent choice, however, for English language learners (ELL). In many classrooms today, there are sometimes six or more languages represented. Teachers can't be expected to master every heritage language spoken by all their pupils every year. In these classrooms, cooperative groups can help as pupils work together on academic tasks. Pupils who speak two languages can help translate and explain lessons to others in the group. Speaking in a smaller group may be less anxiety-provoking for pupils who are learning another language; thus, ELL pupils may get more language practice with feedback in these groups (Smith, 2006).

The Jigsaw cooperative learning strategy (refer back to p. 490) is especially helpful for ELL pupils because they can provide information that another group needs, so they also must talk, explain and interact in their new language. In fact, the Jigsaw approach was developed in response to needs for creating high interdependence in diverse groups. Elliot Aronson and his graduate students invented the 'Jigsaw Classroom' when he was a professor of social psychology (and Anita Woolfolk – co-author of this book – was a student) at the University of Texas at Austin. Some of Anita's friends worked on his research team. Aronson developed the approach: 'as a matter of absolute necessity to help defuse a highly explosive situation' (Aronson, 2000: 137). The Austin schools had just been desegregated by court order. White, African American and Hispanic pupils were together in classrooms for the first time. Hostility and turmoil ensued with fistfights in corridors and classrooms. Aronson's answer was the Jigsaw classroom.

Many European classrooms at the start of the 21st century mirror something of the tensions and hostilities which marked the desegregation of Austin's schools in 1971. Boosted economic migration and the increasing success of *bona fide* and bogus asylum seekers 'parachuting' into European classrooms have created the potential for bewilderment and misunderstandings.

As previously described, in Jigsaw each group member is given part of the material to be learned by the whole group and becomes an 'expert' on his or her piece. Pupils have to teach each other, so everyone's contribution is important. A more recent version, Jigsaw II, adds expert groups in which the pupils who have the same material from each learning group confer to make sure they understand their assigned part and then plan ways to teach the information to their learning group members. Next, pupils return to their learning groups, bringing their expertise to the sessions. In the end, pupils take an individual test covering all the material and also earn extra points for their learning team score. Teams can work for rewards or simply for recognition (Aronson, 2000; Slavin, 1995). In Aronson's eyes, an even greater reward is gained: learning something about respect and compassion.

Years after inventing the Jigsaw strategy in 1992, Elliott Aronson received a letter from a teacher, Judy Pitts, in which she describes a lesson about how to do library research that has a Jigsaw format. The overall project for each group is to educate the class about a different country. Groups have to decide what information to present and how to make it interesting for their classmates. In the library, each group member is responsible for mastering a particular resource (guides, news resources, reference sets, almanacs, etc. – these days that would include digital resources) and teaching other group members how to use it, if the need arises. Pupils learning about each resource meet first in expert groups to be sure all the 'teachers' know how to use the resource.

In this class, pupils confront complex, real-life problems, and not simplified worksheets. They learn by doing and by teaching others. The pupils must take positions and argue for them, whilst being open to the ideas of others. For example, how should a group best inform a class about the political situation in Cyprus? They may encounter different representations of the same information – graphs, databases, maps, interviews

Connect and Extend

Remind yourself now of the *In the Classroom* feature at the start of Chapter 5 and of the responses of our teachers in the corresponding In the Classroom: What Would They Do? feature at the end of the chapter. Did any response mention or hint at the idea of Jigsaw cooperative structure?

Jigsaw

A cooperative structure in which each member of a group is responsible for teaching other members one section of the material.

or encyclopedia articles – and have to integrate information from different sources. This lesson exemplifies many of the characteristics of constructivist approaches described in Chapter 9. The pupils have a good chance of learning how to do library research by actually doing it.

The Classroom Community

David and Roger Johnson (1999) describe three Cs for safe and productive schools: cooperative community, constructive conflict resolution and civic values. At the heart of the community is the idea of positive interdependence – individuals working together to achieve mutual goals. We have spent several pages talking about cooperation in learning. Now let's consider the other two Cs – constructive conflict resolution and civic values.

Constructive conflict resolution

Connect and Extend

The need for belonging is the third level of Maslow's hierarchy, discussed in Chapter 10 (p. 441).

Constructive conflict resolution is essential in the community because conflicts are inevitable and even necessary for learning. Piaget's theory of development and the research on conceptual change teaching (Chapter 2, p. 38) tell us that deep learning requires cognitive conflict. Our pupils playing, doing and being in groups will have interpersonal conflicts, which also can lead to learning. Table 11.5 shows how academic and interpersonal conflicts can be positive forces in a learning community. One study of 15-year-olds found that pupils who were wrong, but for

Handling conflict can be difficult for young people. Studies have shown that many conflicts amongst secondary school pupils are either resolved in destructive ways or never at all

Table 11.5   Academic and interpersonal conflict and learning

Conflict, if handled well, can support learning. Academic conflicts can lead to critical thinking and conceptual change. Conflicts of interest are unavoidable, but can be handled so no one is the loser.

Academic controversy	**Conflicts of interest**
One person's ideas, information, theories, conclusions and opinions are incompatible with those of another, and the two seek to reach an agreement.	The actions of one person attempting to maximise benefits prevents, blocks or interferes with another person maximising her or his benefits.
Controversy procedure	*Integrative (problem-solving) negotiations*
Research and prepare positions	Describe wants
Present and advocate positions	Describe feelings
Refute opposing position and refute attacks on own position	Describe reasons for wants and feelings
Reverse perspectives	Take other's perspective
Synthesise and integrate best evidence and reasoning from all sides	Invent three optional agreements that maximise joint outcomes
	Choose one and formalise agreement

Source: From 'The three Cs of school and classroom management' by D. Johnson and R. Johnson. In H. J. Freiberg (ed.), *Beyond Behaviorism: Changing the Classroom Management Paradigm.* Boston: Allyn and Bacon. Copyright © 1999 by Allyn and Bacon.

different reasons, were sometimes able to correct their misunderstandings if they argued together about their conflicting wrong answers (Schwarz, Neuman and Biezuner, 2000).

Peer harassment

One common form of conflict in schools involves teasing and harassment – bullying (Chapter 3 has more information). Teachers tend to underestimate the amount of bullying that takes place in schools. For example, in one survey of 13-year-olds, 60% of the pupils said that they had been harassed by a bully, but teachers in their schools estimated the number would be about 16% (Barone, 1997). Another national survey found that about 33% of 11- to 15-year-olds had been involved in moderate or frequent bullying (Nansel *et al.*, 2001) and a survey of English schools in 2000 reported the persistence of a culture of silence with 30% of 10- to 14-year-old victims telling no one of the bullying (Smith and Shu, 2000). The need to maintain relationships is strong. This co-author was reminded of this when his son, Tom, complained of being forced to stay in the corner of a social area by two boys and this happened every break and lunch time. As a father, he couldn't understand why Tom kept going back to that social area. Tom's explanation was that they were his friends, and 'I'd rather be with them than be by myself.' Some friends! The line between good-natured exchanges and hostile teasing may seem thin (robust nonetheless), but a rule of thumb is that teasing someone who is less powerful or less popular or using any racial, ethnic or religious slur should never be tolerated.

Table 11.6 Dos and don'ts about teasing

Teasing has led to some tragic situations. Talk about what to do in your class.

Do:

1. Be careful of other's feelings.

2. Use humour gently and carefully.

3. Ask whether teasing about a certain topic hurts someone's feelings.

4. Accept teasing from others if you tease.

5. Tell others if teasing about a certain topic hurts your feelings.

6. Know the difference between friendly, gentle teasing and hurtful ridicule or harassment.

7. Try to read others' 'body language' to see if their feelings are hurt – even when they don't tell you.

8. Help a weaker student when he or she is being ridiculed.

Don't:

1. Tease someone you don't know well.

2. [If you are a boy] tease girls about sex.

3. Tease about a person's body.

4. Tease about a person's family members.

5. Tease about a topic when a pupil has asked you not to.

6. Tease someone who seems agitated or whom you know is having a bad day.

7. Be thin-skinned about teasing that is meant in a friendly way.

8. Swallow your feelings about teasing – tell someone in a direct and clear way what is bothering you.

Source: From *Secondary Classroom Management: Lessons from Research and Practice* (3rd ed.) by C. S. Weinstein and A. J. Mignano, Jr. Published by McGraw-Hill. Copyright © 2003 by McGraw-Hill. Adapted with permission from The McGraw-Hill Companies.

Connect and Extend

For guidelines and concrete actions for achieving cooperation in classrooms see the Companion Website (Web Link 11.3).

Connect and Extend

For details of other strategies to integrate pupils into conflict resolution see Cowie, H. and Hutson, N. (2005), 'Peer support: a strategy to help bystanders challenge school bullying', *Pastoral Care in Education*, 23(2) (June), pp. 40–44.

What can teachers do?

In every community there are conflicts. Learning to resolve them is an important life skill. In fact, a two-year longitudinal study that followed a representative sample of five- to 11-year-olds found that aggressive children whose teachers taught them conflict management strategies were diverted from a future of aggression and violence (Aber, Brown and Jones, 2003). However, when teachers are silent about aggression and teasing, pupils may 'hear' agreement with the insult (Weinstein, 2003). Table 11.6 presents a list of dos and don'ts about teasing in schools.

Handling conflict is difficult for most of us – and for young people it can be even harder. Given the public's concern about violence in schools, it is surprising how little we know about conflicts among pupils (Webb and Vulliamy, 2002; Miller *et al.*, 2000; Rose and Gallup, 2001).

There is some evidence that in primary schools, conflicts most often centre on disputes over resources (school stationery, computers, sports equipment or toys) and over preferences (which activity to do first or what game to play). Over 30 years ago, a large study of more than 8,000 secondary school pupils and 500 teachers from three major cities concluded that 90% of the conflicts among pupils are resolved in destructive ways or are never resolved at all (DeCecco and Richards, 1974). The few studies conducted since that time have reached similar conclusions. Avoidance, force and threats seem to be the major strategies for dealing with conflict (Johnson *et al.*, 1995). But there are better ways – peer mediation and negotiation strategies that teach lifelong lessons.

Peer mediation and negotiation

David Johnson and his colleagues (1995) provided conflict resolution training to 227 pupils aged seven to ten. Pupils learned a five-step negotiating strategy:

1. *Jointly define the conflict.* Separate the person from the problem and the actions involved, avoid win–lose thinking, and get both parties' goals clear.

2. *Exchange positions and interests.* Present a tentative proposal and make a case for it; listen to the other person's proposal and feelings; and stay flexible and cooperative.

3. *Reverse perspectives.* See the situation from the other person's point of view and reverse roles and argue for that perspective.

4. *Invent at least three agreements that allow mutual gain.* Brainstorm, focus on goals, think creatively, and make sure everyone has power to invent solutions.

5. *Reach an integrative agreement.* Make sure both sets of goals are met. If all else fails, flip a coin, take turns or call in a third party – a mediator.

Connect and Extend

For details of the strategies, see the *Theory into Practice* issue on 'Conflict Resolution and Peer Meditation' edited by David and Roger Johnson (2004).

In addition to learning conflict resolution, all pupils in Johnson and Johnson's study were trained in mediation strategies. The role of the mediator was rotated – every day the teacher chose two pupils to be the class mediators and to wear the mediators' T-shirts. Johnson and his colleagues found that pupils learned the conflict resolution and mediation strategies and used them successfully, both in school and at home, to handle conflicts in a more productive way.

Cunningham and his colleagues (1998) examined the effects of a pupil-mediated conflict resolution programme on primary school playground aggression. Mediation teams of ten- to 11-year-old pupils participated in 15 hours of training according to the model developed by Cunningham, Cunningham and Martorelli (1997) and mediation was introduced onto the playgrounds of three schools. Mediators successfully resolved approximately 90% of the playground conflicts in which they intervened and physically aggressive playground behaviour was reduced by up to 65%. These effects were sustained at one-year follow-up observations. Teacher and pupil-mediator questionnaires provided strong support for the impact, feasibility and acceptability of this programme.

Connect and Extend

For a discussion of some barriers to including children in mediation see Soar, K. *et al.* (2005), 'Pupil involvement in special educational needs disagreement resolution: some perceived barriers to including children in mediation', *British Journal of Special Education, 32*(1), pp. 35–41.

Civic values

The last C is civic values – the understandings and beliefs that hold the community together. Values are learned through direct teaching, modelling, reading literature, engaging in group discussions and sharing concerns. At classroom level, some teachers have a 'Concerns Box' where pupils can put written concerns and comments. The box is opened once a week at a class meeting and the concerns are discussed. Johnson and Johnson (1999) give the example of a class meeting about respect. One pupil tells her classmates that she felt hurt during playtime the day before because no-one listened when she was trying to teach them the rules to a new game. The pupils discussed what it means to be respectful and why respect is important. Then the pupils shared personal experiences of times when they felt respected and times when they did not feel respected.

Connect and Extend

For an evaluation of a violence prevention programme see Kelder, S. *et al.* (2000), 'Outcome evaluation of a multi-component violence-prevention program for middle schools: the Students for Peace project', *Health Education Research, 15*(1), pp. 45–58.

At other times teachers need to draw on the growing political literacy of their pupils to address difficult local, national and international issues. Although few topics should be viewed as no-go areas, sensitivity and care needs to be taken when dealing with topics where views amongst the children, their parents and the governing body of the school are polarised and fiercely held.

STOP AND THINK

Consider this situation, described by Deuchar and Maitles (2004: 171). As part of a citizenship lesson to ten- and 11-year-old pupils, the teacher opens a discussion about leadership. The children start talking about President George Bush and Prime Minister Tony Blair and the war in Iraq. Some controversial views are being expressed. How should the teacher handle this situation?

Connect and Extend

For a complete discussion of the debate about character education, see Abbeduto, L. (ed.) (2002), *Taking Sides: Clashing on Controversial Issues in Educational Psychology*, pp. 128–155. Guilford: McGraw-Hill/Duskin.

An example of discussion during a citizenship lesson

In Figure 11.3 are some excerpts from a class discussion of Scottish pupils aged ten and 11 with comments and interpretations from the two researchers, Ross Deuchar and Henry Maitles. We have quoted at length as the outcomes are important indicators of the potential for learning civic values, cooperation and community in classroom contexts. The children are identified using anonymised initial capital letters.

The Advisory Group on Citizenship's (1998) 'essential elements' for preparing pupils for citizenship in adult life are listed in Table 11.7.

A class discussion of Scottish pupils aged 10 and 11 with comments and interpretations from the two researchers, Ross Deuchar and Henry Maitles.

'President Bush . . . there's some ways he's enterprising and some ways he's stupid as well. He has to talk in front of millions and millions of people in his country . . . but I don't think he should go to war with Iraq . . . he's power crazy.' (T)

'Some people say he's (George Bush) quite power-hungry.' (L)

'It's a case that if George Bush goes into something, Tony Blair has always got to be right behind him.' (T)

These initial discussions led to further debate among pupils about the reasons for Britain and America going into the war, and the pros and cons of the conflict taking place. Some pupils felt that the outbreak of war was inevitable because Saddam Hussein 'had bombs' and was 'trying to do what Hitler was trying to do – rule the world'. However, others had quite different opinions:

'I think George Bush is the one that's really wrong. I think he's bonkers and he's the one that's trying to complete what Hitler was trying to do and not Saddam . . . and he's getting Britain to help him.' (J)

'It's because of oil – because Iraq stole oil off of Spain and now Britain's not daft . . . they want it.' (T)

'Why are they bombing innocent Iraqis? He was after Bin Laden and then all of a sudden Saddam Hussein popped up out of nowhere and he started with him.' (T2)

Some pupils appeared passionate about key events during the war, such as the emotions they had experienced on the day that they had seen the Iraqi people celebrate as they helped tear down Saddam Hussein's statue in Baghdad:

'I felt happy that they were getting their freedom back, I just didn't feel right because they didn't have enough food and water, and all the fires that were going on round the town and all the burgling – they were just breaking into shops and stealing stuff.' (J)

'I had mixed emotions about the day, because I felt happy for them that they felt happy taking the statue of Saddam Hussein down . . . but I felt sad because how could they go with the British soldiers that have been bombing them? . . . causing so much destruction to them?' (T)

'I think it was the right thing to do by celebrating because he's been hurting innocent people for no reason and he's been very cruel to the people and I think that celebrating was the right idea because they're free of him and they don't know where he is so they may as well celebrate in the time that they've got left.' (S)

When asked about the peace protests that had taken place throughout the UK at the beginning of the war, including those involving school pupils, pupils had mixed views. While some pupils felt that it was not appropriate for school children to be involved in protests because 'it's not their responsibility', others felt that everyone had the right to 'protest against the war'. Some pupils felt that it was rather a pointless exercise, or perhaps agreed with it in principle but were unsure how to justify it:

'I don't really think it was a good idea because the people that are protesting are not very sure of what's going on over in Iraq. It's actually not even happening in Scotland, it's happening in Iraq so there's no point in wasting your time.' (S2)

'The people that were protesting weren't daft, but it was a wrong idea to do it because they're away in Iraq and we're only in Glasgow . . . and Iraq's away over the other side of the world.' (L)

'I think it was a good idea . . . I don't really think anything about that, I just don't like the whole thing about war.' (J)

With reference to the Advisory Group on Citizenship's (1998) 'essential elements' for preparing pupils for citizenship in adult life, the pupils clearly displayed a rich knowledge of topical and contemporary issues at international levels, as well as an awareness of the nature of democracy and the way in which the future of Iraq could and should be decided. Their concern for humanitarian issues surrounding the Iraq War clearly displayed a growing understanding of the nature of diversity, social conflict and a concern for the common good. In addition, their reflective comments about the underlying causes of the war illustrated their ability to engage in a critical approach to the evidence presented to them via the mass media. These pupils appeared to have a strong concern for human dignity, equality and the need to resolve conflict diplomatically, and were increasingly able to recognise forms of manipulation that may be used by political leaders in their attempts to justify the need for war.

Figure 11.3
A discussion about leadership

Source: Deuchar, R. and Maitles, H. (2004). 'I just don't like the whole thing about war!: encouraging the expression of political literacy among primary pupils as a vehicle for promoting education for active citizenship'. Paper presented at the European Conference on Educational Research, University of Crete, 22–25 September 2004.

Character education

Some educators believe that civic values are best taught through character education but not everyone agrees that character should be taught in schools, as you can see in the Discussion Point on p. 510.

Table 11.7 Essential elements for preparing pupils for citizenship in adult life to be reached by the end of compulsory schooling

Key concepts	Values and dispositions	Skills and aptitudes	Knowledge and understanding
<ul><li>democracy and autocracy</li><li>cooperation and conflict</li><li>equality and diversity</li><li>fairness, justice, the rule of law, rules, law and human rights</li><li>freedom and order</li><li>individual and community</li><li>power and authority</li><li>rights and responsibilities</li></ul>	<ul><li>concern for the common good</li><li>belief in human dignity and equality</li><li>concern to resolve conflicts</li><li>a disposition to work with and for others with sympathetic understanding</li><li>proclivity to act responsibly: that is care for others and oneself; premeditation and calculation about the effect actions are likely to have on others; and acceptance of responsibility for unforeseen or unfortunate consequences</li><li>practice of tolerance</li><li>judging and acting by a moral code</li><li>courage to defend a point of view</li><li>willingness to be open to changing one's opinions and attitudes in the light of discussion and evidence</li><li>individual initiative and effort</li><li>civility and respect for the rule of law</li></ul>	<ul><li>ability to make a reasoned argument both verbally and in writing</li><li>ability to cooperate and work effectively with others</li><li>ability to consider and appreciate the experience and perspective of others</li><li>ability to tolerate other view points</li><li>ability to develop a problem-solving approach</li><li>ability to use modern media and technology critically to gather information</li><li>a critical approach to evidence put before one and ability to look for fresh evidence</li><li>ability to recognise forms of manipulation and persuasion</li><li>ability to identify, respond to and influence social, moral and political challenges and situations</li></ul>	<ul><li>topical and contemporary issues and events at local, national, EU, Commonwealth and international levels</li><li>the nature of democratic communities, including how they function and change</li><li>the interdependence of individuals and local and voluntary communities</li><li>the nature of diversity, dissent and social conflict</li><li>legal and moral rights and responsibilities of individuals and communities</li><li>the nature of social, moral and political challenges faced by individuals and communities</li><li>Britain's parliamentary political and legal systems at local, national, European, Commonwealth and international level, including how they function and change</li><li>the nature of political and voluntary action in communities</li></ul>

Table 11.7   *(Continued)*

Key concepts	Values and dispositions	Skills and aptitudes	Knowledge and understanding
	• determination to act justly • commitment to equal opportunities and gender equality • commitment to active citizenship • commitment to voluntary service • concern for human rights • concern for the environment		• the rights and responsibilities of citizens as consumers, employees, employers and family and community members • the economic system as it relates to individuals and communities • human rights charters and issues • sustainable development and environmental issues

Source: FEFC (2000) Citizenship for 16–19-year-olds in Education and Training. REP/1056/00. Appendix A p. 30. © FEFC 2000.

Teaching civic values through the curriculum: an example of global citizenship and resolving conflict (through participation)

Bourne Community College has included Citizenship studies through its Personal Social and Health Education (PSHE) curriculum. For pupils aged 13–14 it is usually in the form of large projects which involve a broad range of integrated civic values.

One such project focuses on the global dimension, involving contemporary examples of conflict, the role of international organisations (political and voluntary aid), the examination of resolution and active fundraising to support victims of conflict. Consequently, pupils use research, planning, enquiry, communication, participation and reflection skills in the process.

Pupils research the nature, history and role of the UN and Human Rights (and associated vocabulary) through books, the web, quizzes and discussion about media examples. They then identify a specific conflict in groups (perhaps a limited number for one class) and use formal homework time to investigate it more deeply. They prepare presentations in writing (media articles/video) and orally (in front of the class/assemblies) using ICT and graphics skills covering:

- What is the conflict about (motives and perspectives)?
- Is it being resolved/what solutions are there (conflict resolution)?

Connect and Extend

For more ideas on the use of literature 'as a bridge' between pupils' affective and cognitive learning experiences read Pellegrini, A. D. *et al.* (1995), 'The nexus of social and literacy experiences at home and school: Implications for primary school oral language and literacy', *British Journal of Educational Psychology, 65*(3), pp. 273–285.

Connect and Extend

For case studies of many ways to develop civic values and citizenship through the curriculum see the Companion Website (Web Link 11.4).

- Are there any refugees or asylum seekers (consequences of conflict)?
- Which international organisations are trying to help (work of voluntary organisations)?

Pupils are then challenged to raise funds to support a voluntary aid organisation involved with that conflict. 'It makes me feel lucky, and I feel better about myself because I'm doing something about it (global conflict)' (Laurence, aged 14). (Taken from: http://www.teachernet.gov.uk/casestudies/)

Getting started on community

Connect and Extend

See the March 2003 issue of *Educational Leadership* for several articles on 'Creating Caring Schools' and the September 2003 issue of *Educational Leadership* for several articles on 'Building Classroom Relationships'.

Learning and knowing something about civic values, citizenship and cooperation is part of the first steps in setting up and maintaining a community. Many people argue you can't have a community without an agreed way of behaving towards each other – a set of rules or a charter. The Elton Report (DES, 1989: 72) recommends establishing 'bottom-line' ground rules from the very first lesson and McNamara and Moreton say the process:

should ideally be undertaken at the start of a year, or when a group is just forming, and should be returned to if there is a problem with one particular rule being broken at any point in the year (1995: 54).

An example lesson to establish a classroom charter

Ian Hedley (1997) provides an example of working with a group of lower-ability 13- and 14-year-old maths pupils:

One fifty-minute lesson is spent with the pupils in the school's conference room. We sit in a circle and I explain everything agreed to by the group will be acted upon but:

- *some rules, national laws and whole school rules, cannot be negotiated; and*
- *remember you come to mathematics lessons to learn.*

   Pupils form random groups of four and have a pen and a large sheet of paper. They draw a large circle on the paper and inside the circle write everything they would like to be happening in a good mathematics lesson, outside the circle everything they would not like. Then everybody returns to the circle to discuss their ideas.
   After this discussion the groups reform to think about the rules needed to make their ideal lessons happen. They are only allowed to put 'Do' (positive) rules. If they have time, they put ideas for sanctions too.
   The lesson finishes with a discussion of their rules, focussing on areas where all the groups agree and attempting to resolve areas where there is little agreement.
   After the negotiation lesson I take all the sheets of paper and combine the rules to make the classroom charter. This is displayed in the classroom and a copy given to every pupil, their homework being to look at the charter and make sure it was as they had agreed, and let me know if it was not. So far no-one has asked for changes to be made. An example of the end result is shown below [in Figure 11.4].

Building a classroom community also takes daily attention to showing that each pupil is respected, that individual's cares and worries are acknowledged and that they bring special needs to the class community which they join each morning. An

In maths lessons we will all (including Mr Hedley) do our best to:

- work together when we need to;

- work as hard as we can;

- work quietly;

- get homework done on time;

- make sure we have the correct equipment (pen, pencil, rule, calculator); and

- be polite and pleasant to each other at all times.

Mr Hedley will do his best to:

- make sure we have enough time to do our homework;

- not lose his temper;

- help everybody as much as possible;

- plan more practical lessons;

- find some maths videos to watch;

- end the week with a maths game; and

- plan more group and pair work.

Figure 11.4
A classroom charter

Source: From 'Evaluating Classroom Charters' by Ian Hedley, Dorset 1997, Section 2.2. http://homepage.ntlworld.com/i.hedley/sen/chartstudy.htm

example of respect for pupils and their lives comes from Esme Codell. 'Madame Esme' (the name she preferred) had a morning classroom ritual:

> In the morning, three things happen religiously. I say good morning . . . to every single child and make sure they say good morning back. Then I collect 'troubles' in a 'Trouble Basket,' a big green basket into which the children pantomime unburdening their home worries so they can concentrate on school. Sometimes a kid has no troubles. Sometimes a kid piles it in, and I in turn pantomime bearing the burden. This way, too, I can see what disposition the child is in when he or she enters. Finally, before they can come in, they must give me a word, which I print . . . and keep in an envelope. It can be any word, but preferably one that they heard and don't really know or one that is personally meaningful. We go over the words when we do our private reading conferences (Codell, 2001: 30).

Esme Codell is not just showing respect for her pupils and their lives, she is also teaching compassion and tolerance. Some would argue that this is not what schools are for and that many aspects of character and morality are best taught in the home. See the Discussion Point below for some contrasting opinions.

More about belonging

When pupils perceive their schools are competitive places where they are treated differently based on race, gender or ethnicity, then they are more likely to act out or

DISCUSSION POINT

Should schools teach character and compassion?

Not all educators believe that schools should teach compassion, tolerance or other aspects of character and morality. Here are the two contrasting opinions.

Agree: Yes, schooling should include character education

Proponents of character education point to violence in the schools, teenage pregnancy and drug use amongst young people as evidence that educators need to address issues of morality and virtue. They argue that families are no longer doing a good job in this area, so schools must assume the burden. Thomas Lickona (2002) describes character education as the deliberate effort to cultivate personal qualities such as wisdom, honesty, kindness and self-discipline. The goals of character education are to produce good people (who can work and love), good schools (that are caring and conducive to learning), and a good society (that deals effectively with problems such as violence and poverty). To accomplish these goals, Lickona believes that pupils need knowledge and moral reasoning capabilities, emotional qualities such as self-respect and empathy, and skills such as cooperation and communication. Character education strategies include modelling kindness and cooperation, creating a classroom community that is democratic and supportive, using cooperative learning strategies, including reflection on moral issues in the curriculum, and teaching conflict resolution.

Disagree: No, character education is ineffective and dangerous

Alfie Kohn (2002) cautions that the term 'character education' has two meanings. The first is the general concern shared by most parents and educators that pupils grow into good, caring, honest people. The second is a narrow set of programmes and strategies for teaching a particular set of values. Few people disagree with the general concern, but there is disagreement about the narrower programmes. For example, Kohn says:

> *What goes by the name of character education nowadays is, for the most part, a collection of exhortations and extrinsic inducements designed to make children work harder and do what they're told. Even when other values are also promoted – caring or fairness, say – the preferred method of instruction is tantamount to indoctrination. The point is to drill pupils in specific behaviours rather than engage them in deep, critical reflection about certain ways of being (2002: 138).*

Kohn suggests that rather than try to 'fix' pupils' character, we should fix the structure of schools to make them more just and caring.

WHAT DO YOU THINK?

Agree or Disagree? Vote online at www.pearsoned.co.uk/woolfolkeuro.

withdraw altogether. But when they feel that they have choices, that the emphasis is on personal improvement and not comparisons, and when they feel respected and supported by teachers, pupils are more likely to bond with schools (Osterman, 2000). We have talked in other chapters (use the index to review these topics) about encouraging pupil engagement and promoting positive attitudes towards education. We saw that culturally responsive teaching can provide access to learning for more pupils. We looked at authentic tasks and problem-based learning as ways to connect with pupils' lives and interests. We examined the TARGET model for ideas about building motivation to learn. Here we consider research that specifically examines what helps pupils, particularly adolescents, feel connected to school.

Pupils are more likely to have a sense of belonging in school when they believe their teachers care about them. We saw in Chapter 3 that caring can be both academic and personal. When Kathryn Wentzel (1998, 2002) asked pupils how they knew that their teachers cared about them, they talked about teachers who tried to make classes interesting, who were fair and honest with them, who made sure they understood the materials, and who asked if something was wrong when they seemed upset. In other research, pupils describe teachers who notice when they are absent and ask why. Pupils believe teachers care when disciplinary procedures are fair and respectful and when the teachers use humour to connect with their pupils. In other words, the teachers trust and respect their pupils and care about them as learners and as people (Coldron *et al.*, 2002; Cullingford, 2002).

Violence in Schools

STOP AND THINK

Think back to the tragic events of April 2002 when 18 people lost their lives in a school shooting in the German city of Erfurt? Perhaps pupils in your class show you the Internet BBC News Report (shown in Figure 11.5). What would you say to them? How do you think this grievous event should be best dealt with in school?

Extreme violence in schools is very rare in schools in the US and Europe but in the past decade there have been some terrible tragedies that saddened and angered us as members of our world community.

Of real concern is the amount of knives now being taken into our schools and being used by pupils on each other and on teachers. In November 2003, 14-year-old Luke Walmsley was stabbed through the chest by a 15-year-old at his Lincoln school – the latest in a series of knifings in schools across England. A 30-minute BBC Radio 1 documentary 'Knives Out' looked into why children as young as five are carrying knives and find out if stabbings of musicians like Dizzee Rascal have any impact on the culture of young people carrying knives on the streets and in our schools. You can listen to the documentary online at http://www.bbc.co.uk/radio1/onelife/personal/safety/knives_doc.shtml or follow the link from www.pearsoned.co.uk/woolfolkeuro.

Connect and Extend

To read about violent crime in London schools access Neill, S. R. St-J (2006), 'Knives and other weapons in London schools', *International Journal on School Disaffection, 3*(2), pp. 27–32; see also Petit, G. S. and Dodge, K. A. (2003), 'Violent Children: Special Issue', *Developmental Psychology, 39*(2).

Figure 11.5
BBC News Report on Erfurt shooting

Source: BBC News Report at http://news.bbc.co.uk/1/hi/world/europe/1952869.stm

Friday, 26 April, 2002, 21:32 GMT 22:32 UK

Eighteen dead in German school shooting

Eighteen people died when an expelled former pupil went on a shooting spree at his school in the eastern German city of Erfurt. Masked and dressed in black, the gunman walked through classrooms killing 14 teachers, two schoolgirls and one of the first policemen on the scene before taking his own life. Pupils of the Gutenberg School spent four hours trapped inside before police could declare the building safe.

The German authorities have not given the name of the Erfurt killer but they said he was a 19-year-old who had been expelled from the school several months earlier and told he could not sit his university entrance exam.

'We were sitting in class doing our work and we heard a shooting sound,' said eyewitness Filip Niemann. 'We joked about it and the teacher smiled,' said Niemann. 'The teacher let us go out and see what was happening and when we left the classroom, three to four metres in front of us, there was a masked person in black holding his gun at his shoulder.'

Niemann saw a teacher being shot and fled with other pupils as the killer stalked the classrooms, searching for more teachers. After a caretaker alerted the police, two officers appeared at the school around noon, only to find dead bodies as they entered.

Connect and Extend

To read how school-based interventions can make a difference for children on the path to violence, see Aber, J. L., Brown, J. L. and Jones, S. M. (2003), 'Developmental trajectories towards violence in middle childhood: Course, demographic differences, and response to school-based intervention', *Developmental Psychology, 39*, pp. 324–348.

Connect and Extend

To understand one modern perspective on how school violence may be one function of violence permeating the wider community read Astore, R. A. *et al.* (2006), 'Arab and Jewish elementary school students' perceptions of fear and school violence: understanding the influence of school context', *British Journal of Educational Psychology, 76*(1), pp. 91–118.

Violence in schools does not have to be of such an extreme manifestation. In 22 years of working in schools this co-author was attacked three times: a couple of half-hearted punches from angry fathers and a very hard slap across the face from a very angry mother. This led me to formulate a somewhat insubstantial theory that the best way of keeping violence out of our schools was to ban all parents from the premises.

Most teachers will face some sort of violent threat or action during their careers but extreme violence is very rare and we would be unwise to think of schools as violent places. By and large American and European schools are decent, calm, safe and relatively secure places to be for both teachers and pupils. We are right to be alarmed when things go very wrong.

Even though extreme violence in schools is relatively rare, interpersonal violence among our young people is a concern for both parents and teachers (Lowry *et al.*, 1995). Young people ages 12 to 24 are the most likely victims of nonfatal violence, and many of these attacks take place on school property. About one-third of all injury-related deaths are the result of interpersonal violence – and young people are often the victims or the attackers in these violent acts (Peterson and Newman, 2000). This problem has many causes; it is a challenge for every element of society. What can the schools do? The guidelines shown in the following Focus in Practice will help you to think about how to react in difficult circumstances.

Prevention

The best answer to school violence is prevention. As a teacher, you may have little to say about violence on television, metal detectors or knife ownership amongst young people – but you have much to say about the way pupils treat each other and the sense of community created in your classes. You can teach acceptance

FOCUS ON PRACTICE

Handling potentially explosive situations

Move slowly and deliberately towards the problem situation

Examples
1. Walk slowly, then be as still as possible.
2. Establish eye-level position.

Be respectful

Examples
1. Keep a reasonable distance.
2. Do not crowd the pupil. Do not get 'in the pupil's face'.
3. Speak respectfully. Use the pupil's name.
4. Avoid pointing or gesturing.

Be brief

Examples
1. Avoid long-winded statements or nagging.
2. Stay with the agenda. Stay focused on the problem at hand. Do not get side-tracked.
3. Deal with less severe problems later.

Avoid power struggles

Examples
1. Speak privately if possible.
2. Do not get drawn into 'I won't, you will' arguments.
3. Don't make threats or raise your voice.

Inform the pupil of the expected behaviour (and the negative consequence) as a choice or decision for the pupil to make. Then withdraw from the pupil and allow some time for the pupil to decide

Examples
1. 'Michael, you need to return to your desk, or you will have to go to the "support suite". You have a few seconds to decide.' The teacher then moves away, perhaps attending to other pupils.
2. If Michael does not choose the appropriate behaviour, deliver the negative consequences. ('You are choosing to go to the "support suite"'). Follow through with the consequence and have the errant Michael escorted to the support suite with some work and a note for the staff on duty there.

For more ideas, see http://www.njcap.org/templated/Programs.html.

Source: From *Secondary Classroom Management: Lessons from Research and Practice* (3rd ed.) by C. S. Weinstein and A. J. Mignano Jr. Published by McGraw-Hill.

Connect and Extend

To read about violence in South African schools see Fraser, W. J. (1996), 'Reflections on the causes and manifestations of violence in South African schools', *Prospects, 26*(2), pp. 249–278.

Connect and Extend

Study of the causes of gang membership and for the existence of gangs in schools can be found in a number of useful studies including Torrance, D. A. (1997), 'Do you want to be in my gang?: a study of the existence and effects of bullying in a primary school class', *British Journal of Special Education, 24*(4), pp. 158–162.

Connect and Extend

To explore problems related to school gang violence, read Parks, C. P. (1995), 'Gang behavior in the schools: myth or reality?', *Educational Psychology Review, 7*, pp. 41–68.

and compassion through direct and indirect means. You can create a culture of belonging for all your pupils. Yet, sometimes it might feel like 'swimming against the tide' because schools exist in a context which have many factors seemingly outside of a teacher's influence. Some studies have argued that poor parental supervision, school staff victimisation of pupils, location of school and particularly gang involvement, are the main factors contributing to school violence (Sumer and Cetinkaya, 2004) and that teachers can have little influence.

Yet a philosophy of despair simply will not do. We know teachers and schools that do make a difference; that do provide stability and a safe environment despite poor parental supervision; that cut out and police any victimisation of pupils; that gain the support of the community in locations where detrimental socioeconomic factors could be a problem; and that successfully protect their pupils from the influence of the street gangs. But why do teenagers in particular turn to the excitements and dangers of the street (and school) gangs in the first place?

Some urban gang members reported that they turned to gang activities when their teachers insulted them, called them names, humiliated them publicly, belittled their culture, ignored them in class or blamed all negative incidents on particular pupils. The pupils reported joining gangs for security and to escape teachers who treated them badly or expected little of them because of their ethnicity (Parks, 1995). Another two-year study found that gang members respected teachers who insisted in a caring way that they focus on academic performance (Huff, 1989). Anita Woolfolk – co-author of this text – once asked a gifted secondary school teacher which teachers were most effective with the really tough pupils. He said there are two kinds, teachers who can't be intimidated or fooled and expect their pupils to learn, and teachers who really care about the pupils. When Anita asked, 'Which kind are you?' he answered, 'Both!' He is an example of a 'warm demander', as you will see in the next section.

Teachers and pupils need to know the warning signs of potential dangers. Table 11.8 describes two kinds of signs – immediate warning and potential problems.

Respect and Protect

One system that has been developed to combat violence in the schools is *Respect and Protect*. The programme is founded on five ideas: First, everyone is obliged to respect and protect the rights of others. Second, violence is not acceptable. Third, the programme targets the violence-enabling behaviours of staff, pupils and parents such as denying, rationalising, justifying or blaming others for violence. Fourth, there is a clear definition of what constitutes violence that distinguishes two kinds of violence – bully/victim violence and violence that arises from normal conflicts. Finally, the programme has both adult-centred prevention that improves the school climate and pupil-centred interventions that give pupils choices and clear consequences (Rembolt, 1998). Table 11.9 gives an overview of the levels of choices and consequences.

Another approach that builds respect and acceptance moves outside the classroom – community service learning.

Table 11.8   Recognising the warning signs of violence

The following lists were developed by the American Psychological Association. Other resources are available at http://helping.apa.org/warningsigns/

If you see these immediate warning signs, violence is a serious possibility:

- loss of temper on a daily basis
- frequent physical fighting
- significant vandalism or property damage
- increase in use of drugs or alcohol
- increase in risk-taking behaviour
- detailed plans to commit acts of violence
- announcing threats or plans for hurting others
- enjoying hurting animals
- carrying a weapon

If you notice the following signs over a period of time, the potential for violence exists:

- a history of violent or aggressive behaviour
- serious drug or alcohol use
- gang membership or strong desire to be in a gang
- access to or fascination with weapons, especially guns
- threatening others regularly
- trouble controlling feelings like anger
- withdrawal from friends and usual activities
- feeling rejected or alone
- having been a victim of bullying
- poor school performance
- history of discipline problems or frequent run-ins with authority
- feeling constantly disrespected
- failing to acknowledge the feelings or rights of others

Source: From 'Warning Signs'. Copyright © 1999 by the American Psychological Association. Adapted with permission of the APA. For more information, consult the website – http://apahelpcenter.org/featuredtopics/feature.php?id=38.

Community Service Learning

Community service learning is another approach to combining academic learning with personal and social development for secondary and college pupils (Fredricks, 2003; Woolfolk Hoy, Demerath and Pape, 2002). There are several characteristics of successful community service learning (http://www.csuchico.edu/ psed/servicelearning/). Successful service learning activities:

Community service learning
An approach to combining academic learning with personal and social development.

- are organised and meet actual community needs;
- are integrated into the pupils' curriculum;
- provide time to reflect about the service experience;
- provide opportunities to apply newly learned academic skills and knowledge;
- enhance both academic learning and a sense of caring for others.

Table 11.9   Respect and Protect

This overview of choices, consequences and contracts shows measured responses to each level of violence.

Violence level*	Level one	Level two	Level three	Level four	Level five
Violation	Rule Violation (Minor infraction)	Misuse of Power (Repeat violation)	Abuse of Power (Serious)	Continued Abuse (Severe)	Pathology (Intractable)
Staff action	Confront behaviour Stop violence Deal with problem File intervention report Review No Violence rule Suggest anger management, conflict resolution, peer mediation or class meeting	Confront behaviour Stop violence Refer to office File intervention report Try to assess type of conflict Evaluate for talk with parent	Confront behaviour Stop violence Refer to office File intervention report Try to assess type of conflict Parent conference Suggest parenting programme	Confront behaviour Stop violence Refer to office File intervention report Assess type of conflict Do psychosocial evaluation Hold parent conference Mandate parenting programme Suggest family counselling	Confront behaviour Stop violence Refer to office File intervention report Follow psychosocial recommendations Hold parent conference Mandate parenting programme Suggest intensive therapy or treatment for pupil
Pupil consequences	Review of activity for violence Parent notified (optional) Restitution Legal action	Office referral Life Skills worksheet Parent notified Restricted until worksheet finished Restitution Legal action	Office referral Parent notified Minimum time-out Violence Group Anger management Connections Empowerment Restitution Legal action	Office referral Parent notified Maximum time-out Violence Group Reconnections Restitution Legal action	Office referral Parent notified Maximum time-out Placement into an alternative setting Restitution Legal action
Contracts**	Verbal Promise	Simple Contract	Turf Contract I	Turf Contract II	Bottom-Line Contract

*Pupils are placed at Levels 1–5 depending on the frequency and severity of their violent behaviour. Any violent act that is racial, sexual, involves physical fighting or is committed against staff results in the pupil being placed immediately at Level 3 or higher. The programme manual provides lists of behaviours that correlate with each level of violence.

**See source for a complete description of the different contracts.

Source: From Rembolt, C. (1998) 'Making violence unacceptable' *Educational Leadership, 56*(3), p. 36. Reprinted with permission. The Association for Supervision and Curriculum Development is a worldwide community of educators advocating sound policies and sharing best practices to achieve the success of each learner. To learn more visit ASCD at www.ascd.org.

Community service learning (sometimes shortened to service learning) activities may involve direct service (tutoring, serving meals at homeless shelters), indirect service (collecting food for shelters, raising money) or advocacy (design and distribute posters about a food collection, write newspaper articles) (Johnson and Notah, 1999). Service learning also could be a form of problem-based learning, described in Chapter 9 (p. 420), where the problem involves how to serve an identified need in the community.

Participation in community service learning promotes political and moral development for young people of all ages. Through service learning projects, adolescents in particular experience their own competence and influence by working with others in need. Pupils see themselves as political and moral agents, rather than as merely good citizens (Youniss and Yates, 1997). In addition, community service learning can help pupils think in new ways about their relationships with people who are unlike them, and thus can lead them to become more tolerant of difference (Tierney, 1993). Finally, service learning experiences foster an 'ethic of care' that can result in a growing commitment to confront difficult social problems (Rhodes, 1997). In this sense, pupil involvement in community service learning can motivate and empower adolescents to critically reflect on their role in society (Woolfolk Hoy, Demerath and Pape, 2002; Claus and Ogden, 1999).

Studies of service learning have produced mixed results. Some studies have found modest gains on measures of social responsibility, tolerance for others, empathy, attitude towards adults and self-esteem (Solomon *et al.*, 2001). A case study at an urban parochial secondary school describes a successful service-learning experience (Yates and Youniss, 1999). In the class, pupils examined the moral implications of current events such as homelessness, poverty, exploitation of immigrant labourers and urban violence. Pupils also were required to serve four times (approximately 20 hours) at an inner-city soup kitchen. The researchers concluded that pupils emerged from the course with 'a deeper awareness of social injustice, a greater sense of commitment to confront these injustices, and heightened confidence in their abilities overall' (Yates and Youniss, 1999: 64).

Consider the following Focus on Practice, some examples are taken from Richard Sagor (2003) and Elias and Schwab (2006).

FOCUS ON PRACTICE

Using service learning

The service should be ongoing, not just a brief project

Examples
1. Instead of having a two-week food collection with a party for the class that collected the most, involve pupils in a longer commitment to cook or serve food at shelters for homeless families.
2. Contact local organisations to identify real needs that your pupils could address or search online by postcode. The Salvation Army is a good starting place.

Consider virtual volunteering. See http://www.csv.org.uk/

Examples

1. Translate a document into another language.
2. Provide multimedia expertise, such as preparing a MS PowerPoint or other computer-based presentations.
3. Design a newsletter or brochure, or copyedit a publication or proposal.
4. Proofread drafts of paper and online publications.
5. Research and write articles for brochures, newsletters, websites.
6. Design a logo for an organisation or programmme, or fill other illustration needs.

Make sure learning is at the heart of community service learning

Examples

1. Have clear learning objectives for the service learning projects.
2. Examine National Curriculum programmes of study in science, history, health, literature, and so on to see how some might be met through service projects – for example, how might concepts in biology be learned though designing a nutrition education project for senior citizens or pre-school pupils?
3. Have pupils reflect over time about their experiences, keep diaries, write or draw or film what they have learned, and include these reflections in class discussions.

Make sure the service draws on the pupils' talents and skills so that it is actually valuable to the recipients, and the pupils gain a sense of accomplishment and usefulness from applying their skills to help others

Examples

1. Pupils who have artistic talents might help redecorate a game room at a senior citizens' centre.
2. Pupils who are good storytellers could work with children at a mothers and toddlers group or in a specialist children's clinic or hospital ward.
3. Pupils who are bilingual might help teachers translate school newsletters for parents or serve as translators at local events.

For more ideas, see http://www.do-it.org.uk/ or http://www.saintorsinner.org.uk/.

Connections

What are the connections between behavioural, emotional, social and cognitive engagement in schools? The research on school-based youth development and problem prevention programmes points to *three factors for success*. Successful programmes focus on enhancing pupils' social and emotional competence, connections to others, and contributions to their communities (Greenberg *et al.*, 2003). These factors parallel the major sections of this chapter – cooperating in classroom groups, creating classroom communities and connecting to communities outside the school. After reading this chapter and studying the suggested reading and identified research, can you begin to see how attention to the *three factors for success* help teachers effectively engage pupils together in their own learning and in the learning of their classmates? The next chapter will help to consolidate your learning on how teachers create learning environments.

SUMMARY TABLE

Social Processes in Learning (pp. 483–485)

What are some of the social factors that influence learning in school?

Peers, parents and teachers influence norms and values about school achievement. Children tend to select friends that share their orientations and interests, and these peer groups, in turn, influence children's academic motivation. But parents and teachers play a role, too. Pupils with authoritative parents are more likely to choose positive peer groups and to resist peer pressure for antisocial behaviours such as drug use. If pupils have few or no friends, being liked by the teacher can be especially important.

Collaboration and Cooperation (pp. 485–500)

What are the differences between collaboration and cooperation?

One view is that cooperation is a philosophy about how to relate to others – how to learn and work. Cooperation is a way of dealing with people that respects differences, shares authority and builds on the knowledge that is distributed among other people. Collaboration, on the other hand, is a way of working together with others to attain a shared goal.

What are the learning theory underpinnings of cooperative learning?

Learning can be enhanced in cooperative groups through rehearsal and elaboration (information processing theories), creation and resolution of disequilibrium (Piaget's theory), or scaffolding of higher mental processes (Vygotsky's theory).

Describe five elements that define true cooperative learning

Pupils *interact face-to-face* and close together, not across the room. Group members experience *positive interdependence* – they need each other for support, explanations and guidance. Even though they work together and help each other, members of the group must ultimately demonstrate learning on their own – they are held *individually accountable* for learning, often through individual tests or other assessments. If necessary, the *collaborative skills* important for effective group functioning, such as giving constructive feedback, reaching consensus and involving every member, are taught and practised before the groups tackle a learning task. Finally, members monitor *group processes* and relationships to make sure the group is working effectively and to learn about the dynamics of groups.

How should tasks match design in cooperative learning?

A relatively structured task works well with a structured technique; extrinsic rewards can enhance motivation, effort and persistence under these conditions; roles, especially roles that focus attention on the work to be accomplished, also may be productive. On the other hand, strategies that encourage extended and productive interactions are appropriate when the goal is to develop higher-order thinking and problem solving. The use of rewards may well divert the group away from the goal of in-depth cognitive processing. When the goal of peer learning is enhanced social skills or increased inter-group understanding and appreciation of diversity, the assignment of specific roles and functions within the group might support communication. Rewards probably are not necessary and may actually get in the way because the goal is to build community, a sense of respect and responsibility for team members.

What are some possible strategies for cooperative learning?

Strategies include reciprocal questioning, scripted cooperation, Jigsaw and many others described by Spencer Kagan.

The Classroom Community (pp. 500–511)

What are Johnson and Johnson's three Cs of establishing a classroom community?

The three Cs are cooperative community, constructive conflict resolution and civic values. Classroom management begins by establishing a community based on cooperative learning. At the heart of the community is the idea of positive interdependence – individuals working together to achieve mutual goals. Constructive conflict resolution is essential in the community because conflicts are inevitable and even necessary for learning. But, teachers often underestimate the amount of peer conflict and bullying that happens in schools. Peer mediation is one good possibility for dealing with peer harassment. The steps for peer mediation are: (1) Jointly define the conflict. (2) Exchange positions and interests. (3) Reverse perspectives. (4) Invent at least three agreements that allow mutual gain. (5) Reach an integrative agreement. The last C is civic values – the understandings and beliefs that hold the community together. Values are learned through direct teaching, modelling, reading literature, engaging in group discussions and sharing concerns.

How do teachers get started on a caring community?

To get started on building community, teachers should make expectations for both academic work and pupils' behaviours clear. Respect for pupils' needs and rights should be at the centre of class procedures. Pupils know that their teachers care about them when teachers try to make classes interesting, are fair and honest with them, make sure they understand the materials and have ways to cope with pupils' concerns and troubles.

Violence in the Schools (pp. 511–515)

What can be done about violence in schools?

Incidents such as school shootings bring attention from the media. But young people ages 12 to 24 are the most likely group to be victims of nonfatal violence – often on school property. Possibilities to deal with violence include preventing violence by creating compassionate, respectful classrooms. It is especially important to respect the cultural heritages of the pupils while also maintaining high expectations for learning, School-wide programmes such as *Respect and Protect* may provide the support teachers' need to deal with violence.

Community Service Learning (pp. 515–518)

What is community service learning?

Community service learning activities are organised and meet actual community needs. They are integrated into the pupils' curriculum, and provide time for the pupil to reflect about the service experience and to apply newly learned academic skills and knowledge. It is critical that both aspects of service learning are accomplished – both giving a valuable service and supporting the learning of pupils.

Glossary

Collaboration: Working together and in parallel with others to reach a shared goal.

Community service learning: An approach to combining academic learning with personal and social development.

Cooperation: A way of dealing with people that respects differences, shares authority and builds on the combined knowledge of self and others.

Cooperative learning: Arrangement in which pupils work in groups and make gains in learning on the basis of the success of the group.

Jigsaw: A cooperative structure in which each member of a group is responsible for teaching other members one section of the material.

Reciprocal questioning: Approach where groups of two or three pupils ask and answer each other's questions after a lesson or presentation.

Scripted cooperation: A learning strategy in which two pupils take turns summarising material and critiquing the summaries.

CHECK YOUR LEARNING!   WEB

In the Classroom: What Would They Do?

You will remember that 'In the Classroom' there had been reports of pupils bringing knives into school and that a gang culture was developing. This had all come to light because Emily's mother had complained that her daughter's attitude had worsened considerably. In these circumstances what should teachers do, how should they respond to Emily's mother and what should be the school's response to the concerns of teachers and other parents?

Here is how some practising teachers responded:

Lisbeth Jonsson, primary school teacher, Sweden

Bullying and intimidation are growing problems in Sweden too. Which pupil dares to tell teachers or parents what is going on? We had a case in south Sweden quite recently, where the school closed for two weeks. Many pupils were afraid to go to school and the situation was getting out of hand. The gang members were taken out of this particular school and placed in other schools – not together of course. In some schools the 'victim' of bullying had to change school, which was a very bad solution. We need a united front of parents and school staff to avoid this kind of problem. But the weak link is often the parents, so why not start 'teaching' them?

Lizzie Meadows, deputy head teacher, The Park Primary School, Kingswood, Bristol

My immediate response to Emily's mother would be to reassure her that I would endeavour to find out whether there is anything that may be causing this change in Emily. I would explore with her mother whether the change has been gradual or was sudden and whether there was anything happening at home that may have upset her. I would ask her to monitor her behaviour at home and I would likewise do it at school. I would also reassure her that if there is any suspicion of bullying that the school would do its best to get to the bottom of it and take a very hard line. I would arrange to ring her in a week to compare notes. As a class teacher I would take my concerns to management and in the meantime document anything that arouses suspicion. As a manager of the school, I would be extremely concerned about this issue. In the short term I would ensure high presence and visibility around the school of all senior staff at all times of the day. I would also engage the police in discussions concerning gangs and knives. A longer term issue has to be promoting academic success and learning as a good thing, and gradually break down the negative image of 'the keener' and also finding a way to channel those that want to be in gangs. I would ensure that all staff are on board with this notion and that they work hard with the parents to promote learning as the key to success.

Lee Card, primary school teacher, Bosbury Church of England Primary School, Herefordshire

As a class teacher, my priority would be to look out for the welfare and safety of the child when in the classroom itself. If the gang are from older year groups then she should feel that her classroom is a safe and reassuring place to be. In such a delicate situation, full school support and a consistent approach is needed. I would be inclined to ensure that the Head is party to all conversations or meetings involving Emily's parents or Emily herself (perhaps keeping a log book). Emily's mother needs to feel that the school will consistently deal with any situation quickly and effectively and good communication throughout is essential if this is to be achieved. Again, I would hope for guidance and leadership from the Head in looking into the situation further. It seems like the younger 'target' children would be the best way into finding out about the gangs and how they are operating in school.

Tessa Herbert, English teacher, John Masefield High School, Ledbury

If only there was any easy answer to bullying! The immediate response to Emily's mother might be that Emily is probably growing up, but that the school has been alerted to a possible problem and is dealing with it. If there is a rumour, names are probably known. These girls must be taken out individually and the consequences of their actions clearly spelt out, not only to them but also to their parents. There is no need to tie these conversations to any specific informant. Any evidence of gang problems in school should be dealt with immediately and firmly. Exclusions have to be considered. A 'listening group' of pupils could be very useful to support the vulnerable and to the keep staff in touch with what is happening on the ground, without betraying individual confidences. Such a group of Year 10 pupils at my school, undertaking an NVQ, have proved very valuable as 'confidantes' for younger pupils.

PART **3** Teaching and Assessing

Overview

This chapter looks at ways teachers create social and physical environments for learning by examining classroom management – one of the main concerns of teachers, particularly newly qualified teachers. The nature of schooling, teaching and young people makes good classroom management a critical ingredient of success; we will investigate why this is true. Successful teachers create more time for learning, involve more pupils and help pupils to become self-managing.

A positive learning environment must be established and maintained throughout the year. One of the best ways to do this is to try to prevent problems from occurring at all. However, when problems arise – as they always do – an appropriate response is important. What should a teacher do when openly challenged by pupils, when one pupil asks for advice on a difficult personal problem, or when another withdraws from all participation? We will examine the ways that teachers can communicate effectively with their pupils in these and many other situations.

By the time you have completed this chapter, you should be able to answer the following questions:

- **What are the special managerial demands of classrooms and the needs of pupils of different ages?**
- **How should a teacher establish procedures and a list of class rules?**
- **How should a teacher arrange the physical environment of a classroom to fit learning goals and teaching methods?**
- **How should a teacher manage computers in the classroom to fit learning goals and teaching methods?**
- **What are Kounin's suggestions for preventing management problems?**
- **How should a teacher respond to a pupil who seldom completes work?**
- **What are two different approaches for dealing with a conflict between a teacher and a pupil?**

In the Classroom

You are visiting a school and being shown around by two very well-dressed pupils who are both knowledgeable and proud of their school. It is the start of the day and most pupils are sitting at their desks getting on with their work. There is a calm atmosphere around the school and as you go in to some of the classrooms you are greeted by the teachers, and pupils are keen to show you what they are doing. The design of the building includes windows between the corridors and the classrooms, so you don't have to go into every classroom to see what is happening. You are particularly impressed with how the pupils are working in the computer room, the music room and the library. However, one corridor seems very noisy and you are surprised to find one pupil standing outside a classroom door.

The teacher is having a difficult time. Pupils are calling out, talking and teasing each other, leaning back on their chairs and throwing things across the room when the teacher's back is turned. It is clear that very little learning is taking place.

When you return to the school office the head teacher asks how you have enjoyed the visit. 'Very

much', you say. 'You obviously run a tight ship here, so I was surprised to see the way the children were behaving in classroom 4.' The head teacher suddenly looks very worried. 'Oh dear,' he replies, 'that's our Mr Jones. He's very new and some of the children are taking advantage of his inexperience. I'm doing everything I can to support him. You obviously caught him at a bad time. I'll have a word with his mentor, who is our school professional tutor.'

How should the school professional tutor support Mr Jones and ensure that his behaviour management improves? Why do you think the pupils in Mr Jones class are behaving in a very different way to the other pupils in the school? What can the head teacher do to help?

Group Activity

With another member of your group, role play a discussion between the school professional tutor and Mr Jones. What is your plan to deal with this situation?

The Need for Organisation

In study after study of the factors related to pupil achievement, classroom management stands out as the variable with the largest impact (Marzano and Marzano, 2003). Knowledge and expertise in classroom management are marks of expertise in teaching and conversely, stress and exhaustion from managerial difficulties are precursors of burn-out in teaching (Emmer and Stough, 2001). What is it about classrooms that make management so critical?

Connect and Extend

Some educators object to the metaphor of teacher as manager. They suggest that the image brings with it notions of manipulation and detachment. What other metaphors can you suggest for teachers acting to maintain order? My research in this area suggests that images of group leaders, problem solvers and nurturers are common.

Classrooms are particular kinds of environments. They have distinctive features that influence their inhabitants no matter how the pupils or the desks are organised or what the teacher believes about education (Dorman and Adams, 2004; Ghaith, 2003; Roth *et al.*, 1999). Classrooms are multi-dimensional. They are crowded with people, tasks and time pressures. Many individuals, with differing goals, preferences and abilities, must share resources, accomplish various tasks, use and re-use materials without losing them, move in and out of the room, and so on. In addition, actions can have multiple effects. Asking questions of low-ability pupils may encourage their participation and thinking, but may slow the discussion and lead to management problems if the pupils cannot answer. Actions and events occur simultaneously – things happens at once, the pace is fast and teachers have hundreds of exchanges with pupils during a single day.

In this rapid-fire existence, events are unpredictable. Even when plans are carefully made, the digital whiteboard painstakingly prepared, and the demonstration is ready, a burned-out bulb in the projector or a loud, angry discussion right outside the classroom can still interrupt the lesson. Classrooms are public spaces, so the way the teacher handles these unexpected intrusions is seen and judged by all. Pupils are always noticing if the teacher is being 'fair'. Is there favouritism? What happens when a rule is broken? Finally, classrooms have histories. The meaning of a particular teacher's or pupil's actions depends in part on what has happened before in the classroom. The fifteenth time a pupil arrives late requires a different response from the teacher than the first late arrival. In addition, the history of the first few weeks of a new academic year affects life in the class all year.

Connect and Extend

Motivation and classroom management are closely related. The motivational strategies described in Chapter 10 (p. 468) are good first steps in effective class management.

The basic task: gain their cooperation

No productive activity can take place in a group without the cooperation of all members. This obviously applies to classrooms. Even if some pupils don't participate, they must allow others to do so. (We all have seen one or two pupils bring an entire class to a halt.) So the basic management task for teachers is to achieve order and harmony by gaining and maintaining pupil cooperation in class activities (Gillies, 2006; Pollard, 1985). Given the multi-dimensional, simultaneous, fast-paced, unpredictable, public and historical nature of classrooms, this is quite a challenge.

Gaining pupil cooperation means much more than dealing effectively with misbehaviour. It means planning activities, having materials ready, making appropriate behavioural and academic demands on pupils, giving clear signals, accomplishing transitions smoothly, foreseeing problems and stopping them before they start, selecting and sequencing activities so that flow and interest are maintained – and much more. Also, different activities require different managerial skills. For example, a new or complex activity may be a greater threat to classroom management than a familiar or straightforward activity and appropriate pupil participation varies across different activities. For example, loud pupil comments during a hip-hop reading of Green Eggs and Ham are indications of engagement and cooperation, not disorderly calling-out (Doyle, 2006).

The basic management task for teachers is to achieve order and harmony by gaining and maintaining pupil cooperation in class activities

Obviously, gaining the cooperation of young children is not the same task as gaining the cooperation of 13- to 16-year-olds. Jere Brophy and Carolyn Evertson (1978) identified four general stages of classroom management, defined by age-related needs. During nursery and the first few years of primary school, direct teaching of classroom rules and procedures is important. For children in the middle primary years, many classroom routines have become relatively automatic, but new procedures for a particular activity may have to be taught directly, and the entire system still needs monitoring and maintenance.

Towards the end of primary school, some pupils begin to test and defy authority. The challenges for teachers at this stage are to deal productively with these disruptions and to motivate pupils who are becoming less concerned with teachers' opinions and more interested in their social lives. By the end of secondary school, the challenges are to manage the curriculum, fit academic material to pupils' interests and abilities, and help pupils become more self-managing. The first few classes each term or year are devoted to teaching particular procedures for using materials and equipment, or for keeping track of and submitting assignments and coursework. By this stage most pupils know what is expected of them.

The goals of classroom management

STOP AND THINK

Write three principles of effective classroom management. You can review these principles when you have read the rest of the chapter.

Classroom management

Techniques used to establish and maintain a positive and safe learning environment, relatively free of behaviour problems.

The aim of classroom management is to maintain a positive, productive learning environment but the imposition of such order for its own sake is an empty goal. As we discussed in Chapter 6, it is unethical to use classroom management techniques just to keep pupils docile and quiet. So what, then, is the point of working so hard to manage classrooms? There are at least three reasons.

1. More time for learning

Imagine using a stopwatch to time the various parts of a television quiz show. As well as the usual interruptions of commercial breaks, there are the introductions of the host and the contestants, and the descriptions of prizes. Time is taken to move contestants to different parts of the set, to spin a wheel or move into the 'safe zone', to check the scores or remind everybody about the rules. Actually, very little quizzing takes place. If you used a similar approach in classrooms, timing all the different activities throughout the day, you might be surprised by how little actual teaching takes place. When observing trainee teachers I often do a simple tick list of their utterances in two columns: teaching utterances (e.g. questions, explanations, responses) and managing utterances (requests, commands, admonishments etc.). The latter often outnumbers the former by anything up to five to one. Try the same exercise yourself when next you have the opportunity to observe somebody teaching. Many minutes each day are lost through interruptions, disruptions, late starts and poorly managed lesson transitions (Ackers and Hardman, 2001; Pollard *et al.*, 1994).

Obviously, pupils can only learn what they encounter. Almost every study examining time and learning has found a significant relationship between time spent on content and pupil learning (Hinger, 2006; Van Dalen *et al.*, 1999; Berliner, 1988). In fact, pupils complain that they have insufficient time to accomplish schoolwork and the correlations between time spent and pupil learning are usually larger than the correlations between specific teacher behaviours and pupil learning (Alerby, 2003). One large study in London schools estimated that the total time that pupils spend in compulsory schooling – time spent at school – is 15,000 hours (Rutter *et al.*, 1979). Thus, if there is plenty of time in school one important goal of classroom management is to expand the sheer number of minutes available for learning. This is sometimes called allocated or available time. One current approach to maximising available time is to develop policies and practices in e-learning; 'any time–any place–anywhere' learning (Pittard, 2004).

Allocated or available time

Time set aside for learning.

Engaged time

Time spent being active with some task, or talking to or listening to others.

Time on task

Time spent actively engaged in the learning offered by the task at hand.

Simply making more time for learning will not automatically lead to achievement. To be valuable, time must be used effectively. As you saw in the chapters on cognitive learning, the way pupils process information is a central factor in what they learn and remember. Basically, pupils will learn what they practice and think about (Doyle, 1983). Time spent actively involved in specific learning tasks often is called engaged time or sometimes time on task (Veenman *et al.*, 2000). Table 12.1 shows the amount of time on task by school children in 12 Scottish primary schools. The research was based on detailed classroom observation of pupils aged five, eight and 11 years, and their teachers. Overall, pupils were engaged on task for two-thirds of the available time.

Successful learning time

Time when pupils are actually succeeding at the learning task.

Again, however, spending time on task doesn't guarantee learning. Pupils may be struggling with material that is too difficult or using the wrong learning strategies. When pupils are working with a high rate of success – really learning and understanding – we call the time spent successful learning time. Much of the psychology of education and psychological research into what happens in classrooms, and which underpins this book, seeks to establish how teachers provide pupils with successful learning time.

Table 12.1 Percentage of available time spent in various kinds of activity, by age and overall

Pupil activity	Age 5	Age 8	Age 11	Overall
Engaged on task	67	71	63	67
Managing task	11	9	9	10
Assessment	0	1	0	1
Distracted	4	6	10	7
Waiting	8	9	7	8
Filling in	1	1	1	1
Out of the room	7	5	8	7

Source: Adapted from McPake, J., Harlen, W., Powney, J. and Davidson, J. (1999). Teachers' and Pupils' Days in the Primary Classroom. The Scottish Council for Research in Education (now part of The Faculty of Education, University of Glasgow). Research Report No. 93, p. 20. December 1999.

Table 12.2 Percentage of time spent by pupils in various forms of interaction, by age and overall

Pupil interaction	Age 5	Age 8	Age 11	Overall
One-to-one interaction with class teacher	2	3	2	2
Interaction with group – on task	9	6	7	7
Interaction as part of whole-class teaching	32	35	28	32
Overall percentage of time spent interacting	43	44	37	41

Source: Adapted from McPake, J., Harlen, W., Powney, J. and Davidson, J. (1999). *Teachers' and Pupils' Days in the Primary Classroom.* The Scottish Council for Research in Education (now part of The Faculty of Education, University of Glasgow). Research Report No. 93, p. 24. December 1999.

A second goal of class management is to increase successful learning time by keeping pupils actively engaged in worthwhile, appropriate activities through interaction about their learning with teachers and fellow pupils. Social constructivist theories (see Chapter 9, p. 411) 'share two main ideas: that learners are active in constructing their own knowledge and that social interactions are important to knowledge construction' (Bruning *et al.*, 2004: 195). Table 12.2 is also drawn from the findings of the classroom study in Scottish primary schools (McPake *et al.*, 1999: 23). Overall, pupils on task were interacting for 41% of their time.

The surprise here is the small amount of time available on task when pupils are interacting with their fellow pupils in collaborative, cooperative learning tasks. Furniture in the classrooms were 'arranged to facilitate group work rather than whole class work' (McPake *et al.*, 1999: 23) so there does seem to be a disproportionate amount of interaction time spent as part of whole-class teaching methods.

Getting pupils engaged in learning early in their school careers can make a big difference. Several studies have shown that teachers' rating of pupils' on-task, persistent engagement by five-year-olds predicts achievement test score gains for nine-year-olds and, alarmingly, provides an accurate prediction of a decision to drop out of full-time education before 18 (Fredricks, Blumenfeld and Paris, 2004).

2. Access to learning

Each classroom activity has its own rules for participation. Sometimes these rules are clearly stated by the teacher, but often they are implicit and unstated. Teacher and pupils may not even be aware that they are following different rules for different activities (Berliner, 1983). For example, in a reading group, pupils may have to raise their hands to make a comment, but in circle time in the same class, they may simply have to catch the teacher's eye.

As we saw in Chapter 5, the rules defining who can talk, what they can talk about, and when, to whom and how long they can talk are often called participation structures. In order to participate successfully in a given activity, pupils must understand the participation structure. Some pupils, however, seem to come to school less able to participate than others. The participation structures they learn at home in interactions with siblings, parents and other adults do not match the participation structures of school activities (Bernhard *et al.*, 2004). Yet teachers are not necessarily aware of this conflict. Instead, the teachers see that a child doesn't quite fit in, always seems to say the wrong thing at the wrong time, or is very reluctant to participate, and they are not sure why.

What can we conclude? To reach the second goal of good classroom management – giving all pupils access to learning – you must make sure everyone knows how to participate in class activities. The key is awareness. What are your rules and expectations? Are they understandable, given your pupils' cultural backgrounds and home experiences? What unspoken rules or values may be operating? Are you clearly signalling appropriate ways to participate? For some pupils, particularly those with behavioural and emotional challenges, direct teaching and practising of the important behaviours may be required (Emmer and Stough, 2001).

An example of being sensitive to participation structures was documented by Adrienne Alton-Lee and her colleagues in a classroom in New Zealand (2001). As a critical part of a unit on children in hospitals, the teacher, Ms Nikora, planned to have one of her pupils, a Maori girl named Huhana, describe a recent visit to the hospital. Huhana agreed. However, when the time came and the teacher asked her to come to the front of the class and share her experiences, Huhana looked down and shook her head. Rather than confront or scold Huhana, the teacher simply said, 'All right. If we sit in a circle . . . Huhana might be able to tell us about what happened.' When pupils were in a circle, the teacher said, 'All right, Huhana, after Ms Nikora called your mum and she . . . Where did she take you to?' As Huhana began to share her experience, the teacher scaffolded her participation by asking questions, providing reminders of details the teacher had learned in previous conversations with Huhana, and waiting patiently for the pupil's responses. Rather than perceiving the child as lacking competence, the teacher saw the situation as hindering competent expression.

Participation structures

Rules defining how to participate in different activities.

STOP AND THINK

What are the differences in the verbal and non-verbal ways that pupils show respect, pay attention and bid for a turn in conversation? How can social differences in interaction styles and expectations make classroom management more challenging?

3. Management for self-management

The third goal of any management system is to help pupils become better able to manage themselves. If teachers focus on pupil compliance, they will spend much of the teaching/learning time monitoring and correcting. Pupils come to see the purpose of school as just following rules, not constructing deep understanding of academic knowledge. And complex learning structures such as cooperative or problem-based learning require pupil self-management. Compliance with rules is not enough to make these learning structures work (McCaslin and Good, 1998).

The movement from demanding obedience to teaching self-management and self-control is a fundamental shift in discussions of classroom management today (Kaplan *et al.*, 2002). Without teaching for self-control, many low-frequency, low-level disruptive behaviours continue to take place with a deleterious effect on learning. Garry Squires, an educational psychologist working for a county psychological service in England, writes about using psychological methods to improve self-control of behaviour.

Connect and Extend

Many computer programs exist to help teachers manage their own activities both inside and outside the classroom. Typical activities include online standard forms, IEPs, pupil home and school databases, pupil reports, letters to parents, archiving and locating information, electronic mail, financial planning and scheduling. Can you find any of these online standard forms?

> *It's a typical day for Josh (fictional name only) in Anytown High School; he's in trouble again! A shout of protest from the back of the class, 'Miss, Josh kicked me.' 'Why did you do that?' his teacher asks. As usual, he doesn't know, or at least that's what he tells his teacher. This happens about once a day, often outside of the classroom. Josh is not the only one like this.*
>
> *Many schools have pupils like Josh. They present low-frequency behavioural difficulties that interfere with learning outcomes or cause disruption to the smooth running of the school. The low frequency of the behaviour makes it difficult to apply a standard behaviourist framework of collecting information about antecedents and applying contingencies to aid learning of alternative and more acceptable behaviours.*
>
> *This is further confounded by the unpredictability of where the behaviour will occur and, often, it is away from adults, making the application of rewards and sanctions more difficult. Yet the persistence of the behaviour over a long time makes it wearing on pastoral staff and gradually leads the young person on the path towards exclusion, or for teachers to want to 'pass him or her on' to someone else to deal with (i.e. an educational psychologist).*
>
> *For some of these pupils, it is their emotional responses to events in school that leads to their emotional over-reaction. The result is unacceptable behaviour that gets the child into 'trouble'. Many children like Josh fall into recognisable categories: they may be over-anxious, aggressive, be considered to be a bully, or be a victim of bullying (Squires, 2001).*

Tom Savage says simply, 'the most fundamental purpose of discipline is the development of self-control. Academic knowledge and technological skill will be of little consequence if those who possess them lack self-control' (1999: 11). Through self-control, pupils demonstrate *responsibility* – the ability to fulfill their own needs without interfering with the rights and needs of others or without jeopardising the moral or psychological well-being of their peers (Lawson and Comber, 2000). Pupils learn self-control by making choices and dealing with the consequences, setting goals and priorities, managing time, collaborating to learn, mediating disputes and making peace, and developing dependable relations with trustworthy teachers and classmates (Danielson, 2002; Ronen, 2004).

Encouraging self-management requires extra time, but teaching pupils how to take responsibility is an investment well worth the effort. When primary and secondary teachers have very effective class management systems but neglect to set pupil self-management as a goal, their pupils often find that they have trouble working independently after they move on from these 'well-managed' classes.

Self-management

Management of your own behaviour and acceptance of responsibility for your own actions.

Creating a Positive Learning Environment

Connect and Extend

In Chapter 13 you will learn about the importance of careful planning and clear objectives. Good planning is an important aspect of classroom management.

In making plans for your class, much of what you have already learned in this book should prove helpful. You know, for example, that problems are prevented when individual variations, such as those discussed in Chapters 2, 3, 4 and 5, are taken into account in curriculum, unit and lesson planning. Sometimes pupils become disruptive because the work assigned is too difficult. Also, pupils who are bored by lessons well below their ability levels may be interested in finding more exciting activities to fill their time.

In one sense, teachers prevent discipline problems whenever they make an effort to motivate pupils. A pupil engaged in learning is usually not involved in a clash with the teacher or other pupils at the same time. All plans for motivating pupils are steps towards preventing problems.

Some research results

What else can teachers do? For several years, educational psychologists have focused on the impact of new approaches to classroom management. Researchers in Israel (Shechtman and Leichtentritt, 2004) explored the impact of 'affective teaching' (valuing pupil attitudes, feelings and beliefs, and encouraging pupils to discuss their personal interests and experiences) on pupil behaviour. They compared the approach with 'cognitive teaching' (which focused on providing information and explaining concepts).

Fifty-two student teachers taught special education classes in primary and secondary schools (each containing around eight pupils) three lessons using both teaching methods – cognitive teaching for the first half of the lesson and affective teaching for the second half. The researchers' statistical analysis showed a decrease in misbehaviour and an increase in positive behaviours during the affective teaching units compared with the cognitive units. The different effects of the teaching approaches were found at both primary and secondary level.

The researchers concluded that the affective teaching approach encouraged pupils' personal growth, supported their mental health and promoted pro-social skills in a natural way and recommended that teachers include elements of affective teaching into their lessons to complement cognitive teaching.

A study by Theodora Papatheodorou (2000) was undertaken in Greece to investigate the management approaches employed by nursery teachers to deal with children's behaviour problems. The findings showed that teachers appear to mainly attend to and deal with conduct problems which cause greater disturbance in the classroom. However, emotional and developmentally related problems were also addressed revealing teachers' concerns about their pupils' well-being and development. Teachers seemed to mainly use positive ways in dealing with children's behaviour problems, but they did deliver punishments as well.

The quality of relationships between beginning teachers and pupils is considered in a Scottish study (McNally *et al.*, 2005) which illustrates trainee teachers' attempts to gain a deeper understanding of classroom behaviour, to explore connections between theory and practice and to identify the contribution made by other teachers. It was argued that trainees at the first stages of classroom teaching experiences are, despite the inevitable anxieties in their new encounters, starting to make deeper sense of classroom behaviour theories than can be provided by tips on discipline.

In 1996, an interesting study at the University of Rome (Taeschner *et al.*, 1998) found that successful behaviour managers had something 'magic' which the others did not. Explicitly, that successful teachers (magic teachers!) used non-verbal methods to gain and hold attention (teachers' gaze) rather than breaking from their narration to use exhortative verbal behaviour: the teachers' narrative flow was not continually interrupted by managerial statements or commands. Think back to my two tick lists of 'teaching' and 'management' utterances.

What else do teachers do? What else can they do? Between 1980 and 2006, teams of researchers led by Ed Emmer (Emmer and Stough, 2001; Emmer *et al.*, 1980; Emmer and Gerwels, 2006) looked at a large number of classrooms, making frequent observations of the first weeks of school and less frequent visits later in the year. After several months, there were dramatic differences among the classes. Some had very few management problems, while others had many. The most and least effective teachers were identified on the basis of the quality of classroom management and pupil achievement later in the year.

Next, the researchers looked at their observation records of the first weeks of the academic year to see what strategies were used by effective teachers. Other comparisons were made between the teachers who ultimately had harmonious, high-achieving classes, and those classes fraught with problems. On the basis of these comparisons, the researchers developed management principles (e.g. having planned procedures and rules for coping with common behaviours and incidents). They then taught these principles to a new group of teachers, and the results were quite positive. Teachers who applied the principles had fewer problems; their pupils spent more time learning and less time disrupting; and achievement was higher (Emmer *et al.*, 2006; Evertson *et al.*, 2003).

> ### Connect and Extend
>
> For a description of a study that tested the Emmer/Evertson management principles along with other approaches, such as reinforcement strategies with adolescents in several schools, see Gottfredson, D. C. *et al.* (1993), 'Managing adolescent behavior: A multiyear, multischool study', *American Educational Research Journal*, *30*, pp. 179–217.

Rules and procedures required

> ### STOP AND THINK
>
> Rules are different to principles. What are the three or four most important rules for any classroom?

At the primary school level, teachers must lead 30 or so pupils of varying abilities through many different activities each day. Without efficient rules and procedures, a great deal of time is wasted answering the same question over and over: 'My pencil broke. How can I do my maths?'; 'I'm finished my story. What should I do now?'; 'I left my homework at home. What should I do?'

At the secondary-school level, teachers typically deal daily with over 150 pupils who use dozens of materials and often change rooms for each class. Secondary-school pupils are also more likely to challenge teachers' authority. The effective managers studied by Emmer, Evertson and their colleagues had planned procedures and rules for coping with these situations.

Procedures

How will materials and pupils' work be distributed and collected? Under what conditions can pupils leave the room? How will marking take place? What are the special routines for handling equipment and supplies in science, in art, in physical education or design technology lessons? Procedures (often called routines) describe how activities

Procedures

Prescribed steps for an activity.

Figure 12.1
Standard classroom procedures

Source: Edited from Peterhead Academy
Behaviour Policy, p. 5.
http://www.peterheadacademy.
aberdeenshire.sch.uk/assets/pdf/pages_
policies_parents_001.pdf

These are the standard classroom procedures published by the Peterhead Academy in Aberdeenshire, Scotland.

We wish to establish general classroom routines with which both staff and pupils are comfortable and fair. These are:

Punctuality – Staff and pupils will make every effort to arrive on time for classes.

Arrival at classroom – Pupils will line up quietly in the corridor, at the classroom door, as close to the wall as possible.

Welcome to class – Teachers will greet pupils at the door of the classroom.

Entry to classroom – The teacher will decide when the class is ready to enter the classroom and the order in which pupils will enter.

Start of lesson – Pupils will sit down quietly, remove outdoor clothing and take out jotters, books, pen, pencil, etc. ready to start the lesson.

Class register – The teacher will check the class register either at the start of the lesson or when the class is working.

Seating plan – Each class will have a seating plan, available on the teacher's desk for the use of cover teachers; the teacher will decide who sits in which seat.

Lesson plan – The teacher will explain how the lesson will work and what the pupils are expected to do.

End of lesson – The teacher will gather the class before the end of the lesson to review the work which has been completed.

Ready to leave the classroom – Pupils will show that they are ready to leave the classroom by sitting quietly in their places.

Departure from the classroom – The teacher will decide when the class is ready and will stand at the door to supervise the corridor during class changeover.

are accomplished in classrooms, but they are seldom written down; they are simply the ways of getting things done in class. The establishment of standard and acceptable routines is important to each classroom to maximise the amount of available time, time on task and time interacting in teaching and learning activities with the teacher. School improvement measures, particularly in secondary schools, often include the establishment and maintenance of standard procedures which apply to all classrooms and learning spaces whilst accepting that there will be additional routines in some learning spaces (e.g. science laboratories and sports halls). Figure 12.1 shows standard classroom procedures published by the Peterhead Academy in Aberdeenshire, Scotland.

STOP AND THINK

Efficient procedures and routines reduce confusion and opportunities for misbehaviour and they save time that can be devoted to learning tasks. Think about frequent activities or classroom events that would benefit from well-structured procedures or routines (the following Focus on Practice should help you). What methods should teachers adopt for establishing procedures and routines so that pupils are likely to observe them.

FOCUS ON PRACTICE

Establishing class procedures

Determine procedures for pupils' care of furniture, classroom equipment and other facilities

Examples
1. Set aside a tidy-up time each day or once a week in 'self-contained' classes.
2. Demonstrate and have pupils practise how to push chairs under the desk, take and return materials stored on shelves, sharpen pencils, use the sink or water fountain, assemble equipment, and so on.
3. Develop a rotating system of monitors to take charge of equipment or materials.

Decide how pupils will be expected to enter and leave the room

Examples
1. Have a procedure for pupils to follow as soon as they enter the room. Some teachers have a standard task ('Have your homework out and be checking it over.' 'Try the short quiz on the board.').
2. Inform pupils under what conditions they can leave the room, and make sure they understand when they need to ask for permission to do so.
3. Tell pupils what they should do if they enter the classroom late.
4. Set up a policy about class dismissal. Many teachers require pupils to be in their places and quiet before they can leave at the end of lesson. The teacher, not the bell, dismisses the class – a few at a time.

Establish signals and teach them to your pupils

Examples
1. In the classroom use a animated countdown signal on the whiteboard, move to a particular spot in the classroom and stare silently at the class, use a phrase like 'Pens down, Eyes, front'. Make executive commands short and distinct and herald them with a warning: 'Aaaaand – Stop Work'.
2. In the corridors, raise a hand or use some other signal to indicate 'Stop'.
3. On the playground, use a whistle to indicate 'Line up'.

Set procedures for pupil participation in class

Examples
1. Decide whether you will have pupils raise their hands for permission to speak or simply require that they wait until the speaker has finished.

2. Determine a signal to indicate that you want everyone to respond at once. Some teachers raise a cupped hand to their ear. Others end the question with 'Everyone . . .'
3. Make sure you are clear about differences in procedures for different activities: reading groups, collaborative projects, discussion, teacher presentation, silent working, watching TV and video, peer study groups, library and computer room sessions, and so forth.
4. Establish how many pupils at a time can be at the pencil sharpener, teacher's desk, sink, bookshelves, reading corner or toilet.

Determine how you will communicate, collect and return pupils' work

Examples

1. Establish a place for listing the work. Some teachers reserve a particular corner of the board. Others write set work in coloured chalk or pens. For younger pupils, it may be better to prepare worksheets in folders, colour-coding them as a maths workbook, reading record and science kit.
2. Be clear about how and where pupils' work should be collected. Some teachers collect classwork and homework in a box or tray; others have a pupil collect work while they introduce the next activity.

For ideas about involving pupils in developing rules and procedures follow the links from www.pearsoned.co.uk/woolfolkeuro.

Rules

Rules

Statements specifying expected and forbidden behaviours; dos and don'ts.

Rules specify expected and forbidden actions in the class. They are the dos and don'ts of classroom life. Unlike procedures, rules are often written down and displayed. When establishing rules, teachers should consider what kind of atmosphere they want to create. What pupil behaviours will help them teach effectively? What limits do the pupils need to guide their behaviour? The rules individual teachers set should be consistent with school rules, and also in keeping with principles of learning. For example, we know from the research on small-group learning that pupils benefit when they explain work to peers; they 'learn as they teach'. A rule that forbids pupils to help each other may be inconsistent with good learning principles or a rule that says, 'No rubbing-out when writing' may make pupils focus more on preventing mistakes than on communicating clearly in their writing (Emmer and Stough, 2001).

Rules should be positive and observable (raise your hand to ask a question or give an answer). Having a few general rules (with a ceiling of five or six) that cover many specifics is better than listing all the dos and don'ts. One benefit of discussing and re-drafting rules with the class is that they can be written in a language which the pupils understand and use. Also, any personal element of confrontation between teacher and a miscreant pupil can be minimised by reminding the rule-breaker that these were the rules that everybody 'signed up' to. However, responsibility for setting rules remains with the teachers and the school. If specific actions are forbidden, such as leaving the school during a session or smoking at school, then a specific school rule should make this clear (O'Brien, 1998).

Connect and Extend

Visit primary school classes and note the rules displayed by different teachers at the same age level. Identify rules that are common to all or most classes, as well as those that are unusual. What 'progression' happens as the children get older?

Rules for primary school

Evertson and her colleagues (2006) give four examples of general rules for primary school classes:

1. *Respect and be polite to all people.* Give clear explanations of what you mean by 'polite', including not hitting, fighting or teasing. Examples of polite behaviour include waiting your turn, saying 'please' and 'thank you', and not calling names. This applies to behaviour towards adults (including supply teachers, classroom assistants and special needs support staff) and other pupils.

2. *Be prompt and prepared.* This rule highlights the importance of the teaching and learning work in the class. Being prompt includes the beginning of the day and during transitions between activities.

3. *Listen quietly while others are speaking.* This applies to the teacher and other pupils, in both whole-class lessons or group discussions.

4. *Obey all school rules.* This reminds pupils that all school rules apply in your classroom. Then pupils cannot claim, for example, that they thought it was all right to chew sweets or listen to a MP3 in your lesson, even though these are against school rules, 'because we never made a rule about it for us'.

Whatever the rule, pupils need to be taught the behaviours that the rule includes and excludes. Examples (test cases), practice and discussion will be needed before understanding and acceptance is complete.

STOP AND THINK

Fair, consistently enforced rules can have a positive effect on motivation to learn by promoting a safe and warm classroom environment. Describe how to establish and maintain effective rules. Keep in mind age-related concerns.

As you've seen, different activities often require different rules. This can be confusing for primary school pupils until they have thoroughly learned all the rules. To prevent confusion, you might consider making posters or digital 'slides' that list the rules for each type of activity. Then, before the activity, you can display the appropriate poster as a reminder. This provides clear and consistent cues about participation structures so all pupils, not just the 'well-behaved', know what is expected. Of course, these rules must be explained and discussed before the posters can have their full effect.

Consequences

As soon as teachers decide on rules and procedures, they must consider what they will do when a pupil breaks a rule or does not follow a procedure. It is too late to make this decision after the rule has been broken. For many infractions, the logical consequence is going back to 'do it right'. Pupils who run in the corridor may have to return to where they started and walk properly. Incomplete worksheets can be finished. Materials left out can be put back (Charles, 2002b). Some tips for using consequences are shown in Figure 12.2.

Figure 12.2
Tips for using consequences

Source: Adapted with permission. From *Rediscovering Hope: Our Greatest Teaching Strategy* by Richard Curwin. Copyright 1992 by Solution Tree (formerly National Educational Service), 304 West Kirkwood Avenue, Bloomington, Indiana, 47404, 800-733-6786, www.solution-tree.com.

1. Always implement a consequence when a rule is broken.
2. Select the most appropriate consequence from the list of alternatives, taking into account the offence, situation, pupil involved and the best means of helping that pupil.
3. State the rule and consequence to the offending pupil. Nothing more need be said.
4. Be private. Only the pupil(s) involved should hear.
5. Do not embarrass the pupil.
6. Do not think of the situation as win–lose. This is not a contest. Do not get involved in a power struggle.
7. Control your anger. Be calm and speak quietly, but accept no excuses from the pupil.
8. Sometimes it is best to let the pupil choose the consequence.

Natural or logical consequences

Instead of punishing, have pupils redo, repair or in some way face the consequences that naturally flow from their actions.

Teachers can also use natural or logical consequences to support social/emotional development by doing the following (Elias and Schwab, 2006):

- Teacher responses should separate the deed from the doer – the problem is the behaviour, not the pupil.

- Emphasise to pupils that they have the power to choose their actions and thus avoid losing control.

- Encourage pupil reflection, self-evaluation and problem solving – avoid teacher lecturing.

- Help pupils identify and give a rationale for what they could do differently next time in a similar situation.

Sometimes, consequences are more complicated. In their case studies of four expert primary school teachers, Weinstein and Mignano (2003) found that the teachers' negative consequences fell into seven categories, as shown in Table 12.3. The main point here is that decisions about penalties (and rewards) must be made early on, so pupils know before they break a rule or use the wrong procedure what this will mean for them. We encourage our trainee-teachers as early as possible in a new school placement to get a copy of the school rules, the class rules and the policy and procedures for dealing with pupils who break the rules.

Rights, responsibilities, rules, routines and consequences

You might consider setting rules and consequences within a framework of rights and responsibilities for pupils, teachers and other adults working in the school. Developing rights and responsibilities rather than just rules and routines makes a very important point to pupils. 'Teaching children that something is wrong because there is a rule against it is not the same as teaching them that there is a rule against it because it is wrong, and helping them to understand why this is so' (Weinstein, 1999: 154). Pupils should understand that the rules are developed so that everyone can work and learn together.

Table 12.3 Seven categories of penalties for pupils

1. *Expressions of disappointment.* If pupils like and respect their teacher, then a serious, sorrowful expression of disappointment may cause pupils to stop and think about their behaviour.

2. *Loss of privileges.* Pupils can lose free time. If they have not completed homework, for example, they can be required to do it during free.

3. *Exclusion from the group.* Pupils who distract their peers or fail to cooperate can be separated from the group until they are ready to cooperate. Some teachers give a pupil a pass for 10 to 15 minutes. The pupil must go to another class, where the other pupils and teachers ignore the offending pupil for that time.

4. *Written reflections on the problem.* Pupils can write in journals, write essays about what they did and how it affected others, or write letters of apology – if this is appropriate. Another possibility is to ask pupils to describe objectively what they did; then the teacher and the pupil can sign and date this statement. These records are available if parents or managers need evidence of the pupils' behaviour.

5. *Detentions.* Detentions can be very brief meetings after school, during free time, or at lunch. The main purpose is to talk about what has happened. (In secondary school, detentions are often used as punishments; suspensions and expulsions are available as more extreme measures.)

6. *Visits to the head teacher's office.* Expert teachers tend to use this penalty rarely, but they do use it when the situation warrants. Some schools require pupils to be sent to the office for certain offences, such as fighting. If you tell a pupil to go to the office and the pupil refuses, you might call the office saying the pupil has been sent. Then the pupil has the choice of either going to the office or facing the head teacher's penalty for 'disappearing' on the way.

7. *Contact with parents.* If problems become a repeated pattern, most teachers contact the pupils' family. This is done to seek support for helping the pupil, not to blame the parents or punish the pupil.

Source: Adapted from *Elementary Classroom Management* (3rd ed.) by C. S. Weinstein and A. J. Mignano, Jr. New York: McGraw-Hill. Copyright © 2003 by The McGraw-Hill Companies. Adapted with permission.

Bill Rogers (an Australian educational consultant and teacher trainer) asserts that an agreed code of rights, responsibilities, rules and routines (sometimes referred to as the 4Rs) underpins behaviour management and discipline within and throughout a school. A 'right' might be thought of a reasonable expectation enjoyed when people are acting responsibly. Yet, teaching pupils to think about other people's rights and their own responsibilities is not as easy as it sounds, even when considering certain essential or non-negotiable rights: to feel safe at school; to be treated with dignity and respect; to learn with the best of support (Rogers, 2000).

The 4 Rs
An agreed code of rights, responsibilities, rules and routines.

So, if teachers are going to involve pupils in setting rules or creating a constitution of rights and responsibilities, they may need to wait a little while until they have established a sense of community in the classroom. Some people believe that before pupils can contribute meaningfully to the class rules, they need to trust the teacher and the situation (Elias and Schwab, 2006). Others, including the authors of this book, believe that discussing, framing, establishing and maintaining the 4Rs helps to create a sense of community, builds trust and provides a framework for developing motivation, self–management and responsible behaviour.

As well as planning for routines and rules we need to consider another kind of planning that affects the learning environment; designing the physical arrangement of the class furniture, materials and learning tools.

Planning spaces for learning

Spaces for learning should invite and support the activities planned for the classroom, and they should respect the inhabitants of the space. This respect begins at the classroom door for young children by helping them identify their class. One school that won awards for its architecture painted each classroom door a different bright colour, so young children can find their 'home' (Herbert, 1998). Once inside, spaces can be created that invite quiet reading, group collaboration or independent research. If pupils are to use materials, they should be able to reach them. In an interview with Marge Scherer, Herb Kohl (a distinguished teacher and author) describes how he creates a positive environment in his classes.

What I do is put up the most beautiful things I know – posters, games, puzzles, challenges – and let the children know these are provocations. These are ways of provoking them into using their minds. You have to create an environment that makes kids walk in and say, 'I really want to see what's here. I would really like to look at this' (1999: 9).

In terms of classroom arrangement, there are two basic ways of organising space: shared interest areas and personal/group spaces. These types of organisation are not mutually exclusive; many teachers use a design that combines the two types of space. Groups of individual pupil's desks – their spaces – are placed in the centre, with shared interest areas in the back or around the periphery of the room. This allows the flexibility needed for whole class, group, small-group, paired and individual activities. Figure 12.3 shows a primary classroom that combines shared interest areas and personal/group spaces.

Shared interest areas

The design of shared interest areas can influence the way the areas are used by pupils. For example, working with a classroom teacher, Carol Weinstein (1977) was able to make changes in shared interest areas that helped the teacher meet her objectives of having more girls involved in the science area and having all pupils experiment more with a variety of manipulative materials. In a second study, changes in a library corner led to more involvement in literature activities throughout the class (Morrow and Weinstein, 1986). When you design shared interest areas for your class, keep the following Focus on Practice in mind.

Personal spaces

Can the physical setting influence teaching and learning in classrooms organised by spaces? Front-seat location does seem to increase participation for pupils who are predisposed to speak in class, whereas a seat in the back will make it more difficult to

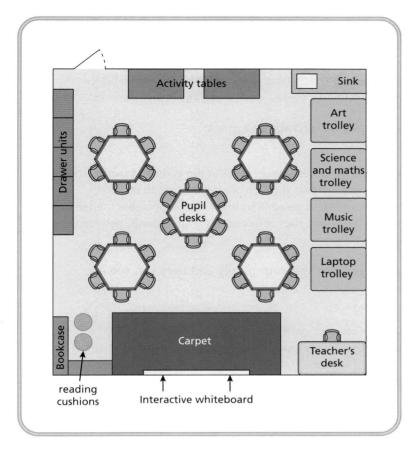

Figure 12.3
A primary school classroom arrangement

This teacher of eight- and nine-year-olds has designed a space that allows teacher presentation and demonstrations, group work, maths and science enquiry activities, informal reading, art and other projects without requiring constant rearrangements.

FOCUS ON PRACTICE

Designing learning spaces

Note the fixed features and plan accordingly

Examples

1. Remember that the interactive whiteboard and computers need electrical outlets and connection to the internet point. Cable runs should never cross a classroom pathway. Whiteboards must be at a height for pupils to reach to the top of the board. You might have to put a robust platform below the board.
2. Keep art supplies near the sink, small-group work by a whiteboard.

Create easy access to materials and a well-organised place to store them

Examples

1. Make sure materials and resources are well-signed, easy to reach and visible to pupils.
2. Have enough shelves so that materials need not be stacked.

Provide pupils with clean, convenient surfaces for studying

Examples
1. Put bookshelves next to the reading area, games by the games table.
2. Prevent fights by avoiding crowded work or storage retrieval spaces.

Make sure work areas are private and quiet

Examples
1. Make sure there are no tables or work areas in the middle of traffic lanes; a person should not have to pass through one area to get to another.
2. Keep noisy activities as far as possible from quiet ones. Increase the feeling of privacy by placing partitions, such as bookcases or pegboards, between areas or within large areas.

Arrange things so you can see your pupils and they can see all presentations

Examples
1. Make sure you can see over partitions.
2. Design seating so that pupils can see you without moving their chairs or desks.

Avoid dead spaces and 'racetracks'

Examples
1. Don't have all the interest areas around one side of the room, leaving a large dead space elsewhere.
2. Avoid placing a few items of furniture right in the middle of any large space, creating a 'racetrack' around the furniture.

Provide choices and flexibility

Examples
1. Establish private cubicles for individual work, open tables for group work, and cushions on the floor for whole-class meetings and individual reading time.
2. Give pupils a place to keep their personal belongings. This is especially important if pupils don't have personal desks incorporating storage.

Try new arrangements, then evaluate and improve

Examples
1. Have a 'two-week arrangement', then evaluate.
2. Enlist the aid of your pupils, particularly at the beginning of the year. They have to live in the room, too, and designing a classroom can be a very challenging educational experience.

Try http://ngfl.northumberland.gov.uk/ict/qca/ks2/unit5A/default.htm, or follow the link from www.pearsoned.co.uk/woolfolkeuro, for an application that pupils (and teachers!) can use to plan their classroom.

participate and easier to sit back and daydream (Woolfolk and Brooks, 1983). But the action zone where participation is greatest may be in other areas such as on one side or near a particular shared area (Good, 1983; Lambert, 1994). To 'spread the action around', Weinstein and Mignano (2003) suggest that teachers move around the room when possible, establish eye contact with and direct questions to pupils seated far away, and vary the seating so the same pupils are not always consigned to the back. Staying to the outside of the room and using 'circle and scan' techniques helps to keep pupils on task and 'connected' to the learning intentions of the lesson.

Many, and in some schools most or all, classrooms are now equipped with large interactive digital display boards, broadband connected to the internet. The use of interactive whiteboards (IWBs) is developing as large, colourful, dynamic, audio-enabled performance spaces for teachers and pupils. The display capabilities are being widely used, but less well developed is the use of the 'capture' facilities of the technology (Hughes and Longman, 2005). The introduction of IWBs to classrooms has meant a change to classroom layouts to facilitate the central focus the board provides. Figure 12.4 shows a 'U'-shaped classroom layout for pupils aged ten to 14 years, designed to take account of the interactive whiteboard.

Action zone

Area of a classroom where the greatest amount of interaction takes place, increasingly the area around the interactive digital whiteboard.

Connect and Extend

For one example of a research study into the impact of the use of interactive whiteboards on teaching and classroom management read Smith, F. *et al.* (2006), 'The impact of interactive whiteboards on teacher–pupil interaction in the National Literacy and Numeracy Strategies', *British Educational Research Journal, 32*(3) pp. 443–457.

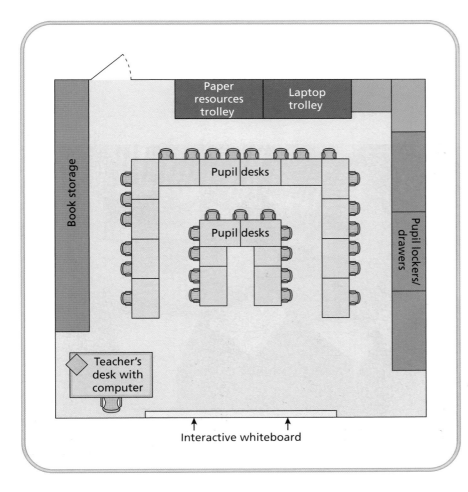

Figure 12.4
The arena classroom arrangement for 10- to 14-year-olds

This teacher has designed a space that allows teacher and pupil presentations and demonstrations using the interactive digital whiteboard, small group work by turning chairs around, computer interactions, practical activities, display and other projects, without requiring constant rearrangements. The classroom was designed for children aged 10 to 14 years old although it is very useful for seminars in higher education.

Connect and Extend

Read three case studies describing how teachers planned the physical environments in their rooms, see Pointon, P. and Kershner, R. (2000) 'Making decisions about organizing the primary classroom as a context for learning: The views of three experienced teachers and their pupils', *Teaching and Teacher Education, 16*, pp. 117–127.

Connect and Extend

For one example of the impact of computers on teaching and classroom management read Grant, M. *et al.* (2005), 'Computers on wheels: an alternative to "each one has one"', *British Journal of Educational Technology, 36*(6), pp. 1017–1034.

Horizontal rows share many of the advantages of the traditional row and column arrangements. Both are useful for independent seatwork and teacher, pupil or media presentations; they encourage pupils to focus on the presenter and simplify housekeeping. Horizontal rows also permit pupils to work more easily in pairs. However, this is a poor arrangement for large-group discussion.

Clusters of four or circle arrangements are best for pupil interaction. Circles are especially useful for discussions, but still allow for independent seatwork. Clusters permit pupils to talk, help one another, share materials and work on group tasks. Both arrangements, however, are poor for whole-group presentations and may make class management more difficult.

The fishbowl or stack special formation, where pupils sit close together near the focus of attention (the back row may even be standing), should be used only for short periods of time, because it is not comfortable and can lead to discipline problems. On the other hand, the fishbowl can create a feeling of group cohesion and is helpful when the teacher wants pupils to watch a short demonstration, brainstorm on a class problem or see a small visual aid.

The arena formation (see Figure 12.4) establishes a focus on the teacher and the interactive whiteboard whilst allowing for chairs to be turned for group work and discussion. The U-shape of desks which creates the arena formation is very inclusive, and means that a teacher in the performance space is only two rows of desks away from any pupil in the class. Teachers can still use the 'circle and scan' techniques discussed earlier and is less tempted to see the grouping of personal spaces as an opportunity for unnecessary ability grouping. The use of digital slate technologies in relation to the interactive whiteboard also allows for continuous change in the position of the action zone or zones within the classroom.

Using computers effectively brings with it particular management challenges

Planning for computer uses

Many classrooms today have computers. Some classes have only one, others have several, and some rooms are equipped with a computer for every pupil or one between two pupils. Using computers effectively brings with it particular management challenges. Computers can be used to connect to powerful knowledge bases around the world; to act as tools for writing, drawing, calculating and designing; to simulate scientific experiments or life in other times and places; to collaborate and communicate with people across the hall or across the ocean; to publish work or make presentations; and to keep track of projects, collaborative tasks or learning targets. To get the greatest benefits from computers in your classroom, teachers must have good management systems. Table 12.4 summarises some strategies for managing computer rooms.

Most classrooms will not have a computer for every pupil. In fact, many have only one computer or none at all. The following Focus on Practice discusses using computers in classrooms.

Table 12.4 Ideas for managing a computer room

These ideas adapted from those of Cheryl Bolick and James Cooper (2006).

- Always run through a lesson in the computer room before presenting it to the class, and always have a back-up lesson prepared in case the technology fails.
- Type instructions for frequently used computer operations – opening programs, inserting images, printing documents – on reminder posters displayed near to each workstation.
- If you have many classes moving in and out of the computer room each day and have little or no time to set up between classes, arrange for older pupils to help. End your lesson five minutes early and get pupils to set up for the next class.
- Make it a class rule that pupils can help each other but cannot ever touch another pupil's computer.
- Keep a red plastic cup at each computer. When a pupil needs help, have them place the highly visible signal on top of their monitor. For flat screens use another signalling device.
- Place different coloured sticker dots on the left and right bottom corners of each monitor. Use these to indicate which side of the screen you are talking about and to determine whose turn it is if pupils share a computer.
- When addressing the whole class, pupils must switch off their monitors and remove any headphones.
- Use an interactive whiteboard or other display device for demonstrations.
- Create a folder in the Start Menu, and place any programs you use with pupils in that folder. Pupils never have to click Programs – everything they use is in one folder.
- When working on a network, ask the Technology Manager to set up a shared folder for internet resources. Then, when you are planning an internet lesson, save a shortcut to the website in that folder. During a lesson in the computer room, pupils can go to the shared folder, double-click the link, and go straight to the site without typing the URL. This saves time and prevents stress for both pupils and teachers.

Source: *Handbook of Classroom Management: Research, Practice and Contemporary Issues* by C. Mason Bolick and J. M. Cooper. Copyright 2006 by Lawrence Erlbaum Associates Inc–Books [T]. Reproduced with permission of Lawrence Erlbaum Associates Inc–Books [T] in the format Textbook via Copyright Clearance Center.

FOCUS ON PRACTICE

Using computers: management issues

If you have only one computer in your classroom: Provide convenient access

Examples
1. Find a central location if the computer is used to display material for the class.
2. Find a spot on the side of the room that allows seating and a 'multi-view' of the screen, but does not crowd or disturb other pupils if the computer is used as a workstation for individuals or small groups.

Be prepared

Examples
1. Check to be sure software needed for a lesson or assignment is installed and working.
2. Make sure instructions for using the software or doing the assignment are in an obvious place and clear. You might prepare a prompt sheet to assist pupils to stay on task.
3. Provide a worksheet to focus attention on successful learning time.

Create 'trained experts' to help with computers

Examples
1. Train pupil experts and rotate experts.
2. Use other adults – classroom support staff, parents, grandparents or older siblings.

Develop systems for using the computer

Examples
1. Make up a timetable to ensure that all pupils have access to the computer and so no pupils monopolise the time.
2. Create standard ways of saving pupil work.

If you have more than one computer in your classroom, plan the arrangement of the computers to fit your instructional goals

Examples
1. For cooperative groups, arrange so pupils can cluster around their group's computer.
2. For different projects at different computer stations, allow for easy rotation from station to station.

Experiment with other models for using computers

Examples

1. Navigator Model – four pupils per computer. One pupil is the (mouse and keyboard) driver, another is the 'navigator'. 'Back-seat driver 1' manages the group's progress and 'back-seat driver 2' serves as the timekeeper. The navigator attends a 10- to 20-minute training session in which the facilitator provides an overview of the basics of particular software. Navigators cannot touch the mouse. Driver roles are rotated.
2. Facilitator Model – six pupils per computer. The facilitator has more experience, expertise or training and serves as the guide or teacher.
3. Collaborative Group Model – seven pupils per computer. Each small group is responsible for creating some component of the whole group's final product. For example, one part of the group writes a report, another creates a map and a third uses the computer to gather and graph census data.

For more ideas, see www.internet4classrooms.com/one_computer.htm.

Getting started: the first weeks

Determining a room design, rules and procedures are the first steps towards having a well-managed class, but how do effective teachers gain pupils' cooperation in those early critical days and weeks? One study carefully analysed the first weeks' activities of effective and ineffective primary school teachers, and found striking differences (Emmer, Evertson and Anderson, 1980). By the second or third week of school, pupils in the ineffective teachers' classrooms were more and more disruptive, and less and less on task.

Effective class managers for primary pupils

In the effective teachers' classrooms, the very first day was well organised. Name badges were ready and there was something interesting for each child to do straightaway. Materials and resources were set up and teachers had planned carefully to avoid any last-minute tasks that might take them away from their pupils. These teachers dealt with the children's pressing concerns first. 'Where do I put my things?' 'How do I pronounce my teacher's name?' 'Can I whisper to my neighbour?' 'Where is the toilet?' The effective teachers were explicit about their expectations. They had a workable, easily understood set of rules and taught the pupils the most important rules right away. They taught the rules like any other subject – with lots of explanation, examples and practice.

Throughout the first weeks, the effective teachers continued to spend quite a bit of time teaching rules and procedures. Some used guided practice to teach procedures; others used rewards to shape behaviour. Most taught pupils to respond to an audio or visual signal to gain their attention. These teachers worked with the class as a whole on enjoyable learning activities. They did not rush to get pupils into small groups or to get them started in readers. This whole-class work gave the teachers a better opportunity to continue monitoring all pupils' learning of the rules and procedures. Misbehaviour was stopped quickly and firmly, but not harshly.

In the poorly managed classrooms, the first weeks were quite different. Rules were not workable; they were either too vague or very complicated. For example, one teacher made a rule that pupils should 'be in the right place at the right time'. Pupils were not told what this meant, so their behaviour could not be guided by the rule. Neither positive nor negative behaviours had clear, consistent consequences. After pupils broke a rule, ineffective managers might give a vague criticism, such as 'Some of my children are too noisy', or issue a warning, but not follow through with the threatened consequence.

In the poorly managed classrooms, procedures for accomplishing routine tasks varied from day to day and were never taught or practised. Instead of dealing with these obvious needs, ineffective managers spent time on procedures that could have waited. For example, one teacher had a class fire drill practice on the first day, but left unexplained other procedures that would be needed every day. Pupils wandered around the classroom aimlessly and had to ask each other what they should be doing. Often the pupils talked to one another because they had nothing productive to do. Ineffective teachers frequently left the room. Many became absorbed in paperwork or in helping just one pupil. They had not made plans for how to deal with pupils who arrived late, unexpectedly or for other kinds of interruptions. One ineffective classroom manager tried to teach pupils to respond to a bell as a signal for attention, but later let the pupils ignore it. All in all, the first weeks in these classrooms were disorganised and filled with surprises for teachers and pupils alike.

Connect and Extend

Five excellent and very practical discussions of classroom behaviour management are shown on the  Companion Website (Web Link 12.1).

Effective classroom managers for secondary pupils

What about getting started in a secondary school class? It appears that many of the differences between effective and ineffective primary school teachers hold at the secondary level as well. Again, effective classroom managers focus on establishing rules, procedures and expectations on the first day. These standards for academic work and class behaviour are clearly communicated to pupils and consistently enforced during the first weeks of term. Pupil behaviour is closely monitored and infractions of the rules are dealt with quickly. In classes with lower-ability pupils, work cycles are shorter; pupils are not required to spend long, unbroken periods on one type of activity. Instead, during each period, they are moved smoothly through several different tasks. In general, effective teachers carefully follow each pupil's progress, so pupils cannot avoid work without facing consequences (Emmer and Evertson, 1982).

With all this close monitoring and consistent enforcement of the rules, you may wonder if effective secondary teachers have to be grim and humourless. There is that old staff room saying, 'Don't smile before Christmas!' and even a book with that title (Ryan and Cranfield, 1970)! Not at all. As any experienced teacher can tell you, there is much more to smile about when the class is cooperative and classes are more willing to be cooperative if you smile at them. I've just been through a stack of books about classroom behaviour management. Almost all the writers shy away from even mentioning humour because, perhaps, people's sense of humour is idiosyncratic and opportunities for a successful joke can rarely be predicted. It's difficult to write it into your lesson plan. Yet the humour of incongruence and the absurd begins at a very early age and we never lose it (Loizou, 2005).

Maintaining a Good Environment for Learning

In the last section we compared the different ways in which effective and ineffective classroom managers organised their class in the first weeks of teaching. The evidence is clear that making a good start really helps. However, a good start is just that – a beginning. Effective teachers build on this beginning. They maintain their management system by preventing problems and keeping pupils engaged in productive learning activities. We have discussed several ways to keep pupils engaged. In the chapter on motivation, for example, we considered stimulating curiosity, relating lessons to pupil interests, establishing learning goals instead of performance goals and having positive expectations. What else can teachers do?

Encouraging engagement

The format of a lesson affects pupil involvement. In general, as teacher supervision increases, pupils' engaged time also increases (Emmer and Evertson, 1981). One study, for example, found that primary pupils working directly with a teacher were on task 97% of the time, whereas pupils working on their own were on task only 57% of the time (Frick, 1990). This does not mean that teachers should eliminate independent work for pupils. It simply means that this type of activity usually requires careful planning and monitoring.

When the task provides continuous cues for the pupil about what to do next, involvement will be greater. Activities with clear steps are likely to be more absorbing, because one step leads naturally to the next. When pupils have all the materials they need to complete a task, they tend to stay involved. If their curiosity is piqued, pupils will be motivated to continue seeking an answer and, as you now know, pupils will be more engaged if they are involved in authentic tasks – activities that have connections to real life. Also, activities are more engaging when the level of challenge is higher and when pupils' interests are incorporated into the tasks (Emmer and Gerwels, 2006).

Of course, teachers can't supervise every pupil all the time, or rely on curiosity. Something else must keep pupils working on their own. In their study of primary and secondary teachers, Evertson, Emmer and their colleagues found that effective classroom managers at both phases had well-planned systems for encouraging pupils to manage their own work (Emmer, Evertson and Worsham, 2006; Evertson, Emmer and Worsham, 2006). The following Focus on Practice is based on their findings.

Connect and Extend

A principle of educational psychology is that the more pupils are cognitively engaged in an activity, the more they are likely to learn. Use an internet search to find what tactics teachers can employ to maximise their pupils' cognitive engagement during learning tasks?

FOCUS ON PRACTICE

Keeping pupils engaged

Make basic work requirements clear

Examples

1. Specify and display the routine work requirements for headings, paper size, pen or pencil use and neatness.

2. Establish and explain rules about late or incomplete work. If a pattern of incomplete work begins to develop, deal with it early; speak with parents if necessary.
3. Make 'hand-in' times reasonable, and stick to them unless the pupil has a very good excuse for lateness.

Communicate the specifics of assignments

Examples
1. With younger pupils, have a routine procedure for handing in work. Write or display the details of any work on the board in the same place each day.
2. Remind pupils of deadlines.
3. With more complex long-term projects, give pupils a prompt sheet describing what to do, what resources are available, due dates, and so on. Pupils should also be told your marking criteria.
4. Demonstrate how to do the work, do the first few questions together, or provide a sample worksheet.

Monitor work in progress

Examples
1. When you start the class work, make sure each pupil gets started correctly. If you check only pupils who raise their hands for help, you will miss those who think they know what to do but don't really understand, those who are too shy to ask for help, and those who don't plan to do the work at all.
2. Check progress periodically. In discussions, make sure everyone has a chance to respond.
3. Give frequent feedback about the progress of the work, not just how pupils are behaving.

Give timely feedback

Examples
1. Primary pupils should get work back the day after they are handed in.
2. Good work can be displayed in class and sent home to parents each week.
3. Pupils of all ages can keep a record of their achievements, projects completed and extra credits earned.
4. For older pupils, break up long-term assignments into several phases, giving feedback at each point.

Prevention is the best medicine

To help promote pupil engagement teachers have to manage any problems that arise. The ideal way to manage problems, of course, is to prevent them in the first place. In a classic study, Jacob Kounin (1970) examined classroom management by comparing effective teachers, whose classes were relatively free of problems, with

Movement management refers to keeping lessons and pupils moving at an appropriate pace with smooth transitions, as activities and location for those activities change throughout the day

ineffective teachers, whose classes were continually plagued by chaos and disruption. Observing both groups in action, Kounin found that they were not very different in the way they handled discipline once problems arose. The difference was that the successful managers were much better at preventing problems. Kounin concluded that effective classroom managers were especially skilled in four areas: 'withitness', overlapping activities, group focusing and movement management. More recent research confirms the importance of these factors (Emmer and Stough, 2001; Evertson, 1988).

Withitness

Withitness means communicating to pupils that you are aware of everything that is happening in the classroom – that you aren't missing anything. 'With-it' teachers seem to have eyes in the back of their heads. They avoid becoming absorbed or interacting with only a few pupils, because this encourages the rest of the class to wander. They are always scanning the room, making eye contact with individual pupils, so the pupils know they are being monitored (Charles, 2002a; Richardson and Fallona, 2001). These teachers prevent minor disruptions from becoming major. They also know who instigated the problem, and they make sure they deal with the right people. In other words, they do not make what Kounin called timing errors (waiting too long before intervening) or target errors (blaming the wrong pupil and letting the real perpetrators escape responsibility for their behaviour).

If two problems occur at the same time, effective managers deal with the more serious one first. For example, a teacher who tells two pupils to stop whispering, but ignores even a brief shoving match at the pencil sharpener communicates a lack of awareness. Pupils begin to believe they can get away with almost anything if they are clever (Charles, 2002b).

Withitness

According to Kounin, awareness of everything happening in a classroom.

Overlapping

Overlapping

Supervising several activities at once.

Overlapping means keeping track of and supervising several activities at the same time. For example, a teacher may have to check the work of an individual and at the same time keep a small group working by saying, 'Right, go on,' and stop an incident in another group with a quick 'look' or reminder (Burden, 1995; Stephen and Crawley, 1994).

Group focus

Group focus

The ability to keep as many pupils as possible involved in activities.

Maintaining a group focus means keeping as many pupils as possible involved in appropriate class activities and avoiding narrowing in on just one or two pupils. All pupils should have something to do during a lesson. For example, the teacher might ask everyone to write the answer to a question, then call on individuals to respond while the other pupils compare their answers. Responses might be required while the teacher moves around the room to make sure everyone is participating (Myhill, 2002). To encourage individual answers from large groups, pupils can hold up small whiteboards or number fans. This is one way teachers can ensure that all pupils are involved and that everyone understands the material.

Movement management

Movement management

Keeping lessons and the group moving at an appropriate (and flexible) pace, with smooth transitions and variety.

Movement management means keeping lessons and the group moving at an appropriate (and flexible) pace, with smooth transitions and variety. The effective teacher avoids abrupt transitions, such as announcing a new activity before gaining the pupils' attention or starting a new activity in the middle of something else. In these situations, one-third of the class will be doing the new activity, many will be working on the old lesson, several will be asking other pupils what to do, some will be taking the opportunity to have a little fun, and most will be confused. Another transition problem Kounin noted is the *slowdown*, or taking too much time to start a new activity. Sometimes teachers give too many directions. Problems also arise when teachers have pupils work one at a time while the rest of the class waits and watches.

Caring relationships: connections with school

When pupils and teachers have positive, trusting relationships, many management problems never develop. Pupils respect teachers who maintain their authority without being rigid, harsh or unfair and whose creative teaching style 'makes learning fun'. Pupils also value teachers who show personal caring by acting themselves (not just as teachers), sharing responsibility, minimising the use of external controls or threats, including everyone, searching for pupils' strengths, communicating effectively, and showing an interest in their pupils' lives and pursuits (Beattie, 2002; Woolfolk Hoy and Weinstein, 2006). All efforts at building positive relationships and classroom community are steps towards preventing management problems. Pupils who feel connected with school are happier, more self-disciplined and less likely to engage in dangerous behaviours such as substance abuse, violence and early sexual activity (Slap *et al.*, 2003; Rasmussen *et al.*, 2005; Renold, 2003; McNeely *et al.*, 2002).

Pupil social skills as prevention

But what about the pupils? What can they do? When pupils lack social and emotional skills such as being able to share materials, read the intentions of others or handle frustration then classroom management problems often follow. So all efforts to teach social and emotional self-regulation are steps for preventing management problems. Over the short and medium term, educators can teach and model these skills, then give pupils increasing responsibility for their learning and their 'behaviour for learning'. Over the long term, teachers can help to change attitudes that value aggression over cooperation and compromise (Nyroos *et al.*, 2004). Chapters 3 and 11 gave ideas for teaching social and emotional skills and competencies.

Dealing with discipline problems

Being an effective manager does not mean publicly correcting every minor infraction of the rules. This kind of public attention may actually reinforce the misbehaviour, as we saw in the 'Coping with undesirable behaviour' section of Chapter 6 (p. 262). Teachers who frequently correct pupils do not necessarily have the best-behaved classes (Irving and Martin, 1982). The temptation is to show far more disapproval of pupils than approval of good behaviour. Some studies show 80% of teachers' comments to pupils about behaviour were disapproving statements (Harrop and Swinson 2000). The key is being aware of what is happening in your classroom and knowing what is important so you can prevent problems.

Most pupils comply quickly when the teacher gives a desist order (a 'stop doing that') or redirects behaviour. But some pupils are the targets of more than their share of desists. One study found that these disruptive pupils seldom complied with the first teacher request to stop. Often, the disruptive pupils responded negatively, leading to an average of four to five cycles of teacher desists and pupil responses before the pupil complied (Nelson and Roberts, 2000). Emmer and colleagues (2006) and Levin and Nolan (2000) suggest seven simple ways to stop misbehaviour quickly, moving from least to most intrusive. You can check these in the following Focus on Practice.

Connect and Extend

For a description of an extensive research project examining how teachers cope with problem behaviours, see Brophy, J. and McCaslin, M. (1992), 'Teachers' reports of how they perceive and cope with problem pupils', *Elementary School Journal, 93,* pp. 3–68.

FOCUS ON PRACTICE

Seven ways to stop misbehaviour

1. *Make eye contact* with, or move closer to, the offender. Other nonverbal signals, such as pointing to the work pupils are supposed to be doing, might be helpful. Make sure the pupil actually stops the inappropriate behaviour and gets back to work. If you do not, pupils will learn to ignore your signals.

2. Try *verbal hints* such as 'name-dropping' (simply insert the pupil's name into the lecture), asking the pupil a question or making a humorous (not sarcastic) comment such as, 'I must be hallucinating. I swear I heard someone shout out an answer, but that can't be because I haven't called on anyone yet!'

3. Ask pupils *if they are aware* of the negative effects of their actions or send an 'I message', described later in the chapter.

4. If they are not performing a class procedure correctly, *remind the pupils* of the procedure and have them follow it correctly. You may need to quietly collect a

toy, comb, magazine or note that is competing with the learning activities, while privately informing the pupils that their possessions will be returned after class.

5. In a calm, unhostile way, *ask the pupil to state the correct rule or procedure* and then to follow it. Glasser (1969) proposes three questions: 'What are you doing? Is it against the rules? What should you be doing?'

6. Tell the pupil in a clear, assertive and unhostile way to *stop the misbehaviour.* (Later in the chapter we will discuss assertive messages to pupils in more detail.) If pupils 'talk back', simply repeat your statement.

7. *Offer a choice.* For example, when a pupil continued to call out answers no matter what the teacher tried, the teacher said, 'John, you have a choice. Stop calling out answers immediately and begin raising your hand to answer or move your seat to the back of the room and you and I will have a private discussion later. You decide' (Levin and Nolan, 2000: 177).

Many teachers prefer the use of logical consequences, described earlier, as opposed to penalties. For example, if one pupil has harmed another, you can require the offending pupil to make an 'Apology of Action', which includes a verbal apology plus somehow repairing the damage done. This helps offenders develop empathy and social perspective taking as they think about what would be an appropriate 'repair' (Elias and Schwab, 2006).

If you must impose penalties, the Focus on Practice below, taken from Weinstein (2003) and Weinstein and Mignano (2003), give ideas about how to do it. The examples are taken from the actual words of the expert teachers described in their book.

There is a caution about penalties. Never use lower achievement status (moving to a lower maths group, giving a lower mark, giving excess homework) as a punishment for breaking class rules. These actions should be done only if the benefit of the action outweighs the possible risk of harm. As Carolyn Orange notes, 'Effective, caring teachers would not use low achievement status, grades or the like as a means of discipline. This strategy is unfair and ineffective. It only serves to alienate the pupil' (2000: 76).

Connect and Extend

Read about the 24 other mistakes teachers make that can cause pupils anxiety and trauma, see Orange, C. (2000), *25 biggest mistakes teachers make and how to avoid them.* Thousand Oaks, CA: Corwin.

Special problems with secondary pupils

STOP AND THINK

Zero tolerance, as an approach to behaviour management, has been reported as being applied by the police in town centres and by head teachers in schools. What do you think about zero tolerance of poor behaviour in schools? Would you be able to support such a policy?

FOCUS ON PRACTICE

Imposing penalties

Delay the discussion of the situation until you and the pupils involved are calmer and more objective

Examples
1. Say calmly to a pupil, 'Sit there and think about what happened. I'll talk to you in a few minutes,' or, 'I don't like what I just saw. Talk to me during your free time today.'
2. Say, 'I'm really angry about what just happened. Everybody take out jotters; we are going to write about this.' After a few minutes of writing, the class can discuss the incident.

Impose penalties privately

Examples
1. Make arrangements with pupils privately. Stand firm in enforcing arrangements.
2. Resist the temptation to 'remind' pupils in public that they are not keeping their side of the bargain.
3. Move close to a pupil who must be disciplined and speak so that only the pupil can hear.

After imposing a penalty, re-establish a positive relationship with the pupil immediately

Examples
1. Send the pupil on an errand or ask him or her for help.
2. Compliment the pupil's work or give a real or symbolic 'pat on the back' when the pupil's behaviour warrants. Look hard for such an opportunity.

Set up a graded list of penalties that will fit many occasions

Examples
1. For not handing in homework: (1) receive reminder; (2) receive warning; (3) hand homework in before close of school day; (4) stay after school to finish work; (5) participate in a teacher–pupil–parent conference to develop an action plan.

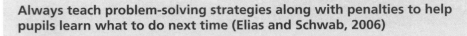

Always teach problem-solving strategies along with penalties to help pupils learn what to do next time (Elias and Schwab, 2006)

Examples

1. Use 'Problem Diaries', where pupils record what they were feeling, identify the problem and their goal, then think of other possible ways to solve the problem and achieve the goal.

2. Try Keep Calm 5-2-5: At the first physical signs of anger, pupils say to themselves: 'Stop. Keep Calm', then take several slow breaths, counting to five breathing in, two holding breath, and five breathing out.

For more ideas, see http://www.stopbullyingnow.com or http://www.cfchildren.org.

Connect and Extend

Even the most well-managed classroom will have instances of pupil misbehaviour. Explain the principles for dealing with common pupil misbehaviours. Use an internet search to find out about the strategies teachers employ to deal fairly and effectively with common behavioural problems.

Some common behavioural problems

Many secondary pupils never complete their work. Besides encouraging pupil responsibility, what else can teachers do to deal with this frustrating problem? Pupils at this age have a good deal of homework or examination coursework to complete and teachers have many pupils. Therefore, both teacher and pupils may lose track of what has and has not been completed. Some pupils use a daily organiser – paper or electronic – and, in addition, the teacher must keep accurate records. The most important thing is to enforce the established consequences for incomplete work. Pupils need to know that the choice is theirs: they can do the work and succeed, or they can refuse to do the work and face the consequences. The teacher might also ask, in a private moment, if there is anything interfering with the pupil's ability to finish the work.

There is also the problem of pupils who continually break the same rules, always forgetting materials, for example, or getting into fights. What should the teacher do? Often teachers seat these pupils away from others who might be influenced by them, or try to catch them before they break the rules. However, if rules are broken, teachers must be consistent in applying established consequences, and not accept promises to do better next time (Levin and Nolan, 2000). Pupils must be taught how to monitor their own behaviour and some of the self-management techniques described in Chapter 6 (p. 278) should be helpful. Finally, effective teachers remain friendly with their pupils, try to catch them in a good moment so they can talk to them about something other than their rule-breaking.

A defiant, hostile pupil can pose serious problems. If there is an outburst, the teacher should try to get out of the situation as soon as possible, because everyone loses in a public power struggle. One possibility is to give the pupil a chance to save face and cool down by saying, 'It's your choice to cooperate or not. You can take a minute to think about it.' If the pupil complies, both teacher and pupil can talk later about controlling the outbursts. If the pupil refuses to cooperate, the teacher can tell him or her to wait in the corridor until the class starts work, then step outside for a private talk. If the pupil refuses to leave, the teacher should send another class member for a more senior member of staff. Again, it is important to follow through with the consequences of such behaviour. Even if the pupil complies before help arrives, the teacher should not let him or her off the hook. If outbursts occur frequently, a conference can be arranged with the head of year, parents or other teachers. If the problem is an irreconcilable clash of personalities, the pupil should be transferred to another teacher. In the Stop and Think about zero-tolerance for rule-breaking you may have realised that there are two sides to the argument about implementing zero-tolerance in schools. The following Discussion Point looks at both sides.

Schools find it useful to keep records of outbursts by logging the pupil's name, words and actions, date, time, place and teacher's response. These records may help identify patterns and can prove useful in meetings with parents or school support services (Burden, 1995). Some teachers have pupils sign entries to verify the incidents and others ask pupils to record their own behaviour and to action plan for improvement through self-management.

Violence or destruction of property is a difficult and potentially dangerous problem. The first step a teacher should take is to send for help and get the names of participants and witnesses. Often teachers get rid of any crowd that may have gathered; an audience will only make things worse. Staff should never try to break up a fight without help but should always make sure the school office is aware of the incident; usually the school has a policy for dealing with these kinds of situations.

DISCUSSION POINT

Is zero tolerance a bad idea?

In a response to very visible violence in society today, some schools have instituted 'zero-tolerance' policies for rule breaking. One result? Two eight-year-old boys were suspended for making 'terrorist threats'. They had pointed paper guns at their classmates while playing. Do zero-tolerance policies make sense?

Agree: Yes, zero tolerance means zero common sense

Zero tolerance stems from the work of Wilson and Kelling (1982) who argued that allowing a climate of disorder to develop leads to more serious crimes. For example, leaving a broken window in a building and not repairing it will inspire some individuals to vandalise the rest of the building. From small beginnings, people turn to more serious crimes. Of course, it makes good sense to remove a damaged book from circulation or chair from use, to immediately remove any graffiti and to deal swiftly and decisively with cases of bullying. However, zero-tolerance of quite normal behaviours such as playing with 'guns' or observing the exact detail of a uniform code in schools can lead to bad decisions.

There are many stories available on the internet. In researching this Discussion Point we read that pupils have been suspended for playing with water pistols, carrying key ring fobs that look like guns, using their fingers as pretend guns in a game and drawing pictures of guns.

A general zero tolerance means a one size fits all mentality that may bring some short-term gains but doesn't change the causes and therefore the long-term incidence of misbehaviour in schools. Finally, many of the popular zero-tolerance interventions such as security guards in schools, corridor monitors, and the introduction of metal detectors have no apparent effect on the incidence of school bullying (Hyman *et al.*, 2006; NCES, 2003).

Disagree: No, zero tolerance is necessary for now

The arguments for zero tolerance focus on school safety and the responsibilities of schools and teachers to protect the pupils and themselves. Of course, many of the extreme incidents reported in the news seem like overreactions to childhood pranks or worse, over-zealous application of zero tolerance to innocent mistakes or lapses of memory. So how do school managers separate the innocent from the dangerous?

As this co-author goes from school to school examining practice of his trainee teachers, he sees worsening levels of low-level classroom disruptive behaviour and many teachers and schools seem powerless to do anything about it. It appears to be normal for pupils to call out, to move around the room at will, to throw pencils and paper around the room, to back-chat the teachers, to demand attention and to refuse to complete the work that is set. Trainee teachers resort to low-level mundane tasks so that the pupils cannot say they don't understand or can't do it, and to bribing the pupils to behave with sweets and chocolate.

Ignoring and allowing poor behaviour is to condone that behaviour and is an abrogation of teacher and school responsibility. Successful school improvement measures almost always include a zero tolerance approach to behaviour carried out by all members of staff, supervised and led by highly visible and active senior teachers and school managers. Put simply, if a pupil gets away with something, one thing, just once, *publicly* then it is human nature to attempt the same behaviour again and for others to follow suit.

WHAT DO YOU THINK?

Agree or Disagree? Vote online at www.pearsoned.co.uk/woolfolkeuro.

Reaching every pupil: school-wide positive behaviour supports

In Chapter 6 (p. 266) we discussed two important ideas for supporting positive behaviour throughout a school: functional behavioural analysis and positive behaviour supports (PBS). In England positive behaviour support is provided through behavioural supports plans (BSPs), which are required under the Education Act 1997, and individual education plans (IEPs) for pupils with special educational needs including emotional and behavioural difficulties. IEPs are supported by behavioural supports plans and so contribute to a school-wide programme. At the school level, the teachers and managers:

- agree on a common approach for supporting positive behaviours and correcting problems;

- develop a few positively stated, specific behavioural expectations and procedures for teaching these expectations to all pupils;

- identify a continuum of ways (from small and simple, to more complex and stronger) to acknowledge appropriate behaviours and correct behavioural errors;

- integrate the behavioural support plan procedures with the schools' discipline policy.

At the classroom level, teachers are encouraged to use such preventive strategies as precorrection, which involves identifying the context for a pupil's misbehaviour, clearly specifying the alternative expected behaviour, and modifying the situation to make the problem behaviour less likely. For example, moving the pupil away from tempting distractions, then rehearsing the expected positive behaviours in the new context and providing powerful reinforcers should the problem behaviour recur. There is an emphasis on keeping pupils engaged, providing a positive focus, consistently enforcing school/rules, correcting disruptive behaviour proactively, and planning for smooth transitions (Blandford, 1998; McClean *et al.*, 2005).

Research on behavioural supports plans is limited, but results have been promising. The development of new curricula opportunities is often part of BSPs , especially the development of vocational and work experience placements. Many schools have clearly felt relief that they were now free from some of the perceived constraints of the English National Curriculum, which, it is argued, is rarely viewed as relevant to many pupils with emotional and behavioural difficulties. BSPs usually stress the advantages of using specialist staff to support preventative measures in schools (prevention being always better than cure) but the reality seems to be that specialist advisory and support teachers could often not escape a 'fire-fighting' role. Nevertheless, the BSPs showed local managers seeking to move towards more inter-agency working, early identification and preventative interventions which would encourage inclusive practice and lessen the needs for alternative provision outside of mainstream schooling (Cole *et al.*, 2003).

Precorrection

A way of preventing serious behaviour problems of pupils who have been labelled at risk by directing the pupils towards more appropriate actions.

The Need for Communication

STOP AND THINK

A pupil says to a teacher, 'That book you've given us is really stupid – I'm not reading it!' What should the teacher say?

Message sent–message received

Communication between teacher and pupils is essential when problems arise. Communication is more than 'teacher talks – pupil listens'. It is more than the words exchanged between individuals. We communicate in many ways. Our actions, movements, voice tone, facial expressions and many other non-verbal behaviours send messages to our pupils. Many times, the messages we intend to send are not the messages our pupils receive. Look at the following examples of the differences between the message sent and the message received.

Example 1

Teacher: Carl, where is your homework?

Carl: I left it in my dad's car this morning.

Teacher: Again? You will have to bring me a note tomorrow from your father saying that you actually did the homework or you will be in homework detention for the rest of the week.

Message Carl receives: I can't trust you. I need proof you did the work.

Example 2

Teacher: Sit at every other desk. Put all your things under your desk. Jane and Laurel, you are sitting too close together. One of you move!

Message Jane and Laurel receive: I expect you two to cheat on this test.

Example 3

A new pupil comes to Ms Lincoln's class. The child is messy and unwashed. Ms Lincoln puts her hand lightly on the girl's shoulder and says, 'It's nice to see you' but the teacher's muscles tense, and she leans away from the child.

Message pupil receives: I don't like you. I think you are bad.

In all interactions, a message is sent and a message is received. Sometimes teachers believe they are sending one message, but their voices, body positions, choices of words and gestures may communicate a different message.

Pupils may hear the hidden message and respond to it. For example, a pupil may respond with hostility if she or he feels insulted by the teacher (or by another pupil), but may not be able to say exactly where the feeling of being insulted came from. Perhaps it was in the teacher's tone of voice, not the words actually spoken. However, the teacher feels attacked for no reason. The first principle of communication is that people respond to what they think was said or meant, not necessarily to the speaker's intended message or actual words.

Paraphrase rule

Policy whereby listeners must accurately summarise what a speaker has said before being allowed to respond.

One method of checking that the message received is accurate is to use the paraphrase rule. Before any participant, including the teacher, is allowed to respond to any other participant in a class discussion, he or she must summarise what the previous speaker said. If the summary is wrong, indicating the speaker was misunderstood, the speaker must explain again. The respondent then tries again to paraphrase. The process continues until the speaker agrees that the listener has heard the intended message.

Paraphrasing is more than a classroom exercise. It can be the first step in communicating with pupils. Before teachers can deal appropriately with any pupil problem, they must know what the real problem is. A pupil who says, 'This book is really stupid! Why did we have to read it?' may really be saying, 'The book is too difficult for me. I can't read it, and I feel stupid.'

Diagnosis: whose problem is it?

As a teacher, you may find some pupil behaviours unacceptable, unpleasant or troubling. It is often difficult to stand back from these problems, take an objective look and decide on an appropriate response. According to Thomas Gordon (1981), the key to good teacher–pupil relationships is determining why you are troubled by a particular behaviour and who 'owns' the problem. The answer to these questions is critical. If it is really the pupil's problem, the teacher must become a coach and supporter, helping the pupil find his or her own solution. However, if the teacher 'owns' the problem, it is the teacher's responsibility to find a solution through problem solving with the pupil.

> ### STOP AND THINK
>
> A well-managed classroom requires a two-way communication style between a teacher and the pupils. What are the various communication styles that teachers employ when interacting with pupils? Can you suggest how those styles affect pupil behaviour?

Diagnosing who owns the problem is not always straightforward. Let's look at three troubling situations to get some practice in this skill:

1. A pupil writes obscene words and draws sexually explicit illustrations in a school encyclopedia.
2. A pupil tells you that his parents had a bad fight and he hates his father.
3. A pupil quietly reads a computer magazine at the back of the room.

Why are these behaviours troubling? If a teacher cannot accept the pupil's behaviour because it has a serious effect – if a teacher is prevented from reaching their professional goals by the pupil's action – then the teacher owns the problem. It is the teacher's responsibility to confront the pupil and seek a solution. A teacher-owned problem appears to be present in the first situation described above – the young artist – because teaching materials are damaged.

If the teacher feels annoyed by the behaviour because it is getting in the pupil's own way or because of embarrassment for the child, but the behaviour does not directly interfere with teaching, then it is probably the pupil's problem. The fact that a pupil who hates his father would not prevent teaching and learning, even though one might wish the pupil felt differently. The problem is really the pupil's, and he must find his own solution.

The third situation is more difficult to diagnose. One argument is that the teacher is not interfered with in any way, so it is the pupil's problem. However, teachers might find the pupil reading the magazine distracting during a lesson, so it is their problem, and they must find a solution. In a 'grey area' such as this, the answer probably depends on how the teacher actually experiences the pupil's behaviour. Having decided who owns the problem, it is time to act.

Connect and Extend

Read about how children respond to ambiguous communications in D. B. Bugental, *et al.* (1999), 'Children "tune out" in response to the ambiguous communication style of powerless adults', *Child Development, 70,* pp. 214–230.

Counselling: the pupil's problem

Let's pick up the situation in which the pupil found the reading book 'stupid'. How might a teacher handle this positively?

Pupil: This book is really stupid! Why did we have to read it?

Teacher: You're pretty upset. This seems a waste of time to you. [Teacher paraphrases the pupil's statement, trying to hear the emotions as well as the words.]

Pupil: Yeah! Well, it is a waste of time. I mean, I don't know if it is. I don't understand all of it.

Teacher: Some of it is hard to read and that bothers you?

Pupil: Sure, I don't like feeling stupid. I know I can write a good essay, but not about a book this hard.

Teacher: I think I can give you some hints that will make the book easier to understand. Can you see me after school today?

Pupil: Okay.

Empathetic listening

Hearing the intent and emotions behind what another says and reflecting them back by paraphrasing.

Here the teacher used empathetic listening to allow the pupil to find a solution. (As you can see, this approach relies heavily on paraphrasing.) By trying to hear the pupil and by avoiding the tendency to jump in too quickly with advice, solutions, criticisms, reprimands or interrogations, the teacher keeps the communication lines open. Here are a few *unhelpful* responses the teacher might have made:

- I chose the book because it is the best example of the author's style in our library. You will need to have studied it before your English Literature exam next year. (The teacher justifies the choice; this prevents the pupil from admitting that this reading book is too difficult.)

- Did you really read it? I bet you didn't do the work, and now you can't do the essay. (The teacher accuses; the pupil hears, 'The teacher doesn't trust me!' and must either defend herself or himself or accept the teacher's view.)

- Your job is to read the book, not ask me why you need to. (The teacher pulls rank, and the pupil hears, 'You can't possibly decide what is good for you!' The pupil can rebel or passively accept the teacher's judgement.)

Empathetic, active listening is more than a parroting of the pupil's words; it should capture the emotions, intent and meaning behind them. Sokolove *et al.* (1986: 241) have summarised the components of active listening: (1) blocking out external stimuli; (2) attending carefully to both the verbal and non-verbal messages; (3) differentiating between the intellectual and the emotional content of the message; and (4) making inferences regarding the speaker's feelings. Howieson and Semple (2000) emphasise the need for empathetic listening to be an authentic part of the communication between pupils and teachers – not an exercise in looking as if you are trying to understand what a pupil is saying.

When pupils realise they really have been heard and not judged negatively for what they have said or felt, they begin to trust the teacher and to talk more openly. Sometimes the true problem surfaces later in the conversation.

Confrontation and assertive discipline

Now let's assume a pupil is doing something that actively interferes with teaching. The teacher decides the pupil must stop. The problem is the teacher's. Confrontation, not counselling, is required.

'I' messages

Gordon (1981) recommends sending an 'I' message in order to intervene and change a pupil's behaviour. Basically, this means telling a pupil in a straightforward, assertive and nonjudgemental way what she or he is doing, how it affects you as a teacher, and how you feel about it – the last sometimes implied rather than directly expressed. The pupil is then free to change voluntarily, and often does so. Here are two 'I' messages:

- 'If you leave your bags in the aisles, I might trip and hurt myself.'

- 'When you all call out, I can't concentrate on each answer, and that means I can't understand what people are saying.'

'I' message

Clear, non-accusatory statement of how something is affecting you.

Assertive discipline

Education consultants, Lee and Marlene Canter (1992; Canter, 1996) suggest other approaches for dealing with a teacher-owned problem. They call their method of providing clear, firm, non-hostile responses, assertive discipline. Audrey Osler (2000), research professor at the University of Leeds, discusses assertive discipline in the context of children's rights, responsibilities and their understanding of school discipline. One important observation is that many teachers are ineffective with pupils because they are either 'wishy-washy' and passive, or hostile and aggressive (Charles, 2002a).

Instead of telling the pupil directly what is the right thing to do, passive teachers tell, or often ask, the pupil to try to think about the appropriate action. The passive teacher might comment on the problem behaviour without actually telling the child what to do differently: 'Why are you doing that? Don't you know the rules?' or 'Sam, are you disturbing the class?' Or teachers may clearly state what should happen, but never follow through with the established consequences, giving the pupils 'one more chance' every time. Finally, passive teachers ignore behaviour that should receive a response or they may wait too long before responding.

A *hostile response style* involves different mistakes. Teachers make 'you' statements that condemn the pupil without stating clearly what the pupil should be doing: 'You should be ashamed of the way you're behaving!' or 'You never listen!' or 'You are acting like a baby!' Teachers may also threaten pupils angrily, but follow through too seldom, perhaps because the threats are too vague – 'You'll be very sorry you did that when I get through with you!' – or too severe. For example, a teacher tells a pupil in a physical education class that he will have to 'sit on the bench for *three weeks*'. A few days later, a team is short of one member and the teacher lets the pupil play, never returning him to the bench to complete the three-week sentence. Often a teacher who has been passive becomes hostile and explodes when pupils persist in misbehaving.

In contrast with both the passive and hostile styles, an assertive response communicates to the pupils that you care too much about them and the process of learning to allow inappropriate behaviour to persist. Assertive teachers clearly state what they expect. To be most effective, the teachers often look into a pupil's eyes when speaking and address the pupil by name. Assertive teachers' voices are calm, firm and confident. They are not sidetracked by accusations such as 'You just don't understand!' or 'You don't like me!' Assertive teachers do not get into a debate about the fairness of the rules. They expect changes, not promises or apologies.

Not all educators believe that assertive discipline is useful. Earlier critics questioned the penalty-focused approach and emphasised that assertive discipline undermined pupil self-management (Render *et al.*, 1989). John Covaleskie (1992) observed 'What

Assertive discipline

Clear, firm, non-hostile response style.

Connect and Extend

Read more about power and discipline in D. B. Bugental, *et al.* (1999), 'In charge but not in control: The management of teaching relationships by adults with low perceived power', *Developmental Psychology, 35*, pp. 1367–1378.

helps children become moral is not knowledge of the rules, or even obedience to the rules, but discussions about the reasons for acting in certain ways' (p.56). These critics have had an impact. More recent versions of assertive discipline focus on teaching pupils 'in an atmosphere of respect, trust, and support, how to behave responsibly' (Charles, 2002a: 47).

Confrontations and negotiations

If 'I' messages or assertive responses fail and a pupil persists in misbehaving, teacher and pupil are in a conflict. Several pitfalls now loom large. The two individuals become less able to perceive each other's behaviour accurately. Research has shown that the more angry you get with another person, the more you see the other as the villain and yourself as an innocent victim. If you feel the other person is in the wrong, and he or she feels just as strongly that the conflict is your entire fault then very little mutual trust is possible. A cooperative solution to the problem is almost impossible. In fact, by the time the discussion has gone on a few minutes, the original problem is lost in a storm of charges, countercharges and self-defence (Baron and Byrne, 2003).

Connect and Extend

Read Zay, D. (2005) 'Preventing school and social exclusion: a French–British comparative study', *European Educational Research Journal, 4*(2) or see the Companion Website (Web Link 12.2).

There are three methods of resolving a conflict between teacher and pupil. One is for the teacher to impose a solution. This may be necessary during an emergency, as when a defiant pupil refuses to leave the classroom to discuss a public outbreak, but it is not a good solution for most conflicts. The second method is for the teacher to give in to the pupil's demands. You might be convinced by a particularly compelling pupil argument, but again, this should be used sparingly. It is generally a bad idea to be talked out of a position, unless the position was wrong in the first place. Problems arise when either the teacher or the pupil gives in completely.

Gordon (1981) recommends a third approach, which he calls the 'no-lose method'. Here, the needs of both the teacher and the pupils are taken into account in the solution. No one person is expected to give in completely; all participants retain respect for themselves and each other. The no-lose method is a six-step, problem-solving strategy:

1. Define the problem. What exactly are the behaviours involved? What does each person want? (Use active listening to help pupils pinpoint the real problem.)
2. Generate many possible solutions. Brainstorm, but remember, don't allow any evaluations of ideas yet.
3. Evaluate each solution. Any participant may veto any idea. If no solutions are found to be acceptable, brainstorm again.
4. Make a decision. Choose one solution through consensus – no voting. In the end, everyone must be satisfied with the solution.
5. Determine how to implement the solution. What will be needed? Who will be responsible for each task? What is the timetable?
6. Evaluate the success of the solution. After trying the solution for a while, ask, 'Are we satisfied with our decision? How well is it working? Should we make some changes?'

Connect and Extend

For an excellent analysis of the literature relating to management in urban schools, see Keys, W. *et al.* (2003), *Successful Leadership of Schools in Urban and Challenging Contexts: a Review of the Literature.* Nottingham: NCSL

To this point we have concentrated on dealing with conflicts between teachers and pupils but many of the conflicts in classrooms are between pupils. Without attempting to create unnecessary conflicts between pupils such 'opportunities' can be important learning experiences for all concerned.

Research on management approaches

In this chapter we have considered the results of a number of important studies and their potential impact on the quality of classroom management. For example, right at the beginning of the chapter we talked about the work of Marzano and Marzano (2003) in identifying the 'key to classroom management'. But what of classroom management itself? Just how important is it to pupils' learning?

Classroom management received perhaps its strongest endorsement in a encyclopedic study by Margaret Wang, Geneva Haertel and Herbert Walberg (1994). They synthesised the results of three previous studies. The first study drew on content analysis of 86 chapters from research reviews, 44 book chapters, 11 journal articles and 20 commissioned and government reports. This produced a list of 228 variables that impact on pupil attainment. The second study asked 134 education experts to rate each of the 228 variables in terms of the relative strength of impact. The third study involved an analysis of 91 major research syntheses.

Results of the meta-research were used to create a 28-category conceptual framework – models of schooling that influenced learning. By combining the results from the content analysis, the research synthesis and the survey of experts, an average score was obtained for each of the 28 categories, and each of the 28 categories was listed according to its relative influences on learning.

The 'attitude towards the subject matter' was ranked seventh. 'Teacher and pupil academic interactions' was ranked 14th. 'Management decision making' (actively concerned with the teaching programme) was ranked 23rd. 'Home environment/ parental support' is listed as the fourth most influential influence; the key factor of parental support in influencing learning, according to this analysis, is parents ensuring their children complete their homework! Overall, classroom management (strategies that maintain active pupil participation) was ranked first.

> **Connect and Extend**
>
> Miller, A., Ferguson, E. and Moore, E. (2002). 'Parents' and pupils' causal attributions for difficult classroom behaviour', *British Journal of Educational Psychology*, 72(1), pp. 27–40.

Integrating ideas

If we have established classroom management as one of the most important factors (or according to Wang *et al.*, the most important factor) contributing to pupils' achievement, what factors most contribute to successful classroom management? In a study conducted in Australia, Ramon Lewis (2001) found that pupils taking greater responsibility for their own learning was associated with:

- recognising and rewarding appropriate pupil behaviours;
- talking with pupils about how their behaviour affects others;
- involving pupils in class discipline decisions; and
- providing non-directive hints and descriptions about unacceptable behaviours.

Lewis also concluded paradoxically that teachers find using these interventions difficult when pupils are aggressive – and most in need of the approaches. When teachers feel threatened over a period of time, it can be difficult to do what pupils need, but that may be the most important time to act positively. So, who is best placed to support teachers to act positively and whose support is most important to teachers establishing and maintaining a positive classroom environment in which all pupils can flourish?

Communicating with families about classroom management

As we have seen throughout this book, most recently in Wang, Haertel and Walberg's meta-analysis, families are important partners in education. This statement applies to classroom management as well. When parents and teachers share the same expectations and support each other, they can create a more positive classroom environment and more time for learning. The following Focus on Practice provides ideas for working with families and the community.

Besides prevention, schools can also establish mentoring programmes, conflict resolution training, social skills training, more relevant curricula, and parent and community involvement programmes (Padilla, 1992; Parks, 1995). One intervention that seems to be helpful is peer mediation, discussed in Chapter 11. Now is a good time to review the main ideas of this chapter and to reflect on how teachers might establish and maintain a positive learning environment in classrooms.

FOCUS ON PRACTICE

Classroom management

Make sure families know the expectations and rules of your class and school

Examples

1. At a school open evening have some pupils do lighthearted skits about the rules – how to follow them and what breaking them 'looks like' and 'sounds like'.
2. Make a poster for the refrigerator at home that describes, in a light way, the most important rules and expectations.
3. For older pupils, give families a list of dates for the assessments and major assignments, along with tips about how to encourage quality work by pacing the effort – avoiding last minute panic.
4. Communicate in appropriate ways – use the family's first language when possible. Tailor messages to the reading level of the home.

Make families partners in recognising good citizenship

Examples

1. Send positive notes home when pupils work well in the classroom, especially pupils who have had trouble with classroom behaviour.
2. Give ideas for ways any family, even those with few economic resources, can celebrate accomplishment – a favourite food; the chance to choose a video to rent; a comment to a special person such as an aunt, grandparent or minister; the chance to read to a younger sibling.

Identify talents in the community to help build a learning environment in your class

Examples

1. Have pupils write letters to carpet and furniture stores asking for donations of remnants to carpet a reading corner.

2. Find family members who can build shelves or room dividers, paint, sew, laminate resources, write stories, re-pot plants or network computers.
3. Contact businesses for donations of computers, printers or other equipment.

Seek cooperation from families when behaviour problems arise

Examples
1. Talk to families over the phone or by e-mail messaging. Keep good records about the problem behaviour.
2. Listen to family members and let them know they are not part of the problem but a big part of the solution.

For more ideas see http://www.dundee.ac.uk/fedsoc/research/projects/parentsineducation/.

SUMMARY TABLE

The Need for Organisation (pp. 526–531)

What are the challenges of classroom management?

Classrooms are by nature multi-dimensional, full of simultaneous activities, fast-paced and immediate, unpredictable, public and affected by the history of pupils' and teachers' actions. A teacher must juggle all these elements every day. Productive classroom activity requires pupils' cooperation. Maintaining cooperation is different for each age group. Young pupils are learning how to 'go to school' and need to learn the general procedures of school. Older pupils need to learn the specifics required for working in different subjects. Working with adolescents requires teachers to understand the power of the adolescent peer group.

What are the goals of good classroom management?

The goals of effective classroom management are to make ample time for learning; improve the quality of time use by keeping pupils actively engaged; make sure participation structures are clear, straightforward and consistently signalled; and encourage pupil self-management, self-control and responsibility.

Creating a Positive Learning Environment (pp. 532–548)

Distinguish between rules and procedures

Rules are the specific dos and don'ts of classroom life. They usually are written down or posted. Procedures cover administrative tasks, pupil movement, housekeeping, routines for accomplishing lessons, interactions between pupils and teachers, and interactions among pupils. Rules can be written in terms of rights and pupils may benefit from participating in establishing these rules. Consequences should be established for following and breaking the rules and procedures so that the teacher and the pupils know what will happen.

Distinguish between personal spaces and interest areas

There are two basic kinds of organisation, personal work spaces (the traditional classroom arrangement) and functional (dividing space into interest or work areas). Flexibility is often the key. Access to materials, convenience, privacy when needed, ease of supervision and a willingness to re-evaluate plans are important considerations in the teacher's choice of physical arrangements.

What management issues do computers raise in the classroom?

Clear procedures are especially important when there are computers in the classroom. Whether teachers have one, several or a room full of computers, they need to think through what pupils will need to know, teach procedures and provide easy-to-find and follow written instructions for common tasks. Pupils or parent volunteers can be trained as expert support. Different role structures can make management of computer tasks easier.

Contrast the first school week of effective and ineffective classroom managers

Effective classroom managers spent the first days of class teaching a workable, easily understood set of rules and procedures by using lots of explanation, examples and practice. Pupils were occupied with organised, enjoyable activities and learned to function cooperatively in the group. Quick, firm, clear and consistent responses to infractions of the rules characterised effective teachers. The teachers had planned carefully to avoid any last-minute tasks that might have taken them away from their pupils. These teachers dealt with the children's pressing concerns first.

Maintaining a Good Environment for Learning (pp. 548–559)

How can teachers encourage engagement?

In general, as teacher supervision increases, pupils' engaged time also increases. When the task provides continuous cues for the pupil about what to do next, involvement will be greater. Activities with clear steps are likely to be more absorbing, because one step leads naturally to the next. Making work requirements clear and specific, providing needed materials and monitoring activities all add to engagement.

Explain the factors identified by Kounin that prevent management problems in the classroom

To create a positive environment and prevent problems, teachers must take individual differences into account, maintain pupil motivation and reinforce positive behaviour. Successful problem preventers are skilled in four areas described by Kounin: 'withitness', overlapping, group focusing and movement management. When penalties have to be imposed, teachers should impose them calmly and privately. In addition to applying Kounin's ideas, teachers can prevent problems by establishing a caring classroom community and teaching pupils to use social skills and emotional self-regulation skills.

Describe seven levels of intervention in misbehaviour

Teachers can first make eye contact with the pupil or use other non-verbal signals, then try verbal hints such as simply inserting the pupil's name into the lecture. Next the teacher asks if the offender is aware of the negative effects of the actions, then reminds the pupil of the procedure and has her or him follow it correctly. If this does not work, the teacher can ask the pupil to state the correct rule or procedure and then to follow it, and then move to telling the pupil in a clear, assertive and unhostile way to stop the misbehaviour. If this fails too, the teacher can offer a choice – stop the behaviour or meet privately to work out the consequences.

What are some special problems and challenges in secondary classrooms?

Teachers working in secondary schools should be prepared to handle pupils who don't complete school work, repeatedly break the same rule or openly defy teachers.

The Need for Communication (pp. 559–567)

What is meant by 'empathetic listening'?

Communication between teacher and pupil is essential when problems arise. All interactions between people, even silence or neglect, communicate some meaning. Empathetic, active listening can be a helpful response when pupils bring problems to teachers. Teachers must reflect back to the pupils what they hear them saying. This reflection is more than a parroting of words; it should capture the emotions, intent and meaning behind them.

Distinguish among passive, hostile and assertive response styles

The *passive style* can take several forms. Instead of telling the pupil directly what to do, the teacher simply comments on the behaviour, asks the pupil to *think about* the appropriate action, or threatens but never follows through. In a *hostile response style,* teachers may make 'you' statements that condemn the pupil without stating clearly what the pupil should be doing. An *assertive response* communicates to the pupils that the teacher cares too much about them and the process of learning to allow inappropriate behaviour to persist. Assertive teachers clearly state what they expect.

Glossary

Action zone: Area of a classroom where the greatest amount of interaction is taking place, increasingly the area around the interactive digital whiteboard.

Allocated or available time: Time set aside for learning.

Assertive discipline: Clear, firm, non-hostile response style.

Classroom management: Techniques used to establish and maintain a positive and safe learning environment, relatively free of behaviour problems.

Empathetic listening: Hearing the intent and emotions behind what another says and reflecting them back by paraphrasing.

Engaged time: Time spent being active with some task, or talking to or listening to others.

Group focus: The ability to keep as many pupils as possible involved in activities.

'I' message: Clear, non-accusatory statement of how something is affecting you.

Movement management: Keeping lessons and the group moving at an appropriate (and flexible) pace, with smooth transitions and variety.

Natural or logical consequences: Instead of punishing, have pupils redo, repair or in some way face the consequences that naturally flow from their actions.

Overlapping: Supervising several activities at once.

Paraphrase rule: Policy whereby listeners must accurately summarise what a speaker has said before being allowed to respond.

Participation structures: Rules defining how to participate in different activities.

Precorrection: A way of preventing serious behaviour problems of pupils who have been labelled at risk by directing the pupils towards more appropriate actions.

Procedures: Prescribed steps for an activity.

Rules: Statements specifying expected and forbidden behaviours; dos and don'ts.

Self-management: Management of your own behaviour and acceptance of responsibility for your own actions.

Successful learning time: Time when pupils are actually succeeding at the learning task.

The 4 Rs: An agreed code of rights, responsibilities, rules and routines.

Time on task: Time spent actively engaged in the learning offered by the task at hand.

Withitness: According to Kounin, awareness of everything happening in a classroom.

CHECK YOUR LEARNING!

 WEB

In the Classroom: What Would They Do?

Here is how some practising teachers responded to the questions about how the school professional tutor should support Mr Jones and ensure that his behaviour management improved.

Tessa Herbert, English teacher, John Masefield High School, Ledbury

A strategy adopted by our school involves carefully analysing the class in terms of identifying the key players in the disruption. The professional mentor should sit down with Mr Jones and ask him to break the group into sub-groups: the compliant (no matter what), those who usually cooperate with Mr Jones, those who will follow the strongest and those, probably only a relatively small number, who are deliberately sabotaging the lesson.

Mr Jones should always be ready to greet the whole class as they arrive, by name and with good humour. The plan is then to concentrate absolutely on the first two groups, giving them positive attention and feedback, noticing and rewarding the fact that they are working well. The hope is that Mr Jones will gradually draw in the waverers who wish to be noticed and can be for their good work. The small final group will then be isolated without support and should, with firm reminders of the classroom rules, start to see that it is in their interest to comply. The trick is to hold your nerve. Not always easy and the process is as long as a piece of string.

Jackie Day, special needs co-ordinator, The Ridge Primary School, Yate

The professional tutor should ensure that Mr Jones is familiar with the school's behaviour policy, which should be based on rights, responsibilities, routines and rules, and should contain the list of rewards and sanctions used throughout the school. He should observe what is happening in Mr Jones' classroom to see whether the children's poor behaviour is indeed due to Mr Jones' inexperience, or perhaps whether there are children in the class with undetected special needs. Some 90% of pupils behave well in a structured environment with clear boundaries. It may be that Mr Jones has not yet established appropriate class rules, which should be drawn up with the children, and be based on maintaining the rights of all children to learn and to be safe. He should check for clear routines in the classroom, and that Mr Jones' teaching is appropriately differentiated. Mr Jones may need help with his own body language, tone of voice and in using the language of choice with children. He should understand that none of us can force children to behave well, but we can encourage them to make the right choices by keeping calm and spelling out the consequences of wrong choices. The head teacher could help by observing him teach, giving feedback on his behaviour management, and making it easy for Mr Jones to ask for advice if he needs it.

Lisbeth Jonsson, primary school teacher, Sweden

The problems you mention are very familiar to us all. To try to solve Mr Jones' difficulties we would separate the 'naughtiest' pupils from the class and let the professional tutor work with them for some time. Meanwhile, the head teacher should support Mr Jones by having serious talks with the other pupils together with Mr Jones, making clear how much it can influence their future studies if the classroom teaching doesn't work. After taking the separated pupils back into the class, it would be of importance for Mr Jones to have the support and help from the tutor in the classroom. Unfortunately it is not easy to change a bad start into a good relation between pupils and teacher. Pupils have a tendency to 'take over' when a teacher is nervous and insecure and doesn't have enough self-esteem. So – can Mr Jones change his way of behaviour? If so, it would be better to let him start in another class together with a fellow teacher and 'work his way up' to a class of his own. Mr Jones has to regain his self-esteem under new conditions. It is also important to handle the situation without delay, otherwise Mr Jones' problem could spread to other classes.

Lizzie Meadows, deputy head teacher, The Park Primary School, Kingswood, Bristol

The school needs to take a very proactive approach to the difficulties that Mr Jones is currently experiencing. Initially they will need to convene a meeting between him, his mentor and the head teacher. While being supportive of Mr Jones and emphasising his strengths, the head teacher needs to be very clear about the expectations of the school and also explore with him reasons for any current difficulties and possible solutions. Second, they need to establish a structured programme of support that not only looks at behaviour management but also the learning opportunities in Mr Jones' classroom. This could involve peer observations and feedback, training opportunities both internally and externally and very specific targets for Mr Jones to meet. Third, the head teacher and senior management need to have a very high profile in Mr Jones' corridor and find as many excuses to pop into his room as they can, without of course undermining him in front of the pupils.

Lee Card, primary school teacher, Bosbury Church of England Primary School, Herefordshire

The support of the head and the mentor, in this case the professional tutor, is essential in this situation in ensuring Mr Jones' success. The children have obviously taken advantage of an inexperienced teacher who may not have given clear enough boundaries or guidelines to his class. Sometimes, in wanting to be 'liked' as a teacher, this is the first thing to go and children are very quick in pushing the boundaries further each day. It is, of course, possible that Mr Jones has a particularly challenging class in terms of behaviour. Either way, he is struggling and needs guidance and support quickly and regularly.

The mentor should be given time by the head to observe Mr Jones. This will hopefully enable him or her to pin down what the crux of the problem is. Feedback to Mr Jones must happen quickly and should result in a short-term, easily achievable target (e.g. setting up a reward system such as 'team points' to praise good behaviour). This would need to continue regularly until the situation has improved.

If the observation process is exacerbating the problem, perhaps Mr Jones finds this an intimidating experience; a further support would be for the head to allow Mr Jones opportunities to view more experienced practitioners with their classes. Seeing positive behaviour management in action beats hearing or reading about it any day, and will give Mr Jones practical ideas to use in his class.

Go to the Companion Website (www.pearsoned. co.uk/woolfolkeuro) for additional case studies and examples of classroom rules and routines.

Overview

Much of this book has been about learning and learners. In this chapter, we focus on teachers and teaching. We look first at how teachers plan, including how to use learning objectives or themes as a basis for planning. With this foundation of knowing how to set goals and make plans, we move to a consideration of some general teacher-centred strategies: whole-class teaching, individual classwork, homework, questioning, one-to-one support and group discussion.

What else do we know about teachers? Are there particular characteristics that distinguish effective from ineffective teachers, other than simply the differing amount of progress made by pupils in their classes? We will explore research on whole-class teaching which points to the importance of several factors that contribute to effective teaching. In the final section of this chapter, we will focus on pupil-centred approaches and identify the implications for teaching.

By the time you have completed this chapter, you should be able to answer the following questions:

- **When and how should teachers use learning objectives?**
- **In what situations would each of the following formats be most appropriate: whole-class teaching, individual work and homework, one-to-one support and group discussion?**
- **What are the characteristics of effective teachers?**
- **How can teachers' expectations affect pupil learning?**
- **How does the teacher's role vary in direct and constructivist teaching approaches?**

In the Classroom

On a training day before term begins, a new teacher is handed curriculum documents showing a detailed framework of learning objectives associated with pupils being able to reach the expected levels of achievement in the national assessment tests. The new teacher is told that the school is 'in special measures', because pupils have not made adequate yearly progress for the past two years. This year the pupils must reach the required standard and that teaching styles must reflect the school's aspiration that all pupils will reach the expected levels of achievement. The programmes of study are comprehensive and appropriate but the school seems to have no strategy for teaching, other than drill and practice on facts and skills that might be on the national assessment tests. How should the teacher plan to arouse pupils' curiosity and interests about the topics and skills that will be tested, and establish the value of learning this material? How should a new teacher engage pupils in 'real learning' about the topics?

Group Activity

With three or four others, identify a key concept in a chosen subject that is likely to be on a national assessment. Plan a lesson to teach that will engage pupils in 'real learning'; to understand, remember and apply the concept.

The First Step: Planning

STOP AND THINK

Teacher-educator Greta Morine-Dershimer (2003) asks which of the following are true about teacher planning:

- Time is of the essence.
- Plans are made to be broken.
- Don't look back.

- A little goes a long way.
- You can do it yourself.
- One size fits all.

What do you think each of these mean and do you think they are completely or partly true?

When you thought about the In the Classroom feature at the beginning of this chapter, you were *planning*. In the past few years, educational researchers have become very interested in teachers' planning, because of a growing understanding of the importance of planning and preparation to effective classroom practice. Researchers have interviewed teachers about how they plan, asked teachers to 'think out loud' while planning or to keep journals describing their plans, and even studied teachers intensively for months at a time. What do you think they have found?

Here are the results of research. First, planning influences what pupils will learn, because planning transforms the available time and curriculum materials into activities, assignments and tasks for pupils – *time is of the essence* when planning. This is the first point in the Stop and Think above – look out for the others in the text that follows. When a teacher decides to devote seven hours to language learning and 15 minutes to science in a given week, the pupils in that class will learn more language than science. In fact, differences as dramatic as this do occur, with some teachers dedicating twice as much time as others to certain subjects (Boyle and Bragg, 2006; Galton, 2000). Planning done in preparation for the coming academic year is particularly important, because many daily and weekly routines and patterns, such as subject time allocations, are established early. So, *a little planning does go a long way* in terms of what will be taught and what will be learned.

Second, teachers engage in several levels of planning – by the year, term, unit, week and day, and all these levels must be coordinated. Conversely, accomplishing the year's plan requires breaking the work into terms, the terms into units, and the units into weeks and days. For experienced teachers, unit planning seems to be the most important level, followed by weekly and then daily planning. As teachers gain experience in teaching, it seems easier to coordinate these levels of planning and incorporate National Curriculum objectives and standards as well (Morine-Dershimer, 2006).

Third, plans reduce – but do not eliminate – uncertainty in teaching. Planning must allow flexibility. There is some evidence that when teachers 'overplan' – fill every minute and stick to the plan no matter what – their pupils do not learn as much as pupils whose teachers are flexible (Beatriz de Ganzalez *et al.*, 2004; Cowley and Williamson, 1998). So *plans are NOT made to be broken* – but sometimes they need to be 'bent a little'.

The plans of beginning teachers sometimes don't work because they lack knowledge about the pupils or the subject – they can't estimate how long it will take pupils to complete an activity or they stumble when asked for an explanation or a different example (John, 2006; Veenman and Denessen, 2001; Calderhead, 1996).

FOCUS ON PRACTICE

Characteristics of good planners

In order to plan creatively and flexibly, teachers need to:

- have wide-ranging knowledge about pupils, their interests and their abilities;
- have wide-ranging and deep knowledge of the subjects being taught;
- know alternative ways to teach and assess understanding;
- understand how best to work with groups and individuals;
- know the expectations and limitations of the school and community;
- to know how to apply and adapt materials and texts; and
- be able to pull all this knowledge together into meaningful activities.

In planning, *you can do it yourself* – but collaboration is better. Working with other teachers and sharing ideas is one of the best experiences in teaching. Some educators think that a collaborative approach to planning used in Japan called *kenshu* or 'mastery through study' is one reason why Japanese pupils do so well on international tests (PISA, 2003). A basic part of the *kenshu* process involves a small group of teachers developing a lesson, then videotaping one of the group members teaching the lesson. Next, all members review the tape, analyse pupils' responses, and improve the lesson further. Other teachers try the revised lesson and more improvements follow. At the end of the school year, all the study groups may publish the results of their work. To learn about this approach, search the internet using the keywords 'lesson study'. While you are out there in cyberspace, explore some of the lesson plans available using the keywords 'lesson plans', or search by subject or age group – for example, 'maths lesson plans'.

Connect and Extend

For an explanation of lesson study, see the Companion Website (Web Link 13.1). You can also search the internet using the keywords 'lesson study'.

 WEB

In planning, you can go it alone, but collaboration is better. Sharing ideas with colleagues can be one of the best experiences in teaching

But even great lesson plans taken from a terrific website have to be adapted to a particular context. Some of the adaptation comes before teaching and some comes after. In fact, much of what experienced teachers know about planning comes from looking back – reflecting – on what worked and what didn't, and therefore growing professionally in the process. Collaborative reflection and revising lessons are major components of the lesson study approach to planning.

Finally, there is no one model for effective planning. *One size does NOT fit all* in planning. Planning is a creative problem-solving process for experienced teachers. These teachers know how to accomplish many lessons and how to teach parts of lessons effectively. They know what to expect and how to proceed, so they don't necessarily continue to follow the detailed lesson-planning models they learned during their initial teacher-training programmes. Planning is more informal – 'in their heads'. However, the connection has been explored between the effectiveness of many experienced teachers planning and the detailed system for planning they learned during their training programmes (John, 2006).

No matter how teachers plan, they must have learning objectives in mind. In the next section, we consider the range of objectives that teachers might have for their pupils.

Objectives for learning

We hear much today about aims, purposes, visions, goals, outcomes and standards. At a very general, abstract level are the great, grand goals society may have for the education system such as the two principal aims to the National Curriculum introduced into England, Wales and Northern Ireland in 1988:

- **Aim 1:** The school curriculum should aim to provide opportunities for all pupils to learn and to achieve.

- **Aim 2:** The school curriculum should aim to promote pupils' spiritual, moral, social and cultural development and prepare all pupils for the opportunities, responsibilities and experiences of life.

In Scotland, *A Curriculum for Excellence* was published in November 2004, which provides explicit statements of the aims of education in Scotland. In summary, the purposes of education are to enable all young people to become:

- successful learners
- confident individuals
- responsible citizens
- effective contributors.

However, very general goals are meaningless as potential guidelines for teaching so we need curriculum subject documents to provide general learning statements linked to age groups. For example, in the Renewed Framework (2006) for the teaching of mathematics for pupils in England, we find that pupils aged 11 and 12 years are expected to 'Consolidate and extend mental methods of calculation to include decimals, fractions and percentages'. More detailed statements (from the same document) of what pupils will learn or will be taught such as 'Use bracket keys and the memory of a calculator to carry out calculations with more than one step; use the square root key' (DfES, 2006), are close to being learning objectives.

Objectives are the performances pupils are expected to demonstrate after teaching, to show that they have learned what was expected of them. Objectives written by people with behavioural views focus on observable and measurable

---

Lesson study

As a group, teachers develop, test, improve and re-test lessons until they are satisfied with the final version.

Learning objectives

Clear statements of what pupils are intended to learn.

Connect and Extend

To read about the Renewed Framework for literacy and mathematics and the Primary National Strategy, and explore the online planning tools see the Companion Website (Web Link 13.2).

changes in the learner. Behavioural objectives use terms such as *list, define, add* or *calculate.* Cognitive objectives, on the other hand, emphasise thinking and comprehension, so they are more likely to include words such as *understand, recognise, create* or *apply.* Let's look at one well-developed method of writing specific objectives.

STOP AND THINK

Do you think behavioural objectives are really objectives in themselves, or are they a 'means to an end'?

Mager: start with the specific

Robert Mager – educational psychologist – developed a very influential system for writing instructional objectives (Mager, 1975). His idea is that objectives ought to describe what pupils will be doing when demonstrating their achievement and how teachers will know they are doing it, so these are generally regarded as behavioural objectives. According to Mager, a good objective has three parts. First, it describes the intended *pupil behaviour.* What must the pupil do? Second, it lists the *conditions* under which the behaviour will occur: how will this behaviour be recognised or tested? Third, it gives the *criteria* for acceptable performance on the test. For example, an objective in social studies might be: 'Given a recent article from the local newspaper [conditions], the pupil will mark each statement with an F for fact or an O for opinion ([observable pupil behaviour], with 75% of the statement correctly marked [criteria].' With this emphasis on final behaviour, Mager's system requires a very explicit statement. Mager contends that often pupils can teach themselves if they are given well-stated objectives.

> **Behavioural objectives**
>
> Learning objectives stated in terms of observable behaviours.

Gronlund: start with the general

Norman Gronlund – an expert in the assessment of pupil achievement – offers a different approach (2004), which is often used for writing cognitive objectives. He believes that an objective should be stated first in general terms (*understand, solve, appreciate,* etc.). Then the teacher should clarify by listing a few sample behaviours that would provide evidence that the pupil has attained the objective. Look at the example in Table 13.1. The goal here really is presenting and defending a research project. A teacher could never list all the behaviours that might be involved in 'presenting and defending', but stating an initial, general objective along with specific examples makes the purpose clear.

> **Cognitive objectives**
>
> Learning objectives stated in terms of higher-level thinking operations.

Flexible and creative plans – using taxonomies

STOP AND THINK

Think about some recent assignments you have completed. What kind of thinking is involved in doing the assignments?

- Remembering facts and terms?
- Understanding key ideas?
- Applying information to solve problems?
- Analysing a situation, task or problem?
- Making evaluations or giving opinions?
- Creating or designing something new?

What kind of thinking is involved in answering this Stop and Think question?

Table 13.1 Gronlund's combined method for creating objectives

General objective
Presents and defends the research project before a group.

Specific examples
1. Describes the project in a well-organised manner.
2. Summarises the findings and their implications.
3. Uses display materials to clarify ideas and relationships.
4. Answers group members' questions directly and completely.
5. Presents a report that reflects careful planning.
6. Displays sound reasoning ability through presentation and answers to questions.

Source: Gronlund Norman, *How to Write and Use Instructional Objectives* (6th ed.), © 2000 pp. 74–75. Reprinted by permission of Pearson Education, Inc., Upper Saddle River, NJ.

Taxonomy

Classification system.

Fifty years ago, a group of experts in educational evaluation led by Benjamin Bloom set out to improve college and university examinations. The impact of their work has touched education at all levels around the world (Turcsányi-Szabó *et al.*, 2007; Lam and McNaught, 2006; Bennet, 2001). Bloom and his colleagues developed a taxonomy, or classification system, of educational objectives. Objectives were divided into three domains: cognitive, affective and psychomotor. A handbook describing the objectives in each area was eventually published. In real life, of course, behaviours from these three domains occur simultaneously. While pupils are writing (psychomotor), they are also remembering or reasoning (cognitive), and they are likely to have some emotional response to the task as well (affective).

STOP AND THINK

Taxonomies influence every aspect of instruction from textbook design to lesson planning. As you read the next section, stop at the end of each section and try to list from memory the major objectives of each of the taxonomies, and describe the focus of each objective. Then go back and check out your lists.

The cognitive domain

Cognitive domain

In Bloom's taxonomy, memory and reasoning objectives.

Six basic objectives are listed in Bloom's taxonomy of the thinking or cognitive domain (Bloom *et al.*, 1956):

1. *Knowledge:* Remembering or recognising something without necessarily understanding, using or changing it.
2. *Comprehension:* Understanding the material being communicated without necessarily relating it to anything else.
3. *Application:* Using a general concept to solve a particular problem.
4. *Analysis:* Breaking something down into its parts.

5. *Synthesis:* Creating something new by combining different ideas.
6. *Evaluation:* Judging the value of materials or methods as they might be applied in a particular situation.

It is common in education to consider these objectives as a hierarchy, each skill building on those below, but this is not always accurate. Some subjects, such as mathematics, do not fit this structure very well (Kreitzer and Madaus, 1994). Still, you will hear many references to *lower-level* and *higher-level objectives*, with knowledge, comprehension and application considered lower-level, and the other categories considered higher-level. As a rough way of thinking about objectives, this can be helpful (Gronlund, 2004). The taxonomy of objectives can also be helpful in planning assessments because different procedures are appropriate for objectives at the various levels, as you will see in Chapter 15 (p. 663).

Bloom's taxonomy

Bloom's taxonomy has guided educators for over 50 years and is considered by some to be one of the most significant educational writings of the 20th century (Paul, 1985). In 2001, a group of educational researchers published the first major revision of the taxonomy (Anderson and Krathwohl, 2001). The new version retains the six basic levels in a slightly different order, but the names of three levels have been changed to indicate the cognitive processes involved. The six cognitive processes are remembering (knowledge), understanding (comprehension), applying, analysing, evaluating and creating (synthesising). In addition, the revisers have added a new dimension to the taxonomy to recognise that cognitive processes must process something – you have to remember or understand or apply some form of knowledge. If you look at Table 13.2, you will see the result. We now have six processes – the cognitive acts of remembering, understanding, applying, analysing, evaluating and creating. These processes act on four kinds of knowledge = factual, conceptual, procedural and metacognitive.

> **Connect and Extend**
>
> For an in depth look at how taxonomies can help us understand how we acquire our most basic concepts read Ghiselin, M. T. (1998), 'Etiological classification and the acquisition and structure of knowledge', *Behavioral and Brain Sciences, 21*(1), pp. 72–73.

Table 13.2 A revised taxonomy in the cognitive domain

The knowledge dimension	The cognitive process dimension					
	1. Remember	2. Understand	3. Apply	4. Analyse	5. Evaluate	6. Create
A. Factual knowledge						
B. Conceptual knowledge						
C. Procedural knowledge						
D. Metacognitive knowledge						

Source: From *A Taxonomy for Learning, Teaching, and Assessing* by Lorin W. Anderson and David R. Krathwohl. Published by Allyn and Bacon, Boston, MA. Copyright © 2001 by Pearson Education.

Consider how this revised taxonomy might suggest objectives for history lessons. An objective that targets *analysing conceptual knowledge* is:

After reading an historical account of the Battle of the Boyne, pupils will be able to recognise the author's point of view or bias.

An objective (in the same historical context) for evaluating metacognitive knowledge might be:

Pupils will reflect on their strategies for identifying the biases of the author.

The affective domain

Affective domain

Objectives focusing on attitudes and feelings.

The objectives in the taxonomy of the affective domain or domain of emotional response, have not yet been revised from the original version. These objectives run from least to most committed (Krathwohl, Bloom and Masia, 1964). At the lowest level, a pupil would simply pay attention to a certain idea. At the highest level, the pupil would adopt an idea or a value and act consistently with that idea. There are five basic objectives in the affective domain:

1. *Receiving:* Being aware of or attending to something in the environment. This is the 'I'll-listen-to-the-concert-but-I-won't-promise-to-like-it' level.
2. *Responding:* Showing some new behaviour as a result of experience. At this level, a person might applaud after the concert or hum some of the music the next day.
3. *Valuing:* Showing some definite involvement or commitment. At this point, a person might choose to go to a concert instead of a film.
4. *Organisation:* Integrating a new value into one's general set of values, giving it some ranking among one's general priorities. This is the level at which a person would begin to make long-range commitments to concert attendance.
5. *Characterisation by value:* Acting consistently with the new value. At this highest level, a person would be firmly committed to a love of music and demonstrate it openly and consistently.

Like the basic objectives in the cognitive domain, these five objectives are very general. To write specific learning objectives, you must state what pupils will actually be doing when they are receiving, responding, valuing, and so on. For example, an objective for a food sciences unit of lessons at the valuing level (showing involvement or commitment) might be stated:

After completing the unit on food contents and labeling, pupils will decide to join a junk-food boycott by giving up sweets.

The psychomotor domain

Psychomotor domain

Physical ability and coordination objectives.

Until recently, the psychomotor domain, or realm of physical ability objectives, has been mostly overlooked by teachers not directly involved with physical education. There are several taxonomies in this domain (e.g. Harrow, 1972; Simpson, 1972) that generally move from basic perceptions and reflex actions to skilled, creative movements. James Cangelosi (1990) provides a useful way to think about objectives in the psychomotor domain as either (1) voluntary muscle capabilities that require endurance, strength, flexibility, agility or speed, or (2) the ability to perform a specific skill.

Objectives in the psychomotor domain should be of interest to a wide range of educators including those in fine arts, vocational-technical education and special education. Many other subjects, such as chemistry, physics and biology also require specialised movements and well-developed hand–eye coordination. Using lab equipment, the computer mouse or art materials means learning new physical skills. Here are two psychomotor objectives:

Four minutes after completing a 1500 kilometre run in eight minutes or under, your heart rate will be below 120 beats per minute.

Use a computer mouse effectively to 'drag and drop' files.

Whatever the scope of the learning objectives for pupils, Terry TenBrink (2006: 57) suggests these criteria to judge how well the learning objectives are framed. Objectives should be:

1. Pupil-oriented (emphasis on what the pupil is expected to do).
2. Descriptive of an appropriate learning *outcome* (both developmentally appropriate and appropriately sequenced, with more complex objectives following prerequisite objectives).
3. Clear and understandable (not too general or too specific).
4. Observable (avoid outcomes you can't see such as 'appreciating' or 'realising').

The Focus on Practice below should help you understand how teachers use objectives for lesson and assignment planning.

Connect and Extend

Read Taneja, V. *et al.* (2002), 'Not by bread alone: impact of a structured 90-minute play session on development of children in an orphanage', *Child: Care Health and Development*, *28*(1), pp. 95–100. What learning objectives are set?

FOCUS ON PRACTICE

Using learning objectives

Avoid hyperbole – phrases that sound noble and important, but say very little, such as 'Pupils will become deep thinkers.'

Examples
1. Keep the focus on specific changes that will take place in the pupils' knowledge or skills.
2. Ask pupils to explain the meaning of the objectives. If they can't give specific examples of what is meant, the objectives are not communicating learning intentions to the pupils.

Suit the activities to the objectives

Examples
1. If the goal is to memorise vocabulary, give the pupils memory aids and practice exercises.
2. If the goal is the ability to develop well-thought-out positions, consider position papers, debates, projects or mock trials.
3. If pupils are to become better writers, give many opportunities for writing and rewriting.

Make sure tests are related to your objectives

Examples
1. Write objectives and rough drafts for tests at the same time – revise these drafts of tests as the units unfold and objectives change.
2. Weight the tests according to the importance of the various objectives and the time spent on each.

For additional ideas, see http://alto.aber.ac.uk/caa/helpsheets/learning-objectives.pdf or websites at www.pearsoned.co.uk/woolfolkeuro.

Another view: planning from a constructivist perspective

STOP AND THINK

Think about recent assignments you have completed. Well-constructed assignments can help you to 'piece together' some big ideas from the area of study. What are the big ideas that run through your recent assignments? What other ways could you learn about those big ideas besides preparing for and doing the assignments?

Constructivist approach

View that emphasises the active role of the learner in building understanding and making sense of information.

Traditionally, it has been the teacher's responsibility to do most of the detailed planning for teaching, but new ways of planning are developing. In constructivist approaches, planning is shared and negotiated. The teacher and pupils together make decisions about content, activities and approaches. Rather than having specific pupil behaviours and skills as objectives, the teacher has over-arching goals – 'big ideas' – that guide planning. These goals are understandings or abilities that the teacher returns to again and again.

An example of constructivist planning

Vito Perrone – a leading teacher educator – has these goals for his secondary history pupils (1994). He wants his pupils to be able to:

- use primary sources, formulate hypotheses and engage in systematic study;
- handle multiple points of view;
- be close readers and active writers; and
- pose and solve problems.

The next step in the planning process is to create a learning environment that allows pupils to move towards these goals in ways that respect their individual interests and abilities. Perrone suggests identifying 'those ideas, themes, and issues that provide the depth and variety of perspective that help pupils develop significant understandings' (1994: 12). For a secondary history course, a theme might be 'democracy and revolution', 'fairness', or 'slavery'. In maths or music at any age group, a theme might be 'patterns'; or in literature, 'personal identity' might be the theme. Perrone

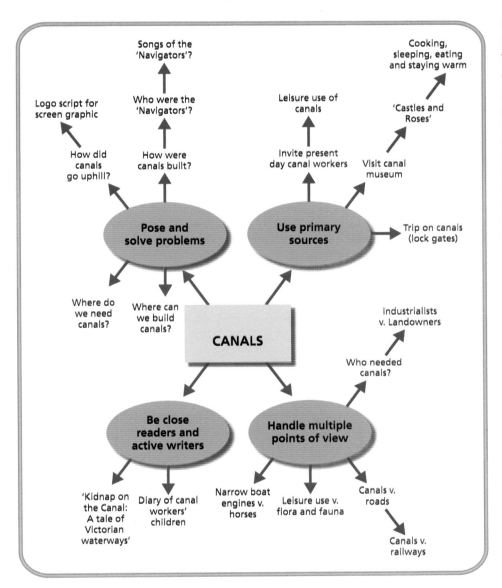

**Figure 13.1
Planning with a
topic map**

With this map of the topic 'Canals' teachers can identify themes, issues and areas for study based on the big ideas of pose and solve problems, use primary sources, be close readers and active writers, and handle multiple points of view.

suggests mapping the topic as a way of thinking about how the theme can generate learning and understanding. An example of a topic map, using the theme of 'Canals', is shown in Figure 13.1. You may remember reading about mindmaps in Chapter 8 (p. 343 and p. 379) and might like to revisit the ideas of mindmaps to compare them with the topic map.

With this topic map as a guide, teacher and pupils can work together to identify activities, materials, projects and performances that will support the development of the pupils' understanding and abilities – the overarching goals of the class. The teacher spends less time planning specific presentations and assignments and more time gathering a variety of resources and facilitating pupils' learning. The focus is not so much on pupils' products as on the processes of learning through enquiry and the thinking behind the products.

> ### STOP AND THINK
>
> Contrast the uses and outcomes of using mindmaps and topic maps for planning and for assessment.

Integrated and thematic plans

The planning or topic map in Figure 13.1 shows a way to use the theme of canals to integrate issues in a unit of lessons based on the big ideas the teacher has for the learning objectives of the unit. Teaching through themes and integrated content are increasingly major elements in planning and designing lessons and units. For example, pupils aged 11–14 in England will follow integrated courses in 'Crime', 'Human Rights', 'Britain – a diverse society', 'Leisure and sport in the local community', 'Why is it so difficult to keep the peace in the world today?' and 'How do we deal with conflict?' The units integrate and explore ideas taken from a variety of subject disciplines under the general area of Citizenship education.

> ### STOP AND THINK
>
> Thematic learning units that integrate two or more content areas have become more common in modern classrooms. What might be some of the challenges in working in this way and how might planning in integrated units help engage learners (Chapter 11) and encourage complex cognitive processes of learning (Chapter 8)?

In the system of primary schooling found in the UK (where pupils spend much of the week with one teacher providing most of the taught curriculum) there are many more opportunities to plan in integrated ways than in secondary school settings. In primary classrooms, there is no reason to work on spelling skills, then listening skills, then writing skills, and then humanities or science. All these abilities can be developed together if pupils work to solve authentic problems. Some example topics for integrating themes with younger children are 'people', 'friendship', 'communications', 'habitats', 'communities' and 'patterns'. Some possibilities for older children are given in Table 13.3.

Let's assume you have an idea of *what* you want pupils to understand, but *how* do you teach to encourage understanding? You still need to decide what's happening on Monday. You still need to design teaching that is appropriate for the objectives.

Teaching

How would you go about identifying the keys to successful teaching? (The In the Classroom feature in Chapter 1 highlights how even relatively inexperienced teachers are sometimes asked to identify successful teaching amongst their colleagues). You might ask pupils, head teachers or school inspectors, university teacher-trainers or experienced teachers to list the characteristics of successful teachers. You might observe

Table 13.3 Some themes for integrated planning for older children

Courage	Time and space
Mystery	Groups and institutions
Survival	Work
Human interaction	Motion
Communities of the future	Cause and effect
Communication/language	Probability and prediction
Human rights and responsibilities	Change and conservation
Identity/coming of age	Diversity and variation
Interdependence	Autobiography

Source: Adapted from *Toward a Coherent Curriculum* by J. A. Beane (ed.), 1995, Alexandria, VA: Association for Supervision and Curriculum Development; *Interdisciplinary High School Teaching* by J. H. Clarke and R. M. Agne, 1997, Boston: Allyn and Bacon; and *Teaching through Themes* by G. Thompson, 1991, New York: Scholastic.

classrooms, rate different teachers on certain characteristics, and then see which characteristics were associated with teachers whose pupils either achieved the most or were the most motivated to learn. (To do this, of course, you would have to decide how to assess achievement and motivation.) You could identify teachers whose pupils, year after year, learned more than pupils working with other teachers; then you could watch the more successful teachers and note what they do. You might also train teachers to apply several different strategies to teach the same lesson and then determine which strategy led to the greatest pupil learning. You could videotape teachers, then ask them to view the tapes and report what they were thinking about as they taught and what influenced their decisions while teaching. You might study transcripts of classroom dialogue to learn what helped pupils understand.

Effective teachers know how to transform their knowledge into examples, explanations, illustrations and activities

STOP AND THINK

Whole-class teaching is often thought of as the 'traditional' approach to teaching. In what situations is this teaching format most effective? What are the basic steps involved in carrying out this form of teaching?

All these approaches and more have been used to investigate teaching (Cohen, Mannion and Morrison, 2007). Often, and over the past 30 years, researchers have used the relationships identified between teaching and learning as the basis for developing teaching approaches and testing these approaches in design experiments (Brown, 1992; DfEE, 2000; Mortimer *et al.*, 1988; Galton and Simon, 1980; Rutter *et al.*, 1979; Bennett, 1976). Let's examine some of the specific knowledge about teaching gained from these projects.

Characteristics of effective teachers

STOP AND THINK

Think about the most effective teacher you ever had – the one that you learned the most from. What were the characteristics of that person? What made that teacher so effective?

Some of this early research on effective teaching focused on the personal qualities of the teachers themselves. Results revealed some lessons about three teacher characteristics: knowledge, clarity and warmth.

Teachers' knowledge

Do teachers who know more about their subject have a more positive impact on their pupils? It depends on the subject. Secondary school pupils appear to learn more mathematics from teachers with degrees or significant coursework in mathematics (Wayne and Youngs, 2003). When we look at teachers' knowledge of facts and concepts in other subjects, as measured by A-level grades (exams taken at the age of 18 in England and Wales) and university degree classifications, the relationship to pupil learning is unclear and may be indirect. Teachers who know more facts about their subject do not necessarily have pupils who learn more. But teachers who know more may make clearer presentations and recognise pupil difficulties more readily. They are ready for any pupil questions and do not have to be evasive or vague in their answers. Indeed, we know from Linda Darling-Hammond's (2000) work that the quality of teachers – as measured by whether the teachers were fully qualified and that their degree or a major part of their degree was in their teaching field – is related to pupil performance. Thus, knowledge is necessary (but not sufficient) for effective teaching because being more knowledgeable helps teachers be clearer and more organised.

Clarity and organisation

Teachers who provide clear presentations and explanations tend to have pupils who learn more (Roager *et al.*, 2007; Rodrigues, 2001), are less anxious about assessments

(Myhill, 2003) and who rate their teachers more positively (Holfve-Sabel, 2006). Teachers with more knowledge of the subject tend to be less vague in their explanations to the class. The less vague the teacher, the more the pupils learn (Norwich, 1999). See the Focus on Practice below for ideas about how teachers can be clear and organised in their teaching.

FOCUS ON PRACTICE

Teaching effectively

Organise your lessons carefully

Examples
1. Provide objectives that help pupils focus on the purpose of the lesson.
2. Begin lessons by writing a brief outline on the board, or work on an outline with the class as part of the lesson.
3. If possible, break the presentation into clear steps or stages.
4. Review periodically.

Anticipate and plan for difficult parts in the lesson

Examples
1. Do the exercises beforehand and anticipate pupil problems.
2. Have definitions ready for new terms, and prepare several relevant examples for concepts.
3. Think of analogies that will make ideas easier to understand.
4. Organise the lesson in a logical sequence; include checkpoints that incorporate oral or written questions or problems to make sure the pupils are following the explanations.

Strive for clear explanations

Examples
1. Avoid vague words and ambiguous phrases: Steer clear of *the somes* – 'something', 'someone', 'sometime', 'somehow'; *the not verys* – 'not very much', 'not very well', 'not very hard', 'not very often'; and other unspecific fillers, such as 'sort of', 'and so on', 'as you know', 'I guess', 'in fact', 'or whatever', and 'more or less'.
2. Use specific (and, if possible, colourful) names instead of 'it', 'them' and 'thing'.
3. Refrain from using pet phrases such as 'You know', 'like' and 'Okay?' Another idea is to record a lesson on tape to check yourself for clarity.
4. Give explanations at several levels so all pupils will understand.
5. Focus on one idea at a time and avoid digressions.

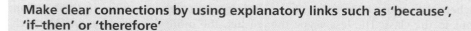

Make clear connections by using explanatory links such as 'because', 'if–then' or 'therefore'

Examples

1. 'The North had an advantage in the Civil War because its economy was based on manufacturing.'
2. Explanatory links are also helpful in labelling visual material such as graphs, concept maps or illustrations.

Signal transitions from one major topic to another with phrases

Examples

1. 'The next area', 'Now we will turn to' or 'The second step is'.
2. Outline topics, listing key points or drawing concept maps on the board.

Communicate an enthusiasm for your subject and the day's lesson

Examples

1. Tell pupils why the lesson is important. Have a better reason than 'This will be on the test' or 'You will need to know it next year'. Emphasise the value of the learning itself.
2. Be sure to make eye contact with the pupils.
3. Demonstrate ideas and connections using gestures.
4. Vary pace, pitch and volume in speaking. Use silence for emphasis.

Warmth and enthusiasm

As you are well aware, some teachers are much more enthusiastic than others. Some studies have found that ratings of teachers' enthusiasm for their subject are correlated with pupil achievement gains (Fischman *et al.*, 2006; Condie and Simpson, 2004; Moyles, 2001). Warmth, friendliness and understanding seem to be the teacher traits most strongly related to pupil attitudes (Klein, 2004; Hufton *et al.*, 2002; Murray, 1983). In other words, teachers who are warm and friendly tend to have pupils who like them and the class in general. But notice, these are descriptive or correlational studies. The results do not tell us that teacher enthusiasm causes pupil learning or that warmth causes positive attitudes, only that the two variables tend to occur together. Teachers trained to demonstrate their enthusiasm have pupils who are more attentive. The Focus on Practice above includes some ideas for communicating warmth and enthusiasm.

Beyond these general characteristics, how can teachers plan teaching? The following sections describe formats or strategies – building blocks that can be used to construct lessons and units. We begin with the strategy many people associate most directly with teaching: explanation and presentation.

Connect and Extend

Read Debra Myhill (2006), 'Talk, talk, talk: teaching and learning in whole-class discourse', *Research Papers in Education*, 21(1), pp. 19–41.

Explanation and presentation

Some studies have found that teachers' presentations take up about 20% of all classroom time and that there is more whole-class teaching when the teacher is using an interactive whiteboard (Smith *et al.*, 2006). Teacher explanation is appropriate for communicating a large amount of material to many pupils in a short period of time, introducing a new topic, giving background information or motivating pupils to learn more on their own. Teacher presentations are therefore most appropriate for cognitive and affective objectives at the lower levels of the taxonomies described earlier: for remembering, understanding, receiving, responding and valuing (Myhill, 2006; Smith *et al.*, 2004; Arends, 2001).

Whole-class teaching

In the 1980s and 1990s, there was a good deal of research in the UK and other European countries that focused on effective teaching. The results of all this work identified a model of whole-class teaching – whole-class interactive teaching – which was related to improved pupil learning.

The whole-class interactive teaching model fits a specific set of circumstances because it was derived from a particular approach to research. Researchers identified the elements of whole-class interactive teaching by comparing teachers whose pupils learned more than expected based on base-line assessments (assessments of pupils' achievement before teaching – e.g. at the start of formal schooling) with teachers whose pupils performed at an expected or average level (Tymms, 1999). The researchers focused on existing practices in European classrooms (Reynolds and Muus, 1999). There was a particular focus on teaching methods that would engage the full ability range within the classroom, minimise differences in attainment and attempt to ensure that no child was 'left behind'. There was particular interest in contexts where there was minimum emphasis on resources for teaching and learning, other than the teacher (Calder, 2000; Szalontai, 2000).

Effective teaching was usually defined as that which could be seen to correlate with average improvement in standardised test scores for a whole class or school. So the results hold for large groups, but not necessarily for every pupil in the group. Even when the average achievement of a group improves, the achievement of some individuals may decline (Good, 1996; Shuell, 1996). For this and other reasons the research supporting the official endorsement of whole-class interactive teaching as one main methodology for delivering higher standards in schools is questioned (Brown *et al.*, 1998).

Official endorsement of 'interactive whole-class teaching' was based on a belief that interactive whole-class teaching was as an 'active teaching' model which would promote high quality dialogue and discussion between teachers and pupils. Pupils were expected to play an active part in discussion by asking questions, contributing ideas and explaining and demonstrating their thinking to the class.

Research findings (Smith *et al.*, 2004) suggest that at best traditional patterns of whole-class interaction have not been dramatically transformed by the adoption of whole-class interactive teaching as the best-practice model for whole-class explanation and presentation. Where some change has been observed, the adoption of whole-class interactive teaching 'encourages teachers to use more directive forms of teaching with little opportunities for pupils to explore and elaborate on their ideas' (Hardman, 2003).

Given these findings, you can see that whole-class teaching seems to apply best to the teaching of basic skills – clearly structured knowledge and essential skills, such as science facts, mathematics computations, reading vocabulary and grammar rules (Kjellin and Granlund, 2006). These skills involve tasks that are relatively unambiguous; they can be taught step-by-step and tested by standardised tests. The teaching approaches described below are not necessarily appropriate for objectives such as helping pupils to write creatively, solve complex problems or mature emotionally. However, in some contexts researchers have described successful uses of interactive

Whole-class teaching

Teaching characterised by high levels of teacher explanation, demonstration and interaction with all the pupils at the same time.

Basic skills

Clearly structured knowledge that is needed for later learning and that can be taught step by step.

whole-class teaching to make whole-group teaching 'more motivating and able to keep the attention of the students in relatively higher levels throughout the lecture. Furthermore, students felt that they had made important gains in transferable problem solving skills' (Gülpinar and Yegen, 2005: 590).

Franz Weinert and Andreas Helmke describe effective whole-class teaching as having the following features:

> *(a) the teacher's classroom management is especially effective and the rate of pupil interruptive behaviours is very low; (b) the teacher maintains a strong academic focus and uses available teaching time intensively to initiate and facilitate pupils' learning activities; (c) the teacher ensures that as many pupils as possible achieve good learning progress by carefully choosing appropriate tasks, clearly presenting subject-matter information and solution strategies, continuously diagnosing each pupil's learning progress and learning difficulties, and providing effective help through remedial instruction (1995: 138).*

How would a teacher turn these themes into actions? We can turn to the following Focus on Practice for a comprehensive list of strategies revealing the essence of whole-class interactive teaching as recommended by 'The Mathematics Enhancement Project' (MEP) developed for the Centre for Innovation in Mathematics Teaching (CIMT) at the University of Exeter, UK.

These strategies are not steps to be followed in a particular order, but all of them are elements of effective whole-class teaching. For example, feedback, review or reteaching should occur whenever necessary and should match the abilities of the pupils. Also, keep in mind the age and prior knowledge of pupils. The younger or the less

FOCUS ON PRACTICE

Strategies for interactive whole-class teaching in mathematics

1. Prepare everything before the lesson
2. Begin by reviewing homework
3. Warm up with mental arithmetic
4. Tell pupils the aim of the lesson
5. Give clear, precise instructions
6. Work through examples on the board interactively
7. Encourage as many pupils as possible to work at the board
8. Vary the mathematical precision in oral and written work
10. Correct mistakes and misconceptions as they arise
11. Monitor the progress of every pupil
12. Vary the pace and activities
13. Use enthusiasm and humour
14. Praise pupils
15. Summarise the lesson
16. Set homework clearly (should be linked to the next lesson)

Source: Based on Burghes, D. (2000), *Mathematics Enhancement Programme (MEP), The First Three Years,* CIMT, University of Exeter.

prepared the pupils, the briefer the explanations should be. Teachers following these strategies use more and shorter cycles of presentation, guided practice, feedback and correction. The Focus on Practice on pp. 587–588 gives you further ideas for applying the best of whole-class teaching.

Why does whole-class teaching work?

What aspects of whole-class teaching might explain its success? Linda Anderson from the English Literature Department at the Open University, UK suggests that lessons that help pupils perceive links among main ideas will help them construct accurate understandings (1989). Well-organised presentations, clear explanations, the use of explanatory links, and reviews as described in the Focus on Practice on pp. 587–588 can all help pupils perceive connections among ideas. If done well, therefore, a whole-class teaching lesson could be a resource that pupils use to construct understanding. For example, reviews activate prior knowledge, so the pupil is ready to understand. Brief, clear presentations and guided practice avoid overloading the pupils' information processing systems and taxing their working memories. Numerous examples and explanations give many pathways and associations for building networks of concepts. *Work through examples on the board interactively* can also give the teacher a snapshot of the pupils' thinking as well as their misconceptions, so these can be addressed directly as misconceptions rather than simply as 'wrong answers'.

Every subject, not just mathematics or language learning, can require some direct instruction. Noddings (1990) reminds teachers that pupils may need some direct instruction in how to use various manipulative materials to get the possible benefits from them. Pupils working in cooperative groups may need guidance, modelling and practice in how to ask questions and give explanations. For example, to solve difficult problems, pupils may need some regular direct instruction in possible problem-solving strategies.

Evaluating whole-class teaching

Whole-class teaching, particularly when it involves extended teacher presentations or lectures, has some disadvantages. Some pupils have trouble listening for more than a few minutes at a time and they simply shut teachers out. Teacher presentations can put the pupils in a passive position by doing much of the cognitive work for them and may prevent pupils from asking or even thinking of questions (Freiberg and Driscoll, 2005).

Scripted cooperation is one way of incorporating active learning into whole-class teaching. Several times during the presentation, the teacher asks pupils to work in pairs. For example, one person is the summariser of a section of the presentation that has just been delivered and the partner critiques the summary. This gives pupils a chance to check their understanding, organise their thinking and translate ideas into their own words. Other possibilities are described in Table 13.4.

Critics also claim that whole-class teaching is based on the *wrong* theory of learning. In this 'wrong theory', teachers break material into small segments, present each segment separately, and reinforce or correct, thus *transmitting* understandings from teacher to pupil. The pupil is seen as an 'empty vessel' waiting to be filled with knowledge, rather than an active constructor of knowledge (Berg and Clough, 1991; Driscoll, 2005). These criticisms of an over reliance on whole-class teaching echo the criticisms of behavioural learning theories.

However, there is further ample evidence, that whole-class teaching and explanation can help pupils learn actively, not passively (Jones and Tanner, 2002; Whitburn, 2001). For younger and less prepared learners, pupil-controlled learning without teacher direction and instruction can lead to systematic deficits in the

Scripted cooperation

Learning strategy in which two pupils take turns summarising material and criticising the summaries.

Connect and Extend

Review your understanding of pupils as 'empty vessels' by reviewing the section 'Pupils understanding of how they are learning' in Chapter 8 (p. 374) and by reading Hans van der Meij (2003), 'Minimalism revisited', *Document Design*, 4(3), pp. 212–233.

Table 13.4   Active learning and teacher presentations

Here are some ideas for keeping pupils cognitively engaged in lessons. They can be adapted for many ages.

Question, all write: Pose a question, ask everyone to jot an answer, then ask, 'How many pupils would be willing to share their thoughts?'

Outcome sentences: After a segment of presentation, ask pupils to finish a sentence such as 'I learned . . ., I'm beginning to wonder . . . , I was surprised. . . .' Share as above. Pupils may keep their outcome sentences in a learning log or portfolio.

Underexplain with learning pairs: Give a brief explanation, then ask pupils to work in pairs to figure out the process or idea.

Voting: Ask 'How many of you . . .' questions and take a count. 'How many of you agree with Raschon?' 'How many of you are ready to move on?' 'How many of you got 48 on this problem?'

Choral response: Have the whole class restate in unison important facts and ideas, such as 'The environment is one whole system' or 'A ten-sided polygon is called a decagon.'

Speak-write: Tell pupils you will speak for three or four minutes. They are to listen, but not take notes. At the end of the time, ask them to write the main ideas, a summary, or questions they have about what you said.

Source: From Harmin, M. (1994) *Inspiring Active Learning: A Handbook for Teachers.* Alexandria, Virginia: ASCD. Reprinted with permission. The Association for Supervision and Curriculum Development is a worldwide community of educators advocating sound policies and sharing best practices to achieve the success of each learner. To learn more, visit ASCD at www.ascd.org.

pupils' knowledge. Without guidance, the understandings that pupils construct can be incomplete and misleading (Yates, 2005; Weinert and Helmke, 1995).

Individual classwork and homework

> **STOP AND THINK**
>
> Think back to your school days. Do you remember any homework? What sticks in your mind about the homework you were set?

Connect and Extend

Does discovery learning produce more meaningful learning than direct instruction or is this a fundamental misconception? Read Gregory Yates (2005), '"How Obvious": Personal reflections on the database of educational psychology and effective teaching research', *Educational Psychology, 25*(6), pp. 681–700.

There is little research on the effects of independent individual classroom work, but it is clear that this technique is often used. Typically, primary school children will spend about half of their time working by themselves, reading, writing, drawing or using equipment, compared to about a third of their time listening. Older pupils listen less and write more (McPake *et al.*, 1999).

Individual classwork

Individual classwork should follow up whole-class or group teaching and give pupils supervised practice. It should not be the main form of activity. Unfortunately, many textbook pages and worksheets do little to support the learning of important objectives. So, before teachers set work they should ask themselves, 'Does doing this work help pupils learn anything that matters?' Pupils should see the connection between the individual classwork and what they have been taught. The objectives and the purpose should be clear, all the materials that might be needed should be provided, and the work should be matched to the ability of the pupils well enough that pupils can succeed on their own. Success rates should be high – near 100%. When individual classwork is too difficult, pupils often resort to guessing or copying just to finish (Anderson, 1985).

Homework

In contrast to the limited research on the efficacy of individual classwork, educators have been studying the effects of homework for some considerable time (Cooper, 2004; Cooper and Valentine, 2001; Corno, 2000; Trautwein and Koller, 2003). As you can see from the Discussion Point below there continues to be a debate about the value of homework.

To benefit from individual classwork or homework, pupils must stay engaged and do the work. The first step towards engagement is getting pupils started by making sure they understand what is expected of them. It may help to do the first few questions as a class and to clear up any misconceptions. This is especially important for homework because pupils may have no one at home to consult if they have a problem. A second way to keep pupils involved is to hold them accountable for completing the work correctly, not just for 'filling in the gaps'. This means the work should be checked as soon after completion as possible, and pupils given an opportunity to correct errors or improve the work.

Connect and Extend

Try a web search using the term 'overuse of worksheets'. This phrase is often used by school inspectors concerned about unsatisfactory lessons or standards of teaching in a school. Research the inspection reports to find connections between the overuse of worksheets and exercises from textbooks, and unsatisfactory teaching.

Individual classwork

Independent classroom work set to be completed during lessons.

DISCUSSION POINT

Is homework a valuable use of time?

Like so many aspects of education, homework has moved in and out of favour. It was seen as too much pressure on pupils during the more educationally progressive 1960s. By the 1980s and 1990s, homework was 'in' again as a way to improve the standing of children compared to pupils around the world (Cooper and Valentine, 2001). Everyone has done homework – were those hours well spent?

Agree: Yes, well-planned homework can work for many pupils

Harris Cooper and Jeffrey Valentine reviewed many studies of homework. Although they concluded that there is little relationship between homework and learning for young pupils, the relationship between homework and achievement grows progressively stronger for older pupils. There is evidence that amounts of time on homework had a positive association with academic achievement (Holmes and Croll, 1989). Pupils in secondary school who do more homework (and watch less television after school) achieve higher results, even when other factors such as gender, grade level, ethnicity, SES and amount of adult supervision are taken into consideration (Cooper and Valentine, 2001; Cooper et al., 1999). Consistent with these findings, the UK Government's Department for

Education and Science (1998) made these recommendations. The guidelines for primary school pupils are:

- pupils aged 5 and 6 years, 1 hour per week;
- 7–9 years, 1.5 hours per week;
- 10–11 years, 30 minutes a day.

The guidelines for secondary school pupils are:

- 11–12 years, 45 to 90 minutes per day;
- 12–14 years, 1 to 2 hours per day;
- 15–16 years, 1.5 to 2.5 hours per day.

Disagree: No, homework does not help pupils learn

No matter how interesting an activity is, pupils will eventually get bored with it – so why give them work both in and out of school? They will simply grow weary of learning and important opportunities are lost for community involvement or leisure activities that would create well-rounded citizens. When parents help with homework, they can do more harm than good – sometimes confusing their children or teaching them incorrectly. Interview data from families with teenagers described homework as a significant site of parent–teenager tensions (Solomon, Warin and Lewis, 2002; Smith, 2000) and between parents and schools.

Pupils from poorer families often must work, so they miss doing the homework; then the learning discrepancy between the rich and poor grows even greater. Besides, the research is inconsistent about the effects of homework. For example, one study found that in-class work was better than homework in helping primary school pupils learn (Cooper and Valentine, 2001).

WHAT DO YOU THINK?

Agree or Disagree? Vote online at www.pearsoned.co.uk/woolfolkeuro.

Connect and Extend

Joy Faulkner and Carolyn Blyth – educational psychologists – feel the evidence of research suggests that the setting of homework can be a valid component of the learning process. Read their article 'Homework: is it really worth all the bother?', *Educational Studies, 21*(3), pp. 447–454.

Making classwork and homework valuable

Individual classwork requires careful monitoring and being available to help pupils when they need it. To be available, teachers should move around the class and avoid spending too much time with one or two pupils. Short, frequent contacts are best (Brophy and Good, 1986). Sometimes teachers may be working with a small group while other pupils do individual work. In these situations, it is especially important for pupils to know what to do if they need help. Expert teachers establish rules like: 'Ask three, then me.' Pupils have to consult three classmates before seeking help from the teacher. Expert teachers also spend time early in the year showing pupils *how* to help each other – how to ask questions and how to explain (Weinstein and Mignano, 2003).

What about monitoring homework? If pupils get stuck on homework, they need help at home, someone who can scaffold their work without just 'giving the answer' (Pressley, 1995). Yet many parents don't know how to help (Hoover-Dempsey *et al.*, 2001). The Focus on Practice below gives ideas for how teachers can help parents 'help with homework'.

FOCUS ON PRACTICE

Homework

Make sure families know what pupils are expected to learn

Examples

1. At the beginning of a year or term, send home a list of the main learning objectives, examples of major projects, key due dates, a homework 'calendar', and a list of resources available at libraries or on the internet.
2. Provide a clear, concise description of your homework policy; consequences for late, forgotten or missing homework, etc.

Help families find a comfortable and helpful role in their child's homework

Examples

1. Remind families that 'helping with homework' means encouraging, listening, monitoring, praising, discussing, brainstorming – not necessarily teaching and **never** doing the work for their child.
2. Encourage families to set aside a quiet time and place for everyone in the family to study. Make this time a regular part of the daily routine.
3. Have some homework assignments that are fun and involve the whole family – puzzles, family albums, watching a television programme together and doing a 'review'.
4. During parent–teacher consultations, ask families what they need to play a more helpful role in their child's homework. More detailed information? Websites? Explanations of study skills?

Solicit and use suggestions from families about homework

Examples

1. Find out what responsibilities the child has at home – how much time is available for homework.
2. Periodically, have a 'homework hotline' for questions and suggestions.

If no-one is at home to help with homework, set up other support systems

Examples

1. Assign 'study buddies' who can be available over the phone.
2. If pupils have computers, provide lists of internet help lines.
3. Locate free help in public libraries and make these resources known.

> Take advantage of family and community 'funds of knowledge' to connect homework with life in the community and life in the community with lessons in school
>
> *Examples*
> 1. Create a class lesson about how family members use maths and reading in dress making and in housing construction (Epstein and Van Voorhis, 2001).
> 2. Design interactive homework projects that families do together to evaluate products for the home, for example, deciding on the best buy on shampoo or DVDs.
>
> For more ideas, see
> - www.bbc.co.uk/schools/parents/work/secondary/homework/homework_how_much.shtml
> - www.parentscentre.gov.uk/whatchildrenlearn/learningathomeoutsideschool/homework

Questioning and recitation

Studies of whole-class teaching in the UK by Edwards and Westgate (1994) show that classroom discourse across all stages of schooling is dominated by what Tharp and Gallimore (1988) call 'the recitation script'. Teachers pose questions, pupils answer. This form of teaching, sometimes called *recitation*, has been with us for many years. Drawing on UK classrooms, Sinclair and Coulthard (1975) first demonstrated a typical form of recitation. It consists of three phases: an *initiation*, usually in the form of a teacher question (often closed), a *response* (usually brief) in which a pupil attempts to answer the question, and a *follow-up* move, in which the teacher provides some form of feedback (mostly superficial praise) to the pupil's response. This three-part exchange, or IRF structure emphasises recalling information rather than genuine exploration of a topic. These steps are repeated over and over. Such questioning therefore seeks predictable correct answers and only rarely are teachers' questions used to support pupils to a more complete understanding. However, in recent years, a number of studies have highlighted the potential of classroom talk that sounds more like a dialogue between peers. For example, a European study (Alexander, 2000) pinpoints patterns of teacher–pupil interactions which support active pupil participation, particularly amongst Russian and French pupils.

Connect and Extend

Effective questioning skills are among the most valuable skills that a teacher can possess – and among the more difficult to develop. See the Companion Website (Web Link 13.3).

Let us consider the heart of recitation, the initiation or *questioning* phase. Effective questioning techniques may be among the most powerful tools that teachers employ during lessons. An essential element of innovations such as cognitive apprenticeships, peer learning techniques, authentic learning activities, and nearly all other contemporary learning techniques is keeping pupils cognitively engaged – and that is where skilful questioning strategies are especially effective. Questions play several roles in cognition. They can help pupils rehearse information for effective recall. They can work to identify gaps in pupils' knowledge base, and provoke curiosity and long-term interest. They can initiate cognitive conflict and promote the disequilibrium (Ben-Peretz, 2002), provoking the learner to find new insights by 'rocking the cognitive boat' or unsettling the way an individual is currently making sense of the world around them. Pupils as well as teachers should learn to question effectively. This co-author tells his psychology and teacher-training students that the first step in doing a good classroom research project is asking a good question.

For now, we will focus on teachers' questions, to make them as helpful as possible for pupils. Many beginning teachers are surprised to discover how valuable good questions can be and how difficult they are to create.

STOP AND THINK

Think back to your most recent set of lectures. What kinds of questions did your lecturer ask? What sort of thinking was required to answer the questions? Remembering, understanding, applying, analysing, evaluating or creating? How long does the lecturer wait for an answer?

Kinds of questions

Some educators have estimated the typical teacher asks between 30 and 120 questions an hour, or about 1,5000,000 questions over a teaching career (Sadker and Sadker, 2006). What are these questions like? Many can be categorised in terms of Bloom's taxonomy of objectives in the cognitive domain. Table 13.5 offers examples of questions at the different levels. (Also, revisit p. 376.)

Another way to categorise classroom questioning is in terms of convergent questions (only one right answer) or divergent questions (many possible answers). Questions about concrete facts are convergent: 'Who ruled England in 1540?', 'Who wrote the original Peter Pan?' Questions dealing with opinions or hypotheses are divergent: 'In this story, which character is most like you and why?', 'In 100 years, which of the past five Prime Ministers will be most admired?'

Quite a bit of space in education textbooks has been devoted to urging teachers to ask a greater number of higher-level (analysing, evaluating and creating) and divergent questions. Is this really a better way of questioning? Research has provided several surprises.

Connect and Extend

Review the sections on open, closed and structured questions in Chapter 8 and Figure 8.8.

Convergent questions

Questions that have a single correct answer.

Divergent questions

Questions that have no single correct answer.

Fitting the questions to the pupils

Both high- and low-level questions can be effective (Burns and Myhill, 2004; Redfield and Rousseau, 1981). Different patterns seem to be better for different pupils, however. The best pattern for younger pupils and for lower-ability pupils of all ages is simple questions that allow a high percentage of correct answers, ample encouragement, help when the pupil does not have the correct answer and praise. For high-ability pupils, the successful pattern includes harder questions at both higher and lower levels and more critical feedback (Good, 1988).

Whatever their age or ability, all pupils should have some experience with thought-provoking questions and, if necessary, help in learning how to answer them. As we saw in Chapter 8, to master critical thinking and problem-solving skills, pupils must have a chance to practise the skills. They also need time to think about their answers. But research shows that teachers wait an average of only one second for pupils to answer (Rowe, 1974). Consider the following slice of classroom life (Sadker and Sadker, 2006: 130–131):

Teacher: Who wrote the poem 'Stopping by Woods on a Snowy Evening'? Tom?

Tom: Robert Frost.

Teacher: Good. What action takes place in the poem? Sally?

Table 13.5   Classroom questions for objectives in the cognitive domain

Questions can be posed that encourage thinking at every level of Bloom's taxonomy in the cognitive domain. Of course, the thinking required depends on what has gone before in the discussion.

Category	Type of thinking expected	Examples
Knowledge (remembering)	Recalling or recognising information as learned	Define . . . What is the capital of . . . ? What did the text say about . . . ?
Comprehension (understanding)	Demonstrating understanding of the materials; transforming, reorganising or interpreting	Explain in your own words . . . Compare . . . What is the main idea of . . . ? Describe what you saw . . .
Application (applying)	Using information to solve a problem with a single correct answer	Which principle is demonstrated in . . . ? Calculate the area of . . . Apply the rule of . . . to solve . . .
Analysis (analysing)	Critical thinking; identifying reasons and motives; making inferences based on specific data; analysing conclusions to see if supported by evidence	What influenced the writings of . . . ? Why was Stockholm chosen . . . ? Which of the following are facts and which are opinions . . . ? Based on your experiment, what is the chemical . . . ?
Synthesis (creating)	Divergent, original thinking; original plan, proposal, design or story	What's a good name for . . . ? How could we raise money for . . . ? What would Britain be like if Germany had won . . . ?
Evaluation (evaluating)	Judging the merits of ideas, offering opinions, applying standards	Which member of parliament is the most effective? Which painting do you believe to be better? Why? Why would you favour . . . ?

Source: Cooper, James, *Classroom Teaching Skills*, Third Edition. Copyright © 1986 by Houghton Mifflin Company.

Sally: A man stops his sleigh to watch the woods get filled with snow.

Teacher: Yes. Emma, what thoughts go through the man's mind?

Emma: He thinks how beautiful the woods are (She pauses for a second.)

Teacher: What else does he think about? Joe?

Joe: He thinks how he would like to stay and watch. (Pauses for a second.)

Teacher: Yes – and what else? Rita? (Waits half a second.) Come on, Rita, you can get the answer to this. (Waits half a second.) Well, why does he feel he can't stay there indefinitely and watch the woods and the snow? Sarah?

Sarah: Well, I think it might be—. (Pauses a second.)

Teacher: Think, Sarah. (Teacher waits for half a second.) All right then – Mike? (Waits again for half a second.) John? (Waits half a second.) What's the matter with everyone today? Didn't you do the reading?

Very little thoughtful responding can take place in this situation. When teachers learn to pose a question, then wait at least three to five seconds before calling on a pupil to answer, pupils tend to give longer answers; more pupils are likely to participate, ask questions and volunteer appropriate answers; pupil comments involving analysis, synthesis, inference and speculation tend to increase; and the pupils generally appear more confident in their answers (van Zee *et al.*, 2001; Rowe, 1974; Sadker and Sadker, 2006). Unfortunately, the earlier classroom interaction about Robert Frost's poem is far more typical (Myhill and Dunkin, 2005).

This seems like a simple improvement in teaching, but five seconds of silence is not that easy to handle. It takes practice. Pupils could jot down ideas or even discuss the question with another pupil and formulate an answer together. This makes the wait more comfortable and gives pupils a chance to think. Of course, if it is clear that pupils are lost or don't understand the question, waiting longer will not help. When a question is met with blank stares, teachers should rephrase the question or ask if anyone can clarify it. Teachers can also 'park the question' and come back to it later. The most important thing to remember is allowing pupils an adequate length of *wait time* to answer the question seems to lead to better quality of answers (Slavin, 1991).

A word about selecting pupils to answer questions or targeting. If you only select volunteers, then you may get the wrong idea about how well pupils understand the material. Also, the same people volunteer over and over again. Many expert teachers have some systematic way of making sure that they include as many pupils as possible. One possibility is to put each pupil's name on an index card, then shuffle the cards and go through the deck as you call on people. Teachers also use the card to make notes about the quality of pupils' answers or any extra help pupils seem to need. More usually, expert teachers seem to successfully keep a mental note of who they have asked and how successful they were in matching questions to the target pupils.

Targeting

The way teachers select pupils to answer questions and matching the questions to the pupils.

Responding to pupil answers

What do you do after the pupil answers? The most common response, occurring about 50% of the time in most classrooms, is simple acceptance – 'OK' or 'Uh-huh' (Sadker and Sadker, 2006). But there are better reactions, depending on whether the pupil's answer is correct, partially correct or wrong. If the answer is quick, firm and correct, then accept the answer or ask another question. If the answer is correct but hesitant, give the pupil feedback about why the answer is correct: 'That's right, Susan, water at the surface of the pond freezes first because . . .'. This allows you to explain the material again. If this pupil is unsure, others may be confused as well. If the answer is partially or completely wrong but the pupil has made an honest attempt, you should probe for more information, give clues, simplify the question, review the previous steps or reteach the material. If the pupil's wrong answer is silly or careless, however, it is better to correct the answer and go on.

Of course, question-and-answer interactions occur with groups and individuals as well as the whole class and next we look at the importance of organising group discussion to focus on learning intentions, but first it is worth reflecting on Chris Kyriacou's (a teacher trainer who focuses on the psychological aspects of teaching) summary of what we have said in the last section.

Effective handling by a teacher of question-and-answer interactions with pupils is probably one aspect of teaching which most powerfully contributes to establishing a classroom climate in which pupils feel positively about themselves as learners and are motivated to participate actively in the academic tasks which take place (1995: 125).

Group discussion helps pupils learn to express themselves clearly, to justify opinions and to tolerate different views

Group discussion

Group discussion

Conversation in which the teacher does not have the dominant role; pupils pose and answer their own questions.

Group discussion is in some ways similar to the recitation strategy, but it should be more like the instructional conversations described in Chapter 9 (Tharp and Gallimore, 1991). A teacher may pose questions, listen to pupil answers, react and probe for more information, but in a true group dialogue, the teacher does not have a dominant role. Pupils ask questions, answer each other's questions and respond to each other's answers (Beck *et al.*, 1996; Parker and Hess, 2001).

There are many advantages to group discussions. The pupils are directly involved and have the chance to participate. Group discussion helps pupils learn to express themselves clearly, to justify opinions and to tolerate different views. Group discussion also gives pupils a chance to ask for clarification, examine their own thinking, follow personal interests and assume responsibility by taking leadership roles in the group. Thus, group discussions help pupils evaluate ideas and synthesise personal viewpoints. Discussions are also useful when pupils are trying to understand difficult concepts that go against common sense. As we saw in Chapters 8 and 9, many scientific concepts, such as the role of light in vision or Newton's laws of motion, are difficult to grasp because they contradict commonsense notions. By thinking together, challenging each other, and suggesting and evaluating possible explanations, pupils are more likely to reach a genuine understanding.

Of course, there are disadvantages. Class discussions are quite unpredictable and may easily digress into exchanges of ignorance. Some members of the group may have great difficulty participating and become anxious if forced to speak. In addition, you may have to do a good deal of preparation to ensure that participants have a background of knowledge on which to base the discussion. In many cases, a few pupils will dominate the discussion while the others become disengaged (Nardi and Steward, 2003).

The following Focus on Practice gives some ideas for preparing for and supporting productive group discussion. While we are focusing on the teacher, there is one more characteristic that affects pupil learning – the teacher's beliefs about the pupils.

Connect and Extend

For an interesting study on leading classroom discussions with young children read Linda Farr Darling (2002), 'Moles, porcupines, and children's moral reasoning: unexpected responses', *Early Years: An International Journal of Research and Development*, 22 (2), pp. 91–103.

FOCUS ON PRACTICE

Productive group discussions

Invite shy children to participate

Examples

1. 'What's your opinion, Joel?' or 'Does anyone have another opinion?'
2. Don't wait until there is a deadly silence to ask shy pupils to reply. Most people, even those who are confident, hate to break a silence.

Direct pupil comments and questions back to another pupil

Examples

1. 'That's an unusual idea, Steve. Kim, what do you think of Steve's idea?'
2. 'That's an important question, John. Moiya, do you have any thoughts about how you'd answer that?'
3. Encourage pupils to look at and talk to one another rather than talk directly to you.

Make sure that you understand what a pupil has said. If you are unsure, other pupils may be unsure as well

Examples

1. Ask a second pupil to summarise what the first pupil said; then the first pupil can try again to explain if the summary is incorrect.
2. 'Karen, I think you're saying . . . Is that right, or have I misunderstood?'

Probe for more information

Examples

1. 'That's a strong statement. Do you have any evidence to back it up?'
2. 'Did you consider any other alternatives?'
3. 'Tell us how you reached that conclusion. What steps did you go through?'

Bring the discussion back to the subject

Examples

1. 'Let's see, we were discussing . . . and Sarah made one suggestion. Does anyone have a different idea?'
2. 'Before we continue, let me try to summarise what has happened so far.'

Give time for thought before asking for responses

Examples

1. 'How would your life be different if television had never been invented? Jot down your ideas on paper, and we will share reactions in a minute.' After a minute: 'Helen, will you tell us what you wrote?'

When a pupil finishes speaking, look around the group to judge reactions

Examples
1. If other pupils look puzzled, ask them to describe why they are confused.
2. If pupils are nodding assent, ask them to give an example of what was just said.

Teacher Expectations

Pygmalion effect

Exceptional progress by a pupil as a result of high teacher expectations for that pupil; named after the mythological king, Pygmalion, who made a statue, then caused it to be brought to life.

Self-fulfilling prophecy

An expectation (sometimes groundless) that is confirmed because it has been expected.

Nearly 40 years ago, a study by Robert Rosenthal and Lenore Jacobson (1968) captured attention in a way that few studies by psychologists have since then. The study also caused great controversy within the professional community. Debate about the meaning of the results continues (Babad, 1995; Rosenthal, 1995; Snow, 1995).

What did Rosenthal and Jacobson say that caused such a stir? They chose several pupils at random in a number of primary school classrooms, and then told the teachers that these pupils probably would make significant intellectual gains during the year. The pupils did indeed make larger gains than normal that year. The researchers presented data suggesting the existence of a 'Pygmalion effect', one kind of self-fulfilling prophecy in the classroom. A self-fulfilling prophecy is an expectation (sometimes groundless) that leads to behaviours that then make the original expectation come true (Merton, 1948). An example is a false belief that a bank is failing, leading to a rush to withdraw money that then causes the bank to fail as expected (you may remember the scene from *Mary Poppins*).

Two kinds of expectation effects

> **STOP AND THINK**
>
> When you thought about the most effective teacher you ever had, was one of the characteristics that the teacher believed in you or demanded the best from you? How did the teacher communicate that belief?

Sustaining expectation effect

Pupil performance maintained at a certain level because teachers don't recognise improvements.

Actually, two kinds of expectation effects can occur in classrooms. In the self-fulfilling prophecy described above, the teacher's beliefs about the pupils' abilities have no basis in fact, but pupil behaviour comes to match the initially inaccurate expectation. The second kind of expectation effect occurs when teachers are fairly accurate in their initial reading of pupils' abilities and respond to pupils appropriately. So far, so good. There is nothing wrong with forming and acting on accurate estimates of pupil ability. The problems arise when pupils show some improvement, but teachers do not alter their expectations to take account of the improvement. This is called a sustaining expectation effect, because the teacher's unchanging expectation sustains the pupil's achievement at the expected level. The chance to raise expectations, provide more appropriate teaching and thus encourage greater pupil achievement is lost. In practice, self-fulfilling prophecy effects seem to be stronger in the early grades, and sustaining effects are more likely in the later grades (Kuklinski and Weinstein, 2001). Some pupils are more likely than others to be the recipients of sustaining expectations. For example, withdrawn children provide little information about themselves, so teachers may sustain their expectations about these children because of the seeming lack of new information (Jones and Gerig, 1994).

↔ Connect and Extend

Read Babad, E. (1995), 'The "Teacher's Pet" phenomenon, pupils' perceptions of differential behavior, and pupils' morale', *Journal of Educational Psychology, 87*, pp. 361–374.

Sources of expectations

There are many possible sources of teachers' expectations. Intelligence test scores are an obvious source, perhaps of an error in expectations if teachers do not interpret the scores appropriately. Gender also influences teachers; most teachers expect more behaviour problems from boys than from girls (Papatheodorou and Ramasut, 1993) and may have higher academic expectations for girls (Jones and Myhill, 2004). The notes from previous teachers and the medical or psychological reports found in cumulative folders (permanent record files) are another obvious source of expectations. Knowledge of ethnic background also seems to have an influence (Rubie-Davies *et al.*, 2006), as does prior experience of older brothers and sisters. Teachers hold higher expectations for attractive pupils (Babad, 1995). Previous achievement, socioeconomic status and the actual behaviours (Eraut, 2002) of the pupil are also often used as sources of information. Even the pupil's after-school activities can be a source of expectations. Teachers tend to hold higher expectations for pupils who participate in extra-curricular activities than for pupils who do nothing after school (Van Matre, Valentine and Cooper, 2000).

> ### STOP AND THINK
>
> Should teachers read pupils' cumulative files at the beginning of the school year? If so, how can you keep from forming low expectations? Is there any reason why teachers should not have high expectations for all of their pupils? What about the distinction between 'high expectations' and 'reasonable expectations'?

Expectations and beliefs focus attention and organise memory (Eraut, 2002), so teachers may pay attention to and remember the information that fits the initial expectations (Black, 2004; Fiske, 1993). Even when pupil performance does not fit expectations, the teacher may rationalise and attribute the performance to external causes beyond the pupil's control. For example, a teacher may assume that the low-ability pupil who did well on a test must have cheated and that the high-ability pupil who failed must have been upset that day. In both cases, behaviour that seems out of character is dismissed. It may take many instances of supposedly uncharacteristic behaviour to change the teacher's beliefs about a particular pupil's abilities. Thus, expectations often remain in the face of contradictory evidence (Rubie-Davies *et al.*, 2006; Brophy, 1998).

Do teachers' expectations really affect pupils' achievement?

The answer to this question is more complicated than it might seem. There are two ways to investigate the issue. One is to give teachers unfounded expectations about

Connect and Extend

Do teachers expect boys to misbehave? Read Myhill D. and Jones, S. (2006), '"She doesn't shout at no girls": pupils' perceptions of gender equity in the classroom', *Cambridge Journal of Education*, *36*(1) pp. 99–113.

their pupils and note if these baseless expectations have any effects. The other approach is to identify the naturally occurring expectations of teachers and study the effects of these expectations. The answer to the question of whether teacher expectations affect pupil learning depends in part on which approach is taken to study the question.

The 1968 Rosenthal and Jacobson experiment (p. 601) used the first approach – giving teachers groundless expectations and noting the effects. The study was criticised for the experimental and statistical methods the researchers used (Snow, 1995). A careful analysis of the results revealed that even though six- to 11-year-old pupils participated in the study, the self-fulfilling prophecy effect could be traced to dramatic changes in just five pupils aged six and seven. When other researchers tried to replicate the study, they did not find evidence of a self-fulfilling prophecy effect, even for children in these lower grades (Claiborn, 1969). After reviewing the research on teacher expectations, Raudenbush (1984) concluded that these expectations have only a small effect on pupil IQ scores (the outcome measure used by Rosenthal and Jacobson) and only in the early years of a new school setting – in the first years of prmary school and then again in the first years of secondary school.

But what about the second approach – naturally occurring expectations? Research shows that teachers do indeed form beliefs about pupils' capabilities. Many of these beliefs are accurate assessments based on the best available data and are corrected as new information is collected. Even so, some teachers do favour certain pupils (Babad, 1995). For example, in a study of 110 pupils followed from age four to 18, Jennifer Alvidrez and Rhona Weinstein (1999) found that teachers tended to overestimate the abilities of pre-school children they rated as independent and interesting and to underestimate the abilities of children perceived as immature and anxious. Teachers' judgements of pupil ability at age four predicted pupil academic achievement at age 18. The strongest predictions were for pupils whose abilities were *underestimated*. If teachers decide that some pupils are less able, and if the teachers lack effective strategies for working with lower-achieving pupils, then pupils may experience a double threat – low expectations and inadequate teaching (Good and Brophy, 2003). The power of the expectation effect depends on the age of the pupils (generally speaking, younger pupils are more susceptible) and on how differently a teacher treats high- versus low-expectation pupils, an issue we turn to next (Kuklinski and Weinstein, 2001).

Teaching strategies

As we have seen, different grouping processes may well have a marked effect on pupils. Some teachers leave little to the imagination; they make their expectations all too clear. For example, Alloway (1984) recorded comments such as these directed to low-achieving groups:

- 'I'll be over to help you slow ones in a minute.'

- 'The blue group will find this hard.'

In these remarks the teacher not only tells the pupils that they lack ability, but also communicates that finishing the work, not understanding, is the goal.

Once teachers assign pupils to ability groups, they usually assign different learning activities. To the extent that teachers choose activities that challenge pupils and increase achievement, these differences are probably necessary. Activities become inappropriate, however, when pupils who are ready for more challenging work are not given the opportunity to try it because teachers believe they cannot handle it. This is an example of a sustaining expectation effect.

Teacher–Pupil Interactions

However the class is grouped and whatever the assignments, the quantity and the quality of teacher–pupil interactions are likely to affect the pupils. Table 13.6 shows six dimensions of teacher communication towards pupils that may be influenced by expectations. These dimensions include both teaching practices and interpersonal interactions. Pupils who are expected to achieve tend to be asked more and harder questions, to be given more chances and a longer time to respond, and to be interrupted less often than pupils who are expected to do poorly. Teachers also give these

Table 13.6 Teacher expectations and the dimensions of classroom interactions

Interactions	Low teacher expectations	High teacher expectations
Managerial – pupils' position and resources	*'Line up quietly in two's at the door.'* Using commands Frequent monitoring and re-enforcement	*'I've got to get to a meeting. Last one out, switch the light off.'* Light touch Autonomy provided Trusting
Conforming	*'Do that again and you're for it.'* Confrontational Rules driven with overt threat of sanctions	*'That really made me feel very uncomfortable.'* Humane, concerned Seek causes and solutions.
Question and answer	*Who wrote Hard Times?* Right/Wrong Behaviourist Closed and convergent	*'What's important to you in this debate?'* High wait-time Conversational – an exchange of ideas Open, probing and divergent
Explanation	*'Remember, the three angles of every triangle add up to 180 degrees.'* Tell Pupil as 'empty vessel' Teacher as infallible expert	*'If that is true, what would it mean for the angles in the triangle?'* Selling ideas Constructing arguments Making connections Co-learners
Assessing	*'Don't worry if you can't do them all – just do what you can.'* Multiple choice Fill-in the missing word Marks for presentation	*'I'm looking for something special here. I'll leave you to it.'* Problem solving Following lines of enquiry
Social	*'How did Man U do on Saturday?'* Feigned interest Stilted Out of context	*'That's just what my daughter Emily thinks – she's bonkers as well!'* Genuine, warm Following things in common

high-expectation pupils cues and prompts, communicating their belief that the pupils can answer the question (Burns, 2006; Lyster, 2004; Allington, 1980). When an answer on a test is 'almost right', the teacher is more likely to give the benefit of the doubt (and thus the better grade) to high-achieving pupils (Finn, 1972). Teachers tend to smile at these pupils more often and to show greater warmth through such non-verbal responses as leaning towards the pupils and nodding their heads as the pupils speak (Wang *et al.*, 2001; Woolfolk and Brooks, 1983, 1985).

In contrast, with low-expectation pupils, teachers ask easier questions, allow less time for answering, and are less likely to give prompts. Teachers are more likely to respond with sympathetic acceptance or even praise to inadequate answers from low-achieving pupils, but to criticise these same pupils for wrong answers. Even more disturbing, low-achieving pupils receive less praise than high-achieving pupils for similar correct answers. This inconsistent feedback can be very confusing for low-ability pupils. Imagine how hard it would be to learn if your wrong answers were sometimes praised, sometimes ignored and sometimes criticised, and your right answers received little recognition (Burnett, 2002; Good 1983).

Of course, not all teachers form inappropriate expectations or act on their expectations in unconstructive ways (Chin, 2006; Babad *et al.*, 1982) but avoiding the problem may be more difficult than it seems. In general, low-expectation pupils also tend to be the most disruptive pupils. (Of course, low expectations can reinforce their desire to disrupt or misbehave.) Teachers may ask these pupils less often for a response, wait a shorter time for their answers, and give them less praise for right answers, partly to avoid the wrong, careless or silly answers that can cause disruptions, delays and digressions (Cooper, 1979). The challenge is to deal with these very real threats to classroom management without communicating low expectations to some pupils or fostering their own low expectations of themselves. Sometimes, low expectations become part of the culture of the school – beliefs shared by teachers and head teachers alike (Haynes *et al.*, 2006; Weinstein, Madison and Kuklinski, 1995). The following Focus on Practice may help you avoid some of these problems.

> ### Connect and Extend
>
> Are low expectations of pupils a psychological or social phenomenon? Read Haynes, J. *et al.* (2006), 'The barriers to achievement for White/Black Caribbean pupils in English schools', *British Journal of Sociology of Education*, 27(5), pp. 569–583.

FOCUS ON PRACTICE

Avoiding the negative effects of teacher expectations

Use information about pupils from tests, cumulative folders and other teachers very carefully

Examples
1. Avoid reading cumulative folders at the beginning of the year except vital health or family information.
2. Be critical and objective about the reports you hear from other teachers.

Be flexible in your use of grouping strategies

Examples
1. Review work of pupils often and experiment with new groupings.
2. Use different groups for different subjects.
3. Use mixed-ability groups in cooperative exercises.

Make sure all the pupils are challenged

Examples
1. Don't say, 'This is easy, I know you can do it.'
2. Offer a wide range of problems and encourage all pupils to try a few of the harder ones for extra praise. Find something positive about these attempts.

Be especially careful about how you respond to low-achieving pupils during class discussions

Examples
1. Give them prompts, cues and time to answer.
2. Give ample praise for good answers.
3. Call on low achievers as often as high achievers.

Use materials that show a wide range of ethnic groups

Examples
1. Check readers and library books. Is there ethnic diversity?
2. If few materials are available, ask pupils to research and create their own, based on community or family sources.

Make sure that your teaching does not reflect racial, ethnic or sexual stereotypes or prejudice

Examples
1. Use a mental or physical checking system to be sure you call on and include all pupils.
2. Monitor the content of the tasks you assign. Do boys get the 'hard' maths problems to work at the board? Do you avoid having pupils with limited English give oral answers?

Be fair in evaluation and disciplinary procedures

Examples
1. Make sure equal offences receive equal punishment. Find out from pupils in an anonymous questionnaire whether you seem to be favouring certain individuals.
2. Try to mark pupil work without knowing the identity of the pupil. Ask another teacher to give you a 'second opinion' from time to time.

Communicate to all pupils that you believe they can learn – and mean it

Examples
1. Return classwork and homework that does not meet standards with specific suggestions for improvements.
2. If pupils do not have the answers immediately, wait, probe and then help them think through an answer.

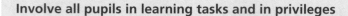

Involve all pupils in learning tasks and in privileges

Examples

1. Use some system to make sure you give each pupil practice in reading, speaking and answering questions.
2. Keep track of who gets to do what job. Are some pupils always on the list while others seldom make it?

Monitor your non-verbal behaviour

Examples

1. Do you lean away or stand farther away from some pupils? Do some pupils get smiles when they come into the classroom while others get only frowns?
2. Does your tone of voice vary with different pupils?

Many of the characteristics of effective teachers we have discussed in this chapter are those that members of the community which teachers serve would recognise as those of a good teacher. We have discussed the notion of the good teachers before in the teaching section of this chapter (p. 584) yet pupils' perspectives are always exciting and none more so than in the context of teachers' expectations of their pupils. So what are pupils' expectations of their teachers and what for pupils makes for a 'good teacher'. Figure 13.2 is one example of how some pupils from Feniton Primary School in Devon, UK see the mix of characteristics and qualities that for them makes for a good teacher. This figure visually and figuratively places the teacher at the centre of effective practice and we should remember that this chapter has been about teachers and teaching for learning, rather than about learners. However, teachers seldom place themselves at the centre of what they do. Many place their pupils at the centre of their professional practice and this is called pupil-centred teaching practice.

Pupil-Centred Teaching

Neither high expectations nor the appropriate use of any teaching format can *ensure* that pupils will understand. To help pupils reach this goal, Eleanor Duckworth believes that teachers must pay very close attention to understanding their pupils' understandings (Meek, 1991). The final two chapters of this book are reserved for important ideas of how teachers understand what children know and understand by using classroom assessment and standardised tests. How else would teachers know their pupils' learning needs? One way of describing teachers placing pupils' learning needs at the heart of planning, of having high expectations of pupils, and of effectively delivering a vivid, matched and relevant curriculum is to talk about child-centred or pupil-centred teaching. What do we know about good practice in pupil-centred teaching? Table 13.7 lists some key themes of pupil-centred teaching practices.

It may sound as if placing importance in the learning needs of pupils might, in some way, devalue the importance of teachers 'knowing their stuff' about what they

Pupil-centred teaching

Involves placing pupils' learning needs at the heart of planning, of having high expectations of pupils, and of effectively delivering a vivid, matched and relevant curriculum.

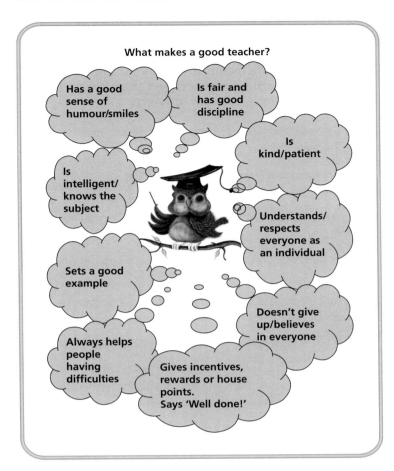

Figure 13.2
What makes a good teacher?

Source: http://www.feniton.
devon.sch.uk/projects/teacher.htm

are teaching. On the contrary, it is clear that a teacher's enthusiasm for and knowledge of the subject is critical for teaching (Daly, 2004; Hedges and Cullen, 2005). Part of that knowledge is pedagogical content knowledge, or knowing how to teach a subject to your particular pupils (Hashweh, 2005). In the past decade, psychologists have made further progress towards understanding how pupils learn (Bullock and Muschamp, 2006). Based on these findings, many approaches have been developed to teach reading, writing, mathematics, science, social studies and all the other subjects. Often these approaches reflect the constructivist perspectives described in Chapter 9 and pupil-centred teaching practices you have explored in this section.

Beyond the debates to outstanding teaching

In spite of the debates we have explored in this chapter, there is no one best way to teach. Different aims and pupil needs require different teaching methods. Whole-class teaching, supported by well-structured and matched classwork and homework often leads to better performance on achievement tests, whereas the more 'informal' methods such as discovery learning or inquiry approaches are associated with better performance on tests of creativity, abstract thinking and problem solving. In addition, the more informal methods are better for improving attitudes

Connect and Extend

Now is a good time to explore the subject or subjects that most interest you. You might want to investigate what constitutes effective teaching for a particular age group such as early years, a particular curriculum subject such as science or music, or an area of curriculum provision such as vocational training. Use an online journals service and links from professional sites to connect to the debates and to extend your understanding of effective teaching.

Table 13.7   Key themes of pupil-centred teaching practices

Key theme	Reference in *Psychology in Education*	These questions are meant to focus your thinking on pupil-centred teaching practices and there are no right or wrong answers – just your answers!
Motivation	Chapter 10 (p. 468)	How might teachers support self-determination and autonomy in pupil-centred teaching practices?
Play	Chapter 2 (p. 60)	What more should we have said about play? See http://www.montessori.org.uk/about.php
Creativity	Chapter 8 (p. 364)	How might pupil-centred teaching practices (PCTP) encourage creativity?
Self-concept	Chapter 3 (p. 105)	Self-concept is what individuals . . . about themselves? So what for PCTP?
Discovery learning	Chapter 8 (p. 343)	Why might *guided discovery* be one of the most important key themes in PCTP?
Constructivism	Chapter 9 (p. 411)	Think of five reasons why Vygotsy might have approved of a 21st-century Montessori school?
Learning and thinking skills	Chapter 7 (p. 319)	How would you answer the friend who argued metacognition is only for normal children, not pupils with learning disabilities?
Inclusion	Chapter 4 (p. 150)	Should 'mainstreaming' pupils with learning disabilities emphasise commonality not difference?
Moral and values education	Chapter 3 (p. 113)	Would a class discussion of a world tragedy be compatible with pupil-centred teaching practices?
Pupils learn differently	Chapter 5 (p. 187)	What are the main differences (PCTP) between an integrated and a multi-cultural classroom?
Problem solving	Chapter 11 (p. 489)	Should pupils work in groups in PCTP? What kinds of groups might be appropriate?
Self-management	Chapter 12 (p. 531)	Do girls or boys do better at schools which practice pupil-centred teaching practices?

towards school and for stimulating curiosity, cooperation among pupils and social relation with classmates (Holfve-Sabel, 2006). According to these conclusions, when the goals of teaching involve problem solving, creativity, understanding and mastering processes, many approaches besides whole-class teaching should be effective. These guidelines are in keeping with the conclusion that teaching becomes less direct as pupils mature (Kember, 2001) and when the goals involve affective development and problem solving or critical thinking (Good, 1983). Every pupil may require direct, explicit teaching for some learning objectives, some of the time, but every pupil also needs to experience more open, constructivist, pupil-centred teaching as well.

What can be said is that effective teachers know their subjects deeply and with affection, that they know their pupils and how best each of them learns. Moreover, effective teachers plan for learning not just for activity, deliver the planned curriculum using a variety of teaching strategies, are adaptable and fluent, focus on learning, and make the learning experiences of pupils as relevant and vivid as possible within the resources available. Some teachers hone these skills to such an extent that they become outstanding practitioners and learn to share their outstanding practice with their colleagues and beginning teachers. Part of becoming an outstanding teacher is to know how well pupils are doing and to plan for them accordingly. In the final two chapters we will explore how teachers assess their pupils.

SUMMARY TABLE

The First Step: Planning (pp. 574–584)

What are the levels of planning and how do they affect teaching?

Teachers engage in several levels of planning – by the year, term, unit, week and day. All the levels must be coordinated. Accomplishing the year's plan requires breaking the work into terms, the terms into units and the units into weeks and days. The plan determines how time and materials will be turned into activities for pupils. There is no single model of planning, but all plans should allow for flexibility. Planning is a creative problem-solving process for experienced teachers. They know how to accomplish many lessons and how to teach segments of lessons. They know what to expect and how to proceed, so they don't necessarily continue to follow the detailed lesson-planning models they learned during their teacher-preparation programmes. Planning is more informal – 'in their heads'.

What are learning objectives?

A learning objective is a clear and unambiguous description of your educational intentions for your pupils. Mager's influential system for writing behavioural objectives states that a good objective has three parts – the intended pupil behaviour, the conditions under which the behaviour will occur, and the criteria for acceptable performance. Gronlund's alternative approach suggests that an objective should be stated first in general terms, then the teacher should clarify by listing sample behaviours that would provide evidence that the pupil has attained the objective. The most recent research on instructional objectives tends to favour approaches similar to Gronlund's.

Describe the three taxonomies of educational objectives

Bloom and others have developed taxonomies categorising basic objectives in the cognitive, affective and psychomotor domains. In real life, of course, behaviours from these three domains occur simultaneously. A taxonomy encourages systematic thinking about relevant objectives and ways to evaluate them. Six basic objectives are listed in the cognitive domain: knowing, understanding, applying, analysing, evaluating and creating. A recent revision of this taxonomy adds that these processes can act on four kinds of knowledge – factual, conceptual, procedural and metacognitive. Objectives in the affective domain run from least committed to most committed. At the lowest level, a pupil would simply pay attention to a certain idea. At the highest level, the pupil would adopt an idea or a value and act consistently with that idea. Objectives in the psychomotor domain generally move from basic perceptions and reflex actions to skilled, creative movements.

Describe teacher-centred and pupil-centred planning

In teacher-centred approaches, teachers select learning objectives and plan how to get pupils to meet those objectives. Teachers control the 'what' and 'how' of learning. In contrast, planning is shared and negotiated in pupil-centred, or constructivist, approaches. Rather than having specific pupil behaviours as objectives, the teacher has overarching goals or 'big ideas' that guide planning. Integrated content and teaching with themes are often part of the planning. Assessment of learning is ongoing and mutually shared by teacher and pupils.

Teaching (pp. 584–602)

What methods have been used to study teaching?

For years, researchers have tried to unravel the mystery of effective teaching using classroom observation, case studies, interviews, experimentation with different methods, stimulated recall (teachers view videotapes and explain their teaching), analysis of lesson transcripts and other approaches to study teaching in real classrooms.

What are the general characteristics of good teaching?

Teacher knowledge of the subject is necessary but not sufficient for effective teaching because being more knowledgeable helps teachers be clearer and more organised. Teachers who provide clear presentations and explanations tend to have pupils who learn more and who rate their teachers more positively. Teacher warmth, friendliness and understanding seem to be the traits most strongly related to positive pupil attitudes.

What is whole-class teaching?

Whole-class teaching is appropriate for teaching basic skills and explicit knowledge. It includes the teaching functions of review/overview, presentation, guided practice, feedback and correctives (with reteaching if necessary), independent practice and periodic reviews. The younger or less able the pupils, the shorter the presentation should be with more cycles of practice and feedback.

Individual classwork and homework

Individual classwork should follow up whole-class or group teaching and give pupils supervised practice. It should not be the main form of activity. The evidence of research suggests that the setting of homework, which is both appropriate to the subject and correctly administered, can be a valid component of the learning process.

Distinguish between convergent and divergent and high-level versus low-level questions

Convergent questions have only one right answer. Divergent questions have many possible answers. Higher-level questions require analysis, synthesis and evaluation – pupils have to think for themselves. The best pattern for younger pupils and for lower-ability pupils of all ages is simple questions that allow a high percentage of correct answers, ample encouragement, help when the pupil does not have the correct answer and praise. For high-ability pupils, the successful pattern includes harder questions at both higher and lower levels and more critical feedback. Whatever their age or ability, all pupils should have some experience with thought-provoking questions and, if necessary, help in learning how to answer them.

How can wait time affect pupil learning?

Teacher responses to answers should not be too hasty in most cases and should provide appropriate feedback. When teachers learn to pose a question, then wait at least three to five seconds before calling on a pupil to answer, pupils tend to give longer answers; more pupils are likely to participate, ask questions and volunteer appropriate answers; pupil comments involving analysis, synthesis, inference and speculation tend to increase; and the pupils generally appear more confident in their answers.

What are the uses and disadvantages of group discussion?

Group discussion helps pupils participate directly, express themselves clearly, justify opinions and tolerate different views. Group discussion also gives pupils a chance to ask for clarification, examine their own thinking, follow personal interests and assume responsibility by taking leadership roles in the group. Thus, group discussions help pupils evaluate ideas and synthesise personal viewpoints. However, discussions are quite unpredictable and may easily digress into exchanges of ignorance.

Teacher Expectations (pp. 602–608)

What are some sources of teacher expectations?

Sources include intelligence test scores, gender, notes from previous teachers and the medical or psychological reports found in cumulative folders, ethnic background, knowledge of older brothers and sisters, physical characteristics, previous achievement, socioeconomic status and the actual behaviours of the pupil.

What are the two kinds of expectation effects and how do they happen?

The first is the self-fulfilling prophecy; the teacher's beliefs about the pupils' abilities have no basis in fact, but pupil behaviour comes to match the initially inaccurate expectation. The second is a sustaining expectation effect; teachers are fairly accurate in their initial reading of pupils' abilities and respond to pupils appropriately. The problems arise when pupils show some improvement but teachers do not alter their expectations to take account of the

improvement. When this happens, the teacher's unchanging expectation can sustain the pupil's achievement at the expected level. In practice, sustaining effects are more common than self-fulfilling prophecy effects.

What are the different avenues for communicating teacher expectations?

Some teachers tend to treat pupils differently, depending on their own views of how well the pupils are likely to do. Differences in treatment towards low-expectation pupils may include setting less challenging tasks, focusing on lower-level learning, giving fewer choices, providing inconsistent feedback, and communicating less respect and trust. Pupils may behave accordingly, fulfilling teachers' predictions or staying at an expected level of achievement.

Pupil-Centred Teaching (pp. 608–611)

Key themes of pupil-centred approaches are motivation, play, creativity, self-concept, discovery learning, constructivism, integration, moral and values education, pupils learn differently, learning and thinking skills, problem solving and self-management. Whole-class teaching supported by individual classwork and homework and pupil-centred approaches may be appropriate at different times.

Glossary

Affective domain: Objectives focusing on attitudes and feelings.

Basic skills: Clearly structured knowledge that is needed for later learning and that can be taught step by step.

Behavioural objectives: Learning objectives stated in terms of observable behaviours.

Cognitive domain: In Bloom's taxonomy, memory and reasoning objectives.

Cognitive objectives: Learning objectives stated in terms of higher-level thinking operations.

Constructivist approach: View that emphasises the active role of the learner in building understanding and making sense of information.

Convergent questions: Questions that have a single correct answer.

Divergent questions: Questions that have no single correct answer.

Group discussion: Conversation in which the teacher does not have the dominant role; pupils pose and answer their own questions.

Individual classwork: Independent classroom work set to be completed during lessons.

Learning objectives: Clear statement of what pupils are intended to learn.

Lesson study: As a group, teachers develop, test, improve and re-test lessons until they are satisfied with the final version.

Psychomotor domain: Physical ability and coordination objectives.

Pupil-centred teaching: Involves placing pupils' learning needs at the heart of planning, of having high expectations of pupils, and of effectively delivering a vivid, matched and relevant curriculum.

Pygmalion effect: Exceptional progress by a pupil as a result of high teacher expectations for that pupil; named after the mythological king, Pygmalion, who made a statue, then caused it to be bought to life.

Scripted cooperation: Learning strategy in which two pupils take turns summarising material and criticising the summaries.

Self-fulfilling prophecy: An expectation (sometimes groundless) that is confirmed because it has been expected.

Sustaining expectation effect: Pupil performance maintained at a certain level because teachers don't recognise improvements.

Targeting: The way teachers select pupils to answer questions and matching the questions to the pupils.

Taxonomy: Classification system.

Whole-class teaching: Teaching characterised by high levels of teacher explanation, demonstration and interaction with all the pupils at the same time.

CHECK YOUR LEARNING! WEB

In the Classroom: What Would They Do?

You will remember from the start of this chapter that a new teacher has been handed curriculum planning documents that have an exclusive focus on preparing pupils for national testing arrangements. How should the teacher plan to arouse pupils' curiosity and interests about the topics and skills that will be tested, and establish the value of learning this material? How should a new teacher engage pupils in 'real learning' about the topics? Here is how some practitioners have responded to these questions:

Lee Card, class teacher, seven- to eight-year-olds, Bosbury Church of England Primary School, Herefordshire

Irrelevant of context, at the heart of everything that happens in and out of this teacher's classroom must be a belief that learning for the *sake* of learning isn't learning at all. It is merely regurgitating fragmented particles of knowledge that will ultimately be lost in experience. Learning cannot be taught, nor can it be forced in some ritualistic drill of terror! Learning is a living, breathing organism that needs to be fuelled, nurtured, encouraged and inspired to grow, to live and to thrive.

The teacher must find a way to make the learning *meaningful*, which, for me, means taking the programmes of study and mapping them into groups of topics/themes that make sense to teach alongside each other. Even better, would be to adapt the units to fit in with others being taught at the same time. The objectives and outcomes remain, the way they are taught is where the meaning and where the enjoyment comes in! Teaching art, literacy and science units through a Viking theme is magic.

The teacher must find a way to make the learning *real*. For me, this means getting to know your children. Adapt teaching units to 'play on' their passions or interests and find ways to make the learning applicable to *their* lives. If they can see their learning in action, it is a mighty powerful tool for recall and enthusiasm to do more! (An example of what I mean from my classroom: 22 Year 7s writing passionately; complaining to a giant book publisher about an unpublished text they have read, by a local author they have met, is way beyond fun!)

I'm not the idealistic fool I sound. There is a time and a place for teaching the facts and the skills to answer test questions. I just wish there wasn't.

Jackie Day, special needs co-ordinator, The Ridge Primary School, Yate

Learning is for life and not *just* for passing tests. When introducing a topic the teacher should plan to connect the learning with the pupils' own experience. Curiosity might be aroused by questioning, pictures, an outside visit or artefacts brought into the classroom. Children should reflect on what they already know and consider what they would like to find out about. Some choice can be given in areas of research and in methods of presentation, to encourage 'ownership' of the learning. At the end of the topic, learning should be reviewed so that pupils can appreciate and celebrate their own progress. Appropriate support and differentiation must be given to ensure that everyone has the basic skills necessary to access the learning, and the more able will need suitable challenges.

Individual lessons should be planned with clear learning objectives, making explicit what is being learnt and why. Teacher-input should be brief and multi-sensory. The 'I do, We do, You do,' teaching strategy works well. The teacher models the skill or concept, and then guides the pupils through a learning activity before they demonstrate their learning by working independently. The plenary is an opportunity for recalling what has been learnt. Marking should give clear feedback on success in meeting the learning objective and show how to improve.

Above all, I believe children are inspired to learn by imaginative teachers who are really interested in both their subject and the children they teach. They can even make the 'drill and practice' fun!

Tessa Herbert, English teacher, John Masefield High School, Ledbury

Teaching for learning and teaching for examination success often seem to be at variance with each other. In some ways, the teacher has to have faith that a pupil who understands a unit will be able to interpret a question and give a fresh response. However, pupils still need to practise the necessary techniques that will make their answer 'tick the boxes'.

In Shakespeare, for example, character and theme, drama and atmosphere, can all be explored through practical work, encapsulating key moments and lines in pairs or small groups. Modern media forms can be used to discuss issues raised (e.g. the chat show). In this way pupils discover characters are 'real people' and their dilemmas are relevant. They still need to learn the skill of making a point, quoting to support it and making a comment on it.

Reading texts that are appropriate to the pupils' interests is important when practising for the reading paper; they are more likely to analyse something that interests them than an obvious exam text.

Have the courage to go out on a limb sometimes so that pupils become both the questioners and the discoverers.

Lisbeth Jonsson, primary school teacher, Skepperviks, Sweden

To help you with this task, I would have to write a chapter of my own. But concerning first language teaching (in my case Swedish) I have found that pupils have great fun at correcting one another's language errors (anonymously of course) and they try very hard to write correctly, when they know they will be corrected by their class mates. Concerning maths – there are so many ways to teach 'in reality'!

It is a very odd scenario though! How could one new teacher turn that old ship, without creating bad feelings among the colleagues?

Go to the Companion Website www.pearsoned.co.uk/woolfolkeuro for additional case studies.

Overview

Would it surprise you to learn that published tests, such as GCSEs, A levels and IQ tests, are creations of the 20th century? In the 19th and early 20th centuries, university entrance was generally based on recommendations by head teachers or housemasters, and on essays and interviews with tutors. From your own experience, you know that testing has come a long way since then – too far, say some critics. They want to revise testing as a means to an end of reshaping the curriculum and reforming education and schooling. We will explore these new ideas in this chapter.

In spite of criticisms that there is too much testing in our schools, teachers still administer many standardised tests to their pupils, more than is required by the national system of tests at the end of Key Stages or phases of schooling. The move to more testing is principally about the multi-use of test results. As Patricia Broadfoot (Professor of Education at Bristol University) says:

> educational assessment is not just about judging *individual* potential and performance. It has always been just as much about judging *institutional* quality (1996: 7).

Every year, the work and worth of every state school is evaluated based on pupils' scores on standardised tests. Schools that fail year-on-year to increase the number of pupils who 'pass' these tests, are deemed to be failing schools and so face severe consequences, including the replacement of staff or possible closure. Therefore, teachers must be knowledgeable about testing. This chapter focuses on preparing for standardised tests and interpreting the results. Understanding how standardised test scores are determined, what they really mean and how they can be used (or misused) provides you with a framework for ensuring that you are expert in preparing pupils for such tests and using any results with circumspection.

First, we consider testing in general, including the various methods of interpreting test scores. Then, we look at the different kinds of standardised tests used in schools. Finally, we examine the criticisms of testing and the alternatives being proposed.

By the time you have completed this chapter, you should be able to answer the following questions:

- **How do you calculate mean, median, mode and standard deviation?**
- **What are percentile ranks, standard deviations, *z* scores, *T* scores and stanine scores?**
- **How can you improve reliability and validity in testing?**
- **What do results of achievement, aptitude and diagnostic tests tell teachers?**
- **How would you prepare pupils (and yourself) for standardised tests?**
- **What are the strengths and weaknesses of alternative forms of assessment such as portfolios?**

In the Classroom

It is nearing the end of the school year, the national testing results are finally in and the parents' report form went home last Friday. On Monday morning during preparation and planning time, a class teacher is asked to go to the head teacher's office. The parents of one pupil are in the office and have asked to speak with the class teacher and the head teacher immediately. The father is a prominent businessman and the mother is a lawyer. Their daughter received a Level 5 on her standardised maths tests. This would place her in the top 18% of the percentile ranking. The school is aware that she has been privately tutored in mathematics for much of the year.

The school uses an alpha grade system to inform pupils and parents how well they are doing and recently the girl has been marked with Bs and Cs in the class – she seldom completes homework and has trouble with the enquiry approach to maths. She just wants to know the 'steps' to solve the problems so she can finish. The teacher has tried several times to get the parents to come in to talk about ways to support the girl's learning, but they never seem to have had the time – until today.

The father says, 'Well, you can see from our daughter's scores that you have been totally wrong in the grades you have given her this year. We thought she was just weak in maths, but now it is clear you have something against her! Or maybe you just don't know how to teach maths to bright girls.'

The mother chimes in, 'Yes, we expect you to reconsider her report grades for the year in light of her clear abilities. In fact,' she glances at the head teacher and then glares at the class teacher, 'we believe she should get a recommendation from you for her to join the gifted and talented set for maths next year, because she obviously knows the material already.' What should the teacher say to the parents? What do teachers need to know about tests to deal with this kind of situation? How should the school approach working with this pupil?

Group Activity

With three other members of your group, role-play this scenario.

Measurement and Assessment

STOP AND THINK

A pupil does poorly in the arithmetic reasoning section of a standardised test. Interpretation of the results differ if the test were a criterion-referenced type as opposed to a norm-referenced type. Note down what you think are the differences between criterion-referenced and norm-referenced tests.

Teaching involves making many kinds of judgements – decisions based (hopefully) on professional values: 'Should we use a different text this year?', 'Is this film appropriate for my pupils?' 'Will Jacob do better if he drops a set?' 'Should Terry get a B– or a C+ on the project?' Straight away, professional values begin to mix with measures of pupil attainment.

Measurement is quantitative – the description of an event or characteristic using numbers. Measurement tells how much, how often or how well by providing scores, ranks or ratings. Instead of saying, 'Sarah doesn't seem to understand addition,' a teacher might say, 'Sarah answered only two of the 15 problems correctly in her addition homework.' Measurement also allows a teacher to compare one pupil's performance on one particular task with either a standard performance or the performances of the other pupils. This is the start of understanding the idea of norm-referencing.

Not all the decisions made by teachers involve measurement. Some decisions are based on information that is difficult to express numerically: pupil preferences, information from parents, previous experiences, even intuition. However, measurement does play a large role in many classroom decisions and, when properly done, it can provide unbiased data for decision making.

We tend to use the term assessment to describe the process of gathering information about pupils' learning. Assessment is broader than testing and measurement because it includes all kinds of ways to sample and observe pupils' skills, knowledge and abilities. Assessment can be any one of many procedures used to evaluate pupil performance (Broadfoot, 1996). Assessments can be formal, such as unit tests, or informal, such as observing who emerges as a leader during group work. Assessments can be designed by classroom teachers or by national agencies on behalf of government departments. Today, assessments can go well beyond paper-and-pencil exercises to observations of performances, the appraisal of developed portfolios or the evaluation of created artifacts (Popham, 2005a). In this chapter, we focus on formal assessments designed by groups and agencies outside the classroom. These assessments usually involve testing and the reporting of scores.

The scores given on any type of test have no meaning by themselves; we must make some kind of comparison in order to interpret test results. There are two basic types of comparison. In the first, a test score is compared to the scores obtained by other people who have taken the same test. This is called a norm-referenced comparison.

Some statisticians might argue that a teacher-made class test, where scores are placed in rank order and a pupil's position is compared to a mean average score, or a median position, is a form of norm-referencing – and they would be right to say this. However, such a small scale comparative measure is unlikely to give an accurate indicator of a pupil's attainment compared to other pupils of the same age group. Therefore,

Measurement

An evaluation expressed in quantitative (statistical) terms.

Assessment

Procedures used to obtain information about pupil performance.

Norm-referenced comparison

Testing in which scores are compared with the mean average performance of others.

a much larger group of pupils (perhaps many thousands) must take the same test for the average comparator to be considered typical for that age group. Get 30 11-year-olds to take a spelling test of the same ten words and you can say that a pupil's score of 8 can be referenced to the norm of those 30 pupils, but this is a very small norm group and therefore, the interpretation of a score of 8 out of 10 is only interesting in comparison with the scores of that small group. National testing of many thousands of pupils of the same age group would give a more typical average against which to compare a pupil's score on the spelling test. We might then be able to say with more confidence that he or she is a better than average speller (but only, of course, of those particular ten words).

The second type of comparison is criterion-referenced comparison. Here the comparison is to a fixed standard or banded passing score linked to a hierarchical curriculum framework which provides a link between pupils' scores and specific curriculum objectives. If a pupil achieves a particular score, then he or she shows attainment of the referenced curriculum objectives, and this measure of attainment is not a comparison made with the scores of other pupils. Actually, the same test can be interpreted either in a norm-referenced or criterion-referenced way.

Norm-referenced test interpretations

As we have said, in norm-referenced testing, the people who have taken the test provide the norms for determining the meaning of a given individual's score. You can think of a norm as being the typical level of performance for a particular group. By comparing the individual's raw score (the actual number correct) to the norm, we can determine if the score is above, below or around the mean average for that group. There are at least three types of norm groups (comparison groups) in education – the class or school itself, the local authority and national samples. National norm groups used for large-scale assessment programmes are tested one year and then the scores for that group serve as comparisons or norms every year for several years. The norm groups are selected so that all social and economic status (SES) groups are included in the sample. Because high-SES pupils tend to

Norm groups
A group whose mean average score serves as a standard for evaluating any pupil's score on a test.

Criterion-referenced comparison
Testing in which scores are compared to a set performance standard.

Connect and Extend
Use your library access to electronic journals to find Freeman, E. and Miller, M. (2001), 'A norm-referenced, criterion-referenced, and dynamic assessment: what exactly is the point?', *Educational Psychology in Practice, 17*(1), pp. 3–16.

Norm reference tests are useful in measuring overall achievement but are not necessarily useful to predict pupils' readiness to move on to more advanced work

do better on many standardised tests, a high-SES school district will almost always have higher scores compared to the norm group, because the norm group had a larger proportion of low-SES pupils.

Norm-referenced tests tend to cover a wide range of general objectives. They are especially useful in measuring the overall achievement of pupils who have come to understand complex material by different routes. Norm-referenced tests are also appropriate when only the top few candidates can be successful in a selection process.

However, norm-referenced measurement has its limitations. The results of a norm-referenced test do not tell you whether pupils are ready to move on to more advanced material. For instance, knowing that a pupil is in the top 3% of the class on a test of algebraic concepts will not tell you if he or she is ready to move on to advanced maths; everyone in the class may have a limited understanding of algebraic concepts.

Nor are norm-referenced tests particularly appropriate for measuring affective and psychomotor (the connection between mental and physical activity) objectives. To measure individuals' psychomotor learning, you need a clear description of standards. (Even the best gymnast in school performs certain exercises better than others and needs specific guidance about how to improve.) In the affective area, attitudes and values are personal; comparisons among individuals are not really appropriate. For example, how could we measure an 'average' level of moral values or opinions? Finally, norm-referenced tests tend to encourage competition and comparison of scores. Some pupils compete to be the best. Others, realising that being the best is impossible, may compete to be the worst, and both goals have their casualties. It could be argued that the interpretation of criterion-referenced tests by those who are taking them is less likely to encourage competition and comparison of scores.

Criterion-referenced test interpretations

When test scores are compared, not to those of others as in norm-referencing, but to a given criterion or standard of performance, this is criterion-referenced testing. To decide who should be allowed to drive a car, it is important to determine just what standard of performance is appropriate for selecting safe drivers. It does not matter how your test results compare to the results of others. If your overall performance on the test was in the top 10% but you consistently drove through red lights, you would not be a good candidate for receiving a full licence, even though your score was high.

Criterion-referenced tests measure the mastery of very specific objectives. The results of a criterion-referenced test should tell the teacher exactly what the pupils can and cannot do, at least under certain conditions. For example, a criterion-referenced test would be useful in measuring the ability to add two three-digit numbers. A test could be designed with 20 different problems, and the standard for mastery could be set at 17 correct out of 20. (The standard is often somewhat arbitrary and may be based on such things as the teacher's experience.) If two pupils receive scores of 7 and 11, it does not matter that one pupil did better than the other because neither met the standard of 17. Both need more help with addition. Sometimes standards for meeting the criterion must be set at 100% correct. You would not like to have your appendix removed by a surgeon who left surgical instruments inside the body only 10% of the time.

In teaching basic skills, there are many instances where comparison to a preset standard is more important than comparison to the performance of others. It is not very comforting to know, as a parent, that your child is better in reading than most of the pupils in her class if none of the pupils is reading at the level expected for their age group.

However, criterion-referenced tests are not appropriate for every situation. Some subjects are less straightforward to break down into sets of discrete objectives, despite

Table 14.1 Two kinds of test interpretation

Norm-referenced test interpretation may work best when you are:

- Measuring general ability (strengths and weaknesses) in certain areas, such as English, algebra or science
- Assessing the range of abilities in a large group
- Selecting top candidates when only a few openings are available.

Criterion-referenced tests may work best when you are:

- Measuring mastery of basic skills
- Determining if pupils have prerequisites to start a new unit
- Testing affective and psychomotor objectives
- Providing evidence that pupils have met learning standards
- Grouping pupils for instruction.

the best intentions of those who write programmes of study for wide-ranging national curricula. For example, we would argue that many creative subjects, including creativity itself, are less easily divided up in a hierarchical way. Moreover, although standards are important in criterion-referenced testing, they can often be arbitrary, as we have already seen. When deciding whether a pupil has mastered the addition of three-digit numbers comes down to the difference between 16 or 17 correct answers, it seems difficult to justify one particular standard over another. Finally, at times, it is valuable to know how the pupils in your class compare to other pupils of the same age group both locally and nationally. Table 14.1 offers a comparison of norm-referenced and criterion-referenced tests. You can see that each type of test is well suited for certain situations, but each also has its limitations.

What Do Test Scores Mean?

Standardised tests are those official-looking pamphlets and piles of forms sent to or purchased by schools and administered to pupils. More specifically, the tests are called standardised because they are administered, scored and interpreted in a standard manner – same directions, time limits and scoring for all (Popham, 2005a). Standard methods of developing questions, administering the test, scoring it and reporting the scores are all implied by the term standardised test.

Standardised tests

Tests given, usually nationwide, under uniform conditions and scored according to uniform procedures.

Basic concepts

> **STOP AND THINK**
>
> Guess the mean, median and mode for these two sets of scores:
>
> 50, 45, 55, 55, 45, 50, 50   Mean _____   Median _____   Mode _____
>
> 100, 0, 50, 90, 10, 50, 50   Mean _____   Median _____   Mode _____
>
> Which set of scores has the largest standard deviation?

In standardised testing, the test items and instructions have been tried out to make sure they work and then rewritten and retested as necessary. When norm-referenced interpretations are used, the final version of the test is administered to a norming sample, a large sample of subjects as similar as possible to the pupils who will be taking the test throughout the country. This norming sample serves as a comparison group for all pupils who take the test. In some national tests the first 10% of all test papers are scored quickly by teams of markers and sent to the national agency so that grade or level boundaries can be determined from the scores of the selected 10%. In these circumstances the population taking the test contains the norming sample.

The test publishers provide one or more ways of comparing each pupil's raw score (number of correct answers) with the norming sample. Let's look at some of the concepts on which comparisons and interpretations are based.

Frequency distributions

A frequency distribution is simply a listing of the number of people who obtain each score or fall into each range of scores on a test or other measurement procedure. For example, on a spelling test, 19 pupils received these scores: 100, 95, 90, 85, 85, 85, 80, 75, 75, 75, 70, 65, 60, 60, 55, 50, 50, 45, 40. A graph, in this case a bar chart of the spelling test scores, is shown in Figure 14.1 where one axis (the *x*-axis or horizontal axis) indicates the possible scores and the other axis (the *y*-axis or vertical axis) indicates the number of pupils who attained each score.

Measurements of central tendency and standard deviation

You have probably had a great deal of experience with means. A mean is simply the arithmetical average of a group of scores. To calculate the mean, you add the scores and divide the total by the number of scores in the distribution. For example, the total of the 19 spelling scores is 1,340, so the mean is 1,340 divided by 19, or 70.53. The mean offers one way of measuring central tendency, a score that is typical or representative of the whole distribution of scores. Very high or very low scores may affect the mean so it becomes less typical or representative of the distribution.

Two other measures of central tendency are the median and the mode. The median is the middle score in the distribution, the point at which half the scores are larger

Norming sample

Large sample of pupils serving as a comparison group for scoring standardised tests.

Frequency distribution

Record showing how many scores fall into set groups.

Bar chart

Graph of a frequency distribution using vertical or horizontal bars.

Mean

Arithmetic average.

Central tendency

Typical score for a group of scores.

Median

Middle score in a group of scores.

Mode

Most frequently occurring score.

Figure 14.1
Bar chart of a frequency distribution

This bar chart shows the number of people who earned each score on a test. You can quickly see, for example, that three people earned a 75 and three people earned an 85.

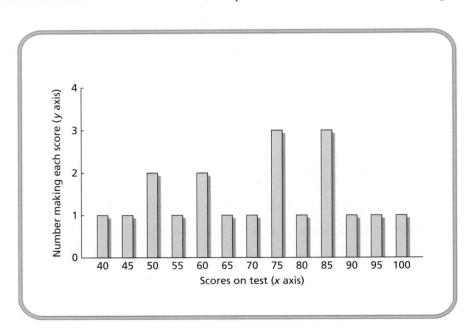

and half are smaller. The median of the 19 spelling scores is 75. Nine scores in the distribution are greater than or equal to 75, and nine are less. When there are a few very high or low scores, the median may be a better representative of the central tendency of a group. The mode is the score that occurs most often. The distribution in Figure 14.1 actually has two modes, 75 and 85, because each of these scores occurred three times. This makes it a bimodal distribution.

The measure of central tendency gives a score that is representative of the group of scores, but it does not tell you anything about how the scores are distributed. Two groups of scores may both have a mean of 50, but be alike in no other way. One group might contain the scores 50, 45, 55, 55, 45, 50, 50; the other group might contain the scores 100, 0, 50, 90, 10, 50, 50 – the groups in the Stop and Think box on p. 621. In both cases, the mean, median and mode are all 50, but the distributions are quite different.

STOP AND THINK

At a parents' association meeting, parents were complaining because half of the pupils in the area scored below the area average on the achievement tests that were given. Is this a valid complaint? What would you say?

The standard deviation is a measure of how widely the scores vary from the mean. The larger the standard deviation, the more spread out the scores are in the distribution. The smaller the standard deviation, the more the scores are clustered around the mean. For example, in Distribution A (50, 45, 55, 55, 45, 50, 50) the standard deviation is much smaller than in Distribution B (100, 0, 50, 90, 10, 50, 50). See the worked example below in Table 14.2. Another way of saying this is that distributions with very small standard deviations have less variability in the scores.

The standard deviation is relatively easy to calculate if you remember your secondary school maths. It does take time, however. The process is similar to taking an average, but you use square roots. To calculate the standard deviation, you follow the steps in Table 14.2. Distribution B on Table 14.2 shows a standard deviation almost 10 times that of Distribution A, yet the mean, the median and the mode are 50. You should now be able to check your calculations to the last Stop and Think question.

Standard deviation

Measure of how widely scores vary from the mean.

Variability

Degree of difference or deviation from a mean.

STOP AND THINK

With other factors similar, which maths class, A or B, is probably easier to teach, judging from the following standard score results (50 = national average)?
Class A: Mean = 55, SD = 13 or Class B: Mean = 53, SD = 4.*

Knowing the mean and the standard deviation of a group of scores gives you a better picture of the meaning of an individual score. For example, suppose you received a score of 78 on a test. You would be very pleased with the score if the mean of the test were 70 and the standard deviation were 4. In this case, your score would be 2 standard deviations above the mean, a score well above average.

Consider the difference if the mean of the test had remained at 70, but the standard deviation had been 20. In the second case, your score of 78 would be less than 1 standard deviation from the mean. You would be much closer to the middle of the group,

Answer: Probably Class B because the range of achievement levels is not as great as in Class A.

Table 14.2 Calculation of the standard deviation

Method	Distribution A	Distribution B
1. Calculate the mean (written as $\bar{X}$) of the scores.	50 + 45 + 55 + 55 + 45 + 50 + 50 = 350 350 ÷ 7 = 50	100 + 0 + 50 + 90 + 10 + 50 + 50 = 350 350 ÷ 7 = 50
2. Subtract the mean from each of the scores. This is written as $(X - \bar{X})$.	50 − 50 = 0 45 − 50 = −5 55 − 50 = 5 55 − 50 = 5 45 − 50 = −5 50 − 50 = 0 50 − 50 = 0	100 − 50 = 50 0 − 50 = −50 50 − 50 = 0 90 − 50 = 40 10 − 50 = −40 50 − 50 = 0 50 − 50 = 0
3. Square each difference (multiply each difference by itself). This is written $(X - \bar{X})^2$. (This removes the negative values)	$0^2 = 0$ $-5^2 = 25$ $5^2 = 25$ $5^2 = 25$ $-5^2 = 25$ $0^2 = 0$ $0^2 = 0$	$50^2 = 2500$ $-50^2 = 2500$ $0^2 = 0$ $40^2 = 1600$ $40^2 = 1600$ $0^2 = 0$ $0^2 = 0$
4. Add all the squared differences. This is written $\Sigma(X - \bar{X})^2$.	0 + 25 + 25 + 25 + 25 + 0 + 0 = 100	2500 + 2500 + 0 + 1600 + 1600 + 0 + 0 = 8200
5. Divide this total by the number of scores. This is written $\dfrac{\Sigma(X - \bar{X})^2}{N}$.	100 ÷ 7 ≅ 14.29	8200 ÷ 7 ≅ 1171.42
6. Find the square root. This is written $\sqrt{\dfrac{\Sigma(X - \bar{X})^2}{N}}$, which is the formula for calculating the standard deviation.	√14.29 ≅ 3.78	√1171.42 ≅ 34.23

Range

Distance between the highest and the lowest scores in a group.

with a score above average, but not high. Knowing the standard deviation tells you much more than simply knowing the range of scores. No matter how the majority scored on the tests, one or two pupils may do very well or very poorly and thus make the range very large.

The normal distribution

Normal distribution

The most commonly occurring distribution, in which scores are distributed evenly around the mean.

Standard deviations are very useful in understanding test results. They are especially helpful if the results of the tests form a normal distribution. You may have encountered the normal distribution before. It is the bell-shaped curve, the most well known frequency distribution because it describes many naturally occurring physical and social phenomena. Many scores fall in the middle, giving the curve its 'puffed' appearance. You find fewer and fewer scores as you look out towards the end points, or *tails*, of the distribution. The normal distribution has been thoroughly analysed by statisticians. The mean of a normal distribution is also its midpoint. Half the scores are above the mean and half are below it. In a normal distribution, the mean, median and mode are all the same point. This is one useful way of defining the normal distribution.

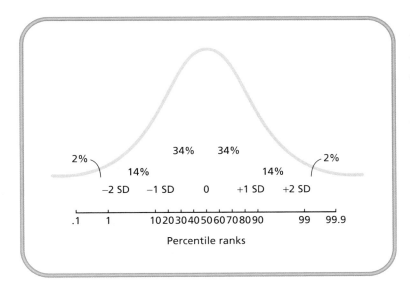

Figure 14.2
The normal distribution

The normal distribution or bell-shaped curve has certain predictable characteristics. For example, 68% of the scores are clustered within 1 standard deviation below to 1 standard deviation above the mean.

Another convenient property of the normal distribution is that the percentage of scores falling within each area of the curve is known, as you can see in Figure 14.2. A person scoring within 1 standard deviation of the mean obviously has a lot of company because many scores squash up here. In fact, 68% of all scores are located in the area from 1 standard deviation below to 1 standard deviation above the mean. About 16% of the scores are higher than 1 standard deviation above the mean. Of this higher group, only 2% are better than 2 standard deviations above the mean. Similarly, only about 16% of the scores are less than 1 standard deviation below the mean, and of that group only about 2% are worse than 2 standard deviations below the mean. At 2 standard deviations from the mean in either direction, the score is an outlier.

In day-to-day life you can make much use of normal distribution, in many cases without even realising it. If you went into a large department store and observed that everybody in the store was over 2 metres tall, you would more than likely be a little surprised. (Unless you then observed that this was a department providing for taller people!) You would have expected most people to be around the 'average' height, perhaps spotting just one or two people in the shop that would be taller than 2 metres. There are numerous things that occur with a normal distribution including shoe size, IQ score, diameter of trees and body temperature. What other phenomena would you expect to occur with a normal distribution and what phenomena would definitely not match the definition of a normal distribution curve?

Types of scores

STOP AND THINK

At a parent consultation evening following a set of tests, a mother and father are concerned about their child's percentile rank of 86. They say that they expect their child to 'get close to 100%. We know she should be able to do that because her National Curriculum Level is one higher than the expectation for her age.' What should the teacher say?

Now you have enough background for a discussion of the different kinds of scores you may encounter in reports of results from standardised tests – scores these parents don't seem to understand.

Percentile rank scores

The concept of ranking is the basis for one very useful kind of score reported on standardised tests, a percentile rank score. In percentile ranking, each pupil's raw score is compared with the raw scores of the pupils in the norming sample. The percentile rank shows the percentage of pupils in the norming sample that scored at or below a particular raw score – sometimes the mean average. If a pupil's score were the same as or better than three-quarters of the pupils in the norming sample, the pupil would score in the 75th percentile or have a percentile rank of 75. You can see that this does not mean that the pupil had a raw score of 75 correct answers or even that the pupil answered 75% of the questions correctly. Rather, the 75 refers to the percentage of people in the norming sample whose scores on the test were equal to or below this pupil's score. A percentile rank of 50 means that a pupil has scored as well as or better than 50% of the norming sample and has achieved an average score. Why is this an average score? Because the 50% (percentile rank) coincides with the mean average of the norming sample.

Figure 14.3 illustrates one caution in interpreting percentile scores. Differences in percentile ranks do not mean the same thing in terms of raw score points in the middle of the scale as they do at the fringes. The graph shows Joan's and Alice's percentile scores on a fictitious 'Test of Excellence in Language and Arithmetic'. Both pupils are about average in arithmetic skills. One equalled or surpassed 50% of the norming sample; the other, 60%. However, because their scores are in the middle of the distribution, this difference in percentile ranks means a raw score difference of only a few points. Their raw scores were actually 75 and 77. In the language test, the difference in percentile ranks seems to be about the same as the difference in arithmetic, since one

Percentile rank

Percentage of those in the norming sample who scored at or below an individual's score.

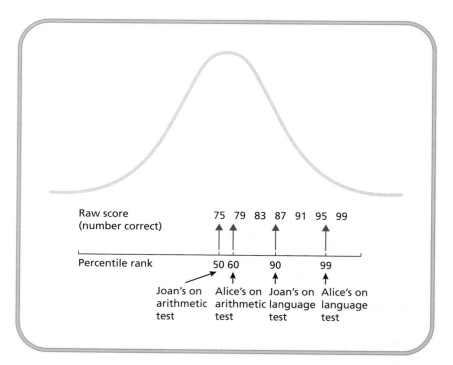

Figure 14.3
Percentile ranking on a normal distribution curve

Percentile scores have different meanings at different places on the scale. For example, a difference of a few raw score points near the mean might translate into a 10-point percentile difference, while it would take 6 or 7 points to make a 10-point percentile difference farther out on the scale.

ranked at the 90th percentile and the other at the 99th. Yet the difference in their raw scores on the language test is much greater. It takes a greater difference in raw score points to make a difference in percentile rank at the extreme ends of the scale. On the language test the difference in raw scores is about 10 points.

Age-equivalent scores

Age-equivalent scores are generally obtained from separate norming samples for each age group. The average of the scores of all the 11-year-olds in the norming sample defines the equivalent score for the level typically awarded to 11-year-olds. Suppose the raw-score average of the norming sample of 11-year-olds is 38. Any pupil who attains a raw score of 38 (or some score within a defined band around 38) on that test will be assigned a level-equivalent score for 11-year-olds (say Level 4). Level-equivalent scores are sometimes listed in numbers such as 3a, 4b, 7c, and so on. The number gives the level, the letter stands for a fraction of a level, i.e. a, b or c is working to the first, second or third part of the level.

> **Level-equivalent score**
>
> Measure of level based on comparison with norming samples from each age group.

Suppose a pupil with the level-equivalent score of 6 is aged 11. Should this pupil be accelerated immediately, to be taught with 13- and 14-year-olds? Probably not! Different forms of tests are used at different ages, so the 11-year-old may not have had to answer questions that would be given to 14-year-olds. The high score may represent superior mastery of material taught to 11-year-olds rather than a capacity for doing advanced work. Even though an average 14-year-old could do as well as our 11-year-old on this particular test, a 14-year-old would certainly know much more than this test covered. Also, level-equivalent score units do not mean the same thing at every age. For example, a 7-year-old reading at a 5-year-old level would have more difficulty in school than a 16-year-old who reads at the 14-year-old level equivalent.

Level-equivalent scores are misleading and are often misinterpreted, especially by parents, therefore most educators and psychologists strongly believe they should not be used at all. There are several other forms of reporting available that are more appropriate.

Standard scores

As you may remember, one problem is that differences in percentile ranks do not mean the same thing in terms of raw score points in the middle of the scale as they do at the fringes. So, a discrepancy of a certain number of raw-score points has a different meaning at different places on the scale. With standard scores, on the other hand, a difference of 10 points is the same everywhere on the scale.

> **Standard scores**
>
> Scores based on the standard deviation.

Standard scores are based on the standard deviation. A very common standard score is called the z score. A z score tells how many standard deviations above or below the average a raw score is. In the example described earlier, in which you were fortunate enough to get a 78 on a test where the mean was 70 and the standard deviation was 4, your z score would be +2, or 2 standard deviations above the mean. If a person were to score 64 on this test, the score would be 1.5 standard deviation units *below* the mean, and the z score would be −1.5. A z score of 0 would be no standard deviations above the mean – in other words, right on the mean.

> **z score**
>
> Standard score indicating the number of standard deviations above or below the mean.

To calculate the z score for a given raw score, subtract the mean from the raw score and divide the difference by the standard deviation. The formula is:

$$z = \frac{\text{Raw Score} - \text{Mean}}{\text{Standard Deviation}}$$

As it is often inconvenient to use negative numbers, other standard scores have been devised to eliminate this potential inconvenience. The T score has a mean of 50

> **T score**
>
> Standard score with a mean of 50 and a standard deviation of 10.

and uses a standard deviation of 10. Thus, a *T* score of 50 indicates average performance. If you multiply the *z* score by 10 (which eliminates the decimal) and add 50 (which gets rid of the negative number), you get the equivalent *T* score as the answer. The person whose *z* score was −1.5 would have a *T* score of 35.

First multiply the *z* score by 10: $-1.5 \times 10 = -15$
Then add 50: $-15 + 50 = 35$

Before we leave this section on types of scores, we should mention one other widely used method. Stanine scores (the name comes from 'standard nine') are standard scores. There are only nine possible scores on the stanine scale, the whole numbers 1 to 9. The mean is 5, and the standard deviation is 2. Each unit from 2 to 8 is equal to half a standard deviation.

Stanine scores

Whole number scores from 1 to 9, each representing a wide range of raw scores.

Stanine scores provide a method of considering a pupil's rank, because each of the nine scores includes a specific range of percentile scores in the normal distribution. For example, a stanine score of 1 is assigned to the bottom 4% of scores in a distribution. A stanine of 2 is assigned to the next 7%. Of course, some raw scores in this 7% range are better than others, but they all get a stanine score of 2.

Each stanine score represents a wide range of raw scores. This has the advantage of encouraging teachers and parents to view a pupil's score in more general terms instead of making fine distinctions based on a few points. Figure 14.4 compares the three types of standard scores we have considered, showing how each would fall on a normal distribution curve.

STOP AND THINK

You may find it useful to review the last section on standard scores in order to be clear about the differences between *z* scores, *T* scores and *stanine* scores.

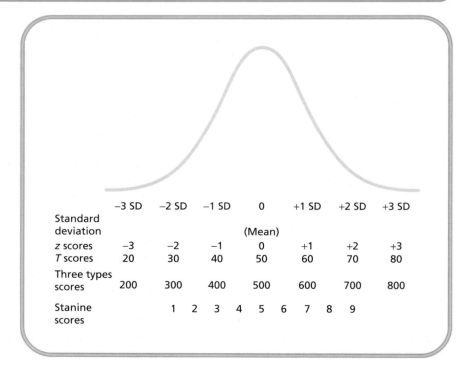

Figure 14.4
Four types of standard scores on a normal distribution curve

Using this figure, you can translate one type of standard into another.

	−3 SD	−2 SD	−1 SD	0	+1 SD	+2 SD	+3 SD
Standard deviation				(Mean)			
z scores	−3	−2	−1	0	+1	+2	+3
T scores	20	30	40	50	60	70	80
Three types scores	200	300	400	500	600	700	800
Stanine scores		1 2	3 4	5 6	7 8	9	

Interpreting test scores

One of the most common problems with the use of tests is misinterpretation of scores. This often happens because of the belief that numbers are precise measurements of a pupil's ability. No test provides a perfect picture of a person's abilities; a test is only one small sample of behaviour. Three factors are important in developing good tests and interpreting results: reliability, validity and absence of bias.

Reliability of test scores

If you took a standardised test on Monday, then took the same test again a week later, and you received about the same score each time, you would have reason to believe the test scores were reliable. If 100 people took the test one day, then repeated it the following week, and the ranking of the individual scores was about the same for both tests, you would be even more certain the test scores were reliable. (Of course, this assumes that no one looks up answers or studies before the second test.) Scores are reliable if a test gives a consistent and stable 'reading' of a person's ability from one occasion to the next, assuming the person's ability remains the same. A reliable thermometer works in a similar manner, giving you a reading of 100°C each time you measure the temperature of boiling water. Measuring reliability this way, by giving the test on two different occasions, indicates stability or test–retest reliability. If a group of people takes two equivalent versions of a test and the scores on both tests are comparable, this indicates alternate-form reliability.

Reliability can also refer to the internal consistency or the precision of a test. This type of reliability, known as split-half reliability, is calculated by comparing performance on half of the test questions with performance on the other half. If, for example, someone did quite well on all the odd-numbered items and not at all well on the even-numbered items, we could assume that the items were not very consistent or precise in measuring what they were intended to measure.

There are several ways to compute reliability, but all the possibilities give values between 0.0 and 1.0 like a correlation coefficient. Above 0.9 is considered very reliable; 0.8 to 0.9 is good, and below 0.8 is not very good reliability for standardised tests (Haladyna, 2002). The most effective way to improve reliability is to add more items to a test. Generally speaking, longer tests are more reliable than shorter ones (Mehrens and Lehmann, 1978).

Error in scores

All tests are imperfect estimators of the qualities or skills they are trying to measure in part because there are bound to be errors in every testing situation. There are sources of error related to the pupil such as mood, motivation, test-taking skills or even cheating. Sometimes the errors are in your favour and you score higher than your ability might warrant; perhaps you reviewed a key section just before the test. Sometimes the errors go against you – you are sick, sleepy or mis-read the instructions. There are also sources of error related to the test itself – the directions are unclear, the reading level is too high, the items are ambiguous or the time limits are wrong.

The score each pupil receives always includes some amount of error. How can error be reduced? As you might guess, this returns us to the question of reliability. The more reliable the test scores are, the less error there will be in the score actually obtained. On standardised tests, test developers take this into consideration and make estimations of how much the pupils' scores would probably vary if they were tested repeatedly. This estimation is called the standard error of measurement. Thus, a reliable test can also be defined as one with a small standard error of measurement. In their interpretation of tests, teachers must also take into consideration the margin for error.

Reliability

Consistency of test results measured by looking at the comparability of scores on two different occasions or of two equivalent versions.

Standard error of measurement

Hypothetical estimate of variation in scores if testing were repeated.

Confidence interval

Confidence interval

Range of scores within which an individual's particular score is likely to fall.

Never base an opinion of a pupil's ability or achievement on the exact score the pupil obtains. Many test companies now report scores using a confidence interval or 'standard error band' that encloses the pupil's actual score. This makes use of the standard error of measurement and allows a teacher to consider the range of scores that might include a pupil's true score – the score the pupil would get if the measurement were completely accurate and error-free.

Let us assume, for example, that two pupils in your class take a standardised achievement test in English. The standard error of measurement for this test is 5. One pupil receives a score of 79 and the other, a score of 85. At first glance, these scores seem quite different. But when you consider the standard error bands around the scores, not just the scores alone, you see that the bands overlap. The first pupil's true score might be anywhere between 74 and 84 (that is, the actual score of 79 plus and minus the standard error of 5). The second pupil's true score might be anywhere between 80 and 90. It is crucial to keep in mind the idea of standard error bands when selecting pupils for special educational provision. No child should be rejected simply because the obtained score missed the cut-off by one or two points. The pupil's true score might well be above the cut-off point.

True score

The score the pupil would get if the measurement were completely accurate and error-free.

Validity

Validity

Degree to which a test measures what it is intended to measure.

If test scores are sufficiently reliable, the second criterion is whether the scores are valid, or more accurately, whether the judgements and decisions about a person's abilities based on the results of the test are valid. To have validity, the decisions and inferences based on the test must be supported by evidence. This means that validity is judged in relation to a particular use or purpose, that is, in relation to the actual decision being made and the evidence for that decision (Lambert and Lines, 2000; Popham, 2005a). A particular test might be valid for one purpose, but not for another.

Connect and Extend

Messick, S. (1995). 'Standards of validity and the validity of standards in performance assessment', *Educational Measurement: Issues and Practice*, 14(4), pp. 5–8.

There are different kinds of evidence to support a particular judgement. If the purpose of a test is to measure the skills covered in a course or unit, then we would hope to see test questions on all the important topics and not on extraneous information. If this condition is met, we would have content-related evidence of validity. Have you ever taken a test that dealt only with a few ideas from one lecture or just a few pages of a textbook? Then decisions based on that test (like your grade) certainly lacked content-related evidence of validity.

Some tests are designed to predict outcomes. A-levels for example (examination taken at the age of 18, the results of which are often used to select pupils for university places) are intended to predict performance in university. If A-level scores correlate with academic performance in university as measured by, say, marks average in the first year, then we have criterion-related evidence of validity for the use of A-levels in admissions decisions.

Most standardised tests are designed to measure some psychological characteristic or 'construct' such as reasoning ability, reading comprehension, motivation, intelligence, creativity and so on. (Psychologists call these attributes constructs because they are constructions of different human behaviours.) It is a bit more difficult to gather construct-related evidence of validity, yet this is a very important requirement – probably the most important. Indeed, Cronbach (1980) and Messick (1989) identify construct validity as the unifying concept underlying all validity. Construct-related evidence of validity is gathered over many years and is indicated by a pattern of scores. For example, older children can answer more questions on intelligence tests than younger children can. This fits with our construct of intelligence. If the average five-year-old answered as many questions correctly on a test as the average 13-year-old, we would doubt that the test really measured intelligence. Construct-related evidence for validity can also be demonstrated when the results of a test correlate with the results of other well-established, valid measures of the same construct.

To summarise, many psychologists suggest that construct validity is the unifying category and that gathering content- and criterion-related evidence is another way of determining if the test measures the construct it was designed to measure. In short, is the test a good measure of the characteristic it is assumed to assess?

A test must be reliable in order to be valid. For example, if, over a few months, an intelligence test yields different results each time it is given to the same child, then by definition it is not reliable. Certainly, it couldn't be a valid measure of intelligence because intelligence is assumed to be fairly stable, at least over a short period of time. However, reliability will not guarantee validity. If that intelligence test gave the same score every time for a particular child, but didn't predict school achievement, speed of learning or other characteristics associated with intelligence, then performance on the test would not be a true indicator of intelligence. The test would be reliable – but invalid. As you will see in the next chapter, reliability and validity are issues with all assessments, not just standardised tests. Classroom tests should yield scores that are reliable, as free from error as possible and accurately indicate what they are supposed to measure. The Focus on Practice below should help you understand and checkout the reliability and validity of the standardised tests you give.

FOCUS ON PRACTICE

Increasing reliability and validity

Make sure the test actually covers the content of the unit of study

Examples
1. Compare test questions to unit learning objectives. Make sure that there is good overlap.
2. Use local achievement tests and local norms when possible.
3. Check to see if the test is long enough to cover all important topics.
4. Find out if there any difficulties your pupils experience with the test, such as not enough time, too difficult a level of reading, and so on. If there are, discuss these problems with appropriate curriculum and assessment managers.

Make sure pupils know how to use all the test materials

Examples
1. Several days before the testing, do a few practice questions with a similar format.
2. Demonstrate the use of the answer sheets, especially computer-scored answer sheets.
3. Check with new pupils, shy pupils and pupils who have difficulty reading to make sure they understand the questions and the instructions.
4. Make sure pupils know if and when guessing is appropriate.

Follow instructions for administering the test exactly

Examples
1. Practise giving the test before you actually use it.
2. Follow the time limits exactly.

Make pupils as comfortable as possible during testing

Examples
1. Do not create anxiety by making the test seem like the most important event of the year.
2. Help the class relax before beginning the test, perhaps by telling a joke or having everyone take a few deep breaths. Don't be tense yourself!
3. Make sure the room is quiet.
4. Discourage cheating by monitoring the room. Don't become absorbed in your own paperwork.

Remember that no test scores are perfect

Examples
1. Interpret scores using bands instead of a single score.
2. Ignore small differences between scores.

For more information on Bias in Testing and how to avoid it, see http://www.fairtest.org/ For a good explanation of reliability and validity, see http://seamonkey.ed.asu.edu/~alex/teaching/assessment/reliability.html or follow the links from http://www.pearsoned.co.uk/woolfolkeuro.

Assessment bias

Assessment bias

Qualities of an assessment instrument that offend or unfairly penalise a group of pupils because of the pupils' gender, SES, race, ethnicity, etc.

Earlier we said that three factors are important in developing good tests and interpreting results. The first two are reliability and validity and we now turn to the third, absence of bias. Assessment bias 'refers to qualities of an assessment instrument that offend or unfairly penalize a group of pupils because of the pupils' gender, ethnicity, socioeconomic status, religion, or other such group-defining characteristic' (Popham, 2005a: 77). Biases are aspects of the test such as content, language or examples that might distort the performance of a group – either for better or for worse. For example, if a reading test used passages that described boxing or football scenarios, we might expect males on average to do better than females.

Two forms of assessment bias are unfair penalisation and offensiveness. The reading assessment with heavy sports content is an example of unfair penalisation – girls may be penalised for their lack of boxing or football knowledge. Offensiveness occurs when a particular group might be insulted by the content of the assessment. Offended, angry pupils may not perform at their best if, for example, the content of a comprehension test assumes that many British muslims supported the London suicide bombings of July 2005.

Are tests such as the individual measures of intelligence or formal examinations at 16 and 18 fair assessments for minority-group pupils? This is a complex question.

Research on test bias shows that most standardised tests predict school achievement equally well across all groups of pupils. Items that might appear on the surface to be biased against minority-group pupils are not necessarily more difficult for them to answer correctly (Sattler, 2001). But even though standardised aptitude and achievement tests are not biased in predicting school performance, many people believe that the tests still can be unfair to some groups. Tests may not have *procedural fairness;* that is, some groups may not have an equal opportunity to show what they know on the test. Here are a few examples:

1. The language of the test and the test writer is often different from the languages of the pupils.

2. Answers that support the marker's middle-class values are often rewarded with more points.

3. On individually administered intelligence tests, being very verbal and talking a lot is rewarded. This favours pupils who feel comfortable in that particular situation.

Also, tests may not be fair, because different groups have had different *opportunities to learn* the material tested. The questions asked tend to centre on experiences and facts more familiar to the dominant culture than to minority-group pupils. Consider this test question for 8-year-olds adapted from Popham (2005a: 336):

> My uncle's *field* is computer programming

Look at the sentences below. In which sentence does the word *field* mean the same as it does in the boxed sentence above?

A. The bowler knew she had to *field* the bowling crease.

B. They prepared the *field* by spraying and ploughing it.

C. I know the *field* I plan to enter when I finish university.

D. The doctor used a wall chart to examine my *field* of vision.

Items like this are on most standardised tests. But not all families describe their work as a *field* of employment. If your parents work in professional fields such as computers, medicine, law or education, the item might make sense because the 'talk' of the home might include reference to working in a professional field, but what if your parents worked at a grocery store or a tyre and exhaust centre? Are these fields? Life outside class has prepared some pupils, but not others for this question.

Concern about cultural bias in testing has led some psychologists to try to develop culture-fair or culture-free tests. Two examples of interest are the Porteus Maze test, where, as the name suggests, the test is to draw routes through a series of mazes, and Raven's Progressive Matrices where a figure is selected to complete a matrix. Both tests were originally validated by correlating scores with traditional IQ tests. However, neither test proved culture-free as, in the case of the maze test, lack of familiarity with streets and cul-de-sacs put Australian Aborigines at a complete disadvantage, leading to biased and defamatory judgements being made about the intelligence of Aborigines (Gipps and Murphy, 1994). When you think about it, how can you separate culture from cognition? Every pupil's learning is embedded in his or her culture and every test question grows from some kind of cultural knowledge.

Today, most standardised tests are checked carefully for assessment bias, but teacher-made tests may have biased content as well. It makes sense for beginning teachers to have colleagues check tests for bias (Popham, 2005a).

Culture-fair or culture-free test

A test without cultural bias.

Connect and Extend

Using and adapting the Focus on Practice on page 635, prepare a testing guide sheet. Focus on a particular age group.

STOP AND THINK

Teachers, learning specialists and school psychologists use a variety of tests. Distinguish between achievement, diagnostic and aptitude tests. Describe the purposes for each.

Types of Standardised Tests

Connect and Extend

What kinds of tests do pupils take during their time in school? See the Companion Website (Web Link 14.1). What tests are missing from this list?

Several kinds of standardised tests are used in schools today. If you have seen school portfolio records of achievement that include testing records for individual pupils over several years, then you know the many ways pupils are tested. There are three broad categories of standardised tests: achievement, diagnostic and aptitude (including interest). As a teacher, you will probably encounter achievement and aptitude tests most frequently.

Achievement tests: what has the pupil learned?

STOP AND THINK

Do you remember the first reading tests you took? This co-author's began: 'tree, little, milk, egg, book'. (He took the same test twice a year for seven years!) From the score on this test his teachers would work out his reading age. How did that work?

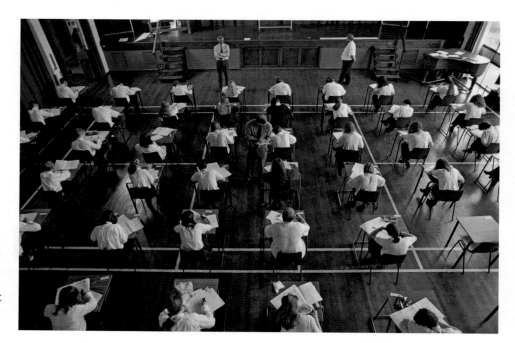

Standardised tests used in education usually fit three broad categories: achievement, diagnostic and aptitude (including interest)

FOCUS ON PRACTICE

Becoming an expert test-taker

Use the night before the test effectively

Examples
1. Study the night before the exam, ending with a final look at a summary of the key points, concepts and relationships.
2. Get a good night's sleep. If you know you generally have trouble sleeping the night before an exam, try getting extra sleep on several previous nights.

Set the situation so you can concentrate on the test

Examples
1. Give yourself plenty of time to eat or go to the toilet before going to the classroom.
2. Don't sit near a friend. It may make concentration difficult. If your friend leaves early, you may be tempted to do so, too.

Make sure you know what the test is asking

Examples
1. Read the directions carefully. If you are unsure, ask the teacher or invigilator for clarification.
2. Read each question carefully to spot tricky words, such as *not, except, all of the following but one.*
3. On an essay test, read every question first, so you know the size of the job ahead of you and can make informed decisions about how much time to spend on each question. Note your timings down.
4. On a multiple-choice test, read every alternative, even if an early one seems right. Remember the examiners tend to include a close-to-call alternative.

Use time effectively

Examples
1. Begin working right away and move as rapidly as possible while your energy is high.
2. Do the easy questions first.
3. Don't get stuck on one question. If you are stumped, mark the question so you can return to it easily later, and go on to questions you can answer more quickly.
4. If you are unsure about a question, answer it, but mark it so you can go back if there is time.

5. On a multiple-choice test, if you know you will not have time to finish, fill in all the remaining questions with the same letter if there is no penalty for guessing.
6. If you are running out of time on an essay test, do not leave any questions blank. Briefly outline a few key points to show the instructor you knew the answer but needed more time.

Know when to guess on multiple-choice or true-false tests

Examples
1. Always guess when only right answers are scored.
2. Always guess when you can eliminate some of the alternatives.
3. Don't guess if there is a penalty for guessing, unless you can confidently eliminate at least one alternative.
4. Does the grammar give the right answer away or eliminate any alternatives?

Check your work

Examples
1. Even if you can't stand to look at the test another minute, reread each question to make sure you answered the way you intended.
2. If you are using a machine-scored answer sheet, check occasionally to be sure the number of the question you are answering corresponds to the number of the answer on the sheet.

On essay tests, answer as directly as possible

Examples
1. Avoid flowery introductions. Answer the question in the first sentence and then elaborate.
2. Don't save your best ideas till last. Give them early in the answer.
3. Unless the instructions require complete sentences, consider listing points, arguments and so on by number in your answer. It will help you organise your thoughts and concentrate on the important aspects of the answer.

Learn from the testing experience

Examples
1. Pay attention when the teacher reviews the answers. You can learn from your mistakes, and the same question may reappear in a later test.
2. Notice if you are having trouble with a particular kind of item; adjust your study approach next time to handle this type of item better.

For more test-taking strategies see http://www.testtakingtips.com/.

The most common standardised tests given to pupils are achievement tests. These are meant to measure how much a pupil has learned in specific content areas such as reading recognition or de-coding, reading comprehension, language usage, computation, science, social studies, mathematics and logical reasoning. There are achievement tests for both individuals and groups. These tests vary in their reliability and validity. Group tests can be used for screening – to identify children who might need further testing or as a basis for grouping pupils according to achievement levels. Individual achievement tests are given to determine a child's academic level more precisely, or to help form a profile of missed learning.

Diagnostic tests: what are the pupil's strengths and weaknesses?

Achievement tests, both standardised and teacher-made, identify weaknesses in academic content areas such as mathematics, computation or reading. Individually administered diagnostic tests identify weaknesses in learning processes. If teachers want to identify specific learning problems, they may need to refer to results from the various diagnostic tests that have been developed to assess these learning processes. Most diagnostic tests are given to pupils individually by a trained professional. The goal is usually to identify the specific problems a pupil is having. There are diagnostic tests to:

- assess the ability to hear differences among sounds;
- remember spoken words or sentences;
- recall a sequence of symbols;
- separate figures from their background;
- express relationships;
- coordinate eye and hand movements;
- describe objects orally;
- blend sounds to form words;
- recognise details in a picture;
- coordinate movements; and
- many other abilities needed to learn, remember and communicate learning.

Primary school teachers are more likely than secondary school teachers to receive information from diagnostic tests. Secondary school pupils are more likely to take aptitude tests.

Achievement tests

Standardised tests measuring how much pupils have learned in a given content area.

Connect and Extend

Use EbscoHost Electronic Journals Service or similar to access Topping, K. J. and Fisher, A. M. (2003), 'Computerised formative assessment of reading comprehension: field trials in the UK', *Journal of Research in Reading, 26*(3), pp. 267–279.

Connect and Extend

Accurate information from the teacher is essential for pupils' academic progress. The ERIC Digest *Explaining Test Results to Parents* might help with this task. See the Companion Website (Web Link 14.2).

Diagnostic tests

Individually administered tests to identify special learning problems.

Aptitude tests

Tests meant to predict future performance.

STOP AND THINK

Choose a partner to role-play a parent–teacher consultation. Using the examples of Terry and Jasveer below, 'the teacher' should interpret the scores to 'the parent' and make judgements or recommendations about the child's future educational experiences. 'The parent' should feel free to ask questions concerning the interpretation and the recommendations.

Terry: Seven years old, scores based on national norm
Maths Computation: 6.0 (age-equivalent score)
Maths Reasoning: 3.5 (age-equivalent score)

Reading Vocabulary: 85th percentile
Reading Comprehension: 53rd percentile
Group IQ score: 79 (The test was given the day before Terry's birthday – why might this be important?)

Jasveer: 15 years old, scores based on local norms
Maths Computation: 5 (stanine score)
Maths Reasoning: 4 (stanine score)
Reading Vocabulary: 53 (*T* score)
Reading Comprehension: 38 (*T* score)
Individual intelligence test: 125

Aptitude tests: how well will the pupil do in the future?

> **STOP AND THINK**
>
> What aptitude tests have you taken? Did they correctly predict how well you can learn in the future? If you are not sure what an aptitude test is you may need to return to this after you have studied this section.

Both achievement and aptitude tests measure developed abilities. Achievement tests may measure abilities developed over a short period of time, such as during a four-lesson unit on map reading, or over a longer period of time, such as a term. Aptitude tests are meant to measure abilities developed over many years and to predict how well a pupil will learn unfamiliar material in the future. The greatest difference between the two types of tests is that they are used for different purposes. Achievement tests measure final performance and aptitude tests predict how well people will do in future courses at university or in vocational courses (Anastasi, 1988).

IQ and scholastic aptitude

In Chapter 4, we discussed one of the most influential aptitude tests of all, the IQ test. The IQ test as we know it could well be called a test of scholastic aptitude. Now that you understand the concept of standard deviation, you will be able to appreciate several statistical characteristics of the tests. For example, the IQ score is really a standard score with a mean of 100 and a standard deviation of 15 or 16, depending on the test. Thus, about 68% of the global population would score between $+1$ and -1 standard deviations from the mean, or between about 85 and 115.

A difference of a few points between two pupils' IQ scores should not be viewed as important. Scores between 90 and 109 are within the average range. In fact, scores between 80 and 119 are considered within the range of low average to high average. To see the problems that may arise, consider the following conversation:

Parent: We came to speak with you today because we are shocked at our son's IQ score. We can't believe he has only a 99 IQ when his sister scored much higher on the same test. We know they are about the same. In fact, Sam has better achievement grades than Lauren did in Class 5.

Teacher: What was Lauren's score?

Parent: Well, she did much better. She scored a 103!

Clearly, brother and sister have both scored within the average range. Although the standard error of measurement on most IQ tests varies slightly from one age group to the next, the average standard error for the total score is usually about 3. So the bands around Sam's and Lauren's IQ scores – about 96 to 102 and 100 to 106 – are overlapping. Either child could have scored 100, 101 or 102.

Discussing test results with families

At times, you will be expected to explain or describe test results to your pupils' families. The Focus on Practice below gives some ideas.

FOCUS ON PRACTICE

Explaining and using test results

Be ready to explain, in non-technical terms, what each type of score on the test report means

Examples
1. If the test is norm-referenced, know if the comparison group was national or local. Explain that the child's score shows how he or she performed *in relation to* the other pupils in the comparison group.
2. If the test is criterion-referenced, explain that the child's scores show how well he or she performs in specific areas.

If the test is norm-referenced, focus on the percentile scores. They are the easiest to understand

Examples
1. Explain that percentile scores tell what percent of pupils in the comparison group made the same score or lower – higher percentiles are better and 99 is as high as you can get. 50 is average.
2. Remind parents that percentile scores do not tell the 'percent correct', so scores that would be bad on a classroom test (say 65% to 75% or so) are above average – even good – as percentile scores.

Avoid using age-equivalent scores

Examples
1. If parents want to focus on the 'level' of their child, tell them that high level-equivalent scores reflect a thorough understanding of the current work and *not* necessarily the capacity to do higher level work.
2. Tell parents that the same level-equivalent score has different meanings in different subjects – reading and mathematics, for example.

Be aware of the error in testing

Examples

1. Encourage parents to think of the score not as a single point, but as a range or band that includes the score.
2. Ignore small differences between scores.
3. Note that sometimes individual skills on criterion-referenced tests are measured with just a few (two or three) items. Compare test scores to actual class work in the same areas.
4. Use the consultation time to plan a learning goal for the child that families can support.

Examples

1. Have example questions, similar to those on the test, to show parents what their child can do easily and what kinds of questions he or she found difficult.
2. Be prepared to suggest an important skill to target.

For more help explaining tests to parents, see http://pareonline.net/getvn.asp?v=1&n=1.

Issues in Standardised Testing

STOP AND THINK

As part of the interview process for a job in a primary school, a teacher is asked 'What should we do to raise national attainment test scores in this school so we can reach our targets?' How should the teacher respond?

Connect and Extend

Since their inception, there have been controversies regarding the use of standardised tests in schools. Familiarise yourself with the major issues that underlie these controversies by web-searching using 'standardised testing' as your search terms. Explain the positions of the different camps in these controversies.

For this co-author's entire teaching career (he began teaching in 1975) policy makers have been concerned about the test performance of pupils, and have associated 'raising standards' in schools with improving those test performances. This comparatively recent emphasis upon testing in UK schools and perhaps further afield in the world, may have had its roots in a post-modern anti-liberalism, anti-progressive movement adopted by politicians of both main UK parties. The political movement to hold the institution of education to account can be traced back, beginning in 1969, to the Black papers of Brian Cox and A. E. Dyson, and later Rhodes Boyson, which mounted an attack on what was seen as the excesses of experimental progressive ideas.

What transpired, was a system of statutory national testing of a National Curriculum, delivered according to successful styles of teaching observed in the classrooms of competitor nations higher in the international league tables of educational performance, and policed by a powerful inspection regime, established as the Office for Standards in Education (OfSTED). The aggregated results of standard assessment tests (SATs) taken at seven, 11 and 14 were used, along with public examination results at 16 (GCSEs) and 18 (A-levels) to create league tables of schools.

Statutory reporting to parents included information that allowed them to compare the test results achieved by their children with the rest of the school, with pupils of the same age in the area and with national statistics. It also enabled parents and the wider community to compare the results of schools. Targets were set nationally, locally, for classes and groups and for individual children. Targets were seen as the key to pushing up standards and schools that exceeded the targets were seen as successful schools. However, schools whose percentages of pupils at seven, 11, 14, 16 and 18 years did not achieve the national targets were by definition 'failing schools' and liable to special measures and closure.

Attempts were made to make the whole regime 'fairer' with the introduction of value-added measures of school performance. These included base-line assessments (so called, because they provided a starting measure) at the beginning of formal schooling, profiling of younger pupils in early years settings and the testing of pupils at any stage when they moved school. This also included batteries of tests attempting to compare individual and class performance with individual potential and contextual factors. These tests are known as PIPS (Performance Indicators in Primary Schools), PIMS (Performance Indicators in Middle Schools) and YELLIS (not performance indicators in secondary schools but rather the **YE**ar **11** **I**nformation **S**ystem).

The reaction of many head teachers to these national and local policy moves to associate testing with raising standards has been to impose a regime of testing (and reaction to the results of that testing) on the schools that they led. For example, take a look at the testing, recording, reporting and target-setting regime established by one school in the north-west of England and used as an exemplar case study on the UK Government 'Qualifications and Curriculum Authority' website (see Figure 14.5).

Remember what Patricia Broadfoot wrote in 1996 (quoted in part in the introduction to this chapter):

educational assessment is not just about judging individual *potential and performance. It has always been just as much about judging* institutional *quality (1996: 7).*

Whether it is 'just as much about' or 'more or less about' judging institutional quality than about individual children, it is clear that there is a good deal of testing going on in our schools. Given all this testing, how are the results used?

Accountability and high-stakes testing

STOP AND THINK

How has standardised testing affected your life so far? What life opportunities have been opened or closed to you based on test scores? Was the process fair?

Tests are not simply procedures used in research. Every day there are many decisions made about individuals that are based on the results of tests. Should Emily be issued a driver's licence? How many and which pupils at 13 would benefit from an accelerated programme in science? Who needs extra tutoring? Who will be admitted to university or law school? Test scores may affect admission to school and to sixth form, access to 'gifted and talented' programmes, placement in special education classes, to teacher qualification and advancement, and to school funding.

Connect and Extend

For more discussion of high stake testing see the Companion Website (Web Link 14.3).

The school

Staining Church of England VC Primary School is a school situated in a village outside Blackpool, Lancashire, UK. It draws from a wide range of backgrounds and the number of children with special needs and free school meals entitlement are both average. Children's attainment upon joining the school is average. The 2001 OfSTED inspection report recognised that the children achieve very well and attain standards that are much higher than children in similar schools. The school has used a wide range of assessment and analysis tools in the past and has now settled on a combination of tools:

Performance Indicators in Primary Schools (PIPS) are used in all years (twice in Reception) following the recommended schedule. Results are held on paper and in a Microsoft Excel database and are discussed by teachers, subject coordinators, the special educational needs coordinator (SENCO), the head teacher and the deputy head teacher. The School Governors' Committees discuss composite results, trends and value-added analysis. PIPS 'chances graphs' are used to support setting targets for each individual child for Key Stage 1 and Key Stage 2.

National Foundation for Educational Research (NFER) reading tests are taken by Years 2 to 6 in May and June. Reading ages and standardised scores are recorded in Schools Information Management System (SIMS) Assessment Manager and a report is produced to track progress. The standardised scores are particularly useful for establishing target groups of children, for example those with scores in the 95–100 range to be given additional support. Each half-term, all years from 1 to 6 have a piece of unaided writing formally assessed by the teacher. The results are recorded in Assessment Manager. NFER Richmond tests (across a wide range of curriculum subjects) are taken by Years 4, 5 and 6 early in the spring term. Results are held on paper and in an Excel database.

Each term, teacher assessments are collected for every child and progress towards the agreed targets is recorded and discussed. The Qualifications and Curriculum Authority (QCA) optional tests are taken by Years 3, 4, and 5 in the same week in May that Years 2 and 6 sit the statutory tests. Results are recorded in SIMS Assessment Manager and summaries are produced for each class. After the National Curriculum and optional tests the school enters the results for every child into the QCA diagnostic software (now Pupil Achievement Tracker). The school uses the analysis provided by the diagnostic software in a number of ways.

The question-by-question results and the analysis of 'missed out' questions are very useful to the class teacher to inform planning. The 'web graphs' produced for each child are also a very useful facility. It also uses summary analysis in its discussions, for example the breakdown of the results by attainment target and by gender. It then imports this data into the Pupil Achievement Tracker (PAT). The value-added graphs are particularly useful in the discussion of the progress of groups and individual children.

Each July, the head teacher, the current teacher and the prospective teacher for the following year, with subject coordinators and the SENCO as appropriate, meet to discuss each class. All the above data is available to support these discussions and it is considered alongside the teacher's regular assessment. For each child, current National Curriculum levels (for English, mathematics and science) are agreed and targets are set for the end of the following year. Numerical targets are currently not shared with parents and children, except in Year 6, but curriculum targets are shared with both by the teacher. Each year the head teacher prepares a summary of the performance and assessment (PANDA) results provided by the Office for Standards in Education (OfSTED) and of the school results and targets for the governors.

Figure 14.5
One example of a testing regime in a UK primary school

Source: www.qca.org.uk/9115_9288.html

In making these decisions, it is important to distinguish between the quality of the test itself and the way the test is used. Even the best assessments can be, and have been, misused. In earlier years, for example, using otherwise valid and reliable individual intelligence tests, many pupils were inappropriately identified as having mental retardation (Snapp and Woolfolk, 1973). The problem was not with the tests, but with the fact that the test score was the only information used to classify pupils. Much more information is always needed to make this type of placement decision.

Behind all the statistics and terminology are issues related to values and ethics. Who will be tested? What are the consequences of choosing one test over another for a particular purpose with a given group? What is the effect of the testing on the pupils? How will the test scores of minority-group pupils be interpreted? What do we really mean by intelligence, competence and scholastic aptitude? Do our views agree with those implied by the tests we use to measure these constructs? How will test results be integrated with other information about the individual to make judgements? Answering these questions requires choices based on values, as well as accurate information about what tests can and cannot tell us. Keep these values issues in mind as we examine testing uses and decisions.

Because the decisions affected by test scores are so critical, many educators call this process high-stakes testing. As we have observed, one of the high-stakes uses for test results is to hold teachers, schools and head teachers accountable for pupil performance. For example, teachers promotion or advancement through salary bar points might be tied to their pupils' achievement, or a schools' funding or very existence may be affected by test results. The pupils in 'failing schools' can and are encouraged to transfer. If the school's scores against targets don't improve, the school's management and/or teaching staff can be replaced or the school closed. High-stakes testing is precisely that and no-one should underestimate the potential impact of the use of such testing on national systems, schools and teachers, classes and individual pupils (James, 2000)

Not just teachers and head teachers have their jobs on the line. In 1997, the then UK Government's Secretary of State for Education, David Blunkett, said that by 2002 he wanted 80% of 11-year-olds to reach the expected levels (measured by national testing) in English and 75% in mathematics. He promised to resign if the targets were not met by 2002. The results of national tests for 11-year-olds in 2002 reported 75% reached the standard expected for their age in English and 73% reached that level for mathematics. By then, Mr Blunkett had moved to the Home Office where he subsequently resigned.

Is it reasonable to hold teachers and schools accountable for pupil achievement? The Discussion Point below compares two opposing points of view.

No matter how good the test, some uses of high-stakes tests are not appropriate. Table 14.3 describes these problem uses.

The dangers and possibilities of high-stakes testing

The teachers we work with are frustrated that results of standardised tests often come too late in the year to help them plan catch-up or booster lessons for their current pupils. They are also troubled by the amount of time that testing takes – to prepare for the tests and to give them; and more, they complain that some national tests cover material that the curriculum does not include. Are they right?

Documented problems with high-stakes testing

When so much rides on the results of a test, you would assume that the test actually measured what had been taught and the way it had been taught. In the past, this match has been a problem. When national tests in mental arithmetic were first

High-stakes testing

Standardised tests whose results have powerful influences when used by school managers, other officials or employers to make decisions.

Accountable

Making teachers and schools responsible for pupil learning, usually by monitoring learning with high-stakes tests.

➡ Connect and Extend

See Harlen, W. (2003), 'The inequitable impacts of high stakes testing', *Education Review, 17*(1), pp. 43–50 and Wall, D. (2000), 'The impact of high-stakes testing on teaching and learning: can this be predicted or controlled?' *28*(4), pp. 499–509.

DISCUSSION POINT

Should tests be used to hold teachers accountable?

There are two possible meanings for accountability. The first has to do with gathering information so that we can make good educational decisions about programmes, policies and resources. The second is holding someone responsible for pupil learning – usually the school or the teacher (Haladyna, 2002).

Agree: Yes, the public needs information

The argument for this kind of accountability is that the public has a right to know how their schools are doing, especially because public money is used to finance schools. Testing may help to raise expectations for the lowest-performing schools and give managers the information they need to target support in their schools (Doherty, 2002). UK government policy on raising standards in school (and therefore enhancing life chances for pupils) depended upon public information about how schools and local education authorities (LEAs) were doing. In a speech made to the North of England Education Conference, January 1998, the then School Standards Minister Stephen Byers said:

'Today we publish targets for every LEA to reach by the end of this Parliament and with them our promise to monitor their performance annually. There will be no hiding place for under-performance – every parent will know these figures and will judge LEAs on how they meet them.

We want no excuse for failure. Many LEAs are in deprived areas, but poverty is no excuse for underachievement – it is a reason for targeted support. There is clear evidence that some schools in depressed areas are already reaching above the national average – if they can improve, all schools can improve.

Disagree: No, using test scores to hold teachers and schools accountable does not make sense

Will results of standardised tests really give parents information about the quality of their children's schools or the work of LEAs? If the test matches important objectives of the curriculum, is given to pupils who actually studied the curriculum for a reasonable period of time, is free of bias, fits the pupils' language capabilities and was administered properly, then test results provide some information about the effectiveness of schools. But as James Popham notes, 'Unfortunately, the scores on most of today's large-scale accountability exams reflect pupils' socio-economic status much more accurately than they do teachers' skills' (2005b: 80). If we rank all the schools by achievement test scores, the order would be virtually the same as if we ranked the schools by the average income of the pupils' families (Noguera, 2005).

There is another problem with holding teachers and schools accountable for all pupils reaching a particular standard, a problem that the UK government was willing to admit to in 2004 and reported in the *Times Educational Supplement*:

Government admits to league table flaws

Value-added and traditional league tables exaggerate differences between schools and can be an unreliable indicator of their performance, the Government admitted this week. Most variation in schools' test results is caused by factors such as deprivation, prior attainment and special needs rather than differences in effectiveness, a Department for Education and Skills analysis of exam results found.

The report, published on the department's website www.dfes.gov.uk, is a startling admission from a government which has put tables at the heart of its standards agenda and used them to set numerous targets for schools. It will be seized upon by opponents of league tables as evidence that the Government's insistence on publishing them is unfair to schools and is bad politics.
(John Slater, TES, 6 August 2004)

Finally, it is foolish to require all pupils to learn the same things and judge them by the same standards when they haven't had the same opportunity to learn the material. The high-stakes accountability process seems to assume that 'public humiliation is enough to get schools to improve. I see no evidence that that works' (Noguera, 2005: 15).

WHAT DO YOU THINK?
Agree or Disagree? Vote online at www.pearsoned.co.uk/woolfolkeuro.

introduced into England as part of the statutory assessment tests for pupils aged 11, pupils were not allowed to make any marks on their paper other than the answer. Indeed, marks were deducted even if the pupils got the right answer but noted down an amount to assist their memory. This penalising of children for making informal notes was completely out of kilter with the teaching strategies being encouraged in this context. Even where teachers make criteria-referenced judgements about attainment of seven-year-olds in English, there can be a significant misalignment between the programmes of study the teachers follow with their children on the run up to the assessment, and the level descriptors the teachers use to award attainment levels to the children (Hall, 2001). Recently, the overlap between curriculum content and teaching methods, and what is tested, has been improving, but it still makes sense to be aware of possible mismatches.

What about time? There are any number of research studies in the literature (e.g. Sturman, 2003; Wilkins *et al.*, 2003; Remedios *et al.*, 2005; Conner, 2003) that suggest disproportionate amounts of time are spent in schools testing children and preparing children to be tested. Harry Torrance from the Institute of Education, Manchester (UK) Metropolitan University asserted in a professorial lecture delivered at the University of Sussex, 11 June 2002 (subsequently published in 2003):

All international research evidence, gathered over many years, not to mention personal experience and common sense, suggests that this is what happens when 'high stakes' tests are encountered in educational systems; i.e. when teachers and students are faced with tests which carry significant consequences for student life chances and teacher accountability, very significant time and energy will be devoted to test preparation.

 **Connect and Extend**

Check out Gregory, K. and Clark, M. (2003). 'High Stakes Assessment in England and Singapore', *Theory in Practice*, pp. 66–74, and Jones, L. (2001). 'Assessing achievement versus high-stakes testing: A crucial contrast', *Educational Assessment*, 7(1), pp. 21–28.

Table 14.3 Inappropriate uses for high-stakes test results

Beware of some uses for standarised test results. Tests were not designed for these purposes:

Pass/fail decisions	In order to label pupils as pass or fail (as meeting or not meeting the expected standard for children of seven, 11 or 14) there must be strong evidence that the test is valid, reliable and free of bias. Some tests, for example the Standard Assessment Tests in England have been challenged as not meeting these standards, and many tests are even less well-placed to be the basis for pass/fail decisions.
Country-to-country comparisons	You cannot really compare countries using standarised test scores. Countries do not have the same curriculum, tests, resources or challenges. If comparisons are made, they usually tell us what we already know – some countries have more funding for schools and more families with higher incomes or education levels.
Evaluation of teachers or schools (league tables)	Many influences on test scores – family and community resources – are outside the control of teachers and schools. Often pupils move from school to school, so many pupils taking a test in spring may have been in the school only for a few weeks.
Identifying where to buy a house	Generally speaking, the schools with the highest test scores are in the neighbourhoods where families have the highest levels of education and income. They may not be the 'best schools' in terms of teaching, programmes for children with specific or general learning difficulties, or leadership for inclusive education, but they are the schools lucky enough to have the 'right' pupils.

Source: Adapted from *Essentials of Standarised Achievement Testing: Validity and Accountability* by T. H. Haladyna. Copyright © 2002 by Pearson Education.

Connect and Extend

What about psychological assessment of pupils? How can schools promote good testing practices? In 2001, Jose Muniz and his colleagues studied the opinions of psychologists across Europe. Examine the results in Muniz, J. *et al.* (2001), 'Testing practices in European countries', *European Journal of Psychological Assessment, 17*(3), pp. 201–11.

Another unintended consequence of the early high-stakes testing in primary schools is to identify pupils who have not reached the expected standard or 'failed'. Pupils then 'self-identify' themselves as failures and believe they are going to fail in the future. Children's attitudes to failure are complex but it is an essentially human reaction to see personal failure as a predictor of future performance. If children fail (particularly high-stakes test or task), they think they will fail next time (Seegers *et al.*, 2002) and continue to fail until they achieve success. Until they prove to themselves that they are capable of not failing, they see no point in continuing to attend school or working hard at their lessons (Hoyle, 1998; Elliott, 1999). This effect has been seen as more marked in pupils from minority ethnic groups (Kalmijn and Kraaykamp, 2003).

Using high-stakes testing well

To be valuable, testing programmes must have a number of characteristics. Of course, the tests used must be reliable, valid and fit for purpose, and free of bias. In addition, a testing programme must:

1. Match the content standards of the curriculum – this is a vital part of validity.
2. Make sure all pupils taking the test have adequate opportunities to learn the material being tested.

3. Be part of the larger assessment plan. No individual test provides all the necessary information about pupil achievement. It is critical that schools avoid making pass/fail decisions based on a single test.

4. Test complex thinking, not just skills and factual knowledge.

5. Take into account the pupil's language. Pupils who have difficulty reading or writing in English will not perform well on tests that require English proficiency.

6. Include all pupils in the testing, but also provide informative reports of the results that make the pupils' situations clear if they have special challenges or circumstances such as disabilities.

7. Provide alternative assessment strategies for pupils with identifiable disabilities.

8. Provide opportunities for early re-testing when the stakes are high.

9. Provide appropriate support when pupils fail.

This is important, so we make no apology for repeating it: high-stakes standardised achievement tests must be chosen so that test items actually measure knowledge gained in lessons and set homework tasks. Also, pupils must have the necessary skills to take the test. If pupils score low on a science test, not because they lack knowledge about science, but because they have difficulty reading the questions, don't speak English, or have too little time to finish, then the test is not a valid measure of science achievement for those pupils.

Connect and Extend

See Linn, R. (2003), 'Accountability: Responsibility and reasonable expectations', *Educational Researcher, 32*(7), pp. 3–13.

Preparing for tests

Two types of preparation can make a difference in test scores. One type helps pupils become familiar with the procedures of standardised tests. Pupils who have extensive experience with standardised tests do better than those who do not. Some of this advantage may be the result of greater self-confidence, less tendency to panic, familiarity with different kinds of questions (e.g. analogies such as hot : cold and ? : white), and practice with the various answer sheets (Anastasi, 1988). Even brief introductions about how to take tests can help pupils who lack familiarity and confidence.

A second type of preparation that appears to be very promising is instruction in general cognitive skills such as solving problems, analysing questions, considering all alternatives, noticing details and deciding which are relevant, avoiding impulsive answers and checking work. These are kinds of metacognitive and study skills we have discussed before in Chapter 7 and which find application in all phases and domains of education (Arabsolghar and Elkins, 2001; Atkinson *et al.*, 2006; McEwen *et al.*, 2001). The teaching and acquisition of powerful metacognitive and study skills is really important to all learners but none more than those with disabilities and learning difficulties.

Reaching every pupil: helping pupils with disabilities prepare for high-stakes tests

Erik Carter and his colleagues (2005) tested a procedure for preparing pupils with learning disabilities, mild intellectual disabilities and language impairments for high-stakes tests. The pupils were ages 15 to 19; over half were African American males and all had individual educational programmes (see Chapter 4) to guide their education. None had passed the required achievement tests. Over six lessons the pupils were taught the strategies presented in Table 14.4.

The good news is that after completing the preparation lessons, pupils improved their scores significantly on the tests. However, the bad news is that the increases were not large enough to bring most of the pupils to the passing level.

Connect and Extent

Chapter 15 deals with many issues including the important notion of 'Assessment for Learning' (AfL). See the Companion Website (Web Link 14.4). What research informs the 'Assessment for Learning' agenda? Can you trace the origin of the ten principles of AfL?

 WEB

Table 14.4 Helping pupils with learning disabilities, mild intellectual disabilities and language impairments prepare for high-stakes testing

Strategy	Objectives
Bubble sheet comparison and timing	Fills in bubbles completely
	Be aware of how much available time is remaining
	Pace yourself when taking a test
	Answer all problems before time expires
Sorting problems	Sort problems by differentiating between easier and more difficult ones
	Complete the easy problems on a test prior to attempting the more difficult ones
	Sort problems based on similarity in content
Estimation	Estimate answers in maths problems by using rounding
Substitution and backsolving	Substitute the answers provided on a multiple choice test into the question being asked to find the one correct answer
Recopying problems	Rewrite problems in a more familiar form to make them easier to solve
Underlining and reading all answers	Identify exactly what the question is asking you do to
	Read all questions carefully to make better answer choices
	Underline key words and phrases in the question
Elimination	Eliminate absurd multiple choice questions
	Eliminate answers with redundant or similar information
	Eliminate answers with extreme qualifiers

Source: *Preventing School Failure, 49*(2), p. 58, 2005. Reprinted with permission of the Helen Dwight Reid Educational Foundation. Published by Heldref Publications, 1319 Eighteenth St., NW, Washington DC 20036-1802. Copyright © 2005.

The authors recommend that preparation for testing should occur much earlier for pupils with disabilities. The pupils in this study, at an average age of 16, were already discouraged. The strategies taught should be closely aligned with the specific types of problems that the pupils will encounter on the test and should be embedded in good content instruction. Finally, pupils with disabilities are often especially anxious about the negative consequences of failing – not passing public examinations, no access to college or university. The best way to deal with this anxiety is to better equip the pupils with the academic skills they will need to succeed (Carter *et al.*, 2005).

New Directions in Assessment

Standardised tests continue to be controversial. In response to dissatisfaction with traditional forms of assessment, new approaches have emerged to deal with some of the most common testing problems. As the public and government demanded greater accountability in education in the 1980s and 1990s and as new standardised tests became the basis for high-stakes decisions, pressure to do well led many teachers and schools to 'teach to the test'. This tended to focus pupil learning on basic skills and facts. Even more troubling, say critics, the new standardised tests assess skills that have little equivalent in the real world. Pupils are asked to solve problems or answer questions they will probably never encounter again (except in another school test); they are expected to solve problems or answer questions alone, without relying on any tools or resources and while working under extreme time limits. Real life just isn't like this. Important problems take time to solve and often require using resources, consulting other people, and integrating basic skills with creativity and high-level thinking (Kirst, 1991a; Wolf *et al.*, 1991).

In response to these criticisms, the authentic assessment movement was born. The goal was to create standardised tests that assess complex, important, real-life outcomes. The approach is also called direct assessment or alternative assessment. These terms refer to procedures that are alternatives to traditional multiple-choice standardised tests because they directly assess pupil performance on 'real-life' tasks (Hambleton, 1996; Popham, 2005a). For example, the specialist publishing organisation 'Be a mathematician' (BEAM) is founded on the belief that children are assessed most effectively through problem solving which is authentic to real-world behaviours – investigation, enquiry and discussion – and that such assessment contributes to learning and children's mathematical thinking. BEAM's resources and training have been developed with this in mind. Go to http://www.beam.co.uk/ to see the performance tasks for Foundation Stage through to Year 9. You can select tasks by year level. Tasks come with directions for pupils, a guide for teachers, examples of pupils' work, and an assessment guide or rubric. See Chapter 15 for a fuller discussion about authentic assessment in the classroom.

Improvements in standardised testing

Many of the suggestions for improving standardised tests will require new forms of testing, more thoughtful and time-consuming scoring, and perhaps new ways of judging the quality of the tests themselves. Standardised tests of the future may be more like a writing or interview exercise you may have submitted for university entrance and less like the multiple-choice standardised tests you may have taken at school as part of public examinations. Newer tests will feature more constructed-response formats. This means that pupils will create responses (essays, problem solutions, graphs, diagrams), rather than simply selecting the (one and only) correct answer. This will allow tests to measure higher-level and divergent thinking.

In the midst of all of the excitement about authentic assessment, it is important to be sensible. Just being different from traditional standardised tests will not guarantee that the alternative tests are better. Many questions have to be answered. Assume, for example, that a new assessment requires pupils to complete a hands-on science project. If the pupil does well on one science project, does this mean the pupil 'knows' science and would do well on other projects? One study found that pupils' performance on three different science tasks was quite variable: a pupil who did well on the absorbency experiment, for example, might have trouble with the electricity task. Thus, it was hard to generalise about a pupil's knowledge of science based on just the three tasks. Many more tasks would be needed to get a good sense of science knowledge, but a performance assessment with many different tasks would be expensive and time-consuming (Shavelson, Gao and Baxter, 1993).

Connect and Extend

You might be engaged with 'Psychology in Education' in a distance learning environment that includes online assessment tasks (see the Companion Website – Web Link 14.4). What constitutes authentic on-line tasks?

Authentic assessment

Measurement of important abilities using procedures that simulate the application of these abilities to real-life problems.

Connect and Extend

Chapter 15 also includes a discussion of alternative methods for authentic assessment, including portfolios and exhibitions.

Connect and Extend

Read Herrington, J. *et al.* (2006). 'Authentic tasks online: A synergy among learner, task, and technology', *Distance Education*, 27(2), pp. 233–247.

Constructed-response format

Assessment procedures that require the pupil to create an answer instead of selecting an answer from a set of choices.

In many subjects the most reliable test is to demonstrate the ability to produce a finished product

In addition, if high-stakes decisions are based on performance assessments, will teachers begin to 'teach to the assessment' by giving pupils practice in these particular performances? Will being a good writer bias judges in favour of a performance? Will this make performance assessments even more prone to discriminate against some groups and how will the projects be judged? Does evaluation of more 'authentic assessment tasks' lead to problems with reliability and consistency? Will different judges agree on the quality?

By way of an example, Barootchi and Keshavarz (2002) studied portfolio assessment scores used as assessment tools on 'English as a Foreign Language' courses in Iran. They found that portfolio assessment scores correlated significantly with those of teacher-made achievement test, and high inter-rater reliability was also achieved. Therefore it was concluded that portfolio assessment, as a promising testing and teaching tool for teachers in EFL classes, could be used in conjunction with teacher-made tests to provide the continuous, ongoing measurement of students' growth needed for formative evaluation and for planning instructional programmes. Elizabeth Girot at the University of the West of England questioned 'graduateness' in the context of nurse education and the use of portfolios as a method of assessment. She concludes that: 'Clearly much more work needs to be done to produce a tool that would present a valid and reliable way of determining the achievement of "fitness for practice"' (2000: 334).

Furthermore, John Pitts, Colin Coles and Peter Thomas reported on a project to assess a series of portfolios of participants in general medical practice trainers. Reliability (consistency) of individual assessors' judgements was moderate but inter-marker reliability did not reach a level that could support making a safe summative judgement. They conclude that: 'while portfolios might be valuable as resources for learning, as assessment tools they should be treated as problematic' (2001).

In other words, will judgements based on alternative assessments be reliable, valid and free from bias? Will the assessment results generalise to tasks beyond those on the test itself? Will the new assessments have a positive effect on learning or will the reverse be true? To date, the most typical impact of high-stakes testing and examinations on pupils' motivation for learning and on teachers and the curriculum, reveals some seriously detrimental effects (Harlen, 2005). Because authentic assessment is a comparatively new area, it will take time to develop high-quality alternative national assessments in which appropriate accommodations (see Table 14.5) can be made for children of all backgrounds and abilities. Until more is known, it may be best to focus on authentic assessment at the classroom level, as we will discuss in the next chapter.

And finally, time for a test . . .

Some of the largest scale international comparative testing of school children is reported in the findings of the Organization for Economic Co-operation and Development (OECD) Programme for International Student Assessment (PISA). It is a three-yearly collaborative effort on the part of member countries (42 countries in 2003 with an additional 11 countries in 2006) of the OECD to measure how well pupils at age 15 are prepared to meet the challenges of today's societies. Take a look at the chart in Figure 14.6 that is taken from the results of tests completed by 4,500 to

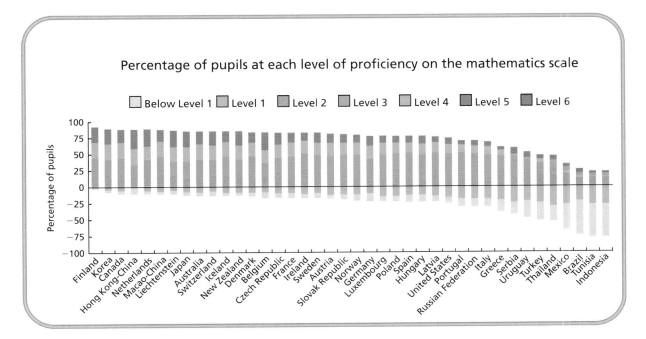

Figure 14.6
Results of tests completed by pupils, PISA 2003.

Source: OECD PISA 2003 database, Table 2.5a, http://www.oecd.org. Copyright OECD, 2003.

Table 14.5 Accommodations in testing

Accommodations in testing may be made in the setting of the test, timing and scheduling, test presentation and pupil response modes. Schools have to keep good records about what is done, because these accommodations have to be documented. Here are some examples of possible accommodations taken from Spinelli, 2002 (pp.151–152).

Examples of setting accommodations

Conditions of setting

- Minimal distractive elements (e.g. books, artwork, window views)
- Special lighting
- Special acoustics
- Adaptive or special furniture
- Individual pupil or small group of pupils rather than large group

Location

- Study carrel
- Separate room (including special education classroom)
- Seat closest to test administrator (e.g. teacher)
- Home
- Hospital
- Correctional institution

Examples of timing accommodations

Duration

- Changes in duration can be applied to selected subtests of an assessment or to the assessment overall
- Extended time (i.e. extra time)
- Unlimited time

Organisation

- Frequent breaks during parts of the assessment (e.g. during subtests)
- Extended breaks between parts of assessment (e.g. subtests) so that assessments can be administered in several sessions

Examples of scheduling accommodations

Time

- Specific time of day (e.g. morning, midday, afternoon, after ingestion of medication)
- Specific day of week
- Over several days

Organisation

- In a different order from that used for most pupils (e.g. longer subtest first, shorter later; maths first, English later)
- Omit questions that cannot be adjusted for an accommodation (e.g. graph reading for pupil using Braille) and adjust for missing scores

Examples of presentation accommodations

Format alterations

- Braille edition
- Large-print version
- Larger bubbles on answer sheet
- One complete sentence per line in reading passage
- Bubbles to side of choices in multiple-choice exams
- Key words or phrases highlighted
- Increased spacing between lines
- Fewer number of items per page

Procedure changes

- Use sign language to give directions to pupil
- Reread directions
- Write helpful verbs in directions on board or on separate piece of paper
- Simplify language, clarify or explain directions
- Provide extra examples
- Prompt pupil to stay focused on test, move ahead, read entire item
- Explain directions to pupil during test

Assistive devices

- Audiotape of directions
- Computer reads directions and/or items
- Magnification device
- Amplification device (e.g. hearing aid)
- Noise buffer
- Templates to reduce visible print
- Markers or masks to maintain place
- Dark or raised lines
- Pencil grips

Table 14.5   (Continued)

Examples of response accommodations

Format alterations
- Mark responses in test booklet rather than record on separate page
- Respond on different paper, such as graph paper, wide-lined paper, paper with wide margins

Procedural changes
- Use reference materials (e.g. dictionary, arithmetic tables)

- Give response in different mode (e.g. pointing, oral response to tape recorders, sign language)

Assistive devices
- Word processor or computer to responses
- Amanuensis (proctor-scribe writes pupil responses)
- Slant board or wedge
- Calculator or abacus
- Brailler or other communication device (e.g. symbol board)
- Spell checker

10,000 pupils in each country. Following your reading of this chapter, can you make sense of the chart? Are there any surprises? More importantly, what questions spring to mind when looking at these results? How could we make this exercise into an authentic test of your understanding of this chapter?

SUMMARY TABLE

Measurement and Assessment (pp. 618–621)

Distinguish between measurement and assessment

Measurement is the description of an event or characteristic using numbers. Assessment includes measurement, but is broader because it includes all kinds of ways to sample and observe pupils' skills, knowledge and abilities.

Distinguish between norm-referenced and criterion-referenced tests

In norm-referenced tests, a pupil's performance is compared to the average performance of others. In criterion-referenced tests, scores are compared to a pre-established standard. Norm-referenced tests cover a wide range of general objectives. However, results of norm-referenced tests do not tell whether pupils are ready for advanced material, and they are not appropriate for affective and psychomotor objectives.

Criterion-referenced tests measure the mastery of very specific objectives.

What Do Test Scores Mean? (pp. 621–634)

Describe the key features of a standardised test

Standardised tests are most often norm-referenced. They have been pilot-tested, revised and then administered in final form to a norming sample, which becomes the comparison group for scoring.

What are mean, median, mode and standard deviation?

The mean (arithmetical average), median (middle score) and mode (most common score) are all measures of central tendency. The standard deviation reveals how scores spread out around the mean. A normal distribution is a frequency distribution represented as a bell-shaped curve.

Many scores cluster in the middle; the farther from the midpoint, the fewer the scores.

Describe different kinds of scores

There are several basic types of standardised test scores: percentile rankings, which indicate the percentage of others who scored at or below an individual's score; age-equivalent scores, which indicate how closely a pupil's performance matches average scores for a given age group; and standard scores, which are based on the standard deviation. *T* and *z* scores are both common standard scores. A stanine score is a standard score that incorporates elements of percentile rankings.

What is test reliability?

Some tests are more reliable than others; that is, they yield more stable and consistent estimates. Care must be taken in the interpretation of test results. Each test is only a sample of a pupil's performance on a given day. The score is only an estimate of a pupil's hypothetical true score. The standard error of measurement takes into account the possibility for error and is one factor of test reliability.

What is test validity?

The most important consideration about a test is the validity of the decisions and judgements that are based on the test results. Evidence of validity can be related to content, criterion or construct. Construct-related evidence for validity is the broadest category and encompasses the other two categories of content and criterion. Tests must be reliable to be valid, but reliability does not guarantee validity.

What is absence of bias?

Tests must be free of assessment bias. Bias occurs when tests include material that offends or unfairly penalises a group of pupils because of the pupils' gender, SES, race or ethnicity. Culture-fair tests have not proved to solve the problem of assessment bias.

Types of Standardised Tests (pp. 634–640)

What are three kinds of standardised tests?

Three kinds of standardised tests are used frequently in schools: achievement, diagnostic and aptitude. Profiles from norm-referenced achievement tests can also be used in a criterion-referenced way. Diagnostic tests usually are given individually to primary-school pupils when learning problems are suspected. Aptitude tests are designed to predict how a pupil will perform in the future.

Issues in Standardised Testing (pp. 640–648)

What are some current issues in testing?

Controversy over standardised testing has focused on the role and interpretation of tests, the widespread use of tests to evaluate schools, the problems with accountability based on test scores and the testing of teachers. If the test matches important objectives of the curriculum, is given to pupils who actually studied the curriculum for a reasonable period of time, is free of bias, fits the pupils' language capabilities and was administered properly, then test results provide some information about the effectiveness of the school. However, studies of the actual tests in action show troubling consequences such as narrowing the curriculum and pushing some pupils out of school early. Teachers should use results to improve instruction, not to stereotype pupils or to justify lowered expectations.

Can pupils become better test-takers? How?

Performance on standardised tests can be improved if pupils gain experience with this type of testing and are given training in study skills and problem solving. Many pupils can profit from direct teaching about how to prepare for and take tests. Involving pupils in designing these test preparation programmes can be helpful. Pupils with learning challenges may benefit from intensive and ongoing preparation for taking tests, particularly if the test-taking strategies are tied to specific problems, and content learned and tested.

New Directions in Assessment (pp. 648–653)

What is authentic assessment?

Authentic assessments are procedures that assess pupils' abilities to solve important real-life problems, think creatively and act responsibly. Such approaches assume that assessment should reveal the potential for future learning and help identify interventions for realising that potential. Standardised tests of the future will be more varied and will use more constructed-response formats, requiring pupils to generate (rather than select) answers.

Improvements in standardised testing

Many of the suggestions for improving standardised tests will require new forms of testing, more thoughtful and time-consuming scoring, and new ways of judging the quality of the tests themselves. The use of portfolios may be an attractive option but not all educators are convinced as problems have been found with consistency between markers and therefore the reliability of the assessment.

Glossary

Accountable: Making teachers and schools responsible for pupil learning, usually by monitoring learning with high-stakes tests.

Achievement tests: Standardised tests measuring how much pupils have learned in a given content area.

Aptitude tests: Tests meant to predict future performance.

Assessment: Procedures used to obtain information about pupil performance.

Assessment bias: Qualities of an assessment instrument that offend or unfairly penalise a group of pupils because of the pupils' gender, SES, race, ethnicity, etc.

Authentic assessment: Measurement of important abilities using procedures that simulate the application of these abilities to real-life problems.

Bar chart: Graph of a frequency distribution using vertical or horizontal bars.

Central tendency: Typical score for a group of scores.

Confidence interval: Range of scores within which an individual's particular score is likely to fall.

Constructed-response format: Assessment procedures that require the pupil to create an answer instead of selecting an answer from a set of choices.

Criterion-referenced comparison: Testing in which scores are compared to a set performance standard.

Culture-fair or culture-free test: A test without cultural bias.

Diagnostic tests: Individually administered tests to identify special learning problems.

Frequency distribution: Record showing how many scores fall into set groups.

High-stakes testing: Standardised tests whose results have powerful influences when used by school managers, other officials or employers to make decisions.

Level-equivalent score: Measure of level based on comparison with norming samples from each age group.

Mean: Arithmetical average.

Measurement: An evaluation expressed in quantitative (statistical) terms.

Median: Middle score in a group of scores.

Mode: Most frequently occurring score.

Norm groups: A group whose mean average score serves as a standard for evaluating any pupil's score on a test.

Normal distribution: The most commonly occurring distribution, in which scores are distributed evenly around the mean.

Norming sample: Large sample of pupils serving as a comparison group for scoring standardised tests.

Norm-referenced comparison: Testing in which scores are compared with the mean average performance of others.

Percentile rank: Percentage of those in the norming sample who scored at or below an individual's score.

Range: Distance between the highest and the lowest scores in a group.

Reliability: Consistency of test results measured by looking at the comparability of scores on two different occasions or of two equivalent versions.

Standard deviation: Measure of how widely scores vary from the mean.

Standard error of measurement: Hypothetical estimate of variation in scores if testing were repeated.

Standard scores: Scores based on the standard deviation.

Standardised tests: Tests given, usually nationwide, under uniform conditions and scored according to uniform procedures.

Stanine scores: Whole number scores from 1 to 9, each representing a wide range of raw scores.

***T* score:** Standard score with a mean of 50 and a standard deviation of 10.

True score: The score the pupil would get if the measurement were completely accurate and error-free.

Validity: Degree to which a test measures what it is intended to measure.

Variability: Degree of difference or deviation from a mean.

***z* score:** Standard score indicating the number of standard deviations above or below the mean.

CHECK YOUR LEARNING!   WEB

In the Classroom: What Would They Do?

Here is how some practising teachers would respond to the In the Classroom feature at the start of Chapter 14. Remember the parents expected that the teacher would reconsider their daughter's report grades for the year 'in light of her clear abilities', and sought a recommendation from the teacher that their daughter should 'join the gifted and talented set for maths next year, because she obviously knows the material already'.

Lisbeth Jonsson, primary school teacher, Sweden

We have discussed the matter and asked ourselves, whether it is relevant what status the parents´ have or not. And of course it is! These are not the only parents who react in this way – unfortunately. We think, the teacher should explain to the parents how the tests are made and what they are supposed to show. The teacher has to be aware of the different kinds of testing to be able to explain it properly. We think that the teacher and the head teacher should offer this pupil to be tested by another teacher/ teachers (perhaps even with the parents present).

Lizzie Meadows, deputy head teacher, The Park Primary School, Kingswood, Bristol

Firstly, the teacher needs to reassure the girl's parents that she has nothing against her daughter and that she is a valued member of the class. The teacher should however point out that there is an issue with homework and ask the parents if they are aware that she rarely does it and explore reasons for this. The teacher needs to explain about the way the girl is approaching mathematics how she is in effect going through the motions to get the right answers but that there is limited understanding in some areas. The teacher could offer to show the parents some of the tests and explain how a Level 5 could be achieved without a deeper understanding of some of the concepts, and that their daughter's current issues with an enquiry based approach is going to hamper her progress in the gifted and talented set. The teacher could show the parents the girl's work and explain why she has been a B/C student in terms of continuous assessment. It would be worth offering to meet with the tutor in order to move the girl's learning forward by supporting the work done in school, and asking the parents for their full support in homework. The teacher could then offer to communicate regularly with the parents over issues of progress and homework.

Lee Card, primary school teacher, Bosbury Church of England Primary School

In this scenario, it appears the teacher in question actually *did* know how to teach able pupils in mathematics! In looking to progress her learning to the enquiry based approach in mathematics, the teacher has made steps in preparing her for future learning. The teacher could mention this to the parents, although I fear the mood in the room has been set for a rather frosty response! However, it is essential in this situation for the teacher, with the backing of the head teacher, to justify their grading system. The parents need to be informed as to why the B and C grades were given and the criteria by which they were allocated. A teacher in such a scenario would need a detailed knowledge of national testing in mathematics to explain how grades are arrived at. Under no circumstances should the grades be altered, as this would undermine the entire school system. In conveying to the parents that they have the child's *future* learning at heart, and that this is influencing the style of teaching she is receiving.

Jackie Day, special educational needs co-ordinator, Ridge Junior School, Yate

The teacher should be positive about the child's Level 5, and the effort put in to achieve it. However, it should be explained that test results are not the whole story. Reasonably bright children can be coached to learn algorithms and remember facts by rote (such as ¼ = 0.25) without understanding the relevant maths. Furthermore, they can be tutored to pass tests by practising on past papers, as similar questions tend to come up. Exceptional ability in maths is shown by the child who makes connections before being taught methods, and is able to investigate maths problems systematically and independently. The school should help this pupil to solve problems by getting her to talk through her mathematical thinking, and perhaps use concrete models to check the extent of her understanding.

Go to www.pearsoned.co.uk/woolfolkeuro for additional case studies.

Overview

If I had to reduce all of educational psychology to just one principle I would say this: the most important single factor influencing learning is what the learner already knows. Ascertain this and teach him accordingly.   *(Ausubel, 1968)*

In this chapter, we will look at both tests and grades, focusing not only on the effects they are likely to have on pupils, but also on practical ways to develop more efficient methods for assessing what learners already know, understand or can do.

We begin with a consideration of the many types of tests teachers prepare each year and approaches to assessment that don't rely on traditional testing. Then, we examine the effects grades are likely to have on pupils, and because there are so many grading systems, we also spend some time identifying the advantages and disadvantages of one type of classroom assessment over another. Finally, we turn to the very important topic of communication with pupils and parents. How will you justify the grades you give?

By the time you have completed this chapter, you should be able to answer the following questions:

- **How do teachers test pupils on a curriculum unit?**
- **How can teachers evaluate tests that are included in bought resources?**
- **How can teachers create multiple-choice and 'essay' tests?**
- **How do teachers use 'authentic' assessment approaches, including portfolios, performances, presentations and scoring rubrics?**
- **What are the potential positive and negative effects of grades on pupils?**
- **What are examples of criterion-referenced and norm-referenced grading systems?**
- **What do teachers need to know to explain a grading system to parents who do not understand their child's report?**

In the Classroom

A school requires that each teacher give letter grades to their pupils. Teachers can use any method as long as one of A, B, C, D or F appears for each of the subject areas on every pupil's report. Some teachers are using worksheets, quizzes, homework and class tests for pupils to gain credit towards end-of-year grades. Others are setting group work and asking for pupil portfolios. A few teachers are grading on progress and effort more than final attainment. Some are trying contract approaches and experimenting with longer-term projects, while others are relying almost completely on daily class work. Two teachers who use group work are considering giving credit towards grades for making a 'good contribution to the group' and competitive bonus points for a top-scoring group. Others are planning to use improvement points for class rewards, but not for grades. There is a small group of staff who object to the use of grades and only want to use written comments and a traffic light approach (green, amber or red) to record

whether pupils met, are close to meeting or have not met particular learning objectives. The school want to develop a common system that is fair and manageable, encourages learning not just performance, and gives the pupils feedback they can use to prepare for the national tests. Should teachers include credit for behaviours such as group participation or effort? How would they put all the assessment elements together to determine a grade for every pupil? How would the school justify such a grading system to the parents? How will these issues affect different age groups?

Group Activity

With two or three other members of your group develop a section of a class handbook that describes a grading policy. Be prepared to defend the policy.

Formative and Summative Assessment

Connect and Extend

Think back to Chapter 14 and what you learned about formative assessment methods. What are some specific ways in which formative evaluation can be implemented in classrooms?

Formative assessment

Ungraded testing used before or during teaching to aid in planning and diagnosis.

Pretest

Formative test for assessing pupils' knowledge, readiness and abilities.

Diagnostic test

Formative test used during teaching to determine pupils' areas of weakness and possible causes.

Summative assessment

Testing that follows teaching and assesses achievement.

Teachers may have little to say about the grading system for their school. Many schools have a standard approach to grading. Nevertheless, teachers will have choices about how they use a grading system and how they assess pupils' learning. Should they give tests? How many? What kinds? Will pupils do projects or keep portfolios of their work? How will homework influence grades? What if pupils do not have support at home for the completion of their homework?

There are two general uses or functions for assessment: formative and summative. Formative assessment occurs before or during teaching. The purposes of formative assessment are to guide the teacher in planning and to help pupils identify areas that need work. In other words, formative assessment helps *form* teaching. Often pupils are given a formative test prior to teaching, a pretest that helps the teacher determine what pupils already know (think back to Ausubel's assertion quoted at the top of this chapter). Sometimes a test is given during teaching to see what areas of weakness remain and to uncover the reasons for under-performance so teaching can be directed towards the problem areas. This is generally called a diagnostic test, but should not be confused with the standardised diagnostic tests of more general learning abilities discussed in the previous chapter. A classroom diagnostic test identifies a pupil's areas of achievement and weakness in a particular subject and at best gives the teachers some idea of the causes of the difficulties the pupil is experiencing. Older pupils are often able to apply the information from diagnostic tests to 're-teach' themselves. Pretests and diagnostic tests are not graded and because formative tests do not count towards the final grade, pupils who tend to be very anxious about 'high-stakes' tests may find this low-pressure practice in test-taking especially helpful.

Summative assessment occurs at the end of instruction. Its purpose is to let the teacher and the pupils know the level of accomplishment attained. Summative assessment, therefore, provides a *summary* of accomplishment. The final exam is a classic example.

The distinction between formative and summative assessment is based on how the results are used. Any kind of assessment – traditional, performance, project, oral, portfolio, and so on – can be used for either formative or summative purposes. If the goal is to obtain information about pupil learning for planning purposes, the assessment is formative. If the purpose is to determine final achievement (and help to determine a grade), the assessment is summative. In fact, the same assessment could be used as a formative evaluation at the beginning of the unit and as a summative evaluation at the end.

STOP AND THINK

Check your understanding of the **purposes** of formative and summative assessment. Explain how teachers and pupils can make effective use of the information generated by each type of test.

The formative uses of assessment are really the most important in teaching. James Popham believes that, 'Unfortunately, too many teachers still think that the chief role of classroom tests is the assignment of grades. But any teacher who uses tests dominantly to determine whether pupils get high or low grades should receive

The final exam is a classic example of a summative assessment. This type of assessment occurs at the end of instruction and provides a summary of accomplishment

a solid F in classroom assessment' (2005: 262). Tests and all assessments should be used to help teachers make better decisions about teaching. Table 15.1 gives some examples.

Diagnostic assessment

Before moving on to think about traditional classroom assessment we need to deal with the thorny subject of diagnostic assessment. When teachers have problems matching tasks to pupils' attainments the usual cause is the 'misdiagnosis or non-diagnosis of pupils' skills and knowledge. When mismatching was observed by teachers, . . . they rarely went back to isolate the pupil's cognitive problems' (Bennett *et al.*, 1984: 185).

Here is a typical scenario. A maths teacher has explained how to multiply two two-digit numbers together in a column algorithm (24 × 13), demonstrating the process and reciting the same verbal patter or incantation, the self-same teacher had been

---

Table 15.1   Using tests to make decisions about teaching

The best use of assessment is to plan, guide and target teaching. Here are some decisions that can benefit from assessment results

Decision category	Typical assessment strategy	Decision options
What to teach in the first case	Pre-assessment before teaching	Whether to provide teaching for specific objectives
How long to keep teaching towards a particular learning objective	'En route' assessments of pupils' progress	Whether to continue or cease teaching for a learning objective either for an individual or for the whole class
How effective was a teaching sequence?	Comparing pupil's post-test to pre-test performances	Whether to retain, discard or modify a given teaching sequence the next time it is due to be used

Source: Adapted from *Classroom Assessment: What Teachers Need to Know* (4th ed.) by J. W. Popham. Published by Allen and Bacon, Boston, MA. Copyright © 2005 by Pearson Education.

---

taught when they were nine or ten years old. It goes something like this: 'Nought down, once four is four, one two is two; three fours are twelve, carry two; two threes are six, add one is seven; two and zero makes two, four and seven makes eleven, carry one; two and one make three.' (Perhaps you learned a different algorithm so just try 24 × 13 to remind yourself about the chant you learned.)

There is a line of pupils at the teacher's desk waiting to get their answers checked. Bernard has got every 'sum' wrong. What does the teacher do? The teacher repeats the same patter whilst doing the 'sum' in the pupil's exercise book, only this time a little slower and a little louder. '**NOUGHT DOWN**, ONCE FOUR IS **FOUR**, ONE TWO IS **TWO**; THREE FOURS ARE **TWELVE, CARRY TWO**; TWO THREES ARE **SIX**, ADD ONE IS . . .' You get the idea! At the end of the second demonstration, the teacher asks 'Now do you understand?' and the pupil nods enthusiastically (anything to get away from the teacher's desk).

Not only in this scenario is there a mismatch between what the pupil was capable of doing and the set task, but no attempt is made to diagnose why that mismatch had taken place.

So what should the teacher have done? There is only one appropriate response to a pupil's misinterpretations: that is to diagnose their source on the pupil's construction of knowledge, skills and understandings. However, diagnostic interviewing (which includes probing questioning and getting children to demonstrate their understanding until their understanding breaks down) takes time, and time in the classroom is at a premium. It could be argued that teachers cannot afford such time yet, given the evidence of the long-term effects of allowing misconceptions to fester it should be asserted that teachers *cannot* afford *not* to ascertain pupil's misconceptions as soon as possible (Bennett *et al.*, 1984). Perhaps part of the solution to this seemingly intractable problem is to get the most from traditional classroom testing.

↔ Connect and Extend

Much of Neville Bennett's and his colleagues book, *The Quality of Pupil Learning Experiences* (1984) London: Lawrence Erlbaum, is to do with matching learning tasks to learner's abilities. Chapter 9 on the Quality of Teacher Diagnosis is a worthwhile and timely read at this point in your study of classroom assessment.

Getting the Most from Traditional Assessment

STOP AND THINK

Think back to your most recent test. What was the format? Did you feel that the test results were an accurate reflection of your knowledge or skills? What makes a good test? What makes a fair test? Did taking the test promote your learning? Did you want to work harder (and therefore do better next time) after you received the results?

When most people think of assessment, they usually think of testing. As you will see shortly, teachers today have many other options, but testing is still a significant activity in many classrooms. So let's consider options for assessing pupils using the traditional testing approach. In this section we will examine how to plan effective tests, evaluate the tests that accompany standard curriculum materials and write test questions.

Planning for testing

One result of high-stakes testing (refer to Chapter 14 for more information) is that teachers now have more classroom assessments and reviews focused on the standards behind the high-stakes tests. These assessments need to be well organised and planned. With a good plan, teachers are in a better position to judge the tests provided in bought resources and to develop their own class assessments.

High-stakes testing

Standardised tests whose results have powerful influences when used by school administrators, other officials or employers to make decisions.

When to test?

Frank Dempster (1991) examined the research on reviews and tests and reached these useful conclusions for teachers:

1. Frequent testing encourages the retention of information and appears to be more effective than a comparable amount of time spent reviewing and studying the material.

2. Tests are especially effective in promoting learning if pupils are given a test on the material soon after they learn it, then retest on the material later. Retestings should be spaced further and further apart.

3. The use of 'cumulative' questions on tests is a key to effective learning. Cumulative questions ask pupils to apply information learned in previous units to solve a new problem.

Other educationalists are not so convinced about the value of testing. In a recent pamphlet for the *Demos* think-tank, Paul Skidmore challenges the idea that testing promotes learning:

The view that testing raises standards of educational achievement rests on the assumption that increasing the transparency of performance motivates teachers and pupils to put more effort in to their teaching and learning. When we are shown that our performance is inadequate, our response (so the argument runs) is to declare, like Boxer the industrious horse in Animal Farm *[Orwell, 1951], 'I will work harder.' Yet, however intuitively*

Connect and Extend

Reading tests are used widely. Start connecting into the research on the testing of reading by accessing an interesting study by Erik De Corte *et al.* where the effects of the learning environment were measured using a pretest- post-test-retention design. (2001) 'Improving text comprehension strategies in upper primary school children: A design experiment', *British Journal of Educational Psychology, 71*(4), pp. 531–559.

Connect and Extend

Objective and essay tests continue to have important roles in effective assessment and evaluation. Describe the appropriate uses of these types of tests. Identify the advantages and limitations of each.

appealing this logic may seem, it rests on a largely fictional – or at best very elitist – account of what motivates us to learn (2003: 54).

Skidmore goes on to attack testing as demotivating (particularly low-achievers), overly concerned with performance goals rather than learning, accentuates the difference in performers between high and low achievers, distorts teachers' classroom practice by tempting teachers to 'teach to the test', to adopt a 'transmission' model and, most seriously, testing can damage children's physical and mental well-being.

Frank Dempster also argues (and is probably on much safer ground) that pupils will learn more if the curriculum includes fewer topics, but explores those topics in greater depth and allows more time for review, practice, testing and feedback (Dempster, 1993).

Judging textbook tests

Most primary and secondary school resources today come complete with supplemental materials such as teaching notes, worksheet masters and ready-made tests. Using these tests can save time, but is this good teaching practice? The answer depends on the learning objectives for pupils, the way the material is taught and the quality of the tests provided. If the textbook test is of high quality, matches the assessment plan and accords with the teaching provided for pupils, then it may be the right test to use. It is always important to check the reading level of the test items provided and be prepared to revise/improve them (Airasian, 2005; McMillan, 2004). All too often a test in maths problem solving, historical or scientific enquiry becomes little more than a test in reading comprehension. Table 15.2 gives key points to consider in evaluating textbook tests.

What if there are no tests available for the material you want to cover, or the tests provided in your bought resources are not appropriate for your pupils? Then it's time for you to create your own tests. We will consider the two major kinds of traditional tests – objective and essay.

Table 15.2 Key points to consider in judging textbook tests

1. The decision to use a textbook test or pre-made standard achievement test must come after a teacher identifies the learning objective(s) that he or she has taught and now wants to assess.

2. Textbook and standard tests are designed for a 'typical' classroom, but since few classrooms are typical, most teachers deviate somewhat from the text in order to accommodate for their pupils' needs.

3. The more classroom teaching deviates from the textbook, the less valid the textbook tests are likely to be.

4. The main consideration in judging the adequacy of the textbook or standard achievement test is the match between its test questions and what the pupils were taught in class:

   a. Are questions similar to the teacher's learning objectives and teaching emphases?

   b. Do questions require pupils to perform the behaviours they were taught?

   c. Do questions cover all or most of the important objectives taught?

   d. Is the language level and terminology appropriate for pupils?

   e. Does the number of items for each objective provide a sufficient sample of pupils' performance?

Source: Adapted from *Classroom Assessment: Concepts and Applications* (5th ed.) by P. W. Airasian (2005). New York: McGraw-Hill, p. 161. Copyright © 2005 by the McGraw-Hill Companies.

Objective testing

Multiple-choice questions, matching exercises, true/false statements and short-answer or fill-in items are all types of objective testing. The word 'objective' in relation to testing means 'not open to many interpretations' or 'not subjective'. The scoring of these types of items is relatively straightforward compared to the scoring of essay questions because the answers are more clear-cut than essay answers.

Objective testing

Multiple-choice, matching, true/false, short-answer and fill-in tests; scoring answers requires little interpretation.

How should you decide which item format is best for a particular test? Use the one that provides the most direct measure of the learning outcome you intended for pupils (Gronlund, 2003). In other words, if you want to see how well pupils can write a letter, have them write a letter, don't ask multiple-choice questions about letters. However, if many different item formats will work equally well, then use multiple-choice questions because they are easier to score fairly and can cover many topics. Switch to other formats if writing good multiple-choice items for the material is not possible or appropriate. For example, if related concepts such as terms and definitions need to be linked, then a matching item is a better format than multiple-choice. If it is difficult to come up with several wrong answers for a multiple-choice item, try a true/false question instead. Alternatively, ask the pupil to supply a short answer that completes a statement (fill in the blank). Variety in objective testing can lower pupils' anxiety because the entire grade does not depend on one type of question that a particular pupil may find difficult. We will now look closely at the multiple-choice format because it is the most versatile – and the most difficult to use well.

Using multiple-choice tests

Multiple-choice questions are assuredly the most versatile type of objective question which, if skilfully constructed can reliably test recall of facts, comprehension, ability to apply knowledge in new contexts, and understanding of drawings, calculations and graphs. More complex versions of multiple-choice tests can use question groups and permutation sets to minimise the impact of guesswork (Ward, 1981) and well-constructed and tested questions can contribute to valid assessments (when the questions are deeply connected to the forms of understanding and knowledge).

The use of multiple-choice questions is also very popular with those responsible for organising the testing of large groups of learners. This is because of the ease and speed of marking which these test items offer (Gipps and Murphy, 1994) but there are questions about the validity of assessments made exclusively using this type of objective testing. Gipps and Murphy (1994) argue that the exclusive use of such tests tends to advantage boys, particularly boys at the lower end of the ability range (Willingham and Cole, 1997).

STOP AND THINK

Note down one or two possible reasons why the exclusive use of multiple-choice tests tends to advantage boys, particularly boys at the lower end of the ability range. Check out your ideas by referring to the Companion Website (Web Link 15.1).

WEB

We tend to associate extensive use multiple-choice questions with standardised tests of the form used in national and international testing programmes. In fact, many schools require teachers to give pupils experience answering multiple-choice tests in order to prepare them for high-stakes testing (McMillan, 2004) so teachers need to know how to use these tests well. Of course, whilst multiple-choice items efficiently test facts, questions can assess more than recall and recognition if they require the pupil to deal with new material by *applying* or *analysing* the concept or principle being tested (Gronlund, 2003; McMillan, 2004). For example, the following multiple-choice item is designed to assess pupils' ability to recognise unstated assumptions, one of the skills involved in analysing an idea.

An educational psychology lecturer states, 'A z score of $+1$ on a test is equivalent to a percentile rank of approximately 84.' Which of the following assumptions is the lecturer making?

1. The scores on the test range from 0 to 100.

2. The standard deviation of the test scores is equal to 3.4.

3. The distribution of scores on the test is normal.

4. The test is valid and reliable.

Writing multiple-choice questions

All test items require skilful construction, but good multiple-choice items are a real challenge. Some pupils jokingly refer to multiple-choice tests as 'multiple-guess' tests – a sign that these tests are often poorly designed. Your goal in writing test items is to design them so that they measure pupil achievement, not test-taking and guessing skills.

The stem of a multiple-choice item is the part that asks the question or poses the problem. The choices that follow are called alternatives. The wrong answers are called distractors because their purpose is to distract pupils who have only a partial understanding of the material. If there were no good distractors, pupils with only a vague understanding would have no difficulty in finding the right answer.

The following Focus on Practice should make writing multiple-choice and other objective test questions easier.

Stem

The question part of a multiple-choice item.

Alternatives

All the answers offered which include the correct answer and the distractors.

Distractors

Wrong answers offered as choices in a multiple-choice item.

FOCUS ON PRACTICE

Writing multiple-choice test items

The stem should be clear and simple, and present only a single problem. Unessential details should be left out

Open to improvement
There are several different kinds of standard or derived scores. An IQ score is especially useful because . . .

Better
Which of the following is an advantage of an IQ score?

The problem in the stem should be stated in positive terms. Negative language is confusing. If you must use words such as *not, no* or *except*, underline them or use capitals.

Open to improvement
Which of the following is not a standard score?

Better
Which of the following is NOT a standard score?

Do not expect pupils to make extremely fine discrimination among answer choices.

Open to improvement
What is the percentage of area in a normal curve falling between +1 and −1 standard deviations?
a. 66%   b. 67%   c. 68%   d. 69%.

Better
What is the percentage of area in a normal curve falling between +1 and −1 standard deviations?
a. 14%   b. 34%   c. 68%   d. 95%.

As much wording as possible should be included in the stem so that phrases will not have to be repeated in each alternative.

Open to improvement
A percentile score:
a. indicates the percentage of items answered correctly
b. indicates the percentage of correct answers divided by the percentage of wrong answers
c. indicates the percentage of people who scored at or above a given raw score
d. indicates the percentage of people who scored at or below a given raw score.

Better
A percentile score indicates the percentage of:
a. items answered correctly
b. correct answers divided by the percentage of wrong answers
c. people who scored at or above a given raw score
d. people who scored at or below a given raw score.

Each alternative answer should fit the grammatical form of the stem, so that no answers are obviously wrong

Open to improvement
The Stanford-Binet test yields an
a. IQ score   c. vocational preference
b. reading level   d. mechanical aptitude.

Better
What does the Stanford-Binet test assess?
a. intelligence   c. vocational preference
b. reading level   d. mechanical aptitude.

Categorical words such as *always, all, only* or *never* should be avoided unless they can appear consistently in all the alternatives. Most smart test takers know that categorical answers are usually wrong

Open to improvement
A pupil's true score on a standardised test is:
a. never equal to the obtained score
b. always very close to the obtained score
c. always determined by the standard error of measurement
d. usually within a band that extends from +1 to −1 standard errors of measurement on each side of the obtained score.

Better
Which one of the statements below would most often be correct about a pupil's true score on a standardised test?
a. It equals the obtained score
b. It will be very close to the obtained score
c. It is determined by the standard error of measurement
d. It could be above or below the obtained score.

You should also avoid including two distractors that have the same meaning. If only one answer can be right and if two answers are the same, then these two must both be wrong. This narrows down the choices considerably

Open to improvement
What is the term for the most frequently occurring score in a distribution?
a. mode   c. arithmetic average
b. median   d. mean

Better
What is the term for the most frequently occurring score in a distribution?
a. mode   c. standard deviation
b. median   d. mean

Avoid using the exact wording found in the textbook

Poor pupils may recognise the answers without knowing what they mean.

Avoid overuse of 'all of the above' and 'none of the above'

Such choices may be helpful to pupils who are simply guessing. In addition, using *all of the above* may trick a quick pupil who sees that the first alternative is correct and does not read on to discover that the others are correct, too.

Obvious patterns on a test also aid pupils who are guessing

The position of the correct answer should be varied, as should its length.

> **Incorrect alternatives should reflect common pupil misunderstandings**
>
> Be careful, however, that the wrong alternatives are not so obviously wrong that pupils don't even consider them.
>
> For a good summary on writing test items of many different forms, see Clausen-May, T. (2001). *An Approach to Test Development.* Slough: NFER.
>
> Source: Adapted from Clausen-May (2001), Satterly (1989) Gronlund (2003), Popham (2005), and Smith, Smith and De Lisi (2001).

The correct answer, and therefore the assumption made by the lecturer to the question posed earlier: 'A z score of $+1$ on a test is equivalent to a percentile rank of approximately 84.' was alternative 3. 'The distribution of scores on the test is normal'. If you struggled with this question and the questions in the Focus on Practice above you might like to review some of the work and reading you did for Chapter 14.

Essay testing

The best way to measure some learning objectives is to require pupils to create answers on their own and an essay question is appropriate in these cases. The most difficult part of essay testing is judging the quality of the answers, but writing good, clear questions is not particularly easy, either. We will look at writing, administering and grading essay tests, with most of the specific suggestions taken from Satterley (1989), Desforges (1990) and Gronlund (2003). We will also consider factors that can bias the scoring of essay questions and ways you can overcome these problems.

> **STOP AND THINK**
>
> Evaluate these two essay questions from Popham (2005: 172–173):
>
> 1. (Secondary school level) 'You have just viewed a videotape containing three widely seen television commercials. What is the one classic propaganda technique present in all three commercials?'
>
> 2. (Middle school level) 'Thinking back over the mathematics lessons and homework of the past 12 weeks, what conclusions can you draw? Take no more than one page for your response.'

Constructing essay tests

When evaluating the two essay questions in the Stop and Think feature you may have written about the amount of time that essay tests take to do. One view is that, because answering takes time, true essay tests cover less material than objective tests. Thus, for efficiency, essay tests should be limited to the assessment of more complex learning outcomes.

An essay question should give pupils a clear and precise task and should indicate the elements to be covered in the answer. (Are the questions above clear and precise?) The pupils should know how extensive their answer should be and about how much time they should spend on each question. Question 2 above gives a page limit, but would you know what is being asked?

Pupils should be given ample time for answering. If more than one essay is being completed in the same class period, you may want to suggest time limits for each question. Remember, however, that time pressure increases anxiety and may prevent accurate assessment of some pupils. Whatever your approach, do not try to make up for the limited amount of material an essay test can cover by including a large number of essay questions. It would be better to plan on more frequent testing than to include more than two or three essay questions in a single class period. Combining an essay question with a number of objective items is one way to avoid the problem of limited sampling of course material (Gronlund, 2003).

Evaluating essays: dangers

In 1912, Starch and Elliot began a classic series of experiments that shocked educators into critical consideration of subjectivity in testing. These researchers wanted to find out the extent to which teachers were influenced by personal values, standards and expectations in scoring essay tests. For their initial study, they sent copies of English examination papers written by two secondary-school pupils to English teachers in 200 secondary schools. Each teacher was asked to score the papers according to his or her school's standards. A percentage scale was to be used, with 75% as a pass mark.

The results? Neatness, spelling, punctuation and communicative effectiveness were all valued to different degrees by different teachers. The scores on one of the papers ranged from 64% to 98%, with a mean of 88.2. The average score for the other paper was 80.2, with a range between 50% and 97%. The following year, Starch and Elliot (1913a, 1913b) published similar findings in a study involving history and geometry papers. The most important result of these studies was the discovery that the problem of subjectivity in grading was not confined to any particular academic area. The main difficulties were the individual standards of the grader and the unreliability of scoring procedures. Before thinking about how teachers can avoid problems of subjectivity and inaccuracy we need to think about how teachers can ensure greater reliability. Reliability in marking essay type questions stems from being clear about the purpose of the exercise. Charles Desforges (1990) contrasts two essay questions. First: 'Explain in not more than 400 words how a fire extinguisher works'; and second, 'Explain how the soda/acid fire extinguisher works. Show in your explanation the equations describing the chemical actions which take place when the extinguisher is used.'

In the first example, what will count as an explanation? Do they want operating instructions? What are the general principles for putting fires out? Does the marker want general principles stated? What type of fire extinguisher should the writer choose? What about physical and chemical changes? There are just too many decisions for pupils to make and because pupils will make very different choices, this makes marking very difficult. We will consider advantages and disadvantages of constructed tests (another name for essay type questions) a little later but first, check out the following Focus on Practice on the construction of essay titles. How can we retain the advantages of constructed responses but at the same time elicit clearly defined mental processes which, like well-constructed multiple-choice questions, 'are deeply connected to the forms of understanding and knowledge' the essays set out to test?

Marking essays: methods

Gronlund (2003) offers several strategies for marking essays that avoid problems of subjectivity and inaccuracy. When possible, a good first step is to construct a set of scoring criteria or a rubric (more on this later) and share it with pupils. Even when

FOCUS ON PRACTICE

Writing essay-type test items

These examples show how you can connect essay titles to forms of understanding and knowledge and defined mental processes. Examples are in no particular order and with no particular age range in mind.

a. *Understanding cause and effect*
Give three reasons why more cars are sold in Britain than in Iceland.

b. *Summarising*
Summarise the story of Beowulf in 100 words or less.

c. *Decision for or against*
Should the death penalty be restored for terrorist murders? Defend your answer.

d. *Application of rules or principles*
Where would you weigh more, on the moon or on Mars? Explain your answer.

e. *Analysis*
Why is there so much violence on football terraces?

f. *Formulating questions*
Two children stole a packet of biscuits from a supermarket. What questions should the teacher ask before deciding whether to punish them?

g. *Criticism of the adequacy or relevance of a statement*
Criticise or defend the statement: 'The central conflict in *Far from the Madding Crowd* is between Boldwood and Troy'.

h. *Giving examples or illustrating principles*
Name three examples of the use of the lever in your home.

i. *Making comparisons*
Compare trawling and drifting as methods of catching fish.

j. *Explanation*
Macbeth says 'Life's but a walking shadow, a poor player, that struts and frets his hour upon the stage'. Explain the meaning of this statement.

Items of this kind can provide quite a stringent test of a variety of teaching objectives. Care needs to be given to the key words (e.g. *compare, explain, defend, summarise*) which indicate specifically the process required.

Some general considerations in presenting essay test items

1. Be fair to your pupils. Children cannot write many essays in a fixed period of time. Whereas one or two badly constructed objective test items may not have very serious consequences, a badly thought-out essay title can be counter-productive.

2. Write the question in such a way that it indicates the level of response you are looking for. Titles that are wide open are inappropriate especially for children in primary and middle schools. Try to ensure that the title makes clear what you are looking for in the answer, or provide a structure (headings) to aid organisation.

3. With children in primary and middle schools it is preferable to use a number of questions which require short answers rather than a few which involve long answers.

4. Avoid questions of the 'who' or 'what' variety: these can usually be dealt with more effectively by the objective item.

5. Remember that some of the advantages claimed for the essay test are less applicable to the level of maturity expected in children of primary and middle school age ranges than for older pupils. Adapt the length of the response to what may reasonably be expected of pupils of the age range being assessed. There are considerable limitations in the younger child's ability to conceptualise and organise information in free response and whilst children learn to write by writing, do not expect too much.

6. If the essay item is being used in norm-referenced testing do not provide optional questions. No comparisons of achievement are possible if children in a class tackle heterogeneous items of differing levels of difficulty.

7. Do allow time for pupils to write their answers. There is little justification for measuring handwriting speed under the guise of an essay test.

Source: Adapted from David Satterly (1989) *Assessment in Schools* (2nd ed). Oxford: Blackwell.

pupils are given some choice in testing, teachers can decide what type of information should be in any answer. Here is an example from TenBrink (2003: 326):

Question: Defend or refute the following statement: Civil wars are necessary to the growth of a developing country. Cite reasons for your argument, and use examples from history to help substantiate your claim.

Scoring Rubric: All answers, regardless of the position taken, should include (1) a clear statement of the position, (2) at least five logical reasons, (3) at least four examples from history that clearly substantiate the reasons given. (NB: the choice of five reasons and four examples would be made on the basis of an appropriate expectation given the substance of the question.)

Once expectations are set for answers, points are assigned to the various parts of the essay. Points might also be given for the organisation of the answer and the internal consistency of the essay. Grades can be assigned to marks bands such as 1 to 5 or A, B, C, D and F, and papers sorted into piles by grade. As a final step, papers in each pile should be skimmed to see if they are comparable in quality. These techniques will help ensure fairness and accuracy in grading.

When grading essay tests with several questions, it makes sense to grade all responses to one question before moving on to the next. This helps prevent the quality of a pupil's answer to one question from influencing your reaction to the pupil's other

Table 15.3 Advantages and disadvantages of different kinds of test items

No kind of item is perfect. A mix of kinds may be the best approach

Type	Advantages	Disadvantages
Short answer	Can test recall of many facts in a short time. Fairly easy to score. Excellent format for maths. Tests recall.	Difficult to measure complex learning. Often ambiguous.
Essay	Can test complex learning. Can assess thinking process and creativity.	Difficult to score objectively. Uses a great deal of testing time. Subjective.
True/False	Tests the most facts in shortest time. Easy to score. Tests recognition. Objective.	Difficult to measure complex learning. Difficult to write reliable test items. Subject to guessing.
Matching	Excellent for testing associations and recognition of facts. Although terse, can test complex learning (especially concepts). Objective.	Difficult to write effective items. Subject to process of elimination.
Multiple choice	Can assess learning at all levels of complexity. Can be highly reliable, objective. Tests fairly large knowledge base in short time. Easy to score.	Difficult to write. Somewhat subject to guessing.

Source: Cooper, James, *Classroom Teaching Skills* (7th ed.). Copyright © 2003 by Houghton Mifflin Company. Adapted with permission.

answers. Between questions shuffle the papers so that no pupil ends up having all their questions marked first (when markers may be taking more time to give feedback or are applying stricter standards, for example) or last (when markers may be tired of writing feedback or more lax in standards). Greater objectivity may be achieved if you ask pupils to put their names on the back of the paper, so that marking is anonymous. A final check on fairness is to have another teacher who is equally familiar with the learning objectives and subject matter mark the tests without knowing what grades have been awarded. This can give you valuable insights into areas of bias in your marking practices.

Now that we have examined both objective and essay testing, we can compare examples of the different approaches. Table 15.3 presents a summary of the advantages and disadvantages of each.

Alternatives to Traditional Assessments

We have been considering how to make traditional testing (objective tests including multiple-choice and essay writing) more effective; now, let's look at a few alternative approaches to classroom assessment. One of the main criticisms of standardised tests – that they control the curriculum, emphasising recall of facts instead of thinking and problem solving – is also a major criticism of classroom tests. Few teachers would dispute these criticisms. Even if you follow the guidelines we have been discussing, traditional testing can be limiting. So what can be done? Should alternatives in classroom assessment make traditional testing obsolete? The following Discussion Point addresses this question.

DISCUSSION POINT

Are authentic assessments always better than traditional tests?

We have seen the advantages and disadvantages of standardised tests, but what about classroom testing? Are traditional multiple-choice and essay tests useful in classroom assessment?

Agree: Yes, traditional tests are a poor basis for classroom assessment

In his booklet, *Beyond Measure. Why educational assessment is failing the test,* Paul Skidmore (2003) argues for a very different kind of educational assessment; one in which higher standards of learning should not equate higher scores on multiple-choice tests. Furthermore, when scores on traditional tests become the standard against which society judges pupils, teachers and schools, the message to pupils and teachers is that only right answers matter and the thinking behind the answers is unimportant. Skidmore notes:

> *Assessment systems need to be fundamentally redesigned to test deep understanding rather than just content knowledge. Many assessments currently fail to determine properly whether knowledge is conditionalised or whether it remains 'inert', i.e. whether learners understand when and how to activate it.*

> *We have a great opportunity to recast assessment not simply as a way of certifying learning, but of actively contributing to it. Assessment has become so synonymous with external testing at the end of the programme of study that we have lost sight of the crucial role that appropriately designed (and delivered) forms of assessment can play in improving the quality of classroom teaching and learning (2003: 59–60).*

Skidmore continues to argue for assessment that makes sense, that test knowledge as it is applied in real-world situations. Understanding cannot be measured by tests that ask pupils to use skills and knowledge out of context. There are real problems with both the validity and reliability of traditional classroom assessment techniques:

> *The solution will almost certainly lie in diversifying the methods by which assessment is conducted. Team-based projects and exercises, computer simulations, presentations and orals, hands-on experiments and so on could*

help to make assessment more authentic, by widening the range of skills and competencies that a learner can demonstrate, and so potentially make the inferences drawn from it more valid. In the interests of reliability, it would be important that these kinds of assessment take place more frequently, and less intrusively, than a conventional timed paper-and-pencil test (2003: 73).

Disagree: No, traditional tests can play an important role

Most psychologists and educators would agree with Skidmore that setting clear, authentic assessment tasks is important, but many also believe that traditional tests are useful in this process. Learning may be more than knowing the right answers, but right answers are important. While schooling is about learning to think and solve problems, it is also about knowledge. Pupils must have something to think about – facts, ideas, concepts, principles, theories, explanations, arguments, images, opinions. Well-designed traditional tests can evaluate pupils' knowledge effectively and efficiently (Airasian, 2005; Kirst, 1991). Some educators believe that traditional testing should play an even greater role than it currently does. Educational policy analysts (e.g. OECD PISA 2003, see pp. 651–653) suggest that pupils in the UK and America, compared to pupils in many other developed countries, lack essential knowledge because our schools have moved to emphasise process – critical thinking, self-esteem, problem solving – more than content. In order to teach more about content, teachers will need to determine how well their pupils are learning the content, and traditional testing provides useful information about content learning.

Tests are also valuable in motivating and guiding pupils' learning. There is research evidence that frequent testing encourages learning and retention. In fact, pupils generally learn more in classes with more rather than fewer tests (Dempster, 1991).

Source: Paul Skidmore (2003) *Beyond Measure. Why educational assessment is failing the test.* London: Demos.

WHAT DO YOU THINK?

Agree or Disagree? Vote online at www.pearsoned.co.uk/woolfolkeuro.

One solution that has been proposed to solve the testing dilemma is to apply the concept of authentic assessment to classroom testing.

Authentic classroom assessment

Authentic assessments ask pupils to apply skills and abilities as they would in real life. For example, they might use fractions to enlarge or reduce recipes. Grant Wiggins made this argument almost 20 years ago:

> *If tests determine what teachers actually teach and what pupils will study for – and they do – then the road to reform is a straight but steep one: test those capabilities and habits we think are essential, and test them in context. Make [tests] replicate, within reason, the challenges at the heart of each academic discipline. Let them be – authentic (1989: 41).*

Authentic assessments

Assessment procedures that test skills and abilities as they would be applied in real-life situations.

Connect and Extend

Check out Herrington J. *et al.* (2006), 'Authentic tasks online: A synergy among learner, task, and technology', *Distance Education,* 27(2), pp. 233–247. This article describes a model for the development of authentic tasks that can assist in designing environments of increased, rather than reduced, complexity.

Pupil presentations are a type of performance test that requires them to use good communication and are likely to involve many hours of preparation

Wiggins goes on to say that if our learning goals for pupils include the abilities to write, speak, listen, create, think critically, do research, solve problems or apply knowledge, then our tests should ask pupils to write, speak, listen, create, think, research, solve and apply. How can this happen?

Many educators suggest we look to the arts and sports for analogies to solve this problem. If we think of the 'test' as being the recital, presentation, game, mock court trial or other performance, then teaching to the test is just fine. All coaches, artists and musicians gladly 'teach' to these 'tests' because performing well on these tests is the whole point of teaching. Authentic assessment asks pupils to perform. The performances may be thinking performances, physical performances, creative performances or other forms. So performance assessment is any form of assessment that requires pupils to carry out an activity or produce a product in order to demonstrate learning (Airasian, 2005). Remember from earlier in the chapter that one of the key parts of diagnostic testing is to get pupils to perform up to the point that their understanding, skill or knowledge breaks down.

It may seem odd to talk about thinking as a performance, but there are many parallels. Serious thinking is risky, because real-life problems are not well defined. Often, the outcomes of our thinking are public – others evaluate our ideas. Like a dancer auditioning for a West End show or a sculptor looking at a lump of clay, we must cope with the consequences of our performance being evaluated. A pupil facing a difficult problem must experiment, observe, redo, imagine and test solutions; apply both basic skills and inventive techniques; make interpretations; decide how to communicate results to the intended audience; accept criticism and improve the initial solution (Eisner, 1999; Herman, 1997). Table 15.4 lists some characteristics of authentic tests.

Portfolios and presentations

The concern with authentic assessment has led to the development of several approaches based on the goal of *performance in context*. Instead of circling answers to 'factual' questions about non-existent situations, pupils are required to solve real

Performance assessments

Any form of assessment that requires pupils to carry out an activity or produce a product in order to demonstrate learning

Connect and Extend

For ideas about how classroom assessment is blended into a whole school policy see the Companion Website (Web Link 15.3). Also search the web for an example from a secondary school or college. What are the phase specific issues?

WEB

Table 15.4   Characteristics of authentic tests

A. Structure and logistics

1. Are more appropriately public; involve an audience, a panel, and so on.
2. Do not rely on unrealistic and arbitrary time constraints.
3. Offer known, not secret, questions or tasks.
4. Are more like portfolios or a *season* of games (not one-shot).
5. Require some collaboration with others.
6. Recur – and are *worth* practising for, rehearsing and retaking.
7. Make assessment and feedback to pupils so central that school timetables, structures and policies are modified to support them.

B. Intellectual design features

1. Are 'essential' – not needlessly intrusive, arbitrary, or contrived to 'manufacture' a grade.
2. Are 'enabling' – constructed to point pupils towards more sophisticated use of the skills or knowledge.
3. Are contextualised, complex intellectual challenges, not 'atomised' tasks, corresponding to isolated 'outcomes'.
4. Involve the pupil's own research or use of knowledge, for which 'content' is a means.
5. Assess pupils' habits and repertoires, not mere recall or plug-in skills.
6. Are *representative* challenges – designed to emphasise *depth* more than breadth.

7. Are engaging and educational.
8. Involve somewhat ambiguous ('ill-structured') tasks or problems.

C. Grading and scoring standards

1. Involve criteria that assess essentials, not easily counted (but relatively unimportant) errors.
2. Are graded not on a 'curve' but in reference to performance standards (criterion-referenced, not norm-referenced).
3. Involve demystified criteria of success that appear to *pupils* as inherent in successful activity.
4. Make self-assessment a part of the assessment.
5. Use a multifaceted scoring system instead of one aggregate grade.
6. Exhibit harmony with shared whole school aims.

D. Fairness and equity

1. Ferret out and identify (perhaps hidden) strengths.
2. Strike a *constantly* examined balance between honouring achievement and natural skill or fortunate prior training.
3. Minimise needless, unfair and demoralising comparisons.
4. Allow appropriate room for pupils' learning styles, aptitudes and interests.
5. Can be – should be – attempted by *all* pupils, with the test 'scaffolded up', not 'dumbed down', as necessary.

Source: From 'Characteristics of authentic tests' by G. W. Wiggins, April 1989, *Educational Leadership*, *46*(7), p. 44. Reprinted with permission.

problems. Facts are used in a context where they apply – for example, the pupil uses grammar facts to write a persuasive letter to a software company requesting donations for the school computer suite. Here is another example of a test of performance:

> *Many local supermarkets claim to have the lowest prices. But what does this really mean? Does it mean that every item in their store is priced lower, or just some of them? How can you really tell which supermarket will save you the most money? Your assignment is to design and carry out a study to answer this question. What items and prices will you compare and why? How will you justify the choice of your 'sample'? How reliable is the sample, etc.? (Wolf et al., 1991: 61)*

Pupils completing this 'test' will use mathematical facts and procedures in the context of solving a real-life problem. In addition, they will have to think critically and write persuasively.

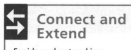

Connect and Extend

For ideas about making classroom assessment better, see the Companion Website (Web Link 15.3).

Portfolios and presentations are two approaches to assessment that require performance in context. With these approaches, it is difficult to tell where instruction stops and assessment starts because the two processes are interwoven (Smith, Smith and De Lisi, 2001).

Portfolios

For years, photographers, artists, models and architects have had portfolios to display their skills and often to get jobs. A portfolio is a systematic collection of work, often including work in progress, revisions, pupil self-analyses and reflections on what the pupil has learned (Popham, 2005). One pupil's self-reflection is presented in Figure 15.1.

Written work or artistic pieces are common contents of portfolios, but pupils might also include graphs, diagrams, snapshots of displays, peer comments, audio- or videotapes, laboratory reports and computer printouts – anything that demonstrates learning in the area being taught and assessed (Belanoff and Dickson, 1991; Camp, 1990; Wolf *et al.*, 1991). There is a distinction between process portfolios and final or 'best work' portfolios. The distinction is similar to the difference between formative and summative evaluation. Process portfolios document learning and show progress. Best work portfolios showcase final accomplishments (Johnson and Johnson, 2002). Table 15.5 shows some examples for both individuals and groups.

Presentations

A presentation (sometimes called an exhibition) is a performance test that has two additional features. First, it is public, so pupils preparing presentations must take the audience into account; communication and understanding are essential. Second, a presentation often requires many hours of preparation, because it is often the culminating experience of a whole unit of work. Thomas Guskey and Jane Bailey (2001) suggest that exhibits help pupils understand the qualities of good work and recognise

Portfolio

A collection of the pupil's work in an area, showing growth, self-reflection and achievement.

Presentation

A performance test or demonstration of learning that is public and usually takes an extended time to prepare.

Figure 15.1
A pupil reflects on learning: self-analysis of work in a portfolio

Not only has this pupil's writing improved, but the pupil has become a more self-aware and self-critical writer.

Source: From 'What makes a portfolio a portfolio?' by F. L. Paulson, P. Paulson and C. Meyers (1991) *Educational Leadership*, 48(5), p. 63. Reprinted with permission.

> 2
>
> Today I looked at all my stories in my writing folder I read some of my writing since September I noticed that I've improved some stuff Now I edit my stories, and revise Now I use periods, quotation mark Sometimes my stories are longer I used to miss pell my words and now I look in a dictionary or ask a friend and now I write exciting and scary stories and now I have very good endings. Now I use capitals I used to leave out words and write short simple stories.

Table 15.5 Process and best works portfolios for individuals and groups

The process portfolio

Subject area	Individual pupil	Co-operative group
Science	Documentation (running records or logs) of using the scientific method to solve a series of laboratory problems	Documentation (observation checklists) of using the scientific method to solve a series of laboratory problems
Mathematics	Documentation of mathematical reasoning through double-column mathematical problem solving (computations on the left side and running commentary explaining thought processes on the right side)	Documentation of complex problem solving and use of higher-level strategies
Language	Evolution of compositions from early notes through outlines, research notes, response to others' editing and final draft	Rubrics and procedures developed to ensure high-quality peer editing

The best works portfolio

Subject area	Individual pupil	Cooperative group
Language	The best compositions in a variety of styles – expository, humour/satire, creative (poetry, drama, short story), journalistic (reporting, editorial columnist, reviewer) and advertising copy	The best dramatic production, video project, TV broadcast, newspaper, advertising display
Social studies	The best historical research paper, opinion essay on historical issue, commentary on current event, original historical theory, review of a historical biography, account of participation in academic controversy	The best community survey, essay resulting from academic controversy, oral history compilation, multidimensional analysis of historical event, 'journalist' interview with historical figure
Arts	The best creative products such as drawings, paintings, photographs, sculptures, pottery, poems, acting performances	The best creative products such as murals, plays written and performed, inventions thought of and built

Source: From *Meaningful Assessment: A Meaningful and Cooperative Process* by D. W. Johnson and R. T. Johnson. Published by Allyn and Bacon, Boston, MA. Copyright © 2002 by Pearson Education.

those qualities in their own productions and performances. Pupils also benefit when they select examples of their work to exhibit and articulate their reasons for making the selections. Being able to judge quality can encourage pupil motivation by setting clear goals.

The following Focus on Practice give some ideas for using portfolios and pupil presentations in teaching.

FOCUS ON PRACTICE

Creating portfolios

Pupils should be involved in selecting the pieces that will make up the portfolio

Examples
1. During the unit or term, ask each pupil to select work that fits certain criteria, such as 'my most difficult problem,' 'my best work,' 'my most improved work,' or 'three approaches to'.
2. For their final submissions, ask pupils to select pieces that best show how much they have learned.

A portfolio should include information that shows pupil self-reflection and self-criticism

Examples
1. Ask pupils to include a rationale for their selections.
2. Have each pupil write a 'guide' to his or her portfolio, explaining how strengths and weaknesses are reflected in the work he or she has included.
3. Include self- and peer critiques, indicating specifically what is good and what might be improved.
4. Model self-criticism of your own productions.

The portfolio should reflect the pupils' activities in learning

Examples
1. Include a representative selection of projects, writings, drawings, and so forth.
2. Ask pupils to relate the goals of learning to the contents of their portfolios.

The portfolio can serve different functions at different times of the year

Examples
1. Early in the year, it might hold unfinished work or 'problem pieces'.
2. At the end of the year, it could contain only what the pupil is willing to make public.

Portfolios should show growth

Examples
1. Ask pupils to make a 'history' of their progress along certain 'dimensions' and to illustrate points in their growth with specific works.
2. Ask pupils to include descriptions of activities outside class that reflect the growth illustrated in the portfolio.

Teach pupils how to create and use portfolios

Examples
1. Keep models of very well done portfolios as examples, but stress that each portfolio is an individual statement.
2. Examine your pupils' portfolios frequently, especially early in the year when they are just getting used to the idea. Give constructive feedback.

For more ideas about using portfolios and some examples of assessed portfolios, see www.qca.org.uk/6447.html or use the link from the website at http://www. pearsoned.co.uk/woolfolkeuro.

Evaluating portfolios and performances

Checklists, rating scales and scoring rubrics are helpful when you assess performances, because assessments of performances, portfolios and presentations are criterion-referenced, not norm-referenced. In other words, the pupils' products and performances are compared to established standards, not ranked in relation to other pupils' work (Cambourne and Turbill, 1990; Wiggins, 1991). For example, Figure 15.2 gives three alternatives – numerical, graphic and descriptive – for rating an oral presentation.

Connect and Extend

For a further discussion on portfolios go to *Enhancing student self-assessment competencies through academic portfolios and student-parent conferences in middle schools* by Paul Camic and Lynda Cafasso (see the Companion Website – Web Link 15.4).

WEB

Numerical rating scale

Directions:
Indicate how often the pupil performs each of these behaviours while giving an oral presentation. For each behaviour circle **1** if the pupil **always** performs the behaviour, **2** if the pupil **usually** performs the behaviour, **3** if the pupil **seldom** performs the behaviour, and **4** if the pupil **never** performs the behaviour.

Physical expression

A. Stands straight and faces audience.
    1 2 3 4
B. Changes facial expression with change in the tone of the presentation.
    1 2 3 4

Graphic rating scale

Directions:
Place an **X** on the line that shows how often the pupil did each of the behaviours listed while giving an oral presentation.

Physical expression

A. Stands straight and faces audience.

    always   usually   seldom   never

B. Changes facial expression with change in the tone of the presentation.

    always   usually   seldom   never

Figure 15.2
Three ways of
rating an oral
presentation

Source: From *Classroom
Assessment: Concepts
and Applications*
(5th ed.) by P. W. Airasian
(2005). New York:
McGraw-Hill, p. 251.
Copyright © 2005 by The
McGraw-Hill Companies.

Descriptive rating scale

Directions:

Place an **X** on the line at the place that best describes the pupil's performance of each behaviour.

Physical expression

A. Stands straight and faces audience.

| stands straight, always looks at audience | weaves, fidgets, eyes roam from audience to ceiling | constant, distracting movements, no eye contact with audience |

B. Changes facial expression with change in the tone of the presentation.

| matches facial expressions to content and emphasis | facial expressions usually appropriate, occasional lack of expression | no match between tone and facial expression; expression distracts |

Scoring rubrics

Rules that are used to
determine the quality of a
pupil performance.

Connect and Extend

Read about the impact of digital portfolios on teachers and learners in Wall, K., *et al.* (2006), 'Developing digital portfolios: investigating how digital portfolios can facilitate pupil talk about learning', *Technology, Pedagogy and Education, 15* (3), pp. 261–273.

Connect and Extend

For information about every aspect of the use of scoring rubrics in the classroom as well as an extensive collection of rubrics that can be used or adapted by teachers see the

 Companion Website (Web Link 15.5).

Scoring rubrics

A checklist or rating scale gives specific feedback about elements of a performance. Scoring rubrics are rules that are used to determine the quality of a pupil performance (Mabry, 1999). For example, a rubric describing an excellent oral presentation might be:

Pupil consistently faces audience, stands straight and maintains eye contact; voice projects well and clearly; pacing and tone variation appropriate; well-organised; points logically and completely presented; brief summary at end (Airasian, 1996: 155).

Performance assessment requires careful judgement on the part of teachers and clear communication to pupils about what is good and what needs improving. In some ways, the approach is similar to the clinical method first introduced by Alfred Binet to assess intelligence (see the section in Chapter 4, Measuring intelligence). It is based on observing the pupil perform a variety of tasks and comparing his or her performance to a standard. Just as Binet never wanted to assign a single number to represent the child's intelligence, teachers who use authentic assessments do not try to assign one score to the pupil's performance. Even if rankings, ratings and grades have to be given, these judgements are not the ultimate goals – improvement of learning is. Some of the following Focus on Practice for developing rubrics are taken from Goodrich (1997) and Johnson and Johnson (2002).

FOCUS ON PRACTICE

Developing a rubric

1. *Look at models:* Show pupils examples of good and not-so-good work. Identify the characteristics that make the good ones good and the not-so-good, not-so-good.

2. *List criteria:* Use the discussion of models to begin a list of what counts in quality work.

3. *Articulate gradations of quality:* Describe the best and worst levels of quality, then fill in the middle levels based on your knowledge of common problems and the discussion of not-so-good work.

4. *Practise on models:* Have pupils use the rubrics to evaluate the models you gave them in Step 1.

5. *Use self- and peer assessment:* Give pupils their task. As they work, stop them occasionally for self- and peer-assessment.

6. *Revise:* Always give pupils time to revise their work based on the feedback they get in Step 5.

7. *Use teacher assessment:* Use the same rubric pupils used to assess their work yourself.

8. A number of *websites* provide examples of rubrics in different subjects and grades or will allow teachers to generate their own rubrics. Use the links from http://www.shambles.net/pages/staff/rubrics/ or use the link from the website at http://www.pearsoned.co.uk/woolfolkeuro.

Note: Step 1 may be necessary only when you are asking pupils to engage in a task with which they are unfamiliar. Steps 3 and 4 are useful but time-consuming; you can do these on your own, especially when you've been using rubrics for a while. A class experienced in rubric-based assessment can streamline the process so that it begins with listing criteria, after which the teacher writes out the gradations of quality, checks them with the pupils, makes revisions, then uses the rubric for self-, peer and teacher assessment.

It is often helpful to have pupils join in the development of rating scales and scoring rubrics. When pupils participate, they are challenged to decide what quality work looks or sounds like in a particular area. They know in advance what is expected. As pupils gain practice in designing and applying scoring rubrics, their work and their learning often improve. Figure 15.3 is an evaluation form for self- and peer assessment of contributions to cooperative learning groups.

Connect and Extend

Adapt the *Focus on Practice* above for developing rubrics specific to a particular age group.

Reliability, validity, generalisability

Because judgement plays such a central role in evaluating performances, issues of reliability, validity and generalisability are critical considerations. When examiners are experienced and scoring rubrics are well developed and refined, reliability can be good (Herman and Winters, 1994; LeMahieu, Gitomer and Eresh, 1993). Some of this confidence in reliability occurs because a rubric focuses the examiners' attention on a few dimensions of the work and gives limited scoring levels to choose from. If scorers can give only a rating of 1, 2, 3 or 4, they are more likely to agree than if they could score based on a 100-point scale. So the rubrics may achieve reliability not because they capture underlying agreement among raters, but because the rubrics limit options and thus limit variability in scoring (Mabry, 1999).

In terms of validity, there is some evidence that pupils who are classified as 'good' writers on the basis of portfolio assessment are judged less capable using standard writing assessments. Which form of assessment is the best reflection of

Figure 15.3
Self- and peer
evaluation of
group learning

Source: Adapted from
'The role of cooperative
learning in assessing and
communicating student
learning' by D. W.
Johnson and R. T.
Johnson. In *ASCD
1996 Yearbook:
Communicating Student
Learning* (p. 41),
T. Guskey (ed.).
Alexandria, Virginia,
ASCD. Reprinted with
permission.

Pupil self- and peer evaluation form

This form will be used to assess the members of your learning group. Fill in one form on yourself and then one form for each member of your group. During the group discussion, give each member the form you have filled out for him or her. Compare the way you rated yourself with the ways your group members have rated you. Ask for clarification when your rating differs from the ratings given by other members of the group. Each member should set a goal for increasing his or her contribution to the academic learning of all group members.

Person being rated: _____

Write the number of points earned by the group member:

(4 = excellent, 3 = good, 2 = OK, 1 = not-so-good)

☐ On time for lessons

☐ Arrives prepared for lessons

☐ Reliably completes all work on time

☐ Work is of a high quality

☐ Contributes to group learning every day

☐ Asks for help when it is needed

☐ Gives step-by-step explanations

☐ Builds on others' reasoning

☐ Relates what is being learned to previous knowledge

☐ Helps draw or construct a model of what is being learned

☐ Looks for ways to extend a task

---

enduring qualities? There is so little research on this question, it is hard to say (Herman and Winters, 1994). In addition, when rubrics are developed to assess specific tasks, the results of applying the rubrics may not predict performance on anything except very similar tasks, so we do not know whether the pupils' performance on the specific task will generalise to the larger area of study (Haertel, 1999; McMillan, 2004).

Diversity and equity in performance assessment

Equity is an issue in all assessment and no less so with performances and portfolios. With a public performance, there could be bias effects based on a pupil's appearance and speech, or the pupil's home access to expensive ICT resources. Performance assessments have the same potential as other tests to discriminate unfairly against pupils who are not wealthy or who are culturally different (McDonald, 1993). And the extensive group work, peer editing and out-of-class time devoted to portfolios means that some pupils may have access to more extensive networks of support and outright help. Many pupils come from families that have sophisticated graphics and desktop publishing capabilities. Others may have little support from home. These differences can be sources of bias and inequity.

Connect and Extend

See Chapter 6 for a discussion of how to use praise effectively. The ideas in Chapter 6 apply to written feedback as well.

Informal assessments

Informal assessments are ungraded (formative) assessments that gather information from multiple sources to help teachers make decisions (Banks, 2005). Early on in the unit, assessments should be formative (provide feedback, but not count towards a grade), saving the summative assessments (and any required grading) for later in the unit when all pupils have had the chance to learn the material (Tomlinson, 2005a). Some examples of informal assessment are pupil observations and checklists, questioning, journals and pupil self-assessment.

> **Informal assessments**
>
> Ungraded (formative) assessments that gather information from multiple sources to help teachers make decisions.

Journals are very flexible and widely used informal assessments. Pupils usually have personal or group journals and write in them on a regular basis. In their study, Michael Pressley and his colleagues (2001) found that excellent literacy teachers of five- and six-year-olds used journals for three purposes:

> **Connect and Extend**
>
> Read Boudett, K. P. *et al.* (2005). 'Teaching educators how to use pupil assessment data to improve instruction', *Phi Delta Kappa, 86*, pp. 700–706.

- As communication tools that allowed pupils to express thoughts and ideas.

- As an opportunity to apply what they have learned.

- As an outlet to encourage fluency and creative expression in language usage.

Teachers may use journals to learn about their pupils in order to better connect their teaching to the pupils' concerns and interests. Often, journals focus on academic learning, usually through responses to prompts. For example, Banks (2005) describes one secondary-school physics teacher who asked his pupils to respond to these three questions in their journals:

1. How can you determine the coefficient of friction if you know only the angle of the inclined plane?

2. Compare and contrast some of the similarities and the differences between magnetic, electronic and gravitational fields.

3. If you were to describe the physical concept of sound to your best friend, what music would you use to demonstrate this concept?

When he read the pupils' journals, the teacher realised that many of the pupils' basic assumptions about friction, acceleration and velocity came from personal experiences and not from scientific reasoning. His approach to teaching had to change to reach the pupils. The teacher never would have known to make changes without reading the journals (Banks, 2005).

There are many other kinds of informal assessments – keeping notes and observations about pupil performance, rating scales and checklists. Every time teachers ask questions or watch pupils perform skills, the teachers are conducting informal assessments. Look at Table 15.6. It summarises the possibilities and limitations of aligning different assessment tools with targets. One major message in this chapter is to match the type of assessment tools used to the target – what is being assessed.

Table 15.6 Aligning different assessment tools with targets

Different learning outcomes require different assessment methods

Target to be assessed	Assessment method			
	Selected response	Essay	Performance assessment	Personal communication
Knowledge mastery	Multiple choice, true/false, matching and fill-in can sample mastery of elements of knowledge	Essay exercises can tap understanding of relationships among elements of knowledge	Not a good choice for this target – three other options preferred	Can ask questions, evaluate answers, and infer mastery – but a time-consuming option
Reasoning proficiency	Can assess understanding of basic patterns of reasoning	Written descriptions of complex problem solutions can provide a window into reasoning proficiency	Can watch pupils solve some problems and infer about reasoning proficiency	Can ask pupil to 'think aloud' or can ask follow-up questions or probe reasoning
Skills	Can assess mastery of the prerequisites of skilful performance – but cannot tap the skill itself	Can assess mastery of the prerequisites of skilful performance – but cannot tap the skill itself	Can observe and evaluate skills as they are being performed	Strong match when skill is oral communication proficiency; also can assess mastery of knowledge prerequisite to skilful performance
Ability to create products	Can assess mastery of knowledge prerequisite to the ability to create quality products – but cannot assess the quality of the products themselves	Can assess mastery of knowledge prerequisite to the ability to create quality products – but cannot assess the quality of the products themselves	A strong match can assess: (a) proficiency in carrying out steps in product development and (b) attributes to the products itself	Can probe procedural knowledge and knowledge of attributes or quality products – but not product quality

Source: From 'Where is our assessment future and how can we get there?' by R. J. Stiggins. In R. W. Lissitz and W. D. Schafer (eds), *Meaningful Assessment: A Meaningful and Cooperative Process*. Published by Allyn and Bacon, Boston, MA. Copyright © 2002 by Pearson Education.

Connect and Extend

For important and influential ideas about making classroom assessment better, see Black, P. *et al.* (2004), 'Working inside the black box: Assessment for learning in the classroom', *Phi Delta Kappan, 86*, pp. 8–21.

Involving pupils in assessments

One way to connect teaching and assessment while developing pupils' sense of efficacy for learning (that pupils understand and appreciate how a particular approach – in this context, an assessment method – will help achieve a higher grade) is to involve the pupils in the assessment process. Pupils can keep track of their own progress and assess their improvement. The following Focus on Practice gives ideas for how to help pupils judge their own work and participate in assessing their own learning.

FOCUS ON PRACTICE

Involving pupils in classroom assessment

Here are a dozen ways of using assessment in the service of pupil learning

1. Engage pupils in reviewing good and not-so-good samples to determine attributes of good performance or product.
2. Before a discussion with the teacher or partner, pupils identify their own perceptions of strengths and weaknesses on a specific aspect of the work.
3. Pupils practise using criteria to evaluate anonymous good and not-so-good work.
4. Pupils work in pairs to revise an anonymous sample they have just evaluated.
5. Pupils write a process report, detailing the processes they went through to create a product or a performance. In it they reflect upon the problems they encountered and how they solved them.
6. Pupils develop practice tests based on their understanding of the intended learning targets and essential concepts in the material to be learned.
7. Pupils generate and answer questions they think might be on the end of unit test, based on their understanding of the content/processes/skills they were responsible for learning.
8. A few days before the test, pupils discuss answers to questions such as: 'Why am I taking this test? Who will use the results? What is it testing? How do I think I will do? What do I need to study? Who would make a good study partner?
9. Teacher identifies specific learning targets on the test and prepares a 'test analysis' chart for pupils, with three boxes: 'My strengths'; 'Quick review' and 'Further study'. Upon receipt of the corrected test, pupils identify learning targets they have mastered and write them in 'My strengths' box. Next, pupils categorise their wrong answers as either 'simple mistake' or 'further study', then list them in the appropriate box.
10. Pupils review a collection of their work over time and reflect on their growth. 'I have become a better reader this term. I used to . . ., but now I . . .'
11. Pupils use a collection of their self-assessments to summarise their learning and set goals for future learning: 'Here is what I have learned . . . here is what I need to work on . . .'
12. Pupils select and annotate evidence of achievement for a portfolio.

Source: Adapted from 'Using student-involved classroom assessment to close achievement gaps' by R. J. Stiggins and J. Chappuis, *Theory into Practice, 44,* 2005, p. 16.

Effects of Grading on Pupils

STOP AND THINK

Think back on your school reports and grades over the years. Perhaps you might be able to 'root them out' from your personal files. Did you receive a grade that was lower than you expected? How did you feel about yourself, the teacher, the subject and school in general as a result of the lower grade? What could the teacher have done to help you understand and profit from the experience?

When we think of grades, we often think of competition. Competition may be particularly hard on anxious pupils, pupils who lack self-confidence and pupils who are less prepared. So, although high standards and competition do tend to be generally related to increased academic learning, it is clear that a balance must be struck between high standards and a reasonable chance to succeed. Rick Stiggins and Jan Chappuis observe:

> From their very earliest school experiences, our pupils draw life-shaping conclusions about themselves as learners on the basis of the information we provide to them as a result of their teachers' classroom assessments. As the evidence accumulates over time, they decide if they are capable of succeeding or not. They decide whether the learning is worth the commitment it will take to attain it. They decide . . . whether to risk investing in the schooling experience. These decisions are crucial to their academic well-being (2005: 11).

Effects of failure

It may sound as though low grades and failure should be avoided in school. But the situation is not that simple.

The value of failing?

After reviewing many years of research on the effects of failure from several perspectives, Margaret Clifford (1990, 1991) concluded:

> It is time for educators to replace easy success with challenge. We must encourage pupils to reach beyond their intellectual grasp and allow them the privilege of learning from mistakes. There must be a tolerance for error-making in every classroom, and gradual success rather than continual success must become the yardstick by which learning is judged (1990: 23).

Some level of failure may be helpful for most pupils, especially if teachers help the pupils see connections between hard work and improvement. Efforts to protect pupils from failure and to guarantee success may be counterproductive. In fact, the more able your pupils are, the more challenging and important it will be to help them learn to 'fail successfully' (Foster, 1981). Carol Tomlinson, an expert on differentiated teaching, puts it this way: 'Pupils whose learning histories have caused them to believe that excellence can be achieved with minimal effort do not learn to expend effort, and yet perceive that high grades are an entitlement for them' (2005b: 266).

Pupils often need help working out why their answers are incorrect; without such timely feedback they are likely to make the same mistakes again and again

In my classroom we talk about the 'learning zone' that school pupils (then) and higher education students (now) gain instant access to when they get something wrong. That's the best thing about getting something wrong, you are rewarded with the chance to learn something new and then get the buzz of getting it right. Such approaches chime with the notion of 'successful' or constructive failure.

Effects of feedback

The results of several studies of feedback fit well with the notion of 'successful' or constructive failure. These studies have concluded that it is more helpful to tell pupils *why* they are wrong so they can learn more appropriate strategies (Bangert-Drowns *et al.*, 1991). Pupils often need help figuring out why their answers are incorrect. Without such feedback, they are likely to make the same mistakes again. Yet this type of feedback is rarely given. In one study, only about 8% of the teachers noticed a consistent type of error in a pupil's arithmetic computation and informed the pupil (Bloom and Bourdon, 1980).

What are the identifying characteristics of effective written feedback? With older pupils (late primary and secondary school), written comments are most helpful when they are personalised and when they provide constructive criticism. This means the teacher should make specific comments on errors or faulty strategies, but balance this criticism with suggestions about how to improve, as well as comments on the positive aspects of the work (Butler and Nisan, 1986; Guskey and Bailey, 2001). Working with teachers, Maria Elawar and Lyn Corno found that feedback was dramatically improved when the teachers used these four questions as a guide: 'What is the key error? What is the probable reason the pupil made this error? How can I guide the pupil to avoid the error in the future? What did the pupil do well that could be noted?' (1985: 166). Here are some examples of the type of teachers' written comments that proved helpful (adapted from Elawar and Corno, 1985: 164):

> *Saj, you know how to calculate a percentage, but the computation is wrong in this instance. Can you see where? (Teacher has underlined the location of errors.)*

> *You know how to solve the problem – the formula is correct – but you have not demonstrated that you understand how one fraction multiplied by another can give an answer that is smaller than either ($\frac{1}{2} \times \frac{1}{2} = \frac{1}{4}$).*

Comments like these should help pupils to correct errors and recognise good work, progress and increase skill.

STOP AND THINK

Given the various roles of evaluation, what are the disadvantages of a teacher giving a test and not returning the results until several weeks later? What is the disadvantage of merely displaying the result without returning the actual test? What is the disadvantage of returning the pupils' scored answer sheets without reviewing the correct answers?

Grades and motivation

Connect and Extend

Can grades be used as motivators for all pupils? What determines whether a grade is motivating? How can a teacher use grades so that they tend to be motivating instead of discouraging? Check in Chapter 10 for the possible motivational effects of success and failure.

If you are relying on grades ('I want you to get an A for your next homework') to motivate pupils, you had better think again (Smith, Smith and De Lisi, 2001). The assessments you give should support pupils' motivation to learn – not just to work for a grade. Is there really a difference between working for a grade and working to learn? The answer depends in part on how a grade is determined. As a teacher, you can use grades to motivate the kind of learning you intend pupils to achieve in your course. If you test only at a simple but detailed level of knowledge, you may force pupils to choose between complex learning and a good grade but when a grade reflects meaningful learning, working for a grade and working to learn become the same thing. Finally, while high grades may have some value as rewards or incentives for meaningful engagement in learning, low grades generally do not encourage greater efforts. Pupils receiving low grades are more likely to withdraw, blame others, decide that the work is 'stupid,' or feel responsible for the low grade but helpless to make improvements. Pupils go through a downward spiral of receiving low grades: 'The test was stupid, the teacher is stupid, the subject is stupid, school is stupid and (worse of all) I'm stupid.' They give up on themselves or on school (Tomlinson, 2005b). Rather than give a failing grade, you might consider the work incomplete and give pupils support in revising or improving. Maintain high standards and give pupils a chance to reach them (Guskey, 1994; Guskey and Bailey, 2001).

The following Focus on Practice summarises the effects grades can have on pupils.

FOCUS ON PRACTICE

Minimising the detrimental effects of grading

Avoid awarding high grades and high praise for answers that conform to your ideas or to those in the textbook

Examples
1. Give extra points for correct and creative answers.
2. Withhold your opinions until all sides of an issue have been explored.
3. Praise pupils for disagreeing in a rational, productive manner.
4. Give partial credit for partially correct answers.

Make sure each pupil has a reasonable chance to be successful, especially at the beginning of a new task

Examples
1. Pre-test pupils to make sure they have pre-requisite abilities.
2. When appropriate, provide opportunities for pupils to re-test to raise their grades, but make sure the re-test is as difficult as the original.
3. Consider 'failing efforts' as 'incomplete' and encourage pupils to revise and improve.
4. Base grades more on work at the end of the unit of work, set un-graded work in the beginning of the unit.

Balance written and oral feedback

Examples
1. Consider giving short, lively written comments with younger pupils and more extensive written comments with older pupils.
2. When a grade is lower than the pupil might have expected, be sure the reason for the lower grade is clear.
3. Tailor comments to the individual pupil's performance; avoid writing the same phrases over and over.
4. Note specific errors, possible reasons for errors, ideas for improvement and work done well.

> **Make grades as meaningful as possible**
>
> *Examples*
> 1. Tie grades to the mastery of important learning objectives.
> 2. Give un-graded assignments to encourage exploration.
> 3. Experiment with performances and portfolios.
>
> **Base grades on more than just one criterion**
>
> *Examples*
> 1. Use essay questions as well as multiple-choice items on a test.
> 2. Grade oral reports and class participation.

Grading and Reporting: Nuts and Bolts

STOP AND THINK

Think about the other modules you are taking this term besides this one. How are your marks calculated in those courses? Do you know how your marks and grades will be calculated in this course?

Connect and Extend

For a summary of the use of formative assessment see Threfall, J. (2005), 'The formative use of assessment information in planning – the notion of contingent planning', *British Journal of Educational Studies*, *53*(1), pp. 54–65.

Criterion-referenced grading

Assessment of each pupil's mastery of learning objectives.

Norm-referenced grading

Assessment of pupils' achievement in relation to one another.

To determine a final grade from the marks awarded, the teacher must make a major decision. Should a pupil's grade reflect the amount of material learned and how well it has been learned, or should the grade reflect the pupil's status in comparison with the rest of the class? In other words, should grading be criterion-referenced or norm-referenced?

Criterion-referenced versus norm-referenced grading

In criterion-referenced grading, the grade represents a list of accomplishments. If clear objectives have been set for the course, the grade may represent a certain number of objectives met satisfactorily. When a criterion-referenced system is used, criteria for each grade generally are spelled out in advance. It is then up to the pupil to earn the grade she or he wants to receive. Theoretically, in this system, all pupils can achieve an 'A' if they reach the criteria. Criterion-referenced grading has the advantage of relating judgements about a pupil to the achievement of clearly defined learning objectives. Some schools have developed reporting systems where school reports list objectives along with judgements about the pupil's attainment of each. The middle school report card shown in Figure 15.4 demonstrates a relationship between assessment and the learning objectives.

In norm-referenced grading, the major influence on a grade is the pupil's standing in comparison with others. If a pupil studies very hard and almost everyone else does too, the pupil may receive a disappointing grade, perhaps a C or D. One

Linsdale Middle School, Boughton Lizzard, Hamfordshire   Date_____

Pupil   Form   Form tutor   Head teacher

_____   _____   _____   _____

_____   _____   _____   _____

E = Excellent   S = Satisfactory   P = Making progress   N = Needs improvement

READING

__ Reads with understanding

__ Can write about what is read

__ Completes reading group work on time

__ Shows an interest in reading

Reading skills

__ Decodes new words

__ Understands new words

Independent reading level

Below/At Year Level/Above

Language

__ Uses oral language effectively

__ Listens attentively

__ Learns weekly spellings

Writing skills

__ Understands writing as process

__ Creates a rough draft

__ Makes meaningful revisions

__ Creates edited, legible final version

MATHEMATICS

Problem solving

__ Solves teacher-generated problems

__ Solves self-pupil-generated problems

__ Can create story problems

Interpreting problems

__ Uses appropriate strategies

__ Can use more than one strategy

__ Can explain strategies in writing

__ Can explain strategies orally

Maths concepts

Understands place value

Beginning/Developing/Refined

Number facts

Beginning/Developing/Refined

Calculation

Beginning/Developing/Refined

Shape, space and measure

Beginning/Developing/Refined

HUMANITIES

__ Understands subject matter

__ Shows curiosity and enthusiasm

__ Contributes to class discussions

__ Uses map skills

__ Interprets text

Topics covered:_____

_____

_____

SCIENCE

__ Shows curiosity

__ Asks thoughtful questions

__ Uses scientific methods to set up and run experiments

__ Makes good scientific observations

__ Researches scientific topics

WORKING SKILLS

__ Listens carefully

__ Follows directions

__ Works neatly and carefully

__ Checks work

HOMEWORK

__ Completes work on time

__ Completes work to standard required

__ Extends homework tasks

PRESENTATIONS

_____

_____

_____

_____

_____

_____

SOCIAL SKILLS

__ Shows courtesy

__ Respects rights of others

__ Shows self-control

__ Interacts well with others

__ Shows a cooperative and positive attitude in class

__ Shows a cooperative attitude when asked to work with other pupils

Editing skills

__ Uses capital letters correctly

__ Punctuates correctly

__ Uses complete sentences

__ Uses paragraphs

__ Demonstrates dictionary skills

Writing skill level

Below/At Year Level/Above

Goals:

_____

_____

_____

Data Handling

Beginning/Developing/ Refined

Overall maths skill level

Below/At Year Level/Above

Attitude/work skills

__ Welcomes a problem

__ Persistent

__ Takes advantage of learning from others

__ Listens to others

__ Participates in discussion

Goals:

_____

_____

__ Completes work on time

__ Uses time wisely

__ Works well independently

__ Works well in a group

__ Takes risks in learning

__ Welcomes a challenge

Goals:

_____

_____

_____

__ Is willing to help other pupils

__ Works well with other adults

Goals:

_____

_____

_____

Attendance

Present _____

Absent _____

Late _____

Figure 15.4
A criterion-referenced school report

This is one example of a criterion-referenced school report. All criterion-referenced reports indicate pupils' progress towards specific learning goals

Source: Adapted from 'Reporting Methods in Grades K-8' by K. Lake and K. Kafka in *ASCD 1996 Yearbook: Communicating Student Learning,* Alexandria, Virginia, ASCD (p. 104) T. Guskey (ed). Reprinted with permission.

Grading on the curve

Norm-referenced grading that compares pupils' performance to an average level.

common type of norm-referenced grading is called grading on the curve. (Check out Chapter 14's section on the normal distribution.) How you feel about this approach probably depends on where your grades generally fell along that 'curve'. There is good evidence that this type of grading damages the relationships among pupils and between teachers and pupils and also diminishes motivation for most pupils (Krumboltz and Yeh, 1996). When you think about it, if the curve arbitrarily limits the number of good grades that can be given, then, in the game of grading, most pupils will be losers (Guskey and Bailey, 2001; Haladyna, 2002; Kohn, 1996). Over 25 years ago, Benjamin Bloom (of Bloom's taxonomy) pointed out the fallacy of grading on the curve:

There is nothing sacred about the normal curve. It is the distribution most appropriate to chance and random activity. Education is a purposeful activity, and we seek to have pupils learn what we have to teach. If we are effective in our teaching, the distribution of achievement should be very different from the normal curve. In fact, we may even insist that our educational efforts have been unsuccessful *to the extent that the distribution of achievement approximates the normal distribution (1981: 52–53).*

Connect and Extend

For an international perspective read Håkan Andersson's paper presented at the European Conference on Educational Research in 2004. See the Companion Website (Web Link 15.6).

STOP AND THINK

Can you define criterion- and norm-referenced grading systems, identify examples of each, and explain the advantages and disadvantages of each system? Describe the possible effects of grades on pupils of adopting criterion- and norm-referenced grading systems. Again refer back to Chapter 10 for ideas on intrinsic and extrinsic motivational factors.

Let's examine a few popular systems for calculating grades.

The point system and percentage grading

One popular system for combining grades from many assignments is a point system. Each test or assignment is given a certain number of total points, depending on its importance. A test worth 40% of the grade could be worth 40 points. A paper worth 20% could be worth 20 points. Points are then awarded on the test or paper, based on specific criteria. An A+ paper, one that meets all the criteria, could be given the full 20 points; an average paper might be given 10 points. If tests of comparable importance are worth the same number of points, are equally difficult, and cover a similar amount of material, this system can be fair and practical. However, in many schools, these points still must be converted into some form of final grade. So the teacher has to decide the standards for assigning grades. What process might teachers have adopted for awarding grades in the term report example provided in Figure 15.5?

Using another approach, percentage grading, the teacher can assign grades based on how much knowledge each pupil has mastered – what percentage of the total knowledge he or she understands. To do this, the teacher might score tests and other class work with percentage scores (based on how much is correct – 50%, 85%, etc.) and then average these scores to reach a unit/term/year score. These scores can then be converted into letter grades according to pre-determined bands. Any number of pupils can earn any grade. School systems often establish equivalent percentage categories for As, Bs, and so on. The percentages vary from school to school. An A grade might be 70% to 100% in one school but 80% to 100% in another.

Even though it is quite common, this approach has problems. Can we really say what is the total amount of knowledge available in, for example, science for 13- and 14-year-olds? Are we sure we can accurately measure what percentage of this body of knowledge each pupil has attained? To use percentage grading appropriately, we would have to know exactly what there was to learn and exactly how much of that knowledge each pupil had learned (Popham, 2005). These conditions are seldom met, even though teachers use the bands to assign grades as if measurement were so accurate that a one-point difference was meaningful. What happens at the boundaries between grade bands is always a matter of some debate. Does Figure 15.5 solve any of these dilemmas?

> **Percentage grading**
>
> System of converting class performances to percentage scores and assigning grades based on predetermined bands.

Profiling

Don't be fooled by the seeming security of points or absolute percentages. Teachers' grading philosophy will continue to operate, even in the most tightly run assessment systems. However, because there is more concern today with specifying objectives and criterion-referenced assessment, especially at the primary school phase, several alternative methods for evaluating pupil progress against predetermined criteria have evolved including profiling.

A norm-referenced school report

Linsdale Middle School, Boughton Lizzard, Hamfordshire   Date_____

Pupil   Form   Form tutor   Head teacher

Key to grades: Effort 1 = Tries hard all the time   **2** = Usually tries   **3** = Tries sometimes   **4** = Seldom tries

Attainment A = Usually achieves at a level in the top 5% of the year group
B = Usually achieves at a level in the top 25% of the year group
C = Usually achieves at a level in the middle 50% of the year group
D = Usually achieves at a level in the bottom 25% of the year group
E = Usually achieves at a level in the bottom 5% of the year group

Mathematics	Effort _____	**French**	Effort _____
	Attainment _____		Attainment _____
English	Effort _____	**Art and Design**	Effort _____
	Attainment _____		Attainment _____
Science	Effort _____	**Music**	Effort _____
	Attainment _____		Attainment _____
History	Effort _____	**Physical Education**	Effort _____
	Attainment _____		Attainment _____
Geography	Effort _____	**Technology**	Effort _____
	Attainment _____		Attainment _____
Religious Education	Effort _____	**Personal, Social and Health Education**	Effort _____
	Attainment _____		Attainment _____

Figure 15.5
A school report awarding grades for effort and attainment

This is one example of a norm-referenced school report. All norm-referenced reports indicate pupils' attainment in relation to peers.

Notes: As in Fig. 15.4 *A criterion-referenced report,* not all grades are awarded on the basis of the main assessment model. In this case, the effort grade is related to a time/effort function that provides a criteria standard.

One excellent example of profiling is the Foundation Profile, which is the record of assessments made of English children aged three to five years. The Foundation Stage was introduced as a distinct phase of education for children aged three to five years in September 2000. In preparation, *Curriculum Guidance for the Foundation Stage* was distributed in May 2000. This curriculum guidance sets out six areas of learning (Early Learning Goals) which form the basis of the Foundation Stage curriculum. These areas are:

- Personal, social and emotional development
- Communication, language and literacy
- Mathematical development
- Knowledge and understanding of the world
- Physical development
- Creative development.

Each Early Learning Goal has a set of related early learning goals or strands. When the Education Act 2002 extended the National Curriculum to include the Foundation Stage, the Early Learning Goals became statutory, and the Act specified that there should be strands for each of the areas.

During any activity each child's developments and achievements can be noted and recorded on assessment scales found in the Foundation Stage Profile which have been derived from the 'Stepping Stones' and 'Early Learning Goals'. There is a copy of the Foundation Stage Profile for each child in the class. It is available as a booklet or an e-profile. More details of the use of the Foundation Stage Profile can be found in the QCA Sure Start handbook, which you can download from the website at http://www.qca.org.uk/ or follow the link from the website at www.pearsoned.co.uk/woolfolkeuro.

The Foundation Stage Profile captures the early learning goals as a set of 13 assessment scales, each of which has nine points. The first three points describe a child who is still progressing towards the achievements described in the early learning goals, and are based mainly on the stepping stones in the curriculum guidance. Most children will achieve all of these three points before they achieve any of the early learning goals. The next five points are drawn from the early learning goals themselves. These are presented in approximate order of difficulty. However, the points are not necessarily hierarchical and a child may achieve a later point without having achieved some or all of the earlier points. The final point in each scale describes a child who has achieved all the points from 1–8 on that scale, has developed further both in breadth and depth, and is working consistently beyond the level of the early learning goals.

Practitioners build up their assessments throughout the year on a cumulative basis, from ongoing learning and teaching activities. The Profile has been designed to reflect this process using the evidence from ongoing assessment, to record the achievement of particular items in the scales. From the Profile, it is possible to see which items a child has achieved in the autumn, spring and summer terms. This will assist practitioners who wish to use the Profile as part of their approach to assessment for learning. The Foundation Stage Profile forms the basis for reports to parents and for information to be passed on to the child's next teacher.

Profiles are powerful ways of assessing pupils' achievements but one potential problem remains in even the best assessment system; engaging pupils with the assessment process. Contract systems and grading rubrics can help with this.

> **STOP AND THINK**
>
> How would you solve the following problem? As part of using a contract system in a class, one requirement for an A grade is 'to write a book critique'. However, some pupils are reporting on books that they read last year, and some are handing in short, superficial critiques. How can the teacher structure the contract system to raise the standard of pupils' work?

The contract system and grading rubrics

Contract system

System in which each pupil works for a particular grade according to agreed-upon standards.

When applied to the whole class, the contract system indicates the type, quantity and quality of work required for each number or letter grade in the system. Rubrics describe the performance expected for each level. Pupils agree, or 'contract', to work for particular grades by meeting the specified requirements and performing at the level specified. For example, the following standards might be established:

F: Not completing or handing in the required work.

D: Completing or handing in the required work.

C: Completing or handing in the required work and receiving a mark on all assignments to indicate they are satisfactory.

B: Completing or handing in the required work and receiving a mark on all assignments with at least three that achieve a mark indicating higher achievement.

A: As above, plus a successful oral or written report on one of the books listed for supplementary reading.

This example calls for more subjective judgement than would be ideal. However, such contract systems can reduce pupil anxiety about grades. The contract system can be applied to individual pupils, in which case it functions much like an independent study plan.

> ⬅➡ **Connect and Extend**
>
> See Chapter 6 for a discussion of behaviour management contracts.

Unfortunately, the system can lead to overemphasis on the quantity of work. Teachers may be too vague about the standards that differentiate acceptable from unacceptable work. This is where scoring rubrics for each assignment can be helpful. If clear and well-developed rubrics describe the performances expected for each assignment, and if pupils learn to use the rubrics to evaluate their own work, then quality, not quantity, will be at the centre of grading. You can modify the contract system by including a revise option. This system allows pupils to improve their work, but also should reward pupils for getting it right the first time. The Focus on Practice below give ideas for using any grading system in a fair and reasonable way.

Revise option

In a contract system, the chance to revise and improve work.

Other issues in grading

Grading on effort and improvement

Grading on effort and improvement is not really a complete grading system, but rather a theme that can run through most grading methods. Should teachers grade pupils based on how much they learn or on the final level of learning? One problem with using improvement as a standard for grading is that the best pupils improve the least, because they are already the most competent. Do you want to penalise these pupils because they knew quite a bit initially, and the teaching and testing have limited how

FOCUS ON PRACTICE

Using any grading system

Explain grading policies to pupils and remind them of the policies regularly

Examples

1. Give older pupils a handout describing the assignments, tests, grading criteria and timetable.
2. Explain to younger pupils in a low-pressure manner how their work will be evaluated.

Base grades on clearly specified, reasonable standards

Examples

1. Specify standards by developing a rubric with pupils – have anonymous examples of excellent, good and not-so-good work from previous classes.
2. Discuss workload and grading standards with more experienced teachers.
3. Give a few first to gauge the difficulty of the test and to estimate the time pupils will need.

Base your grades on as much objective evidence as possible

Examples

1. Plan in advance how and when the test will take place.
2. Keep a portfolio of pupil work. This may be useful in parent conferences.

Be sure pupils understand test directions

Examples

1. Outline the directions on the board.
2. Ask several pupils to explain the directions.
3. Go over a sample question first.

Correct, return and discuss test questions as soon as possible

Examples

1. Have pupils who wrote good answers read their responses for the class; make sure they are not the same pupils each time.
2. Discuss why wrong answers, especially popular wrong choices, are incorrect.
3. As soon as pupils finish a test, give them the answers to questions and the page numbers where answers are discussed in the text.

As a rule, do not change a grade

Examples
1. Make sure you can defend the grade in the first place.
2. Do change any clerical or calculation errors.

Guard against bias in grading

Examples
1. Ask pupils to put their names on the backs of their papers.
2. Use an objective point system or model papers when grading essays.

Give pupils the benefit of the doubt. All measurement techniques involve error

Examples
1. Give the higher grade in borderline cases, unless there is a very good reason not to.
2. If a large number of pupils miss the same question in the same way, revise the question for the future and consider not aggregating scores for that question with the rest of the test.

Source: From *Problems in Middle and High School Teaching: A Handbook for Pupil Teachers and Beginning Teachers* (pp. 182–187) by A. M. Drayer, 1979, Boston: Allyn and Bacon. Copyright © 1979 by Allyn and Bacon.

much learning they can demonstrate? After all, unless you assign extra work, these pupils will run out of things to do (Airasian, 2005; Guskey and Bailey, 2001).

STOP AND THINK

Think about your philosophy of teaching. What do you believe about testing and grading? How will you assign grades? (Consult the Focus on Practice above for ideas and review the learning intentions for this chapter.)

Individual learning expectation (ILE)

Pupils earn improvement points on tests or assignments for scoring above their personal base (average) score or for making a perfect score.

One solution is to use the individual learning expectation (ILE) system. With this system, pupils earn improvement points on tests or assignments for scoring above their personal base (average) score or for making a perfect score. The teacher can count these improvement points when figuring a final grade or simply use them as a basis for giving other classroom rewards. Another option is to recognise good pupil effort through oral or written comments, notes to parents or other recognition.

Cautions: being fair

The attributions a teacher makes about the causes of pupil successes or failures can affect the grades that pupils receive. Teachers are more likely to give higher grades for effort (a controllable factor) than for ability (an uncontrollable factor). Lower grades are more likely when teachers attribute a pupil's failure to lack of effort instead of lack of ability (Weiner, 1979). It is also possible that grades can be influenced by a halo effect – that is, by the tendency to view particular aspects of a pupil based on a general impression, either positive or negative. As a teacher, you may find it difficult to avoid being affected by positive and negative halos. A very pleasant pupil who seems to work hard and causes little trouble may be given the benefit of the doubt (B− instead of C+), whereas a very difficult pupil who seems to refuse to try might be a loser at grading time (D instead of C−).

There is another aspect of fairness. If pupils' grades are affected by unclear directions, difficulty reading the test or assignment questions, low grades for missing homework, a test that did not measure what was taught, time pressures, or other factors that are not related to the skills being assessed, then 'grade pollution' has occurred. When flowery language or an artistic cover inflates a pupil's grade, we have more grade pollution. Grades should reflect what a pupil knows, understands, or can do related to the learning objective specified (Tomlinson, 2005b).

Connect and Extend

Individual learning expectations can be part of an individual learning plan. Read about developing ILPs in a Further Education (16–19 years) context via the Companion Website (Web Link 15.7).

Halo effect

The tendency for a general impression of a person to influence our perception of any aspect of that person.

Beyond Grading: Communicating with Families

No number or letter grade conveys the totality of a pupil's experience in a class or course. Pupils, parents and teachers sometimes become too focused on the end point – the grade. But communicating with families should involve more than just sending home grades. There are a number of ways to communicate with and report to families. Many teachers I know have a beginning-of-the-year newsletter or pupil handbook that communicates homework, behaviour and grading policies to families. Other options described by Guskey and Bailey (2001) are:

- notes attached to reports
- phone calls, especially 'Good News' calls
- school open evenings
- conferences, including pupil-led conferences
- portfolios or exhibits of pupil work
- homework hotlines
- school or class web pages
- home visits.

Here is an example of a 'Good News Call' based on Guskey and Bailey (2001). A primary school head teacher carries her phone with her as she walks through the corridors, visits the dining room, supervises the playground and observes teachers' classes. When she sees a pupil performing well in class, assisting a classmate or helping to improve the school, she immediately calls that pupil's parent or carer on her phone and announces, 'Hello, this is Ms Johnson, the head teacher at Judd Primary School. I just saw Tonya . . . .' After explaining what she observed and complimenting the child, she hands the phone to the child so that he or she can talk briefly with the parent or carer. Everyone leaves with a big smile. One caution – if a family member didn't answer, it would be a bad idea to leave a call back message because the message recipients might fear that their children were sick or injured.

Connect and Extend

Read Munk, D. D. and Bursuck, W. D. (2001), 'Preliminary findings on personalised grading for middle school pupils with learning disabilities', *Exceptional Children, 67*, pp. 211–234.

When asked about calls to parents concerning pupil problems, Ms Johnson explains, 'Those I save for after school. Often, I have to think more carefully about what I'm going to say and what strategies I'm going to recommend. When I see a child doing something wonderful, however, I want to let the parents know about that right away. I never have to weigh my words and I think it means more to the child.'

The head teacher's phone calls have completely altered the culture of this school. Parent involvement and participation in school events is at an all-time high, and their regard for Ms Johnson and the school staff is exceptionally positive. It's a small thing, but it has made a big difference.

Consultations with parents are expected of teachers in primary and secondary schools. Clearly, the more skilled teachers are at communicating, the more effective they will be at conducting these consultations. Listening and problem-solving skills such as those discussed in Chapter 12 can be particularly important. When dealing with parents or pupils who are angry or upset, teachers need to hear the concerns of the participants, not just their words. The atmosphere should be friendly and unrushed. Any observations about the pupil should be as factual as possible, based on observation or information from assignments. Information gained from a pupil or a parent should be kept confidential. The Focus on Practice below offers some helpful ideas for planning and conducting consultations.

FOCUS ON PRACTICE

Consultations

Plan ahead

Examples
1. What are your goals?
2. Problem solving?
3. Sharing test results?
4. Asking questions that you want answered?
5. Providing information you want to share? Emphasise the positive.
6. Describing your 'next steps' in the classroom?
7. Making suggestions for use at home?

Begin with a positive statement

Examples
1. 'Jacob has a great sense of humour.'
2. 'Giselle really enjoys materials that deal with animals.'
3. 'Yesim is sympathetic when somebody has a problem.'

Listen actively

Examples
1. Empathise with the parents.
2. Accept their feelings: 'You seem to feel frustrated when Lee doesn't listen.'

Establish a partnership

Example

1. Ask parents to follow through on class targets at home: 'If you ask to see the home/school link book and go over it at home with Iris, I'll review it and check her progress at school.'

Plan follow-up contacts

Examples

1. Write notes or make phone calls to share successes.
2. Keep parents informed *before* problems develop.

End with a positive statement

Examples

1. 'Joseph has made several friends this year.'
2. 'Ashanti should be a big help in the social studies play that her group is developing.'

Beyond Grading: Qualitative Knowledge of What Pupils Can Do

In this chapter we have explored a range of assessment techniques including profiling, testing (traditional and 'authentic') and grading by which pupils and parents can not only compare achievements against criteria – hopefully the learning intentions – but also against other pupils in the class. 'I got a B. What did you get?' National testing regimes (see Chapter 14) have changed the way in which teachers go about classroom assessment and many pupils are subject to testing regimes that include a good deal of pencil and paper and computer tests of the multiple-choice format.

This chapter has reflected this move to grading of pupils on an 'A to F' model and the leveling of pupils' attainments against the criteria set by the National Curriculum Levels. We have also tried to show that the move to the use of more multiple-choice question formats on computer systems (e.g. SuccessMaker from Research Machines) requires teachers to be properly critical of poorly constructed multiple-choice tests.

In part this is because we all have a wish for high-quality assessment techniques that enable teachers to know their pupils as learners, their preferred learning styles, their strengths and the reasons for their weaknesses. It is also because we think the use of traditional multiple-choice questions (favoured in national and international testing regimes) does little to provide the kind of quality assessment of pupils as individual learners.

Here is an example of what we mean; a story quoted by Desmond Nuttall at a presentation to the Centre for Policy Studies Conference in 1993 (Murphy *et al.*, 1995). The story highlights what is thought to be a common problem with an

Connect and Extend

Find out about SuccessMaker. See the Companion Website (Web Link 15.8). What do you think of such individual integrated learning systems?

over-use of multiple-choice testing techniques, that learners lose the ability to write full text answers.

> *The Americans now realise the harm done by their extensive use of multiple-choice questions and are seeking to develop much broader assessment devices – portfolios, practical activities and so forth. This allows me to tell the story of three Americans arriving at London Heathrow. They had duly ticked the boxes on the immigration forms, but the first had only been able to put a cross where the form required his signature. The second had put two crosses and, when questioned about this by the immigration officer, explained that the first cross stood for her first name and the second for her last name. The third had put three crosses and explained that the first stood for his first name, the second for his last name, and the third for his PhD (Harvard) (1995: 240).*

Reaching every pupil

Classroom assessment should, first and foremost, support pupil learning. However, stereotypes and biases can interfere with assessment. In assigning and reporting grades, how do teachers make accommodations for pupils with special needs? Table 15.7 gives some options.

It may be up to the teacher to decide how to calculate the grades of pupils with special needs and pupils whose first language is not English, but teachers need to check whether there are school policies already in place. Also, some schools now offer families a choice of the languages for the report itself. The form is the same; just the language is different (Guskey and Bailey, 2001).

Cultural bias

Several studies have found that teachers may hold lower expectations for ethnic minority pupils and these biases can influence teaching and assessment (Banks, 2005). For example, Lipman (1997) found that teachers of ethnically diverse classes are less innovative and more traditional in their instruction. These lower expectations can show up in giving higher grades to pupils for lower-quality work.

Biases can be subtle. For example, in the tests that you write, will you incorporate language and experiences that are familiar to your pupils? James Popham, now an expert in assessment, describes his first teaching job at a rural secondary school in a small agricultural town with a population of 1,500:

> *I had grown up in a fairly large city and had no knowledge about farming or ranching. To me, a 'range' was a kitchen appliance on which one cooked meals. In retrospect, I am certain that many of my classroom test items contained 'city' content that might have confused my pupils. I'll bet anything that many of my early test items unfairly penalised some of the boys and girls who had rarely, if ever, left their farms or ranches to visit more metropolitan areas (2005: 86).*

Connect and Extend

Connect to issues of cultural fairness in testing by reading Gordon Stobart's paper, 'Fairness in multicultural assessment systems' (2005) *Assessment in Education: Principles, Policy and Practice, 12*(3), pp. 275–287. Also review the key ideas in Chapter 5 relating to assessment.

Think of the range of differences in experiences of your pupils if they are from other countries or speak other languages. The Focus on Practice below, developed by several professional organisations, could guide your thinking about classroom assessment (Banks, 2005: 82).

Quality teaching and quality assessment share the same basic principles and these principles hold for all pupils. Carol Tomlinson suggests that good instruction and good grading both depend on a teacher who:

- is aware of and responds to pupil differences;

- specifies clear leaning outcomes;

| **Table 15.7** Possible grading accommodations for pupils with special needs | |

Adaptation	**Example**
Change grading criteria	
Vary assessment with different activities or products	Increase participation in classroom group activities and decrease amount of essay examinations
Grade on improvement	Give a high effort grade if the pupil's total points have increased significantly from the previous term
Modify or individualise curriculum expectations	Indicate in the IEP that the pupil will work on subtraction whilst other pupils work on division
Use contracts and modified course requirements for quality, quantity and timelines	State in the contract that the pupil will receive a B for completing all assignments at 80% quantity and timelines, accuracy and for completing a catch-up programme
Provide supplementary information	
Add comments to clarify details about the criteria used	Write on the report that the pupil's grade reflects performance on IEP objectives and not on the ordinary classroom curriculum
Add information from your pupil activity log	Note that whilst the pupil's grade was the same as last term, daily records show the pupils completed more maths exercises with less teacher assistance
Add information about effort, progress and achievement from portfolios or performance-based assignments	State that the pupil's written language showed an increase in word variety, sentence length and quality of ideas
Use other grading options	
Use checklist of skills and show the number or percentage of objectives met	Attach a checklist to the report indicating that during the term, the pupils mastered addition facts, two-digit addition with regrouping and counting change

Source: Adapted from *Developing Grading and Reporting Systems for Student Learning* (p.118) by T. R. Guskey and J. M. Bailey, 2001.

- uses pre-tests and formative assessments to monitor pupil progress towards learning goals;

- adapts instruction in a variety of ways to ensure, as much as possible, that each pupil continues to progress;

- makes sure pupils know the criteria for success on summative assessments that are tightly aligned to the stated learning goals;

- provides varied forms of assessment to ensure that pupils have an unobstructed opportunity to express what they have learned (2005b: 265–266).

FOCUS ON PRACTICE

Standards for educational and psychological testing

Assessments should be as fair as possible for pupils from diverse gender, race or ethnic backgrounds

Examples
1. Avoid any slang expressions that might be offensive.
2. Eliminate items with stereotypes that might offend, such as Eurocentric views of history that assume Columbus 'discovered' America – there were many people ahead of him who discovered and lived in America.

Assessments should relate only to the instruction given and not to background knowledge that might penalise pupils from diverse backgrounds

Examples
1. Review standardised and classroom assessments to see if some questions require knowledge not available to certain groups, such as questions about some sports (may penalise females), travel (may penalise pupils from low-income families) or driving holidays (may penalise pupils from families without cars).
2. Make sure certain answers don't favour particular social or political ideas.

Don't let assessments become a measure of language proficiency unless language is the focus of the test

Examples
1. Make special accommodations for English Language Learners such as extra time or the use of dictionaries.
2. Make sure maths tests are not really reading proficiency tests.

Source: Based on Banks, S. R. (2005). *Classroom Assessment: Issues and Practice*. Boston: Allyn and Bacon, p. 82.

A legal framework

The Education (Individual Pupils Achievement) Regulations 1996 entitles parents in England (there are corresponding statutory instruments for other parts of the UK) to specific information relating to their child's academic progress. This must be sent to parents at least once a year. Also the Data Protection Act (1998) which came into force on 1 March 2000 establishes the rights of pupils along with parents to obtain copies of educational records. If a record contains information that pupils or parents believe is incorrect, they can challenge such entries and have the information removed if they win the challenge. This means that the information in a pupils' records must be based on firm, defensible evidence. Tests must be valid and reliable. Pupils' grades must be justified by thorough assessment and observation, and any comments and anecdotes about pupils must be accurate and fair.

Formative and Summative Assessment (pp. 660–662)

What are two kinds of classroom assessment?

Most teachers must assess pupils and assign grades. Many schools have established policies about testing and grading practices, but individual teachers decide how these practices will be carried out. In the classroom, assessment may be formative (ungraded, diagnostic) or summative (graded). Formative assessment helps form teaching and summative assessment summarises pupils' achievements.

Getting the Most from Traditional Assessment (pp. 663–673)

How should teachers plan for assessment?

Assessment requires planning. Learning is supported by frequent testing using cumulative questions that ask pupils to apply and integrate knowledge. With the goals of assessment in mind, teachers are in a better position to design their own tests or evaluate the tests provided by textbook publishers.

Describe two kinds of traditional testing

Two traditional formats for testing are the objective test and the essay test. Objective tests, which can include multiple-choice, true/false, fill-in, and matching items, should be written with specific guidelines in mind. Writing and scoring essay questions requires careful planning, in addition to criteria to discourage bias in scoring.

Alternatives to Traditional Assessments (pp. 673–687)

What is authentic assessment?

Critics of traditional testing believe that teachers should use authentic assessment procedures.

Authentic assessment requires pupils to perform tasks and solve problems that are similar to the real-life performances that will be expected of them outside of school.

Describe portfolios and presentations

Portfolios and presentations are two examples of authentic assessment. A portfolio is a collection of the pupil's work, sometimes chosen to represent growth or improvement or sometimes featuring 'best work'. Presentations are public performances of the pupil's understandings. With portfolios and presentations, there is an emphasis on performing real-life tasks in meaningful contexts.

What are the issues of reliability, validity and equity with portfolios and performance assessment?

Using authentic assessments does not guarantee reliability, validity and equity (absence of bias). In fact, without clear standards and training, examiners can reach very different conclusions about portfolios and performances. Using rubrics is one way to make assessment more reliable and valid. But the results from assessment based on rubrics may not predict performance on related tasks. Also, examiner bias based on the appearance, speech or behaviour of minority-group pupils or a lack of resources may place minority-group pupils at a disadvantage in performance assessments or projects.

Effects of Grading on Pupils (pp. 688–692)

How can failure support learning?

Pupils need experience in coping with failure, so standards must be high enough to encourage effort. Occasional failure can be positive if appropriate feedback is provided. Pupils who never learn how to cope with failure may give up quickly when their first efforts are unsuccessful.

Can feedback, including grades, promote learning and motivation?

Written or oral feedback that includes specific comments on errors or faulty strategies, but that balances this criticism with suggestions about how to improve, along with comments on the positive aspects of the work, increases learning. Grades can encourage pupils' motivation to learn if they are tied to meaningful learning.

Grading and Reporting: Nuts and Bolts (pp. 692–701)

Describe two kinds of grading

Grading can be either criterion-referenced or norm-referenced. Criterion-referenced reports usually indicate how well the individual pupil has met each of several objectives.

What is the point system?

Tests and papers are often scored on a point system. Many schools use percentage grading systems, but the difficulty of the tests and the scoring criteria often influence the results. The difference between a B and a C may only be a matter of one or two points on paper, but the effect of the difference can be large for a pupil.

Describe some alternatives to traditional grading

Alternatives to traditional grading are the contract and individual learning expectation (ILE). Whatever system is used, teachers have to decide whether to grade on effort, improvement or some combination and whether to limit the number of good grades available.

What are some sources of bias in grading?

Many factors besides quality of work can influence grades. For example, the teacher's beliefs about the pupil's ability or effort or the pupil's general classroom behaviour. There are many appropriate accommodations that teachers can make to ensure that grading is fair.

Beyond Grading: Communicating with Families (pp. 701–703)

How can communications with families support learning?

Not every communication from the teacher needs to be tied to a grade. Communication with pupils and parents can be important in helping a teacher understand pupils and present effective instruction by creating a consistent learning environment. Pupils and parents have a legal right to see all the information in the pupils' records, so the contents of files must be appropriate, accurate and supported by evidence.

Beyond Grading: Qualitative Knowledge of What Pupils Can Do (pp. 703–706)

Reaching every pupil

Classroom assessment should, first and foremost, support pupil learning. However, stereotypes and biases can interfere with assessment.

Cultural bias

Several studies have found that teachers may hold lower expectations for ethnic minority pupils and these biases can influence teaching and assessment (Banks, 2005). Quality teaching and quality assessment share the same basic principles and these principles hold for all pupils.

A legal framework

The Education (Individual Pupils Achievement) Regulations 1996 entitles parents in England (there are corresponding statutory instruments for other parts of the United Kingdom) to specific information relating to their child's academic progress. Tests must be valid and reliable. Pupils' grades must be justified by thorough assessment and observation, and any comments and anecdotes about pupils must be accurate and fair.

Glossary

Alternatives: All the answers offered which include the correct answer and the distractors.

Authentic assessments: Assessment procedures that test skills and abilities as they would be applied in real-life situations.

Contract system: System in which each pupil works for a particular grade according to agreed-upon standards.

Criterion-referenced grading: Assessment of each pupil's mastery of learning objectives.

Diagnostic test: Formative test used during teaching to determine pupils' areas of weakness and possible causes.

Distractors: Wrong answers offered as choices in a multiple-choice item.

Formative assessment: Ungraded testing used before or during teaching to aid in planning and diagnosis.

Grading on the curve: Norm-referenced grading that compares pupils' performance to an average level.

Halo effect: The tendency for a general impression of a person to influence our perception of any aspect of that person.

High-stakes testing: Standardised tests whose results have powerful influences when used by school administrators, other officials or employers to make decisions.

Individual learning expectation (ILE): Pupils earn improvement points on tests or assignments for

scoring above their personal base (average) score or for making a perfect score.

Informal assessments: Ungraded (formative) assessments that gather information from multiple sources to help teachers make decisions.

Norm-referenced grading: Assessment of pupils' achievement in relation to one another.

Objective testing: Multiple-choice, matching, true/false, short-answer and fill-in tests; scoring answers requires little interpretation.

Percentage grading: System of converting class performances to percentage scores and assigning grades based on predetermined bands.

Performance assessments: Any form of assessment that requires pupils to carry out an activity or produce a product in order to demonstrate learning.

Portfolio: A collection of the pupil's work in an area, showing growth, self-reflection and achievement.

Presentation: A performance test or demonstration of learning that is public and usually takes an extended time to prepare.

Pretest: Formative test for assessing pupils' knowledge, readiness and abilities.

Revise option: In a contract system, the chance to revise and improve work.

Scoring rubrics: Rules that are used to determine the quality of a pupil performance.

Stem: The question part of a multiple-choice item.

Summative assessment: Testing that follows teaching and assesses achievement.

CHECK YOUR LEARNING!

 WEB

In the Classroom: What Would They Do?

Think back to the teaching situation (In the Classroom) provided at the beginning of this chapter. You may remember that a school required each teacher to give letter grades to their pupils. How would teachers put all the assessment elements together to determine a grade for every pupil? How would the school justify such a grading system to the parents? How will these issues affect different age groups? Here is how some practising teachers responded to the teaching situation presented at the beginning of this chapter about setting up a system to give letter grades.

Jackie Day, special educational needs co-ordinator, The Ridge Primary School, Yate

A consistent approach that is clearly understood is essential. Grades A–F represent points gained for progress towards learning objectives and effort (A = 5, B = 4, C = 3, D = 2, F = 1).

Award 3 points for a learning objective met, 2 points for being close, and 1 for not yet meeting it. Award one extra point for outstanding progress, and one for exceptional effort and/or interest, shown in discussions, group projects or homework. Children must be set appropriate learning targets, and parents made aware whether their child is working at, above or below the expected level for their age group. Thus a C grade could be gained by a bright underachiever, whilst a diligent child with SEN might score a B by meeting appropriate learning objectives (possibly from a previous Key Stage). This would be inclusive, whilst giving appropriate feedback to pupils and parents.

Tessa Herbert, English teacher, John Masefield High School, Ledbury

If the curriculum is balanced between practical, co-operative and formal tasks, there should not be a big problem as they will all have been assessed using the school's chosen method and the final grade/level can be an average of the year's grades. For example, in English, a group might do an individual speaking task, group discussions, a project involving writing, design, planning and speaking, written assessments, assessment and progress profiles, and perhaps an end of year examination. All these tasks will have been marked using the same method so an overall mark will be apparent. On a report, there should be a place for a comment on effort, homework, organisation, etc. (e.g. excellent, good, satisfactory, poor). This should apply to any age group.

Lee Card, primary school teacher, Bosbury Church of England Primary School

Using such a letter grade system can be a clear, manageable way of reporting to both parents and pupils, as well as being useful for whole school tracking of attainment. The teachers in this scenario have differing ideas as to what success criteria should be taken into account. For me, a whole school common approach is not just desirable but essential in creating a worthwhile and equal system of assessment and recording. In order for it to 'encourage learning', it would have to include some form of pupil input or feedback. This causes problems when working with such a simple grading system, as a child attaining consistent 'F' grades will inevitably become disillusioned with the process. I believe the grading system should be based solely upon academic achievement against individual curriculum areas' success criteria. These can be shared with the pupils at the start of the unit, and drawn upon throughout to ensure they are aware of how they will be graded. This system allows for each pupil to build up a series of grades for each curriculum area, the allocation of which being clear and consistent for all involved. At the end of the academic year, a 'mean' grade may be allocated or a 'best fit' taking into account the grades attained.

Lizzie Meadows, deputy head teacher, The Park Primary School, Kingswood, Bristol

This is a whole school issue of consistency. The school needs to work on, with the teachers across the year groups, a common and consistent approach to assessment based on an assessment for learning model. The system needs to be understood and implemented by all of the teachers to ensure that the pupils are fully aware of their next steps for learning. As for credits for behaviour and group participation, this should be part of the behaviour management policy and system and linked to rewards and sanctions that the school have in place.

Glossary

A

Absence seizure: A seizure involving only a small part of the brain that causes a child to lose contact briefly.

Academic tasks: The work the pupil must accomplish, including the content covered and the mental operations required.

Accommodation: Altering existing schemes or creating new ones in response to new information.

Accountable: Making teachers and schools responsible for pupil learning, usually by monitoring learning with high-stakes tests.

Achievement tests: Standardised tests measuring how much pupils have learned in a given content area.

Acronym: Technique for remembering names, phrases or steps by using the first letter of each word to form a new, memorable word.

Action research: Systematic observations or tests of methods conducted by teachers or schools to improve teaching and learning for their learners.

Action zone: Area of a classroom where the greatest amount of interaction is taking place, increasingly the area around the interactive digital whiteboard.

Adaptation: Adjustment to the environment.

Adolescent egocentrism: Assumption that everyone else shares one's thoughts, feelings and concerns.

Advance organiser: Statement of inclusive concepts to introduce and sum up material that follows.

Affective domain: Objectives focusing on attitudes and feelings.

Agency: The capacity to coordinate learning skills, motivation and emotions to reach your goals.

Algorithm: Step-by-step procedure for solving a problem; a prescription for solutions.

Allocated or available time: Time set aside for learning.

Alternatives: All the answers offered which include the correct answer and the distractors.

Analogical instruction: Teaching new concepts by making connections (analogies) with information that the pupil already understands.

Analogical thinking: Heuristic in which one limits the search for solutions to situations that are similar to the one at hand.

Anorexia nervosa: Eating disorder characterised by very limited food intake.

Antecedents: Events that precede an action.

Anxiety: General uneasiness, a feeling of tension.

Applied behaviour analysis: The application of behavioural learning principles to understand and change behaviour.

Appropriate: Internalise or take for yourself knowledge and skills developed in interaction with others or with cultural tools.

Aptitude tests: Tests meant to predict future performance.

Arousal: Physical and psychological reactions causing a person to feel alert, excited or tense.

Articulation disorders: Any of a variety of pronunciation difficulties, such as the substitution, distortion or omission of sounds.

Asperger's syndrome: Includes many of the characteristics of autism, but greatest problems lie in social relations.

Assertive discipline: Clear, firm, non-hostile response style.

Assessment: Procedures used to obtain information about pupil performance.

Assessment bias: Qualities of an assessment instrument that offend or unfairly penalise a group of pupils because of the pupils' gender, SES, race, ethnicity, etc.

Assimilation: Fitting new information into existing schemes.

Assisted learning: Providing strategic help in the initial stages of learning, gradually diminishing as learners gain independence.

Attachment: The emotional bond between an infant and a caregiver.

Attention: Focus on a stimulus.

Attention-deficit hyperactivity disorder (ADHD): Current term for disruptive behaviour disorders marked by over activity, excessive difficulty sustaining attention or impulsiveness.

Attribution theories: Descriptions of how individuals' explanations, justifications and excuses influence their motivation and behaviour.

Authentic assessment: Measurement of important abilities using procedures that simulate the application of these abilities to real-life problems.

Authentic assessments: Assessment procedures that test skills and abilities as they would be applied in real-life situations.

Authentic task: Tasks that have some connection to real-life problems the learners will face outside the classroom.

Autism or autism spectrum disorders: Developmental disability significantly affecting verbal and nonverbal communication and social interaction, generally evident before age 3 and ranging from mild to major.

Automated basic skills: Skills that are applied without conscious thought.

Automaticity: The result of learning to perform a behaviour or thinking process so thoroughly that the performance is automatic and does not require effort.

Autonomy: Independence.

Availability heuristic: Judging the likelihood of an event based what is available in your memory, assuming those easily remembered events are common.

Aversive: Irritating or unpleasant.

B

Barchart: Graph of a frequency distribution using verticle or horizontal bars.

Basic skills: Clearly structured knowledge that is needed for later learning and that can be taught step by step.

Behavioural learning theories: Explanations of learning that focus on external events as the cause of changes in observable behaviours.

Behaviour modification: Systematic application of antecedents and consequences to change behaviour.

Behavioural objectives: Learning objectives stated in terms of observable behaviours.

Being needs: Maslow's top-level needs, sometimes called growth needs.

Belief perseverance: The tendency to hold on to beliefs, even in the face of contradictory evidence.

Bilingualism: Speaking two languages fluently.

Bioecological model: Bronfenbrenner's theory describing the nested social and cultural contexts that shape development. Every person develops within a *microsystem,* inside a *mesosystem,* embedded in an *exosystem,* all of which are a part of the *macrosystem* of the culture.

Blended families: Parents, children and stepchildren merged into families through remarriages.

Bottom-up processing: Perceiving based on noticing separate defining features and assembling them into a recognisable pattern.

Brainstorming: Generating ideas without stopping to evaluate them.

Bulimia: Eating disorder characterised by overeating, then getting rid of the food by self-induced vomiting or laxatives.

C

CAPS: A strategy that can be used in reading literature: *Characters, Aim* of story, *Problem, Solution.*

Case study: Intensive study of one person or one situation.

Central executive: The part of working memory that is responsible for monitoring and directing attention and other mental resources.

Central tendency: Typical score for a group of scores.

Cerebral palsy: Condition involving a range of motor or coordination difficulties due to brain damage.

Chain mnemonics: Memory strategies that associate one element in a series with the next element.

Chunking: Grouping individual bits of data into meaningful larger units.

Classical conditioning: Association of automatic responses with new stimuli.

Classification: Grouping objects into categories.

Classroom management: Techniques used to establish and maintain a positive and safe learning environment, relatively free of behaviour problems.

Cmaps: Tools for concept mapping developed by the Institute for Human Machine Cognition that are connected to many knowledge maps and other resources on the Internet.

Co-constructed process: A social process in which people interact and negotiate (usually verbally) to create an understanding or to solve a problem. The final product is shaped by all participants.

Code-switching: Successful switching between cultures in language, dialect or nonverbal behaviours to fit the situation.

Cognitive apprenticeship: A relationship in which a less experienced learner acquires knowledge and skills under the guidance of an expert.

Cognitive behaviour modification: Procedures based on both behavioural and cognitive learning principles for changing your own behaviour by using self-talk and self-instruction.

Cognitive development: Gradual orderly changes by which mental processes become more complex and sophisticated.

Cognitive domain: In Bloom's taxonomy, memory and reasoning objectives.

Cognitive evaluation theory: Suggests that events affect motivation through the individual's perception of the events as controlling behaviour or providing information.

Cognitive objectives: Learning objectives stated in terms of higher-level thinking operations.

Cognitive view of learning: A general approach that views learning as an active mental process of acquiring, remembering and using knowledge.

Collaboration: Working together and in parallel with others to reach a shared goal.

Collective monologue: Form of speech in which children in a group talk but do not really interact or communicate.

Community of practice: Social situation or context in which ideas are judged useful or true.

Community service learning: An approach to combining academic learning with personal and social development.

Compensation: The principle that changes in one dimension can be offset by changes in another.

Complex learning environments: Problems and learning situations that mimic the ill-structured nature of real life.

Concept: A general category of ideas, objects, people or experiences whose members share certain properties.

Concept mapping: Pupil's diagram of his or her understanding of a concept.

Concrete operations: Mental tasks tied to concrete objects and situations.

Conditional knowledge: 'Knowing when and why' to use declarative and procedural knowledge.

Conditioned response (CR): Learned response to a previously neutral stimulus.

Conditioned stimulus (CS): Stimulus that evokes an emotional or physiological response after conditioning.

Confidence interval: Range of scores within which an individual's particular score is likely to fall.

Confirmation bias: Seeking information that confirms our choices and beliefs, while disconfirming evidence.

Conscience: Includes information about those things viewed as bad by parents and society punishes with guilt.

Consequences: Events that follow an action.

Conservation: Principle that some characteristics of an object remain the same despite changes in appearance.

Constructed-response format: Assessment procedures that require the pupil to create an answer instead of selecting an answer from a set of choices.

Constructivism: View that emphasises the active role of the learner in building understanding and making sense of information.

Constructivist approach: View that emphasises the active role of the learner in building understanding and making sense of information.

Context: The physical or emotional backdrop associated with an event.

Contiguity: Association of two events because of repeated pairing.

Contingency contract: A contract between the teacher and a learner specifying what the learner must do to earn a particular reward or privilege.

Continuous reinforcement schedule: Presenting a reinforcer after every appropriate response.

Contract system: System in which each pupil works for a particular grade according to agreed-upon standards.

Convergent questions: Questions that have a single correct answer.

Convergent thinking: Narrowing possibilities to a single answer.

Cooperation: A way of dealing with people that respects differences, shares authority and builds on the combined knowledge of self and others.

Cooperative learning: Arrangement in which pupils work in groups and make gains in learning on the basis of the success of the group.

Correlations: Statistical descriptions of how closely two variables are related.

Creativity: Imaginative, original thinking or problem solving.

Criterion-referenced grading: Assessment of each pupil's mastery of learning objectives.

Criterion-referenced comparison: Testing in which scores are compared to a set performance standard.

Critical thinking: Evaluating conclusions by logically and systematically examining the problem, the evidence and the solution.

Crystallised intelligence: Ability to apply culturally approved problem-solving methods.

Cueing: Providing a stimulus that 'sets up' a desired behaviour.

Cultural deficit model: A model that explains the school achievement problems of ethnic minority pupils by assuming that their culture is inadequate and does not prepare them to succeed in school.

Cultural tools: The real tools (computers, scales, rulers etc.) and symbol systems (numbers, language, graphs) that allow people in a society to communicate, think, solve problems and create knowledge.

Culturally relevant pedagogy: Excellent teaching for pupils from ethnic minorities that includes academic success, developing/maintaining cultural competence, and developing a critical consciousness to challenge the status quo.

Culturally responsive school: Schools that provide culturally diverse pupils equitable access to the teaching-learning process.

Culture: The knowledge, values, attitudes and traditions that guide the behaviour of a group of people and allow them to solve the problems of living in their environment.

Culture-fair/culture-free test: A test without cultural bias.

D

Decay: The weakening and fading of memories with the passage of time.

Decentring: Focusing on more than one aspect at a time.

Declarative knowledge: Verbal information; facts; 'knowing that' something is the case.

Deductive reasoning: Drawing conclusions by applying rules or principles; logically moving from a general rule or principle to a specific solution.

Deficiency needs: Maslow's four lower-level needs, which must be satisfied first.

Defining attributes: Distinctive features shared by members of a category.

Descriptive studies: Studies that collect detailed information about specific situations, often using observation, surveys, interviews, recordings or a combination of these methods.

Development: Orderly, adaptive changes we go through from conception to death.

Developmental crisis: A specific conflict whose resolution prepares the way for the next stage.

Deviation IQ: Score based on statistical comparison of an individual's performance with the average performance of others in that age group.

Diagnostic test: Formative test used during teaching to determine pupils' areas of weakness and the possible causes.

Diagnostic tests: Individually administered tests to identify special learning problems.

Dialect: Rule-governed variation of a language spoken by a particular group.

Digital divide: The disparities in access to technology between poor and more affluent pupils and families.

Disability: The inability to do something specific such as walk or hear.

Discovery learning: Bruner's approach, in which pupils work on their own to discover basic principles.

Discrimination: Treating or acting unfairly towards particular categories of people.

Disequilibrium: In Piaget's theory, the 'out-of-balance' state that occurs when a person realises that his or her current ways of thinking are not working to solve a problem or understand a situation.

Dis-identification: Recognition of a sub-persona of self-image, which may or may not be used according to social context.

Disorder: A broad term meaning a general disturbance in physical or mental functioning.

Distractors: Wrong answers offered as choices in a multiple-choice item.

Distributed practice: Practice in brief periods with rest intervals.

Distributive justice: Beliefs about how to divide materials or privileges fairly among members of a group; follows a sequence of development from equality to merit to benevolence.

Divergent questions: Questions that have no single correct answer.

Divergent thinking: Coming up with many possible solutions.

Domain-specific knowledge: Information that is useful in a particular situation or that applies mainly to one specific topic.

Domain-specific strategies: Consciously applied skills to reach goals in a particular subject or problem area.

Dyscalculia: A condition that affects the ability to acquire arithmetical skills.

E

Educational psychology: Refers to the broad area of training and work of educational psychologists who apply psychological theories, research and techniques to help children and young people who may have learning difficulties, emotional or behavioural problems.

Ego: Responsible for dealing with reality and meeting needs of the id in a socially acceptable way.

Egocentric: Assuming that others experience the world the way that you do.

Ego-ideal: Includes standards of good, desirable behaviour approved by parents and society – rewarded with feelings of pride.

Ego-involved learner: Learners who focus on how well they are performing and how they are judged by others.

Elaboration: Adding and extending meaning by connecting new information to existing knowledge.

Elaborative rehearsal: Keeping information in working memory by associating it with something else you already know.

Emotional and behavioural disorders: Behaviours or emotions that deviate so much from the norm that they interfere with the child's own growth and development and/or the lives of others – inappropriate behaviours, unhappiness or depression, fears and anxieties and trouble with relationships.

Emotional intelligence (EQ): The ability to process emotional information accurately and efficiently.

Empathetic listening: Hearing the intent and emotions behind what another says and reflecting them back by paraphrasing.

Engaged time: Time spent being active with some task, or talking to or listening to others.

English as a second language (ESL): Designation for programmes and classes to teach English to pupils who are not native speakers of English.

English as an additional language (EAL): Designation for programmes and classes to teach English to pupils who are not native speakers of English and may have other additional languages.

English language learners (ELL): Pupils whose primary or heritage language is not English.

Enquiry learning: Approach in which the teacher presents a puzzling situation and pupils solve the problem by gathering data and testing their conclusions.

Entity view of ability: Belief that ability is a fixed characteristic that cannot be changed.

Epilepsy: Disorder marked by seizures and caused by abnormal electrical discharges in the brain.

Episodic memory: Long-term memory for information tied to a particular time and place, especially memory of the events in a person's life.

Epistemological beliefs: Beliefs about the structure, stability and certainty of knowledge and how knowledge is best learned.

Equilibration: Search for mental balance between cognitive schemes and information from the environment.

Ethnicity: A cultural heritage shared by a group of people.

Ethnography: A descriptive approach to research that focuses on life within a group and tries to understand the meaning of events to the people involved.

Executive control processes: Processes such as selective attention, rehearsal, elaboration and organisation that influence encoding, storage and retrieval of information in memory.

Exemplar: A specific example of a given category that is used to classify an item.

Expectancy D7 value theories: Explanations of motivation that emphasise individuals' expectations for success combined with their valuing of the goal.

Experimentation: Research method in which variables are manipulated and the effects recorded.

Expert teachers: Experienced, effective teachers who have developed solutions for common classroom problems. Their knowledge of the teaching process and content is extensive and well organised.

Explicit memory: Long-term memories that involve deliberate or conscious recall.

Expository teaching: Ausubel's method – teachers present material in complete, organised form, moving from broadest to more specific concepts.

Extinction: The disappearance of a learned response.

Extrinsic motivation: Motivation created by external factors such as rewards and punishments.

F

Failure-accepting learners: Learners who believe their failures are due to low ability and there is little they can do about it.

Failure-avoiding learners: Learners who avoid failure by sticking to what they know, by not taking risks or by claiming not to care about their performance.

First wave constructivism: A focus on the individual and psychological sources of knowing, as in Piaget's theory.

Fixated: A person remains fixed at a certain psychosexual stage and their personality reflects this throughout life.

Flashbulb memories: Clear, vivid memories of emotionally important events in your life.

Fluid intelligence: Mental efficiency, non-verbal abilities grounded in brain development.

Flynn effect: Because of better health, smaller families, increased complexity in the environment and more and better schooling, IQ test scores are steadily rising.

Formal operations: Mental tasks involving abstract thinking and coordination of a number of variables.

Formative assessment: Ungraded testing used before or during teaching to aid in planning and diagnosis.

Frequency distribution: Record showing how many scores fall into set groups.

Functional behavioural assessment (FBA): Procedures used to obtain information about antecedents, behaviours and consequences to determine the reason or function of the behaviour.

Functional fixedness: Inability to use objects or tools in a new way.

Funds of knowledge: Knowledge that families and community members have in many areas of work, home and religious life that can become the basis for teaching.

G

Gender biases: Different views of males and females, often favouring one gender over the other.

Gender-role identity: Beliefs about characteristics and behaviours associated with one sex as opposed to the other.

Gender schemas: Organised networks of knowledge about what it means to be male or female.

General knowledge: Information that is useful in many different kinds of tasks; information that applies to many situations.

Generalised seizure/tonic-clonic seizure: A seizure involving a large portion of the brain.

Generativity: Sense of concern for future generations.

Gestalt: German for *pattern* or *whole.* Gestalt theorists hold that people organise their perceptions into coherent wholes.

Gifted learner: A very bright, creative and talented pupil.

Goal: What an individual strives to accomplish.

Goal-directed actions: Deliberate actions towards a goal.

Goal orientations: Patterns of beliefs about goals related to achievement in school.

Goal structure: The way learners relate to others who are also working towards a particular goal.

Good behaviour game: Arrangement where a class is divided into teams and each team receives a black mark or demerit points for breaking agreed-upon rules of good behaviour.

Grading on the curve: Norm-referenced grading that compares pupils' performance to an average level.

Group consequences: Rewards or punishments given to a class as a whole for adhering to or violating rules of conduct.

Group discussion: Conversation in which the teacher does not have the dominant role; pupils pose and answer their own questions.

Group focus: The ability to keep as many pupils as possible involved in activities.

Guided discovery: An adaptation of discovery learning, in which the teacher provides some direction.

H

Halo effect: The tendency for a general impression of a person to influence our perception of any aspect of that person.

Handicap: A disadvantage in a particular situation, sometimes caused by a disability.

Heritage language: The language spoken in the learner's home or by members of the family.

Heuristic: General strategy used in attempting to solve problems.

Hierarchy of needs: Maslow's model of levels of human needs, from basic physiological requirements to the need for self-actualisation.

High-road transfer: Application of abstract knowledge learned in one situation to a different situation.

High-stakes testing: Standardised tests whose results have powerful influences when used by school managers, other officials or employers to make decisions.

Hostile aggression: Bold, direct action that is intended to hurt someone else; unprovoked attack.

Humanistic interpretation: Approach to motivation that emphasises personal freedom, choice, self-determination and striving for personal growth.

Hypothetico-deductive reasoning: A formal-operations problem-solving strategy in which an individual begins by identifying all the factors that might affect a problem and then deduces and systematically evaluates specific solutions.

I

'I' message: Clear, non-accusatory statement of how something is affecting you.

Id: The instinctive needs and desires of a person present from birth.

Identity: Principle that a person or object remains the same over time.

Identity achievement: Strong sense of commitment to life choices after free consideration of alternatives.

Identity diffusion: Uncentredness; confusion about who one is and what one wants.

Identity foreclosure: Acceptance of parental life choices without consideration of options.

Images: Representations based on the physical attributes – the appearance – of information.

Implicit memory: Knowledge that we are not conscious of recalling, but influences behaviour or thought without our awareness.

Importance/attainment value: The importance of doing well on a task; how success on the task meets personal needs.

Improvements in standardised testing: Many of the suggestions for improving standardised tests will require new forms of testing, more thoughtful and time-consuming scoring, and new ways of judging the quality of the tests themselves. The use of portfolios may be an attractive option but not all educators are convinced as problems have been found with consistency between markers and therefore the reliability of the assessment.

Incentive: An object or event that encourages or discourages behaviour.

Inclusion: The integration of all learners, including those with severe disabilities, into mainstream classes.

Incremental view of ability: Belief that ability is a set of skills that can be changed.

Individual classwork: Independent classroom work set to be completed during lessons.

Individual Education Plan (IEP): This builds on the curriculum that a child with learning difficulties or disabilities is following and is designed to set out the strategies being used to meet each child's identified needs.

Individual learning expectation (ILE): Pupils earn improvement points on tests or assignments for scoring above their personal base (average) score or for making a perfect score.

Inductive reasoning: Formulating general principles based on knowledge of examples and details.

Industry: Eagerness to engage in productive work.

Informal assessments: Ungraded (formative) assessments that gather information from multiple sources to help teachers make decisions.

Information processing: The human mind's activity of taking in, storing and using information.

Initiative: Willingness to begin new activities and explore new directions.

Insight: The ability to deal effectively with novel situations.

Instructional conversation: Situation in which individuals learn through interactions with teachers and/or peers.

Instrumental aggression: Strong actions aimed at claiming an object, place or privilege – not intended to harm, but may lead to harm.

Integrity: Sense of self-acceptance and fulfilment.

Intellectual disabilities: Significantly below-average intellectual and adaptive social behaviour, evident before age 18.

Intelligence: Ability or abilities to acquire and use knowledge for solving problems and adapting to the world.

Intelligence quotient (IQ): Score comparing mental and chronological ages.

Interference: The process that occurs when remembering certain information is hampered by the presence of other information.

Intermittent reinforcement schedule: Presenting a reinforcer after some but not all responses.

Internalise: Process whereby children adopt external standards as their own.

Intersubjective attitude: A commitment to build shared meaning with others by finding common ground and exchanging interpretations.

Interval schedule: Length of time between reinforcers.

Intrinsic motivation: Motivation associated with activities that are their own reward.

Intrinsic or interest value: The enjoyment a person gets from a task.

Intuitive thinking: Making imaginative leaps to correct perceptions or workable solutions.

J

Jigsaw: A cooperative structure in which each member of a group is responsible for teaching other members one section of the material.

K

Keyword method: System of associating new words or concepts with similar-sounding cue words and images.

KWL: A strategy to guide reading and inquiry: Before – What do I already *know*? What do I *want* to know? After – What have I *learned*?

L

Language disorders: A marked deficit in the ability to understand and express language.

Lateralisation: The specialisation of the two hemispheres (sides) of the brain cortex.

Learned helplessness: The expectation, based on previous experiences with a lack of control, that all one's efforts will lead to failure.

Learning: Process through which experience causes permanent change in knowledge or behaviour.

Learning difficulty disability: Problem with acquisition and use of language; may show up as difficulty with reading, writing, reasoning and mathematics.

Learning objectives: Clear statement of what pupils are intended to learn.

Learning preferences: Preferred ways of studying and learning, such as using pictures instead of text, working with other people versus alone, learning in structured or in unstructured situations, and so on.

Learning strategies: General plans for approaching learning tasks.

Learning styles: Characteristic approaches to learning and studying.

Learning tactics: Specific techniques for learning, such as using mnemonics or outlining a passage.

Learning zone: A part of a lesson or activity where a pupil is open to new learning. It is usually signalled by the pupil acknowledging that he or she doesn't know or understand something.

Legitimate peripheral participation: Genuine involvement in the work of the group, even if your abilities are undeveloped and contributions are small.

Lesson study: As a group, teachers develop, test, improve and re-test lessons until they are satisfied with the final version.

Level-equivalent score: Measure of level based on comparison with norming samples from each age group.

Levels of processing theory: Theory that recall of information is based on how deeply it is processed.

Loci method: Technique of associating items with specific places.

Locus of causality: The location – internal or external – of the cause of behaviour.

Long-term memory: Permanent store of knowledge.

Long-term working memory: Holds the strategies for pulling information from long-term memory into working memory.

Low-road transfer: Spontaneous and automatic transfer of highly practised skills.

M

Maintenance rehearsal: Keeping information in working memory by repeating it to yourself.

Massed practice: Practice for a single extended period.

Mastery experiences: Our own direct experiences – the most powerful source of efficacy information.

Mastery goal: A personal intention to improve abilities and learn, no matter how performance suffers.

Mastery-oriented learners: Learners who focus on learning goals because they value achievement and see ability as improvable.

Maturation: Genetically programmed, naturally occurring changes over time.

Mean: Arithmetical average.

Meaningful verbal learning: Focused and organised relationships among ideas and verbal information.

Means-ends analysis: Heuristic in which a goal is divided into subgoals.

Measurement: An evaluation expressed in quantitative (statistical) terms.

Median: Middle score in a group of scores.

Melting pot: A metaphor for the absorption and assimilation of immigrants into the mainstream of society so that ethnic differences vanish.

Mental age: In intelligence testing, a score based on average abilities for that age group.

Metacognition: Knowledge about our own thinking processes.

Metalinguistic awareness: Understanding about one's own use of language.

Microgenetic studies: Detailed observation and analysis of changes in a cognitive process as the process unfolds over a several-day or week period of time.

Minority group: A group of people who have been socially disadvantaged – not always a minority in actual numbers.

Mnemonics: Techniques for remembering; also, the art of memory.

Mode: Most frequently occurring score.

Modelling: Changes in behaviour, thinking or emotions that occur through observing another person – a model.

Moral dilemmas: Situations in which no choice is clearly and indisputably right.

Moral realism: Stage of development wherein children see rules as absolute.

Moral reasoning: The thinking process involved in judgments about questions of right and wrong.

Morality of cooperation: Stage of development wherein children realise that people make rules and people can change them.

Moratorium: Identity crisis; suspension of choices because of struggle.

Motivation: An internal state that arouses, directs and maintains behaviour.

Motivation to learn: The tendency to find academic activities meaningful and worthwhile and to try to benefit from them.

Movement management: Keeping lessons and the group moving at an appropriate (and flexible) pace, with smooth transitions and variety.

Multicultural education: Education that promotes equity in the schooling of all pupils.

Multiple representations of content: Considering problems using various analogies, examples and metaphors.

Myelination: The process by which neural fibres are coated with a fatty sheath called myelin which makes message transfer more efficient.

N

Natural or logical consequences: Instead of punishing, have pupils redo, repair or in some way face the consequences that naturally flow from their actions.

Need for autonomy: The desire to have our own wishes, rather than external rewards or pressures, determine our actions.

Negative correlation: A relationship between two variables in which a high value on one is associated with a low value on the other. Example: height and distance from top of head to the ceiling.

Negative reinforcement: Strengthening behaviour by removing an aversive stimulus when the behaviour occurs.

Neo-Piagetian theories: More recent theories that integrate findings about attention, memory and strategy use with Piaget's insights about children's thinking and the construction of knowledge.

Neurons: Nerve cells that store and transfer information.

Neutral stimulus: Stimulus not connected to a response.

Norm groups: A group whose mean average score serves as a standard for evaluating any pupil's score on a test.

Normal distribution: The most commonly occurring distribution, in which scores are distributed evenly around the mean.

Norming sample: Large sample of pupils serving as a comparison group for scoring standardised tests.

Norm-referenced comparison: Testing in which scores are compared with the mean average performance of others.

Norm-referenced grading: Assessment of pupils' achievement in relation to one another.

O

Objective testing: Multiple-choice, matching, true/false, short-answer and fill-in tests; scoring answers requires little interpretation.

Object permanence: The understanding that objects have a separate, permanent existence.

Observational learning: Learning by observation and imitation of others.

Operant conditioning: Learning in which voluntary behaviour is strengthened or weakened by consequences or antecedents.

Operants: Voluntary (and generally goal-directed) behaviours emitted by a person or an animal.

Operations: Actions a person carries out by thinking them through instead of literally performing the actions.

Organisation: Ongoing process of arranging information and experience into mental systems or categories.

Organisation: Ordered and logical network of relations.

Overgeneralisation: Inclusion of non-members in a category; overextending a concept.

Overlapping: Supervising several activities at once.

Overlearning: Practising a skill past the point of mastery.

Overt aggression: A form of hostile aggression that involves physical attack.

P

Paraphrase rule: Policy whereby listeners must accurately summarise what a speaker has said before being allowed to respond.

Parenting styles: The ways of interacting with and disciplining children.

Participant observation: A method for conducting descriptive research in which the researcher becomes a participant in the situation in order to better understand life in that group.

Participants/subjects: People or animals studied.

Participation structures: Rules defining how to participate in different activities.

Part learning: Breaking a list of rote learning items into shorter lists.

Peg-type mnemonics: Systems of associating items with cue words.

Percentage grading: System of converting class performances to percentage scores and assigning grades based on predetermined bands.

Percentile rank: Percentage of those in the norming sample who scored at or below an individual's score.

Perception: Interpretation of sensory information.

Performance assessments: Any form of assessment that requires pupils to carry out an activity or produce a product in order to demonstrate learning.

Performance goal: A personal intention to seem competent or perform well in the eyes of others.

Personal development: Changes in personality that take place as one grows.

Perspective-taking ability: Understanding that others have different feelings and experiences.

Phonological loop: Part of working memory. A memory rehearsal system for verbal and sound information of about 1.5 to 2 seconds.

Physical development: Changes in body structure and function over time.

Plasticity: The brain's tendency to remain somewhat adaptable or flexible.

Portfolio: A collection of the pupil's work in an area, showing growth, self-reflection and achievement.

Positive behavioural supports (PBS): Interventions designed to replace problem behaviours with new actions that serve the same purpose for the learner.

Positive correlation: A relationship between two variables in which the two increase or decrease together. Example: calorie intake and weight gain.

Positive practice: Practicing correct responses immediately after errors.

Positive reinforcement: Strengthening behaviour by presenting a desired stimulus after the behaviour.

Pragmatics: The rules for when and how to use language to be an effective communicator in a particular culture.

Precorrection: A way of preventing serious behaviour problems of pupils who have been labelled at risk by directing the pupils towards more appropriate actions.

Prejudice: Prejudgment or irrational generalisation about an entire category of people.

Premack principle: Principle stating that a more-preferred activity can serve as a reinforcer for a less-preferred activity.

Preoperational: The stage before a child masters logical mental operations.

Presentation: A performance test or demonstration of learning that is public and usually takes an extended time to prepare.

Presentation punishment: Decreasing the chances that a behaviour will occur again by presenting an aversive stimulus following the behaviour; also called Type I punishment.

Pretest: Formative test for assessing pupils' knowledge, readiness and abilities.

Priming: Activating a concept in memory or the spread of activation from one concept to another.

Principle: Established relationship between factors.

Private speech: Children's self-talk, which guides their thinking and action. Eventually, these verbalisations are internalised as silent inner speech.

Problem: Any situation in which you are trying to reach some goal and must find a means to do so.

Problem-based learning: Methods that provide learners with realistic problems that don't necessarily have 'right' answers.

Problem solving: Creating new solutions for problems.

Procedural knowledge: Knowledge that is demonstrated when we perform a task; 'knowing how'.

Procedural memory: Long-term memory for how to do things.

Procedures: Prescribed steps for an activity.

Processing activities: Types of activities that encourage children to process the information in the same way rather than re-present subject knowledge they have found.

Productions: The contents of procedural memory; rules about what actions to take, given certain conditions.

Prompt: A reminder that follows a cue to make sure the person reacts to the cue.

Propositional network: Set of interconnected concepts and relationships in which long-term knowledge is held.

Prototype: A best example or best representative of a category.

Psychoanalytic theory: Based upon the work of Sigmund Freud.

Psychology of education: The discipline concerned with teaching and learning processes; applies the methods and theories of psychology to teaching and learning and has its own methods and theories as well.

Psychomotor domain: Physical ability and coordination objectives.

Psychosexual stages: The stages through which humans pass as they develop their adult personality.

Psychosocial: Describing the relation of the individual's emotional needs to the social environment.

Puberty: The physiological changes during adolescence that lead to the ability to reproduce.

Punishment: Process that weakens or suppresses behaviour.

Pupil-centred teaching: Involves placing pupils' learning needs at the heart of planning, of having high expectations of pupils, and of effectively delivering a vivid, matched and relevant curriculum.

Pygmalion effect: Exceptional progress by a pupil as a result of high teacher expectations for that pupil; named after the mythological king, Pygmalion, who made a statue, then caused it to be brought to life.

R

Race: A group of people who share common biological traits that are seen as self-defining by the people of the group.

Racial and ethnic pride: A positive self-concept about one's racial or ethnic heritage.

Radical constructivism: Knowledge is assumed to be the individual's construction; it cannot be judged right or wrong.

Random: Without any definite pattern; following no rule.

Range: Distance between the highest and the lowest scores in a group.

Ratio schedule: Reinforcement based on the number of responses between reinforcers.

READS: A five-step reading strategy: *Review* headings; *Examine* boldface words; *Ask,* 'What do I expect to learn?'; *Do* it – Read; *Summarise* in your own words.

Reciprocal determinism: An explanation of behaviour that emphasises the mutual effects of the individual and the environment upon each other.

Reciprocal questioning: Approach where groups of two or three pupils ask and answer each other's questions after a lesson or presentation.

Reconstruction: Recreating information by using memories, expectations, logic and existing knowledge.

Reflective: Thoughtful and inventive. Reflective teachers think back over situations to analyse what they did and why and to consider how they might improve learning for their pupils.

Regress: A person returns to an earlier stage of development when in stressful situations.

Reinforcement: Use of consequences to strengthen behaviour.

Reinforcer: Any event that follows a behaviour and increases the chances that the behaviour will occur again.

Relational aggression: A form of hostile aggression that involves verbal attacks and other actions meant to harm social relationships.

Reliability: Consistency of test results measured by looking at the comparability of scores on two different occasions or of two equivalent versions.

Removal punishment: Decreasing the chances that a behaviour will occur again by removing a pleasant stimulus following the behaviour; also called Type II punishment.

Representativeness heuristic: Judging the likelihood of an event based on how well the events match your prototypes – what you think is representative of a category.

Reprimands: Criticisms for misbehaviour; rebukes.

Resilience: The ability to adapt successfully in spite of difficult circumstances and threats to development.

Resistance culture: Group values and beliefs about refusing to adopt the behaviours and attitudes of the majority culture.

Respondents: Responses (generally automatic or involuntary) elicited by specific stimuli.

Response: Observable reaction to a stimulus.

Response cost: Punishment by loss of reinforcers.

Response set: Rigidity; tendency to respond in the most familiar way.

Restructuring: Conceiving of a problem in a new or different way.

Retrieval: Process of searching for and finding information in long-term memory.

Reversibility: A characteristic of Piagetian logical operations – the ability to think through a series of steps, then mentally reverse the steps and return to the starting point; also called reversible thinking.

Reversible thinking: Thinking backwards, from the end to the beginning.

Revise option: In a contract system, the chance to revise and improve work.

Reward: An attractive object or event supplied as a consequence of a behaviour.

Ripple effect: 'Contagious' spreading of behaviours through imitation.

Rote learning: A type of memorisation by repetition to facilitate automatic and accurate recall of, for example, number facts, historical dates or lines from a Shakespeare sonnet.

Rote memorisation: Remembering information by repetition without necessarily understanding the meaning of the information.

Rules: Statements specifying expected and forbidden behaviours; dos and don'ts.

S

Satiation: Requiring a person to repeat a problem behaviour past the point of interest or motivation.

Scaffolding: Support for learning and problem solving. The support could be clues, reminders, encouragement, breaking the problem down into steps, providing an example, or anything else that allows the individual to grow in independence as a learner.

Schema-driven problem solving: Recognising a problem as a 'disguised' version of an old problem for which one already has a solution.

Schemas (singular, **schema**): Basic structures for organising information; concepts.

Schemes: Mental systems or categories of perception and experience.

Scoring rubrics: Rules that are used to determine the quality of a pupil performance.

Script: Schema or expected plan for the sequence of steps in a common event such as buying groceries or ordering take-away pizza.

Scripted cooperation: Learning strategy in which two pupils take turns summarising material and criticising the summaries.

Second wave constructivism: A focus on the social and cultural sources of knowing, as in Vygotsky's theory.

Secure base: The attachment figure provides a safe foundation for the child to explore the world.

Self-actualisation: Fulfilling one's potential.

Self-concept: Individuals' knowledge and beliefs about themselves – their ideas, feelings, attitudes and expectations.

Self-efficacy: A person's sense of being able to deal effectively with a particular task.

Self-esteem: The value each of us places on our own characteristics, abilities and behaviours.

Self-fulfilling prophecy: An expectation (sometimes groundless) that is confirmed because it has been expected.

Self-instruction: Talking oneself through the steps of a task.

Self-management: Management of your own behaviour and acceptance of responsibility for your own actions.

Self-management: Use of behavioural learning principles to change your own behaviour.

Self-regulated learning: A view of learning as skills a combination of academic learning skills and self-control.

Self-regulation: Process of activating and sustaining thoughts, behaviours and emotions in order to reach goals.

Self-reinforcement: Controlling your own reinforcers.

Semantic memory: Memory for meaning.

Semilingual: Not proficient in any language; speaking one or more languages inadequately.

Semiotic function: The ability to use symbols – language, pictures, signs or gestures – to represent actions or objects mentally.

Sensitive responsiveness: A mother/caregiver's ability to respond accurately, promptly and appropriately to an infant's needs.

Sensorimotor: Involving the senses and motor activity.

Sensory memory: System that holds sensory information very briefly.

Serial-position effect: The tendency to remember the beginning and the end but not the middle of a list.

Seriation: Arranging objects in sequential order according to one aspect, such as size, weight or volume.

Setting: Ability grouping for part of the school timetable or for a particular activity and therefore to different academic experiences based on achievement.

Sexual identity: A complex combination of beliefs and orientations about gender roles and sexual orientation.

Shaping: Reinforcing each small step of progress towards a desired goal or behaviour.

Short-term memory: Component of memory system that holds information for about 20 seconds.

Single-subject experimental studies: Systematic interventions to study effects with one person, often by applying and then withdrawing a treatment.

Situated learning: The idea that skills and knowledge are tied to the situation in which they were learned and difficult to apply in new settings.

Social cognitive theory: Theory that adds concern with cognitive factors such as beliefs, self-perceptions and expectations to social learning theory.

Social conventions: Agreed-upon rules and ways of doing things in a particular situation.

Social development: Changes over time in the ways we relate to others.

Social goals: A wide variety of needs and motives to be connected to others or part of a group.

Social isolation: Removal of a disruptive member of the class for 5 to 10 minutes.

Social learning theory: Theory that emphasises learning through observation of others.

Social negotiation: Aspect of learning process that relies on collaboration with others and respect for different perspectives.

Social persuasion: A 'pep talk' or specific performance feedback – one source of self-efficacy.

Sociocultural theory: Emphasises the role in development of cooperative dialogues between children and more knowledgeable members of society. Children learn the culture of their community (ways of thinking and behaving) through these interactions.

Sociocultural views of motivation: Perspectives that emphasise participation, identities and interpersonal relations within communities of practice.

Socioeconomic status (SES): Relative standing in the society based on income, power, background and prestige.

Sociolinguistics: The study of the formal and informal rules for how, when, about what, to whom, and how long to speak in conversations within cultural groups.

Spasticity: Overly tight or tense muscles, characteristic of some forms of cerebral palsy.

Speech disorder: Inability to produce sounds effectively for speaking.

Spiral curriculum: Bruner's structure for teaching that introduces the fundamental structure of all subjects early in the school years, then revisits the subjects in more and more complex forms over time.

Spreading activation: Retrieval of pieces of information based on their relatedness to one another. Remembering one bit of information activates (stimulates) recall of associated information.

Stand-alone thinking skills programmes: Programmes that teach thinking skills directly without need for extensive subject matter knowledge.

Standard deviation: Measure of how widely scores vary from the mean.

Standard error of measurement: Hypothetical estimate of variation in scores if testing were repeated.

Standard scores: Scores based on the standard deviation.

Standardised tests: Tests given, usually nationwide, under uniform conditions and scored according to uniform procedures.

Stanine scores: Whole number scores from 1 to 9, each representing a wide range of raw scores.

Statistically significant: Not likely to be a chance occurrence.

Stem: The question part of a multiple-choice item.

Stereotype: Schema that organises knowledge or perceptions about a category.

Stereotype threat: The extra emotional and cognitive burden that your performance in an academic situation might confirm a stereotype that others hold about you.

Stimulus: Event that activates behaviour.

Stimulus control: Capacity for the presence or absence of antecedents to cause behaviours.

Story grammar: Typical structure or organisation for a category of stories.

Streaming: Ability grouping for the whole school timetable and therefore to different academic experiences based on achievement.

Streaming/between-class ability grouping: System of grouping in which learners are assigned to classes based on their measured ability or their achievements.

Successful learning time: Time when pupils are actually succeeding at the learning task.

Successive approximations: Small components that make up a complex behaviour.

Summative assessment: Testing that follows teaching and assesses achievement.

Superego: Holds all the moral principles and ideals acquired from parents and society.

Sustaining expectation effect: Pupil performance maintained at a certain level because teachers don't recognise improvements.

Synapses: The tiny space between neurons – chemical messages are sent across these gaps.

Syntax: The order of words in phrases or sentences.

T

***T* score:** Standard score with a mean of 50 and a standard deviation of 10.

Tacit knowledge: Knowing how rather than knowing that – knowledge that is more likely to be learned during everyday life than through formal schooling.

Targeting: The way teachers select pupils to answer questions and matching the questions of the pupils.

Task analysis: System for breaking down a task hierarchically into basic skills and subskills.

Task-involved learners: Learners who focus on mastering the task or solving the problem.

Taxonomy: Classification system.

Teachers' sense of efficacy: A teacher's belief that he or she can reach even the most difficult pupils and help them learn.

The 4 Rs: An agreed code of rights, responsibilities, rules and routines.

Theory: Integrated statement of principles that attempts to explain a phenomenon and make predictions.

Theory of mind: An understanding that other people are people too, with their own minds, thoughts, feelings, beliefs, desires and perceptions.

Theory of multiple intelligences: In Gardner's theory of intelligence, a person's eight separate abilities: logical-mathematical, linguistic, musical, spatial, bodily-kinesthetic, interpersonal, intrapersonal and naturalist.

Time on task: Time spent actively engaged in the learning offered by the task at hand.

Time out: Technically, the removal of all reinforcement. In practice, isolation of a learner from the rest of the class for a brief time.

Token reinforcement system: System in which tokens earned for academic work and positive classroom behaviour can be exchanged for some desired reward.

Top-down processing: Perceiving based on the context and the patterns you expect to occur in that situation.

Transfer: Influence of previously learned material on new material.

Triarchic theory of successful intelligence: A three-part description of the mental abilities (thinking processes, coping with new experiences and adapting to context) that lead to more or less intelligent behaviour.

True score: The score the pupil would get if the measurement were completely accurate and error-free.

U

Unconditioned response (UR): Naturally occurring emotional or physiological response.

Unconditioned stimulus (US): Stimulus that automatically produces an emotional or physiological response.

Undergeneralisation: Exclusion of some true members from a category; limiting a concept.

Utility value: The contribution of a task to meeting one's goals.

V

Validity: Degree to which a test measures what it is intended to measure.

Variability: Degree of difference or deviation from mean.

Verbalisation: Putting your problem-solving plan and its logic into words.

Vicarious experiences: Accomplishments that are modelled by someone else.

Vicarious reinforcement: Increasing the chances that we will repeat a behaviour by observing another person being reinforced for that behaviour.

Visuospatial sketchpad: Part of working memory. A holding system for visual and spatial information.

Voicing problems: Inappropriate pitch, quality, loudness and intonation.

Volition: Willpower; self-discipline; work styles that protect opportunities to reach goals by applying self-regulated learning.

W

Whole-class teaching: Teaching characterised by high levels of teacher explanation, demonstration and interaction with all the pupils at the same time.

Within-class ability grouping: System of grouping in which learners in a class are divided into two or three groups based on ability in an attempt to accommodate individual differences.

Withitness: According to Kounin, awareness of everything happening in a classroom.

Work-avoidant learners: Learners who don't want to learn or to look smart, but just want to avoid work.

Working-backward strategy: Heuristic in which one starts with the goal and moves backward to solve the problem.

Working memory: The information that you are focusing on at a given moment.

Z

z score: Standard score indicating the number of standard deviations above or below the mean.

Zone of proximal development: Phase at which a child can master a task if given appropriate help and support.

Chapter 1

Ball, D. L. (1997). What do students know? Facing challenges of distance, context, and desire in trying to hear children. In B. J. Biddle, T. L. Good and I. F. Goodson (eds), *The International Handbook of Teachers and Teaching* (pp. 769–818). Dordrecht, The Netherlands: Kluwer.

Brophy, J. E. (2003). An interview with Jere Brophy by B. Gaedke and M. Shaughnessy. *Educational Psychology Review, 15*, 199–211.

Coleman, J. S. (1966). *Equality of Educational Opportunity.* Washington DC: U.S. Government Printing Office.

Dee, J. R. and Henkin, A. B. (2002). Assessing dispositions toward cultural diversity among preservice teachers. *Urban Education, 37*(1), 22–40.

Demie, F. (2004). Achievement of Black Caribbean pupils: good practice in Lambeth schools. *British Educational Research Journal, 32*(4), August 2005, 481–508.

DfES (2004). *Every Child Matters: Change for Children.* www.everychildmatters.gov.uk links to a downloadable version of this paper, accessed 2 May 2007.

Gage, N. L. (1991). The obviousness of social and educational research results. *Educational Researcher, 20*(A), 10–16.

Graham, S. and Weiner, B. (1996). Theories and principles of motivation. In D. Berliner and R. C. Calfee (eds), *Handbook of Educational Psychology* (pp. 63–84). New York: Macmillan.

Hogan, T., Rabinowitz, M. and Craven, J. A. III. (2003). Representation in teaching: Inferences from research of expert and novice teachers. *Educational Psychologist, 38*, 235–247.

Hudson, B. (2002). Holding complexity and searching for meaning: teaching as reflective practice. *Journal of Curriculum Studies, 34*(1), 43–57.

Kirk, S., Gallagher, J. J. and Anastasiow, N. J. (1993). *Educating Exceptional Children* (7th ed.). Boston: Houghton Mifflin.

Landrum, T. J. and Kauffman, J. M. (2006). Behavioral approaches to classroom management. In C. M. Evertson and C. S. Weinstein (eds), *Handbook of Classroom Management: Research, Practice, and Contemporary Issues.* Mahwah, NJ: Erlbaum.

Larrivee, B. (2000). Transforming teaching practice: becoming the critically reflective teacher. *Reflective Practice, 1*(3), 293–307.

Leinhardt, G. (2001). Instructional explanations: A commonplace for teaching and location for contrasts. In V. Richardson (ed.), *Handbook of Research on Teaching* (4th ed.), 333–357. Washington, DC: American Educational Research Association.

Madsen, C. H., Becker, W. C., Thomas, D. R., Koser, L. and Plager, E. (1968). An analysis of the reinforcing function of sit down commands. In R. K. Parker (ed.), *Readings in Educational Psychology.* Boston: Allyn and Bacon.

Mullen, C. (2000). Teaching and learning through critical reflective practice. *Teacher Development, 4*(3), 437–454.

Ogden, J. E., Brophy, J. E. and Evertson, C. M. (1977, April). *An experimental investigation of organization and management techniques in first-grade reading groups.* Paper presented at the annual meeting of the American Educational Research Association, New York.

Parker, K., Hannah, E. and Topping, K. J. (2006). Collective teacher efficacy, pupils' attainment and socio-economic status in primary schools. *Improving Schools, 9*(2), 111–129.

Pintrich, P. R. (2000). Educational psychology at the millennium: A look back and a look forward. *Educational Psychologist, 35,* 221–226.

Polanyi, M. (1962). *Personal Knowledge: Towards a Post-critical Philosophy.* Chicago: University of Chicago Press.

Pressley, M. and Roehrig, A. D. (2003). Educational psychology in the modern era: 1960 to the present. In B. J. Zimmerman and D. H. Schunk (eds), *Educational Psychology: A Century of Contributions* (pp. 333–366). Mahwah, NJ: Lawrence Erlbaum.

Russell, T. (2005). Can reflective practice be taught? *Reflective Practice, 6*(2), 199–204.

Rutter, M., Maughan, B., Mortimore, P. and Ouston, J. (1979). *Fifteen Thousand Hours: Secondary Schools and their Effects on Children.* London: Open Books.

Schon, D. (1983). *The Reflective Practitioner.* New York: Basic Books.

Shulman, L. S. (1987). Knowledge and teaching: Foundations of the new reform. *Harvard Educational Review, 19*(2), 4–14.

Siegler, R. S. and Crowley, K. (1991). The microgenetic method: A direct means for studying cognitive development. *American Psychologist, 56,* 606–620.

Sousa, D. R. (1995). *How the Brain Learns.* Reston, VA: NASSP (National Association of Secondary School Principles).

Stanovich, K. E. (1992). *How to Think Straight About Psychology* (3rd ed.). Glenview, IL: Scott, Foresman.

TES (2006). *My best teacher,* TES magazine 24.11.06.

Tierney, R. J., Readence, J. E. and Dishner, E. K. (1990). *Reading Strategies and Practices: A Compendium* (3rd ed.). Boston: Allyn and Bacon.

Times Education Supplement Magazine 24.11.06 'Best/worse lesson', p. 4.

Times Education Supplement Magazine 08.12.06 'Best/worse lesson', p. 4.

Tutt, R. (2006). Reconciling the irreconcilable: coping with contradictory agendas. *Forum: For promoting 3–19 Comprehensive Education, 48*(2).

Vygotsky, L. (1962). *Thought and Language.* Trans. E. Hanfmann and G. Vakar. Mass: MIT Press.

Warin, J., Maddock, M., Pell, A. and Hargreaves, L. (2006). Resolving identity dissonance through reflective and reflexive practice in teaching. *Reflective Practice, 7*(2), 233–245.

Wittrock, M. C. (ed.) (1986). *Handbook of Research on Teaching* (3rd ed.). New York: Macmillan.

Wittrock, M. C. (1992). An empowering conception of educational psychology. *Educational Psychologist, 27,* 129–142.

Wong, L. (1987). Reaction to research findings: Is the feeling of obviousness warranted? *Dissertation Abstracts International,* 48/12, 3709B (University Microfilms #DA 8801059).

Chapter 2

Anderson, P. J. and Graham, S. M. (1994). Issues in second-language phonological acquisition among children and adults. *Topics in Language Disorders, 14,* 84–100.

Anderson, R. C., Nguyen-Jahiel, K. and McNurlen, A. (2001). The snowball phenomenon: spread of ways of talking and ways of thinking across groups of children. *Cognition and Instruction, 19*(1), 1–46.

Baker, C. (1993). *Foundations of Bilingual Education and Bilingualism.* Clevedon, England: Multilingual Matters.

Bakerman, R., Adamson, L. B., Koner, M. and Barr, R. G. (1990). !Kung infancy: The social context of object exploration. *Child Development, 61,* 794–809.

Baillargeon, R. (1999). Yong infants' expectations about hidden objects: A reply to three challenges. *Developmental Psychology, 2,* 115–132.

Berger, K. S. (2006). *The Developing Person through Childhood and Adolescence* (6th ed.). New York: Worth Publishers.

Berk, L. E. (1992). Children's private speech: An overview of theory and the status of research. In R. Diaz and L. Berk (eds) *Private Speech: From Social Interaction to Self-regulation.* Hillsdale, NJ: Erlbaum.

Berk, L. E. (2005). *Infants, Children, and Adolescents* (5th ed.). Boston: Allyn and Bacon.

Berk, L. E. and Spuhl, S. T. (1995). Maternal interaction, private speech, and task performance in preschool children. *Early Childhood Research Quarterly, 10,* 145–169.

Bhatia, T. K. and Richie, W. C. (1999). The bilingual child: Some issues and perspectives. In W. C. Richie and T. K. Bhatia (eds), *Handbook of Child Language Acquisition.* San Diego: Academic Press.

Bialystok, E. (1999). Cognitive complexity and attentional control in the bilingual child. *Child Development, 70,* 636–644.

Bransford, J. D., Brown, A. L. and Cocking, R. R. (2000). *How People Learn: Brain, Mind, Experience, and School.* Washington, DC: National Academy Press.

Brown, R. and Hanlon, C. (1970). Derivational complexity and order of acquisition in child speech. In J. R. Hayes (ed.), *Cognition and the Development of Language.* New York: Wiley.

Bruer, John T. (1999). In search of . . . brain-based education. *Phi Delta Kappan, 80,* 648–657.

Bruner, J. (1983). *Child Talk.* New York: Norton.

Byrnes, J. P. and Fox, N. A. (1998). The educational relevance of research in cognitive neuroscience. *Educational Psychology Review, 10,* 297–342.

Case, R. (1985). A developmentally-based approach to the problem of instructional design. In R. Glaser, S. Chipman and J. Segal (eds), *Teaching Thinking Skills, 2,* 545–562. Hillsdale, NJ: Lawrence Erlbaum.

Case, R. (1992). *The Mind's Staircase: Exploring the Conceptual Underpinnings of Children's Thought and Knowledge.* Mahwah, NJ: Lawrence Erlbaum.

Case, R. (1998). The development of conceptual structures. In D. Kuhn and R. S. Siegler (eds), *Handbook of Child Psychology: Vol. 2: Cognition, Perception, and Language* (pp. 745–800). New York: Wiley.

Ceci, S. J. and Roazzi, A. (1994). The effects of context on cognition: Postcards from Brazil. In R. J. Sternberg (ed.), *Mind in Context* (pp. 74–101). New York: Cambridge University Press.

Chomsky, N. (1957). *Syntactic Structures.* The Hague: Mouton and Co.

Confrey, J. (1990). A review of the research on students' conceptions in mathematics, science, and programming. *Review of Research in Education, 16,* 3–56.

Cook, J. L. and Cook, G. (2005). *Child Development: Principles and Perspectives*. Boston: Allyn and Bacon.

Cummins, J. (1984). *Bilingualism and Special Education*. San Diego: College Hill Press.

Cummins, J. (1994). The acquisition of English as a second language. In K. Spangenberg-Urbschat and R. Prichard (eds), *Kids Come in all Languages: Reading Instruction for ESL Students* (pp. 36–62). Newark, DE: International Reading Association.

Cunningham, P. (2006). Early years teachers and the influence of Piaget: evidence from oral history. *Early Years*, 26(1), 5–16.

Das, J. P. (1995). Some thoughts on two aspects of Vygotsky's work. *Educational Psychologist, 30*, 93–97.

Delpit, L. (1995). *Other People's Children: Cultural Conflict in the Classroom*. New York: The New Press.

Delpit, L. (2003). Educators as 'seed people': Growing a new future. *Educational Researcher, 7*(32), 14–21.

DfEE/QCA, (2000). *Teaching in England: the Foundation Stage*. Viewed at http://www.teachernet.gov.uk/teachinginengland/detail.cfm?id=167

Diaz-Rico, L. T. and Weed, K. Z. (2002). *The Crosscultural, Language, and Academic Development Handbook* (2nd ed.). Boston: Allyn and Bacon.

Driscoll, M. P. (2005). *Psychology of Learning for Instruction* (3rd ed.). Boston: Allyn and Bacon.

Duncan, R. M. and Cheyne, J. A. (1999). Incidence and functions of self-reported private speech in young adults: A self-verbalization questionnaire. *Canadian Journal of Behavioural Sciences, 31*, 133–136.

Edelman, G. M. (1992). *Bright Air, Brilliant Fire: On the Matter of the Mind*. New York: Basic Books.

Elkind, D. (1981). Obituary: Jean Piaget (1896–1980). *American Psychologist, 36*, 911–913.

Emerson, M. J. and Miyake, A. (2003). The role of inner speech in task switching: A dual-task investigation. *Journal of Memory and Language, 48*, 148–168.

Fischer, K. W. and Pare-Blagoev, J. (2000). From individual differences to dynamic pathways of development. *Child Development, 71*, 850–853.

Flavell, J. H., Miller, P. H. and Miller, S. A. (2002). *Cognitive Development* (4th ed.). Upper Saddle River, NJ: Prentice-Hall.

Galambos, S. J. and Goldin-Meadow, S. (1990). The effects of learning two languages on metalinguistic development. *Cognition, 34*, 1–56.

Garcia, E. E. (1992). 'Hispanic' children: Theoretical, empirical, and related policy issues. *Educational Psychology Review, 4*, 69–94.

Geary, D. C. (1998). What is the function of mind and brain? *Educational Psychologist, 10*, 377–388.

Geary, D. C. and Bjorklund, D. F. (2000). Evolutionary developmental psychology. *Child Development, 7*, 57–65.

Gelman, R. (2000). The epigenesis of mathematical thinking. *Journal of Applied Developmental Psychology, 21*, 27–37.

Gelman, R. and Cordes, S. A. (2001). Counting in animals and humans. In E. Dupoux (ed.), *Essay in Honor of Jacques Mehler*. Cambridge, MA: MIT Press.

Glassman, M. (2001). Dewey and Vygotsky: Society, experience, and inquiry in educational practice. *Educational Researcher, 30*(4), 3–14.

Gredler, M. E. (2005). *Learning and Instruction: Theory into Practice* (5th ed.). Boston: Allyn and Bacon.

Hallahan, D. P. and Kauffman, J. M. (2006). *Exceptional Learners: Introduction to Special Education* (10th ed.). Boston: Allyn and Bacon.

Hunt, J. McV. (1961). *Intelligence and Experience*. New York: Ronald.

John-Steiner, V. and Mahn, H. (1996). Sociocultural approaches to learning and development: A Vygotskian framework. *Educational Psychologist, 31*, 191–206.

Karpov, Y. V. and Bransford, J. D. (1995). L. S. Vygotsky and the doctrine of empirical and theoretical learning. *Educational Psychologist, 30*, 61–66.

Karpov, Y. V. and Haywood, H. C. (1998). Two ways to elaborate Vygotsky's concept of mediation implications for instruction. *American Psychologist, 53*, 27–36.

Kolb, G. and Whishaw, I. Q. (1998). Brain plasticity and behavior. In J. T. Spence, J. M. Darley and D. J. Foss (eds), *Annual Review of Psychology* (pp. 43–64). Palo Alto, CA: Annual Reviews.

Kozulin, A. (1990). *Vygotsky's Psychology: A Biography of Ideas*. Cambridge, MA: Harvard University Press.

Kozulin, A. (ed.). (2003). *Vygotsky's Educational Theory in Cultural Context*. Cambridge, UK: Cambridge University Press.

Kozulin, A. and Presseisen, B. Z. (1995). Mediated learning experience and psychological tools: Vygotsky's and Feuerstein's perspectives in a study of student learning. *Educational Psychologist, 30*, 67–75.

Leat, D. and Nichols, A. (1997). *Scaffolding Children's Thinking – Doing Vygotsky in the Classroom with National Curriculum Assessment*. Paper presented at the British Educational Research Association Annual (September 11–14, 1997): University of York. Viewed at http://www.leeds.ac.uk/educol/documents/000000383.htm

Lehman, D. R. and Nisbett, R. E. (1990). A longitudinal study of the effects of undergraduate training on reasoning. *Developmental Psychology, 26*, 952–960.

Lenneberg, E. (1967). *Biological Foundations of Language*. New York: Wiley.

Marinova-Todd, S., Marshall, D. and Snow, C. (2000). Three misconceptions about age and L2 learning. *TESOL Quarterly, 34*(1), 9–34.

Markman, E. M. (1992). Constraints on word learning: Speculations about their nature, origins, and domain specificity. In M. Gunnar and M. Maratsos (eds), *Minnesota Symposium on Child Psychology*, *25*, 59–101. Hillsdale, NJ: Lawrence Erlbaum.

McCafferty, S. G. (2004). Introduction. *International Journal of Applied Linguistics*, *14*(1), 1–6.

McCaslin, M. and Hickey, D. T. (2001). Self-regulated learning and academic achievement: A Vygotskian view. In B. Zimmerman and D. Schunk (eds), *Self-regulated learning and academic achievement: Theoretical perspectives* (2nd ed., pp. 227–252). Mahwah, NJ: Lawrence Erlbaum.

McDonald, L. and Stuart-Hamilton, I. (2002). Egocentrism in older adults – Piaget's Three Mountains Task Revisited. *Educational Gerontology*, *28*(1), 35–43.

Mears, T. (1998). Saying 'Si' to Spanish. *Boston Globe*, April 12.

Meece, J. L. (2002). *Child and Adolescent Development for Educators* (2nd ed.). New York: McGraw-Hill.

Meesook, K. (2003). Cultural and school-grade differences in Korean and American children's narrative skills. *International Review of Education*, *49*(1), 177–190.

Miller, P. H. (2002). *Theories of Developmental Psychology* (4th ed.). New York: Worth.

Moll, L. C., Amanti, C., Neff, D. and Gonzalez, N. (1992). Funds of knowledge for teaching: Using a qualitative approach to connect homes and classrooms. *Theory into Practice*, *31*, 132–141.

Moore, M. K. and Meltzoff, A. N. (2004). Object permanence after a 24-hr delay and leaving the locale of disappearance: the role of memory, space, and identity. *Developmental Psychology*, *40*, 606–620.

Moshman, D. (1997). Pluralist rational constructivism. *Issues in Education: Contributions from Educational Psychology*, *3*, 229–234.

Mussen, P., Conger, J. J. and Kagan, J. (1984). *Child Development and Personality* (6th ed.). New York: Harper and Row.

Nelson, C. A. (2001). The development and neural bases of face recognition. *Infant and Child Development*, *10*, 3–18.

O'Boyle, M. W. and Gill, H. S. (1998). On the relevance of research findings in cognitive neuroscience to educational practice. *Educational Psychology Review*, *10*, 397–410.

Orlando, L. and Machado, A. (1996). In defense of Piaget's theory: A reply to 10 common criticisms. *Psychological Review*, *103*, 143–164.

Palincsar, A. S. (1998). Social constructivist perspectives on teaching and learning. In J. T. Spence, J. M. Darley and D. J. Foss (eds), *Annual Review of Psychology* (pp. 345–375). Palo Alto, CA: Annual Reviews.

Perry, B. D. and Pollard, R. (1997). *Altered brain development following global neglect in early childhood*. Proceedings from the Annual Meeting of the Society for Neuroscience, New Orleans.

Piaget, J. (1954). *The Construction of Reality in the Child* (M. Cook, Trans.). New York: Basic Books.

Piaget, J. (1962). *Comments on Vygotsky's Critical Remarks concerning 'The Language and Thought of the Child' and 'Judgment and Reasoning in the Child.'* Cambridge, MA: MIT Press.

Piaget, J. (1963). *Origins of Intelligence in Children*. New York: Norton.

Piaget, J. (1964). Development and learning. In R. Ripple and V. Rockcastle (eds), *Piaget Rediscovered* (pp. 7–20). Ithaca, NY: Cornell University Press.

Piaget, J. (1969). *Science of Education and the Psychology of the Child*. New York: Viking.

Piaget, J. (1970a). Piaget's Theory. In P. Mussen (ed.), *Handbook of Child Psychology* (3rd ed.) (Vol. 1, pp. 703–732). New York: Wiley.

Piaget, J. (1970b). *The Science of Education and the Psychology of the Child*. New York: Orion Press.

Piaget, J. (1974). *Understanding Causality* (D. Miles and M. Miles, Trans.). New York: Norton.

Pressley, M. (1996). *Getting beyond whole language: Elementary reading instruction that makes sense in light of recent psychological research*. Paper presented at the Annual meeting of the American Psychological Association, Toronto.

Price, W. F. and Crapo, R. H. (2002). *Cross-cultural Perspectives in Introductory Psychology* (4th ed.). Pacific Grove, CA: Wadsworth.

Rathus, S. A. (1988). *Understanding Child Development*. New York: Holt, Rinehart and Winston.

Rauscher, F. H. and Shaw, G. L. (1998). Key components of the Mozart effect. *Perceptual and Motor Skills*, *86*, 835–841.

Reich, P. A. (1986). *Language Development*. Englewood Cliffs, NJ: Prentice-Hall.

Ricciardelli, L. A. (1992). Bilingualism and cognitive development: Relation to threshold theory. *Journal of Psycholinguistic Research*, *21*, 301–316.

Rogoff, B. (1990). *Apprenticeship in Thinking: Cognitive Development in Social Context*. New York: Oxford University Press.

Rogoff, B. (2003). *The Cultural Nature of Human Development*. New York: Oxford University Press.

Rogoff, B. and Morelii, G. (1989). Perspectives on children's development from cultural psychology. *American Psychologist*, *44*, 343–348.

Rosenshine, B. and Meister, C. (1992). *The uses of scaffolds for teaching less structured academic tasks.* Paper presented at the annual meeting of the American Educational Research Association, San Francisco.

Roskos, K. and Neuman, S. B. (1993). Descriptive observation of adults' facilitation of literacy in young children's play. *Early Childhood Research Quarterly, 8,* 77–98.

Roskos, K. and Neuman, S. B. (1998). Play as an opportunity for literacy. In O. N. Saracho and B. Spodek (eds), *Multiple Perspectives on Play in Early Childhood Education* (pp. 100–115). Albany: State University of New York Press.

Rosser, R. (1994). *Cognitive Development: Psychological and Biological Perspectives.* Boston: Allyn and Bacon.

Schunk, D. H. (2004). *Learning Theories: An Educational Perspective* (4th ed.). Columbus, OH: Merrill/Prentice-Hall.

Shaywitz, B. A. *et al.* (2004). Development of left occipitotemporal systems for skilled reading in children after a phonologically-based intervention. *Biological Psychiatry, 55,* 926–933.

Siegler, R. S. (1998). *Children's Thinking* (3rd ed.). Upper Saddle River, NJ: Prentice-Hall.

Siegler, R. S. (2000). The rebirth of children's learning. *Child Development, 71,* 26–35.

Skinner, B. F. (1957). *Verbal Learning.* New York: Appleton-Century-Crofts.

Stanovich, K. E. (1998). Cognitive neuroscience and educational psychology: What season is it? *Educational Psychology Review, 10,* 419–426.

Steele, K. M., Bass, K. E. and Crook, M. D. (1999). The mystery of the Mozart effect: Failure to replicate. *Psychological Science, 10,* 366–368.

Sulzby, E. and Teale, W. (1991). Emergent literacy. In R. Barr, M. L. Kamil, P. B. Mosenthal and P. D. Pearson (eds), *Handbook of Reading Research, Vol. II* (pp. 727–758). New York: Longman.

Sylvester, R. (2003). *A Biological Brain in a Cultural Classroom* (2nd ed.). Thousand Oaks, CA: Sage.

Tharp, R. G. and Gallimore, R. (1988). *Rousing Minds to Life: Teaching, Learning, and Schooling in Social Context.* New York: Cambridge University Press.

Tomasello, M., Kruger, A. C. and Ratner, H. H. (1993). Cultural learning. *Behavioral and Brain Sciences, 16,* 495–552.

Tomlinson, C. A. (2005). Differentiating instruction. *Theory Into Practice, 44*(3).

Vygotsky, L. S. (1978). *Mind in Society: The Development of Higher Mental Process.* Cambridge, MA: Harvard University Press.

Vygotsky, L. S. (1986). *Thought and Language.* Cambridge, MA: MIT Press.

Vygotsky, L. S. (1987a). The genetic roots of thinking and speech. In R. W. Rieber and A. S. Carton (eds), *Problems of General Psychology, Vol. 1. Collected Works* (pp. 101–120). New York: Plenum. (Work originally published in 1934.)

Vygotsky, L. S. (1987b). *Problems of General Psychology.* New York: Plenum.

Vygotsky, L. S. (1993). *The Collected Works of L. S. Vygotsky: Vol. 2* (J. Knox and C. Stevens, Trans.). New York: Plenum.

Vygotsky, L. S. (1997). *Educational Psychology* (R. Silverman, Trans.). Boca Raton, FL: St. Lucie.

Weinberger, D. (2001, March 10). A brain too young for good judgment. *New York Times,* p. A13.

Wertsch, J. V. (1991). *Voices of the Mind: A Sociocultural Approach to Mediated Action.* Cambridge, MA: Harvard University Press.

Wertsch, J. V. and Tulviste, P. (1992). L. S. Vygotsky and contemporary developmental psychology. *Developmental Psychology, 28,* 548–557.

Whitehurst, G. J., Epstein, J. N., Angell, A. L., Payne, A. C., Crone, D. A. and Fischel, J. E. (1994). Outcomes of an emergent literacy program in headstart. *Journal of Educational Psychology, 86,* 542–555.

Wink, J. and Putney, L. (2002). *A Vision of Vygotsky.* Boston: Allyn and Bacon.

Winsler, A., Carlton, M. P. and Barry, M. J. (2000). Age-related changes in preschool children's systematic use of private speech in a natural setting. *Journal of Child Language, 27,* 665–687.

Winsler, A. and Naglieri, J. A. (2003). Overt and covert verbal problem-solving strategies: Developmental trends in use, awareness, and relations with task performance in children age 5 to 17. *Child Development, 74,* 659–678.

Wood, D., Bruner, J. and Ross, S. (1976). The role of tutoring in problem solving. *British Journal of Psychology, 66,* 181–191.

Wood, S. E., Wood, E. G. and Boyd, D. (2005). *The World of Psychology* (5th ed.). Boston: Allyn and Bacon.

Zhou, Z., Peverly, S. T., Beohm, A. E. and Chongde, L. (2001). American and Chinese children's understanding of distance, time, and speed interrelations. *Cognitive Development, 15,* 215–240.

Chapter 3

Aber, J. L., Brown, J. L. and Jones, S. M. (2003). Developmental trajectories toward violence in middle childhood: Course, demographic differences, and response to school-based intervention. *Developmental Psychology, 39,* 324–348.

Ainsworth, M. and Wittig, B. (1969). Attachment and the exploratory behaviour of one-year-olds in a strange situation. In B. M. Foss (ed.) *Determinants of Infant Behaviour, 4*, 113–136, London: Methuen.

Altermatt, E. R., Pomerantz, E. M., Ruble, D. N., Frey, K. S. and Greulich, F. K. (2002). Predicting changes in children's self-perceptions of academic competence: A naturalistic examination of evaluative discourse among classmates. *Developmental Psychology, 38*, 903–917.

Amato, L. F., Loomis, L. S. and Booth, A. (1995). Parental divorce, marital conflict, and offspring well-being during early adulthood. *Social Forces, 73*, 895–915.

Amato, P. R. (2001). Children of divorce in the 1990s: An update of the Amato and Keith (1991) meta-analysis. *Journal of Family Psychology, 15*, 355–370.

Anderman, E. M. and Midgley, C. (2004). Changes in self-reported academic cheating across the transition from middle school to high school. *Contemporary Educational Psychology, 29*, 499–517.

Anderson, C. A. and Bushman, B. J. (2001). Effects of violent video games on aggressive behavior, aggressive cognition, aggressive affect, physiological arousal, and prosocial behavior: A meta-analytic review of the scientific literature. *Psychological Science, 12*, 353–359.

Arbona, C. Jackson, R., McCoy, A. and Blakely, C. (1999). Ethnic identity as a predictor of attitudes towards fighting. *Journal of Early Adolescence, 19*(3), 323–340.

Archer, S. L. and Waterman, A. S. (1990). Varieties of identity diffusions and foreclosures: An exploration of the subcategories of the identity statuses. *Journal of Adolescent Research, 5*, 96–111.

Arnold, M. L. (2000). Stage, sequence, and sequels: Changing conceptions of morality, post-Kohlberg. *Educational Psychology Review, 12*, 365–383.

Bandura, A. (1997). *Self-efficacy: The Exercise of Control.* New York: Freeman.

Bandura, A., Ross, D. and Ross, S. (1963). Imitation of film-mediated aggressive models. *Journal of Abnormal and Social Psychology, 66*, 3–11.

Baumrind, D. (1991). Effective parenting during early adolescent transitions. In P. A. Cowan and M. Hetherington (eds), *Family Transitions* (pp. 111–165). Hillsdale, NJ: Lawrence Erlbaum.

BBC News (2005). 'Six-year-olds "want to be thin"'. Viewed at http://news.bbc.co.uk/1/hi/health/4319105.stm March 2005.

Beat (Beating eating disorders) (2007). *Understanding Eating Disorders.* Viewed at http://www.b-eat.co.uk/Search/w_search_searchresultspage_pav_e?SearchableText=statistics

Bee, H. L. (1981). *The Developing Child.* USA: Harper & Row.

Beezer, B. (1985). Reporting child abuse and neglect: your responsibilities and your protections. *Phi Delta Kappan, 66*, 434–436.

Berger, K. (2006). *The Developing Person Through Childhood and Adolescence* (7th ed.) New York: Worth.

Berger, K. S., and Thompson, R. A. (1995). *The Developing Person Through Childhood and Adolescence.* New York: Worth.

Berk, L. E. (2005). *Infants, Children, and Adolescents* (5th ed.). Boston: Allyn and Bacon.

Boom, J., Brugman, D. and van der Heijden, P. G. (2001). Hierarchical structure of moral stages assessed by a sorting task. *Child Development, 72*, 535–548.

Bosworth, K. (1995). Caring for others and being cared for. *Phi Delta Kappan, 76*(9), 686–693.

Bowlby, J. (1951). *Maternal Care and Mental Health.* World Health Organization Monograph (Serial No.2).

Brazleton, T. B., Tronick, E., Adamson, L., Als, H. and Wise, S. (1975). Early mother infant reciprocity. *Ciba Found Symposium* (33):137–154.

Brazelton, T. B. and Cramer, B. G. (1991). *The Earliest Relationship.* London: Karnac Books.

Brazelton, T. B. and Nugent, J. K. (1995). *The Neonatal Behavioural Assessment* Scale (3rd ed.). MacKeith Press, London.

Broidy, L. M., Nagin, D. S., Tremblay, R. E., Bates, J. E., Brame, B., Dodge, K., Ferguson, D., Horwood, J., Loeber, R., Laird, R., Lynam, D., Moffitt, T., Pettit, G. S. and Vitaro, F. (2003). Developmental trajectories of childhood disruptive behaviors and adolescent delinquency: A six site, cross-national study. *Developmental Psychology, 39*, 222–245.

Bronfenbrenner, U. (1989). Ecological systems theory. In R. Vasta (ed.), *Annals of Child Development* (Vol. 6, pp. 187–249). Boston: JAI Press, Inc.

Bronfenbrenner, U. and Evans, G. W. (2000): Developmental science in the 21st century: Emerging theoretical models, research designs, and empirical findings. *Social Development, 9*, 115–125.

Brooks-Gunn, J. (1988). Antecedents and consequences of variations in girls' maturational timing. In M. D. Levin and E. R. McAnarney (eds), Early Adolescent Transitions (pp. 101–121). Lexington, MA: Lexington Books.

Buckingham, D. (2005). Violent imagery 'harms children'. BBC News, viewed at http://news.bbc.co.uk/I/hi/health/4275131.stm February 2005.

Burton, R. V. (1963). The generality of honesty reconsidered. *Psychological Review, 70*, 481–499.

Byrne, B. M. (2002). Validating the measurement and structure of self-concept: Snapshots of past, present, and future research. *American Psychologist, 57*, 897–909.

Byrne, B. M. and Shavelson, R. J. (1996). On the structure of social self-concept for pre-, early, and late adolescents: A test of the Shavelson model. *Journal of Personality and Social Psychology, 70,* 599–613.

Byrne, B. M. and Worth Gavin, D. A. (1996). The Shavelson model revisited: Testing for structure of academic self concept across pre-, early, and late adolescents. *Journal of Educational Psychology, 88,* 215–229.

Carpendale, J. I. M. (2000). Kohlberg and Piaget on stages and moral reasoning. *Developmental Review, 20,* 181–205.

Chapman, J. W., Tunmer, W. E. and Prochnow, J. E. (2000). Early reading-related skills and performance, reading self-concept, and the development of academic self-concept: A longitudinal study. *Journal of Educational Psychology, 92,* 703–708.

Children's Defense Fund. (2005). *Child Poverty.* Available online at http://www.childrensdefense.org/familyincome/childpoverty/default.aspx. Accessed May 19, 2005.

Cline, T., de Abreu, G., Fihosy, C., Gray, H., Lambert, H. C. and Neale, J. (2002). Minority Ethnic Pupils in Mainly White Schools', Report for the Department of Education and Skills. Viewed at http://www.dfes.gov.uk/research/data/uploadfiles/RR365.pdf

Coie, J. D. and Dodge, K. A. (1998). Aggression and antisocial behavior. In N. Eisenberg (ed.), *Handbook of Child Psychology: Vol. 3. Social, Emotional, and Personality Development* (5th ed.) (pp. 779–862). New York: Wiley.

Coie, J. D., Terry, R., Lenox, K., Lochman, J. and Hyman, C. (1995). Childhood peer rejection and aggression as predictors of stable patterns of adolescent disorder. *Development and Psychopathology, 7,* 697–714.

Cole, D. A., Martin, J. M., Peeke, L. A., Seroczynski, A. D. and Fier, J. (1999). Children's over- and underestimation of academic competence: A longitudinal study of gender differences, depression, and anxiety. *Child Development, 70,* 459–473.

Cook, J. L. and Cook, G. (2005). *Child Development: Principles and Perspectives.* Boston: Allyn and Bacon.

Cooper, C. R. (1998). *The Weaving of Maturity: Cultural Perspectives on Adolescent Development.* New York: Oxford University Press.

Coplan, R. J., Prakash, K., O'Neil, K. and Armer, M. (2004). Do you 'want' to play? Distinguishing between conflicted shyness and social disinterest in early childhood. *Developmental Psychology, 40,* 244–258.

Cota-Robles, S., Neiss, M. and Rowe, D. C. (2002). The role of puberty in violent and nonviolent delinquency among Anglo-American, Mexican-American and African-American boys. *Journal of Adolescent Research, 17,* 364–376.

Cothran, D. J. and Ennis, C. D. (2000). Building bridges to student engagement: Communicating respect and care for students in urban high school. *Journal of Research and Development in Education, 33*(2), 106–117.

Covington, M. V. (1992). *Making the Grade: A Self-Worth Perspective on Motivation and School Reform.* New York: Holt, Rinehart and Winston.

Crandell, L. E. and Hobson, R. P. (1999). Individual differences in young children's IQ: A social-developmental perspective. *Journal of Child Psychology and Psychiatry and Allied Disciplines, 40,* 455–464.

Crick, N. R., Casas, J. F. and Mosher, M. (1997). Relational and overt aggression in preschool. *Developmental Psychology, 33,* 579–588.

Crisci, P. E. (1986). The quest national centre: a focus on prevention of alienation. *Phi Delta Kappan, 67,* 440–442.

Crocker, J. and Park, L. E. (2004). Reaping the benefits of pursuing self-esteem without the costs. *Psychological Bulletin, 130,* 392–414.

Cumberbatch, G. (2004). Villain or victim? A review of the research evidence concerning violence and its effects in the real world with additional reference video games. A report prepared for the Video Standards Council. Viewed at www.videostandards.org.uk/sections/downloads/pdfs/Video%20**Violence**%202004.

Damon, W. (1994). Fair distribution and sharing: The development of positive justice. In B. Puka (ed.), *Fundamental Research in Moral Development* (pp. 189–254). *Moral Development: A Compendium, Vol. 2.* New York: Garland Publishing.

Darcey, J. S. and Travers, J. F. (2006). *Human Development Across the Lifespan* (6th ed.). New York: McGraw-Hill.

Davis, H. A. (2003). Conceptualizing the role and influence of student–teacher relationships on children's social and cognitive development. *Educational Psychologist, 38,* 207–234.

Davis-Kean, P. E. and Sandler, H. M. (2001). A meta-analysis of measures of self-esteem for young children: A framework for future measurers. *Child Development, 72,* 887–906.

Deci, E. L. and Ryan, R. M. (1985). *Intrinsic Motivation and Self-Determination in Human Behavior.* New York: Plenum.

Dodge, K. A. and Pettit, G. S. (2003). A biopsychosocial model of the development of chronic conduct problems in adolescence. *Developmental Psychology, 39,* 349–371.

Dohnt, H. and Tiggemann, M. (2005). Peer influences on body dissatisfaction and dieting awareness in young girls. *British Journal of Developmental Psychology, 23,* 103–116.

Eccles, J., Wigfield, A. and Schiefele, U. (1998). Motivation to succeed. In W. Damon (Series ed.) and N. Eisenberg (Volume ed.), *Handbook of Child Psychology: Vol. 3. Social,*

Emotional, and Personality Development (5th ed., pp. 1017–1095). New York: Wiley.

Egan, S. K., Monson, T. C. and Perry, D. G. (1998). Social-cognitive influences on change in aggression over time. *Developmental Psychology, 34,* 996–1006.

Eisenberg, N. and Fabes, R. A. (1998). Prosocial development. In W. Damon (Series ed.) and N. Eisenberg (Vol. ed.), *Handbook of Child Psychology: Vol. 3. Social, Emotional, and Personality Development* (5th ed., pp. 701–778). New York: Wiley.

Eisenberg, N., Martin, C. L. and Fabes, R. A. (1996). Gender development and gender effects. In D. Berliner and R. Calfee (eds), *Handbook of Educational Psychology* (pp. 358–396). New York: Macmillan.

Eisenberg, N., Shell, R., Pasernack, J., Lennon, R., Beller, R. and Mathy, R. M. (1987). Prosocial development in middle childhood: A longitudinal study. *Developmental Psychology, 23,* 712–718.

Elias, M. J. and Schwab, Y. (2006). From compliance to responsibility: Social and emotional learning and classroom management. In C. Evertson and C. S. Weinstein (eds), *Handbook for Classroom Management: Research, Practice and Contemporary Issues.* Mahwah, NJ: Lawrence Erlbaum.

Entwisle, D. R. and Alexander, K. L. (1998). Facilitating the transition to first grade: The nature of transition and research on factors affecting it. *The Elementary School Journal, 98,* 351–364.

Erikson, E. H. (1963). *Childhood and Society* (2nd ed.). New York: Norton.

Erikson, E. H. (1968). *Identity, Youth, and Crisis.* New York: Norton.

Erikson, E. H. (1980). *Identity and the Life Cycle* (2nd ed.). New York: Norton.

Eysenck, H. J. and Wilson, G. (1973). *The Experimental Study of Freudian Theories.* London: Methuen.

Feldman, R. S. (2004). *Child Development* (3rd ed.). Upper Saddle River, NJ: Prentice-Hall.

Flavell, J. H., Miller, P. H. and Miller, S. A. (2002). *Cognitive Development* (4th ed.). Upper Saddle River, NJ: Prentice-Hall.

Frank, S. J., Pirsch, L. A. and Wright, V. C. (1990). Late adolescents' perceptions of their parents: Relationships among deidealization, autonomy, relatedness, and insecurity and implications for adolescent adjustment and ego identity status. *Journal of Youth and Adolescence, 19,* 571–588.

Frankel, K. and Bates, J. (1990). Mother-toddler problem-solving: Antecedents in attachment, home behaviour and temperament. *Child Development, 61,* 810–819.

Fredricks, J. A., Blumenfeld, P. C., Paris, A. H. (2004). School engagement: Potential of the concept, state of the evidence. *Review of Educational Research, 74,* 59–109.

Freud, A. (trans. Barbara Low) (1931). *Introduction of Psychoanalysis for Teachers.* London: Allen and Unwin.

Freud, A. (trans. B. Low) (1963). *Psycho-analysis for Teachers and Parents.* New York: W.W.Norton.

Freud, S. (1953). *The Standard Edition of the Complete Psychological Works of Sigmund Freud.* London: Hogarth Press.

Freud, S. (1962). *Three Essays on the Theory of Sexuality,* trans. James Strachey. New York: Basic Books.

Galbraith, A. and Alexander, J. (2005). Literacy, self-esteem and locus of control. *Support for Learning, 20*(1), 28–34.

Garbarino, J. and deLara, E. (2002). *And Words Can Hurt Forever: How to Protect Adolescents From Bullying, Harassment, and Emotional Violence.* New York: Free Press.

Garner, P. W. and Spears, F. M. (2000). Emotion regulation in low-income preschool children. *Social Development, 9,* 246–264.

Garrod, A., Beal, C. and Shin, P. (1990). The development of moral orientation in elementary school children. *Sex Roles, 22,* 13–27.

Gehlbach, H. (2004). A new perspective on perspective taking: A multidimensional approach to conceptualizing an aptitude. *Educational Psychology Review, 16,* 207–234.

Gilligan, C. (1982). *In a Different Voice: Psychological Theory and Women's Development.* Cambridge, MA: Harvard University Press.

Gilligan, C. and Attanucci, J. (1988). Two moral orientations: Gender differences and similarities. *Merrill-Palmer Quarterly, 34,* 223–237.

Glasgow, K. L., Dornbusch, S. M., Troyer, L., Steinberg, L. and Ritter, P. L. (1997). Parenting styles, adolescents' attributions, and educational outcomes in nine heterogeneous high schools. *Child Development, 68,* 507–523.

Goodchild, S. (2006). Dying to be thin: Why one in 100 young women suffer from eating disorders. *The Independent,* 22 November.

Graham, S. (1996). How causal beliefs influence the academic and social motivation of African-American children. In G. G. Brannigan (ed.), *The Enlightened Educator: Research Adventures in the Schools,* pp. 111–126. New York: McGraw-Hill.

Graham, S. (1998). Self-blame and peer victimization in middle school: An attributional analysis. *Developmental Psychology, 34,* 587–599.

Greenberg, R. P. (1986). The case against Freud's cases. *Behavioral and Brain Sciences, 9,* 240–241.

Grossman, H. and Grossman, S. H. (1994). *Gender Issues in Education.* Boston: Allyn and Bacon.

Grotevant, H. D. (1998). Adolescent development in family contexts. In N. Eisenberg (ed.), *Handbook of Child*

Psychology: Vol. 3. Social, Emotional, and Personality Development (5th ed.) (pp. 1097–1149). New York: Wiley.

Guay, F., Larose, S. and Boivin, M. (2004). Academic self-concept and educational attainment level: A ten-year longitudinal study. *Self and Identity, 3*, 53–68.

Hagborg, W. J. (1993). Rosenberg self-esteem scale and Harter's self-perception profile for adolescents: A concurrent validity study. *Psychology in Schools, 30*, 132–136.

Hallahan, D. P. and Kauffman, J. M. (2006). *Exceptional Learners: Introduction to Special Education* (10th ed.). Boston: Allyn and Bacon.

Harris, J. R. (1998). *The Nurture Assumption: Why Children Turn Out The Way They Do; Parents Matter Less Than You Think and Peers Matter More.* New York: Free Press.

Harter, S. (1998). The development of self-representations. In N. Eisenberg (ed.), *Handbook of Child Psychology: Vol 3. Social, Emotional, and Personality Development* (5th ed., pp. 553–618). New York: Wiley.

Harter, S. (2003). The development of self-representation during childhood and adolescence. In M. R. Leary and J. P. Tangney (eds), *Handbook of Self and Identity* (pp. 610–642). New York: Guilford.

Hartup, W. W. and Stevens, N. (1999). Friendships and adaptation across the lifespan. *Current Directions in Psychological Science, 8*, 76–79.

Helms, J. E. (1995). An update of Helms's White and People of Color racial identity models. In J. G. Ponterotto, J. M. Casas, L. A. Suzuki and C. M. Alexander (eds), *Handbook of Multicultural Counseling* (pp. 181–198). Thousand Oaks, CA: Sage.

Helwig, C. C., Arnold, M. L., Tan, D. and Boyd, D. (2003). Chinese adolescents' reasoning about democratic and authority-based decision making in peer, family, and school contexts. *Child Development, 74*, 783–800.

Herman, M. (2004). Forced to choose: Some determinants of racial identification in multi-racial adolescents. *Child Development, 75*, 730–748.

Hetherington, E. M. (1999). Should we stay together for the sake of the children? In E. Hetherington (ed.), *Coping with Divorce, Single-Parenting, and Remarriage: A Risk and Resilience Perspective* (pp. 93–116). Hillsdale, NJ: Lawrence Erlbaum.

Hetherington, E. M. and Kelly, J. (2002). *For Better or For Worse: Divorce Reconsidered.* New York: W. W. Norton.

Hodges, E. V. E. and Perry, D. G. (1999). Personal and interpersonal antecedents and consequences of victimization by peers. *Journal of Personality and Social Psychology, 76*, 677–685.

Hoffman, M. L. (2000). *Empathy and Moral Development.* New York: Cambridge University Press.

Hoffman, M. L. (2001). A comprehensive theory of prosocial moral development. In A. Bohart and D. Stipek (eds), *Constructive and Destructive Behavior* (pp. 61–86). Washington, DC: American Psychological Association.

Hoge, D. R., Smit, E. K. and Hanson, S. L. (1990). School experiences predicting changes in self-esteem of sixth- and seventh-grade students. *Journal of Educational Psychology, 82*, 117–126.

Huesmann, L. R., Moise-Titus, J., Podolski, C. P. and Eron, L. D. (2003). Longitudinal relations between children's exposure to TV violence and their aggressive and violent behavior in young adulthood: 1977–1992. *Developmental Psychology, 39*, 201–221.

Isabella, R. and Belsky, J. (1991). Interactional synchrony and the origins of infant–mother attachment: A replication study. *Child Development, 62*, 373–384.

James, W. (1890). *The Principles of Psychology* (Vol. 2). New York: Holt.

James, W. H., Kim, G. K. and Armijo, E. (2000). The influence of ethnic identity on drug use among ethnic minority adolescents. *Journal of Drug Education, 30*(3), 265–280.

Jarrett, R. (1995). Growing up poor: The family experiences of socially mobile youth in low-income African-American neighborhoods. *Journal of Adolescent Research, 10*, 111–135.

Jensen, L. A., Arnett, J. J., Feldman, S. S. and Cauffman, E. (2002). It's wrong but everybody does it: Academic dishonesty among high school and college students. *Contemporary Educational Psychology, 27*, 209–228.

Jones, D. C. (2004). Body image among adolescent girls and boys: A longitudinal study. *Developmental Psychology, 40*, 823–835.

Kaltiala-Heino, R., Marttunen, M., Rantanen, P. and Rimpela, M. (2003). Early puberty is associated with mental health problems in middle adolescence. *Soc Sci Med 57*(6), 1055–1064.

Katz, S. R. (1999). Teaching in tensions: Latino immigrant youth, their teachers, and the structures of schooling. *Teachers College Record, 100*(4), 809–840.

Kim, K. M. (1998). Korean children's perceptions of adult and peer authority and moral reasoning. *Developmental Psychology, 5*, 310–329.

Klein, M. (1959). Our adult world and its roots in infancy. In *Envy and Gratitude and Other Works*, 1946–63. New York: Delta, 1977, pp. 247–263.

Kling, K. C., Hyde, J. S., Showers, C. J. and Buswell, B. N. (1999). Gender differences in self-esteem: A meta-analysis. *Psychological Bulletin, 125*, 470–500.

Kohlberg, L. (1963). The development of children's orientations toward moral order: Sequence in the development of moral thought. *Vita Humana, 6*, 11–33.

Kohlberg, L. (1975). The cognitive-developmental approach to moral education. *Phi Delta Kappan, 56,* 670–677.

Kohlberg, L. (1981). *The Philosophy of Moral Development.* New York: Harper and Row.

Kokko, K. and Pulkkinen, L. (2000). Aggression in childhood and long-term unemployment in adulthood: A cycle of maladaptation and some protective factors. *Developmental Psychology, 36,* 463–472.

Kroger, J. (2000). *Identity Development: Adolescence Through Adulthood.* Thousand Oaks, CA: Sage.

Leming, J. S. (1981). Curriculum effectiveness in value/moral education. *Journal of Moral Education, 10,* 147–164.

Livingstone, S. and Bovill, M. (eds) (2001). *Children and Their Changing Media Environment.* Lawrence Eribaum Associates.

Lyons-Ruth, K., Easterbrooks, M. and Cibelli, C. (1997). Infant attachment strategies, infant mental lag and maternal depression symptoms: Predictors of internalizing and externalizing problems at age 7. *Developmental Psychology, 33*(4), 681–692.

Ma, X. and Kishor, N. (1997). Attitude toward self, social factors, and achievement in mathematics: A meta-analytic review. *Educational Psychology Review, 9,* 89–120.

Marcia, J. E. (1987). The identity status approach to the study of ego identity development. In T. Honess and K. Yardley (eds), *Self and Identity: Perspectives Across the Life Span* (pp. 161–171). London: Routledge and Kegan Paul.

Marcia, J. E. (1991). Identity and self development. In R. Lerner, A. Peterson and J. Brooks-Gunn (eds), *Encyclopedia of Adolescence* (Vol. 1). New York: Garland.

Marcia, J. E. (1994). The empirical study of ego identity. In H. Bosma, T. Graafsma, H. Grotebanc and D. DeLivita (eds), *The Identity and Development.* Newbury Park, CA: Sage.

Marcia, J. E. (1999). Representational thought in ego identity, psychotherapy, and psychosocial development. In I. E. Sigel (ed.), *Development of Mental Representation: Theories and Applications.* Mahwah, NJ: Lawrence Erlbaum.

Markstrom-Adams, C. (1992). A consideration of intervening factors in adolescent identity formation. In G. R. Adams, R. Montemayor and T. Gullotta (eds), *Advances in Adolescent Development: Vol. 4. Adolescent Identity Formation* (pp. 173–192). Newbury Park, CA: Sage.

Marsh, H. W. (1990). Influences of internal and external frames of reference on the formation of math and English self-concepts. *Journal of Educational Psychology, 82,* 107–116.

Marsh, H. W. and Ayotte, V. (2003). Do multiple dimensions of self-concept become more differentiated with age? The differential distinctiveness hypothesis. *Journal of Educational Psychology, 95,* 687–706.

Marsh, H. W. and Craven, R. (2002). The pivotal role of frames of reference in academic self-concept formation: The Big Fish Little Pond Effect. In F. Pajares and T. Urdan (eds), *Adolescence and Education* (Vol. II, pp. 83–123). Greenwich, CT: Information Age.

Marsh, H. W. and Hau, K.-T. (2003). Big-Fish-Little-Pond effect on academic self-concept. *American Psychologist, 58,* 364–376.

Marsh, H. W. and Holmes, I. W. M. (1990). Multidimensional self-concepts: Construct validation of responses by children. *American Educational Research Journal, 27,* 89–118.

Marsh, H. W. and Yeung, A. S. (1997). Coursework selection: Relation to academic self-concept and achievement. *American Educational Research Journal, 34,* 691–720.

Matas, L., Arend, R. and Stroufe, L. (1978). Continuity of adaptation in the second year: the relationship between quality of attachment and later competence. *Child Development, 49,* 547–556.

Mediascope (1996). *National Television Violence Study: Executive Summary 1994–1995.* Studio City, CA: Author.

Meece, J. L. (2002). *Child and Adolescent Development for Educators* (2nd ed.). New York: McGraw-Hill.

Meins, E. (1997*). Security of Attachment and the Social Development of Cognition.* Hove, England: Psychology Press.

Miller, P. H. (2002). *Theories of Developmental Psychology* (4th ed.). New York: Worth.

Milner, H. R. (2003). Teacher reflection and race in cultural contexts: History, meaning, and methods in teaching. *Theory into Practice, 42*(3), 173–180.

Murdock, T. B., Hale, N. M. and Weber, M. J. (2001). Predictors of cheating among early adolescents: Academic and social motivations. *Contemporary Educational Psychology, 26,* 96–115.

Murdock, T. B. and Miller, A. (2003). Teachers as sources of middle school students' motivational identity: Variable-centered and person-centered analytic approaches. *Elementary School Journal, 103,* 383–399.

Murray, L. and Trevarthen, C. (1985). Emotional regulations of interactions between two-month-olds and their mothers. In T. M. Field and N. A. Fox (eds), *Social Perception in Infants* (pp. 177–197). Norwood, NJ: Ablex.

Nelson, G. (1993). Risk, resistance, and self-esteem: A longitudinal study of elementary school-aged children from mother-custody and two-parent families. *Journal of Divorce and Remarriage, 19,* 99–119.

Noguera, P. (2005). The racial achievement gap: How can we assume an equity of outcomes? In L. Johnson, M. E. Finn and R. Lewis (eds), *Urban Education With an Attitude.* Albany, NY: SUNY Press.

Nucci, L. P. (2001). *Education in the Moral Domain*. New York: Cambridge Press.

Nurmi, J. (2004). Socialization and self-development: Channeling, selection, adjustment, and reflection. In R. Lerner and L. Steinberg (eds), *Handbook of Adolescent Psychology*. New York: Wiley.

Pajares, F. and Schunk, D. H. (2001). Self-beliefs and school success: Self-efficacy, self-concept, and school achievement. In R. Riding and S. Rayner (eds), *Perception* (pp. 239–266). London: Ablex Publishing.

Pajares, F. and Schunk, D. H. (2002). Self and self-belief in psychology and education: an historical perspective. In J. Aronson and D. Cordova (eds), *Psychology of Education: Personal and Interpersonal Forces*, pp. 1–19. New York: Academic Press.

Paris, S. G. and Cunningham, A. E. (1996). Children becoming students. In D. Berliner and R. Calfee (eds), *Handbook of Educational Psychology* (pp. 117–146). New York: Macmillan.

Patterson, G. R. (1997). Performance models for parenting: A social interactional perspective. In J. Grusec and L. Kuczynski (eds), *Parenting and the Socialization of Values: A Handbook of Contemporary Theory* (pp. 193–235). New York: Wiley.

Pavri, S. (2003). Loneliness in children with disabilities: How teachers can help. In K. Freiberg (ed.), *Annual Editions: Educating Exceptional Children 03/04* (pp. 154–160). Guilford, CT: McGraw-Hill/Duskin.

Pavri, S. and Luftig, R. L. (2000). The social face of inclusive education: Are students with disabilities really included? *Preventing School Failure, 45*, 8–14.

Pellegrini, A. D., Bartini, M. and Brooks, F. (1999). School bullies, victims, and aggressive victims: Factors relating to group affiliation and victimization in early adolescence. *Journal of Educational Psychology, 91*, 216–224.

Penuel, W. R. and Wertsch, J. V. (1995). Vygotsky and identity formation: A sociocultural approach. *Educational Psychologist, 30*, 83–92.

Phelan, P., Davidson, A. L. and Cao, H. T. (1992). Speaking up: Students' perspectives on school. *Phi Delta Kappan, 73*(9), 695–704.

Phinney, J. (2003). Ethnic identity and acculturation. In K. Chun, P. Ball and G. Marin (eds), *Acculturation: Advances in Theory, Measurement, and Applied Research* (pp. 63–81). Washington, DC: American Psychological Association.

Phinney, J. S. (1990). Ethnic identity in adolescents and adults: Review of research. *Psychological Bulletin, 108*(3), 499–514.

Phinney, J. S. and Devich-Navarro, M. (1997). Variations in bicultural identification among African-American and Mexican-American adolescents. *Journal of Research on Adolescence, 7*, 3–32.

Piaget, J. (1965). *The Moral Judgment of the Child*. New York: Free Press.

Pintrich, P. R. and Schunk, D. H. (2002). *Motivation in Education: Theory, Research, and Applications* (2nd ed.). Upper Saddle River, NJ: Merrill/Prentice-Hall.

Posada, G., Jacobs, A., Richmond, M., Carbonell, O. A., Alzate, G., Bustamante, M. R. and Quiceno, J. (2002). Maternal care giving and infant security in two cultures. *Developmental Psychology, 38*, 67–78.

Price, L. F. (2005). The biology of risk taking. *Educational Leadership, 62*(7), 22–27.

Reinke, W. M. and Herman, K. C. (2002a). A research agenda for school violence prevention. *American Psychologist, 57*, 796–797.

Reinke, W. M. and Herman, K. C. (2002b). Creating school environments that deter antisocial behaviors in youth. *Psychology in the Schools, 39*, 549–560.

Rosenberg, M. (1979). *Conceiving the Self*. New York: Basic Books.

Rotherham-Borus, M. J. (1994). Bicultural reference group orientations and adjustment. In M. Bernal and G. Knight (eds), *Ethnic Identity*. Albany, NY: State University of New York Press.

Rudolph, K. D., Lambert, S. F., Clark, A. G. and Kurlakowsky, K. D. (2001). Negotiating the transition to middle school: The role of self-regulatory processes. *Child Development, 72*, 926–946.

Ryan, A. (2001). The peer group as a context for development of young adolescents' motivation and achievement. *Child Development, 72*, 1135–1150.

Selman, R. L. (1980). *The Growth of Interpersonal Understanding*. New York: Academic Press.

Skoe, E. E. A. (1998). The ethic of care: Issues in moral development. In E. E. A. Skoe and A. L. von der Lippe (eds), *Personality Development in Adolescence* (pp. 143–171). London: Routledge.

Slaby, R. G., Roedell, W. C., Arezzo, D. and Hendrix, K. (1995). *Early Violence Prevention*. Washington, DC: National Association for the Education of Young Children.

Smetana, J. G. (2000). Middle-class African-American adolescents' and parents' conceptions of parental authority and parenting practices: A longitudinal investigation. *Child Development, 71*, 1672–1686.

Sobesky, W. E. (1983). The effects of situational factors on moral judgment. *Child Development, 54*, 575–584.

Spencer, M. B. and Markstrom-Adams, C. (1990). Identity processes among racial and ethnic-minority children in America. *Child Development, 61*, 290–310.

Sprenger, M. (2005). Inside Amy's brain. *Educational Leadership, 62*(7), 28–32.

Steinberg, L. (2005). *Adolescence* (7th ed.). New York: McGraw-Hill.

Stice, E. and Shaw, H. (2004). Eating disorder prevention programs: A meta-analytic review. *Psychological Bulletin, 130,* 206–227.

Stinson, S. W. (1993). Meaning and value: Reflections on what students say about school. *Journal of Curriculum and Supervision, 8*(3), 216–238.

Stormshak, E. A., Bierman, K. L., Bruschi, C., Dodge, K. A., Coie, J. D., *et al.* (1999). The relation between behavior problems and peer preference in different classrooms. *Child Development, 70,* 169–182.

Tesser, A., Stapel, D. A. and Wood, J. V. (2002). *Self and Motivation: Emerging Psychological Perspectives.* Washington, DC: American Psychological Association.

Theodorakou, K. and Zervas, Y. (2003). The effects of the creative movement teaching method and the traditional teaching method on elementary school children's self-esteem. *Sport, Education and Society, 8*(1), 91–104.

Timmer, S. G., Eccles, J. and O'Brien, K. (1988). How children use time. In F. Juster and F. Stafford (eds), *Time, Goods, and Well-Being.* Ann Arbor, MI: Institute for Social Research, University of Michigan.

Turiel, E. (1998). The development of morality. In W. Damon (series ed.) and N. Eisenberg (vol. ed.), *Handbook of Child Psychology: Vol. 3. Social, Emotional, and Personality Development* (5th ed., pp. 863–932). New York: Wiley.

Twenge, J. M. and Campbell, W. K. (2001). Age and birth cohort differences in self-esteem: A cross temporal meta-analysis. *Journal of Personality and Social Psychology Review, 5,* 321–344.

Underwood, J. and Szabo, A. (2003). Academic offences and e-learning: individual propensities in cheating. *British Journal of Educational Technology, 34,* 467–477.

Valentine, J. C., DuBois, D. L. and Cooper, H. (2004). The relations between self-beliefs and academic achievement: A systematic review. *Educational Psychologist, 39,* 111–133.

van den Boom, D. C. and Hoeksma, J. B. (1994). The influence of temperament and mothering on attachment and exploration: An experimental manipulation of sensitive responsiveness among lower-class mothers with irritable infants. *Child Development, 65*(6), 1457–1477.

Vispoel, W. P. (1995). Self-concept inartistic domains: An extension of the Shavelson, Hubmner, and Stanton (1976) model. *Journal of Educational Psychology, 87,* 134–153.

Walker, L. J. (1991). Sex differences in moral reasoning. In W. M. Kurtines and J. L. Gewirtz (eds), *Handbook of Moral Behavior and Development* (Vol. 2, pp. 333–362). Hillsdale, NJ: Lawrence Erlbaum.

Walker, L. J. and Pitts, R. C. (1998). Naturalistic conceptions of moral maturity. *Developmental Psychology, 34,* 403–419.

Walker, L. J., Pitts, R. C., Hennig, K. H. and Matsuba, M. K. (1995). Reasoning about morality and real-life moral problems. In M. Killen and D. Hart (eds), *Morality in Everyday Life: Developmental Perspectives* (pp. 371–407). Cambridge, UK: Cambridge University Press.

Waters, E. (1978). The reliability and stability of individual differences in infant-mother attachment. *Child Development, 49,* 483–494.

Waters, H. F. (1993). Networks under the gun. *Newsweek,* 64–66, 12 July.

Wentzel, K. R. (1997). Student motivation in middle school: The role of perceived pedagogical caring. *Journal of Educational Psychology, 89*(3), 411–419.

Wentzel, K. R., Barry, C. M. and Caldwell, K. A. (2004). Friendships in middle school: Influences on motivation and school adjustment. *Journal of Educational Psychology, 96,* 195–203.

Wigfield, A., Eccles, J., MacIver, D., Rueman, D. and Midgley, C. (1991). Transitions at early adolescence: Changes in children's domain-specific self-perceptions and general self-esteem across the transition to junior high school. *Developmental Psychology, 27,* 552–565.

Wigfield, A., Eccles, J. S. and Pintrich, P. R. (1996). Development between the ages of 11 and 25. In D. Berliner and R. Calfee, (eds), *Handbook of Educational Psychology* (pp. 148–185). New York: Macmillan.

Wilgenbusch, T. and Merrell, K. W. (1999). Gender differences in self-concept among children and adolescents: A meta-analysis of multidimensional studies. *School Psychology Quarterly, 14,* 101–120.

Williams, C. and Bybee J. (1994). What do children feel guilty about? Developmental and gender differences. *Developmental Psychology, 30,* 617–623.

Woolfolk Hoy, A., Davis, H. and Pape, S. (2006). Teachers' knowledge, beliefs, and thinking. In P. A. Alexander and P. H. Winne (eds), *Handbook of Educational Psychology* (2nd ed.). Mahwah, NJ: Lawrence Erlbaum.

Woolfolk Hoy, A. and Weinstein, C. S. (2006). Students' and teachers' perspectives about classroom management. In C. Evertson and C. S. Weinstein (eds), *Handbook for Classroom Management: Research, Practice, and Contemporary Issues.* Mahwah, NJ: Lawrence Erlbaum.

Yeung, A. S., McInerney, D. M., Russell-Bowie, D., Suliman, R., Chui, H. and Lau, I. C. (2000). Where is the hierarchy of academic self-concept? *Journal of Educational Psychology, 92,* 556–567.

Zelli, A., Dodge, K. A., Lochman, J. E. and Laird, R. D. (1999). The distinction between beliefs legitimizing aggression and deviant processing of social cues: Testing measurement validity and the hypothesis that biased processing mediates the effects of beliefs on aggression. *Journal of Personality and Social Psychology, 77,* 150–166.

Chapter 4

Barklay, R. A. (2002). International consensus statement on ADHD. *Clinical Child and Family Psychology Review, 5*(2), 89–111.

Baron, R. A. (1998). *Psychology* (4th ed.). Boston: Allyn and Bacon.

Basic Skills Agency (1997). *International Numeracy Survey: A Comparison of the Basic Numeracy Skills of Adults 16–60 in Seven Countries.* BSA, London.

Benn, C. and Chitty, C. (1996). *Thirty Years On: Is Comprehensive Education Alive and Well or Struggling to Survive?* London: David Fulton.

Berk, L. E. (2005). *Infants, Children, and Adolescents* (5th ed.). Boston: Allyn and Bacon.

Biggs, J. (2001). Enhancing learning: A matter of style of approach. In R. Sternberg and L. Zhang (eds), *Perspectives on Cognitive, Learning, and Thinking Styles* (pp. 73–102). Mahwah, NJ: Lawrence Erlbaum.

Bloom, B. S. (1982). The role of gifts and markers in the development of talent. *Exceptional Children, 48,* 510–522.

Boaler, J. (1997a). Setting, social class and survival of the quickest. *British Educational Research Journal, 23,* 575–595.

Boaler, J. (1997b). When even the winners are losers: evaluating the experiences of 'top set' students. *Journal of Curriculum Studies, 29,* 165–182.

Boaler, J. (1997c). *Experiencing School Mathematics: Teaching Styles, Sex and Setting.* Buckingham: Open University Press.

Boaler, J., William, D. and Brown, M (2000). Students' experiences of ability grouping – disaffection, polarisation and construction of failure. *British Educational Research Journal, 26*(5), 631–648.

British Institute of Learning Disabilities (BILD) (2004). Factsheet – what is a learning disability? Kidderminster: BILD. Available at www.bild.org.uk

British Psychological Society (BPS) (2000). *Learning Disability: Definitions and Contexts.* Leicester: British Psychological Society.

Brookes, L. (1997). *Dyslexia: 100 years on brain research and understanding.* Available at http://www.dyslexia-inst.org.uk/articles/100_years.htm

Butterworth (2002). Cited in Dowker, A. (2004). 'Dyscalculia in children: its characteristics and possible interventions'. (Paper presented at OECD Literacy and Numeracy Network Meeting, El Escorial, Spain, March 2004).

Byrnes, J. P. and Fox, N. A. (1998). The educational relevance of research in cognitive neuroscience. *Educational Psychology Review, 10,* 297–342.

Callahan, C. M., Tomlinson, C. A. and Plucker, J. (1997). *Project STATR using a multiple intelligences model in identifying and promoting talent in high-risk students.* Storrs, CT: National Research Center for Gifted and Talented. University of Connecticut Technical Report.

Carroll, J. B. (1993). *Human Cognitive Abilities: A Survey of Factor Analytic Studies.* Cambridge, England: Cambridge University Press.

Carroll, J. B. (1997). The three-stratum theory of cognitive abilities. In D. P. Flanagan, J. L. Genshaft and P. L. Harrison (eds), *Contemporary Intellectual Assessment: Theories, Tests, and Issues* (pp. 122–130). New York: Guilford.

Castle, S., Deniz, C. B. and Tortora, M. (2005). Flexible grouping and student learning in a high-needs school. *Education and Urban Society, 37,* 139–150.

Cattell, R. B. (1963). Theory of fluid and crystallized intelligence: A critical experiment. *Journal of Educational Psychology, 54,* 1–22.

Ceci, S. J. (1991). How much does schooling influence intelligence and its cognitive components? A reassessment of the evidence. *Developmental Psychology, 27,* 703–720.

Centre for Studies on Inclusive Education (CSIE) (2005). *Assessments and statements.* Available at http://csie.org.uk

Coffield, F. J., Moseley, D. V., Hall, E. and Ecclestone, K. (2004). *Learning Styles and Pedagogy in Post-16 Learning: A systematic and critical review.* London: Learning and Skills Research Centre/University of Newcastle upon Tyne.

Current Directions in Psychological Science. (1993). Special Section: Controversies, *2,* 1–12.

Daley, T. C., Whaley, S. E., Sigman, M. D., Espinosa, M. P. and Neumann, C. (2003). IQ on the rise: The Flynn Effect in rural Kenyan children. *Psychological Science, 14*(3), 215–219.

Department of Health (2001). *Valuing People: A new strategy for learning disability for the 21st century.* London: DH Publications. Available at http://www.archive.official-documents.co.uk/document/cm50/5086/5086.pdf

DfEE/QCA (1999). *The National Curriculum for England.* London: HMSO.

DfES (2001a). *Special educational needs code of practice.* Available at http://www.teachernet.gov.uk/_doc/3724/SENCodeOfPractice.pdf

DfES (2001b). *Promoting children's mental health within early years and school settings.* Available at http://www.teachernet.gov.uk/_doc/4619/mentalhealth.pdf

DfES (2002). *Guidance on teaching gifted and talented pupils.* Available at http://www.nc.uk.net/gt/

DfES (2004a). *National Statistics First Release: Special Educational Needs in England, January, 2004.* London: National Statistics. Available at http://www.dfes.gov.uk/rsgateway/DB/SFR/s000537/SFR44-2004v4.pdf

DfES (2004b). *Drugs: Guidance for Schools.* Viewed at http://publications.teachernet.gov.uk/eOrderingDownload/DfES%200092%20200MIG373.pdf

DfES (2005). *Learning and teaching for dyslexic children.* London: DfES Publications Centre. Available at http://www.standards.dfes.gov.uk/primary/publications/inclusion/1170961/pns_incl1184-2005dyslexia_s2.pdf

DfES (2006). *Statistical First Release: Special Educational Needs in England, January, 2006.* London: National Statistics. Available at http://www.dfes.gov.uk/rsgateway/DB/SFR/s000661/SFR23-2006v2.pdf

Diller, L. (1998). *Running on Ritalin.* New York: Bantam Books.

DirectGov (2006). *Education and Learning.* Available at http://www.direct.gov.uk/EducationAndLearning/Schools/SpecialEducationalNeeds/SpecialEducationalNeedsArticles/fs/en?CONTENT_ID=4000690&chk=TKdRrF

Doggett, A. M. (2004). ADHD and drug therapy: Is it still a valid treatment? *Child Health Care, 8,* 69–81.

Dowker, A. (2004). *Dyscalculia in children: its characteristics and possible interventions.* Paper presented at OECD Literacy and Numeracy network meeting, Spain, March, 2004. Available at www.brookes.ac.uk/schools/education/rescon/ocnef/dyscalculia.doc

Dunn, R., Beaudry, J. S. and Klavas, A. (1989). Survey of research on learning styles. *Educational Leadership, 47*(7), 50–58.

Dunn, R., Dunn, K. and Price, G. E. (2000). *Learning Style Inventory.* Lawrence, KS: Price Systems.

Dunn, R. and Griggs, S. (2003). *Synthesis of the Dunn and Dunn Learning-Style Model Research: Who, what, when, where, and so what?* New York: St. John's University.

Dusenbury, L. and Falco, M. (1995). Eleven components of effective drug abuse prevention curricula. *Journal of School Health, 65,* 420–425.

Dyson, A., Farrell, P. and Polat, F. (2004). *Inclusion and Pupil Achievement.* Nottingham: DfES publications.

EADSNE (European Agency for Development in Special Needs Education) (2003). *Special needs education in Europe: Inclusive policies and practices.* Available at www.european-agency.org/site/info/publications/agency

EUMAP (2005). *Rights of people with intellectual disabilities: access to education and employment,* UK. Open Society Institute. Available at http://www.learningdisabilities.org.uk/html/content/rights_people_intellectual_disabilities.pdf

European Commission Health and Consumer Protection (2005). *Some elements about the prevalence of Autism Spectrum Disorders (ASD) in the European Union.* Available at ec.europa.eu/health/ph_information/dissemination/diseases/autism_

EURYDICE (European Commission Directorate General for Education and Culture) at NFER (National Foundation for Educational Research) (2002). *Eurofocus on Transition from primary to secondary education in European countries.* Available at http://www.nfer.ac.uk/eurydice/briefingseurope/transfer-from-primary-to-secondary-education.cfm

Eyre, D. (2002). Introduction: Effective schooling for the gifted and talented. In D. Eyre and H. Lowe (eds). *Curriculum Provision for the Gifted and Talented in the Secondary School.* London: NACE/Fulton.

Feshbach, N. (1997). Empathy: The formative years – Implications for clinical practice. In A. Bohart and L. Greenberg (eds), *Empathy Reconsidered: New Directions in Psychotherapy* (pp. 33–59). Washington, DC: American Psychological Association.

Feshbach, N. (1998). Aggression in the schools: Toward reducing ethnic conflict and enhancing ethnic understanding. In P. Trickett and C. Schellenbach (eds), *Violence Against Children in the Family and the Community* (pp. 269–286). Washington, DC: American Psychological Association.

Finkel, D., Reynolds, C. A., McArdle, J. J., Gatz, M. and Pedersen, N. L. (2003). Latent growth curve analyses of accelerating decline in cognitive abilities in adulthood. *Developmental Psychology, 39,* 535–550.

Finlan, M. (1994). *Learning Disabilities: The Imaginary Disease.* Westport, CT: Gergin and Garvey.

Forness, S. R. and Knitzer, J. (1992). A new proposed definition and terminology to replace 'Serious Emotional Disturbance' in individuals with Disabilities Education Act. *School Psychology Review, 21,* 12–20.

Fox, L. H. (1981). Identification of the academically gifted. *American Psychologist, 36,* 1103–1111.

Freeman, J. (1998). *Educating the very able: current international research.* OFSTED Review of Research. London: HMSO.

Friend, M. (2006). *Special Education: Contemporary Perspectives for School Professionals.* Boston: Allyn and Bacon.

Friend, M. and Bursuck, W. D. (2002). *Including Students with Special Needs* (3rd ed.). Boston: Allyn and Bacon.

Fuchs, L. S., Fuchs, D., Hamlett, C. L. and Karns, K. (1998). High-achieving students' interactions and performance on complex mathematical tasks as a function of homogeneous and heterogeneous pairings. *American Educational Research Journal, 35,* 227–268.

Galindo-Ruada, F. and Vignoles, A. (2005). *The heterogeneous effect of selection in secondary schools:*

Understanding the changing role of ability. London School of Economics: Centre for the economics of education. Available at http://scholar.google.com/scholar?hl= en&lr=&q=cache:XaXoJ3MIFKAJ:cee.lse.ac.uk/cee%2520dps/ ceedp52.pdf+selective+secondary+education+11%2B+ exam+UK+end

Gardner, H. (1983). *Frames of Mind: The Theory of Multiple Intelligences*. New York: Basic Books.

Gardner, H. (1998). Reflections on multiple intelligences: Myths and messages. In A. Woolfolk (ed.), *Readings in Educational Psychology* (2nd ed.) (pp. 61–67). Boston: Allyn and Bacon.

Gardner, H. (2003, April 21). *Multiple intelligence after twenty years*. Paper presented at the American Educational Research Association, Chicago, Illinois.

Garmon, A., Nystrand, M., Berends, M. and LePore, P. C. (1995). An organizational analysis of the effects of ability grouping. *American Educational Research Journal, 32,* 687–715.

Goleman, D. (1995). *Emotional Intelligence*. New York: Bantam.

Graham, S. (1996). How causal beliefs influence the academic and social motivation of African-American children. In G. G. Brannigan (ed.), *The enlightened educator: Research adventures in the schools* (pp. 111–126). New York: McGraw-Hill.

Gregorc, A. F. (1982). *Gregorc Style Delineator: Development, technical, and administrative manual*. Maynard, MA: Gabriel Systems.

Grigorenko, E. L. and Sternberg, R. J. (2001). Analytical, creative, and practical intelligence as predictors of self-reported adaptive functioning: A case study in Russia. *Intelligence, 29,* 57–73.

Guilford, J. P. (1988). Some changes in the Structure-of-Intellect model. *Educational and Psychological Measurement, 48,* 1–4.

Gustafsson, J-E. and Undheim, J. O. (1996). Individual differences in cognitive functioning. In D. Berliner and R. Calfee (eds), *Handbook of Educational Psychology* (pp. 186–242). New York: Macmillan.

Haddon, M. (2003). *The Curious Incident of the Dog in the Night-Time*. London: Random House Children's Books.

Hallahan, D. P. and Kauffman, J. M. (2006). *Exceptional Learners: Introduction to Special Education* (10th ed.). Boston: Allyn and Bacon.

Hallahan, D. P., Lloyd, J. W., Kauffman, J. M., Weiss, M. P. and Martinez, E. A. (2005). *Introduction to Learning Disabilities* (5th ed.). Boston: Allyn and Bacon.

Hallowell, E. M. and Ratey, J. J. (1994). *Driven to Distraction*. New York: Pantheon Books.

Hardman, M. L., Drew, C. J. and Egan, M. W. (2005). *Human Exceptionality: Society, School, and Family (8th ed.)*. Boston: Allyn and Bacon.

Health Promoting Schools (2005). *Choices: it's up to you*. Health Promoting Schools, Derbyshire.

HMSO (2001). Special Educational Needs and Disability Act. Available at http://www.opsi.gov.uk/acts/acts2001/ 20010010.htm

Ho, Anita (2004). To be labelled, or not to be labelled: that is the question. *British Journal of Learning Disabilities, 32*(2), 86–92.

Holahan, C. and Sears, R. (1995). *The Gifted Group in Later Maturity*. Stanford, CA: Stanford University Press.

Horn, J. L. (1998). A basis for research on age differences in cognitive capabilities. In J. J. McArdle and R. W. Woodcock (eds), *Human Cognitive Theories in Theory and Practice* (pp. 57–87). Mahwah, NJ: Lawrence Erlbaum.

Howe, M. J. A., Davidson, J. W. and Sloboda, J. A. (1998). Innate talents: Reality or myth? *Behavioral and Brain Sciences, 21,* 399–406.

Hunt, E. (2000). Let's hear it for crystallized intelligence. *Learning and Individual Differences, 12,* 123–129.

Hunt, N. and Marshall, K. (2002). *Exceptional Children and Youth: An Introduction to Special Education* (3rd ed.). Boston: Houghton Mifflin.

Ireson, J. and Hallam, S. (1999). Raising standards: Is ability grouping the answer? *Oxford Review of Education, 25*(3), 343–358.

Izard, C. E. (2001). Emotional intelligence or adaptive emotions? *Emotion, 1,* 249–257.

Jackson, B. (1964). *Streaming: An Education System in Miniature*. London, UK: Routledge and Kegan Paul.

Jones, E. D. and Southern, W. T. (1991). Conclusions about acceleration: Echoes of a debate. In W. Southern and E. Jones (eds), *The Academic Acceleration of Gifted Children* (pp. 223–228). New York: Teachers College Press.

Kanaya, T., Scullin, M. H. and Ceci, S. J. (2003). The Flynn effect and U.S. policies: The impact of rising IQ scores on American society via mental retardation diagnoses. *American Psychologist, 58,* 1–13.

Keefe, J. W. (1982). Assessing student learning styles: An overview. In *Student Learning Styles and Brain Behavior*. Reston, VA: National Association of Secondary School Principals.

Keefe, J. W. and Monk, J. S. (1986). *Learning Style Profile Examiner's Manual*. Reston, VA: National Association of Secondary School Principals.

Keill, S. and Clunies-Ross, L. (2003). *Survey of educational provision for blind and partially sighted children in England, Scotland and Wales in 2002*. London: RNIB.

Kendall, L., O'Donnell, L. Golden, S. *et al.* (2005). *Excellence in Cities: the national evaluation of a policy to raise standards in urban schools 2000–200.* London: HMSO. Available at http://www.renewal.net/Documents/RNET/Research/Excellencecitiesnational.

Kerckhoff, A. C. (1986). Effects of ability grouping in British secondary schools. *American Sociological Review, 51,* 842–858.

Kirby, A. and Townsend, M. A. R. (2005). Conversations with accelerated and non-accelerated gifted students. *New Zealand Journal of Gifted Education,* 14(1), pp. 1–9 Available at www.education.auckland.ac.nz/uoa/fms/default/education/docs/pdf/research/FoEdAnnualReport2005.pdf

Kirk, S., Gallagher, J. J. and Anastasiow, N. J. (1993). *Educating Exceptional Children* (7th ed.). Boston: Houghton Mifflin.

Kolb, D. (1985). *Learning Style Inventory.* Boston, MA: McBer and Company.

Kulik, J. A. and Kulik, C. C. (1984). Effects of accelerated instruction on students. *Review of Educational Research, 54,* 409–425.

Kulik, J. A. and Kulik, C. L. (1997). Ability grouping. In N. Colangelo and G. Davis (eds), *Handbook of Gifted Education* (2nd ed., pp. 230–242). Boston: Allyn and Bacon.

Landerl, K., Bevan, A. and Butterworth, B. (2004). Developmental dyscalculia and basic numerical capacities: a study of 8–9 year students. *Cognition,* 93, pp. 99–125.

Law, J., Boyle, J., Harris, F., Harkness, A. and Nye, C. (1998). Screening for speech and language delay: a systematic review of the literature. *Health Technology Assessment, 9,* pp. 1–184.

Leonard, L. (1997). *Children with Specific Language Impairment.* Cambridge: The MIT press.

Lerner, R. M. and Galambos, N. L. (1998). Adolescent development: Challenges and opportunities for research, programs, and policies. In J. T. Spence, J. M. Darley and D. J. Foss (eds), *Annual Review of Psychology* (pp. 413–446). Palo Alto, CA: Annual Reviews.

Lewinsohn, P. M., Rohde, P. and Seeley, J. R. (1994). Psychological risk factors for future attempts. *Journal of Consulting and Clinical Psychology, 62,* 297–305.

Lindsay, G., Dockrell, J., Mackie, C. and Letchford, B. (2005). The roles of specialist provision for children with speech and language difficulties in England and Wales: a model for inclusion? *Journal of Research in Special Educational Needs, 5*(3), 88–96.

Lip Chap S. (2002). Public images of mathematics. *Philosophy of Mathematics Journal,* 15 (2002). Available at http://www.people.ex.ac.uk/PErnest/pome15/public_images.htm

Louis, B., Subotnik, R. F., Breland, P. S. and Lewis, M. (2000). Establishing criteria for high ability versus selective admission to gifted programs: Implications for policy and practice. *Educational Psychology Review, 12,* 295–314.

Lovelace, M. K. (2005). Meta-analysis of experimental research based on the Dunn and Dunn Model. *Journal of Educational Research, 98,* 176–183.

Loveless, T. (1998). The tracking and ability grouping debate. *Fordham Report, 2*(88), 1–27.

Lovett, M. W., *et al.* (2000). Components of effective remediation for developmental disabilities: Combining phonological and strategy-based instruction to improve outcomes. *Journal of Educational Psychology, 92,* 263–283.

Maker, C. J. (1987). Gifted and talented. In V. Richardson-Koehler (ed.), *Educators' Handbook: A Research Perspective* (pp. 420–455). New York: Longman.

Male, D. B. (1999). Research Report: Learned helplessness in children with severe learning difficulties. *SLD (Severe Learning Difficulties) Experience, 24,* 16–17.

Mayer, J. D. and Cobb, C. D. (2000). Educational policy on emotional intelligence: Does it make sense? *Educational Psychology Review, 12,* 163–183.

Mayer, J. D. and Salovey, P. (1997). What is emotional intelligence? In P. Salovey and D. Sluyter (eds), *Emotional Development, Emotional Literacy, and Emotional Intelligence.* New York: Basic Books.

Mayer, R. E. and Massa, L. J. (2003). Three facets of visual and verbal learners: Cognitive ability, cognitive style and learning preference. *Journal of Educational Psychology, 95*(4), 833–846.

McArdle, P., O'Brien, G. and Kolvin, I. (1995). Hyperactivity: prevalence and relationship with conduct disorder. *Journal of Child Psychology and Psychiatry, 36,* 279–303.

McClelland, D. C. (1993). Intelligence is not the best predictor of job performance. *Current Directions in Psychological Science, 2,* 5–6.

McNemar, Q. (1964). Lost: Our intelligence? Why? *American Psychologist, 19,* 871–882.

Meece, J. L. (2002). *Child and Adolescent Development for Educators* (2nd ed.). New York:McGraw-Hill.

MENCAP (The National Society for Mentally Handicapped Children and Adults) (2004). *People with profound and multiple learning disabilities.* Available at www.mencap.org.uk/html/campaigns/pmld/

Merrell C. and Tymms P. (2001). Inattention, hyperactivity and impulsiveness: Their impact on academic achievement and progress. *British Journal of Educational Psychology;* 71(Pt 1): 43–56.

Mills, J. R. and Jackson, N. E. (1990). Predictive significance of early giftedness: The case of precocious reading. *Journal of Educational Psychology, 82,* 410–419.

Mind (2006). *Suicide* fact sheet. Available at http://www.mind.org.uk/Information/Factsheets/Suicide/#Top

Mitchell, B. M. (1984). An update on gifted and talented education in the U.S. *Roeper Review, 6,* 161–163.

NAGTY (National Academy for Gifted and Talented Youth) (2006). *Launch of National Register for gifted and talented students.* Available at http://www.nagty.ac.uk/about/media_room/gifted_and_talented/national_register_launch.aspx

National Autistic Society (2006). *How many people have autistic spectrum disorders?* Available at http://www.nas.org.uk/nas/jsp/polopoly.jsp?d=299&a=3527

National Literacy Trust (2006). *Streaming and setting does it make a difference to achievement?* Available at www.literacytrust.org.uk

National Statistics (2006). *Statistics on Young People and Drug Abuse*: England, 2006. Available at http://www.ic.nhs.uk/pubs/youngpeopledrugmisuse2006/youngpeopledrugmisusefull/file

Neisser, U., Boodoo, G., Bouchard, A., Boykin, W., Brody, N., Ceci, S. J., Halpern, D. F., Loehlin, J. C., Perloff, R., Sternberg, R. J. and Urbina, S. (1996). Intelligence: Knowns and unknowns. *American Psychologist, 51,* 77–101.

Nestor-Baker, N. S. (1999). *Tacit knowledge in the superintendency: An exploratory analysis.* Unpublished doctoral dissertation, The Ohio State University, Columbus, OH.

NIASA (National Initiative for Autism: Screening and Assessment) (2003). *National Autism plan for children.* The National Autistic Society. Available at http://www.cafamily.org.uk/NAPExec.pdf#search=%22interventions%20children%20ASD%22

Nylund, D. (2000). *Treating Huckleberry Finn: A new narrative approach to working with kids diagnosed ADD/ADHD.* San Francisco: Jossey-Bass.

Ofsted (2002a). *The National Literacy Strategy: the first four years 1998–2002.* Available via www.ofsted.gov.uk

Ofsted (2002b). *The National Numeracy Strategy: the first three years 1999–2002.* Available via www.ofsted.gov.uk

Ofsted (2006). *Setting in Primary Schools,* London: OFSTED Publications Centre.

Owens, R. (1999). *Language Disorders: A Functional Approach to Assessment and Intervention* (3rd ed.). Boston: Allyn and Bacon.

Panksepp, J. (1998). Attention deficit hyperactivity disorders, psychostimulants, and intolerance of playfulness: A tragedy in the making? *Current Directions in Psychological Science, 7,* 91–98.

Paris, S. (1988, April). *Fusing Skill and Will: The integration of cognitive and motivational psychology.* Paper presented at the annual meeting of the American Educational Research Association, New Orleans.

Parliamentary Office of Science and Technology (POST) (2004). *Dyslexia and Dyscalculia.* July 2004, No. 226, London: POST.

Petrides, K. V., Frederickson, N. and Furnham, A. (2004). The role of trait emotional intelligence in academic performance and deviant behaviour at school. *Personality and Individual Differences, 36,* 277–293.

Petrill, S. A. and Wilkerson, B. (2000). Intelligence and achievement: A behavioral genetic perspective. *Educational Psychology Review, 12,* 185–199.

Pintrich, P. R. and Schrauben, B. (1992). Students' motivational beliefs and their cognitive engagement in academic tasks. In D. Schunk and J. Meece (eds), *Students' Perceptions in the Classroom: Causes and Consequences* (pp. 149–183). Hillsdale, NJ: Lawrence Erlbaum.

Purdie, N., Hattie, J. and Carroll, A. (2002). A review of the research on interventions for Attention Deficit Hyperactivity Disorder: What works best? *Review of Educational Research, 72,* 61–99.

QCA (no date). *Guidance on teaching gifted and talented pupils.* Available at http://www.nc.net/gt

Range, L. M. (1993). Suicide prevention: Guidelines for schools. *Educational Psychology Review, 5,* 135–154.

Reid, M. K. and Borkowski, J. G. (1987). Causal attributions of hyperactive children: Implications for teaching strategies and self control. *Journal of Educational Psychology, 79,* 296–307.

Reis, S. M., Kaplan, S. N., Tomlinson, C. A., Westberg, K. L., Callahan, C. M. and Cooper, C. R. (2002). Equal does not mean identical. In L. Abbeduto (ed.), *Taking Sides: Clashing on Controversial Issues in Educational Psychology* (pp. 31–35). Guilford, CT: McGraw-Hill/Duskin.

Renzulli, J. S. and Reis, S. M. (2003). The schoolwide enrichment model: Developing creative and productive giftedness. In N. Colangelo and G. A. Davis (eds). *Handbook of Gifted Education* (pp. 184–203). Boston: Allyn and Bacon.

Reynolds, D., Sullivan, M. and Murgatroyd, S. (1987). *The Comprehensive Experiment: A Comparison of the Selective and Non-Selective System of School Organisation.* London: Falmer Press.

Rice, F. P. and Dolgin, K. G. (2002). *The Adolescent: Development, Relationships, and Culture* (10th ed.). Boston: Allyn and Bacon.

Richardson, T. M. and Benbow, C. P. (1990). Long-term effects of acceleration on the social-emotional adjustment of mathematically precocious youths. *Journal of Educational Psychology, 82,* 464–470.

RNIB (2006). *See it right* guidelines. Viewed at http://www.rnib.org.uk/xpedio/groups/public/documents/publicWebsite/public_seeitright.hcsp

RNID (Royal National Institute for the Deaf) (2006). *Information and Resources*. Available at http:www.rnid.org.uk/information_resources/factsheets/education/factsheets

Roberts, R. D., Zeidner, M. and Matthews, G. (2001). Does emotional intelligence meet traditional standards for an intelligence? Some new data and conclusions. *Emotion, 1,* 196–231.

Robinson, A. and Clinkenbeard, P. R. (1998). Giftedness: An exceptionality examined. In J. T. Spence, J. M. Darley and D. J. Foss (eds), *Annual Review of Psychology* (pp. 117–139). Palo Alto, CA: Annual Reviews.

Roid, G. H. (2003). *Stanford–Binet Intelligence Scales, Fifth Edition.* Itasca, IL: Riverside Publishing.

Rosenfeld, M. and Rosenfeld, S. (2004). Developing teacher sensitivities to individual learning differences. *Educational Psychology, 24,* 465–486.

Samaritans (1998). *Exploring the Taboo.* Samaritans.

Sattler, J. M. (2001). *Assessment of Children: Cognitive Applications* (4th ed.). San Diego, CA: Jerome M. Sattler, Inc.

Sawyer, R. J., Graham, S. and Harris, K. R. (1992). Direct teaching, strategy instruction, and strategy instruction with explicit self-regulation: Effects on the composition skills and self-efficacy of learning disabled students. *Journal of Educational Psychology, 84,* 340–352.

Scheerens, J., Nanninga, H. and Pellgrum, W. (1989). Generalizability of instructional and school effectiveness indicators across nations; preliminary results of a secondary analysis of the IEA second mathematics study. In B. P. M. Creemers, T. Peters and D. Reynolds (eds). *School effectiveness and school improvement. Proceedings of the second international congress, Rotterdam* (Lisse, Swets and Zeitlinger).

Scottish Executive (2006). *Literature review of educational provision for pupils with additional support needs.* Available at http:www.scotland.gov.uk/Publications/2006/10/19104601/3

Seligman, M. E. P. (1975). Helplessness: On depression, development, and death. San Francisco: Freeman.

Shoda, Y., Mischel, W. and Peake, P. K. (1990). Predicting adolescent cognitive and self-regulatory competencies from preschool delay of gratification. *Developmental Psychology, 26,* 978–986.

Sisk, D. A. (1988). Children at risk: The identification of the gifted among the minority. *Gifted Education International, 5,* 138–141.

Smith, D. D. (1998). *Introduction to Special Education: Teaching in an Age of Challenge* (3rd ed.). Boston: Allyn and Bacon.

SNAP (Special Needs Assessment Profile (2006). *Dyscalculia: School support.* Available at http://www.snapassessment.com/INFdyscal.htm

Snider, V. E. (1990). What we know about learning styles from research in special education. *Educational Leadership, 48*(2), 53.

Snow, R. E., Corno, L. and Jackson, D. (1996). Individual differences in affective and cognitive functions. In D. Berliner and R. Calfee (eds), *Handbook of Educational Psychology* (pp. 243–310). New York: Macmillan.

Spearman, C. (1927). *The Abilities of Man: Their Nature and Measurement.* New York: Macmillan.

Stahl, S. A. (2002). Different strokes for different folks? In L. Abbeduto (ed.), *Taking Sides: Clashing on Controversial Issues in Educational Psychology* (pp. 98–107). Guilford, CT: McGraw-Hill/Duskin.

Stanovich, K. E. (1994). Constructivism in reading. *Journal of Special Education, 28,* 259–274.

Steer, C. R. (2005). Managing attention deficit/hyperactivity disorder: unmet needs and future directions. *Archives of Diseases in Childhood,* 90:i19–i25.

Steinberg, L. (2005). *Adolescence* (7th ed.). New York: McGraw-Hill.

Sternberg, R. J. (1985). *Beyond IQ: A Triarchic Theory of Human Intelligence.* New York: Cambridge University Press.

Sternberg, R. J. (1997). *Successful intelligence.* New York: Plume.

Sternberg, R. J. (2000). *Handbook of Human Intelligence.* New York: Cambridge University Press.

Sternberg, R. J. (2002). Raising the achievement of all students: Teaching for successful intelligence. *Educational Psychology Review, 14,* 383–393.

Sternberg, R. J. (2004). Culture and intelligence. *American Psychologist, 59,* 325–338.

Sternberg, R. J. and Detterman, D. L. (eds). (1986). *What is Intelligence? Contemporary Viewpoints on its Nature and Definition.* Norwood, NJ: Ablex.

Sternberg, R. J. and Wagner, R. K. (1993). The geocentric view of intelligence and job performance is wrong. *Current Directions in Psychological Science, 2,* 1–5.

Sternberg, R. J., Wagner, R. K., Williams, W. M. and Horvath, J. A. (1995). Testing common sense. *American Psychologist, 50,* 912–927.

Stevenson, H. W. and Stigler, J. (1992). *The Learning Gap.* New York: Summit Books.

Stoll, L. Fink, D. and Earl, L. (2004). *It's About Learning [and It's About Time].* London: Routledge Falmer.

Suknanda, L. and Lee, B. (1998). *Streaming, setting and grouping by ability: a review of the literature,* Slough: NFER.

Tait, H. and Entwistle, N. J. (1998). Identifying students at risk through ineffective study strategies. *Higher Education, 31,* 97–116.

Taylor, E. (1998). Clinical foundation of hyperactivity research. *Behavioural Brain Research, 94,* 11–24.

Taylor, E., Sandberg, S., Thorley, G. and Giles, S. (1992). *The Epidemiology of Childhood Hyperactivity.* Maudsley Monograph. London: Oxford University Press.

Taylor, R. L., Richards, S. B. and Brady, M. P. (2005). *Mental Retardation: Historical Perspectives, Current Practices, and Future Directions.* Boston: Allyn and Bacon.

Teaching in England (2006a). Individual Education Plan. Available at www.teachernet.gov.uk/teachinginengland/detail.cfm?id=393-16k

Teaching in England (2006b). Special Educational Needs. Available at http://www.teachernet.gov.uk/teachinginengland/detail.cfm?id=378

Terman, L. M., Baldwin, B. T. and Bronson, E. (1925). Mental and physical traits of a thousand gifted children. In L. M. Terman (ed.), *Genetic Studies of Genius* (Vol. 1). Stanford, CA: Stanford University Press.

Terman, L. M. and Oden, M. H. (1947). The gifted child grows up. In L. M. Terman (ed.), *Genetic Studies of Genius* (Vol. 4). Stanford, CA: Stanford University Press.

Terman, L. M. and Oden, M. H. (1959). The gifted group in mid-life. In L. M. Terman (ed.), *Genetic Studies of Genius* (Vol. 5). Stanford, CA: Stanford University Press.

Thorndike, E. L. (1920). Intelligence and its uses. In Petrides, K. V., Frederickson, N. and Furnham, A. (2004). The role of trait emotional intelligence in academic performance and deviant behaviour at school. *Personality and Individual Differences, 36,* 277–293.

Tobler, N. and Stratton, H. (1997). Effectiveness of school-based drug prevention programs: A metaanalysis of the research. *Journal of Primary Prevention, 18,* 71–128.

Tong, B. (2002). *The Challenge of the Exceptional Child in the Classroom.* Bernetby: Desktop Publications.

Torrance, E. P. (1986). Teaching creative and gifted learners. In M. Wittrock (ed.), *Handbook of Research on Teaching* (3rd ed., pp. 630–647). New York: Macmillan.

van Kraayenoord, C. E., Rice, D., Carroll, A., Fritz, E., Dillon, L. and Hill, A. (2001). *Attention Deficit Hyperactivity Disorder: Impact and Implications for Queensland.* Queensland, Asutralia: Queensland Disability Services, (available online at www.families.qld.gov.au).

Vassilas, C. A. and Morgan, H. G. (1997). Suicide in Avon. *British Journal of Psychiatry, 170,* 453–455.

Vygotsky, L. S. (1997). *Educational Psychology* (R. Silverman, Trans.). Boca Raton, FL: St. Lucie.

Wallace, B. (2000). *Teaching the Very Able Child: Developing a Policy and Adopting Strategies for Provision.* London: NACE/Fulton.

Weinberg, R. A. (1989). Intelligence and IQ. *American Psychologist, 44,* 98–104.

Westberg, K. L., Archambault, F. X., Dodyns, S. M. and Slavin, T. J. (1993). The classroom practices observation study. *Journal of the Education of the Gifted, 16*(2), 120–146.

White, J. (2004). Howard Gardner: the myth of Multiple Intelligences. Lecture at Institute of Education, University of London, 17 November. Available at http://k1.ioe.ac.uk/schools/mst/LTU/phil/HowardGardner_171104.pdf.]

Willcutt, E. G., Pennington, B. F., Boada, R., Ogline, J. S., Tunick, R. A., Chhabidas, N. A. and Olson, R. K. (2001). A comparison of the cognitive deficits in reading disability and attention-deficit/hyperactivity disorder. *Journal of Abnormal Psychology, 110,* 157–172.

Williams, W., Blythe, T., White, N., Li, J., Sternberg, R. and Gardner, H. (1996). *Practical Intelligence in School.* New York: HarperCollins.

Winner, E. (2000). The origins and ends of giftedness. *American Psychologist, 55,* 159–169.

Winner, E. (2003). Musical giftedness. *Bulletin of Psychology and the Arts, 4,* 1, 2–5.

Wintergerst, A. C., DeCapua, A. and Itzen, R. C. (2001). The construct validity of one learning styles instrument. *System, 29*(3), 385–403.

Wood, S. E. and Wood, E. G. (1999). *The World of Psychology* (3rd ed.). Boston: Allyn and Bacon.

World Health Organization International Classification of Diseases (1992). *Hyperkinetic disorders.* F90. Geneva. Available at http://www.mentalhealth.com/icd/p22-ch01.html

Chapter 5

Aboud, F. E. (2003). The formation of in-group favoritism and out-group prejudice in young children: Are they distinct attitudes? *Developmental Psychology, 39,* 48–60.

Alleyne, B. (2002). An idea of community and its discontents: towards a more reflexive sense of belonging in multicultural Britain. *Ethnic and Racial Studies, 25*(4), 607–627.

Anderson, S. M., Klatzky, R. L. and Murray, J. (1990). Traits and social stereotypes: Efficiency differences in social information processing. *Journal of Personality and Social Psychology, 59,* 192–201.

Andriessen, I. and Phalet, K. (2002). Acculturation and school success: a study among minority youth in the Netherlands. *Intercultural Education, 13*(1), 21–36.

Anyon, J. (1980). Social class and the hidden curriculum of work. *Journal of Education, 162,* 67–92.

Archer, L. and Yamashita, H. (2003). Theorising inner-city masculinities: 'race', class, gender and education. *Gender and Education, 15*(2), 115–132.

Armand, F., Lefrançois, P., Baron, A., Gomez, M-C. and Nuckle, S. (2004). Improving reading and writing learning in underprivileged pluri-ethnic settings. *British Journal of Educational Psychology, 74*(3), 437–459.

Aronson, J. (2002). Stereotype threat: Contending and coping with unnerving expectations. In J. Aronson and D. Cordova (eds), *Improving Education: Classic and Contemporary Lessons from Psychology* (pp. 279–301). New York: Academic Press.

Aronson, J., Steele, C. M., Salinas, M. F. and Lustina, M. J. (1999). The effect of stereotype threat on the standardized test performance of college pupils. In E. Aronson (ed.), *Readings About the Social Animal* (8th ed.). New York: Freeman.

Attewell, P. and Battle, J. (1999). Home computers and school performance. *The Information Society, 15*(1), 1–10.

Au, K. H. (1980). Participation structures in a reading lesson with Hawaiian children: Analysis of a culturally appropriate instructional event. *Anthropology and Education Quarterly, 11,* 91–115.

Bailey, J. and Pillard, R. (1991). A genetic study of male sexual orientation, *Arch Gen Psychiatry, 48,* 1089–1096.

Baker, D. (1986). Sex differences in classroom interaction in secondary science. *Journal of Classroom Interaction, 22,* 212–218.

Baker, P. and Eversley, J. (eds) (2000). *Multilingual Capital,* London: Battlebridge.

Banks, J. A. (1993). Multicultural education: Development, dimensions, and challenges. *Phi Delta Kappan, 75,* 22–28.

Banks, J. A. (2002). *An Introduction to Multicultural Education* (3rd ed.). Boston: Allyn and Bacon.

Barber, T. (2002). 'A Special Duty of Care': exploring the narration and experience of teacher caring. *British Journal of Sociology of Education, 23*(3), 383–395.

BBC News (2005). At http://news.bbc.co.uk/1/hi/england/london/4740015.stm accessed 23 March 2006.

Bell, J. F. (2001). Investigating gender differences in the science performance of 16-year-old pupils in the UK. *International Journal of Science Education, 23*(5), 469–486.

Benenson, J. F. (1993). Greater preference among females than males for dyadic interaction in early childhood. *Child Development, 64,* 544–555.

Berk, L. E. (2005). *Infants, Children, and Adolescents* (5th ed.). Boston: Allyn and Bacon.

Berndt, T. J. and Keefe, K. (1995). Friends' influence on adolescents' adjustment to school. *Child Development, 66,* 1312–1329.

Blackledge, A. (1993). 'We can't tell our stories in English': Language, story and culture in the primary school. *Language, Culture and Curriculum, 6*(2), 129–141.

Blackledge, A. (2001a). Literacy, schooling and ideology in a multilingual state. *Curriculum Journal, 12*(3), 291–312.

Blackledge, A. (2001b). The wrong sort of capital? Bangladeshi women and their children's schooling in Birmingham, U.K. *International Journal of Bilingualism, 5*(3), 345–369.

Blair, M. (2002). Effective school leadership: The multi-ethnic context. *British Journal of Sociology of Education, 23*(2), 179–191.

Blatchford, P., Bassett, P., Goldstein, H. and Martin. C. (2003). Are class size differences related to pupils' educational progress and classroom processes? Findings from the Institute of Education class size study of children aged 5–7 years. *British Educational Research Journal, 29*(5), 709–730.

Boaler, J. (1994). When do girls prefer football to fashion? An analysis of female underachievement in relation to 'realistic' mathematics context. *British Educational Research Journal, 20,* 551–564.

Boaler, J. (1997a). *Experiencing School Mathematics – Teaching Styles, Sex and Setting.* Buckingham: Open University Press.

Boaler, J. (1997b). Reclaiming school mathematics: the girls fight back, *Gender and Education, 9,* 285–305.

Boaler, J. (1997c). When even the winners are losers: evaluating the experiences of top set students. *Journal of Curriculum Studies, 29*(2), 165–182.

Boaler, J. (1998). Open and closed mathematics: student experiences and understandings. *Journal for Research in Mathematics Education, 29,* 41–63.

Boaler, J., William, D. and Brown, M. (2000). Students' experiences of ability grouping – disaffection, polarization and the construction of failure. *British Educational Research Journal, 26,* 631–648.

Borman, G. D. and Overman, L. T. (2004). Academic resilience in mathematics among poor and minority pupils. *Elementary School Journal, 104,* 177–195.

Brannon, L. (2002). *Gender: Psychological Perspectives* (3rd ed.). Boston: Allyn and Bacon.

Brice, A. E. (2002). *The Hispanic Child: Speech, Language, Culture and Education.* Boston: Allyn and Bacon.

Brooker, L. (2003). Learning how to learn: parental ethnotheories and young children's preparation for school. *International Journal of Early Years Education, 11*(2), 117–128.

Brown, M. (1953). On a definition of culture. *Psychological Review, 60,* 215.

Bruer, John T. (1999). In search of . . . brain-based education. *Phi Delta Kappan, 80,* 648–657.

Bryan, B. (2004). Jamaican Creole: In the process of becoming. *Ethnic and Racial Studies, 27*(4), 641–659.

Bryant, C. G. A. (1997). Citizenship, national identity and the accommodation of difference: reflections on the German, French, Dutch and British cases. *New Community*, *23*(2), 157–172.

Burgess, R. G. (1983). *Experiencing Comprehensive Education: A Study of Bishop McGregor School.* London: Methuen.

Burtonwood, N. (2002). Political philosophy and the lessons for faith-based schools. *Educational Studies*, *28*(3), 239–252.

Byrnes, J. P. (2003). Factors predictive of mathematics achievement in White, Black, and Hispanic 12th graders. *Journal of Educational Psychology*, *95*, 316–326.

Cairney, T. C. (2000). Beyond the classroom walls: The rediscovery of the family and community as partners in education. *Educational Review*, *52*(2), 163–174.

Campbell, J. and Mandel, F. (1990). Connecting math achievement to parental influences. *Contemporary Educational Psychology*, *15*, 64–74.

Castellano, J. A. and Diaz, E. I. (eds). (2002). Gifted and talented education for culturally and linguistically diverse pupils. *Reaching new horizons.* Boston: Allyn and Bacon.

Chawla, D. (2003). Two journeys. *Qualitative Inquiry*, *9*(5), 785–804.

Chisholm, I. (1998). Six elements for technology integration in multicultural classrooms. *Technology, Pedagogy and Education*, *7*(2), 247–268.

Chitty, C. (1995). Diversity and excellence: a recipe for confusion. *Forum (for Promoting 3–19 Comprehensive Education)*, *37*(3), 92–93.

CILT (2006). The national centre for languages Research Brief RBX3/01 on DfES 2001 http://www.cilt.org.uk/faqs/langspoken.htm downloaded 23 March 2006.

Cokley, K. O. (2002). Ethnicity, gender, and academic self-concept: A preliminary examination of academic dis-identification and implications for psychologists. *Cultural Diversity and Ethnic Minority Psychology*, *8*, 378–388.

Colding, B., Hummelgaard, H. and Husted, L. (2005). How studies of the educational progression of minority children are affecting education policy in Denmark. *Social Policy and Administration*, *39*(6), 684–696.

Cole, M. (2003). Ethnicity, 'status groups' and racialization: A contribution to a debate on national identity in Britain. *Ethnic and Racial Studies*, *26*(5), 962–969.

Colley, H. and Hodkinson, P. (2001). Problems with bridging the gap: The reversal of structure and agency in addressing social exclusion. *Critical Social Policy*, *21*(3), 335–359.

Collier, V. (1987). Age and rate of language acquisition of second language for academic purposes. *TESOL* Quarterly, *21*(4), 617–641.

Connell, R. W. (1996). Teaching the boys: New research on masculinity, and gender strategies for schools. *Teachers College Record*, *98*, 206–235.

Cooper, M., Lloyd-Reason, L. and Wall, S. (2003). Social deprivation and educational underachievement: lessons from London. *Education and Training*, *45*(2), 79–88.

Craig, A. P. (2003). Culture and the individual. *Theory and Psychology*, *13*(5), 629–650.

Crandall, C. S., D'Anello, S., Sakalli, N., Lazarus, E., Wieczorkowska, G. and Feather, N. T. (2001), An attribution-value model of prejudice: Anti-fat attitudes in six nations. *Personality and Social Psychology Bulletin*, *27*(1), 30–37.

Croizet, J.-C., Després, G., Gauzins, M.-E., Huguet, P., Jacques-Philippe Leyens, J.-P. and Méot, A. (2004). Stereotype threat undermines intellectual performance by triggering a disruptive mental load. *Personality and Social Psychology Bulletin*, *30*(6), 721–731.

Cross, B. (2003). 'Watch mi eyes': the predicament of visual and scribal literacy choices, as explored with rural Jamaican adolescent boys. *Compare*, *33*(1), 65–83.

Crozier, G. (2003). School, family and community relationships, with reference to families of Bangladeshi origin in the North East of England. Paper presented at the British Educational Research Association Annual Conference, Heriot-Watt University, Edinburgh, 11–13 September 2003; at the European Conference on Educational Research, University of Hamburg, 17–20 September 2003; and at the European Research Network About Parents and Education, University of Gdansk, Poland, 4 September 2003.

Cullingford, C. (1999). *The Causes of Exclusion: Home, School and the Development of Young Criminals.* London: Kogan Page.

Dandy, J. and Nettelbeck, T. (2002). A cross-cultural study of parents' academic standards and educational aspirations for their children. *Educational Psychology*, *22*(5), 621–627.

Davies, B. and Kerry, T. (1999). Improving student learning through calendar change. *School Leadership and Management*, *19*(3), 359–371.

Deacon, A. (2003). 'Levelling the playing field, activating the players': New Labour and 'the cycle of disadvantage'. *Policy and Politics*, *31*(2), 123–137.

Deaux, K. (1993). Commentary: Sorry, wrong number: A reply to Gentile's call. *Psychological Science, 4,* 125–126.

Delpit, L. (1995). *Other People's Children: Cultural Conflict in the Classroom.* New York: The New York Press.

Delpit, L. (2003). Educators as 'Seed People': Growing a new future. *Educational Researcher, 7*(32), 14–21.

Demie, F. (2001). Ethnic and gender differences in educational achievement and implications for school improvement strategies. *Educational Research*, *43*(1), 91–106.

DfEE – Department For Education and Employment (1999). All Our Futures: creativity, culture and education. Sudbury, Suffolk: DfEE Publications.

DfES – Department for Education and Skills (2005a). Ethnicity and education: the Evidence on Minority Ethnic Pupils. Research Topic Paper, January 2005.

DfES – Department for Education and Skills (2005b). School Workforce in England: Provisional Teacher Sickness Absence in 2004 and Teacher Ethnicity 2005. SFR 20/2005, 26 May 2005.

DfES – Department for Education and Skills (2006). Ethnicity and Education: the Evidence on Minority Ethnic Pupils aged 5–16. Research topic paper 0208-2006DOM-EN.

Dobzhansky, T. (1937). *Genetics and the Origin of Species.*

Doll, B., Zucker, S. and Brehm, K. (2005). *Resilient Classrooms: Creating Healthy Environments for Learning.* New York: Guilford.

Dore, A. (1995). Heard the one about . . . , *Times Educational Supplement*, 31 March, 3–4.

Dostert, S. (2004). Sometimes I feel as if there's a big hole in my head where English used to be! – Attrition of L1 English. *International Journal of Bilingualism, 8*(3), 383–387.

Duncan, G. J. and Brooks-Gunn, J. (2000). Family poverty, welfare reform, and child development. *Child Development, 71*, 188–196.

ECPC (2006). Key Facts http://www.ecpc.org.uk/keyfacts.asp accessed 17 March 2006.

Elrich, M. (1994). The stereotype within. *Educational Leadership, 51*(8), 12–15.

Errasti, M. P. S. (2003). Acquiring writing skills in a third language: The positive effects of bilingualism. *International Journal of Bilingualism, 7*(1), 27–42.

Evans, G. W. (2004). The environment of childhood poverty. *American Psychologist, 59*, 77–92.

Evans, L. and Davies, K. (2000). No sissy boys here: A content analysis of the representation of masculinity in elementary school reading texts. *Sex Roles, 42*, 255–270.

Fagot, B. I. and Hagan, R. (1991). Observations of parent reactions to sex-stereotyped behaviours: Age and sex effects. *Child Development, 62*, 617–628.

Fagot, B. I., Hagan, R., Leinbach, M. D. and Kronsberg, S. (1985). Differential reactions to assertive and communicative acts of toddler boys and girls. *Child Development, 56*, 1499–1505.

Fawcett, A. J., Nicolson, R. I. Moss, H., Nicolson, M. K. and Reason, R. (2001). Effectiveness of reading intervention in junior school. *Educational Psychology, 21*(3), 299–312.

Feiler, A. and Webster, A. (1999). Teacher predictions of young children's literacy success or failure. *Assessment in Education: Principles, Policy and Practice, 6*(3), 341–356.

Fennema, E. and Peterson, P. (1988). Effective teaching for boys and girls: The same or different? In D. Berliner and B. Rosenshine (eds), *Talks to Teachers* (pp. 111–127). New York: Random House.

Fillmore, L. W. and Snow, C. (2000). What teachers need to know about language. [Online]. Available: http://www.cal.org/ericcll/teachers.pdf

Flaherty, J., Veit-Wilson, J. and Dornan, P. (2004). *Poverty: The Facts.* London: CPAG.

Flynn, M. K. (2001). Constructed identities and Iberia. *Ethnic and Racial Studies, 24*(5), 703–718.

Ford, T. E., Ferguson, M. A., Brooks, J. L. and Hagadone, K. M. (2004). Coping sense of humor reduces effects of stereotype threat on women's math performance. *Personality and Social Psychology Bulletin, 30*(1), 643–653.

Forrester, G. (2005). All in a day's work: primary teachers 'performing' and 'caring'. *Gender and Education, 17*(1), 271–287.

Gamoran, A. (1986). Instructional and institutional effects of ability grouping, *Sociology of Education, 59*, 185–198.

Gamoran, A. (1987). The stratification of high school learning opportunities. *Sociology of Education, 60*, 135–155.

Garcia, E. E. (2002). *Student Cultural Diversity: Understanding the Meaning and Meeting the Challenge.* Boston: Houghton Mifflin.

Garcia, R. L. (1991). *Teaching in a Pluralistic Society: Concepts, Models, and Strategies.* New York: HarperCollins.

Garcia-Lopez, R. and Sales-Ciges, A. (1998). Teacher training with a view towards developing favourable attitudes regarding intercultural education and cultural diversity. *European Journal of Intercultural Studies, 9*(1), 63–77.

Gardner, H. (1983). *Frames of Mind: The Theory of Multiple Intelligences.* New York: Basic Books.

Gardner, H. and Hatch, T. (1989). Multiple intelligences go to school: Educational implications of the theory of multiple intelligences. *Educational Researcher, 18*(8), 4–9.

Garnets, L. (2002). Sexual orientations in perspective. *Cultural Diversity and Ethnic Minority Psychology, 8*, 115–129.

Gay, G. (2000). *Culturally Responsive Teaching: Theory, Research, and Practice.* New York: Teachers College Press.

Geary, D. C. (1995). Sexual selection and sex differences in spatial cognition. *Learning and Individual Differences, 7*, 289–303.

Geary, D. C. (1999). Evolution and developmental sex differences. *Current Directions in Psychological Science, 8*, 115–120.

Georgiou, St. (1997). Parental involvement: definition and outcomes. *Social Psychology of Education, 1*(3), 189–209.

Gersten, R. (1996). Literacy instruction for language-minority pupils: The transition years. *Elementary School Journal, 96*, 217–220.

Ghosn, I. K. (2002). Four good reasons to use literature in primary school ELT. *ELT Journal, 56*(2), 172–179.

Ghuman, S. P. A. (2002). South-Asian adolescents in British schools: a review. *Educational Studies, 28*(1), 47–59.

Gilbert, D. (2004). Racial and religious discrimination: the inexorable relationship between schools and the individual. *Intercultural Education, 15*(3), 253–266.

Goldenberg, C. (1996). The education of language-minority pupils: Where are we, and where do we need to go? *Elementary School Journal, 96,* 353–361.

Goodey, J. (2001). The criminalization of British Asian youth: Research from Bradford and Sheffield. *Journal of Youth Studies, 4*(4), 429–450.

Gordon, E. W. (1991). Human diversity and pluralism. *Educational Psychologist, 26,* 99–108.

Grant, N. (1997). Some problems of identity and education: A comparative examination of multicultural education. *Comparative Education, 33*(1), 9–28.

Gregory, E., Williams, A. and Kelly, C. (2001). Home to school and school to home: Syncretised literacies in linguistic minority communities. *Language, Culture and Curriculum, 14*(1), 9–25.

Grimley, L. K. and Bennett, J. (2000). Beginning school ready to learn: An international perspective. *School Psychology International, 21*(3), 322–335.

Guha, S. (2006). Using mathematics strategies in early childhood education as a basis for culturally responsive teaching in India. *International Journal of Early Years Education, 14*(1), 15–34.

Gupta, A. S. and O'Brien-Friederichs, J. (1995). International education in a multicultural environment: an analysis of the impact on individual identity and group relations and a discussion of the important agents. *European Journal of Intercultural Studies, 1995, 6*(1), 25–36.

Gurian, M. and Henley, P. (2001). *Boys and Girls Learn Differently: A Guide for Teachers and Parents.* San Francisco: Jossey-Bass.

Haan, M-de and Elbers, E. (2004). Minority status and culture: local constructions of diversity in a classroom in the Netherlands. *Intercultural Education, 15*(4), 441–453.

Hakuta, K. (1986). *Mirror of Language: The Debate on Bilingualism.* New York: Basic Books.

Hakuta, K. and Gould, L. J. (1987). Synthesis of research on bilingual education. *Educational Leadership, 44*(6), 38–45.

Halmari, H. (2005). 'I'm forgetting both': L1 maintenance and codeswitching in Finnish-English language contact. *International Journal of Bilingualism, 9*(3), 397–433.

Halpern, D. F. (2000). *Sex Differences in Cognitive Abilities.* Mahwah, NJ: Lawrence Erlbaum.

Halpern, D. F. (2004). A cognitive-process taxonomy for sex differences in cognitive abilities. *Current Directions in Psychological Science, 13,* 135–139.

Hargreaves, D. H. (1967). *Social Relations in a Secondary School.* London: Tinling.

Heemskerk, I. (2005). Inclusiveness and ICT in education: A focus on gender, ethnicity and social class. *Journal of Computer Assisted Learning, 21*(1), 1–16.

Heller, M. (1992). The politics of codeswitching and language choice. *Journal of Multilingual and Multicultural Development, 13*(1), 123–142.

Hennink, M., Diamond, I. and Cooper, P. (1999). Young Asian women and relationships: traditional or transitional? *Ethnic and Racial Studies, 22*(5), 867–891.

Hess, R., Chih-Mei, C. and McDevitt, T. M. (1987). Cultural variation in family beliefs about children's performance in mathematics: Comparisons among People's Republic of China, Chinese-American, and Caucasian-American families. *Journal of Educational Psychology, 79,* 179–188.

HM Treasury (1999). Tackling poverty and extending opportunity: The modernisation of Britain's tax and benefit system, no 4. London. HMSO

Hodkinson, A. (2004). The social context of learning and the assimilation of historical time concepts: an indicator of academic performance or an unreliable metric? *Research in Education, 71,* 50–66.

Holliday, A. (1999). Small cultures. *Applied Linguistics, 20*(2), 237–264.

Horgan, D. D. (1995). *Achieving Gender Equity: Strategies for the Classroom.* Boston: Allyn and Bacon.

Hughes, A. and Trudgill, P. (1987). *English Accents and Dialects.* London: Edward Arnold.

Jackson, K. (2002). Making the reality match the mission statement: Infusing diversity in the life of your school. *International Schools Journal, 21*(2), 60–68.

Jackson, S. and Martin, P. Y. (1998). Surviving the care system: Education and resilience. *Journal of Adolescence, 21,* 569–583.

Johnson, A. M., Mercer, C. H., Erens, B. *et al.* (2001). Sexual behaviour in Britain: Partnerships, practices and HIV risk behaviours. *Lancet, 358,* 1835–1842.

Johnson, L. S. (2003). The diversity imperative: Building a culturally responsive school ethos. *Intercultural Education, 14*(1), 17–30.

Jones, S. M. and Dindia, K. (2004). A meta-analytic perspective on sex equity in the classroom. *Review of Educational Research, 74,* 443–471.

Joshee, R. (2003). A framework for understanding diversity in Indian education. *Race, Ethnicity and Education, 6*(3), 283–297.

Keller, J. and Dauenheimer, D. (2003). Stereotype threat in the classroom: Dejection mediates the disrupting threat effect on women's math performance. *Personality and Social Psychology Bulletin, 29*(3), 371–381.

Knapp, M., Turnbull, B. J. and Shields, P. M. (1990). New directions for educating children of poverty. *Educational Leadership, 48*(1), 4–9.

Koda, K. (1998). The role of phonemic awareness in second language reading. *Second Language Research, 14*(2), 194–215.

Ladson-Billings, G. (1990). Like lightning in a bottle: Attempting to capture the pedagogical excellence of successful teachers of Black pupils. *Qualitative Studies in Education, 3,* 335–344.

Ladson-Billings, G. (1992). Culturally relevant teaching: The key to making multicultural education work. In C. A. Grant (ed.), *Research and Multicultural Education* (pp. 106–121). London: Falmer Press.

Ladson-Billings, G. (1995). But that is just good teaching! The case for culturally relevant pedagogy. *Theory Into Practice, 34,* 161–165.

Lamb, S. (1994). Dropping out of school in Australia, *Youth and Society, 26*(2), 194–210.

Lambert, A. J. (1995). Stereotypes and social judgment: The consequences of group variability. *Journal of Personality and Social Psychology, 68,* 388–403.

Leach, C. W., Peng, T. R. and Vockens, J. (2000). Is racism dead? Comparing (expressive) means and (structural equation) models. *British Journal of Social Psychology, 39*(3), 449–465.

Lee, R. M. (2005). Resilience against discrimination: Ethnic identity and other-group orientation as protective factors for Korean Americans. *Journal of Counseling Psychology, 52,* 36–44.

Lemmer, E. M. (2002). *Schools reaching out: comprehensive parent involvement in South African primary schools.* Paper presented at the European Conference on Educational Research, University of Lisbon, 11–14 September 2002.

Lemmer, E. and Squelch, J. (1993). *Multicultural Education. A teacher's manual.* Pretoria: Sigma Press.

Lenga, R. and Short, G. (2002). Jewish primary schools in a multicultural society: responding to diversity? *Journal of Beliefs and Values, 23*(1), 43–54.

Le Roux, J. (2001). Effective schooling is being culturally responsive. *Intercultural Education, 12*(2001), 41–50.

Le Roux, J. (2002). Effective educators are culturally competent communicators. *Intercultural Education, 13*(1), 37–48.

Lewontin, R. C. (1972). 'The apportionment of human diversity', *Evolutionary Biology, 6,* 391–398.

Liben, L. S. and Signorella, M. L. (1993). Gender-schematic processing in children: The role of initial interpretations of stimuli. *Developmental Psychology, 29,* 141–149.

Lidz, C. S. and Macrine, S. L. (2001). An alternative approach to the identification of gifted culturally and linguistically diverse learners: The contribution of dynamic assessment. *School Psychology International, 22*(1), 74–96.

Linn, M. C. and Hyde, J. S. (1989). Gender, mathematics, and science. *Educational Researcher, 18,* 17–27.

Liu, W. M., Ali, S. R., Soleck, G., Hopps, J., Dunston, K. and Pickett, T., Jr. (2004). Using social class in counseling psychology research. *Journal of Counseling Psychology, 51,* 3–18.

Maccoby, E. E. (1998). *The Two Sexes: Growing Up Apart, Coming Together.* Cambridge, MA: Belknap/Harvard University Press.

Macrae, C. N., Milne, A. B. and Bodenhausen, C. V. (1994). Stereotypes as energy-saving devices: A peek inside the cognitive toolbox. *Journal of Personality and Social Psychology, 66,* 37–47.

Macrae, S., Maguire, M. and Milbourne, L. (2003). Social exclusion: exclusion from school. *International Journal of Inclusive Education, 7*(2), 89–101.

Madela, E. N. and Poggenpoel, M. (1993). The experience of a community characterized by violence: implications for nursing. *Journal of Advanced Nursing, 18*(5), 691–700.

Maqsud, M. (1993). Relationships of some personality variable to academic attainment of secondary school pupils. *Educational Psychology, 13*(1), 11–18.

Marlowe, M. (2006). Torey Hayden's teacher lore: A pedagogy of caring. *Journal of Education for Teaching: International Research and Pedagogy, 32*(1), 93–103.

Mason, L. (2003). High school students' beliefs about maths, mathematical problem solving, and their achievement in maths: A cross-sectional study. *Educational Psychology, 23*(1), 73–85.

McLoyd, V. C. (1998). Economic disadvantage and child development. *American Psychologist, 53,* 185–204.

Meo, A. and Parker, A. (2004). Teachers, teaching and educational exclusion: Pupil Referral Units and pedagogic practice. *International Journal of Inclusive Education, 8*(1), 103–120.

Mifflin, M. (1999). Singing the pink blues. Mothers who think. Retrieved 16 March2002, from http://www.salon.com/mwt/feature/1999/12/13/toys/

Mills, M. (2000). Troubling the 'failing boys' discourse. *Discourse, 21*(2), 237–246.

Mills, M. (2003). Shaping the boys' agenda: the backlash blockbusters. *International Journal of Inclusive Education, 7*(1), 57–73.

Morrow, L. M. (1983). Home and school correlates of early interest in literature. *Journal of Educational Research, 76,* 221–230.

Mullis, I. V. S., Martin, M. O., Gonzalez, E. and Kennedy, A. M. (2003), *PIRLS 2001 International report: IEA's study of*

reading literacy achievement in primary schools.
http://timss.bc.edu/pirls2001i/PIRLS2001_Pubs_IR.html
downloaded 23 March 2006.

Myers, D. G. (2005). *Exploring Psychology* (6th ed. in modules). New York: Worth.

Nesdale, D. (2001). Language and the development of children's ethnic prejudice. *Journal of Language and Social Psychology, 20*(1), 90–110.

Nesdale, D., Maass, A., Durkin, K. and Griffiths, K. (2005). Group norms threat and children's racial prejudice. *Child Development, 76*(3).

Newcombe, N. and Baenninger, M. (1990). The role of expectations in spatial test performance: A meta-analysis. *Sex Roles, 16,* 25–37.

Noble, G. and Watkins, M. (2003). So, how did Bourdieu learn to play tennis? Habitus, consciousness and habituation. *Cultural Studies, 17*(3–4), 520–539.

O'Brien, L. T. and Crandall, C. S. (2003). Stereotype threat and arousal: Effects on women's math performance. *Personality and Social Psychology Bulletin, 29*(6), 782–789.

Office for National Statistics (2002). Annual Local Area Labour Force Survey 2001/02.

OECD (2004). Learning for Tomorrow's World. First Results from PISA 2003. http://www.pisa.oecd.org/dataoecd/1/60/34002216.pdf downloaded 23 March 2006.

Okagaki, L. (2001). Triarchic model of minority children's school achievement. *Educational Psychologist, 36,* 9–20.

Ovando, C. J. (1989). Language diversity and education. In J. Banks and C. McGee Banks (eds), *Multicultural Education: Issues and Perspectives* (pp. 208–228). Boston: Allyn and Bacon.

Page, R. N. (1984). *Perspectives and Processes: the negotiation of educational meaning in high school classes for academically unsuccessful students* (unpublished PhD dissertation) University of Wisconsin.

Parry, O. (1997). 'Schooling is Fooling': Why do Jamaican boys underachieve in school? *Gender and Education, 9*(2), 223–232.

Patterson, C. (1995). http://www.apa.org/pi/parent.html downloaded 2/7/2005.

Picaroni, B. (2004). When teaching makes a difference: A case study on language teaching in the final primary year. *Improving Schools, 7*(3).

Pomeroy, E. (1999). The teacher–student relationship in secondary school: Insights from excluded students. *British Journal of Sociology of Education, 20*(4), 465–482.

Preece, P. F. W., Skinner, N. C. and Riall, R. A. H. (1999). The gender gap and discriminating power in the National Curriculum Key Stage three science assessments in England and Wales. *International Journal of Science Education, 21*(9), 979–987.

Prosser, H., Hutchison, D. and Wedge, P. (1979). The prediction of educational failure. *Educational Studies, 5*(1), 73–82.

Rassool, N. (2004). Exploring the construction of social class in educational discourse: the rational order of the nation state versus global uncertainties. *Pedagogy, Culture and Society, 12*(1), 121–139.

Rennie, L. J. and Parker, L. H. (1987). Detecting and accounting for gender differences in mixed-sex and single-sex groupings in science lessons. *Educational Review, 39*(1), 65–73.

Renold, E. (2001). 'Square-girls', femininity and the negotiation of academic success in the primary school. *British Educational Research Journal, 27*(5), 577–588.

Reynolds, M., McCartan, D. and Knipe, D. (2003). Traveller culture and lifestyle as factors influencing children's integration into mainstream secondary schools in West Belfast. *International Journal of Inclusive Education, 7*(4), 403–414.

Rivière, D. (2005). Identities and intersectionalities: performance, power and the possibilities for multicultural education. *Research in Drama Education, 10*(3), 341–354.

Robinson, P. (2001). Individual differences, cognitive abilities, aptitude complexes and learning conditions in second language acquisition. *Second Language Research, 17*(4), 368–392.

Rop, C. (1997/1998). Breaking the gender barrier in the physical sciences. *Educational Leadership, 55*(4), 58–60.

Sadker, M. and Sadker, D. (1984). *Failing at Fairness: How America's Schools Cheat Girls.* New York: Scribner.

Sadker, M., Sadker, D. and Klein, S. (1991). The issue of gender in elementary and secondary education. *Review of Research in Education, 17,* 269–334.

Salisbury, J., Rees, G. and Gorard, S. (1999). Accounting for the differential attainment of boys and girls at school. *School Leadership and Management, 19*(4), 403–426.

Savage, Mike (2003). A new class paradigm? *British Journal of Sociology of Education, 24*(4), 535–541.

Savickiené, I. and Kalédaité, V. (2005). Cultural and linguistic diversity of the Baltic States in a new Europe. *Journal of Multilingual and Multicultural Development, 26*(5), 442–452.

Schleiner, A-M. (2001). Does Lara Croft wear fake polygons? Gender and gender-role subversion in computer adventure games. *Leonardo, 34*(3), 221–226.

Schwartz, F. (1981). Supporting or subverting learning: Peer groups patterns in four tracked schools, *Anthropology and Education Quarterly, 12,* 99–121.

Segall, M. H. (1984). More than we need to know about culture, but are afraid to ask. *Journal of Cross-Cultural Psychology, 15*(2), 153–162.

Sewell, T. (1997). *Black Masculinity and Schooling: How black boys survive modern schooling*, Stoke-on-Trent: Trentham Books.

Sewell, T. (1998). Loose canons: exploding the myth of the 'black macho' lad. In D. Epstein, J. Elwood, V. Hey and J. Maw (eds) *Failing Boys Issues in Gender and Achievement*. Buckingham: Open University Press.

She, H. S. (2000). The interplay of a biology teacher's beliefs, teaching practices and gender-based student-teacher classroom interaction. *Educational Research*, *42*(1), 100–111.

Sheets, R. H. (2005). *Diversity Pedagogy: Examining the Role of Culture in the Teaching-Learning Process*. Boston: Allyn and Bacon.

Skelton, C. and Hall, E. (2001). The development of gender roles in young children. Department of Education, University of Newcastle for The Equal Opportunities Commission at http://www.eoc.org.uk/PDF/gender_roles.pdf downloaded 23 March 2006.

Slater, P. J. B. (2001). There's CULTURE and 'Culture'. *Behavioral and Brain Sciences*, *24*(2), 356–357.

Smith, Z. (2004). *The Observer,* 12 September P. 18. London: Guardian Newspapers Limited.

Social Exclusion Unit (1998). *Truancy and School Exclusion*, Cm.3957. London: HMSO.

Solomon, Y., Warin, J. and Lewis, C. (2002). Helping with homework? Homework as a site of tension for parents and teenagers. *British Educational Research Journal*, *28*(4), 603–622.

Sommer, K. L. and Baumeister, R. F. (2002). Self-evaluation, persistence, and performance following implicit rejection: The role of trait self-esteem. *Personality and Social Psychology Bulletin*, *28*(7), 926–938.

Song, I. and Hattie, J. (1984). Home environment, self-concept and academic achievement: A causal modelling approach. *Journal of Educational Psychology, 76,* 1269–1281.

Soori, H. and Bhopal, R. S. (2002). Parental permission for children's independent outdoor activities. *European Journal of Public Health*, *12*(2), 104–109.

Sotillo, S. M. (2002). Finding our voices, finding ourselves: Becoming bilingual and bicultural. In G. S. Boutte (ed.), *Resounding Voices: School Experiences of People from Diverse Ethnic Backgrounds* (pp. 275–307). Boston: Allyn and Bacon.

Sowden, C. (2003). Understanding academic competence in overseas students in the UK. *ELT Journal*, *57*(4), 377–385.

Spencer, M. B., Noll, E., Stoltzfus, J. and Harpalani, V. (2001). Identity and school adjustment: Questioning the 'acting white' assumption. *Educational Psychologist, 36*(1), 21–30.

Stainthorp, R. and Hughes, D. (2000). Parents, teachers and able readers in Key Stage 1: Conversations with parents. *Reading (now called Literacy)*, *34*(3), 124–129.

Starkey, H. and Osler, A. (2001). Language learning and antiracism: Some pedagogical challenges. *Curriculum Journal*, *12*(3), 313–345.

Stevenson, D. and Baker, D. (1987). The family-school relation and the child's school performance. *Child Development, 58,* 1348–1357.

Stone, J. (2003). Self-consistency for low self-esteem in dissonance processes: The role of self-standards. *Personality and Social Psychology Bulletin*, *29*(7), 846–858.

Stuart, D. and Volk, D. (2002). Collaboration in a culturally responsive literacy pedagogy: Educating teachers and Latino children. *Reading (now called Literacy)*, *36*(3), 127–134.

Stumpf, H. (1995). Gender differences on test of cognitive abilities: Experimental design issues and empirical results. *Learning and Individual Differences, 7,* 275–288.

Suzuki, B. H. (1983). The education of Asian and Pacific Americans: An introductory overview. In D. Nakanishi and M. Hirano-Nakanishi (eds), *The Education of Asian and Pacific Americans: Historical Perspectives and Prescriptions for the Future* (pp. 1–14). Phoenix, AZ: Oryx Press.

Svoboda, J. S. (2001). Review of *Boys and girls learn differently.* The Men's Resource Network. Retrieved 3 May, 2007 from http://mensightmagazine.com/reviews/Svoboda/boysandgirls.htm

Tharp, R. G. (1989). Psychocultural variables and constants: Effects on teaching and learning in schools. *American Psychologist, 44,* 349–359.

Timperley, H. S. and Phillips, G. (2003). Changing and sustaining teachers' expectations through professional development in literacy. *Teaching and Teacher Education*, *19*(6), 627–641.

Tsouroufli, M. (2002). Gender and teachers' classroom practice in a secondary school in Greece. *Gender and Education*, *14*(2), 135–147.

Tubbs, C. Y., Roy, K. M. and Burton, L. M. (2005). Family ties: Constructing family time in low-income families. *Family Process*, *44*(1), 77–91.

TUC (2002). Black and Excluded, 12 April. London: Trades Union Council.

Uline, C. L. and Johnson, J. F. (2005). Closing the achievement gap: What will it take? Special Issue of *Theory Into Practice, 44*(1), Winter.

Van-Galen, J. A. (2004). Seeing classes: Toward a broadened research agenda for critical qualitative researchers. *International Journal of Qualitative Studies in Education, 17*(5), 663–684.

Vardill, R. and Calvert, S. (2000). Gender imbalance in referrals to an educational psychology service. *Educational Psychology in Practice, 16*(2), 213–223.

Vasquez, J. A. (1990). Teaching to the distinctive traits of minority pupils. *The Clearing House, 63,* 299–304.

Venkatakrishnan, H. and Dylan, W. (2003). Tracking and mixed-ability grouping in secondary school mathematics classrooms: A case study. *British Educational Research Journal, 29*(2), 189–204.

Vitaro, F., Dobkin, P. L., Carbonneau, R. and Tremblay, R. E. (1996). Personal and familial characteristics of resilient sons of male alcoholics. *Addiction, 91*(8), 1161–1178.

Vitaro, F., Larocque, D., Janosz, M. and Tremblay, R. E. (2001). Negative social experiences and dropping out of school. *Educational Psychology, 21*(4), 401–415.

Vonk, R. (2002). Effects of stereotypes on attitude inference: Outgroups are black and white, ingroups are shaded. *British Journal of Social Psychology, 41*(1), 157–167.

Walker, R. (1998). The Americanisation of British welfare: A case-study of policy transfer, *Focus, 19*(3), 32–40.

Ward, L. M. (2004). Wading through the stereotypes: Positive and negative associations between media use and Black adolescents' conception of self. *Developmental Psychology, 40,* 284–294.

Warrington, M. and Younger, M. (2000). The other side of the gender gap. *Gender and Education, 12*(4), 493–508.

Webster, A. and Feiler, A. (1999). Teacher predictions of young children's literacy success or failure. *Assessment in Education, 6*(3), 341–356.

Whitelaw, S. Milosevic, L. and Daniels, S. (2000). Gender, behaviour and achievement: A preliminary study of pupil perceptions and attitudes. *Gender and Education, 12*(1), 87–113.

Woolfolk Hoy, A., Demerath, P. and Pape, S. (2002). Teaching adolescents: Engaging developing selves. In T. Urdan and F. Pajares (eds), *Adolescence and Education* (pp. 119–169). Vol. I. Greenwich, CT: Information Age Publishing.

Wright, S. C. and Taylor, D. M. (1995). Identity and the language of the classroom: Investigating the impact of heritage versus second language instruction on personal and collective self-esteem. *Journal of Educational Psychology, 87,* 241–252.

Yarhouse, M. A. (2001). Sexual identity development: The influence of valuative frameworks on identity synthesis. *Psychotherapy, 38*(3), 331–341.

Yee, A. H. (1992). Asians as stereotypes and pupils: Misperceptions that persist. *Educational Psychology Review, 4,* 95–132.

Zsolnai, A. (2002). Relationship between children's social competence, learning motivation and school achievement. *Educational Psychology, 22*(3), 317–329.

Chapter 6

Alber, S. R. and Heward, W. L. (1997). Recruit it or lose it! Training students to recruit positive teacher attention. *Intervention in School and Clinic, 32,* 275–282.

Alber, S. R. and Heward, W. L. (2000). Teaching students to recruit positive attention: A review and recommendations. *Journal of Behavioral Education, 10,* 177–204.

Alberto, P. and Troutman, A. C. (2006). *Applied Behavior Analysis for Teachers: Influencing Student Performance* (7th ed.). Saddle River, NJ: Prentice-Hall/Merrill.

Baccus, J. R., Baldwin, M. W. and Packer, D. J. (2004). Increasing Implicit Self-Esteem Through Classical Conditioning. *Psychological Science, 15*(7), 498–502.

Bandura, A. (1965). Influence of models' reinforcement contingencies on the acquisition of imitative responses. *Journal of Personality and Social Psychology, 1,* 589–595.

Bandura, A. (1977). *Social Learning Theory.* Englewood Cliffs, NJ: Prentice-Hall.

Bandura, A. (1986). *Social Foundations of Thought and Action.* Englewood Cliffs, NJ: Prentice-Hall.

Bandura, A. (1997). *Self-Efficacy: The exercise of control.* New York: Freeman.

Barnhill, G. P. (2005). Functional behavioral assessment in schools. *Intervention in School and Clinic, 40,* 131–143.

Brophy, J. E. (1981). Teacher praise: A functional analysis. *Review of Educational Research, 51,* 5–21.

Cameron, J. and Pierce, W. D. (1994). Reinforcement, reward, and intrinsic motivation: A meta-analysis. *Review of Educational Research, 64,* 363–423.

Capstick, J. (2005). Pupil and staff perceptions of rewards at a pupil referral unit. *Emotional and Behavioural Difficulties, 10*(2), 95–117.

Chance, P. (1992). The rewards of learning. *Phi Delta Kappan, 73,* 200–207.

Chance, P. (1993). Sticking up for rewards. *Phi Delta Kappan, 74,* 787–790.

Cowley, S. (2003a). *Sue Cowley's Teaching Clinic.* London: Continuum.

Cowley, S. (2003b). *How to Survive Your First Year in Teaching* (2nd ed.). London: Continuum.

Cowley, S. (2006). *Getting the Buggers to Behave* (3rd ed.). London: Continuum.

Crone, D. A. and Horner, R. H. (2003). *Building Positive Behavior Support Systems in Schools: Functional Behavioral Assessment.* New York: The Guilford Press.

Deci, E. L. (1975). *Intrinsic Motivation.* New York: Plenum.

Deci, E. L. and Ryan, R. M. (1985). *Intrinsic Motivation and Self-determination in Human Behavior.* New York: Plenum.

Deci, E. L., Koestner, R. and Ryan, R. M. (1999). A meta-analytic review of experiments examining the effects of extrinsic rewards on intrinsic motivation. *Psychological Bulletin, 125,* 627–668.

Eisenberg, R., Pierce, W. D. and Cameron, J. (1999). Effects of rewards on intrinsic motivation – negative, neutral, and positive: Comment on Deci, Koestner, and Ryan (1999). *Psychological Bulletin, 125,* 677–691.

Embry, D. D. (2002). The good behavior game: A best practice candidate as a universal behavior vaccine. *Clinical Child and Family Psychology Review, 5,* 273–297.

Epanchin, B. C., Townsend, B. and Stoddard, K. (1994). *Constructive Classroom Management: Strategies for Creating Positive Learning Environments.* Pacific Grove, CA: Brooks/Cole.

Fulk, C. L. and Smith, P. J. (1995). Students' perceptions of teachers' instructional and management adaptations for students with learning or behavior problems. *Elementary School Journal, 95,* 409–419.

Gibbs, J. W. and Luyben, P. D. (1985). Treatment of self-injurious behavior: Contingent versus noncontingent positive practice overcorrection. *Behavior Modification, 9,* 3–21.

Harris, K. R. (1990). Developing self-regulated learners: The role of private speech and self-instruction. *Educational Psychologist, 25,* 35–50.

Harris, K. R., Graham, S. and Pressley, M. (1991). Cognitive-behavioral approaches in reading and written language: Developing self-regulated learners. In N. N. Singh and I. L. Beale (eds), *Learning Disabilities: Nature, Theory, and Treatment* (pp. 415–451). New York: Springer-Verlag.

Harris, K. R. and Pressley, M. (1991). The nature of cognitive strategy instruction: Interactive strategy construction. *Exceptional Children, 57,* 392–404.

Hayes, S. C., Rosenfarb, I., Wulfert, E., Munt, E. D., Korn, Z. and Zettle, R. D. (1985). Self-reinforcement effects: An artifact of social standard setting? *Journal of Applied Behavior Analysis, 18,* 201–214.

Hill, W. F. (2002). *Learning: A Survey of Psychological Interpretations* (7th ed.). Boston: Allyn and Bacon.

Houghton, S., Wheldall, K., Jukes, R. and Sharpe, A. (1990). The effects of limited private reprimands and increased private praise on classroom behaviour in four British secondary school classes. *British Journal of Educational Psychology, 60,* 255–265.

Kaplan, J. S. (1991). *Beyond Behavior Modification* (2nd ed.). Austin, TX: Pro-Ed.

Kazdin, A. E. (1984). *Behavior Modification in Applied Settings.* Homewood, IL: Dorsey Press.

Kazdin, A. E. (2001). *Behavior Modification in Applied Settings* (6th ed.). Belmont, CA: Wadsworth.

Kohn, A. (1993). Rewards versus learning: A response to Paul Chance. *Phi Delta Kappan, 74,* 783–787.

Kohn, A. (1996). By all available means: Cameron and Pierce's defense of extrinsic motivators. *Review of Educational Research, 66,* 1–4.

Kounin, J. S. (1970). *Discipline and Group Management in Classrooms.* New York: Holt, Rinehart and Winston.

Landrum, T. J. and Kauffman, J. M. (2006). Behavioral approaches to classroom management. In C. M. Evertson and C. S. Weinstein (eds), *Handbook of Classroom Management: Research, Practice, and Contemporary Issues.* Mahwah, NJ: Erlbaum.

Lane, K., Falk, K. and Wehby, J. (2006). Classroom management in special education classrooms and resource rooms. In C. M. Evertson and C. S. Weinstein (eds), *Handbook of Classroom Management: Research, Practice, and Contemporary Issues.* Mahwah, NJ: Erlbaum.

Lavond, D., Kim, J. and Thompson, R. (1993). Mammalian brain substrates of aversive classical conditioning. *Annual Review of Psychology, 44,* 317–342.

Lepper, M. R. and Greene, D. (1978). *The Hidden Costs of Rewards: New Perspectives on the Psychology of Human motivation.* Hillsdale, NJ: Erlbaum.

Lepper, M. R., Keavney, M. and Drake, M. (1996). Intrinsic motivation and extrinsic reward: A commentary on Cameron and Pierce's meta-analysis. *Review of Educational Research, 66,* 5–32.

Lewis, T. J., Sugai, G. and Colvin, G. (1998). Reducing problem behavior through a school-wide system of effective behavioral support: Investigation of a school-wide social skills training program and contextual interventions. *School Psychology Review, 27,* 446–459.

Locke, E. A. and Latham, G. P. (1990). *A Theory of Goal Setting and Task Performance.* Englewood Cliffs, NJ: Prentice-Hall.

Locke, E. A. and Latham, G. P. (2002). Building a practically useful theory of goal setting and task motivation: A 35-year odyssey. *American Psychologist, 57,* 705–717.

Maag, J. W. and Kemp, S. E. (2003). Behavioral intent of power and affiliation: Implications for functional analysis. *Remedial and Special Education, 24,* 57–64.

Mace, F. C., Belfiore, P. J. and Hutchinson, J. M. (2001). Operant theory and research on self-regulation. In B. Zimmerman and D. Schunk (eds), *Self-regulated Learning and Academic Achievement: Theoretical Perspectives* (2nd ed.). Mahwah, NJ: Erlbaum.

Manning, B. H. and Payne, B. D. (1996). *Self-talk for Teachers and Students: Metacognitive Strategies for Personal and Classroom Use.* Boston: Allyn and Bacon.

Mayhew, J. (1997). *Psychological Change: A Practical Introduction.* London: Macmillan.

McGoey, K. E. and DuPaul, G. J. (2000). Token reinforcement and response cost procedures: Reducing disruptive behavior of children with attention-deficit/hyperactivity disorder. *School Psychology Quarterly, 15*, 330–343.

McKenzie, T. L. and Rushall, B. S. (1974). Effects of self-recording on attendance and performance in a competitive swimming training environment. *Journal of Applied Behavior Analysis, 7*, 199–206.

Meichenbaum, D. (1977). *Cognitive Behavior Modification: An Integrative Approach.* New York: Plenum.

Menzies, R. (1937). Conditioned vasomotor responses in human subjects. *Journal of Psychology 4*, 75–120.

Miller, R. B. (1962). Analysis and specification of behavior for training. In R. Glaser (ed.), *Training Research and Education: Science Edition.* New York: Wiley.

Mueller, C. M. and Dweck, C. S. (1998). Praise for intelligence can undermine children's motivation and performance. *Journal of Personality and Social Psychology, 75*, 33–52.

Murdock, S. G., O'Neill, R. E. and Cunningham, E. (2005). A comparison of results and acceptability of functional behavioral assessment procedures with a group of middle school students with emotional/behavioral disorders (E/BD). *Journal of Behavioral Education, 14*, 5–18.

O'Leary, S. (1995). Parental discipline mistakes. *Current Directions in Psychological Science, 4*, 11–13.

Ollendick, T. H., Dailey, D. and Shapiro, E. S. (1983). Vicarious reinforcement: Expected and unexpected effects. *Journal of Applied Behavior Analysis, 16*, 485–491.

Papatheodorou, T. (2000). Management approaches employed by teachers to deal with children's behaviour problems in nursery classes. *School Psychology International, 21*(4), 415–440.

Parlor, I. P. (1927). *Conditioned Reflexes: An Investigation of the Physiological Activity of the Cerebral Cortex.* Translated and edited by G. V. Anrep. London: Oxford University Press. Available at http://psychclassics.yorku.ca/Parlor/

Pfiffner, L. J. and O'Leary, S. G. (1987). The efficacy of all positive management as a function of the prior use of negative consequences. *Journal of Applied Behavior Analysis, 20*, 265–271.

Pintrich, P. R. and Schunk, D. H. (2002). *Motivation in Education: Theory, Research, and Applications* (2nd ed.). Upper Saddle River, NJ: Merrill/Prentice-Hall.

Premack, D. (1965). Reinforcement theory. In D. Levine (ed.), *Nebraska Symposium on Motivation, 13*, 123–180. Lincoln, NE: University of Nebraska Press.

Rachlin, H. (1991). *Introduction to Modern Behaviorism* (3rd ed.). New York: W. H. Freeman.

Rachlin, H. (2000). *The Science of Self-control.* Cambridge, MA: Harvard University Press.

Reeve, J. (1996). *Motivating Others: Nurturing Inner Motivational Resources.* Boston: Allyn and Bacon.

Rogers, B. (2000). *Behaviour Management: A Whole School Approach.* London: Chapman.

Rogers, B. (ed.) (2002). *Teacher Leadership and Behaviour Management.* London: Paul Chapman.

Rogers, B. (ed.) (2004). *How to Manage Children's Challenging Behaviour.* London: Paul Chapman.

Rogers, B. (2006). *Classroom Behaviour* (2nd ed.). London: Paul Chapman.

Ryan, R. M. and Deci, E. L. (1996). When paradigms clash: Comments on Cameron and Pierce's claim that rewards do not undermine intrinsic motivation. *Review of Educational Research, 66*, 33–38.

Schunk, D. H. (2004). *Learning Theories: An Educational Perspective* (4th ed.). Columbus, OH: Merrill/Prentice-Hall.

Schunk, D. H. and Hanson, A. R. (1985). Peer models: Influence on children's self-efficacy and achievement. *Journal of Educational Psychology, 77*, 313–322.

Schwartz, B., Wasserman, E. A. and Robbins, S. J. (2002). *Psychology of Learning and Behavior* (5th ed.). New York: W. W. Norton.

Siasoco, R. V. (2006). *Lolita's bad role models.* Available at http://www.feministezine.com/feminist/modern/Lolitas-Bad-RoleModels.html

Skinner, B. F. (1950). Are theories of learning necessary? *Psychological Review, 57*, 193–216.

Skinner, B. F. (1953). *Science and Human Behavior.* New York: Macmillan.

Skinner, B. F. (1989). The origins of cognitive thought. *American Psychologist, 44*, 13–18.

Slider, N., Noell, G. and Williams, K. (2006). Providing practising teachers classroom management professional development in a brief self-study format. *Journal of Behavioural Education, 15*(4), 215–228.

Soodak, L. C. and McCarthy, M. R. (2006). Classroom management in inclusive settings. In C. M. Evertson and C. S. Weinstein (eds), *Handbook of Classroom Management: Research, Practice, and Contemporary Issues.* Mahwah, NJ: Erlbaum.

Sullivan, M. A. and O'Leary, S. G. (1990). Maintenance following reward and cost token programs. *Behavior Therapy, 21*, 139–149.

Sweeney, W. J., Salva, E., Cooper, J. O. and Talbert-Johnson, C. (1993). Using self-evaluation to improve difficult to read handwriting for secondary students. *Journal of Behavioral Education, 3*, 427–443.

Theodore, L. A., Bray, M. A., Kehle, T. J. and Jenson, W. R. (2001). Randomization of group contingencies and reinforcers for reduce classroom disruptive behavior. *Journal of School Psychology, 39,* 267–277.

Umbreit, J. (1995). Functional analysis of disruptive behavior in an inclusive classroom. *Journal of Early Intervention, 20*(1), 18–29.

Van Houten, R. and Doleys, D. M. (1983). Are social reprimands effective? In S. Axelrod and J. Apsche (eds), *The Effects of Punishment on Human Behavior.* San Diego: Academic Press.

Walker, J. E., Shea, T. M. and Bauer, A. M. (2004). *Behavior Management: A Practical Approach for Educators.* Upper Saddle River, NJ: Merrill/Prentice Hall.

Wasserman, E. A. and Miller, R. R. (1997). What's elementary about associative learning. In J. T. Spence, J. M. Darley and D. J. Foss (eds), *Annual Review of Psychology* (pp. 573–607). Palo Alto, CA: Annual Reviews.

Wheldall, K. and Merrett, F. (1992). Effective classroom behaviour management: positive teaching. In K. Wheldall (ed.), *Discipline in Schools. Psychological Perspectives on the Elton Report.* London: Routledge.

Wilson, C. W. and Hopkins, B. L. (1973). The effects of contingent music on the intensity of noise in junior high home economics classes. *Journal of Applied Behavior Analysis, 6,* 269–275.

Winett, R. A. and Winkler, R. C. (1972). Current behavior modification in the classroom: Be still, be quiet, be docile. *Journal of Applied Behavior Analysis, 15,* 499–504.

Woodruff-Pak, D. and Steinmetz, J. (eds) (2000). *Eyeblink Classical Conditioning: Human.* Boston: Kluwer Academic.

Zimmerman, B. J. and Schunk, D. H. (eds) (2003). *Educational Psychology: A Century of Contributions.* A Project of Division 15 (Educational Psychology) of the American Psychological Association. Mahwah, NJ: Erlbaum.

Chapter 7

Alexander, P. A. (1992). Domain knowledge: Evolving themes and emerging concerns. *Educational Psychologist, 27,* 33–51.

Alexander, P. A. (1996). The past, present, and future of knowledge research: A reexamination of the role of knowledge in learning and instruction. *Educational Psychologist, 31,* 89–92.

Alexander, P. A. (1997). Mapping the multidimensional nature of domain learning: The interplay of cognitive, motivational, and strategic forces. *Advances in Motivation and Achievement, 10,* 213–250.

Anderson, J. R., Reder, L. M. and Simon, H. A. (1996). Situated learning and education. *Educational Researcher, 25,* 5–11.

Anderson, J. R. (1995a). *Cognitive Psychology and its Implications* (4th ed.). New York: Freeman.

Anderson, J. R. (1995b). *Learning and Memory.* New York: John Wiley and Sons.

Anderson, J. R. (2005). *Cognitive Psychology and its Implications* (6th ed.). New York: Worth.

Anderson, J. R., Reder, L. M. and Simon, H. A. (1996). Situated learning and education. *Educational Researcher, 25,* 5–11.

Ashcraft, M. H. (2002). *Cognition* (3rd ed.). Upper Saddle River, NJ: Prentice-Hall.

Ashcraft, M. H. (2006). *Cognition* (4th ed.). Upper Saddle River, NJ: Prentice-Hall.

Atkinson, R. C. and Shiffrin, R. M. (1968). Human memory: A proposed system and its control processes. In K. Spence and J. Spence (eds), *The Psychology of Learning and Motivation* (Vol. 2, pp. 89–195). New York: Academic Press.

Atkinson, R. K., Levin, J. R., Kiewra, K. A., Meyers, T., Atkinson, L. A., Renandya, W. A. and Hwang, Y. (1999). Matrix and mnemonic text-processing adjuncts: Comparing and combining their components. *Journal of Educational Psychology, 91,* 242–257.

Ausubel, D. P. (1963). *The Psychology of Meaningful Verbal Learning.* New York: Grune and Stratton.

Baddeley, A. D. (1986). *Working Memory.* Oxford, UK: Clarendon Books.

Baddeley, A. D. (2001). Is working memory still working? *American Psychologist, 56,* 851–864.

Bargh, J. A. and Chartrand, T. L. (1999). The unbearable automaticity of being. *American Psychologist, 54,* 462–479.

Black, P. and Wiliam, D. (1998). Assessment and classroom learning. *Assessment in Education, 5*(1), 7–71.

Black, P. and Wiliam, D. (2002). *Inside the Black Box: Raising Standards through Classroom Assessment.* London: NFER Nelson.

Bransford, J. D., Brown, A. L. and Cocking, R. R. (2000). *How People Learn: Brain, Mind, Experience, and School.* Washington, DC: National Academy Press.

Brown, A. (1987). Metacognition, executive control, self-regulation, and other more mysterious mechanisms. In F. Weinert and R. Kluwe (eds), *Metacognition, Motivation, and Understanding* (pp. 65–116). Hillside, NJ: Lawrence Erlbaum.

Brown, A. L., Bransford, J., Ferrara, R. and Campione, J. (1983). Learning, remembering, and understanding. In P. Mussen (ed.), *Handbook of Child Psychology* (Vol. 3, pp. 515–629). New York: Wiley.

Bruner, J. S., Goodnow, J. J. and Austin, G. A. (1956). *A Study of Thinking.* New York: Wiley.

Bruning, R. H., Schraw, G. J., Norby, M. M. and Ronning, R. R. (2004). *Cognitive Psychology and Instruction* (4th ed.). Columbus, OH: Merrill.

Carney, R. N. and Levin, J. R. (2000). Mnemonic instruction, with a focus on transfer. *Journal of Educational Psychology, 92,* 783–790.

Carney, R. N. and Levin, J. R. (2002). Pictorial illustrations *still* improve students' learning from text. *Educational Psychology Review, 14,* 5–26.

Clark, J. M. and Paivio, A. (1991). Dual coding theory and education. *Educational Psychology Review, 3,* 149–210.

Collins, A., Brown, J. S. and Newman, S. E. (1989). Cognitive apprenticeship: Teaching the crafts of reading, writing, and mathematics. In L. B. Resnick (ed.), *Knowing, Learning, and Instruction: Essays in Honor of Robert Galser* (pp. 453–494). Hillsdale, NJ: Lawrence Erlbaum.

Craik, F. I. M. and Lockhart, R. S. (1972). Levels of processing: A framework for memory research. *Journal of Verbal Learning and Verbal Behavior, 11,* 671–684.

Danielsdottir, G., Sigurgeirsdottir, S., Einarsdottir, H. R. and Haraldsson, E. (1993). Interrogative suggestibility in children and its relationship with memory and vocabulary. *Personality and Individual Differences, 14,* 499–502.

Driscoll, M. P. (2005). *Psychology of Learning for Instruction* (3rd ed.). Boston: Allyn and Bacon.

Ericsson, K. A. and Kintsch, W. (1994). *Long-term Working Memory.* Boulder, Colorado: Institute of Cognitive Science, University of Colorado.

Farnham-Diggory, S. (1994). Paradigms of knowledge and instruction. *Review of Educational Research, 64,* 463–477.

Fitts, P. M. and Posner, M. I. (1967). *Human Performance.* Belmont, CA: Brooks Cole.

Gagne, E. D. (1985). *The Cognitive Psychology of School Learning.* Boston: Little, Brown.

Gagne, E. D., Yekovich, C. W. and Yekovich, F. R. (1993). *The Cognitive Psychology of School Learning* (2nd ed.). New York: HarperCollins.

Garner, R. (1990). When children and adults do not use learning strategies: Toward a theory of settings. *Review of Educational Psychology, 60,* 517–530.

Gathercole, S. E., Pickering, S. J., Ambridge, B. and Wearing, H. (2004). The structure of working memory from 4 to 15 years of age. *Developmental Psychology, 40,* 177–190.

Gentner, D. (1975). Evidence for the psychological reality of semantic components: The verbs of possession. In D. Norman and D. Rumelhart (eds), *Explorations in Cognition* (pp. 211–246). San Francisco: Freeman.

Gray, P. (2002). *Psychology* (4th ed.). New York: Worth.

Greeno, J. G., Collins, A. M. and Resnick, L. B. (1996). Cognition and learning. In D. Berliner and R. Calfee (eds), *Handbook of Educational Psychology* (pp. 15–46). New York: Macmillan.

Hall, J. W. (1991). More on the utility of the keyword method. *Journal of Educational Psychology, 83,* 171–172.

Herbert, D. and Burt, J. (2004). What do students remember? Episodic memory and the development of schematization. *Applied Cognitive Psychology, 18*(2), 77–88.

Hernshaw, L. S. (1987). *The Shaping of Modern Psychology: A Historical Introduction from Dawn to Present Day.* London: Routledge and Kegan Paul.

Hunt, R. R. and Ellis, H. C. (1999). *Fundamentals of Cognitive Psychology* (6th ed.). New York: McGraw-Hill College.

Iran-Nejad, A. (1990). Active and dynamic self-regulation of learning processes. *Review of Educational Research, 60,* 573–602.

James, W. (1912). *Talks to Teachers on Psychology: And to Students on Some of Life's Ideals.* New York: Holt.

Jones, M. S., Levin, M. E., Levin, J. R. and Beitzel, B. D. (2000). Can vocabulary-learning strategies and pair-learning formats be profitably combined? *Journal of Educational Psychology, 92,* 256–262.

Kintsch, W. (1998). *Comprehension: A Paradigm for Cognition.* New York: Cambridge University Press.

Kirk, S. A., Gallagher, J. J., Anastasiow, N. J. and Coleman, M. R. (2006). *Educating Exceptional Children* (11th ed.). Boston: Houghton Mifflin.

Koriat, A., Goldsmith, M. and Pansky, A. (2000). Toward a psychology of memory accuracy. In S. Fiske (ed.), *Annual Review of Psychology* (pp. 481–537). Palo Alto, CA: Annual Reviews.

Kosslyn, S. M. and Koenig, O. (1992). *Wet Mind: The New Cognitive Neuroscience.* New York: Free Press.

Lachter, J., Forster, K. I. and Ruthruff, K. I. (2004). Forty-five years after Broadbent (1958): Still no identification without attention. *Psychological Review, 111,* 880–913.

Levin, J. R. (1994). Mnemonic strategies and classroom learning: A twenty-year report card. *Elementary School Journal, 94,* 235–254.

Lindsay, P. H. and Norman, D. A. (1977). *Human Information Processing: An Introduction to Psychology* (2nd ed.). New York: Academic Press.

Locke, J. (1690). An essay concerning human understanding. In Goldie, M. (1997). *Locke: Political Essays.* Cambridge: Cambridge University Press.

Loftus, E. and Palmer, J. C. (1974). Reconstruction of automobile destruction: An example of the interaction between language and memory. *Journal of Verbal Learning and Verbal Behavior, 13,* 585–589.

Masoura, E. and Gathercole, S. (2005). Contrasting contributions of phonological short-term memory and long-term knowledge to vocabulary learning in a foreign language. *Memory, 13*(3/4), 422–429.

Matlin, M. W. and Foley, H. J. (1997). *Sensation and Perception* (4th ed.). Boston: Allyn and Bacon.

Mautone, P. D. and Mayer, R. E. (2001). Signaling as a cognitive guide in multimedia learning. *Journal of Educational Psychology, 93,* 377–389.

Mayer, R. E. (1996). Learners as information processors: Legacies and limitations of educational psychology's second metaphor. *Journal of Educational Psychology, 31,* 151–161.

Mayer, R. E. (1999). Multimedia aids to problem-solving transfer. *International Journal of Educational Research, 31,* 611–623.

Mayer, R. E. (2001). *Multimedia Learning.* New York: Cambridge University Press.

Mayer, R. E. and Gallini, J. K. (1990). When is an illustration worth ten thousand words? *Journal of Educational Psychology, 82,* 715–726.

Mayer, R. E. and Sims, V. K. (1994). For whom is a picture worth a thousand words? Extensions of a dual-coding theory of multimedia learning. *Journal of Educational Psychology, 86,* 389–401.

Meichenbaum, D., Burland, S., Gruson, L. and Cameron, R. (1985). Metacognitive assessment. In S. Yussen (ed.), *The Growth of Reflection in Children* (pp. 1–30). Orlando, FL: Academic Press.

Mendell, P. R. (1971). Retrieval and representation in long-term memory. *Psychonomic Science, 23,* 295–296.

Metcalfe, J. and Shimamura, A. P. (eds) (1994). *Metacognition: Knowledge about Knowing.* Cambridge, MA: MIT Press.

Miller, G. A. (1956). The magical number seven, plus or minus two: Some limits on our capacity for processing information. *Psychological Review, 63,* 81–97.

Miller, G. A., Galanter, E. and Pribram, K. H. (1960). *Plans and the Structure of Behavior.* New York: Holt, Rinehart and Winston.

Morris, P. F. (1990). Metacognition. In M. W. Eysenck (ed.), *The Blackwell Dictionary of Cognitive Psychology* (pp. 225–229). Oxford, UK: Basil Blackwell.

Mumford, M. D., Costanza, D. P., Baughman, W. A., Threlfall, V. and Fleishman, E. A. (1994). Influence of abilities on performance during practice: Effects of massed and distributed practice. *Journal of Educational Psychology, 86,* 134–144.

Myers, D. G. (2005). *Exploring Psychology* (6th ed. in Modules). New York: Worth.

Neisser, U. (1976). *Cognition and Reality.* San Francisco: Freeman.

Nelson, K. (1986). *Event Knowledge.* Hillsdale, NJ: Lawrence Erlbaum.

Nelson, T. O. (1996). Consciousness and metacognition. *American Psychologist, 51,* 102–116.

Nicolson, R. and Fawcett, A. (1994). *Spelling Remediation for Dyslexic Children: A Skills Approach.* Chichester: Wiley.

Ofsted (2006). *Evaluation of the manageability of the joint area review and corporate assessment process.* Available at www.ofsted.gov.uk/publications

Paivio, A. (1971). *Imagery and Verbal Processes.* New York: Holt, Rinehart and Winston.

Paivio, A. (1986). *Mental Representations: A Dual-coding Approach.* New York: Oxford University Press.

Paris, S. G. and Cunningham, A. E. (1996). Children becoming students. In D. Berliner and R. Calfee (eds), *Handbook of Educational Psychology* (pp. 117–146). New York: Macmillan.

Paris, S. G., Lipson, M. Y. and Wixson, K. K. (1983). Becoming a strategic reader. *Contemporary Educational Psychology, 8,* 293–316.

Perkins, D. N. and Salomon, G. (1989). Are cognitive skills context-bound? *Educational Researcher, 18,* 16–25.

Perner, J. (2000). Memory and theory of mind. In E. Tulving and F. I. M. Craik (eds), *The Oxford Handbook of Memory* (pp. 297–312). New York: Oxford.

Pressley, M. (1991). Comparing Hall (1988) with related research on elaborative mnemonics. *Journal of Educational Psychology, 83,* 165–170.

Pressley, M. and Woloshyn, V. (1995). *Cognitive Strategy Instruction That Really Improves Children's Academic Performance.* Cambridge, MA: Brookline Books.

Reder, L. M. (1996). Different research programs on metacognition: Are the boundaries imaginary? *Learning and Individual Differences, 8,* 383–390.

Rumelhart, D. and Ortony, A. (1977). The representation of knowledge in memory. In R. Anderson, R. Spiro and W. Montague (eds), *Schooling and the Acquisition of Knowledge* (pp. 99–135). Hillsdale, NJ: Lawrence Erlbaum.

Rummel, N., Levin, J. R. and Woodward, M. M. (2003). Do pictorial mnemonic text-learning aids give students something worth writing about? *Journal of Educational Psychology, 95,* 327–334.

Schunk, D. H. (2000). *Learning Theories: An Educational Perspective* (3rd ed.). Columbus, OH: Merrill/Prentice-Hall.

Schunk, D. H. (2004). *Learning Theories: An Educational Perspective* (4th ed.). Columbus, OH: Merrill/Prentice-Hall.

Schwartz, B., Wasserman, E. A. and Robbins, S. J. (2002). *Psychology of Learning and Behavior* (5th ed.). New York: W. W. Norton.

Semb, G. B. and Ellis, J. A. (1994). Knowledge taught in school: What is remembered? *Review of Educational Research, 64,* 253–286.

Sherman, J. W. and Bessenoff, G. R. (1999). Stereotypes as source-monitoring cues: On the interaction between episodic and semantic memory. *Psychological Science, 10,* 106–110.

Shuell, T. J. (1986). Cognitive conceptions of learning. *Review of Educational Research, 56,* 411–436.

Shuell, T. J. (1990). Phases of meaningful learning. *Review of Educational Psychology, 60,* 531–548.

Smith, F. (1975). *Comprehension and Learning: A Conceptual Framework for Teachers.* New York: Holt, Rinehart and Winston.

Smith, S. M., Glenberg, A. and Bjork, R. A. (1978). Environmental context and human memory. *Memory and Cognition, 6,* 342–353.

Sperling, G. (1960). The information available in brief visual presentations. *Psychological Monographs, 74* (11, Whole No. 498).

Sternberg, R. J. (1999). A propulsion model of types of creative contribution. *Review of General Psychology, 3,* 83–100.

Sweller, J., van Merrienboer, J. J. G. and Paas, F. G. W. C. (1998). Cognitive architecture and instructional design. *Educational Psychology Review, 10,* 251–296.

Von Restorff, H. (1933). Über die Wirkung von Bereichsbildungen im Spurenfeld (The effects of field formation in the trace field). *Psychologie Forschung, 18,* 299–334.

Wang, A. Y. and Thomas, M. H. (1995). Effects of keywords on long-term retention: Help or hindrance? *Journal of Educational Psychology, 87,* 468–475.

Wang, A. Y., Thomas, M. H. and Ouellette, J. A. (1992). Keyword mnemonic and retention of second-language vocabulary words. *Journal of Educational Psychology, 84,* 520–528.

Warren A., Hulse-Trotter, K. and Tubbs, E. C. (1991). Inducing resistance to suggestibility in children. *Law and Human Behaviour, 15,* 273–285.

Willoughby, T., Porter, L., Belsito, L. and Yearsley, T. (1999). Use of elaboration strategies by grades two, four, and six. *Elementary School Journal, 99,* 221–231.

Wilson, M. (2001). The case for sensorimotor coding in working memory. *Psychonomic Bulletin and Review, 8,* 44–57.

Wittrock, M. C. (1982). *Educational implications of recent research on learning and memory.* Paper presented at the annual meeting of the American Educational Research Association, New York.

Chapter 8

Adeyemi, M. B. (2002). An investigation into the status of the teaching and learning of the concept of democracy at the junior secondary school level in Botswana. *Educational Studies, 28*(4), 385–401.

Ahlberg, M. (2004). *Varieties of Concept Mapping/ Variedades de Mapas Conceptuales.* Poster presentation at First International Conference on Concept Mapping/Primer Congreso Internacional Sobre Mapas Conceptuales Pamplona, Spain/España Sept. 14–17.

Alexander, P. A. (1992). Domain knowledge: Evolving themes and emerging concerns. *Educational Psychologist, 27,* 33–51.

Alexander, P. A. (1996). The past, present, and future of knowledge research: A reexamination of the role of knowledge in learning and instruction. *Educational Psychologist, 31,* 89–92.

Amabile, T. M. (1996). *Creativity in Context.* Boulder, CO: Westview Press.

Anderson, J. R. (1993). Problem solving and learning. *American Psychologist, 48,* 35–44.

Anderson, J. R. (1995). *Cognitive Psychology and its Implications* (4th ed.). New York: Freeman.

Atkinson, R. K., Renkl, A. and Merrill, M. M. (2003). Transitioning from studying examples to solving problems: Combining fading with prompting fosters learning. *Journal of Educational Psychology, 95,* 774–783.

Ausubel, D. P. (1963). *The Psychology of Meaningful Verbal Learning.* New York: Grune and Stratton.

Ausubel, D. P. (1977). The facilitation of meaningful verbal learning in the classroom. *Educational Psychologist, 12,* 162–178.

Ausubel, D. P. (1982). Schemata, advance organizers, and anchoring ideas: A reply to Anderson, Spiro, and Anderson. *Journal of Structural Learning, 7,* 63–73.

Baer, J. (1997). *Creative Teachers, Creative Students.* Boston: Allyn and Bacon.

BEA (1997). American Psychological Association's Board of Educational Affairs: *Learner-Centered Psychological Principles: A Framework for School Redesign and Reform* http://www.apa.org/ed/lcp.html#%20Individual%20Differences accessed May 2006.

Benjafield, J. G. (1992). *Cognition.* Englewood Cliffs, NJ: Prentice-Hall.

Berk, L. E. (2001). *Awakening Children's Minds: How Parents and Teachers can Make a Difference.* New York: Oxford University Press.

Berk, L. E. (2005). *Infants, Children, and Adolescents* (5th ed.). Boston: Allyn and Bacon.

Betres, J., Zajano, M. and Gumieniak, P. (1984). Cognitive styles, teacher methods and concept attainment in the social studies. *Theory and Research in Social Education, 12*(2), 1–18.

Bjorklund, D. F. (1989). *Children's Thinking: Developmental Function and Individual Differences*. Pacific Grove, CA: Brooks/Cole.

Bloom, B. S., Engelhart, M. D., Frost, E. J., Hill, W. H. and Krathwohl, D. R. (1956). *Taxonomy of Educational Objectives. Handbook I: Cognitive Domain*. New York: David McKay.

Bonotto, C. and Basso, M. (2001). Is it possible to change the classroom activities in which we delegate the process of connecting mathematics with reality? *International Journal of Mathematical Education in Science and Technology, 32*(3), 385–399.

Bransford, J. D. and Schwartz, D. (1999). Rethinking transfer: A simple proposal with multiple implications. In A. Iran-Nejad and P. D. Pearson (eds), *Review of Research in Education, 24*, 61–100. Washington, DC: American Educational Research Association.

Bransford, J. D. and Stein, B. S. (1993). *The IDEAL Problem Solver: A Guide for Improving Thinking, Learning, and Creativity* (2nd ed.). New York: Freeman.

Branson, R. (2007). http://virgin.com/aboutvirgin/ allaboutvirgin/richardsautobiography/ accessed 9 August 2007.

Bridges, D. (1993). Transferable skills: A philosophical perspective. *Studies in Higher Education, 18*(1), 43–51.

Brown, A. L. and DeLoache, J. S. (1978). Skills, plans and self-regulation. In R. Siegler (ed.), *Children's Thinking: What Develops*. Hillsdale, New Jersey: Erlbaum.

Bruner, J. S. (1960). *The Process of Education*. New York: Vintage Books.

Bruner, J. S. (1973). *Beyond the Information Given: Studies in the Psychology of Knowing*. New York: Norton.

Bruner, J. S., Goodnow, J. J. and Austin, G. A. (1956). *A Study of Thinking*. New York: Wiley.

Buehler, R., Griffin, D. and Ross, M. (1994). Exploring the 'planning fallacy': Why people underestimate their task completion times. *Journal of Personality and Social Psychology, 67*, 366–381.

Bulgren, J. A., Deshler, D. D., Schumaker, J. B. and Lenz, B. K. (2000). The use and effectiveness of analogical instruction in diverse secondary content classrooms. *Journal of Educational Psychology, 92*, 426–441.

Byrnes, J. P. (1996). *Cognitive Development and Learning in Instructional Contexts*. Boston: Allyn and Bacon.

Campbell, J. I. D. and Austin, S. (2002). Effects of response time deadlines on adults' strategy choices for simple addition. *Memory and Cognition, 30*(6), 988–994.

Carroll, J. M. (1990). *The Nurnberg Funnel*. Cambridge, Mass: MIT Press.

Chan, C. K. and Sachs, J. (2001). Beliefs about learning in children's understanding of science texts. *Contemporary Educational Psychology, 26*, 192–210.

Chen, Z. and Mo, L. (2004). Schema induction in problem solving: A multidimensional analysis. *Journal of Experimental Psychology: Learning, Memory, and Cognition, 30*, 583–600.

Cheng, P. C-H. and Shipstone, D. M. (2003). Supporting learning and promoting conceptual change with box and AVOW diagrams. Part 1: Representational design and instructional approaches. *International Journal of Science Education, 25*(2), 193–204.

Chi, M. T. H. (1978). Knowledge structures and memory development. In R. Siegler (ed.), *Children's Thinking: What Develops?* (pp. 73–96). Hillsdale, NJ: Lawrence Erlbaum.

Chi, M. T. H., Glaser, R. and Farr, M. (eds) (1988). *The Nature of Expertise*. Hillsdale, NJ: Lawrence Erlbaum.

Conlon, T. (2004). *But is Our Concept Map any Good?: Classroom Experiences with the Reasonable Fallible, Analyser/'Pero ¿Está Bueno Nuestro Mapa Conceptual?': Experiencias con el Analizador Razonable y Falible*. Paper at First International Conference on Concept Mapping/Primer Congreso Internacional Sobre Mapas Conceptuales Pamplona, Spain/España. 14–17 Sept.

Cooper, G. and Sweller, J. (1987). Effects of schema acquisition and rule automation on mathematical problem-solving transfer. *Journal of Educational Psychology, 79*, 347–362.

Corkill, A. J. (1992). Advance organizers: Facilitators of recall. *Educational Psychology Review, 4*, 33–67.

Counsell, C. (2000). Why was Becket murdered? Teaching pupils to sort, classify and analyse. *Teaching Thinking, 1*.

Cummins, D. D. (1991). Children's interpretation of arithmetic word problems. *Cognition and Instruction, 8*, 261–289.

De Corte, E. (2003). Transfer as the productive use of acquired knowledge, skills, and motivations. *Current Directions in Psychological Research, 12*, 142–146.

De Corte, E. and Verschaffel, L. (1985). Beginning first graders' initial representation of arithmetic word problems. *Journal of Mathematical Behavior, 4*, 3021.

Derry, S. J. (1989). Putting learning strategies to work. *Educational Leadership, 47*(5), 4–10.

Dinnel, D. and Glover, J. A. (1985). Advance organisers: Encoding manipulations. *Journal of Educational Psychology, 77*, 514–522.

Doctorow, M., Wittrock, M. C. and Marks, C. (1978). Generative processes in reading comprehension. *Journal of Educational Psychology, 70*, 109–118.

Duncker, K. (1945). On solving problems. *Psychological Monographs, 58* (5, Whole No. 270).

Eggen, P. D. and Kauchak, D. P. (2001). *Strategies for Teachers: Teaching Content and Thinking Skills* (4th ed.). Boston: Allyn and Bacon.

Ellis, J. A., and Whitehill, B. V. (1996). The effects of explanations and pictures on learning, retention, and transfer of a procedural assembly task. *Contemporary Educational Psychology, 21*(2), 129–148.

Ericsson, K. A. (1999). Expertise. In R. Wilson and F. Keil (eds), *The MIT Encyclopedia of the Cognitive Sciences* (pp. 298–300). Cambridge, MA: MIT Press.

Ericsson, K. A. and Charness, N. (1999). Expert performance: Its structure and acquisition. In S. Ceci and W. Williams (eds), The nature-nurture debate: The essential readings. *Essential readings in developmental psychology.* Malden, MA: Blackwell.

Escribe, C. and Huet N. (2005). Knowledge accessibility, achievement goals, and memory strategy maintenance. *British Journal of Educational Psychology, 75*(1), 87–104.

Feldman. J. (2003). The simplicity principle in human concept learning. *Current Directions in Psychological Science, 12*, 227–232.

Flavell, J. (1976). Metacognitive aspects of problem-solving. In L. Resnick (ed.), *The Nature of Intelligence*. Hillsdale, NJ: Erlbaum Assoc.

Fleith, D. (2000). Teacher and student perceptions of creativity in the classroom environment. *Roeper Review, 22*, 148–153.

Freud, S. (1959). Creative writers and daydreaming. In J. Strachey (ed.), *The Standard Edition of the Complete Psychological Works of Sigmund Freud* (Vol. 9). London: Hogarth Press.

Friend, M. and Bursuck, W. (1996). *Including Students with Special Needs: A Practical Guide for Classroom Teachers.* Boston: Allyn and Bacon.

Gagné, E. D., Yekovich, C. W. and Yekovich, F. R. (1993). *The Cognitive Psychology of School Learning* (2nd ed.). New York: HarperCollins.

Gardner, H. (1993a). *Creating Minds: An anatomy of creativity seen through the lives of Freud, Einstein, Picasso, Stravinsky, Elliot, Graham, and Gandhi.* New York: Basic Books.

Gardner, H. (1993b). The relationship between early giftedness and later achievement. Ciba Foundation. The origins and development of high ability, 175–186. viii. Oxford, England: John Wiley & Sons.

Gardner, R., Brown, R., Sanders, S. and Menke, D. J. (1992). 'Seductive details' in learning from text. In K. A. Renninger, S. Hidi and A. Krapp (eds), *The Role of Interest in Learning and Development* (pp. 239–254). Hillsdale, NJ: Lawrence Erlbaum.

Gentner, D., Loewenstein, J. and Thompson, L. (2003). Learning and transfer: A general role for analogical encoding. *Journal of Educational Psychology, 95*, 393–408.

Gick, M. L. (1986). Problem-solving strategies. *Educational Psychologist, 21*, 99–120.

Gleitman, H., Fridlund, A. J. and Reisberg, D. (1999). *Psychology* (5th ed.). New York: Norton.

Goldstone, R. L., Steyvers, M. and Rogosky, B. J. (2003). Conceptual interrelatedness and caricatures. *Memory and Cognition, 31*(2), 169–180.

Hamilton, R. J. (1985). A framework for the evaluation of the effectiveness of adjunct questions and objectives. *Review of Educational Research, 55*, 47–86.

Hamman, D., Berthelot, J., Saia, J. and Crowley, E. (2000). Teachers' coaching of learning and its relation to students' strategic learning. *Journal of Educational Psychology, 92*, 342–348.

Hampton, J. A. and Cannon, I. (2004). Category-based induction: An effect of conclusion typicality. *Memory and Cognition, 32*(2), 235–243.

Hardiman, P. T., Dufresne, R. and Mestre, J. P. (1989). The relation between problem categorization and problem solving among experts and novices. *Memory and Cognition, 17*, 627–638.

Haughton, E. (1999). Making History (Education Guardian) http://education.guardian.co.uk/software/story/0,5500, 84473,00.html accessed May 2006.

Haydn, T. (1997). Why and how we teach history in schools: The case of the Roman Soldier. *Teaching History, 86* (January), 27.

Hofer, B. K. and Pintrich, P. R. (1997). The development of epistemological theories: Beliefs about knowledge and knowing and their relation to learning. *Review of Educational Research, 67*, 88–140.

Irwin, J. W. (1991). *Teaching Reading Comprehension* (2nd ed.). Boston: Allyn and Bacon.

Jonassen, D. H. (2003). Designing research-based instruction for story problems. *Educational Psychology Review, 15*, 267–296.

Joyce, B. R., Weil, M. and Calhoun, E. (2006). *Models of Teaching* (7th ed.). Boston: Allyn and Bacon.

Kail, R. and Hall, L. K. (1999). Sources of developmental change in children's word-problem performance. *Journal of Educational Psychology, 91*, 600–668.

Kalyuga, S., Chandler, P., Tuovinen, J. and Sweller, J. (2001). When problem solving is superior to studying worked examples. *Journal of Educational Psychology, 93*, 579–588.

Kardash, C. M. and Howell, K. L. (2000). Effects of epistemological beliefs and topic-specific beliefs on undergraduates' cognitive and strategic processing of dual-positional text. *Journal of Educational Psychology, 92*, 524–535.

Keogh, B. (1999). Concept cartoons, teaching and learning in science: An evaluation. *International Journal of Science Education, 21*(4), 431–446.

Kiewra, K. A. (1985). Investigating notetaking and review: A depth of processing alternative. *Educational Psychologist, 20,* 23–32.

Kiewra, K. A. (1988). Cognitive aspects of autonomous note taking: Control processes, learning strategies, and prior knowledge. *Educational Psychologist, 23,* 39–56.

Kiewra, K. A. (1989). A review of note-taking: The encoding storage paradigm and beyond. *Educational Psychology Review, 1,* 147–172.

Klausmeier, H. J. (1992). Concept learning and concept teaching. *Educational Psychologist, 27,* 267–286.

Korf, R. (1999). Heuristic search. In R. Wilson and F. Keil (eds), *The MIT Encyclopedia of the Cognitive Sciences* (pp. 372–273). Cambridge, MA: MIT Press.

Koschmann, T. (2005). Concepts and Categories. *Journal of the Learning Sciences, 14*(1), 111–113.

Krathwohl, D. R. T. (2002). A revision of bloom's taxonomy: An overview. *Theory into Practice, 41*(4), 212–218.

Langan-Fox, J., Waycott, J. L. and Albert, K. (2000). Linear and graphic organizers: Properties and processing. *International Journal of Cognitive Ergonomics, 4*(1), 19–34.

Leat, D. and Lin, M. (2003). Developing a pedagogy of metacognition and transfer: Some signposts for the generation and use of knowledge and the creation of research partnerships. *British Educational Research Journal, 29*(3), 383–414.

Lee, A. Y. and Hutchinson, L. (1998). Improving learning from examples through reflection. *Journal of Experimental Psychology: Applied, 4,* 187–210.

Levine, D. (1985). *Improving Student Achievement Through Mastery Learning Programs.* San Francisco: Jossey-Bass.

Lorch, R. F., Lorch, E. P., Ritchey, K., McGovern, L. and Coleman, D. (2001). Effects of headings on text summarization. *Contemporary Educational Psychology, 26,* 171–191.

Luiten, J., Ames, W. and Ackerson, G. (1980). A meta-analysis of the effects of advance organisers on learning and retention. *American Educational Research Journal, 17,* 211–218.

Lye, J. (1997). *The Problem of Meaning in Literature* at http://www.brocku.ca/english/jlye/meaning.html accessed 22 May 2006.

Maier, N. R. F. (1933). An aspect of human reasoning. *British Journal of Psychology, 24,* 144–155.

Mayer, R. E. (1983). *Thinking, Problem Solving, Cognition.* San Francisco: Freeman.

Mayer, R. E. (1984). Twenty-five years of research on advance organisers. *Instructional Science, 8,* 133–169.

Mayer, R. E. and Wittrock, M. C. (1996). Problem-solving transfer. In D. Berliner and R. Calfee (eds), *Handbook of Educational Psychology* (pp. 47–62). New York: Macmillan.

Mirel, B. and Allmendinger, L. (2004). Visualizing complexity: Getting from here to there in ill-defined problem landscapes. *Information Design Journal, 12*(2), 141–151.

Mller-Freienfels, R. (1935). On the psychology of psychology. *Acta Psychologica* (The Hague), 157–174.

Moreau, S. and Coquin-Viennot, D. (2003). Comprehension of arithmetic word problems by fifth-grade pupils: Representations and selection of information. *British Journal of Educational Psychology, 73*(1), 109–121.

Morin, V. A. and Miller, S. P. (1998). Teaching multiplication to middle school students with mental retardation. *Education and Treatment of Children, 21,* 22–36.

Myers, D. G. (2005). *Exploring Psychology* (6th ed. in modules). New York: Worth.

Nakamura, J. and Csikszentmihalyi, M. (2001). Catalytic creativity: The case of Linus Pauling. *American Psychologist, 56,* 337–341.

Nelson, T. O. and Narens, L. (1996). Why investigate metacognition? In Metcalfe, J. and Shimamura, A. P. (ed.). *Metacognition: Knowing about Knowing.* Cambridge, Massachusetts: MIT Press.

Norton, P. and Sprague, D. (2001). *Technology for Teaching.* Boston: Allyn and Bacon.

Novak, J. D. and Gowin, D. B. (1984). *Learning How to Learn.* New York: Cambridge University Press.

O'Brien, T. (1998). *Promoting Positive Behaviour.* London: David Fulton.

Ormrod, J. E. (2004). *Human Learning* (4th ed.). Columbus, OH: Merrill/Prentice-Hall.

Osborn, A. F. (1963). *Applied Imagination* (3rd ed.). New York: Scribner's.

Palincsar, A. S. and Brown, A. L. (1984). Reciprocal teaching of comprehension-fostering and monitoring activities. *Cognition and Instruction, 1,* 117–175.

Perkins, D. N. and Salomon, G. (1989). Are cognitive skills context-bound? *Educational Researcher, 18,* 16–25.

Peverly, S., Brobst, K., Graham, M. and Shaw, R. (2003). College adults are not good at self-regulation: A study on the relationship of self-regulation, note-taking, and test-taking. *Journal of Educational Psychology, 95,* 335–346.

Phye, G. D. (1992). Strategic transfer: A tool for academic problem solving. *Educational Psychology Review, 4,* 393–421.

Phye, G. D. (2001). Problem-solving instruction and problem-solving transfer: The correspondence issue. *Journal of Educational Psychology, 93,* 571–578.

Phye, G. D. and Sanders, C. E. (1994). Advice and feedback: Elements of practice for problem solving. *Contemporary Educational Psychology, 17,* 211–223.

Pintrich, P. R., Marx, R. W. and Boyle, R. A. (1993). Beyond cold conceptual change: The role of motivational beliefs and classroom contextual factors in the process of conceptual change. *Review of Educational Research, 63,* 167–199.

Plucker, J. A., Beghetto, R. A. and Dow, G. T. (2004). Why isn't creativity more important to educational psychologists? Potential pitfalls and future directions in creativity research. *Educational Psychology, 39*(2), 83–96.

Posner, M. I. (1973). *Cognition: An Introduction.* Glenview, IL: Scott, Foresman.

Raudsepp, E. and Haugh, G. P. (1977). *Creative Growth Games.* New York: Harcourt Brace Jovanovich.

Reid, D. J. and Beveridge, M. (1986). Effects of text illustration on children's learning of a school science topic. *British Journal of Educational Psychology, 56*(3), 294–303.

Resnick, L. B. (1981). Instructional psychology. *Annual Review of Psychology, 32,* 659–704.

Robbins, S. B., Lauver, K., Davis, H. L., Davis, D., Langley, R. and Carlstrom, A. (2004). Psychosocial and study skill factors predict college outcomes? A meta-analysis. *Psychological Bulletin, 130,* 261–288.

Robbins, S. B., Le, L. and Lauver, K. (2005). Promoting successful college outcomes for all students: Reply to Weissberg and Owen (2005). *Psychological Bulletin, 131,* 410–411.

Robinson, D. H. and Kiewra, K. A. (1995). Visual argument: Graphic outlines are superior to outlines in improving learning from text. *Journal of Educational Psychology, 87,* 455–467.

Robinson, D. H. (1998). Graphic organisers as aids to test learning. *Reading Research and Instruction, 37,* 85–105.

Rose, J. (2006). Independent Review of the Teaching of Early Reading: Final Report. Nottingham: DfES Publications.

Ruscio, J., Whitney, D. M. and Amabile, T. M. (1998). Looking inside the fishbowl of creativity: Verbal and behavioral predictors of creative performance. *Creativity Research Journal, 11*(3), 243–263.

Ruthven, K. (1998). The use of mental, written and calculator strategies of numerical computation by upper-primary pupils within a 'calculator-aware' number curriculum. *British Educational Research Journal, 24*(1), 21–42.

Salomon, G. and Perkins, D. N. (1989). Rocky roads to transfer: Rethinking mechanisms of a neglected phenomenon. *Educational Psychologist, 24,* 113–142.

Sattler, J. M. (1992). *Assessment of Children* (3rd ed. rev.). San Diego: Jerome M. Sattler.

Schneider, W. and Bjorklund, D. F. (1992). Expertise, aptitude, and strategic remembering. *Child Development, 63,* 416–473.

Schommer, M. (1997). The development of epistemological beliefs among secondary students: A longitudinal study. *Journal of Educational Psychology, 89,* 37–40.

Schraw, G. and Olafson, L. (2002). Teachers' epistemological world views and educational practices. *Issues in Education, 8,* 99–148.

Schunk, D. H. (2004). *Learning Theories: An Educational Perspective* (4th ed.). Columbus, OH: Merrill/Prentice-Hall.

Scott, C. L. (1999). Teachers' biases toward creative children. *Creativity Research Journal, 12,* 321–337.

Seegers, G., Putten, C. M. van and Brabander, C. J. de (2002). Goal orientation, perceived task outcome and task demands in mathematics tasks: Effects on students' attitude in actual task settings. *British Journal of Educational Psychology, 72*(3), 365–384.

Shuard, H., Walsh, A., Goodwin, J. and Worcester, V. (1991), *Calculators, Children and Mathematics.* London: Simon and Schuster.

Shuell, T. J. (1990). Phases of meaningful learning. *Review of Educational Psychology, 60,* 531–548.

Simon, D. P. and Chase, W. G. (1973). Skill in chess. *American Scientist, 61,* 394–403.

Simon, H. A. (1995). The information-processing view of mind. *American Psychologist, 50,* 507–508.

Simonton, D. K. (2000). Creativity: Cognitive, personal, developmental, and social aspects. *American Psychologist, 55,* 151–158.

Singley, K. and Anderson, J. R. (1989). *The Transfer of Cognitive Skill.* Cambridge, MA: Harvard University Press.

Snowman, J. (1984). Learning tactics and strategies. In G. Phye and T. Andre (eds), *Cognitive Instructional Psychology* (pp. 243–275). Orlando, FL: Academic Press.

Taber, K. (2005). The limits to discovery learning: An open letter to a headmaster. *Physics Education, 40*(6), 496–497.

Tan, O. S. (2002). Lifelong learning through a problem-based learning approach, in A. S. C. Chang, A. S. C. and Goh, C. C. M. (eds), *Teachers' Handbook on Teaching Generic Thinking Skills.* Singapore, Prentice Hall.

TIMSS – Third International Mathematics and Science Study (1998). Washington, DC: National Center for Educational Statistics. Available online at http://nces.ed.gov/timss/

Torrance, E. P. (1972). Predictive validity of the Torrance tests of creative thinking. *Journal of Creative Behavior, 6,* 236–262.

Torrance, E. P. and Hall, L. K. (1980). Assessing the future reaches of creative potential. *Journal of Creative Behavior, 14,* 1–19.

Tsai, M-T. and Tsai, L-L. (2005). The critical success factors and impact of prior knowledge to nursing students when transferring nursing knowledge during nursing clinical practise. *Journal of Nursing Management, 13*(6), 459–466.

UK Labour Force Survey: Employment status by occupation and sex (Spring 2003–Spring 2005) http://www.statistics.gov.uk/downloads/theme_labour/, accessed 10 May 2006.

Van Meter, P. (2001). Drawing construction as a strategy for learning from text. *Journal of Educational Psychology, 93,* 129–140.

Van Meter, P., Yokoi, L. and Pressley, M. (1994). College students' theory of note-taking derived from their perceptions of note-taking. *Journal of Educational Psychology, 86,* 323–338.

Volman, M. and Ten Dam, G. (2000). Qualities of instructional-learning episodes in different domains: The subjects Care and Technology. *Journal of Curriculum Studies, 32*(5), 721–741.

Vosniadou, S. and Schommer, M. (1988). Explanatory analogies can help children acquire information from expository text. *Journal of Educational Psychology, 80,* 524–536.

Vygotsky, L. S. (1962). *Thought and Language.* USA: Massachusetts Institute of Technology.

Waits, B. K. and Demana, F. (2000). Calculators in mathematics teaching and learning: Past, present, future. In M. J. Burke and F. R. Curcio (eds), *Learning Mathematics for a New Century: NCTM 2000 Yearbook* (pp. 51–66). Reston, VA: National Council of Teachers of Mathematics.

Walsh, B. (1998). Why Gerry likes history now: The power of the word processor. *The Historical Association: Teaching History, 93,* 6–15.

Weisberg, R. W. (1993). *Creativity: Beyond the Myth of Genius.* New York: W. H. Freeman.

Willoughby, T., Porter, L., Belsito, L. and Yearsley, T. (1999). Use of elaboration strategies by grades two, four, and six. *Elementary School Journal, 99,* 221–231.

Winner, E. (2000). The origins and ends of giftedness. *American Psychologist, 55,* 159–169.

Zimmerman, B. J. and Schunk, D. H. (eds). (2001). *Self-regulated Learning and Academic Achievement: Theoretical Perspectives* (2nd ed.). Mahwah, NJ: Lawrence Erlbaum.

Chapter 9

Albanese, M. A. and Mitchell, S. A. (1993). Problem-based learning: A review of literature on its outcomes and implementation issues. *Academic Medicine, 68,* 52–81.

Alexander, P. A. (2006). *Psychology in Learning and Instruction.* Upper Saddle River, NJ: Merrill/Prentice-Hall.

Anderson, J. R., Reder, L. M. and Simon, H. A. (1996). Situated learning and education. *Educational Researcher, 25,* 5–11.

Arends, R. I. (2004). *Learning to Teach* (6th ed.). New York: McGraw-Hill.

Atherton, J. S. (2003). *Learning and Teaching: Problem-based Learning.* Available: http://146.227.1.20/~jamesa//teaching/pbl.htm. Accessed: 31 August 2006.

Bandura, A. (1982). Self-efficacy mechanisms in human agency. *American Psychologist, 37,* 122–147.

Bandura, A. (1986). *Social Foundations of Thought and Action.* Englewood Cliffs, NJ: Prentice-Hall.

Bandura, A. (1993). Perceived self-efficacy in cognitive development and functioning. *Educational Psychologist, 28,* 117–148.

Bandura, A. (1997). *Self-Efficacy: The Exercise of Control.* New York: Freeman.

Bereiter, C. (1997). Situated cognition and how I overcome it. In D. Kirshner and J. A. Whitson (eds), *Situated Cognition: Social, Semiotic, and Psychological Perspectives* (pp. 281–300). Mahwah, NJ: Lawrence Erlbaum.

Boekaerts, M. (1999). Self-regulated learning: Where we are today. *International Journal of Educational Research, 31*(6), 445–457.

Brown, M. and Askew, M. (1997). In a Class of Their Own. *Times Educational Supplement,* Extra Mathematics (pII).

Bruner, J. S. (1966). *Toward a Theory of Instruction.* New York: Norton.

Bruning, R. H., Schraw, G. J., Norby, M. M. and Ronning, R. R. (2004). *Cognitive Psychology and Instruction* (4th ed.). Columbus, OH: Merrill.

Capa, Y. (2005). *Novice Teachers' Sense of Efficacy.* Doctoral dissertation, The Ohio State University, Columbus, OH.

Capon, N. and Kuhn, D. (2004). What's so good about problem-based learning? *Cognition and Instruction, 22,* 61–79.

Cobb, P. and Bowers, J. (1999). Cognitive and situated learning: Perspectives in theory and practice. *Educational Researcher, 28*(2), 4–15.

Cole, M. (1985). The zone of proximal development: Where culture and cognition create each other. In J. V. Wertsch (ed.), *Culture, Communication, and Cognition: Vygotskian*

Perspectives (pp. 146–161). Cambridge: Cambridge University Press.

Collins, A., Brown, J. S. and Holum, A. (1991). Cognitive apprenticeship: Making thinking visible. *American Educator, 15*(3), 38–39.

Collins, A., Brown, J. S. and Newman, S. E. (1989). Cognitive apprenticeship: Teaching the crafts of reading, writing, and mathematics. In L. B. Resnick (ed.), *Knowing, Learning, and Instruction: Essays in Honor of Robert Galser* (pp. 453–494). Hillsdale, NJ: Lawrence Erlbaum.

Corno, L. (1992). Encouraging students to take responsibility for learning and performance. *Elementary School Journal, 93,* 69–84.

Corno, L. (1995). The principles of adaptive teaching. In A. Ornstein (ed.), *Teaching: Theory into Practice* (pp. 98–115). Boston: Allyn and Bacon.

Corno, L. and Snow, R. E. (1986). Adapting teaching to individual differences in learners. In M. Wittrock (ed.), *Handbook of Research on Teaching* (3rd ed., pp. 605–629). New York: Macmillan.

Cunningham, D. J. (1992). Beyond educational psychology: Steps toward an educational semiotic. *Educational Psychology Review, 4,* 165–194.

Dawes, L., Mercer, N. and Wegerif, R. (2000). *Thinking Together: A Programme of Activities for Developing Thinking Skills at KS2.* Birmingham: Questions Publishing.

De Corte, E., Greer, B. and Verschaffel, L. (1996). Mathematics learning and teaching. In D. Berliner and R. Calfee (eds), *Handbook of Educational Psychology* (pp. 491–549). New York: Macmillan.

De Kock, A., Sleegers, P. and Voeten, J. M. (2004). New learning and the classification of learning environments in secondary education. *Review of Educational Research, 74,* 141–170.

Derry, S. J. (1992). Beyond symbolic processing: Expanding horizons for educational psychology. *Journal of Educational Psychology, 84,* 413–419.

DfES (2005). *Harnessing Technology: Transforming Learning and Children's Services.* Nottingham: DfES Publications.

Driscoll, M. P. (2005). *Psychology of Learning for Instruction* (3rd ed.). Boston: Allyn and Bacon.

Echevarria, M. (2003). Anomalies as a catalyst for middle school students' knowledge construction and scientific reasoning during science inquiry. *Journal of Educational Psychology, 95,* 357–374.

Evensen, D. H., Salisbury-Glennon, J. D. and Glenn, J. (2001). A qualitative study of six medical students in a problem-based curriculum: Toward a situated model of self-regulation. *Journal of Educational Psychology, 93,* 659–676.

Fisher, P. (ed.) (2001). *Thinking Through History.* Cambridge: Chris Kington Publishing.

Fives, H. R., Hamman, D. and Olivarez, A. (2005). *Does burnout begin with student teaching? Analyzing efficacy, burnout, and support during the student-teaching semester.* Paper presented at the Annual Meeting of the America Educational Research Association, Montreal, CA.

Flammer, A. (1995). Developmental analysis of control beliefs. In A. Bandura, (ed.), *Self-efficacy in Changing Societies* (pp. 69–113). New York: Cambridge University Press.

Fredricks, J. A., Blumenfeld, P. C., and Paris, A. H. (2004). School engagement: Potential of the concept, state of the evidence. *Review of Educational Research, 74,* 59–109.

Fuchs, L. S., Fuchs, D., Prentice, K., Burch, M., Hamlett, C. L., Owen, R. and Schroeter, K. (2003). Enhancing third-grade students' mathematical problem solving with self-regulated learning strategies. *Journal of Educational Psychology, 95*(2), 306–315.

Galbraith, A. and Alexander, J. (2005). Literacy, self-esteem and locus of control. *Support for Learning, 20*(1), 28–34.

Garrison, J. (1995). Deweyan pragmatism and the epistemology of contemporary social constructivism. *American Educational Research Journal, 32,* 716–741.

Geary, D. C. (1995). Sexual selection and sex differences in spatial cognition. *Learning and Individual Differences, 7,* 289–303.

Gergen, K. J. (1997). Constructing constructivism: Pedagogical potentials. *Issues in Education: Contributions from Educational Psychology, 3,* 195–202.

Gibbons, P. (2002). *Scaffolding Language, Scaffolding Learning: Teaching Second Language Learners in the Mainstream Classroom.* Portsmouth, NH: Heinemann.

Graham, S. and Weiner, B. (1996). Theories and principles of motivation. In D. Berliner and R. C. Calfee (eds), *Handbook of Educational Psychology* (pp. 63–84). New York: Macmillan.

Greeno, J. G., Collins, A. M. and Resnick, L. B. (1996). Cognition and learning. In D. Berliner and R. Calfee (eds), *Handbook of Educational Psychology* (pp. 15–46). New York: Macmillan.

Hall, K. and Harding, A. (2003). A Systematic Review of Effective Literacy Teaching in Mainstream Schools.

Higgins, S. (2001). *Thinking Through Primary Teaching.* Cambridge: Chris Kington Publishing.

Hmelo-Silver, C. E. (2004). Problem-based learning: What and how do students learn? *Educational Psychology Review, 16,* 235–266.

Holmes, B. and Greik, L. (1998). *Views of the Mountain from the Valley: A rural community assessment of the*

Japanese education system. The 43rd International Conference of Eastern Studies. Tokyo: 22–23 May.

Hoy, W. K. and Woolfolk, A. E. (1993). Teachers' sense of efficacy and the organizational health of schools. *Elementary School Journal, 93,* 355–372.

Hung, D. W. L. (1999). Activity, apprenticeship, and epistemological appropriation: Implications from the writings of Michael Polanyi. *Educational Psychologist, 34,* 193–205.

Keyser, V. and Barling, J. (1981). Determinants of children's self-efficacy beliefs in an academic environment. *Cognitive Therapy and Research, 5,* 29–40.

Kiewra, K. A. (2002). How classroom teachers can help students learn and teach them how to learn. *Theory Into Practice, 41,* 71–80.

Lajoie, S. P. and Greer, J. E. (1995). Establishing an argumentation environment to foster scientific reasoning with Bio-World. In D. Jonnassen and G. McCalla (ed.). *Proceedings of the International Conference on Computers in Education*. Singapore: 5–8 December, 89–96.

Lashley, T. J., II, Matczynski, T. J. and Rowley, J. B. (2002). *Instructional Models: Strategies for Teaching in a Diverse Society* (2nd ed.). Belmont, CA: Wadsworth/Thomson Learning.

Lave, J. (1997). The culture of acquisition and the practice of understanding. In D. Kirshner and J. A. Whitson (eds), *Situated Cognition: Social, Semiotic, and Psychological Perspectives* (pp. 17–35). Mahwah, NJ: Lawrence Erlbaum.

Lave, J. and Wenger, E. (1991). *Situated Learning: Legitimate Peripheral Participation*. Cambridge, MA: Cambridge University Press.

Leat, D. (1998). *Thinking Through Geography*. Cambridge: Chris Kington Publishing.

Magnusson, S. J. and Palincsar, A. S. (1995). The learning environment as a site of science reform. *Theory Into Practice, 34,* 43–50.

Marshall, H. H. (ed.) (1992). *Redefining Student Learning: Roots of Educational Change*. Norwood, NJ: Ablex.

Marshall, H. H. (1996). Implications of differentiating and understanding constructivist approaches. *Journal of Educational Psychology, 31,* 235–240.

Martinez-Pons, M. (2002). Parental influences on children's academic self-regulatory development. *Theory Into Practice, 41,* 126–131.

Mayer, R. E. (1996). Learners as information processors: Legacies and limitations of educational psychology's second metaphor. *Journal of Educational Psychology, 31,* 151–161.

Mayer, R. E. (2004). Should there be a three-strikes rule against discovery learning? A case for guided methods of instruction. *American Psychologist, 59,* 14–19.

Mayer, R. E. and Wittrock, M. C. (1996). Problem-solving transfer. In D. Berliner and R. Calfee (eds), *Handbook of Educational Psychology* (pp. 47–62). New York: Macmillan.

McCaslin, M. and Good, T. (1996). The informal curriculum. In D. Berliner and R. Calfee (eds), *Handbook of Educational Psychology* (pp. 622–670). New York: Macmillan.

McCaslin, M. and Hickey, D. T. (2001). Self-regulated learning and academic achievement: A Vygotskian view. In B. Zimmerman and D. Schunk (eds), *Self-regulated Learning and Academic Achievement: Theoretical Perspectives* (2nd ed., pp. 227–252). Mahwah, NJ: Lawrence Erlbaum.

McCombs, B. L. and Marzano, R. J. (1990). Putting the self in self-regulated learning: The self as agent in integrating skill and will. *Educational Psychologist, 25,* 51–70.

McGuinness, C. (1999). *From Thinking Skills to Thinking Classrooms: A review and evaluation of approaches for developing pupils' thinking*. London: DFEE Research Report RR115.

Miller, P. H. (2002). *Theories of Developmental Psychology* (4th ed.). New York: Worth.

Moshman, D. (1982). Exogenous, endogenous, and dialectical constructivism. *Developmental Review, 2,* 371–384.

Moshman, D. (1997). Pluralist rational constructivism. *Issues in Education: Contributions from Educational Psychology, 3,* 229–234.

Murphy, P. K. and Alexander, P. A. (2000). A motivated exploration of motivation terminology. *Contemporary Educational Psychology, 25,* 3–53.

NALDIC (2006). *Supporting Language and Cognitive Development*. Available at http://www.naldic.org.uk/ITTSEAL2/teaching/SupportingLanguageandCognitivedevelopment.cfm

Needles, M. and Knapp, M. (1994). Teaching writing to children who are undeserved. *Journal of Educational Psychology, 86,* 339–349.

Neuman, S. B. and Roskos, K. A. (1997). Literacy knowledge in practice: Contexts of participation for young writers and readers. *Reading Research Quarterly, 32,* 10–32.

Nichol, J. and Turner-Bisset, R. (2006). Cognitive apprenticeship and teachers' professional development. *Journal of In-Service Education, 32*(2), 149–169.

Pajares, F. (1997). Current directions in self-efficacy research. In M. L. Maehr and P. R.

Palincsar, A. S. (1998). Social constructivist perspectives on teaching and learning. In J. T. Spence, J. M. Darley and D. J. Foss (eds), *Annual Review of Psychology* (pp. 345–375). Palo Alto, CA: Annual Reviews.

Palincsar, A. S., Magnuson, S. J., Marano, N., Ford, D. and Brown, N. (1998). Designing a community of practice:

Principles and practices of the GIsML community. *Teaching and Teacher Education, 14,* 5–19.

Paris, S. G. and Ayres, L. R. (1994). *Becoming Reflective Students and Teachers: With Portfolios and Authentic Assessment.* Washington, DC: American Psychological Association.

Paris, S. G., Byrnes, J. P. and Paris, A. H. (2001). Constructing theories, identities, and actions of self-regulated learners. In B. J. Zimmerman and D. H. Schunk (eds), *Self-regulated Learning and Academic Achievement: Theoretical Perspectives* (2nd ed., pp. 253–287). Mahwah, NJ: Lawrence Erlbaum.

Pasch, M., Sparks-Langer, G., Gardner, T. G., Starko, A. J. and Moody, C. D. (1991). *Teaching as Decision Making: Instructional Practices for the Successful Teacher.* New York: Longman.

Perkins, D. N., Jay, E. and Tishman, S. (1993). New conceptions of thinking: From ontology to education. *Educational Psychologist, 28,* 67–85.

Perry, N. E. and Drummond, L. (2002). Helping young students become self-regulated researchers and writers. *The Reading Teacher, 56,* 298–310.

Perry, N. E., Phillips, L. and Dowler, J. (2004). Examining features of tasks and their potential to promote self-regulated learning. *Teachers College Record, 106,* 1854–1878.

Perry, N. E., VandeKamp, K. O., Mercer, L. K. and Nordby, C. J. (2002). Investigating teacher-student interactions that foster self-regulated learning. *Educational Psychologist, 37,* 5–15.

Peterson, P. L., Fennema, E. and Carpenter, T. (1989). Using knowledge of how students think about mathematics. *Educational Leadership, 46*(4), 42–46.

Phillips, D. (1997). How, why, what, when, and where: Perspectives on constructivism and education. *Issues in Education: Contributions from Educational Psychology, 3,* 151–194.

Piaget, J. (1971). *Biology and Knowledge.* Edinburgh, UK: Edinburgh Press.

Pintrich, P. R. and Schunk, D. H. (2002). *Motivation in Education: Theory, Research, and Applications* (2nd ed.). Upper Saddle River, NJ: Merrill/Prentice-Hall.

Pintrich, P. R. and Zusho, A. (2002). The development of academic self-regulation: The role of cognitive and motivational factors. In A. Wigfield and J. Eccles (eds), *Development of Achievement Motivation* (pp. 249–284). San Diego: Academic Press.

Polson, P. G. and Jeffries, R. (1985). Instruction in general problem-solving skills: An analysis of four approaches. In J. Segal, S. Chipman and R. Glaser (eds), *Thinking and Learning Skills* (Vol. 1, pp. 417–455). Mahwah, NJ: Lawrence Erlbaum.

Prawat, R. S. (1991). The value of ideas: The immersion approach to the development of thinking. *Educational Researcher, 20,* 3–10.

Prawat, R. S. (1992). Teachers' beliefs about teaching and learning: A constructivist perspective. *American Journal of Education, 100,* 354–395.

Prawat, R. S. (1996). Constructivism, modern and postmodern. *Issues in Education: Contributions from Educational Psychology, 3,* 215–226.

Pressley, M. (1995). More about the development of self-regulation: complex, long-term, and thoroughly social. *Educational Psychologist, 30,* 207–212.

Putnam, R. T. and Borko, H. (1997). Teacher learning: Implications of new views of cognition. In B. J. Biddle, T. L. Good and I. F. Goodson (eds), *The International Handbook of Teachers and Teaching* (Vol. 2, pp. 1223–1296). Dordrecht, the Netherlands: Kluwer.

Puustinen, M. and Pulkkinen, L. (2001). Models of self-regulated learning: A review. *Scandinavian Journal of Educational Research, 45,* 269–286.

Rogoff, B. (1995). Observing sociocultural activity on three planes: Participatory appropriation, guided participation, and apprenticeship. In J. Wertsch, P. del Rio and A. Alverez (eds), *Sociocultural Studies of Mind* (pp. 139–164). Cambridge, England: Cambridge University Press.

Rogoff, B. (1998). Cognition as a collaborative process. In W. Damon (Series Ed.) and D. Kuhn and R. S. Siegler (Vol. Eds), *Handbook of Child Psychology: Vol. 2* (5th ed., pp. 679–744). New York: Wiley.

Rohrkemper, M. and Corno, L. (1988). Success and failure on classroom tasks: Adaptive learning and classroom teaching. *Elementary School Journal, 88,* 297–312.

Romney, D. M. and Samuels, M. T. (2001). A Metaanalytic Evaluation of Feurstein's Instrumental Enrichment Program. *Education and Child Psychology, 18*(4), 19–34.

Roth, W-M. and Bowen, G. M. (1995). Knowing and interacting: A study of culture, practices, and resources in a grade 8 open-inquiry science guided by an apprenticeship metaphor. *Cognition and Instruction, 13,* 73–128.

Schoenfeld, A. H. (1989). Teaching mathematical thinking and problem solving. In L. B. Resnick and L. E. Klopfer (eds), *Toward the Thinking Curriculum: Current Cognitive Research* (pp. 83–103). Alexandria, VA: ASCD.

Schoenfeld, A. H. (1994). *Mathematics Thinking and Problem Solving.* Hillsdale, NJ: Lawrence Erlbaum.

Schunk, D. H. (2000). *Learning Theories: An Educational Perspective* (3rd ed.). Columbus, OH: Merrill/Prentice-Hall.

Schunk, D. H. (2004). *Learning Theories: An Educational Perspective* (4th ed.). Columbus, OH: Merrill/Prentice-Hall.

Schwarzer, R. and Schmitz, G. S. (2005). *Perceived self-efficacy and teacher burnout: a longitudinal study in ten schools.* Research paper. Freie Universitat Berlin, Germany.

Serpell, R. (1993). Interface between sociocultural and psychological aspects of cognition. In E. Forman, N. Minick and C. A. Stone (eds), *Contexts for Learning: Sociocultural Dynamics in Children's Development* (pp. 357–368). New York: Oxford University Press.

Shuell, T. J. (1996). Teaching and learning in a classroom context. In D. Berliner and R. Calfee (eds), *Handbook of Educational Psychology* (pp. 726–764). New York: Macmillan.

Siegler, R. S. (1993). Adaptive and non-adaptive characteristics of low-income children's mathematical strategy use. In B. Penner (ed.), *The Challenge in Mathematics and Science Education: Psychology's Response* (pp. 341–366). Washington, DC: American Psychological Association.

Sigurborsdottir, I. (1998). Philosophy with children in Foldaborg. *International Journal of Early Childhood 30*(1), 14–16.

Snow, R. E., Corno, L. and Jackson, D. (1996). Individual differences in affective and cognitive functions. In D. Berliner and R. Calfee (eds), *Handbook of Educational Psychology* (pp. 243–310). New York: Macmillan.

Spiro, R. J., Feltovich, P. J., Jacobson, M. L. and Coulson, R. L. (1991). Cognitive flexibility, constructivism, and hypertext: Random access instruction for advanced knowledge acquisition in ill-structured domains. *Educational Technology, 31*(5), 24–33.

Sprod, T. (1998). 'I can change your opinion on that': Social constructivist whole class discussions and their effect on scientific reasoning. *Research in Science Education, 28*(4), 463–480.

Tangney, B., FitzGibbon, A., Savage, T., Mehan, S. and Holmes, B. (2001). Communal constructivism: Students constructing learning for as well as with others. In C. Crawford *et al.* (eds), *Proceedings of Society for Information Technology and Teacher Education International Conference 2001* (pp. 3114–3119). Chesapeake, VA: AACE.

Tishman, S., Perkins, D. and Jay, E. (1995). *The Thinking Classroom: Creating a Culture of Thinking.* Boston: Allyn and Bacon.

Toth, E., Klahr, D. and Chen, Z. (2000). Bridging research and practice: A cognitively based classroom intervention for teaching experimentation to elementary school children. *Cognition and Instruction, 18,* 423–459.

Tschannen-Moran, M. and Woolfolk Hoy, A. (2001). Teacher efficacy: Capturing an elusive construct. *Teaching and Teacher Education, 17,* 783–805.

Turner, J. C. (1997). Starting right: Strategies for engaging young literacy learners. In J. T. Guthrie and A. Wigfield (eds), *Reading Engagement: Motivating Readers through Integrated Instruction* (pp. 183–204). Newark, DL: International Reading Association.

Turner, J. C. and Paris, S. G. (1995). How literacy tasks influence students' motivation for literacy. *The Reading Teacher, 48,* 662–673.

Valentine, J. C., DuBois, D. L. and Cooper, H. (2004). The relations between self-beliefs and academic achievement: A systematic review. *Educational Psychologist, 39,* 111–133.

Vera, A. H. and Simon, H. A. (1993). Situated action: A symbolic interpretation. *Cognitive Science, 17,* 7–48.

Wallace, B. and Adams, H. B. (1993). *TASC: Thinking Actively in a Social Context.* Oxford: AB Academic Publishers.

Wang, M. C. and Palincsar, A. S. (1989). Teaching students to assume an active role in their learning. In M. Reynolds (ed.), *Knowledge Base for the Beginning Teacher* (pp. 71–84). New York: Pergamon.

Weinstein, C. E. (1994). Learning strategies and learning to learn. *Encyclopedia of Education.*

Wharton-McDonald, R., Pressley, M., Rankin, J., Mistretta, J., Yokoi, L. and Ettenberger, S. (1997). Effective primary-grades literacy instruction = Balanced literacy instruction. *The Reading Teacher, 50,* 518–521.

Wheatley, K. F. (2002). The potential benefits of teacher efficacy doubts for educational reform. *Teaching and Teacher Education, 18,* 5–22.

Windschitl, M. (2002). Framing constructivism in practice as the negotiation of dilemmas; An analysis of the conceptual, pedagogical, cultural, and political challenges facing teachers. *Review of Educational Research, 72,* 131–175.

Winne, P. H. (1995). Inherent details in self-regulated learning. *Educational Psychologist, 30,* 173–188.

Winne, P. H. and Hadwin, A. F. (1998). Studying as self-regulated learning. In D. J. Hacker, J. Dunlosky and A. C. Graesser (eds), *Metacognition in Educational Theory and Practice* (pp. 277–304). Mahwah, NJ: Lawrence Erlbaum.

Winne, P. H. and Perry, N. E. (2000). Measuring self-regulated learning. In P. Pintrich, M. Boekaerts and M. Zeidner (eds), *Handbook of Self-regulation* (pp. 531–566). Orlando, FL: Academic Press.

Woods, B. S. and Murphy, P. K. (2002). Thickening the discussion: What can William James tell us about constructivism? *Educational Theory, 52,* 443–449.

Woolfolk Hoy, A. and Burke-Spero, R. (2005). Changes in teacher efficacy during the early years of teaching: A comparison of four measures. *Teaching and Teacher Education, 21,* 343–356.

Woolfolk, A. E., Winne, P. and Perry, N. (2006). *Educational Psychology.* (3rd Canadian ed.). Toronto, CA: Pearson.

Zimmerman, B. J. (2002). Becoming a self-regulated learner: An overview. *Theory Into Practice, 41,* 64–70.

Chapter 10

Ainley, M., Hidi, S. and Berndorf, D. (2002). Interest, learning, and the psychological processes that mediate their relationship. *Journal of Educational Psychology, 94,* 545–561.

Alexander, P. A. and Murphy, P. K. (1998). The research base for APA's Learner-Centered Psychological Principles. In N. Lambert and B. McCombs (eds), *How Students Learn: Reforming schools through learner-centered education* (pp. 33–60). Washington, DC: American Psychological Association.

Alloy, L. B. and Seligman, M. E. P. (1979). On the cognitive component of learned helplessness and depression. *Journal of Learning and Motivation, 13,* 219–276.

Ames, C. (1992). Classrooms: Goals, structures, and student motivation. *Journal of Educational Psychology, 84,* 261–271.

Ames, R. and Lau, S. (1982). An attributional analysis of student help-seeking in academic settings. *Journal of Educational Psychology, 74,* 414–423.

Anderman, E. M. and Maehr, M. L. (1994). Motivation and schooling in the middle grades. *Review of Educational Research, 64,* 287–310.

Anderson, C. W., Holland, J. D. and Palincsar, A. S. (1997). Canonical and sociocultural approaches to research and reform in science education: The story of Juan and his group. *Elementary School Journal, 97,* 359–384.

Anderson, L. M., Brubaker, N. L., Alleman-Brooks, J. and Duffy, G. G. (1985). A qualitative study of seatwork in first-grade classrooms. *Elementary School Journal, 86,* 123–140.

Bandura, A. (1993). Perceived self-efficacy in cognitive development and functioning. *Educational Psychologist, 28,* 117–148.

Bandura, A. (1997). *Self-efficacy: The Exercise of Control.* New York: Freeman.

Baumeister, R. F. and Leary, M. R. (1995). The need to belong: Desire for interpersonal attachments as a fundamental human motivation. *Psychological Bulletin, 117,* 497–529.

Beane, J. A. (1991). Sorting out the self-esteem controversy. *Educational Leadership, 49*(1), 25–30.

Berlyne, D. (1966). Curiosity and exploration. *Science, 153,* 25–33.

Blumenfeld, P. C., Puro, P. and Mergendoller, J. R. (1992). Translating motivation into thoughtfulness. In H. Marshall (ed.), *Redefining Student Learning: Roots of Educational Change* (pp. 207–240). Norwood, NJ: Ablex.

Boekaerts, M. (2002). *Motivation to learn.* Education Practice Series. International Bureau of Education (UNESCO). Available at http://www.ibe.unesco.org/publications/EducationalPracticesSeriesPdf/prac10e.pdf#search=%22social%20goals%20motivation%20Europe%22

Brophy, J. E. (1985). Teacher–student interaction. In J. Dusek (ed.), *Teacher Expectancies* (pp. 303–328). Hillsdale, NJ: Lawrence Erlbaum.

Brophy, J. E. (1988). On motivating students. In D. Berliner and B. Rosenshine (eds), *Talks to Teachers* (pp. 201–245). New York: Random House.

Brophy, J. E. (2003). An interview with Jere Brophy by B. Gaedke and M. Shaughnessy.

Brophy, J. E. and Good, T. (1986). Teacher behavior and student achievement. In M. Wittrock (ed.), *Handbook of Research on Teaching* (3rd ed.) (pp. 328–375). New York: Macmillan.

Butler, R. and Neuman, O. (1995). Effects of task and ego achievement goals on help-seeking behaviors and attitudes. *Journal of Educational Psychology, 87,* 261–271.

Cassady, J. C. and Johnson, R. E. (2002). Cognitive anxiety and academic performance. *Contemporary Educational Psychology, 27,* 270–295.

Clifford, M. M. (1990). Students need challenge, not easy success. *Educational Leadership, 48*(1), 22–26.

Clifford, M. M. (1991). Risk taking: Empirical and educational considerations. *Educational Psychologist, 26,* 263–298.

Cordova, D. I. and Lepper, M. R. (1996). Intrinsic motivation and the process of learning: Beneficial effects of contextualization, personalization, and choice. *Journal of Educational Psychology, 88,* 715–730.

Covington, M. V. (1992). *Making the Grade: A Self-worth Perspective on Motivation and School Reform.* New York: Holt, Rinehart and Winston.

Covington, M. V. and Mueller, K. J. (2001). Intrinsic versus extrinsic motivation: An approach/avoidance reformulation. *Education Psychology Review, 13,* 157–176.

Covington, M. V. and Omelich, C. (1987). 'I knew it cold before the exam': A test of the anxiety-blockage hypothesis. *Journal of Educational Psychology, 79,* 393–400.

Cowley, G. and Underwood, A. (1998, June 15). Memory. *Newsweek, 131*(24), 48–54.

deCharms, R. (1983). Intrinsic motivation, peer tutoring, and cooperative learning: Practical maxims. In J. Levine and M. Wang (eds), *Teacher and Student Perceptions: Implications for Learning* (pp. 391–398). Hillsdale, NJ: Lawrence Erlbaum.

Deci, E. L., Koestner, R. and Ryan, R. M. (1999). A meta-analytic review of experiments examining the effects of extrinsic rewards on intrinsic motivation. *Psychological Bulletin, 125,* 627–668.

Deci, E. L. and Ryan, R. M. (1985). *Intrinsic Motivation and Self-determination in Human Behavior.* New York: Plenum.

Deci, E. L. and Ryan, R. M. (eds). (2002). *Handbook of Self-determination Research.* Rochester: University of Rochester Press.

Deci, E. L., Vallerand, R. J., Pelletier, L. G. and Ryan, R. M. (1991). Motivation and education: The self-determination perspective. *Educational Psychologist, 26,* 325–346.

Dewey, J. (1913). *Interest and Effort in Education.* Cambridge, MA: Houghton-Mifflin.

Dolezal, S. E., Welsh, L. M., Pressley, M. and Vincent, M. (2003). How do nine third-grade teachers motivate their students? *Elementary School Journal, 103,* 239–267.

Dweck, C. S. (1999). *Self-theories: Their Role in Motivation, Personality, and Development.* Philadelphia: Psychology Press.

Dweck, C. S. (2000). *Self-theories: Their Role in Motivation, Personality, and Development.* Philadelphia: Routledge Press.

Dweck, C. S. (2002). The development of ability conceptions. In A. Wigfield and J. Eccles (eds), *The Development of Achievement Motivation.* San Diego, CA: Academic Press.

Dweck, C. S. and Bempechat, J. (1983). Children's theories on intelligence: Consequences for learning. In S. Paris, G. Olson and W. Stevenson (eds), *Learning and Motivation in the Classroom* (pp. 239–256). Hillsdale, NJ: Lawrence Erlbaum.

Dyson, A. H. (1997). *Writing Superheroes: Contemporary Childhood, Popular Culture, and Classroom Literacy.* New York: Teachers College Press.

Eccles, J. and Wigfield, A. (1985). Teacher expectations and student motivation. In J. Dusek (ed.), *Teacher Expectancies* (pp. 185–226). Hillsdale, NJ: Lawrence Erlbaum.

Eccles, J. and Wigfield, A. (2001). Teacher expectations and student motivation. In J. Dusek (ed.), *Teacher Expectancies* (pp. 185–226). Hillsdale, NJ: Lawrence Erlbaum.

Eccles, J., Wigfield, A. and Schiefele, U. (1998). Motivation to succeed. In W. Damon (Series Ed.) and N. Eisenberg (Vol. Ed.), *Handbook of Child Psychology: Vol. 3. Social, Emotional, and Personality Development* (5th ed., pp. 1017–1095). New York: Wiley.

Elliott, J., Hufton, N., Anderman, E. and Illushin, L. (2000). The psychology of motivation and its relevance to educational practice. *Educational and Child Psychology, 17,* 121–137.

Feather, N. T. (1982). *Expectations and Actions: Expectancy-Value Models in Psychology.* Hillsdale, NJ: Lawrence Erlbaum.

Flink, C. F., Boggiano, A. K. and Barrett, M. (1990). Controlling teaching strategies: Undermining children's

self-determination and performance. *Journal of Personality and Social Psychology, 59,* 916–924.

Freud, S. (1990). *Beyond the Pleasure Principle.* New York: W. W. Norton and Company.

Furrer, C. and Skinner, E. (2003). Sense of relatedness as a factor in children's academic engagement and performance. *Journal of Educational Psychology, 95*(11), 148–161.

Gaedke, B. and Shaughnessy, M. F. (2003). An interview with Jere Brophy. *Educational Psychology Review, 15,* 199–211.

Garner, R. (1998). Choosing to learn and not-learn in school. *Educational Psychology Review, 10,* 227–238.

Graham, S. (1991). A review of attribution theory in achievement contexts. *Educational Psychology Review, 3,* 5–39.

Graham, S. and Barker, G. (1990). The downside of help: An attributional developmental analysis of helping behavior as a low ability cue. *Journal of Educational Psychology, 82,* 7–14.

Graham, S. and Weiner, B. (1996). Theories and principles of motivation. In D. Berliner and R. C. Calfee (eds), *Handbook of Educational Psychology* (pp. 63–84). New York: Macmillan.

Grolnick, W. S., Gurland, S. T., Jacob, K. F. and DeCourcey, W. (2002). The development of self-determination in middle childhood and adolescence. In A. Wigfield and J. Eccles (eds), *Development of Achievement Motivation* (pp. 147–171), New York: Academic Press.

Guthrie, J. T. and Alao, S. (1997). Designing contexts to increase motivations of reading. *Educational Psychologist, 32,* 95–105.

Guthrie, J. T., Cox, K. E., Anderson, E., Harris, K., Mazzoni, S. and Rach, L. (1998). Principles of integrated instruction for engagement in reading. *Educational Psychology Review, 10,* 227–238.

Harackiewicz, J. M., Barron, K. E., Pintrich, P. R., Elliot, A. J. and Thrash, T. M. (2002). Revision of achievement goal theory: Necessary and illuminating. *Journal of Educational Psychology, 94,* 562–575.

Harp, S. F. and Mayer, R. E. (1998). How seductive details do their damage: A theory of cognitive interest in science learning. *Journal of Educational Psychology, 90,* 414–434.

Hickey, D. T. (2003). Engaged participation vs. marginal non-participation: A stridently sociocultural model of achievement motivation. *Elementary School Journal, 103*(4), 401–429.

Hiroto, D. S. and Seligman, M. E. P. (1975). Generality of learned helplessness in man. *Journal of Personality and Social Psychology, 31,* 311–327.

Hufton, N., Elliott, J. and Illushin, L. (2002). Educational motivation and engagement: qualitative accounts from three countries. *British Educational Research Journal, 28*(2), 265–289.

Johnson, D. W. and Johnson, R. T. (1999). *Learning Together and Alone: Cooperation, Competition, and Individualization* (5th ed.). Boston: Allyn and Bacon.

K2- E-Learning made in Europe (2004). *Fifth Dimension: Local learning communities in a global world*. Available at http://www.know2.org/index.cfm?PID=62&ProjID=25435&action1=display&action2=public

Lave, J. and Wenger, E. (1991). *Situated Learning: Legitimate Peripheral Participation.* Cambridge, MA: Cambridge University Press.

Locke, E. A. and Latham, G. P. (2002). Building a practically useful theory of goal setting and task motivation: A 35-year odyssey. *American Psychologist, 57,* 705–717.

Lowenstein, G. (1994). The psychology of curiosity: A review and reinterpretation. *Psychological Bulletin, 117,* 75–98.

Malone, T. W. and Lepper, M. (1987). Making learning fun: A taxonomy of intrinsic motivations for learning. In R. E. Snow and M. J. Farr (eds), *Aptitude, Learning and Instruction. Volume 3: Cognitive and Affective Process Analysis* (pp. 223–253). Hillsdale, NJ: Lawrence Erlbaum.

Maslow, A. H. (1968). *Toward a Psychology of Being* (2nd ed.). New York: Van Nostrand.

Maslow, A. H. (1970). *Motivation and Personality* (2nd ed.). New York: Harper and Row.

McClelland, D. (1985). *Human Motivation.* Glenview, IL: Scott, Foresman.

Meijer, A. M. and Wittenboer, G. L. H. van den (2004). The joint contribution of sleep, intelligence and motivation to school performance, *Personality and Individual Differences, 37,* 95–106.

Midgley, C. (2001). A goal theory perspective on the current status of middle level schools. In T. Urdan and F. Pajares (eds), *Adolescence and Education* (pp. 33–59). Volume I. Greenwich, CT: Information Age Publishing.

Midgley, C., Kaplan, A. and Middleton, M. (2001). Performance-approach goals: Good for what, for whom, under what circumstances, and at what cost? *Journal of Educational Psychology, 93,* 77–86.

Miller, G. A., Galanter, E. and Pribram, K. H. (1960). *Plans and the Structure of Behavior.* New York: Holt, Rinehart and Winston.

Miller, P. H. (2002). *Theories of Developmental Psychology* (4th ed.). New York: Worth.

Mitchell, M. (1993). Situational interest: Its multifaceted structure in the secondary school mathematics classroom. *Journal of Educational Psychology, 85,* 424–436.

Murphy, P. K. and Alexander, P. A. (2000). A motivated exploration of motivation terminology. *Contemporary Educational Psychology, 25,* 3–53.

Naveh-Benjamin, M. (1991). A comparison of training programs intended for different types of test-anxious students: Further support for an information-processing model. *Journal of Educational Psychology, 83,* 134–139.

Naveh-Benjamin, M., McKeachie, W. J. and Lin, Y. (1987). Two types of test-anxious students: Support for an information processing model. *Journal of Educational Psychology, 79,* 131–136.

Nicholls, J. (1984). Achievement motivation: Conceptions of ability, subjective experience, task choice, and performance. *Psychology Review, 91,* 328–346.

Nicholls, J., Cobb, P., Wood, T., Yackel, E. and Patashnick, M. (1990). Assessing student's theories of success in mathematics: Individual and classroom differences. *Journal for Research in Mathematics Education, 21,* 109–122.

Nicholls, J. G. and Miller, A. (1984). Conceptions of ability and achievement motivation. In R. Ames and C. Ames (eds), *Research on Motivation in Education. Vol. 1: Student Motivation* (pp. 39–73). New York: Academic Press.

Ortony, A., Clore, G. L. and Collins, A. (1988). *The Cognitive Structure of Emotions.* Cambridge, UK: Cambridge University Press.

Osterman, K. F. (2000). Students' need for belonging in the school community. *Review of Educational Research, 70,* 323–367.

Paulman, R. G. and Kennelly, K. J. (1984). Test anxiety and ineffective test taking: Different names, same construct? *Journal of Educational Psychology, 76,* 279–288.

Pekrun, R., Goetz, T., Titz, W. and Perry, R. P. (2002). Academic emotions in students' self-regulated learning and achievement. A program of qualitative and quantitative research. *Educational Psychologist, 37,* 91–105.

Pintrich, P. R. (2003). A motivational science perspective on the role of student motivation in learning and teaching. *Journal of Educational Psychology, 95,* 667–686.

Pintrich, P. R., Marx, R. W. and Boyle, R. A. (1993). Beyond cold conceptual change: The role of motivational beliefs and classroom contextual factors in the process of conceptual change. *Review of Educational Research, 63,* 167–199.

Pintrich, P. R. and Schunk, D. H. (2002). *Motivation in Education: Theory, Research, and Applications* (2nd ed.). Upper Saddle River, NJ: Merrill/Prentice-Hall.

QCA (Qualifications and Curriculum Agency) (2006). *INCA: International Review of Curriculum and Assessments Framework*. Available at http://www.inca.org.uk/

Reeve, J. (1996). *Motivating Others: Nurturing Inner Motivational Resources.* Boston: Allyn and Bacon.

Reeve, J., Bolt, E. and Cai, Y. (1999). Autonomy-supportive teachers: How they teach and motivate students. *Journal of Educational Psychology, 91,* 537–548.

Reeve, J., Deci, E. L. and Ryan, R. M. (2004). *Self-determination Theory: A dialectical framework for understanding the sociocultural influences on motivation and learning: Big theories revisited* (Vol. 4, pp. 31–59). Greenwich, CT: Information Age Press.

Reeve, J., Nix, G. and Hamm, D. (2003). The experience of self-determination in intrinsic motivation and the conundrum of choice. *Journal of Educational Psychology, 95,* 347–392.

Reisberg, D. and Heuer, F. (1992). Remembering the details of emotional events. In E. Winograd and U. Neisser (eds), *Affect and Accuracy in Recall: Studies of 'Flashbulb' Memories.* Cambridge, England: Cambridge University Press.

Renninger, K. A., Hidi, S. and Krapp, A. (eds). (1992). *The Role of Interest in Learning and Development.* Hillsdale, NJ: Lawrence Erlbaum.

Rogers, C. R. and Freiberg, H. J. (1994). *Freedom to Learn* (3rd ed.). Columbus, OH: Charles E. Merrill.

Rogoff, B., Turkanis, C. G. and Bartlett, L. (2001). *Learning Together: Children and Adults in a School Community.* New York: Oxford.

Ryan, A. (2001). The peer group as a context for development of young adolescents' motivation and achievement. *Child Development, 72,* 1135–1150.

Ryan, R. M. and Deci, E. L. (1996). When paradigms clash: Comments on Cameron and Pierce's claim that rewards do not undermine intrinsic motivation. *Review of Educational Research, 66,* 33–38.

Ryan, R. M. and Deci, E. L. (2000). Intrinsic and extrinsic motivation: Classic definitions and new directions. *Contemporary Educational Psychology, 25,* 54–67.

Schraw, G. and Lehman, S. (2001). Situational interest: A review of the literature and directions for future research. *Educational Psychology Review, 13,* 23–52.

Schunk, D. H. (2000). *Learning Theories: An Educational Perspective* (3rd ed.). Columbus, OH: Merrill/Prentice-Hall.

Schutz, P. A. and Davis, H. A. (2000). Emotions and self-regulations during test-taking. *Educational Psychologist, 35,* 243–256.

Seligman, M. E. P. (1975). *Helplessness: On Depression, Development, and Death.* San Francisco: Freeman.

Smith, C. (2005). *Pupil motivation inquiry: response from members of the eppi review of motivation group.* Available at http://www.scottish.parliament.uk/business/committees/education/inquiries/pmi/University%20of%20Glasgow.pdf

Solomon, D., Battistich, V., Watson, M., Schaps, E. and Lewis, C. (2000). A six-district study of educational change:

Direct and mediated effects of the Child Development Project. *Social Psychology of Education, 4,* 3–51.

Stepien, W. and Gallagher, S. (1993). Problem-based learning: As authentic as it gets. *Educational Leadership, 50*(7), 25–28.

Stipek, D. J. (1993). *Motivation to Learn* (2nd ed.). Boston: Allyn and Bacon.

Stipek, D. J. (2002). *Motivation to Learn: Integrating Theory and Practice* (4th ed.). Boston: Allyn and Bacon.

Sztefka, B. (2002). *A case study on the teaching of culture in a foreign language.* Available from http://www.beta-iatefl.hit.bg/pdfs/case_study.pdf.

Tollefson, N. (2000). Classroom applications of cognitive theories of motivation. *Education Psychology Review, 12,* 63–83.

Urdan, T. C. and Maehr, M. L. (1995). Beyond a two-goal theory of motivation and achievement: A case for social goals. *Review of Educational Research, 65,* 213–243.

van Laar, C. (2000). The paradox of low academic achievement but high self-esteem in African American students: An attributional account. *Educational Psychology Review, 12,* 33–61.

Vroom, V. (1964). *Work and Motivation.* New York: Wiley.

Wade, S. E., Schraw, G., Buxton, W. M. and Hayes, M. T. (1993). Seduction of the strategic reader: Effects of interest on strategies and recall. *Reading Research Quarterly, 28,* 3–24.

Webb, N. M. and Palincsar, A. (1996). Group processes in the classroom. In D. C. Berliner and R. C. Calfee (eds), *Handbook of Educational Psychology* (pp. 841–876). New York: Macmillan.

Weiner, B. (1979). A theory of motivation for some classroom experiences. *Journal of Educational Psychology, 71,* 3–25.

Weiner, B. (1986). *An Attributional Theory of Motivation and Emotion.* New York: Springer.

Weiner, B. (1992). *Human Motivation: Metaphors, Theories, and Research.* Newbury Park, CA: Sage.

Weiner, B. (1994a). Ability versus effort revisited: The moral determinants of achievement evaluation an achievement as a moral system. *Educational Psychologist, 29,* 163–172.

Weiner, B. (1994b). Integrating social and persons theories of achievement striving. *Review of Educational Research, 64,* 557–575.

Weiner, B. (2000). Interpersonal and intrapersonal theories of motivation from an attributional perspective. *Educational Psychology Review, 12,* 1–14.

Weiner, B. and Graham, S. (1989). Understanding the motivational role of affect: Lifespan research from an attributional perspective. *Cognition and Emotion, 4,* 401–419.

Wenger, E. (1998). *Communities of Practice: Learning, Meaning, and Identity.* New York: Cambridge University Press.

Wigfield, A. and Eccles, J. (1989). Test anxiety in elementary and secondary school students. *Educational Psychologist, 24,* 159–183.

Wigfield, A. and Eccles, J. S. (2002). Students' motivation during the middle school years. In J. Aronson (ed.), *Improving Academic Development: Impact of Psychological Factors in Education.* New York: Academic Press.

Williams, G. C., Wiener, M. W., Markakis, K. M., Reeve, J. and Deci, E. L. (1993). Medical students' motivation for internal medicine. *Annals of Internal Medicine.*

Wolters, C. A., Yu, S. L. and Pintrich, P. R. (1996). The relation between goal orientation and students' motivational beliefs and self-regulated learning. *Learning and Individual Differences, 8,* 211–238.

Yerkes, R. M. and Dodson, J. D. (1908). The relation of strength of stimulus to rapidity of habit formation. *Journal of Comparative Neurology, 18,* 459–482.

Young, A. J. (1997). I think, therefore I'm motivated: The relations among cognitive strategy use, motivational orientation, and classroom perceptions over time. *Learning and Individual Differences, 9,* 249–283.

Zeidner, M. (1995). Adaptive coping with test situations. *Educational Psychologist, 30,* 123–134.

Zeidner, M. (1998). *Test Anxiety: The State of the Art.* New York: Plenum.

Chapter 11

Aber, J. L., Brown, J. L. and Jones, S. M. (2003). Developmental trajectories toward violence in middle childhood: Course, demographic differences, and response to school-based intervention. *Developmental Psychology, 39,* 324–348.

Abrami, P. C., Lou, Y., Chambers, B., Poulsen, C. and Spence, J. C. (2000). Why should we group students within-class for learning? *Educational Research and Evaluation, 6*(2), 158–179.

Aronson, E. (2000). *Nobody Left to Hate: Teaching Compassion after Columbine.* New York: Worth.

Aunola, K. and Nurmi, J. (2005). The role of parenting styles in children's problem behaviour. *Child Development, 76*(6), 1144–1159.

Barone, F. J. (1997). Bullying in school: It doesn't have to happen. *Phi Delta Kappan, 79,* 80–82.

Battistich, V., Solomon, D. and Delucci, K. (1993). Interaction processes and student outcomes in cooperative groups. *Elementary School Journal, 94,* 19–32.

Battistich, V., Watson, M., Solomon, D., Lewis, C. and Schaps, E. (1999). Beyond the three R's: A broad agenda for school reform. *Elementary School Journal, 99,* 415–432.

Bevington, J. and Wishart, J.G. (1999). The influence of classroom peers on cognitive performance in children with behavioural problems. *British Journal of Educational Psychology, 69*(1), 19–32.

Bowlby, J. (1988). *A Secure Base.* London: Routledge.

Brabant, C., Bourdon, S. and Jutras, F. (2003). Home education in Quebec: Family first. *Evaluation and Research in Education, 17*(2–3), 112–131.

Bruner, J. S. (1986). *Actual Minds, Possible Worlds.* Cambridge, MA: Harvard University Press.

Casanova, P., García-Linares, C., de la Torre, M. and de la Villa, C. (2005). Influence of family and socio-demographic variables on students with low academic achievement. *Educational Psychology, 25*(4), 423–435.

Charlton, T. and David, K. (1993). *Managing Misbehaviour in Schools.* London: Routledge.

Claus, J. and Ogden, C. (1999). Service learning for youth empowerment and social change: An introduction. In J. Claus and C. Ogden (eds), *Service Learning for Youth Empowerment and Social Change.* New York: Peter Lang.

Codell, E. R. (2001). *Educating Esme: Diary of a Teacher's First Year.* Chapel Hill, NC: Algonquin Books.

Cohen, E. G. (1986). *Designing Group Work: Strategies for the Heterogeneous Classroom.* New York: Teachers College Press.

Cohen, E. G. (1994). *Designing Group Work* (2nd ed.). New York: Teachers College Press.

Coldron, J., Coldwell, M., Logie, A., Povey, H., Radice, M. and Stephenson, K. (2002). *We just talk things through and then she helps me: relationships of trust and mediation.* Paper presented at the Annual Conference of the British Educational Research Association, University of Exeter, England, 12–14 September. The text is in the Education-line internet document collection at: <http://www.leeds.ac.uk/educol/documents/00002412.htm>, p. 27.

Collins, W. A., Maccoby, E. E., Steinberg, L., Hetherington, E. M. and Bornstein, M. H. (2000). Contemporary research on parenting: The case for nature and nurture. *American Psychologist, 55,* 218–232.

Committee on Increasing High School Pupils' Engagement and Motivation to Learn (2004). *Engaging schools: Fostering high school pupils' motivation to learn.* Washington, DC: The National Academies Press.

Cullingford, C. (2002). *The happiest days of their lives? Pupils and their learning styles.* Paper presented at the European Conference on Educational Research, University of Lisbon, 11–14 September. The text is in the Education-line internet document collection at: <http://www.leeds.ac.uk/educol/documents/00002279.htm>, p. 27.

Cunningham, C. E., Cunningham, L. J. and Martorelli, V. (1997). *Coping with Conflict at School: The Collaborative Student Mediation Project Manual*. Hamilton, Canada: COPE Works.

Cunningham, C. E., Cunningham, L. J., Martorelli, V., Tran, A., Young, J. and Zacharias, R. (1998). The effects of primary division, student-mediated conflict resolution programs on playground aggression. *Journal of Child Psychology and Psychiatry* (formerly *Journal of Child Psychology and Psychiatry and Allied Disciplines*), *39*(5), 653–662.

Dansereau, D. F. (1985). Learning strategy research. In J. Segal, S. Chipman and R. Glaser (eds), *Thinking and Learning Skills. Vol. I: Relating Instruction to Research* (pp. 209–239). Hillsdale, NJ: Lawrence Erlbaum.

DeCecco, J. and Richards, A. (1974). *Growing Pains: Uses of School Conflicts*. New York: Aberdeen.

DES (1989). Discipline in Schools: Report of the Committee of Enquiry chaired by Lord Elton, 'The Elton Report'. London: HMSO.

Deuchar, R. and Maitles, H. (2004). *I just don't like the whole thing about war!: Encouraging the expression of political literacy among primary pupils as a vehicle for promoting education for active citizenship*. Paper presented at the European Conference on Educational Research, University of Crete, 22–25 September.

de Winter, M., Kroneman, M. and Baerveldt, C. (1999). The social education gap report of a Dutch peer-consultation project on family policy. *British Journal of Social Work, 29*(6), 903–914.

Durbin, D. L., Darling, N., Steinberg, L. and Brown, B. B. (1993). Parenting style and peer group membership among European-American adolescents. *Journal of Research on Adolescence, 3*, 87–100.

Elias, M. J. and Schwab, Y. (2006). From compliance to responsibility: Social and emotional learning and classroom management. In C. Evertson and C. S. Weinstein (eds), *Handbook for Classroom Management: Research, Practice, and Contemporary Issues*. Mahwah, NJ: Lawrence Erlbaum.

Elliott, R. and Leonard, C. (2004). Peer pressure and poverty: exploring fashion brands and consumption symbolism among children of the 'British poor'. *Journal of Consumer Behaviour, 3*(4), 347–359.

Elliott, J. G., Huflon, N., Illushin, L. and Lauchlin, F. (2001). Motivation in the junior years: International perspectives on children's attitudes, behaviour and their relationship to educational achievement. *Oxford Review of Education, 27*(1), 37–68.

Feldman, N. (1986). Effects of a reciprocal questioning procedure on the reading comprehension of learning disabled children. *Dissertation Abstracts International, 47*(6-A), p. 2098.

Fredericks, L. (2003). *Making the Case for Social and Emotional Learning and Service-learning*. Denver, CO: Education Commission of the States.

Fredricks, J. A., Blumenfeld, P. C. and Paris, A. H. (2004). School engagement: Potential of the concept, state of the evidence. *Review of Educational Research, 74*, 59–109.

Gage, N. L. (1991). The obviousness of social and educational research results. *Educational Researcher, 20*(A), 10–16.

Gillies, R. (2003). The behaviors, interactions, and perceptions of junior high school pupils during small-group learning. *Journal of Educational Psychology, 96*, 15–22.

Gillies, R. (2004). The effects of cooperative learning on junior high school pupils during small group learning. *Learning and Instruction, 14*, 197–213.

Graham, S. and Weiner, B. (1996). Theories and principles of motivation. In D. Berliner and R. C. Calfee (eds), *Handbook of Educational Psychology* (pp. 63–84). New York: Macmillan.

Greenberg, M. T., Weissberg, R. P., O'Brien, M. U., Zins, J. E., Fredericks, L., Resnik, H. and Elias, M. J. (2003). *American Psychologist, 58*(6/7), 466–474.

Hedley, I. (1997). *Personal essay: Evaluating Classroom Charters*. At http://homepage.ntlworld.com/i.hedley/sen/chartstudy.htm. Accessed 28 September 2006.

Huff, C. R. (1989). Youth gangs and public policy. *Crime and Delinquency, 35*, 524–537.

Huitt, W. (2003). The information processing approach to cognition. *Educational Psychology Interactive*. Valdosta, GA: Valdosta State University.

Jackson, C. (2006), 'Wild' girls? An exploration of 'ladette' cultures in secondary schools. *Gender and Education, 18*(4), 339–360.

Johnson, A. M. and Notah, D. J. (1999). Service learning: History, literature, review, and a pilot study of eighth graders. *Elementary School Journal, 99*, 453–467.

Johnson, D. W. and Johnson, R. T. (1999). *Learning Together and Alone: Cooperation, Competition, and Individualization* (5th ed.). Boston: Allyn and Bacon.

Johnson, D. W., Johnson, R. T., Dudley, B., Ward, M. and Magnuson, D. (1995). The impact of peer mediation training on the management of school and home conflicts. *American Educational Research Journal, 32*, 829–844.

Jordan, E. (2001). Exclusion of Travellers in state schools. *Educational Research, 43*(2), 117–132.

Kagan, S. (1994). *Cooperative Learning*. San Juan Capistrano, CA: Kagan Cooperative Learning.

Kalmijn, M. and Kraaykamp, G. (2003). Dropout and downward mobility in the educational career: An event-history anaylsis of ethnic schooling differences in the Netherlands. *Educational Research and Evaluation, 9*(3), 265–287.

King, A. (1994). Guiding knowledge construction in the classroom: Effects of teaching children how to question and how to explain. *American Educational Research Journal, 31*, 338–368.

King, A. (2002). Structuring peer interactions to promote high-level cognitive processing. *Theory Into Practice, 41*, 31–39.

Kirk, S., Gallagher, J. J. and Anastasiow, N. J. (1993). *Educating Exceptional Children* (7th ed.). Boston: Houghton Mifflin.

Kirk, S. A., Gallagher, J. J., Anastasiow, N. J. and Coleman, M. R. (2006). *Educating Exceptional Children* (11th ed.). Boston: Houghton Mifflin.

Kohn, A. (2002). How not to teach values. In L. Abbeduto (ed.), *Taking Sides: Clashing Views on Controversial Issues in Educational Psychology* (pp. 138–153). Guilford, CT: McGraw-Hill/Duskin.

Kutnick, P., Blatchford, P. and Baines, E. (2002). Pupil groupings in primary school classrooms: Sites for learning and social pedagogy? *British Educational Research Journal, 28*(2), 187–206.

Landrum, T. J. and Kauffman, J. M. (2006). Behavioral approaches to classroom management. In C. M. Evertson and C. S. Weinstein (eds), *Handbook of Classroom Management: Research, Practice, and Contemporary Issues*. Mahwah, NJ: Erlbaum.

Leach, F. (2003). Learning to be violent: The role of the school in developing adolescent gendered behaviour. *Compare, 33*(3), 385–400.

Leask, M. and Younie. S. (2001). Communal constructivist theory: information and communications technology pedagogy and internationalisation of the curriculum. *Journal of Information Technology for Teacher Education, 10*(1–2), 117–134.

Lee, F. W-L. and Ip, F. M-L. (2003). Young school dropouts: Levels of influence of different systems. *Journal of Youth Studies, 6*(1), 89–110.

Lickona, T. (2002). Character education: Seven crucial issues. In L. Abbeduto (ed.), *Taking Sides: Clashing on Controversial Issues in Educational Psychology* (pp. 130–137). Guilford, CT: McGraw-Hill/Duskin.

Loeber, R. and Stouthamer-Loeber, M. (1986). Family factors as correlates and predictors of juvenile conduct problems and delinquency. In M. Tonry and N. Morris (eds), *Crime and Justice, 7*. Chicago: University of Chicago Press.

Lowry, R., Sleet, D., Duncan, C., Powell, K. and Kolbe, L. (1995). Adolescents at risk for violence. *Educational Psychology Review, 7*, 7–40.

Madsen, C. H., Becker, W. C., Thomas, D. R., Koser, L. and Plager, E. (1968). An analysis of the reinforcing function of 'sit down' commands. In R. K. Parker (ed.), *Readings in Educational Psychology*. Boston: Allyn and Bacon.

Mason, L. H. (2004). Explicit self-regulated strategy development versus reciprocal questioning: Effects on expository reading comprehension among struggling readers. *Journal of Educational Psychology, 96*(2), 283–296.

McCaslin, M. and Good, T. (1996). The informal curriculum. In D. Berliner and R. Calfee (eds), *Handbook of Educational Psychology* (pp. 622–670). New York: Macmillan.

McCord, J. (1979). Some child-rearing antecedents of criminal behaviour in adult men. *Journal of Personality and Social Psychology, 37*, 1477–1486.

McNamara, S. and Moreton, G. (1995). *Changing Behaviour: Teaching Children with Emotional and Behavioural_Difficulties in Primary and Secondary Classrooms*. London: David Fulton.

Meehan, S., Holmes, B., and Tangney, B. with senior students of St Brigid's National School (2001). Who wants to be a teacher? An exploration of the theory of communal constructivism at the chalk face. *Teacher Development, 5*(2), 177–190.

Miller, A., Ferguson, E. and Byrne, I. (2000). Pupils' causal attributions for difficult classroom behaviour. *British Journal of Educational Psychology, 70*(1), 85–96.

Miller, N. and Harrington, H. J. (1993). Social categorization and intergroup acceptance: Principles for the development an design of cooperative learning teams. In R. Hertz-Lasarowitz and N. Miller (eds), *Interaction in Cooperative Groups: The Theoretical Anatomy of Group Learning* (pp. 203–227). New York: Cambridge University Press.

Nansel, T. R., Overbeck, M., Pilla, R. S., Ruan, W. J., Simons-Morton, B. and Schiedt, P. (2001). Bullying behavior among US youth: Prevalence and association with psychosocial adjustment. *Journal of the American Medical Association, 285*(16), 2094–2100.

O'Donnell, A. M. (ed.). (2002). Promoting thinking through peer learning. Special issue of *Theory Into Practice, 61*(1).

O'Donnell, A. M. and O'Kelly, J. (1994). Learning from peers: Beyond the rhetoric of positive results. *Educational Psychology Review, 6*, 321–350.

Osterman, K. F. (2000). Pupils' need for belonging in the school community. *Review of Educational Research, 70*, 323–367.

Palincsar, A. S. and Brown, A. L. (1984). Reciprocal teaching of comprehension-fostering and monitoring activities. *Cognition and Instruction, 1*, 117–175.

Palincsar, A. S. and Herrenkohl, L. R. (2002). Designing collaborative learning contexts. *Theory Into Practice, 61*, 26–32.

Pallante, J. A. and Lindsey, J. D. (1991). Questioning and reciprocal dialogue: two major concerns for reading educators in the 1990s. *Education Today, 41*(3), 29–36.

Panitz, T. (1996). *A definition of collaborative vs cooperative learning*. Available online at http://www.city.londonmet.ac.uk/deliberations/collab.learning/panitz2.html (downloaded 1 April, 2005).

Parks, C. P. (1995). Gang behavior in the schools: Myth or reality? *Educational Psychology Review, 7*, 41–68.

Peterson, J. L. and Newman, R. (2000). Helping to curb youth violence: The APA-MTV 'Warning Signs' initiative. *Professional Psychology: Research and Practice, 31*, 509–514.

Piaget, J. (1985). *The Equilibrium of Cognitive Structures: The central problem of intellectual development* (T. Brown and K. L. Thampy, Trans.). Chicago: University of Chicago Press.

Puncochar, J. and Fox, P. W. (2004). Confidence in individual and group decision-making: When 'two heads' are worse than one. *Journal of Educational Psychology, 96*, 582–591.

Rembolt, C. (1998). Making violence unacceptable. *Educational Leadership, 56*(3), 32–38.

Rhodes, R. A. (1997). Community service and higher learning: Explorations of the caring self. Albany: State University of New York Press.

Riding, R. J. and Fairhurst, P. (2001). Cognitive style, home background and conduct behaviour in primary school pupils. *Educational Psychology, 21*(1), 115–124.

Riley, D. and Shaw M. (1985). *Parental Supervision and Juvenile Delinquency*. London: HMSO.

Rose, L. C. and Gallup, A. M. (2001). The 33rd annual Phi Delta Kappa/Gallup Poll of the public's attitude toward the public schools. *Phi Delta Kappan, 83*(1), 41–58.

Rosenshine, B. and Meister, C. (1994). Reciprocal teaching: A review of the research. *Review of Educational Research, 64*, 479–530.

Ross, J. A. and Raphael, D. (1990). Communication and problem solving achievement in cooperative learning groups. *Journal of Curriculum Studies, 22*, 149–164.

Sagor, R. (2003). *Motivating Students and Teachers in an Era of Standards*. Alexandria, VA: Association for Supervision and Curriculum Development.

Schwarz, B. B., Neuman, Y. and Biezuner, S. (2000). Two wrongs may make a right . . . if they argue together! *Cognition and Instruction, 18*, 461–494.

Siegler, R. S. and Crowley, K. (1991). The microgenetic method: A direct means for studying cognitive development. *American Psychologist, 56*, 606–620.

Slavin, R. E. (1995). *Cooperative Learning* (2nd ed.). Boston: Allyn and Bacon.

Smith, D. D. (2006). *Introduction to Special Education: Teaching in an Age of Opportunity* (5th ed.). Boston: Allyn and Bacon.

Smith, P. K. and Shu, S. (2000). What good schools can do about bullying: Findings from a survey in English schools after a decade of research and action. *Childhood, 7*(2), 193–212.

Solomon, D., Watson, M. S. and Battistich, V. A. (2001). Teaching and schooling effects on moral/prosocial development. In V. Richardson (ed.), *Handbook of Research on Teaching* (4th ed., pp. 566–603). Washington, DC: American Educational Research Association.

Stanovich, K. E. (1992). *How to Think Straight about Psychology* (3rd ed.). Glenview, IL: Scott, Foresman.

Sumer, Z. and Cetinkaya, E. (2004). *Student, teacher, and parent perceptions regarding violence in school: a qualitative investigation*. Paper presented at the European Conference on Educational Research, University of Crete, 22–25 September. The text is in the Education-line internet document collection at: http://www.leeds.ac.uk/educol/documents/00003876.htm, p. 13.

Tierney, R. J., Readence, J. E. and Dishner, E. K. (1990). *Reading Strategies and Practices: A Compendium* (3rd ed.). Boston: Allyn and Bacon.

Tierney, W. G. (1993). *Building Communities of Difference: Higher Education in the Twenty-first Century*. Westport, CT: Bergin and Garvey.

Tinklin, T. (2003). Gender differences and high attainment. *British Educational Research Journal, 29*(3), 307–325.

Veenman, S., Kenter, B. and Post, K. (2000). Cooperative learning in Dutch primary classrooms. *Educational Studies, 26*(3), 281–302.

Vitaro, F., Larocque, D., Janosz, M. and Tremblay, R. E. (2001). Negative social experiences and dropping out of school. *Educational Psychology, 21*(4), 401–415.

Warrington, M., Younger, M. and Williams. J. (2000). Student attitudes, image and the gender gap. *British Educational Research Journal, 26*(3), 393–407.

Webb, N. M. (1985). Verbal interaction and learning in peer-directed groups. *Theory Into Practice, 24*, 32–39.

Webb, N. M., Farivar, S. H. and Mastergeorge, A. M. (2002). Productive helping in cooperative groups. *Theory Into Practice, 41*, 13–20.

Webb, N. M. and Mastergeorge, A. M. (2003). The development of pupils' helping behavior and learning in peer-directed small groups. *Cognition and Instruction, 21*, 361–428.

Webb, N. M. and Palincsar, A. (1996). Group processes in the classroom. In D. C. Berliner and R. C. Calfee (eds), *Handbook of Educational Psychology* (pp. 841–876). New York: Macmillan.

Webb, R. and Vulliamy, G. (2002). The social work dimension of the primary teacher's role. *Research Papers in Education*, *17*(2), 165–184.

Weinstein, C. S. (2003). *Secondary Classroom Management: Lessons from Research and Practice* (2nd ed.). New York: McGraw-Hill.

Wentzel, K. R. (1998). Social relationships and motivation in middle school: The role of parents, teachers, and peers. *Journal of Educational Psychology, 90*(2), 202–209.

Wentzel, K. R. (2002). Are effective teachers like good parents? Teaching styles and student adjustment in early adolescence. *Child Development, 73,* 287–301.

Wentzel, K. R. and Battle, A. A. (2001). Social relationships and school adjustment. In T. Urdan and F. Pajares (eds), *Adolescence Education: General Issues in the Education of Adolescents* (Vol. 1, pp. 93–118). Greenwich, CT: Information Age.

Wilson, H. (1980). Parental supervision: a neglected aspect of delinquency. *British Journal of Criminology, 20,* 203–235.

Wong, L. (1987). Reaction to research findings: Is the feeling of obviousness warranted? *Dissertation Abstracts International*, 48/12, 3709B (University Microfilms #DA 8801059).

Woolfolk Hoy, A., Demerath, P. and Pape, S. (2002). Teaching adolescents: Engaging developing selves. In T. Urdan and F. Pajares (eds), *Adolescence and Education* (pp. 119–169). Volume I. Greenwich, CT: Information Age Publishing.

Woolfolk Hoy, A. and Tschannen-Moran, M. (1999). Implications of cognitive approaches to peer learning for teacher education. In A. O'Donnell and A. King (eds), *Cognitive Perspectives on Peer Learning* (pp. 257–284). Mahwah, NJ: Lawrence Erlbaum.

Yates, M. and Youniss, J. (1999). Promoting identity development: Ten ideas for school-based service-learning programs. In J. Claus and C. Ogden (eds), *Service Learning for Youth Empowerment and Social Change* (pp. 43–67). New York: Peter Lang.

Youniss, J. and Yates, M. (1997). *Community Service and Social Responsibility in Youth*. Chicago: University of Chicago Press.

Chapter 12

Ackers, J. and Hardman, F. (2001). Classroom interaction in Kenyan primary schools. *Compare*, *31*(2), 245–261.

Alerby, E. (2003). 'During the break we have fun': A study concerning pupils' experience of school. *Educational Research*, *45*(1), 17–28.

Alton-Lee, A., Diggins, C., Klenner, L., Vine, E. and Dalton, N. (2001). Teacher management of the learning environment during a social studies discussion in a new-entrant classroom in New Zealand. *Elementary School Journal, 101,* 549–566.

Baron, R. A. and Byrne, D. (2003). *Social Psychology* (10th ed.). Boston: Allyn and Bacon.

Beattie, M. (2002). Educational leadership: modeling, mentoring, making and re-making a learning community. *European Journal of Teacher Education*, *25*(2–3) 199–221.

Berliner, D. C. (1983). Developing concepts of classroom environments: Some light on the T in studies of ATI. *Educational Psychologist, 18,* 1–13.

Berliner, D. C. (1988). Simple views of effective teaching and a simple theory of classroom instruction. In D. Berliner and B. Rosenshine (eds), *Talks to Teachers* (pp. 93–110). New York: Random House.

Bernhard, J. K., Freire, M., Bascunan, L., Arenas, R., Nury Rugeles Verga, N. R. and Gana, D. (2004). Behaviour and misbehaviour of Latino children in a time of zero tolerance: mothers' views. *Early Years: An International Journal of Research and Development*, *24*(1), 49–62.

Blandford, S. (1998). *Managing Discipline in Schools*. London: Routledge.

Brophy, J. E. and Evertson, C. (1978). Context variables in teaching. *Educational Psychologist, 12,* 310–316.

Bruning, R. H., Schraw, G. J., Norby, M. M. and Ronning, R. R. (2004). *Cognitive Psychology and Instruction* (4th ed.). Columbus, OH: Merrill.

Burden, P. R. (1995). *Classroom Management and Discipline: Methods to Facilitate Cooperation and Instruction*. White Plains, NY: Longman.

Canter, L. (1996). First the rapport – then the rules. *Learning, 24*(5), 12.

Canter, L. and Canter, M. (1992). *Lee Canter's Assertive Discipline: Positive behavior management for today's classroom*. Santa Monica: Lee Canter and Associates.

Charles, C. M. (2002a). *Essential Elements of Effective Discipline*. Boston: Allyn and Bacon.

Charles, C. M. (2002b). *Building Classroom Discipline* (7th ed.). Boston: Allyn and Bacon.

Cole, E., Daniels, H. and Visser, J. (2003). Patterns of provision for pupils with behavioural difficulties in England: A study of government statistics and behaviour support plan data. *Oxford Review of Education*, *29*(2), 187–205.

Covaleskie, J. F. (1992). Discipline and morality: Beyond rules and consequences. *Educational Forum, 56*(2), 56–60.

Danielson, P. (2002). Learning to cooperate: Reciprocity and self-control. *Behavioural and Brain Sciences, 25*(2), 256–257.

Dorman, J. and Adams, J. (2004). Associations between pupils' perceptions of classroom environment and academic efficacy in Australian and British secondary schools. *Westminster Studies in Education, 27*(1), 69–85.

Doyle, W. (1983). Academic work. *Review of Educational Research, 53,* 159–200.

Doyle, W. (2006). Ecological approaches to classroom management. In C. Evertson and C. S. Weinstein (eds), *Handbook for Classroom Management: Research, Practice, and Contemporary Issues.* Mahwah, NJ: Lawrence Erlbaum.

Elias, M. J. and Schwab, Y. (2006). From compliance to responsibility: Social and emotional learning and classroom management. In C. Evertson and C. S. Weinstein (eds), *Handbook for Classroom Management: Research, Practice, and Contemporary Issues.* Mahwah, NJ: Lawrence Erlbaum.

Emmer, E. T. and Evertson, C. M. (1981). Synthesis of research on classroom management. *Educational Leadership, 38,* 342–345.

Emmer, E. T. and Evertson, C. M. (1982). Effective classroom management at the beginning of the school year in junior high school classes. *Journal of Educational Psychology, 74,* 485–498.

Emmer, E. T., Evertson, C. M. and Anderson, L. M. (1980). Effective classroom management at the beginning of the school year. *Elementary School Journal, 80,* 219–231.

Emmer, E. T., Evertson, C. M. and Worsham, M. E. (2006). *Classroom Management for Secondary Teachers* (7th ed.). Boston: Allyn and Bacon.

Emmer, E. T. and Gerwels, M. C. (2006). Classroom management in middle school and high school classrooms. In C. Evertson and C. S. Weinstein (eds), *Handbook for Classroom Management: Research, Practice, and Contemporary Issues.* Mahwah, NJ: Lawrence Erlbaum.

Emmer, E. T. and Stough, L. M. (2001). Classroom management: A critical part of educational psychology with implications for teacher education. *Educational Psychologist, 36,* 103–112.

Evertson, C. M. (1988). Managing classrooms: A framework for teachers. In D. Berliner and B. Rosenshine (eds), *Talks to Teachers* (pp. 54–74). New York: Random House.

Evertson, C. M., Emmer, E. T. and Worsham, M. E. (2003). *Classroom Management for Elementary Teachers* (6th ed.). Boston: Allyn and Bacon.

Evertson, C. M., Emmer, E. T. and Worsham, M. E. (2006). *Classroom Management for Secondary Teachers* (7th ed.). Boston: Allyn and Bacon.

Fredricks, J. A., Blumenfeld, P. C., and Paris, A. H. (2004). School engagement: Potential of the concept, state of the evidence. *Review of Educational Research, 74,* 59–109.

Frick, T. W. (1990). Analysis of patterns in time: A method of recording and quantifying temporal relations in education. *American Educational Research Journal, 27,* 180–204.

Ghaith, G. (2003). The relationship between forms of instruction, achievement and perceptions of classroom climate. *Educational Research, 45*(1), 83–93.

Gillies, R. M. (2006). Teachers' and pupils' verbal behaviours during cooperative and small-group learning. *British Journal of Educational Psychology, 76*(2), 271–287.

Glasser, W. (1969). *Schools Without Failure.* New York: Harper and Raw.

Good, T. L. (1983). Classroom research: A decade of progress. *Educational Psychologist, 18,* 127–144.

Gordon, T. (1981). Crippling our children with discipline. *Journal of Education, 163,* 228–243.

Harrop, H. and Swinson, J. (2000). Natural rates of approval and disapproval in British infant, junior and secondary classrooms. *British Journal of Educational Psychology, 70*(4), 473–483.

Herbert, E. A. (1998). Design matters: How school environment affects children. *Educational Leadership, 56*(1), 69–71.

Hinger, B. (2006). The distribution of instructional time and its effect on group cohesion in the foreign language classroom: A comparison of intensive and standard format courses. *System* (Elsevier) 34.1, 233–255.

Howieson, C. and Semple, S. (2000). The evaluation of guidance: listening to pupils' views. *British Journal of Guidance and Counselling, 28*(3), 373–387.

Hughes, M. W. H. and Longman, D. (2005). *Interactive digital display boards and class teaching: interactive or just another epidiascope?* Paper presented at the annual conference of the British Educational Research Association. University of Glamorgan, Wales 15–17 September.

Hyman, I., Kay, B., Tabori, A., Weber, M., Mahon, M. and Cohen, I. (2006). Bullying: Theory, research and interventions about student victimization. In C. Evertson and C. S. Weinstein (eds), *Handbook for Classroom Management: Research, Practice, and Contemporary Issues.* Mahwah, NJ: Lawrence Erlbaum.

Irving, O. and Martin, J. (1982). Withitness: The confusing variable. *American Educational Research Journal, 19,* 313–319.

Kaplan, A., Gheen, M. and Midgley, C. (2002). Classroom goal structure and student disruptive behaviour. *British Journal of Educational Psychology, 72*(2), 191–211.

Kounin, J. S. (1970). *Discipline and Group Management in Classrooms.* New York: Holt, Rinehart and Winston.

Lambert, N. M. (1994). Seating arrangement in classrooms. *The International Encyclopedia of Education* (2nd ed.) 9, 5355–5359.

Lawson, T. and Comber, C. (2000). Censorship, the Internet and schools: A new moral panic? *Curriculum Journal, 11*(2), 273–285.

Levin, J. R. and Nolan, J. F. (2000). *Principles of Classroom Management: A Professional Decision-making Model.* Boston: Allyn and Bacon.

Lewis, R. (2001). Classroom discipline and pupil responsibility: The pupils' view. *Teaching and Teacher Education, 17,* 307–319.

Loizou, E. (2005). Infant humor: The theory of the absurd and the empowerment theory. *International Journal of Early Years Education, 13*(1), 43–53.

Marzano, R. J. and Marzano, J. S. (2003). The key to classroom management. *Educational Leadership, 61*(1), 6–13.

McCaslin, M. and Good, T. L. (1998). Moving beyond management as sheer compliance: Helping pupils to develop goal coordination strategies. *Educational Horizons, 76,* 169–176.

McClean, B., Dench, C., Grey, I., Shanahan, S., Fitzsimons, E., Hendler, J., Corrigan, and Person, M. (2005). Focused training: A model for delivering positive behavioural supports to people with challenging behaviours. *Journal of Intellectual Disability Research, 49*(5), 340–352.

McNally, J., I'Anson, J., Whewell, S. and Wilson, G. (2005). 'They think that swearing is okay': First lessons in behaviour management. *Journal of Education for Teaching: International Research and Pedagogy, 31*(3), 169–185.

McNeely, C. A., Nonnemaker, J. M. and Blum, R. W. (2002). Promoting school connectedness: Evidence from the National Longitudinal Study of Adolescent Health. *Journal of School Health, 72*(4), 138–146.

McPake, J., Harlen, W., Powney, J and Davidson, J. (1999). *Teachers' and Pupils' Days in the Primary Classroom.* Scottish Council for Research in Education. Research Report No. 93, December 1999.

Morrow, L. M. and Weinstein, C. (1986). Encouraging voluntary reading: The impact of a literature program on children's use of library centers. *Reading Research Quarterly, 21,* 330–346.

Myhill, D. (2002). Bad boys and good girls? Patterns of interaction and response in whole class teaching. *British Educational Research Journal, 28*(3), 339–352.

National Center for Educational Statistics. (2003). Indicators of school crime and safety 2002. Retrieved 22 January 2004 from http://nces.ed.gov/pubs2003/schoolcrime/6.asp?nav=1.

Nelson, J. R. and Roberts, M. L. (2000). Ongoing reciprocal teacher-pupil interactions involving disruptive behaviours in general education classrooms. *Journal of Emotional and Behavioural Disorders, 4,* 147–161.

Nyroos, M., Ranberg, L. and Kundahl, L. (2004). A matter of timing: Time use, freedom and influence in school from a pupil perspective. *European Educational Research Journal, 3*(4), 743–758.

O'Brien, T. (1998). *Promoting Positive Behaviour.* London: David Fulton.

Orange, C. (2000). *25 Biggest Mistakes Teachers Make and How to Avoid Them.* Thousand Oaks, CA: Corwin.

Osler, A. (2000). Children's rights, responsibilities and understandings of school discipline. *Research Papers in Education, 15*(1), 49–67.

Padilla, F. M. (1992). *The Gang as an American Enterprise.* New Brunswick, NJ: Rutgers University Press.

Papatheodorou, T. (2000). Management approaches employed by teachers to deal with children's behaviour problems in nursery classes. *School Psychology International, 21*(4), 415–440.

Parks, C. P. (1995). Gang behaviour in the schools: Myth or reality? *Educational Psychology Review, 7,* 41–68.

Pittard, V. (2004). Evidence for e-learning policy. *Technology, Pedagogy and Education, 13*(2), 181–194.

Pollard, A. (1985). *The Social World of the Primary School.* (pp. 158–71). London: Cassell.

Pollard, A., Broadfoot, P., Osborne, M. and Abbott, D. (1994). *Changing English Primary Schools?* (pp. 178–82) London: Cassell.

Rasmussen, M., Damsgaard, M. T., Holstein, B. E., Poulsen, L. H. and Due, P. (2005). School connectedness and daily smoking among boys and girls: The influence of parental smoking norms. *European Journal of Public Health, 15*(6), 607–612.

Render, G. F., Padilla, J. N. M. and Krank, H. M. (1989). What research really shows about assertive discipline. *Educational Leadership, 46*(6), 72–75.

Renold, E. (2003). 'If you don't kiss me, you're dumped': Boys, boyfriends and heterosexualised masculinities in the primary school. *Educational Review, 55*(2), 179–194.

Richardson, V. and Fallona, C. (2001). Classroom management as method and manner. *Journal of Curriculum Studies, 33*(6), 705–728.

Rogers, W. (2000). *Behaviour Management.* London: Paul Chapman Publishing Ltd.

Ronen, T. (2004). Imparting self-control skills to decrease aggressive behaviour in a 12-year-old boy: A case study. *Journal of Social Work, 4*(3), 269–288.

Roth, W-M., Boutonne, S., McRobbie, C. J. and Lucas, K. B. (1999). One class, many worlds. *International Journal of Science Education, 21*(1), 59–75.

Rutter, M, Maughan, B., Mortimore, P. and Ouston, J. (1979). *Fifteen Thousand Hours. Secondary Schools and their Effects on Children.* London: Open Books.

Ryan, K. and Cranfield, J. (1970). *Don't Smile Until Christmas: Accounts of the First Year of Teaching.* Chicago: University of Chicago Press.

Savage, T. V. (1999). *Teaching Self-control Through Management and Discipline.* Boston: Allyn and Bacon.

Scherer, M. (1999). The discipline of hope: A conversation with Herb Kohl. *Educational Leadership, 56*(1), 8–13.

Shechtman, Z. and Leichtentritt, J. (2004). Affective teaching: A method to enhance classroom management. *European Journal of Teacher Education, 27*(3), 323–333.

Slap, G. B., Lot, L., Huang, B., Daniyam, C. A., Zink, T. M. and Succop, P. A. (2003). Sexual behaviour of adolescents in Nigeria: Cross-sectional survey of secondary school students. *BMJ (British Medical Journal), 326*(7379), 15.

Sokolove, S., Garrett, J., Sadker, D. and Sadker, M. (1986). Interpersonal communications skills. In J. Cooper (ed.), *Classroom Teaching Skills: A Handbook* (pp. 233–278). Lexington, MA: D. C. Heath.

Squires, G. (2001). Using cognitive behavioural psychology with groups of pupils to improve self-control of behaviour. *Educational Psychology in Practice, 17*(4), 317–335.

Stephen, P. and Crawley, T. (1994). *Becoming an Effective Teacher.* Cheltenham. Stanley Thornes.

Taeschner, T., Testa, P., Cacioppo, M. and Lucchese, F. (1998). *Analyzing behavior in the classroom.* Poster presented at Measuring Behavior '98, 2nd International Conference on Methods and Techniques in Behavioral Research, 18–21 August 1998, Groningen, The Netherlands.

Van Dalen, J., Van Hout, J. C. H. M., Wolfhagen, H. A. P., Scherpbier, A. J. J. A. and Van Der Vleuten, C. P. M. (1999). Factors influencing the effectiveness of communication skills training: programme contents outweigh teachers' skills. *Medical Teacher, 21*(3), 308–310.

Veenman, S., Kenter, B. and Post, K. (2000). Cooperative learning in Dutch primary classrooms. *Educational Studies, 26*(3), 281–302.

Wang, M. C., Haertel, G. D. and Walberg, H. J. (1994). What helps students learn? *Educational Leadership, 51*(4), 74–79. (ERIC Document Reproduction Service No. ED461694).

Weinstein, C. S. (1977). Modifying pupil behaviour in an open classroom through changes in the physical design. *American Educational Research Journal, 14,* 249–262.

Weinstein, C. S. (1999). Reflections on best practices and promising programs: Beyond assertive classroom discipline. In H. J. Freiberg (ed.), *Beyond Behaviourism: Changing the Classroom Management Paradigm* (pp. 147–163). Boston: Allyn and Bacon.

Weinstein, C. S. (2003). *Secondary Classroom Management: Lessons from Research and Practice* (2nd ed.). New York: McGraw-Hill.

Weinstein, C. S. and Mignano, A. (2003). *Elementary Classroom Management: Lessons from Research and Practice* (3rd ed.). New York: McGraw-Hill.

Woolfolk, A. E. and Brooks, D. (1983). Nonverbal communication in teaching. In E. Gordon (ed.), *Review of Research in Education* (Vol. 10, pp. 103–150). Washington, DC: American Educational Research Association.

Woolfolk Hoy, A. and Weinstein, C. S. (2006). Pupils' and teachers' perspectives about classroom management.

In C. Evertson and C. S. Weinstein (eds), *Handbook for Classroom Management: Research, Practice, and Contemporary Issues.* Mahwah, NJ: Lawrence Erlbaum.

Chapter 13

Alexander, R. (2000). *Culture and Pedagogy: International Comparisons in Primary Education.* Oxford: Blackwell.

Allington, R. (1980). Teacher interruption behaviours during primary-grade oral reading. *Journal of Educational Psychology, 71,* 371–377.

Alloway, N. (1984). *Teacher Expectations.* Paper presented at the meetings of the Australian Association for Research in Education, Perth, Australia.

Alvidrez, J. and Weinstein, R. S. (1999). Early teacher perceptions and later student academic achievement. *Journal of Educational Psychology, 91,* 731–746.

Anderson, L. M. (1985). What are pupils doing when they do all that seatwork? In C. Fisher and D. Berliner (eds), *Perspectives on Instructional Time* (pp. 189–202). New York: Longman.

Anderson, L. M. (1989). Classroom Instruction. In M. C. Reynolds (ed.), *Knowledge Base for the Beginning Teacher.* Oxford: Pergamon Press.

Anderson, L. W. and Krathwohl, D. R. (eds). (2001). *A Taxonomy for Learning, Teaching, and Assessing: A revision of Bloom's taxonomy of educational objectives.* New York: Longman.

Arends, R. I. (2001). *Learning to Teach* (5th ed.). New York: McGraw-Hill.

Babad, E. Y. (1995). The 'teachers' pet' phenomenon, pupils' perceptions of differential behavior, and pupils' morale. *Journal of Educational Psychology, 87,* 361–374.

Babad, E. Y., Inbar, J. and Rosenthal, R. (1982). Pygmalion, Galatea, and the Golem: Investigations of biased and unbiased teachers. *Journal of Educational Psychology, 74,* 459–474.

Beatriz de Gonzalez, C., Hernandez, T., Kusch, J. and Ryan, C. (2004). Planning as action research. *Educational Action Research, 12*(1), 59–76.

Beck, I. L., McKeown, M. G., Worthy, J., Sandora, C. A. and Kucan, L. (1996). Questioning the author: A yearlong classroom implementation to engage pupils with text. *Elementary School Journal, 96,* 385–414.

Bennett, J. (2001). Practical work at the upper high school level: the evaluation of a new model of assessment. *International Journal of Science Education, 23*(1), 97–110.

Bennett, S. N. (1976). *Teaching Styles and Pupil Progress.* London: Open Books.

Ben-Peretz, M. (2002). Retired teachers reflect on learning from experience. *Teachers and Teaching: Theory and Practice, 8*(3), 313–323.

Berg, C. A. and Clough, M. (1991). Hunter lesson design: The wrong one for science teaching. *Educational Leadership, 48*(4), 73–78.

Black, L. (2004). Teacher–pupil talk in whole-class discussions and processes of social positioning within the primary school classroom. *Language and Education, 18*(5), 347–360.

Bloom, B. S., Engelhart, M. D., Frost, E. J., Hill, W. H. and Krathwohl, D. R. (1956). Taxonomy of educational objectives. *Handbook I: Cognitive Domain.* New York: David McKay.

Boyle, B. and Bragg, J. (2006). A curriculum without foundation. *British Educational Research Journal, 32*(4), 569–582.

Brophy, J. E. (1998). *Motivating Pupils to Learn.* New York: McGraw-Hill.

Brophy, J. E. and Good, T. (1986). Teacher behaviour and pupil achievement. In M. Wittrock (ed.), *Handbook of Research on Teaching* (3rd ed.) (pp. 328–375). New York: Macmillan.

Brown, A. L. (1992). Design experiments: Theoretical and methodological challenges in creating complex interventions in classroom settings. *Journal of the Learning Sciences, 2,* 141–178.

Brown, M., Askew, M., Baker, D., Denvir, H. and Millet, A. (1998). Is the National Numeracy Strategy research-based? *British Journal of Educational Studies, 46*(4), 362–385.

Bullock, K. and Muschamp, Y. (2006). Learning about learning in the primary school. *Cambridge Journal of Education, 36*(1), 49–62.

Burnett, P. (2002). Teacher praise and feedback and students' perceptions of the classroom environment. *Educational Psychology, 22*(1), 5–16.

Burns, C. and Myhill, D. (2004). Interactive or inactive? A consideration of the nature of interaction in whole-class teaching. *Cambridge Journal of Education, 34*(1), 35–49.

Burns, E. (2006). Pause, prompt and praise – peer tutored reading for pupils with learning difficulties. *British Journal of Special Education, 33*(2), 62–67.

Calder, P. (2000). Learning from Romania and Hungary, *Mathematics Teaching, 171.*

Calderhead, J. (1996). Teacher: Beliefs and knowledge. In D. Berliner and R. Calfee (eds), *Handbook of Educational Psychology* (pp. 709–725). New York: Macmillan.

Cangelosi, J. S. (1990). *Designing Tests for Evaluating Student Achievement.* New York: Longman.

Chin, C. (2006). Classroom interaction in science: Teacher questioning and feedback to students' responses.

International Journal of Science Education, 28(11), 1315–1346.

Claiborn, W. L. (1969). Expectancy effects in the classroom: A failure to replicate. *Journal of Education Psychology, 60,* 377–383.

Cohen, L., Mannion, L. and Morrison, K. (2007). *Research Methods in Education* (6th ed.). London: Routledge Falmer.

Condie, R. and Simpson, M. (2004). The impact of ICT initiatives in Scottish schools: cultural issues. *European Journal of Teacher Education, 27*(1), 73–82.

Cooper, H. M. (1979). Pygmalion grows up: A model for teacher expectation communication and performance influence. *Review of Educational Research, 49,* 389–410.

Cooper, H. M. (2004). Special Issue: Homework. *Theory Into Practice, 43*(3).

Cooper, H. M. and Valentine, J. C. (eds). (2001). Special Issue: Homework. *Educational Psychologist, 36*(3), Summer.

Cooper, H. M., Valentine, J. C., Nye, B. and Kindsay, J. J. (1999). Relationships between five after-school activities and academic achievement. *Journal of Educational Psychology, 91,* 369–683.

Corno, L. (2000). Looking at homework differently. *Elementary School Journal, 100,* 529–548.

Cowley, T. and Williamson, J. (1998). A recipe for success? Localised implementation of a (flexible) National Curriculum. *Curriculum Journal, 9*(1), 79–94.

Daly, C. (2004). Trainee English teachers and the struggle for subject knowledge. *Changing English: Studies in Culture and Education, 11*(2), 189–204.

Darling-Hammond, L. (2000). Teacher quality and student achievement: A review of state policy evidence. *Educational Policy Analysis Archives, 8,* 1–48. Retrieved 20 January, 2002 from http://epaa.asu.edu/epaa/v8n1/

DfEE (2000). *Research into Teacher Effectiveness.* London: The Stationery Office.

DfES (1998). *Homework: Guidelines for Primary and Secondary Schools.* London: The Stationery Office.

DfES (2006). *Primary Framework for Literacy and mathematics.* Primary National Strategy. http://www.standards.dfes.gov.uk/primaryframeworks/downloads/PDF_Special/textversion.pdf accessed 09.04.2007

Driscoll, M. P. (2005). *Psychology of Learning for Instruction* (3rd ed.). Boston: Allyn and Bacon.

Edwards, A. D. and Westgate, D. P. G. (1994). *Investigating Classroom Talk* (2nd ed.). London: Falmer Press.

Epstein, J. L. and Van Voorhis, F. L. (2001). More than minutes: Teachers' roles in designing homework. *Educational Psychologist, 36,* 181–193.

Eraut, M. (2002). Menus for choosy diners. *Teachers and Teaching: Theory and Practice, 8*(3), 371–379.

Finn, J. (1972). Expectations and the educational environment. *Review of Educational Research, 42,* 387–410.

Fischman, W., DiBara, J. and Gardner, H. (2006). Creating good education against the odds. *Cambridge Journal of Education, 36*(3), 383–398.

Fiske, S. T. (1993). Social cognition and social perception. *Annual Review of Psychology, 44,* 155–194.

Freiberg, H. J. and Driscoll, A. (2005). *Universal Teaching Strategies* (4th ed.). Boston: Allyn and Bacon.

Galton, M. (2000). The National Curriculum balance sheet for Key Stage 2: A researcher's view. *Curriculum Journal, 11*(3), 323–341.

Galton, M. and Simon, B. (eds) (1980). *Progress and Performance in the Primary Classroom.* London: Routledge and Kegan Paul.

Good, T. L. (1983). Classroom research: A decade of progress. *Educational Psychologist, 18,* 127–144.

Good, T. L. (1988). Teacher expectations. In D. Berliner and B. Rosenshine (eds), *Talks to Teachers* (pp. 159–200). New York: Random House.

Good, T. L. (1996). Teaching effects and teacher evaluation. In J. Sikula (ed.), *Handbook of Research on Teacher Education* (pp. 617–665). New York: Macmillan.

Good, T. L. and Brophy, J. (2003). *Looking in Classrooms* (9th ed.). Boston: Allyn and Bacon.

Gronlund, N. E. (2004). *Writing Instructional Objectives for Teaching and Assessment* (7th ed.). Upper Saddle River, NJ: Prentice-Hall.

Gülpinar, M. and Yegen, B. (2005). Interactive lecturing for meaningful learning in large groups. *Medical Teacher, 27*(7), 590–594.

Hardman, F., Smith, F. and Wall, K. (2003). 'Interactive whole-class teaching' in the National Literacy Strategy, *Cambridge Journal of Education, 33*(2).

Harrow, A. J. (1972). *A Taxonomy of the Psychomotor Domain: A guide for developing behaviour objectives.* New York: David McKay.

Hashweh, M. (2005). Teacher pedagogical constructions: a reconfiguration of pedagogical content knowledge. *Teachers and Teaching: Theory and Practice, 11*(3), 273–292.

Haynes, J., Tikly, L. and Caballero, C. (2006). The barriers to achievement for White/Black Caribbean pupils in English schools. *British Journal of Sociology of Education, 27*(5), 569–583.

Hedges, H. and Cullen, J. (2005). Subject knowledge in early childhood curriculum and pedagogy: Beliefs and practices. *Contemporary Issues in Early Childhood, 6*(1), 66–79.

Holfve-Sabel, M. (2006). A comparison of student attitudes towards school, teachers and peers in Swedish comprehensive schools now and 35 years ago. *Educational Research, 48*(1), 55–75.

Holmes, M. and Croll, P. (1989). Time spent on homework and academic achievement. *Educational Research, 31*(1), 36–45.

Hoover-Dempsey, K. V., Battiato, A. C., Walker, J. M. T., Reed, R. P., DeJong, J. M. and Jones, K. P. (2001). Parental involvement in homework. *Educational Psychologist, 36,* 195–209.

Hufton, N., Elliott, J. and Illushin, L. (2002). Educational motivation and engagement: Qualitative accounts from three countries. *British Educational Research Journal, 28*(2), 265–289.

John, P. (2006). Lesson planning and the pupil teacher: Re-thinking the dominant model. *Journal of Curriculum Studies, 38*(4), 483–498.

Jones, M. G. and Gerig, T. M. (1994). Silent sixth-grade pupils: Characteristics, achievement, and teacher expectations. *Elementary School Journal, 95,* 169–182.

Jones, S. and Tanner, H. (2002). Teachers' interpretations of effective whole-class interactive teaching in secondary mathematics classrooms. *Educational Studies, 28*(3), 265–274.

Jones, S. and Myhill, D. (2004). 'Troublesome boys' and 'compliant girls': Gender identity and perceptions of achievement and underachievement. *British Journal of Sociology of Education, 25*(5), 547–561.

Kember, D. (2001). Beliefs about knowledge and the process of teaching and learning as a factor in adjusting to study in higher education. *Studies in Higher Education, 26*(2), 205–221.

Kjellin, M. and Granlund, M. (2006). Children's engagement in different classroom activities. *European Journal of Special Needs Education, 21*(3), 285–300.

Klein, J. (2004). Who is most responsible for gender differences in scholastic achievements: Pupils or teachers? *Educational Research, 46*(2), 183–193.

Krathwohl, D. R., Bloom, B. S. and Masia, B. B. (1964). *Taxonomy of Educational Objectives. Handbook II: Affective domain.* New York: David McKay.

Kreitzer, A. E. and Madaus, G. F. (1994). Empirical investigations of the hierarchical structure of the taxonomy. In L. W. Anderson and L. A. Sosniak (eds), *Bloom's Taxonomy: A forty-year retrospective.* Ninety-third yearbook for the National Society for the Study of Education: Part II (pp. 64–81). Chicago: University of Chicago Press.

Kuklinski, M. R. and Weinstein, R. S. (2001). Classroom and developmental differences in a path model of teacher expectancy effects. *Child Development, 72,* 1554–1578.

Kyriacou, C. (1995). Direct teaching. In Desforges, C. (ed.). *An Introduction to Teaching: Psychological Perspectives.* Oxford: Blackwell.

Lam, P. and McNaught, C. (2006). Design and evaluation of online courses containing media-enhanced learning materials. *Educational Media International, 43*(3), 199–218.

Lyster, R. (2004). Differential effects of prompts and recasts in form-focused instruction. *Studies in Second Language Acquisition, 26*(3), 399–432.

Mager, R. (1975). *Preparing Instructional Objectives* (2nd ed.). Palo Alto, CA: Fearon.

McPake, J., Harlen, W., Powney, J. and Davidson, J. (1999). Teachers' and pupils' days in the primary classroom. Scottish Council for Research in Education, SCRE Research Report No 93. The Scottish Council for Research in Education.

Meek, A. (1991). On thinking about teaching: A conversation with Eleanor Duckworth. *Educational Leadership, 50*, 30–34.

Merton, R. K. (1948). The self-fulfilling prophecy. *Antioch Review, 8*, 193–210.

Morine-Dershimer, G. (2003). Instructional planning. In J. Cooper (ed.), *Classroom Teaching Skills* (7th ed., pp. 19–51). Boston: Houghton-Mifflin.

Morine-Dershimer, G. (2006). Instructional planning. In J. Cooper (ed.), *Classroom teaching skills* (7th ed., pp. 19–51). Boston: Houghton-Miffin.

Mortimer, P., Sammons, P., Lewis, D. and Ecob, R. (1988). *School Matters*. London: Open Books.

Moyles, J. (2001). Passion, paradox and professionalism in early years education. *Early Years: An International Journal of Research and Development, 21*(2), 81–95.

Murray, H. G. (1983). Low inference classroom teaching behaviour and pupil ratings of college teaching effectiveness. *Journal of Educational Psychology, 75*, 138–149.

Myhill, D. (2003). Principled understanding? Teaching the active and passive voice. *Language and Education, 17*(5), 355–370.

Myhill, D. (2006). Talk, talk, talk: teaching and learning in whole-class discourse. *Research Papers in Education, 21*(1), 19–41.

Myhill, D. and Dunkin, F. (2005). Questioning learning. *Language and Education, 19*(5), 415–427.

Nardi, E. and Steward, S. (2003). Is mathematics T.I.R.E.D? A profile of quiet disaffection in the secondary mathematics classroom. *British Educational Research Journal, 29*(3), 345–366.

Noddings, N. (1990). Constructivism in mathematics education. In R. Davis, C. Maher and N. Noddings (eds), *Constructivist Views on the Teaching and Learning of Mathematics* (pp. 7–18). Monograph 4 of the National Council of Teachers of Mathematics, Reston, VA.

Norwich, B. (1999). Pupils' reasons for learning and behaving and for not learning and behaving in English and maths lessons in a secondary school. *British Journal of Educational Psychology, 69*(4), 547–569.

Papatheodorou, T. and Ramasut, A. (1993). Teachers' attitudes towards children's behaviour problems in nursery classes in Greece. *International Journal of Early Years Education, 1*(3), 35–48.

Parker, W. C. and Hess, D. (2001). Teaching with and for discussion. *Teaching and Teacher Education, 17*, 273–289.

Paul, R. W. (1985). Bloom's taxonomy and critical thinking instruction. *Educational Leadership, 42*, 36.

Perrone, V. (1994). How to engage students in learning. *Educational Leadership, 51*(5), 11–13.

PISA (2003). Program for International Student Assessment results at www.pisa.oecd.org

Pressley, M. (1995). More about the development of self-regulation: Complex, long-term, and thoroughly social. *Educational Psychologist, 30*, 207–212.

Raudenbush, S. (1984). Magnitude of teacher expectancy effects on pupil IQ as a function of the credibility of expectancy induction: A synthesis of findings from 18 experiments. *Journal of Educational Psychology, 76*, 85–97.

Redfield, D. L. and Rousseau, E. W. (1981). A meta-analysis of experimental research on teacher questioning behavior. *Review of Educational Research, 51*, 181–193.

Reynolds, D. and Muus, D. (1999). The effective teaching of mathematics: A review of research. *School Leadership and Management, 19*(3), 273–288.

Rodger, S., Murray, H. and Cummings, A. (2007). Effects of teacher clarity and student anxiety on student outcomes. *Teaching in Higher Education, 12*(1), 91–104.

Rodrigues, S. and Thompson, I. (2001). Cohesion in science lesson discourse: clarity, relevance and sufficient information. *International Journal of Science Education, 23*(9), 929–940.

Rosenthal, R. (1995). Critiquing Pygmalion: A 25-year perspective. *Current Directions in Psychological Science, 4*, 171–172.

Rosenthal, R. and Jacobson, L. (1968). *Pygmalion in the Classroom.* New York: Holt, Rinehart, Winston.

Rowe, M. B. (1974). Wait-time and rewards as instructional variables: Their influence on language, logic, and fate control. Part 1: Wait-time. *Journal of Research in Science Teaching, 11*, 81–94.

Rubie-Davies, C., Hattie, J. and Hamilton, R. (2006). Expecting the best for students: Teacher expectations and academic outcomes. *British Journal of Educational Psychology, 76*(3), 429–444.

Rutter, M., Maughan, B., Mortimore, P. and Ouston, J. (1979). *Fifteen Thousand Hours.* London: Open Books.

Sadker, M. and Sadker, D. (2006). Questioning skills. In J. Cooper (ed.), *Classroom Teaching Skills* (8th ed., pp. 104–150). Boston: Houghton-Mifflin.

Shuell, T. J. (1996). Teaching and learning in a classroom context. In D. Berliner and R. Calfee (eds), *Handbook of Educational Psychology* (pp. 726–764). New York: Macmillan.

Simpson, E. J. (1972). The classification of educational objectives in the psychomotor domain. *Psychomotor Domain*. Vol. 3. Washington: Gryphon House.

Sinclair, J. and Coulthard, M. (1975). *Towards an Analysis of Discourse: The English Used by Teachers and Pupils.* London: Oxford University Press.

Slavin, R. E. (1991). *Educational Psychology* (3rd ed.). Boston: Allyn and Bacon.

Smith, F., Hardman, F., Wall, K. and Mroz, M. (2004). Interactive whole-class teaching in the National Literacy and Numeracy Strategies. *British Educational Research Journal, 30*(3), 395–411.

Smith, F., Hardman, F. and Higgins, S. (2006). The impact of interactive whiteboards on teacher–pupil interaction in the National Literacy and Numeracy Strategies. *British Educational Research Journal, 32*(3), 443–457.

Smith, R. (2000). Whose childhood? The politics of homework. *Children and Society, 14*(4), 316–325.

Snow, R. E. (1995). Pygmalion and intelligence. *Current Directions in Psychological Science, 4,* 169–171.

Solomon, Y., Warin, J. and Lewis, C. (2002). Helping with homework? Homework as a site of tension for parents and teenagers. *British Educational Research Journal, 28*(4), 603–622.

Szalontai, T. (2000). Facts and Tendencies in Hungarian Maths Teaching (pp. 1–2) http://www.ex.ac.uk/cimt/ijmtl/tshungmt.pdf

TenBrink, T. D. (2006). Assessment. In J. Cooper (ed.), *Classroom Teaching Skills* (8th ed., pp. 55–78). Boston: Houghton-Mifflin.

Tharp, R. G. and Gallimore, R. (1988). *Rousing Minds to Life: Teaching, Learning and Schooling in Social Context.* Cambridge UK: Cambridge University Press.

Tharp, R. G. and Gallimore, R. (1991). *The Instructional Conversation: Teaching and Learning in Social Activity.* Washington, DC: National Center for Research on Cultural Diversity and Second Language Learning.

Trautwein, U. and Koller, O. (2003). The relationship between homework and achievement – still a mystery. *Educatonal Psychology Review, 15,* 115–145.

Turcsányi-Szabó, M., Bedo, A. and Pluhár, Z. (2007). Case study of a TeaM challenge game – e-PBL revisited. *Education and Information Technologies,* Preprint (January 2007), pp. 1–15.

Tymms, P. (1999). Baseline Assessment and Monitoring in Primary Schools: Achievements, Attitudes, and Value-added Indicators. London: David Fulton.

Van Matre, J. C., Valentine, J. C. and Cooper, H. (2000). Effect of pupils' after-school activities on teachers' academic expectations. *Contemporary Educational Psychology, 25,* 167–183.

van Zee, E., Iwasyk, M., Kurose, A., Simpson, D. and Wild, J. (2001). Student and teacher questioning during conversations about science. *Journal of Research in Science Teaching, 38*(2), 159–190.

Veenman, S. and Denessen, E. (2001). The coaching of teachers: Results of five training studies. *Educational Research and Evaluation, 7*(4), 385–417.

Wang, X-L., Bernas, R. and Eberhard, P. (2001). Effects of teachers' verbal and non-verbal scaffolding on everyday classroom performances of students with Down syndrome. *International Journal of Early Years Education, 9*(1), 71–80.

Wayne, A. J. and Youngs, P. (2003). Teacher characteristics and pupil achievement gains: A review. *Review of Educational Research, 73,* 89–122.

Weinert, F. E. and Helmke, A. (1995). Learning from wise mother nature or big brother instructor: The wrong choice as seen from an educational perspective. *Educational Psychologist, 30,* 135–143.

Weinstein, C. S. and Mignano, A. (2003). *Elementary Classroom Management: Lessons from Research and Practice* (3rd ed.). New York: McGraw-Hill.

Weinstein, R. S., Madison, S. M. and Kuklinski, M. R. (1995). Raising expectations in schools: Obstacles and opportunities for change. *American Educational Research Journal, 32,* 121–159.

Whitburn, J. (2001). Effective classroom organisation in primary schools: Mathematics. *Oxford Review of Education, 27*(3), 411–428.

Woolfolk, A. E. and Brooks, D. (1983). Nonverbal communication in teaching. In E. Gordon (ed.), *Review of Research in Education* (Vol. 10, pp. 103–150). Washington, DC: American Educational Research Association.

Woolfolk, A. E. and Brooks, D. (1985). The influence of teachers' nonverbal behaviours on pupils' perceptions and performance. *Elementary School Journal, 85,* 514–528.

Yates, G. (2005). 'How obvious': Personal reflections on the database of educational psychology and effective teaching research. *Educational Psychology, 25*(6), 681–700.

Chapter 14

Anastasi, A. (1988). *Psychological Testing* (6th ed.). New York: Macmillan.

Arabsolghar, F. and Elkins, J. (2001). Teachers' expectations about students' use of reading strategies, knowledge and behaviour in Grades 3, 5 and 7. *Journal of Research in Reading*, *24*(2), 154–162.

Atkinson, C., Regan, T. and Williams, C. (2006). Working collaboratively with teachers to promote effective learning. *Support for Learning*, *21*(1), 33–39.

Barootchi, N. and Keshavarz, M. H. (2002). Assessment of achievement through portfolios and teacher-made tests. *Educational Research*, *44*(3), 279–288.

Broadfoot, P. M. (1996). *Education Assessment and Society*. Buckingham: Open University Press.

Carter, E. W., Wehby, J., Hughes, C., Johnson, S. M., Plank, D. R., Barton-Arwood, S. M. and Lunsford, L. B. (2005). Preparing adolescents with high-incidence disabilities for high-stakes testing with strategy instruction. *Preventing School Failure, 49*(2), 55–62.

Connor, M. J. (2003). Pupil stress and standard assessment tasks (SATs): An Update. *Emotional and Behavioural Difficulties, 8*(2), 101–107.

Cronbach, L. J. (1980). Vakidity on parole: How can we go straight? *New Directions for Testing and Measurement, 5*, 99–108.

Doherty, K. M. (2002). Assessment. *Education Week on the Web*. Retrieved 5 August from http://edweek.org/context/topics/issuespage.cmf?id=41

Elliott, J. G. (1999). Practitioner review: School refusal: Issues of conceptualisation, Assessment, and Treatment. *Journal of Child Psychology and Psychiatry (formerly Journal of Child Psychology and Psychiatry and Allied Disciplines), 40*(7), 1001–1012.

Gipps, C. and Murphy, P. (1994). *A Fair Test? Assessment, Achievement and Equity*. Buckingham: Open University Press.

Girot, E. A. (2000). Assessment of graduates and diplomates in practice in the UK – are we measuring the same level of competence? *Journal of Clinical Nursing, 9*(3), 330–337.

Haladyna, T. H. (2002). *Essentials of Standardised Achievement Testing: Validity and Accountability*. Boston: Allyn and Bacon.

Hall, K. (2001). Level descriptions and curriculum relatedness in English at Key Stage 1. *Educational Review, 53*(1), 47–56.

Hambleton, R. K. (1996). Advances in assessment models, methods, and practices. In D. C. Berliner and R. C. Calfee (eds), *Handbook of Educational Psychology* (pp. 899–925). New York: Macmillan.

Harlen, W. (2005). Teachers' summative practices and assessment for learning – tensions and synergies. *Curriculum Journal, 16*(2), 207–223.

Hoyle, D. (1998). Constructions of pupil absence in the British education service. *Child and Family Social Work, 3*(2), 99–111.

James, M. (2000). Measured lives: The rise of assessment as the engine of change in English schools. *Curriculum Journal, 11*(3), 343–364.

Kalmijn, M. and Kraaykamp, G. (2003). Dropout and downward mobility in the educational career: An event-history anaylsis of ethnic schooling differences in The Netherlands. *Educational Research and Evaluation, 9*(3), 265–287.

Kirst, M. (1991). Interview on assessment issues with Lorrie Shepard. *Educational Researcher, 20*(2), 21–23.

Lambert, D. and Lines, D. (2000). *Understanding Assessment: Purposes, Perceptions, Practice*. London: Routledge Falmer.

McEwen, A., McGuinness, C. and Knipe, D. (2001). Teaching and cognitive outcomes in A-levels and advanced GNVQs: Case studies from science and business studies classrooms. *Research Papers in Education, 16*(2), 199–222.

Mehrens, W. A. and Lehmann, I. J. (1978). *Measurement and Evaluation in Education and Psychology*. London: Holt, Rinehart and Winston.

Messick, S. (1989). Validity. In Linn, R. L. (ed.) *Educational Measurement*, 3rd ed. New York: John Wiley.

Noguera, P. (2005). The racial achievement gap: How can we assume an equity of outcomes. In L. Johnson, M. E. Finn and R. Lewis (eds), *Urban Education with an Attitude*. Albany, NT: SUNY Press.

Pitts, J., Coles, C. and Thomas, P. (2001). Enhancing reliability in portfolio assessment: 'shaping' the portfolio. *Medical Teacher, 23*(4), 351–356.

Popham, W. J. (2005a). *Classroom Assessment: What Teachers Need to Know* (4th ed.). Boston, MA: Allyn and Bacon.

Popham, W. J. (2005b). Instructional quality: Collecting credible evidence. *Educational Leadership, 62*(6), 80–81.

Remedios, R., Ritchie, K. and DaLieberman, D. A. (2005). I used to like it but now I don't: The effect of the transfer test in Northern Ireland on pupils' intrinsic motivation. *British Journal of Educational Psychology, 75*(3), 435–452.

Sattler, J. M. (2001). *Assessment of Children: Cognitive Applications* (4th ed.). San Diego, CA: Jerome M. Sattler, Inc.

Seegers, G., van Putten, C. M. and de Brabander, C. J. (2002). Goal orientation, perceived task outcome and task demands in mathematics tasks: Effects on students' attitude in actual task settings. *British Journal of Educational Psychology, 72*(3), 365–384.

Shavelson, R. J., Gao, X. and Baxter, G. (1993). *Sampling variability of performance assessments.* CSE Technical

Report 361. Los Angeles: UCLA Center for the Study of Evaluation.

Snapp, M. and Woolfolk, A. E. (1973). *An examination of children in special education over a thirteen-year period*. Paper presented at the National Association of School Psychologists, 5th Annual Meeting, New York.

Spinelli, C. G. (2002). *Classroom Assessment for Students with Special Needs in Inclusive Classrooms*. Upper Saddle River, NJ.: Merrill/Prentice-Hall.

Sturman, L. (2003). Teaching to the test: Science or intuition? *Educational Research, 45*(3), 261–273.

Torrance, H. (2003). National assessment in England. In Kellaghan T. and Stufflebeam D. (eds). *International Handbook of Educational Evaluation*. Kluwer.

Wilkins, J. L. M., Graham, G., Parker, S., Westfall, S., Fraser, R. G. and Tembo, M. (2003). Time in the arts and physical education and school achievement. *Journal of Curriculum Studies, 35*(6), 721–734.

Wolf, D., Bixby, J., Glenn, J., III and Gardner, H. (1991). To use their minds well: New forms of pupil assessment. *Review of Research in Education, 17*, 31–74.

Chapter 15

Airasian, P. W. (1996). *Assessment in the Classroom*. New York: McGraw-Hill.

Airasian, P. W. (2005). *Classroom Assessment: Concepts and Applications* (5th ed.). New York: McGraw-Hill.

Ausubel, D. P. (1968). *Educational Psychology: A Cognitive View*. New York: Holt, Rinehart and Winston.

Bangert-Drowns, R. L., Kulik, C. C., Kulik, J. A. and Morgan, M. (1991). The instructional effect of feedback in test-like events. *Review of Educational Research, 61*, 213–238.

Banks, S. R. (2005). *Classroom Assessment: Issues and Practice*. Boston: Allyn and Bacon.

Belanoff, P. and Dickson, M. (1991). *Portfolios: Process and Product*. Portsmouth, NH: Heinemann, Boynton/Cook.

Bennett, N., Desforges, C., Cockburn, A. and Wilkinson, B. (1984). *The Quality of Pupil Learning Experiences*. London: Lawrence Erlbaum.

Bloom, B. S. (1981). *All our Children Learning: A Primer for Parents, Teachers, and Other Educators*. New York: McGraw-Hill.

Bloom, R. and Bourdon, L. (1980). Types and frequencies of teachers' written instructional feedback. *Journal of Educational Research, 74*, 13–15.

Butler, R. and Nisan, M. (1986). Effects of no feedback, task-related comments, and grades on intrinsic motivation and performance. *Journal of Educational Psychology, 78*, 210–224.

Cambourne, B. and Turbill, J. (1990). Assessment in whole-language classrooms: Theory into practice. *Elementary School Journal, 90, 337*–349.

Camp, R. (1990). Thinking together about portfolios. *Quarterly of the National Writing Project, 27*, 8–14.

Clausen-May, T. (2001). *An Approach to Test Development*. Slough: NFER.

Clifford, M. M. (1990). Students need challenge, not easy success. *Education Leadership, 48*(1), 22–26.

Clifford, M. M. (1991). Risk Taking: Empirical and Educational Considerations. *Educational Psychologist, 26*, 263–298.

Dempster, F. (1991). Synthesis of research on reviews and tests. *Educational Leadership, 48*(7), 71–76.

Dempster, F. N. (1993). Exposing our pupils to less should help them learn more. *Phi Delta Kappan, 74, 432*–437.

Desforges, C. (1990). *Testing and Assessment*. London: Cassell Education.

Eisner, E. W. (1999). The uses and limits of performance assessments. *Phi Delta Kappan, 80*, 658–660.

Elawar, M. C. and Corno, L. (1985). A factorial experiment in teachers' written feedback on pupil homework: Changing teacher behavior a little rather than a lot. *Journal of Educational Psychology, 77*, 162–173.

Foster, W. (1981). *Social and emotional development in gifted individuals*. Paper presented at the Fourth World Conference on Gifted and Talented, Montreal.

Gipps, C. and Murphy, P. (1994). A fair test? *Assessment, Achievement and Equity*. Buckingham: Open University Press.

Goodrich, H. (1997). Understanding rubrics. *Educational Leadership, 54*(4), 14–17.

Gronlund, N. E. (2003). *Assessment of Pupil Achievement* (7th ed.). Boston: Allyn and Bacon.

Guskey, T. R. (1994). Making the grade: What benefits pupils? *Educational Leadership, 52*(2), 14–21.

Guskey, T. R. and Bailey, J. M. (2001). *Developing Grading and Reporting Systems for Student Learning*. Thousand Oaks, CA: Corwin Press.

Haertel, E. H. (1999). Performance assessment and educational reform. *Phi Delta Kappan, 80*, 662–666.

Haladyna, T. H. (2002). *Essentials of Standardized Achievement Testing: Validity and Accountability*. Boston: Allyn and Bacon.

Herman, J. (1997). Assessing new assessments: How do they measure up? *Theory Into Practice, 36*, 197–204.

Herman, J. and Winters, L. (1994). Portfolio research: A slim collection. *Educational Leadership, 52*(2), 48–55.

Johnson, D. W. and Johnson, R. T. (2002). *Meaningful Assessment: A Meaningful and Cooperative Process*. Boston: Allyn and Bacon.

Kirst, M. (1991). Interview on assessment issues with James Popham. *Educational Researcher, 20*(2), 24–27.

Kohn, A. (1996). By all available means: Cameron and Pierce's defence of extrinsic motivators. *Review of Educational Research, 66,* 1–4.

Krumboltz, J. D. and Yeh, C. J. (1996). Competitive grading sabotages good teaching. *Phi Delta Kappan, 78,* 324–326.

LeMahieu, P., Gitomer, D. H. and Eresh, J. T. (1993). *Portfolios in large-scale assessment: Difficult but not impossible.* Unpublished manuscript, University of Delaware.

Lipman, P. (1997). Restructuring in context: A case study of teacher participation and the dynamics of ideology, race, and power. *American Educational Research Journal, 34,* 3–37.

Mabry, L. (1999). Writing to the rubrics: Lingering effects of traditional standardized testing on direct writing assessment. *Phi Delta Kappan, 80,* 673–679.

McDonald, J. P. (1993). Three pictures of an presentation: Warm, cool, and hard. *Phi Delta Kappan, 6,* 480–485.

McMillan, J. H. (2004). *Classroom Assessment: Principles and Practice for Effective Instruction* (3rd ed.). Boston: Allyn and Bacon.

Murphy, R., Nuttall, D. L. and Broadfoot, P. (1995). Quoting Nuttall in a Presentation at Centre for Policy Studies Conference, 21 September 1993. *Effective Assessment and the Improvement of Education. A Tribute to Desmond Nuttall.* London: Falmer.

Orwell, G. (1951). *Animal Farm.* Harmondsworth: Penguin.

Popham, W. J. (2005). *Classroom Assessment: What Teachers Need to Know* (4th ed.). Boston, MA: Allyn and Bacon.

Pressley, M., Wharton-McDonald, R., Allington, R., Block, C. C., Morrow, L., Tracey, D., Baker, K., Brooks, G., Cronin, J., Nelson, E. and Woo, D. (2001). A study of effective first-grade literacy instruction. *Scientific Studies of Reading, 5,* 35–58.

Satterly, D. (1989). *Assessment in Schools* (2nd ed.). Oxford: Blackwell.

Skidmore, P. (2003). *Beyond Measure: Why Educational Assessment is Failing the Test.* London: Demos.

Smith, J. K., Smith, L. F. and De Lisi, R. (2001). *Natural Classroom Assessment: Designing Seamless Instruction and Assessment.* Thousand Oaks, CA: Corwin Press.

Starch, D. and Elliot, E. C. (1912). Reliability of grading high school work in English. *Scholastic Review, 20,* 442–457.

Starch, D. and Elliot, E. C. (1913a). Reliability of grading work in history. *Scholastic Review, 21,* 676–681.

Starch, D. and Elliot, E. C. (1913b). Reliability of grading work in mathematics. *Scholastic Review, 21,* 254–259.

Stiggins, R. J. and Chappius, J. (2005). Using student-involved classroom assessment to close achievement gaps. *Theory into Practice, 44,* 11–18.

TenBrink, T. D. (2003). Assessment. In J. Cooper (ed.) *Classroom Teaching Skills* (7th ed., pp. 311–353). Boston: Houghton-Mifflin.

Tomlinson, C. A. (2005a). Grading and differentiation: Paradox or good practice? *Theory Into Practice, 44,* 262–269.

Tomlinson, C. A. (2005b, Summer). Differentiating instruction. *Theory Into Practice, 44*(3).

Ward, C. (1981). *Preparing and Using Objective Questions.* Cheltenham: Stanley Thornes.

Weiner, B. (1979). A theory of motivation for some classroom experiences. *Journal of Educational Psychology, 71,* 3–25.

Wiggins, G. (1991). Standards, not standardization: Evoking quality pupil work. *Educational Leadership, 48*(5), 18–25.

Willingham, W. W. and Cole, N. S. (1997). *Gender and Fair Assessment.* Mahwah, NJ: Lawrence Erlbaum.

Wolf, D., Bixby, J., Glenn, J., III and Gardner, H. (1991). To use their minds well: New forms of pupil assessment. *Review of Research in Education, 17,* 31–74.

Index

Note: Page references in bold refer to terms included in the Glossary